ISBN 978-0-365-60360-3
PIBN 11258611

FB &c Ltd, Dalton House, 60 Windsor Avenue, London, SW19 2RR.
Company number 08720141. Registered in England and Wales.

For support please visit www.forgottenbooks.com

THE MAGAZINE FOR ARMY ENGINEERS

Spring 1982

BRIGHT STAR 82

The Engineer Story

BRIGHT STAR 82

The Engineer Story

UNITED STATES ARMY ENGINEER CENTER AND FORT BELVOIR, VA

COMMANDER/COMMANDANT
Maj. Gen. James N. Ellis

DEPUTY COMMANDANT
Col. Alvin G. Rowe

CHIEF OF STAFF/DEPUTY INSTALLATION COMMANDER
Col. David O. Cooksey

COMMAND SERGEANT MAJOR
CSM Marvin L. Knowles

DIRECTORATES

DIRECTORATE OF ENGINEER FORCE MANAGEMENT
Lt. Col. Charles S. Nichols

DIRECTORATE OF COMBAT DEVELOPMENTS
Col. Phillip R. Hoge

DIRECTORATE OF TRAINING DEVELOPMENTS
Col. John W. Devens

DIRECTORATE OF TRAINING AND DOCTRINE
Col. Stanley R. Johnson

UNITS

ENGINEER CENTER BRIGADE
Col. Robert A. Dey

ENGINEER TRAINING BRIGADE
Col. Peter J. Groh

PUBLIC AFFAIRS OFFICER
Maj. James E. Kiley Jr.

EDITOR
John Florence

ASSOCIATE EDITOR
Sp5 N. P. Lang

COVER ILLUSTRATION
designed by 1st Lt. Stephen J. Ressler.

Ellis Named Engineer School Commandant

Maj. Gen. James N. Ellis

Maj. Gen. James N. Ellis assumed command in March of the U.S. Army Engineer Center and Fort Belvoir from Maj. Gen. Max W. Noah who becomes director of Program Analysis and Evaluation, Office of the Chief of Staff of the Army.

Ellis comes to Fort Belvoir from Atlanta where he served as division engineer of the South Atlantic Division, U.S. Army Corps of Engineers (COE).

A U.S. Military Academy graduate, Ellis has a master's degree in civil engineering from the University of Illinois, is airborne and ranger qualified and is a graduate of the Army War College.

He served two tours in Vietnam; commanded companies twice in the 82d Airborne Division; was commander of the 4th Engineer Battalion, 4th Infantry Division (Mechanized); and rose to the rank of associate professor of earth, space and geographic sciences at the U.S. Military Academy.

His COE assignments include district engineer, Louisville District; executive director, Office of the Chief of Engineers; and division engineer, Middle East Division.

Ellis is a native of Cape Girardeu, Mo; he and his wife, Mareth, have three children.

VOLUME 12 SPRING 1982 NUMBER 1

FEATURES

:t Belvoir, Va. Unless specifically stated, material ap-
iny agency of the U.S. Army. All photographs contained
rinting this publication was approved by Headquarters
given to ENGINEER and the author. • **ENGINEER OBJECTIVES** are to provide a forum for the exchange of ideas, to inform and motivate and to promote the professional development of all members of the Army engineer family. • **DIRECT CORRESPONDENCE** with ENGINEER is authorized and encouraged. Inquiries, letters to the editor, manuscripts, photographs and general correspondence should be sent to: Editor, ENGINEER, U.S. Army Engineer Center, Fort Belvoir, Va. 22060. Telephone Autovon 354–3082. If a return of manuscripts or material is desired, a self-addressed envelope is required. • **SUBSCRIPTIONS** to ENGINEER are available through the Superintendent of Documents, U.S. Government Printing Office, Washington, D.C. 20402. A check or money order payable to Superintendent of Documents must accompany all subscription requests. Rates are $8.00 domestic (including APO and FPO addresses) and $10.00 for foreign addresses. Individual copies are available at $2.75 per copy to domestic addresses and $3.45 for foreign addresses. • **SECOND CLASS** postage paid at Fort Belvoir, Va. and Riverdale, Md. ISSN 0046-1989

UNITED STATES ARMY ENGINEER CENTER AND FORT BELVOIR, VA

COMMANDER/COMMANDANT
Maj. Gen. James N. Ellis

DEPUTY COMMANDANT
Col. Alvin G. Rowe

CHIEF OF STAFF/DEPUTY INSTALLATION COMMANDER
Col. David O. Cooksey

COMMAND SERGEANT MAJOR
CSM Marvin L. Knowles

DIRECTORATES

DIRECTORATE OF ENGINEER FORCE MANAGEMENT
Lt. Col. Charles S. Nichols

DIRECTORATE OF COMBAT DEVELOPMENTS
Col. Phillip R. Hoge

DIRECTORATE OF TRAINING DEVELOPMENTS
Col. John W. Devens

DIRECTORATE OF TRAINING AND DOCTRINE
Col. Stanley R. Johnson

UNITS

ENGINEER CENTER BRIGADE
Col. Robert A. Dey

ENGINEER TRAINING BRIGADE
Col. Peter J. Groh

PUBLIC AFFAIRS OFFICER
Maj. James E. Kiley Jr.

EDITOR
John Florence

ASSOCIATE EDITOR
Sp5 N. P. Lang

COVER ILLUSTRATION
designed by 1st Lt. Stephen J. Ressler.

Ellis Named Engineer School Commandant

Maj. Gen. James N. Ellis

Maj. Gen. James N. Ellis assumed command in March of the U.S. Army Engineer Center and Fort Belvoir from Maj. Gen. Max W. Noah who becomes director of Program Analysis and Evaluation, Office of the Chief of Staff of the Army.

Ellis comes to Fort Belvoir from Atlanta where he served as division engineer of the South Atlantic Division, U.S. Army Corps of Engineers (COE).

A U.S. Military Academy graduate, Ellis has a master's degree in civil engineering from the University of Illinois, is airborne and ranger qualified and is a graduate of the Army War

VOLUME 12 SPRING 1982 NUMBER 1

FEATURES

DEPARTMENTS

ENGINEER is an authorized publication of the U.S. Army Engineer Center and Fort Belvoir, Va. Unless specifically stated, material appearing herein does not necessarily reflect official policy, thinking or endorsement by any agency of the U.S. Army. All photographs contained herein are official U.S. Army photographs unless otherwise credited. Use of funds for printing this publication was approved by Headquarters Department of the Army, July 22, 1981. Material herein may be reprinted if credit is given to ENGINEER and the author. • **ENGINEER OBJECTIVES** are to provide a forum for the exchange of ideas, to inform and motivate and to promote the professional development of all members of the Army engineer family. • **DIRECT CORRESPONDENCE** with ENGINEER is authorized and encouraged. Inquiries, letters to the editor, manuscripts, photographs and general correspondence should be sent to: Editor, ENGINEER, U.S. Army Engineer Center, Fort Belvoir, Va. 22060. Telephone Autovon 354–3082. If a return of manuscripts or material is desired, a self-addressed envelope is required. • **SUBSCRIPTIONS** to ENGINEER are available through the Superintendent of Documents, U.S. Government Printing Office, Washington, D.C. 20402. A check or money order payable to Superintendent of Documents must accompany all subscription requests. Rates are $8.00 domestic (including APO and FPO addresses) and $10.00 for foreign addresses. Individual copies are available at $2.75 per copy to domestic addresses and $3.45 for foreign addresses. • **SECOND CLASS** postage paid at Fort Belvoir, Va. and Riverdale, Md. ISSN 0046–1989

by Maj. Gen. Max W. Noah

Sharing the responsibility for training developments

We often hear that finding answers to the question, "How and with what do we fight?" is the business of the Engineer School's Directorate of Combat Developments, and most of us tend to leave that issue to the designated "thinkers" in our ranks. In peacetime, a natural and vital additional question is, "How and with what do we *train* to fight?" When we look for answers to this question, we enter the world of training development. This is the milieu of the Army Training and Evaluation Program (ARTEP), *Soldier's Manual, Trainer's Guide* (formerly called *Commander's Manual*), *Job Book,* Skill Qualification Test (SQT), Training Extension Course (TEC), etc., etc., . . . all of the materials designed to help you and me plan, conduct and evaluate the training of the soldiers and units for whom we are responsible. Because we all share training responsibility to one degree or another, we need to be familiar with this world of training development. Accordingly, I'd like to discuss several points regarding some of our common training concerns.

The ARTEP

As a unit leader, the ARTEP has to be your guide for evaluating and training your unit on *most* of the tasks expected of it in combat. There may very well be additional tasks required of your unit by specific operations plans or other situations unique to your parent command. If your unit has specific combat tasks assigned to it which are not in your ARTEP, include them in your training program by all means. If you need our help in training these tasks, please let us know.

The ARTEP for most units contains a greater number of tasks than the unit can realistically train on or maintain proficiency during the course of a normal training year. Accordingly, commanders, you are expected to use the ARTEP task lists as a menu and to select from them training tasks most critical to your unit. It is a chain-of-command function to determine the criticality of tasks and training priorities. If you have any question about which tasks are critical for your unit, see your boss.

We all know that most commands use the external evaluation feature of the ARTEP as a test of unit training readiness and sometimes this bothers unit commanders. It is true that the ARTEP itself was designed as a diagnostic tool, but commanders may want to use selected elements from it for tests. Hopefully, however, such use does not inhibit use of the ARTEP for its broader, designated purposes.

Soldier's Manuals

Documenting the tasks expected of each soldier and the conditions and standards by which they are to be performed is an extremely ambitious undertaking. I recognize that the size and number of these manuals are formidable obstacles to their intended use. We are looking for your ideas on how manuals can be streamlined and still fill their intended purposes. *The Common Task Soldier's Manual* was published in June 1981. Thereafter, new or revised soldier's manuals will not duplicate the tasks contained in the common task manual. This should reduce the size of our manuals considerably.

One of the frustrations frequently expressed by unit trainers is that the soldier coming out of the training base isn't "MOS qualified." At a minimum, unit trainers need to look in the *Trainer's Guide* to find out the tasks in which the soldier should have been trained at the training base and the training tasks for which the unit is responsible. We know that the soldier coming out of the training base isn't "MOS qualified" because he has yet to be trained in all the tasks of his MOS. He, however, should be proficient in those tasks indicated as a training base responsibility in the *Trainer's Guide*. Resource constraints preclude training the new soldier to a higher level of proficiency at the training base. As a general rule, you can expect the new soldier arriving in your unit from the training base to be about 40–50 percent MOS qualified. The remaining 50–60 percent is the training job for unit commanders.

Another frustration of unit trainers is that there is no ready way to correlate the collective (unit) tasks in the unit's ARTEP with the individual tasks in the *Soldier's Manual*. If this could be done, it would make it simpler for units to concurrently train on specific individual and collective tasks, thereby making better use of precious training time. These needed "crosswalks" between collective and individual tasks are being developed, and we are furnishing them to the units concerned as they become available. Some of these crosswalks have been provided to us by field units, and we appreciate them sharing the fruits of their efforts. By the way, National Guard and Reserve units seem to be the leaders in this effort.

SQT

We, as a community, undoubtedly spend more time and effort developing and administering SQTs than on anything else in our training system. The SQT is one of the more controversial features of the system. Our common challenge, within the constraints of the SQT system, is to make the SQT supportive of the training needs of the unit as well as the individual. Ideally, I would like to see our soldiers—at all skill levels, and officers, too—demonstrate battlefield survivability skills, with each commander being able to select most of the tasks to be evaluated based on the situation in his or her particular unit.

Making Things Better

I'll be the first to admit that all of our training development products could be improved and that some of them, in fact, contain errors. We at the Engineer School don't want to be in the business of suggesting that you do something "dumb" in training your unit or your soldiers. If you find something in our products that doesn't make sense, then don't do it that way. (Unless, of course, your boss says otherwise. In that case, you have a problem with your boss, not with the product.) Please don't keep potential training improvements a secret. We're never going to get our training development products healthy if you don't let us know what is wrong with them and share your suggestions for improvements. We may not be able to make all the changes you suggest, but I guarantee that they will be given honest consideration. Address your comments to:

Commandant
U.S. Army Engineer School
ATTN: ATZA-TD
Fort Belvoir, VA 22060

or call us on the Engineer Hotline.

This is my final article as commandant. My year-and-a-half at the School has been much too short, but we have a number of new initiatives started in the combat engineering arena which you out there in the Army need to push. Doctrine and training is the business of all of us. Mobility and countermobility is our game. Topographic information is an important piece. And all this needs to be more up front where the shooting is. Fast, survivable, deployable—that's what we need. Your Army deserves no less. Let's "Clear the Way!"

Noah
Engineer

ENGINEER HOTLINE

Engineer related problems, questions and comments can be addressed telephonically to the U.S. Army Engineer School's "Engineer Hotline." The Hotline's auto-answer recorder operates 24 hours a day, seven days a week. Callers should state their name, address and telephone number, followed by a concise question or comment.

The School's Coordination and Review Branch, part of the Training Literature Division, Directorate of Training Developments, has experts analyze your problem and reply directly to you within three to 15 days. The Hotline is not intended as a receiving agency for formal requests.

Call commercial (703) 664–3646; WATS 800–336–3095, extension 3646; or AV 354–3646.

NEW BRIDGE REINFORCEMENT SYSTEM

The U.S. Army Mobility Equipment Research and Development Command (MERADCOM) has awarded $370,050 to Fiber Materials, Inc., to develop a bridge reinforcement system using organic composite materials. The contractor will design a reinforcement system, test the system according to MERADCOM standards, develop a pilot production line and produce 20 composite tensile elements from the pilot production line.

The new reinforcement system is similar to the one currently developed as part of the Bridging For The 80s program. Use of graphite epoxy composites, however, will reduce the system's weight from 95 pounds for the developed steel version to 26 pounds for the new design. Delivery of the reinforcement sets is scheduled for September 1982.

MSgt. Boyd Crawford displays the inert training round he developed with the help of the Fort McCoy, Wis., Training Aids Services Office.

INERT ROUND DEVELOPED FOR CEV

MSgt. Boyd Crawford, U.S. Army Readiness Group, Fort McCoy, Wis., and the post's Training Aids Services Office (TASO), have developed an inert practice round for the combat engineer vehicle (CEV) main gun.

The dummy round, made of elastomer polyurethane plastic, costs about $70 and weighs 41 pounds. A live round weighs 65.5 pounds; the weight of the inert round can be increased if necessary.

The Wisconsin Army National Guard's 32d Engineer Company, 32d Infantry Brigade (Mech), Onalaska, Wis., reports the round shows almost no wear after more than two months testing.

Contact MSgt. Crawford at (608) 388–3991 for more information.

RDF TO RECEIVE WATER PURIFIERS

A $4.5 million contract for water purification units for the Rapid Deployment Joint Task Force has been awarded to Cosmodyne, Inc. by the U.S. Army Mobility Equipment Research and Development Command. Cosmodyne, a division of Avel Corp., is producing 14 reverse osmosis water purification units each capable of purifying 150,000 gallons of water per day. The commercial units will be used until larger militarized systems are developed.

The first finished units were expected to be delivered in February.

ENGINEER WET GAP TRAINING

Selecting a CONUS wet gap training site for engineer units is in its final stages. The leading contender seems to be the Arkansas River wet gap training site at Fort Chaffee, Ark. Although final selection and site development are several months away, the area is now available for use by active, Reserve, or National Guard units year round.

The area has one mile of frontage and 2,500 acres of maneuver area, with access routes to the river but no prepared launch sites yet. Water gap width ranges from 750 to 1,000 feet, with an average depth of 25 feet. The water runs three-to-eight feet per second; the near shore is sandy and the far shore is riprap.

Plans call for construction of three tactical crossing sites during summer 1982. Road net and bivouac areas can be improved/constructed as required by training units. Barracks are available year-round. Contact Lt. Col. Richard L. Brown, AV 962–2840, for further information.

ENGINEER DINNER DATE IS SET

Active and retired engineer officers worldwide are cordially invited to celebrate the Corps' 207th anniversary at the 115th Annual Engineer Dinner at Fort Belvoir, Va., May 14.

Highlight of the evening will be the annual presentation of the Itschner Awards to the year's most outstanding engineer company of the active Army, Reserve and National Guard, and the Sturgis Award to the Corps' preeminent enlisted soldier.

The dinner begins at 6:30 p.m. at Mackenzie Hall (post officers' club). Spouses of attending officers are invited to the 6th Annual Counterpart Dinner scheduled concurrently at the Fort Belvoir Main Club (NCO club).

Theme for the counterpart dinner is "Das Heidleberger Schloss" and attendees will be treated to a performance of "The Student Prince."

Following the dinners, at 10 p.m., is the Castle Ball at Mackenzie Hall.

Tickets for the engineer dinner are $14 each and available in advance by sending a check or money order, payable to the 115th Annual Engineer Dinner, to Post Office Box 552, U.S. Army Engineer Center, Fort Belvoir, Va., 22060.

Tickets for the counterpart dinner cost $10.50 each; $5 each for the Castle Ball. For tickets, send check or money order payable to Annual Counterpart Dinner and/or Castle Ball to Mrs. John T. Miller, 9813 Doulton Court, Fairfax, Va., 22030.

Reservations and ticket purchases for all events must be made by May 7.

CORPS TO CONSTRUCT SINAI INSTALLATIONS

The U.S. Army Corps of Engineers has been designated construction agent for the Multinational Force and Observers (MFO), an international peacekeeping force established as a result of the 1979 Camp David Accords between Israel and Egypt.

Construction for the MFO includes two base camps, one in northern Sinai at Eitam Air Base and one in the south near Sharm el Sheikh. The base camps will support a force of about 2,500.

Under the terms of the Camp David Accords, the Sinai is to be demilitarized by April 25, 1982; the peacekeeping force must be in place prior to that date.

Col. William E. Lee Jr., the contracting officer, has assumed command of the Sinai Construction Office in Tel Aviv, Israel, with a resident engineer office established at each of the two construction sites.

GEOTECHNICAL LAB DEDICATED TO CASAGRANDE BY CHIEF

The new $4.6 million geotechnical laboratory at the U.S. Army Engineer Waterways Experiment Station (WES), Vicksburg, Miss., has been dedicated the Arthur Casagrande Building by Chief of Engineers Lt. Gen. Joseph K. Bratton.

The 82,000 sq. ft. building houses research facilities for soil mechanics, geology and rock mechanics, earthquake engineering, pavement systems, and both the soils testing facility and the soils research center. The laboratory also includes a center of mobility expertise.

Casagrande was recognized as the world's foremost specialist in soil mechanics and foundation engineering and their application to civil engineering works. He served as a teacher and consultant to the Corps of Engineers for 46 years and was a Gordon McKay Professor in soil mechanics and foundation engineering at Harvard University until his recent death.

AIRBORNE ENGINEERS WALK ON WATER

(photo by Richard E. Sharp)

With help from a "no visible means of support" bridge, soldiers of the 3rd platoon, Company B, 307th Engineer Battalion, 82d Airborne Division, walk on water.

Responding to a challenge from their battalion commander, the men rappelled into an area near Fort Bragg's McArthur Lake, conducted a mock river assault and, after securing both shores, began this uniqúe bridge construction task.

Twelve-foot 'deadmen' on both shores served as anchors and three cables were stretched across a 150 foot wet gap. To them was attached a continuous ribbon of aluminum mats. The finished product provided an invisible bridge for ¼-ton trucks, and supported the weight of a Gamma Goat.

BERRY IS NAMED MISSOURI YOUNG ENGINEER

Reserve Capt. Robert T. Berry has been named 1981 Missouri Young Engineer of the Year by the Missouri Society of Professional Engineers.

Berry, a civil engineer on the Kansas City Survey Team, an element of the 416th Engineer Command (USAR), previously served with the 471st Engineer Company (USAR), Rolla, Mo. During four years of active duty, he served in Germany with the 317th Engineer Battalion (Combat) and with the 1st Engineer Battalion (Combat), Fort Riley, Kan.

He currently works for a Kansas City engineering company as project manager for wastewater facilities, design and construction and other public works.

Berry received a degree in civil engineering from the University of Missouri and a master's in engineering management from Boston University. Additionally, he has a M.S. in environmental health engineering and a doctorate of engineering degree from the University of Kansas.

NEW RIFLE RANGE FOR RAMSTEIN

A $400,000 rifle and pistol range was constructed by the 1st platoon, Company C, 79th Engineer Battalion (Combat) (Heavy), for the 86th Tactical Fighter Wing (USAF), at Ramstein, West Germany.

The facility includes a 25-meter pistol range, 50 and 100-meter rifle ranges and a 50-meter track mounted, moveable targets system range. The ranges will be used by the U.S. Air Force and Army, the German polizei special weapons teams and by enthusiastic sportsmen in the Kaiserslautern area.

CAPSTONE CONFERENCE

Key participants in a major CAPSTONE training conference sponsored recently by the 264th Engineer Group, Wisconsin Army National Guard, included, from left, in photo below, Col. Richard Polo, commander, 7th Engineer Brigade, USAREUR; Maj. Gen. Raymond Matera, Wisconsin Guard adjutant general; and Col. Jerome Berard, commander, 264th Engineers.

The two-day conference brought together in Eau Claire, Wis., representatives from 23 active and reserve component (RC) units.

Also present were syndics from FORSCOM, the Engineer School, two readiness and mobilization regions, two reserve maneuver training commands, and readiness group personnel from four states.

Unit commanders were briefed on relationships and training priorities while RC staff personnel were able to coordinate directly with their active Army counterparts.

The CAPSTONE program provides planning and training association between active and RC units to expedite wartime deployment.

TRAPPED!

An antitank ditch constructed by the 15th Engineers, 9th Infantry Division, snags a M-60 tank from the division's 2/72d Armor during a Fort Lewis, Wash., FTX.

USAR UNITS MAY WEAR ACTIVE PATCHES

Army Reserve units having training affiliations with an active Army unit are now authorized to wear the shoulder sleeve insignia of the active component unit.

DA Uniform Board officials have noted that local approval to wear the insignia is subject to mutual agreement between the reserve unit's Major U.S. Army Reserve Command and the active Army unit commander.

The new policy is included in an interim change to AR 670–1, which was published last fall.

Previously, only Army National Guard units were authorized to wear the patches of their affiliated units.

ENGINEERS CONSTRUCT AIR STRIP AT A.P. HILL

The 618th Engineer Company (LE)(ABN) recently parachuted into Fort A.P. Hill, Va., along with 29 pallet-loads of equipment to begin a 12-day, around-the-clock marathon to construct a 5,000-ft. assault air strip. Commanded by Capt. George D. Mitroka, the unit is attached to the 307th Engineer Battalion (CBT)(ABN), 82d Airborne Division.

Assisted by the 11th Engineer Battalion (CBT)(HVY), Fort Belvoir, Va., the strip was completed three days ahead of schedule. The strip allows units to be airlifted to Fort A.P. Hill, avoiding time consuming truck convoying.

Air Force pilots will use the strip to practice landings and takeoffs from unimproved facilities.

—*FORUM*—

"Pro-Pay" For Degrees?

by Capt. Robert L. McClure

With the Reagan administration's increase in defense spending, an interesting possibility for Engineer officers has appeared. It may now become feasible to pay Army engineers and scientists for their talents, much the same as is now done with military doctors. The reason cited for doing so is to combat the low retention rate for such officers in all services. While the Air Force and Navy may have problems unique to them that only money will solve, paying Army Engineers extra is a mistake.

To deny that the services don't need scientists and "hard core" engineers is foolish. The Air Force definitely needs aeronautical engineers and scientists for its highly technical equipment. With the civil works mission in the Army Corps of Engineers, those of us with castles on our collars also fully recognize the need for career officers with a formal engineer education. Even though it is possible to have a successful career in the Engineers without a PE or engineering degree, the perception still exists that to get a battalion command or choice district assignment one needs to be a certified engineer. The perception, especially from the company grade officer, is that only certified engineers (engineering or PE) make it to "the top" in the Corps. At the least, they believe certain assignments will forever elude those officers not "hard core" engineers.

But the Corps of Engineers isn't *all* technical and engineer intensive. Anyone who has served in a combat engineer battalion knows that constructing a tank ditch does not require a civil engineering degree from Georgia Tech. This is one reason the Army accepts into the Corps so many officers without engineering degrees.

Recent Engineer Officer Basic Course classes have averaged from 40 to 60 percent "hard core" engineers in terms of education. The remainder have included officers with a variety of degrees ranging from music to biology to history.

While the need for an engineering degree at the junior officer level is not critical, its importance increases above the rank of major. This is when the percentage of assignments requiring an engineer background rises due to the district and research missions given the Corps. Today a rejuvenated civilian engineer job market hires away "hard core" Engineer officers at a high rate, while the need for such talent in the Army has not decreased. To cover the shortfall, some officers from other branches (Infantry, Armor, etc.) now have a Skill Code (SC) 21 additional specialty. Usually their educational background has earned them assignments to a variety of civil works districts. However, this practice of assigning SC 21 as an additional specialty still fails to address the *retention* problem for engineer skilled officers.

The foregoing begs the obvious question: Why not pay officers with engineering and science degrees a bonus to help stem the tide of resignations? Combat engineer purists abhor the idea. For the past several years, we Engineers have tried hard to be a combat arm and have done a fairly good job. In war, engineers will be critical on the battlefield; the infantry and armor will not be able to move and to survive without us, it's that simple. Army, not Engineer, doctrine has us a member of the combined arms team—where we belong. In war, we have a battlefield, not a technical mission. If for no other reason, the teamwork demanded of combined arms operations says no branch is more equal than the other. In such a situation, why should the engineer be paid more than the artilleryman?

Leaving that argument aside for a minute, let's examine this "pro-pay." Who should we pay? Obviously not all Engineers because not everyone has an engineering degree. Perhaps a performance standard is desired. To receive the bonus, an Engineer officer would need a technical degree (of a type to be specified) and a professional engineer license. This sounds logical, but what impact would it have on promotion/selection boards? It would probably exacerbate the already perceived split between those with and without engineer credentials.

How about creating a new specialty code? This would be an additional specialty meant primarily for those interested in district engineer assignments, facilities engineering, or specialized research connected with their degree. To get the bonus, an officer must have the required education/credentials *and* work in a specified job. A new specialty code would also address another problem vexing personnel managers. Currently with SC 21 used as both an initial *and* additional specialty, it is (theoretically) possible for an Infantry officer with an SC 21 additional specialty to command an engineer battalion. A new specialty code would solve this problem by reserving SC 21 for exclusive use as an initial entry specialty.

With the real problem being engineer retention, could we not make other incentives available rather than money? Instead of spending money buying "hard core" engineers, let's transfer that money into increased educational opportunities for the junior officer. More education earlier may increase the number of Engineer officers that stay beyond their initial term of service, thereby slowing the resignation rate. Let's face it, the Army needs "hard core" engineers but is not retaining them at an acceptable rate. Simply throwing money at the problem will not solve it. I contend that paying bonuses to Engineer officers is inappropriate and would be a mistake.

Capt. Robert L. McClure is a graduate of the U.S. Military Academy and the Engineer Officer Advanced Course. He completed airborne and ranger training and served in Germany with the 12th Engineer Battalion as a platoon leader and company commander. Capt. McClure is currently assigned to Headquarters, U.S. Army Engineer Center, Fort Belvoir, Va.

Nonjudicial punishment

Company Commande As Judge and Jury

When it comes to handling minor military offenses and misconduct, one of the most valuable aids to the unit commander is nonjudicial punishment. The president of the United States grants commanders the authority to punish in accordance with Article 15 of the *Uniform Code of Military Justice* (as stated in the *Manual for Courts-Martial*), however, *proper use* of the Article 15 is the key to a successful command.

The Article 15 is not always the answer, and commanders must know when and whether to use it. The following discussion considers proper actions commanders should take, beginning with the discovery of an offense through the imposition of punishment, including the effects of punishment on the individual soldier and his unit.

"Why did this offense take place?" "What could have been done to prevent it?" These questions continually plague commanders. However, leadership and true concern for the individual soldier will normally reduce the number of offenses within a unit. Absent without leave (AWOL), for example, is a specific offense often preventable. Sincere, positive and concerned leadership is the most important element in the prevention of AWOL.[1] Good leadership in the military is important, especially at lower command echelons where it directly interacts with individual soldiers. A good leader, one who knows and cares for his subordinates and keeps them informed, can prevent many offenses frequently punished under Article 15. But when misconduct does occur, commanders must carefully consider the evidence before deciding what course of action to take. Evidence must be complete and valid.

by Maj. Raymond F. Powell

Will the evidence stand up in a court of law? Inexperienced leaders often request punishment based on evidence that is biased, unfounded or where the rights of the individual were violated. The severity of the offense and the record of the individual must be judiciously considered.

Punishment must be understood by the commander. Punishment only maintains minimum standards by motivating behavior up to a minimally acceptable level. It should be used when an individual fails to respond to positive incentives or for a lack of motivation, not a lack of ability or training. Punishment is not always the solution. If an individual has failed, but tried hard, and was punished, he will not try again. Lack of ability should be corrected by means such as extra training, most probably on the individual's own time.[2]

Alternatives to punishment have a greater corrective impact than punishment. Extra training, reprimands, suspension of privileges and formal counseling all have their effect. The main point is that the individual is aware of his misconduct. He knows his superior is aware, and he knows that recurring actions will be dealt with more severely. A basic leadership point is that a minor offense does not have to go to the commander, but may be corrected with alternatives at the lowest level appropriate.

The commander should decide how to handle alleged misconduct after reviewing evidence and the recommendations of his subordinates. Throughout this detailed process, the individual still has the right to a speedy trial and delays cannot be tolerated. The commander should review alternatives to punishment, and especially, learn what subordinate leaders have previously done to prevent the alleged misconduct.

The commander deciding to use nonjudicial punishment (Article 15), must do it properly, as in a court of law. Legal advice may be necessary. The charges must be prepared explicitly in accordance with the *Manual For Courts-Martial.* Charges must be able to stand in a court-martial; if they cannot, punishment under the provisions of Article 15 should not be imposed. There are specific rules and guidance to follow for the imposition of Article 15 punishment. Further guidance is to use common sense leadership and human relations.

At Article 15 proceedings, the commander is both judge and jury, and his office is the court room. Proceedings must be held in a professional manner with military bearing and dignity. Distractions such as telephone calls and clutter on a desk should be eliminated. The individual's chain-of-command should be present not only to tell their side but to hear exactly what the commander tells the individual. Every proceeding should be considered a counseling session, not just as a time set aside for the imposition of punishment. If witnesses or other evidence are required, the proceedings should be recessed and properly completed later to ensure the full rights of the individual are respected.

The judge/commander must communicate in a fair and equitable manner without playing favorites. He must listen to the facts and to the individual and must remove any prejudices or preconceived notions he may have. He must *prove* the soldier guilty (if, in fact, he is guilty), not just try to see if he is innocent. The most important part of the proceeding is that the commander must communicate with the individual. Barriers to communication will definitely hinder any results. As with any good form of leadership activity, there is no room for profanity, which is only an excuse for poor language and communication abilities. The entire process is centered around communication and respect.

"Fourteen days extra duty, reduction to grade E-3..." The actual imposition of punishment, no matter to what degree, should be completely thought out. The purpose of punishment under Article 15 should be corrective in nature.[3] The goals of punishment should be to protect society against a repetition of the offense, to reform the individual so he will be less likely to repeat the offense, and to deter others from considering and undertaking such an offense.[4] The commander must make the punishment fit the crime and the individual, plus set the example for others. He must also evaluate the probable effects of the punishment upon the individual and the unit. Care should be taken not to compound existing problems. Properly used, suspension of punishment provides a behavioral incentive to the offender and an excellent opportunity to evaluate the individual during the period of suspension.[5] With well considered and explained punishment, the individual knows why he is being punished. He also perceives that the punishment and his hearing were fair and will think twice about committing the offense again.

There are many benefits of properly conducted proceedings, including that the individual gains respect for the commander and supervisors despite punishment. This infectious respect along with the group's knowledge of the commander's standard will result in a unit with fewer problems. Individual soldiers should be allowed to progress upon completion of punishment, the purpose being to help them improve as soldiers and to motivate them to do their jobs without carrying the burden of a previous punishment. Many times a good soldier is left improperly punished, without a chance to improve and a potential is therefore lost by the military.

The commander's job is vast with administering nonjudicial punishment under Article 15 only one of his responsibilities. However, the number of offenses he must review will be reduced when they are properly and expeditiously handled. With fewer offenses, all leaders within the chain-of-command will have more positive time for the individual soldier, creating a more harmonious and stronger Army.

Maj. Raymond F. Powell is a graduate of the Engineer Officer Advanced Course and Command and General Staff College. He graduated from Rutgers University with a B.S. in engineering and the University of Missouri at Rolla with an M.S. in engineering management. He served two tours in Vietnam, including duty as an aviation platoon leader and as the S-3 of Engineer Region III. Other duty includes company commands with the 75th and 5th Engineer Battalions, assistant PMS at Princeton University and XO of the 43rd Engineer Battalion. He is currently on the staff of the Command and General Staff College.

FOOTNOTES:

1. U.S. Army FM 22-100, *Military Leadership*, page 16-3.
2. U.S. Army FM 22-100, *Military Leadership*, page 8-5.
3. *Manual for Courts-Martial*, 1969, U.S. Government Printing Office, page 26-3.
4. U.S. Army FM 27-1, *Legal Guide for the Commander*, page 8-1.
5. *Manual for Courts-Martial*, 1969, U.S. Government Printing Office, page 26-3.

Your Unparalleled Heritage

Secretary of the Army John O. Marsh Jr. speaks to Engineer Officer Basic Course 7-81.

Last month, the nation marked the 200th anniversary of the battle where our independence was won—Yorktown. The freedom and independence declared in Philadelphia was won after six and one-half years of war on a peninsula in Virginia. Those great words—life, liberty and the pursuit of happiness—were given real meaning.

The last line of that declaration pledged the lives, fortunes and sacred honor of the signers. Washington, our first commander-in-chief, did not sign the Declaration of Independence because he had resigned from the Continental Congress to take command of the Army. If that document could have been submitted to him, along with the surrender agreement, the same comment he placed on the surrender agreement with his signature he might have penned on the bottom of the declaration: "Done in the trenches before Yorktown, October 19, 1781".

Many times the Army has gone into the trenches to achieve or preserve freedom. The final victory in the Revolution was the result of a great operation by the engineers of Washington and Rochambeau, who employed in a classic way the techniques of siege engineering.

The engineers are a key part of our Revolutionary history and go back to the founding of the Army. This Revolution led to the establishment of a school of engineering which in 1802 became the United States Military Academy. The rationale for educating officers focused on training engineers. The need to train engineers led to the establishment of the Virginia Military Institute and Norwich University.

After the Revolution, two great events further emphasized the importance of Army engineers; the Louisiana Purchase in 1803 and the Mexican War. With them came vast land areas to be explored and surveyed, roads to be opened and canals to be built.

The War Between the States, or the Civil War, has been called the first of the modern wars. Also, it was a war of firsts:

- The first to use the railroads. This impacted on logistics and troop movements;
- The first to employ the telegraph which collapsed time and distance in communications;
- The first to employ ironclads;
- The first to use aerial reconnaissance; and,
- The first to be recorded photographically thanks to Mathew Brady.

It was the first war of modern engineering. Legendary feats were undertaken by the engineers in both armies. The war saw constructed one of the first, and also the longest, pontoon bridges ever built. It crossed the James River and its span was 2,200 feet. History records that on one occasion Union engineers built a 2,000 foot pontoon bridge in seven hours. This type of bridging over major rivers was commonplace by both armies during that struggle.

Today, the role of the Corps of Engineers continues to be unique. It has a dual mission—one military and one civil. The civil mission goes back to the earliest days of the republic when the country looked to the Corps for engineering experience as America moved west. This took the Corps into rivers and harbors, flood control, dredging, dams, canals and other significant construction projects. You have a great heritage of building America, and your monuments are to be found in every state. This experience in the civilian sector makes available a trained force, constantly ready to meet mission requirements of a wartime environment.

We live in a critical time where readiness not only of the Corps but the Army and of our sister services is essential. I will not cite the many problem areas that are so prevalent around the globe, but let me say there are seven major geographical areas of concern. These areas are:

Europe. Where NATO forces are counter-poised to prevent aggression by the Warsaw Pact;
Africa. That continent that is the scene of great instability and political crosscurrents, but is so vital to the West because of its resources;
The Middle East. What at times appears to be a tinderbox of conflict;
Southwest Asia. Where we find Soviet combat forces in Afganistan;
Northeast Asia. Where U.S. forces, along with our Korean allies, safeguard the Korean peninsula;
Southeast Asia. Which is still gripped by oppression; and,
Latin America. Where we see instability in parts of our own hemisphere.

To an audience such as this, it is not necessary for me to dwell on the challenges we face, or the need for a strong defense. You are aware of this. Wherever U.S. forces may be deployed—as the president has noted—it is our purpose to prevent conflict and deter war through a strong strategic and conventional capability. Fundamental to this strength is the Corps of Engineers. That strength is directly related to you and the kind of person you are and the officer you become.

As you pursue your career, let me make several suggestions which I hope will stand you in good stead. Some of these are drawn from an examination of the life of George Marshall—chief of staff of the Army, secretary of defense, secretary of state and Nobel Prize winner.

Throughout his military career, from the time he entered the Virginia Military Institute as a cadet, until his retirement from active service in 1945, his life was one of training, self-learning and self-discipline.

The American poet, Longfellow, wrote:

"Lives of great men all re-

mind us
We can make our lives sublime,
And departing, leave behind us
Footprints on the sands of time."

Marshall had the ability to select priorities and pursue them with perseverence. Early in his career he developed a sense of cost discipline and the careful management of resources. He developed the ability to take a complex matter and reduce it to a simple, understandable, workable plan. The secret to this is thoroughness which produced understanding and mastery of a subject.

Marshall was also receptive to new ideas. He was innovative and creative and was willing to take risks with new ideas. Time for Marshall was a resource. Because you are young, you may not realize that time is a resource. Longfellow, wrote:

"The heights by great men reached and kept,
Were not attained by sudden flight,
But they while their companions slept,
Were toiling upward in the night."

Because time is a resource, there are four areas in which I would like to see you devote more of your time. They are in the nature of s.lf-improvement and study.

First, I urge you to acquire a greater knowledge of geography so that you have a better understanding of place and people, terrain and resources. This takes you into demographics and economic geography. A greater understanding by Americans of the world's people and where resources are located is important.

A second area in which I would like for you to invest time is developing a language capability. In a world that is not only competitive, but also one in which there is a great need for cooperation, Americans and American interests are handicapped by the lack of this ability.

I would like for you to place greater emphasis on writing and the ability to present your thoughts cogently, with clarity and understanding in written form. This is a difficult task. However I was once told that hard writing makes easy reading.

Lastly, you should develop a program for maintaining physical fitness. It will require self-discipline.

Essential to the Corps are the young officers who provide leadership. In your ranks have marched such American military leaders as Robert E. Lee and George Meade, who commanded opposing armies at Gettysburg.

You have an unparalleled heritage. It was an Army engineer who, at the request of the Russian czar in 1842, built the first railroad in Russia from Saint Petersburg to Moscow.

It was men in the 11th Engineer Regiment—today the 11th Engineer Battalion stationed at Fort Belvoir—that took the first casualties in World War I as they sought to make a passageway across no-man's land for an Allied assault.

It was U.S. combat engineers that landed at Normandy and Utah Beach on D-Day an hour before the first wave of American infantry.

In World War II, the Corps of Engineers, under the most adverse terrain and climate conditions, built the Alcan Highway which was 1,500 miles in length. It took only eight months to complete.

Army engineers, under Col. George Goethals, constructed one of the great engineering marvels of the world when they built the Panama Canal—a task which the builders of the Suez Canal failed to achieve in seven years time, and cost the lives of 22,000 workers.

It might surprise you to know after the War Between the States, it was Army engineers who redesigned and completed the construction of the Washington Monument.

If you were to ascend the steps of the Washington Monument, you would find placed in the sides of the monument, stones taken from various states, reminders that ours is a union of many. At about the 500 foot level, you can see a white, polished stone taken from the ruins of ancient Carthage.

Other than an identification of the donor who gave the stone during the last century, there is nothing to indicate why, in a monument that is uniquely American, there is displayed a stone taken from a city the 20th century does not know. Carthage once flourished on the southern shores of the Mediterranean Sea; prosperous in trade and in commerce, and material wealth, it was the pride and envy of the ancient world. But, Carthage was destroyed by Rome.

Could it be this stone from that great but forgotten city was placed there to remind us that material wealth and progress are never substitutions for national will?

However, this is not the end of the story. Remember something else when you see that monument. I mentioned to you earlier that the Army engineers redesigned and finished the construction of the Washington Monument. At the peak of the monument, the capstone, is a small pyramid made of 100 ounces of aluminum—the largest piece of aluminum that had been cast up to that time. It was placed there on the 6th day of December 1884. Inscribed on its base are these words:

"Chief Engineer and Architect,
Colonel Thomas Lincoln Casey,
Corps of Engineers."

Today is a time of farewells. Shortly, you will go your separate ways. Some to the Regulars, some to the Reserves, some to the Guard. Wherever duty takes you, I am proud you are officers in the Army. I thank you for your service to our country.

Emerson wrote:

"So nigh is granduer to our dust,
So close is God to man;
When duty whispers low thou must,
The youth replies, I can."

And, I know that is the reply of this graduating class today.

Secretary of the Army John O. Marsh Jr., an infantry officer with U.S. occupation forces in Germany following World War II, is a law school graduate of Washington and Lee University. He served in the U.S. House of Representatives from 1963–71 and was Vice President Ford's assistant for national security in 1974. As a Virginia Army National Guardsman, he completed airborne and jumpmaster schools, and retired from the Guard as a Lt. Col. in 1976. His son, Scot, was a graduate of EOBC 7–81.

BRIGHT STAR

The Engineer Perspective.

by Lt. Col. Raymond E. Knell

Remember those recruiting posters that promised to show you the world? Remember hoping that your unit would be selected for a special off-post exercise? For the members of Task Force Tiger, those dreams came true during Joint Training Exercise (JTX) Bright Star 82, the second in a series of deployment and training exercises in Southwest Asia sponsored by the Rapid Deployment Joint Task Force (RDJTF).

JTX Bright Star 82 was conducted in November-December, 1981, in Egypt, Sudan, Oman and Somalia. While the operations in Egypt were widely publicized, the exercise in Somalia was particularly important to engineers. The RDJTF mission to the 20th Engineer Brigade (Combat) (Airborne) of XVIII Airborne Corps at Fort Bragg, N.C., was to form a task force of engineers, accompanied by medical teams, military police and terminal port personnel, to deploy by air and sea to Berbera, a small village on the north coast of Somalia. Once deployed, the unit would conduct a logistical assessment of the area.

The 20th Engineer Brigade, in turn, tasked its 27th Engineer Battalion (Combat) (Airborne) to organize, train, equip and to deploy a self-contained joint task force (JTF) by air and sea to the vicinity of Berbera; to exist in an unknown, harsh desert environment; to be good guests in a foreign land; to gather medical and terrain information; to train in a realistic mission environment; to complete quick, visible, high-impact action projects as a token and remembrance of our presence; to redeploy, debrief, and disband; and to capture and disseminate terrain information and lessons learned.

The mission was historic. This would be the first significant U.S. military presence in Somalia since the Russians were expelled in 1977. Somalia is the horn of Africa; to the north lies the Gulf of Aden and the narrow straits to the Red Sea, to the east the Indian Ocean. Berbera is a small village with a deepwater port. In the mid-1970's the Soviet Union initiated a massive construction program near Berbera building a 400 bed hospital, a water distribution system, a desalination plant, a causeway and pier, a POL tank farm and jetty, a missile support and maintenance area and an airfield capable of handling any aircraft in the world.

When the Somalis demanded that the Russians leave the country, the Soviets left in extreme haste, leaving most of the construction program unfinished.

The JTF, dubbed Task Force Tiger for the 27th's nickname, the Tiger Battalion, was a composite, short-term, self-sustaining organization. Some 35 different company-sized units were represented. Elements of the 20th Engineer Brigade's 27th and 548th Engineer Battalions provided the general engineer capability of the force. Cartographers, terrain analysts, bridge specialists and surveyors represented the remaining units of the brigade. The Air Force's Air-Land Control Element, Red Horse and Prime Beef teams as well as elements of the Army's 7th Transportation Group, 16th Military Police Brigade and Fort Bragg medical teams provided airhead, port, security and field hospital capability. A Joint Services Communication Element (JSCE) satellite communications terminal provided Task Force Tiger access to reliable communications by teletype and voice with the RDJTF exercise headquarters near Cairo, Egypt. Task Force Tiger was capable of sustained independent operation, requiring only air resupply of rations and local procurement of raw water and fuel.

JTX Bright Star units in Egypt experienced many of the problems of desert warfare, including severe sandstorms. This was not the case for Task Force Tiger. Although there was heat and sand, the climate was not severe. The terrain near Berbera is a desert coastal plain; the soil is sandy silt with angular rock fragments up to the size of a fist. The top 4 to 6 inches of soil is extremely dry and appears to be porous, but is not. Below the dry surface, the soil is the same composition but very densely packed. Significant time and effort are required to dig sumps, latrines, or fighting positions with hand tools; entrenching tools are almost useless. Scrub trees up to 20 feet tall dot the plain, providing concealment from ground-level observation for up to 2½-ton trucks. The trees provide no concealment for vehicles from aerial observation. The coastal plain ends 10 to 20 miles inland, becoming a highland plateau. Weather and terrain data vary drastically between the coastal plain and the highlands; data from one area cannot be used for the other area.

In the June-August hot season, the temperature in Berbera reaches 115 F in the shade, and a stiff wind is routine. The coastal weather during the exercise, however, was sunny, with highs in the upper 80s, lows in the upper 60s and a light 5 to 8 knot breeze.

The exercise provided the engineers unique challenges in planning the deployment, coordinating among task force members and with other agencies, deploying to a strange area and conducting training and operations with their Somali hosts.

Planning for the exercise was based on only limited knowledge of the exercise area. Although a RDJTF and 20th Engineer Brigade survey team visited Berbera for a few hours in September, detailed information about the area was scarce. The most critical planning task was defining the task force organization and mission. Simultaneous planning for the Somali portion of JTX Bright Star occurred at RDJTF headquarters, at XVIII Airborne Corps and at the multiple units represented in Task Force Tiger. Daily, vigorous coordination was necessary to keep abreast of new initiatives.

Operational security also influenced planning and coordination. The location and dates of the exercise were classified until immediately prior to deployment. Initially, soldiers knew that they were deploying to Southwest Asia. Only key leaders, however, knew the country and deployment schedule. Most of the soldiers believed that they were going to Egypt. Immediately prior to deployment, the task force was assembled and isolated in a secure "lock-in" area, and operational briefings revealed the destination and schedule.

Heavy equipment for Task Force Tiger arrives in Berbera by sea from Savannah, Ga.

Many of the preparations for the deployment were normal procedures for members of the Rapid Deployment Force or for other units whose contingencies call for overseas deployment. Medical and personnel records review, immunization update, equipment preparation and personnel roster reconciliation were all normal preparations for overseas exercises. The only special training required was for operation of the new 600-gallon-per-hour reverse osmosis water purification unit (ROWPU) and the water chiller attachment for the 400-gallon water trailer.

The development of deployment load plans on the other hand, posed unique challenges. Limited information was available about the area, and the absence of previous exercises in Somalia meant that no after-action reports were available to help determine what to take and how to move it. The task force was allocated one C5A and a fixed amount of deck space on the roll-on/roll-off ship *Cygnus* for oversized equipment, and nine C141 aircraft for troops and the remaining equip-

TASK FORCE TIGER

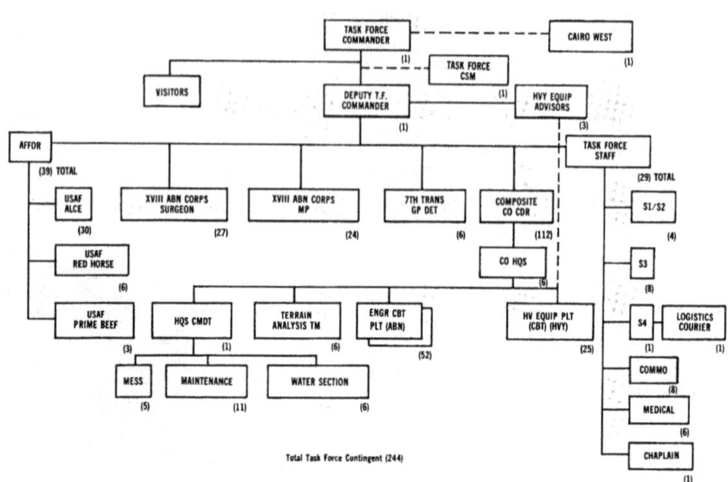

ment. What should go by ship? How should the remainder be distributed among the aircraft? Would the first plane to take off be the first to land? What prime movers had to be available at Berbera to unload non-motorized equipment? Deployment load plans were the greatest challenge of the exercise. Four constraints were adopted for all load plans.

(1) Only bulk amounts of petroleum, oils and lubricants (POL) and raw water would be available from the Somalis. Everything else had to fit on available transportation.

(2) Food and drinkable water would accompany the soldiers on each aircraft to sustain them until the ROWPU and the food resupply cycle from Egypt were operational.

(3) The troop and equipment list would be general enough to provide for reasonable changes in the mission after arrival in Somalia.

(4) The loss or delayed arrival of any one piece of equipment would not endanger mission accomplishment.

Equipment for the sea shipment left Fort Bragg on October 16 and the *Cygnus* sailed from Savannah, Ga., on October 19. With one intermediate stop at Alexandria, Egypt, and a day-long delay through the Suez Canal, the *Cygnus* arrived at Berbera on November 17. The air deployment left Pope Air Force Base (adjacent to Fort Bragg) on November 14 and 15 and arrived on the 15th and 16th. Although some aircraft took longer to arrive than the planned 18 hours and the sequence of arrival differed from that of departure, all sorties arrived at Berbera by the scheduled end of the airflow. The planning for out-of-sequence arrival paid off; there was temporary inconvenience but no mission or safety reduction.

Once in country, all elements of Task Force Tiger moved quickly to accomplish their mission. Teams designed to gather medical and terrain information found many opportunities to improve U.S. knowledge of the local facilities and terrain. A terrain analysis team from the 283d Engineer Detachment at Fort Bragg spent most of its time on the road, gathering data for map revisions and verifications, such as the new major highway linking Berbera and Mogadishu which replaces significant portions of the route currently shown on 1:250,000 scale maps. Preventive medicine teams gathered water samples from each of the fresh water sources for Berbera. No harmful bacteria or virus was found in any sample.

Specific Projects

Engineer projects were designed to leave behind a lasting reminder of United States assistance. At the water stand for all nearby military garrisons, water tankers had made a mudhole of the area. Combat engineers placed a concrete pad under the spout and ditched a runoff channel. Combat heavy engineers repaired water erosion on an older portion of the road linking Berbera and Mogadishu where over half of the road surface had been eaten away. Engineers replaced and recompacted the soil, added a six-inch layer of rock from local quarries, and applied an asphalt and rock-chip surface treatment to extend the life of the road.

The Air Force Prime Beef team from Wright-Patterson AFB painted the unmarked runway to international standards using hundreds of gallons of special paint mixed with over 13,000 pounds of reflective glass beads.

All elements of Task Force Tiger participated in desert training and in joint training with Somali military forces stationed at Berbera. Somali soldiers rigged and detonated American 40-pound

American Sappers in Somalia

by Capt. Kerry K. Pierce

Objectives for Task Force Tiger in Bright Star 82 placed heavy emphasis upon survival and security, a mission requiring excellent training in tactical wire and bunker construction. Soldiers from Charlie Company, 27th Engineer Battalion (Combat) (Airborne) erected over 900 meters of half-apron and cattle fencing to provide a minimum security boundary for the bivouac. Two reinforced bunkers for machine guns were also constructed at critical points on the perimeter. During the excavation of the bunkers, the engineers received their first experiences with the "desert sand" of Somalia. Along the coastal plain, the soil appeared loose and fine; however, it proved to be mostly silt which was compacted to the consistency of concrete just a few inches below the surface. All digging was an extreme challenge for both hand tools and the light, airborne engineer equipment. Addition of water only made the soil harder.

With the establishment of the base camp, the Composite Engineer Company focused upon construction and training opportunities. Somali units around Berbera were eager to interact with their American guests. During the first week, for example, a joint inspection of host-nation Soviet-built vehicles, air defense weapons and communications equipment was arranged. The engineers were able to examine the equipment, to send messages over the wireless and to perform actual crew drill on antiaircraft guns.

Much of the subsequent training involved teaching Somali soldiers American techniques and doctrine. A good example was the joint demolitions training which began with demonstrations of standard explosives and expedient charges. The U.S. engineers went on to conduct hands-on training in the use of det cord, electric and nonelectric priming and the use of expedient cratering charges (ammonium nitrate). This was the Somali soldiers first experience with demolitions. The Americans learned valuable lessons on the effectiveness of cratering techniques in the desert—subsoil hardness resulted in more favorable blast results than expected.

Maintaining physical conditioning was also a key part of the training in Somalia. Twice Charlie Company conducted rucksack marches and on their second march, were accompanied by a platoon of Somali marines.

Just prior to redeployment, a joint weapons exercise was organized. The combat engineers first demonstrated basic marksmanship with the .45 caliber pistol, M-16, M-203, and M-60 to Somali marines, then coached them in actual firing. The Americans then got

As part of their physical training regimen, task force personnel participated in rucksack marches.

the rare opportunity to engage targets with the AK-47 assault rifle, which was impressive in its semiautomatic accuracy but proved inferior to the M-16 when fired on automatic.

The training experiences in Somalia left the engineers confident in their basic skills. JTX Bright Star 82 validated numerous techniques and procedures in the different environment of Southwest Asia and revealed other combat engineer training needs to support the RDF mission.

Capt. Kerry K. Pierce is commander of Co. C, 27th Engineer Battalion (CBT) (ABN). During Bright Star 82 he was Composite Company commander. A 1974 U.S. Military Academy graduate, he is a registered professional engineer in Virginia.

shaped charges, and Somali marines learned new skills as medical aidmen. Other joint training included firing U.S. and Soviet weapons and operation of other Soviet equipment. The Air Force fire truck team from Ramstein AFB, Germany, taught the Somalis to fill and to operate two local

The 244 task force troops were issued desert camouflaged fatigues and Vietnam style bush hats.

Fiat fire trucks. The proof of their learning came before the task force departure when, according to the Somali commander, both trucks were used to assist the town of Berbera in extinguishing a warehouse fire.

ROWPU Success

The two new items of water treatment equipment performed well in Somalia. The ROWPU made excellent potable water from both fresh and salt water. At the Berbera port, the ROWPU processed salt water which was twice as salty as the maximum for which the ROWPU was designed to process, yet easily met both water quality and quantity standards. The five-day shakedown and training period at Fort Bragg prior to deployment was a key factor in the performance of the ROWPU. Although the maximum air temperature of 91 to 93 F did not tax the capability of the water chiller to reduce water temperature from 120 to 60 F, the unit reliably produced pleasantly cool water, even without the special water-tank cover.

Redeployment from Berbera to Fort Bragg was far easier than the deployment. Everything had already fit together on the way over and it was obvious what had to be returned. The *Cygnus* was reloaded on November 24 and airflow commenced from Berbera the same day. All aircraft arrived at Pope AFB by November 27, the *Cygnus* off-loaded at Savannah on December 13 and the task force was completely closed at home stations on December 16.

In assessing lessons from JTX Bright Star 82, some caution must be used in extrapolating the accomplishments of Task Force Tiger for future exercises. The exercise in Somalia was a logistical exercise in the coolest period of the year and there was no significant off-road movement. Temperatures were similar to those the units experienced at Fort Bragg. The force remained within a 25-mile radius of base camp and on level terrain. No rain fell; no flash flooding was experienced.

On the other hand, some of the lessons of the exercise in Somalia are applicable to future deployments of composite units to an unfamiliar overseas area. The task force demonstrated that a small force can enter by air an area where no prior basing exists and establish a support base. The organization and staffing levels of the task force proved to be well founded. Good people from many units took less than two days to develop

Canabalized remnants of a Soviet truck serve as a reminder of an earlier Russian presence.

SOPs and cohesion. Equipment proved reliable as well—the ROWPU and chiller worked extremely well. Units encountered no trafficability problems in the area with current equipment. FM radios transmitted clearly at normal operating ranges. The 250 cfm air compressor was very valuable in preparing for redeployment: it blew off dust, leaving little required washing. One important note for anyone planning a future exercise—B-rations take more cooks and KPs than A-rations; more preparation is also required.

The accomplishments of Task Force Tiger were significant and every member of the force has great pride in those successes. The task force organized, deployed, lived, learned, trained and redeployed without accident, incident, lost time or heat injury.

Lt. Col. Raymond E. Knell commands the 27th Engineer Battalion (CBT) (ABN). A 1964 U.S. Military Academy graduate, he has completed airborne and ranger training, Command and General Staff College, and has a master's degree in civil engineering from the University of Illinois. He is a registered professional engineer in Illinois and has served on the engineering department faculty, U.S. Military Academy. Other assignments include the 168th and 23d Engineer Battalions; 159th Engineer Group; Seattle Engineer District and the Office of the Secretary of the Air Force.

The Critical Path Method

Is It Time To Change?

By Capt. Andrew Hamlin, Capt. Robert J. Huff and 1st Lt. Michael J. Harris

The "critical path method" (CPM) is widely recognized as a powerful management tool. The CPM allows supervisors to effectively allocate their available resources throughout the planning, scheduling and controlling phases of a construction project. The Engineer School has taught a traditional version of CPM called "activity-on-the-arrow (AOA)," for over fifteen years. This form of CPM has been a reliable workhorse for shaping the thought process of young engineer officers and it has helped speed countless construction projects through to timely completion.

However, the School is considering a less traditional version of CPM called "precedence diagraming (PD)" or "activity-on-the-node." This article will discuss concepts of network analysis systems in general, then address specific advantages and disadvantages of CPM (activity-on-the-arrow) versus PD (activity-on-the-node). Reader comments or suggestions are welcome and can be directed to the address or telephone number at the end of this article.

Although network analysis systems vary in format and usefulness, the general approach to solving management problems is the same. The initial step involves breaking the project into component parts (activities) and developing a network model. This network graphically depicts the logical interrelationships of activities which make up an entire project. In this initial step, the manager constructs the network as if he has unlimited resources, and therefore no consideration is given to constraining factors such as men and equipment. Manpower or equipment conflicts are eventually resolved as the construction schedule is developed, and this is the real strength of a network analysis system. The manager is able to proceed in a systematic fashion, developing a feasible construction schedule without becoming overwhelmed by a complicated project in the early stages of planning.

The key to a successful construction schedule is the manager's ability to obtain reasonably accurate estimates of material, manpower and equipment requirements for each activity in the network. This analysis will lead to an estimate of how long each activity will take to accomplish (activity duration).

At this point the manager begins a time analysis of the network. By knowing the logic relationships and activity durations, the following time data can be calculated for each activity:

Early start and early finish times,
late start and late finish times
and total float.

Critical activities and activities which cannot be delayed without extending the overall project duration can now be identified. These critical activities form one or more continuous paths through the network and dictate the minimum project duration. The information acquired up to this point is then placed on an early start schedule, so-called because the constraining factors of men and equipment have not yet been considered. This final, most difficult step to master, is to "resource constrain" the early start schedule and original logic diagram. If the resources demanded by the early start schedule exceed the resources available to the manager, a modification to the schedule and network results. The resequencing of activities on the schedule and network is accomplished by establishing resource relationships between activities. On the network, these new relationships appear as resource arrows. Resource arrows can have a profound impact on the time analysis and therefore alter the critical path(s).

When the final construction schedule is developed, it should be used throughout the remainder of the construction project. The manager is constantly required to provide data on the current project status and often must make decisions on how better to employ his resources. If the network analysis system is properly updated and the data provided is understood, the manager has an invaluable tool to assist him in accomplishing his mission.

The use of a network analysis system should be considered for complicated projects which can be broken into well defined activities. It should be used when resource constraints are expected and when the manager is prepared to keep his construction schedule updated and accurate.

A network analysis system is not a panacea to be used in all situations. For example, a network should not be used for simple projects of short duration. For these projects, some other management technique, such as a bar chart, would be just as effective and less time-consuming. A network analysis system may be inappropriate when activities cannot be easily defined or are difficult to estimate accurately, or in projects where the same cycle of activities is performed daily or periodically. Here, a representative flow diagram may be a better management tool. Most importantly, a network analysis system is not useful to a manager who does not understand the system in sufficient detail or to one who is unwilling/unable to properly update the schedule throughout the course of the construction.

When the manager decides a network analysis system is appropriate he must choose which technique to use. Two popular systems of CPM are activity-on-the-arrow and activity-on-the-node. To explain the differences, a sample project is visualized and plotted using both techniques.

The Critical Path Method, AOA, was developed by the DuPont Corp. in the late 1950s. The network diagram is produced using three graphic symbols: "solid" activity narrows, "broken" dummy arrows, and circular event nodes. The familiar representations are shown in Figure 1. Note the effect added resource relationships have on the critical path.

The Critical Path Method, activity-on-the-node, which will be referred to for the remainder of this article as PD (precedence diagraming), was developed by J.W. Fondahl of Stanford University. This modification of the original CPM is not a recent development. It is widely used and often brought up when the subject of future trends in construction management is discussed. The precedence diagram is produced using, primarily, two graphic symbols, activity nodes and

ACTIVITY-ON-THE-ARROW

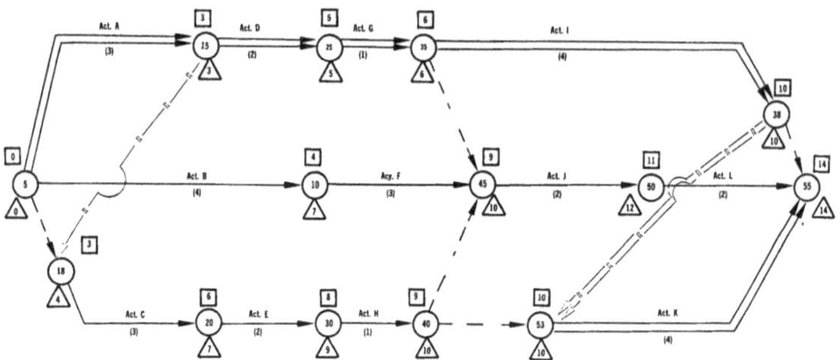

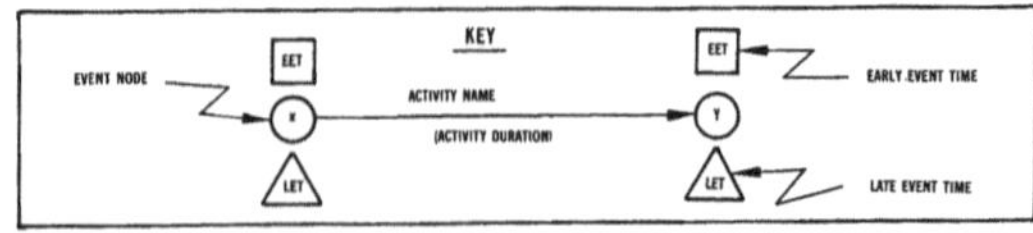

FIGURE 1.

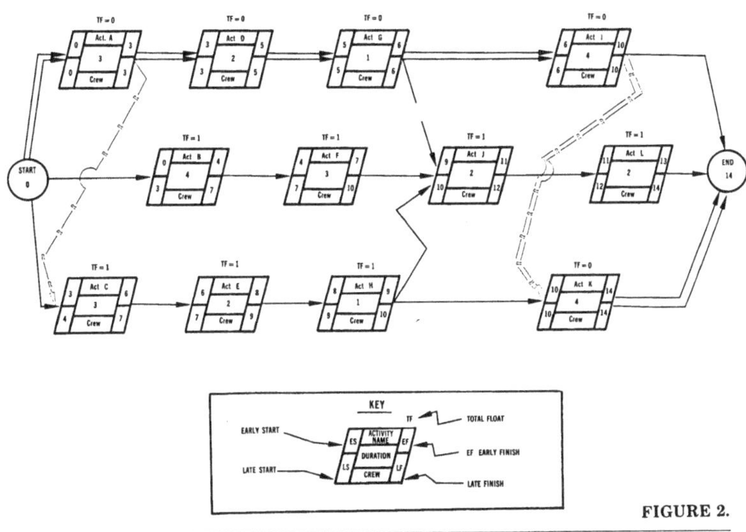

FIGURE 2.

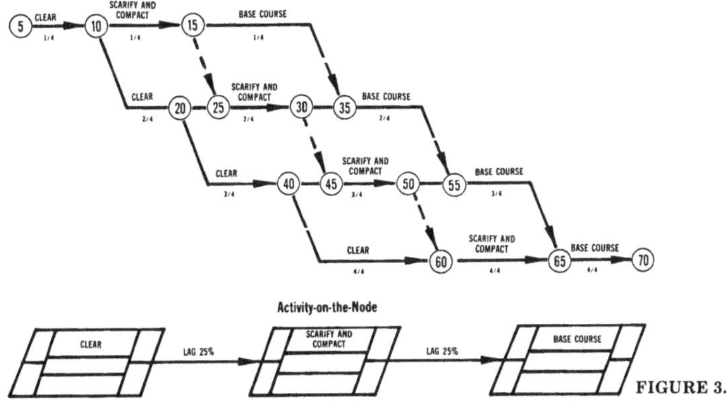

FIGURE 3.

relationship arrows. The project now takes on a different appearance, as shown in Figure 2.

Before comparing the merits of each system, the reader is encouraged to study Figures 1 and 2. The glossary of terms on the right should clarify data within each figure.

The precedence diagram presents a simpler, cleaner logic diagram than the AOA diagram. There is no need for dummy arrows in the precedence network, eliminating a major source of confusion for the less experienced managers of network analysis systems. The PD is less cluttered than the AOA diagram and relationships between activities are more readily apparent. The PD is also more goal or "milestone" oriented and is therefore easier to learn and understand.

Information on an activity's early start, late finish, early finish, late start and total float is easily accessible on the precedence network. The information for each activity is consolidated at the node representing that activity. In an AOA diagram only the early start and late finish times are on the diagram. To find these, the user must refer to both the head and tail of the activity arrow. The early finish, late start and total float are not listed on the AOA diagram. They can, however, be quickly calculated and listed on a separate tabulation sheet. As the project progresses, it often becomes necessary to update the logic diagram. Since the information for an activity is on the node in precedence diagraming, blank preprinted or computer printed nodes with the updated information can be placed over the original node, causing minimal draftsmanship problems.

Resource constraining an AOA diagram often requires the use of several new nodes and dummy arrows, in addition to the resource arrow. This is done to avoid overconstraining other activities in the network. In a PD, there is one resource arrow for each resource relationship. The diagram remains concise and the resource relationships clear.

Sometimes an activity can begin before a related preceding activity has been completely finished. Therefore, two activities that are related can actually overlap each other. These "leads" or "lags" can be represented in both systems, as seen in Figure 3. One of the real strengths of precedence diagraming is its ability to handle these lead and lag factors. The graphic representation is less involved and still depicts the main activities. The lead or lag factor can be entered into a computer with much less difficulty than in AOA.

Precedence diagraming has many avid supporters in the construction arena. However, this system is not seen as being superior to AOA by every management expert. PD can be difficult to update manually if lag factors or other "wrinkles" are used by the manager. This can be a seri-

'erms

ins the start of any activity leaving it until the necessary preceding activities have been pleted. An event node occurs when all preceding activities have been accomplished. The proed occurrence of event nodes is indicated by early and late event times associated with a node.

at: This is the amount of time an activity can lelayed before it begins to impact on the overproject duration (total float). The amount of e an activity can be delayed before it impacts the early start of other activities is called free t and is a component of total float. The reining component of total float is called erfering float. An activity delayed into this e period will interfere with the early start of er activities but will not extend the project ation.

ationship arrow: These arrows are used in cedence diagrams and show how the activity es interact. Relationship arrows do *not* represent activities.

source arrow: These relationship arrows inate how the initial logic of the network has n modified to insure that the available rerces for the project are not exceeded. They are d in both AOA and PD.

source constrained schedule: This is the fi- construction schedule which the manager pares. It is a modified early start schedule and ures that the available resources for the proj- are not exceeded.

te event time: This time represents the latest e an event node can occur without delaying overall project duration.

te finish: This time indicates when an activity st be finished in order to keep it from exding the project duration. In an AOA diagram, late finish is found by referring to the late nt time below the head node of a particular ivity.

h instructors of engineer management at the gineer School. Harris is a Cornell University iduate who recently served as platoon leader of . A, 11th Engineer Battalion, Fort Belvoir. pt. Hamlin formerly served as a platoon leader d company commander with the 9th Engineer ttalion, Germany.

ous drawback. The manager has no simple way to check a computer-assisted project. The potential for this problem is also present, to some degree, when using AOA.

It is recognized that neither technique is totally superior to the other and that each system has its advantages and disadvantages in different situations. If the Engineer School adopts precedence diagraming as *the* primary construction management technique, AOA will have to remain visible, as it will be regularly encountered by managers for years to come.

One obvious impact of the transition from AOA to PD is that of a break in communication between incoming officers/NCOs who understand the PD system and their chain-of-command who are more familiar with AOA. This is not as significant a problem as a first impression may indicate. Precedence diagraming is very similar to AOA in many areas. Whether using AOA or PD, the manager is responsible for providing a certain amount of review and reeducation to his subordinate supervisors to insure the plan and schedule are correctly followed.

How will a change in instruction influence existing Army literature, regulations, ARTEPs, soldier's manuals, TMs and SOPs? Precedence diagraming is still a critical path method. Any references to this management technique will remain applicable with little if any modification. TM 5-333, *"Construction Management,"* provides a discussion of both AOA and PD.

The Engineer School would emphasize PD not because it has overwhelming advantages over AOA, but because precedence diagraming has certain merits over AOA for managing smaller projects which are not supported by computers. Since the bulk of projects managed by the recently graduated Engineer School students are not complex, they normally contain a limited number of activities and are managed without the aid of computers. As a result, PD is a logical choice. Precedence diagraming is preferred for managers just learning to use a network analysis system. As more experience is gained, the engineer manager becomes familiar with both systems. Since both AOA and PD are valid and effective management tools, senior managers can choose the technique they feel most comfortable with.

Comments from the field are encouraged. Managers with experience in one or both of the systems should express their viewpoints to the USAES project officer, Capt. A. Hamlin, at the following address:

United States Army Engineer School
Department of Military Engineering
ATTN: ATZA-DTE-EM
Fort Belvoir, Virginia 22060

Phone: AUTOVON 354-3272

And Company Maintenance

by Capt. Merrit P. Drucker

Army units occupy a large number of facilities of varying ages and conditions and these facilities represent an important, extremely valuable asset. Every effort should be made to maintain them in the best condition possible.

Current doctrine holds that facilities maintenance begins with and is the responsibility of the installation commander. This is indeed correct since failure to give facility maintenance command attention leads to run-down barracks, mess halls and motor pools; lowered morale; and ultimately, to decreased combat effectiveness.

Army Regulation 420–22, *Preventive Maintenance and Self-Help Programs,* defines preventive maintenance as the systematic care, servicing and inspection of equipment utility plants and systems, buildings, structures, and grounds facilites to detect and correct incipient failures and to accomplish minor maintenance. Although most preventive maintenance is handled by the post facility engineers, self-help programs allow military personnel and occupants of family/troop housing to themselves accomplish limited maintenance, repair work and to make minor improvements. This article explains how the company-level self-help program fits into the Army Real Property Maintence System and suggests ways to make self-help programs more effective.

Effective facilities maintenance is difficult to accomplish without the support of the installation commander and all subordinate leaders. When a company commander inventories unit equipment prior to assuming command, for example, he should also inspect and inventory the buildings, maintenance areas and grounds assigned to the company. Commanders sign for their buildings on DA Form 2062, *Hand ReceiptAnnex No*; authorized repairs are made by unit personnel or, as required, reported to the facility engineer.

The facilities maintenance plan should be an integral part of the total leadership plan for the unit. Maintenance of facilities at company level is a direct responsibility of the enlisted chain-of-command; first sergeants, platoon sergeants and squad leaders should be held accountable for the maintenance of their assigned facilities. Each soldier, in turn, should be responsible for performing minor repairs in his assigned area. The commander should hand-receipt individual rooms to the soldiers who occupy them. All inspections by the chain-of-command should also include inspection of buildings and grounds.

Most units find it necessary to appoint one individual to perform authorized minor repairs, to draw supplies and equipment and to serve as unit representative to the facility engineer. This soldier, usually known as the "self-help NCO," must be chosen carefully. The soldier selected should be competent, motivated, capable of working with tools and able to work with little or no supervision. It may be advantageous to make this an additional duty. Many installations conduct a short school which self-help NCOs must attend. If the training is available, commanders should consider sending one individual per platoon to the school. This will enable the company to distribute the maintenance workload and will enhance the unit's overall maintenance program.

Most company-sized units have an adequate supply of tools available to the self-help NCO; a review of the unit Table of Organization and Equipment will indicate the location and type of tools available. Usually, the appropriate tool sets will be located in the company headquarters section. The engineer squad tool box, the general mechanic's tool set or the No. 1 common tool set, will contain the tools needed to perform building maintenance. All tools must be properly hand-receipted and accounted for. Items such as paint brushes, paint, putty, hardware and glass may be obtained from the Self-Service Center or through the facility engineer. Expendable supplies must be carefully controlled to prevent loss or theft.

It is absolutely critical for the self-help NCO to maintain communications with the supporting facility engineer. Problems beyond the capabilities of the unit must be reported to the facility engineer promptly. A log should be maintained of telephonic service orders and of work requests submitted on forms. The service order number or document number for each job should be readily available to the commander or to anyone inspecting the unit. The log should be updated and purged regularly so it can be used as an effective management tool.

The commander should instill in members of the company a sense of responsibility for assigned facilities. Almost without exception, soldiers can be trained to maintain their facilities in an outstanding manner. If troops are provided with materials, leadership and strong command emphasis, facilities can be maintained in an above average condition. Troop involvement promotes an attitude of personal responsibility for the barracks.

In any given company, there are usually several soldiers who have been carpenters, plumbers, painters or electricians in civilian life. These soldiers are an asset to the unit since they can do a significant amount of repair and maintenance work. Projects like regrouting latrines and showers or installing tile floors and sidewalks can be done quite professionally by unit members if such projects are authorized by the facility engineer. Authorization for such projects is mandatory since they are out of the realm of self-help and into the area of minor construction.

There are many things a commander can do to improve facilities. The company charge-of-quarters can be used to inspect the barracks and orderly room and make a list of problems so the unit self-help personnel can start correcting problems without having to inspect the entire facility. When the mess officer or staff duty officer inspects the dining facility, the building and installed fixtures should be thoroughly inspected, too. If problems are identified on a daily basis, they can be corrected before becoming severe.

Another opportunity for increased building maintenance occurs when the company goes off post or to the field leaving a detachment behind. The rear detachment should be responsible for securing, inspecting, cleaning and maintaining the unit's facilities. The detachment should have specific, identified missions regarding the facilities. For example, this is an ideal time to do painting without disrupting the entire unit; maintenance involving turning off water, gas or electricity is also easier to accomplish. Motor pool maintenance, such as repairing pavement, painting lines or cleaning, is also easier since most of the vehicles may be out of the motor pool.

Building exteriors deserve special attention; many times cracked walls, broken electrical outlets or stopped up drains are overlooked. The outside of buildings must be maintained to prevent the elements from damaging the interior, to conserve energy and to present a good appearance. The roof of a building should be inspected regularly by facility engineer personnel for leaks, water damage, cracks and stopped up rain gutters.

Another often neglected facility is a structure located distant from the company or in an isolated area. These facilities must be checked periodically and repairs made rapidly. Buildings in areas where the temperature falls below freezing must be winterized when not used, a task normally accomplished by the facility engineer. If buildings are unoccupied for a short period during freezing weather, they should be inspected daily to check for frozen pipes.

Grounds, fences, sidewalks, roads, curbs, parking lots, culverts and street lights within company boundries should be inspected regularly and work orders initiated as required. Many repairs in these areas will have to be made by the facility engineer. The company can help by reporting problems promptly and by not allowing practices which damage the grounds, such as driving vehicles over sidewalks and grounds. Gutters and culverts should be kept free of debris and consideration should be given to erosion control. Maintaining adequate ground cover is one method of controlling erosion. The drainage of water from large paved areas, drain pipes and culverts should be checked to insure that soil erosion is not taking place.

The battalion S-4 has staff responsibility for facilities maintenance. There are several things the S-4 can do to assist the company maintenance program. The S-4 should hand-receipt facilities from the installation and then, in turn, hand-receipt the facilities to company commanders. The S-4 should supervise the inspection, inventory and transfer of buildings to new company commanders. The S-4 self-help NCO can draw supplies and equipment for the battalion or supervise composite details from companies to accomplish specific self-help missions. The battalion self-help NCO should conduct frequent inspection and assistance visits to the companies. These visits should stress teaching, coaching and helping the company self-help personnel to maintain and repair their facilities. If properly selected and trained, the battalion self-help NCO can handle most of the S-4's facilities management responsibilities.

Some units operate a consolidated battalion self-help program with each company designating one soldier to work for the battalion self-help NCO. Such centralization can greatly increase the efficiency and effectiveness of the self-help program. The decision to consolidate depends upon the specific unit situation and is made by the battalion commander.

Fire prevention, safety, physical security, sanitation and energy conservation are all interrelated areas and each is dependent, to some degree, upon well maintained facilities. Every effort should be made to integrate these areas with the unit facilities maintenance program. Communication must be maintained between those who have responsibilities in these areas, and effective planning is required to prevent conflicts or duplication of effort.

"The (service order) log should be updated and purged regularly . . ."

Of the five functional logistical areas—supply, maintenance, transportation, services and facilities—facilities is equal in importance to the other four. The type and condition of a unit's facilities have a distinct impact upon the effectiveness and morale of the unit. A well maintained, functional, clean barracks or vehicle maintenance building is an indicator of an organized and disciplined unit.

Additional information on self-help programs can be obtained from AR 420–22, *Preventive Maintenance and Self-Help Programs*, and TM 5–610, *Preventive Maintenance, Facilities Engineering—Buildings and Structures*.

Capt. Merrit P. Drucker is an infantry officer and instructor in the Command and Leadership Branch, U.S. Army Engineer School, Fort Belvoir, Va. A graduate of St. John's University, the Infantry Officer Advanced Course and the Supply Management Officer Course, he has served in several command and staff positions with the 1/508th Infantry, 82d Airborne Division. He has had articles published in Army Logistician *and* Infantry *and has been selected for instructor duty at the U.S. Military Academy.*

A Different Kind Of Training Project

by Capt. Douglas D. Gransberg

Let's set the scene. The XYZ Engineer Battalion (Combat) (Heavy) is planning a battalion field training exercise (FTX). The S-3, Major Oakleaf, and his assistant, Second Lieutenant Goldbar, are discussing their plans.

Major O: "Well, we've got the line company construction missions set. Now what are we going to do to keep the A Company equipment platoon busy?"

Lieutenant G: "No sweat, sir! They can send their dozers to the B Company tank ditch. C Company will probably request all their dump trucks and bucket loaders for the haul mission. S-4 always needs a forklift and a light set, and the rest of them can pull security around the battalion TOC."

Sound familiar? As those who served in the Alpha Company of a combat heavy battalion know, it's often the same old story on FTXs; piecemeal employment of the 62E and 62F equipment operators and endless hours of guard duty for the 62H asphalt/concrete specialists and the 62G quarrymen. However, with a little imagination and some easily obtainable construction materials, the equipment platoon can be assigned a small project challenging their construction abilities and utilizing every Military Occupational Specialty in the platoon.

The mission given the equipment platoon, A Company, 864th Engineer Battalion, was to construct a field expedient "de-drumming plant." When bituminous material is issued, it often comes in fifty-five gallon drums. This requires the bitumen to be emptied out of the drums (hence the name "de-drumming") into a machine that heats it to a temperature at which it can be pumped. The skid-mounted, 750 gallon-per-hour asphalt melter is the ideal machine for this purpose. Furthermore, when the melters are placed at a height that permits gravity flow into the distributor trucks, a great deal of minor maintenance hassles are eliminated.

Constructing a de-drumming plant was the idea of the junior NCOs of the equipment platoon and consisted of four phases. The first phase was site preparation. A trench 2 feet deep was cut and lined with polyethylene sheeting. Two inches of sand was placed above and below the sheeting to protect it from punctures and the trench was backfilled with a granular material. This provided a spillage protected lane in which the distributors could be loaded. Additionally, the remainder of the area was compacted. Phase two consisted of erecting an elevated platform on which to set the melters. Six timber piles per melter were driven to refusal and cut off 10 feet above the ground. A timber framework was then installed on top of the piles. A timber headwall was constructed on the front side of the structure and backfilled to a depth of 3 feet. The third phase involved installing, leveling and plumbing the melters on top of the platform; an earthfill ramp was built behind the platform as the final phase. Once the

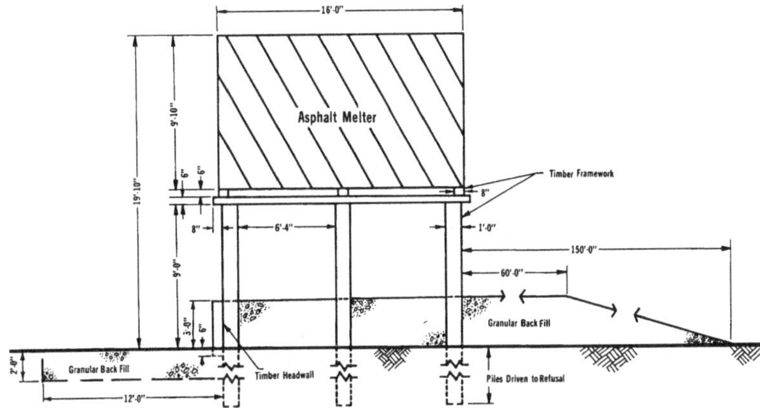

The equipment platoon, A Company, 864th Engineer Battalion, Fort Lewis, Wash., constructed this field expedient "de-drumming" plant during two FTXs. The training project provided an excellent opportunity to evaluate the platoon's capabilities to perform a realistic construction mission under tactical conditions.

ramp was completed, de-drumming could begin utilizing a forklift on the ramp to lift the drums to a height at which they could be emptied into the melter.

Half the project was completed during a battalion FTX in late March 1981, and the other half was done during the battalion ARTEP in April 1981. This enabled the unit to be evaluated on ARTEP Task 14-1, *Conduct Piledriving Operations*, for the first time in eight years and allowed the equipment platoon to be evaluated on its ability to function as a single unit. The entire project was accomplished under tactical conditions with much of the work done during the hours of darkness. The total process took approximately three days during each week-long exercise. Inexperience at piledriving was the primary factor lengthening the time to completion; however, simulated enemy threat, NBC play, inclement weather and minor maintenance problems took their toll as well.

The following describes which tasks were performed in each MOS:

• 62G, Quarryman: The quarry section was required to open and to operate a borrow pit to provide fill for the ramp. Additionally, they operated their 75 ton-per-hour crusher continuously to

The ENGINEER Problem

The following portland cement mix proportion was provided to you.

Water-cement ratio = 5.5 gallons/sack
Cement factor = 6.5 sacks/cubic yard

Fine aggregates
- Specific gravity = 2.60
- Proportion by volume = 40%
- Absorption = 0.6%
- Total moisture content = 6.0%

Coarse aggregates
- Specific gravity = 2.70
- Proportion by volume = 60%
- Absorption = 0.5%
- No free-surface moisture

Air content = 6.0%

Determine the weights of the fine and coarse aggregates and the water added to batch 1 cubic yard of concrete.

Lifting and loading specialists, MOS 62F, drove piles and used cranes and forklifts during the battalion FTX. (Photos by Robert J. Walz.)

provide granular backfill for the trench as well as to stockpile gravel for later use by the battalion.

•62H, Asphalt Concrete Specialist: The asphalt section was required to compact the site using their 10–14 ton steel wheel roller. They installed the plastic sheeting, spread the protective sand blanket and installed the melters when the platform was completed.

•62F, Lifting and Loading Specialist: The primary task given the 62Fs was driving the piles. Additionally, they utilized the cranes and forklifts to lift timber framework to the top of the piles and to set the melters.

•62E, Construction Equipment Operator: The 62Es operated both the bulldozers and bucketloaders at the project site, the borrow pit and the quarry.

•62J, General Construction Machine Operator: A 250 cfm air compressor and pneumatic tool set were used for several purposes. First, the pneumatic chain saw was used to cut the timbers for the framework and the headwall, then it was used to cut the piles to the appropriate height. Both the jackhammer and the pneumatic drill were used to pin the timbers to the piles. The 62Js were also given the responsibility to provide lighting at the project site, the borrow pit and the quarry.

•64C, Vehicle Operator: The dump truck drivers utilized both the 5-ton and 20-ton dump trucks throughout the project.

•Additionally, both engineer (62B) and ordnance (63B) mechanics were used during the project.

In all, fourteen ARTEP tasks were evaluated as a result of the project. The task numbers from ARTEP 5-115, dated 1 October 1980, were: 3-4, 4-4, 4-7, 4-8, 4-13, 11-12, 12-2, 13-2, 13-7, 13-8, 13-11, 13-20 and 14-1.

General construction machine operators, MOS 62J, pinned timbers to piles and provided lighting to various project sites.

The de-drumming plant construction project proved a useful training endeavor. Allowing the equipment platoon to maintain unit integrity enhanced the morale and efficiency of the unit. It also allowed the equipment platoon leadership to coordinate the efforts of the platoon in concert. Best of all, the project provided a great deal of valuable experience in little used construction skills.

Capt. Douglas D. Gransberg is commander of Company A, 864th Engineer Battalion (Combat) (Heavy), Fort Lewis, Wash. He served previously with the 78th Engineer Battalion, and later this spring will join the St. Paul District. Capt. Gransberg has a master's degree in civil engineering from Oregon State University and is a registered professional engineer in Oregon.

The ENGINEER Solution

The absolute volume method is used to solve this problem.

$$\text{Absolute volume} = \frac{\text{Weight of a material}}{(\text{Specific gravity})\ (62.4\ \text{lbs/cu ft})}$$

CEMENT

Weight of cement	= (6.5 sacks/cu yd) (94 lbs/sack)	= 611 lbs
Absolute volume	$= \dfrac{611\ \text{lbs}}{(3.15)\ (62.4\ \text{lbs/cu ft})}$	= 3.1 cu ft

WATER (Unadjusted for aggregate moisture)

Weight of water	= (6.5 sacks/cu yd) (5.5 gals/sack) (8.33 lbs/gal)	= 298 lbs
Absolute volume	$= \dfrac{298\ \text{lbs}}{(1)\ (62.4\ \text{lbs/cu ft})}$	= 4.8 cu ft

AIR

Volume of air	= (0.06) (27 cu ft/cu yd)	= 1.6 cu ft
VOLUME SUBTOTAL	= 3.1 + 4.8 + 1.6	= 9.5 cu ft
VOLUME OF AGGREGATES IN A 1 CUBIC YARD BATCH	= (27 cu ft) − (9.5 cu ft)	= 17.5 cu ft

FINE AGGREGATES

Absolute volume	= (0.40) (17.5 cu ft)	= 7.0 cu ft
Weight (dry)	= (7.0 cu ft) (2.60) (62.4 lbs/cu ft)	= 1136 lbs
Weight (wet)	= (1136 lbs) (1.06)	= 1204 lbs

COARSE AGGREGATES

1st Lt. Thomas Baltazar, commander, 86th Engineer Detachment (Diving), 30th Engineer Battalion, is assisted from the icy Potomac River by 2d class diver Sp5 Andre Simbeck during operations to recover a crashed jetliner. The plane crashed into the river near Washington, D.C., during a January snowstorm.

(photo by Mary Storms)

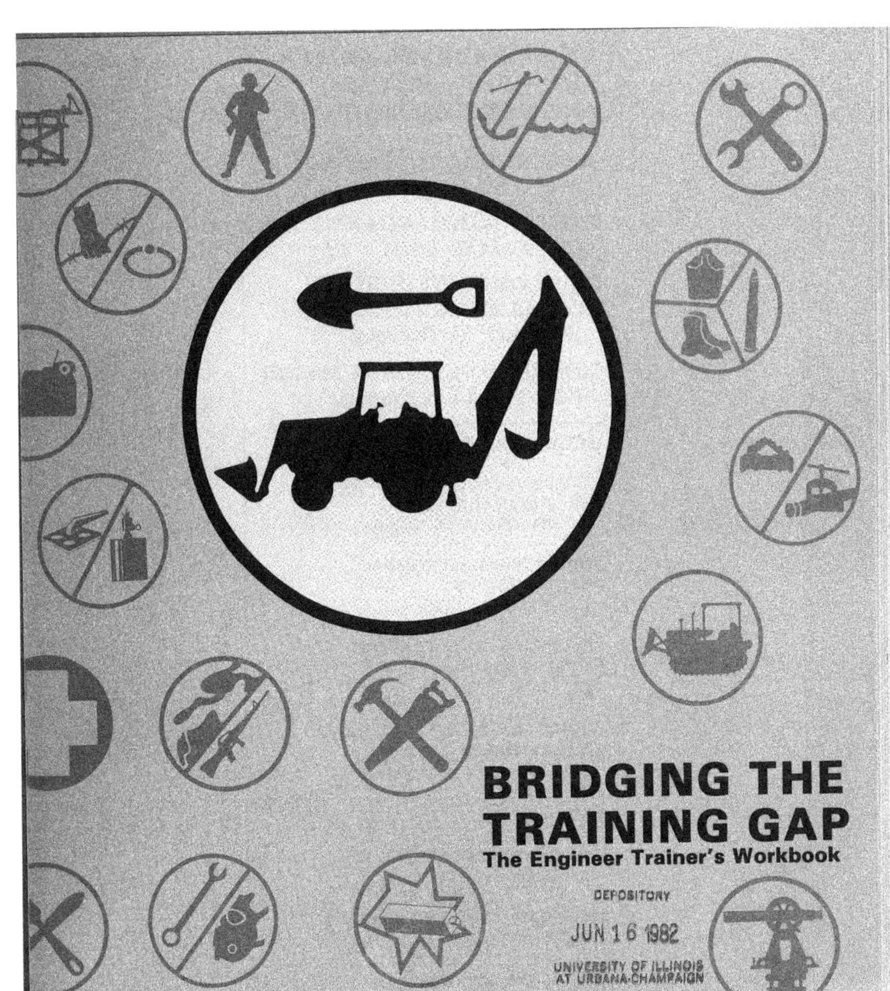
BRIDGING THE
TRAINING GAP
The Engineer Trainer's Workbook

UNITED STATES ARMY ENGINEER CENTER AND FORT BELVOIR, VA

COMMANDER/COMMANDANT
Maj. Gen. James N. Ellis

DEPUTY COMMANDANT
Col. Alvin G. Rowe

CHIEF OF STAFF/DEPUTY INSTALLATION COMMANDER
Col. David O. Cooksey

COMMAND SERGEANT MAJOR
CSM Marvin L. Knowles

DIRECTORATES

DIRECTORATE OF ENGINEER FORCE MANAGEMENT
Lt. Col. Charles S. Nichols

DIRECTORATE OF COMBAT DEVELOPMENTS
Col. Phillip R. Hoge

DIRECTORATE OF TRAINING DEVELOPMENTS
Col. John W. Devens

DIRECTORATE OF TRAINING AND DOCTRINE
Col. Stanley R. Johnson

UNITS

ENGINEER CENTER BRIGADE
Col. Robert A. Dey

ENGINEER TRAINING BRIGADE
Col. Peter J. Groh

PUBLIC AFFAIRS OFFICER
Maj. James E. Kiley Jr.

EDITOR
John Florence

ASSOCIATE EDITOR
Sp5 N. P. Lang

VOLUME 12 SUMMER 1982 NUMBER 2

FEATURES

DEPARTMENTS

ENGINEER is an authorized publication of the U.S. Army Engineer Center and Fort Belvoir, Va. Unless specifically stated, material appearing herein does not necessarily reflect official policy, thinking or endorsement by any agency of the U.S. Army. All photographs contained herein are official U.S. Army photographs unless otherwise credited. Use of funds for printing this publication was approved by Headquarters, Department of the Army, July 22, 1981. Material herein may be reprinted if credit is given to ENGINEER and the author. • **ENGINEER OBJECTIVES** are to provide a forum for the exchange of ideas, to inform and motivate and to promote the professional development of all members of the Army engineer family. • **DIRECT CORRESPONDENCE** with ENGINEER is authorized and encouraged. Inquiries, letters to the editor, manuscripts, photographs and general correspondence should be sent to: Editor, ENGINEER, U.S. Army Engineer Center, Fort Belvoir, Va., 22060. Telephone Autovon 354-3082. If a return of manuscripts or material is desired, a self-addressed envelope is required. • **SUBSCRIPTIONS** to ENGINEER are available through the Superintendent of Documents, U.S. Government Printing Office, Washington, D.C. 20402. A check or money order payable to Superintendent of Documents must accompany all subscription requests. Rates are $8.00 domestic (including APO and FPO addresses) and $10.00 for foreign addresses. Individual copies are available at $2.75 per copy to domestic addresses and $3.45 for foreign addresses. • **SECOND CLASS** postage paid at Fort Belvoir, Va., and Riverdale, Md. ISSN 0046-1989.

by Maj. Gen. James N. Ellis

Three Key Activities

As the new Engineer School commandant, I welcome this opportunity to continue "Clear the Way." I think it is critically important that I continue the tradition of my predecessor, Maj. Gen. Max W. Noah, in providing you the School perspective on the many issues affecting the Engineer community.

I welcome your comments and will endeavor to highlight those issues most important to the military engineer. In future issues of ENGINEER, I will address matters with which we should share perspectives. These initial comments, however, reflect my personal support of three critical areas here at the School.

First, and I believe, one of the most significant activities at the Engineer School, is our Mission Area Analysis (MAA). This process began with a mobility-countermobility-survivability Systems Program Review (SPR) conducted at Fort Belvoir in April 1981. Maj. Gen. Noah reported to you on the SPR a year ago. During that review, Engineers assessed our concepts, organizations, training, and material needed to do our job. That was followed by an action plan which analyzed the shortcomings in our system and identified the means to correct them and to accomplish our job more effectively. Many of the items identified last fall in that action plan are now under way.

In November, we moved to the preparation of the formal MAA. The Engineer portion (one of eight analyzing the entire Army mission) is called Combat Support, Engineering and Mine Warfare. In this analysis, we shall break down every task and subordinate mission within the Corps of Engineers' responsibility and, again, in even more detail, assess our capability to accomplish those jobs. This is a very important effort from the standpoint of the time and number of people required to accomplish it. But more important is its significance to the character of the Engineer mission of the future. One can say, from a mission standpoint, in terms of our total relationship to the Army, this MAA may well be the most important project we will undertake in this decade.

A second very important activity here concerns the doctrinal literature program. The Army, as a whole, has reassessed how it is to fight in the future, based upon a modern concept called the Airland Battle. Stemming from that concept, a new keystone manual, FM 100–5, *Operations,* containing the basic doctrine for the future has evolved. We and the other TRADOC schools have reviewed that doctrine and are preparing first, our respective keystone and then, the supporting field manuals. The first field manual for combat engineers is FM 5–100, *Engineer Combat Operations,* which has been published in a coordinating draft for review by Engineers and other members of the combat arms team worldwide. It contains many changes from what we are familiar with in current manuals. We will next consolidate many of the other doctrinal manuals into seven or eight supporting manuals based on FM 5–100. I will keep you advised on the status of this important effort as it progresses, and I encourage you to consider this doctrine effective upon receipt of these new manuals.

The third critical activity demanding our attention is the responsibility for proponency. I am excited about this particular mission of the Engineer School because it is people oriented, and our involvement is essential to the total career development of Engineer soldiers. Accordingly, I believe a discussion of proponency in my first column would be appropriate and timely. This insight should serve to explain our present posture and future direction.

On October 1, 1981, the Engineer School became the specialty proponent for the Corps of Engineers. As commandant, I advise and assist the deputy chief of staff for personnel (DCSPER) and MILPERCEN on personnel management policies and programs affecting Engineer officers (SC 21 and 22), warrant officers (MOS 310A, 621A, 811A, 821A, 833A, and 841A), and enlisted personnel (CMF 12, 51, and 81).

The Engineer Proponency Steering Committee (EPSC) has been organized to assist me on policy recommendations. The EPSC reviews issues and provides recommended actions or policy changes. My recommendations are then forwarded to the appropriate office or agency; such as DA, DCSPER or MILPERCEN.

The Directorate of Evaluation and Standardization, currently the Directorate of Engineer Force Management (Provisional) (DEFM(P)), is the principal action agency for Engineer specialty proponency. The DEFM(P) prioritizes and evaluates proponency issues for the commandant and EPSC. They coordinate directly with TRADOC, MILPERCEN, OCE, Soldier Support Center, and ODCSPER. The DEFM(P) has its own evaluation teams and receives much of its information from the field.

Although the proponency mission is relatively new to the School, many issues are already being reviewed. Some of these include: professional development, force alignment, AERB requirements, educational requirements, accession/retention, combat exclusion policy for women, engineer and scientific continuation pay, and additional specialties for commissioned officers. Other issues are constantly surfacing for evaluation and appropriate action. The following highlights some of the issues:

The Engineer officer specialty code was restructured on March 1, 1982. All topographic Engineer officer positions were designated as SC 22—a new specialty code. New Special Skill Identifiers (SSI) were designated for the remaining SC 21 positions. The EPSC has expressed concern that the restructured SC 21 may require additional fine tuning to insure Engineer officers receive adequate professional development. Accordingly, development evaluations are currently underway to address this problem.

Another area of interest to officers is the engineering and scientific career continuation pay (ESCCP) which the Air Force requested from Congress. While DA endorsed the concept, the Army Officer Personnel Management System is not comparable to the Air Force's system. Since specific degrees are mandatory for most Air Force officer specialties, it is relatively easy to determine academic shortages. Due to the wide variety of degrees in any one Army specialty, implementation of a bonus program for the Army is not feasible at this time.

Force alignment has been in the news recently. Promotion policies are changing to facilitate aligning the force. The FY 82 E–7 selection board selected E–6 soldiers for promotion by MOS for the first time. The Army, with input from the Engineer School on Engineer MOSs, selected the number of soldiers necessary to fill known or anticipated Engineer job vacancies. Clearly, promotion opportunities for those in a critically needed skill, or MOS, were much higher than for soldiers in overage skills. By placing a direct correlation between the numbers of promotions given to the various MOSs, and the strength status of those MOSs, the Army has taken a giant step forward in aligning the total enlisted force. The after-action report from the board has been received by the School, and evaluation of the report and board results will determine which policy changes will enhance professional development and career potential for our enlisted soldiers.

The DA Women in the Army study group is conducting a total review of units and positions to determine where women can be effectively utilized. The physical demands of MOSs and the combat probability of a unit will be the basis of this determination. The Engineer School is developing the raw data for the study.

Most proponency issues are multifaceted. Education, specialty structure and professional development are all intertwined. Whenever a new material system is introduced, personnel requirements change. This, in turn, affects the structure of the specialty and makes demands upon the training system. In the past, the full personnel impact of new material introduction was often not apparent until years later. Specialty proponency provides discipline to the personnel process by insuring the system can support these changes.

Proponency is both a responsibility and an opportunity. As the new commandant, I accept the challenge of the responsibility and look forward to the opportunity for the positive change we can affect. Let us have your ideas, *"Clear the Way."*

JNE

News & Notes

A 9th Infantry Division soldier uses a UNIMOG to dig an individual defensive position during a Fort Lewis FTX.

UNIMOG IS TESTED AT FORT LEWIS

The UNIMOG is one candidate being tested as a small emplacement excavator (SEE). The UNIMOG has a German chasis with attachments added by Case Equipment, Inc. As part of the 9th Infantry Division's High Technology Test Bed, the UNIMOG is being rated on its ability to meet operational requirements. Its performance is being evaluated by the Army's Mobility Equipment Research and Development Command (MERADCOM), Fort Belvoir. According to MERADCOM, initial test reports have validated the concept of using a UNIMOG-type piece of equipment to dig small forward area emplacements.

OCAR REMINDS RESERVISTS: DRESS RIGHT!

The new decoration and service ribbons authorized by DA should be worn by qualified reservists, too, Office of the Chief, Army Reserve, reports.

The Army Service Ribbon is worn by all officers and enlisted personnel following successful completion of the resident basic/orientation course or initial MOS producing course.

The Army Achievement Medal may be awarded to all but general officers, for meritorious service or achievement. The NCO Professional Development Ribbon is awarded for successful completion of designated NCO professional development courses.

The Overseas Service Ribbon is awarded for successful completion of overseas tours with numerals used to denote second and subsequent awards. The OSR will not be awarded for overseas service already recognized with another service medal, such as the Vietnam Service Medal.

No orders will be published for these awards, so check AR 672-5-1 with changes or consult your unit personnel officer to make sure you're dressed right. You may also want to update your official photo.

92d TRAINS FOR JUNGLE

A detachment from the 92d Engineer Battalion (Combat) (Heavy), Fort Stewart, Ga., recently accompanied the 1st Battalion (Ranger), 75th Infantry, on a 21-day jungle training course in Panama.

The 92d, which supports the 1-75th in the event of the Rangers deployment, learned jungle tactics including training in water operations, jungle survival, placing booby traps and land navigation.

In addition to weapons maintenance classes and physical training, the soldiers received instruction in poncho flotation rafts; using rope bridges and in vertical extraction, an airborne operation that lifts up to four men, suspended by ropes, out of an area of helicopter.

FORCE ALIGNMENT EFFECTS REENLISTMENT

The Army's new Force Alignment Program may make it harder for some soldiers to reenlist. Recent success in meeting reenlistment goals has enabled the Army to look more closely at soldiers who reenlist and the skills for which they reenlist. Force alignment is designed to improve MOS balance, eliminate poor performers and to support modernization of the force.

Particularly effected are prior service enlistees who will be allowed to reenter only into critical skills. Additionally, soldiers must now be in grade E-4 or above to reenlist at all. Soldiers in grade E-5 and below at the time of reenlistment will be allowed to sign up for their present MOS or an understrength MOS only.

Commanders are advised by MILPERCEN to reenlist only those soldiers who will be productive in a changing Army, who are potential NCOs or senior technicians and those who are willing to serve where the Army needs them.

HAND-HELD CALCULATOR

Six combat planning tasks are being programmed into a new hand-held calculator for engineers. Classroom and field testing will be done during FY 83. The six programs are: minefield and wire obstacle logistics, demolitions and cratering calculations, bridge classifications, and the critical path method. To write software, first obtain documentation standards by writing to: U.S. Army Engineer School, ATTN: ATZA-TDC-A (Calculator), Fort Belvoir, Va., 22060.

ENGINEERS NEEDED AS GERMAN LINGUISTS

Staff Sergeants in MOS 51H30 (Construction Supervisor) or SFCs in MOS 51T30 (Technical Engineering Supervisor) are needed for assignments as German linguists. Interested NCOs who are *not qualified* linguists may apply if they score 89 or better on the Defense Language Aptitude Battery (DLAB) Test available at local education centers.

Applicants should submit their name, MOS and test results (if needed) to MILPERCENs Engineer Branch (DAPC-EPL-E), 2461 Eisenhower Ave., Alexandria, Va.

Selected NCOs will attend a nine-month German course at the Defense Language Institute Foreign Language Center, Monterey, Cal. Call Mrs. Scott at Engineer Branch for more information, AV 221-7710.

W. VA. GUARD GETS ENGINEERS

A new Army National Guard engineer detachment was recently formed at West Virginia's only military reservation. Camp Dawson, near Kingwood, W. Va., is now home for the 229th Engineer Detachment (Utility) commanded by Capt. David M. Davison. Senior detachment NCO is SFC Edward M. Gatens.

The 35-soldier detachment will provide maintenance, minor construction and rehabilitation of Camp Dawson facilities.

News & Notes

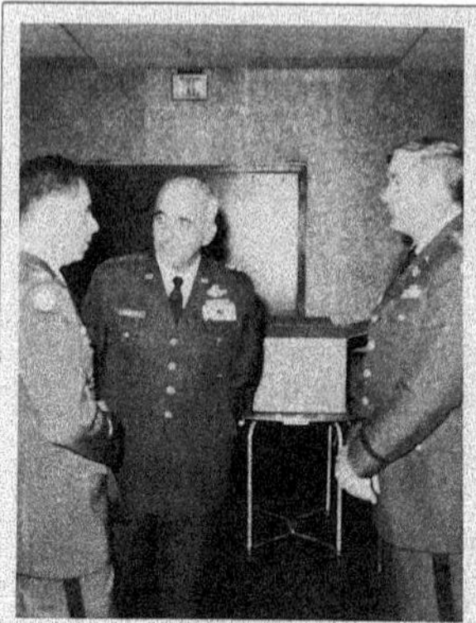

Chaplain (Capt.) Nicholas J. Kusevich, 17th Engineer Battalion, 2d Armored Division, conducts a field mass wearing olive drab vestments made from an Army parachute. Kusevitch is one of only 10 Eastern Orthodox priests in the Army. Developed in Eastern Europe, the religion includes Greeks, Ukrainians, Romanians, and Russians. There are over six million of the Eastern Orthodox faith in the United States. (Photo by Mark Vitullo)

DA AWARD FOR ENGINEER TOPO LAB

The Engineer Topographic Laboratories (ETL), Fort Belvoir, Va., has received the 1981 Department of the Army Most Improved Laboratory of the Year Award.

Commended for the first successful interface between a photo interpreter analyzing high-resolution aerial photography and a digital computer supporting a geographic information system, ETL was selected for the award above 35 other Army labs.

ETL, the largest topographic research and development organization of its kind, specializes in mapping, geodesy, point positioning and military geographic information. The laboratory commander/director is Col. Edward K. Wintz.

CERAMIC ANODE IS BREAKTHROUGH FOR CERL

A breakthrough in corrosion-prevention technology has been made by the U.S. Construction Engineering Research Laboratory (CERL) at Champaign, Ill., with development of the ceramic anode.

The invention makes corrosion prevention available at one-fourth the cost and in a size reduction—500 times by weight—that permits installation in areas previously too small. Yet the ceramic anode has the same life as the relatively heavy and bulky silicon-iron or graphite anodes used in cathodic protection for the past 30 years. The ceramic anode is about the size of a dime.

The consumption rate of conducting ceramic materials such as ferrites is 500 times less than the currently used silicon-iron and graphite anodes. However, ceramics are extremely brittle and cannot be fabricated. To overcome these problems, CERL plasma-sprayed ferrite on valve metal (titanium or niobium) which can be fabricated to any shape. The niobium anode was designed specifically for salt-water use due to its resistance to pitting.

An application in civil works for the CERL ceramic anode will be on lock gates. At Army installations, the anode will be used on elevated water-storage tanks and underground pipes. Examples of potential use are with submarines and ships, and on off-shore structures such as oil-drilling platforms.

PROFESSIONAL ENGINEER/ ENGINEER-IN-TRAINING ASSISTANCE

The U.S. Army Engineer School provides information regarding registration of military officers and DoD civilians as "Professional Engineers" and as "Engineers-in-Training." The School also provides study materials for PE and EIT exams. For more information on the PE and EIS programs, call Capt. Phil Jones or Mr. Bob Baldwin, (703) 664-2889/2527, FTS 554, AVN 354. Send written queries to: Commandant, U.S. Army Engineer School, ATTN: ATZA-DTE-RA (PE/EIT Coordinator), Fort Belvoir, VA 22060. If you are writing for study materials only, substitute attention line: ETM Division (Bldg. 215).

The Command Sergeant Major

by Gen. Bruce C. Clarke, USA (Ret.)

In the fall of 1940, the chief of the armed force sent a group of four officers to England to learn all they could about the actions in France by the British units that had recently escaped from Dunkerque. I was one of those officers and was assigned to the British 1st Armored Division which was re-equipping and retraining south of London.

In a couple of months, I learned to know the British concept of organization, training, command and leadership. I was impressed by the British regimental system, which seemed to rely little on the centralized control of personnel in the War Office. The key enlisted man of the regiment (our battalion) was the sergeant major.

He was a very imposing man and was the walking authority on the history, ethics, soldierly standards and information of the regiment. When a new recruit was ready to be taken before the sergeant major, he was well turned out and formally presented. The sergeant major sat very militarily behind his desk and the recruit stood at rigid attention. The sergeant major covered briefly the long, glorious history of the regiment. He then covered several things that all men in that regiment did, and several things that they didn't do. He informed the new soldier, still at rigid attention, that if he violated these rules a noncommissioned officer would speak to him; if he did it repeatedly, he would speak to him again himself. With that, the young soldier was dismissed.

This established the basic of peer discipline in the unit. No formal command instructions would take its place in its effect upon a new soldier. When Lt. Col. Creighton W. Abrams was commanding the 37th Tank Battalion in World War II, I heard one of his sergeants one day shout to a soldier who had violated some rule or order, "Soldier, you don't do that in Abe's battalion." This was prompt and adequate corrective action.

In 1949, Maj. Gen. I.D. White, the commanding general of the U.S. Constabulary in Germany, directed me, one of his brigade commanders, to create an NCO academy for the constabulary. With that, the present 7th Army NCO Academy was born.

It has had a profound effect on the Army's noncommissioned officer corps. Its duplicates have covered our Army and the Korean Army over the past 30 years. From this, has evolved the E–8 and E–9 ranks in our Army. The latter is the rank of command sergeant major; the top enlisted man in a unit in our Army.

Before the first class at the Constabulary NCO Academy, I made this statement, "There never has been a good Army without a good noncommissioned officer corps." I repeated it before a graduating class in November 1981, some 32 years later. If anything it is more important today in our Army.

When, soon after World War II, the Army deputy chief of staff for personnel presented the proposed post-war titles of the then seven grades of enlisted men to General of the Army/Chief of Staff Omar N. Bradley, he started with E–7 master sergeant; E–6 sergeant first class. When the chief of staff approved these, he then recommended that the E–5 be a sergeant second class. Gen. Bradley strongly disapproved, and directed that a new title be found. The title of staff sergeant was the result. Gen. Bradley then went on to say that he wanted no 'second class' sergeants in his Army. A command sergeant major has a lot to do to prevent this.

Over 30 years later we find our country with soldiers in Korea, in Europe and elsewhere supporting our national foreign relations programs by providing the basis from which our military and diplomatic efforts are carried on. Frederick the Great once said, "Diplomacy without the military is like an orchestra without instruments." This realistic concept makes every military man overseas an important person and an important member of our diplomatic-military team. The same goes for those who are prepared to augment and to support our forces overseas in an emergency.

The morale of a soldier comes from three things: A feeling that he has an important job to do, a feeling that he is trained to do it well, and a feeling that his good work is recognized and appreciated.

The command sergeant major is the principal enlisted staff assistant to his commander. As such, he makes suggestions and recommendations to his commander as called for and as is appropriate. But he is more; he sets the standards in leadership, performance of duty, conduct, discipline, morale and community relations for the noncommissioned officers of his unit.

His importance to his unit and to his commander is only limited by his ability, energy and imagination. His field of influence for good among the enlisted men in his unit knows no bounds.

AFGHA

The Soviet

by James H. Hansen

After nearly two years of conflict in Afghanistan, there has been remarkably little public discussion of the Soviet methods for dealing with the Moslem insurgency there. This is indeed unfortunate, because the analysis of Soviet tactics in Afghanistan is a useful method of assessing the qualitative effectiveness of Soviet military forces. A study of Soviet tactics in Afghanistan indicates certain weaknesses in the Soviet military style, some of which Moscow's planners have tried to correct. It is now apparent that the Soviet military has adopted counterinsurgency as one of its permanent missions. Moreover, the U.S.S.R. is using Afghanistan as a test ground for new weapons, and much can be learned from a look at the arms which are in operational service now against the Moslem guerrilla forces.

The Application of Lessons Learned

Several months after the initial Soviet invasion of Afghanistan, Moscow's military planners recognized that their forces would have to adapt to the type of war being fought in that unforgiving theater. As early as March 1980, it was apparent that armored forces were generally useless against an enemy whose presence on the battlefield was sudden and fleeting. In general, Soviet ground forces were slow to react to rapidly changing tactical situations, and Soviet air power was used with little effect.

During mid-1980, however, a changeover in Soviet tactics was underway. The Soviet contingent in Afghanistan introduced armored fighting vehicles to replace many of the tanks. The Soviet forces now rely primarily on armored vehicles such as the BMP armored fighting vehicle, its airborne BMD cousin, the BRDM armored reconnaissance vehicle, and the ubiquitous BTR-60 armored personnel carriers. In addition, motorized rifle divisions were deployed in smaller maneuver units to pursue guerrillas with greater effect. Soviet divisions now frequently operate in brigade and battalion-sized units. The Soviet contingent in Afghanistan, moreover, has placed ever-increasing reliance on air power. The U.S.S.R. has now deployed a stead-

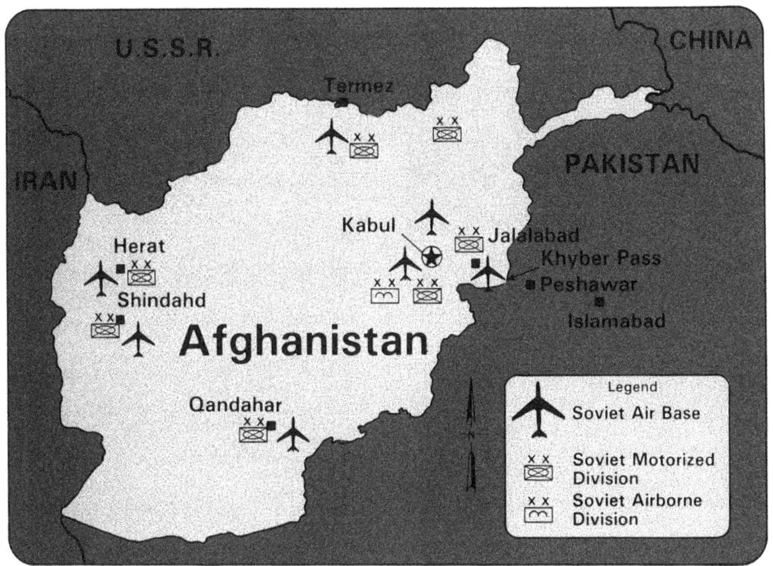

tions of all kinds: airborne operations, use of helicopters, motorized rifle company tactics, river crossings, cliff scaling techniques, etc. The Soviet aviation journal *Aviatsiya i Kosmonavtika* (Aviation and Cosmonautics) has featured summaries of operations in Afghanistan as well.[5]

Tactical Trump Cards

Some of the more sensitive, and presumably effective, Soviet tactics do not appear in Russian-language military journals. Reference is made to the employment of chemical munitions as well as the use of special operations forces.

Reports of Soviet use of chemical weapons in Afghanistan predate the introduction of Soviet combat forces in December 1979. A U.S. State Department publication released in August 1980 noted that the Soviets have employed chemical weapons in half of Afghanistan's 28 provinces, largely those in the east where the most intense fighting has occurred.[6] So far three general types of chemical munitions are being used: a type of lethal chemical, which apparently is a nerve agent; a so-called "knockout" gas which leaves the victims unconscious for several hours, during which time Soviet troops land and conduct unopposed operations; and a concentrated CS tear gas, which appears to be the most widely used of all the Soviet chemical agents.[7] Chemical munitions could be very effective against guerrillas who are dug into mountainous areas and are difficult to dislodge with conventional firepower.[8]

The Soviets have also introduced significant numbers of elite special operations units into the campaign. These are called *spetsnaz* (for "special designation") units, forces which are roughly comparable to U.S. Army Ranger units. The U.S.S.R. appears to put a great deal of stock in such troops—to a greater degree than is commonly appreciated in the West.[9] These helicopter-borne commandos spearhead various types of counter-guerilla thrusts, and are backed up by columns of motorized rifle troops. Analysis of the Afghan campaign thus far suggests that motorized rifle units provide most of the "cordoning" forces in cordon-and-search operations, while the elite forces provide many of the effective hunter-killer units.

Soviet elite forces include the airborne units, which are heavily involved in the combat. The only major airborne force now believed to be in the country is the 105th Guards Airborne Division, which was one of the spearhead elements in December 1979. Analysis of the campaign suggests a pronounced qualitative difference between the

The Soviet BMP armored fighting vehicle, shown here in a Red Square parade, has been even more useful than the tank in Afghanistan operations.

combat performance of Soviet airborne units and the more pedestrian performance of motorized rifle divisions, of which seven remain in the country.

The Cost to Both Sides

The Soviet troops have paid a moderately heavy price since December 1979, as suggested by the preliminary analysis of available casualty figures. Based on American estimates of casualty figures, the monthly Soviet casualty rate (both dead and wounded) is running at several hundred men per month, with no more than 100 men killed each month on the average. This figure is scaled down from earlier estimates, and the rate will prove to be acceptable to Soviet planners, so long as Soviet forces continue to inflict several times as many casualties as they take.

The Afghan civilian population has paid a very heavy price, because Soviet tactical operations have been aimed increasingly at the population. This is suggested by reports of Soviet units leveling villages which are believed to harbor guerrilla fighters. In one two-week period in mid-1980, Soviet ground and air forces "reduced to rubble" some 50–60 Afghan villages.[10] As of mid-1981, about half a million Afghan citizens had been killed or wounded by Soviet military action, and over two million people have fled the country, according to a former Afghan government official.

In this context, the Afghanistan campaign has produced numerous atrocity stories, told by both sides. In this type of war, it is clear that Soviet commanders do not view atrocities as war crimes, but as calculated tactics in an ongoing effort to intimidate or coerce the population. In this category of "tactics," one must also include mass reprisals as well as institutionalized terror.

The Soviet counterinsurgency campaign should not be viewed in the military context alone. Instead one should examine all the other measures which the Soviets are employing in their effort to subdue the armed opposition. Soviet strategic doctrine recognizes that the military civilian effort should be interconnected, and population control is a critical element in the U.S.S.R.'s overall strategy in Afghanistan.

By now, the KGB apparently has penetrated the *Mujahideen* after stepping up its operations in Afghanistan.[11] Many KGB personnel there probably are associated with the Third Directorate, which is responsible for counterintelligence within the Soviet armed forces.

At the same time, the Soviet occupiers are also recasting the Afghan legal system after that of the U.S.S.R. The Afghan educational system is being transformed along Soviet lines as well. Many thousands of Soviet officials have entered Afghanistan to assist in the day-to-day functioning of Afghan government ministries.[12] The exact distribution of Soviet officials within the ministries remains unknown for now.

On the military side, many thousands of Afghan government troops are receiving training in the U.S.S.R.—now about 10,000 NCO's in the country for a six-month training period. The effort to reconstitute the pre-1978 Afghan armed forces is a major component of the Soviets' overall strategy, although Moscow probably is not banking on this program alone for the long-term stability of the country.

An Afghan People's Militia has been operating against the guerrillas since at least early 1980. This force appears to be the same type of paramilitary adjunct which has been established in other states after a communist takeover: in Ethiopia, to name one recent example. People's Militia battalions made up of young recruits are entrusted with maintaining law and order in the cities, and also with countering the rebels who are active on the highways. As such, the People's Militia battalions are tasked with escorting convoys between the cities.[13]

The U.S.S.R. is in the midst of a wide-ranging program to expand the lines of communication between Soviet Central Asia and Afghanistan, an effort which could greatly assist the overall Soviet logistics and resupply plan. One permanent bridge has been built over the Amu Darya (Oxus) River at Termez. A second permanent bridge is reportedly under construction across the same river. The Soviets are considering the construction of a rail line into Kabul which would link up with the Soviet railway system (there are currently no rail lines in Afghanistan). The U.S.S.R. also has ambitious plans to build air cushion vehicle cargo platforms to link the Soviet river port of Termez with the Afghan cities of Shir-Kahn and Khayratan. The flotilla of air cushion vehicles, some with carrying capacities of up to 40 tons, will be built at a shipyard in Chardzou in the Soviet Turkmen SSR. In addition, the U.S.S.R. is upgrading some of Afghanistan's 36 existing airfields, and is constructing some new ones as well. One new military airfield has been built at Dasht-e-Atishan, some 40 kilometers east of the Iranian border in Herat Province.[14]

The Air War

Except for the assault helicopter's standout role, Soviet aviation fire support to ground forces has not been an important factor in the campaign against the rebels. One source notes that this aviation fire support (called *aviatsionnaya podderzhka* in Russian) has a "long way to go" before it can be considered effective.[15] This is largely due to three reasons. First, the Moslem rebels do not appear to be vulnerable to air operations. They are an elusive enemy for the Soviets, and any early warning of an impending air strike negates the effects of that strike. The second reason is that the mountainous terrain has inhibited the effectiveness of air-to-ground fire from jet aircraft. Air strikes in the desert regions of western Afghanistan would have more effect against the rebel forces, but most of the fighting has occurred in the eastern provinces adjacent to Pakistan. The third reason is that the Soviets have deployed few jet ground attack aircraft in Afghanistan. The overwhelming percentage of the Soviet tactical combat aircraft in the country are relatively old MIG-21's, which are best suited for air-to-air combat.[16] Soviet planners have thus far not perceived the need to deploy relatively advanced ground attack aircraft, such as the SU-24 Fencer or the MIG-27 Flogger D and J models.

On the other hand, the MI-24 Hind D helicopter gunship has proven to be a highly effective weapons platform. Its capabilities have been tested to the utmost: from transporting squad-sized units to dropping chemical bombs. By many accounts, the Hind D is the weapon most feared by the Moslem guerrillas, and its performance in combat has been described as "devastating."

The Soviets maintain a force of well over 200 assault helicopters in Afghanistan, reportedly split into small squadrons.[17] They often use two-ship or four-ship formations in combat, but elements of eight or more have been reported.

The assault helicopters, both the MI-24 Hind D/E series and the MI-8 Hip C/E series, represent the vital component of a new concept that is being tested in Afghanistan, the tactical airborne landing. In this maneuver, a motorized rifle unit, quite often a battalion of 400–500 men, is airlifted by helicopter to the enemy rear area where it operates in cooperation with the troops advancing from the front. A helicopter-borne assault may occur as far as 50 kilometers ahead of the front lines, although the linkup with the main body of troops should occur within two or three hours.[18]

Colonel M. Belov, perhaps the most tireless advocate of Soviet assault helicopter capabilities, has characterized this type of operation by its "strict coordination, surprise and dynamism of troop actions." Such operations are also known for their "fast overcoming of large distances, irrespective of natural obstacles and obstructions. . . ." Soviet military doctrine recognizes that the airborne force must be highly active and maneuverable in action, take the enemy by surprise, and show "resolve and daring."[19] It would first appear that only special operations *(spetsnaz)* forces and airborne troops are ideally suited to carry out such operations, but some regular motorized rifle battalions have also been trained for this type of mission.

If anything, Soviet units in Afghanistan have become overly dependent on helicopters. Whenever a Soviet troop column or supply convoy moves into guerrilla territory, it is accompanied by Hinds. While half of them remain overhead, watching for rebel activity, the others land troops in crests ahead of the advancing column. These troops provide security until the column has passed, after which time the process is repeated further along the route. This type of leapfrogging tactic generally would make it difficult for the Afghan rebels to halt Soviet offensives by striking at supply lines.

Ground Forces Structure

The Soviet ground troops have been split up into seven distinct commands. These areas are under the *de facto* control of Soviet generals, despite the presence of local Afghan political leaders. The exact boundaries between the seven commands have not yet been reported, but the number would correspond to the number of motorized rifle (MR) divisions believed to be in country, with each MR division having responsibility for certain territory.

If there are indeed seven fully manned MR divisions in Afghanistan, each with an average strength of 12,500 men, then total Soviet manpower there would be higher than the often-repeated figure of 85,000. The seven MR divisions alone would account for some 87,500 troops. The addition of a fully-manned airborne division, the 7,500-man 105th Guards Airborne Division, would bring total ground forces manpower to some 95,000. Headquarters and support units in the Kabul area could account for another 5,000 men. Moreover, at least 5,000 aviation personnel would be required to man and maintain the jet combat aircraft and helicopters in the country. This all suggests that total troop strength in Afghanistan would be over 100,000, provided that ground divisions there were manned to their authorized strength. Instead, it is likely that the Soviets have sent some nonessential divisional component units back to their garrisons in the U.S.S.R.

An examination of this troop strength reveals some surprising similarities between the Central

Group of Forces (CGF) in Czechoslovakia and the Soviet contingent in Afghanistan. The CGF was formed from the remaining units which invaded Czechoslovakia in 1968, and is comparable in size with the Soviet force in Afghanistan. There are

The Soviets were shuttling in elite units to give them maximum combat experience.

some 73,000 ground troops in Czechoslovakia, along with about 150 combat aircraft, according to most accounts published in the West.[20] In the event of general war in Europe, the CGF probably would merge into a larger *front* (the largest type of Soviet military organization). Likewise, in the event of general hostilities in South Asia or the Persian Gulf area, the Soviet contingent in Afghanistan could also merge into a wartime *front*, in a force available for operations in the immediate area.

The Enduring Counterinsurgency Mission

A discussion of Soviet operations in Afghanistan strongly suggests that counterinsurgency has become a permanent mission of the Soviet armed forces. This is all the more apparent when one considers the continuing Soviet support to the pro-Communist pacification efforts in Angola and in Ethiopia. So long as Soviet and pro-Soviet forces continue to participate in local conflicts, it is likely that the U.S.S.R. will attain additional expertise in counterinsurgency.

There is further supporting evidence that the Soviets have adopted the counterinsurgency mission. In December 1980, reports reaching the West indicated that the Soviets were shuttling in elite units in order to give them maximum combat experience in Afghanistan. In January 1981, Soviet military spokesmen noted that the scale of tasks being undertaken by the Soviet General Staff has "expanded," thus suggesting that counterinsurgency is becoming an increasingly fashionable career field within the Soviet military structure.[21]

Soviet military doctrine has also evolved over the past few years. One major change is a greater emphasis on civil wars and on national liberation struggles, as well as a stated willingness to assist in "defensive" campaigns in order to counter pro-Western efforts to restore capitalism in newly-established socialist nations. Colonel K. Vorobiev,

this equipment, as well as the associated tactics, could eventually be used against U.S. or NATO forces in the future. The U.S.S.R. closely monitored U.S. military operations during the Vietnam conflict, and drew its own conclusions with the goal of enhancing the potential effectiveness of Soviet forces should they ever directly face American combat units. There is a paramount need for the U.S. to do the same vis-a-vis the Soviet campaign in Afghanistan. Indeed, the Soviet *proverka* in Afghanistan should not be viewed through a narrow and cloudy window. American fighting men have too much to lose if the Soviets apply their new weapons and "lessons learned" against them at some time in the future, without some foreknowledge on our part.

As a final observation, the analysis of the Soviet approach to the counterinsurgency campaign in Afghanistan occasionally reminds one of earlier campaigns against outgunned tribesmen, at a time when the issues all seemed much simpler. In the mid-1930's, Vittorio Mussolini was candid enough to give his eyewitness account of the Italian effort against the Ethiopians:

I still remember the effect I produced on a small group of Galla tribesmen massed around a man in black clothes. I dropped an aerial torpedo right in the center, and the group opened up like a flowering rose. It was most entertaining.[25]

Footnotes

1. Zalmay Khalilzad, "Soviet-Occupied Afghanistan," *Problems of Communism*, November-December 1980, p. 32. See also *Aviation Week & Space Technology*, September 7, 1981, p. 29. The number of helicopters varies over time.
2. Alfred L. Monks, *The Soviet Intervention in Afghanistan* (Washington, D.C.: American Enterprise Institute for Public Policy Research, 1981), p. 41.
3. Stuart Auerbach, "Soviets in Kabul Said to Sell Arms On Black Market," *Washington Post*, February 6, 1981, pp. A1, A26. Soviet troops are also using hashish in place of vodka, which is relatively scarce.
4. David C. Isby, "Afghanistan's Winter War," *Soldier of Fortune*, April 1981, p. 43.
5. Colonel A. Khorobykh, "V Nebe nad Gindukushem" (In the Sky over the Hindu Kush), *Aviatsiya i Kosmonavtika*, No. 8, 1980.
6. U.S. Department of State, *Reports of the Use of Chemical Weapons in Afghanistan, Laos and Kampuchea*, August 1980, p. 5.
7. *ibid.*, passim. See also Isby, *op. cit.*, p. 44.
8. Very early during the post-invasion campaigns in 1980, it appeared that the Soviets were going to employ chemical weapons on a fairly wide scale. See James Hansen, "USSR–Afghanistan: Perspectives on the Conflict," *Military Intelligence*, April-June 1980, p. 43.
9. See Frederick Wiener, *The Armies of the Warsaw Pact Nations*. Second Edition. (Vienna, Austria: Carl Ueberreuter Publishers, 1978).
10. Stuart Auerbach, "Soviet Strikes Reportedly Level Afghan Villages," *Washington Post*, July 15, 1980, p. A8.
11. Isby, *op. cit.*, p. 43.
12. Donald E. Fink, "Afghan Invasion Linked to 1968 Action," *Aviation Week & Space Technology*, July 14, 1980, p. 23. The population of the Soviet civilian enclave in Kabul is said to have jumped from 1,800 before the invasion to between 6,000 and 7,000.
13. "Pravada Reports Afghan Militia Operations," *FBIS Daily Report* for U.S.S.R., July 10, 1981, p. D1.
14. See Khalilzad, *op. cit.*, p. 33, concerning the bridges. See also "Air Cushion Freighters to Service Afghan Route," *FBIS Daily Report* for U.S.S.R., July 24, 1981, p. D6. See also "USSR Troop Increase on Afghan-Iranian Border Noted," *FBIS Daily Report* for China, July 25, 1981, p. F3, concerning the new airfield.
15. Galen L. Geer, "Prayers Replace Pushups," *Soldier of Fortune*, November 1980, p. 42.
16. Khalilzad, *op. cit.*, p. 32.
17. "Armed Forces," *U.S.S.R. Facts & Figures Annual* (Gulf Breeze, Florida: Academic International Press, 1981), p. 74.
18. U.S. Army Intelligence and Threat Analysis Center (ITAC), *Soviet Army Operations*. IAG–13–U–78, August 11, 1978, pp. 7–6 to 7–8.
19. Colonel Yu. Chernyshov, "A Tactical Airborne Landing," *Soviet Military Review*, No. 5, 1980.
20. Lothar Ruehl, "The Slippery Road to MBFR," *Strategic Review*, Winter 1979–1980, p. 28. See also Weiner, *op. cit.*, passim.
21. Colonel P. Mochalov and Engineer-Colonel B. Lyapkalo, "Improving Command and Control," *Krasnaya Zvezda*, January 7, 1981.
22. Monks, *op. cit.*, p. 42.
23. *ibid.*, p. 42.
24. See *Soldier of Fortune* for September 1980, October 1980, November 1980, April 1981, and May 1981 for reports of various types of weapons being used in Afghanistan.
25. Henry Davidoff, *The Pocket Book of Quotations* (New York: Simon & Schuster, 1942), p. 424.
26. The map is taken from Khalilzad, *op. cit.*, p. 25. Sincere thanks to *Problems of Communism* for permission to use the map in this publication.

James H. Hansen is an employee of the BDM Corporation of McLean, Va., where he leads and participates in research projects relating to Soviet/Warsaw Pact military capabilities. He served in the CIA until 1978. He is a frequent contributor to National Defense and to other defense and foreign policy publications. The CIA has reviewed this article to eliminate classified information, but that review neither constitutes CIA authentication of factual material nor implies its endorsement of the views expressed.

Reprinted courtesy of *National Defense* magazine

Recovery of Flight 90

An Engineer Battalion's Contribu

by Capt. David R. Gallay

Less than a minute after becoming airborne during a Washington, D.C., snowstorm, January 13, 1982, Air Florida Flight 90 lost altitude, struck five cars and a truck on the 14th Street Bridge and crashed into the icy Potomac River. Aboard the Boeing 737 were 74 passengers and a crew of five, bound from Washington's National Airport to Tampa, Fla. Five persons survived the crash.

Within minutes of the accident, the Federal Aviation Administration implemented its airport disaster plan. At Fort Belvoir, Va., one of the first activities alerted was the 30th Engineer Battalion (Topographic) (Army), Engineer Center Brigade. Its two attached diving detachments, the 86th and 511th, were placed on standby, and a two-week operation that affected nearly every man and woman of the 30th began.

Early January 14th, Engineer Center Brigade units were set to support recovery and salvage operations. Their mission focused on recovery of the flight and voice recorders, recovery of bodies and salvage of the aircraft. Battalion divers entered the water for the first time late the morning of the 14th.

As the diving situation developed, the battalion sought additional ways to contribute to the operation. The 30th's 584th Engineer Company (Cartographic), for example, took an old copy of a U.S. Department of Transportation pictomap and produced a line map that was subsequently used for site planning. The cartographers also enlarged and printed an existing map of the area on a clear film base. This map was particularly useful to the District of Columbia's Metropolitan Police in planning and controlling rerouted automobile traffic near the cash site.

"Underwater visibility was frequently less than 30 centimeters."

Additionally, surveyors of the battalion's 82d Engineer Company (Survey) were needed to fix the locations of buoys set out by divers marking pieces of wreckage. The surveyors also sited the navigational aids used by remote sensing technicians of the Corps of Engineers' Cold Regions Research Engineering Laboratory (CRREL). These technicians scanned the river bottom by radar and developed profiles indicating wreckage locations (Figure 1). To assist in plotting debris locations, the 584th placed a grid and scaled drawing of the downed aircraft onto the original line map.

At the end of each day, divers, surveyors, CRREL technicians and cartographers, gathered in the 30th's on-site reproduction van to compare notes. There, an updated situation map was prepared and reproduced for use in planning and controlling subsequent dives.

The divers were central to the operation. The battalion's 18 divers, working alongside Coast Guard, Navy and D.C. police divers, recovered all victims and essential wreckage despite extremely adverse weather conditions. Air temperatures were

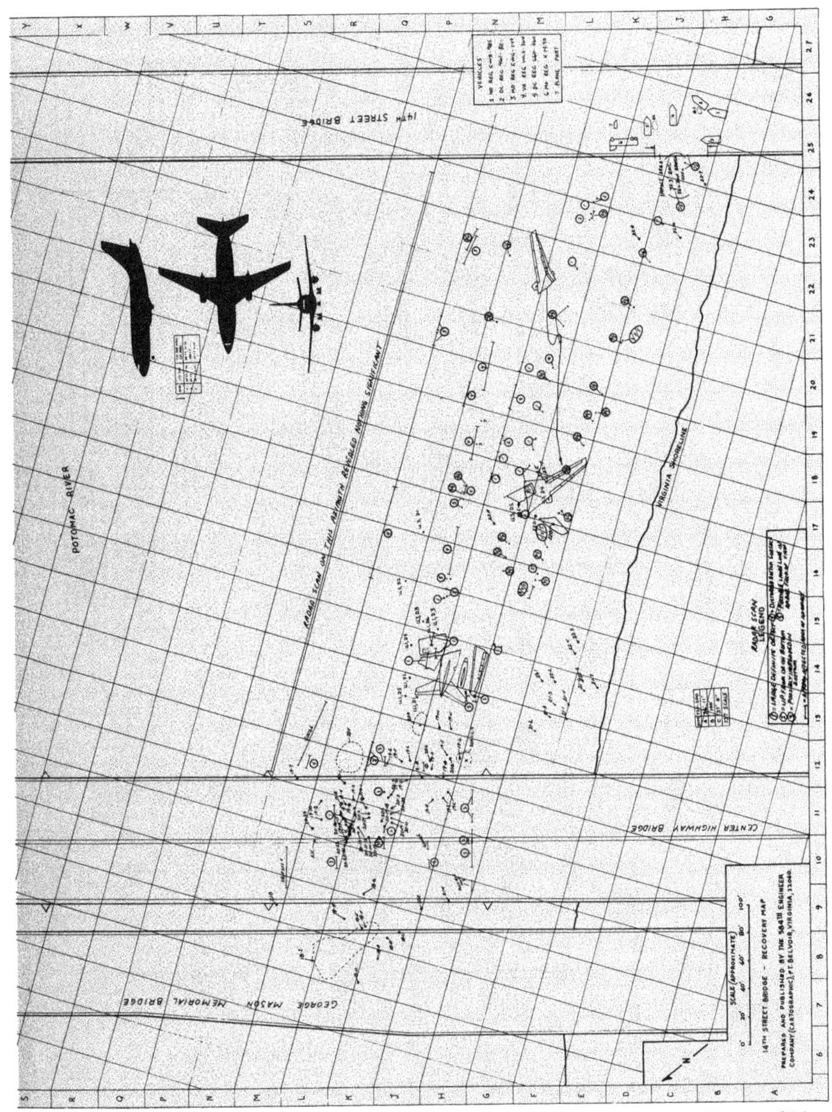

'igure 1. A reproduction of the actual recovery map prepared by the 854th Engineer Company (Cartographic)

FEDERAL EMERGENCY MANAGEMENT AGENCY

US PARK POLICE

DC METROPOLITAN POLICE

NATIONAL TRANSPORTATION SAFETY BOARD

DEPARTMENT OF TRANSPORTATION

DIRECTOR OF MILITARY SUPPORT (DOD EXECUTIVE AGENT)

U.S. ARMY CORPS OF ENGINEERS

ARMY OPERATIONS CENTER

POTOMAC ELECTRIC AND POWER COMPANY

CHESAPEAKE AND POTOMAC TELEPHONE COMPANY

MILITARY DISTRICT OF WASHINGTON

DEPUTY CHIEF OF STAFF OPERATION

U.S. ARMY TRAINING AND DOCTRINE COMMAND

U.S. ARMY FORCES COMMAND

CHIEF OF NAVAL OPERATIONS (OP 64)

CINC U.S. ATLANTIC FLEET

COMMANDER SURFACE FORCES U.S. ATLANTIC FLEET

COMMANDER SURFACE GROUP TWO

COMMANDER SURFACE SQUAD

CHIEF NAVAL MATERIAL

NAVAL SEA SYSTEMS COMMAND

HEADQUARTERS U.S. AIR FORCE

TACTICAL AIR COMMAND

1776th AIRLIFT DIVISION

U.S. ARMY ENGINEER CENTER AND FORT BELVOIR

1st U.S. ARMY

80th DIVISION

NOTE
ORGANIZATIONS ACTUALLY AT CRASH SITE ARE DEPICTED BELOW THIS LINE

US PARK POLICE

DC METROPOLITAN POLICE

NAVAL ON SCENE COMMANDER

SUPERVISOR OF SALVAGE U.S.N.

89th FIELD MAINT SQUADRON

FEDERAL EMERGENCY MANAGEMENT AGENCY

SECRETARY OF THE ARMY PUBLIC AFFAIRS OFFICE

MILITARY DISTRICT OF WASHINGTON SITE OIC

464th TRANSPORTATION BOAT CO LCM

LCM 8144

LCM 8379

LCM 8004

ON SCENE DIVING MEDICAL SUPPORT

ASST OSC/ SALVAGE MASTER

COAST GUARD GROUP BALT.

COAST GUARD AIR STATION NATIONAL AIRPORT

USA AVC (PHOTOGRAPHY)

ENGINEER CENTER BRIGADE

BALTIMORE ENGINEER DISTRICT

CHAPLAIN

BOAT OFFICER SUPERVISOR OF DIVING OPCON

USCGC CAPSTAN

THIRD INFANTRY (OLD GUARD)

U.S. ARMY COMMUNICATIONS CENTER

COLD REGIONS REASEARCH & ENGR LABORATRY

DIVING TEAM NO 3

DIVING TEAM NO 2

DIVING TEAM NO 1

30th ENGINEER BATTALION (TOPOGRAPHIC)

11th ENGINEER BATTALION (COMBAT HEAVY)

EXPLOSIVES ORDINANCE DISPOSAL INDIAN HEAD (NAVY)

HARBOR CLEARANCE UNIT NO 2 (NAVY)

COAST GUARD DIVERS

902nd ENGINEER CO (FLOAT BRIDGE)

DIVERS

DIVERS

DIVERS

NAVAL SURFACE WEAPONS CENTER DIVE TEAM

82nd ENGINEER CO (SURVEY)

15th COMBAT SUPPORT HOSPITAL

584th ENGINEER COMPANY (CARTOGRAPHIC)

86th ENGINEER DETACHMENT (DIVING)

511th ENGINEER DETACHMENT (DIVING)

PHOTOMAPPING PLT

REPRODUCTION PLT

LEGEND

SUPPORT AND COORDINATION

OPERATIONAL CONTROL

OPERATIONAL RESPONSIBILITY

COMMAND

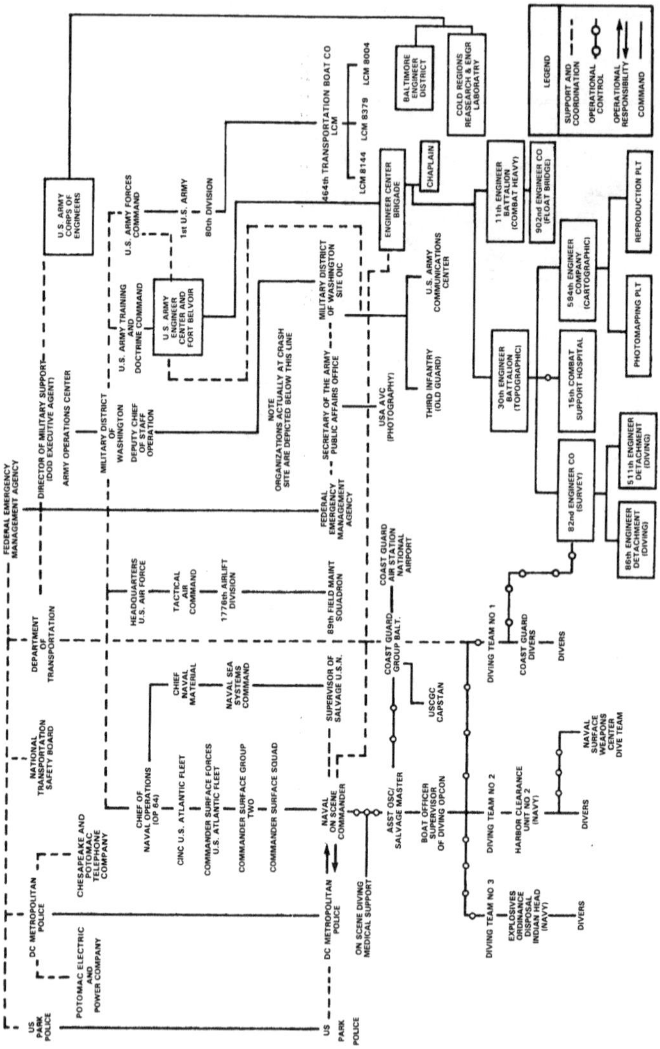

Computer Graphics For Automated Drafting

Huntsville revolutionizes designing, planning and mapping

by M. R. Stevens

In the old days, it might take an architect-engineer or draftsman 20 hours to draw or design a project on a drawing board, depending upon the difficulty of the design. However, with today's modern technology of computer graphics, the same job can be done in just five hours.

The Office of the Chief of Engineers (OCE) has been using computer graphics for several years, but the Huntsville Division and the St. Louis District pioneered development of automated drafting for the Corps. While all three organizations have implemented large, turnkey computer graphics systems for automated drafting and computer-aided design and drafting (CADD), this article features the Huntsville operation.

During a nine-month survey by the Huntsville Division, automated drafting outperformed the manual method four-to-one. During the study, engineers using automated drafting produced 1,521 drawings in only 2,863 manhours. The same drawings produced manually would have required 12,697 manhours.

While automated drafting covers a broad spectrum of applications, at the Huntsville Division, primary interest is in civil design; management, project planning and scheduling; and in mapping. Huntsville has been using automated drafting units since 1978.

Civil design using computer graphics was used recently by Huntsville personnel at the North and South Sinai Peacekeeping Camps. Engineers were provided "as built" drawings of existing facilities, such as utilities, roads, buildings, structures and topographic features drawn on a skewed (not accurate) metric scale. To manually convert the drawings to the English units used by American contractors would have taken approximately four weeks, however, using CADD through automatic-electronic tracing at a computer graphic work-station, the job was completed by a single technician in just 24 manhours.

Within the Huntsville Division, one of the most important uses of computer graphics is in management, project planning and scheduling. Using the critical path method (CPM) and the data management retrieval system (DMRS), project managers are able to set up the system to produce complete packages in a fraction of the time it takes to do the same job manually.

Using the manual method, an engineer makes original drawings, encoding the activities for key punching so a "batch process analysis" can be performed by conventional computer. Any changes in tasks or times would mean more drawings to reflect the changes. With computer graphics, however, the engineer can time-scale his network drawing. He can draw a chart that shows months of the year and the period during which each task should be performed. He can even color-code the schedules to make it more comprehensive for the project manager. If there is a change in task or schedule, he does not have to start over as the draftsman does; he can make corrections or edit the plot on the computer graphics screen. Should there be a change in design, he can retrieve the plot from the data retrieval system and draw the change into the original plot in a matter of minutes. He can edit, change schedules, make additions or correct mistakes as they occur.

Once the package is completed, it remains in the computer disk file for retrieval or update, or it can be put on a small reel of tape and stored for future use. This is a real advantage, considering the large amount of space it takes to store manually produced drawings. It is also possible to telephonically transfer entire packages to other divisions or districts with comparable computer systems.

In mapping, computer graphics is used to update maps in the central file, thus eliminating many errors that occur when updates are made on one document but not on others.

With manual systems, the length of time it

Civil engineer Dale C. King uses a computer graphics terminal and the critical path method to prepare time scheduling charts. (Photo by M.R. Stevens.)

takes to get up-to-date copies of maps or specific areas is a frequent problem. Now, however, one can pick areas and boundaries to be mapped as well as the level of detail required. Once the information is specified, the system selects appropriate data from the file to produce an up-to-date, hardcopy map. Manually changing the scale of maps has always presented problems, too, because the maps usually have to be redrawn. But with computer graphics, scales can be changed almost instantaneously. The entire base map is displayed on the graphics screen, an area is magnified and the operator selects the desired detail. Once detail and scale are established, a hardcopy of the map can be automatically reproduced.

Using computer graphics, information and related data from maps is readily available and the job of manually reviewing maps is eliminated. Engineers list the information needed and the system scans the map file, printing requested information to the engineer's standards. In addition to providing quick and accurate reports, the system automatically revises the map file when maps are updated.

Map revision is a time consuming task. for draftsmen or engineers because it involves overlays, notes, insertions and deletions that tend to clutter the original, and, if the revision has errors, it must be corrected again. With computer graphics, the map is displayed on the screen so engineers or draftsmen can make direct changes. Specific areas or whole sections can be changed, rearranged or corrected on the screen which eliminates redrawing. Map revision can be completed in a fraction of the time it takes to make changes manually. Computer graphics can also be used to standardize the shape, size and symbols used on maps.

While the Huntsville Division currently uses computer graphics in only three major areas (civil design; management, project planning and scheduling; and mapping) the system can be expanded as the Corps becomes involved in new and different projects. As more personnel are trained in the use of computer graphics, potential for standardization between divisions and districts becomes more attainable. And, while Corps-wide standardization is still in the future, for the organizations using computer graphics now, the future is today.

Writer's Guidelines

In response to queries from prospective authors, we pass along the following ENGINEER writer's guidelines:

TOPIC—Although our focus is upon combat engineering, any subject of professional interest to the Corps is welcome. It is always best to query first since an article similar to yours may have appeared already or may be scheduled for a future issue. Please title your article.

LENGTH—Length is not as important as content. Let your subject matter dictate length. Most ENGINEER articles range from 1,000 to 3,000 words. One caution, however: if it appears your article will be exceptionally lengthy, please call or write so we can let you know if sufficient space will be available.

PHOTOGRAPHS AND ARTWORK—Photos and drawings strengthen your article, and in some cases are vital graphic aids to conveying your message. Photos should be black and white, glossy, and, preferably, at least 5" × 7". Drawings must be legible but need not be "camera ready."

COVER LETTER—Please include a cover letter with your name, address, a phone number at which you can be contacted, a brief (one or two paragraph) description of your article, and biographical data on yourself.

NEWS & NOTES—We're always looking for contributions here, especially those with photographs. Your TASC or public affairs officer will be able to provide you photographic support.

Finally, we'll work with you on polishing your writing skills. The most important criteria for an ENGINEER article is the story it tells and the professional growth it stimulates in your fellow Engineers.

We look forward to seeing your article in a future issue of ENGINEER.

Geofabrics in Military Construction

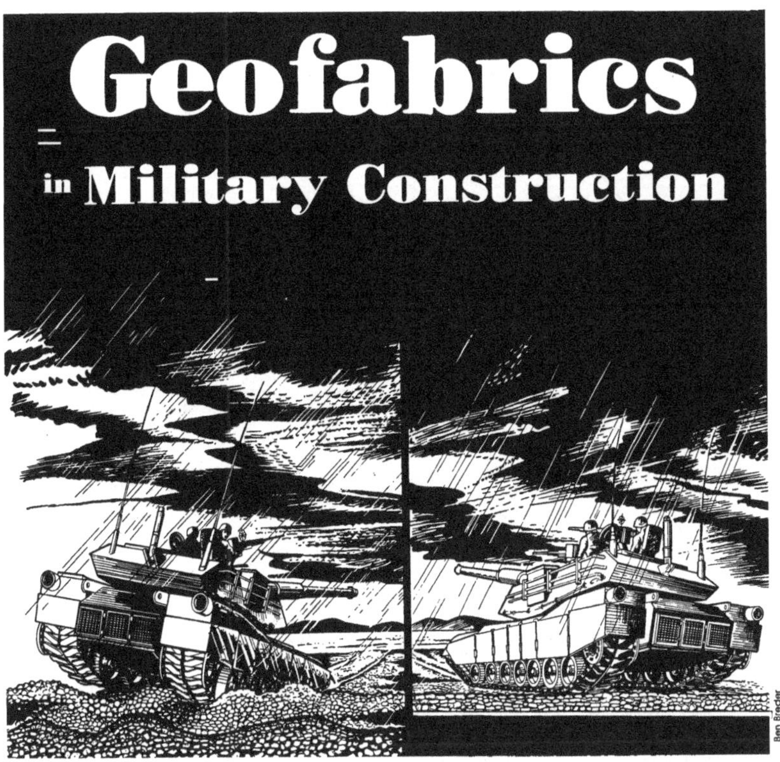

Without Fabric With Fabric

by Capt. Stephen L. Gerecke and Capt. Philip M. Jones

Geotextiles and geomembranes (both called geofabrics) have gained wide acceptance in civilian construction practice. They are employed in a number of methods to take advantage of their structural properties. Those methods most applicable to the military engineer are:

Reinforcement—spreads a vehicle load over a larger area, "bridges over" soft spots, and slows development of ruts.

Separation—prevents intrusion and mixing at the interface of the base aggregate and subgrade, and the resultant loss of strength.

Drainage—allows removal (passage) of water without the build up of high pore pressure and the resultant loss of soil strength.

Reinforcement may be further defined as:

Subgrade restraint—the prevention or reduction of soil movement and strain by fabric confinement.

Earth reinforcement—the use of a fabric to increase the strength of a soil-fabric system.

This paper will address subgrade restraint and soil reinforcement of roads leading to tactical bridges, stream crossings, fording sites and other areas where poor trafficability exists. Consideration is given to the

Secant Modulus Curve

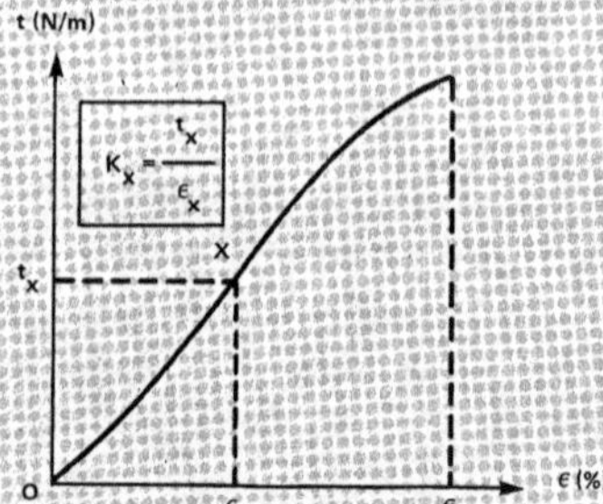

Figure 1—Typical tension-elongation curve of geotextile (E_F = elongation at failure; E_x = elongation at point x; t_x = tension at point x; and K_x = secant modulus at point x).

construction fabrics normally available to theater of operations engineers and to conservation of time and materiel.

Military Use of Construction Fabrics

The trafficability of soils near tactical bridges and stream crossings is often a problem, particularly after repeated passages of military vehicles. The in-place California bearing ratio (CBR) value may be as low as five to 15 percent prior to any traffic, providing the soil and root mat are undisturbed. However, once vehicle traffic begins to churn and blend the cover material, the CBR value may drop below one percent.

The standard solution is to remove the mud and replace it with dry, trafficable materials (usually crushed stone). However, the next rain will probably reduce the area to its original condition if traffic continues. This is true regardless of the type of cover material used, unless excessive quantities are placed.

Adequate drainage is needed, plus something to keep the poor quality subgrade from mixing with the better quality cover material. This is where the geofabric is most valuable. The quantity of aggregate needed to support traffic over low strength subgrades can be reduced by up to 50 percent through the use of a fabric interface.

Geofabrics are composed of two types of materials, *geotextiles* and *geomembranes*. The most basic difference between them is that geotextiles are permeable, while geomembranes are impermeable. Both may be either woven or non-woven, however, the geomembrane will have a second layer of impervious material bonded to the fabric base to prevent passage of fluids.

There are presently hundreds of fabrics on the commercial market. The profusion of these products and the manufacturers' claims about them make it difficult to judge their usefulness. However the "secant modulus" seems the best method for comparison of different fabrics.

The secant modulus is a key property of geofabrics designed for soil reinforcement. The modulus is the ratio of the tension on the fabric to the elongation of the fabric caused by a standard test load. A high modulus means a low stretch while a low modulus would indicate more stretch, thus less ultimate strength.

The modulus of a fabric is determined by plotting the amounts of elongation and the tensile force used to effect that elongation (strain). A sample curve showing the secant modulus, K, is given. The value of K is generally taken at elongations of ten percent. While the ten percent value is not by itself significant, its use does allow for ready comparison with other fabrics.

Results of tests have shown that geofabrics under a loaded surface will significantly reduce elongation at the interface of the aggregate and the subgrade. This reduction results from the geofabrics confinement of both the soil and aggregate. The reduction is greater with higher values of secant moduli. A high modulus fabric is easier to roll out, walk on, and will carry a higher traffic load than a fabric of lower secant modulus. (Reference 1).

It has also been found that the tensile/elastic modulus of the geofabric has a pronounced effect on the strains within the aggregate layer above the fabric. The greater the fabric's resistance to deformation, the lower the strains will be in the aggregate layer above the fabric. The greater the fabric's resistance to deformation, the lower the strains will be in the aggregate layer above the fabric. This results in lower stress being passed to the subgrade and less rutting of the road. (Reference 2).

Using the secant modulus, K, for comparing fabrics is difficult since there is currently no industry standard for reporting the modulus of the fabric. Table 1 gives K values for the more common fabrics. Depending upon fabric construction, i.e., woven or non-woven, spun bonded, needle punched, etc., it may have different elongation properties in different directions. A manufacturer may choose to report the stronger of the two moduli for directional fabrics, the weaker, or the average. Published literature is generally nonspecific about the direction of the test, or the type of test done on each fabric. (Reference 3). There are two test methods for use with directional and non-directional fabrics: the uniaxial for woven fabrics, and the biaxial for nonwoven fabrics. The results obtained from a uniaxial test for a woven fabric are not much different from those using a biaxial test. However, with nonwoven fabrics the difference is important, and the biaxial test is strongly recommended. A review of Table 1 shows the increased value for K using the biaxial test for nonwoven fabrics. (Reference 4).

Data published by manufacturers often has information on grab tensile strength and elongation. However, to permit accurate comparisons the results listed must state the test method used and the percent elongation at which the measurements were taken. The preferred elongation for secant moduli data is ten percent.

Design Using Geofabrics

Extensive work by the Woodward-Clyde consultant firm and the Corps of Engineers' Waterways Experiment Station (WES) at Vicksburg, Miss., has resulted in the development of a very useful graph. Given the anticipated vehicle requirements and the available materials, e.g., number of passages of vehicles, in-place CBR of the soil and type(s) of fabric(s), the reduction of the cover aggregate can be determined for that section of road. The reduction is relative to the same

Fabric Trade Name and Secant Modulus Values

Fabric Trade Name	*Woven (W) or Nonwoven (N)*	*Uniaxial Text* kN/m	*Biaxial Text* kN/m
Bay Mills 196–380	W	700	
Nicolon 66475	W	633	
Polyfilter–X	W	180	
Advance Type I	W	188	
Nicolon 66186	W	190	
Permealiner M–1195	W	124	
Bidim C–42	N	39	198
Advance Type II	W	126	
Terrafix NA 330	N/W	85	
Polyfilter–GB	W	72	
Bidim C–38	N	24	122
Filter–X	W	60	
Bidim C–34	N	18	97
Lotrak 16/15	W	64	
Nicolon 66530	W	60	
Typar 3601	N	68	64
Bidim C–28	N	12	76
Stablienka	N	48	
Supac	N	13	
Monofelt N–5500–01	N	13	
Bidim C–22	N	16	54
Typar 3401	N	39	44
Mirafi 140	N	26	
Stabilenka	N	30	
International Paper 503	N	12	
Stabilenka T–80	N	12	
Enkamat 7020	N	5	
Enkamat 7010	N	1	

All of the above were tested at 10% elongation. The two listed below were tested at the percent elongation shown (%).

Reeves T–16	W	200	(10%)
Reeves T–17	W	426	(15%)

All uniaxial tests are in the warp (long direction) plane, and all values are given in kilo-Newtons per meter.
(1 lbf/in = 0.175 kN/m)

Table 1

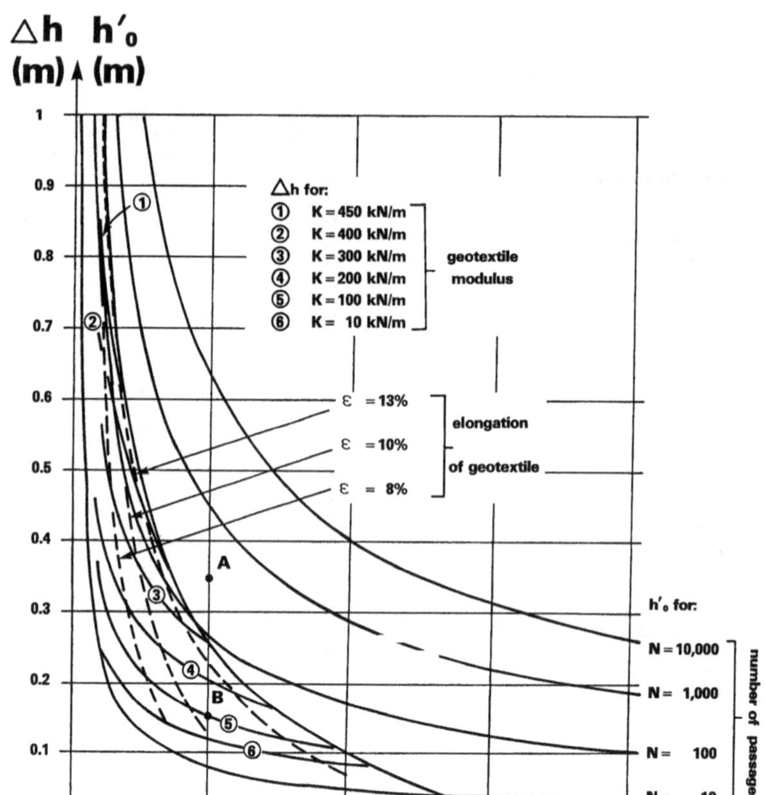

Figure 2. Aggregate thickness h'_o (case without geotextile when traffic is taken into account) and possible reduction of aggregate thickness Δh resulting from the use of a geotextile vs subgrade soil cohesion.

road without fabric. The key to determining that reduction is the K value of the fabric placed between the in-place soil and the cover aggregate. The graph, shown on page 22, was developed through numerical analysis which correlated the following factors: soil strength, wheel loads, fabric strength and the soil-fabric system. Two facts were used to minimize the number of variables and charts. The first was that the thickness of the aggregate using CBR and number of passages does not depend upon the fabric to be used. On the graph, this value is represented as h_o'. The second fact was that the reduction of cover aggregate does not depend upon the traffic. This value is represented by Δh. These two facts permitted both h_o' vs CBR and Δh vs CBR to be plotted on the one graph. Both curves are actually families relating various vehicle passages and geofabric moduli, respectively. (Reference 4)

The graph was set up for a standard 18 kip single-axle, dual wheel load and the formation of all 11 inch deep rut. It appears to be in general conformity with test results generated by WES and will assist military engineers in the trial design and aggregate reduction determination of theater of operation roads.

The following is a sequence of steps to determine the aggregate reduction using a geofabric.

1) Evaluate the CBR value of the subgrade at the anticipated time of construction. This should include any degradation caused by prior traffic and construction equipment. The cone penetrometer and airfield index may be used to find this value.

2) Estimate the number of passages, in equivalent 18 kip single-axle vehicle units (see Figure 3).

3) Using Table 1, find the value for secant modulus for the fabric on hand, or select best if several are available. If the fabric is not listed on the table, its value of K may be calculated from the manufacturer's data.

4) Enter the graph (Figure 2) at the in-place CBR value and read up to the number of passages. Read to

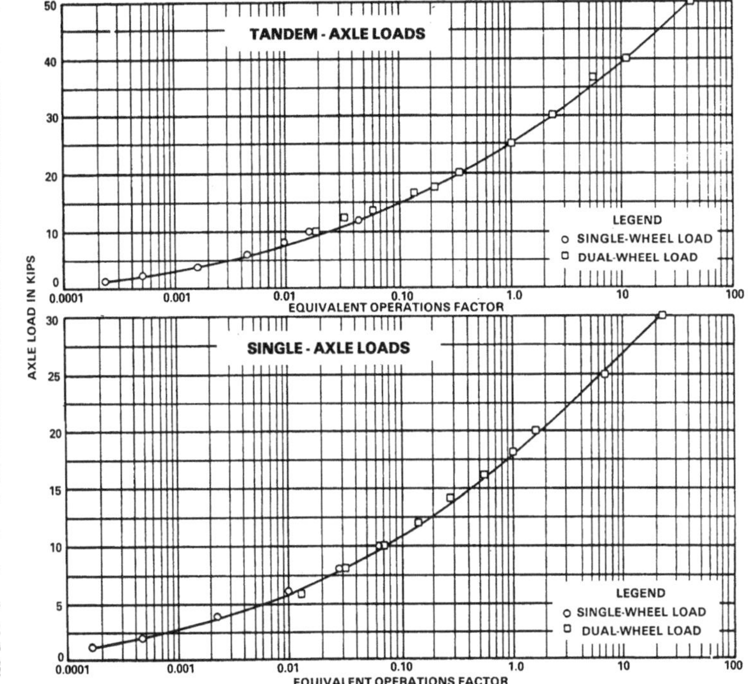

Figure 3. Flexible pavement design curves for roads, equivalent operations factor for tandem-axle and single-axle loads. Taken from TM5-330/AFM 86-3, Vol II.

the left, the thickness of aggregate required, H'_o, without fabric. Record and save for step 6.

5) Enter the graph (Figure 2) at the in-place CBR value and read up to the approximate K value of the fabric, in kN/m. Read to the left the Δh value for reduction of aggregate.

6) Subtract the value found in step 5 from that found in step 4. This is the required aggregate depth when the fabric is first placed on the subgrade. As traffic passages accumulate, it may be necessary to add aggregate to weaker portions of the road as spot fill.

Equivalent 18 kip single-axle vehicle passages can be determined through the use of Figure 3, *Equivalent Operations Factor*. This procedure equates all vehicles to an equivalent vehicle for use on the aggregate reduction graph, Figure 2. The anticipated traffic is estimated by type and load, and an equivalent operations factor is selected from Figure 2. The sum of the daily traffic equivalent operations is multiplied by the planned life of the road in days. This will give the total vehicle passages for the planned road.

Example

a. Equivalent vehicle passages
Given: vehicle load, operations per day and planned life of the road; the operation factor, equivalent operations per day and the total passages may be calculated.

Axle or gross load in pounds	*Type vehicle by axle*	*Operations per day*
1,000	single	200
5,000	tandem	175
10,000	single	100
10,000	tandem	200
20,000	tandem	90

Planned life of road is 26 weeks.

Axle or gross load (pounds)	*Operation factor (from Figure 3)*	*Operations per day*	*Equivalent operations per day*
		Single-axle	
1,000	0.00016	200	0.032
10,000	0.007	100	0.70
		Tandem-axle	
5,000	0.003	175	0.5295
10,000	0.024	200	4.80
20,000	0.360	90	32.40

Total equivalent operations per day (EO/D) 38.4615.

Planned life of road, 26 weeks with 7 days per week. Total passages = (weeks) × (days/week) × (EO/D) i.e., (26) × (7) × (38.4615) = 6,999.99 ≈ 7,000.

b) *Aggregate Reduction*
Given: vehicle passages = 7,000,
In-place CBR = 1%,
Fabric: Reeves T-17 w/k = 426 kN/m.*

*Reeves T-17 is currently available in the military supply system.

Enter Figure 2 at the bottom with the CBR value of 1 percent. Read up to the point of passages, then read to the left the value for h'_o of 0.57 m. For the fabric enter the figure at CBR of 1 and read up to the K value of 426 kN/m, read to the left the Δh value of 0.25 m. The required thickness is 0.57—0.25 m giving 0.32 m or approximately 12½ inches. The savings is approximately 10 inches , or 44%.

c) To calculate the secant modulus of a fabric
Given: grab tensile strength of 102.8 lbf/in at 10% elongation. Secant Modulus = (gbs) ÷ (el), thus K = (102.8) ÷ (0.10) = 1028 lbf/in.

To convert to SI units, 1 lbf/in = 0.175 kN/m, so (1,028 lbf/in) × (0.175) = 179.9 kN/m. This value may be used to enter Figure 3 to determine aggregate reduction.

The aggregate reduction example showed a savings of about 10 inches. If this were a T/O road 23 feet in width and one mile in length, the aggregate saved would be approximately 3,750 cubic yards. Additional savings would be realized through reduced maintenance of that section of road.

It has been suggested by both Mr. Giroud, (Reference 4) and Mr. Webster, (Reference 1), that a fabric with a very high secant modulus would make possible a limited passage road with *no* cover aggregate. This could be applicable for a hasty road with planned low traffic volume and a very short term requirement.

Table 1 lists some of the geofabrics that are, or have been available commercially, as well as two (Reeves T-16 and T-17) which are available in the military supply system. The values shown were derived from a variety of sources, and may not reflect the current products on the market today. The K value will assist in selecting either the best fabric from those on hand, or in ordering one which will suit the requirements for the project. The table will also permit the determination of the aggregate reduction for that fabric.

Installation

Installation of geofabrics is not a difficult task bu should be done with care to avoid tearing the material There is also a requirement to overlap the ends and/o sides at joints. The five steps below will assist in th proper placement of fabrics for road and airfield use:

1) The area to be covered should be cleared of al sharp objects which might tear the material. Any larg objects which might cause deformations in the materi al as fill is placed should be removed.

2) If possible, the site should be rough graded an compacted. A significant increase in strength will result when the subgrade is compacted even marginally.

3) The fabric is almost always supplied on rolls. This permits the fabric to be unrolled over the area to be covered. This may be done either by hand or machine, depending upon the subgrade. In cases where the subgrade is covered by a mud blanket, the fabric should be only partially unrolled. As fill is placed on the fabric it will cause the mud to push out ahead of the fabric. The

object is to avoid trapping pockets of mud under the fabric. When using equipment to spread the roll, it is best to operate the machinery directly on the subgrade and not on the fabric. This will help in preventing tears in the fabric.

4) At the end of each roll, and if two sections are placed side by side, an overlap must be made. The amount of overlap is dependent upon the subgrade, the expected traffic, the depth of fill and the fabric being used. As a general rule, the following overlaps are recommended, based on the CBR of the in-place soil:

CBR, percent	20	15	10	8	6	4	2
Overlap, percent of roll width	10	12	14	15	18	22	25

(Reference 5)

The use of fabrics will not cure a poor design, nor will their employment turn soup into concrete. The minimum CBR value which will support an aggregate-fabric system has not yet been determined and is beyond the scope of this article. However, fabric without aggregate covering has been used successfully in some cases. It is noteworthy that the value of fabrics drop considerably with CBR values above five percent. The higher strength soils will be aided by the separation action of the fabrics, and their use for that function may be cost justified.

There are other areas of fabric properties that may affect field performance which have not been discussed in this article. The use of the secant modulus and the graph developed by Mr. Giroud (Reference 7) will establish a base for fabric performance through K values.

The military engineer can now design a theater of operations road over a low strength soil with reasonable confidence in the performance of the end product and can now work towards the full utilization of his limited construction materials.

References

1. U.S. Army Engineer Waterways Experiment Station, *Investigation of Construction Techniques for Tactical Bridge Approach Roads Across Soft Ground.* Technical Report S-77-1, (Vicksburg, Miss., 1977).

2. Carroll, R.G.; *The Role of Geotextile Modulus in the Behavior and Design of Soil-Geotextile-Aggregate Systems.* ASCE Geotechnical Conference, Session A-4.

3. Law Engineering Testing Company, *Guidelines for Design of Flexible Pavements Using Mirafi Woven Stabilization Fabrics.* (Houston, Texas.)

4. Giroud, J.P. and Noiray, L. "Geotextile-Reinforced Unpaved Road Design," *Journal of The Geotechnical Engineering Division*, ASCE, (Vol. 107, No. GT9, September 1981).

5. Koerner, R.M. and Walsh, J.P.: *Construction and Geotechnical Engineering Using Synthetic Fabrics,* (New York, 1980).

6. University of Illinois, Department of Civil Engineering; *Design Procedures for Soil Fabric-Aggregate Systems with Mirafi 500X Fabric.* (Urbana, Ill., 1980.)

7. Williamson, J.S. and Mohney, J.; *Guidelines for Use of Fabrics in Construction and Maintenance of Low-Volume Roads.* Report No. FHWA-TS-78-205, (Washington, D.C., 1978).

8. Department of the Army Technical Manual 5-330, *Planning and Design of Roads, Airbases and Heliports in the Theater of Operations,* September 1968.

Capt. Stephen L. Gerecke is assigned to the Directorate of Engineering and Housing, Stuttgart, Germany. As a civilian engineer, he worked on geotechnical projects in Louisiana and California. He has served as the 565th Engineer Battalion S-4 and commander, 93rd Float Bridge Company (MAB). He has a bachelor of science degree in civil engineering from the University of Texas at Austin.

Capt. Philip Jones is a senior instructor of soils and equipment utilization for the Roads and Airfields Branch, U.S. Army Engineer School, Fort Belvoir, Va. He is a graduate of the U.S. Military Academy and has served as S-3, 565th Engineer Battalion and as commander of A Company, 78th Engineer Battalion. He has a master of science degree in civil engineering from the University of California at Berkeley.

The ENGINEER Problem

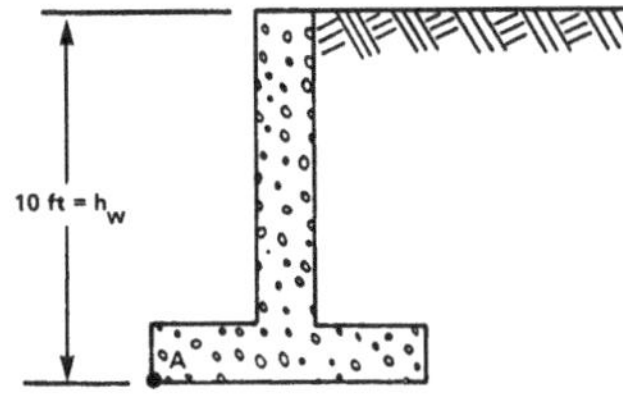

A retaining wall is to be constructed as shown. What resisting moment must be developed per foot of the wall to keep it from overturning about point A? The density of the soil (γs) is 130 lbs/ft^3 with an internal angle of friction ($\emptyset$) of 33.5. There will be no traffic on top of the wall or the soil.

PANAMA
Keeping the Canal on Track

by Capt. Frederick R. Ferrin

One of the Army's smallest and most unique units is the U.S. Army Element, Panama Canal Commission. A company grade officer's assignment to the Commission is normally an advanced civil school utilization tour, and from the moment your sponsor tells you to leave your uniforms in storage and to stock up on light clothing, you know this will be no ordinary assignment.

ew works to expose rail soon to be re-ed using the "alternate tie" method. il now, the Panama Canal's tow track em has had few improvements since nstallation in 1913. (Photos by Capt. lerick Ferrin.)

History

The U.S. Army Corps of Engineers' long and illustrious history in Panama began before the year 1900, when various Engineer officers, including the Chief of Engineers, were appointed to investigative committees evaluating the feasibility of excavating a canal across the Isthmus of Panama. The Corps' legacy continued with the appointment of Lt. Col. George W. Goethals, an Army Engineer who replaced chief engineer John Stevens under whose masterful direction the first phases of canal construction were completed. Two other Engineers, Maj. David D. Gaillard and Maj. William Sibert, once roommates at West Point, were chosen to direct the most difficult construction efforts of the Panama Canal—the 100,000,000 cubic yard excavation between Lake Gatun and the Pacific entrance, and the massive concrete structures of Gatun Dam and Gatun Locks.

After the canal opened in August 1914, George Goethals remained as governor of the Canal Zone, and until the zone ceased to exist (by order of the Panama Canal Treaty of 1979) the position of governor was traditionally a Corps of Engineers assignment.

The duty environment at the canal is unique because of its tropical setting, unusual political status and because the canal itself is so unusual. Officers assigned to this project gain experience few others share. Americans and Panamanians, military and civilian; each doing their part to keep the canal open to world shipping. Additionally, most officers acquire a working knowledge of Spanish in order to effectively communicate with their Spanish-speaking co-workers.

The U.S. Army Element, Panama Canal Commission, is currently comprised of four Engineer officers commanded by Maj. Michael Bates. The commander also serves as director of the Engineering and Construction Bureau, which employs 2,480 civilians within its five divisions of engineering, electrical, maintenance, dredging and industrial.

In January 1981, the maintenance division began renovation of the ship tow track system at the three sets of canal locks. The project, expected to be completed by 1985, will possibly be one of the last, major in-house projects undertaken by the commission before transfer of the canal to the Republic of Panama in the year 2000.

Few improvements have been made to the original tow track system, installed circa 1913 during construction of the locks. Much of the system has become badly worn, and the weight of today's powerful towing locomotives and the lateral loads induced by larger ships have dramatically increased stresses to the system.

The towing system consists of two 90-pound crane rails, a continuous slotted rack with which the towing locomotive's quill gear meshes and a 440-volt conductor slot which provides power to the locomotives.

The track renovations call for repair or replacement of system components as necessary; and at a minimum, the 90-pound rail closest to the lock chamber must be replaced with 105-pound rail and new, high-strength attachment hardware will be installed.

The most important criterion of the project is that replacement of the rail system must not effect normal canal operations. Any disruption of this strictly programmed and vitally important commercial enterprise causes worldwide repercussions in the shipping industry. The project engineer, therefore, must make maximum use of the time between the passing of each day's last and first ships. It is only during this daily "window" that rail may actually be removed. However, if a lane at one of the locks is placed out of service for routine or planned maintenance, the track renovation engineers will use the time to accelerate the normal renovation schedule.

Unique Repair Method

The method currently used to repair the locks' tow track system was developed several years ago by the engineering division of the Panama Canal Commission. The procedure, dubbed the "alternate tie method," is novel in that it can be performed during regular towing operations without adverse effect upon freshly placed concrete.

The towing locomotive rails are supported every eighteen inches by alternating short and long ties. A long tie supports both the waterside and landside rails, passing below the slotted rack between the rails. The short ties are, as the name implies, much shorter and support only one rail. Both the long and short ties rest on and in concrete.

Renovation begins when the concrete encasing the ties is demolished down to the ties' bottom flange. A 2½ inch hole is drilled into the concrete at the waterside end of each long tie, and a 2 inch schedule 80 pipe, driven into the hole until refusal, is then welded to the long tie. This pipe provides temporary support to the long tie as concrete below the long and short ties is demolished. The short ties are removed and repaired, and the old 90-pound rail is replaced by new 105-pound crane rail. The repaired short ties are returned

NCO Training For German Engineers

by SGM Dieter Helmig

Noncommissioned officer training and advancement in the West German Army is quite unlike the typical NCO paths in the American Army, and, as one would expect, these variations reflect some of the cultural differences of our two countries. In Germany, for example, all men from the ages of 18-28 may be drafted. Women serve in the German Army only as medical doctors, pharmacists or dentists.

After finishing intermediate school (at age 15 or 16), both male and female students receive vocational training to qualify them for their later career. This training lasts two-to-three and one-half years and could be in any skill from salesman to mechanic. By law, vocational training ends with a formal, state examination.

In the German Army, soldiers enlist in two ways—as volunteers through recruiting offices or as draftees who wish to enlist for longer terms; draftees have the opportunity to enlist anytime during their 15 months of active service. Although soldiers enlist for various terms, they may reenlist—extend their enlistment—at any time. All German soldiers fit into one of three categories. He is either a draftee, a short-term volunteer (2-15 years) or career soldier.

If an enlistee desires to serve as an NCO, he is tested before he enlists. If he passes the test, he is identified as an NCO candidate and takes basic training for three months along with draftees and those identified as officer candidates.

In the German Army, basic training is given by the division to which the soldier will be assigned. After basic, the NCO candidate, draftee and officer candidate begin six months of advanced training. In the case of engineer soldiers, common military skills are covered, as is engineer training. If he is doing excellent work, the advanced training graduate is promoted to GEFREITER (private E-2). At this point, he has been on active duty for nine months.

The NCO candidate now attends UNTEROFFIZIERGRUNDLEHRGANG TEIL I & II (NCO Basic Course Part I & II) for a total of six months. The NCO Basic Course II for engineers is given in Munich, Bavaria, and trains the soldier to be a leader, a supervisor, a specialist with expert knowledge, and an instructor. If the NCO candidate had enlisted for at least four years, he will also attend for one month a supplementary course emphasizing principles of human leadership.

After completing the NCO Basic Course and supplemental course (if applicable), the candidate must pass a test consisting of written, oral and practical portions. The test is required by German law. After returning to his unit, the successful NCO candidate is promoted to UNTEROFFIZIER (sergeant).

The German sergeant serves as a squad leader and instructor. The requirements for the sergeant grade are high, and he must be able to lead, to motivate, and to train his squad using all the principles of modern leadership.

The Senior NCO

In the German Army Corps of Engineers, many platoon leaders are senior NCOs with the rank of HAUPTEFELDWEBEL (master sergeant or sergeant major). The engineer platoon is the smallest independent element in the company, and, especially in the armored engineer company, it has a high degree of autonomy. Accordingly, it is vital that the platoon leader be able to accomplish assigned missions using his own judgment and initiative. He must be able to follow the reasoning of his superiors. He has command authority and must not wait for orders if a situation demands immediate action. It should be noted that in the German Army, commanders at all levels are given considerable latitude on *how* to accomplish a mission. When the company commander assigns his engineer platoon leader a mission, the platoon leader determines *on his own* the method and resources required to accomplish the task.

To assist him the NCO platoon leader normally has another senior NCO or deputy, and three jun-

German engineers are identified by this badge worn on a red beret.

ior NCO squad leaders. How is the NCO platoon leader prepared to be an instructor, superior and leader? The answer is through the FELDWEBELLEHRGANG (Advanced NCO Training Course). To attend the course, an NCO must: be a STABSUNTEROFFIZIER (staff sergeant), have at least four years of service, have enlisted for at least eight years, and meet specified physical fitness and professional skill levels.

The Advanced NCO Course lasts 16-23 weeks. The NCOs receive training as an instructor and are placed in command positions. Sand table instruction is an important part of this course. A large part of the course is devoted to leadership training and to civic education. After completing the course, the NCO has mastered:

- the principles of command and control
- command organization
- command and control
- logistics

All graduates are licensed to perform demolition work and to act as demolition OICs. NCOs going to ribbon bridge, AVLB or CEV platoons become licensed examiners and are authorized to issue operator permits for all engineer equipment in their platoon. To graduate, all NCOs must pass a written, oral and practical exam, as required by German law.

After the NCO Advanced Course, the NCO returns to his unit and serves an "internship." When his probationary period is over (that is dependent upon his supervisor's evaluation), he is promoted to FELDWEBEL (sergeant first class).

Completion of the NCO Advanced Course gives him the credits required to become a career NCO (who stays on active duty until age 53) or to be selected to be a FACHOFFIZIER (specialist officer)* in his seventh year of service.

* The fachoffizier is similar to the U.S. Army's warrant officer, but there are important differences. A fachoffizier, for example, may command a specialized unit; a U.S. warrant officer does not serve in command positions.

The Engineer Workbook

Bridging the Training Gap

by John Florence

"It is the most outstanding training management method I've ever seen. It does more to help the unit commander than any training document I've come across," says Col. Claude W. Biehn, former deputy director, Training Management Study of the Reserve Components, Office of the Deputy Assistant Secretary of Defense.

Indeed it is an impressive document. In 1,058 pages, the new *Engineer Trainer's Workbook* defines training objectives *and* supplies complete ARTEP training plans; training evaluation standards; and a plenary, Army-wide reference listing for all engineer ARTEP missions. The prodigious workbook is the culmination of a six-year effort by the 579th Engineer Battalion (Combat) (Corps), California Army National Guard, to produce explicit guidelines implementing the philosophy of the Battalion Training Management System (BTMS).

The document is being published by the U.S. Army Training and Doctrine Command (TRADOC) and distributed by late spring to all active Army and reserve component combat engineer battalions. The workbook will be bound as a loose-leaf document to encourage trainers to use it for its intended purpose—as a *work*book. Appropriate pages can be easily removed for reference or photocopied and used by trainers for planning or recording training notes.

MISSION LIST - SECTION TASKS TRAINING GUIDE #10

CONSTRUCTION

TASK	DESCRIPTION	PAGE	SECTION TASKS - IDT	SECTION TASKS - AT	FUTURE TRAINING YEAR	POST MOBILIZATION	TASKS CURRENTLY PROFICIENT
4-13	SECURE WORKSITE		OCT ✓			✓	
4-30	INSTALL HASTY PROTECTIVE MINEFIELD		JUN ✓		✓		
6-25	CONSTRUCT TRACKED VEHICLE FIGHTING POSITIONS		APR ✓		✓		
6-26	CONSTRUCT ARTILLERY EMPLACEMENTS		MAY ✓		✓		
6-31	CONSTRUCT LOG CRIB						✓
6-32	CONSTRUCT AN ABATIS						✓
8-3	CONSTRUCT A 30 FOOT, CLASS 20, SINGLE LANE TIMBER TRESTLE BRIDGE		SEP ✓		✓		
8-5	REINFORCE BRIDGE WITH PIER/BENT				✓		
11-12	REACT TO ENEMY CONTACT (SQUAD)		OCT ✓			✓	
13-22	CONSTRUCT CULVERTS		JAN ✓	✓			
13-29	CONSTRUCT HASTY HELICOPTER LANDING ZONE		[illegible] ✓		✓		
14-3	CONSTRUCT PREFABRICATED METAL BUILDING		OCT ✓				
14-8	CONSTRUCT TENT FRAMES		NOV ✓	✓		✓	
14-9	CONSTRUCT A CONCRETE PAD						✓
14-10	CONSTRUCT A VERTICAL WALL		FEB ✓				
14-12	INTALL ELECTRICAL EQUIPMENT AND FIXTURES		AUG ✓	✓		✓	
14-17	INSTALL PLUMBING AND FIXTURES		MAR ✓			✓	
14-18	INSTALL HEATING AND VENTING EQUIPMENT		JUL ✓			✓	

MISSION LIST

Figure 1. ARTEP tasks are grouped into mission lists to aid planners in preparing training forecasts.

Background

The version of the workbook distributed by TRADOC traces its lineage back to 1976 when its originators, Maj. Jerrald Jurin and Capt. Jim Combs set out to upgrade unit training.

Combs at the time was commanding B Company and Jurin recently finished his command time in A Company (where Combs had served as a platoon leader). The two men shared a desire to ameliorate training quality by providing better training guidance to their NCOs. "If our training guidance is vague or shallow," Combs says, "then results are the same. As managers, we (the officer corps) have been very effective at setting training goals, but very ineffective at providing trainers the vehicle needed to arrive at those goals."

So six years ago, Combs devised his own train-

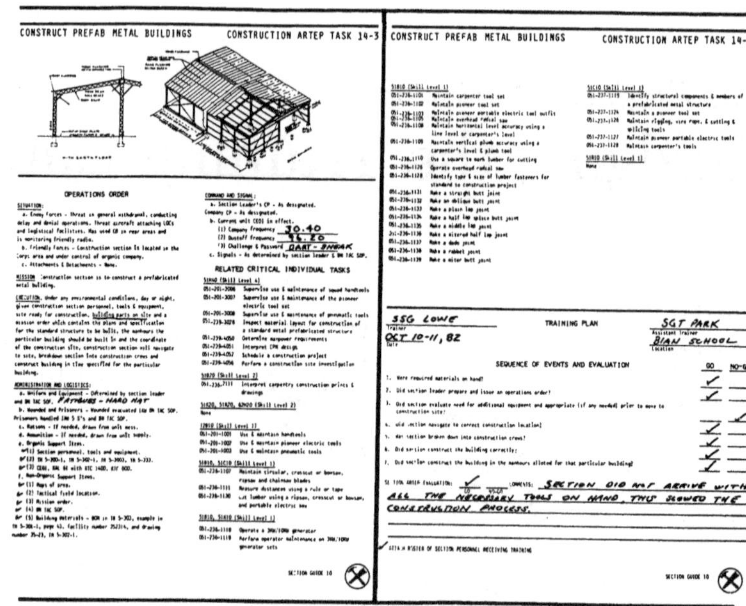

CONSTRUCT PREFAB METAL BUILDINGS — CONSTRUCTION ARTEP TASK 14-3

OPERATIONS ORDER

RELATED CRITICAL INDIVIDUAL TASKS

SECTION GUIDE 10

CONSTRUCT PREFAB METAL BUILDINGS — CONSTRUCTION ARTEP TASK 14-3

SSG LOWE (Trainer) — TRAINING PLAN — SGT PARK (Assistant Trainer)

OCT 10-11, 82 (Date) — BIAN SCHOOL (Location)

SEQUENCE OF EVENTS AND EVALUATION

	GO	NO-GO
1. Were required materials on hand?	✓	
2. Did section leader prepare and issue an operations order?	✓	
3. Did section evaluate need for additional equipment and appropriate (if any needed) prior to move to construction site?		✓
4. Did section navigate to correct construction location?	✓	
5. Was section broken down into construction crews?	✓	
6. Did section construct the building correctly?	✓	
7. Did section construct the building in the manhours alloted for that particular building?	✓	

SECTION ARTEP EVALUATION: ✓ GO ___ NO-GO COMMENTS: SECTION DID NOT ARRIVE WITH ALL THE NECESSARY TOOLS ON HAND. THIS SLOWED THE CONSTRUCTION PROCESS.

✓ ATTACH ROSTER OF SECTION PERSONNEL RECEIVING TRAINING

SECTION GUIDE 10

Figure 2. Every engineer ARTEP task is presented in an operations order format, followed by a list of related tasks, a training and evaluation plan and (not shown) a list of applicable trainin references.

ing vehicle, the "packet training program," which proved successful at company level and was adopted by the battalion. But while it was a significant improvement to the 579th's training program, it still was not the single-source training document Combs and Jurin envisioned.

Jurin and Combs set out to simply revise the packet training program, but their three-year effort proved so extensive that an entirely new document emerged. Jurin during this time was battalion XO and was employed in a full-time manning position at the battalion headquarters at Santa Rosa. Combs quit his successful scuba diving equipment sales job to also accept a full-time manning slot at the battalion, reasoning that he could then more conveniently collaborate with Jurin on the workbook. Because their technician jobs kept them busy during the day, efforts on the workbook were reserved for nights and weekends. In February 1981, TRADOC learned of the project, provided $14,000 in funding and asked for the completed document by March 1982.

Jurin and Combs launched a whirlwind effor to complete the workbook within the 13 mont suspense. Janet Jurin, Maj. Jurin's wife and graphic artist, worked on the project full-tim without pay for those 13 months, purchasing out of-pocket most of her equipment and supplies. Often working as much as 16 hours a day, she created from scratch a readable and functiona design for the workbook, procured or prepared illustrations, and researched and designed a system of logos graphically identifying each of th mission areas in the workbook. She prepared al the dummy pasteups, all camera ready pasteup and handled other production duties.

Other key personnel assisting Combs and Juri were SSG Peggy Custer of the 579th and SF Ronald Wiese, the battalion's active Army trair ing advisor. By the time the workbook was read to go to TRADOC, in just 13 months over 2,60 documented volunteer manhours had been con tributed to the project. Over a four-year term

14TH ENGINEERS

Patrons of the Engineer Workbook

According to the 579th Engineer Battalion (Combat) (Corps), California Army National Guard, the keystone in their ability to produce the *Engineer Trainer's Workbook* was the strong support of Lt. Col. Clair F. Gill and his 14th Engineer Battalion (Combat)(Corps) at Fort Ord, Calif.

The 579th-14th Engineers nexus is the Reserve Deployment Enhancement Program (RDEP). The 14th Engineers is the only active Army unit having direct experience with the workbook. Because of their affiliation under RDEP, the two units frequently train together and cooperate on jointly beneficial projects, such as the recent coproduction of the new battalion tactical SOP now used by both units.

Regarding the *Engineer Trainer's Workbook*, the 14th supported the Guardsmen with advice, manpower and served as a test bed for certain portions of the workbook. 14th Engineers making significant individual contributions to the workbook include 1st Lt. Thomas Curran who spent three months at 579th headquarters in Santa Rosa. Curran was praised by Gill and by the 579th for his long hours of painstaking research in producing reference lists for every ARTEP mission in the workbook. SFC Thomas Austin also assisted the 579th from Fort Ord as a program writer-developer.

According to Gill, 80 percent of the workbook is directly applicable to active Army engineer battalions. Gill says that so far, the workbook has been most beneficial to the 14th in preparing the training and evaluation outlines required under the Battalion Training Management System (BTMS) prior to conducting ARTEPs. Maj. Donald Holzwarth, S-3 for the 14th, cites preparation of last October's four simultaneous, company-sized, external ARTEPs as an example of the workbook's value.

Using a draft copy of the workbook, Holzwarth says his office prepared the ARTEPs in *one-fifth* the time normally required. Personnel from the 7th Infantry Division's 13th Engineer Battalion served as ARTEP evaluators and, according to Gill, "they were ecstatic" over the convenience and utility of the evaluation forms with which they were provided. The forms came from the *Engineer Trainer's Workbook.*

Although the workbook will be helpful to training planners at all levels, Gill says the primary trainer, the squad leader, will ultimately benefit most because the workbook will provide him a complete list of references for each ARTEP task. "In the past", Gill says, "we had so many references in so many different places, that it took a magician to pull them together."

If the *Engineer Trainer's Workbook* lives up to its billing, it will add its own magic to engineer training.

$22,185 of personal funds were spent on the program, most of it contributed by Combs and the Jurins.

A key supporter who Jurin credits with injecting sustaining lifeblood into the endeavor was Lt. Col. Clair F. Gill, commander of the 14th Engineer Battalion (Combat) (Corps), Fort Ord. The 14th and the 579th are linked under the Reserve Deployment Enhancement Program, and, accordingly, the two battalions often train together.

Gill provided advice, personnel, and the 14th field tested specific training programs described in the workbook. (Details on the 14th's contributions to the workbook are noted above).

COMPOSITION OF THE WORKBOOK

The workbook is divided into four chapters:

- *Chapter One* includes an introduction, general workbook overview and chapter index.
- *Chapter Two* contains key training documents including mission lists, operations orders, training plans, and a consolidated reference list for each mission area.
- *Chapter Three* is a complete training program for the headquarters company and headquarters platoons. Included are documents to plan, resource, conduct and to evaluate common task training, section training and MOS training.
- *Chapter Four* supplies professional development training plans for officers and NCOs in mission related leadership tasks and administrative duties.

The utility of the Engineer Trainer's Workbook begins with preparing annual training forecasts. Each mission category (construction, for example) is covered by a "training packet." The first page of the training packet is the *mission list* showing the task number, title, and page location of each ARTEP task described within the packet. The mission list serves as an important planning tool since it identifies the applicable task level (squad-platoon-company) and provides space for the training planner to indicate when the unit will train in each skill area (see Figure 1). For example, referring to the construction mission list, a National Guard company commander might schedule Task 13-22, *Construct Culverts,* to be covered during annual training; Task 4-3, *Secure Worksite,* might be planned for a weekend drill, and Task 14-17, *Install Plumbing and Fixtures,* may be programmed for post mobilization. Tasks at which the unit is already proficient are also noted. According to Jurin, by using the workbook, the 579th's yearly training forecast can be completed in three-to-four hours; preworkbook planning required entire drill weekends for several months.

Using the mission list and accompanying training packet, planners can review, in a single source, all pertinent information about training a particular task, then decide the most appropriate time to conduct the training. To benefit the primary trainer, every training packet contains a complete list of applicable references ranging from manuals to TV tapes to correspondence courses.

Critics have suggested that such extensive training assistance stifles trainer initiative and denies to them the experience of fully preparing their classes. Jurin and Combs strongly disagree, saying that the trainer's mission is to present high quality training, not to become a part-time librarian prospecting for suitable reference material. In a National Guard or reserve unit, Combs notes, time is an especially precious quantity. Unit training must be prepared quickly, accurately and presented professionally.

Op Order Format

Along with the mission list and reference inventory, each training packet presents an ARTEP task as an operations order. Jurin says they departed from the usual BTMS task-conditions-and standards format because the workbook offered a valuable opportunity to encourage troop and trainer familiarity the operations order. According to Jurin, "The operations order is a proven document; it works. We want it so ingrained in our people, that they're always thinking in terms of op orders."

Following the operations order, is the *training plan* which includes a sequence of tasks for trainees to perform and a section for the training supervisor to list a go/no-go status. There is also space to indicate a pass/fail status on the overall task, an area to record the names of attending personnel and room for remarks regarding individual strong or weak points (see Figure 2).

In the three years that the 579th has been using exclusively the concepts in the trainer's workbook, Combs says that unit training quality has markedly improved and has manifested in measurably better performance during annual training. Col. Biehn, now with the Office of Policy and Liaison, National Guard Bureau, says that during his visit to the 579th last year, NCOs had high praise for the workbook. Combs says the 579th's improved training quality has led to higher unit morale and carried the battalion's retention rate to third best in the California Army Guard.

The *Engineer Trainer's Workbook* was written for reserve component engineer battalions, but active units can easily perform the minor changes necessary to make the workbook fully suited to their needs. The book should be a boon to planners, to trainers and ultimately to the troops themselves as they benefit from better planned, better organized training programs.

As Jurin says of the workbook, "I like to think of this as a life insurance policy for the soldier."

Platoon Inventory

by Maj. Curtis R. Rogers

After meeting his commander and receiving a briefing on the unit, a newly assigned lieutenant faces his first real challenge—conducting a 100 percent inventory of his platoon's equipment. His signature on that inventory will mark the final step in his full assumption of responsibility for his platoon, and he should take care to do it right.

His first step in the inventory process should be to get together with the experts—the battalion S4 or the property book officer, the company executive officer, and the company supply sergeant. Thirty minutes with an expert can unravel what at first may look like an insurmountable problem. During the discussion, he should ask them about any recent change or problem that could affect the inventory.

At the same time, he should obtain from them the current technical manuals, supply bulletins, supply catalogs, and any other publications he will need to conduct the inventory. In addition, he must make certain that the appropriate TM for each piece of equipment, along with its publication date, appears on the master hand receipt.

These publications are essential; without them an inventory is a waste of time, because they describe the equipment through photographs and equipment listings. The major components of the equipment must be reviewed with reference to both the descriptive pictures and the BII (basic issue items) list.

This advice cannot be stressed too strongly. Failure to use the current publications in the inventory process is probably the most common mistake a new platoon leader makes, and the most costly. He should therefore follow the rule: "If you ain't got the book, don't look."

Once he is satisfied that he is sufficiently educated and equipped, the lieutenant can begin the formal inventory process.

A change of command inventory is a joint mission. It should be done with both the outgoing and the incoming officers present; it should not be conducted if one or the other is absent. A sufficient amount of time should be set aside for the inventory, and the entire process should be well organized. Unrelated tasks must be set aside until the inventory has been finished.

All items that are to be inventoried—that must be counted—should be put out in the open where both parties can see them. The front of the company's area is probably as good a place as any. All of the platoon's equipment must be made available; otherwise, those taking the inventory will spend a lot of time trying to chase down the missing items.

When physically counting equipment, both platoon leaders must be certain of the actual accountable quantity. For example, a unit may have been issued or may have turned in items since its last master hand receipt was made. (If the unit is using the division logistics systems (DLOGS), a computerized list will be provided.) Normally, the master hand receipt is updated before the inventory, and this should eliminate any need to review "sub-hand receipts." But a platoon may have equipment signed out to its members; if so, it must be turned in before—not during—the inventory and then re-issued. This simple formula can be used to insure a correct balance sheet: Hand receipt count, plus issues and minus turn-ins, minus equipment in maintenance, equals the accountable quantity.

One critical aspect of accounting for the equipment that is in maintenance is to make sure the complete item is turned in. Although this is normally required, sometimes components are turned in but not some of the other end items.

The identification of equip-

Supply discipline is a high priority . . .

ment may be difficult, too, but the new platoon leader must stick with it. He may even have to measure, weigh, and compare certain items carefully. Above all, he must be certain of the presence and composition of every item of his equipment.

During the inventory, equipment should also be checked for its serviceability. If it is badly worn and a replacement can be ordered, it should be done at that time. Any missing items should be reported immediately to the commander and to the S4 or property book officer, and supply actions should be started to remedy the shortages. This equipment should not appear on the hand receipt.

At the same time, any excess equipment must be turned in to the supply people; this is as much a moral problem as it is a physical and monetary one. It may be found, also, that certain items no longer serve a purpose within a unit, and with the commander's approval, they should be turned in as well.

If any problem arises during the inventory that seems impossible to resolve, the platoon leader should go back to the experts and insist on a detailed explanation. Often the problem will turn out to be simple administrative errors on hand receipts—even experts can make mistakes!

Finally, the new platoon leader should be sure that the master hand receipt he signs reflects things as they really are. To discover otherwise later can be professionally and financially devastating.

After the new platoon leader has signed for his platoon's equipment, he should make it a point to continue to inventory and inspect that equipment throughout his tenure in that unit. In fact, the semi-annual inventory is as important as the initial one. He must pay special attention to any items that might be added to the BII after his initial inventory and see that they are put on the hand receipt.

At the end of his tour, h must conduct a final 100 pe cent inventory with his su cessor.

Supply discipline and equi ment accountability are hig priorities for today's unit lea er. A 100 percent inventory ma not be as exciting as a comb patrol or a platoon raid, but it at least as important. And an platoon leader—either a ne one or an old one—owes it t himself to do it right. (R printed from *Infantr Magazine.*)

Maj. Curtis R. Rogers was co missioned through Officer Ca didate School in 1969 an served as a rifle company co mander and a battalion S4 wit the 193d Infantry Brigade i Panama. He is a 1977 gradua of the University of Tampa an recently completed the Foreig Area Officer Course. He is no assigned to the Rapid Deplo ment Joint Task Force at McDi Air Force Base, Fla.

The ENGINEER Solution

The horizontal force of the backfilled soil (H_b) varies proportionately with the depth of the soil. The loading diagram is shown below. The entire loading system can be resolved into one force H_b. Its point of application divides the loading triangle into equal halves. This occurs at 1/3 its height (hw/3) or 10/3 feet from its base.

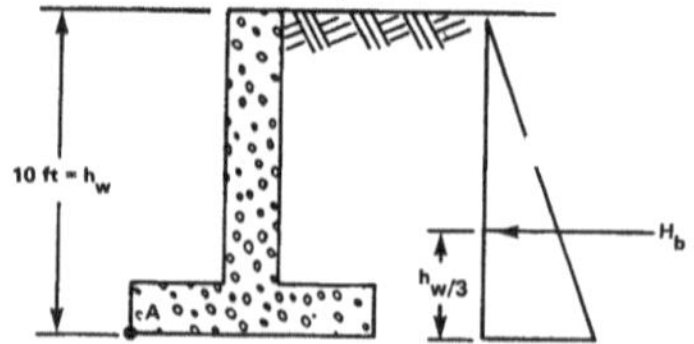

The force created by the soil is proportional to the density, the internal angle of friction and the height of the wall.

$$H_b = (Ka \cdot \gamma s \cdot hw)\ hw/2$$

where Ka = the coefficient of active earth pressure

$$Ka = \tan^2 (45-\phi/2) = \tan^2 (45—33.5/2) = .289$$

H_b= (.289) (130) (10) (10/2) = 1879 lbs per foot of wall

The moment arm about point A is hw/3 or 3.33 feet. Therefore, the wall must create resisting moment of M = 1879 (3.33) = 6257 ft-lbs clockwise.

APPLE TO THE RESCUE

No Seeds. No Pits. No Errors.

Since adding an Apple II Plus microcomputer to their maintenance shop, the 14th Engineer Battalion (Combat) (Corps) at Fort Ord is producing maintenance reports and other documents in only a fraction of the time previously required. According to CW2 Steven Gardner, battalion equipment repair technician, a single Apple operator now completes in less than an hour deadline reports that used to take four TAMMS clerks an entire day.

Besides saving time, Gardner says the computer printouts are virtually error free and not being handwritten, are always legible.

Genesis of the program was Gardner and then Battalion Motor Officer Capt. Richard H. MacCombie deciding that their maintenance management system needed streamlining. When the decision was made to computerize, MacCombie moved his personal microcomputer, a TRS-80 Model I, into the maintenance shop. Gardner then determined which tasks most needed attention, and MacCombie did the programming.

Meanwhile, Battalion Commander Lt. Col. Clair F. Gill formally requested a microcomputer system from FORSCOM. MacCombie's replacement, 1Lt. James Roberts, kept the pressure on FORSCOM until the 14th finally received an Apple II Plus with Monitor III display screen and Epson MX-80 F/T printer.

The battalion currently uses the Apple to prepare daily (and other periodic) company and consolidated deadline reports directly onto DA Form 2406, *Material Condition Status Report.* The computer is also used to prepare printouts of the battalion's scheduled maintenance reports, and Gardner plans to add replacement parts record keeping to the Apple inventory since the 14th is under SAILS (Standard Army Intermediate Level Supply Subsystem).

In the case of daily deadline reports, each morning the company motor sergeants provide to the battalion maintenance shop vehicle and equipment status reports. The Apple operator then adjusts the previous day's deadline report according to the new information, receives a printout, and an hour later the motor sergeants pick up their copy of the revised document. The company reports are consolidated for the overall battalion picture with all reports including a final percentage figure showing the amount of mission essential equipment operational.

The Apple system is also used for selected administrative tasks, specifically for the battalion's "good guy", "bad guy" reports.

PFC Se Ho Kim prepares a maintenance report on the 14th Engineers' Apple II microcomputer.

Battalion maintenance personnel routinely conduct spot vehicle inspections in the motor pool and battalion area. If his vehicle and log book are in proper condition, the operator receives, through his company commander, a letter from Gill acknowledging the good performance. If his vehicle fails the inspection, the operator receives a less cheery epistle. In either case, the Apple operator simply enters the vehicle driver's name and unit, and the Apple prints a programmed letter onto a DF ready for Gill's signature and the company commander's endorsement.

The 14th offers to assist other engineer units desiring to computerize maintenance operations by supplying to them copies of the paperwork required to secure the computer. The 14th will also transfer programming if they are supplied a blank 5/4-inch floppy diskette. The program will be compatible only with another Apple II Plus, 48K. For more information call CW2 Steven Gardner at (408) 242-2050, AV 929.—*John Florence*

A 27-foot erection boat pulls a ribbon bridge built by Company E, 2nd Engineer Battalion, 2nd Infantry Division, during Team Spirit exercises in the Republic of Korea.
(Photo by David Polewski)

UNITED STATES ARMY ENGINEEER CENTER AND FORT BELVOIR, VA

COMMANDER/COMMANDANT
MG James N. Ellis

DEPUTY COMMANDANT
COL Alvin G. Rowe

CHIEF OF STAFF/DEPUTY INSTALLATION COMMANDER
COL Paul J. Higgins

COMMAND SERGEANT MAJOR
CSM Marvin L. Knowles

DIRECTORATES

DIRECTORATE OF ENGINEER FORCE MANAGEMENT
LTC Arthur S. Brown

DIRECTORATE OF COMBAT DEVELOPMENTS
COL Phillip R. Hoge

DIRECTORATE OF TRAINING DEVELOPMENTS
COL Stanley R. Johnson

DIRECTORATE OF TRAINING AND DOCTRINE
COL Ralph T. Rundle

UNITS

ENGINEER CENTER BRIGADE
COL Don W. Barber

ENGINEER TRAINING BRIGADE
COL Peter J. Groh

PUBLIC AFFAIRS OFFICER
MAJ James E. Kiley Jr.

EDITOR
John Florence

ASSISTANT EDITOR
SSG Bernard W. Tate

ART DIRECTOR
John Florence

Engineer

VOLUME 12 FALL 1982 NUMBER 3

FEATURES

Lessons learned  *p. 20*

Tests at Belvoir  *p. 29*

"Outstanding job" *p. 36*

DEPARTMENTS

ENGINEER is an authorized publication of the U.S. Army Engineer Center and Fort Belvoir, Va. Unless specifically stated, material appearing herein does not necessarily reflect official policy, thinking or endorsement by any agency of the U.S. Army. All photographs contained herein are official U.S. Army photographs unless otherwise credited. Use of funds for printing this publication was approved by Headquarters, Department of the Army, July 22, 1981. Material herein may be reprinted if credit is given to ENGINEER and the author. • **ENGINEER OBJECTIVES** are to provide a forum for the exchange of ideas, to inform and motivate and to promote the professional development of all members of the Army engineer family. • **DIRECT CORRESPONDENCE** with ENGINEER is authorized and encouraged. Inquiries, letters to the editor, manuscripts, photographs and general correspondence should be sent to: Editor, ENGINEER, U.S. Army Engineer Center, Fort Belvoir, Va., 22060. Telephone Autovon 354-3082. If a return of manuscripts or material is desired, a self-addressed envelope is required. • **SUBSCRIPTIONS** to ENGINEER are available through the Superintendent of Documents, U.S. Government Printing Office, Washington, D.C., 20402. A check or money order payable to Superintendent of Documents, must accompany all subscription requests. Rates are $8.50 domestic (including APO and FPO addresses,) and $10.65 for foreign addresses. Individual copies are available at $4.50 per copy to domestic addresses and $5.65 for foreign addresses. • **SECOND CLASS** postage paid at Fort Belvoir, Va., and Riverdale, Md. ISSN 0046–1989.

A new plan for ENGINEER

BY MG JAMES N. ELLIS
Commandant, U.S. Army Engineer School

MG Ellis

As you know, ENGINEER depends upon its readers to supply the majority of articles and information in each issue. This allows each of us the opportunity to positively influence the quality and content of our branch journal. It is important to take advantage of that opportunity.

New Program

For our part, we at the Engineer School are working to enhance the content of the magazine. In civilian terms, I would be considered the ENGINEER publisher so it is appropriate that I review for you the highlights of our new editorial plan.

First of all, ENGINEER remains a quarterly publication and will continue focusing upon combat engineering. Beginning with the next issue, however, each edition of ENGINEER will be "sponsored" by one of the School's four directorates (Combat Developments, Engineer Force Management, Training Developments and Training and Doctrine). The sponsoring directorate will have space for several feature articles that support a general directorate theme. We hope this will give you greater insight into the major issues and concerns at the School. This is important because, ultimately, many of these topics become translated into policies that directly affect your career or how you perform your job. In addition to sponsoring one issue per year, each directorate and the Defense Mapping School will have a news and information column in every ENGINEER.

News From MILPERCEN

There are other changes you'll see in the next issue. I'm very pleased that LTC(P) Paul Chinen at the Engineer Officer Personnel Management Directorate and LTC Liston Edge at the Enlisted Personnel Management Directorate (both at MILPERCEN) will supply personnel news for us in every issue. Many of you in the field have asked ENGINEER to expand its coverage of personnel news. This is one of the ways we are meeting that need.

CSM Column

The Engineer Center command sergeant major will also have a regular column beginning with the winter issue; a welcome complement to "Clear the Way," and one tailored specifically for the NCO. The USAEC CSM is my principle advisor on all engineer enlisted personnel matters but focuses primarily on the NCO corps.

Another change begins in this issue. Professor David Skaggs of Bowling Green State University has given us the first in our new military history series. His article, "Washington's Legacies to the Modern Army," is appropriate to initiate the series. As a young surveyor, Washington began his first surveying expedition from Belvoir on grounds now part of the Engineer School. In the traditional sense, we like to claim General Washington as one of the Corps. Future articles in the history series will concentrate specifically on engineer history. The study of military history should be high on your professional development agenda. The world's great military leaders have invariably been serious students of military history. I urge you to tap this same resource. We will help.

Bright Ideas

And finally, I'm requesting your support for a new department called "Bright Ideas." One of the biggest favors we can do for ourselves is to review and adopt, if appropriate, the innovations and creative problem-solving techniques others have used successfully. The first step, though, is to get those bright ideas out into the open where all engineers can examine them. I'm talking about pointers on a better way to organize training, combat engineer/construction tips, or improving unit administrative or supply procedures. What we want here are pithy items; a few lines to several paragraphs. Include an address and phone number so readers can obtain details directly from the individual or unit concerned. If your bright idea is article length, then it's in a different category and will be welcomed as a feature story. I hope you will agree this new department could become one of the most valuable sections of the magazine. I look forward to reading about your bright ideas in ENGINEER.

As ENGINEER Magazine evolves under this new editorial plan, we hope you will find the journal even more meaningful. We look forward to your continued support as we . . .

CLEAR THE WAY

JNE

1981 ITSCHNER & STURGIS WINNERS HONORED

Congratulations to the 1981 Itschner Award winners, recognized at the 115th Annual Engineer Dinner held at Fort Belvoir, Va., last May. Also honored at the dinner was the recipient of the 1981 Sturgis Medal.

The Sturgis Medal is presented each year to an active duty enlisted engineer in recognition of outstanding contributions to military troop construction or base maintenance. This year's winner was SSG Jackie L. Thomas, Headquarters, 79th Engineer Battalion (Combat) (Heavy), 18th Engineer Brigade, Germany.

The Itschner Awards recognize the most outstanding engineer company of the active Army, Army Reserve and Army National Guard, for engineering construction and community service. The 1981 winners were:

Active Army: C Company, 78th Engineer Battalion (Combat), 7th Engineer Brigade, VII Corps, Germany.

Army Reserve: D Company, 844th Engineer Battalion (Combat) (Heavy), Kingsport, Tenn.

Army National Guard: B Company, 262d Engineer Battalion (Combat) (Corps), Belfast, Maine.

ENGINEERS BUILD WORLD'S FAIR BRIDGE

Photo by David Luttrell

A community service project by the Army Reserve's 844th Engineer Battalion (Combat) (Heavy) made life a little more pleasant for thousands of visitors to the 1982 World's Fair in Knoxville, Tenn.

The 844th constructed a 290 foot triple-single Bailey bridge for pedestrian traffic so visitors could reach the Tennessee Valley Authority's energy exhibit without having to cross a heavily traveled roadway.

The bridge was constructed in three sections, and a crane was used to place them because of insufficient room for normal construction and launching.

The 844th's D Company was among this year's Itschner Award winners (see above).

News & Notes

READY RESERVISTS AID ARMY FROM HOME

The Engineer School found a unique way to combat manpower and fund shortages when preparing training packets for instructors and students at USAR schools. Qualified members of the Individual Ready Reserve were contacted and asked if they would prepare, at home, instructional units related to their specialty in return for retirement points.

Because Individual Ready Reservists are not assigned to troop units, they form a ready manpower pool. The Office of the Chief, Army Reserve, reports that of 100 Reservists contacted, about 30 expressed an interest. The Reservists were sent an administrative packet specifying the end product desired, specific learning objectives for each course and supporting reference materials. The Reservists also had access to the Engineer Hotline for guidance, problem-solving or administrative support.

Army Regulation 140–185 outlines the procedures for such ventures. Basically, the Individual Ready Reservist earns one retirement point for each four hours of work performed.

According to a spokesman at the Engineer School, the project was a great success and high quality results were obtained. Agencies or individuals interested in starting similar programs may contact MAJ Jerry L. Crowder at the School. Call AV 354-6190 or 800–336-3095.

SCHOOL'S TUDOR AWARD TO CPT MICHAEL PELKEY

Congratulations to CPT Michael P. Pelkey, recipient of the Engineer School's Tudor Award for academic achievement in military engineering.

The award, in honor of Ralph A. Tudor, a 1923 graduate of the U.S. Military Academy, is presented annually to the Engineer Officer Advanced Course (EOAC) student with the most outstanding achievements in academics, physical fitness, class effectiveness and contributions to the school.

Among Pelkey's accomplishments while attending EOAC class 1–81 were a grade point average of 97 and a score of 298 out of a possible 300 on the Army Physical Readiness Test. Additionally, Pelkey competed in the Washington, D.C., Marine Corps Marathon; passed the Virgina Professional Engineer examination; was a member of the class football team and served as a full-time trainer for 40 Engineer Officer Basic Course students.

Pelkey is assigned to HHC, 18th Engineer Brigade, Karlsruhe, Germany.

ENGINEERS PREPARE GALLANT EAGLE SITE

Soldiers of D Company, 864th Engineer Battalion, Presidio of San Francisco, Cal., literally paved the way for units participating in Gallant Eagle 82. The soldiers deployed early to grade 50 miles of roadway, repair aircraft landing strips, clear a helipad site and construct 12 miles of antitank ditches.

An estimated 1,300 fixed-wing aircraft, 450 helicopters, 1,100 wheeled vehicles and 800 tracked vehicles were used in the training, with D Company providing a 320,000-gallon fuel-storage depot site and a 140-tent cantonment complete with shower points.

Gallant Eagle 82, a United States Readiness Command sponsored exercise held at Fort Irwin, Cal., last spring, involved nearly 40,000 soldiers and civilians in the largest Rapid Deployment Force field exercise yet.

LEGISLATION SEEKS PROMOTION OF RESERVISTS ON ACTIVE DUTY

The Department of the Army has proposed legislation allowing promotion of certain Reserve officers serving in Active Guard/Reserve (AGR) assignments.

Under existing interpretations of the law, Army Reserve officers on active duty who are promoted to a Reserve grade higher than that held when ordered to active duty, may not serve in the higher grade while on active duty. The Reservist must either leave active duty or accept appointment in the Army of the United States in a temporary grade equal to the grade in which he served before the promotion.

The legislative proposal would effect non-obligated Reserve officers serving on active duty whose promotions have been postponed. These delays have made it increasingly difficult to attract and retain quality officers for the expanding AGR program, the Office of the Chief, Army Reserve reports.

If Congress approves the proposal, these officers would still be subject to the grade limitations of Section 524 of the Defense Officer Personnel Management Act (DOPMA).

Under the proposal, a Reserve officer on active duty selected for promotion would be eligible to be reordered to active duty in the higher grade, provided there was a vacancy in that grade available under DOPMA grade table limits for AGR officers. If no vacancy exists, the officer would continue to serve in the lower grade until a vacancy occurred, or until he completed his tour and was released from active duty. At that time, he would be promoted to the higher grade, with his date of rank retroactive to the date on which he was eligible to be promoted.

Chaplain (CPT) Nicholas J. Kusevich, 17th Engineer Battalion, 2d Armored Division, conducts a field mass wearing olive drab vestments made from an Army parachute. Kusevich is one of only 10 Eastern Orthodox priests in the Army. Developed in Eastern Europe, the religion includes Greeks, Ukrainians, Romanians and Russians. There are more than six million of the Eastern Orthodox faith in the United States. (Photo by Mark Vitullo)

DIVERS NEEDED FOR RIBBON BRIDGE COMPANIES

Seven-man diving sections will be added to nondivisional ribbon bridge companies (TOE 5–79H) in early fiscal year 1983.

Divers, MOS OOB, will support bridging and ferry operations by performing approach and river bottom reconnaissance, building bridge protection systems, repairing bridges and recovering sunken equipment. Some sections will conduct SCUBA (self-contained underwater breathing apparatus) operations.

Soldiers E2 through E4 can volunteer for deep sea diving training if they are less than 30 years old, pass the Navy swim test and will have 21 months service remaining after the 12-week diving course.

Contact the CMF 51 assignment officer at MILPERCEN (AV 221–7710) for additional information.

—*FORUM*—

THE SOVIET SOLDIER

Is Ivan really 10 feet tall?

by Les Aspin

The Pentagon normally reduces comparisons of Soviet and American military power to "bean counts," to use its own term. In the standard news magazine chart, this boils down to a row of Soviet tanks and a shorter row of American tanks. This chart usually includes a row of Soviet soldiers in silhouette and a shorter row of American soldiers in silhouette.

The bean count approach overlooks the more crucial question of quality. This is especially true of manpower. The United States Army tends to be dismissed by liberals and conservatives alike as a collection of misfits and dummies. The Soviet Army on the other hand, consistently comes off as a corps of tough, if not brutal, professionals—almost superhuman.

Military attachés with the United States liaison mission in West Germany have visited Soviet forces in East Germany and come away to write with amazement at the tremendous physical specimens filling that force. Their evidence: not one single soldier was seen wearing eyeglasses. These observa tions have been quoted approvingl dozens of times without anyone's mentioning that the Soviet Army does not issue eyeglasses and that, therefore, many of those soldiers can't see well enough to aim their rifles.

Those who tout the wonders of the Soviet military tend to be neai sighted, too.

Life in the Red Army is tough—not Marine Corps tough, but concentration camp tough. The evidence is available from a variet of sources. Some of the most interesting comes from American and European interviews with Soviet émigrés. The themes that run through their descriptions of Sovie military life paint a far different picture from that usually held by Americans:

- Alcoholism is rampant, dwarfing the drug problem faced b the United States armed forces.
- Food is poor. Young recruits are often denied all but table scraps.
- Physical brutality is the norm, with senior soldiers freely allowed to get their "kicks" by assaulting younger soldiers.

The composite picture is perhaps most dramatically summed up by the results of a survey by Richard A. Gabriel, author of *The New Rec Legions*, in which 113 Soviet émigrés were asked: "Did anyone in your unit ever attempt to commit suicide?" More than 53 percent answered yes. That points to something considerably different from tough training.

The Soviet military is far from the classless society that ideology decrees. The men in each unit are in effect divided into two distinct classes. The upper class—those who have been in uniform more than a year—are allowed to unleash a reign of terror on the lowei class.

Kirill Podrabinek, a conscript who served in an infantry unit in Turkmenistan in the mid-1970s, graphically described conditions in a letter smuggled out of the Soviet Union in 1976 to émigrés in West Germany. He said that younger troops were beaten from the first day they arrived in the unit. The senior troops "instill terror right away," he wrote.

It's not just physical assault that causes demoralization. As many émigrés have said, the food in the barracks is poor—when there is food. Lieutenant Viktor Belenko, who flew his MIG to Japan in 1976, said, "I think if we took a pig from a good *kholkhoz* (state farm) and put it in a mess hall, that pig would faint."

A little overdrawn, perhaps. But Podrabinek describes how younger troops are deprived of food. First-year soldiers sit at the end of the table away from the pot of food. Senior soldiers are served first. "It is understood that if there is something worth looking at in the pot, let's say potatoes, and not just barley gruel, the person at the foot of the table may not get any. At the foot sits the weakest youngster or the one who has received the worst maltreatment."

Another former soldier, Aleksandr Makushechev, a sergeant, has described how brutality and deprivation of food cause friction between the two classes of soldiers. Interviewed on Radio Liberty, he said that first-year soldiers were often denied cartridges on the rifle range for fear they might shoot their seniors.

In the United States, the military worries about alcohol abuse. In the Red Army, they no longer bother to worry. Alcoholism defines Soviet society as apple pie defines American society, so the fact that drinking is endemic in the military is not surprising. Soviet soldiers, paid the equivalent of about $1.50 a week, go to considerable trouble to find free alcohol. Lieutenant Belenko described how his mates would steal, sell or drink the alcohol intended for the coolant systems of MIG fighters. Others tell of sneaking into army tanks to extract brake fluid in order to drink it.

Soviet leaders frown on drug abuse. Despite this, Soviet émigrés report growing use of *plan* (made from opium), *anasha* (a form of hashish) and *chefir* (a stimulant made by boiling tea leaves), not to mention medicines stolen from medical units.

When we look at the Soviet Army and see a 10-foot-tall hardened soldier, we may be looking at a "Potemkin village." In fact, the Soviet Army once literally created a Potemkin military unit to ensure a perfect performance for the hierarchy, the pseudonymous Viktor Suvorov, a former tank company commander, relates in his book, *The Liberators*. In 1967, officers were assembled and dressed as privates to make sure that everyone involved in the exercise performed well. In a real war, however, that option for mobilizing quality troops does not present itself.

The two keys to the effectiveness of a fighting unit are cohesion and leadership.

Cohesion stems from pride and mutual respect among the troops, who fight because to do otherwise would be to forfeit the esteem of their comrades. But comradeship is an element no longer found in quantity in the Soviet forces. The system of two classes among the troops doesn't generate cohesion; it militates against it. In Professor Gabriel's survey of former soldiers, a remarkable 30 percent said they had not made even one close friend in the service. You cannot have cohesion without the bonds of friendship. Some think that tough living conditions produce a tough soldier. Podrabinek says that's nonsense: "It makes them cowards. A slave who has accepted his lot is always cowardly."

Unmasking the Soviet soldier: How good is he?

Leadership is the second key element in forming a real fighting force. The quality of that leadership is indicated by the failure of Soviet officers to address the brutality, the drug and alcohol abuse, the food deprivation and the many other unsavory characteristics of Soviet military life.

This failure is built into the system. Soviet military regulations require commanders to report offenses by subordinates to the next higher headquarters. But the regulations also hold the commander responsible for the subordinate's conduct. The result is that at every level breaches are ignored. Even the Soviet press has acknowledged that reports to headquarters are often little more than "eyewash" as officers seek to cover up indiscipline.

There is a danger of overstating this case. Not every Soviet soldier is beneath contempt. We should not replace the myth of the 10-foot-tall hardened Russian infantryman with yet another myth of a three-foot-tall starving coward holding an empty cartridge case.

What is needed is a better perspective when Soviet and American armed forces are compared to each other.

Is the American military filled with too many "dummies"? The United States armed forces will not accept the least intelligent one-seventh of the population. Soviet law provides no such exemption. Perhaps the Soviet Army takes in young men from the country's minorities who have only the barest acquaintance with the Russian language. Furthermore, as the birth rate falls among Russians and rises among, say, Uzbeks, Kazakhs and other minorities, the proportion of these peoples who do not speak Russian will rise to one-third of all recruits, according to a United States Census Bureau analysis of Soviet census data.

Are we suffering an absence of experienced sergeants because "only" one-third of those finishing their tours of duty re-enlist? In the Soviet military, only one percent re-enlist, and the military doesn't really have any corps of experienced noncommissioned officers.

The Soviet Army does present a serious threat. But we only fool ourselves and threaten to undermine our own morale when we exaggerate the qualities of the Soviet military.

Les Aspin, (D–Wis.), is a member of the House Armed Services Committee. *Reprinted from the* **New York Times,** *June 8, 1982.*

A Materially Different Military Bridge

by Richard W. Helmke

The material isn't new, but its application to military bridge structures is. The material is generally referred to as "composite material," a high strength continuous fiber in conjunction with epoxy resin.

A prototype military bridge system produced by the Trilateral (U.S., U.K., F.R.G.) Design and Analysis Group, resulted in the U.S. Army Mobility Equipment Research and Development Command, Fort Belvoir, Va., erecting a test bed for comparison of conventional and composite material bridge components.

The approach to testing was to replace individual metallic elements within the test bed bridge with composite material elements. While this technique penalized the design slightly at connection points, it provided side by side comparison under duplicate load conditions. A 31-meter dry gap support bridge (later expanded to 52 meters, Figure 1) served as the test bed bridge.

The conversion to composite materials design for bridge structures is considerably more involved than just the substitution of one material for another on a property by property basis. Probably the most outstanding difference in the design approach to composite materials, is that the module of elasticity (E) of the material is now a variable, and as such, subject to specification much as we now specify the physical properties of common construction materials (hardness, yield strength, etc.) The effect of this variable for a given material composition allows us to stiffen and relax structural elongations without adding or reducing the amount of material used.

In the test bed bridge, the application of composite materials was demonstrated in the bottom chord sandwich panel, the traversing beam, the bridge tensile reinforcement system and the wound web module.

The Bottom Chord

The area most sensitive to improvements in strength and stiffness, is the bottom surface of the test bed bridge. The old bottom surface was a 24 inch wide, five-eighths of an inch thick, aluminum plate. The new composite bottom is also 24 inches wide and five-eighths inches thick, but is a layered plate of aluminum, graphite-epoxy and aluminum.

The sandwich panel is made up of a one-eighth inch thick aluminum sheet, a three-eighths of an inch thick sheet of graphite-epoxy, and another one-eighth inch thick aluminum sheet, fully bonded as shown in Figure 2. This encapsulates and protects the brittle graphite with ductile aluminum, and the sandwich configuration retains 80 percent of the traverse stiffness of the all aluminum plate it replaces. Transverse stiffness is required for bank support in a military bridge since the location of the bridge reaction can fall anywhere on the bottom chord.

To take full advantage of the fluid plastic state through which the composite material passes during part fabrication, the manufacturing method was developed concurrently with the structural design. A piece of composite material 20 inches wide by .375 inches thick by seven meters long, was needed for

stress to the metallic components. The new bottom panels offer another bonus—they are 30 percent lighter than the solid aluminum plates. A stronger, lighter bridge, with no changes to the physical geometry. It's almost magic!

The Traversing Beam

The traversing beam is the structural element used to emplace and recover the bridge at the bridging site. The beam traverses back and forth within the bridge structure but never leaves its location between the treadways. Since it is totally supported within the cross braces of the bridge, it deflects the same elastic curve as the bridge does when the bridge is loaded. In other words, the beam sees both launching loads and bridge loads. The current all aluminum beam weighs 110 pounds per foot, and constitutes 25 percent of the entire bridge structure. The all composite beam weighs 35 pounds per foot and due to its increased stiffness carries more of the bridge load. The seven meter long test bed beams were pinned at each end to produce as much traversing beam as there was bridge. They were fabricated using many of the same techniques as used for the sandwich chord. A simplified fabrication sequence is:

- *Wind a seven meter tubular mandrel with graphite/epoxy at +45°/90°/−45° plys.*
- *Wind continuous graphite loops (longos) around steel spools on seven meter centers.*
- *Lay the longo on the box winding both top and bottom sandwiches together to form multi-fingered shear joints. Note that the longos are longitudinally staggered to produce the desired male/female pin joints.*
- *Spacers, sandwich core and previously wound slider tracks are laid on the mandrel at the desired location.*
- *The entire winding/layup is now over-wound with several plys of graphite/epoxy completing the cross-section.*
- *The entire bundle is then inserted into a mold and oven cured to produce a final configuration which requires neither joining nor machining.*

This application uses medium modules graphite material. Although it is more costly (three times) than the metallic element it replaces, the projected energy savings due to the reduction in mass (7,500 pounds) which must be transported, justifies the high production cost.

Bridge Reinforcement

A third area of our test bed common to other military bridges, was the long span reinforcement system. We used a cable/bar tensile system suspended beneath the main bridge structure. The variable concern in this system is the stretch or deflection of the cable system, which in turn controls the deflection and load seen by the main bridge structure. The stretch or deflection of the cable for any given length of cable is proportional to the cross-sectional area (A) and the modulus of elasticity (E). By using a composite material with a very high E, such as 55 mpsi graphite, it is easy to reduce the cable area (since the cable load is low) and, therefore, the weight of the cable.

The overall effect of the change in cable material is to transform a steel tensile element that weighs 200 pounds and requires four men to emplace, into a composite (kevlar or graphite) element that weighs 50 pounds and can be emplaced by one man in half the time.

The method of production for this element is, again, continuous wet winding of the composite into a continuous loop. This continuous loop, folded end to end, is given a 90 degree twist and then molded into a rigid link. Each 3.5 meter link is interthreaded to the next, with pin connections required only at the king post and bridge termination.

The Web Module

The web structure used in the test bed bridge was a dimple plate web configuration. The dimple plate is made by pressing rows and columns of dimples into sheets of aluminum, placing the dimples nose to nose and spot welding each

52 METER DRYGAP SUPPORT BRIDGE WITH CABLE REINFORCEMENT

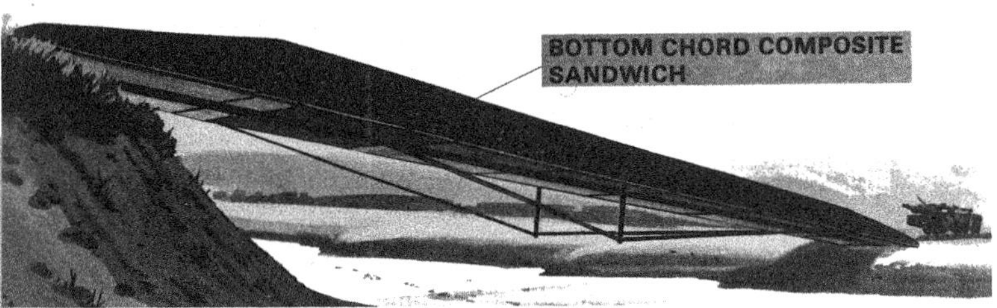

Figure 1. Test bed bridge showing location of bottom chord sandwich panel and bridge reinforcement system.

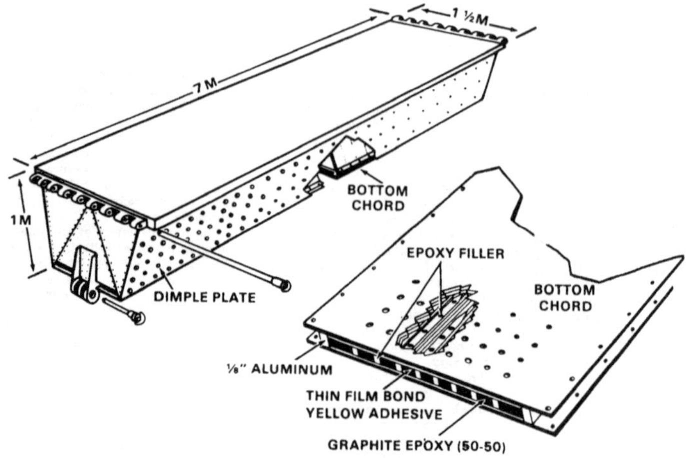

Figure 2. The bottom chord sandwich panel consists of a .125 inch 7075–T63 aluminum face sheet bonded to 50 million psi modulus graphite-epoxy composite.

dimple. In theory, this produces a stiff, stable, thin skinned web which is water tight and easily weld repaired. In reality, the thickness of the aluminum sheet (.08 inches) was controlled by the thinnest section that could be welded, and not by structural considerations which would have required less than half this thickness. The installation of the dimple plate webs requires 27 feet of weld per foot of treadway—and that does not count the 3,000 spot welds also required.

The component that replaced the dimple plate in the test bed bridge, was the web module. The special composite material feature to be exploited here, is the fluid plastic consistancy of the fabricated part prior to final configuration set. Simply stated, we can mold and shape it without machining. The method of fabrication for each web module is:

- *Inflate a flexible mandrel (long hollow tube).*
- *Wind the tube with composite.*
- *Lay on web spacers (built in stiffeners.)*
- *Wind it again with composite.*
- *Deflate the mandrel slightly and insert it into the mold shape desired. Reinflate.*

The result of this procedure is a bridge web configuration which duplicates the geometric constraints of the dimple system—a totally sealed, hollow-celled, stiff web structure which can be either bolted or bonded (probably both) to the top deck and to the bottom composite chord.

We are only beginning to test the applications of composite technology in military bridge structures. Although some of the designs proposed have been found to be less than optimal, the message seems clear. Composite materials are ready to enter the Army.

The material must be carefully placed to efficiently use its desirable characteristics. An increased number of material property variables are managed in design, and the fabrication techniques must be mastered in production, however, the opportunity for real innovation makes the additional mechanics worthwhile.

The common disclaimer, "that stuff is just too expensive," does not really apply to composite materials anymore. The basic raw material prices for graphite are expected t recede as demand and productio increases, while inflation is drivin up the cost of conventional materi als. If we discard the "dollars pe pound" block for a more realisti "dollars per product," we find tha many applications are suprisingl cost effective right now. Composit materials have reached the bridg site and their impact will be felt i the 1980s.

Mr. Richard W. Helmke is chie Concepts and Composites Branc Marine and Bridge Laborator U.S. Mobility Equipment Researc and Development Command, Fo Belvoir, Va. Since 1959, he ha served in various civil service pos tions, including as the Army's chi designer for mobile bridge system with assault, floating and tactic applications. Mr. Helmke chairs t Trilateral (U.S., U.K. and F.R.G Design and Analysis Group whic gathered data for the recently pu lished **Design and Test Code fc Military Bridge Structures.** *He a registered graduate profession engineer in Virginia.*

Predicting Concrete Quality

CERL's new Concrete Control Monitor determines quality 15 minutes after concrete is placed.

by Debbie J. Lawrence

The Corps of Engineers' new Concrete Quality Monitor (CQM) two-test system evaluates water and cement percentages in fresh concrete samples to predict the 28-day compressive and flexural strength potential of the mix. Currently, strengths of concrete cannot be predicted until seven days after placement, with final strength predictions made 28 days after placement. The CQM test of fresh concrete can be completed in 15 minutes.

The water test consists of mixing a known weight of concrete with a known volume and concentration of salt solution, then determining the salt concentration of the intermixed salt solution using a chloride meter. The free water in the concrete dilutes the salt solution, thus changing the salt concentration. The strength of the intermixed salt solution is directly related to the water in the concrete sample.

The concrete test separates the aggregate from the cement portion of a concrete sample, then uniformly suspends the cement in a fixed volume of water. A fixed volume sample of the suspended cement is dissolved in diluted nitric acid, and the calcium strength of the dissolved solution is determined using a calcium analyzer.

Because cement is mainly composed of calcium compounds, the calcium content of the dissolved solution is linearly proportional to the cement content of the mix.

Author uses the monitor.

Recent laboratory and field test results show the system can determine the water and cement content of concrete to ±5- to 7-percent, and estimate both compressive and flexural strength potentials to within 10- to 15-percent. The approximate equipment cost is $6,800.

The Corps' CQM has several significant advantages over other test methods. This system, and its predecessors the Kelly/Vail and CERL/KV systems, are the only systems that rapidly (within 10 to 15 minutes) determine both water and cement content in fresh concrete. However, the CQM system is easier to use than the Kelly/Vail and CERL/KV systems (which require precision preparation of a significant quantity and number of reagents). CQM testing relies on instrumental analysis and associated small quantites of prepackaged reagents.

The CQM system is also easy to transport and calibrate. The equipment may be disassembled and packed in crates small enough to be sent as excess baggage on commercial airlines. The system is calibrated by conducting a standard CQM cement content test which takes less than 10 minutes.

In addition to these advantages, the CQM system is versatile and cost effective. It can be used to determine the lime and cement content of stabilized soils, mixer efficiencies and the presence and concentration of chlorides in concrete. The cost of operating the system (on a per-test basis) is significantly less than conventional concrete cylinder testing.

The CQM is being used by the Corps of Engineers' Tulsa District on soil cement stabilization, by the Walla Walla District on roller compacted concrete at the Willow Creek Dam project, and the American Society of Testing and Materials is developing a tentative standard test procedure based on the CQM and CERL/KV systems.

Debbie J. Lawrence, a chemical engineer at the Army Construction Engineering Research Laboratory, Champaign, Ill., is the principal investigator for the quality control/quality assurance program. She worked in construction for the Illinois Department of Transportation and as a quality engineer for General Electric before coming to the Corps. A graduate of the University of Illinois with a B.S. degree in chemical engineering, she is working on a Master's degree in chemical engineering.

Washington's Legacies

To The Modern Army©

by David Curtis Skaggs, Ph.D.

A nineteenth-century biographer once described George Washington as "bolder than Alexander, more crafty than Hannibal, wiser than Caesar, more prudent than Gustavas Adolphus, more resourceful than Frederick, more sagacious than Napoleon and more successful than Scipio."

Surely no commander has exhibited all these virtues. However, neither do I subscribe to Gore Vidal's theory, stated in his novel, *Burr,* that "had (either Horatio) Gates or (Charles) Lee been placed in command of the Army, the war would have ended three years sooner."

Thus we are faced with a dual image of the commander of the Continental Army, and from this there is much to learn. For this purpose, I shall group his legacies into two categories—tactical and personal.

The best known of his tactical legacies is his use of surprise. "Surprise," wrote Douglas MacArthur, "is the most vital element for success in war." Few have exploited this "vital element" more successfully than George Washington. The victories at Trenton, Princeton, Stony Point and Yorktown provide examples all commanders should remember.

Surprise cannot be achieved without developing to a fine art the skills of military intelligence and deception. Washington's talents in

these associated areas were excellent. His intelligence agents were legion but none exceeded the fact that the leading Loyalist journalist in British-held New York City was in his spy network. No enemy disposition or movement occurred without the American commander knowing of it. Deception of his own movements was critical in holding the main British army in Trenton while he undertook a forced march to Princeton. Both there and at Yorktown, His Majesty's generals were defeated due to surprise combined with vital intelligence and crafty deception.

Concurrent with surprise was the tactic of peripheral attack. After bitter defeats finally taught him otherwise, General Washington sought to attrit a superior enemy force through attacks at outposts. Trenton, Germantown, Paulus Hook, Stony Point and Yorktown epitomize this type operation. It is here that the modern Army has the most to learn from him. Since the age of Grant, American generals have sought the main enemy armed force and grappled with it until our superior firepower and manpower destroyed the opponent's will to resist.

Certainly we cannot expect such conditions to exist in possible war in Central Europe. George Washington learned what FM 100–5 seeks to teach us all: the U.S. Army must prepare its units to fight outnumbered and win. Washington's example of skillful concentration of force at decisive points is essential for all modern commanders to learn. Washington, wrote Douglas Southall Freeman, "was a bargain hunter. He always sought the largest gain for the least gore." Peripheral operations achieved this and allowed the Americans to control most of the North American land area despite many losses from Quebec to Charleston.

A third tactical legacy is Washington's use of defense. Modern strategy places extraordinary emphasis on offensive operations, almost to the exclusion of the critical role defense plays in forcing the enemy into situations that make him vulnerable. For Engineer officers, General Washington's skillful use of defensive fortifications cannot be overemphasized. Nowhere is this more apparent to contemporary Americans than by walking up to Fort Putnam above West Point and surveying the combination of defense in depth and mutual support that Thaddeus Kosciuszko designed to create the Hudson citadel from which Washington operated from 1778–83.

We need to learn more about the importance of tactical strong points and their significance to modern battle. We need not adopt a Maginot Line mentality to comprehend that the defense of Europe requires use of every civilian bulldozer, backhoe and cement mixer to provide the hostile strongholds that threaten the flanks and rear of any Warsaw Pact force. Moreover, from such positions can be made the type of peripheral attacks that Washington utilized at Stormy Point and Paulus Hook.

His final tactical legacy involves the use of combined operations. While our first commanding general was most inept at combined arms tactics (his failure to use cavalry and dragoons is a mystery to most commentators), his repeated plans to exploit the French Navy in the American theater is a study in frustration until it finally worked at Yorktown. From Newport, Rhode Island, to Savannah, Georgia, Washington's attempts from 1778 to 1780 to isolate a British garrison with a combination of land and naval forces failed. A less resolute commander would have given up, but not George Washington. With a persistence that modern commanders must emulate, he tried a fourth time. This time it worked. Such grand tactics are absolutely necessary on the modern battlefield and must be emulated despite our frustrations. Otherwise we cannot expect victory. The successful modern commander must be as much a diplomat as he is a general.

Examine Washington's most illustrious campaign—the Chesapeake encirclement of 1781. Here we see defense, surprise, peripherial attack and combined operations in exquisite execution.

The winter of 1780–81 represents the nadir of the American war effort. Inflation eroded the economy to where several hundred Continental dollars equaled one English pound. Mutiny in the ranks of the Continental Army threatened to destroy the only national institution existing in the country. Militarily the previous year saw the defeat of two "armies" sent to stop General Sir Henry Clinton's effort to destroy the rebellion by attacking its soft underbelly in the South. Defeats at Charleston and Camden left Georgia and most of South Carolina in British hands. Lord Cornwallis stood poised to invade North Carolina and Clinton sent a raiding party into Virginia. To stop this threatened loss of the whole South, Washington could only send a few Continentals under Nathanael Greene to the Carolinas and even fewer under Frederick von Steuben to Virginia. By mid-February the situation was desperate. One of Greene's reconnaissance forces under Daniel Morgan inflicted heavy losses to one of Cornwallis' flanking commands, but the act seemed only to enrage the British commander who promptly chased Greene across North Carolina. Meanwhile, newly commissioned British Brigadier Benedict Arnold led 1,500 redcoats up the James River to Richmond. Steuben seemed helpless to stop him and was replaced by Lafayette.

In May, Washington confided in his diary, "In a word—instead of having everything in readiness to take the field, we have nothing—and instead of having the prospect of a glorious offensive campaign before us, we have a bewildered, and gloomy defensive one—unless we should receive a powerful aid of ships—land troops and money from our generous allies and these, at present, are too contingent to build upon."

It was these contingencies that the success of the rebellion depended, and Washington sought to secure from his "generous allies" the troops, ships, and money necessary to wage a "glorious offensive campaign" against the center of British power in North America—New York City. Washington hoped that the new French naval commander Comte Francois de Grasse, then in the West Indies, and General Comte Jean Baptiste de Rochambeau's army at Newport would combine with the Continental Army to take New York. To this end, Generals Rochambeau and Washington met at Wethersfield, Conn., the last week of May 1781.

Rochambeau ostensibly agreed to the attack on Clinton's force beginning at Staten Island. Since such a move would place the French army on the west bank of the Hudson, Rochambeau was willing to accept this plan because from eastern New

Jersey he could more easily march toward the Chesapeake where he hoped to entrap Cornwallis' smaller force. Informing Admiral de Grasse of the Wethersfield decisions, he indicated his preference for the southern operation. Deploring the sorry state of the Continental Army, the French general urged de Grasse to bring enough ships, troops, and money to insure success against Cornwallis.

To few foreigners does the United States owe a more lasting debt than Admiral de Grasse. He did more than a weak ally could expect. He ignored explicit instructions from Paris to escort a West Indian merchant convoy to France. He secured 3,000 French troops from the Santo Domingo garrison, and not only received Governor Bernado de Galvez's permission to postpone a Franco-Spanish expedition against Jamacia, but also borrowed gold from His Catholic Majesty's coffers in Havana. When word of his pending expedition for the Chesapeake reached Washington, the American commander dropped his preference for New York and joined in the greatest combined operation in military history before the landing on Normandy.

If Washington's predilection for attacking New York deviated from his pattern of peripheral attack, his willingness to modify his plans indicates a flexibility characteristic of all great commanders. Moreover, he skillfully used his original plan as a deceptive cover for the Chesapeake operation, for surprise was a key to success. Clinton must feel threatened and Cornwallis must feel secure in order that the two not cooperate and ruin the opportunity.

Nowhere else do the tactical traits of Washington's generalship find better expression than in the Chesapeake encirclement. Secure in Fortress West Point, he had a defensive position unassailable by an 18th century army. Skillful in compromising his own inclinations for the locus of attack, he conducted a combined operation involving the movement of thousands of troops, hundreds of miles toward a single objective despite numerous obstacles to success. Managing a deception of two British generals, he achieved surprise that forced a significant defeat over an army which a mere 20 years earlier stood unchallenged in North America. Finally, he recognized that while attacking Cornwallis might not achieve a decisive victory over the British main force, the loss of such an important segment of His Britannic Majesty's army could force a major reassessment of the desirability of continuing the war by the leaders at Whitehall. Nowhere else can a modern Army officer find better examples of the interaction of defense, peripheral attack, surprise and joint operations, than in this episode.

Washington had character. No other attribute is so indefinable, yet so essential to military success . . .

Like all successful captains, George Washington had character. No other behavioral attribute is so indefinable, but none so essential to military success, than to be seen by one's associates and subordinates as having a force of personality that distinguishes the great leader from others. Washington had this trait.

Part of it undoubtedly derived from his superb physical condition. He survived eight years as commanding general without a day of leave and only three brief periods of sickness. He regularly rode horseback, often covering 15 miles before breakfast. He set an example of endurance unequaled by the heartiest Continental. Moreover, his well-proportioned, over six-foot physique, gave the image of the ideal leader.

But character involves more than appearance and physical condition. It requires a moral courage that is understood by all one's subordinates. His leadership was by example. Washington disciplined with justice and consideration, he promoted on the basis of talent, he solicited and respected

accepted the failures of others so long as they contributed to the subordinate's development into a better leader.

While no two great captains exhibit character in the same manner, George Washington exemplified how conscious integrity, patriotism, and responsibility constitute the essential ingredients of leadership. No modern captain can duplicate his personality, nor would one want to, but all leaders need those essential ingredients of character to inspire those who follow them through the trials of camp and combat.

A second ingredient of his personality was persistence. Like all warriors, he desired a short war. It became quickly obvious this would not be the case and he undertook those activities necessary for prolonged warfare. He raised a regular Army and avoided decisive conflict that might eliminate the Continental Army and its existence as the symbol of American nationhood. He grew with experience and persisted to the end despite defeat, discouragement, and defection.

A modern commentator may feel the Army has gone too far from persistence. The siren song of "win the first battle" may symbolize a revolution in our strategic thought antagonistic to the Washington legacy. Sure we would like to win the opening round, but frankly we must win the last. There will be those who argue that the first battle may be the last, but seldom has there been a one battle war—ask Hannibal, ask Napoleon, ask Hitler or Yamamoto about first battle victories. Persistence pays off, as Scipio, Wellington, Eisenhower and MacArthur can well testify. We must prepare not merely to win the first battle, but also to continue the fight. Persistence is a virtue writers of modern doctrine should not ignore. It is also a trait as essential to the garrison Army as to the one in the field.

The final Washington legacy is both the most difficult and the most important—subordination of military to civilian control. Dr. Richard Kohn called this the "ultimate greatness of Washington . . . No matter how difficult the times, desperate his own situation, or great his disagreements with Congress or the states, Washington never undermined civil authority or threatened with his vast prestige to overturn the government."

No event so nicely combines his three personality traits of character, persistence and subordination than the often forgotten Newburgh Conspiracy and Washington's response known as the Newburgh Address. Washington's finest hour, his most important legacy to each of you and all his countrymen, was not on the fields of Trenton, Princeton or Yorktown, not during the bitter winter encampments at Valley Forge or Morristown; rather it occurred during those frustrating months between the surrender of Cornwallis and the conclusion of peace. With Congress unable to meet either its pay or pension obligations and with the value of Continental currency and bonds sinking out of sight, a combination of nationalists, financial interests and disgruntled Army officers threatened a coup d'etat.

Washington played his cards carefully. He maneuvered it so that he would address a meeting of officers before the conspirators could act. In what was undoubtedly the most important speech of his career, Washington described how a coup would "overturn the liberties of our country, and . . . open the flood gates of civil discord and deluge our rising empire in blood." He concluded his prepared statement with an appeal for order and temperate action that reminds modern readers of Winston Churchill: "And you will by the dignity of your conduct, afford occasion for posterity to say, . . . had this day been wanting, the world had never seen the last stage of perfection to which human nature is capable of attaining."

No generation of soldiers deserved more and received less from their countrymen.

As he finished, he reached into his pocket and produced a letter from a congressman who described the difficulties of the situation. As he tried to read it, he paused in bewilderment and, after fumbling in his waistcoat pocket, produced something only a few members of his staff knew about. There was a bit of melancholy in his voice as he explained: "Gentlemen, you will permit me to put on my spectacles, for I have not only grown gray, but almost blind in the service of my country."

The effect of this tender statement in contrast with the civil war, treason and ruination of the ideals for which they fought and which he had earlier predicted, was immediate. Some officers wept. Virtually all recoiled at the idea of a coup d'etat. Washington read the letter, left the meeting, and the conspirators' plans were destroyed by the response to his charismatic leadership.

While I urge you consider and apply to your career all the legacies of Washington's generalship, both tactical and personal, I cannot overemphasize the need for you to follow the last one. No generation of soldiers deserved more and received less from its countrymen than that which fought for our independence. General Washington could easily have justified seizing the reigns of civil authority on grounds of national policy. He had examples from Caesar to Cromwell to imitate. But he refused. He sacrificed the immediate welfare of his officers and men on the altar of republicanism. It was a noble sacrifice. When next time a modern politician cancels the pet weapons system, manpower increase, pay raise or military policy you advocate, recall this final legacy of General Washington. Remain faithful to his ideal of republican virtue—the mythic Roman citizen-soldier Cincinnatus—and ignore the easy way out—symbolized by the classic case of Julius Caesar.

Dr. David Curtis Skaggs, an Army Reserve LTC, is on active duty to attend the Army War College, Carlisle Barracks, Pa. He is a professor of history at Bowling Green State University, Bowling Green, Ohio.

U.S. vs. Soviet Engineer Training

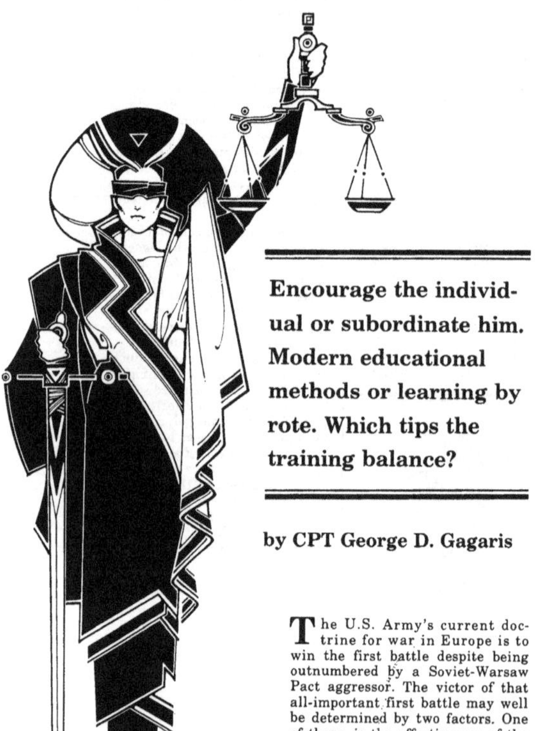

Encourage the individual or subordinate him. Modern educational methods or learning by rote. Which tips the training balance?

by CPT George D. Gagaris

The U.S. Army's current doctrine for war in Europe is to win the first battle despite being outnumbered by a Soviet-Warsaw Pact aggressor. The victor of that all-important first battle may well be determined by two factors. One of these, is the effective use of the combined arms team. Both American and Soviet armies rely on this concept as their tactical cornerstone.

An integral part of this team is the combat engineer, who is locat well forward with the maneuv forces. The combat engineer pr vides these committed forces wi essential mobility, countermobili and survivability support.

Another factor that may dete mine the victor of the next war the state of individual milita training within the two opposi forces. This training poses eno mous challenges for U.S. and Wa saw Pact armies, especially wi the introduction of sophisticat equipment, weapons and tacti Without meeting this individu training challenge, other milita training goals are difficult accomplish.

Field Manual 100–5, *Operation* and military strategists, agree th these factors may be critical el ments in determining the victor the next war. By developing an i depth understanding of these fa tors in peacetime, U.S. soldiers all levels will be better prepared win the first battle. This may l done by comparing U.S. and Sovi Warsaw Pact initial entry traini for combat engineers.

For U.S. combat engineers, i tial entry training is conducted the U.S. Army Training Center E gineer, Fort Leonard Wood, M The 2d Training Brigade conduc One Station Unit Training (OSU for most soldiers entering Care Management Field (CMF) 12. Th includes combat engineers, Mi tary Occupational Specialty (MO 12B; and bridge specialists, MC 12C. The atomic demolitions mur tions (ADM) specialist, MOS 12 also trains at Fort Leonard Woo but after graduation attends tl ADM course at Fort Belvoir, Va., qualify for his MOS.[1]

The purpose of the combat engineer (CE) OSUT program, is to provide a smooth transition from civilian to military life, and to qualify the new soldier in an engineer MOS. The 13-week program includes all program of instruction (POI) elements for basic combat training, as well as MOS 12B and 12C advanced individual training.[2]

The integration of these two POIs permits early introduction of MOS related skills, followed by reinforcement training that ensures soldier proficiency. CE-OSUT uses one unit and one cadre at one station to complete the training necessary to produce a soldier qualified for assignment in an engineer company. This arrangement also allows more accurate assessment of individual ability and potential, and for swift elimination of unproductive soldiers.

The U.S. soldier's normal training day is at least a full 16 hours and is designed to challenge him physically and mentally. Physical readiness training (PRT) is conducted daily and makes up approximately 10 percent of the soldier's total training.

Although PRT is based on a baseline physical training program, the overall program differs slightly from unit to unit because company commanders establish unit goals. The commander also determines the PRT schedule of activities for his unit.[3] A unit's daily PRT will include some sort of exercise, such as the 'daily dozen,' or a grass or rifle drill and a run. Additional physical training comes from road marches of up to 15 miles, negotiating obstacle or confidence courses and playing team sports, all of which toughen soldiers physically and mentally.

Engineer OSUT is basically divided into three phases: survivability, countermobility and mobility. In addition to these phases, the first few weeks of training are spent under a program of "total control," to aid in establishing obedience and discipline. During "total control," a new soldier is constantly supervised by unit drill sergeants who indoctrinate the military way of life. The sergeants also introduce soldiers to general information about the Corps of Engineers and Army combat engineering.

The first five weeks of the training cycle develop the soldier's ability to survive on the battlefield. Instruction during this phase concentrates on physical training, basic rifle marksmanship, obstacles, communications, rigging and first aid.

In the next four weeks, instruction centers on countermobility. This includes studying demolitions, land mine warfare, the M60 machine gun, the M203 grenade launcher and the light antitank weapon. During this phase, soldiers also receive instruction in map reading, communications, engineer tools and physical training.

The last four weeks compose the mobility phase, with soldiers learning offensive skills, such as fixed and float bridging, river assault operations and infantry squad tactics with assault demolitions. Also during the final phase, soldiers participate in a week-long field exercise known as "Engineer Week." The week is devoted to Army Training and Evaluation Program 5–35, *Squad and Platoon Missions,* which allows the soldier to apply new skills in a tactical scenario.

The foundation of the entire CE-OSUT program is its performance oriented, or, "hands-on" training. The soldier learns by doing a task under minimum supervision, and is later evaluated using diagnostic tests that check his progress through military, physical and combat engineer training. These diagnostic tests are: the End of Course Test, given in the seventh week to measure mastery of common soldier skills; the Army Physical Readiness Test, during the 10th week; and the Combat Engineer Test, given in the 11th week to assure overall proficiency before assignment to an engineer unit. A soldier must pass each of these tests to graduate from CE-OSUT and to qualify for either MOS 12B or 12C. ADM specialists study an additional 17 days before receiving MOS 12E.

By comparison, Soviet combat engineer initial military training is quite different. The reasons for this disparity are beyond the scope of this article, however, certain general considerations provide a better understanding of the overall Soviet military training program.

One of these considerations is that the Soviet Union regards military training, and military service, as vital to the nation's existence. This concern is apparent in the 1967 *Law on Universal Military Service,* which provides for "the mandatory conscription of eighteen-year-old males in semi-annual increments, and also governs the system of drafting of young men into the armed forces."[4] The U.S. Army, of course, relies on an all-volunteer force during peacetime and drafts only during mobilization.

Besides conscription, the 1967 *Law on Universal Military Service*

Combat engineer OSUT emphasizes teamwork but differs from Soviet training by also stressing personal achievement. (OSUT photos by Vicky Lipps)

U.S. soldiers learn by doing a task under minimum supervision.

establishes mandatory military training for all Soviet citizens, beginning at age 16. In contrast, there is no mandatory military training for the United States general population.

Finally, consider the upbringing of the Soviet children. These children are taught at an early age to relinquish their individuality to the group and to subordinate themselves to authority. Strict discipline and obedience is developed throughout the school system, and even earlier, in state-owned nurseries and kindergartens.[5] These values set apart the Soviet soldier from his American counterpart, whose *individual* achievements are repeatedly stressed.

The Soviet Union's unique military training cycle can be broken into three phases: civilian premilitary training, in-service training and reserve training.[6] Only the Soviet civilian premilitary training and a part of the in-service training can be considered comparable to U.S. initial entry training. The remainder of Soviet in-service training might be compared to the training performed by our TO&E units. Soviet reserve training is conducted much like training in the U.S. Army Reserve or National Guard. In general, the Soviet Ministry of Defense oversees the entire training process, establishing the goals, political subjects and training programs for the coming year.[7]

Soviet premilitary training is a result of the 1967 *Law on Universal Military Service,* which established "a compulsory system of premilitary training for all young men and women between the ages of 16 and 18, inclusive."[8] The program, begun in 1968, attempts to make the transition from civilian to soldier quicker and easier for new draftees. Premilitary training is general in nature, showing no regard for individual military specialities. The program provides young people with the basic military skills, including awareness of military organization and regulations, use of small arms (including antitank weapons) and civil defense training. They receive 140 hours of training during the standard preinduction program. Training also includes various field exercises lasting from five to 15 days. In addition, the program provides for selected youths to receive special training in their second year. This technical training ranges from driving a truck to operating a radar scope.

The benefits of preinduction training are open to argument, and some Soviet leaders have expressed displeasure with the program.[9] One noticeable problem is that the quality of training varies greatly from unit to unit. Many new soldiers must be retrained in the basic skills upon induction. This retraining process significantly reduces the time available for conducting essential in-service level military training.

Twice each year, a quota of men who have reached their 18th birthday are notified to report for active duty. At this point the commissarists, or draft board, "assign the inductees to the various branches, arms and services of the component forces."[10] These assignments are based on the individual's abilities, job specialties or specialties learned during preliminary training. On a specific day, inductees are taken to their assigned units to begin their active duty, or in-service, training.

The new soldier immediately begins an intensive four week training period known as the "Course of the Young Soldier."[11] This course is used to politically indoctrinate the new soldier and to complete the basic training started during preinduction. The soldier must successfully complete this period of training before he may take the military oath of allegiance and begin the remainder of his military training. The unit officers, warrant officers and noncommissioned officers supervise most of this specialty training, which begins with elementary skill instruction.

In the case of the engineer sol

PROGRAM OF INSTRUCTION

Combat Engineer One Station Unit Training

Engineer training (mines, tools, rigging, bridging, demolitions and Engineer Week) vehicle operations and maintenance and camouflage	243.5
Combat skills (first aid, tactics, chemical/biological and radiological warfare, foot marching) map reading, squad tactics and bivouac	226
Basic soldiering (inspections, drill, military subjects) and unit taught subjects	132
Weapons (M16A1 rifle, grenades, M60 machine gun, light antitank weapon)	90
Physical Readiness Training (Army Physical Readiness Test, confidence courses, team sports)	85
Administrative time (miscellaneous processing)	70
Testing	20
TOTAL	**866.5 hours**

Training for Soviet engineers (above) is packaged differently from a U.S. engineer's (below), but the biggest difference may be training leadership.

dier, he will be required to "master one specialty and be adequately prepared to perform one or two other related engineering tasks so as to make the engineer special sub-units less vulnerable to losses of trained men."[12] On the average, it will take the soldier six months of training to become proficient in his speciality. There are no distinct breaks in the training to differentiate the progression from elementary skills to more advanced skills. However, sometime during that initial six month period, the Soviet soldier will "graduate," much like his American counterpart does at the end of CE-OSUT.

A typical Soviet training day is similar to one in CE-OSUT.[13] At least six hours of each training day is set aside for military instruction. The training is very repetitious, and learning is by rote. Except for political indoctrination, classroom instruction is minimal, with field training under realistic combat conditions the norm. Soviet instruction relies heavily on simulators instead of actual pieces of equipment. This practice extends the life of actual equipment and keeps repair and replacement costs low.

Physical fitness for the Soviet soldier, as well as for the Soviet citizen, is a part of everyday life. Participation in a formal physical conditioning program starts at age 10, progressing through five stages up to age 60 for men and age 55 for women. Active duty military PRT is geared to prepare soldiers for combat and for the heavy work associated with military service. Training includes unarmed combat, negotiating obstacle courses, various long and short distance runs, gymnastics, swimming, ski racing, forced marches and team sports play. As in the U.S. Army, "each unit commander is responsible for the physical conditioning of his men" and for the functioning of the PRT program.[14]

Although Soviet initial entry training is somewhat different in structure, it is basically on the same level as training conducted for U.S. soldiers in CE-OSUT. The primary impression is that any military training program is only as good as the leaders responsible for it.

Footnotes

1. Information concerning CE-OSUT is based on the author's personal experience.
2. Second Training Brigade (OSUT) *Information Folder,* 2d Training Brigade, Fort Leonard Wood, Mo., p. 8.
3. *Initial Entry Training,* "On the Trail to Better Leadership," 1979, Fort Leonard Wood, Mo., p. 18.
4. Defense Intelligence Agency, *Handbook on the Soviet Armed Forces,* February 1978, p. 5–1.
5. Office of the Assistant Chief of Staff for Intelligence, *Understanding Soviet Military Development,* April 1977, p. 35.
6. DIA, op cit., p. 6–1.
7. David J. Foley and Frank Stone, "The Soviet Ground Forces Training Program," *Defense Intelligence Report,* April 1978, p. 8.
8. DIA, op cit., p. 6–1.
9. DIA, op cit., p. 6–2.
10. DIA, op cit., p. 5–2.
11. DIA, op cit., p. 6–8.
12. C.N. Donnely, 'Combat Engineers of the Soviet Army," *International Defense Review,* Vol. 11, No. 2, April 1978, p. 194.
13. DIA, op cit., p. 1–8.
14. David J. Foley and Frank Stone, "Physical Training of the Soviet Soldier," *Defense Intelligence Report,* April 1978, p. 10.
15. Office of the Assistant Chief of Staff for Intelligence, op cit., p. 36.

CPT George Gagaris is a graduate of the U.S. Military Academy and the Engineer Officer Basic and Advanced Courses. He served as a training officer and company commander with the 2d Training Bde., U.S. Army Training Center Engineer, Ft. Leonard Wood, Mo. He is now stationed in Germany.

ENGINEER HOTLINE

Engineer related problems, questions and comments can be addressed telephonically to the U.S. Army Engineer School's "Engineer Hotline." The Hotline's auto-answer recorder operates 24 hours a day, seven days a week. Callers should state their name, address and telephone number, followed by a concise question or comment. You'll receive a reply within three to 15 days. The Hotline is not intended as a receiving agency for formal requests.

Call commercial (703) 664-3646; WATS 800-336-3095, extension 3646; or AV 354-3646.

Engineers from TF Simoneaux move to new defensive positions during the Ft. Hunter Liggett FTX.

ENGINEERS AS INFANTRY

"Fight as infantry when required"—that is an important secondary mission of combat engineers. It is a wartime mission often assumed at a critical time and at a critical place. But, how often does the combat engineer command a combined arms team in peacetime?

by LTC James M. Cullem

The troops of two engineer battalions duck down deeper into their foxholes as artillery rounds whistle overhead, winging their way toward attacking enemy formations in the open field ahead. The friendly artillery support is comforting to the defenders dug-in on the high ground. But in quick response, enemy guns initiate counterfires causing friendly casualties, decimating troops and equipment still in the open. Amidst smoke and confusion, battle is joined between attacking infantry and defending engineers.

So went the opening event of a 7th Infantry Division field training exercise (FTX) at Fort Hunter Liggett, Cal., a unique FTX in that two combat engineer battalions, reorganized as infantry under a brigade headquarters, were engaged in a "defend" mission.

Concept

The scenario for the FTX reflected a classical battle plan. A friendly nation with which the U.S. had treaty commitments, "Dagon," possessed rich uranium mines coveted by its northern neighbor, "Ur." Ur invaded Dagon, scored significant early successes, and the United States sent the 7th Infantry Division to assist Royal Dagonian forces.

The 1st Brigade, 7th Infantry Division, played the Urian forces, and the 2d Brigade, 7th Infantry Division, played the lead elements of the 7th Division. Since the 7th Division is a "roundout" unit with only two active brigades, no other infantry troops were available to play the Dagonian forces.

LTC Clair P. Gill's 14th Engineer Battalion (Corps) (Combat) of three line companies and a headquarters company was available, as was the divisional 13th Engineer Battalion (Combat) commanded by LTC Joseph A. Simoneaux. The latter unit consisted of two active duty line companies and a headquarters company. The division artillery (DIVARTY), with a doctrinal role as alternate division command post, served as the Royal Dagonian Brigade headquarters.

Combat engineers fighting as infantry is not unique. In December 1944, during the Battle of the Bulge, the 1278th, 299th, 35th, and 158th Engineer Battalions fought side by side as infantry defending the approaches to Bastogne. The 51st Engineer Battalion played a key role in holding positions to the northwest of Bastogne and won a Presidential Unit Citation for its performance. These battalions and other engineer units, fighting as infantry, won the praise of Maj. Gen. Troy H. Middleton, the VII Corps commander.[1]

The 14th Engineer Battalion, among others, fought as infantry in Korea, especially during the defense of the Pusan perimeter in 1950.[2] Since the end of the Korean War, however, there has been little opportunity for combat engineers to train as infantry forces. The Hunter Liggett FTX, then, was an unusual engineer training opportunity.

Preparations

In February and March 1980, the 13th and 14th Engineer Battalions conducted training in infantry tactics and employing artillery and mortar fire, close air support and TOW missiles. Officers from the 7th Division's 3/32 and 2/32 Infantry Battalions, the division Air Force liaison office and DIVARTY provided instruction.

Field exercises in March and April gave both engineer battalions good opportunities to debug their communications procedures, practice rapid deployment of the command post and to improve camouflage techniques. Several TEWTs (tactical exercises without troops), and a ground and air reconnaissance of the battle area were conducted at Fort Hunter Liggett.

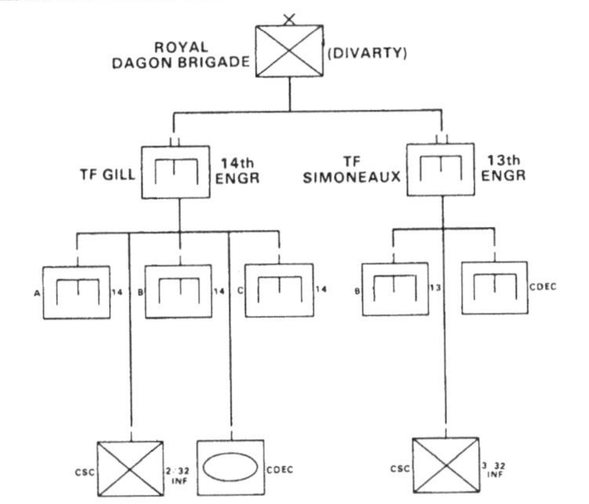

Task organization for the engineers-as-infantry FTX.

Task Organization

Not equipped with organic TOWs, armor, scouts or mortars, the engineers had to be provided these weapons and personnel to accomplish their mission. The initial task organization is shown in Figure 1. The combat support company (CSC) of the 2/32 Infantry Battalion and a company (−) of tanks from the Combat Development Experimentation Command (CDEC) were attached to the 14th Engineers. The CSC of the 3/32 Infantry and the engineer company of CDEC were attached to the 13th Engineers. A Company, 13th Engineers, remained in its traditional role with the 1st Brigade, the Urian forces. Both engineer battalions were supported by artillery fire support teams (FIST), tactical air control parties (TACP), and forward maintenance support teams. Helicopters from the 1/10th Air Cavalry, Redeye and Vulcan gun sections from the division air defense artillery (ADA) battalion, and ground surveillance radar (GSRs) teams were also in support. As per battalion SOPs, heavy equipment, trucks and most engineer tools and kits were sent to the field trains area as soon as the battle began.

Each engineer task force was named after its commander. The units were deployed to Fort Hunter Liggett on April 30 and the task forces were organized in place by May 3.

fighting positions, aerial drops of barrier materials to the initial positions of both engineer battalions were made by C130 aircraft on May 4. The airdrop provided excellent training in Air Force resupply operations in the forward combat zone. These materials were used to construct obstacles forward of initial task force positions. Organic engineer dozers and backhoes dug in the tank and TOW positions. Close coordination between engineer and attached infantry and armor troops yielded optimum weapon, obstacle and fighting position interaction.

The Ft. Hunter Liggett area of operations.

The Battle Area

The terrain at Fort Hunter Liggett consists largely of treeless plains and open valleys which provide maneuver room for small tank forces. There are also areas of rocky mountains, grassy hills, lakes, streams and wooded areas conducive to dismounted infantry operations. Though the total size of the maneuver area was limited, it was nonetheless ideal for the FTX. Both task forces (TF) were to defend well forward in their sectors. TF Gill, the larger, was on the left flank defending a sector five kilometers wide which included the major mechanized avenues of approach. Smaller TF Simoneaux defended a narrower sector, two and one-half kilometers wide, on the right flank with higher and more mountainous terrain. The terrain in both task force sectors provided a series of natural delay positions.

Although restricted access to the battle area prior to the exercise precluded the installation of a maximum number of obstacles and

Attack, Counterattack

The DIVARTY's live-fire preparation on May 5 was made as realistic as possible so the troops could experience friendly artillery fire passing overhead and impacting to the front. The positioned engineers had full view of the artillery preparation and gained a heightened appreciation for the effectiveness of artillery and the need for well built foxholes with overhead cover. Following the artillery preparation, Urian forces began daylight probes along the entire Royal Dagon Brigade front. Friendly ambush patrols, outposts, and CSC scouts screening in front of Dagon positions proved invaluable in "seeing the battlefield" during the early engagements. Also, the initial placement of obstacles and battle positions paid large dividends in tilting initial combat ratios in favor of the defenders.

However, a battalion-sized night assault against the Dagon left flank company was successful after a long and confusing battle. Team A, TF Gill, withdrew under pressure and the flanking maneuver by the enemy penetrated several kilometers into friendly territory. At the same time, on the Dagon right, the TF Simoneaux's CDEC was attacked by dismounted infantry and an airmobile assault force, but the company was able to hold its position. In addition, an artillery attack on the TF Gill tactical operations center (TOC) resulted in personnel losses to the battalion staff.

At this critical time, the Dagonian Brigade commander (DIVARTY commander) ordered a counterattack. TF Tidwell, led by the commander, CSC, 2/32 Infantry, was formed. From all the scouts of both the 2/32 and 3/32 CSCs and the CDEC tank company (eight tanks) which had been originally attached to B Company, TF Gill. A platoon of engineer troops on 5-ton trucks was detached from C Company, TF Gill. This mobile force was assembled and in position by 0400 hours. TF Tidwell was to thrust across the TF Gill sector behind the strongly held B and C Company positions and strike the enemy column. The counterattack was launched at 0445 hours supported by artillery, attack helicopters and tactical aircraft. It was a total success.

Early Lessons Learned

The first major engagements of the "war" provided some very useful lessons. Probably the most significant was the need to anticipate the unexpected, and look for it to happen at night. Although the low valley approaches in the center were obviously the major avenues of approach, the enemy forces massed against the flanks in a night attack and bypassed the strongly defended center. Only a dogged defense and a preplanned counterattack saved the day.

The active defense envisioned in mechanized warfare requires quick lateral and reinforcing movement of troops on the FEBA (forward edge of the battle area). Dismounted infantry, however, have a difficult time disengaging, and cannot move laterally across the battlefield quickly enough to react to a penetration. As opposed to the current philosophy of mechanized warfare where most available forces are committed to likely avenues of approach, an engineer battalion, reorganized as dismounted infantry, ought to keep a reserve of at least one platoon. Trucks or other vehicles must be available for transportation, and supporting arms such as scout jeeps, armor, and artillery need to be earmarked once the reserve is committed.

The inherent vulnerability of the TOC to artillery fire became evident the first day. The best alternate TOC is the combat support company headquarters because the CSC has adequate radio communications and usually has the TOC backup mission in an infantry battalion. Care must be taken to conceal the TOC's location from the enemy. TOCs should be moved at least once every 12 hours. It must be well dug in and be located away from hilltops, crossroads or other locations likely to be targeted by enemy artillery. The terrain should be used to mask signal emissions.

Action The Second Day

On the second day of the war, the engineer troops engaged in a delaying action all along the front. Despite Dagonian successes the previous night, Urian forces again penetrated the left flank and continued to advance. The rate of movement of these forces set the pace of the delay as TF Gill sought to avoid envelopment on the left. Contact between TF Gill and TF Simoneaux was maintained during the delay and precluded Urain forces from slipping between the two units. Because TF Simoneaux's movement was slowed by the rugged terrain, an airmobile operation was used to move the engineers from their second to their third position.

It was during this phase of the operation that Murphy's Law came into full play and a most significant communications problem developed. The loss of the TOC (and switchboard) on the first day, coupled with a defensive battle that turned into a delaying action, caused a complete breakdown of communications. During movement, engineer company teams were unable to tie into pre-laid wire and FM communications were severely hindered by the terrain, by unskilled operators, and by a lack of radios at the company level. Radio communications were lost—laterally and vertically—within TF Gill for a period of about six hours. The direct consequence was loss of control and the opening of serious gaps in the defensive positions along the secondary line of defense.

More Lessons

Units must establish contact with adjacent units on the ground, and must insure radio or wire communications to higher headquarters are maintained at all times. Alternate means of communications, pre-established rally or contact points, use of pyrotechnic signals, etc., must also be agreed to beforehand. Since cryptographic key changes can also cause serious radio problems, they must be anticipated and problems corrected quickly. Every unit must habitually encode its grid coordinate position and send it to higher headquarters. *No* unit should leave a position, especially a critical road block or fortification, until physically replaced by the relieving unit. Fatigue, both physical and mental, took its toll and was reflected in leader's decisions and in the troop's performance. Leaders must find time to sleep and to obtain rest for their men during lulls in the battle or the troops will be close to ineffective after 72 hours of combat.

Serious problems with wire and FM communications led to control problems and defensive gaps.

The Last Day

May 7 was devoted to improving the final defensive line and coordinating for the passage of lines by the 2d Brigade, 7th Infantry Division. More live artillery was fired at 1600 hours to prepare the battlefield. The actual passage of lines took place between 2030 and 2200 hours. Despite extensive coordination during the day, several friendly units exchanged gunfire, a testimony to the difficulty of accomplishing such a maneuver at night in the face of the enemy.

After the passage of lines, TF Simoneaux was reorganized. It released the CDEC engineers and other attachments and placed B Company, 13th Engineers, in direct support of 2d Brigade, 7th Infantry Division. TF Gill also released its attachments and reverted to its corps engineer role. The 13th Engineer Battalion, with A/13th direct support to the 1st Brigade (Urian) and B/13th direct support to the 2d Brigade (7th Infantry Division), remained in the exercise until May 9 accomplishing missions as combat engineers.

Conclusions

Historically, engineer battalions have been reorganized as infantry only when the tactical situation reached a crisis stage. Little in the way of armor, artillery, antiarmor or air support assets are likely to be available. Nevertheless, engineers must know how to employ these assets as a combined arms team. They must continue to apply their special expertise in maximizing the defensive capabilities of the terrain and utilizing available obstacles to optimize the effectiveness of weapons systems. Engineer troops must be capable of fighting a delaying action, whether supporting arms are available or not.

Engineers fighting as infantry are likely to be thinly stretched and opposed by superior forces. Nevertheless, they must somehow retain the ability to counterattack. Contrary to traditional engineer SOPs, enough vehicles must be kept close to the FEBA so troops can move laterally, reinforce or counterattack quickly. Several 5-ton dump trucks at the right time and place can mean the difference between winning and losing.

Friendly forces can expect plenty of incoming artillery so they should be well dug in with covered and concealed positions with protected routes of egress and ingress. This fact warrants a second look at typical engineer reorganization SOPs which program the heavy construction equipment to move to the rear. A better tactic might be to retain the equipment up front until the very last minute to dig positions and create obstacles. Equipment would then withdraw only as far as the next positions and go to work again. Engineer equipment used in this manner can have a great multiplier effect upon the combat power of the fighting forces.

Since infantry operations lend themselves to night fighting in rugged terrain, engineer troops must train in that type of an environment.

If the engineer battalion receives an attachment of armor, it must also receive adequate maintenance and support packages. During the FTX, failure to provide such a package led to fuel or maintenance-related losses of 50 percent of attached armor assets within 72 hours.

From a logistical standpoint, the organization of field trains and combat trains was successful. The field trains contained the bulk of S1/S4 and maintenance assets while the combat trains contained only those S1 and S4 elements needed forward to control the flow of supplies, respond to equipment recovery requests, and to coordinate the flow of replacements and evacuate casualties and refugees. However, the exercise ran too short to determine whether the train's organization, provided from organic assets, could sustain the battalions over an extended period of time. For the most part, the engineers supplied themselves from their initial three-day basic load of ammo and fuel, and required little actual resupply. In addition, as is often the case in training, transportation and logistical capabilities in support of an actual defensive obstacle plan were not tested. Provided that the trucks of the engineer battalion remain available in the battle area, engineers should be able to handle the resupply requirements of an infantry operation.

Operating as part of a brigade requires coordination on a continuous basis. The set-piece nature of the FTX allowed it to work well, but a more free-flowing tactical situation could easily result in serious control problems.

The FTX was a rewarding and challenging experience for the engineers. They had the opportunity to plan and coordinate for the exercise, and to fight as infantry under the direction of a brigade headquarters. Most of the significant lessons learned have already been discussed above. However, two unresolved problems are worthy of a final note.

A price is paid in over all combat effectiveness when engineers are diverted from their primary combat engineer role to perform their secondary infantry role.

Unresolved Problems

1. Communications remain an unsolved problem. By TO&E (table organization and equipment), there are insufficient men and materials to establish telephone communications from battalion to company. The use of wire from company to platoon and from platoon to squad is, however, feasible under current TO&E. Secondly, the currently available radió teletype systems are extremely difficult to put into operation and to maintain. It is recommended that engineer units be augmented with additional radios and communication assets for the infantry mission.

2. A price is paid in overall combat effectiveness when engineers are diverted from their primary combat engineer role to perform their secondary infantry role. Such a reorganization in combat should take place only after the commander has fully considered the consequences of losing engineer combat multipliers. As noted in Hugh M. Cole's *History of the U.S. Army in World War II, the Ardennes: Battle of the Bulge:*

"The magnificent job which Maj. Gen. Middleton later ascribed to the engineers credits them in their role as infantry . . . Nonetheless, the story of the Ardennes barrier lines does make clear that use of engineers in their capacity as

THE GERMAN TERRITORIAL ARMY

An important link between West Germany's military and civilian spheres, and a vital wartime asset to allied forces.

by LTC Hubertus Dunschen

On the face of it, many a soldier in the U.S. Army is tempted to regard the German Territorial Army as a kind of German Army National Guard. Mission and organizational structure, however, are not comparable. Since the German Territorial Army has—among other things—a mediating function with regard to allied NATO forces in Germany, each American officer who is either stationed in Germany or a member of a reinforcement unit would be well advised to familiarize himself to some extent with the characteristics of the German Territorial Army.

Army Structure No. 4

The German Army is composed of three major elements: the Army Field Forces (assigned to NATO), the Territorial Army (under national command) and the General Army Office (national command in charge of central Army agencies and schools). In the late 1970s, following intensive structural studies, the German Army began to adopt a new organization, known as Army Structure No. 4.

The basic organizational structure of the engineers in the Army Field Forces was retained; i.e., one (organic) armored engineer company in each brigade, one engineer battalion per division and one engineer command per corps. The commanders of these regular units at the same time serve as engineer commanders within their respective major formation and as advisors in engineer-related matters to their next higher commander.

Nevertheless, the internal structure, organization and equipment of both engineer battalions and engineer companies were changed and adapted to the overall concept of Army Structure No. 4. All engineer units are fully mobile with the brigade engineers being armored.

The engineers of the Army Field Forces are employed on the battlefield in a direct combat support role. In keeping with the defense concept of the German Armed Forces, their main mission is to impede enemy movements within the scope of operations conducted by the major formations sponsored by them.

The Territorial Army

When setting the objective for the new Army Structure No. 4, the chief of staff of the Army considered it imperative to strengthen the Territorial Army and to make it better suited to fulfill its many missions. Those main tasks of the Territorial Army are:

1. To act as mediator between the military and civilian spheres.
2. To maintain the freedom of operation for NATO forces in the territory of the Federal Republic of Germany by means of:
   - rear area protection
   - military movement control measures
   - supporting river crossing operations
   - NBC defense measures
   - damage repair
   - explosive ordnance disposal
   - psychological defense measures

• establishing and operating communications

Furthermore, the Territorial Army is:

• to assume special command and control, and support tasks
• to ensure readiness of personnel, logistics as well as medical care and support
• to assist in civil defense operations

Thus, the German territorial commander renders direct support to the NATO commander to carry out his mission.

To accomplish its comprehensive mission, the Territorial Army makes use of its territorial headquarters organization, which covers the entire territory of the Federal Republic of Germany, and, its territorial forces which are used for mobile employment.

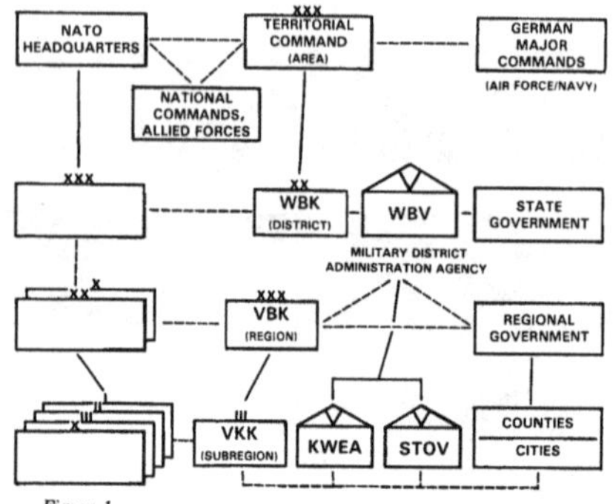

Figure 1.

The Territorial HQ

The territorial headquarters organization is adapted to both the political structure of the Federal Republic of Germany and to the NATO command structure in Central Europe. The organization consists of Territorial Command Schleswig-Holstein, the Territorial Northern Command and the Territorial Southern Command.

Subordinate to these Territorial Commands are the Military District Commands (WBK), which in turn have Military Region Commands (VBK) as subordinate agencies, which in turn command Military Subregion Commands (VKK).

Each Military District has a Military District Administrative Office (WBV) as higher agency of the Federal Armed Forces Administration. Subordinate to these Military District Administrative Offices are a number of Garrison Administrative Offices (STOV) as local agencies of the Federal Armed Forces Administration. This organization of the Federal Armed Forces Administration, however, is not part of the Territorial Army. It is independent of the armed forces and is to cooperate with them to fulfill administrative tasks related to the Bundeswehr. Figure 1 shows the levels of cooperation between the NATO forces, the Territorial Army, the Federal Armed Forces Admi istration and the various levels state and local government in th Federal Republic of Germany.

To ensure smooth cooperation i wartime as well there is a liaiso organization of the Territori Army. Figure 2 illustrates the com plexity of both tasks and coopera tion even at the lowest comman level of the Territorial Army, th Military Subregion Comman (VKK), which is shown as the hu of the liaison network. The sam applies to VBK and WBK with re spect to their allocated levels o cooperation.

Figure 2.

Possible operational links of the German Territorial Army, subregional level.

Territorial Forces

To accomplish the second essen tial part of its mission, to maintai the freedom of operation of NAT(forces on the territory of the Fede al Republic of Germany, the Hom Defense Force and several territo rial service support commands ar placed under the command of th Territorial Army. Both comba power and the number of home de fense units have considerably in creased within the framework o Army Structure No. 4. While al most exclusively consisting of un armored units in the past, mecha nized armored units of the Hom Defense Force have now been acti vated for rear area security/rea area protection.

In addition, the Territorial Arm

commands a number of command and control, combat support and logistic elements as well as special agencies and organizations to fulfill the following tasks:

- military movement control
- engineer support, including area damage control
- NBC defense measures
- communications support
- psychological defense operations
- enforcement of military law and order
- POW
- military geographic and geophysical support
- logistic and medical support for GE and assistance to allied forces
- personnel mobilization and replacement
- public relations
- procurement/use of civilian services/support
- support of civil defense organizations
- information compilation
- liaison

While the Territorial headquarters organization is already fully operational in peacetime, the majority of Territorial Forces consist of cadre-strength or partially cadre-strength units which can be brought up to strength with reservists within a relatively short period of time. Their equipment has already been pre-positioned at mobilization bases.

Host Nation Support

The tasks listed above to some extent coincide with individual host nation support (HNS) functions. The German Territorial Army is therefore an essential carrier, as well as coordinator and mediator, for HNS in peacetime and wartime. The allied forces will submit their requirements within the scope of HNS to the appropriate agencies of the Territorial Army. In this connection, military support is not the main objective of wartime host nation support (WHNS), but rather the provision of both materiel support and services through access to commercial resources.

The subject of wartime host nation support is many-faceted and complex and shall not be detailed here. The roots of WHNS are to be found in the NATO Long-Term Defense Program, and it is designed to make possible the fast redeployment of reserve forces to Europe as well as to increase the conventional deterrence posture of the alliance.

To share the burden and to determine specific commitments, an agreement on WHNS was signed by the United States and the Federal Republic of Germany on April 15, 1982. In accordance with the agreement, Germany assumes considerable capital expenditures and operating costs and has committed itself to provide personnel (military and civilian) on a permanent basis for WHNS tasks already in peacetime. In addition, more than 90,000 men will be made available to support U.S. forces in wartime.

An umbrella organization, to be set up in peacetime, is to assume command and control, logistics and training of the German support forces.

Territorial Army Engineers

Engineer forces form an organic part of the Territorial Forces. It must be emphasized that the engineers of the Territorial Army have also been assigned combat support tasks rather than construction tasks as some elements of the U.S. Army Corps of Engineers. These engineer tasks are primarily related to operations in the rear area, behind the corps. But is it also con-

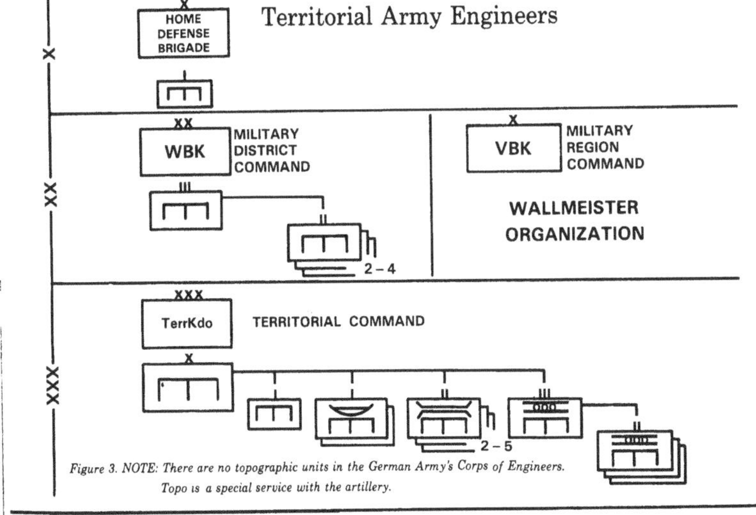

Figure 3. NOTE: There are no topographic units in the German Army's Corps of Engineers. Topo is a special service with the artillery.

ceivable that Territorial Army engineers will be employed in direct support of engineer forces in the Corps area of operations.

The Territorial Northern (GTNC) and Southern Command (GTSC) now have one engineer command each. The commanders of these engineer commands at the same time act as GTNC and GTSC engineer respectively. They are responsible for the employment of all engineer forces of the respective Territorial Command, including necessary preparatory measures. They work closely with the engineer commanders and/or engineer special staff sections of NATO headquarters and the high commands of allied forces as well as with civilian authorities.

The engineer command has the capabilities to ensure the crossing of wide waterways by employing its float bridge battalions and river engineer companies once fixed crossing sites can no longer be used. To ensure crossing of the Rhine River, these battalions and companies are equipped with special river crossing means and bridging equipment which meet the specific requirements of the Rhine.

Relying on its pipeline engineer group as a unit with a logistic mission, the Engineer Command operates fixed facilities and installations of the NATO pipeline system and repairs damaged or destroyed pipeline facilities.

Since the organization of the Territorial Command Schleswig-Holstein (TC S–H) is somewhat different, it shall not be detailed here. The Military District Commands have one engineer group each whose primary mission comprises:

- repairing damage along communications lines and defense-essential infrastructure,
- emplacing barriers, and
- supporting other forces by means of field fortifications.

The Home Defense Brigades as well as the brigades of the Army Field Forces have one organic engineer company each to render direct combat support to the brigade.

The Denial Engineers

The denial engineers (Wallmeister) represent a special engineer organization within the Territorial Army.

The Military Region Commands have varying numbers of denial engineer teams. They conduct reconnaissance with respect to barriers and assist in the installation, control and maintenance of barriers and prechambered targets (target folders). They compile and update engineer intelligence data and advise the units in all matters regarding the planning of barriers and movements.

These denial engineers are experienced senior NCOs of the engineer forces who have received special training for their mission. They carry out their mission in one or several counties *(Landkreise)* and cooperate with the units earmarked for this sector or employed in it.

Since they often hold the sam position for many years, and sinc they frequently are native to thei specific area of responsibility, the are very much familiar with bot aspects of the terrain and the loc population.

Their assistance in preparing e gineer intelligence data (surveys rivers, waterways and adjacent te rain) and their involvement in ba rier infrastructure activities a ready in peacetime (barrie installation/prechambered target makes them local experts who ar often important advisors to the e gineers regarding the fulfillment their mission.

An engineer staff officer in th Military Region Command exe cises command and control over th denial engineer teams.

The Territorial Army, then, is a extensive organization with a wid range of missions. In wartime, ı will provide vital assistance to a lied forces.

LTC Hubertus Dunschen is a gra uate of the University of Cologn and the German Army's Office School and Engineer School. He ha commanded NBC defense, comb engineer and armored enginee companies; served as a battalio and corps operations officer an commanded the 5th Engineer Bat talion. LTC Dunschen is the Ger man Army liaison officer to the U.S Army Engineer School and t MERADCOM at Ft. Belvoir, Va.

The ENGINEER Problem

The factored design load for the upper level floor of a recreation center was calculated to be 1.5 kips per foot. The floor design requires the placement of a continuous beam for 90 feet. The spacing of the supporting columns will enable third-point support of the beam. Adequate lateral bracing will be provided.

Select the most economical wide flange member and calculate the maximum deflection in inches.

Solution on page 41

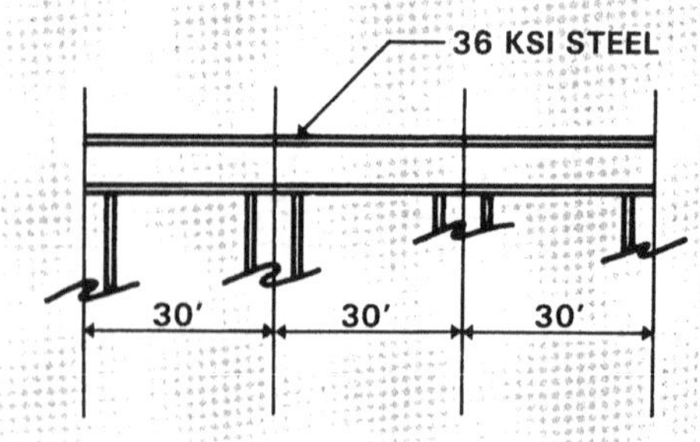

The Engineer Calculator

Mini-computer capabilities & designed specifically for combat engineers.

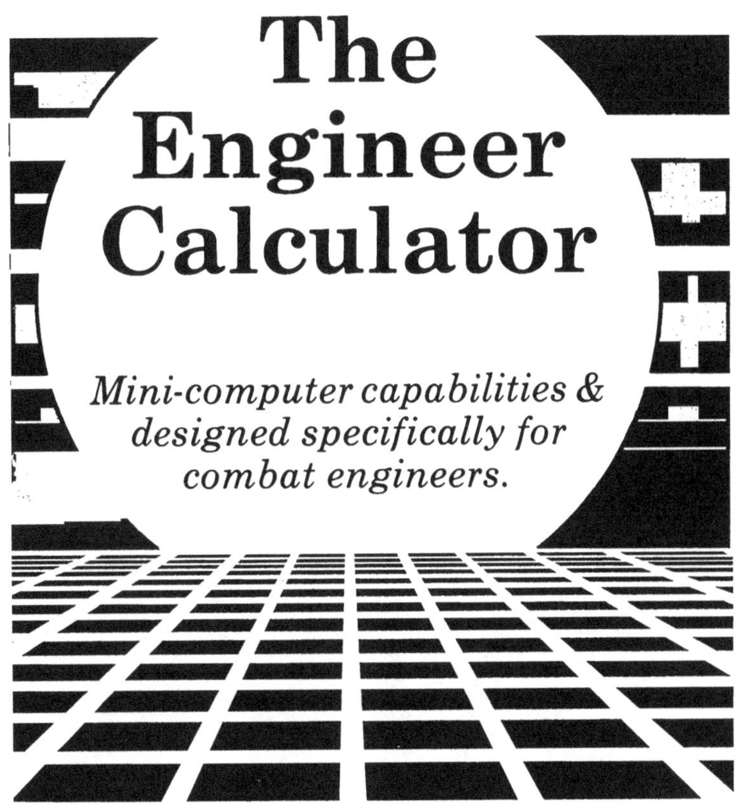

ıhn M. Deponai

ıbat engineers perform a tremendous variety of gineer missions. To complete them successfully, ɘrs often must make complex calculations or fol- ıgthy algorithms to determine logistical re- ents. This fall, the Engineer Programmable ıtor, an experimental training device developed by the U.S. Army Construction Engineering Research Laboratory (CERL) for the Engineer School, will make its debut as a supplement to FM 5-34, *Engineer Field Data*. The benefit of such a device is not in its use as a calculator, but in its use as a powerful, hand-held computer.

Background On Development

Based on feedback from active Army engineer units and detailed analysis by the Engineer School, CERL identified military engineering applications that were suited to automation, and those that if automated, would be highly valued by field troops.

The utility of the particular programs CERL selected was based not only in their specific benefit, but also in their example as to what is possible using an electronic medium like the programmable calculator.

It is hoped that exposure to the programmable calculator will eliminate some of the bias against "thinking automation." Automation is coming! The choice is to be in the vanguard of the inevitable, or to sit back complacently awaiting the day when someone asks, "How come we didn't think of this before?"

Preparing for the future takes a lot of imagination, energy, frustration and initiative. It is impractical to wait for technology to stabilize; the world is changing faster than ever before. New and better hardware and software are forever on the horizon.

The Hardware

The Engineer Programmable Calculator is a Hewlett Packard (HP)-41cv calculator accompanied by a specially programmed, plug-in, read-only-memory (ROM) module, labeled MILENG1/UTIL. This module is smaller than a matchbook, yet can store 8,000 bytes of program information.

The HP-41 has room for four such ROMs—32,000 bytes of information—plus the 2,200 bytes of built-in, read-write memory standard on the HP-41cv model. The HP-41 also has a growing family of peripherals, including a card reader, an optical wand and a thermal printer.

The HP-41 can display alphanumerics. Twelve characters can fit onto the display window and up to 24 characters can be "scrolled" across the window. The alpha characters are printed in blue on the front part of the keys and the alpha mode is accessed simply by pressing the ALPHA key.

Users can assign programs or functions to almost any key on the keyboard; when the calculator is in the user mode (accessed by pressing the USER key), the program assigned to that key will be executed immediately. This is especially convenient when running the same program a number of times.

On the whole, this calculator is very user-friendly. Those who prefer algebraic notation over Reverse-Polish Notation (RPN) may be a little dismayed, but are advised that the programs stored on MILENG1/UTIL require only that the user be able to answer "Y" or "N" and to input values as requested by the program. It is not necessary to know RPN to use the MILENG1/UTIL programs.

Synergy

A major purpose of the demonstration Engineer Programmable Calculator is to show field troops how they can become intelligent partners with the research community in managing change, and not be victims of "the ivory tower."

How the programming conventions used in the Engineer Programmable Calculator evolved, demonstrates how synergism can result from sharing ideas with the

The HP-41c Engineer Programmable Calculator; plug-in, read-only- memory (not visible); card reader (inserted into top of calculator); and thermal printer.

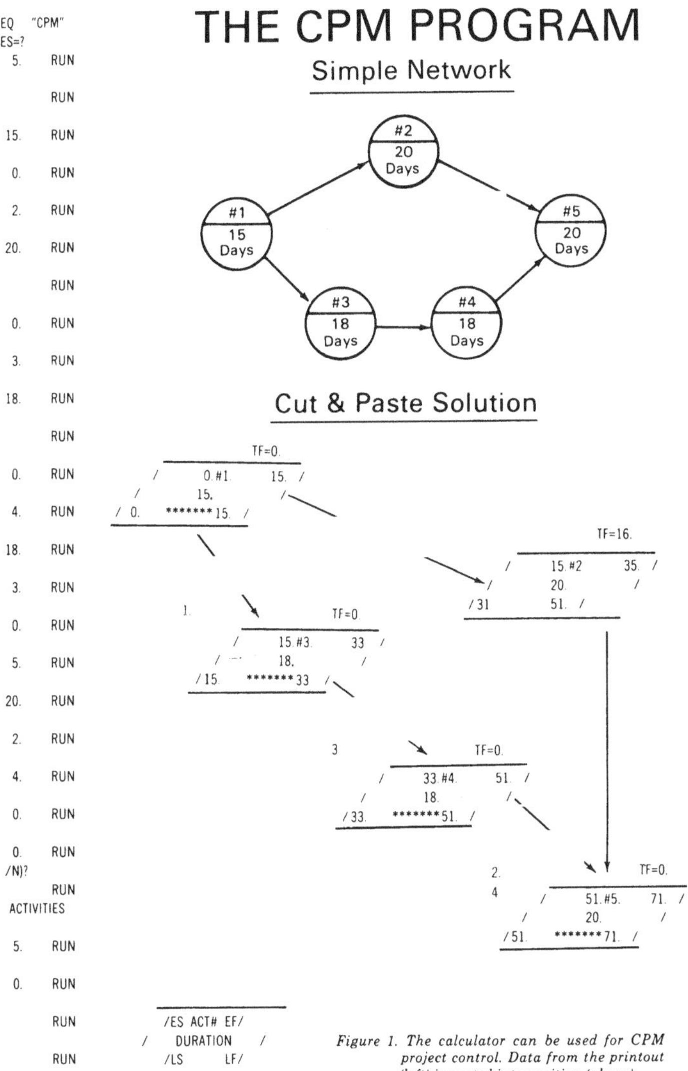

Figure 1. The calculator can be used for CPM project control. Data from the printout (left) is pasted into position (above).

*Figure 2. The following information allows you to program the HP-41cv calculator to provide data regarding preparation of road craters (types). First, execute the built-in routine called "size," then enter "40" to configure the calculator's memory for the program. The program immediately below is an input/output subroutine (*F) which must be entered first. Then enter the road cratering main program (Crater).*

Input/output Subroutine

```
PRP "*F"

01•LBL "*F"
02 7

03•LBL 04
04 CF IND X
05 DSE X
06 GTO 04
07 CF 00
08 RTN

09•LBL "*S"
10 "RESIZE>"
11 1
12 -
13 SF 25
14 RCL IND X
15 FS?C 25
16 RTN
17 FIX 0
18 1
19 +
20 XEQ "*0"
21 STOP

22•LBL "*I"
23 XEQ 13
24 STO 25
25 RDN
26 STO 26

27•LBL 08
28FS? 09
29 RCL IND 24
30 "├="
31 FS? 09
32 ARCL IND 24
33 "├?"
34 CF 22
35 TONE 5
36 AVIEW
37 STOP
38 FS? 22
39 GTO 01
40 FC? 09
41 GTO 00
42 ISG 24
43 STO X
44 RTN

45•LBL 00
46 XEQ 14
47 GTO 08

48•LBL 01
49 "MUST BE"
50 RCL 25
51 X<=Y?
52 GTO 02
53 "├>"

54•LBL 03
55 XEQ "*0"
56 GTO 00

57•LBL 02
58 "├<"
59 RDN
60 RCL 26
61 X<Y?
62 GTO 03
63 RDN
64 STO IND 24
65 ISG 24
66 STO X
67 RTN

68•LBL "*0"
69 "├<"
70 ARCL X

71•LBL "*D"
72 TONE 8
73 TONE 9
74 AVIEW
75 FS? 55
76 PSE
77 FC? 55
78 STOP
79 RTN

80•LBL "*Y"
81 XEQ 13

82•LBL 10
83 "├(Y/N)"
84 SF 10
85 XEQ 05
86 ASTO X
87 "Y"
88 ASTO Y
89 X=Y?
90 RTN
91 CF 10
92 "N"
93 ASTO Y
94 X=Y?
95 RTN
96 XEQ 14
97 GTO 10

98•LBL "*A"
99 XEQ 13

100•LBL 09
101 CF 10
102 "├="
103 FC? 09
104 GTO 05
105 ARCL IND 24
106 ISG 24
107 STO X
108 ARCL IND 24
109 DSE 24
110•LBL 05
111 "├?"
112 CF 23
113 AON
114 TONE 5
115 AVIEW
116 STOP
117 AOFF
118 FS? 10
119 RTN
120 FS? 23
121 GTO 07
122 FS? 09
123 GTO 06
124 XEQ 14
125 GTO 09

126•LBL 07
127 ASTO IND 24
128 ASHF
129 ISG 24
130 STO X
131 ASTO IND 24
132 DSE 24

133•LBL 06
134 CLA
135 ARCL IND 24
136 ISG 24
137 STO X
138 ARCL IND 24
139 ISG 24
140 STO X
141 RTN

142•LBL 13
143 ASTO 20
144 ASHF
145 ASTO 21
146 ASHF
147 ASTO 22
148 ASHF
149 ASTO 23

150•LBL 14
151 CLA
152 ARCL 20
153 ARCL 21
154 ARCL 22
155 ARCL 23
156 RTN

157•LBL "*C"
158 0
159•LBL
160 STO IND
161 ISG Y
162 GTO 1
163 RTN

164•LBL '
165 .99
166 +
167 INT
168 RTN

169•LBL "
170 SF 12
171 "END PROGR
172 TONE
173 TONE
174 AVIEW
175 CF 12
176 ADV
177 ADV
178 ADV
179 ADV
180 RTN
181 "26/C
182 END
```

Main Road Cratering Program

```
PRP "CRATER"

01•LBL "CRATER"

02 40
03 XEQ "*S"
04 CF 00

05•LBL 01
06 FIX 1
07 31.039
08 XEQ "*C"
09 31
10 STO 24
11 "CRATER LENGTH, ("
12 "├FT)"
13 999
14 ENTER↑
15 3
16 XEQ "*I"
17 "USE CRATER CHAR"
18 "├GE"
19 XEQ "*Y"
20 FS? 10
21 ST 00

22•LBL 03
23 "CRATER TYPE:"
24 XEQ "*D"
25 "HASTY"
26 XEQ "*Y"
27 FS? 10
28 GTO 11
29 "DELIBERATE
30 XEQ "*Y"
31 FS? 10
32 GTO 21
33 "RELIEVED FACE"
34 XEQ "*Y"
35 FS? 10
36 GTO 31
37 GTO 03

38•LBL 11
39 XEQ 81
40 33
41 STO 24
42 "CRATER DEPTH, (
43 "├T)"
44 15
45 ENTER↑
```

```
46 7.5
47 XEQ "*I"
48 RCL 33
49 1.5
50 /
51 STO 34
52 10
53 *
54 XEQ "*R"
55 STO 35
56 40
57 /
58 INT
59 RCL 32
60 *
61 STO 36
62 40
63 *
64 STO 38
65 RCL 35
66 RCL 32
67 *
68 —
69 CHS
70 STO 37
71 RCL 38
72 +
73 STO 39
74 ADV
75 FIX 0
76 "#HOLES"
77 RCL 32
78 XEQ "*0"
79 FIX 1
80 "HOLE DEPTH, FT"
81 RCL 34
82 XEQ "*0"
83 FIX 0
84 "EXPLOSIVE, LBS/"
85 "├HOLE"
86 RCL 35
87 XEQ "*0"
88 FS? 00
89 GTO 15
90 GTO 79

91•LBL 15
92 "#CRATER CHG"
93 RCL 36
94 XEQ "*0"
95 "TNT,LBS"
96 RCL 37
97 XEQ "*0"
98 GTO 79
99•LBL 21
100 XEQ 81
101 2
102 /
103 INT
104 1
105 +
106 STO 34
107 RCL 32
108 —
109 CHS
110 STO 35
111 RCL 34
112 2
113 *
114 +
115 STO 36
116 40
117 *
118 STO 39
119 ADV
120 FIX 0
121 "#7FT.HOLES"
122 RCL 34
123 XEQ "*0"
124 "#5FT.HOLES"
125 RCL 35
126 XEQ "*0"
127 FS? 00
128 GTO 23
129 GTO 79

130•LBL 23
131 "#CRATER CHG"
132 RCL 36
133 XEQ "*0"
134 "PRIMER:TNT,LBS"
135 RCL 35
136 XEQ "*0"
137 RCL 39
138 RCL 35
139 +
140 STO 39
141 GTO 79
142•LBL 31
143 RCL 31
144 10
145 —
146 7
147 /
148 XEQ "*R"
149 STO 32
150 1
151 +
152 STO 33
153 40
154 *
155 STO 34
156 RCL 32
157 30
158 *
159 STO 35
160 +
161 STO 39
162 FS? 00
163 GTO 33
164 GTO 35

165•LBL 33
166 RCL 39
167 RCL 33
168 +
169 STO 39

170•LBL 35
171 ADV
172 FIX 0
173 "FRIEND SIDE:"
174 XEQ "*D"
175 "#5FT.HOLES"
176 RCL 33
177 XEQ "*0"
178 FS? 00
179 GTO 36
180 "TNT,LBS"
181 RCL 34
182 XEQ "*0"
183 GTO 37

184•LBL 36
185 "#CRATER CHG"
186 RCL 33
187 XEQ "*0"
188 "PRIMER:TNT,LBS"
189 RCL 33
190 XEQ "*0"

191•LBL 37
192 ADV
193 "ENEMY SIDE:"
194 XEQ "*D"
195 "#4FT.HOLES"
196 RCL 32
197 XEQ "*0"
198 "TNT,LBS"
199 RCL 35
200 XEQ "*0"
201•LBL 79
202 ADV
203 "EXPLO,ΣLB"
204 RCL 39
205 XEQ "*0"
206 "ALSO: NEED SHAP"
207 "├E CHARGES"
208 XEQ "*D"
209 "TO BLAST BOREHO"
210 "├LES!"

211 XEQ "*D"
212 CF 00
213 XEQ "*P"
214 STOP
215 GTO 01

216•LBL 81
217 RCL 31
218 16
219 —

220 5
221 /
222 1
223 +
224 XEQ "*R"
225 STO 32
226 RTN
227 "2/2/82"
228 END
```

Applications Include:

CPM, Bridge Classification, Road Cratering, Demolitions, Minefield Logistics, Obstacles.

field.

Early in its study, CERL researchers worked at developing a set of subroutines to be used by one or more programs. CPT Scott Loomer, an engineer officer at the Defense Mapping School, became aware of the CERL effort and offered to contribute to the work. Working part-time, he developed standard routines that were sound and comprehensive enough to be adopted across the board. He also solved for planners another problem.

Originally, CERL's goal was to make all the calculator's programs fully self-contained so field users would not have to consult reference books to run them. Hampered by this constraint, CERL was unable to find an efficient way to approach the bridge classification problem.

Loomer invented the idea of letting the program tell the user when to use FM 5-34 to extract data from the manual's complex tables or figures. That is, the program would tell the user what table or figure to go to and what entry conditions to use.

The user now extracts and enters the data when prompted by the program. As a result of this innovation, an enormous amount of program memory was saved and the impossible became possible. One soldier's standard subroutines and referencing technique increased the effective capacity of the Engineer Programmable Calculator by about 20 percent. It also let CERL fit two more programs onto the MILENG1/UTIL module.

Here was an example demonstrating the synergistic effect that interaction with the field can create.

Program Conventions

Utility Routines

Six application programs and a set of utility routines are stored on MILENG1/UTIL. Utility routines could be used very effectively by field troops to handle a host of housekeeping chores when writing programs to meet particular needs.

Programs resident on the ROM also use these utility routines. Each program first checks to insure that enough data registers are provided. If not, the program tells the user to RESIZE. A single tone sounds whenever the program requires input. (Differently pitched tones can be used for different program applications.)

A double tone sounds whenever the program outputs information. When a program asks a yes or no question, it will accept only a "Y" or "N" response. Any other response will result in the question being repeated.

When a program asks for a numeric input, the user presses the appropriate number keys, then presses the RUN/STOP (R/S) key to input the data. The program automatically checks that the input is within acceptable range. If not, it tells the user what upper or lower limit must be met and asks for the input again.

The R/S key also is used to input the "Y" or "N" responses and to restart the program after the program outputs information. However, if a printer is attached, the program automatically continues after each output. The format between the "with printer" and "without printer" output differs only in the case of the Critical Path Method (CPM) program.

The Critical Path Method

The CPM program is an efficient way to do the tedious calculations associated with using CPM project control, a management method becoming common in today's Army. The CPM program uses "activity-on-the-node" logic.

Up to 98 activities can be analyzed if the full HP-41cv resident capacity for data storage is used; up to 20 activities can be done on the HP-41c model without memory modules. The "with printer" version prints the output in boxes. The user can cut these out, paste them up and graph logical relationships.

Figure 1 is an example of a simple network. It shows how to input data and how the output looks aft it is cut, pasted and connecte Critical activities have asteris printed in the box. This is a han tool for those who do not have a cess to a minicomputer.

The "without printer" outp must be copied as it is output. Th diagrams can be drawn and ann tated with the correct informatio Note that in the printed versio the preceding activities for each a tivity are noted to the left of ea diagram, so the user will know ho to connect the activities together.

Bridge Classification

The bridge classification progra is used with certain tables in F 5-34 to help the user determi bridge superstructure classific tion. This program may be used f both timber and steel string bridges.

The computer asks the user f the bridge's basic dimensions, e It then refers the user to approp ate tables and figures in FM 5- telling the user what entry val he needs. It asks the user for value of the variables correspo ing to those entry conditions. user extracts the appropriate va from the manual's table or fig and enters it in the calculator.

Road Cratering

The road crater program co putes the amount of explosiv number of cratering charges, a number and depth of holes nee to produce hasty, deliberate or lieved face road craters. Figur shows a sample computation wh the program even determines t two pounds of TNT must be use double prime charges for each fi foot hole.

Demolitions

The demolitions program dresses three common engineer tivities: cutting timber, cutti steel and breaching walls. The p gram lists three timber cutting tions: internal charge placeme external placement and abatis.

The steel cutting option lists fc application areas: railroad rai

Printout Examples

Road Cratering

```
XEQ "CRATER"
CRATER LENGTH, (FT)=?
41.0    RUN
USE CRATER CHARGE (Y/N)?
Y       RUN
CRATER TYPE:
HASTY (Y/N)?
N       RUN
DELIBERATE (Y/N)?
N       RUN
RELIEVED FACE (Y/N)?
Y       RUN

FRIEND SIDE:
#5FT.HOLES=6.
#CRATER CHG=6.
PRIMER:TNT, LBS=6.

ENEMY SIDE:
#4FT.HOLES=5.
TNT,LBS=150.

EXPLO,LB=396.
ALSO: NEED SHAPE CHARGES
TO BLAST BOREHOLES!
END PROGRAM
```

Demolitions

```
XEQ "DEMO"
EXPLOSIVE TYPE:
TNT (Y/N)?
N       RUN
M112 C4(1.25LB)(Y/N)?
Y       RUN
APPLICATION:
CUT TIMBER (Y/N)?
Y       RUN
TIMBER DIA.(IN)=?
24.0    RUN
CHARGE PLACEMENT
ABATIS (Y/N)?
N       RUN
EXTREN (Y/N)?
Y       RUN
REQD. EXPLO.
LBS.=11.3
#EXPLO. UNITS=9
IN OPEN, SAFE DIST.,
M=300
END PROGRAM
```

Minefields

```
XEQ "MINES"
ENTER MINE DENSITY:
#AT/M=?
3.00    RUN
#APF/M=?
4.00    RUN
#APB/M=?
8.00    RUN
IOE CLUSTER COMPOSITION:
#AT=?
1.      RUN
#APF=?
2.      RUN
#APB=?
2.      RUN
DO AT NIGHT(Y/N)?
N       RUN
FIELD LENGTH,(M)=?
400.    RUN
FIELD DEPTH,(M)=?
400.    RUN

TOTAL MINES:
#AT=1,370.
#APF=1,859.
#APB=3,619.
IOE MINES:
#AT=45.
#APF=90.
#APB=90.
MMF MINES:
#AT=1,200.
#APF=1,600.
#APB=3,200.
#IOE CLUSTERS=45.
#STRIPS=9.
2-STRAND,4-SIDE FENCE:
#WIRE(RL)=13.
#SIGNS,PICKETS=165.
#SANDBAGS=3,780.
MANHOURS=962.
END PROGRAM
```

Figure 3.

round steel sections, structural steel sections and carbon steel rods. The breaching applications are used in conjunction with applicable tables in FM 5-34.

Minefield Logistics

The minefield program computes the logistical requirements for installing a standard pattern minefield given the field density, the irregular outer edge cluster composition, the field length and depth, and the conditions under which the work is to be done. A sample printout is shown in Figure 3.

Wire Obstacles

The wire obstacle program computes the logistical requirements for installing any of seven common wire obstacles. The program can also be used to compute the effective length of the obstacle according to its function and location on the battlefield.

If the user already knows the effective length, he would answer "Y" to the first question ("KNOW. EFF.LEN.(Y/N)?") and enter the effective length when asked.

Looking Ahead

By October 1982, 250 copies of MILENG1/UTIL will be produced for testing and evaluation by Engineer Officer Basic Course and NCOES students.

About 150 of these ROMs already are committed to the U.S. Army Engineer School, and to certain engineer battalions that will field test them. The other 100 ROMs will be made available to individual combat engineers who own or have access to an HP-41 calculator.

Written requests for these can be addressed to: CERL-FS, ATTN: John Deponai, P.O. Box 4005, Champaign, Ill., 61820. Include your full name, rank, social security number, current job description and whether or not you have access to an HP-41.

For information, contact Mrs. Gale Smith, the Engineer School's Collective Training and Analysis Division, at (703) 664-4063/3467, AVN 354.

Mr. John M. Deponai leads the Military Engineering Team at the U.S. Army's Construction Engineering Research Laboratory, Champaign, Ill. He is a 1966 graduate of the U.S. Military Academy and served for eight and one-half years on active duty.

ENGINEER SUPPORT TO RANGER OPERATIONS

Rain-soaked 92d Engineers and 1/75th Rangers practice knot tying in Panama. (Photos by John G. Martin)

by 1LT Robert B. Underwood III

The 92d Engineers excel at a unique, demanding mission.

The 1st Battalion (Ranger), 75th Infantry, is an elite unit designed to perform special infantry missions on short notice, anywhere in the world. This mission requires the Rangers to work and to train in many diverse climates and types of terrain. Despite their prodigious capabilities as infantrymen, the Rangers need engineer construction support to prepare for their missions. To meet this need, the 92d Engineer Battalion (Combat) (Heavy) keeps a Ranger Support Element (RSE) ready to be attached to the 1/75th for training exercises or for actual deployment.

to be dispatched and driven to the airfield.

Readiness is always a primary requirement for the company tasked for RSE. When the 1/75th is in a "ready" posture, the RSE platoon members remain at all times where they can be contacted by telephone, and company duty personnel are issued an RSE alert roster with special notification instructions. All RSE personnel are administratively and medically cleared for overseas deployment.

RSE Missions

If alerted, the RSE deploys with the Ranger advanced party to construct and to maintain a Ranger element mobilization base (REMAB), build rehearsal sites, and as time permits, to train.

REMAB construction varies but usually includes organizing and laying out the base, supervising tent erection, constructing latrine facilities, setting up power distribution and lighting, erecting protective fences and establishing a shower point using M12A1 decontamination apparatus.

Rehearsal sites are as unique as the Ranger mission. Camps, buildings, bunkers and their attendant obstacles are often built. These facilities are constructed to resemble as closely as possible actual objective sites and are based on information provided by the Ranger intelligence section. The accuracy of rehearsal sites is critically important to the success of the Ranger operation.

Sometimes, schedules permit the RSE to participate in environmental training with the Rangers. This provides adventure-training opportunities for engineer troops not familiar with advanced infantry skills and working in difficult terrain and climates. Such training naturally supports the engineer secondary mission of fighting as infantry.

RSE Deployments

The 92d Engineers' RSE training deployments have provided a wealth of challenges and exciting training. The major environmental training deployments have been to Panama in December 1981, Fort Bliss/White Sands Missile Range in February 1982 and to Puerto Rico in June 1982.

During the deployment to the Jungle Operations Training Center (JOTC) at Fort Sherman, Republic of Panama, the Rangers received refresher training in individual skills peculiar to a jungle environment. They also trained in platoon and company-sized operations, and held a battalion field training exercise (FTX). The 10-man RSE was integrated as a squad into a Ranger platoon for individual, squad and platoon-level training. All RSE members were awarded the JOTC Jungle Expert Certificate. In many activities, such as the land navigation and nine-event obstacle course, the engineer squad scored comparably to the highly-competitive Ranger squads. The winter being the wet season in Panama, it

92d Engineers lash equipment in a RB15 assault boat while preparing for training on Panama's Chagres River.

"When they saw what we could do, the Rangers went wild."

rained every day during the deployment.

At their request, the RSE during off-duty time received additional JOTC training in helicopter rappelling and in lowering pioneer boxes from a helicopter. The extra training culminated with the RSE rappelling into the jungle and clearing a landing zone using explosives.

These activities were certainly a change of pace for the dozer operators, carpenters, plumbers and draftsmen from the 92d. Besides the JOTC training, the RSE served as the planning and control party to establish a REMAB for the Ranger FTX; objectives and rehearsal sites were built beforehand by the 518th Engineer Company from Fort Kobe, Panama.

Construction Challenge

During the Fort Bliss deployment, the Rangers found out how hard engineers could work and how much could be built in a very limited amount of time.

Although the RSE leader knew some construction tasks were planned, according to RSE OIC 1LT William R. Weeks, the size of the construction mission mushroomed once the RSE deployed. "When they saw what we could do, the Rangers went wild," Weeks said. "They kept asking for more, so we kept giving them more."

During the three-week exercise, the 20-man RSE constructed six mock enemy camps complete with buildings, towers, sandbag positions and protective wire. The RSE used 1,100 2×4×10s, 600 sheets of plywood and 600 pounds of nails.

They also built numerous targets and vehicle silhouettes for live-fire ranges, as well as a protective bunker from which a brave young Ranger (who had been late for formation) could safely operate downrange targets. A MOUT (military operations in urban terrain) site was erected and another rehabilitated. Barracks and offices used by the 1/75th were also rehabilitated.

The construction tasks were made difficult by winds gusting to 50 knots and a prohibition on digging because of the danger of disturbing Indian artifacts. Some structures were secured with wooden footings, but each case of digging required specific, prior approval from the host installation. Several buildings without footings blew down under the severe winds, and the RSE had to rush to repair them before the Ranger assaults began.

RSE members later reported that watching the Rangers in action was one of the exercise's highlights. The group saw several impressive Ranger assaults targeted against engineer construction projects. The attacks were live-fire exercises complete with air strikes and rolling mortar barrages.

Engineers Praised

According to John G. Martin of the Fort Stewart Public Affairs Office, the 92d Engineers were also very impressive. An Army veteran who served in Vietnam with the 5th Special Forces Group, Martin was with the 1/75th during all three RSE deployments. "The engineers did an outstanding job in Panama and Puerto Rico, and they *really* performed well at Fort Bliss," Martin said. "I never heard any complaining; they just kept putting out at a hundred percent and then some. It amazed me how much spirit they had. They showed themselves to be true soldiers."

The Fort Bliss exercise was particularly intense. The RSE worked around-the-clock in 18-hour shifts;

Incessant rain and the rigorous JOTC obstacle course didn't slow the engineer RSE in Panama.

sometimes shifts lasted 24 hours. Exemplifying the 92d Engineers spirit was SSG Johnny Edwards. Serving as the B Company motor sergeant, Edwards was named RSE NCOIC when it appeared that the exercise would duplicate the Panama experience: mostly adventure training and only a few construction tasks. Once the RSE got to Fort Bliss and the construction mission dramatically increased, Edwards found himself on unfamiliar ground as a construction supervisor. His dedication, however, overcame the handicap and he played a key role in successfully managing the construction mission.

During the Fort Bliss deployment, the RSE also trained in mountaineering and patrolling, participated in an airmobile operation, and served as aggressors.

The RSE that accompanied the 1/75th to Puerto Rico encountered a more even mix of training and construction requirements. Rehearsal and objective sites were constructed or rehabilitated, wire erected and obstacles built. Engineers participated in adventure and infantry training similar to what was encountered during the previous deployments.

Valuable Training

The experience and lessons learned by members of the 92d Engineer Battalion during these environmental deployments have been valuable and numerous. The rapid deployment requirement for the RSE keeps the battalion staff and companies sharp on deployment criteria and procedures. The deployments have provided challenging leadership experiences for officers, NCOs and troops. Trips to faraway places have been a definite morale booster for the soldiers fortunate enough to participate.

The program also has provided strong motivation for troops to raise their personal standards since men are chosen for the RSE based on demonstrated daily duty performance. The finer points of living and staying healthy in the field learned from the Rangers have been passed along to buddies and are reflected in better unit performance during field problems.

Most importantly, the 92d Engineers have learned how important and rewarding it is to aggressively support an outstanding infantry unit like the 1/75th Rangers.

*LTC James Keys commanded the 92d during these RSE deployments.

1LT Robert Underwood is an Engineer Officer Advanced Course student at Ft. Belvoir, Va. He served with the 92d Engineer Bn., Ft. Stewart, Ga., as a platoon leader, pipeline engineer and construction officer. 1LT Underwood was RSE OIC on the Panama deployment. He is a graduate of the U.S. Military Academy, Airborne and Ranger Schools.

Engineer Equipment Display

The Engineer Center's Directorate of Combat Developments participated this summer in a "Week of the Eagles" open house and display at Fort Campbell, Ky. The event was sponsored by the 101st Airborne Division (Air Assault).

During the five-day event, thousands of soldiers and civilians saw how divisional engineers might support the combined arms team in the Airland Battle. An Engineer Center survivability display featured several developmental fighting position covers; equipment shown included the M9 Armored Combat Earthmover (ACE), a M180 cratering charge and the Ground Emplaced Mine Scattering System (GEMSS).

Also displayed in the engineer corner was a Marine Corps Mine Clearing Line Charge (MICLIC, M58A1) and a UNIMOG, the West German small emplacement excavator currently being tested at Fort Lewis, Wash.

The engineer display at Ft. Campbell's "Week of the Eagles" included these prototype fighting position covers. (Photo by CPT James E. Burrows)

Paint Problems

by Alfred Beitelman

The Paint Laboratory at the U.S. Army Construction Engineering Research Laboratory (CERL), Champaign, Ill., is responsible for evaluating difficulties in the field application of paints. Over the past several years, lab personnel have visited many field painting operations and have observed specific, recurring problems which reduce coating life and eventually shorten the life expectancy of the painted item.

Many problems that at first glance appear to involve poor paint performance actually reflect a disregard of good painting principles—a disregard evident from basic design to inspection of the painted item. Coatings are the first line of defense against corrosion, but they can only provide their designed protection if they are properly specified, applied and maintained.

When an item needs a paint system for protection or beautification, the coating should be considered in the initial design stages and not left as an afterthought. The size of the item is of little consequence. It may be small enough to hold in the palm of your hand or large enough to span a major river. The basic principles are the same in both cases. The surfaces should be simply configured and must be accessible to allow appropriate surface preparation and coating. In addition, there should be no deep crevices, unnecessary protrusions or sharp corners. Such irregularities are difficult to coat uniformly and are particularly susceptible to physical damage. A surface such as the smooth exterior of an automobile is ideal for painting.

The designer must also be aware of the need to protect concealed surfaces. Inaccessible compartments and complex structural members are major obstacles when coatings are applied.

Proper paint performance depends heavily on adequate surface preparation. It should be obvious that paint will not adhere to a wet or oily surface. Most paints are not designed to adhere to heavy deposits of dirt or chalk. Repainting hard, tile-like surfaces or aged, high-gloss paints also presents potential adhesion problems.

Loose paint is removed from a wood structure during a CERL test.

Unfortunately, surface preparation is often overlooked in painting specifications. And if indeed the required surface preparation is mentioned in a specification, the painting contractor will often minimize the time spent on this operation.

Some contractors tend to belie that a quick coat of paint will cov most defects. Problems resulti from this attitude can be prevent by close inspection and clear written specifications which i clude tasks such as weld spatter r moval, solvent cleaning, glass r moval, removal of corrosi products or poorly adherent co ings, and the treatment of milde

Quality is often compromised the interest of speed, not only du ing surface preparation, but also paint application. Sometimes complete coat is omitted from item; on many painting jobs, giv areas receive fewer coats th specified. To reduce costs for ma rials, some applicators thin t paint too much. Again, detailed i spection could control most of the mistakes.

Effective paint inspection pr grams are usually not consider (much less implemented) wh painting operations are underw If an inspector is present, he oft is not given the appropriate thic ness gauges, pinhole detectors other inspection equipment. He sometimes responsible for all i spection duties on several jobs l ing done simultaneously. To be tr ly effective, he would have to intimately familiar with all co struction items used in the pr ects—from the concrete in t footings to the asphalt on t roof—and he would have to be each project site all the time. Ob ously this is impossible.

If a coating is to be truly eff tive, it must be more than an aft thought in the design proce Painters must think in terms "high-performance protective co ings" rather than "cover it up w a coat of paint," and inspecti must be given high priority to sure a quality product.

Alfred Beitelman, a chemist the Paint Laboratory, U.S. Ar Construction Engineering Resea Laboratory, Champaign, Ill., is principal investigator for ci works and military constructi paint research programs. He ho a B.A. in chemistry from Wartb College, Waverly, Iowa., and h been with the Paint Laboratory 11 years.

The ENGINEER Sc.

1. Assumptions

- Simply supported continuous beam
- Compact section
- Adequate lateral bracing

2. Member Selection

- Using page 2-126 of the 8th Edition, AISC Manual of Steel Construction, calculate the maximum moment and shear due to loading:

$$M_{max} = 0.10\ wl^2 = 0.10(1.5kfp)\ (30\ ft)^2 \qquad M_{max} = \underline{\underline{135.0\ ft\text{-}kips}}$$

$$V_{max} = 0.600wl = 0.60(1.5kfp)\ (30\ ft) \qquad V_{max} = \underline{\underline{27\ kips}}$$

- From page 2-8 of the AISC Manual, select $\underline{\underline{W\ 18 \times 40}}$ with moment capacity of 137.0 ft-kips.

- Additionally, from page 1-8, find the following properties:

$$t_w = 0.315\ w$$
$$d = 17.90\ in$$
$$I = 612\ in^4$$

- Check shear from page 5-65 of the AISC Manual:

$$V_u \leqslant 0.55\ f_y\ t\ d$$
$$\text{where, } V_u = V_{max} \leqslant (0.55)\ (36\ ksi)\ (0.315\ in)\ (17.90\ in)$$
$$27\ k \leqslant 111.64\ k$$

- Shear okay. Use W 18 × 40.

3. Maximum Deflection

- Using the expression from page 2-126 of the AISC Manual, find:

$$\Delta max = 0.0069wl^4/EI$$

- Thus,

$$\Delta max = 0.0069(1.5\ \frac{kip}{ft} \times \frac{1\ ft}{12\ in})\ (30\ ft \times 12\frac{in}{ft})^4/(29{,}000\ ksi \times 612\ in^4)$$

$$= 0.0069\ (0.125\ \frac{kip}{in.})\ (360\ in)^4/(1.7788 \times 10^7\ kip\text{-}in^2)$$

$$\boxed{\bullet\ \Delta max = 0.816\ in}$$

— FORUM —

Equipment Repair Technicians— OUR FORGOTTEN ENGINEERS?

by CW3 Curtis R. Millner

We have a serious problem with assignment and training policies for Engineer warrant officers. Noncommissioned officers coming into the engineer equipment repair field lack relevant experience and training, even though we are getting the cream of the crop.

Jumping from E-7 to WO1 is a great increase in responsibility, but because it's such a small increase in pay, few E-7s apply for warrant duty. As a result, we accept E-6s from related MOSs who show potential and a willingness to learn.

We give these inexperienced warrants a little training in the basic course (not all attend), send them to a unit and expect them to function. The Advanced and Senior Warrant Officer Courses teach a lot about being a staff officer but little in the way of technical material. Unfortunately for the warrant, commanders expect warrant officers (unlike privates and second lieutenants) to be experts, technical experts who can pass along their skills to others in the unit.

Nobody likes to be embarrassed, so what happens is that new warrant officers avoid duty in combat heavy engineer units. They get themselves assigned to support or staff jobs and stay there. There are some solutions to these problems that will help all engineer units, be they combat, combat heavy or bridging units.

First of all, the guidelines in DA Pamphlet 600-11 must be followed more closely. That's where MILPERCEN can help us. Secondly, we've got to take better advantage of training opportunities. There are numerous civilian maintenance schools that offer intense technical courses that directly relate to the duties of an engineer equipment repair technician. These courses are offered (sometimes free of charge) by most equipment manufacturers. This kind of training should be exploited to augment the Army's training programs. Whether it's Army or civilian training, getting our warrants technically qualified must be a Corps-wide priority. Maybe with the proper assignment patterns and good technical training more equipment repair technicians would stay in the Army past 20 years. Longer retention rates would give us greater expertise in maintaining our increasingly complex equipment and reduce our warrant officer procurement needs.

As MG Ellis has stated in "Cle the Way" (Summer 1982), we mu consider the career development engineer soldiers of all ranks. Le be sure we don't forget our warr officers. To have the best Army i the world, we need top-quality maintenance people who have ha the best training available. So fa we haven't done justice to our engineer equipment repair techn cians. That must change because matter how sophisticated our equipment becomes, if it doesn't work, it doesn't fight.

CW3 Curtis R. Millner is the engin equipment maintenance officer HHC, 548th Engineer Bn., Ft. Bra N.C. He was previously assignec the 249th Engineer Bn. in Karlsr Germany. CW3 Millner has co pleted the Basic, Advanced c Senior Warrant Officer Courses, Supply Management Officers Cou and Maintenance Managem Course. He has a B.A. degree in g eral studies from Columbia Coll Columbia, Mo.

Engineer

UME 13 NUMBER 1, 1983

ITED STATES ARMY
GINEER CENTER
D FORT BELVOIR, VA.

MMANDER/COMMANDANT
MG James N. Ellis

PUTY COMMANDANT
COL Alvin G. Rowe

IEF OF STAFF/DEPUTY
TALLATION COMMANDER
COL Paul J. Higgins

MMAND SERGEANT MAJOR
CSM Orville W. Troesch

TOR
hn Florence

ISTANT EDITOR
G Bernard W. Tate

IGN DIRECTOR
n Wilson

the cover:

cover photo shows proto- s of the M9 Armored Combat mover being built at a Pacific and Foundry Co. facility in on, Wash. The M9 is a key of the Army's effort to mod- ze the combat engineers. to courtesy of PACCAR)

FEATURES

DEPARTMENTS

GINEER is an authorized publication of the U.S. Army Engineer Center and Fort Belvoir, Va. Unless specifically stated, material earing herein does not necessarily reflect official policy, thinking or endorsement by any agency of the U.S. Army. All photographs ained herein are official U.S. Army photographs unless otherwise credited. Use of funds for printing this publication was approved Headquarters, Department of the Army, July 22, 1981. Material herein may be reprinted if credit is given ENGINEER and the nor. • ENGINEER OBJECTIVES are to provide a forum for the exchange of ideas, to inform and motivate and to promote the essional development of all members of the Army engineer family. • DIRECT CORRESPONDENCE with ENGINEER is norized and encouraged. Inquiries, letters to the editor, manuscripts, photographs and general correspondence should be sent to: tor, ENGINEER, Directorate of Training Developments (TLD), Stop 16F4, Fort Belvoir, Va. 22060. Telephone (703) 664-3082, N 354. • SUBSCRIPTIONS to ENGINEER are available through the Superintendent of Documents, U.S. Government Printing ce, Washington, D.C., 20402. A check or money order payable to Superintendent of Documents must accompany all subscription uests. Rates are $8.50 domestic (including APO and FPO addresses) and $10.65 for foreign addresses. Individual copies are available 1.50 per copy to domestic addresses and $5.65 for foreign addresses. • SECOND CLASS postage paid at Fort Belvoir, Va., and Va. N 0046-1989.

News & Notes

2d Engineer Bn. soldiers show plenty of spirit as they pound out a 13.1 mile half-marathon.

Engineers tackle half-marathon

"Unlucky thirteen" didn't bother over 500 soldiers of the 2d Engineer Bn. at Camp Casey, Korea, who ran 13.1 miles (a half-marathon) from Uijongbu, a nearby town, to Indianhead Field at Camp Casey.

LTC C. Hilton Dunn Jr., then-battalion commander, wanted the half-marathon to be as much a mental challenge as a physical one. "About 90 percent of you are physically ready now, but only about 60 percent are mentally prepared," Dunn wrote to his soldiers. (Dunn is now director, Department of Military Engineering at Fort Belvoir, Va.)

The engineers met the challenge and took two hours and two minutes to run the distance in platoon formation. They far exceeded Dunn's goal of 90 percent of all runners finishing. He had planned to award trophies to the platoons finishing without any runners dropping out. Five platoons of the 19 entered tied for the honor — S1 Section, HHC 2d Engineers; A Co.'s 1st platoon; C Co.'s 2d and 3d platoons; and E Co.'s 3d platoon. □

Ten MOSs close to women

About 140 women are in the 10 Engineer Military Occupational Specialities (MOSs) closed by the Women In The Army Policy Review Group report. The report was approved by Secretary of the Army John O. Marsh, Jr. Women currently in these MOSs will not be reassigned, according to DA spokesmen. At the end of their tours they will either re-enlist for other MOSs or leave the Army. The vacated slots will be filled by men.

Of the three Engineer Career Management Fields, CMF 51 (General Engineering) is the only one affected. CMF 12 (Combat Engineering) is already closed, and CMF 81 (Topographic Engineering) is still open.

Ten entry-level MOSs in CMF 51 have been closed to women because of the combat exclusion policy, not because of the physical strength tests conducted during the review. The closed MOSs are:

82B — Construction Surveyor
52G — Transportation and Distribution Specialist
00B — Diver
51K — Plumber
51R — Interior Electrician
51B — Carpentry and Masonry Specialist
62H — Concrete and Asphalt Operations
62E — Heavy Construction Equipment Operator

Six entry-level MOSs and four supervisory MOSs are still open to women in CMF 51. They are:

51G — Material Quality Specialist
81B — Technical Drafting Specialist
52E — Prime Power Production Specialist
51M — Firefighter
51C — Structure Specialist
62F — Lifting/Loading Equipment Operator
51T — Technical Engineer Supervisor
51H — Construction Engineer Supervisor
62N — General Engineer Supervisor
51Z — General Engineer Supervisor

Two other engineer MOSs are also open:

51N — Water Treatment Specialist (will soon transfer to Quartermaster)
53B — Industrial Gas Production Specialist (Reserve components only) □

Engineer in NATO olympics

An Army Reserve engineer officer and two teammates captured third place in a NATO military olympics at Fort Meade, Md. The competition was sponsored by the Interallied Confederation of Reserve Officers and held in conjunction with the Reserve Officers of America's annual congress.

2LT Daniel Walker, Boulder, Col., teamed with CPT Jon Nealon, San Antonio, Texas, and Marine Reserve CPT William Pospisil, Sea Girt, N.J., competed against other three-man teams from Canada, Denmark, France, Germany, Italy, the Netherlands, Norway, the United Kingdom, and America. The Norwegians took first place, but less than 50 points separated them from Walker's team.

n 1981, Walker won first place in the ompetition's novice division.

During the first event of the three-ay olympics, the competitors fired he rifle, pistol, and submachine gun f the host army. Walker fired the M3 greasegun" and his team placed econd.

The second day they ran a 500-eter standard NATO obstacle course, en within an hour swam a 50-meter ater obstacle course. Walker's team ok third.

The third day's event was a 15-ilometer obstacle course. One team ember navigated while the others arried the weapons they fired the rst day. Walker was team orienteer, d they placed second. □

alker scrambles up a ladder on the ndard NATO obstacle course. (Jon Fory oto)

It's an easy trip from South Dakota to Nebraska on the first ribbon bridge to cross the Missouri River. (SDARNG Photo)

Army team bridges Missouri River

An old sea chanty sings of longing to "cross the wide Missouri." They didn't find a beautiful Indian maid, but the 200th Engineer Ribbon Bridge Co., South Dakota Army National Guard, and the 509th Engineer Ribbon Bridge Co., Fort Riley, Kan., combined resources near Jefferson, S.D., to build the first ribbon bridge across the Missouri River.

"We asked the 509th to train with us because neither of us has enough bridge sections to do it alone," explained MAJ Arthur K. O'Conner, S-3, 109th Engineer Group. "We chose the Missouri River because it's the best bridging site in the area and its water speed is about the same as the Rhine River in Germany."

The Guardsmen and active soldiers experienced few problems as they bridged the 810-foot river in about 90 minutes. They used two 15-foot towers to anchor the bridge, reinforced by a D7 bulldozer and several heavy trucks. To test the bridge, three self-propelled howitzers from the South Dakota Guard's 147th Field Artillery Bde. totalling about 65 tons were driven across the bridge.

"I was proud of the way the National Guard and regular soldiers teamed up and cooperated to accomplish the mission," said CPT Robert L. Johnson, 509th commander. "I was especially impressed with the National Guard and the job they do. They're thoroughly professional."

About 300 people gathered to watch the exercise, including the South Dakota Adjutant General MG Duane L. Corning, the U.S. Army Readiness Region VIII commander, MG Robert Riscassi, and the 937th Group commander, COL Ralph T. Rundle (now director of Training and Doctrine at Ft. Belvoir, Va.) □

News & Notes

CERL's Portawasher saves money by cleaning dumpsters in place.

CERL cleaner saves big bucks

During the first six months of 1982, Fort Leonard Wood, Mo., saved about $9,240 cleaning dumpsters using the Portawasher designed by the Army Construction Engineer Research Laboratory, Champaign, Ill. The Portawasher uses high-pressure hot water cleaning equipment and a vacuum system to retrieve dirty wash water.

Under the previous contract, Fort Leonard Wood paid $12.50 to truck each dirty dumpster out and a clean dumpster in to replace it. With the Portawasher's in-place cleaning capability, the cost was reduced to $3.26 per dumpster, a 74 percent saving. □

Engineers have best maintenance

Not every Army unit believes logistical readiness is just an individual responsibility. B Co., 54th Engineer Bn. Wildflecken, Germany, turned team and individual logistical readiness into a unit award winner.

B Co. was judged the best unit in the U.S. Army Europe (USAREUR) for the first Department of the Army annual Unit Maintenance Award program in the immediate category.

This award is given to a unit with an outstanding organizational maintenance program using available resources. The winning unit must also maintain an unusually high state of readiness at all times.

The competition was based on accomplishments from Oct. 1, 1981 to Sept. 30, 1982, focusing on training, management, cost and innovation.

B Co. had won the best maintenance posture in the 54th Engineer Bn. in 1982 and they were the brigade's nominee for the Medium Maintenance Company of the Quarter.

One innovation Bravo Company used is the Commander's Certification Program which identifies weak supervisors. Another is their six-month vehicle identification program which tells platoon leaders what vehicles are coming up for service and forecasts the parts needed. With this program, B Company can determine if they have everything to complete the services.

B Co.'s incentive programs include the Mechanic of the Quarter, Driver of the Quarter, and Maintenance Platoon of the Quarter. ■

Pounding swords into plowshears

"They shall pound their swords into plowshears, and their spears into pruning hooks. . ." These words from Isaiah refer to turning combat-related military equipment to peaceful civilian uses, and C Co., 84th Engineer Bn. (Combat) (Heavy) takes the idea seriously. The engineers from Schofield Barracks, Oahu, Hawaii, built a military bridge near the finish line of the Honolulu Marathon for use by civilian and military news media who were photographing runners finishing the grueling 26.2 mile event.

The bridge was an M4T6, commonly used in field situations to span short gaps. ■

Two win Tudor

CPTs David Bedey and Michael Biering have received the 1982 Tudor Award for Academic Achievement in Military Engineering.

The award honors Ralph A. Tudor, a 1923 West Point graduate, who distinguished himself in military and civilian engineering. It is presented annually by the Engineer School to the outstanding graduate of each Engineer Officer Advanced Course year group.

Bedey, Class 1-82, also earned the School's physical fitness award. Biering, Class 5-82, was also a full-time trainer for an Engineer Officer Basic Course platoon.

Both officers had grade averages of over 97 percent and received the Society of American Military Engineers Award of Merit as outstanding graduates of their class. Bedey, a civil engineering graduate from Montana State University, is in the 76th Engineer Battalion (Combat) (Heavy), Fort Drum, N.Y. Biering, a 1978 West Point alumnus, is a graduate student at the Georgia Institute of Technology.

tschner, Sturgis Awards given

Chief of Engineers, LTG Joseph K. Bratton, has announced the winners of the 1982 Itschner and Sturgis Awards.

The Itschner Award, named in honor of a former Chief of Engineers LTG Emerson C. Itschner, is awarded annually to the engineer company which best symbolizes the Corps of Engineers. The Society of American Military Engineers (SAME) gives the award to units in the active Army, Reserve, and National Guard.

Company D, 249th Engineer Bn., 8th Engineer Bde., Karlsruhe, Germany was named the 1982 active Army Itschner Award winner. HHC, 58th Engineer Bn. (Combat) (Corps), Johnstown, Pa., was named as the Reserve winner; and Co. C, 153d Engineer Battalion (Combat), Parkston, S.D., was named as the National Guard winner.

The Sturgis Award, named in honor of LTG Samuel D. Sturgis, is presented annually by the SAME to an outstanding Army enlisted member. This year's award went to SFC(P) Michael L. McGuiggan, Co. D, 802d Engineer Bn., 2d Engineer Gp., Camp Humphreys, Korea.

The awards were presented by Bratton at the 116th Annual Engineer Dinner, May 13, 1983, at Fort Belvoir, Va. □

Correction

"Garbage in, garbage out," they say in the computer business. If your HP41c calculator has ordered you to submerge and launch Trident missiles at Tasmania, you've probably fed it the typographical errors in the programs on page 32 of ENGINEER Magazine, Fall 1982.

Item 69 under the "Input/Output Subroutine" should be "−=". Item 21 under the "Main Road Cratering Program" should be "SF00." □

Low-water crossings make swampy areas at Ft. Polk passable at all times.

Polk engineers fight heat to build

Bad weather, Louisiana heat and field training exercises couldn't stop the 588th Engineer Bn. from building three low-water crossings at Fort Polk.

The engineers took week-long field trips to the Peason Ridge training area to finish the project in three months. They countered the Louisiana heat with standard hot-weather techniques, such as having plenty of water at the work site. They also worked from 6:30 a.m. to 8:30 p.m. with a mid-afternoon break to avoid working during the hottest part of the day.

The low-water crossings they built are concrete roads constructed over culverts in low-lying areas. The culverts drain water that would normally make the areas impassable during rainy weather.

The three crossings in the Peason Ridge training area required 165 soldiers to build. The troops were from all five of the battalion's companies, plus C Co., 34th Engineers, a company permanently assigned to the 588th. The crossings should last 20 years, according to Battalion Commander LTC Philip R. Harris. □

One of "John Henry's Men" helps pull MAB sections. (Betty Bell Photo)

Hell on Water

"Hell on Wheels" raised "Hell on Water" as the soldiers of Co. E, 17th Engineer Bn., 2d Armored Div., launched their Mobile Assault Bridges (MABs) into the Arkansas River.

The ARTEP (Army Training and Evaluation Program) was the final phase of a month-long mission to give the soldiers experience operating MABs in fast rivers like those in Germany.

The ARTEP followed three weeks of intensive training at Fort Chaffee, Ark. During the ARTEP, "John Henry's Men" conducted tactical maneuvers which included operating their amphibious vehicles at night. (The battalion is nicknamed after John Henry, the legendary "steel drivin' man".) □

CLEAR THE WAY

by MG James N. Ellis, Commandant, U.S. Army Engineer School

MODERNIZING THE COMBAT ENGINEER

As we discussed in the last issue, each ENGINEER will have a specific theme of topical interest to all Army engineers. This issue features "Modernizing the Combat Engineers." I think it's a very appropriate topic because the American combat engineer is entering a new era, a time when we will truly have the means to "clear the way" for the maneuver units of Army 86.

We are aggressively addressing engineer force development on all fronts. As you read our theme articles contributed by the School's Directorate of Combat Developments (pages 10 through 24), you will see we are on a clear azimuth toward making engineers an important and integral part of the AirLand Battle force. To keep ahead, we are writing new concepts which lead to doctrine changes. New doctrinal manuals (FM 5-100 *Engineer Combat Operations* series) are already on their way to you, the user. Fielding the M9 Armored Combat Earthmover, the new Ribbon Bridge Erection Boat and the Small Emplacement Excavator are just the beginnings of engineer equipment modernization that will take place in the next 10 years. To keep pace with the equipment modernization we are changing our TOEs.

New Emphasis

Emphasizing the need for engineer modernization to senior Department of the Army personnel has contributed to this engineer resurgence. This highlighting began with the Systems Program Review (SPR) in April, 1981. It developed an "Action Plan" focused o combined arms mobility - countermobility - survivab ity capabilities and deficiencies on the AirLand and contingency battlefield.

Future combat developments are building upon SI results, which provide the foundation for the enginee Mission Area Analysis (MAA). The Engineer School has MAA proponency for combat support, engineeri and mine warfare. The MAA is becoming the definitive statement of the engineer support the Ar needs for the AirLand Battle.

Top Priority

Finishing the analysis has been our top priority, a we completed it early this year. Follow-on publicati are in progress. Virtually the entire engineer comm ity was involved in portions of the analysis—the Cor laboratories, the chief's office, the Engineer Studies Center, all of the School at Fort Belvoir—plus elements of DARCOM and TRADOC.

We believe the analysis will be the basis of our ro map for future engineer combat developments and provide the Army with a pegging point to measure engineer contributions to the total force.

Finally, I emphasize that the thrust of our effort i to enhance total force effectiveness. Our words and actions must demonstrate unity. Our thoughts, plan and modernization process must focus on ensuring engineer readiness on the future battlefield. We nee your assistance and advice as we . . .

CLEAR THE W

/ CSM O.W. Troesch, U.S. Army Engineer Center & School

NEW CHALLENGES FACE NCOs

We noncommissioned officers play a critically important role in the reception, introduction and training required to support the modernization of igineers.

MG Ellis's "Clear The Way" article notes that there ill be new equipment, new doctrine, and new mine arfare techniques introduced in the next few years. 'henever a force modernization effort takes place, it aces a great training burden on us NCOs.

The impact is felt immediately when the new juipment arrives. Doctrinal changes have less effect the NCO and soldier, except in how we train and :ovide support for maneuver units. So our mission as COs and trainers is to "bridge the gap" so our ldiers fully accept new equipment, rapidly learn to se it, and clearly understand its purpose.

etting Ready

The reception phase normally begins when the S4 .forms battalion/company commanders the new juipment is scheduled to arrive. Commanders should ien brief the NCOs about the equipment, so we can repare ourselves and our soldiers for the coming ıanges.

Concurrently, we must start our own training, or articipate with the chain-of-command training, in the se and maintenance the new equipment requires.

We have a large responsibility, not only to train our soldiers to operate and maintain new equipment, but to make sure they understand personnel changes it may cause. In our training effort, we must clearly define the new equipment's benefit to the company, platoon and squad missions. If we don't, soldiers will never understand why the equipment is there and will be reluctant to accept and use it. Fear of the unknown is an area we NCOs must overcome with our training programs. We must ensure the engineer family speaks with one voice.

Dirty Hands

Last but not least, we NCOs must make sure we fully comprehend how to maintain our new equipment. We must be willing to get our hands dirty in the unit maintenance section learning everything that must be tightened, cleaned, and serviced. Then we must train our soldiers to perform this vital function.

As we modernize the Army and the Corps of Engineers, we NCOs have a key mission as both users of new equipment, and trainers of those who use it. I ask all of you to accept the challenges as we move toward the Army of the 1990's. We must prepare ourselves and our soldiers for the AirLand Battle concept. Between equipment developers and the soldiers who use the equipment, we NCOs must . . .

BRIDGE THE GAP

School News

Directorate of Combat Developments

DCD and the Future: The Directorate of Combat Developments (DCD) is helping improve engineer organization and equipment to meet modern battlefield requirements. This thrust is on track due to improved intra-Army communications, top management recognition of engineer needs and a highly dedicated work force.

Featuring DCD activities in this edition of ENGINEER Magazine is a welcome opportunity. Although the feature homes-in on mobility, countermobility and, to some extent, survivability, DCD is actively addressing engineering and topography functions as well. More on these in future editions.

Directorate of Training and Doctrine

ENCOA and EOBC Changes: The Engineer NCO Advanced Course is now 14 weeks and is taught as two courses (CMF 12 and CMF 51). Each has a six-week common phase, an eight-week MOS phase, and small-group practical exercises, including the critical path method, communications and NBC, T/O constructions, and a tactical exercise without troops at Manassas Battlefield. A final two-day engineer stakes problem tests all ENCOA skills.

The Engineer Officer Basic Course now has 77 more training hours. The largest is part of a three-week field phase at Fort A.P. Hill where students learn tactics, mine/countermine warfare, demolitions and weapons, and other subjects. They return to Fort A.P. Hill for one week at the course's end to practice ARTEP tasks.

Directorate of Training Developments

SQT Changes: In February, a comprehensive testing program replaced the three-component SQT. It has a hands-on common task test, a unit hands-on MOS evaluation, and a refined written test.

The hands-on common task SQT is administered to soldiers E-7 and below, and as directed to the Guard and Reserve. The answers are available to commanders for mutual scoring, but results are not used for personnel management. The common task SQT is administered using checklists in the *Soldier's Manual of Common Tasks.* HQDA annually selects tasks for the common task SQT, which can be administered anytime during the year.

The MOS-specific hands-on evaluation contains critical tasks recommended by proponent schools. These hands-on evaluations are administered by the unit using checklists found in the *Soldier's Manual.* Results are not reported to TRADOC or HQDA, so the MOS-specific hands-on evaluation is not part of the soldier's SQT score.

An MOS-specific written test for each MOS skill level determines individual proficiency. It tests representative combat and/or mission-essential tasks, and takes about two hours. The written SQT test period has been shortened

Directorate of Training Developments, cont.

from six to three months. Printed FOUO answers are provided to commanders for all written tests. They permit local scoring for immediate feedback so commanders can correct training weaknesses.

This written test is the SQT score used by promotion selection boards.

Directorate of Engineer Force Management

Enlisted Actions: The Directorate of Engineer Force Management (Provisional) (DEFM) is involved in several actions affecting engineers.

For results of the Women in the Army study and how it affects engineers, see "News & Notes," page 2.

Analysis of enlisted selection board results are going to the field. Command awareness briefings are also being given to EOBC, EOAC, Precommand Course, and ENCOA.

12B NCO Course: A Basic Technical Course is being developed for 51H and 62N.

Combat eligible personnel in MOS 51H, 51B, 51C, 51K and 51R can attend 12B Basic NCO Course.

Physical Profiles: Physical profiles in CMF 51 and 81 have been upgraded. Personnel must meet fitness and weight standards, provide a current photo, and review and update records before the selection boards meet.

Proponency Question Line: Call the Proponency Question Line, (703) 664-4172, AUTOVON 354-4172, with suggestions, questions or comments.

Defense Mapping School

Topo Support Teams: The Army has revised topographic doctrine from scientific terrain studies to quick, combat-oriented analyses. Engineer terrain teams in division, corps and army HQs provide rapid overlays and terrain information for planners.

Direct support division teams, led by a warrant officer (MOS 841A), have five men with a van of equipment. Direct support teams (35 men) and general support theater army teams (27 men) are commanded by majors and provide broader support.

New MOS: In March 1983, new MOS 81Q (terrain analyst) replaced MOS 81CE5. A Basic Terrain Analysis Course (BTAC) will begin in FY84 to train them. An Advanced Terrain Analysis Course (ATAC) began in June 1983 for NCOs.

Warrant Training: In 1979, warrant officer training opened for topographers with the Terrain Analysis Course. Terrain analysis technicians must be terrain analysts, complete the BTAC and ATAC, and apply for warrant officer and MOS 841A.

THE STATE OF THE COMBAT ENGINEER

by COL P.R. Hoge & LTC P. Stevens III

Measuring the state of the American sapper—the combat engineer—requires not just taking his pulse, but measuring his whole system, his job on the battlefield, and the team he supports.

Our most likely battle has two probable characteristics: It will be far away where we are least prepared to go, and it will be much less intense than a battle in Europe. The least likely battle—but the worse case—will be against Warsaw Pact forces in Central Europe. We must be ready for both battles. Their requirements, however, are not only different, but in part mutually exclusive.

The combat engineers' role on these battlefields is precisely what it's always been—altering the ground to our advantage and to the enemy's disadvantage. However, that has new and ominious importance. The Warsaw Pact is organized and trained to overwhelm their foe with massed forces supported by enormous firepower. If we can't use the terrain, we lose a key factor the commander could use to influence the battle's outcome.

Combined Arms Tasks

To describe the combined arms tasks as they relate to the ground, we use the terms mobility, countermobility and survivability. These are not just engineer tasks; they are the business of the whole combined arms team.

Mobility is clearing the way for movement and maneuver. It is breaching minefields, reducing obstacles, and crossing dry and wet gaps.

Countermobility is the reverse—delaying, impeding, or blocking the enemy's movement. Obstacles are created with mechanical or explosive earthworks or minefields.

Survivability is digging in for protection—preparing fighting or protective positions for the maneuver and artillery elements, or for logistic and command activities.

Why are these battle tasks more critical today than in the past? Because the Warsaw Pact's tactics and capabilities are well known. To defeat them, or others using their tactics, requires the total integration of time, troops and equipment through the doctrine called the AirLand Battle. Striking quickly and deeply, seeing the battlefield and slowing the foe to create windows of opportunity are absolutely key to AirLand Battle doctrine. Failing in any one of those areas could result in total mission failure.

Our freedom to maneuver, to delay and block the enemy, and to dig in to survive the first blow and keep figh ing are more important to the Ai Land doctrine than to any oth fighting concept ever practiced l our forces. While the combat eng neer is the principal planner ar actor in the mobility—countermob ity—survivability arena, they mu be practiced by the entire combin arms team because there will simp never be enough engineers to do t job alone. In light of this urgent nee what is the state of the engineer ar the team he supports?

Army Modernization

We are experiencing unparallel hardware modernization. The bo wave of post-Vietnam researc development and acquisition reaching the field. Foremost amo our new weapons stands the M Abrams tank. Its cross-country spe is so great it literally leaves the rest our forces behind. Using the Abran mobility while not forcing it to fig out front alone is an enormous ch lenge. It is a particularly vexi problem to the sapper who must cle the way for the task force.

For example, the Warsaw Pa will make vast use of mines. Add that our own scatterable mines a we find the most insidious proble on the battlefield—countermi operations. We don't have a count mine detection or breaching capability adequate to support armor mobility. Mines do not merely destroy armor; they paralyze the entire attacking force. They require breaching, by-passing or bulling through.

This countermine deficiency is viewed by many as our most serious, but it's not the only one. Consider gap crossing—in highly mobile warfare a simple gap can render our speed useless. The combat force engineer is better equipped here than for countermine but our combined arms hardware is increasingly heavy and appears to have gone away from organic fording or swimming ability.

Breaching obstacles under fire requires equipment suited to the task. The venerable D7 bulldozer on its lowbed transporter is a capable tool for many jobs, but isn't suited to clearing the way in stride and under fire.

Those are just a few areas in which we need to improve. Other problems include obstacle construction, explosives, and digging capability.

Bangalore & Probe

The combat engineer is equipped today much as he was in World War II. Major technological advances are visible in armor, infantry, artillery and aviation, but the sapper still fights with his dump truck, 'dozer, grader, or D-handled shovel. For countermine operations, we still use the probe or bangalore torpedo-type line charges of World War II vintage. This is simply too slow and ineffective for combat breaching under fire.

The Warsaw Pact recognizes the importance of countermine operations and has fielded rollers, plows and rocket propelled line charges mounted on tanks. They have an impressive counterobstacle vehicle—a tank with a moveable blade on the front and an articulated arm on the turret ring to lift and remove obstacles while under fire.

Surprisingly, the U.S. engineer was better off in many respects during World War II than he is today. Then we had rollers, plows, and even rocket-propelled line charges to clear minefields. Obviously, there was a clear need. Why not today?

Engineers lacking the ability to move, operate and to survive on the battlefield results primarily from a lack of priority for these capabilities. Our Army has not fought on a battlefield since the Korean War where extensive countermine, counterobstacle and gap crossing operations were required. Because we haven't *fought* this way, we haven't *trained* this way.

No Gut Feeling

The lack of training in mobility, countermobility and survivability within the combined arms team is more insidious than simple ignorance. An entire generation of maneuver arms officers and NCOs lack the gut feeling for the requirement to do these tasks. As they have advanced in grade, this deficiency in their tactical sense has encouraged ignoring the problem. They don't ignore it maliciously, it's just that they don't understand. So, in the Pentagon's budget drills, the engineer has been a frequent loser. We, the Army, simply haven't funded the research and development or procurement to solve the problem.

Our engineer hardware deficiencies are not totally the result of the Army not appreciating the problem. The engineer has had trouble articulating those needs. For example, countermine operations consist of detection, breaching, proofing and marking. When we argue for building hardware which solves only one aspect of the problem, we've not only failed to meet the need, but also failed to describe the battlefield concept.

To solve the complex problems of mobility, countermobility and survivability, certain combat engineer needs are paramount. He must be quick to keep up with the combined arms team and to do his job in stride and under fire. He must survive to get the job done at all. And he must be strategically deployable to support the light force.

While the picture isn't completely bleak, it needs improvement. One thing is obvious: The combined arms team must train together. Realistic training is fundamental to building a successful team. We can't ignore rivers and assume them away in training. We must place and breach minefields using realistic training mines and battle drills to penetrate them. We must accept such exercise delays because the delays on the battlefield will be more serious. We must build and breach obstacles and not simulate them with tape. And we must dig protective positions and show their benefits to the battle team.

Getting Better & Smarter

On the hardware side, we must be smart and build concept-based equipment fitted to a clear and well-defined need and it must be simple and programmable in the budget.

What, then, is the pulse of the combat engineer? Pretty strong and lively. There's a lot going on; the combined arms team has begun thinking of its mobility, countermobility and survivability needs. This has an impact on both field training and Pentagon budget priorities. So it's a good pulse and the sapper must keep it strong by integrating himself into the combined arms team. The whole team needs to continue to look to its engineers for advice and action. Only then can we be ready to fight and win.

COL P.R. Hoge is the director, Directorate of Combat Developments (DCD), U.S. Army Engineer School. LTC P. Stevens III is a student at the Army War College and served previously as chief, Development Division, DCD.

ENGINEER HOTLINE

Problems, questions, and comments relating to engineer doctrine, training, organization, and equipment can be addressed telephonically to the U.S. Army Engineer School's "Engineer Hotline." The Hotline's auto-answer recorder operates 24 hours a day, seven days a week. Callers should state their name, address and telephone number, followed by a concise question or comment. You'll receive a reply within three to 15 days. The Hotline is not a receiving agency for formal requests.

Call commercial (703) 664-3646; WATTS 800-336-3095, extension 3646; or AV 354-3646.

Determining engineer requirements for the AirLand Battle

THE COMBAT ENGINEER MISSION AREA ANALYSIS

"The analysis will serve as the cornerstone for combat engineering during the next decade."

By MAJ Don A. Shuey

As part of the TRADOC Mission Area Analysis Program, the Engineer School recently conducted a Mission Area Analysis (MAA) examining the combat engineer support required for AirLand Battle operations.

The concept for the MAA originated from Office of Management and Budget (OMB) concerns over the manner in which the defense establishment conducted the materiel acquisition process. Directives from OMB, through the Defense Department, established general guidelines for conducting such analyses. Department of the Army established a set of mission areas and delegated certain areas to TRADOC. Then TRADOC translated these generic DA categories into twelve separate mission areas to be studied by various schools and centers.

The objective of the analyses is to identify what must be done on the 1990 battlefield (missions, functions, and tasks), examine the projected capability to perform these tasks, uncover deficiencies in that capability, and propose corrective actions. Corrective actions are categorized into doctrine, organization, training, and materiel, focusing on the least costly approach.

The Engineer School has responsibility for the Combat Support, Engineering and Mine Warfare (CSEMW) MAA. This title caused some confusion; therefore, the first analysis task developed a clearer understanding of the CSEMW mission area. The CSEMW MAA addresses these actions:

- Mobility operations
- Countermobility operations
- Survivability enhancements
- General engineering
- Topographical services

The topic "Engineers as Infantr[y]" was added because fighting as infa[n]try is the engineer's secondary mi[s]sion. When exercised, it affec[ts] completion of their primary mi[s]sions. The original scope was [to] include only corps and below. Th[is] was extended to include echelo[ns] above corps because of the engine[er] interrelationships required fro[m] corps level and above to support t[he] forward battlefield.

The battlefield missions we[re] examined regarding command a[nd] control, communications, trainin[g], logistics and an area called hum[an] dimensions. The MAA also examin[ed] opportunities to use technologic[al] breakthroughs. The final produ[ct] will be the most comprehensi[ve] analysis of combat engineering [to] date. It will include rank-order[ed] deficiencies and recommended sol[u]tions supporting a development pla[n]. The analysis will serve as a corne[r]stone for the combat engineers for t[he] next decade.

The USAES Directorate of Co[m]bat Developments coordinat[ed] information from not only the En[gi]neer School, but also from TRADO[C], DARCOM, OCE, the Defen[se] Nuclear Agency, the Defense Ma[p]ping Agency, selected MACOM en[gi]neers, and outside experts.

Analytical tools were utiliz[ed] throughout the analysis. Comput[er]

ized force-on-force combat models and wargames such as *Battle* and *Carmonette* became important methods to evaluate combat operations. Combat simulations highlighted deficiencies and compared proposed alternative corrective actions. Tactical exercises without troops provided useful planning information, as did tests at Army schools. Additionally, questionnaires were sent to engineer units, major commands and to general officers to further assist in the results. Specific analyses for CSEWM MAA were conducted at the TRADOC Systems Analysis Agency, Construction Engineer Research Laboratory, Waterways Experimentation Station, and in conjunction with the Close Combat Heavy MAA at Fort Knox. A map exercise at Fort Belvoir with USAES, 9th Infantry Division, and 20th Engineer Brigade (Combat) (Airborne) personnel was also used to enhance and supplement other analyses.

A coordinating draft of the main report (plus an executive summary) was submitted to TRADOC and other interested agencies in January 1983. The draft development plan for implementing MAA initiatives was submitted to TRADOC in March; general distribution of the final report was in May.

"The final product will be the most comprehensive analysis to date of combat engineering."

The Combat Support, Engineering and Mine Warfare MAA provides a coordinated, logical and consistent direction for future engineer planning and programming. It emphasizes which resources must be applied so the Army can fight effectively on the AirLand Battlefield.

Together with the other 11 MAAs, TRADOC will prepare a battlefield development plan to assist the Army in materiel acquisition actions and to influence DA long-range research and development objectives.

MAJ Dan A. Shuey is chief, Evaluation Branch, Evaluation and Analysis Div., Directorate of Combat Developments, U.S. Army Engineer School. He has served as commander of E Co., 10th Engineers, and as S1 of the 2d Engineers in Korea. He has a bachelor's degree in business administration from Park College and is a graduate of the Engineer Officer Advanced Course and Airborne School.

ENGINEER BRANCH TEAM

OFFICER ASSIGNMENTS (l-r)

(Front), LTC Paul Chinen *Branch Chief*
Nina Foster *Administration*
Betty Walsh *Assistant LT Assignments*
Roxanne Smith *Assitant CPT Assignments*
CPT Meredith Temple *LT Assignments*
(Rear), MAJ Charles Rust *MAJ Assignments*
MAJ Lee Gibson *CPT Assignments*
MAJ John Bosilotto *LTC Assignments*
MAJ Edward Harris *Professional Development*

Phone: 2LT-LTC, (202) 325-7504/5/6, AVN 221.

WARRANT OFFICER ASSIGNMENTS

CW4 Edward Walls
Phone: (202) 325-7838/7840, AVN 221.

ENLISTED ASSIGNMENTS (l-r)

MSG James Blair *CMF 81*
SFC Robert Ford *CMF 12*
LTC Liston Edge *Branch Chief*
SGM John Peterson *Branch Sergeant Major*
SFC Billy Ford *CMF 51*

Phone: (202) 325-7710, AVN 221.

ARMY 86

COMBAT ENGINEERS

Army 86 organizes the Army to fight the AirLand Battle. Here is how the engineers fit in.

by MAJ Richard Kanda & CPT Thomas P. Swaim

The Army 86 study is intended to give the Army an improved organizational structure, one tailored to execute AirLand Battle tactical doctrine with advanced weapons and equipment. The study encompasses the entire Army, from the foxhole through theater level.

Such modernization is long overdue. The last major Army reorganization was in the early 1960s when we went from the PENTOMIC to the ROAD organizations. Army 86 organizations are designed to win on the 1990s battlefield.

Army 86 Combat Engineers

After extensive study, including review of previous studies and field reports, some general building blocks have emerged for combat engineer actions in Army 86:

- Take advantage of new technology and integrate new equipment.
- Improve command, control and communications.
- Orient on combat tasks—mobility, countermobility, and survivability—to support maneuver forces.
- Support independent operations forward-orientation, and self-sufficiency.
- Improve our deployability.

When all these factors are combined, we see an Army 86 combat engineer who needs speed, survivability and deployability to support the combined arms team.

Heavy Division 86

Heavy Division 86 was the first Army 86 study and set the stage for all that followed. Heavy Division 86 will replace the current armored and mechanized divisions. Force designs for the organic combat engineer bą talion and its line companies a shown in Figures 1 and 2.

The design's highlights are:

- Equipment systems:
  - Mobility: M9, ROBAT, AVL CEV.
  - Countermobility: GEMSS, CEV.
  - Survivability: SEE, M9, CE
- Organizational changes:
  - Brigade engineer staff secti
  - Water points to DISCOM.

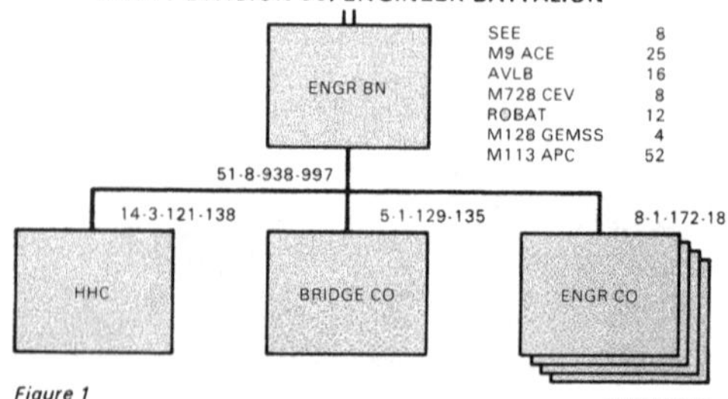

Figure 1

- Equipment from HHC to line companies.
- Mobility/countermobility platoon with new equipment.
- Support platoon provides a maintenance warrant ôfficer.

This new combat engineer organization is a significant improvement because most combat capability and self-sufficiency are forward in the line companies.

The M9 can cut combat trails (mobility), bulldoze an antitank ditch (countermobility), and dig hull-down positions (survivability). It allows us to move and to survive with the force we support.

The new Robotic Obstacle Breaching Assault Tank (ROBAT) and consolidating all divisional AVLBs in the battalion will give us unprecedented capability to breach obstacles. ROBAT allows us to conduct assault breaches of minefields under fire without breaking stride. It can sense a minefield then breach, proof, and mark a path through without operators aboard.

Developmental work is complete on SLUFAE, a standoff minefield breaching system. Current plans are to hold it in a production-ready status, available if war occurs.

Our ability to lay mines with GEMSS makes us much more responsive and productive than with current methods. Also improved is controlling and coordinating combat engineer activities where the battle is being fought.

The Army chief-of-staff approved implementation of this new organization beginning in Fiscal Year 1983. The transition will be phased, based on availability of equipment like the M9 and ROBAT.

Army 86 studies show the need for more host nation support.

Light Division 86

Light Division 86 examines the infantry, airborne and air assault divisions and is still in progress. In December 1981, the Army chief-of-staff ordered a new organization fielded by Fiscal Year 1985 called the High Technology Light Division (HTLD).

The significant features are:

- Mobility: M9, MICLIC, LAB, light equipment package.
- Countermobility: GEMSS, M9, VOLCANO, light equipment package.
- Survivability: SEE, M9, light equipment package.
- Organizational changes: Same as Heavy Division 86, plus:
  - Brigade engineer staff section in maneuver brigade HHC.
  - Bridge company deleted.
  - Light assault company with light equipment package added.
  - Entire battalion C141 transportable.

Many aspects of the HTLD combat engineer battalion were tested by the 9th Infantry Division High Technology Test Bed at Fort Lewis and Yakima, Wash. These tests validated the Small Emplacement Excavator and M9 and provided impetus to accepting the brigade engineer concept. (See page 31 for an in-depth look at the 9th Infantry Division's 15th Engineers.)

VOLCANO, an accelerated development program, provides a lightweight, helicopter or truck-mounted mine emplacement capability.

Combat engineer battalions organic to the Airborne/Air Assault Divsions 86 are just emerging from the conceptual stage; extensive coordination with field commanders is still in progress. These engineer organizations will be standardized as much as possible. Current force designs contain light equipment for assault airstrip work, incorporate developmental equipment for light forces, have staff engineer sections in maneuver brigade HHCs, and consist of four line companies. There is a design constraint of 625 personnel per engineer battalion.

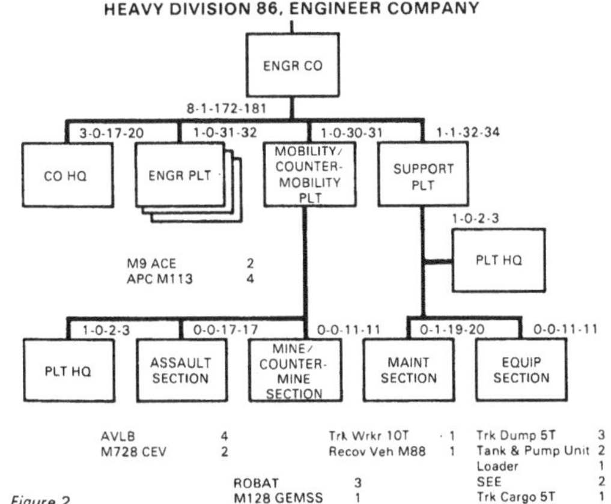

Figure 2

Corps 86

Corps 86 coordinates and sustains the AirLand Battle while the divisions fight it. Heavy Corps 86 organization and structure was based on a European scenario. A Southwest Asia scenario was used in the initial force development for Contingency Corps 86. Four other contingency scenarios will develop a light corps for worldwide deployment.

Army 86 studies and previous analyses support the requirement for five combat engineer battalions per division in a corps. Table of Organization and Equipment 5-45, Combat Engineer Battalion, Corps (Mechanized), was recently approved.

The requirement for this new organization has been long recognized. When fielded, it will improve our combat power. Actual fielding is tied to availability of APCs and other equipment. The unit looks very much like the heavy division engineer battalion minus the bridge company.

When considering a five division corps in the European theater, the required engineer force in Figure 3 results. In contingency situations, there are requirements for critical specialized support, which for forward-deployed forces would be provided by theater army or host nation support.

Deployability constraints dictate an austere force. Trading heavy combat engineer battalions for corps combat battalions plus combat support equipment companies, and introducing an airborne light-equipment company, was dictated by these constraints.

The corps design for engineer support to three light divisions employed in Southeast Asia is shown in Figure 4. Refinement of this force design is continuing with analysis of contingency corps employment in other scenarios.

Echelons Above Corps 86

The Echelons Above Corps (EAC) 86 study examines combat and combat service support at the theater army level. The primary goal is to permit Corps 86 to orient forward to conduct combat operations.

EAC combat engineers support the corps with general engineering in the communications zone (COMMZ) and provide mobility-countermobility-survivability support in the combat zone for maneuver forces. Specialized support required by the logistics support base in the COMMZ is also handled by the EAC engineer force.

Topographic support from division to theater army level is provided by engineers from the EAC 86 engineer topographic battalion.

Results of the EAC 86 study for Europe and emerging results in the contingency corps study, indicate significant engineer shortfalls. Increased use of host nation support and developing contractor support is required. Contract procurement and management by the Corps of Engineers could reduce some shortfalls.

Host nation support is dependent on detailed advance planning and coordination in peacetime to ensure that critical engineering services, equipment, and materials are provided at the right time and place. (Engineer operations at the theater army level are detailed in FM 100-6, *Support Operations (Coordinatin Draft)*, November, 1981.)

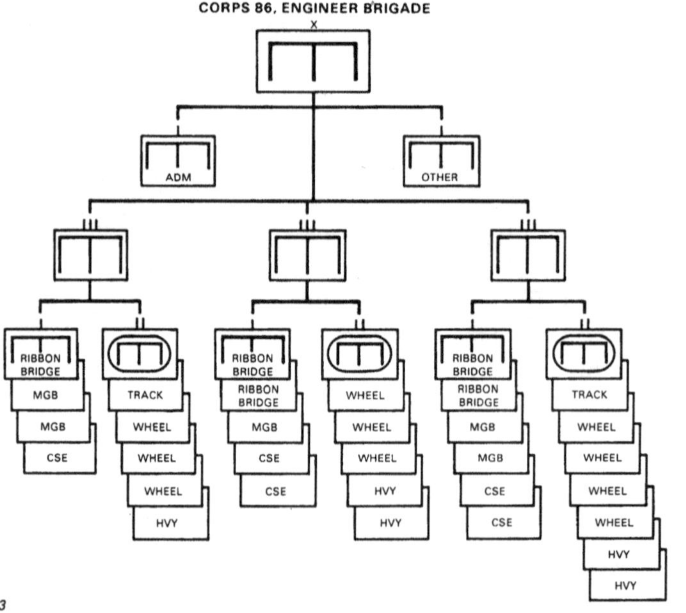

Figure 3

CONTINGENCY CORPS 86, ENGINEER BRIGADE

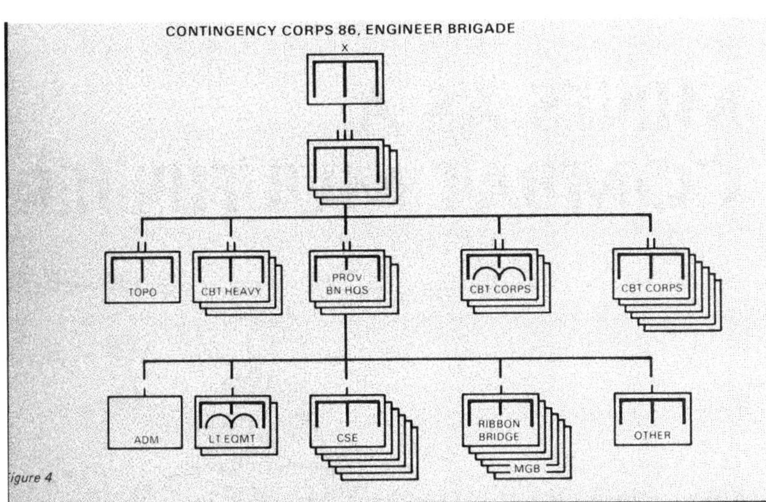

Figure 4

Combat, 1990

Army 86 combat engineer organizations are being designed to meet the challenges of combat in 1990. New equipment will allow us to orient on the critical mobility-survivability tasks. Command and control and self-sufficiency have been improved. As Army 86 engineers, we will be able to keep up with, survive with, and best support the combined arms team.

MAJ Richard Kanda is with the Force Design Branch, Directorate of Combat Developments, U.S. Army Engineer School. He has commanded combat engineer companies in Germany and Vietnam. His last assignment was as the executive officer, 10th Combat Engineer Bn., 3d Infantry Div. (Mech.), Germany. He is a graduate of the Command and General Staff College and has a master's degree in civil engineering.

CPT Thomas P. Swaim is also with the Force Design Branch, Directorate of Combat Developments, U.S. Army Engineer School. He is a graduate of the U.S. Military Academy. His last assignment was as commander of B Co., 52d Engineer Bn., Ft. Carson, Colo. CPT Swaim is a graduate of the Engineer Officer Advanced Course and is a registered professional engineer in Virginia.

Writer's Guidelines

In response to queries from prospective authors, we pass along the following ENGINEER writer's guidelines:

TOPIC—Although our focus is upon combat engineering, any subject of professional interest to the Corps is welcome. It is always best to query first since an article similar to yours may have appeared already or may be scheduled for a future issue. Please title your article.

LENGTH—Length is not as important as content. Let your subject matter dictate length. Most ENGINEER articles range from 1,000 to 3,000 words.

PHOTOGRAPHS AND ARTWORK—Photos and drawings strengthen your article, and in some cases are vital graphic aids to conveying your message. Photos should be black and white, glossy, and, preferably, at least 5" x 7". We can also work from good quality color slides. Drawings must be legible but need not be "camera ready."

COVER LETTER—Please include a cover letter with your name, address and a phone number at which you can be contacted.

NEWS & NOTES—We're always looking for contributions here, especially those with photographs. Your TASO or public affairs officer will be able to provide photographic support.

Finally, we'll work with you on polishing your writing skills. The most important criteria for an ENGINEER article is the story it tells and the professional growth it stimulates in your fellow engineers.

We look forward to seeing your article in a future issue of ENGINEER.

MINES AS A COMBAT MULTIPLIER

A new generation of remotely delivered mines is revolutionizing land-mine warfare.

By MAJ John D. Pawulak
&
CPT James C. Loo

Mine warfare is in a major transition. New high-technology (high-tech) mines have added new dimensions to mine warfare and to the battlefield.

Traditional doctrine of placing large linear minefields between opposing forces at the forward edge of the battle has been replaced by concepts to use mines against enemy units *anywhere* on the battlefield. Remotely delivered high-tech mines could revolutionize land-mine warfare by their on-the-spot capability. These technological advances will complement existing conventional mines and provide commanders greater ability to restrict enemy movement without impeding friendly mobility.

Before Vietnam, our mining capability consisted of antitank (AT) and antipersonnel (AP) mines developed for World War II. These mines still compose most of our land mine inventory. Their size, weight and the time required to emplace them cause logistical and operational burdens. Great tonnage is required for placement, and the manpower and time requirements they demand would be a serious liability during the swift AirLand Battle.

This doesn't mean hand-emplaced mines don't have a place on the battlefield. They are still required during prehostilities in demilitarized zones, and in protective barriers around installations and fighting positions. However, to meet the objectives of land-mine warfare—to fix, delay, disrupt and channelize enemy first-echelon and follow-on forces—more dynamic, rapidly emplaced mines are required.

The M56

During the Vietnam War, mor than 40 new mines were develope but only the M56 Antitank Helico ter Mine Dispensing System wa fielded.

The M56 is a unique concept: mine randomly emplaced and su face exposed. It consists of a contr panel, wiring harness and two exte nally mounted SUU-13 mine di pensers. Each dispenser has 8 antitank mines. The entire system mounted on a utility helicopter. Th mines are ejected and arm on groun impact. Minefield density is dete mined by the dispensing rate and ai craft speed.

While there are advantages to th mine, it does have serious limitation There is no self-destruct option an no antipersonnel capability. M5 mines are pressure fuzed only so th lack full-width kill capability.

Here is a look at the high-tech mines being fielded, in production or under development.

RAAM and ADAM

The Remote AntiArmor Mine System (RAAM) and the Area Denial Artillery Munition (ADAM) systems are each packed into a modified M483 carrier round and fired by 155mm howitzer. Each has factory-set long or short self-destruct times.

A RAAM round base-ejects nine magnetically fuzed AT mines over the target area. Some of them have an anti-disturbance feature and explode if moved.

RAAM and ADAM can be used to attack targets of opportunity or be harassing agents used with other munitions. They are most effective when placed on top of or used in front of enemy units. They may also be used for counterbattery fires and reseeding breached minefields.

RAAM and ADAM have several advantages. They can be delivered deep into enemy territory to disrupt their timetables. The mines' full-width kill capability requires fewer mines to achieve desired densities and, compared with other systems, RAAM and ADAM are low-cost.

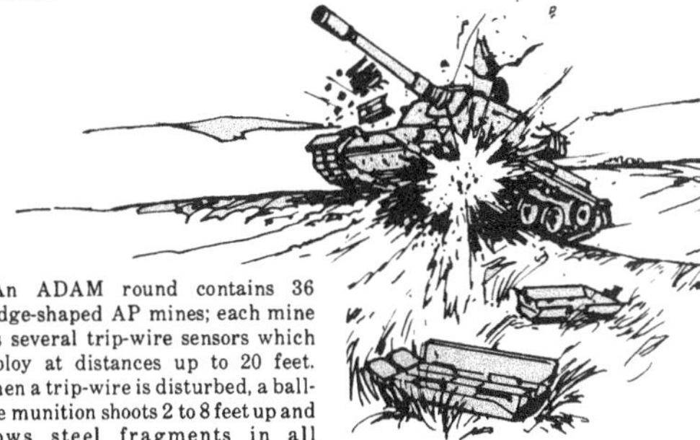

An ADAM round contains 36 wedge-shaped AP mines; each mine has several trip-wire sensors which deploy at distances up to 20 feet. When a trip-wire is disturbed, a ball-like munition shoots 2 to 8 feet up and blows steel fragments in all directions.

Some disadvantages include command and control problems created by using remotely delivered mines. Extensive coordination is required between maneuver elements, engineers and fire support personnel. Also, the mines' short emplacement time and brief self-destruct interval requires rapid reporting to ensure we don't impede our own maneuverability. Competition for artillery will pose a problem, as will logistics.

However, the need to remotely deliver mines significantly outweighs these disadvantages. RAAM and ADAM will provide commanders with a rapid, flexible and effective means of paralyzing enemy forces. Both systems are in the developmental stage.

ADAM

GEMSS and FLIPPER

The M128 Ground Emplaced Mine Scattering System (GEMSS) is in production and will be fielded in Fiscal Year 1984. FLIPPER, an auxiliary GEMSS mine dispenser, is under development.

GEMSS is a trailer-mounted device which arms and dispenses up to 800 mines in 15 minutes. A typical GEMSS mine field consists of three 30 meter wide strips spaced about 500 to 100 meters apart. GEMSS can be used to emplace flank minefields, reinforce existing obstacles or to close gaps or lanes. The system will be issued to corps, heavy and light divisions, armored cavalry regiments and to separate brigade engineer line companies. The unit weighs 7.5 tons (loaded) and can be towed by a 5-ton truck, CEV, M113 APC, M9 ACE or M548 cargo carrier.

FLIPPER is being developed to provide a lightweight, easily operated device to spin-arm, select the self-destruct time, and to dispense M74 and M75 mines. The system will be primarily an auxiliary dispenser for GEMSS mines; four will be issued to each engineer unit authorized a GEMSS dispenser. FLIPPER will be mounted on combat and combat support vehicles.

The M75 and M74 mines each measure 2½ inches high by 4 inches in diameter and weigh about four pounds. Both have operator selected short or long self-destruct times. The AT mines use a magnetic fuze for full-width kill. Antipersonnel mines use four trip-wires for activation. The mine kills by both ground blast and fragmentation.

GEMSS offers rapid, large volume metered mining. The M74 and M75 are smaller than conventional mines, reducing logistical burdens. The most significant disadvantage is GEMSS' size and weight. With the unit weighing 7.5 tons, poor soil conditions could greatly hamper a wheeled prime mover.

GEMSS, however, gives commanders the ability to rapidly emplace large minefields, forcing the enemy to alter his battle plans.

GATOR

GATOR is an air-delivered mine system that dispenses AP and AT mines from tactical and strategic aircraft. It is being developed for either the Air Force CBU-89/B or Navy SUU-66/B dispensers. The Air Force dispenser carries 72 BLU-91/B AT and 22 BLU-92/B AP mines. The Navy dispenser can carry 45 AT and 15 AP mines.

Three self-destruct times are available with each mine. The BLU-91/B AT mine has a magnetic fuze making it a full-width killer. The BLU-92/B AP mine has a blast fragmentary kill mechanism and uses trip-wire sensors.

Both AT and AP mines are about the same weight and shape as a GEMSS mine. They are aerodynamically dispensed when a linear line charge cuts the dispenser's skin. Arming and self-destruct times are automatically set when the dispenser opens. Adapters on the mines aid dispersion and reduce ground impact force.

The system is designed for rapid delivery of interdiction and counter ADA minefields. Denying key terrain, disrupting and paralyzing the enemy are its primary uses. It will be vital in stalling follow-on echelons and will be most effective when used at night.

GATOR is scheduled for fielding in Fiscal Year 1985.

MOPMS

The Modular Pack Mine System (MOPMS) is a compact, easily portable unit which discharges 21 AT or AP mines in a 35 meter semicircle.

The rectangular, 32x23x13 inch unit weighs 150 pounds and can be carried by as few as two men. The M131 version contains 21 AP mines. Each mine deploys four trip-wires which if disturbed, detonates a fragmentary kill mechanism. The M132 module contains 21 AT mines with magnetic fuzes for full-width kill. Future development may include a

GEMSS

mixed module containing both AT and AP mines.

Mines can be dispensed from either module by remote control or standard hardwire. The remote control unit dispenses mines from the

module, recycles self-destruct times or destroys dispensed mines. Hardwire activation only dispenses mines. Self-destruct, recycle and command destruction are not hardwire options.

MOPMS will close gaps and lanes in minefields, reinforce obstacles, and set protective and point minefields. It will be a Class V item for infantry, armor, artillery and engineer units.

The system offers many advantages. Its mines do not have to be dispensed until the last moment and nonactivated units are easily recovered. The mine's recycle capability extends minefield life and reduces logistical burdens. The remote control feature enhances MOPMS as a combat multiplier since several MOPMS can be controlled by a single operator.

MOPMS is currently under development with fielding expected in 1986-87.

VOLCANO

VOLCANO is an interchangeable system which can operate from aircraft or on the ground. It consists of a mine module, dispenser and control unit. GATOR AT and AP mines are being considered for use with VOLCANO. Mine modules will contain AT and AP mines plus a propulsion device.

Air VOLCANO is for combat support aviation companies of all divisions, separate brigades and regiments. Ground VOLCANO will be organic to all division engineer battalions and to the engineer companies of separate brigades and regiments.

When used by aircraft, it will emplace tactical minefields, reinforce obstacles, close lanes and gaps, create mine defiles, protect flanks and deny the enemy key terrain. When used by combat engineer units, VOLCANO will support in the same manner as GEMSS and MOPMS.

VOLCANO's fielding is projected for 1987 (helicopter) and 1990 (ground).

The Future

New high-tech mines will not totally replace conventional hand-emplaced, nonself-destruct mines. Conventional mines will always be required where precise emplacement is necessary, like around installation perimeters. There also are numerous international constraints regarding emplacing remotely-delivered, self-destructing mines prior to hostilities.

Both conventional and high-tech systems have their place on the battlefield. Used together, they provide the maneuver commander with a key combat multiplier.

MAJ John D. Pawulak is a graduate of the University of Maryland and the Engineer Officer Advanced and Army Aviation Rotary Wing Courses. He has served with the 2d Engineer Gp., 76th Engineer Bn, 522d Engineer Co., 222 Aviation Bn., and 54th Infantry Bn. (Mech). He now serves as chief, Countermobility Branch, Directorate of Combat Developments USAES, Ft. Belvoir, Va.

CPT James C. Loo is a graduate of the U.S. Military Academy and the Engineer Officer Basic and Advanced Officer Courses and the Atomic Demolitions Course. He served with the 62d Engineer Bn., Ft. Hood, Texas, as a platoon leader, S1 and company commander. CPT Loo is now aide-de-camp to the director of the Defense Nuclear Agency, Washington, D.C.

COUNTER MINE

for the AirLand Battle

Obsolete, Word War II vintage countermine capabilities have long haunted U.S. engineers. The situation is finally improving.

by LTC Russell L. Fuhrman

Emerging AirLand Battle doctrine has significant engineer implications. To inflict maximum damage on the enemy, maneuver commanders must strike deep. They must use economy of force measures to blunt the enemy penetration while making deep attacks into the enemy's flanks and rear. Engineer countermobility operations will be vital to economy of force operations while mobility operations will help the maneuver commander strike deep.

To give the maneuver commander an AirLand Battle level of mobility, combined arms teams must bypass or breach mined areas in stride and under fire. With increased emphasis on mobility, flexibility and staying power, all units must cope with both remotely delivered and conventio ally emplaced mines on th battlefield.

Soviet mine doctrine, like our uses mines to block the enemy. Sovi forces would use mines extensively offensive and defensive operation They have millions of mines and ca emplace them rapidly with aeri and ground mechanized-delive systems. Soviet combat troops a well trained in land-mine warfar specialized units perform all phas of mine warfare quickly a effectively.

Maintaining mobility against th threat is a challenging problem f the maneuver commander. To st mobile, he must have the capabili to detect, neutralize and ma cleared lanes through minefields.

Unfortunately, our minefiel breaching operations are too slo Explosives and hand-held detecto

The Robotic Obstacle Breaching Assault Tank (ROBAT) is slated for heavy division engineers. ROBAT detects, neutralizes and marks lanes by remote or manual control.

are all we have to counter the mine threat. The Army does have some line charges, but most are in stateside storage, and units are not trained in their employment. Current inventories include about 550 M157 (Diamond Lil) rigid, tank-pushed line charges and 360 rocket-propelled, sled-mounted M173 line charges. Our countermine capability is no better than during World War II.

New Systems

However, several countermine items are under development and can be fielded by 1986-88. These systems give the maneuver commander the mobility required by AirLand Battle doctrine. A critical issue will be Army funding for production. Countermine systems compete for procurement dollars with other systems ranging from the M1 tank to night vision goggles.

Armor units will have an organic countermine capability with the track-width mine roller introduced in Europe during 1982. The roller can detect and neutralize mines and survive the blast of several encounters. Under battle conditions, it can be mounted on the tank in 15 minutes and released remotely within 30 seconds. At a breaching speed of 10 mph, it is 90 percent effective in neutralizing single-impulse, pressure-type mines. Standard issue is three mine rollers per tank battalion.

Like the roller, the track-width plow gives armor units an organic countermine capability. The plow is a relatively lightweight system carried on the tank. It can physically extract, neutralize and remove land mines on the surface or tactically buried 4- to 6-inches deep. A "dogbone" and chain assembly activates any tilt-rod mines between the tracks. The plow can be operated from inside the tank.

SLUFAE & Others

The Surface Launched Unit Fuel Air Explosive (SLUFAE) provides the Army with a significant new countermine capability. SLUFAE allows the maneuver commander to breach a known minefield from more than half a mile away. The system is a 30-tube rocket launcher mounted on a M548 full-tracked cargo carrier. A resupply vehicle with an on-board crane is used to load the rockets and supports the system. The thirty rockets produce a cleared lane 8 meters wide by 240 meters long.

The track-width mine roller was issued to armor units in Europe last year. The roller was reverse engineered from the Soviet PT55/KMT5.

They can be fired individually or in ripples from concealed positions in all weather, day or night.

The Mine Clearing Line Charge (MICLIC) complements SLUFAE in breaching minefields where a "close-in" system is required. The Marine Corps M58A1 trailer-mounted line charge is currently being evaluated to meet this requirement. The MICLIC clears a lane 8 meters wide by 100 meters long. Light forces will receive the first MICLICs procured.

Another line charge being evaluated is the Portable Mine Neutralization System (POMINS). It neutralizes antipersonnel mines, booby traps, and wire obstacles for dismounted infantry. POMINS can be easily set up, fired in less than 30 seconds and will clear a footpath 25 meters long. POMINS is a Class V item for engineers, infantry and armor.

To counter the threat of magnetic mines, the Vehicle Magnetic Signature Duplicator (VEMASID) is being evaluated. A coil device, VEMASID projects a magnetic field forward of the vehicle which creates a tank-like signature, detonating magnetic mines harmlessly in front of the vehicle.

To complete a breach, the cleared lane must be marked for following vehicles. Current marking methods, like using engineer tape or the Hand Emplaced Minefield Marking System (HEMMS), are slow and will not survive in a heavy force environment. The Cleared Lane Marking System (CLAMS) is a mechanical device that will significantly improve our marking capabilities. It attaches to the rear of combat vehicles and uses chemiluminescent markers visible day and night.

The Robotic Obstacle Breaching Assault Tank (ROBAT) is a near-term, affordable solution to the countermine problem for heavy forces. Based on a systems approach, the ROBAT can detect, neutralize and mark a cleared lane by remote or manual control. ROBAT uses existing hardware—an M60 chassis with turret removed and a track-width mine roller or plow on the front. It has two or more protected line charges in the turret well and a marking system on the rear. The ROBAT program is an accelerated, two-year research and development effort with production starting in the third year. Twelve ROBATS will be issued to each heavy division engineer battalion.

This USMC Mine Clearing Line Charge (MICLIC) is being evaluated as a countermine option for light units.

Detecting mined areas and individual mines continues to be a serious shortcoming. There is no current capability to remotely detect minefields and no foreseeable solution until the 1990s. Despite the Army's emphasis on high mobility, minefield detection in the 1980s will be through visual means or encounter.

With new countermine hardware, our capability to breach minefields will significantly improve in the late 1980s. Under cover of suppressive fires and smoke, tank-mounted plows and rollers will breach lanes through lightly defended hasty minefields. Systems like ROBAT and SLUFAE will breach deliberate minefields and establish additional lanes in hasty minefields. With several breached lanes, friendly forces will move through the minefield in stride and under fire. This is a substantial improvement over the slow, labor-intensive capability we currently have. However, our future countermine capability depends on resources committed to these systems.

The Future

With mobility the key to winning the AirLand Battle, an effective countermine capability is vital. Enemy use of mines will be widespread and continuous in an attempt to disrupt and delay our forces and logistics. We can expect threat mines throughout our operational area. We may also have to move through our own minefields. Today, we can't provide the commander that mobility. But field commanders are striving to improve our countermine capability through combined arms battle drills and improvised hardware like armored bulldozers.

This critical hardware deficiency is recognized and a concerted effort is underway by TRADOC and DARCOM to field remedies. The accelerated ROBAT program and buying the Marine Corps M58A1 line charge clearly shows the Army's determination to solve the countermine problem.

LTC Russell L. Fuhrman is commander of the 10th Engineer Bn., Germany. He previously served with the Engineer School's Directorate of Combat Developments in the Development Div. and as chief of the Plans, Programs and Operations Div. He is a graduate of Command and General Staff College and has a master's degree in engineering from Pennsylvania State University.

The 548th Engineers test their readiness (and impress the Navy) with an intense construction exercise.

TASK FORCE PUERTO RICO LIGHT

by LTC John A. Tudela & 1LT Thomas J. Williams

Although U.S. contingency forces are characterized by light, highly mobile units, part of their most important support comes from combat heavy engineers. The 548th Engineer Battalion (Combat) (Heavy) has a contingency mission to deploy an engineer line company in an extremely short time with the remainder of battalion following later.

As part of the 20th Engineer Brigade (Combat) (Airborne Corps), the 548th also supports its home post, Fort Bragg, N. C., and the XVIII Airborne Corps.

This dual mission (combat and construction engineering) attests to the versatility of the combat heavy battalion. However, versatile, well-trained soldiers are an asset only if they can reach their area of operations.

In the past, the 548th sought to maintain its versatility and readiness by convoying annually to Fort Jackson, S.C., for two weeks of combat and construction engineering exercises. The training improved deployability and construction expertise. Also, officers, NCOs and enlisted personnel praised the unit cohesion these exercises generated.

Being a heavy engineer unit, the 548th at times is precluded, or at least inhibited, from being rapidly air transportable because of the large number of C5A aircraft required to move the unit's bulldozers and road-scrapers. So in a rapid deployment situation, the 548th's contingency company would deploy and use local engineering equipment until their own equipment arrived later via ship or aircraft.

Bright Star 81 provided the battalion the opportunity to deploy a heavy equipment platoon by ship to Somalia. The *Cygnus*, a roll-on/roll-off ship, easily accepted the heavy equipment. A few equipment operators sailed with the *Cygnus* on its one-month journey; most other operators were air deployed, timing their arrival to coincide with the ship's. The exercise demonstrated that people, but not heavy equipment, can be quickly air transported. It also highlighted one of the most challenging, but untested, rapid deployment requirements: Deploy without your equipment and still accomplish the mission.

The 548th met that challenge head-on, testing itself by deploying Task

One of the task force's missions was to improve drainage in flood-prone areas. The task force used Guard and Reserve equipment.

Force Puerto Rico Light to the Roosevelt Roads Naval Station, Puerto Rico.

Members of the 548th's Headquarters Company (for administrative and medical support), A Company (for pile driving support), and B Company deployed by air from Pope Air Force Base, N.C. They drew equipment in Puerto Rico and spent two weeks completing a variety of construction tasks.

A two-man advance party preceded the main body by five days to secure engineering support from the Army Reserve's 488th Engineer Battalion at Fort Buchanan, Puerto Rico. A Puerto Rican Army National Guard unit and the 699th Port Construction Company, both at Roosevelt Roads, supplied tactical vehicle support, bridge boats and a crane barge.

The naval station's Public Works Department (PWD, equal to an Army post's Directorate of Engineering and Housing) identified eight projects for the engineers. When the 548th Engineer's capabilities became apparent, the PWD quickly added nine more projects to the original eight.

The first tasks were clearing six flood-prone drainage areas, repairing four miles of road shoulder, installing a security lighting system for the PWD building and clearing 400-foot long vegetation strips for survey operations. The engineers also installed a roof on the Roosevelt Roads Yacht Club, dredged a parasitic-contaminated stream, poured five cubic yards of concrete in a pier upgrading project, and drove 70 20-foot poles (piles) into the ocean floor to support and repair the marina area. There were also other smaller, squad-sized projects.

A small task force detachment went to nearby Vieques Island to work with a Naval mobile construction battalion (SeaBees). They dredged ditches, installed concrete culverts, and built concrete hardwalls and roofing for a Navy weather observation post.

One of the most challenging and rewarding projects was driving the piles at the marina and refurbishing the boat pier decking materials. The PWD said at most only 15 piles could be driven because the pile-driver was on a barge and was subject to wave action and jarring. The Alpha Company pile drivers took the PWD estimate as a challenge to do better. Through sheer determination, they drove 70 piles in 15 days.

Pile driving from a barge required careful monitoring of weather and tides. Decaying pier-poles were removed during low tide and new ones driven at high tide.

Another challenging aspect of the deployment was using local equipment for the missions. The only vehicle brought from Fort Bragg was a contact truck. As planned, using local equipment was one of the chief benefits of the entire mission.

The equipment supplied by the Guard and Reserve was well maintained, but as with any equipment unused for long periods, there were minor problems. Also, operators didn't know their acquired equipment as well as their own at Fort Bragg. The intangible quirks of a machine is an important consideration when using unfamiliar equipment. Increased efforts in preventive maintenance solved many problems in this area.

Although the exercise was intended to practice deploying outside CONUS to an unfamiliar tropical area and in using unfamiliar

Decaying marina pier-poles being removed at low tide. Working from a barge, A Co. put in 70 new piles in 15 days—five times more than the Navy thought possible.

equipment, another valuable benefit came from interacting with the Air Force and Navy SeaBees. Since effective wartime performance depends on interfacing the armed forces, these experiences enhanced the battalion's readiness by strengthening their familiarity with interservice operations.

Task Force Puerto Rico Light tested the battalion's operational flexibility by sending a task force without equipment into unfamiliar country. The primary lesson was that mission completion required flexible integration of all aspects of combat engineering. This operational flexibility required a thorough understanding of mission requirements and detailed planning. Without detailed preparation, flexibility becomes a reaction to circumstances rather than an anticipated response.

Another lesson was the importance of using an advance party when acquiring equipment. There is no substitute for face-to-face coordination.

Regarding medical considerations, immunization for Fort Bragg is identical to the Roosevelt Roads area. Only one threatening medical condition existed inside the base. A small, flood-prone stream required rebanking for flood control, but the water was contaminated with schistosomes (a parasitic infection carried by a certain snail species). A problem arose when a D8 bulldozer broke down while the stream was being rebanked. A maintenance team had to work for about 30 minutes in contaminated water while fixing the 'dozer. Complete preventive measures were taken. Everyone earlier had received a medical-threat briefing so the men were aware of the hazard. A medic at the site saturated with alcohol any skin areas which contacted the water. Because the first phase of schistosomes infection is essentially symptom-free, blood tests were done on all exposed personnel.

Although all personnel knew heat injuries were more likely under the equator sun, there were still several cases of sunburn. These were attributable to failure to use sunscreen. Hydration and adequate rest were strictly enforced; there was only one case of heat cramps and no other heat injuries.

The deployment to Puerto Rico challenged the 548th's ability to move quickly into an unfamiliar environment and to use prepositioned equipment to accomplish a host of demanding missions. The exercise was an exceptionally valuable training tool, one that measurably increased the battalion's readiness to meet rapid deployment contingencies.

LTC John A. Tudela is the Army attache, U.S. Embassy, Mexico City. He commanded the 548th Engineers during the Puerto Rico deployment. He has a bachelor's degree in industrial engineering and a master's in construction engineering, both from Texas A&M. He also has a master's degree in international economics from the Monterey Institute of Foreign Studies and in construction engineering from the Bolivian Engineering College. He had completed Airborne, Special Forces and Foreign Area Officer training; Command and General Staff College; and the Spanish Army War College.

1LT Thomas J. Williams is assigned to the Directorate of Evaluation, Academy of Health Sciences at Ft. Sam Houston, Texas. He served with the 548th Engineers as medical services officer. He has a bachelor's degree from Lincoln University in psychology and a master's from Northeast Missouri State University in community/clinical psychology.

ENGINEER PROBLEM

1. What is the route classification formula?
2. What type of ford is ford #1?
3. What bypass conditions are at the tunnel?
4. What is the minimum radius of curvature in the series of sharp curves?
5. What approach condition is on the left bank of the ford?
6. What is the minimum traveled way width of the underpass?
7. What is the scale of the map used for this overlay?
8. What seasonal limitations does the ford have?
9. What is the percent of the steep grade?
10. What is the turn around time for ferry #1?
11. Is the railroad crossing an obstruction?
12. What type of off route movement/concealment is available along this route?

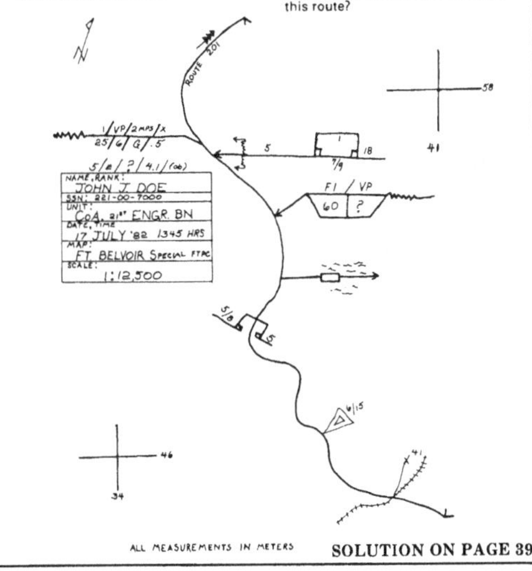

SOLUTION ON PAGE 39

ICE BRIDGING

When the temperature plunges below zero, the 23d Engineer Company puts Mother Nature to work.

by 1LT Mark L. Prahl

It doesn't take magic for a man, a jeep or even a 27-ton bulldozer to cross deep water in winter. All it takes is ingenuity, hard work and some frigid weather to make an ice bridge.

The first step in building an ice bridge is site reconnaissance because there are important location characteristics to consider in positioning the bridge.

The river channel should be straight and fairly wide, more than 60 feet if possible. Areas with unstable currents or temperatures, such as rapids and hot springs, are avoided. Normally, a straight, wide channel will have a slower flow and a level ice surface, and the channel should lie so prevailing winds won't drift snow across the bridge. Routing the bridge between sandbars yields shorter, stronger spans.

The area upstream is also examined. There should be no significant inflow channels directly upstream (closer than 2 km) which may disrupt normal flow.

The bridge should be as close to existing roads as possible because it merely continues those roads. However, for safety, ease of construction and maintenance, the crossing loca-

An ice bridge built in Alaska by the 23d Engineer Co. The 23d built three ice bridges during Brim Frost 83.

tion has a higher selection priority than its distance to roads, as long as the bridge is easily accessible to wheeled vehicles.

A final primary consideration is the near and far banks. A gradual slope to the stream is best because it ensures ease of access by vehicles. If the banks are too steep, ramps are built from the banks to the stream.

After the bridge location has been chosen, the final check before construction is measuring (profiling) the ice. The profile is the most important step in ice bridging and must be conducted diligently and without shortcuts. All safety precautions must be observed and immediate aid ready in case of ice failure while crews are working.

A profile crew is two or more people, with the lead person tied to the rest of the crew by a line. The lead

A profiling crew testing ice thickness.

man bores test holes at 10-foot intervals with an auger or ice-chopper. As he crosses the river, the following persons (the recording crew) belay him and are prepared to assist if he breaks through. Data is recorded for each hole, including its location, ice thickness, snow cover, channel depth and ice quality.

If the profile crew encounters ice 4 inches thick or less, they don skis or snowshoes for safety before continuing. Ice less than 3 inches is too thin; a different site or a standard fixed bridge must be used.

When the profile is complete, all information necessary to decide on accepting the ice bridge location has been collected and construction may begin.

Ice bridge construction is the process of artificially increasing the rate of ice formation on the bridge surface.

The first step is dealing with snow covering the crossing strip. The snow is cleared in a lane 30 meters wide. The roadway is standard military road width, but a 30-meter lane ensures plenty of ice to support it. The snow may be cleared entirely off of the bridge or be compacted to no more than 2 inches thick. Compacting may be done with snowmobiles, skis, or snowshoes. Any snow removed from the bridge must be distrubuted to avoid snow berms higher than 12 inches on the edges of the bridge.

Whether the snow is cleared or compacted, the next step is flooding. Hand-operated or gas-powered ice augers are used to drill 12-inch wide holes in the ice on the downstream side of the bridge. The river or lake becomes the water source for a pumping operation.

"We pump water up from below and flood the ice about an inch deep, let it freeze, then flood it again, until we get the thickness we want," explains SFC Lincoln V. Thompson, operations and training NCO, 23d Engineer Company (Combat) (Heavy), 172d Infantry Brigade. "We've crossed a D7 'cat' on 32 inches of ice and it weighs 54,200 pounds with its bullblade."

The 23d Engineer Company uses three commercial, electric submersible pumps (each powered by a five-kilowatt generator), or gasoline-powered centrifugal pumps to raise layers of water.

"The commercial pumps are better for this job than the centrifugal ones," says Thompson. "The electric

NEAR SHORE APPROACH NEAR SHORE

5'
X - First hole
15'
X - Second hole
30'
X - Third hole
20'
30'
X - Fourth hole
CURRENT
UPSTREAM
PROPOSED CENTERLINE
DOWNSTREAM
30'
X
30'
X
30'
X
15'
X - Last hole
5'

FAR SHORE APPROACH FAR SHORE

TEST HOLE DISTANCES

A typical arrangement of profile holes.

pumps are self-priming and won't freeze in extreme cold. We just drill a hole in the ice, drop it in and start pumping."

"How fast we can build a bridge depends on temperature and how long the bridge must be," explains CPT Christopher M. Turletes, 23d Engineer company commander. "We figure one squad with one pump can freeze 100 feet of bridge per hour at -10°F.

With the slowness of clearing snow and freezing water, ice bridging can't be considered a hasty crossing for combat use.

"Tactically, ice bridges are used on main supply routes and lines of communication," says Turletes. "They are deliberate crossings used when the area beyond is secured and ready to be opened for resupply."

Like the pumps they use, some of the 23d Engineer Company's ice-bridging techniques deviate from standard Army procedure.

"We've built a lot of ice bridges and done considerable research with the Corps' Cold Regions Research Laboratory (CRRL)," explains Turletes. "There's also a lot of research being done commercially on the North Slope with ice bridges, and we've used that, too.

"Figures in TM 5349, *Arctic Construction*, indicate a 200-foot width for ice bridges," Turletes says. "Of course, the wider the bridge, the stronger it is. But the TM tends to be conservative. Our experience and CRRL's research shows that an ice bridge over 14 inches thick is strong enough to resist bending, and that 30 meters is a good width to work with."

Some experts recommend replacing three or four inches of snow on the bridge as a treadway.

"Snow is an insulator and tends to protect the ice bridge from cold air," says Turletes. "After the bridge is constructed, we replace no more than one inch of snow for a wearing surface."

Other experts advocate freezing timbers into the ice to reinforce the bridge.

"Our research and experience shows that logs, planks and straw don't really strengthen an ice bridge," says Turletes. "They are darker, absorb solar heat and could weaken the bridge. We often use logs for ramps and treadways, but not frozen into the ice itself."

After the 23d Engineer Compa builds their ice bridges, they ma tain several safety factors. "When doubt, profile," is the rule. They m sure the ice thickness every eig hours not only to monitor the thi ness of the ice, but also the distance the bottom of the channel. "If the builds up too thick below, the wa dams up behind the bridge and t pressure can cause shears at a weak point," says Thompson.

The 23d Engineer Company bu three ice bridges at Fort Gree Alaska, during exercise Brim Fr 83. Their mission during the exerc was to operate, maintain a upgrade the exercise's main sup route.

1LT Mark L. Prahl is platoon lea of the earthmoving platoon, 23d En neer Co., Ft. Richardson, Alaska. designed airfields for the Corps Engineers, Anchorage District, d ing his previous assignment. He ha bachelor's degree in engineering fr the University of Wisconsin (Ma son), and is a graduate of the Engin Officer Basic Course and the A borne School.

FOR YOUR INFORMATION

TITLE	OFFICE	TITLE	OFFICE
M9 ACE Effectiveness Analysis (Aug 80)	ATZA-CDE	*Poster* FB 123 - Soviet Combat Engineer Tactics, Groupings and Techniques (Jul 82)	ATZA-PAA-A
Countermine Functional Area Analysis (Jun 82)	ATZA-CDE		
Functional Area Analysis of Land-mine Warfare (Jun 82)	ATZA-CDE	*Poster* FB 124 - Soviet Engineer Equipment - Division and Below (Jul 82)	ATZA-PAA-A
Points of Contact (USAES) (Jun 82)	ATZA-CDE	*Poster* FB 125 - Soviet Combat Engineer Organizations Below Divisions (Jul 82)	ATZA-PAA-A
USAES DCD Periodic Intelligence Report (PERINTREP) (Quarterly)	ATZA-CDC		

For information contact: Commandant, USAES, ATTN: ATZA-_____, Ft. Belvoir, Virginia 22060

TITLE	OFFICE	TITLE	OFFICE
TRADOC Pam 525-18, US Army Operational Concept for Countermine Operations (Jun 82)	ATDO-ZD	TRADOC Pam 525-19, US Army Operational Concept for Land-mine Warfare (Jun 82)	ATDO-ZD

For information contact: Commander, TRADOC, ATTN: ATDO-ZD, Ft. Monroe, Virginia 23651

GINEERS

nology

port the infantry brigades, and a deep-strike company supports light-assault missions (compare Figures 1 & 2).

The deep-strike company is a special organization that deploys with a maneuver unit, including on airmobile missions behind enemy lines. Construction of hasty airstrips, building obstacles and digging gun and vehicle emplacements are primary missions.

"The capability to accompany infantry units on airmobile missions and take along the necessary support equipment never realistically existed before now," says LTC James E. Corbin, 15th Engineer Battalion commander. "The deep-strike engineer concept will provide much-needed support to maneuver units assigned such missions."

To support these missions, the battalion is becoming a far-reaching, hard-hitting force to complement HTLD capabilities. Their first combat priority is mobility, followed by survivability and countermobility. Eliminating most large, heavy equipment and sectionalizing items like scrapers and graders helps streamline the battalion.

Using smaller bulldozers and light gap-crossing equipment, the battal-

The Small Emplacement Excavator is a highly prized asset.

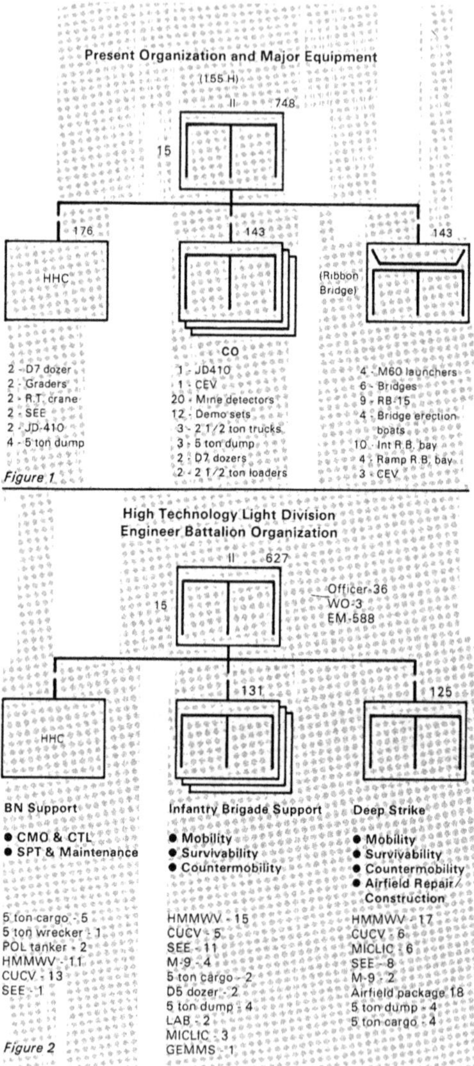

Figure 1

Figure 2

ion will have an airmobile package able to travel with the infantry it supports. The High Mobility Multi-Purpose Wheeled Vehicle, the Mine Clearing Line Charge, the Ground Emplaced Mine Scattering System, and the Light Assault Bridge are all being incorporated into the battalion. However, its most highly prized engineering assets are the Small Emplacement Excavator (SEE) and the M9 Armored Combat Earthmover (ACE).

The SEE is a light, multi-purpose vehicle with a 45 mph road speed. Its four-wheel drive, combined with a differential lock, gives it the power to easily travel through mud and sand. Its two independent hydraulic systems can be used simultaneously. Any of its many attachments can be changed within 30 minutes, allowing one SEE to do a variety of tasks. The battalion has 12 SEEs for concept evaluation.

The M9 ACE can maneuver 200 miles across open terrain without refueling, carry troops, swim and do the jobs of a five-ton dumptruck, 'dozer and grader. It can dig a TOW position in about 10 minutes and M1 tank position in 20-30 minutes.

"The M9 finally puts combat engineers out front, constructing obstacles and preparing TOW and tank positions," says CPT James C. Morris, a former 15th Engineers company commander. "It gives us the same mobility as the infantry we support. With it, we can get in quick, do the job and get out. The M9 frees engineer squads for obstacle construction and demolition missions."

The high-technology engineer battalion revolutionizes the capabilities of combat engineers.

"Now we can lead the way in the attack," says MAJ Emmett Stobbs, battalion executive officer. "In defense or withdrawal, we can do a better job of emplacing mines and building obstacles. Under the new concept, we'll move and fight beside the infantry as an integral part of the combined arms team."

1LT Robert E. L. Titus is the assistant public affairs officer, 9th Infantry Div., Fort Lewis, Wash. He has also served with the division's 3/39 Infantry as a platoon leader and S3 (Air). He is a graduate of Virginia Military Institute.

The CPX AS A TRAINING AID

by MAJ Harley Brinkley & CPT Paul E. Dorr

A well-planned command post exercise (CPX) is an exceptionally valuable training aid. Using a CPX, the battalion commander, for example, can concentrate on training and evaluating his staff and commanders without draining personnel, equipment and monetary resources.

The 875th Engineer Battalion (Combat), Arkansas Army National Guard, participated in two CPXs as preparation for its external Army Training Evaluation Program (ARTEP). The commander of the 875th requested the 95th Division Maneuver Training Command (MTC), Oklahoma City, Okla., to prepare and administer the CPXs and the ARTEP. To establish continuity among the exercises, the 95th MTC developed a three-part, two-year training program.

The CPXs were designed to provide the battalion first-hand experience with the combined arms concept while learning the extent to which combat engineers could be used as a combat multiplier. Each CPX integrated the general scenario guidelines and specific training objectives of the battalion commander. Additionally, objectives and situations entirely new to the battalion were also injected to create a vibrant, intensive training environment. Doctrine and recently published articles were used extensively to develop the missions and situations portrayed to the battalion.

The CPX centered around the European scenario in which the 10th U.S. Corps defends the Fulda Gap in West Germany. Several basic changes were made in the problem to enhance the training potential of the CPX, including:

- The 3d Corps from Fort Hood, Texas, defended the sector to add CAPSTONE realism.
- The covering force mission was given to an armored cavalry regiment (ACR).

The 875th Engineer Battalion was attached to the ACR in the covering force area, making the battalion an important element of a combined arms team located well forward in the defensive area with little time to perform a mammoth mission. This also met the Guard commander's desire to locate the battalion forward of the committed division's rear boundary.

The first CPX, called Pioneer, covered the two days before violation of the international border by opposing forces (OPFOR). The exercise emphasized the planning functions vital to success in the defense. During the second CPX, Pioneer II, the covering force battle was fought. The obstacle and denial plans developed in CPX Pioneer were implemented and the withdrawal of the ACR from the covering force area planned. In the ARTEP, the battalion supported the ACR in the corps rear area as they constructed blocking positions.

For CPX Pioneer; the 875th Engineer's commander established the following training objectives:

- Review command relationships.
- Improve staff coordination.
- Review and practice task planning for engineers in the defense.

The CPX started two hours before the battalion's attachment to the regiment with the engineer battalion commander and his S3 being briefed by the ACR commander. The major tasks assigned to the engineers included:

- Conduct a terrain analysis and recommend changes to phase lines, control points, maneuver routes, unit positions and unit sectors as required.

- Prepare the engineer subparagraph to paragraph three of the ACR's operations order (OPORD), including task organization.

- Assume operational control (OPCON) of the regiment's engineer company.

- Prepare the *Engineer Annex* and the *Obstacle/Denial Annex* to the ACR's OPORD. Coordinate and include all engineer actions down to squadron level to reduce paperwork for squadron commanders.

After analyzing the assigned missions and his unit's capabilities, the 875th commander identified further areas for staff concentration:

- The wheel-mounted engineer battalion did not have the flexibility and maneuver mobility compatible with the regiment.

- The battalion lacked organic capability to communicate throughout the covering force area due to distance, terrain and shortages of equipment.

Perhaps the most unique feature of the CPX over past exercises was the attachment of the engineer battalion to a tactical unit. The engineer commander's responsibility was vastly expanded, for now he had to consider the engineer requirements of a unit four to five times larger than his battalion. When the engineer tasks exceeded his unit's capabilities, he had no engineer group to which he could turn for assistance.

By changing the chain-of-command from engineer to tactical channels, command and support relationships, as well as mobility and communications situations, were practiced and improved. By having a mechanized engineer company OPCON to the battalion, new problems arose for a staff which previously had not deployed "engineers without dump trucks." With a company OPCON to his battalion, companies in direct support of the squadrons and a company in general support of the regiment, the engineer commander and his staff had to understand, in detail, all command and support relationships.

Developing the obstacle plan and and writing the annexes for the ACR's OPORD required detailed coordination. Intra- and interstaff coordination were necessary to ensure that the obstacle plan supported the maneuver concept and that the plan could be supported logistically.

While writing the engineer and obstacle annexes, the engineer battalion planned and coordinated those expressed and implied missions given by the regimental commander. Those missions, by their nature, coincided with the tasks designated by the engineer battalion commander in his training guidance for the exercise, i.e., crater roads and construct vehicle and track defilade positions.

The training benefits from CPX Pioneer were exceptional. The 875th commander developed his next year's training schedule around training deficiencies identified in the CPX. Because of such focused training, the battalion personnel became considerably more qualified to conduct engineer tasks in the defense.

CPX Pioneer II continued the Pioneer scenario with an international border violation. During the exercise, the 875th Engineers performed three major tasks:

- Implemented the obstacle and denial plan prepared during CPX Pioneer.

- Supported the delaying effort of the ACR in the covering force area by preparing fighting and protective positions.

- Planned for the withdrawal under fire of the ACR, including route selection and evaluating potential crossing sites of the Fulda River.

As in CPX Pioneer, Pioneer II provided the battalion commander with the challenge of providing engineer support in a highly mobile defense to a unit whose mobility far exceeded his own. The special areas of concern identified in CPX Pioneer continued to exist, but since they had been iden-

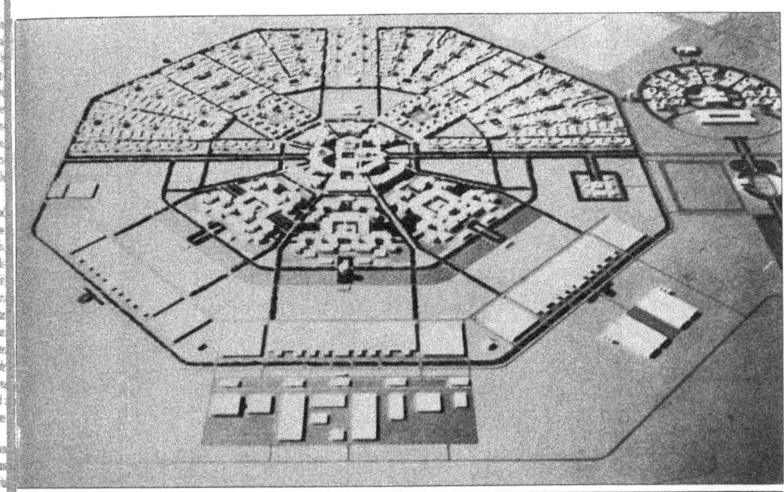

UNDER KKMC

by Donald E. Slater

A remote desert area in the Kingdom of Saudi Arabia is being transformed by the Army Corps of Engineers into a 16 square mile military base for 70,000 military and maintenance personnel and their families.

When completed, the $7 billion King Khalid Military City (KKMC) will be a major cantonment for Saudi troops defending Saudi Arabia's borders. The installation is about 950 kilometers northeast of Jiddah and 450 kilometers north of Riyadh in a remote, sparsely populated desert near the Iraqi border.

The city is octagonal with a Centrum containing the main religious, administrative, and social facilities. All housing is north of the Centrum; all support functions are south. The Saudi Engineer Center and School is west of the city; the parade ground, stadium, race track, hospital, and VIP quarters are to the east. The water supply is also east of the city.

As James Michener began his novel *Centennial* with a description of that town's geology, so the first step in building KKMC was to study the earth that would support the Corps' largest construction project.

Topography

The city is located on a flat, gravelly plain. Relief is in the 7 meter range with a median elevation of about 410 meters. The regional slope is from the northwest with localized depressions. Surface materials consist of lag deposits ("desert pavement") resulting from deflation activity, and surface rock exhibits a film of iron oxide ("desert varnish"). Vegetation is sparse.

Geology

The King Khalid Military City is within a subdivision of the Arabian shelf called the Northern Tuwayq Segment. The area is composed of sedimentary rock from the Paleozoic, Mesozoic, and Cenozoic Ages. The sedimentary rocks are covered in many areas with a thin deposit from the Tertiary and Quaternary Ages.

Rock at the site is sandstone, limestone, and sandstone-conglomerate. The limestone shows evidence of solution activity which formed small caves, pinnacles, and an uneven surface. The solution activity apparently happened before the Quaternary. The sandstone conglomerate is generally weakly-to-moderately cemented. Most of the observed rock exhibits moderately-to-widely spaced, high-angled joints.

Soils

The soils at the site are silty-sands, silts, gravelly-sands, and gravel 0.3 to 3.0 meters deep. The geologic soil age is Quaternary. The gravels are composed of transported subrounded to rounded particles and are mainly igeneous or metamorphic. Soil cementation increases with

The $7 billion King Khalid Military City is the largest construction project ever handled by the Corps. It will be completed late this decade.

depth. The soil's silt component is of low plasticity. There are scattered pockets and layers of gypsum. Permeabilities are low to medium. The soils are moisture-sensitive when remolded during compaction.

Ground Water

Ground water was usually not encountered within the depths explored. However, human activities have caused localized perched water tables. Surface irrigation contributes to forming ground water, as do pipe leaks and sewage disposal areas. Shortly after the city is occupied, ground water will probably become perched on the bedrock, with a water table developing within less than 3 feet of the surface.

Exploration

Subsurface exploration at KKMC was performed in several phases between 1974 and the present. The phases consisted of general exploration for such things as coarse and fine aggregate sources, foundations for structures and specific exploration for facilities like the airfield, stadium, underground storage tanks, and ammunition storage.

Borings ranged in depths between 5 to 15 meters with several extending to 30 meters. Borings were done with truck or trailer-mounted drill rigs using both diamond rotary and hollow stem augers.

Many test pits and test trenches were excavated to depths of up to 5 meters. The test pits were dug with a backhoe to determine the effort required to excavate soil and cemented soil with mechanical equipment. The test trenches were to determine the ripability of surficial rock. Test pits and test trenches both supplied samples of soil and rock for engineering evaluation.

Two types of percolation tests were performed at various locations throughout the site. One type involved a 30-centimeter hole with a 24-hour soak. The other involved a test pit hole with a 24-hour soak. Both were performed to evaluate the rate of water flow into the soil and rock. Extensive laboratory testing was performed on the soil.

Applications

The soil and decomposed rock may be excavated by normal heavy equipment, with blasting required for excavation to any appreciable depths.

"A military engineer must have the ability to improvise. He will have to do his job with what is available on the spot."

Brigadier General (Ret.) Hugh J. Casey

ENG INGE A FADING ART?

by COL Don W. Barber

Any student of military history understands that war places great demands on the military engineer. In wars from antiquity to the 20th century, there are countless examples of engineer ingenuity turning the tide of battle.

Peacetime training, however, places little emphasis on engineer ingenuity and its precursor, reconnaissance. We must rekindle interest in ingenuity during training because the ability to improvise will certainly be a key factor on the next battlefield.

Ingenuity is more than mere technical expertise. It is the engineer leader's ability to assimilate data *and to use it creatively!* The scarcity of resources in combat has frequently driven engineers to ingenious solutions. Moreover, innovative use of locally available materials was the paramount factor in most engineer successes on past battlefields.

Such ingenuity, based on personal reconnaissance, was demonstrated during World War II by then-Colonel Emerson C. Itschner, engineer of the Advanced Section (ADSEC), Communications Zone, Europe.

On Aug. 12, 1944, Itschner took a mission of great importance and difficulty. General Patton, who had broken through the German lines and was racing towards Paris, needed fuel for his tanks and trucks. Itschner had to rebuild the railroad to LeMans in three days.

He faced an immense job. The rail line extended 137 miles, seven bridges were down, and three rail yards were heavily bombed. Few watering and coaling facilities remained. He had 75 hours to do a job requiring several months.

ADSEC's 10,500 engineer troops were scattered throughout Normandy. Itschner had to notify them, assign tasks, and deploy them between Folligny and LeMans.

But first came personal reconnaissance. Itschner flew over the rail net to select lines that could be quickly repaired. He ruled out the most

Captured German equipment is used by engineers of D Co., 332d Engineer Reg., to repair a railroad near Aldenhoven, Germany, during World War II.

direct route because bridges at Pontaubault and Laval were too damaged for quick repair. He decided to use the double-track between LaChapelle Athenaise and LeMans.

The bridge over the Selune River at St. Hilaire-du-Harcourt presented the worst obstacle. The Germans had blown the south end off its abutment. The 347th Engineer General Service (GS) Regiment cut off the damaged end, jacked up the bridge, and rested it on a crib. Men went without sleep so they could complete this task in three days.

When Major General Cecil R. Moore, chief engineer, ETO, flew over the bridge with Itschner six hours before deadline, he saw spelled out in white cement, "Will finish at 2000." And it was.

The first trainload of gasoline left Folligny Aug. 15 and reached LeMans two days later. Thirty trains carrying fuel for Patton followed at 30-minute intervals.

Meanwhile, another general service regiment began repairing bridges at Pontaubault and Laval. When completed by the end of August, they allowed opening a better line to LeMans. Itschner's troops helped speed along the gasoline required for Patton's armor to thrust across Northern France and shorten the European war.

While the LeMans railroad illustrates personal reconnaissance, it doesn't tell all about engineer ingenuity.

The American forces were critically short of bridge materials. In earlier reconnaissances, ADSEC engineers spotted quantities of German-produced meter beams. In an interview conducted by the Office of the Chief of Engineers, Itschner recalled how they were put to use:

All through Europe we found these big meter beams . . . We found other sized beams, too, but the meter beams were the mainstay of the Germans and they were all stamped with the name of a single steelmill—Hadir—located at Differdange, Luxembourg. So we determined right from the start if we ever got into Luxembourg, and we thought we would, we'd head right away for Differdange. And as soon as it was captured we had our people there, and lo and behold, the steelmill was intact. They were badly in need of rubber belts, and of course we didn't have any of them, but we found some others and replaced them, cannibal-

materials spotted during reconnaissance aren't used in a mission. In other words, we aren't fostering battlefield ingenuity.

There are many obstacles to creating a proper training environment—restraints on using locally available materials, prohibitions against cutting trees, training areas without usable materials, and environmental objections.

Many leaders also argue you can't teach ingenuity. That mentality is hogwash. It better be, because we'll need all our ingenuity in the next war.

Engineer leaders should be fostering an innovative spirit. If you have suggestions for improving officer or NCO training or if you tried something in your unit that may improve our curriculum, tell us. Write to USAES, DTAD, Fort Belvoir, Va. 22060. The Engineer School is incorporating the topic of ingenuity into instruction programs.

With military history as a beacon, we can foster a creative spirit by meeting challenges with enthusiasm and imagination. Between those of us at the Engineer School and each of you in the field, we can work together to bring ingenuity back to the forefront in combat engineering.

COL Don W. Barber commands the Engineer Center Brigade at Fort Belvoir. He has completed Engineer Officer Basic and Advanced Courses, Airborne and Ranger training, Command and General Staff College, and the Industrial College of the Armed Forces. He has a master's degree in civil engineering from the University of Tennessee and is a registered professional engineer in Virginia. Past assignments include HQ, U.S. Army Vietnam; Operation Deepfreeze; Operations Personnel Directorate, DCSPER, DA; and command and staff positions in the 7th and 8th Infantry Divisions. Engineer School assignments include director, Directorate of Training and Doctrine and director, Department of Military Engineering.

ENGINEER SOLUTION

1. 5/Z/?/4.1/(OB)

   5-Minimum width encountered was 5 meters.

   Z-Route is type Z anytime a ford or ferry is encountered along a route.

   ?-Lowest Military Load Classification-No bridge along the route and the load classification along the worst section of the route is undetermined.

   4.1-Lowest overhead clearance was encountered at the railroad crossing, 4.1 meters.

   (OB)-Used if any obstructions were encountered, i.e., sharp curves, ferry ford, overhead clearance 4.3 meters, and traveled-way width of underpass.

2. Vehicle/Pedestrian
3. Difficult
4. 15 meters
5. Difficult
6. 6 meters
7. 1:12,500
8. No seasonal limitations
9. 11%
10. 30 minutes
11. Yes-overhead clearance is 4.3 meters
12. Tracked vehicle turn-off with coniferous concealment

Topographic Support:

A new operational concept

by CPT(P) David R. Gallay

Battle graphics, survey data, terrain analysis, updated maps and reproductions—all are products and services required by commanders at all levels. What is the best way to provide those essential services to the light, mobile units of the U.S. Central Command (CENTCOM)?

Fort Belvoir's 30th Engineer Battalion (Topographic) (Army), part of the reactivated Third U.S. Army (which includes CENTCOM), probably would support a CENTCOM deployment. After analyzing the support requirements of likely CENTCOM missions, the 30th has devised a new topographic operational concept.

The analysis defined the battalion's mission in terms of general support—the surveying, mapping, terrain analysis, and map storage/distribution requirements of a light force operation at echelons above corps.

The analysis baseline was predicated on the current Modified Table of Organization and Equipment (Figure 1).

The major objective of the analysis was to develop a self-sufficient and responsive task organization. Self-sufficiency, for analysis purposes, is achieved when an element meets its topographic support requirements without operational backup. Responsiveness is attained when it meets its topographic requirements in the time set in the topographic chapter of the Engineer School's Mission Area Analysis.

The Concept

The battalion's preliminary analysis suggests the organization shown in Figure 2. The analysis also suggests that this organization can provide both general "base-plant" topographic support in rear areas and mobile, combat topographic support.

In concept, the battalion conduct base-plant operations in a semisecur location. Its headquarters compan performs staff and unit housekeep ing functions. The staff is augmente with the major who was the terrai detachment commander under th standard MTOE. With the detac ment ceasing to exist under the ne concept, the major becomes th

CURRENT ORGANIZATION

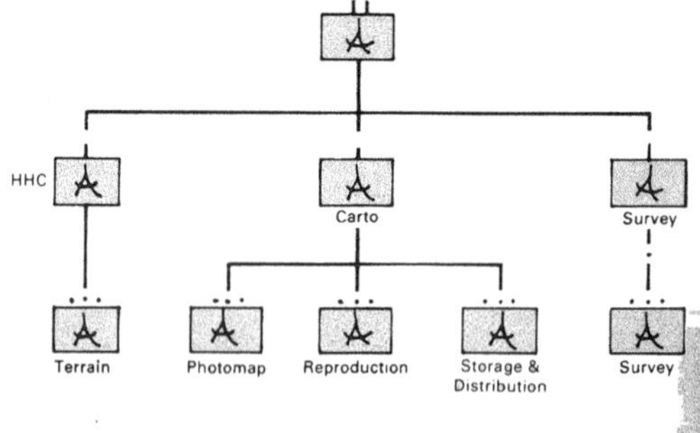

Figure 1. Current MTOE of the 30th Engineer Battalion (Topographic) (Army).

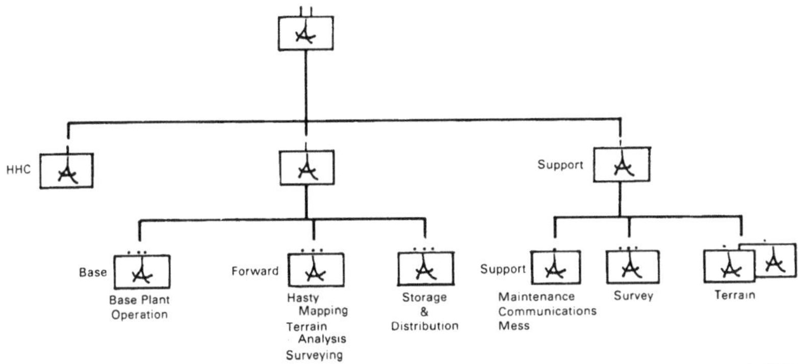

Figure 2. The 30th Engineers' analysis suggests that this organizational structure would best support a CENTCOM deployment.

assistant command topographer. He or she represents the battalion commander and serves as a liaison to higher headquarters.

The new concept shows the topographic company with three platoons: base, forward, and storage/distribution. In the semisecure location, the base platoon performs most mapping missions, while the storage and distribution platoon prepares standard Defense Mapping Agency and nonstandard Army map products for supply-point distribution.

(The Engineer School and others know that storage and distribution functions may be better performed by logistic units using supply support concepts, and that there may be a need for greater Defense Mapping Agency support. However, for the time being, the 30th Engineers will rely on battalion assets.)

As its title implies, the forward platoon isn't confined to a rear area. Its mappers, surveyors, and terrain analysts provide forward combat topographic support to the corps' topographic assets.

The topographic support company is also in the semisecure area. It provides support with specially tailored teams to meet specific requirements. The support platoon, for example, supports the battalion with maintenance, communications and mess resources. The remaining company elements, the survey platoon and two terrain teams, provide general topographic support where needed.

Evaluation and Interpretation

This task organization, plus four alternatives, were evaluated in tactical exercises without troops. Besides the criteria of self-sufficiency and responsiveness, the analysis addressed command and control, communications, logistics, and liaison.

Based on the tests, the task organization's support platoon appears to enhance logistic and communication support. The forward platoon also increases the battalion's operational capabilities. Additionally, the assistant command topographer provides good liaison with both higher and lower headquarters. More importantly, both response time and operational self-sufficiency are improved significantly.

Future Actions

The 30th Engineer Battalion will continue to test the new organization. The plan is to conduct a command post exercise of the battalion's most likely mission. This will be followed by two field training exercises, the first evaluated internally, the second externally. All tests will be compared with the battalion's ARTEP performance when the unit was configured conventionally.

The findings and conclusions of those tests will be consolidated, recommendations prepared, and the entire analysis submitted to the Engineer School. Perhaps a new organizational standard will evolve.

Topographic support to the combined arms team is crucial. The 30th Engineer Battalion's proposed task organization points us in the direction to more effectively support the battlefield commander.

CPT(P) David R. Gallay, XO of the 30th Engineer Battalion, has a bachelor's degree from the U.S. Military Academy, a master's degree in engineering from Purdue University and a master's in management from the University of Southern California. He has commanded engineer companies in Korea and Germany and is a graduate of the Command and General Staff College. He is a registered professional engineer in Virginia.

NONPOLLUTING

WASH FACILITIES

They use up to 99% less water and 86% less energy.

by Joe Matherly & Jerry Benson

A system developed by the Army Construction Engineering Research Laboratory (CERL), Champaign, Ill., cuts time spent washing a mud-caked tank from three hours to 10 minutes. The system also solves attendant wash rack problems of clogging storm drains and polluting adjacent water supplies. CERL's concepts are being successfully applied at Forts Lewis, Wash., and Polk, La.

Fort Lewis completed a one-year pollution abatement project based on CERL recommendations. Project results confirm that the CERL procedures control water pollution from vehicle maintenance areas and reduce time spent on vehicle cleaning.

The Army Environmental Hygiene Agency (AEHA) Western Region Office evaluated the CERL-designed systems at Fort Lewis and found them performing effectively. Better washing equipment, appropriate water pressures, improved station layouts and recycling treated water reduced potable water use by 90 to 95 percent. At a CERL wash facility at Fort Lewis' Yakima Firing Range, washing an M60 tank used only one percent of the water and 14 percent of the energy needed with the previous system.

David Hanke, chief, Sanitation Branch, Utilities Division at Fort Lewis says, "We remove 12,000 cubic feet of dirt from vehicles annually. The wash racks were scattered and storm drains got so clogged they were cleaned once a week. Now there are only two collection facilities to clean. The operation is a dream compared to what it was."

Historically, Fort Lewis has had difficulty meeting pollution-control requirements for water leaving the installation. The primary pollution source was vehicle maintenance activities.

The changes at Fort Lewis motor pools involved eliminating wash racks, constructing vehicle maintenance platforms that use hot-water cleaners, improved waste oil collection/storage, and using overhead cranes. The hot-water cleaners eliminated using vast amounts of detergents, solvents and other aids for cleaning engines and mechanical components. The greatly reduced, simplified waste-water flow is pretreated in small, comparatively inexpensive gravity oil and sediment separators before entering the sewers.

Fort Polk recently began operating a new centralized wash facility using the "tank bath" option. The bath is a water basin with adjustable water levels through which tracked and wheeled vehicles drive. Both entrance and exit areas are equipped with fixed spray guns that an operator plays across the vehicle. The bath's purpose is to wet and quickly remove most soil on the vehicle. The baths also retain the soil, avoiding the costly handling at individual wash-racks.

Jim Kelly, general engineer, Master Planning Branch, Facilities Engineers at Fort Polk, says, "Washing an M60 tank took a crew of four people three to four hours because of the thick clay mud here. Our new facility with the same crew washes it in about 10 minutes; the record is six minutes. This lets soldiers concentrate on training and maintenance, and boosts morale by getting soldiers out of the motor pool and home sooner."

Joe Matherly is the team leader of CERL's Maintenance Facility Pollution Abatement Team. He has a B.S. in chemistry from Eastern Illinois University and a M.S. in environmental engineering from the University of Illinois. He is a registered professional engineer in Illinois.

Jerry Benson is an environmental engineer with CERL's Environmental Division. He has a B.S. in civil engineering from the University of Illinois.

At this new Ft. Polk facility, M60 tanks are washed in 10 minutes.

"Why wasn't I selected?"

by CSM (Ret.) Marvin Knowles

members must base their decisions on the NCO's Official Military Personnel File (OMPF).

Each year, DA announces the dates for all centralized promotion selection boards. Messages alert all NCOs in the zones of consideration to ensure their OMPFs are complete and to verify the information in their promotion packet.

When I sat on a promotion board several years ago, I was shocked at how many OMPFs were incomplete. NCOs must remember that to the board, *your OMPF is you.*

Here are some observations from recent E-7, E-8 and E-9 selection boards:

Physical fitness: Sometimes a service member's height and weight could not be verified. The data was either not posted or not current on the DA Form 2-1. Some official photographs did not correspond to OMPF height and weight statements. In other instances, photos and records showed the NCO was overweight, but no comments or corrective action were noted on EERs. An overweight condition is a major obstacle to being promoted.

Utilization and assignments: Some records revealed an NCO had a profile which logically prevented him from working in his primary MOS. However, the records didn't reflect what action was taken to reclassify him. Sometimes an NCO had spent a considerable amount of time in ROTC, as a recruiter, drill sergeant, instructor, or in an invalid TDA/MTOE position. These "off-line" assignments must be limited. Strive to be assigned to and do well in TOE leadership positions.

Performance and potential: Some EER numerical scores weren't supported by the narrative. On some reports, the rater and indorser recommended promoting the service member, yet the numerical rating was low. Indorsers many times merely parrot rater comments. Comments regarding performance should be specific; an appropriate level of NCOES and future assignments should be recommended.

Board recommendations: NCOs should serve in mainstream assignments and avoid repetitive tours outside the CMF. NCOs must maintain the weight standards listed in AR 600-9, and *must* validate their records before any board. Commanders and leaders need to know the importance of writing EERs which accurately reflect the NCO's performance. Records are important and NCOs must review them conscientiously.

Promotion isn't a reward for past performance; it's recognition of *potential* to serve in a position of greater responsibility. However, judging your potential is based on a review of your file—a file that must be accurate and up-to-date to be fair to you.

CSM (Ret.) Marvin Knowles was command sergeant major of the Engineer Center and School when he retired in 1982. He now lives in Petersburg, Va.

Career Notes

NCO & Enlisted Branch

Tougher Topo: The physical requirements for topographic soldiers have been upgraded to provide the Army with combat-ready field topographic units and to enhance this career management field.

The physical profile serial (PULHES) for MOSs 41B, 81C, 83E, 83F, and 81Z has been changed to ensure these soldiers are able to meet the physical demands of their job.

It should be stressed to commanders and soldiers alike that the physical profile serials listed for MOSs in AR 611-201 are only guidelines.

A common misconception about such changes is that soldiers whose physical profile doesn't meet the new MOS physical standards must be reclassified. This is not always the case.

As long as a soldier with a limiting physical profile can perform his MOS duties, no reclassification is necessary. However, if he can't perform his MOS duties, he should be encouraged to reclassify for medical reasons.

Warrant Officer Branch

Updating Records: Warrant officers must have up-to-date physicals, photographs and Officer Record Briefs (ORBs) for all promotion boards and senior course boards. Recent changes require a photograph for promotion boards.

Phase II Moves: Warrant Officer Advance Course Phase II moved from Fort Belvoir, Va., to Fort Leonard Wood, Mo. in April. Phase I remains at Aberdeen Proving Ground, Md.

Info: For information concerning warrant officer careers, contact CW4 Edward L. Walls, (202) 325-7839/3840; AVN 221.

Commissioned Officers Branch

Company Command: Current DA policy for company command tours of 18 months, plus or minus six months.

Preference Statement: A current preference statement is an important tool for your career manage[ment]. It's especially important that Engineer Branch, MILPERCEN, have you[r] current phone number, and your residence and official mailing address[es]. Also, list any special conditions, e.g., handicapped dependent.

Commissioned Officers, cont.

Official Photographs: DA selection boards use official photos in addition to the ORB and microfiche records. Photos should be updated every four years or after promotion; wear individual awards and a pressed, well-tailored uniform.

Civil School Applications: Officers who desire to compete for civil schools should apply to Engineer Branch. The Civil Schools Selection Board meets in September and March. Applications should be made on DA Form 1618-R. Graduate degree programs are restricted to shortage disciplines in the officer specialties. Applicants must have successful company command and be advanced course graduates.

3R and IG Assignments: Engineer officers captain to lieutenant colonel should plan on at least one ROTC, recruiting, reserve component advisor, or IG assignment.

Tech Jobs for LTs: Lieutenants who do well with troops and have a technical background may qualify for the few technical jobs available to lieutenants. For information, contact the Lieutenants' Assignment Officer.

SC 21 Restructure: DSCPER recently approved the restructuring of Speciality Code 21, "Engineer" for commissioned officers. This change, the culmination of an 18-month study by the Engineer School, separates SC 21 into two clearly defined functional areas: Combat Engineering and Facilities/Contract Management Engineering.

The new SC 21, "Combat Engineer," will encompass positions related to missions involving battlefield mobility, countermobility, survivability, and general engineering tasks. Also included are positions requiring combat engineer expertise. Like the other combat arms specialities, Combat Engineer will be an accession speciality. It will not be available as an additional speciality.

The new SC 23, "Facilities/Contract Construction Management Engineer," will include positions related to Army facilities/family housing support and positions related to civil works and military construction programs. SC 23 will be an additional speciality available to officers of all specialities.

MILPERCEN will review the records of current SC 21 officers and identify those qualified for Combat Engineer and Facilities Construction Management Engineer. Experience, education, and training will be the determining factors in reclassification. Most officers with SC 21 as their initial speciality will be assigned Combat Engineer. About 60 percent of these Combat Engineer officers will also be assigned the additional speciality of Facilities Construction Management Engineer. Officers who now have SC 21 as their additional speciality will generally be reclassified as SC 23.

MILPERCEN will send letters to each officer affected by speciality redesignation. The actual reclassification will occur between April and September, 1984. More details concerning this change will be in future issues of ENGINEER Magazine.

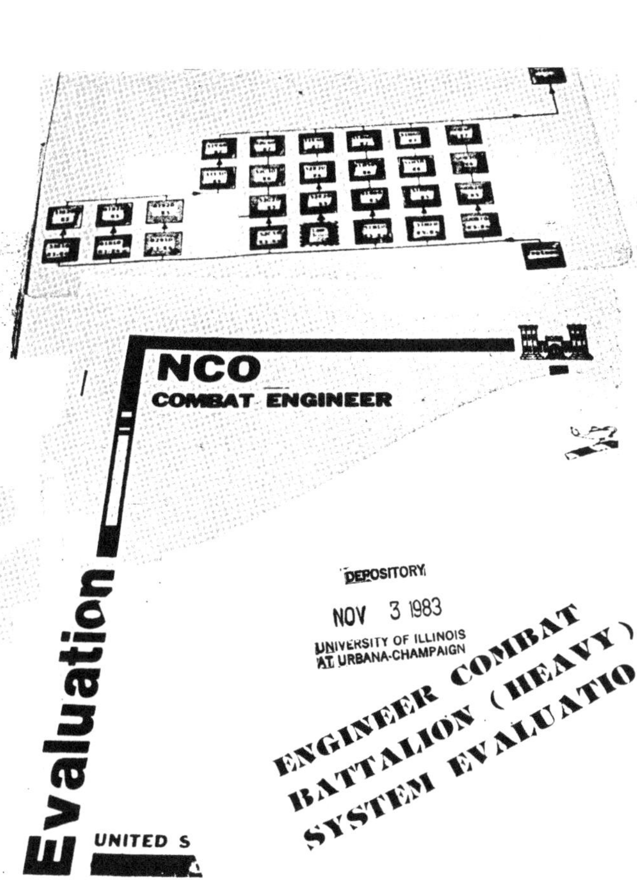
NCO
COMBAT ENGINEER
BC
Evaluation
UNITED S
ENGINEER COMBAT
BATTALION (HEAVY)
SYSTEM EVALUATIO

— FORUM —

BAT: A Better Cratering Tool?

by CPT Randy Lundberg

Despite the usefulness of the M180 Cratering Demolition Kit, the engineer still does not have an adequate system to deny the enemy use of high-speed avenues of approach.

One of our most frequently planned and time consuming countermobility tasks is cratering roads. To provide an easy and rapid method of cratering, development of the XM180 Cratering Demolition Kit was begun in 1964. This resulted in the current M180 system, fielded in 1981, which is effective against most road surfaces.

However, tests at Yuma Proving Ground in 1980 showed that the M180 does not produce an adequate obstacle on autobahn-type pavements.

A second generation cratering munition design study was done in 1982 by the Lawrence Livermore National Laboratory (LLNL) and the Royal Armament Research and Development Establishment (RARDE). The study's chief goal was to devise a hand-emplaced, top-attack munition to destroy concrete bridges by detonating 5 to 7 kg of high explosives .75 meters inside steel reinforced concrete.

Using LLNL's hydrodynamics modeling capability, coupled with technology from the U.S. Air Force's Hard Structures Munition (HSM) and Velocity Augmented Munitions (VAM) programs, the LLNL/RARDE team developed the bridge and tunnel (BAT) munition concept.

The operating principle of the improved system is similar to the M180's. This proposed device is expected to penetrate more than 6 feet of compacted earth or more than 3 feet of concrete, has a gross weight of 80 pounds (half that of the M180), and the only assembly requirement is setting up the tripod.

BAT's versatility is due to a unique arming and fuzing subsystem created by LLNL for the HSM and VAM. A long life, self-contained battery powers fuzes based on LLNL's high-energy slapper detonator technology which replaces blasting caps and does not require primary explosives. All charges and propellants are secondary explosives which have one-third the sensitivity of TNT.

The fuzing system would consist of a programming keyboard with a display that "walks" the operator through several options.

For example BAT could be set for command detonation. Since its power source is self-contained, the present blasting machines or any electrical source could be used to provide the fire signal. Also, its internal timer provides a set-and-forget capability, or it may be set to external control, where several BATs are fired from one programmable fuze.

The fuze also could be prc grammed for a long delay mai charge detonation for a pseudo min option. An anti-tamper mode coul be included. The system has the capa bility to be programmed in a rea area to save time at the demolitio site.

It may appear that a munition lik BAT would require years of mat rial, explosive and electroni research. Fortunately, the circuitr explosives and materials to produc BAT already exist as a result of pr vious work at LLNL. No advances i technology are required to field th system.

The major disadvantage of the sy tem may be that too many options ar available. Limiting the BAT to one c two firing options could simplify th design. This would permit emplo ment by any soldier.

Since only a limited knowledge explosives would be required to use single-mission BAT, covering for personnel could execute selecte reserved road craters to close sa lanes just after passing throug them. This would help reduce th problem of target handoff from th engineers to the covering force an allow a concentrated engineer effo on higher priority missions.

Although the M180 has reache the field, the requirement still exi for a device to rapidly and effective crater all hard surface roads. T engineer must have a reliable, eas emplaced cratering munition accomplish AirLand Battle count mobility tasks. If this same muniti

Please turn to BAT page

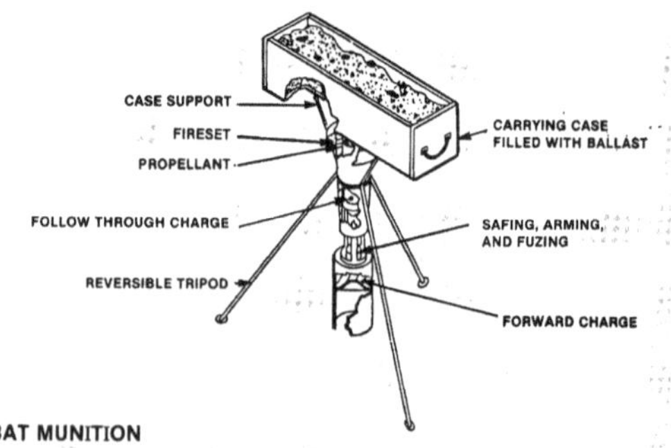

BAT MUNITION

LUME 13 NUMBER 2 SUMMER, 1983

the covers:

nt—Photo by John Florence.

k—CPT Steve Ressler shares his nor and considerable art talent with GINEER readers. A recent advanced rse graduate, CPT Ressler serves h the 12th Engineer Bn., 8th Infantry .

FEATURES

DEPARTMENTS

GINEER is an authorized publication of the U.S. Army Engineer Center and Fort Belvoir, Va. Unless specifically stated, terial appearing herein does not necessarily reflect official policy, thinking or endorsement by any agency of the U.S. Army. • en referring to military personnel in general, the words he, him, and his are used to represent personnel regardless of sex. All tographs contained herein are official U.S. Army photographs unless otherwise credited. Use of funds for printing this lication was approved by Headquarters, Department of the Army, July 22, 1981. Material herein may be reprinted if credit is en ENGINEER and the author. • ENGINEER'S objectives are to provide a forum for the exchange of ideas to inform and ivate and to promote the professional development of all members of the Army engineer family. • Direct correspondence with GINEER is authorized and encouraged. Inquiries, letters to the editor, manuscripts, photographs and general correspondence uld be sent to: Editor, ENGINEER, Directorate of Training Developments (TLD), Stop 16F4, Fort Belvoir, VA, 22060. ephone (703) 664-3082, AVN 354. • Subscriptions to ENGINEER are available through the Superintendent of Documents, U.S. verment Printing Office, Washington, D.C., 20402. A check or money order payable to Superintendent of Documents must ompany all subscription requests. Rates are $8.50 domestic (including APO and FPO addresses) and $10.65 for foreign resses. Individual copies are available at $4.50 per copy for domestic addresses and $5.65 for foreign addresses. • Second Class tage paid at Fort Belvoir, Va., and additional mailing offices. ISSN 0046-1989.

New ETL System For Pershing II

In preparation for the Pershing II missile deployment in Europe, seven noncommissioned, warrant and commissioned officers from CONUS and overseas units met at Ft. Belvoir to learn about a sophisticated mapping system that will accompany the new strategic weapon.

The system, called the Reference Scene Generation Facility (RSGF), was developed by the U.S. Army Engineer Topographic Laboratories (ETL) at Ft. Belvoir. When fielded, it will be used to make reference scenes (machine-readable maps) for Pershing II, the most accurate ballistic missile ever built.

The soldiers, from the 56th Field Artillery Brigade in Germany, the Field Artillery School and the TRADOC System Managers Office at Ft. Sill, Okla., visited ETL to learn how to train other soldiers on using the RSGF. The week-long session was designed to bring the user, the developer and the trainer to a common turf in order to iron out kinks that might crop-up in other soldier training sessions on the RSGF. The soldiers also made a reference scene that was to be used in test-firing the 34-foot missile this summer.

The RSGF was developed by ETL under a contract let to the Goodyear Aerospace Corporation. Test firings in January and February of this year were highly successful and validated the fact that soldiers can make sophisticated scenes by using the facility.

The missile's near-pinpoint accuracy is achieved through a technique called radar area correlation. As the reentry vehicle descends toward a target area, it compares live radar reflection from the target with reference scenes stored in the missile before launch. The reentry vehicle then makes course adjustments based on the comparative readings supplied by the guidance system.

Field artillery soldiers work with ETL's computer (inset); earlier successful test firing of Pershing II missile.

Pershing II is a truck-mounted, highly-mobile, theater nuclear weapon. It's the Army's newest and largest battlefield missile and is part of America's "dual-track" effort to achieve meaningful arms reduction. The missile is scheduled for deployment in Europe in December.

4675th Is #1

The 4675th Engineer Plt., USAR Center, Garden City, Kans., received the Outstanding Small Unit Award at this year's Reserve Officers Assn. convention in Salt Lake City, Utah. The 4675th is commanded by CPT Richard D. West.

ECTC '83: December 2-4, Arlington, Va.

The 1983 Engineer Commander's Training Conference (ECTC) will be held Dec. 2-4 at Stouffer's National Center Hotel in Arlington, Virginia (near Washington National Airport). Hotel reservations may be made toll free at (800) 325-5000.

UT ARNG Spells Relief

The 115th Engineer Group in Utah had a busy summer this year. When heavy snows and rains over a full water table led to massive mud slides and floods, over 100 pieces of equipment and 200 personnel were put to work. But despite some people working 18 to 20 hour shifts and some equipment operating on 24-hour shifts, 94 percent of the equipment functioned without problems.

Helicopters from associated Utah National Guard units were used to transport geologists for observation and testing. Information gained helped direct the engineers' activities. From Farmington (30 miles north of Salt Lake City) to Fillmore (165 miles south of Salt Lake City), homes, farmland, and businesses were rescued or dug-out.

The duties of the 1457th Combat Engineer Battalion were particularly demanding. Engineers from the 1457th convoyed 650 miles to Ft. Carson, Co. for "shake-out" and combined-arms FTXs, and then returned 650 miles to Utah on an emergency recall. Their personnel went into disaster relief service immediately. Their equipment averaged 94 to 97 percent in "up time" during two weeks of round-the-clock operation.

Mayors and county commissioners of the flood and mud-stricken areas expressed great relief at having National Guard assistance. Great appreciation was expressed by many local citizens who brought food and drink to the laboring engineers.

Combat Engineer Game Tourney

The Combat Engineer Game is a board game requiring knowledge of combat engineering and general military subjects. Designed for use by junior NCOs, it involves map reading, resource allocation, and a rank-adjusted scoring system.

The Engineer School is considering the establishment of Army-wide competition. Anyone playing the game can send their scorecard (verified by a supervisor, E6 and above) to USAES, ATZA-TDC-A, Ft. Belvoir, VA 22060, ATTN: 1LT Shafferman. A record of the highest scores will be maintained and published periodically in ENGINEER.

Anyone with ideas on expanding this competition are asked to contact 1LT Arthur Shafferman at the above address or by dialing (703) 664-2498/2384, AVN 354.

Correspondence Course Catalog Out

The Institute for Professional Development (IPD) has distributed the first comprehensive catalog of Army Correspondence Course Program courses and subcourses. The new publication, DA Pam 351-20, was sent to unit training offices, education centers and military occupation specialty (MOS) libraries. There are 490 courses and 3,000 subcourses listed in the 716-page catalog. Dated 1 March 1983, the book replaces all 22 volumes in the previous DA Pam 351-20 series.

All correspondence courses produced by 18 different TRADOC schools, plus four DoD/DA consolidated activities are included. Officers, warrant officers, and enlisted personnel in Active, Reserve, and National Guard components, cadets in ROTC and the National Defense Cadet Corps, authorized federal employees, foreign military personnel, government contractors, and non-U.S. citizens employed by DoD are eligible to study selected correspondence courses. This new catalog does not include correspondence courses offered by the ten DoD/DA non-consolidated activities, which administer their own courses, but it explains how and where to obtain them.

Completion certificates and a limited number of diplomas are awarded. Some courses may be accepted for credit toward a college degree. Questions pertaining to correspondence courses should be addressed to: Institute for Professional Development, U.S. Army Training Support Center, Newport News, VA 23628, or call (804) 878-3085, AVN 927.

CARRY-ON BAGGAGE—*With M203 grenade launcher and chainsaw in hand, SP4 Patrick Hawkins prepares to board a UH60 Black Hawk helicopter during FTX Eagle Strike III. The soldier is from B Co., 326th Engineer Bn. (Air Assault).*

News & Notes

CERL Tests Solar Power

The Energy Systems Division, U.S. Army Construction Engineering Research Laboratory (CERL), Champaign, Ill., recently completed the acceptance test of a 5-kilowatt photovoltaic (direct transfer of solar energy to electricity) power system. The system is installed on the roof of the Holman Guest House at Ft. Huachuca, Ariz., and is part of the Dept. of Energy-funded Federal Photovoltaic Utilization Program. The system, which has 196 photovoltaic panels, operates in parallel with the local utility grid without power storage, the grid providing power at night and during peak periods.

TRY THIS FOR BREAKFAST! *SP5 Joseph Garrido, 84th Engineer Bn. (Cbt)(Hvy), exercises with his M16 during morning PT at Schofield Barracks, Hawaii. The 84th regularly exercises with rifles and runs in combat boots. (Elaine Weil photo)*

Soldiers from C Co. race down an inverted ladder on the team assault course, one of 13 events in the 307th Engineer Bn.'s squad competition. (Marcus Castro photo)

Why Settle For Second?

"They were motivated . . . they gave it their best shot," said SSG Russell G. Smith of his winning squad members. As part of C Co., 307th Engineer Bn., 82nd Airborne Div., Smith's squad participated in a 13-task squad competition.

Included were a 10-kilometer run, emplacing a triple standard concertina fence, conducting a route reconnaissance, negotiating a compass course, setting up a 292 radio antenna and using proper radio procedures, making a target folder, preparing demolitions, making a one-rope bridge, emplacing and removing a hasty minefield, inspecting vehicles, decontaminating equipment, and running through the team assault course.

By winning a combination of key events, Smith's 3rd Sq., 2nd Plt. finished first in the competition. "We knew from the get-go we'd be up there," Smith said of the contest. "Why settle for second when you can be number one?"

LA Guard Takes On Civic Projects

Members of the 527th Engineer Bn., Louisiana Army National Guard sweated-out the summer on civil and military engineering projects that helped communities throughout the state.

Under the Army National Guard's Community Assistance Program, engineer units are able to provide construction equipment and manpower to help complete various civic projects.

The projects included resurfacing a parking lot and constructing sidewalks at the LSU Medical Center in Shreveport, extending a runway at Vivian Airport in Vivian, paving a parking lot in Grambling, building a stock barn at the Rapides Parish Coliseum in Alexandria, and building an animal shelter in Pineville.

Engineer People

FC Gerald Haake hoists a soldier in
aining at Ft. Leonard Wood, Mo.

*AIRBORNE—**PV1 Leland Allison** clears 6'9" in high jump competition. Allison, from B Co., 3rd Engineer Bn., 24th Infantry Div., perched himself 4" above the old record and captured first place in the high jump at the intramural track and field meet at Ft. Stewart, Ga.*

)rill Sgt. Grabs \rmy Award

This year's award for the Army rill Sergeant of the Year was given SFC **Gerald Haake**, a course ıanager at the Drill Sergeant School t Ft. Leonard Wood, Mo. Haake's ward was the culmination of a series f awards that began with Post Drill ergeant of the Year at Ft. Leonard Vood. His other awards included eing named TRADOC Drill Sereant of the Year and NCO of the Ionth, Quarter and Year with the 3th Engineer Bn. at Ft. Ord, Calif., nd with the 4th Bn. (Airborne), 25th Infantry Regt. at Vicenza, taly.

Germany: 23 Yrs.

Most soldiers overseas anxiously await their flight home after a tour of duty, but being stationed in Germany for 23 years suited **CW4 Kenneth L. Griggs** just fine, thank you. Griggs, who retired this summer after over 30 years of service to his country, spent nearly all of his career overseas. He was last assigned to the 82nd Engineer Bn., 7th Engineer Bde.

In 1951, Griggs headed out to his first assignment at Camp Zama, Japan. Since that time, he has served one tour in Korea, two in Vietnam, some miscellaneous time in CONUS, and about 23 years total in Germany.

CW4 (Ret.) Kenneth L. Griggs

Top USAR Re-Up NCO

When **SFC Richard D. Stagman** ook time off from his job as a conıruction foreman to accept the rmy Reserve Reenlistment NCO of ıe Year award for FY82, his boss idn't complain—his boss went with im.

Stagman received his award from ohn O. Marsh, Jr., Secretary of the rmy. Stagman's boss, Richard Iorner, Chairman of the Board for .F. Johnson Co., accompanied him to the Pentagon for the award ceremony.

Since October 1978, Stagman was the reenlistment NCO for the 492nd Engineer Co. of Mankato, Minn. The 492nd is part of the 205th Infantry Bde., 88th ARCOM and 5th Army. Stagman now serves as the reenlistment NCO for the 205th.

Stagman has been credited with yearly retention rates of 80 percent or more.

Engineer People is a new department in ENGINEER presenting items of human interest and spotlighting the personal accomplishments of Army engineers. Please send submissions (typed double-spaced, and noting a point-of-contact) to: Assistant Editor, ENGINEER Magazine, ATZA-TDL Stop 16F4, U.S. Army Engineer School, Ft. Belvoir, VA 22060.

by MG James N. Ellis, Commandant, U.S. Army Engineer School

A Hit or Miss — It's Your Call

Are Engineer School products meeting your needs? We want you to tell us.

The lead articles in this issue (pages 11 to 18) are by the Directorate of Engineer Force Management, Provisional (DEFM).

Despite its high sounding title, DEFM has three down to earth missions: Engineer force personnel proponency, engineer force standardization, and engineer force evaluation. While each of these is equally important, evaluation is perhaps the one least understood. I'd like to focus here on how the evaluation function affects the ability of the engineer force to accomplish its mission, and how it affects the ability of those of us in TRADOC to effectively train the force.

DEFM's articles on the Branch Training Team (page 14) and Training Effectiveness Evaluations (page 15) in this issue cover two key approaches to evaluation, but it is essential to point out the role of evaluation in the Army's training system.

Getting on Target

We should begin by defining what we mean by "evaluation." In the Army's training system, evaluation is the last link in a systematic development chain of analysis, design, development, and implementation. In the application of this process, whether it be for organizations, equipment, training, or manuals, evaluation is the key element. The TRADOC school system, and we here at the Engineer School, consciously involve units, personnel and expertise from the field in our efforts to analyze problems and deficiencies that affect mission accomplishment.

That is only the first step. Once that analysis is complete, and the design, development and implementation of the solutions are accomplished, we need to know how effective we were in producing products that satisfied your needs.

In other words, we need your feedback on whether v hit or missed the target. If we missed, we need to knov by how much and in what direction. That feedback mı come from you—the user in the field. Evaluation does not measure or compare personnel or units. It is not a score sheet or report card on field units. It is, however our only way of measuring how well we are doing in performing our missions for the force. It is our way of determining what is necessary to keep us on target.

The Loop

Feedback from the field can take many forms, all of which are valuable. It can be the results of a formal survey, questionnaire or visit. It can also be an informal discussion by phone, message or letter. The feedback we need can be typed on DA Form 2028, *Recommended Changes to Publications and Blank Forms*, or called to the Engineer Hotline. It can be at the request of the Engineer School, or, more importantly and perhaps least used, on the initiative a unit or person in the field. But most importantly, in whatever form, it must take place. Regardless of how comprehensive our efforts are to be on target the first time, we at the School can assure our success only by adjusting the burst on target. The importance of completing this loop cannot be overemphasized.

You engineer soldiers, NCOs and officers who work in our units, you are the ones who employ our doctrin operate and maintain our equipment, and use our training products. You yourselves are products of our training system. You are the real experts in how well we are doing. Your opinions, comments and suggestions—your feedback and evaluation—are key t our continued success.

I request your support in providing the feedback necessary to continue achieving our mutual goal of excellence in training the engineer force.

USAES Reorganization

I would also like to alert you to the approaching reorganization of the Engineer School. We, along wit all other TRADOC schools, will be reorganizing during FY84 to emphasize even more our mission of training the force. I will provide you more detailed / information in a future issue of ENGINEER.

BRIDGE THE GAP

ꞆSM O.W. Troesch Jr., U.S. Army Engineer Center & School

ive Us Your Two Cents Worth

s NCOs, you work with Engineer School products every day. Your valuation of those products is very important to us.

s noncommissioned officers, you play a vital role in the evaluation process MG Ellis refers to in lear The Way."

ꓥs grass-roots level trainers and maintenance pervisors, you are the Army's first-line users of new uipment, manuals and doctrine. You, more than yone else, know the strengths and weaknesses of ɹr new soldiers coming out of Engineer OSUT.

Each of you is a gold mine of information. Your ꞉edback about Engineer School products is critically nportant to the School's evaluation efforts.

. Good Evaluation

There are several things to keep in mind when ɔing a good evaluation.

First, be objective. Personal criticism based on "this n't the way we did it in my last unit" is not an ⁄aluation. It is sometimes difficult to step back and ·ok at things objectively, but that's what you have ɔt to do. A good evaluation is not based on emotion; good evaluation is based on facts.

Secondly, you'll find it easier to do a complete 'aluation if you try to anticipate what facts the ngineer School must know to improve the product in ıestion. Imagine that you are the person receiving ı evaluation from the field, and that it's your sponsibility to improve the product. You would want know specifics. You would want to know exactly hat was wrong with the product, and you would ɔpreciate specific suggestions on how to correct the 'oblem.

If you approach your evaluation from the ꞉rspectives of being objective and of being complete, ɔur feedback will be accurate and valuable.

Let's walk through a situation in which you, as an NCO in the field, provide an evaluation of a new piece of equipment.

To truly conduct an evaluation of a new piece of equipment, we must first learn all there is to know about it. That includes maintenance, PMCS checks, operation and employment. As a noncommissioned officer, you should be thoroughly trained on your new equipment so that you can train others how to use it and enhance the integration of the new item into the squad, platoon or company. You must be fully knowledgeable of the item if you are going to provide an informative and useful evaluation.

Questions to Ask

The following are some questions you should consider during your evaluation:

- Can the equipment do what we said we wanted it to do?
- Can it be maintained and operated by soldiers, using the operator's manuals provided?
- In what way does it enhance or detract from squad, platoon, or company capabilities?
- What unusual training problems were incurred?
- How could the product be improved?

After an evaluation of a product, system, manual, new piece of equipment or tool, if you're convinced that the product could be improved, write to me here at the Engineer School or tell me in person as I visit engineer units throughout the Army.

We at the Engineer School do not suppose to have all of the answers. It is for that very reason that we encourage your evaluation and feedback. I look forward to discussing this topic and others during my visits. I ask you to help me "bridge the gap" between the school and you, the grass-roots users of Engineer School products.

Directorate of Engineer Force Management

Women In The Army Study: As a result of discussions between MG Ellis and DSCPER, a number of TO positions may be opened or reopened to women. Some units will be partiall opened.

The basis for opening duty positions to women is two-fold: that the positio are behind the brigade rear boundary, and that the individual would not b expected to routinely engage in direct combat. DEFM will do a line-by-lin analysis to determine which Engineer MOSs should be open to women an which should not. The results of the analysis are expected at the end of th year.

Directorate of Training Developments

Supplements for MOS 52D: As a result of refinements to the Skill Qualification Test (SQT) program, th formal SQT will be an annual written test, the results of which will be used fo Enlisted Personnel Management System (EPMS) purposes. Until publicatio of the new 52D Soldier's Manual, a Soldier's Manual Supplement (SMS) wi be available to provide trainers with an informal hands-on evaluation guid and to provide trainers and soldiers holding MOS 52D with revised tas summaries.

Before administering hands-on evaluations during preparation for the 198 SQT, unit commanders, trainers, and soldiers holding MOS 52D should rea the summaries and evaluation material for each task. All copies of the Sold er's Manuals within units should be updated using the information containe in the revised task summaries.

Because of important changes to certain task summaries in the 52D Sold er's Manual, the task summaries must be carefully reviewed and studie before taking the 1984 SQT. The task summaries found in the SMS replac those summaries with the same task number found in the 52D Soldier Manual.

Directorate of Training and Doctrine

EOAC Changes: Officers attending EOAC in FY85 will be confronted with a new, modular ized training strategy. There will also be increased emphasis on computer based educational technology and small-group/experiential learning Situational exercises will be used extensively to have students demonstrat ability to solve problems and gain access to information. By "learning how t learn" and "training to be trainers," students will be better prepared fo continuing their education and training their subordinates after they leav Ft. Belvoir.

TEWT Training: A new aspect of EOAC is a brigade assault river crossing tactical exercis without troops (TEWT) on the Potomac River. By emphasizing ground recon naissance for identification and selection of far shore intermediate objectives development of a deception plan, and selection of crossing sites, the TEW focuses on AirLand Battle operations. The eight-hour day concludes with concept-of-operation briefing, covering all engineer brigade-level respons bilities.

Special Weekend Courses: In a continuing effort to assist Army Reserve and National Guard personnel and units with their training, a series of Special Weekend Courses (SWC) is offered each FY. The courses, taught primarily by DTAD instructors, emphasize combat and construction engineering and tactics. The purpose of the SWC is to improve the skills of training officers and NCOs. POC is Unit Training Section, (703) 664-3008, AV 354.

efense Mapping School

Available Courses: The Defense Mapping Agency provides mapping, charting, and geodetic (MC&G) support to the Secretary of Defense, the Joint Chiefs of Staff, the military departments, and other DoD components. Here is a summary of courses now offered by the Defense Mapping School:

Survey courses: providing accurate horizontal and vertical control for military construction projects (*Construction Survey,* MOS 82B) or for mapping and systems support (*Geodetic Survey,* MOS 82D). Also, DMA teaches *Construction Drafting,* MOS 81B.

Cartographic courses: producing photomaps; compiling and revising maps and map substitutes. *Terrain Analysis* courses (MOS 81Q) and *Graphic Arts* courses (MOS 83E, 83F).

Topographic Instrument Repair (MOS 41B): maintenance of optical surveying and photomapping instruments. *Reproduction Equipment Repair* (MOS 83FJ6): maintaining presses and lithographic equipment.

Analytical Photogrammetric Positioning System (APPS) *Course:* using the system for precise point positioning from aerial photos. *Digital Topographic Data Course:* basic digital mapping.

NCO professional development courses: *Terrain Analysis, Cartography, Geodetic Surveying.* Management courses: *MC&G Officer's Course, MC&G Senior Officer's Course.*

For more information, write: Director, Defense Mapping School, ATTN: TDE, Fort Belvoir, VA 22060.

irectorate of
ombat Developments

MAA Distributed: The U.S. Army Engineer School has published a major new study, the *Combat Support Engineer Mine Warfare Mission Area Analysis (CSEMW MAA).*

The study analyzed the ability of the combat engineer to accomplish the primary missions of mobility, countermobility, survivability, general engineering and topography, as well as the secondary mission of fighting as infantry. The CSEMW MAA produced and identified over 40 major deficiencies, possible corrective actions for each deficiency, and a detailed program to implement the corrective actions. This information was published as the CSEMW MAA Development Plan and will be updated annually. The full report of the CSEMW MAA (the *Executive Summary,* the *Main Report,* the *Supporting Analyses,* and the *Development Plan*) was distributed to (among others) all active engineer commands (battalion and above) and all Army Reserve engineer commands (brigade and above).

Questions or comments regarding the CSEMW MAA should be sent to: Commandant, U.S. Army Engineer School, ATTN: ATZA-CD, Ft. Belvoir, VA 22060.

UPDATE

Feedback from the field indicates that the Army's new SQT system is not well understood.

The new program consists of three parts: A common task test; an informal, local, hands-on evaluation of MOS task performance; and a refined, MOS-specific written test.

Common Task Test

The common task test is a hands-on test, with a written backup test which may be used when equipment is not available. Tasks tested will be taken from the *Soldier's Manual of Common Tasks.* All soldiers E7 and below, will take the common task test. This test may be locally scored, but results must be reported for training diagnostic purposes.

Commanders may use scores as input for EER, local promotion boards, etc. The common task test can be administered at any time during a 12-month period.

Hands-on Evaluation

The informal, local, hands-on evaluation of MOS task performance is administered by the local commander. Using the soldier's manual, the commander selects the tasks to be evaluated and determines where and when the evaluation will take place.

This evaluation may take place anytime during the year and as often as desired. Evaluation score sheets will be in the revised soldier's manuals. Results of this evaluation will not be formally reported.

Written Test

An MOS-specific written test will be developed for each MOS and skill level to measure individual soldier proficiency. The written test will cover soldier's manual tasks representing the entire MOS and skill level, not just current duty position. The test will take about two hours to administer. The period designated for taking the test will be three months long, as prescribed by DA. The test will be given annually in the active component, and every other year in the reserve component.

Local commanders may score skill level one written tests using a printed For Official Use Only answer key provided with the test. All MOS-specific written tests will be centrally scored and used for training decisions and for DA level personnel management purposes in the active component.

SQT feedback reports will be provided to soldiers and commanders. Individual Soldier Reports (IRS) will be sent to soldiers and commanders within 30 days after submission of the test for scoring.

The report will identify those tasks on which a soldier needs additional training. Summary reports will be provided periodically, or upon request, to company through division level commanders. The summary report will contain average SQT scores for all MOS/skill levels tested.

This new SQT system will be phased in through fiscal years 1984 to 1986. During that time, new soldiers manuals are published for most of the 37 Engineer MOSs and 103 skill levels. When fully implemented, the new program will

The Engineer
roponent Program

ciality codes (SC), warrant officer military occupational specialties (MOS), and enlisted Career Management Fields (CMF). The Engineer School also has joint proponent responsibility with the Ordnance School for three MOSs in CMF 63 (Mechanical Maintenance). (See list of SCs and MOSs.)

Within the U.S. Army Engineer School staff, the Directorate of Engineer Force Management, Provisional (DEFM) has been designated to handle proponent matters. However, the responsibility for accomplishing the life cycle personnel management activities remains with the appropriate Engineer School directorate having the functional expertise to resolve a given issue.

Under the Engineer Specialty Proponent System, the USAES can incorporate engineer related considerations into the life cycle personnel management policies, programs, and procedures established subsequently by HQDA.

The engineer proponent is charged with gathering and evaluating information, identifying issues and setting priorities, formulating alternatives, coordinating actions, and causing change in each step of the life cycle personnel management process.

Officer and enlisted engineers are now involved with designing their own personnel management policies. If you have suggestions or concerns in this area, write to the Commandant, U.S. Army Engineer School, ATTN: ATZA-FM, Fort Belvoir, VA 22060.

After your suggestion or information is analyzed, it may be brought before the Engineer Proponency Steering Committee as a potential "initiative." Initiatives approved by the steering committee are developed into recommended policy changes. Through this system, the engineer community can better influence the future of the Corps of Engineers.

Jim Price is a personnel staff officer at DCSPER, HQDA. He has a master's degree in business administration from Central Michigan University and a bachelor's degree from the University of Maryland. He retired from the Army as a command sergeant major and is a graduate of the Sergeants Major Academy.

ENGINEER PROPONENT OFFICER SPECIALTY CODES

21	Combat Engineer
22	Topographic Equipment
23	Facilities/Contract Construction Management Engineer

WARRANT OFFICER MOS

310A0	Utilities Operation and Maintenance Technician
310A5	Power Systems Technician
621A0	Engineer Equipment Repair Technician
621AV	Support Repair Technician
811A0	Survey Technician
833A0	Reproduction Technician
841A0	Terrain Analysis Technician

ENLISTED CMF

12	Combat Engineer
51	General Engineering
81	Topographic Engineering

JOINT PROPONENT WITH ORDNANCE SCHOOL (MOS)

52C	Utilities Equipment Repairer
52D	Power Generator Equipment Repairer
62B	Construction Equipment Repairer

Training the IRR

by MAJ Thomas Binek

How important are reserve component (RC) engineers? The figures speak for themselves. About 63 percent of the Army's engineer officers are assigned to the reserve components: 42 percent in the Army Reserve (USAR) and 21 percent in the Army National Guard. Only 37 percent of our engineer officers are in the active Army.

One of the key missions of the Reserve Components Personnel Administration Center (RCPAC) is to prepare and to mobilize Individual Ready Reservists (IRR). These are reservists in the manpower pool but who are not assigned to a USAR unit. It is RCPAC that manages these men and women, *but it is the active components that must train the IRR.*

Using IRR members to review IG deficiencies, inventory the supply room, or to rewrite a unit fire evacuation plan is not meaningful mobilization training. Such assignments will not help reservists on the battlefield, enhance their professional development, nor motivate them to remain in the USAR.

Special Skills

IRR members have a wide range of military and civilian skills. Besides their engineering expertise, IRR personnel have civilian skills in mathematics, geography, logistics, chemistry, cartography, personnel management, education and other highly technical fields. The active components can use those skills when conducting mobilization exercises, field training exercises, and other essential activities. Just as civilian employers capitalize on military training and education of their employees, the Army must draw on the IRR member's civilian skills.

To understand the active component's role in training the IRR member, it's necessary to briefly discuss how RCPAC supports such training. The RCPAC personnel manager works closely with the individual reservist to identify training needs. A training program is planned, then the personnel manager and the RCPAC Training Coordination Branch find appropriate training opportunities with an active unit. This is one of the most critical phases of the training.

Once a reservist's skills have been identified, good planning is vital. Key players must be identified in the active organization, including the installation director of reserve components (DRC) or USAR advisor, and commanders at all levels. RCPAC identifies an individual and his training needs to the DRC. Then it's the DRC/USAR advisor's duty to contact the reservist, provide him with ai OER/EER support form, and t ensure the individual knows what t expect during the tour of duty.

The best approach is for the activ installation's operations/trainin officer to contact the USAR adviso after the training schedule is complete to determine what IRR personnel assets are required and when the can be productively used. The USAI advisor then submits these requirements to RCPAC as a trainin opportunity.

Deliberate planning is importan and cooperation must exist betwee all key players. The reservist must b trained and be ready to assume hi role during mobilization. Tha responsibility lies squarely upon al of those associated with IRI training.

Shared Effort

The point is that quality IRR train ing results from a shared effor between RCPAC and the activ component.

It is RCPAC's responsibility t plan, coordinate and to manag training opportunities that improv the skills and professional develop ment of IRR members. The activ component, however, must effec tively use IRR personnel by provi ing them training that addresse mobilization requirements.

These principles are best summa ized by Joint Chiefs of Staff Chai

IRR DEMOGRAPHICS

CATEGORIES	OFFICER/WARRANTS	ENLISTED
Grade	78% Company Grade (WO,01-03)	85% Are E-4 or Below
Average Age	35	24
Average AD Service	52% 36 Months or More (44 Months)	58% 36 Months or More (29 Months)
Career Field	CA 33% CS 23% CSS 44%	CA 27% CS 46% CSS 26%
Civilian Education	81% BA/BS Degree or Higher	75% HS/GED or Higher
Combat SVC	27% RVN/DR	.1% RVN/DR
Remaining SVC Obligation	8%	87%
Sex	93% Male	89% Male
Average IRR Service	37.0 Months	15.5 Months

man, General John W. Vessey: "The only true readiness is total force readiness. That's the readiness of the active forces, the Reserve, and the National Guard."

By intelligently tapping the IRR manpower pool, active Army engineer units will benefit from periodic injections of new talent and will make a major contribution to total force readiness.

MAJ Thomas Binek is a personnel management officer at Engineer Branch, RCPAC, and is a member of Ft. Belvoir's Engineer Proponency Steering Committee. He has a bachelor's degree in education from Dickenson State College and has served in several Army Reserve and National Guard engineer units.

HOTLINE Q&A

HOTLINE Q & A is a new department in ENGINEER designed to pass along a sampling of questions received on the Engineer Hotline. For more information on how to use the Hotline see page 14.

Q. How can we obtain copies of the Combat Engineer Game?

A. The Combat Engineer Game (GTA 5-14-1) can be ordered through local TASC offices or by calling 1LT Aurthur Shafferman or Ms. Mariellen Steece at the Engineer School, (703) 664-2384/2498, AVN 354. A second set of mission and question cards for the game will be available in the Spring, 1984.

Q. Is the U.S. Army Engineer School responsible for doctrine and training for water purification units?

A. The Quartermaster School has overall responsibility for doctrine and training for water purification.

Proponency for field water purification and distribution was transferred from the Corps of Engineers to the Quartermaster Corps beginning in 1981. Equipment and personnel changes associated with the transfer are still underway. For the National Guard and Army Reserve, the transfer will not be completed until 1986.

Water source detection and installation water support remains an Engineer responsibility.

Q. We are interested in training our officers in airfield repair. Is there an Air Force manual that outlines the procedures and specifications?

A. The *Interim Planning Guidance for Rapid Runway Repair*, dated December 1981 and published by the Air Force Engineering and Services Center, Tyndall Air Force Base, addresses this area.

Q. What publications address water safety for bridge personnel?

A. AR 385-15, *Water Safety*
TM 385-1-1, *Safety and Health Requirements Manual*
TM 5-210, *Military Floating Bridge Equipment*

Q. What publications can be used by reserve units as a guide in designing an individual training program for the 52G MOS?

A. The soldier's manual and trainer's guide for the 52G MOS will not be out for at least three years. Available at this time is TM 5-765, *Electrical Power Transmission and Distribution;* and *The Lineman's and Cableman's Handbook*, a civilian publication by McGraw Hill.

The Engineer Branch Training Team

by James Scott

What is a Branch Training Team? Another training distractor? Another group of staff weenies coming to the field, making ridiculous demands? Absolutely not!

The Branch Training Team (BTT) establishes important two-way communication between the Engineer School and engineer units. Too often troops in the field feel that everyone at the School is in an ivory tower with little concern or understanding of the problems in the field.

The BTT is a group of representatives from Engineer School directorates that meets with units in the field to discuss changes occurring in the engineer arena. These visits are primarily meetings with engineers from platoon sergeants on up.

Direct Communication

At these meetings, the School representatives give a short presentation on recent changes and developments; then the meeting is opened to questions and comments from unit personnel.

The meetings give individual engineers direct communication with the Engineer School. Many of the questions raised at these sessions are answered on the spot by the team members. Questions the team can't answer are researched at Fort Belvoir and the answers sent back to the unit.

Subjects brought up for discussion during the meetings are later presented to the rest of the School. Such feedback is critical to the operation of the Engineer School. The BTT is a very effective way to obtain information about the quality and effectiveness of Engineer School products.

The Players

The BTT normally includes members from the Directorates of Training Developments, Combat Developments and Engineer Force Management.

The representative from Training Developments discusses skill qualification tests, soldier's manuals, course developments, the Army training and evaluation program, training devices, training extension courses and other training related matters. The Combat Developments representative presents information about material and equipment development, tables of organization and equipment, and organizational changes. The Engineer Force Management team member addresses matters primarily related to personnel management policies.

On some unit visits, representatives from the Engineer Training Center at Fort Leonard Wood will be present to discuss almost any area on which the training center has an impact.

Training Information

The key to the BTT's success is the exchange of information and openly discussing problems and ideas. An equally important factor is disseminating discussion results to the field.

Current plans call for each CONUS engineer battalion to be visited by a BTT once every two years. Engineer units overseas may expect a visit every two or three years, depending on resources.

The Branch Training Team might not actually train anyone, but it is an excellent opportunity for you to talk directly to people at the Engineer School who shape policies that influence your career.

James Scott is chief of the Training Systems Branch, Directorate of Engineer Force Management, U.S. Army Engineer School, Ft. Belvoir.

ENGINEER HOTLINE

Problems, questions, and comments relating to engineer doctrine, training, organization, and equipment can be addressed telephonically to the U.S. Army Engineer School's "Engineer Hotline." The Hotline's auto-answer recorder operates 24 hours a day, seven days a week. Callers should state their name, address and telephone number, followed by a concise question or comment. You'll receive a reply within three to 15 days. **The Hotline is not a receiving agency for formal requests.**

Call commercial (703) 664-3646; WATTS 800-336-3095, extension 3646; or AV 354-3646.

raining ffectiveness valuations

James Scott

he telephone in the battalion S3's office rings. You answer and meone on the other end says people om the Engineer School would like visit your unit as part of a "Train- g Effectiveness Evaluation."

What do you do? Panic? Tell the ller to mind his own business? Do ey want to check out the unit's aining or what? Who are these ɜople?

Relax! A Training Effectiveness valuation (TEE) is not a threat. A EE is simply an effort to determine e effectiveness of Engineer dvanced Individual Training (AIT) nd professional development ourses.

Engineer School courses are deve- ɔped through a complex training evelopment process. This process is ot complete without a post-training valuation. The training develop- ɪent process is a continuous job of pgrading training to ensure that the eeds of the field are being satisfied nd that new courses are aimed in the ight direction.

There are two major questions sked during a TEE: Do the courses n question adequately cover the asks that a skill level one soldier eeds to function in the field? And, if he tasks are covered, are they prop- rly taught? The only real way to etermine this is to go to the field and ee how well the graduates do their ɔbs.

TEEs are done in a variety of ways. Normally, data is collected through a ombination of surveys and inter- iews of skill level one soldiers and heir supervisors. Surveys may be nailed to the unit, to the individual, r taken to the unit during a Branch Training Team visit. Some surveys re done by telephone.

A TEE will not, in most cases, affect a field unit directly, other than the time required for the interviews or survey. In the long run though, the TEE may have a major impact on the quality of OSUT graduates sent to the unit.

It is important that detailed and valid information be collected during the TEEs. It is also important that comments on problem areas be as specific as possible. Many times, the only comments received are that soldiers "aren't able to do anything." This is not only false, but it does not tell the evaluation team where the problem is. Comments, and especially complaints, should be as specific as possible.

So the next time someone from the Directorate of Engineer Force Management at the Engineer School calls and asks if he or she can do a portion of a Training Effectiveness Evaluation at your unit, lend a hand. The evaluator may be able to improve your unit's effectiveness by improving the quality of the graduates you receive. Consider it an investment in your unit's future.

James Scott is chief of the Training Systems Branch, Directorate of Engineer Force Management, U.S. Army Engineer School, Ft. Belvoir.

ENGINEER PROBLEM

Determine the proportions of a 1-cubic yard batch of non-air entrained concrete given the following information:

a. The specified 28-day compressive strength (f'c) has dictated a water-cement ratio (w/c) of .44.

b. Cement is Type I Normal. Specific gravity = 3.15. One sack = 94 pounds.

c. Amount of water and air based on a desired 3-inch slump and 1-inch (-MSA for the cubic yard batch is 300 pounds water and 1.5% entrapped air Water = 8.33#/gallon

d. Sand: Fineness Modulus = 2.6
Specific Gravity = 2.7
Bulk Unit Weight = 110 lbs/cf
2% Free Surface Moisture

e. Gravel: 1" (-) MSA
Specific gravity = 2.65
Bulk Unit Weight = 105 lbs/cf
0% Free Surface Moisture

Volume of Coarse Aggregate Per Unit of Volume of Concrete

Maximum size of aggregate, in.	Volume of dry-rodded coarse aggreate per unit volume of concrete for different fineness moduli of sand			
	2.40	2.60	2.80	3.00
⅜	0.50	0.48	0.46	0.44
½	0.59	0.57	0.55	0.53
¾	0.66	0.64	0.62	0.60
1	0.71	0.69	0.67	0.65
1½	0.75	0.73	0.71	0.69
2	0.78	0.76	0.74	0.72
3	0.82	0.80	0.78	0.76
6	0.87	0.85	0.83	0.87

SOLUTION ON PAGE 27

The Engineer Regimental System

by CPT Dana Bres

Over the next few years, the Corps of Engineers will reorganize into regiments. This regimental system is a key part of the Army's New Manning System, a program to increase unit combat effectiveness by reducing personnel turnover.

Past personnel management policies have focused on the individual. This has caused a considerable number of personnel changes which, in turn, has impeded the development of cohesive, well-trained squads, crews and sections.

Two initiatives—Project COHORT and the regimental system—will help stabilize soldiers in units, and make possible unit replacement and unit homebasing.

COHORT Companies

The key point of the COHORT (Cohesion, Operational Readiness, Training) company is that the soldiers and their leaders will be together for three years, less time for initial entry training (IET).

During this time, no personnel changes will be scheduled. Personnel assigned to a unit at its establishment will remain with that unit for three years. Leaders will have the opportunity to lead and to train without constantly losing personnel due to reassignment. With personnel turnover in Germany currently approaching 40 percent, for example, stabilization should prove a boon to training and espirit.

COHORT soldiers will be stabilized in units from the day they enter the Army. Combat arms soldiers will undergo IET in a company-sized unit. After IET, they will be assigned to a CONUS installation (with cadre) where they will form a stabilized unit. They will remain together throughout their first enlistment.

Deployment Overseas

As part of the regimental system, A COHORT company will deploy overseas (OCONUS) 18 months after IET begins (15 months after the company was activated). The unit will replace OCONUS an identical, paired unit which will be "disbanded."

In other words, when these soldiers have been in the Army for one-half of their initial three-year enlistment, their company will deploy overseas for the remaining 18 months.

The unit overseas being replaced will, in effect, be disbanded. Its first term soldiers will be either discharged or will re-enlist and be sent elsewhere.

To simplify management of the OCONUS-CONUS rotation system, legislation is being drafted which, if enacted, will provide enlistments for a set number of years, plus IET time.

For example, if a combat arms soldier spends three months in IET, then he will enlist for three years and three months. This will make possible equal CONUS and OCONUS tour lengths for the first term soldier.

Cadre Assignments

When an OCONUS unit is disbanded, cadre with family will stay OCONUS to complete a 36-month overseas tour. They probably will be assigned to a battalion or brigade staff, or they could be assigned to an incoming unit to fill a shortage. In some cases, cadre members could be assigned to the community or elsewhere in the theater.

Unaccompanied cadre will return to CONUS after their unit is disbanded. These reassignment procedures will apply to both officer and NCO cadre. Under the regimental system, major personnel changes will occur only when a unit is established in CONUS or disbanded overseas.

The turn around time (TAT) for a member of a regiment would not be under the usual TAT for MOS and grade by more than 12 months. An NCO with a TAT of 36 months, for example, could expect to remain in CONUS for at least 24 months after his return from overseas. The TAT for each MOS and grade will be published periodically by MILPERCEN. The career soldier can expect to serve in his regiment whenever serving the troops. This will provide leaders with a stronger sense of belonging to their unit.

For the Engineers

Differences between the engineers and other combat arms may require adjustments to the basic system, but the Corps of Engineers will be participants in the New Manning System.

The Engineer School has proposed that engineer regiments consist of four-to-six like battalions. Each regiment will represent one of the three engineer enlisted career management fields (CMF) from one or more CONUS installations.

That means there would be combat

PROPOSED ENGINEER REGIMENTS

REGIMENT (HOME)	CONUS	OCONUS
1st EN REGT (RILEY) (CBT)	19th EN BN (KNOX) 1st EN BN (1 ID) *	78th EN BN (FRG) D/1 EN BN (FWD)
2nd EN REGT * (LEWIS) (CBT)	13th EN BN (7 ID) (-) 15th EN BN (9 ID) 326th EN BN (101 ABN)	2nd EN BN (2 ID) 65th EN BN (25 ID) (-)
4th EN REGT (CARSON) (CBT)	4th EN BN (4 ID) 14th EN BN (ORD) 299th EN BN (SILL) (-)	12th EN BN (8 ID) 54th EN BN (FRG) 547th EN BN (FRG)
5th EN REGT (LEONARD WOOD) (CBT)	5th EN BN (LEONARD WOOD) 20th EN BN (CAMPBELL)	9th EN BN (FRG) 82nd EN BN (FRG)
6th EN REGT (STEWART) (CBT)	39th EN BN (DEVENS) 3rd EN BN (24 ID) (-)	317th EN BN (FRG) 10th EN BN (3 ID)
7th EN REGT (POLK) (CBT)	7th EN BN (5 ID) (-) 588th EN BN (POLK)	16th EN BN (1 AD) 237th EN BN (FRG)
8th EN REGT (HOOD) (CBT)	17th EN BN (2 AD) (-) 8th EN BN (1 CAV) * (-)	23rd EN BN (3 AD) D/17 EN BN (FWD)
29th EN REGT * (BELVOIR) (TOPO)	30th EN BN (BELVOIR) 63rd EN CO (BRAGG) 524th EN CO (HOOD)	29th EN BN (HAWAII) 649th EN BN (FRG)
46th EN REGT (BENNING) (CBT HVY)	43rd EN BN (BENNING) 46th EN BN (RUCKER/MCCLELLAN) 34th EN BN (RILEY)	79th EN BN (FRG) 94th EN BN (FRG)
47th EN REGT * (CARSON) (CBT HVY)	11th EN BN (BELVOIR) 52nd EN BN (CARSON/BLISS) 864th EN BN (LEWIS/PRESIDIO)	44th EN BN (ROK) 802nd EN BN (ROK)
84th EN REGT * (BRAGG) (CBT HVY)	76th EN BN (MEADE/DRUM) 548th EN BN (BRAGG/JACKSON)	84th EN BN (HAWAII)
92nd EN REGT (STEWART) (CBT HVY)	92nd EN BN (STEWART/GORDON) 62nd EN BN (HOOD)	293rd EN BN (FRG) (-) 249th EN BN (FRG)
307th EN REGT * (BRAGG) (ABN)	27th EN BN (BRAGG) 307th EN BN (82 ABN)	ABN PLT/509 (ITALY)

* *NON-ROTATING*

MF 12), combat heavy (CMF 51) d topographic (CMF 81) engineer giments.

Combat regiments, for example, uld consist of divisional, divisional echanized), corps and airborne/air sault units.

Regardless of regiment, engineer mpanies would rotate between entical battalions within their regient. For instance, companies from e 4th Engineer Battalion at Fort rson, Colo., would replace like mpanies in the 12th Engineer Bation in Germany. The same type of tation would take place between e 14th Engineer Battalion at Fort d, Calif., and the 54th Engineer ttalion in Germany (see chart).

Enlisted specialties in an engineer company which are not the primary specialty of that company will require management different from the typical COHORT company. Instead of sending these "low-density" MOSs to the company as a package, soldiers of the appropriate specialties will be provided to the CONUS installation where the company is established. These soldiers then will be assigned to COHORT companies based on the organizational needs and the soldier's separation date. The separation date should match the date on which the company will be disbanded overseas.

In organizing regiments, a regimental adjutant will be designated as a liaison between the regiment and MILPERCEN. An honorary position of colonel of the regiment has been considered. The position would be held probably by a distinguished retiree and initially be confined to ceremonial activities.

It is important to remember that the regimental headquarters will serve only as an administrative organization. Present tactical headquarters and commands will not be affected by the regimental system.

CPT Dana Bres is chief of the Operations Systems Evaluations Branch at the Engineer School's Directorate of Engineer Force Management. He is a graduate of the University of Nevada (Reno) and served as a platoon leader and battalion maintenance officer in Germany with the 12th Engineer Bn., 8th Infantry Div.

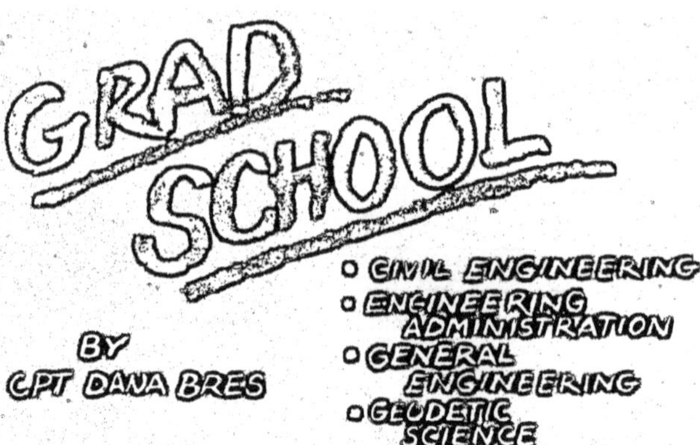

The Army has a number of assignments requiring officers with advanced civil schooling (graduate education). These positions typically are at Department of the Army, major command and installation levels.

Examples of engineer positions requiring graduate education are: Engineer School instructors, engineer district project engineers, installation directors of engineering and housing, or research coordinators at Army research stations.

The requirements for these positions result in annual opportunities for some 500 to 600 officers Army-wide to attend graduate school.

Organizations can request positions be approved (validated) for an officer with graduate education through the Army Educational Requirements Board (AERB). The request and validation process is detailed in AR 621-108, *Military Personnel Requirements for Civilian Education.*

Officers interested in attending graduate school should tell their professional development officer. Typically, the officer must be branch qualified prior to being considered for graduate school. Branch qualification means completing both the Engineer Officer Advanced Course and a successful company command. Officers usually attend graduate school between their sixth and eighth year of service.

As officers are sent to graduate school to fill specific AERB positions, the discipline studied must support Army requirements. In the Corps of Engineers, degrees which most closely match Engineer Branch (SC 21 and 22) requirements are civil engineering, engineering administration, general engineering and geodetic science. These four disciplines constitute over 80 percent of all Engineer positions requested for AERB validation for 1982. MILPERCEN can provide additional information on other disciplines required by the Army.

Usually, an officer can attend graduate school under one of two programs: fully-funded or partially-funded. The fully-funded program provides the officer a permanent change of station move to the school, full pay and allowances, paid tuition and a textbook allowance.

The partially-funded program is a degree completion program which allows the officer time to complete a degree already started. It is similar to the fully-funded program, but the officer must pay for all school related expenses (many officers use veteran's benefits).

Two other programs offer graduate school opportunities for certain officers. The Scientific and Engineering Graduate Schooling for Distinguished Military Graduates Program provides graduate trainin in the physical sciences for a small number of ROTC graduates. The Officer Graduate Training for Top Five Percent Cadets (USMA and ROTC) Program allows outstanding Regular Army graduates of West Point and ROTC to attend graduate school. Further information on these graduate school programs is available in AR 621-1, *Training of Military Personnel at Civilian Institutions.* Career management officers at MILPERCEN can also provide guidance on specific programs.

Normally after graduate schooling, the officer serves an AERB utilization assignment. Further assignments to use graduate skills and training usually follow throughout the officer's career.

CPT Dana Bres is chief of the Operations Systems Evaluation Branch at the Engineer School's Directorate of Engineer Force Management. He is a graduate of the University of Nevada (Reno) and served as a platoon leader and battalion maintenance officer in Germany with the 12th Engineer Bn., 8th Infantry Div.

NEW MIX DESIGN for the CONCRETE MOBILE

by CPT Allen C. Estes

The M919 concrete mobile has vastly improved Army engineers' ability to place large volumes of concrete. Produced by the Barber-Greene Co., the concrete mobile carries its components in separate compartments and mixes the concrete at the job site. The truck can be stopped at any time and the materials stored indefinitely. This is a distinct advantage over most ready-mix trucks which have a set time in which concrete must be deposited before it hardens.

The concrete mobile's capacity is eight cubic yards, roughly equal to a civilian ready-mix truck, and far superior to the 16 cubic foot trailer-mounted mixer it replaces.

This article proposes a revised procedure for computing concrete mobile dial settings. The new procedure eliminates several deficiencies in the existing method and permits better control over the aggregate proportioning and water-cement ratio while mixing concrete.

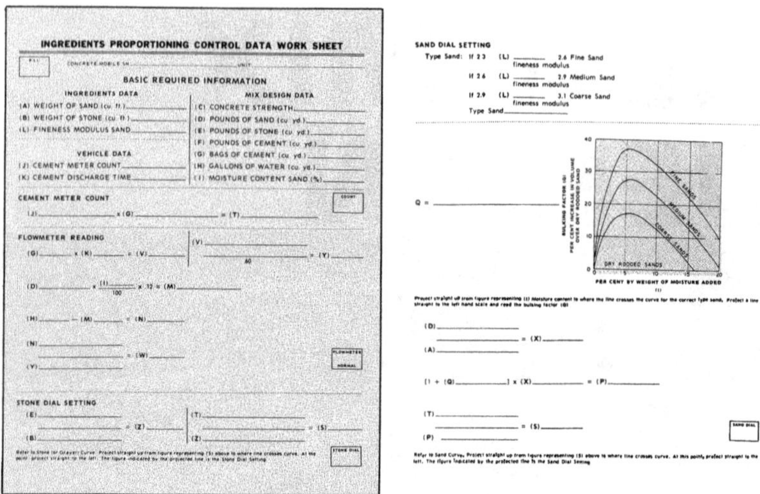

INGREDIENTS PROPORTIONING CONTROL DATA WORK SHEET

CONCRETE MOBILE SN ______ UNIT ______

BASIC REQUIRED INFORMATION

INGREDIENTS DATA	MIX DESIGN DATA
(A) WEIGHT OF SAND (cu. ft.) ______	(C) CONCRETE STRENGTH ______
(B) WEIGHT OF STONE (cu. ft.) ______	(D) POUNDS OF SAND (cu. yd.) ______
(L) FINENESS MODULUS SAND ______	(E) POUNDS OF STONE (cu. yd.) ______
	(F) POUNDS OF CEMENT (cu. yd.) ______
VEHICLE DATA	(G) BAGS OF CEMENT (cu. yd.) ______
(J) CEMENT METER COUNT ______	(H) GALLONS OF WATER (cu. yd.) ______
(K) CEMENT DISCHARGE TIME ______	(I) MOISTURE CONTENT SAND (%) ______

CEMENT METER COUNT

(J) ______ x (G) ______ = (T) ______ COUNT

FLOWMETER READING

(G) ______ x (K) ______ = (V) ______ | (V) ______ / 60 = (Y) ______

(D) ______ x (I) ______ / 100 x 12 = (M) ______

(H) ______ − (M) ______ = (N) ______

(N) ______ / (Y) ______ = (W) ______ FLOWMETER NORMAL

STONE DIAL SETTING

(E) ______ / (B) ______ = (Z) ______ | (T) ______ / (Z) ______ = (S) ______

Refer to Stone (or Gravel) Curve. Project straight up from figure representing (S) above to where line crosses curve. At the point project straight to the left. The figure indicated by the projected line is the Stone Dial Setting. STONE DIAL

SAND DIAL SETTING

Type Sand: If 2.3 (L) ______ fineness modulus 2.6 Fine Sand

If 2.6 (L) ______ fineness modulus 2.9 Medium Sand

If 2.9 (L) ______ fineness modulus 3.1 Coarse Sand

Type Sand ______

Q = ______

Project straight up from figure representing (I) Moisture content to where the line crosses the curve for the correct type sand. Project a line straight to the left hand scale and read the bulking factor (Q)

(D) ______ / (A) ______ = (X) ______

[1 + (Q) ______] x (X) ______ = (P) ______

(T) ______ / (P) ______ = (S) ______ SAND DIAL

Refer to Sand Curve. Project straight up from figure representing (S) above to where line crosses curve. At this point, project straight to the left. The figure indicated by the projected line is the Sand Dial Setting

Figure 1. Suggested replacement for the work sheet in the operator's manual.

Theory

To produce quality concrete with sufficient workability, strength and durability, a mix design must specify the exact amounts of cement, water, aggregate and air to be added. (See the ENGINEER Problem, page 15.)

The concrete mobile can proportion its materials according to a standard dry aggregate mix design. The cement flow is calibrated at the factory and cannot be adjusted. A rotary feed wheel in the cement bin dispenses cement onto a conveyor belt and records the discharged amount on a cement meter at the rear of the truck. The remaining components are adjusted based on the constant flow of cement and the desired mix design.

Old Procedure

The current procedure for calibrating the water flow rate, sand and stone dial settings, and air entraining admixture rates is a simple, step-by-step procedure found in the operator's manual (Figure 1). The current procedure, however, does not consider the fact that wet sand

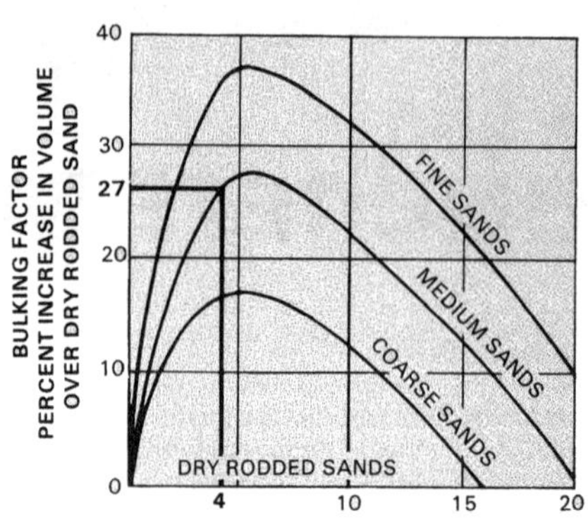

FINENESS MODULUS	
	Fineness Modulus **2.6**
2.30 - 2.59 Fine Sand	Moisture Content **4%**
2.60 - 2.89 Medium Sand	
2.90 - 3.10 Coarse Sand	**BULKING FACTOR 27%**

Figure 2. Bulking factor curve.

CEMENT METER COUNT

$$(J)\ \frac{69}{\text{cement meter count}} \times (G)\ \frac{7.2}{\text{bags of cement per cu yd}} = (T)\ \frac{497}{\text{meter count for one cu yd}}$$

WATER SETTING

$$(G)\ \frac{7.2}{\text{bags of cement per cu yd}} \times (K)\ \frac{28}{\text{cement discharge time}} = (X)\ \frac{202}{\text{seconds per cu yd}}$$

$$(X)\ \frac{202}{\text{seconds per cu yd}} \times 60\ \frac{\text{sec}}{\text{min}} = (Y)\ \frac{3.4}{\text{minutes per cu yd}}$$

$$(D)\ \frac{1092}{\text{pounds of sand}} \times (I)\ \frac{.04}{\text{\% moisture}} \times .12\ \frac{\text{gal}}{\text{lb}} = (M)\ \frac{5.2}{\text{gallons } H_2O \text{ in sand}}$$

$$(H)\ \frac{36}{\text{gallons per cu yd}} - (M)\ \frac{5.2}{\text{gallons in sand}} = (R)\ \frac{30.8}{\text{gallons to be added}}$$

$$(R)\ \frac{30.8}{\text{gallons to be added}} \div (Y)\ \frac{3.4}{\text{minutes per cu yd}} = (Y)\ \frac{9.1}{\text{water setting}}$$

SAND SETTING

Refer to bulking factor curve (Figure 2). Project straight up from figure representing (I) moisture content to where the line crosses the curve for the correct type sand. Project a line straight to the left hand scale and read the bulking factor (Q).

$$(Q) = \frac{.27}{\text{bulking factor}}$$

$$(D)\ \frac{1092}{\text{pounds of sand}} \div (A)\ \frac{110}{\text{unit weight of sand}} = (U)\ \frac{9.9}{\text{saturated surface dry volume of sand}}$$

$$1 + (Q)\ \frac{.27}{\text{bulking factor}} \times (U)\ \frac{9.9}{\text{saturated surface dry volume of sand}}$$

$$= (P)\ \frac{12.6}{\text{wet volume of sand}}$$

$$(T)\ \frac{497}{\text{cement meter count}} \div (P)\ \frac{12.6}{\text{wet volume of sand}} = (S)\ \underline{39.4}$$

Read sand dial setting from the sand curve (Figure 3) entering with your value for (S). Sand dial setting is 3.9.

STONE SETTING

$$(E)\ \frac{1956}{\text{pounds of stone}} \div (B)\ \frac{105}{\text{bulk unit wgt of stone}} = (V)\ \frac{18.6}{\text{volume of stone}}$$

$$(T)\ \frac{497}{\text{cement meter count}} \div (X)\ \frac{18.6}{\text{volume of stone}} = (R)\ \underline{26.7}$$

Read stone dial setting from stone curve entering with your value for (R). (See Figure 4.) Stone dial setting is 6.8.

By setting the sand dial to 3.9, the stone dial to 6.8, the water meter to 9.1 gpm and letting the cement meter run until it reads 497, you should produce one cubic yard of concrete that meets the absolute volume mix design specifications.

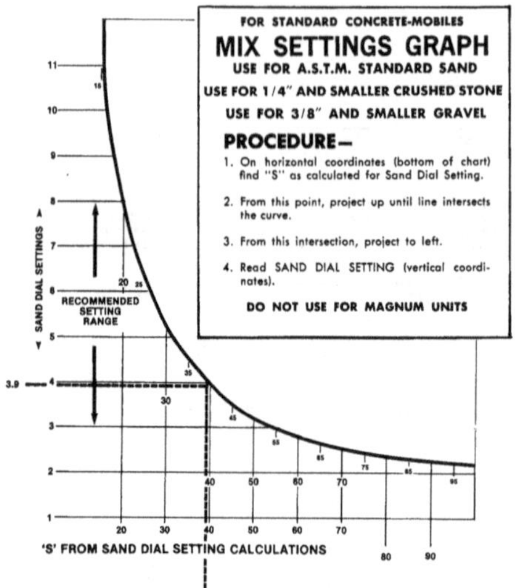

Figure 3. Sand dial graph.

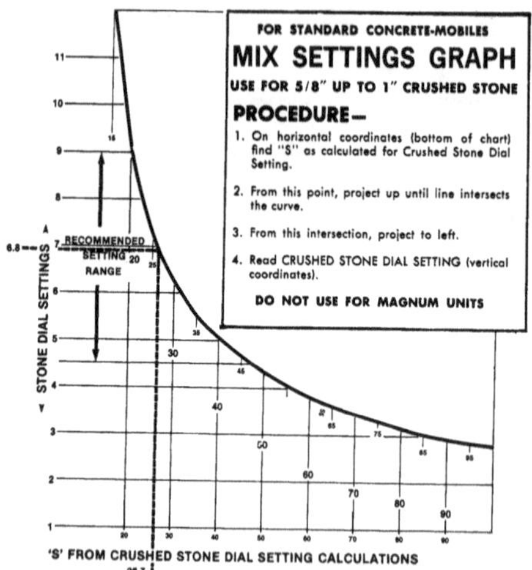

Figure 4. Stone dial graph.

AIRLOADING THE COMBAT HEAVY COMPANY

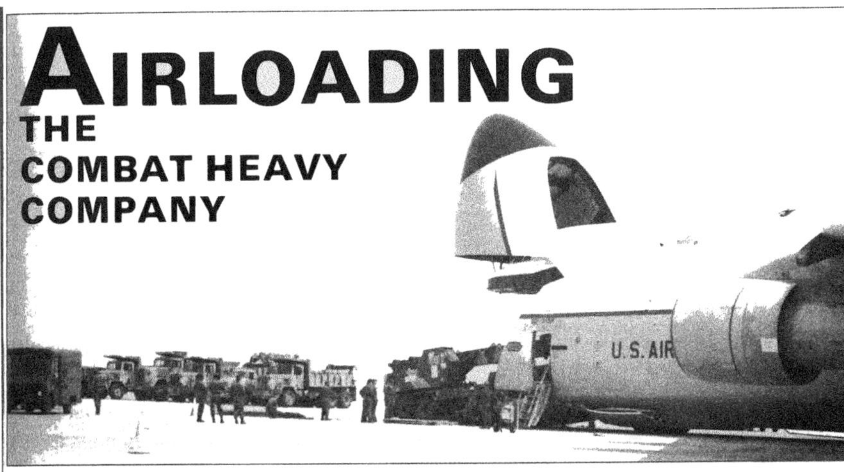

Engineers from Delta Co., 52nd Engineer Bn., load their 25-ton crane onto a C5A Galaxy. (Eric Mogren photos)

by CPT Eric Mogren

The goal: Train D Company, 52nd Engineers, in the techniques and procedures of combat loading aircraft.

Company objectives were to validate unit loading plans; identify problems with loading specific pieces of equipment; verify the time needed to mark, weigh and inspect equipment before loading; and to train crews how to secure vehicles inside aircraft. The C5A aircraft was used for loading large equipment and the C141B was used for the wheeled vehicles and trailers.

First Things First

As with any operation, the keys to success were detailed planning, organization and coordination.

Few of D Company's personnel had participated in an airloading exercise before. It was therefore necessary to train not only the troops, but also the officers and NCOs regarding maintenance and vehicle cleanliness requirements, properly loading tools and equipment onto vehicles, weighing and marking equipment, and moving vehicles onto the aircraft and securing them. It was also necessary to ensure that the airloading plans (MAC Forms 559, 749, and 551) and hazardous material forms (DD Form 1387-2) were properly completed before they were given to the airlift control element (ALCE).

This pre-exercise training was held in the motor pool and classroom, then rehearsed at a C5A mock-up at Biggs Field near Fort Bliss. At Biggs, each aspect of airloading was simulated. Tie-down crews were organized and taught how to secure equipment to the aircraft floor. Vehicles loads were checked to see that they would not shift. An inspection point was set up and manned by unit mechanics who made sure that vehicle met ALCE maintenance requirements. Where necessary, exhaust stacks were removed from trucks and equipment. All vehicles to be loaded were divided in the marshalling area by chalk (plane-load sequence).

The rehearsal proved extremely valuable. Using the mock-up and the detailed planning went a long way toward informing people about what to expect during the actual loading.

Who Are Those Guys?

A few words about the ALCE. It is the coordinating agent between the unit being loaded and the Air Force flight crew. The ALCE ensures that

Take into account the weight of the shoring when planning each chalk. Shoring for heavy equipment can weigh up to 2,000 pounds.

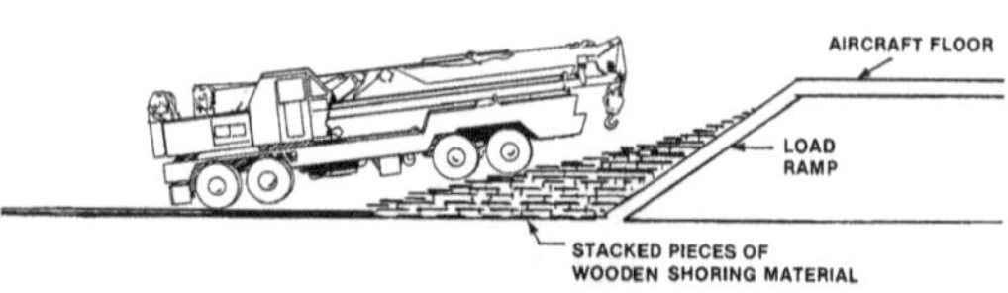

The MT250 crane could not negotiate the sharp angle formed by the loading ramp and runway. The problem was solved by piling up pieces of an old timber-trestle bridge set.

all vehicles and equipment meet Air Force regulations for air transport.

During loading operations, the unit being moved may deal with numerous flight crews, but only with one ALCE. It is important to establish early rapport with ALCE personnel and to understand their requirements. Coordination with the ALCE should be made at least a week prior to loading.

The Real Thing

The actual loading exercise began with each vehicle being weighed and marked to show its center of balance, height, and gross weight. The vehicles then were moved to a holding area near the runway where they were inspected stringently by ALCE personnel for oil leaks, dirt, caked mud or other debris that might fall off during the flight. To check fuel levels, inspectors opened each tank and physically checked the level; simply reading the gauge level was not acceptable. Fuel tanks could be no more than one-half full (or one-quarter full if the vehicle was to be positioned on the ramp).

Next, loading plans and hazardous material forms were turned in and vehicle weights and measurements were spot-checked. To meet height restrictions, exhaust stacks were removed from the M920 tractors, and the cab was removed from the bucket loader. Any vehicle not meeting ALCE standards was not permitted on the aircraft until all deficiencies were corrected.

Once the ALCE completed their inspection, the vehicles were moved onto the runway for loading. The loading was supervised by the aircraft flight crew's loadmaster.

Shoring Requirements

Besides properly restraining equipment inside the aircraft, protecting the aircraft floor was of particular concern. Without protective measures, heavy construction equipment will damage aircraft floor decking. In this case, wooden boards, planks and sheets from an old timber-trestle bridge set were put on the floor as a protective measure. (It is the responsibility of the unit being moved to provide such protective materials.)

To load the dozer, shoring had to be placed from the end of the load ramps to where the vehicle would be tied down. All equipment with metal blades (dozers, road graders, and M830 scrapers) needed three inches of shoring to prevent the cutting edge of the blades from resting directly on the aircraft floor. The biggest shoring challenge, however, involved the 25-ton crane.

The MT250 crane, due to its length, could not negotiate the sharp angle formed between the runway and the ramp (see diagram). The angle was reduced by piling up shoring material between the ramp and the pavement.

A trailer is pushed onto a C5A mock-up during rehearsal. Loading trailers using a truck with a tow pintle mounted on the front saved time.

small for heavy equipment.)

Delta Company vehicles were weighed at a permanent weight station at Fort Bliss. Weighing and marking vehicles is an exacting and time-consuming process. If vehicles are weighed and marked just before being loaded and if anything should go wrong, the entire exercise will be delayed. Weighing operations should be completed no later than the day before the loading operation.

Equipment is secured inside the C5A under Air Force supervision.

As noted earlier, an old timber-trestle bridge set was used for shoring material. The weight of the shoring must be taken into account when planning each chalk. Shoring for heavy equipment, for example, can weigh as much as 2,000 pounds.

Each time a unit conducts airloading training, there will be some untrained people involved, and this will probably cause some early delays. Delta Company now plans at least one and one-half hours to load the first chalk with subsequent chalks being loaded and tied down in 45 minutes for the C5A and within 30 minutes for the C141B.

The static airloading training provided valuable data for contingency planning. Every man in the company responded enthusiastically to the training. In fact, a major factor in the success of the training was the positive attitude and motivation of the individual soldier.

The company later was able to test its new knowledge. An EDRE (emergency deployment readiness exercise) was held with two platoons deploying with equipment to Fort Leonard Wood, Mo., for a week of tactical bridge training. It was a smooth and efficient fly-away due largely to the airloading training.

Every combat engineer unit has an inherent mission to be able to deploy rapidly and efficiently. Static airloading training like D Company conducted helps to provide the skill, confidence and teamwork necessary to effectively carry out an air movement operation.

CPT Eric Mogren commanded D Co., 52nd Bn. (Cbt) (Hvy) during the airloading training. D Co. is assigned to the 70th Ordnance Bn., Ft. Bliss, Texas. CPT Mogren is now working toward a master's degree in civil engineering at the University of Texas, Austin. He served previously with the U.S. Army Sergeants Major Academy, Ft. Bliss, and with the 12th Engineer Bn., 8th Infantry Div.

Haul mines and demolitions with an

Antiarmor Trailer

by LTC Wayne J. Scholl, CPT Byron E. Short Jr., 1LT Thomas E. Peck & Mr. Greg Willis

Combat engineers must be capable of deploying to a theater of operations or contingency area and arrive ready to perform their mission. In most scenarios, this mission initially involves countermobility operations.

A trip to an ammunition supply point is impossible in many contingency areas, so a basic load of demolitions and mines must accompany the deployed unit.

Regardless of the source of class V materiel, it must be quickly hauled forward, along with soldiers, equipment sets and individual gear. Combat engineer units in Europe and Korea have for years assembled trailer loads of demolitions to execute their initial combat missions. These so called "antiarmor trailers" are also a way for CONUS units to quickly and inexpensively load for combat.

Trailer Development

The M796 bolster trailer easily can be modified to serve as an antiarmor trailer capable of hauling 3.5 tons of materiel. With the modified trailers, a combat engineer battalion can deploy with and haul 100 tons of materiel for obstacles—a critical combat multiplier, especially for antiarmor operations.

Charlie Company, 65th Engineer Battalion (Combat), 25th Infantry Division, developed the prototype of

The M796 Bolster trailer easily can be converted to an "antiarmor trailer." Two soldiers can complete the modification in five minutes.

rugged, inexpensive, and locally ricated bolster trailer modifica- . The U.S. Army Defense Ammu- ɔn Center and School (USADACS), tasked by the Military Traffic ıagement Command Transporta- Agency, put the prototype trailer ɔugh demanding performance s to be sure the trailer met specifi- ons for ground, water, and air ısportation.

he Air Force had the toughest ign criteria. Air Force specifica- s required that the trailer accom- date a force resulting from three es the acceleration of gravity in forward and aft directions, two es in the vertical direction and and one half times in the lateral ections. Although that alone was a gh design criteria, the 65th Engi- rs also required that the trailer dification be locally fabricated, be ily maintained and be easily onverted to its original condition.

he trailer passed every test by a e margin and has shown potential Army-wide use. Meanwhile, a ·e efficient design was developed by USADACS which reduced the material requirement, eliminated the need to weld brackets to the trailer and made it easier to build.

The redesigned trailer was then field-tested during the Team Spirit 83 deployment to Korea. The result is a final design that is fully-tested on the performance course and in the field, and is certified for air, sea, and land transport.

Construction Details

Building the components to modify a bolster trailer costs only $200 and includes plywood, 2x4s and 4x4s. About 24 man-hours of construction time are required. All materials can be precut and then constructed in six sections.

To modify a bolster trailer, the floor is set in place first. Front and rear interchangeable bulkheads fit into existing channels in the bolster trailer, thus transferring the shear force to the trailer. After loading by hand or forklift, the interchangeable side walls are inserted, then the cover positioned. Two soldiers can complete the modification in five minutes since each component weighs 165 pounds or less. Nylon tie-down straps carry the momentum forces to the shackles.

The approved construction drawings, including a bill of materials are available from: Director, U.S. Army Defense Ammunition Center and School, ATTN: SARAC-DE (Mr. Greg Willis), Savanna, IL 61704 or contact the Director of Combat Developments, U.S. Army Engineer School, Fort Belvoir, VA 22060.

The antiarmor trailer conversion to the bolster trailer can significantly improve the countermobility potential of CONUS-based combat engineer battalions.

LTC Wayne J. Scholl is commander of the 65th Engineer Bn. (Cbt), 25th Infantry Div. Cpt Byron E. Short Jr. commands C Co., 65th Engineers and 1LT Thomas E. Peck is C Co. XO. Mr. Greg Willis is with the Evaluations Division, U.S. Army Defense Ammunition Center and School, Savanna, Ill.

ENGINEER SOLUTION

Absolute Volume Method

$$\text{Cement} = \frac{1}{w/c}\,(\text{water}) = \frac{1}{.44}\,(300\text{ lbs}) = 681.8\text{ lbs}$$

Gravel (from chart) = .69

$$\text{Wgt}_{\text{gravel}} = .69\,(27\text{ cf/cy})\,(\text{BUW}_{\text{gravel}})$$

$$= .69(27)(105) = 195\text{ lbs}$$

$$\textbf{Absolute Volume} = \frac{\textbf{wgt of material}}{\textbf{specific gravity (62.4)}}$$

$$\text{Cement: } \frac{300\#}{1(62.4\#/\text{cf})} = 3.47\text{ CF}$$

$$\text{Water: } \frac{300\#}{1(62.4\#/\text{cf})} = 4.81\text{ CF}$$

$$\text{Gravel: } \frac{1956\#}{2.65(62.4\#/\text{cf})} = 11.83\text{ CF}$$

$$\text{Air: } .015(27\text{ cf}) = \frac{.41\text{ CF}}{20.52\text{ CF}}$$

Sand: 27CF - 20.52CF = 6.48 CF

$$\text{Wgt}_{\text{sand}} = 6.48\text{ CF}\,(2.7)\,(62.4\#/\text{cf}) = 1092\#$$

$$\text{Adjusted Wgt}_{\text{sand}} = 1.02(1092\#) = 1114\#$$

Adjusted Mix Water = 1092#(.02) = 22#
300# - 22# = 278#

Cement: **682 lbs or 7.2 sacks**
Water: **278 lbs or 33 gallons**
Sand: **1114 lbs**
Gravel **1956 lbs**

Volume of Coarse Aggregate Per Unit of Volume of Concrete

Maximum size of aggregate, in.	Volume of dry-rodded coarse aggreate per unit volume of concrete for different fineness moduli of sand			
	2.40	2.60	2.80	3.00
⅜	0.50	0.48	0.46	0.44
½	0.59	0.57	0.55	0.53
¾	0.66	0.64	0.62	0.60
1	0.71	**0.69**	0.67	0.65
1½	0.75	0.73	0.71	0.69
2	0.78	0.76	0.74	0.72
3	0.82	0.80	0.78	0.76
6	0.87	0.85	0.83	0.87

Career Notes

Commissioned Officer Branch

SC 21 Restructure Update: As announced in the last issue of ENGINEER, restructuring specialty code (SC) 21 (Combat Engineer) for commissioned officers has been approved.

The new SC 21 (Combat Engineer) encompasses positions involved with battlefield mobility, countermobility, survivability, and general engineering. New SC 23 (Facilities/Contract Construction Management Engineer) includes positions associated with Army facilities and housing support, the civil works program, and military construction programs for both the Army and the Air Force. SC 22 (Topographic Engineer) is *not* affected by these changes.

MILPERCEN is reviewing the records of all SC 21 officers to identify those qualified for the new SC 21 and SC 23. Experience, education and training are the factors determining reclassification.

Officers with SC 21 (Engineer) as their initial specialty generally will retain SC 21 (Combat Engineer). About 60 percent of these new SC 21 officers will be assigned SC 23 as an additional specialty. Officers who now have SC 21 as their additional specialty usually will be reclassified as SC 23. About 30 percent of the SC 23 population will be officers from non-Engineer branches.

From January to March 1984, MILPERCEN will send a letter concerning the reclassification process to all dual-specialty officers who have SC 21 (Engineer) as one of their specialties. The letter will explain the reclassification plan and give each officer the opportunity to express his reclassification preferences.

Engineer officers without a second specialty as of January 1984 will not receive a reclassification letter. Instead, their initial specialty will be administratively converted to the new SC 21 (Combat Engineer). Since this conversion will be automatic, it will not be necessary for these officers to contact MILPERCEN. Designation of additional specialties (including SC 23) for these officers will be accomplished under established additional specialty procedures.

All reclassification actions will be done between April and September 1984.

Branch Visits: Engineer Branch makes trips to installations and engineer activities worldwide. The visits give branch personnel an opportunity to provide up-to-date information about the Officer Personnel Management System (OPMS), and give engineer officers the chance to talk face-to-face with their assignment officer.

Some of these trips are scheduled and funded by MILPERCEN, but many visits are requested and funded by units in the field. Requests for an Engineer Branch visit should be sent to: U.S. Army Military Personnel Center, ATTN: DAPC-OPF-E (Branch Chief), 200 Stovall St., Alexandria, VA 22332. Preliminary telephonic inquiries are welcome. Funding for travel, lodging and per diem must be provided by the requesting activity.

During the visit, branch personnel will provide a comprehensive briefing on the OPMS and have an Official Record Brief and microfiche Officer Military Personnel File (OMPF) for each officer in the activity.

During the individual interview (15 to 20 minutes), the assignment officer will discuss promotions, personnel actions, military and civilian schooling, career needs and reassignment. It is also an opportunity to update the OMPF and branch file.

Warrant Officer Branch

W02 Eligibility: E7s and above are now eligible to apply for direct appointment to W02. (No time-in-grade requirements apply.) However, MILPERCEN emphasizes that those selected for appointment to W02 will incur a six-year obligation. Implementation instructions will soon be released to the field. For more information, call CW4 Ed Cole, (202) 325-7839/7840, AV 221.

NCO & Enlisted Branch

Enlisted ASI Management: With the publication of Change 19, AR 611-201, the Army now has 152 authorized additional skill identifiers (ASIs) which can be associated with 115 different MOSs. This represents an increase of 37 ASIs since the Enlisted Personnel Management System began in 1973.

Additional skill identifiers have increased importance when they identify soldiers and positions associated with force modernization. To ensure that the Army receives maximum benefit from its trained personnel, commanders and personnel managers must follow the criteria in AR 600-200; see AR 614-200 for requisitioning guidance.

The requirements for using ASI-qualified soldiers are: (1) soldiers must be employed immediately after ASI training. Duration of the assignment must conform to paragraph 4-6, AR 614-200; (2) ASI-qualified soldiers are improperly used if they are not assigned to a meet a requirement for which they were requisitioned; (3) soldiers with more than one ASI should be used in the requisitioned ASI; (4) soldiers with an ASI and not assigned against an ASI requisition should be in an ASI position if an authorized vacancy exists; and (5) should a unit be assigned more ASI-qualified soldiers than authorized, all authorized positions should be filled with ASI-qualified soldiers.

For more information about enlisted ASI management, call MILPERCEN, (202) 325-8090, AV 221.

ASSIGNMENT CONTACTS

Commissioned Officers:
(202) 325-7504/5/6, AV 221

Branch Chief .... LTC Peter G. O'Neill
Lieutenant Colonels .... MAJ John Basilotto
Majors .... MAJ Steve Rust
Captains .... CPT(P) Tim Wood
Lieutenants .... CPT Bo Temple
SC 49 Assignments .... MAJ Dennis Cochrane
Professional Development .... CPT Philip Jones

Warrant Officers:
(202) 325-7839/7840, AV 221

Assignment Officer .... CW4 Edward Cole

NCO & Enlisted:
(202) 325-7710, AV 221

Branch Chief .... LTC Liston Edge
Branch Sergeant Major .... SGM John Peterson
CMF 81, MOS 12Z (E8s) .... MSG James Blair
CMF 12 .... SFC Richard Markle
Professional Development .... SSG Gary McAllister

THE MECHANIZED COMBAT ENGINEER

CHARACTERIZATION BY CPT STEVE RESSLER

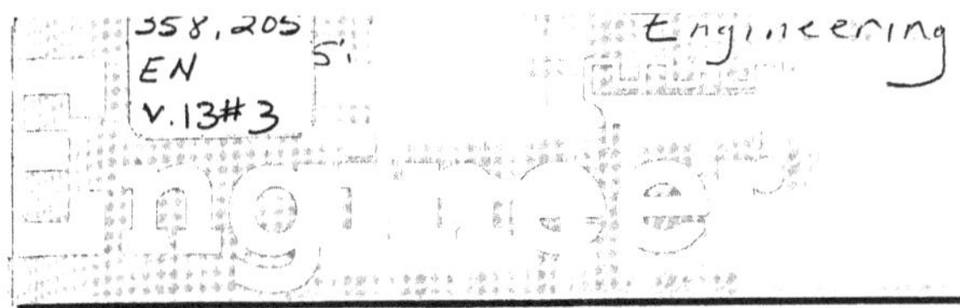

E MAGAZINE FOR ARMY ENGINEERS

FALL 1983

FORUM REBUTTAL

Chief replies: Warrant Officer Training Is Professional and Extensive

by CW4 Eugene F. Thompson

Editor's Note: The following is a response to the Forum article, "Equipment Repair Technicians—Our Forgotten Engineers?" by CW3 Curtis R. Millner, which appeared in ENGINEER/Number 1, 1983.

For the most part, CW3 Curtis R. Millner's comments on the assignment and training policy problems for engineer warrant officers are good. We would be well advised to heed this warning. Exception must be taken, however to his blanket indictment of training provided in the warrant officer basic and advanced courses.

The Basic Course

To understand how the basic course content was derived, one must first understand its purpose. It was never intended that the course replace the prerequisite of being fully qualified for appointment. It should, however, provide the warrant officer with the skills and knowledge required of an officer and technical supervisor. The course should also fill technical knowledge gaps that may exist as a result of specialization in the enlisted ranks.

The qualification requirements for appointment to warrant officer are spelled out in AR 135-100, *Appointment of Commissioned and Warrant Officers of the Army.* The regulation specifies that to be eligible for appointment, each applicant must have education, technical training and practical experience sufficient for the rank. This is further amplified in DA Pamphlet 600-11, *Warrant Officer Professional Development* which says, "Prerequisite to appoint is the prior attainment of full qualification."

The purpose of the basic course, then, is not to be MOS-producing but to supplement or hone existing skills and knowledge. To accomplish this, an 11-week course was developed that covers supply and maintenance management, engines, power trains, construction equipment, power generation equipment, and special purpose equipment.

Obviously, it is not possible to provide training on each of the many systems and pieces of equipment in the engineer inventory. Nor is it possible to develop a course that totally meets all the needs of a student population with varying levels of military experience and expertise. The basic course as presently configured, however, does as much as possible to meet DA training requirements.

What is viewed by CW3 Millner as "a little training" is actually a substantial amount for a newly appointed warrant officer. If a WO1 cannot function satisfactorily in his first assignment, the individual's personal qualifications should be examined, not the Army training he receives as a warrant officer.

It is true that not all newly appointed warrant officers attend the basic course, and this is probably a mistake. Attendance should be mandatory for all warrant officers prior to their first assignment.

The Advanced Course

CW3 Millner's statement regarding the scarcity of technical material in the Warrant Officer Advanced Course was undoubtedly true at one time, but it is no longer the case. Unlike the Warrant Officer Senior Course, which is not MOS related and is, in fact, designed to develop senior warrant officers for high-level staff positions, the Mechanical Maintenance Warrant Officer Advanced Course is technically oriented and is MOS specific. To ensure each mechanical maintenance MOS is adequately covered, the course is divided into two phases.

Phase I is taught at the U.S. Army Ordnance Center and School, Aberdeen Proving Ground, Maryland, and covers both common military subjects and technical subjects that are common to all MOSs in the mechanical maintenance field. Phase II of the course covers technical subjects that pertain to specific MOSs.

The engineer equipment repair technician (MOS 621A) receives five weeks of Phase II training at the U.S. Army Training Center Engineer, Fort Leonard Wood, Missouri. The training is technically oriented with emphasis on support-level maintenance.

(Please turn to page 9.)

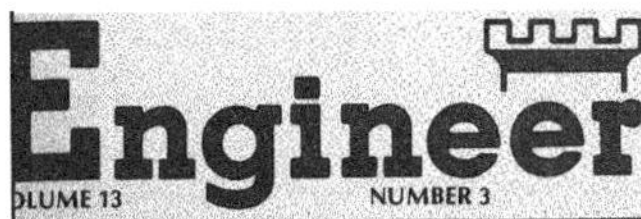

)LUME 13 NUMBER 3 FALL 1983

1 The Cover

\n M9 Bradley infantry fighting ve-
le is transported across Tompkins
in by the 902nd Engineer Co. (Assault
at Bridge) (Ribbon), 11th Engineer
(Combat) (Heavy), Engineer School
e. Photo by SSG Rick Maleck.

FEATURES

DEPARTMENTS

IGINEER is an authorized publication of the U.S. Army Engineer Center and Fort Belvoir, Va. Unless specifically stated, iterial appearing herein does not necessarily reflect official policy, thinking or endorsement by any agency of the U.S. Army. •The rds he, him, and his are used to represent personnel of either sex. •All photographs contained herein are official U.S. Army otographs unless otherwise credited. •The use of funds for printing this publication was approved by Headquarters, Department the Army, on July 22, 1981. •Material herein may be reprinted if credit is given to ENGINEER and the author. •ENGINEER'S iectives are to provide a forum for the exchange of ideas, to inform and motivate and to promote the professional development of all mbers of the Army engineer community. •Direct correspondence with ENGINEER is authorized and encouraged. Inquiries, ters to the editor, commentaries, manuscripts, photographs and general correspondence should be sent to: ENGINEER Magazine, ZA-TDL Stop 16F4, Fort Belvoir, VA 22060. Phone: (703) 664-3082, AV 354. •Subscriptions to ENGINEER are available through Superintendent of Documents, U.S. Government Printing Office, Washington, DC 20402. A check or money order payable to perintendent of Documents must accompany all subscription requests. Rates are $8.50 for domestic (including APO and FPO) dresses and $10.65 for foreign addresses. Individual copies are available at $4.50 per copy for domestic addresses and $5.65 for eign addresses. •Second Class postage paid at Fort Belvoir, Va., and additional mailing offices. ISSN 0046-1989.

Six Engineer MOSs Are Reopened to Women

Female enlisted engineers can now serve in six of ten recently closed military occupational specialties (MOSs).

Earlier this year, ten Engineer MOSs were closed to women as a result of the Army's Women In The Army Policy Review Group report, which was approved by Army Secretary John O. Marsh Jr. But a six-month Army staff review of the direct combat probability coding system has resulted in the reopening of six of the MOSs.

Soldiers who have already taken steps to move from one of the reopened MOSs will be permitted to return if they wish.

Some units that contain the reopened MOSs will still be closed to women. The exclusion is due to those units' high probability of direct combat involvement.

Female soldiers serving in a unit closed to women will be transferred out of the unit during the next several years, in accordance with normal reassignment policies. □

OPEN AGAIN

51B	Carpenter & Masonry Repairer
62E	Heavy Construction Equipment Operator
62G	Quarrying Specialist
62H	Concrete & Asphalt Equipment Operator
62J	General Construction Equipment Operator
82B	Construction Surveyor

STILL CLOSED

00B	Diver
51K	Plumber
51R	Interior Electrician
52G	Transmission & Distribution Specialist

Link Reinforcement Set Extends Length of Medium Girder Bridge

The capability of the medium girder bridge (MGB) is expanding with the aid of a link reinforcement set (LRS).

The LRS was studied recently by test teams from the 264th Engineer Co., Ft. Bragg, N.C. The tests were conducted at Aberdeen Proving Ground, Md.

With the aid of the LRS, the 102-foot MGB can be extended to 163 feet. The bridge is used to transport tanks and other heavy equipment over large terrain depths. The bridge can be quickly erected and dismantled by soldiers under the direction of one senior NCO. □

Engineers In Grenada

The 307th Engineer Bn. (Combat), 82nd Airborne Div., Ft. Bragg, N.C., participated in the recent rescue mission in Grenada. Details will be in the Winter issue of ENGINEER.

A bridge erection boat (shallow draft) transports a section of a ribbon bridge. Modifications to the boat are scheduled for application next year.

Boat Improved

Improvements are being made on the bridge erection boat (shallow draft), following recommendations from the field.

The boat is being refitted to employ the ribbon bridge more efficiently. The boat will decrease launch and retrieval time and offer an operating draft which is more compatible with that of the ribbon bridge. Thus, constraints on the selection of crossing sites will be reduced.

Modifications to the boat consist of a reinforced push knee assembly, a hose kit for out-of-water engine operation, an improved fuel filter pipe, a fore deck grab rail, and rubber sleeving for the cradle stanchions.

The changes are scheduled to appear on the boats in USAREUR by June, and on CONUS-based boats by September 1984.

The 27-foot boat has been fielded since February 1982. Currently, there are about 250 such boats in the U.S. inventory. □

POLE POSITION—*SP4 Russell Dukes (left) and PFC Cedric Archie paint the downtown flagpole in San Francisco, as part of a renovation project. On this site, the first U.S. flag raising in Northern California occurred in 1846. The flagpole is located in the city's Chinatown district. Dukes and Archie serve in D Co., 864th Engineer Bn., Presidio of San Francisco, Calif. (Tim Dewar photo)*

School Route Made Safer

Combat engineers stationed in Korea made a school route safer for children while gaining experience in construction.

Soldiers of 2nd Plt., B Co., 2nd Engineer Bn., 2nd Infantry Div., Camp Casey, Korea recently constructed a stairway along a cliff and a footbridge across a stream near the San Kwang Orphanage in Chunhyon-Myon. The orphanage houses about 80 children who range from toddlers to teens.

Before the bridge was constructed, the children were getting to school by "wading through the stream after scrambling down the cliff," according to SFC James P. Schaller.

The project involved constructing 20 meters of footbridge and pouring 60 meters of concrete for the sidewalk and stairway. Holes were drilled into the face of the cliff and steel bars were used to stabilize the concrete, which was mixed nearby and carried in buckets to the construction site. □

Microcomputer Selection Guide Available to Buyers

Information to assist Army engineers in selecting microcomputers for managing construction activities at field offices has been published by the U.S. Army Construction Engineering Research Laboratory (CERL) in Champaign, Ill.

The Microcomputer Selection Guide for Construction Field Offices is designed to assist managers in deciding what microcomputer systems and software packages should be purchased to improve their operations. According to Glenn Colwell, one of its authors, the selection guide "provides a single source of information on microcomputers for construction managers, many of whom have little time to keep up with the rapidly changing computer field."

The guide takes a prospective purchaser of a microcomputer system through the selection of a system. It presents an overview of microcomputer systems, available software packages, and examples of their use in the field. The guide helps the field manager assess office needs for automation and determine which microcomputer system would meet his needs best. Construction managers can then select a microcomputer system and software from a list of those available.

The microcomputer selection guide will be updated periodically to keep up with changes in the microcomputer field. Copies of the selection guide can be purchased in hard copy or on microfiche from the National Technical Information Center, 5282 Port Royal Road, Springfield, VA 22161, or by contacting the Publications Branch at the U.S. Army Construction Engineering Research Laboratory at (217) 352-6511, ext. 354, FTS 958-7354. Individuals ordering the selection guide from NTIS should identify it by its accession number—ADA130245. The complete bibliographic reference is:

Francois Grobler, Michael J. O'Conner and Glenn E. Colwell, *Microcomputer Selection Guide for Construction Field Offices*, Technical Report P-146 (U.S. Army Construction Engineering Research Laboratory, June 1983). □

by MG James N. Ellis, Commandant, U.S. Army Engineer School

Make A Commitment To NCOES

NCO training is an investment that benefits all of us.

An effective noncommissioned officer corps is central to a ready Army. The level of our NCOs' dedication and the extent of their ability as trainers determine the quality of our Army. Trainers in peacetime and combat leaders in wartime, NCOs are a reflection of the Army's health. They must be the focal point upon which we develop new initiatives and the base upon which we expand during mobilization.

How do NCOs attain these required levels of performance? By experience on the job, supplemented with formal schooling.

Over the past few years, formal schooling for NCOs has evolved into an extensive system of courses called the Noncommissioned Officers Education System (NCOES). The NCOES provides leadership training and MOS specific training. But having a system is not enough. For the quality combat leaders needed to fight and win the AirLand Battle, soldiers and leaders at every level must make a strong *commitment* to supporting the NCOES.

Investing for the Future

The system is only as good as the individual, his associates, and his leaders make it. Investments made today will bring dividends for years to come. As with any investment, some current resource must be saved and a little "pain" felt so that the account can grow. In the case of the NCOES, investments must be made by a number of people. The commander must make the hard decision to reduce his "present-for-duty" strength, while simultaneously competing for training funds and allocations needed for each course. A platoon may lose a ke NCO for a while; other soldiers in the unit will have to pick up the extra work load. Command sergeants major and first sergeants will have t(go that extra mile to recommend the best stude1 for each course, and then assure backfilling of vacant positions during the schooling. An up-tc date order of merit list at unit level is a must. The soldier-student, however, makes one of the biggest investments by attending a distant school away from his family and friends at son cost and hardship.

Selecting and sending a student to an NCOE course is only a part of the unit's responsibility The battalion commander and command sergeant major must ensure that the best NCOs are selected and prepared, both mentally and physically, to attend. Lack of math and readin comprehension, weight problems, and poor physical condition are the most common stude shortcomings. These problems need to be overcome *before* the student leaves for the school.

Courses On-Line

Development of the NCOES is a priority at TRADOC. The article beginning on page 14 provides detailed information about the NCOE

The Engineer School has just launched at Fo Leonard Wood, Missouri, the 51H (Constructio Engineering Supervisor) Basic Technical Cour (BTC). An article about the 51H BTC appears page 13. In about a year, another BTC will begi at Fort Leonard Wood, this one for the 62N (Construction Equipment Supervisor). Other specialized training for engineer tracked vehicl crewmen is under way at the Seventh Army Training Command; similar training will start at Fort Leonard Wood in late 1984. Also, the Defense Mapping School recently began offeri advanced schooling for cartographers and terrain analysts.

The Engineer NCOES is moving forward to lead the way in Army NCO training. The quali of the Engineer NCO Corps, and of the entire Army, will improve in direct proportion to the amount of effort we all put into the system.

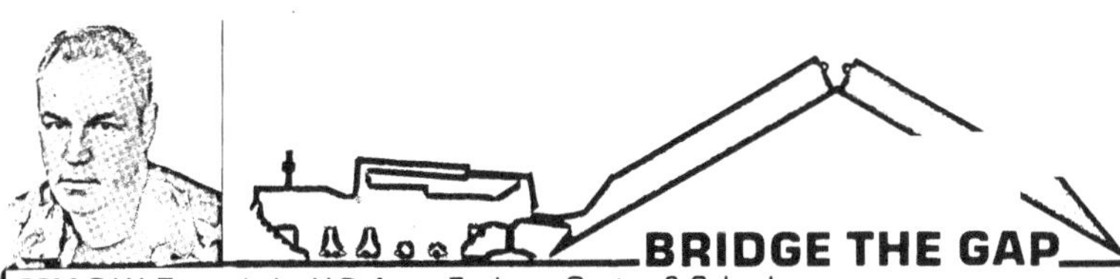

CSM O.W. Troesch Jr., U.S. Army Engineer Center & School

Are We Sending the Right People to NCOES Courses?

ometimes we're not. NCOs must be in the front rank elping to correct the situation.

As the Army moves forward with the velopment of high-technology weapons stems and equipment, there is an increasing ed for a well-trained noncommissioned officer rps to conduct individual soldier training. But e we, as noncommissioned officers, prepared to cept this awesome responsibility and to live up our reputation as the trainers of soldiers?

riority to NCOs

When I visit units, I review unit order of merit sts for NCO professional development hooling at the Primary NCO Course, the rimary Leadership Course, the Basic NCO ourse, the Primary/Basic Technical Courses id other NCOES courses. I continually ask, Vhen will we give attendance priority to oncommissioned officers who, for whatever ason, have never attended NCOES courses?"

Every unit has reasons for not training its oncommissioned officers, reasons ranging from eparing for an upcoming ARTEP or AGI to ome specialists four are better soldiers and serve the opportunity to attend first."

Don't discount these reasons, but rather onsider the reason the Army approved the COES development system and the program's irpose: to train noncommissioned officers to be nall-unit leaders. The NCOES system was set) so NCOs could help soldiers "bridge the gap" om what they learned at Initial Entry and One ation Unit Training to the additional training eded to survive and to win on the battlefield.

If we continue to train the wrong soldier in our COES system, the noncommissioned officer orps will fail to accomplish its second most iportant task, to develop a professional NCO orps.

o Control?

You may say that we NCOs have no control over who goes to NCO schools. I say, not true.

Have we lost the moral courage to stand by our convictions? Are we unable to tell our commanders that we are sending to courses students who do not fill leadership positions, who are not promotable (on a promotion standing list to the pay grade of SGT/SP5), who are overweight, who cannot pass the PT test, who are not qualified with their basic weapons, or who have not mastered at least 70 percent of the tasks in their job books?

Do we look our commander in the eye and say that noncommissioned officers must go to school? Or do we just turn away, as untrained NCOs are promoted and are expected to learn how to be effective leaders and trainers through on-the-job training only?

Are we willing to accept short-term goals as a substitute for the long-term benefit to the Army of a properly trained and professionally developed NCO corps?

If you are a part of the NCO support channel but are not actively involved in selecting NCOES students, then you are shirking one of the responsibilities given to us by the chain-of-command. This responsibility is second in importance to our performance as promotion board members.

If we are to become an Army of excellence and if Engineer branch noncommissioned officers are to continue the tradition of being standard setters for the Army, then we must rededicate ourselves to becoming personally involved with selecting the students sent to NCOES courses and to becoming personally involved with the training of our soldiers and units.

Strive for excellence. In your efforts to educate and to develop junior noncommissioned officers, help them to "bridge the gap" between being a soldier and being a leader of soldiers.

Directorate of Combat Developments (DCD)

Product Improvements Proposals (PIP):

There's good news for users of the ribbon bridge. The TRADOC-DARCOM Spring 1983 Product Improvement Program (PIP) Review conditionally approved PIPs for the bridge. The condition for approval is completion of required coordination and staffing. The PIP includes adding a steel cap to the ramp bay tie-down pin; reducing the size of the roadway dog-bone connector; and elimination of hydraulic fluid leakage from the ramp bay hydraulic system. These improvements address complaints often heard from engineers in the field.

Maneuver Control System (MCS):

An operational capability for automated engineer command and control may be nearing reality. The MCS consists of a tactical computer terminal and tactical computer system. MCS offers a responsive capability for battlefield management of engineer assets, instantaneous situation assessments and immediate transfer of information between the maneuver force and its supporting engineers. Although engineer requirements are not included in the initial MCS buy, they are considered in the follow-on program.

Armored Combat Earthmover (ACE) M9:

The first four M9s of the initial production contract are being assembled at the PACCAR Company plant in Renton, Wash. These M9s will be delivered to Aberdeen Proving Ground, Md., by April 1984 where they will undergo vigorous testing. Successful completion of this testing will lead to a competitive full production contract award in July 1984. The remaining M9s from initial production will be used for force development testing at Ft. Hood during late 1984 and at Fort Lewis during early 1985.

Countermobility-Demolitions:

This fiscal year, DCD focuses attention on engineer operational requirements for demolitions. DARCOM will examine state-of-the-art demolition technology to satisfy engineer requirements for improved one-step systems for producing obstacles.

Already underway is preparation of a requirement document for a bridge, road and tunnel (BRAT) munition. Plans are to review bulk explosives. Atomic demolition munitions (ADM) in the force structure are under review. There is a possibility of identifying a "special conventional" demolition role. Thus, the MOS 12E (ADM specialist) faces the prospect of considerably increased responsibility.

efense Mapping School (DMS)

Terrain Analysis Seminar: The first Terrain Analysis Seminar was held in July at Ft. Belvoir. The working seminar was attended by 99 people, 25 of whom were terrain analysis technicians from theater, corps and division terrain teams from Europe to Korea. The seminar grew out of an idea discussed at the 1982 DoD Mapping, Charting and Geodesy Conference.

The first half of the seminar was devoted to briefings to update the 841A (Training Analysis Technician) personnel on such topics as the Engineer Mission Area Analysis, DMA Production Program, CMF 81 and 841A career fields, topographic equipment, the Topographic Support System, the Digital Topographic Support System, and the quick response multicolor printer.

The second portion of the conference was dedicated to discussions among the terrain analysts on techniques employed in their units to support commanders with terrain analysis, mobility operations on urban terrain, weather effects, and trafficability. By consensus of participants, there will be another terrain analysis seminar in 1984.

irectorate of [raining and Doctrine (DOTD)

Engineer Drills: The Directorate of Training and Doctrine (DOTD) has recently developed 23 engineer drills which initially will be published as three separate field circulars titled Mobility Drills, Countermobility Drills, and General Engineer Drills. After publication as field circulars, these engineer drills will be revised to include comments from the field, and will eventually be incorporated into appropriate field manuals.

Also DOTD is programming to develop survivability and topography drills. The coordinating drafts for mobility and countermobility drills are now in production and should reach field units by the end of December 1983.

Engineer drills are the link between individual and collective proficiency. They are standardized techniques and procedures of engineer training.

Drills include combat, administrative and logistical actions relating to fighting, fueling, fixing and supplying units on the battlefield, as well as other important collective tasks which should be trained repetitively. They also include those few, highly critical actions which must be taken in combat in response to an emergency situation.

Engineer drills provide small units with a courses of action that can be taken immediately without waiting for detailed orders.

Editor's Note:
For information on the :eorganization of the Engineer School, see page 12.

Directorate of Training and Doctrine (continued)

ADSPEC 23 Course: The Facilities/Contract Construction Management Engineer (additional specialty 23) course is available for officers programmed for assignments in facilities engineering or in engineer districts and divisions. The course consists of three modules: the Common Core Module, the Facilities Engineering Management Course (FEMC), and the District/Division Engineer Course.

The Common Core Module is designed to provide training in a variety of engineering disciplines. Both subject matter and practical applications in civil engineering, building construction technology, architectural engineering, electrical engineering, and mechanical engineering are discussed. Emphasis is also placed on construction management techniques, contract administration and other information appropriate to the role of the Facilities/Contract Construction Manager.

Upon completion of the Common Core Module, officers will attend either the FEMC or the District/Division Engineer Course. Those officers who will be assigned to a Directorate of Engineering and Housing attend the FEMC. Officers assigned within the Office of the Corps of Engineers (OCE) attend the District/Division Engineer Course, which is taught by instructors from OCE and the Huntsville District. This course provides detailed information on contract construction administration, how to be a contracting officer's representative, and general inspection techniques and procedures in accordance with OCE specifications and standards.

The next class is scheduled to begin on January 27, 1984.

Directorate of Evaluation and Standardization (DOES)

Follow-Up Training Evaluation: The Engineer School is placing additional emphasis on determining whether the training received by soldiers in OSUT (One Station Unit Training) is meeting the needs of the field. Units in the field can expect to receive questionnaire packets asking the units about the quality of the OSUT graduates they are receiving.

12Es to Recruiting Force: In an effort to provide CONUS stabilization for atomic demolition munitions (ADM) personnel, 12E personnel will become part of the Detailed Recruiting Force in the near future. A total of 22 E6 and 36 E5 12Es will be selected for a three-year tour with Recruiting Command. Personnel may volunteer by submitting a DA Form 4187 to MILPERCEN, ATTN: DAPC-EPL-E, 200 Stovall St., Alexandria, VA 22332.

How to Prepare For Your SQT

Follow these simple guidelines to improve your SQT score.

To prepare for the SQT, you must first know what to study. This information is provided in the SQT notice. The notice identifies all the areas on which you could be tested and lists appropriate references.

Each task listed in the SQT notice identifies the technical manual and/or field manual that explains how to perform the task correctly. The new editions of the soldier's manual also provide a checklist which your supervisor can use to determine your task proficiency.

After you have obtained the correct, current reference publications, the next thing to do is Study! Study! Study! By using the notice and soldier's manual, you can determine which section of the technical manual or field manual applies to the task you are studying. Here is one place where a lot of something may not be the best thing; study only those parts of the manual which are needed for the test. Save the rest for "light reading" when you have free time.

At the test site, make sure you have all the items needed for the test (pencils, scratch paper, test book, etc.) before you begin the test. This will prevent interruptions that might distract you while you are taking the test.

When you receive your test booklet, lightly read over the entire test to get a feel for what types of questions are being asked. Then take the test. Here is where your studying pays off. When you look at the list of possible answers, you will see that one or two of the choices have the least chance of being correct. After you eliminate these, you will narrow your choices to two or three possible answers. Now, select the correct answer. Once you make your selection DO NOT change it! In most cases, the answer you select first is the correct answer.

As you take the test, you will probably come across some questions that you won't be able to answer quickly. Skip these questions for now. By doing this, you won't waste time that you could be using to answer questions you know (remember, this is a timed test).

After you have answered all the easy questions, go back to those that gave you trouble. This is also a good time to check that your question and answer sheet numbers match.

It is a good idea to use most or all of the time allotted. This will prevent you from hurrying through the test and making mistakes. After you have answered all the questions, reread your answers to make sure you have marked the one you intended.

That's all there is to it! If you follow these simple rules, you should find that the time you invested preparing for your SQT really pays off.

Forum, continued

Phase II technical training for the 621A advanced course student is as broad in scope as possible. The student receives instruction on diesel engine repair, including repair of diesel fuel pumps and operation of a diesel fuel pump calibrating stand. The course also covers diagnostic procedures for construction equipment; operational and DA/BS maintenance characteristics (including warranties) of commercial construction equipment; and troubleshooting AC and DC electrical circuits, semi-conductors, and electronic components.

Performance tests and paralleling procedures for power generator sets are also studied at Phase II, along with: water diagnostic maintenance and repairing water purification units; diagnosis and repair of gas turbine engines; and use of test, measurement, and diagnostic equipment, including the simplified test equipment/internal combustion engine. In the area of maintenance management, the student receives instruction on the Army Oil Analysis Program, production control, quality control, material classification, and preparation of a DS/GS maintenance standing operating procedure.

While this list of subjects is not all inclusive, it should be sufficient to indicate the degree of technical training a 621A advanced course student receives during Phase II.

The basic and advanced are under continual review by the Engineer Equipment Committee as part of the effort to improve instruction quality and effectiveness. Feedback from former students and their commanders is an essential ingredient of the improvement program. Your comments are solicited.

CW4 Eugene F. Thompson is chief of the Engineer Equipment Committee, 4th Training Bde., Ft. Leonard Wood, Mo. He was previously assigned as the Battalion Maintenance Officer, 15th Engineer Bn. (CBT), Ft. Lewis, Wash. CW4 Thompson is a graduate of the Warrant Officer Basic Course and Distinguished Graduate of the Warrant Officer Advanced Course. He has an associate's degree in diesel technology from the College of the Redwoods, Eureka, Calif.

Evaluating Soldier Proficiency

by MAJ Thomas J. Aubin

The "old" three-component skill qualification test (SQT) is out. A new program called the Individual Training Evaluation Program (ITEP) has taken its place.

The ITEP uses a three-method system to evaluate a soldier's proficiency: the commander's year-round hands-on evaluation, the common task test, and the MOS-specific SQT.

Commander's Hands-On Evaluation

This part of the ITEP is an informal, local, hands-on evaluation of MOS task performance. The evaluation is given by the local commander. It can be conducted any time during the year and as many times as the commander desires. Tasks and locations for the evaluation are also selected by the commander. The test will be evaluated according to evaluation guides found in the new soldier's manual.

Results of the evaluation will not be formally reported. They are to be used by the local commander as diagnostic tools to evaluate soldier training and to enhance proficiency on MOS tasks.

MOS-Specific SQT

An MOS-specific SQT will be developed for each skill level of every MOS. The SQT will be a written test to measure an individual soldier's MOS proficiency. It will be taken annually during a three-month test period by all Active Component soldiers, E1 through E7. Reserve Component soldiers E1 through E7 will be tested during a six-month test period every two years.

Before each test period, an SQT Notice will be distributed to the unit. The notice lists the number and title of the tasks which may be tested. Only two-thirds of the tasks listed in the notice will actually be tested. There will be no practice questions on the notice. Local commanders will be able to score skill level one written tests using a FOR OFFICIAL USE ONLY printed answer key provided with the test. All MOS-specific written tests will be centrally scored and used for training decisions as well as for DA-level personnel management in the Active Component.

Skill qualification test feedback reports will be provided to soldiers and commanders. Individual Soldier Reports (ISRs) will be sent to soldiers and commanders within 30 days after submission of the test for scoring. This report will identify those tasks on which a soldier needs additional training. Summary reports will be provided periodically, or upon request, to the company through division-level commanders. This report will contain average SQT scores for all MOS skill levels tested.

Common Task Test

The common task test is a hands-on test with a written backup test which may be used when equipment is not available. The common task test is given annually and is used to evaluate the soldier's training on fundamental survival and combat skills. Selection of tasks for the test is based on input from major commands. Th Army Training Support Center pro duces the common task test usin material furnished from the Arm service schools. FM 21-2, *Soldier Manual of Common Tasks*, is th basic publication for training an evaluating common tasks.

All soldiers E7 and below will tak the common task test. The result will be reported for diagnostic us only. However, commanders ar encouraged to use test results whe preparing enlisted evaluatio reports and when making recom mendations for promotions and othe career decisions.

Phase-In

The new Individual Training Eva luation Program will be phased-i during FY 1984-86 as new soldier' manuals are published for most o the Corps of Engineers' 37 MOSs an 103 skill levels. When fully imple mented, the new program will pro vide local feedback for improvin training, as well as a basis for equita ble personnel decisions at DA level For more information about ITEP contact: SQT/QA Branch, Individua Training Division, Directorate o Training and Doctrine, USAES Fort Belvoir, VA 22060; (703) 664 6051, AV 354.

MAJ Thomas J. Aubin is chief of the Engineer School's SQT/QA Branch, Directorate of Training and Doctrine. He served earlier with the School's Directorate of Combat Developments and with Computer Systems Command. He is a graduate of Command and General Staff College and has a bachelor's degree in computer science and statistics from the University of Southern Mississippi.

ENGINEER HOTLINE

Problems, questions, and comments relating to engineer doctrine, training, organization, and equipment can be addressed telephonically to the U.S. Army Engineer School's "Engineer Hotline." The Hotline's auto-answer recorder operates 24 hours a day, seven days a week. Callers should state their name, address and telephone number, followed by a concise question or comment. You'll receive a reply within three to 15 days. **The Hotline is not a receiving agency for formal requests.**

Call commercial (703) 664-3646; WATTS 800-336-3095, extension 3646; or AV 354-3646.

TRAINING MINE IMPROVEMENTS UNDERWAY

by MAJ Joseph G. Papapietro

Training mine deficiencies are among the most serious problems faced by engineers and other members of the combined arms team. The recent Mission Area Analysis (MAA) studies for Close Combat Heavy, and Combat Support Engineering and Mine Warfare highlighted these shortcomings, and the Engineer School is moving as rapidly as possible to provide relief.

First, a brief look at how we arrived at the troublesome position we're in today. There are several problems with currently-fielded training mine devices and the logistical system that supports them.

Most of the training mines used today are inert versions of production line service mines. They are old, many are no longer available, and they have limited training value—especially for collective training tasks.

Plastic molded replica mines were an improvement; but, unfortunately, production was done in a piecemeal fashion, to varying specifications and by different agencies.

The training mine void forced many units to initiate in-house, short-term solutions. However, the lack of standardization and logistical support for these training mines has caused long-term problems.

Finally, and certainly still a problem to overcome, numerous training mine components, including fuzes and smoke grenades, are purchased through ammunition channels. That leads us to the conflict of budgetary priorities between "real" versus training ammunition.

By now you're probably saying, "Enough problems, how about solutions?" We have solutions on the way. The problems noted above identify several needs.

First, we must have mines that are inexpensive and that can be purchased and used in large quantities.

These devices must be responsive, and they should be applicable to both individual and collective tasks. Also, training mines must be easily procured through devices channels, not through ammunition channels.

Meeting all these requirements is a tall order. The solutions are in each of these three major developmental efforts underway at the Engineer School:

- the mine effects simulator (MES),
- the conventional training mine (CTM), and
- the family of scatterable mines (FASCAM) effects simulator (FES).

Mine Effects Simulator

The mine effects simulator (MES) has priority in the Engineer School's training device arena. Embodied as U.S. service mines and Threat mines, the MES is primarily intended for use by engineer and maneuver forces. The MES will provide realistic collective training opportunities for force-on-force, combined arms team training. Also, it will be applicable to both initial institutional and to individual sustainment training.

As experiences at the National Training Center (NTC) and during major combined arms team exercises have shown, the Army is unable to train on real-time employment, breaching and tactical considerations of mine obstacles.

The MES represents a significant advance in adding realism to the battlefield during training. It will cause commanders at all levels to consider the effects of mines. Real-time, real-world casualty assessment will give new emphasis to employment, breaching and tactical considerations. The MES will interact with Multiple Integrated Laser Engagement Systems (MILES) and will have safe, non-pyrotechnic smoke and flash visual detonation cues.

For example, imagine an NTC situation where a mechanized or armored column approaches an area of enemy activity. The column commander sees the telltale engineer tape and, using all his powers of deduction, smartly identifies the area as a minefield. If there are no umpires present, he crosses the area, suffers no casualties nor inconvenience, and receives no training.

The MES, however, will provide a different scenario. Gone will be the engineer tape. Instead, commanders will be forced to "read" the terrain, looking for likely areas in which the enemy might employ mines. If the commander proceeds, he will advance knowing that real-time casualties will be assessed if he errs. He and his men will have to learn to identify mines and minefields and know how to breach or bypass them.

Conventional Training Mine

The conventional training mine (CTM) is designed for use at the other end of the training spectrum. It is for the individual training of all mine users, including engineers, infantry, armor, field artillery, and other personnel with mine related soldier or ARTEP tasks.

The CTM will be a family of devices intended to replace all existing training mines. They will be exact, inert replicas of the M14, M15, M16,

Have a comment?

Developing training mines is the responsibility of the Engineer School's Training Support Branch, Unit Training Division, Directorate of Training and Doctrine. They are always interested in your suggestions and comments. Write to them or call (703) 664-4063/2465, AV 354.

M18A1, M19, and M21 service mines and will provide feedback to student and trainer.

The CTM has several advantages. First, it offers the opportunity to establish a new production base. This will increase availability and reduce costs. Although made of plastic or resin, CTMs will contain enough metal for normal detection and have ballast material for proper weight and feel. Also, a bell or buzzer will alert trainer and trainee of an incorrect arming or disarming procedure or of an unsafe condition.

FASCAM Effects Simulator

The FASCAM effects simulator (FES), like the MES, will give training realism and casualty assessment capability to the family of scatterable mines. The FES system is dependent on the MES's development and the challenge to miniaturize components but retain reliability. The FES is still several years from being fielded.

The mine effects simulator, the conventional training mine and the FASCAM effects simulator will give engineers, along with the rest of the combined arms team, unprecedented realism in mine and countermine training.

MAJ Joseph G. Papapietro is assigned to the Office of the Deputy Chief of Staff for Research Development and Acquisition. He earlier served at the Engineer School as chief, New Equipment Systems Branch, Directorate of Training and Doctrine. He is a graduate of the Command and General Staff College, the Defense Management College and has a master's degree from USC.

THE ENGINEER SCHOOL IS REORGANIZING

The U.S. Army Engineer School and its Engineer Training Brigade (ETB) has begun reorganizing in accordance with Training Doctrine Command's "School Model '83." The reorganization is part of a TRADOC effort to improve the operation of all TRADOC schools. School Model '83 is designed to simplify the training process, to free assets for teaching and writing doctrine, and to make the training departments the focus of the school.

General William Richardson, TRADOC commander, has given top priority to training and also to expanding the responsibilities of school instructors. In addition to teaching, the instructor/subject matter expert will be responsible for writing doctrine and all training development material. Organizational changes at Fort Belvoir are:

- •Consolidation of the Engineer Training Brigade (ETB) with the Engineer Center Brigade (ECB) into one School Brigade.
- •Establishment of a third training department—the Department of Maintenance.
- •Establishment of a school secretary to centrally manage the three training departments and to provide logistical support.
- •Establishment of a Directorate of Evaluation and Standardization (DOES).
- •Establishment of a Proponency Office.

The reorganization at Fort Belvoir began October 1 and should be completed by April 1. These changes should have no effect on the number of military and civilian jobs at Fort Belvoir.

Once complete, the Engineer School will consist of the:

- •Office of the School Secretary
- •Departments of Maintenance, Combined Arms, and Military Engineering
- •Directorates of Training and Doctrine, Evaluation and Standardization, and Combat Developments
- •School Brigade
- •Proponency Office

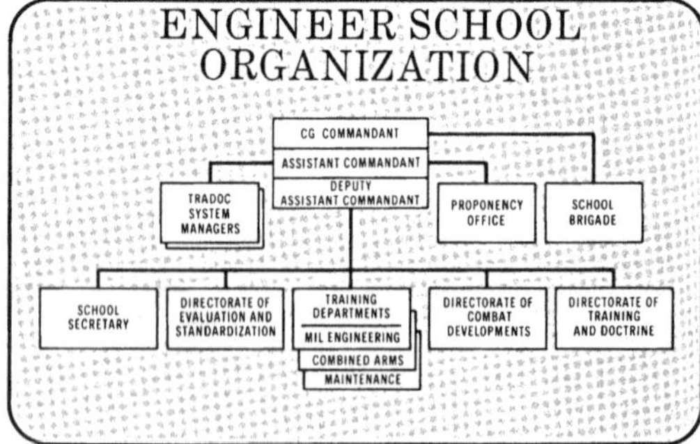

Building Supervisors

A new course begins for 51H Construction Engineering Supervisors

by 1LT Albert G. Marin III

Construction engineers play a vital role in the success of the modern Army. Wherever United States troops are stationed, there is a need for shelter, plumbing, electricity, and storage facilities. Military Occupational Specialties (MOSs) 51B, Carpentry and Masonry Specialist; 51C, Structures Specialist; 51K, Plumber; 51R, Electrician and 51H, Construction Engineering Supervisor exist to satisfy this need. It is important that soldiers with these MOSs be proficient in all aspects of construction engineering.

To help soldiers with MOSs 51B, 51C, 51K, and 51R become construction engineering supervisors (51H), a Basic Technical Course (BTC) has been developed. The 51H BTC is to teach newly, or soon to be, promoted 51Hs the skills necessary to plan, supervise, and inspect vertical construction projects. The BTC is a six-week long course which started this November at Fort Leonard Wood, Missouri.

Course Requirements

Recently (August 1 through September 16, 1983) a 51H BTC pilot course was held. Nineteen students participated in the trial course. The course design proved acceptable; however, the students were deficient in mathematics and reading. Students encountered few problems with the technical aspects of the course, which is explained by the nature of construction engineering.

Carpenters, electricians, and plumbers require only those skills necessary for actual construction or installation. Not so with construction supervisors.

Construction engineering supervisors must be capable readers. Supervising construction projects means dealing with construction directives, construction prints, construction details, bills of materials, and all the other written directives and explanations common to the field. It is important that these documents be read accurately and understood.

Supervisors must also have a good working knowledge of basic mathematics. Addition, subtraction, multiplication, division, ratios, and basic geometry are essential for planning any construction project. Being deficient in either math or reading can hurt your career.

How to Improve Your Skills

To determine your math and reading skills, contact your installation Army Education Center (AEC). Ask to take the Adult Basic Learning Examination (ABLE). The ABLE results will show your strong points and indicate where you may need refresher training.

Based on ABLE results, the AEC will recommend to your unit commander that you participate in the Basic Skills Education Program (BSEP). With approval from your unit commander, the AEC will enroll you in classes to increase your basic mathematical and reading skills. Classes are normally available in the morning or in the afternoon, allowing for a workable agreement between you and your commander.

Before you attend the 51H BTC, or any other noncommissioned officer course, contact your education center to make sure you have the skills needed to complete the course. Don't be caught by surprise; prepare now before it is too late.

1LT Albert G. Marin III is assigned to the Engineer School as MOS team chief of the Construction and Utilities Team, General Engineering Branch, Directorate of Training and Doctrine, Ft. Belvoir. He is a graduate of the University of Maine at Orono and the Engineer Officer Basic Course. He served with the 44th Engineer Bn. (CBT) (HVY) in Korea as a platoon leader and operations officer.

ENGINEER NCOES

A comprehensive listing of NCOES courses for the engineer NCO.

The Noncommissioned Officers Education System (NCOES) provides job related, progressive training for NCOs and specialists throughout their careers. It applies to all enlisted personnel of both Active and Reserve Components. NCOES is an integral part of the Enlisted Personnel Management System.

The objectives as noted in AR-351-1, *Individual Military Education and Training*, are to:

- Prepare NCOs to be trainers and leaders.
- Provide necessary job proficiency training to NCOs.
- Improve unit readiness and collective mission proficiency through individual proficiency of NCOs and subordinate soldiers.

NCOES is divided into four levels: primary, basic, advanced, and senior. NCOES courses focus on training tasks in the next higher skill level. For example, courses at the primary level prepare the skill level one (SL1) soldier (E4) for duty at SL2 (E5). Courses at the basic level prepare the SL2 soldier (E5) for duty at SL3 (E6), etc. Figure 1 shows information about the NCOES courses available for engineer soldiers. Figure 2 shows planned additions to the NCOES.

Reserve Component personnel are eligible to attend all resident NCOES courses, and they may enroll in any available nonresident courses. In addition, members of the Reserve Component may attend NCOES courses conducted by U.S. Army Reserve schools and National Guard NCO academies.

NCOES COURSES FOR ENGINEER SOLDIERS

Course	Purpose	MOS Pre-requisite	Location/ Length	Priority for Attendance	Remarks
Primary NCO Course (PNCOC)	Prepares SL1 combat arms soldiers (E4) for duties at SL2 (E5).	12B, 12C, 12E, 12F	NCO academies CONUS and overseas 4 weeks	E4 selected for promotion to E5, and E5/E6 with no prior leadership training.	Qualified soldiers selected by unit commander to attend.
				E3/E4 performing in E5/E6 leadership positions for which the course is necessary due to unit NCO shortages.	
Primary Leadership Course (PLC)	Prepares SL1 CS/CSS soldiers (E4) for SL2 (E5) and SL3 (E6) supervisor duties.	All CS/CSS MOSs	NCO academies CONUS and overseas 4 weeks	E4 selected for promotion to E5, and E6 with no prior leadership training	Qualified soldiers selected by unit commander to attend.
				E3/E4 performing in E5/E6 leadership positions for which the course is necessary due to unit NCO shortages.	

Figure 1

	Purpose	MOS Pre-requisite	Location/ Length	Priority for Attendance	Remarks
- (PTC)	Trains critical SL2 technical tasks of MOS.	12C	USAES, Ft. Belvoir 5 weeks	Soldiers selected for promotion to E5, or E5s performing in, or assigned to, E6 positions in their MOS.	Commanders nominate to MILPERCEN qualified soldiers to attend.
		52E	Facilities Engr Support Agency, Ft. Belvoir 52 weeks	E3/E4 performing in E5 positions for which the course is necessary due to unit NCO shortages.	
		52G	USAF, Sheppard AFB, 6 weeks		
		00B	USN, Port Hueneme, CA 9 weeks		
		52C	USAES, Ft. Belvoir 11 weeks		
		52D	USAES, Ft. Belvoir 11 weeks		
		62B	USATC, Ft. Leonard Wood 4 weeks		
		82D	DMS, Ft. Belvoir 6 weeks		
neer OC)	Prepares SL2/3 soldiers (E5) for duties at SL3 (E6). Develops SL3 weapons systems and equipment experts who can train and direct subordinates to maintain, operate, and employ weapons and equipment. Develops skilled NCOs who can train and lead subordinates and give and supervise the execution of orders.	12B, 12C, 12E, 51H, 51B, 51C, 51K, 51R	Fts. Bragg, Campbell, Ord, Hood, Polk, Riley, Stewart, Schoefield Bks, 7th ATC. 4 weeks plus 1 week local add-on	Soldiers selected for promotion to E6, and E6s who have not previously attended the course. E4 and E5 performing in E6 positions for which the course is necessary due to unit NCO shortages.	Qualified soldiers selected by unit commander to attend. E4 must be PNCOC graduate. Soldiers in CMF 51 must be combat eligible.
	Trains CEV and AVLB commanders and sergeants	12F	7th ATC, USAREUR 6 weeks	Same as Combat Engr BNCOC	Qualified soldiers selected by unit commander to attend. 12F in USAREUR attend this course in lieu of Combat Engr BNCOC. 12F BNCOC to be established at Ft. Leonard Wood in 4th quarter FY 84.

Figure 1 (continued)

Course	Purpose	MOS Pre-requisite	Location/ Length	Priority for Attendance	Remarks
Basic Technical Course (BTC)	Prepares SL2 (E5) CS/CSS soldiers for supervisory duties at SL3 (E6).	81C	DMS, Ft. Belvoir 7 weeks	Soldiers selected for promotion to E6, or E6 in SL3 positions for which training is designed.	Commanders nominate to MILPERCEN qualified soldiers to attend.
		81Q	DMS, Ft. Belvoir 12 weeks.	E4(P) to E5 performing in E6 positions due to unit NCO shortages.	
		82D	DMS, Ft. Belvoir 14 weeks		
		00B	USN, Panama City, Fl 18 weeks.		
Advanced NCO Course (ANCOC)	Trains SL3/4 soldiers on technical and advanced leadership skills and subjects required to train and lead other soldiers. Prepares SM for duty at SL4 (E7)	All Engineer MOSs CMF 12, 51, 81	USAES, Ft. Belvoir 14 weeks		Selection for attendance made by DA Selection Board.
		62B, 52C, 52D, 52F	USAOS, Aberdeen Proving Ground 12 weeks		CMF 81 soldiers must complete MOS BTC prior to attendance or after completing common engineer track.
					Available through Army Correspondence Course Program.
First Sergeant Course	Prepares SL4 soldiers (E7) and SL5 soldiers (E8) for duty at unit First Sergeant.	All MOSs	USASMA, Ft. Bliss 7th ATC, USAREUR 8 weeks	All 1SG designees (E8, E7(P), E7). 1SG responsible for up to 12 MOSs.	Commanders nominate soldiers to attend.
					Selection made by MACOM, NG, OCAR, MILPERCEN.
Sergeants Major Academy	Train selected soldiers (E8) for positions of highest responsibility throughout the DoD.	All MOSs	USASMA, Ft. Bliss 22 weeks		Selection for attendance made by DA selection board for both resident and non-resident courses.

Figure 1 (continued)

NEW DEVELOPMENTS IN NCOES

Course	MOS	Location/Length	Start Date	Remarks
Primary Leadership Development Course (PLDC)	All MOSs	NCO academies CONUS and overseas 4 weeks	FY 84	Combines PNCOC and PLC.
52F PTC	52F	USAES, Ft. Belvoir 11 weeks	Oct 83	New MOS established in Oct 83.
12E BNCOC Track	12E	7th ATC, Ft. Hood 1 weeks	2d Qtr FY 84	Additional 12E training for students attending Combat Engr BNCOC.
51H BTC	51H, 51B, 51C, 51K, 51R	Ft. Leonard Wood 6 weeks	Nov 83	Course is for newly promoted E6 or E5 promotable to MOS 51H.
62N BTC	62N, 62E, 62F, 62J, 62G, 62H	Ft. Leonard Wood 6 weeks	Oct 84	Course if for newly promoted E6 or E5 promotable to MOS 62N.

Figure 2

51H 62N Between a ROCK and a HARD PLACE

by CPT Charles R. Maggio

"Congratulations on your promotion to E6, SSG Jones, nd good luck at your next assign- ıent." A few months ago Jones was warded that first rocker, the attalion commander shook his and, and Jones felt proud of him- elf. His assignment with the erminal service company had been good assignment for a 62F (Lifting nd Loading Equipment Operator). 'here had been plenty of oppor- unities to operate cranes and fork- ifts. As an operator, he was one of he best.

Now at his new unit as he surveys he the line of dozers, graders, back- ıoes and other earthmoving equip- nent in the combat heavy batta- ion's motor pool, he finds himself in disturbing position. That promo- ion to E6 was more than just a new et of stripes and jump in pay; it was transfer from operator to super- 'isor and a change of MOS from 62F o 62N (Construction Equipment Supervisor). It automatically made ones an "expert" in equipment peration. He would now be expected o supervise projects and to guide oldiers from MOSs 62E, 62F and 32J. Though he possessed an ngineer MOS as a 62F, he was not ıssigned to an engineer unit. Now, n the midst of an engineer battalion, ıe feels at a loss. What can he do? Can anyone help?

The 62N is a "capper" MOS for MOSs 62E, 62F and 62J at the E6 level and for 62G and 62H at the E7 level. These MOSs are grouped together because they are all related to construction equipment operation. Though engineers in each of the 62N feeder MOSs receive specialized training as an operator, there is not yet training for the 62N supervisor.

This dilemma is shared by other cappers in Career Management Field 51. The 51H (Construction Engineering Supervisor) is a capper for MOSs 51B, 51C, 51K and 51R. The 51T is a capper for 51G, 81B and 82B. The supervisors in these cappers are responsible for overseeing the actions of several MOSs of which they may have only general knowledge.

The Engineer School is aware of the supervisors' dilemma and is developing basic technical courses (BTCs) for MOSs 62N and 51H to provide newly promoted E6 and promotable E5 personnel with the technical skills and knowledge to perform as supervisors. The BTCs will focus on training critical skill level three tasks.

Both courses will cover equipment utilization, construction techniques, use of planning documents, and basic supervisory and management techniques. The courses will be held at Fort Leonard Wood, Missouri, beginning with the six-week 51H BTC in November 1983 and the eight-week 62N BTC projected to start in October 1984.

Commanders will nominate to MILPERCEN soldiers qualified to attend resident BTCs within 30 days of the soldier's attaining E6 promotion list status. E6s who have not received the training will be scheduled by commanders for attendance within 30 days of being assigned to supervisory positions. E5s or E4s performing in E6 positions may also become eligible to attend.

So, SSG Jones, you won't be stuck much longer between the proverbial rock and a hard place. Help is on the way. The new 51H and 62N BTCs will help equipment operators make a smoother transition to new duties as supervisors.

Editor's Note: Turn to page 13 for more information about the 51H BTC.

CPT Charles R. Maggio is assigned to the Directorate of Training and Doctrine as a training developer in the General Engineering Branch. He has served as an operations and training officer with D Co., 1st Engineer Bn. and as a platoon leader with the 568th Engineering Co. He is a graduate of Drexel University, the Engineer Officer Basic and Advanced Courses, and the Combined Arms and Services Staff School. CPT Maggio is a registered professional engineer in Virginia.

NTC exercises give combat engineers the chance for realistic countermobility training.

Getting Up To Speed

by LTC John Mennig

Exercises at the National Training Center show ways to make engineer units more effective

The tough, realistic training program at the National Training Center at Fort Irwin, California, has given engineers the opportunity to fine tune their combat support skills. It has also exposed deficiencies shared by many engineer units.

The problem areas are grouped here under the basic combat engineer responsibilities of mobility, countermobility and survivability.

Mobility

Problems with using engineers in mobility operations generally start at the planning phase.

When an offensive operation at task force level is being planned, the supporting engineers, normally led by an engineer platoon leader, should be consulted. Usually, however, there has been no habitual association between the battalion and its special platoons at home station. In such a case, the platoon leader probably has no experience in supporting a maneuver task force in the field, is not sure how to go about it, and is uncomfortable dealing with a battalion commander whom he has never seen before. The result frequently is that the engineers travel behind the task force trail company instead of with the lead company in a direct support (DS) role.

The location of engineers during the attack is up to the task force commander, but the two places engineers probably should not be are leading and trailing. Commanders at NTC who have placed engineers at the front quickly lost their engineer assets to direct and indirect fire, while commanders with engineers to the rear did not have them immediately available when minefields and obstacles stopped their unit's forward momentum.

Although the decision on how to use engineer assets rests with the task force commander, the engineer unit leader is responsible for informing the commander engineer of the capabilities and limitations. That information should be furnished during operations planning and should include all aspects of engineer support, including recommended breaching techniques.

Countermobility

Countermobility operations is the area in which engineers at the NTC have received their most constructive training.

As with mobility operations, countermobility problems begin during the planning phase. Inadequate consideration of the mission, enemy, terrain, troops and time available (METT-T) with respect to engineer support is the root of most problems. It is essential that the task force commander's engineer representative provide professional advice early. That advice could resolve some of these common problems:

- Inadequate barrier planning resulting in a shortage of barrier material.
- Lack of planning for transporting barrier material forward.
- Lack of coordination between the fire support officer and engineer platoon leader about the use of the family of scatterable mines (FASCAM).
- No priorities regarding obstacle construction.
- Time required to construct obstacles not considered.
- Engineer resources not consistently employed throughout the exercise.
- Obstacle completion not reported and minefield reports not made.

These problems may appear simple, but they are the most common. Engineers understand the combat multiplying effect of using engineers correctly (a good article on that subject appeared in the January 1983 issue of *Military Review*). The difficulty comes in making the system work efficiently. There is always more work to be done than engineers available to do it. Lets consider each problem and resolve it as much as possible.

First, before an NTC exercise, consider what material will be available and what influence you can have upon its availability. Then, knowing what you can obtain, plan ahead and coordinate transportation. The only solution may be prepositioning mines and barrier material. In any event, remember that it is much easier to modify an existing plan than to create one from scratch.

The planning stage is also the time to develop procedures for coordinating minefields with the supporting artillery unit. They will be using FASCAM and will be covering obstacles with indirect fire. Know the artillery's capabilities and limitations. If you have thought about these things ahead of time, they usually will not be forgotten during the exercise or in a real combat situation.

Next, when you work with the commander to develop the plan for obstacles, develop priorities. During the exercise, things may happen that prevent you from accomplishing all that you had planned, so have a plan that tells you where the emphasis is needed.

Be certain the commander knows how long it will take to construct obstacles. He has to know what he can expect in the time available. Do not forget to present options. (For example, how much longer could he expect the enemy to be delayed if he supplemented the engineer mine laying effort with infantry? You will not be able to answer that question unless you give it some thought ahead of time.)

Also, plan to use all of your resources. Troops cannot be expected to work 24 hours a day, but reports show that engineers are frequently idle because of a lack of planning. A good plan will keep engineers busy providing the commander with important combat multipliers.

Finally, you must report the obstacles that you emplace. This is important so that passage lanes can be

A poorly constructed antitank ditch is used by OPFOR armor as a fighting position. The tanks are M551s visually modified to resemble Soviet T72 tanks.

controlled and closed at the appropriate time. Lane closing has been a perennial problem at the NTC. Engineers can help remedy this deficiency.

Engineers can prevent another common problem—failure to make minefield reports. Our doctrine dictates that minefield reports will be made, but that has not been happening. The reason for the reports is very simple. We will likely be fighting over the same terrain more than one time, and our mines are just as deadly as theirs!

Survivability

Limited time at the NTC has been devoted to the survivability mission of the engineers. Time during defensive operations is largely spent on countermobility tasks. Most of the time spent on survivability has been to develop earth berms in front of fighting positions. However, limited consideration has been given to how wide a berm must be to provide adequate protection from direct fire weapons. Also, overhead cover and camouflage of berms has been forgotten. It is of little value for a defender to have a berm to his front giving him a false sense of security or one that prominently marks his position for the OPFOR.

Plan & Coordinate

Engineers can be an effective combat multiplier if used properly. Engineers will be used properly if they make their capabilities known ahead of time to the task force commander. It is up to the engineer to provide hi expertise to a very busy commande The engineer must assist with plar ning, and then he must coordinate th engineer operating system to mak sure it works effectively.

LTC John Mennig is the projec manager for Lessons Learned, NT Division, Unit Training Suppor Directorate, Command and Genera Staff College, HQ Combined Arm Center (CAC), Fort Leavenwort Kan. He has a bachelor's degree fro American Technological Universit and is a graduate of Command an General Staff College. He has serve in a variety of command and sta assignments including command o field artillery batteries in the 5th an 25th Divisions and VII Corps.

National Training Center

At the National Training Center (NTC), combat engineers can dig miles of tank ditches and survivable fighting positions, erect miles of barbed wire obstacles, use tons of barrier material and emplace hundreds of mines.

Located at Fort Irwin, California, the 660,000-acre NTC gives combat engineers ample room to train. The center's wide-open spaces and sophisticated training support package gives the Army the opportunity to conduct intense, highly realistic combat training for heavy task forces.

A factor adding realism to the NTC training concept is the opposing force (OPFOR) the task force encounters. The NTC provides a well-trained, numerically superior opposing force using Threat tactics and replicas of Threat vehicles. The OPFOR is organized as a motorized rifle regiment and provides realism on a scale not possible at home stations.

The NTC also increases realism on the training battlefield with the Core Instrumentation System (CIS). Within this system, 500 players and approximately 2,000 weapons equipped with the Multiple Integrated Laser Engagement System (MILES) are electronically monitored by Fort Irwin's main computer system. The system provides continuous position/location, firing information, and radio transmission information for most of the major weapons systems and key players on both the "Red" and "Blue" sides in the training exercise. Data is automatically collected at a number of stations in the engagement simulation area and displayed graphically on screens at the 31 individual control stations.

The system's ability to receive, store, and replay required data at any time is an invaluable tool for trainers. During an after-action review (AAR), the digital input; video input (from mobile televisio cameras and a large, 4,000-millimeter lens camera); plus th observations of 30 observer/controllers are compiled to determin the status of the task force undergoing training.

Sophisticated electronics, a realistic OPFOR unit, and an expansiv maneuver area make the National Training Center the most uniqu training ground in the world.

Need to improve unit training?

Call Your Readiness Group

by LTC James L. Campbell

Limited training resources, little training time, and managing a unit that is often geographically separated, all tax the Reserve Component (RC) engineer commander's ability to give his soldiers quality training.

How does the RC commander train his skill level three, four, and five NCOs? How does he train soldiers in low density MOSs who are the unit's sole representatives of that MOS? And what about individual training for officers? How does he put together a solid training program in NBC survivability skills?

Assistance Available

One solution to these training challenges is to ask your supporting readiness group for assistance.

Readiness groups are made up of branch assistance teams (BATS) for each major specialty such as infantry, artillery and engineer, depending on the type and number of RC units supported.

In addition to the branch-oriented teams, there are several teams that have cross-branch orientations. The administration team provides finance, mess management, supply and administrative support. The "MAIT team" provides maintenance assistance. The Training Management Development Office provides a variety of assistance to all types of units.

Branch assistance teams have several training assistance packages available to support RC engineer units. The more unusual assistance programs of the engineer team, Readiness Group Fort Snelling, are described here in hopes that reservists and guardsmen will call their readiness group and request similar support.

The Fort Snelling programs include the tactical bivouac model, an adaptation of the Combat Engineer Game, obstacle planning, and NBC team training.

Tactical Bivouac Model

Properly setting up a tactical bivouac site is important. Yet, many of us have been in a unit that moved into a bivouac area, set up, then had to tear down and set up again because it wasn't done correctly the first time.

One solution to this problem is to use a model of the terrain, vehicles, weapons and personnel as a walk-through guide for tactical bivouac procedures. The Fort Snelling readiness group uses a 3-foot by 3-foot rubber terrain board with scale model trucks and weapons for this hands-on training exercise.

First, several hours of classes are held to instruct leaders on the organization and mission of the advance party. Then, using the terrain model, the leaders move their equipment into the area and discuss set-up tasks. (The sequence in which the set-up tasks must be performed is described in the soldier's manuals. For instance, the responsibilities of various leaders in setting up defensive sectors are shown as soldier's manual tasks.) This training session for leaders reduced bivouac deficiencies during annual training.

The Combat Engineer Game was developed by the Engineer School and is being redesigned. The initial version was independently reworked by the engineer team, Readiness Group Fort Snelling, into a training device for NCOs. It is designed to train level three, four, and five 12B and 12Z NCOs in certain company, platoon and squad-level engineer ARTEP tasks.

The Combat Engineer Game is played on a small game board that fits into a small case. Markers, symbols and equipment are included for the players. Up to five players can play the game, which lasts two hours. Each player selects a unit mission and starting site on the board. The players state what unit equipment will be required to accomplish the mission. The mode of transportation (air or ground) is also determined by the player.

The players, in turn, begin moving from the starting point to the mission site by answering questions about level one and two, 12B soldier's manual tasks drawn from the movement card pile. When the players answer correctly, they move toward their mission site (via supply or coordination points if the mission requires such intermediate stops).

Once at the mission site, the players, in turn, must answer questions (within one to three minutes) about planning their unit mission, using FM 5-34, *Engineer Field Data*. Each correct answer earns one point. When ten points are accumulated, the player is given 20 minutes to prepare an oral operations order briefing on his unit's mission. If a "go" briefing is presented to the game board manager, the person is declared the winner and play continues to determine the subsequent order of finish.

Typical missions of the game include bridge demolition, Bailey bridge construction, landing site preparation, mine field clearance, and other common engineer tasks. The Combat Engineer Game is a good way to challenge leaders to improve their individual training levels and to review FM 5-34.

Obstacle Planning and Employment

Applying the rules of obstacle placement to form an integrated network of obstacles covered in depth by antitank fires of TOW, DRAGON and tanks is a formidable task for the engineer officer. He rarely gets the chance to see the effects of his obstacle placement. The effects of obstacles with covering fires are demonstrated by using the Dunn-Kempf game terrain board as a training aid.

This eight-hour exercise is intended for the squad leader through company commander. The training begins with a two-hour class on the employment of obstacles. A three-hour, hands-on drill is used to determine the tactics, boundaries, weapon systems location, and obstacle locations on the terrain board. The final three hours are spent playing the Dunn-Kempf game to test how covering fires increase the value of the obstacles sited by the unit leaders. The model affords the opportunity to discuss tactics, targeting priorities and enemy equipment.

This training vehicle is an excellent way to encourage unit leaders to site obstacles in conjunction with the maneuver unit's weapon systems. Using the Dunn-Kempf war game gives the chance to explain the terrain analysis and use allocation techniques of Command and General Staff College Reference Book 100-9. This is an effective way to improve the obstacle planning and employment capability for all engineer units, especially those in the CAPSTONE program.

NBC Team Training

Survival on the "dirty battlefield" mandates a high level of individual NBC proficiency and well-trained NBC teams. Each company-size unit should have four NBC teams. These are the control party, the radiological survey and monitoring team, the chemical detection team, and the decontamination team.

An intensive weekend training program is conducted by the readiness group engineer team to train these NBC teams. The control party spends all weekend training together. Each of the other teams receive eight hours of training in their primary area and then three hours of cross training on each of the two other team responsibilities.

The control party includes an NBC school-trained officer, NCO and an enlisted alternate. The training refamiliarizes the control party with unit NBC equipment; NBC reports; the operational exposure guide (OEG); mission-oriented protective posture (MOPP) tables; and consideration, plotting, and dissemination of NBC information. (*Figure 1* provides a synopsis of key topics that are covered.) A complete analysis and review of the unit's NBC annex to its field SOP completes the weekend of NBC training.

CONTROL PARTY TRAINING ITEMS

- IM93 Radiac Meter with PP1578 Charger
- IM174 Radiac Meter
- AN/PDR27 Radiac Meter
- M15/256 Chemical Detection Kits
- OEG Analysis
- MOPP Analysis/Considerations
- Protective Suits On/Off Procedures
- NBC Reports
- NBC Advice to the Commander
- Ground Survey (T6) Practical Exercise
- Aerial Survey (DVC 3-3) Practical Exercise
- M8 Chemical Alarm
- Equipment Decontamination Station
- Personnel Decontamination Stations
- Team Organization Procedures
- Unit NBC SOP

Figure 1

The radiological survey and monitoring team has an NCOIC, one primary and one alternate operator for each IM174 and AN/PDR27 radiac meter. A review of basic radiation sources, how to conduct radiation surveys and how to use various unit equipment is included in the weekend of training. (The items covered are shown in *Figure 2.*)

The chemical detection team has an NCOIC and a primary and alternate operator for each M15 or M256 kit in the unit. The training familiarizes personnel with chemical and biological weapons' effects, technological background data, and the actions of the chemical detection team. (The equipment covered during the training is noted in *Figure 2.*)

NBC TEAM TRAINING OUTLINE

Radiological Survey Team	Chemical Detection Team	Decontamination Team
Topics:	**Topics:**	**Topics:**
Radiation Sources Review	Chemical Agents Review	Contamination Sources Review
Protective Suits On/Off Procedures	MOPP Modes and Tables Practical Exercise	MOPP Considerations and Practical Exercise
NBC Reports (1, 2, 4)	Protective Suit Practical Exercise	Protective Suits On/Off Procedures
Simplified Fallout Prediction	NBC-3 Report	Operate in Protective Clothing
OEG Analysis and Recommendations	Chemical Contamination Plotting	Equipment Decontamination Station
Team Organization and Procedures	Proper Unmasking Procedures	Personnel Decontamination Station
	Team Organization and Procedures	Team Organization and Procedures
Equipment:	**Equipment:**	**Equipment:**
IM93 Radiac Meter with PP1578 Charger	M15 Chemical Detection Kit	M13 Kit
IM174 Radiac Meter	M256 Chemical Detection Kit	M58 Kit
AN/PDR27 Radiac Meter	M72A2 Chemical Training Kit	M11 Decontamination Apparatus
Aerial Survey Training Set PE (DVC 3-3)	M8 Chemical Alarm	M12A1 Decontamination Apparatus
Ground Survey Training Set PE (T6)		

Figure 2

The decontamination team has an NCOIC and eight enlisted members. The training familiarizes personnel with NBC weapons' effects and the requirements of the decontamination team. (The hands-on training covers the items in *Figure 2*.)

Crew Drills

The low-density MOSs are usually formed into crews such as armored vehicle launched bridge crews, combat engineer vehicle crews and water purification sections. Your readiness group can assist in training these specialized crews. Members of your readiness group BATs are trained in these low-density MOSs.

Challenge Your Readiness Group

Your readiness group exists for one reason—to help train your unit and its leaders. The training assistance available to you is limited only by your imagination. Challenge your readiness group to conduct leader training, low-density MOS training and to help in a variety of ways.

Readiness group training teams are usually busy, so request assistance early. Remember—your readiness group is there to help you.

LTC James L. Campbell commands the 237th Engineer Bn., 7th Engineer Bde., USAREUR. His previous assignment was as chief of the Engineer Team, Readiness Group Fort Snelling, Minn. He has also served in several engineer troop units, with the Engineer Studies Center and with the Engineer Command, Vietnam. LTC Campbell is a graduate of the Command and General Staff College, has a master's degree from Texas A&M University, and is a registered professional engineer.

Hotline Q & A

Q. How can we obtain one of the Engineer Programmable Calculators?

A. The calculator is still being tested, but the read-only-memory chip (ROM) is available from the Construction Engineering Laboratory, CERL-FS, P.O. Box 4005, Champaign, IL 61820.

Q. Has the 155mm artillery round for delivery of the family of scatterable mines (FASCAM) gone into production?

A. The 155mm antitank and antipersonnel mines are in production and are being fielded in Europe.

Q. I need references for the 51M (Firefighter) MOS.

A.
- The *National Fire Protection Agency Handbook*
- TM 5-315, *Firefighting Rescue Procedures in Theaters of Operations*
- TM 5-51M, *Firefighter*
- ARTEP 5-500 *Engineer Cellular Teams*

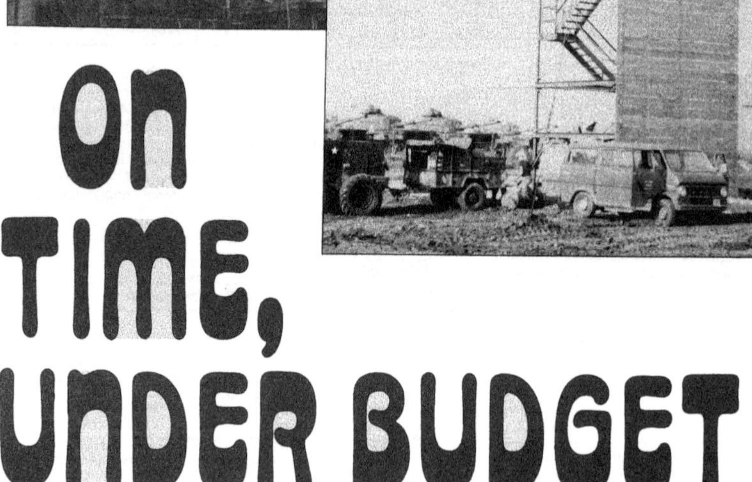

An airfield tower at Ft. Sheridan (left) became a rappelli tower in Joliet, Ill.

On Time, Under Budget

by CPT Frank A. Liebner

What do you do with an extra 30-ton aircraft control tower? Take it apart, move it 80 miles, and reassemble it as a rappelling tower.

When the installation commander at Fort Sheridan, Illinois, asked if the post's obsolete Healy Airfield control tower could be recycled, the answer was yes. The 533rd Engineer Detachment at Fort Sheridan was tasked to move the control tower 80 miles to the U.S. Army Training Area at Joliet, Illinois, and to turn it into a rappelling tower complete with cantilevered top deck for simulated helicopter rappelling.

The project was completed on time, under budget, and using fewer soldiers than anticipated.

The Healey Airfield control tower was made of structural steel with an observation deck cupola of wood and glass. The tower rested on four massive 15.6-foot square concrete footings. Three-quarter inch anchor bolts mounted half-inch thick baseplates at each leg. The main vertical elements were angles (Lx6x6x½), running up continuously 41 feet from the baseplates.

Riveted and bolted splice plates carried additional sections to the top at 62 feet. Horizontal structural elements (W 8x31) were at elevations 12, 25, 38, and 40 feet. One-inch diameter sway braces provided structural rigidity. The observation deck, perched at the 52-foot level, consisted of W 8x31 sections and C 8x11.5 floor joists. The original decking was 2x6xRL tongue and groove oak with a wooden gable roof that had been fitted over a metal parapet at the 62-foot level. Steel stairways and handrails led to the observation deck.

The Planning Process

The recycling project was planned carefully. The 533rd Engineer Detachment commander and the senior engineer construction supervisor developed an operations plan that included working drawings detailing the modifications required, site and movement test models, an activity list, duration estimates, the Critical Path Method (activity-on-the-arrow), the initial construction schedule (resource balancing), equipment lists, bills of material, and required service contracts (i.e., soil testing). All structural design proposals were approved by a civil engineer at the Fort Sheridan Engineer Plans and Services Division, Directorate of Engineering and Housing (DEH).

Time estimates, developed through engineering performance standards (TB 5-420-series), initially called for 45 working days and an average workforce of 23 soldiers. Specialized construction equipment was provided, by DEH and the 863rd Engineer Battalion (Heavy) (USAR).

The project was divided into two phases: administrative and construction. The administrative phase consisted of reviewing and approving final working drawings, material ordering, soil testing, requisitioning equipment from parent organizations, and obtaining budgetary approval.

The construction phase included three concurrent operations: movement operations, Joliet site preparation, and operations at Fort Sheridan. The movement element, which proved to be a limiting factor, involved transporting the major tower structure, delivering materials and moving construction equipment between the two sites.

Preparing the Joliet Site

At the Joliet site, soil analysis identified the requirement for 5x5-foot spread reinforced concrete footings with #4 bar, 6 inch OC x 2. A 2x2-foot square column with eight #6 bars carried the structure from the footings to the design elevation. Baseplates and anchor bolts were duplicated from the original specifications.

Since the proposed 16x52 foot rappelling surface would present wind loading problems, the resulting 70-kip design load required that four deadmen be placed to fix the corners. Concrete cubes 6x6x4 feet, reinforced against the direction of stress, were buried under nine feet of compacted fill. In these were embedded 1½-foot threaded anchor rods (A-36 steel); turnbuckles allowed for 14 inches of linear adjustment. One-inch wire rope tied the turnbuckles to the points of attachment on the tower.

Good site drainage (a project priority) later prevented costly construction delays during several summer storms. A pneumatic sump pump provided an additional capability for incidental water collection in the various excavations.

A crane raises a modular tower section onto a new foundation.

Dismantling Begins

To save time, a modular disassembly process was used. Safety was emphasized. Several existing structures hindered free movement of equipment, and a 5-kva powerline ran overhead. The parapet and the observation deck were freed, intact, from the structure and lowered to the ground. The remaining stairways, swaybraces, and upper angle columns were removed, as required, down to the 41-foot level.

The next step involved an innovative rotational maneuver. Lifting slings were attached to the lower 41 feet of the structure, the anchor bolts were cut free, and the tower was lifted and rotated from the vertical position to the horizontal and onto waiting cribbing.

In the horizontal position, the top 15.5x41-foot "panel" was secured by lifting slings. This enabled the elements of the left and right panels to be disassembled. The tower row was reduced to the upper and lower panels, two deck sections, and miscellaneous beams, stairs, brackets, and braces.

Modification and Transporting

While the tower was on the ground, all components were scraped, primed, and painted (color specification: Engineer red, naturally). Onto one component were mounted three series of channel sections (C 4x5.4) that ran the entire length of the tower on these six lag bolts. Pieces of pressure-treated lumber (2x12x16-feet) were mounted to form the rappelling surface.

The upper and lower panels, deck sections and other elements were loaded onto an M870 semitrailer for transportation to the Joliet site. Since the load approached 16-feet wide and 44-feet long, special road clearance permits and route mapping were obtained from the Illinois State Highway Department. Escort vehicles and a scout vehicle were used. Two additional trips with the tractor-trailer were required to carry the remaining components to the Joliet site.

Reassembling and Completing

Site management was the key at the assembly area. Grade irregularities were first leveled with cribbing. Careful placement of components and equipment siting ensured rapid reassembly of the tower. Before lifting the lower section, two diagonal braces (HP 8x36x16.8 feet) were fixed to the panel baseplates for the required compressive rigidity for the horizontal-to-vertical tilting maneuver. After the lower 41-foot section was set on the baseplates, the vertical alignment was rechecked by both instrument and direct measurement.

The 52-foot level deck was modified while on the ground to accept a 6-foot cantilever section. Steel grating (1 foot by 3/16 inches type 19W4) was welded in place and formed the new deck. Then the top section of the rappelling surface and the remaining two angle columns were married to the deck and secured. The entire subassembly was lifted into place, bolted, and aligned, as before.

The top deck was then completed on two sides with a waist-high safety rail. From three attachment rings, mounted on the deck surface, rappelling ropes would pass over a pipe rail. This rail, which was secured 3 feet from the edge and at a height of 40 inches above the deck, provided a better rope position. On the cantilevered deck, UH1 skid and UH60 door positions were fabricated. Pipes were welded along both deck edges to preclude rope damage. On either side, two sand pits served as landing sites. Finally, chain link fencing was erected to secure the site.

Training Benefits

Besides the troop training value in individual skill development, many personal lessons were learned from the recycling effort. Soldiers had to deal with three-to-four hours of round trip travel daily. Construction techniques were often learn-as-you-go, and soldiers were faced with heat, insects, fatigue, and equipment breakdowns throughout the project.

In spite of these difficulties, the tradesmen-soldiers of the detachment completed the project on time, and $8,500 below the committe budget. A work force of 23 enginee was not needed. Instead, a dedicate crew of eight completed the enti project. The rappelling tow training facility, now in service the U.S. Army Training Area, Joli Illinois, stands as another examp of the esprit of the engineer soldie

CPT Frank A. Liebner is assign to HHC, 130th Engineer Bde., Germany. He served at Fo Sheridan, Ill., as commander of t 533rd Engineer Det. (Utilities) an with the Directorate of Engineeri and Housing. He has also serve with mechanized, heavy and ai borne combat engineer units. CP Liebner has a professional degree architecture from the University Notre Dame, and a master's degr in computer systems and operation management from the University Illinois.

Engineer Problem

Given the following extract from a hasty demolition reconnaissance report, plan the most effective and efficient means of destroying the tunnel and 600 meters of railway leading into the tunnel.

- Explosives available:
  - -100 lbs of TNT
  - -2000 lbs of C4
- Time is not critical.

REQUIRED TASKS: Describe the method, placement and amount of explosives required for destruction of (1) the 600m of track, and (2) the tunnel.

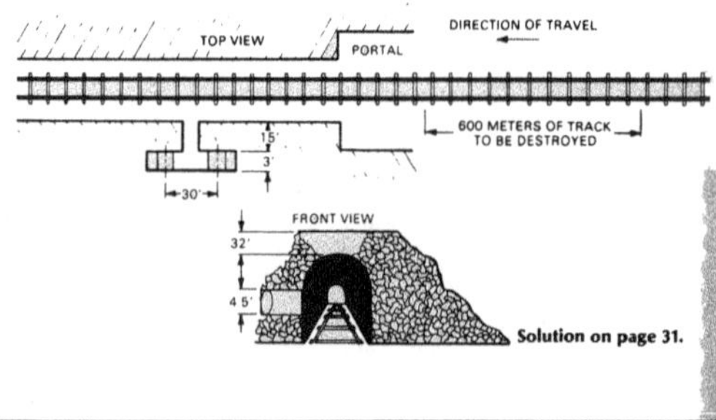

Solution on page 31.

Writing for Publication

by Albert N. Garland
and Marie B. Edgerton

If you are writing for publication (drafting a staff paper or simply preparing a memo), these guidelines will make you a more effective communicator.

First, a prospective author should be aware that in a professional journal of any kind the most important consideration is the subject matter of an article. This is especially true of military publications. Each journal usually has its own particular reason for existing, a stated mission to accomplish through its pages—a specific category of material to cover and a specific group of readers to reach.

A prospective writer, therefore, should study the publication he wants to write for to see what kind of material it normally uses, and then he should write with that publication in mind. Or if he already has an idea for an article on a certain subject, he should look for just the right publication for the article. (In no case should he send it to more than one publication at a time. And he should always send an original manuscript, not a copy.) But how can he find out what kind of material each wants?

He can go to the library, for one thing, and look at various magazines to get a feel for what they normally use. If he doesn't find the magazines there, he can at least get their addresses and write or call the ones he is considering. Most magazines offer sample copies to anyone who is interested, and most also have writer's guides to send along. Most editors are also happy to discuss article ideas by telephone or by mail and to advise a writer on the best approach to use.

While a prospective writer is looking at various magazines to see what subject matter each covers, he should also look at the style of writing in each. Style may not be easy for a new writer to detect, but he can usually tell, for example, whether the writing is formal or informal, serious or light, and whether the magazine uses scenarios, dialogue, or humor, for example.

Once he has done all this, an author also must do his homework. He must become well versed in his subject matter, using the nearest library facilities to fill in any gaps in his own knowledge. And he should not select a subject that is too broad. It is a rare person who can write an article without some preparation; and there is not one who can solve all the world's problems in 2,000 words.

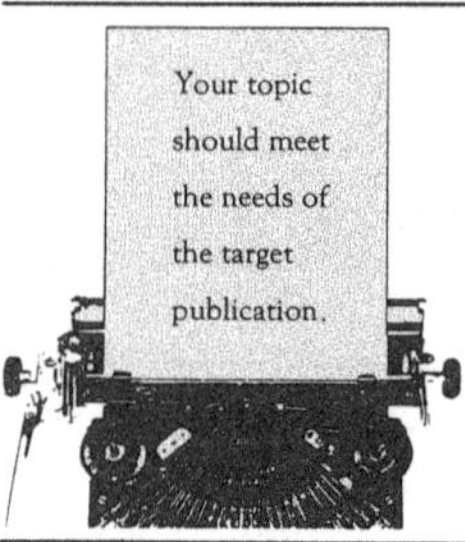

Your topic
should meet
the needs of
the target
publication.

A military writer should be aware, too, that writing for a military publication is not the same as "military writing." The two are quite different, in fact, although we're not sure why that should be. Military writing, unfortunately, is stereotyped and usually follows certain prescribed steps with little deviation permitted. Much of it is filled with meaningless cliches and bureaucratic jargon that together make it essentially unintelligible except to insiders, and often even they find it difficult.

Writing for publication in a military journal, and especially in a civilian magazine, is another matter entirely. The author of a magazine article cannot force another person to read his material as the author of a "military paper" can. The writer must first attract the reader's attention and then work hard to keep it. And he does this by making his writing tight, concise, and interesting—by coming through as a person expressing a human situation, a bit of reality with which a reader can associate himself as a person.

Warnings

Before he begins to write, there are a few more things a writer should know:

- Writing is not easy for most people. A writer's goal should be to make the reading easy; as a famous editor once put it, 'Easy writing makes damn hard reading."
- Writing cannot be hurried. It must flow naturally in its own time. And it must follow the author's thoughts in a logical and progressive way.
- Writing is a lonely job. An author cannot share the experience until he has completed at least one draft of his article. No one else can help him write; it is a task that he must do alone.
- Writing requires patience. It requires the ability to sit at a desk or the dining table, or on the floor, to compose draft after draft. A writer should not expect to produce a finished product on the first try. He has to be ready to rework it again and again. If he does not, he can be sure that an editor somewhere will do it for him—assuming, of course, that the editor sees something valuable enough in the manuscript to bother doing it.

Even then, after all this work, his article may be rejected. Sometimes it will be a good article but at the wrong time or the wrong place. The article may be on a subject that does not appeal to the editor who reads it at that particular time, or the editor may already have accepted a similar article. Rejection is a fact of life in the writing business. But it should not discourage a writer from trying again.

some work to do in preparing an article for publication, an author will stand a better chance of having his article accepted if he will look at it as an editor might. Besides, by doing this, he can often make his thoughts clearer and thus avoid the possibility that the editor may unintentionally change his meaning in the process of doing the editing for him.

Over the years, we have read thousands of manuscripts, ranging from the very good to the very bad. As a result, we have developed a number of writing tips that we think will benefit any military writer—if he uses them properly.

The tips that we have chosen to use here are especially intended to help a prospective author write simply, clearly, and concisely, because too much Army writing is the direct opposite of simple, clear, and concise. The examples used to illustrate these tips have been collected over the years from military writing found in various documents and publications.

Writing Tips

Use the active voice. Although there are times when the passive voice is best—when, for example, the action itself is more important than who does it—the active voice is generally clearer and more concise. "It was ordered that . . .," without saying by whom, may look like a dodge to avoid saying who ordered it. In any case, it certainly does not tell the reader who did it, and getting a real live person into a sentence almost always makes it more interesting and easier to read.

As another example, "The equipment was repaired by the soldiers," does tell who, but "The soldiers repaired the equipment" is shorter and more straightforward. Writers should especially avoid the impersonal, stilted, and typically Army "It is regretted that," saying instead simply "We regret," or "The Army regrets . . ."

The use of the passive voice often leads to monstrous constructions such as this: "The mobilization of all available resources will be made." Although it is somewhat better to say "All available resources will be mobilized," this is still in the passive voice. Much better is the active, "We (or somebody) will mobilize all resources."

Once a writer consciously decides to use the passive voice in a sentence, however, he must be consistent. Switching from the passive to the active in mid-sentence leads to confusion, as this example illustrates: "The senior enemy air defense controller was taken out of the picture by cutting his communication cables." The word "cutting" clearly requires someone to do the cutting, and the enemy air defense controller probably did not cut his own cables to take himself out of the picture.

Be your
own editor.
Use simple,
direct
language.

There are two solutions to this problem: In the passive voice, "The . . . controller was taken out of the picture when his communication cables were cut." Or, in the active voice, "(Someone) took the air defense controller out of the picture by cutting his communication cables."

As this example also illustrates, it is sometimes impossible for an editor to convert a sentence to active voice, because he may not be able to figure out who the doer is supposed to be. Only the author can provide that information.

Make modifiers clear. A word or phrase that is used to modify another word or phrase must be placed so that the relationship between them is clear. This example from a post daily bulletin will illustrate: "Warning: Any toy chest used for storing toys with a hinged lid is a strangulation hazard to a small child." The phrase "with a hinged lid" should go after the word "chest," since the warning is about the chests with hinged lids, not about toys with hinged lids. (Besides, the phrase "used for storing toys" is unnecessary; that is what a toy chest is for. In this case, then, taking out the intruding phrase solves the problem.)

The dangling particple, which has plagued English students throughout their school years, also falls into this category of misplaced or unclear modifiers. For example, "Walking by the motor pool, the truck hit the fence," taken literally means that the truck was walking by the motor pool. But a more likely meaning is, "As I was walking by the motor pool, I saw the truck hit the fence."

Use parallel construction. Parallel construction means putting like elements in a sentence in the same grammatical form. In "preparing, coordination, and evaluation," the word "preparing" does not agree with the others. All should have "tion" endings, or all should have "ing" endings. (The "ing" endings are best, incidentally, because verb forms are generally better to use than nouns.)

In a description of the U.S. flag, "red, white, and blue" are parallel—all adjectives—but "red, white, blue, and made of nylon" are not. The last item in the series is a phrase, not an adjective; therefore, it is not a true series.

This "false series" is the single most common error of parallelism. If three or four items are involved, many writers tend to treat them as a series without analyzing them for logic.

As another example, "He gave them orders, maps, aerial photographs and showed them a sand table of the command post." An "and" before "aerial photographs" to complete that series, "orders, maps, and aerial photographs," would help. (Despite popular belief, there is nothing wrong with using two ands that close together in a sentence as long as it is not hard to read.) Another example, "The new M1 tank runs smoother, faster, and responds easier," is not as easy to solve. It might be better to say, "The new M1 tank is smoothrunning, fast, and responsive."

Faulty parallelism is fairly easy to detect if a writer carefully reads what he has written and applies some logic to it. For example: "His job is developing training, doctrine, materials, and training the officers" presumably means "His job is to develop training doctrine and materials and to train the officers."

Use correct idioms. An idiom is an individual peculiarity of language—a construction that is generally accepted and widely understood but without any real grammatical basis. For example, we say "instead of going" but "rather than go," and even linguists cannot explain why.

Many idiomatically strange constructions have crept into Army writing recently: "Officers are charged to satisfy" and "are responsible to satisfy" appear with some regularity. But the normal idioms are "charged with satisfying" and "responsible for satisfying," and it seems strange to most readers to see them otherwise.

As another example, "to assist the boss to prevent" should be either "to assist the boss in preventing" or, better, "to help him prevent." We normally say, not "acquaint to" but "acquaint with," not "curiosity of" but "curiosity about," not "permeated with" but "permeated by." (Such lists are available in many grammar books and style guides.)

Use transition devices. Transitions are words or phrases that let the reader know what direction the author is taking next. The most common of these are and, but, and for, but there are many others: consequently, therefore, however, nevertheless, subsequently, on the other hand, earlier, later, previously, and so on. Often entire sentences must be used to provide transition. All of these devices help the reader keep track of what the author is saying without having to reread a passage several times. Such devices should be used in sentences, between sentences, between paragraphs, or between major sections of a piece of writing—anywhere there is a shift in the subject.

Be concise. Concise does not mean necessarily brief; it means saying everything that needs to be said to make a point clear but without any unnecessary words or phrases. The examples shown above include redundancies (using two or more words that mean the same thing) and general wordiness (using more words than necessary).

These are only a few of the many

Avoid Wordiness and Redundancies

Instead of	Try
seems apparent	appears
new innovations	innovations (they are new)
many and numerous	many
final and ultimate	final (or) the last
around the perimeter	around (the line that goes around something is its perimeter)
skirt around	skirt (or) go around
important essentials	essentials (important by definition)
serious crisis	crisis (serious by definition)
at this point in time	now
until such time as	until
in the near future	soon
a sufficient amount of	enough
in a timely manner	on time
casual factors	causes
make provision for	provide for
is indicative of	indicates
be cognizant of	know
have the capability	be able
be in agreement	agree
give authorization	authorize
be in possession of	possess
give encouragement	encourage
serve the function of being	be

examples of redundancy and wordiness. To change the habit of writing this way, a writer first has to become aware of the problem; then he has to go back over what he has written to see whether he has used any words that need to be cut.

Use short, familiar words. Part of a writer's task is to choose the right word. And sometimes the longer words, such as those listed on the left below, are best, especially in formal writing. But generally, the shorter, more familiar versions are just as good, and they are more concise. (In formal writing, the longer ones sometimes sound pretentious and stuffy.)

Simple Words Are Best

Instead of	Try
numerous	many
facilitate	ease
the remainder	the rest
individual	man, woman, soldier
sufficient	enough
provide	give
attempt	try
obtain	get
possess	have
desire	want
prior to	before
subsequent to	after
utilize	use
endeavor	try
myriad	many

(On this last item, myriad means many; therefore, a myriad of, which is used so much, makes no sense whatever.)

Above all, a writer should never use a word unless he is sure he knows the meaning of it. (If he really thinks about it, he usually does know; misuse comes more from carelessness than from ignorance.)

It is not uncommon, for example, to see agenda confused with itinerary, defuse with diffuse, glean with gleam, hone with home (one hones skills, homes in on a target), breach with bridge (especially in breaching the gap, which, of course, is already breached), and wreckless with reckless (direct opposites, in fact, when talking about driving.) A pet peeve of ours is the word enhance, which seems to be a favorite these days. Enhance means to increase or augment, but normally it is applied to something that is already good, such as value or beauty. To speak of enhancing lethality (a questionable word in itself) is ludicrous. What's wrong with using increase? Or improve?

Avoid jargon. Many people in the Army (and in other specialty fields as well) become so accustomed to seeing jargon, which is a specialized use of language, that they adopt it for all their writing. But the only time jargon of any kind is acceptable in writing is when the writer knows that all his readers will understand it. When a magazine goes to all kinds of people all over the world, he can be sure that many of them will not understand it. Any writer must therefore make a conscious effort to see that the words and phrases he uses are not only clear and concise but free of specialized uses of words that some will not understand.

Read and practice. Finally, anyone who seriously wants to write for publication should make it a habit to read everything he can. He will not only be stimulated by the ideas of others, he will also be exposed to the way those ideas are put together in writing. This, in turn, should make his own writing come easier.

He might even consider reading some of the many books on writing that are so popular now. One that has always been popular, and one that any writer would recommend, is *The Elements of Style*, by William Strunk Jr., and E. B. White. It is concise and easy to read (its authors practice what they preach).

In addition to reading, a prospective writer should practice writing every chance he gets. Only through practice can he sharpen his skills.

The most important thing about an article is its contents—the message that it has for a magazine's readers. If we see something good enough in a manuscript that is submitted to us, no matter how much help the writing may need, we will help the author get it published, either by giving him specific instructions for rewriting it or by editing it for him.

Our purpose here is to encourage writers, not to discourage them. These tips are designed to help the writer make that "something good" in a manuscript clearer and easier to get at so that an editor somewhere will want to publish it.

This article originally appeared in the September-October 1983 issue of INFANTRY magazine. Albert N. Garland is deputy editor of INFANTRY and Marie B. Edgerton is the associate editor.

Engineer Solution

For destruction of the 600m of track: Given an individual rail length of 7.5m, 80 lbs of TNT would be required to destroy 600m of track.

$$600\text{m} \times \frac{1 \text{ lb TNT}}{7.5\text{m}} = 80 \text{ lbs TNT}$$

The one-pound charges would be placed on alternating connections of both tracks to economize on the amount of explosives used. Tamping is not required but could be used to destroy a longer length of railroad track.

(Reference: FM 5-25, *Explosives and Demolitions*, para 4-40, a, (2), p. 4-56)

For destruction of the tunnel: Given a T-type chamber with a length of 60′, two 750-pound charges of high explosives (C4) should be used for a total of 1500 lbs of C4. Charges should be placed on 30′ centers.

(References: FM 5-25, para 4-41, c, p. 4-58)

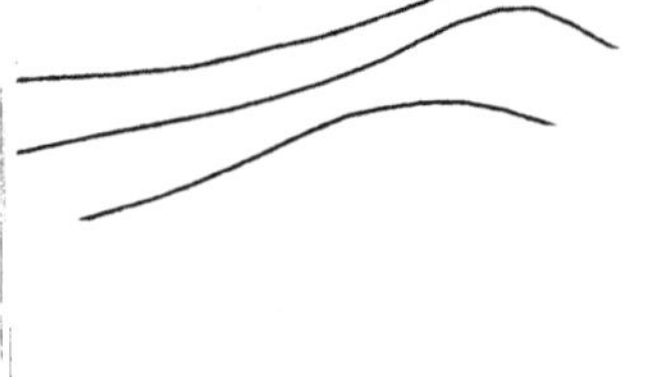

Mapmaking is undergoing revoluntionary change, particularly within the military. The shift from traditional "squint and print" maps and charts to today's semiautomated topographic products is the result of several new surveying, photogrammetric, and cartographic techniques, all employing digital technology.

Today's map is more than a symbolic picture of terrain and man-made features; it is a composite of "digits." These digits are supplied by the military cartographer to support weapon guidance, land navigation, terrain analysis, simulation, and command control systems.

Digital Topographic Data Base

Digits are topographic data that is compiled and converted into computer-compatible form. A collection of organized and evaluated digits make up a digital topographic data base (DTDB). The information for each DTDB is collected by various electronic methods and has recall capabilities for editing and updating.

With the DTDB, military cartographers are supplying digital topographic information for weapon guidance and command and control systems. For example, support system for the Pershing II; Firefinder MX; Airborne Warning and Command System (AWACS); and terrain contour matching (TERCOM) data for cruise missiles all use DTDB information.

Computer Graphics Maps

The traditional paper map has not been replaced; this critical tool will be used for years to come. However, computer-assisted cartography has eliminated many of the time-consuming processes of mapmaking. Some of the advantages are analytical stereoplotters for rapid data collection; interactive editing systems for updating digital information; and innovative programming to allow choice of scale, projection, symbolic detail and grid. There is another recent advantage—use of computer graphics.

In computer graphics, computer impulses are converted into man-readable information and imaged instantaneously on a display device. It offers three-dimensional (3-D) displays with cultural, vegetative tactical and other map-related overlays for terrain and military analysis.

Three dimensional maps (projections) are produced by connecting discrete elevation measurements (from the DTDB) taken at regul intervals along a straight line profile. The resulting fishnet appea ance causes the terrain to "pop u from the page, certainly addin dimension to the extended battl field of the AirLand Battle concep

The 3-D oblique map (Figure 1) i constructed so that projecting ray are parallel, whereas a 3-D shade (color) perspective map's rays com together at a distant point.

These two computer-generated di plays are not maps in the true sens of the word. Even though they repr sent a portion of the earth's surfac they are not drawn to scale. Hov ever, both projections are superior t the standard topographic map whe there is a requirement to visualiz and to analyze the terrain and it effect on military operations.

Terrain is generally analyzed b military commanders in five aspect observation and fire, cover and co cealment, obstacles, key terrain, an avenues of approach. The 3-D maj allow the commander to "see" th channelizing effect of avenues approach, and they clearly emph size key terrain features.

Recommendations for barrier minefields, and other fortificatior can be more easily made with cor

b MAJ David R. Bowen

r maps. Location of observation s, forward observers, and ground ement or flight routes can be lyzed more effectively since ing elevations can be easily . Also, the shaded perspective 's "sunagle" can be altered to uce various shading effects, with er a gray or color-layering poral, to designate graduations in f. This is a particularly valuable acteristic in analyzing terrain rafficability characteristics.

hese two 3-D computer graphic s were produced from digital graphic (elevation) data. Figure an example of manipulating and nstructing aerial photography vs and extract or insert various ation, planimetric (all other coments of a map except relief) or military data.

Today with the combination of 3-D computer graphics, the DTDB, and the original imagery, users can select a specific piece of ground and obtain 3-D oblique or perspective by computer to produce a computer-generated map. This technology, called Digital Image Analysis Laboratory (DIAL), was first developed at the U.S. Army Engineering Topographic Laboratories (ETL), Fort Belvoir, to analyze digitized aerial photography for vegetation information.

For example, the user could request slope information, construct radar masking diagrams or request civil engineering data (e.g., cut and fill requirements and flood-peculiar parameters). The DIAL System is interactive, and depending on the DTDB and other military or engineering data available, unlimited views and combinations of overlay information can be generated in graphic or tabular form.

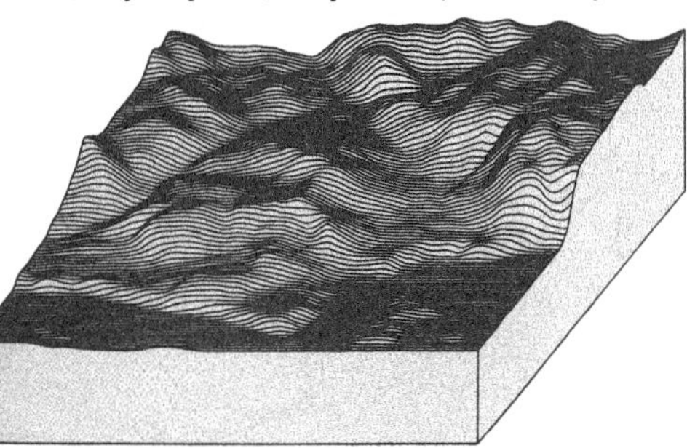

ure 1. 3-D oblique map produced by vector (storage tube) computer phics.

The visual impact that 3-D computer graphic maps offer to enhance terrain analysis is obvious. However, the primary advantage of a computer graphic map over a conventional map is that it can be produced rapidly and offers unlimited fields of view. The noted examples can be produced almost instantly on a display screen, and because of the interactive nature of computer graphics, they can be altered by the user in a matter of seconds.

This interactive advantage allows the user to rotate the map to obtain any desired azimuth and height of view. The commander can "see over the horizon" or visualize how an adversary "sees" his area of responsibility. Also, the DTDB can be accessed to superimpose vegetation, cultural features, grid lines, and other critical military data over the base elevation matrix. Overlaying such data (e.g., vegetation and military units) would certainly assist in the analysis of cover and concealment as well as observation and fire.

Some areas of computer graphic maps may not be visible because of landform obstruction or masking by the terrain. Also, vertical exaggeration could be applied to the display to obtain a desired false differential of elevation. The masking factor

Figure 2. 3-D shaded perspective map produced by raster computer graphics.

can be overcome interactively at the computer graphics terminal by changing direction of view or by elevating the viewer's visual perspective. Vertical exaggeration, if applied, must be to avoid an inaccurate analysis.

The weapon placement plot is an example of the application of five aspects of terrain analysis with computer graphics technology. In this example, (Figure 3), a computer-generated two-dimensional map (contours only) is produced, and a weapon system (M60 machine gun) is placed anywhere on the map to study the effect of terrain on the weapon's characteristics.

The weapon plot, in this case, graphically indicates the weapon's effectiveness. The left and right limits of fire and range are indicated. Also, taking into account the height above ground, the kill zone (shaded area) and dead spaces (open areas in the fan) are displayed. The weapon's orientation and height above the ground can be changed to see various fans of weapon capability. Vegetation and cultural features could be added to the display to increase the realism of the weapon's effectiveness.

The Orthophotomap

An orthophotomap (OPM) is a special topographic map particularly suited for rapid-response mapping requirements. Unlike the conventional line map where total map detail must be transferred from source information, the OPM is an actual picture of the ground with little of the displacement inherent in normal aerial photography.

There are many programs in progress to acquaint the military community with computer graphic mapping. The Field Exploitation of Elevation Data (FEED) system is a demonstration package on computer graphic mapping using a minicomputer-based graphic system. The FEED system is self-contained in a van and has been displayed at several Army and Air Force installations.

The Combined Arms Center, Fort Leavenworth, Kansas, uses a computer graphics system called Battlefield Visualization Graphics (BVG) to produce computer-generated views of terrain for simulation exercises. The computer graphics laboratory at West Point produces computer graphic maps to aid land navigation training. Finally, the National Training Center at Fort Irwin, California, uses a computer graphics display system so instructors and participants can see graphic replays (computer maps overlain with military symbology) of what actually took place during ground exercises.

The computer-generated maps noted in this article, are only a sample of some of the new mapping products being developed and tested.

Computer graphics technology coupled with digital topographic, planimetric, and tactical data offer an innovative, rapid-response tool for the battlefield commander.

MAJ David R. Bowen is executive officer of the 30th Engineer Bn. (Topographic), Ft. Belvoir. He has a master's degree in geography from Arizona State University and is a graduate of the Infantry and Engineer Officer Advanced Courses, the Command and General Staff College, and the Armed Forces Staff College. He served at West Point as assistant professor of cartography and terrain analysis, and was an exchange officer from the Defense Mapping Agency to the Australian Survey Regiment. While serving in Australia, he conducted research in automated cartography and commanded the regiment's cartographic squadron.

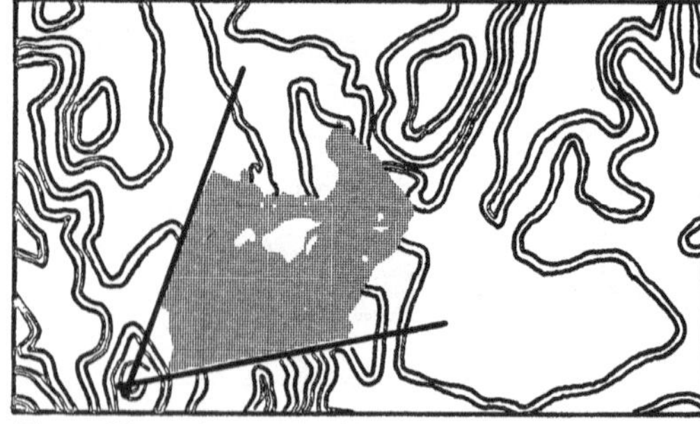

Figure 3. Weapon placement plot with a computer-generated contour map.

Career Notes

Commissioned Officers' Branch

(202) 325-7504/7505/7506, AV 221

LTC Peter G. O'Neill
Branch Chief

MAJ John Basilotto
Lieutenant Colonels

MAJ Steve Rust
Majors

CPT Tim Wood
Captains

CPT Bo Temple
Lieutenants

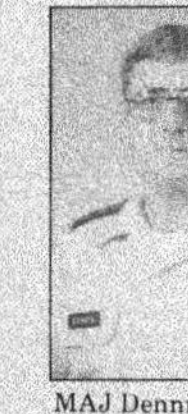

MAJ Dennis Cochrane
SC 49 Assignments

CPT Philip Jones
Professional Development

1983 Promotion Recap:

The results of the 1983 field grade officer promotion boards have been released. Below is a recapitulation of the promotion statistics for SC 21 (Engineer) officers and all Officer Personnel Management Directorate (OPMD) managed officers.

Generally, the promotion rate for SC 21 majors was above the OPMD average, the rate for SC 21 lieutenant colonels was below the average, and the rate for SC 21 colonels was above the average.

SC 21 PROMOTION RECAP (percent selected)

RANK	PC	FTC	PC & FTC	BZ
COL	0	51.8	40.0	3.2
LTC	11.9	68.9	47.0	2.3
MAJ	22.6	81.9	71.9	.8

OPMD PROMOTION RECAP (percent selected)

RANK	PC	FTC	PC & FTC	BZ
COL	6.9	44.6	25.7	2.6
LTC	16.1	71.7	47.8	2.9
MAJ	22.3	78.8	63.9	.5

PC = previously considered
FTC = first time considered
BZ = below the zone

Career Notes

Warrant Officers' Branch

(202) 325-7838/7839, AV 221

Warrant Officers Sought:

CW4 Edward Cole
Warrant Officers

More than 600 enlisted soldiers in combat service suppor specialties could soon exchange their stripes for bars.

The Army is critically short of warrant officers in five technica fields, according to technical service managers at MILPERCEN.

"We need about 600 NCOs in the supply and maintenance fields t fill our critical shortage of warrant officers in those five specialties, said CW4 Lloyd Washer of the Technical Services Branch, Warran Officer Division, Officer Personnel Management Directorat MILPERCEN.

Washer added that interested soldiers, E5 and above, serving i one of the feeder fields, should contact their military personne offices or personnel action centers to apply for appointment a warrant officers. Enlisted service members in the top three grades E7 through E9, can request appointment as a chief warrant office two, incurring a six-year obligation, Washer said.

Warrant specialties to be filled under this program are 310A Utilities Operation/and Maintenance Technician: 621A, Enginee Equipment Repair Technician; 630A, Automotive Repai Technician; 761A, General Supply Technician; and 726A, Suppor Supply Technician.

Feeder skills for the five warrant officer fields include a variety o combat service support military occupational specialties.

The Utilities Operation and Maintenance Technician (310A specialty is open to soldiers serving in these MOSs:

- 51B (Carpentry and Masonry Specialist)
- 51G (Materials Quality Specialist)
- 51H (Construction Engineering Supervisor)
- 51K (Plumber)
- 51R (Interior Electrician)
- 62E (Prime Power Production Specialist)
- 42C (Orthotic Specialist)
- 42D (Dental Lab Specialist)

Soldiers serving in the following specialties are eligible to apply for the 621A warrant officer program as an Engineer Equipment Repair Technician:

- 52C (Utilities Equipment Repairer)
- 52D (Power Generation Equipment Repairer)
- 52F (Turbine-Driven Engine Generation Repairer)
- 62B (Construction Equipment Repairer)

For the 630A, Automotive Repair Technician, field, soldiers serving in the following MOSs may apply:

- 41C (Fire Control Instrument Repairer)
- 41J (Office Machine Repairer)
- 44E (Machinist)

Warrant Officers' Branch (continued)

- 52C (Utilities Equipment Repairer)
- 52D (Power Generation Equipment Repairer)
- 52F (Turbine-Driven Engine Generation Repairer)
- 52K (Tank Turret Repairer)

The following MOSs are feeder skills for the 761A, General Supply Technician, warrant officer program:

- 76C (Equipment Records and Parts Specialist)
- 76J (Medical Supply Specialist)
- 76P (Materiel Control and Accounting Specialist)
- 76V (Materiel Storage and Handling Specialist)
- 76W (Petroleum Supply Specialist)
- 76X (Subsistence Supply Specialist)
- 76Y (Unit Supply Specialist)
- 76Z (Senior Supply Sergeant)

Finally, soldiers in most skills listed for 761A may also apply for the 762A, Support Supply Technician.

Military personnel officials emphasized that soldiers must meet several requirements in addition to their present MOS.

Any soldier serving as an E5 or higher in a skill listed, should contact his or her local military personnel center or personnel actions center to look at AR 635-100 and DA Circular 601-82-13.

NCO & Enlisted Soldiers' Branch

(202) 325-7710, AV 221

Six MOSs are reopened to women; see News & Notes, page 2.

LTC Liston Edge
Branch Chief

SGM John Peterson
Branch Sergeant Major

MSG James Blair
CMF 81, MOS 12Z(E8s)

SFC Richard Markle
CMF 12

SFC John Lane
CMF 51

SFC Gary McAllister
Professional Development

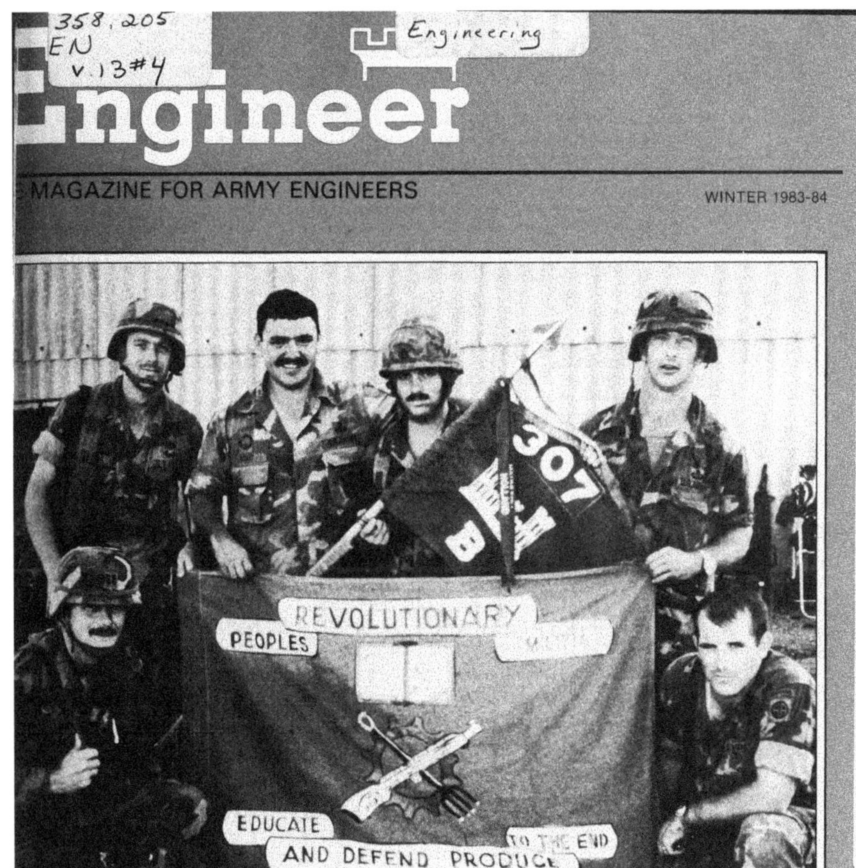

358.205
EN
v.13#4
Engineering
Engineer
MAGAZINE FOR ARMY ENGINEERS
WINTER 1983-84
307
B
REVOLUTIONARY
PEOPLES
EDUCATE
AND DEFEND PRODUCE
TO THE END

By

Leadership is taking the point position when your unit is expecting contact with the enemy or being the last person to abandon ship. Leadership is flying a crippled bomber to the ground when one of your wounded crew members cannot bail out. Leadership is keeping your young soldiers, marines, airmen and sailors alive and never leaving your wounded behind. Leadership is writing a dead trooper's family a personal letter immediately after the battle.

Leadership is not glorifying war. Leadership is not doing "anything" just to get promoted. Leadership is not winning the battle at all costs, nor is it losing a war to avoid casualties. Leadership is not found in the security of a well-fortified command bunker, nor is it found in a plush officers' field mess.

Leadership is rewarding a soldier, sailor, airman, marine, or civilian with the appropriate recognition immediately after an exceptional deed or service. Leadership is commanding and managing. Leadership is establishing, and meeting in priority, specific objectives. Leadership is managing by exception, using job enlargement, and seeking job enrichment.

Starting with this issue, ENGINEER will feature *A Personal Viewpoint*, a replacement to the *Forum* department. This space is provided to give our readers the opportunity to express their personal opinions concerning the Corps of Engineers and the military. This issue features MAJ Wayne L. Dandridge's personal view of leadership.

A leader is humanistic. A leader believes in God, family, and country, in that order. Leadership is treating men and women equally without regard to race, color, creed, religion, age, or custom. Leadership is visiting your wounded and sick frequently. Leadership is knowing and living by the Constitution, the Code of Conduct, the Geneva Convention, and the basic human rights of all mankind. A leader is assertive, but not aggressive.

Leadership is not ruthless nor mindless discipline, but it is the ability to do the right thing at the right time by putting the whole before the parts. Leadership is not a good efficiency report, nor is it paper readiness. Leadership is not a court-martial for every offense nor punishment for every mistake. A good leader is fair, predictable, and consistent.

Giving a superior sound professional advice when you know he or she does not want to hear it is leadership. Leading when you can; following when you should; and getting the hell out of the way when you have nothing to offer, is leadership. Learning the language and customs of a host country is leadership. Staying in top physical condition is leadership.

A leader does not forget that the past is our heritage, the present is our challenge, and the future is our responsibility. Leadership is not being overweight, not smoking, and not drinking alcohol. Leadership is not being right all the time, and it is certainly not being wrong most of the time.

Leadership is a general who

ME 13 NUMBER 4 WINTER 1983-84

On The Cover

Soldiers of B Co., 307th Engineers, display a Marxist flag they captured in Grenada. From left, CPT Don Davis, 2LT Hugh Enicks, SFC Raymond Scott, SSG James Dematteo, 1SG Harold Lockwood, 1LT Scott Snook. Rod Hafemeister photo, courtesy *Soldier of Fortune* magazine.

FEATURES

DEPARTMENTS

GINEER is an authorized publication of the U.S. Army Engineer Center, Fort Belvoir, Va. Unless specifically stated, material earing herein does not necessarily reflect official policy, thinking nor endorsement by any agency of the U.S. Army. The words nim, and his are used to represent personnel of either sex. All photographs contained herein are official U.S. Army photographs ess otherwise credited. The use of funds for printing this publication was approved by the Secretary of the Army on December 983. Material herein may be reprinted if credit is given to ENGINEER and to the author. ENGINEER's objectives are to vide a forum for the exchange of ideas, to inform and motivate and to promote the professional development of all members of Army engineer community. Direct correspondence with ENGINEER is authorized and encouraged. Inquiries, letters to the or, commentaries, manuscripts, photographs and general correspondence should be sent to: ENGINEER Magazine, ATZA-P, Stop 163F, Fort Belvoir, VA 22060. Phone: (703) 664-3082, AV 354. Subscriptions to ENGINEER are available through the erintendent of Documents, U.S. Government Printing Office, Washington, DC 20402. A check or money order payable to erintendent of Documents must accompany all subscription requests. Annual rates are $8.50 for domestic (including APO and)) addresses and $10.65 for foreign addresses. Individual copies are available at $4.50 per copy for domestic addresses and $5.65 foreign addresses. Second Class postage paid at Fort Belvoir, Va., and additional mailing offices. ISSN 0046-1989.

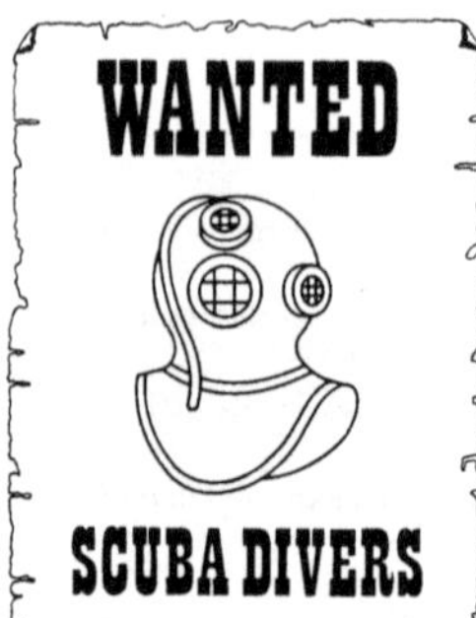

The Army is looking for volunteers to attend scuba training, according to officials at MILPERCEN. Soldiers in primary MOS 12B, Combat Engineer, and 12C, Bridge Crewman are invited to apply if they meet the prerequisites of AR 611-75, *Selection, Qualification, Rating and Disrating of Army Divers:*

- Volunteers for scuba training must be 30 years old or younger and be serving in grades E2 through E5. Soldiers in E6 and E7 grades will be considered as exceptions to policy.
- Aptitude test score minimums are GM 100, GT 110, and APRT 250. (Although AR 611-75 specifies an APRT score of 240, school officials stress that 250 points are required for the scuba program.)
- Applicants must have completed a Type B medical examination, approved by the Department of the Army Surgeon General, according to chapters 7 and 10 of AR 40-501, *Medical Service/Standards of Medical Fitness.*

Enlistment bonuses or selected reenlistment bonuses may be waived for soldiers accepted for the training.

For more information, contact your personnel services NCO or local military personnel office. □

ECTC '83

Experiences in Grenada, the development of training for the 1990s, and Soviet engineer capabilities were among the topics discussed at the recent Engineer Commanders' Training Conference (ECTC) held in Arlington, Va.

The conference is an annual event bringing Active and Reserve Component commanders (battalion level and above) together to exchange ideas and information in a variety of military engineering concerns. The theme of ECTC '83 was "Excellence Starts Here—Training to Fight and Win."

The keynote address was presented by LTG Fred K. Mahaffey, deputy chief of staff for operations and plans, Department of the Army. The general voiced his impressions of several areas of emphasis in Army planning; these included the formation of additional light (10,000 men) divisions,
innovative logistics, development of the capability to fight at night, rapid worldwide deployment, and improvements in weaponry.

The conference included seminars on the new Engineer School model, women in the Army, and the restructuring of Specialty Code 21 (see "Restructuring SC 21" on page 31).

Directorates of the Engineer School, along with other organizations, set up displays which detailed their current programs. Included were a videotaped program on the M9 Armored Combat Earthmover, the new videodisc trainer, and a display of Soviet and Warsaw Pact military clothing and equipment captured in Grenada. □

An ECTC '83 participant peeks through a periscope from a Soviet BTR-60 armored personnel carrier captured in Grenada by B Co., 307th Engineer Bn. (Airborne), 82nd Airborne Div., Ft. Bragg, N.C. *(Dave Arter photo)*

The Videodisc Trainer: More Than A Game

What may appear to be the Army's version of an arcade video game is actually a gunnery training device for the combat engineer vehicle (CEV). It comes complete with indicator lights, sound effects, and a digital readout panel similar to popular video games, but the real points scored translate into Army dollars saved.

Using an idea borrowed from the Armor School at Ft. Knox, Ky., the Engineer School's Directorate of Training and Doctrine (DOTD) is awaiting funding for the DA-approved videodisc trainer, according to 1LT Dexter Barge, a project officer for DOTD's training devices section.

When funded, 72 of the $25,000 videodisc trainers will be sent to CEV-equipped engineer battalions and separate companies. According to Barge, the devices were designed for soldiers in MOS 12F, Engineer Tracked Vehicle Crewman, in conjunction with CEV, AVLB and ACE training.

A programmed videodisc contains vidoetaped segments of realistic situations that could confront engineers in combat environments. Examples are fire missions that call for the destruction of a bridge and an enemy helicopter.

The gunner sits in front of the videodisc trainer and peers through an eyesite while manning the twin hand firing controls. A voice describes the target and fire mission. The target is engaged with the firing controls which permit vertical and horizontal movement of the gunsite. The trainer ticks-off seconds and chalks-up points on the digital display panel. Electronic bells and explosions add excitement and realism to the device.

A soldier tries his hand with the Engineer School's videodisc trainer. Videotaped, simulated combat situations are shown on the monitor while the "gunner" engages his targets with hand-held firing controls. Sound effects and a digital scoreboard make this device fun as well as practical. *(Dave Arter photo)*

The videodisc trainer is a portable combination of a television monitor, a vidoedisc player and a gunner's console. The device permits gunnery training in locations where firing ranges are inaccessible; it can be set-up in the corner of a classroom.

In addition to convenience, the trainer will reduce costs associated with live ammunition training. Barge says that the videodisc trainer and a subcaliber live firing device will allow CEV gun crews to qualify and maintain proficiency with smaller rounds, saving approximately $48,760 per year, per crew. Says Barge of the videodisc trainers, ". . . as you can see, they would soon pay for themselves."

12F BNCOC

A BNCOC (basic NCO course) for MOS 12F, Engineer Tracked Vehicle Crewman, was implemented in USAREUR in 1983; however, only 50 percent of the allocated slots were filled. The course prepares 12F NCOs for the duties and responsibilities of CEV commanders and AVLB section sergeants. There are six student allocations for each six-week cycle of the course. To ensure the continuation of the 12F BNCOC in USAREUR, the allocations must be filled this year. Commanders are urged to get qualified soldiers into the course.

School Wants Your Feedback On MOS Merger

The Engineer School is studying the possibility of combining MOS 82B (Construction Surveyor) and 82D (Topographic Surveyor) into on "Engineer Surveyor" MOS.

The study was prompted because these two MOSs have many similarities, and to a certain degree, a duplication in training and purpose. Combining the MOSs into an "Engineer Surveyor" MOS is probable because both have very small career fields (less than 450 soldiers combined) spread over four skill levels (two in 82B and four in 82D). A future reduction in authorized spaces brought on by new equipment and changing missions would create a severe structure imbalance within the skill levels of both MOSs.

Feedback from field units indicates that combining these two MOSs would come much closer to the "ideal structure" than keeping the MOSs separate.

It would, however, cause an imbalance at the E5-E6 level if these MOSs were combined without a rank redistribution. Therefore a TOE change would be required, possibly adding an E6 survey party chief in combat and dropping an E4 position.

Please send your comments and/or ideas on this study (pro or con) to:
U.S. Army Engineer School
ATTN: ATZA-TD-I-T
Fort Belvoir, VA 22060 □

Have something for News & Notes? Please send your item (with photographs) to ENGINEER Magazine, ATZA-TD-P, Stop 163F, Ft. Belvoir, VA 22060.

SMs In The Works for CMF 81

New soldier's manuals in an evaluative format are being developed at the Engineer School for five of the MOSs in CMF 81 (Topographic Engineering). The manuals for supervisory skill levels include a comprehensive MOS training plan and expedient squad job books.

The remaining MOS in CMF 81, 41B (Topographic Instrument Repair Specialist) is scheduled to have a soldier's manual in the field by December 1986.

TENTATIVE FIELDING DATES

STP	5-83F1 (Photolithographer)	Nov. 1984
STP	5-83F2/3/4/TG (Photolithographer)	
STP	5-82D1/2 (Topographic Surveyor)	Jul. 1985
STP	5-82D3/4/TG (Topographic Surveyor)	
STP	5-83E1/2/TG (Photo and Layout Specialist)	
STP	5-81C (Cartographer)	Nov. 1985
STP	5-81C2/3/4TG (Cartographer)	
STP	5-81Q1 (Terrain Analyst)	
STP	5-81Q2/3/4/TG (Terrain Analyst)	

□

Engineer People

CPT Bill Watkins. (Cynthia Barnes photo)

Summer Games Await Engineer

As all eyes in the world of sports focus their gaze on Los Angeles for the upcoming summer Olympic Games, one Army engineer is busily planning to be there—not as a spectator, but as a participant.

CPT Bill Watkins, recently assigned with the Course Development Div. of the Directorate of Training and Doctrine in the Engineer School at Ft. Belvoir, will be one of five members of America's 100-kilometer road cycling team.

The 29-year-old West Point graduate from Delafield, Wis., joined the Olympic Development Team for bicycling in 1981, along with 99 other national competitors. The five-man 100-kilometer team, which includes Watkins, will be officially announced July 10th at the national olympic time trials in Spokane, Wash. One of the five will be designated as the alternate cyclist for the four-man event. In all, seven American cyclists will compete in the cycling events.

Watkins logs over 350 miles each seven-day training week on his Serotta ten-speed. His training also consists of swimming and exercising with weights. He says he sleeps a minimum of eight hours every night. His diet, dictated by a program called macrobiotics, is low in meat and high in carbohydrates. He eats nuts, seeds and low-calorie protein sources like chicken and fish.

Now training at the National Olympic Training Center in Colorado Springs, his schedule will take him to Austin, Texas, and to pre-olympic competitions in Europe. Watkins predicts that America's toughest cycling foes in the Los Angeles Games will be the Soviet Union, East Germany, Switzerland and Poland. □

Engineer Bagpiper Sounds Off; Plays Pipes for Fun and Relaxation

Amateur musicians abound in the military as in any other field, but CPT Brian Roby, 2nd Bn., 4th Bde., Ft. Leonard Wood, Mo., opts for a more unusual instrument than the usual guitar or trumpet; he plays a set of Scottish bagpipes.

Born of Scottish descent, Roby has played the pipes for six years. "I was in a band at West Point and someone asked me if I wanted to learn how to play the bagpipes," said the USMA graduate, a native of Toledo, Ohio.

Roby bought his first set of bagpipes while assigned to the 12th Engineer Bn. in Dexheim, Germany.

Roby, a recent advanced course graduate, described his instrument as having "wooden reeds, like a clarinet or an oboe. The bag is made from goat's skin and is covered by a wool, plaid cloth. My set has a Scottish, Gordon-Clan plaid pattern covering the bag. And yes, my bagpipes were made in Scotland."

Roby said he plays for relaxation and for enjoyment—usually outdoors and at night, because the pipes are so loud. □

Send submissions for Engineer People to ENGINEER Magazine ATZA-TD-P, Stop 163F, Ft. Belvoir, VA 22060. Please include photographs and a point of contact.

CPT Brian Roby. (Gerry Gillmore photo)

CLEAR THE WAY

by MG James N. Ellis, Commandant, U.S. Army Engineer School

For Success, We Need Strong Leaders

Nothing influences battle as much as a strong leader.

As the Army moves to update its structure, training, tactics, arms, equipment and doctrine to meet the new challenges of the battlefield, so must combat engineers look to the future. As we stiffen the backbone of our combat battalions by introducing new systems such as the M9 ACE, and others, we must not neglect to also develop the soul of the Engineer branch—its leaders.

The accelerated pace, lethality, and decentralized nature of the AirLand Battlefield places a premium on sound and aggressive leadership. As noted by COL Stanley Johnson in his article on page 18, decisions made quickly under the stress of battle can alter the course of an entire campaign. Our leaders, especially at battalion level and lower, must reflect the attributes of what a leader must *be*, *know*, and *do*.

Good Values Build Trust

Character shapes the performance, attitudes and bearing of leaders. Our leaders consistently must think and act in accordance with values such as loyalty, corage, confidence, candor, commitment, responsibility and initiative—all of which determine combat readiness. Behavior inconsistent with these character traits corrodes the trust and confidence soldiers must have in those who lead them in war.

In his article beginning on page 11, COL William Burns defines leadership as "a moral force that is used to inspire individuals to accomplis difficult tasks." That is a good definition, o implying that leaders must go beyond technic and tactical competence. They also must kno human nature. They must understand the nee and emotions of their soldiers and how peop respond to stress. They must understand how t four factors of leadership—follower, leader, co munication, and situation—affect one anothe They must know how to use this knowledge develop cohesion, to foster discipline and to bui individual and team skills. Today, more than ev before in history, determining who controls th battlefield is more a factor of forging a strong wi to fight than of simply fielding new arms an equipment.

Leaders Must Pursue Excellence

Finally, our leaders must plan missions, mak decisions, solve problems, and establish goals a they guide their units to reach and to sustai combat proficiency. To achieve this level o readiness, leaders must communicate high per formance expectations to soldiers; they mus persistently pursue excellence in training, main tenance and troop welfare; and they must ensure united effort by convincing subordinates tha objectives are possible and thus deserve tota dedication.

In this vein, the Engineer School has taken th lead in training and in educating our junio engineer leaders, NCOs and officers. We hav expanded our instruction in ethics and leadershi for students at the NCO advanced course, and a the officer basic and advanced courses. Thi expanded training will provide these engineer with a solid basis for continued leadership development. But the process must not stop there! Onc these students graduate and move on to their units supervisors in the field must take an active personal interest in ensuring that our junio leaders use and expand the skills and knowledg acquired at the Engineer Center. Doing les undermines all of our efforts to prepare for moder battle.

BRIDGE THE GAP

SM O.W. Troesch Jr., U.S. Army Engineer Center & School

e are the vital link ensuring that our ldiers train hard and fight to win

lthough noncommissioned officer leadership is taught from the same leadership ual used for officers, NCO and officer ership must differ because of the needs of the and because of the differences of each group's es.

trait of officer leadership, for example, is ing by reputation. The battalion commander t be with all his soldiers every day. However, if a strong leader, his subordinates know what standards are and what he expects. Those dards are met, even when the commander is present.

s noncommissioned officers, however, we lead iers by daily personal example in everything do or fail to do. We are the catalyst that makes gs happen. We are the indispensible linkage n which the commander depends for his unit to n professionally and to fight hard and win. We ıt develop a brand of personal leadership that inspire soldiers to train hard, to learn well, to be free of bias and prejudice.

Totally Committed

eading today's soldiers takes a total commitıt to duty. We must be willing to inconvenience ıelves to improve our soldiers' training and ipline. As an example, if for some reason a ier fails to master a required task, then we ıt be willing to devote our own personal time—ıts or weekends—to retraining that soldier.

.any times noncommissioned officers must be opular leaders by requiring that soldiers ere to standards, and obey orders and regulas for the good order and discipline of the unit. must resist the temptation to selectively ırce orders or regulations because we don't ıssarily agree with them. Avoiding this tempon is the mark of a good noncommissioned officer and leader, and of a true professional. It is also an instance of leading by example, and of being the linkage to ensure that the commander's standards are reflected at the individual soldier level.

Victor of Statistic?

There is another important reason why we must be strong leaders—winning in war demands it. To win on the battlefield is the only reason our profession exists. Units with strong leaders and motivated, well trained soldiers are the battlefield victors. Units less professional become the battlefield statistics. In wartime, crucial combat engineer tasks will be executed by engineer squads and platoons operating separately from their engineer headquarters. Our young soldiers must be technically, physically and psychologically prepared to perform under the stress of combat. It is no exaggeration to say that an entire battle could hinge on the actions of a single squad of combat engineers.

We are a part of the greatest force modernization effort the Army has ever undertaken, and our soldiers are the highest quality ever. It is incumbent upon us to learn, to develop, and to use leadership techniques that will make our units and soldiers the leading edge in a high-technology Army. More than ever before, our nation needs a professional Army to provide a deterrent to war or, if necessary, to fight and win.

Let us, the noncommissioned officers, be the means by which the Army can "bridge the gap" from today's Army to the Army of the future. Let's rededicate ourselves to providing our soldiers and our engineer units with the strongest, most professional noncommissioned officer corps in the Army. Really strive for excellence. Be all the leader you can be.

Directorate of Combat Developments

Army 21 Engineer Concept: Army 21 is an evolving concept of the engineer system for the ye 1995 through 2030 and is not to be confused with AirLand Ba doctrine. The Concepts Branch is continuing to study the engin mission and capabilities for the 21st century. An engineer comp and regimental engineer section organic to each maneuver regim will provide mobility, countermobility, survivability (M-CM-S) terrain analysis support for the regiment.

At the AirLand Force (ALF) level, engineers organized i companies and battalions under an engineer regiment will prov additional M-CM-S capabilities, the bulk of bridging and gen engineering, and further topographic support. While movi engineer countermine vehicles will be capable of detecting neutralizing mine targets to spearhead armored drives thro enemy-held terrain. Robotic and "intelligent" mine systems supplement the regimental obstacle capabilities.

Tentatively, publication of the Army 21 concept, including Engineer appendix (combat support, engineering and mine warf is scheduled for December 1984. The Engineer School's concept briefed in January at an action officers' workshop at HQ, TRAD

Directorate of Training and Doctrine

New Welding Shop: U.S. Army maintenance facilities in Europe will be receivin new mobile welding shop beginning this Spring. Mounted on a ton trailer, the new welding shop's capabilities are arc, metal ir gas (MIG) and tungsten inert gas (TIG) welding, as well as carbon arc cutting. Additionally, the shop has oxyacetylene cutting welding capabilities. This new item will be issued as a one-for- replacement of the old arc welder with priority given to units wh already have the five-ton trucks required to pull the new weld shop. A skid-mounted version having arc welding capability only go to U.S. forces in Korea.

51H30 BTC: The new 51H30 Basic Technical Course is being offered at Leonard Wood. It is designed to introduce the 51H to the skills of feeder MOSs and to develop construction foremen's skills. The week course is held 12 times annually. Each class has a 25-stud capacity. The course is attended on a TDY or TDY-enroute ba Personnel interested in attending should submit a completed Form 4187 with copies of DA Forms 2 and 201 through comm channels to MILPERCEN, ATTN: DAPC-EPT-F, 200 Stovall Alexandria, VA 22332.

irectorate of valuation and Standardization

Professional Development Pamphlets: The Engineer School completed new professional development pamphlets for both the officer and enlisted ranks. The officer pamphlet updates the current, grey officer professional development pamphlet and covers all specialty codes. The enlisted professional development pamphlet covers information for engineers in grades E1 through E9. Both pamphlets, completed in December 1983, give engineers in the field a current professional development reference.

Name Changes: Effective October 1, 1983, the Directorate of Engineer Force Management (DEFM) became the Directorate of Evaluation and Standardization (DOES), and DEFM's Engineer Force Management Division became a separate office—the Engineer Proponency Office (office symbol is ATZA-EP). A toll-free hotline is open 24 hours a day for proponency related questions. To use it, call 1-800-336-3095, Ext 44172.

efense Mapping School

Digital Topo Data Course: The Defense Mapping School offers a course about digital topographic data three times each year. The course is to help managers understand digital data and what it represents, especially since Army systems are increasingly relying on digital data for guidance and graphic presentation. The course is particularly appropriate for topographic officers and non-engineers involved in weapons or command and control systems acquisition. The six-day course gives military and civilian students a basic understanding of digital mapping, data acquisition, topographic data processing, and the use of digital data in weapon systems, maneuvers, simulations, and command and control.

)epartment of Vilitary Engineering

MOS 12E AIT: The Atomic Demolition Munitions Branch of the Engineer School has revised a TRADOC program of instruction (POI) for the MOS 12E Advanced Individual Training course for skill level 1. The new instructional program covers 18 critical tasks as outlined in the POI.

As before, the course is three weeks (or 103 hours) long. Within the 29 modules are 12 written tests, 21 hands-on performance tests and five practical exercises. The student must score at least 80 percent to receive a "go" for each written test; the performance tests are graded against the soldier's manual and Common Task Test standards.

The POI includes timer calculations; operational, emergency destruction, safety and security procedures; and performance and written tests.

Leadership: A Personal Viewpoint, continued

Teresa, Winston Churchill, Margaret Thatcher, and many other well known figures. Also leaders are Robert Lightle, Herman Perez, Bill Waters, Sandy Dandridge, and thousands of other unknowns.

Leadership can be good or bad, centralized or decentralized, warm or cold, offensive or defensive, macro or micro, or expensive or free. Leadership can be Protestant or Catholic, Jewish or Moslem, Hindu or Morman, atheist or agnostic.

Leadership is guiding. Leadership is legendary. Leadership is foresight. Leadership is absorbent, abstinent, and, unfortunately, at times it is abominable. Leadership is baccalaureate, balanced, basic and too frequently backward and barbaric. Leadership has saved lives, killed, stopped wars, and started wars. Leadership has walked softly and carried a big stick, but it has also been loud and nonviolent.

Leadership is honesty, enthusiasm, loyalty, courage, and wisdom. Taking care of your soldiers', civilians', sailors', airmens', and Marines' dependents is leadership. Leadership includes being a good boss and friend, father or mother, son or daughter, sister or brother, and husband or wife. Knowing that the profession of arms is much more than just a job is leadership.

Leadership is helping, training, encouraging, understanding, motivating, disciplining, crying, laughing, standing firm, giving way, counseling, correcting, giving a second chance, and trying again and again. Leaders are tall, short, thin, heavy, male, female, black, brown, white, yellow, old, young, naturalized and unnaturalized. Leaders are from the city and from the country. Leaders look you in the eye, kick you in the ass, cover your flank, and take your place on the most dangerous mission.

Leadership comes from experience, but experience comes from making mistakes. A leader changes the odds and knows the risks. Leaders develop teamwork. The tides, the channels, the seasons, the winds, the weather, and the best forecast are all known by leaders. Leaders often make good grades i school and have numerous years o formal education and many im portant degrees. But they also hav been known to fail math, Englisl and other equally importar subjects.

Leadership comes from famil friends, teachers, coaches, an pastors. Simple, easy-to-understan orders come from leaders. Comple tasks are changed into short an accurate plans through leadershi Leadership can be learned an taught, but it cannot be forgotte nor bought. Leadership can be seer tasted, smelled, felt, and heard, bu it can come from a blind person wit no hands who cannot hear nor walk

Finally, a leader is so in love wit life that he or she is willing to die t ensure that others' lives will go on!

MAJ Wayne L. Dandridge is member of the Host Country Suppo Team, U.S. Army European Con mand. He has served as a mair tenance test pilot, instructor pilo and in various command and sta positions. He is a graduate of t Armed Forces Staff College and of t Transportation Officer Advance Course. He has a bachelor's degree i aeronautical science from Embr Riddle Aeronautical University an a master's degree from the Florid Institute of Technology.

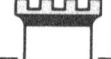

Engineer Problem

You were tasked to relieve a British recon team and destroy a bridge north of your sector. The British team leader hands you a target folder that is only partially filled in. The sketches are accurate but the planned charge placement is inadequate. Your headquarters specified that the bridge demolition create at least a 25-meter gap.

Your company commander arrives to check on your situation. You discuss the problem with him and decide that simply cutting the span will not create the 25-meter gap. The British team prestocked adequate blasting caps, time fuzes, fuze igniters, and detonation cord. However, they did not leave enough explosives. You only have one 2 ½ ton truck (M35A2) to transport additional demolitions and the nearest ammunition supply point is 30 km away (45 minutes one way).

Determine the following: **I.** How much demo and what kind will be required? **II.** How and where will the charges be placed? **III.** Assigning one squad to the mission, how long will it take the squad to bring the target to state of readiness 1? **IV.** How long from state of readiness 1 to state of readiness 2 (Armed)? **V.** Is any special equipment required?

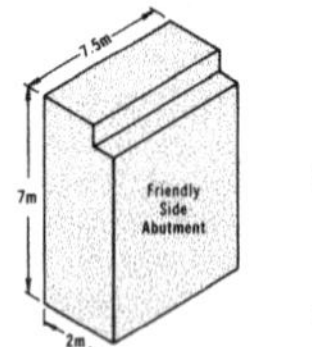

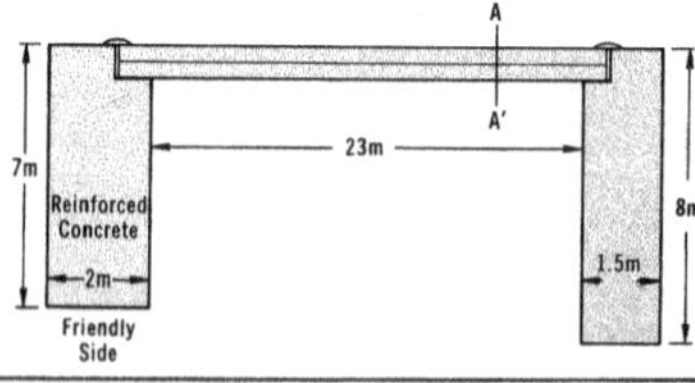

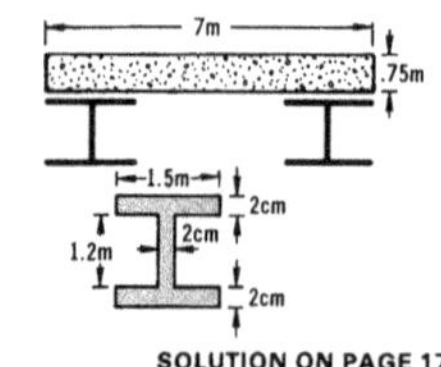

SOLUTION ON PAGE 17.

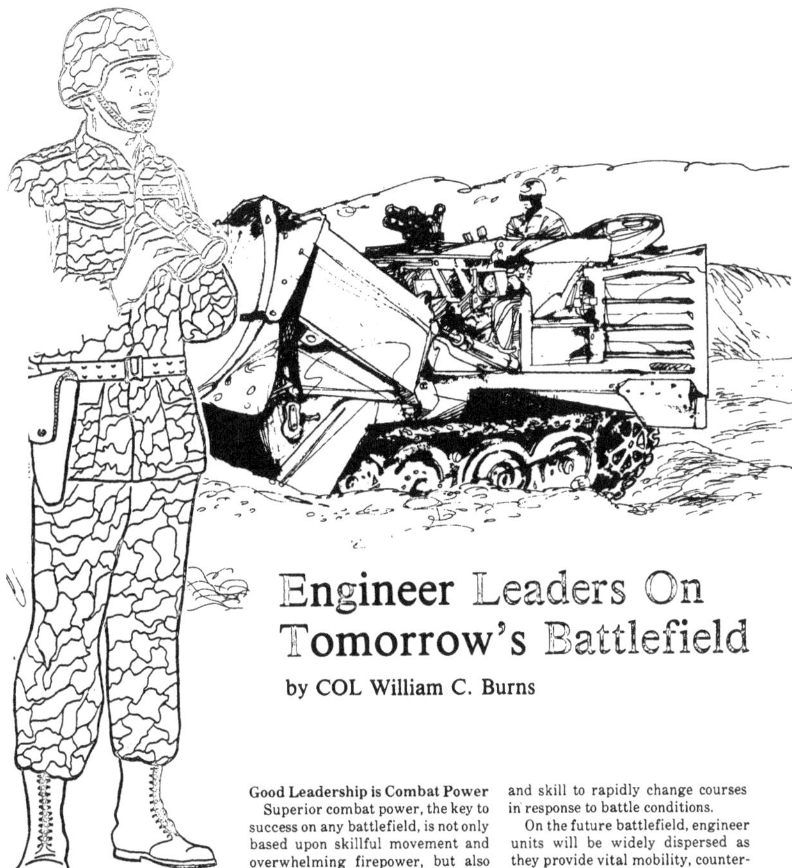

Engineer Leaders On Tomorrow's Battlefield

by COL William C. Burns

Effective leaders. The Army has always had them, but today at need is greater than it has ever en in our history.

Concepts for future battles include battlefield with combat actions nging from behind one's lines rough the enemy's front line units his follow-on forces.

Good Leadership is Combat Power

Superior combat power, the key to success on any battlefield, is not only based upon skillful movement and overwhelming firepower, but also upon the quality of leadership. To win the AirLand Battle of the future, we will need leaders who inspire confidence and the will to win in soldiers. Futhermore, we need leaders, who under extreme stress, can develop new solutions to unexpected problems. The leader must possess both the knowledge to develop sound operational and technical plans and the mental flexibility and skill to rapidly change courses in response to battle conditions.

On the future battlefield, engineer units will be widely dispersed as they provide vital mobility, countermobility, and survivability support to the combined arms team. Good leadership will be imperative at all levels of engineer command. The emphasis, however, will be on platoon and squad level leaders ensuring that their units are effective and carry out their missions in the absence of regular communication from the parent engineer battalion.

The isolation of an active NBC environment will stress units and their leaders. Leaders must be prepared technically, physically and psychologically for such battlefields. The engineer platoon leader must be knowledgeable, innovative, and have the moral courage to see the mission through!

Small Unit Leadership is Important

This issue of ENGINEER focuses on leadership at the platoon level, which is just as critical to accomplishing the engineer's mission as it is to accomplishing the infantry or armor unit's mission.

Although the engineer commander must exercise both leadership and management skills to be successful, leadership is the critical skill. It is the moral force that influences and motivates people to accomplish the assigned task. Leadership is a precious commodity in our Army. Our younger leaders must develop their leadership qualities as well as practice their leadership skills in order for the Army to carryout its mission.

Colonel Gerald Brown's article on page 15 particularly stresses the point that proficiency is a combination of both knowledge and experience.

Education is a continuous process both in and out of the classroom. Captain Ralph Graves' article on page 32 on the new initiatives for the Engineer Officer Advanced Course summarizes the Engineer School's innovative response to providing educational support to the career engineer officer.

Schools, however, only facilitate the opportunity for learning. The leader must be willing to spend many hours on self-education, both on and off "duty time." The military is a most demanding profession. It not only involves competence in the full spectrum of human psychology but of management as well. Meeting this challenge is critical if the leader is going to grow and be ready for the increasing responsibility inherent in a successful military career. In his article on page 20, Captain Willis Lee urges the new lieutenant to develop this self-education habit early in his career. True wisdom, whether you are sergeant, a lieutenant or a colonel, is the knowledge of what we don't know and recognizing the need to learn it. Modern technology has given the military weapons of tremendous destructive potential. We cannot afford to have amateurs leading the soldiers who employ those weapons.

> ***"It is the leader's values that determine the kind of Army we have."***

The Leader's Values

There is a good reason why each of the leadership articles address the qualities or values of a good leader. Skill and knowledge alone are not enough. The Army must operate according to a well defined value system. It is the leader's values that determine the kind of Army we have.

General William R. Richardson, the TRADOC commander, addresses on page 13 the importance of values in his discussion of the importance of commitment, competence, candor and courage. These are the four professional soldierly qualities listed in Chapter 4, FM 100-1, *The Army.*

The leader is on duty twenty-four hours a day and his actions, both professional and personal, establish his values in the eyes of his unit. The experience of senior leaders and countless studies have lead to the same basic truth, first and foremost, that the unit or organization reflects the values demonstrated by its leadership. The values you express and use to guide your actions must be consistent.

Our Most Valuable Asset

Although each author has expressed it differently, a point never to forget is that the ability to do our mission rests ultimately with the individual soldier. It doesn't much matter whether you classify yourself as a commander, leader or manager. What matters is that you recognize that people are our most precious and valuable asset. Without them the Army doesn't exist.

Our prime responsibility as leaders is to ensure that our people are members of a well-led, well-trained, disciplined unit or organization which is properly equipped and supported for its mission. If we as commanders, managers and leaders provide the opportunity for the individual to contribute to the success of the organization, they will to do so to the best of their ability.

Military service offers the opportunity to the individual not only to grow in skills and ability, but to contribute to something larger than himself. If a soldier feels that by making a solid contribution to his unit he has done something important in protecting this nation and the freedom it represents, then he will feel his service time was worthwhile. It is the responsibility of the leader to ensure that this is what happens.

Leadership, in the final analysis, is a moral force that is used to inspire individuals to accomplish difficult tasks that must be done. Successful leadership is firmly based in values and practices which encourage the soldier to succeed and to develop, both as an individual and as a member of his unit.

COL William C. Burns is chief of the Project Management Office, Directorate of Training and Doctrine, U.S. Army Engineer School. He will assume command of the Rock Island Engineer District this summer. COL Burns is a graduate of the U.S. Army War College, has an MBA from Long Island University, a master's degree in operations research from the Naval Post Graduate School, and a bachelor's degree from the U.S. Military Academy. COL Burns is a registered professional engineer in Virginia.

emarks by
General William R. Richardson
at Commissioning Ceremonies
Fort Riley, Kansas, July 1983

4 Fundamentals of Professionalism

There are four basic qualities fundamental to the profession of arms. And it *is* a profession. Make no mistake about that. We are a unique society of individuals with our own professional ethic by which we govern our lives. It is the very foundation which gives us the confidence to meet any test offered us.

First, we believe in commitment. That begins with your oath. Your first leadership assignment is another commitment, both to those you lead and those who lead you and your unit. These commitments never stop. As you gain in rank and experience, you will face commitment to bigger and more far-reaching issues. The commitments you must always remember are those to your nation, your service, your leaders, and those you lead. You will, of course, be committed to excellence at all times. You must strive to improve whatever is in your power to improve. Leave everything with which you are connected better than when you found it.

There are benefits with commitment, too. Commitment is a safe harbor in which to anchor if the storms of disappointment sweep over you. It is a source of strength in the inevitable times when things go wrong or a positive source of confirmation when the good times come your way.

Second, we believe in competence. Lincoln said, "I will study and prepare myself, and someday my chance will come." You must do the same. If you are not competent in a

> *"First, we believe in commitment."*

"Second, we believe in competence."

"Third, we believe in candor."

tactical and technical sense, you will not be qualified to lead. If you're not qualified or not fit to lead, you are a danger to your soldiers. You may expose them to danger needlessly, and they are a precious resource. Even worse, you will destroy their confidence in themselves—and in you.

Remember always that a bad leader with the best troops can be a clear and potential menace to them and to himself. On the other hand, a competent leader—as history has proven time and time again—can take untrained but willing troops and inspire them to do wonders by his example.

The decision point in our profession is the battlefield. We do not *want it* to be so, but it is our duty to spend our lives training for something we hope never to do—wage war at the direction of our civilian leaders.

Soldiers are more aware than anyone of the hazards involved in war. But if we must fight, we must also have people who know what they are doing. There is simply no alternative to this.

Thirdly, we believe in candor. To us, candor means that you have no time or use for lies. You can't abide double meanings. You want communications which are accurate, straightforward, and honest. Let your soldiers see you as honest in all your dealings. Expect the same from them. Let your word be your bond and expect the same from your soldiers. You will rarely find a soldier to whom you cannot safely extend this expression of your regard for him or her. Candor is based on a strong sense of personal honor—a sense of what is right and what is wrong. This is not as easy as it sounds. Find a role model whose honesty and trustworthiness you respect. Watch him or her. You can gain more from understudying a proven leader than in any other way I know.

Finally, we believe in courage. We believe you can develop the physical courage to do your job of leadership under even the most terrifying conditions. If you are competent and confident in your ability and that of your command, you can meet and defeat war. Physical courage is rooted in believing in your unit, your own excellence at leadership, and your devotion to your service and your country.

Moral courage is often another story. It takes as much courage to take and hold an unpopular stand—when it might be easier to blend in with the faceless majority—as it does to face a line of oncoming armor. But if you believe that you are right—after sober and considered judgment—hold your position. When this stand applies to the pursuit of personal or unit excellence, you owe your country nothing less.

The officer corps must possess the highest sense of moral courage if it is to fulfill its purpose of leadership for the American soldier. This will not be easy, nor should it be.

And so, these four qualities symbolize the attributes and values of the American military professional. As

ADVICE for Engineer Lieutenants

by COL Gerald Brown

The theme for this issue of ENGINEER is leadership. ssuming that many readers are nior officers, I shall try to provide dvice on how to achieve success as an ngineer officer in the U.S. Army. Most engineer officers in the rmy today have completed a compressed, yet comprehensive, study in ngineering. For this achievement, I ongratulate you. You have the good rtune to begin your careers at an xciting time. The future is bright in e troop arena and in facilities ngineering.

uccess is . . .?

To be successful, you must first ecide what you mean by success. Do ou aspire to high rank and positions f leadership? Do you desire a eputation as an expert in some articular field? Are you looking for xperience in the Army that will ter help you gain great wealth in fe? Or, are you looking forward to a uiet, useful career in which you can evelop to your maximum potential? ou must look at your career in a ealistic manner and develop realistic bjectives. Everyone can't be a general officer. Everyone can't be a renowned expert in a narrow field. You won't obtain wealth as an Army officer, although you will live comfortably.

Success to you will mean accomplishing your objectives. The best chance of achieving success is through lifelong dedication, perseverance and preparation. A philosophy on professional success was captured by William Jennings Bryan when he wrote:

Destiny is not a matter of chance,
it is a a matter of choice. It is not
a thing to be waited for, it is a
thing to be achieved.

Your degree of success will depend on your intelligence, the amount of general knowledge you acquire, your knowledge of your particular field and your ambition to progress. Also important will be your integrity and your ability to work with others as a team.

What you achieve in your career will be the result of choices you make along the way. The key is constant professional development—to be prepared when opportunity calls.

Keep up with developments in your field. Read professional journals, participate in professional societies and attend continuing education courses.

You may have heard the story of the Nobel Prize winning scientist who was asked how it felt to wake up famous. The scientist replied, "No one wakes up suddenly and finds himself famous. I've been at work night and day for 15 years." In life, the law of cause and effect works this way.

Attributes for Success

You should realize that knowledge and experience are two distinct attributes. Together they can lead you to success. From your first assignment, start to build your experience. Seek positions that will broaden and increase your professional development. One of my college professors, Dr. Ralph Peck of the University of Illinois, studied under the great soils engineer, Karl Terzaghi. Terzaghi told his students that early in one's career, experience is far more important than salary or position. He persuaded young Peck to accept a position in the construction of the Chicago subway system. This job started him on the way to becoming our country's leading foundation engineer.

To gain experience, don't be afraid to request new jobs if your duties fail to absorb your energies completely. Do this primarily during the first five to ten years of your Army career. After that, you should be established in one or two specialty fields. If you change too often, later in your career you risk the reputation of being a rolling stone. Five years from now, make sure you have five years of experience and not one year of experience five times.

Dr. Peck also advised my class to build "engineer judgment." For example, when someone talks about a 600-kip column load, that should create an image in your mind—the size of the column. You should know where to expect such a column—in a parking garage or in the Empire State Building. (In the Empire State Building—right?) When someone tells you that the calculated charge to cut a steel beam is five pounds of C4, you should be able to approximate in your mind what you would expect to see in place. Develop good engineer judgment, and you will be surprised (and dismayed!) at the mistakes you will find on plans and at job sites.

Knowledge and experience are crucial to success in the engineer profession. Both require years of hard work and dedication. Of course, there may be occasions when one's future depends on being at the right place at the right time. Frank Forker, an executive with AMF, Inc., said in a recent article:

> *It may be that life will never present us the real opportunity we seek or desire. But I am determined to so prepare myself that if such an opportunity does come, I shall be ready. I shall have my homework done, the seeds sown and the foundations laid.*

This wisdom is applicable perhaps more in the military than anywhere else. Success is not reached by the easy road. As Disraeli said, "The successful man is the one who has the best information."

The Foundation of Our Profession

Leadership is the foundation of our profession. That is where the greatest contribution is made. Aspire to such positions. Most of you will serve your initial assignment as a platoon leader. Army leadership starts there.

Becoming a leader will not be easy. To get a platoon to follow you without question to clear a lane through a minefield that is under fire is leadership. Develop those skills within yourself. There are some who say that leadership cannot be taught, rather, that leaders are born. They are wrong. Leadership traits can be learned and developed. The essential elements of leadership are knowledge and experience, but leadership also encompasses other traits such as dependability, decisiveness, and selflessness—traits that are commonly known as character.

Here are a few thoughts on some of the qualities required of leaders.

- ***Leaders accept responsibility.*** You cannot exercise the power of leadership without assuming the responsibilities that go with it. These responsibilities will require an extra measure of hard work.
- ***Leaders are courageous.*** They have the moral strength to make decisions and to put thoughts into action. Remember, those who fail are those who never try.
- ***Leaders are decisive.*** Never use the lack of time as a reason not to do something. Leaders must train themselves to make decisions quickly after receiving the facts.
- ***Leaders have vision.*** They have a perspective, a sense of where the organization is, where it is going, and how to get there. Leaders must not become mired in the day-to-day minutiae of the desk "IN" basket.
- ***Leaders are compassionate.*** That does not mean "soft," although empathy certainly is a part of compassion. Compassionate leaders know what is best for subordinates and set them steadfastly on course. Sometimes that means being very tough. Examples of sports leaders come to mind, such as basketball's Bobby Knight of Indiana and football's late "Bear" Bryant of Alabama. Their brand of leadership mixes compassion with toughness. Both are superb leadership examples.
- ***Leaders set and demand high standards of excellence.*** They never accept mediocrity from self or anyone else. They set fair, tough standards and demand excellence in performance.
- ***Leaders must be technically competent.*** One quick way to tarnish leadership is to allow subordinates to discover that their leader doesn't know what he talking about. Leaders never stop learning.
- ***Leaders understand people.*** They are motivators, communicators, listeners, inspirers, and most of all, teachers. The most important quality is consistency. Leaders never waiver from their leadership philosophy. People must know what to do expect

perience, integrity, modesty, sinity, ability to work with others, otion to your work, confidence in r ability, and faith in our country. d, last but not least, you need a ong religious faith to provide the mework for you to decide what is ht, just, and good, and also to ovide you the strength to carry out ur decisions.

COL Gerald Brown commands the Corps of Engineers' Baltimore District. He has served as chief of doctrinal literature management at the Engineer School, as an associate professor of military history at West Point, and commanded the 82nd Engineer Bn., VII Corps, USAREUR.

He is a graduate of the Army War College, has a master's degree in civil engineering from the University of Illinois and has a bachelor's degree from the U.S. Military Academy. COL Brown is a registered professional engineer in Texas.

Engineer Solution

The general approach is to destroy the friendly side abutment. Plan to cut the span once to ensure that the bridge will fall completely into the gaps, leaving no framework for the enemy to use in trying to rebridge the gap.

I. Demo Requirements

A. For destroying abutment:

1. Top of Abutment: $P = R^3\ KC[R = 6.56'; K = 0.54$ (reinforced concrete); $C = 1.0$ (ground placed, tamped)]. Calculation gives 153 1-pound blocks of TNT (or equivalent) per charge. Number of Charges: $N = W/2R$ gives 2 charges required. (Total: 306 1-pound blocks TNT).

2. Bottom/River face of abutment: Use the same calculation with the exception of the tamping factor. Using C=3.6, you find that 549 1-pound blocks of TNT (or equivalent) per charge are required. Again, there will be 2 charges required. (Total: 1,098 1-pound blocks TNT.)

B. For cutting the span:

1. Steel cutting charges for two I beams: cross-sectional area (A) of the steel beam is 840 cm^2 or 130.2 in^2. (Due to the dimensions of the beam, the ribbon charge would not be practical.) $P = \frac{3}{8}A$, $(A = 130.2)$ gives 49-1 pound blocks of TNT/per charge required: There are two beams requiring two charges. (Total: 98-1 pound blocks TNT.)

2. Breaching charges to cut reinforced concrete roadway: $P = R^3$ KC [$(R = 2.46'; C = 1.8$ (untamped)]. Calculation gives 26 1-pound blocks TNT per charge required. Number of charges $N = W/2R$ gives 4.667 or 5 charges required. (Total 130 1-pound blocks of TNT).

II. Location of charges

A. For destroying abutment:

1. Top of abutment: Bury charges behind abutment 2R distance apart at a depth of 2 meters.

2. Bottom/river face of abutment: Place charges 2R distance apart at the base of the abutment.

B. Place charges on each side of each I-beam and on the roadway at A-A', spaced 2R distance apart.

III. You estimate 4 squad hours to prepare the target and bring it to state of readiness 1. This includes travel time for the 2 ½-ton truck to and from the ASP (including loading time—2 hours). You assume that the additional equipment mentioned in V below is available and you can immediately begin cutting holes to place charges behind the abutment.

IV. You estimate 10 minutes to bring the target from state of readiness 1 to state of readiness 2 (Armed). You prime all charges with detonation cord and only caps used will be attached to the ring mains and initiated with a time fuze.

V. Special equipment required.

A. One backhoe to cut behind the abutment and to then backfill over the charges.

B. All other equipment should be carried by the squads in their vehicles as specified in the TOE.

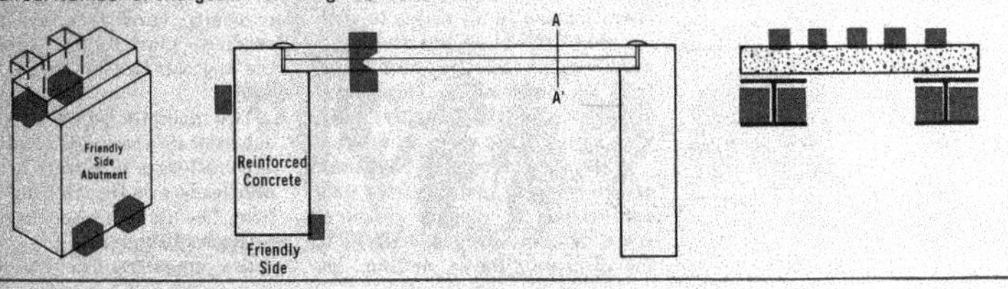

Small-Unit Leadership: Past and Future

by

The outcome of battles and of entire campaigns often rests on the decisiveness of a few small units. Recent experiences in Grenada and the Falkland Islands have confirmed once again the need for resourceful, courageous leadership at the small unit level.

AirLand Battle doctrine places even greater reliance than in the past on the small-unit leader's ability to understand the concept of the operation and on his ability to carry out that concept in the absence of regular communication and guidance from his commander. This is true even more for the engineer leader than for leaders in many other arms.

It has become common practice to detach engineer platoons from their parent unit to support combined arms, battalion-sized task forces. In the AirLand Battle setting, the

the often discussed Remagen idge capture, and the second took ce during the unheralded Aleutian mpaign in Alaska.

s described in *The Last Offensive* Charles B. MacDonald, a classic se of mobility versus counter-bility took place at Remagen. In dition, there was the confrontation the two classic philosophies of mmand—rigid central command the German side) versus gener-zed mission-type orders (on the erican side).

When 2LT Emmet J. Burrows, an fantry platoon leader, emerged m the woods on a bluff over-king Remagen on March 7, 1945, was surprised to see a bridge still anning the Rhine River.

A quick report to his battalion mmander resulted in the order to ove toward the bridge. Quick alysis by BG William M. Hoge, mmander of Combat Command B the 9th Armored Division, was at even though a crossing of the hine at that point didn't fit the rger scheme, the potential benefits r outweighed the risks.

On Hoge's order, an engineer offi-r, Lieutenant Hugh Mott, and two ngineer sergeants, supported by ttacking infantry, worked their ay across the bridge swiftly cut-ng firing wires and dropping the erman explosive charges into the ver. In a short period, the bridge as secured and a bridgehead across e Rhine was established.

The German officers responsible for destroying the bridge were constrained by a rigid directive that written orders were required before a bridge across the Rhine could be destroyed. With the U.S. Army approaching the bridge, a German captain insisted on waiting to destroy the bridge while a lieutenant wrote down the exact timing and wording of the verbal firing order given by the major in charge. This delay, caused by rigid procedures and fear of failure, might have made the difference in the capture of the bridge. This was a case when Americans got "inside the decision loop" of the opposing force, one of the key elements for success in the AirLand Battle. As a result of the decisive action of the manuever unit commander and supporting engi-neers, a bridgehead across the Rhine was gained much earlier, and at far less cost, than might otherwise have been possible.

In the Aleutian Campaign, Army engineers, in extremely harsh cli-matic conditions, accomplished all of the broad range of engineer missions from combat support to airfield construction but it was their capa-bility to fight as infantry that determined the outcome of the cam-paign. In the key battle for control of the island of Attu, the beleaguered Japanese launched a surprise suicidal counterattack to gain control of the U.S. artillery position. The Japanese fought through the infantry line and attacked toward the high ground known as Engineer Hill. Brian Garfield describes in this book, *The Thousand Mile War*, how within minutes the engineers converted to an infantry role.

The Japanese fought their way to the top of Engineer Hill where men of the 50th Engineer Battalion met the charge head-on with bayonets and rifles used as clubs. The Japanese never reached the artillery emplace-ment.

On the point of victory, Hill wrote, *the Americans had come frighteningly close to losing everything they had gained in* (the previous) *three weeks of ferocious, bloody fighting. Only the precarious line of the 50th Engineers, desperate but steadied by discipline, had kept Yamasaki's charge from reaching the all important artillery. But the Engineers had held. It was over.*

The lesson here is that engineers who must work most of the time on traditional tasks—mobility, counter-mobility, survivability and general engineering—are often called upon on short notice in the most crucial of situations to quickly reorganize and fight as infantry.

The engineer small-unit leader of today and tomorrow has the burden of studying and developing his own technical and leadership skills. Con-currently he must assure that his unit is well trained to react quickly, applying their unique skills at the crucial point to assure success of the American effort. The engineer leader who prepares himself and his unit in this manner will be prepared for the demands of the AirLand Battlefield. Entire campaigns can rest on that preparation.

COL Stanley R. Johnson is director of the Directorate of Training and Doctrine, U.S. Army Engineer School.

Be The Expert!

by CPT Willis Lee

Many engineer lieutenants begin their careers as platoon leaders in the engineer battalion of an armored or infantry division. As a combat engineer your mission is to increase the combat effectiveness of the maneuver forces by supplying engineer combat support. As an engineer platoon leader, you face many technical and leadership challenges. There is a lot to learn.

To be successful on the battlefield and in your career you must accomplish your missions. When you accomplish them skillfully, you will save time and effort . . . and lives.

No Time On The Battlefield

As a lieutenant, you have to become more educated to compensate for your lack of experience. To perform effectively you must, at least, know engineer operations. You must be able to forecast, to recommend, and to request engineer materials. You must be able to work with unfamiliar people in unfamiliar places. You must be able to communicate with your company headquarters, which might be 10 to 20 kilometers to the rear. And, you must be proficient in soldiering and leadership. There will not be enough time on the battlefield to master all those things, so begin now.

Presented here are ideas for the engineer platoon leader. They are not of a technical nature; some already may be familiar to you. Hopefully, these thoughts will inspire actions on the part of engineers and maneuver leaders alike.

Difficulties arise daily that inhibit the effective use of the engineer line

the appearance of your soldiers and equipment, in war or peace, as a basis for developing a first and lasting impressions of your platoon. Soldiers who appear undisciplined are usually poorly trained. Vehicles whose appearance and maintenance meet Army standards are usually manned by well-trained, disciplined soldiers.

Training and Teamwork

Use the basics in training. Train yourself first. Don't expect your men to willfully follow you into combat if you can't read a map.

Training resources—especially time—are limited at all levels. On the fluid nuclear and chemical battlefield, your men must move quickly, foresee priority changes, and work without guidance or supervision. Often your platoon will be spread across a task force sector. The ability to give orders on the move by radio is hard to develop, but it is indispensable on the fluid modern battlefield.

Your personnel must have intimate knowledge of the situation and be trained to perform independent operations. Personnel from the newest private to yourself must be able to give concise, essential instructions in obstacle execution to squad leaders and to tank commanders. The lives of your men depend upon the amount of good training they have received.

Emphasize teamwork. While fostering healthy squad competition, continue to work toward a high level of platoon cohesion. It is extremely difficult for a platoon to meet ARTEP Level 1 standards, much less perform well in combat, without a high degree of teamwork.

In most of the tasks you undertake as a leader, you will have to be imaginative and patient. Your results will not always be immediately recognizable. You may have to introduce the concept of teamwork to your platoon, and you may have to force it upon some of your soldiers. Personality conflicts will have to be resolved. Over time, the benefits will far exceed the effort.

FM 100-5, *Operations*, emphasizes that "superior combat power derives from the courage of soldiers, the excellence of their training and the quality of their leadership."

The responsibility you are given when you pin on your green leadership tabs is greater than you can understand at the time. The trust and faith the president embodies in you when you take your commissioning oath is the same trust and faith your men will give you in a disciplined, well-trained unit.

Be Technically Proficient

Establish yourself as an educated engineer and a qualified combat engineer. Know the capabilities of your platoon, your company and your battalion. Know what you can accomplish, what you have to accomplish it with, and how long it will take.

Be knowledgeable of other engineer units. For instance, you should be familiar with the composition of a corps engineer unit that is coming into the task force area of operations. Familiarize yourself with the who, what, where and how of resupply of barrier materials.

Meanwhile, know to whom you can turn for help. Usually, it will be your company commander. Do not hesitate to ask peers, the S3, the commander or anyone else that might help you accomplish your mission and save lives. Become an expert yourself.

Combined Arms

You must establish yourself as a member of the combined arms team. The field manual that covers combat engineer doctrine, FM5-100, *Engineer Combat Operations*, notes, "Engineers move and fight side by side with other combined arms."

How well you can do your job will become evident very quickly. Your expertise will affect the morale and success of your platoon.

Avenues For Professional Development

The following are excellent sources for increasing your military skills.

Army Correspondence Course Program (ACCP): The Army developed this program to enable its members to further their professional education. You can enroll in these courses regardless of the type or location of your unit. Your facility education center will provide the details. You can bite off a big piece like an officer advanced course, or a small piece such as a specific supply course to help you with an additional duty.

People: Your company commander has a wealth of knowledge and experience. He knows where to go for answers, can empathize with your situation, and will talk informally on almost any occasion. For senior platoon leaders, the battalion S3 and the battalion commander also will provide educational assistance.

Your battalion's officer and NCO professional development program may already cover some of the topics discussed in this article. This may provide you with an outline or ideas you can use later in the field with the task force.

Do not discount war stories. Everyone has one, and they can be one more way to increase your knowledge.

Manuals: Principles and doctrine guide the things we do throughout our careers. They are guidelines but each one should be followed to some extent.

FM 71-1, *Tank and Mechanized Infantry Company Team;* and FM 71-2, *Tank and Mechanized Infantry Battalion Task Force,* are easy to read and are used daily in maneuver battalions. TT 71-1/2, *The Abrams Battalion, Division 86,* has been implemented in some units, and the manuals are available.

As you increase your education, seek more specific knowledge of FM 100-5, *Operations;* and FM 71-100, *Armored and Mechanized Division Operations.* All that you can learn of Soviet doctrine, tactics and organization will supplement your soldiers' limited and general knowledge on the enemy. Detailed knowledge of FM 5-100, *Engineer Combat Operations,* and FM 5-34, *Engineer Field Data,* is essential. Finally, don't forget the Soldier's Manuals.

Professional Books: A particularly good place to begin is *The Army Officer's Guide* and DA Pam 600-2, *The Armed Forces Officer.* They are easy to read and though general in nature, both provide a great deal of basic information. They also serve as a quick reference for important data such as branch information and history and proper wear of the uniform.

Professional Journals: If you do not subscribe now, do so. The armed forces arena, especially for the engineer, is too vast and complex for you to keep current by reading general news.

Doctrine, tactics and equipment change. You should keep abreast of new weapons of the 1980s and the AirLand Battle concept. FM 5-100, *Engineer Combat Operations,* notes, "engineers at all levels must be aware of new material developments." Journals also describe the current professional climate in the Army and in the Corps of Engineers.

FM 5-34, *Engineer Field Data,* is yet another useful source, as is the *Engineer Platoon Leader's Handbook.*

munications (C^3) is temporarily lost.

The operations order should also play an important role in preparing your men for the battle. You will have to write the engineer annex to the task force operations, so learn the format. Be detailed but concise.

You should maintain close contact with the individuals that will help you most. Ultimately, you work for the commander. Doctrinally, your guidance and missions will be co-ordinated by the S3. You may also be attached to one of the company teams in the task force. Get to know the commander or S3 as well as possible. If you know how they think, it will aid you in making correct decisions with minimum guidance.

It is to your advantage to get to know the task force personnel. It helps to be able to match faces and personalities with missions. Your platoon will operate with the same maneuver task force during all training exercises. This enables cohesion to develop and helps to solve some of the usual coordination problems.

Certainly each member of the task force influences your mission. The HHC commander and first sergeant are individuals with whom you will work often, and the battalion support platoon leader ensures that the battalion receives fuel, food and ammunition. Those three individuals (among others) have a direct bearing on your mission.

"You must have intimate knowledge of the five-paragraph field order."

Leaders must also continue to learn. Read everything applicable to engineers in the how-to-fight manuals FM 71-1, *Task and Mechanized Infantry Company Team;* FM 71-2, *Tank and Mechanized Infantry Task Force;* and TT 71-1/2, *The Abrams Battalion, Division 86.* You may be surprised to see very few paragraphs about the employing engineers.

Volunteer to give a class to the task force leadership, even if only for 10 minutes following a tactical operations order. Do not attempt to reach only the officers. Use your NCOs to teach their NCOs.

If the task force ever organizes your squads with each of their company teams, use the concept of normal association at squad level. Offer them an opportunity to visit your motor park or assembly area for cross-training and fun. Don't wait for them to offer; ask first. Virtually every commander is willing to show off his unit in front of other soldiers. The cross-training, especially in the engineer's secondary role as infantry will be practicable and fun.

The guidelines presented here are very general. If you get anything from this article, let it be an appreciation for discipline, teamwork, self-improvement, persistence and initiative. *The Army Officer's Guide* says that "engineers can look forward to professional opportunities which are limited only by their own abilities and ambitions."

Whether you plan to make a career in the armed forces or not, the next war (or certainly the next field training exercise) will be your war.

Be the expert!

CPT Willis Lee is an armor officer and ROTC instructor at Kentucky State University, Frankfort. He is a graduate of the Engineer Officer Advanced Course, the U.S. Military Academy, and the Airborne and Ranger schools.

He served in the 1st Armored Division as a tank platoon leader, scout platoon leader, S3(Air) and as a company commander.

Hotline Q & A

Q. I need information on Engineer desert operations.

A. See FM 90-3, *Desert Operations.* Also, your battalion S2 should routinely receive the National Training Center's newsletter, *Red Thrust Star,* which sometimes contains articles on developments in the area of desert operations.

Q. I need material that can be used to teach a class on the hasty protective minefield.

A. Use FM 20-32, *Mine/Countermine Operations at the Company Level;* FM5-102, *Mine Warfare,* and STANAG (Standard of Agreement) 2036, *Land Minefield Laying, Marking, Recording and Report Procedures,* as primary references.

Q. Are there any changes to a non-divisional unit as a result of Division 86 changes in TOEs?

A. Consult the CSEMW MAA (Combat Support, Engineering and Mine Warfare Mission Area Analysis), May 1983, and the Number 1, 1983, issue of ENGINEER which addresses Division 86.

Q. I need a "canned" presentation about the Corps of Engineers. If a presentation is not available, a slide show would do.

A. The Engineer School has neither a briefing nor a slide show about the Corps of Engineers. However, a slide show is being developed and will be fielded sometime in 1984. Meanwhile, slides on the Corps of Engineers can be obtained from Ms. Stanley, Office of the Chief of Engineers (AV 270-0017). You might also want to check with the Corps of Engineers district in your area.

Q. Our engineer battalion is authorized 290M scrapers. Several of them are ready to be "washed out." We are not authorized replacements until the first quarter of FY85. What should we do until the replacements arrive?

A. Call your MACOM to request an exception to policy for extending the repair expenditure limit on 290M scrapers until replacement items are issued.

Divisional Engineer Support During:

OPERATION

by LTC Lawrence L. Izzo

Much of America was settling back for the kickoff of Monday Night Football.

But at 9 p.m. Eastern time on October 24, 1983, the 82nd Airborne Division's 307th Engineer Battalion was beginning to tee up for Operation Urgent Fury—the Grenada rescue mission.

Nineteen hours after the New York Giants and the St. Louis Cardinals began their gridiron combatives, members of the 307th and the infantry they supported were locked in real combat on a Caribbean island five hours flying time from Gifford, Cosell, and home at Fort Bragg.

The Mission

At 11 p.m., on October 24th, the 307th's commander was briefed by the division staff. Two battalions from the division's 2nd Brigade, accompanied by the brigade and division assault command posts (CPs), were deploying to Grenada. They would relieve two Ranger battalions sent to secure the island's important Point Salines airfield in a parachute assault at dawn the next day. The 82nd's two battalions would deploy with their habitual engineer attachments—one platoon each from B Company, with the company commander serving as brigade engineer.

The division task force was to secure the airhead and prepare to rescue American students at the island's St. George's Medical School. Every precaution would be taken to keep the assault secret and to take the enemy by surprise.

Preparing for Combat

By 1 a.m., October 25, combat elements of both battalions were moving to a secure deployment area where they were isolated from the rest of Fort Bragg. Inside the holding area, there were no phones and there was no chance to go back

The 307th Engineer Battalion commander would accompany the task force as the engineer representative in the division CP. His first task on the drop zone would be to assess the condition of the runway and to determine future engineer requirements.

By 9 a.m., troops were loading the C141s. Their parachutes were carried aboard for in-flight rigging during the five-hour trip. Morale was sky high, spurred on in anticipation of the first 82nd Airborne Division combat parachute jump in almost 30 years.

Cuban Counterattack

At 10 a.m., wheels were up and the task force was on its way. During the flight, the division commander received word that the Rangers successfully completed the airfield assault and that the C141s could land. The 82nd would not make a combat jump.

As the first aircraft landed, Cubans launched an abortive counterattack near the end of the Point Salines runway using three Soviet BTR-60 armored personnel carriers. Paratroopers, who had just gotten off of their aircraft, joined in with the Rangers and knocked out two BTR-60s. The third BTR was destroyed by a C130 Spectre gunship. Meanwhile, other C141s circled the airfield waiting for the fighting to die down.

By 4 p.m., the two infantry battalions were on the ground expanding the airhead. Two equipment operators from the 307th who had been attached to a Ranger battalion rejoined their engineer unit. The two men made the airfield parachute assault with the Rangers that morning. In spite of the fighting going on around them, they cleared the runway of construction equipment so the C141s from Fort Bragg could land. These engineers from the 307th were the only paratroopers from the 82nd who made the combat jump.

For the next several days, reinforcements arrived to round out elements of six infantry and two artillery battalions. The 9,000-foot Point Salines airfield runway was in excellent condition. The surface had several lifts of asphalt and could easily handle continuous C141 traffic.

Since the runway was surrounded by construction equipment, bringing in engineer equipment from Fort Bragg was unnecessary. Equipment operators with the first-deployed engineer platoons quickly began using the captured equipment, which included Russian dump trucks and Komatzu bulldozers. As more operators, mechanics and combat engineers arrived, more captured equipment was put into operation.

Escorting Cubans to the new detention center.

Security and Water

Their first night in Grenada, the dozer operators began ditching around the division CP to restrict access and to improve security. Later that night, the dozers served as barricades. Precast concrete blocks surrounding the Point Salines terminal later were stacked to form a truck-proof CP barricade. The 82nd would not chance repeating the Marine's Beirut tragedy which was so fresh in everyone's mind.

Another early engineer requirement was to clear rubble from the concrete apron outside the airport so supplies could be unloaded from C130s flying in from a staging base on Barbados, about 60 miles from Grenada. Completing this task expanded the capacity of the main runway, which was being used for unloading ammunition, food and priority supplies arriving on C141s from Pope AFB. Engineers also dug-in the main refueling point, the ammunition supply point, and cut a road to the field hospital.

On D+1, the first 400 gallon per hour (g.p.h.) erdalator arrived and the 307th established the first of four water points. Later, a corps-level 600 g.p.h. reverse osmosis water purification unit (ROWPU) was brought in. Because of its desalinization capability, the ROWPU was located right next to the ocean near the airfield.

Reinforcements by D+4 brought engineer strength at the airfield to a company (minus) in general support of the division.

They Did It All

A challenge during any airborne operation is reinforcing the task force while simultaneously keeping it supplied. During Urgent Fury, everything had to come by air over thousands of miles. Every aircraft sortie was important. No wasted space on any aircraft was allowed; only the most essential personnel and equipment were deployed.

Hence, the handful of engineers at the airfield in general support found themselves performing many missions. They put Russian generators into operation and provided electricity and lighting to the division CP. Their water-point trucks were used to transport infantry. Engineers helped move beds, blankets and supplies for the field hospital.

They also carried wounded soldiers to evacuation aircraft, dug graves for enemy dead, built latrines, dug garbage pits, repaired plumbing and electricity for the detention compound, distributed water, and erected concertina. They improvised dust suppression equipment for the airfield, cleared landing zones for helicopters, provided local security and gerry-rigged shower points. They accomplished everything asked of them using captured equipment and the barest minimum of hand tools.

Meanwhile, the engineer support for the infantry battalions had grown to six platoons, or the nucleus of two companies. These platoons cleared landing zones, provided demolition support, conducted mine sweeping operations to search for buried weapons, and erected roadblocks.

Engineers also fought alongside their infantry comrades, assisting in airmobile and ground operations. Bravo Company received the mission to secure the largest cache of captured weapons and ammunition on the island, the Frequente warehouse complex. The company repeatedly received sniper fire from the surrounding hills until using ground surveillance radar and key outposts ended the danger. The company inventoried the captured materiel and began moving it to the airfield.

Engineers in Grenada using a captured front loader.

One of the engineers' first tasks was to construct a truck-proof barricade (see arrow) around the division CP.

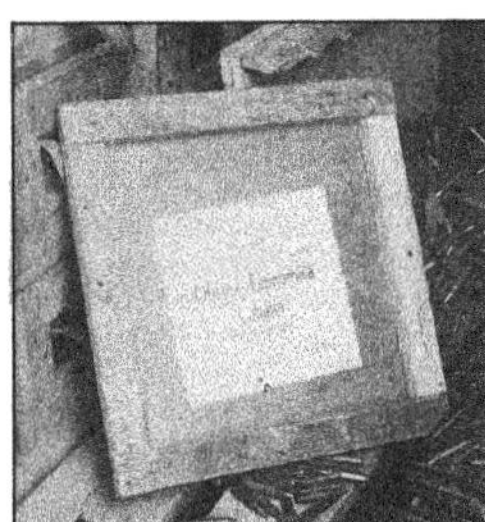
Captured: Soviet 7.62mm ammo labeled "Cuban Economic Office," above. Below, North Korean rocket-propelled grenades.

Urgent Fury
TIME CAPSULE

October 24	
9 p.m.	307th Engineer Bn, 82nd Airborne Div. alerted.
1 a.m.	82nd Airborne Div. task force of two battalions (each with one engineer platoon) moves to predeployment area.
October 25	
Dawn	Rangers (with two heavy equipment operators from the 307th) make a parachute assault onto the Point Salines airfield.
10 a.m.	Wheels up. 82nd Airborne Div. task force on the way.
4 p.m.	Task force lands; abortive Cuban counterattack.
October 26	First of four water points is established.
October 29	Division engineer strength increases to a company (minus).
November 1	307th is tasked to build 1,000-person detention facility.
November 3	Detention facility completed.
November 4	B Co., 307th returns to Fort Bragg.
November 15	C Co., 307th begins returning to Fort Bragg
December 24	Last elements of C Co., 307th return to Fort Bragg.

The Biggest Job

The largest single mission tackled by the division engineers began on D+7 when the division commander told the engineers to construct a new detention facility. The original compound had become overcrowded by the unexpectedly large number of detainees.

With the help of Cuban construction worker volunteers, and with captured equipment, locally purchased materials, tents and other important items rushed in from Fort Bragg, the 307th constructed a 1,000-man camp in 34 hours.

The camp had exterior and interior lighting, 45 GP-medium tents, guard towers, a shower point, plywood latrines, triple standard concertina and segregated interior compounds for the different categories of detainees. On D+9, engineers helped move the prisoners into the new compound.

There were many lessons learned during Urgent Fury. Some key ones for airborne divisional engineers include: the importance of planning for general support of the division rear as well as for supporting forward combat units; understanding and using procedures for purchasing key material locally; planning and coordinating the use of local hires; and most importantly, planning for and making the best use of captured engineer equipment.

With the accomplishment of their mission—rescuing and evacuating all American students, relieving two Ranger battalions and then the Marine ground forces, and capturing or destroying all Cuban forces on the island—the paratroopers of the "All American" 82nd Airborne Division added another chapter to the division's illustrious history.

LTC Lawrence L. Izzo commands the 307th Engineer Battalion, 82nd Airborne Division and was the division engineer for Operation Urgent Fury. Previously he was S3 of the 18th Engineer Brigade, USAREUR. LTC Izzo has an M.S. degree from the Massachusetts Institute of Technology, an M.B.A. degree from Long Island University, and is a licensed professional engineer in Virginia.

COMBAT JUMPERS

Spain, Richardson and the Rangers

For SP4 Charles E. Spain and SP4 William R. Richardson on October 23rd, one hour they were enjoying an off-duty Sunday, the next hour they were on their way to join in the Ranger parachute assault against the Point Salinas airfield in Grenada.

Both men are equipment operators in the 618th Engineer Company (LE), 307th Engineer Battalion, 82nd Airborne Division. They were the only troopers from the 82nd to make the jump in Grenada.

Spain (L) and Richardson now wear wings with a combat star.

For Richardson, it was literally baptism by fire. The parachute assault was his first jump since completing airborne training. It was a jump made under fire, at 500 feet, and with no reserve parachute.

The drop zone was the Point Salinas airfield runway, and it was littered with construction equipment. Spain and Richardson were with the Rangers to move the construction equipment off the runway so the follow-on assault force from Fort Bragg could land.

According to an *Army Times* report, the two engineers worked under sniper fire while the Rangers secured a perimeter around the airfield.

Spain, Richardson and the Rangers jumped at dawn on the 25th. By 1 p.m., they had cleared the runway of equipment. Three hours later the assault force from the 82nd Airborne Division was landing.

Military posters in a Cuban barracks at Pearls Airport.

The Sauteures police station during renovation by C Company, 307th Engineers. (Nancy Ann Zamorski photo.)

Water to the Ankles & No Repair Parts

by SP5 Nancy Ann Zamorski

"Hey, come over here and take a look at this. I went to turn on the water and the faucet broke off in my hand."

That was one of the problems C Company from the 82nd Airborne Division's 307th Engineer Battalion faced while rehabilitating seven police stations in Grenada.

Renovating the stations included painting, electrical rewiring, repairing cell doors, and upgrading the flush toilets and plumbing systems.

"The stations were not damaged from the fighting," said SSG Russel G. Smith Jr., of C Company's 2nd Platoon, 3rd Squad. Smith worked at the abandoned Sauteures police station on the northern tip of the island. "The place was real old. I'd say it dated back to 1900—or at least before the 1930s," he said.

The plumbing in most of the stations was early 1950s vintage, according to one of the engineers.

"We had to put in a new drainage system at the Grenville police station," said Smith. "When we first got there, the water was ankle deep."

Because the plumbing was so old, the engineers had a difficult time finding repair parts. Everything needed for repairs was purchased from stores on the island.

Another problem the engineers had in repairing one of the stations was with electricity.

Inspector Roy Raymond of the Sauteures station is from Grenada. He said that the electricity is shut off in his area, "due to the condition of the generators here." He explained that electricity is shared at different times of the day in the community.

"Because of that," Smith said, "we couldn't work on most of the electrical problems until the evening when the electricity came back on. Once it came back on, I could run a hot wire in.

"We worked with electrical supplies bought on the island that were imported from England," Smith said. "It was difficult for us since the electricity was not the same as back in the states."

The renovated police stations are being used by Grenadian authorities as base areas for security operations now that U.S. troops have left the island.

SP5 Nancy Ann Zamorski is a photojournalist in the XVIII Airborne Corps public affairs office.

Everything Engineers Can Be

by SFC Bob Lentner

The commander of the XVIII Airborne Corps troops in Grenada put them in for a Meritorious Unit Citation, even though they weren't part of the island assault force. They didn't have a chance to fire a shot, but their brigade commander thinks they're some of the best soldiers in the Army.

They're the combat engineers of C Company, 548th Engineer Battalion (Combat). They were soldiers who worked tirelessly as builders and fixers. They improvised detention cells out of packing crates, covered landing strip holes, repaired roofs, kept the dust out of the air on convoy roads, and covered a motor park area with gravel.

And they did a lot more. Shortly after their arrival in Grenada on November 6, 1983, the engineers from Charlie Company, reinforced by two platoons from the 27th Engineer Battalion (Airborne) and six soldiers from the 20th Engineer Brigade's composite engineer battalion, began work on a list of projects that kept them busy around-the clock for almost a month.

The first major project was moving, putting on pallets, and loading all of the weapons and ammunition captured on the island. The Soviet and Cuban arms and munitions were prepared and packaged by the engineers for shipment to stateside receiving points. The task force was also responsible for recovering and destroying explosives found on the island during the invasion.

First sergeant of the engineer task force, SFC Andy Koji, said his men did everything for everybody. "We built a security fence around the radio station, two field PXs, put in lighting at the American embassy, put plumbing and electricity back into the local police stations, and even fed 300 extra people a Thanksgiving meal. We did it all," Koji said.

The commander of C Company and the entire Grenadian engineer task force, CPT Roderick Chisholm, said he couldn't think of a function that his soldiers didn't perform. "They did carpentry, plumbing and electrical work at the island's hospital, built helipads, upgraded prisons, worked on roads and the airstrip, strung a lot of concertina, and even provided security for the airstrip for a while. They did a lot of good work that will last, and they did it together."

The main body of the engineer task force returned to Fort Bragg late on the night of December 7th and were met by families and fellow soldiers at the Green Ramp at Pope Air Force Base. About 20 of the engineers remained in Grenada to complete projects and to prepare equipment for redeployment.

"The soldiers in the task force were great," said COL Daniel R. Schroeder, commander of the 20th Engineer Brigade (Combat) (Airborne Corps). "They did everything we expected of them and more. I'm proud of them. They're everything engineers can be."

SFC Bob Lentener is the public affairs officer of the 20th Engineer Brigade (Combat) (Airborne Corps).

548th Engineers wait for their baggage after returning to Ft. Bragg from Grenada. *(Bob Lentner photo)*

A warehouse full of Soviet-made small arms ammunition. Six arms warehouses were found in Grenada.

A Caribbean Arms Cache

On October 25, 1983, the U.S. military, at the request of the Organization of Eastern Caribbean States, conducted joint operations, code named "Urgent Fury," to protect U.S. and foreign citizens in Grenada and to assist in restoring order and stability in the country.

During the first few days of the operation, more than 600 Cubans were detained in Grenada. Resistance from these well armed military and paramilitary forces belied claims that they were simply "construction crews."

Large amounts of Soviet weapons and equipment, supplied by the Soviets through Cuba to Grenada, were found by the multinational force. Following is a complete list of these weapons and equipment. This weaponry has been estimated to be sufficient to equip two Cuban infantry battalions for 30-45 days of combat.

Rifles and Machine Guns

1,626- Soviet AK-47 assault rifles
1,120- Model 52 (Czech)
58- Enfields
4,074- KS rifles (SKS)
3- MK-3
2- Bren rifles
6- M16s
2,432- Mosin Nagent (7.62mm Soviet rifles
32- M3A1 submachine guns
7- Sterling machine guns
55- M23 submachine guns
17- Sten Mark 2
180- Soviet M1945 Submachine guns
300- Miscellaneous sidearms
31- .22 Caliber rifles
300- Shotguns

Crew Served Weapons

9- Soviet 7.62mm PKM machine guns
8- 73mm SPG-9 recoilless guns
12- ZU-23mm antiaircraft guns
1- DSHQ 12.7mm Machine gun
10- 82mm mortars

Ammunition

5,516,600 RDS- 7.62mm
162 RDS- 73mm
8,962 RDS- 82mm mortar
2,320 RDS- 14.5mm
29,120 RDS- 23mm anti-aircraft gun ammunition
366 RDS- 57mm rocket propelled grenades
940 RDS- 75mm
1200 sticks- Dynamite
24,768- Flares

Miscellaneous Weapons

1,824- Grenades
6- RPG 7 (rocket propelled grenade)
46- RPG 2 (rocket propelled grenade)
8- Tear gas riot guns
8- Flare guns

Vehicles

2- Armored fighting vehicles

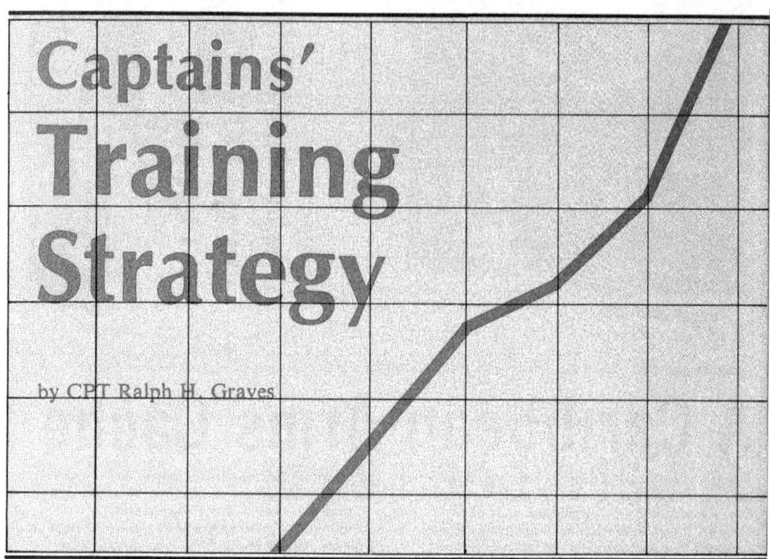

The Engineer School is launching a new Engineer Officer Advanced Course (EOAC) with a combination of features unlike anything the Army has seen before.

Highlights of the 20-week course include grouping lessons into two-week modules, emphasizing experiential training and arranging students into small groups, helping students to incorporate the concept of "wellness" into their professional and personal lives, and using computer based instruction.

The first increment of the new course begins in October 1984. The new course is the result of analyzing field experience, reviewing other courses, and studying the latest educational techniques. The new advanced course's concepts for the near and long terms are called, respectively, Vision 84 and Vision 86.

The Basic Concepts

The fundamental concepts of the new advanced course are:

Scenario/modules: Related lessons will be grouped into two-week modules. Lessons are couched in a scenario format—a setting formulated by the Combined Arms Center at Fort Leavenworth in which notional units perform missions that appear to be taking place in various parts of the world. The scenario format will add realism to instruction and exercises. It also will encourage students to practice solving problems using doctrine as a guide.

Experiential training/small groups: Captains' skills such as planning, managing, and leading are integration skills best taught by doing. The new advanced course will emphasize hands-on training in groups of 10 to 12 students. In addition to small-group practical exercises, each module will include at least one capstone exercise in which the groups perform a number of tasks to accomplish a broad mission.

Wellness: The new course will incorporate the concept of wellness, defined as developing mind, body, and spirit to increase individual potential and satisfaction. Wellness instruction will cover topics such as time management, personal assessment and goal setting, stress management, physical conditioning, control of substance abuse, and diet and nutrition.

Team leaders: Each small group will have a team leader to act as mentor, coach, and facilitator. The team leader will supervise all small-group exercises, evaluate and counsel students, conduct wellness training, and act as role models. Additionally, team leaders will write doctrine, keep the course current, and act as subject matter experts.

Challenge and reward. Rather than emphasize a median or passing standard for test scores, the new course will focus on developing skills for success in the field. The idea is to motivate officers by presenting the challenges of introspective, engineering, and people-related problem solving. An evaluation of group exercise participation and performance counseling by team leaders will supplement traditional evaluation methods.

Computer based instruction (CBI): This concept encourages the student to use the computer terminal to accelerate and personalize instruction. It is particularly applicable to Engineer captains' training because students enter the advanced course with a variety of academic backgrounds. Ultimately, CBI can provide an interactive, worldwide educational network linking all engineer units to the Engineer School.

Core and Functional Courses

The new EOAC will include a 14-week core course followed by functional courses keyed to the student's next assignment. The combined length will be at least 20 weeks, preserving the advanced course as a permanent change-of-station assignment. Reserve Component officers can attend the two-week modules during their Active Duty for Training periods.

Offering the 14-week core course also allows the Engineer School to delete the current 12-week Reserve Component EOAC and to train Reserve and Active Component officers together.

Core Course Requirements

Before attending the core course, each prospective student will take a diagnostic exam. The exam is expected to last four hours, and will be given at education centers or USAR schools. The exam will test military skills covered in the Engineer Officer Basic Course and in initial assignments. Students who do not show an adequate base proficiency will receive special instruction by correspondence or in residence before starting the core course. The diagnostic exam and pre-course will eliminate redundant instruction from the new advanced course.

Course Content

Over 1,000 tasks were reviewed in a scan of Specialty Code (SC) 21 duty positions to determine the course content. Some 600 tasks were identified to be taught in the core course

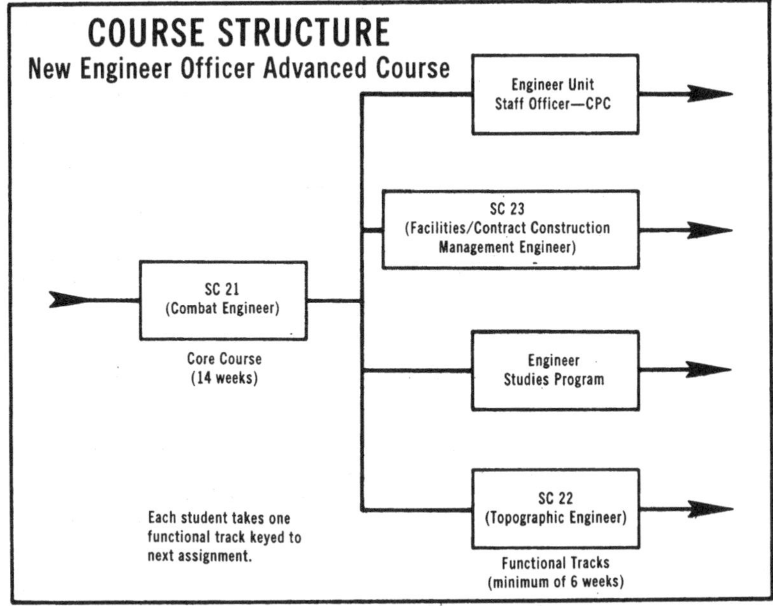

and grouped into lessons within the modules.

The core course scenario will follow a sequence through peacetime, mobilization, deployment, offensive and defensive combat, lines-of-communication and base camp construction, and rapid deployment and counterinsurgency contingencies. The principles of AirLand Battle doctrine and of combined arms employment will be integrated throughout.

Lecture instruction will be reduced greatly in favor of practical exercises. A typical classroom day will run from 7 a.m. to 1 p.m., with the afternoons allocated to out-of-class study and to other activities. Approximately one-third of the instruction will be conducted in small groups.

Functional Courses

The functional courses planned include ADM Mission Officer, SC 23, SC 22, Engineer Unit Staff Officer, the Company Pre-Command Course, and the Engineer Studies Program.

While the core course trains officers in overall planning and execution of combat engineer missions, the Engineer Unit Staff Officer Course prepares officers returning to troop units to serve as battalion staff officers or as engineer staff officers at higher levels. These skills are also applicable to company command. Those who have not yet commanded will attend a Company Pre-Command Course.

At least 10 percent of the instruction in the near term (Vision 84) will be computer based. Subjects taught by computer range from design to tactics. The terminals will be used to assist classroom instruction as well as homework. The system will be used to monitor student progress and to provide course statistical data.

The Network Link

Computer based instruction figures prominently in Vision 86. An educational network is envisioned that would allow students to interact directly with the Engineer School for initial learning, refresher training, problem solving, and communicating by electronic mail, even from remote locations. The bulk of learning could take place through the computer in a non-resident mode. The student would then attend a brief TDY assignment to a core course consisting entirely of experiential training, and to functional courses, either in residence or on the computer, which would prepare the officer for specific duty assignments.

The computer network also could contribute to unit training programs unrelated to the new advanced course. It would be an ideal tool for unit professional development programs and could be used to prepare for upcoming exercises or projects.

Further, the network would enable the Engineer School to publish doctrinal updates rapidly. School and subject matter experts could stay in touch through the network and collaborate on projects. Units facing problems could query the network and benefit from the collective experience of the engineer community. With this network, the Engineer School would become a knowledge base serving engineers throughout the world.

Transition Underway

Work to update the advanced course has been underway since February, 1983, and development of Vision 84 is on schedule for the October 1984 implementation.

Twelve team leaders have been selected, and two classrooms in Humphreys Hall at Fort Belvoir will be modified to accommodate small-group instruction.

Funds have been allotted to buy the hardware to support CBI for Vision 84, and a cell of courseware authors are writing instructional material into the computer.

To facilitate the transition, EOAC 7-84, scheduled to begin on August 20, 1984, will not be held. Components of the new course will be tested in classes 5-84 and 6-84. Students who will attend the first new course, EOAC 1-85, will take the diagnostic test in May 1984. EOAC 1-85, 2-85 and 3-85 will take the course in a format without CBI, to be used as a basis for comparison. EOAC 4-85, beginning on February 18, 1985, will incorporate core and functional courses with a target total of 133 hours of CBI.

Other TRADOC Initiatives

Captains' training is being improved at the Engineer School against a background of other initiatives in the U.S. Army Training and Doctrine Command (TRADOC).

The task analysis performed for Engineer captains' training provided information for development of Military Qualification Standard Level III (MQS III) Common Tasks by the Combined Arms Center at Fort Leavenworth, Kansas. The instructional materials developed for the EOAC core course will be the basis for the MQS III Engineer Specialty Manual.

The 1978 Department of the Army Review of Education and Training for Officers (RETO) study recommended that the time in the advanced courses be reduced. Schools throughout TRADOC soon will be implementing advanced courses with 20-week core courses followed by up to six weeks of functional courses. The new EOAC will reduce student residence time by at least four weeks. Long-term concepts could lead to further reduction.

Implementation of the new captains' training strategy significantly will improve the preparation officers receive for meeting challenges in the field. It can reduce the time officers spend away from units without impairing the quality of officer training. The potential of a computer network linking together the Engineer family is unlimited. Realization of this new vision promises an exciting future for the Corps.

CPT Ralph H. Graves is a member of the Captains' Training Team, Directorate of Training and Doctrine, U.S. Army Engineer School. He is a graduate of the U.S. Military Academy and has a master's degree in engineering from the University of California, Berkeley. He has served in Korea and was assistant division engineer of the 8th Infantry Div., USAREUR.

Restructuring SC 21–

by CPT Bruce H. Reminger

Benefits to the Corps and to The Army

In May 1983, the Army chief of staff approved restructuring officer Specialty Code 21 (Engineer) into SC 21 (Combat Engineer) and SC 23 (Facilities/Contract Construction Management Engineer). With this change, Engineer branch officers can become more proficient in combat engineering and in facilities/contract construction management, without being required to become fully qualified in another additional specialty.

Problems with Old SC 21

In accordance with the Officer Personnel Management System (OPMS), commissioned officers must have two specialties, an "accession" or initial specialty (INSPEC) and an additional specialty (ADSPEC). The INSPEC is assigned upon commissioning, and the ADSPEC is designated at about the fifth through eighth years of service.

The Corps of Engineers is a unique branch, one with both military and civil missions. Under the old SC 21, Engineer officers performed a diversity of assignments—a diversity which sometimes did not promote meaningful career progression in either combat engineering or in facilities/contract construction management. There was simply not enought time available to become fully qualified in all aspects of the branch and in an ADSPEC.

A second problem with the former SC 21 regarded the projected field grade officer shortage. Four to nine years from now, approximately one-third of all Corps of Engineers field grade requirements would have to have been filled by ADSPEC 21 officers. The shortage would be due to the number of SC 1 officers required to work in their ADSPEC and thus be unavailable for duty in SC 21 positions.

The restructure creates a new SC 21 (Combat Engineer) which is an INSPEC only, designated upon commissioning. Typical duty positions are company commander, battalion/group/brigade staff officer, military engineering instructor, Reserve Component advisor, and recruiting commander.

Since new SC 21 is an INSPEC only, all positions will be held by Corps of Engineers officers. All Corps of Engineers officers are being automatically reclassified as (new) INSPEC 21s. Those officers from other branches currently holding ADSPEC 21 will be awarded new ADSPECs during FY 84.

SC 23 (Facilities/Construction Management Engineer) is an ADPSEC only. Typical positions are facilities engineer, director of engineering and housing, district engineer, and project engineer.

Currently, members of Year Group (YG) 77 are receiving their ADSPEC designation. In the designation process (or reclassification process for SC 21 officers senior to YG 77), MILPERCEN is considering the following criteria, in order of priority:

- Prior experience in a position now coded as SC 23
- Engineering degree
- Individual officer preferences

The ADSPEC designation process for YG 77 should be complete by the end of FY 84.

Benefits of the Restructure

The restructure helps to solve the Corps' officer force structure problems by converting a large number of SC 21 positions to SC 23. This allows Engineer officers to satisfy the OPMS requirement to become proficient in their ADSPEC while fulfilling an Engineer branch position requirement. Since more Engineer officers will be available to work within the branch, fewer ADSPEC engineers from branches will be required.

Officers are eligible for command selection, advanced schooling, and promotion by specialty, not by branch. With more time available for both combat engineering and facilities/contract construction management assignments, chances are that Engineer officers will be better qualified in either specialty—or both. This is much better than attempting to qualify everyone in all aspects of the Corps of Engineers, and then having them compete against those who are well qualified in more narrowly defined specialties. Those Engineer officers who do not desire SC 23 as their ADSPEC may choose a different ADSPEC. This will provide good career options for Engineer officers without engineering degrees, or for those who do not desire assignments in the facilities or contract management arenas.

The restructure is also good news for the officer corps as a whole because it diminishes the need to force individuals from other branches to serve as ADSPEC engineers. Since new SC 21 is an INSPEC only, all SC 21 positions will be held by Corps of Engineers officers. About 70 percent of the SC 23 population will be made up of SC 21/23 officers.

The change also benefits women in the Corps. Because all positions in SC 23 are open, women can participate fully in the specialty and have the same variety of opportunities men have.

SC 22, Topographic Engineer, is not affected by the restructure of SC 21.

CPT Bruce H. Reminger is a personnel management officer in the Engineer School's Proponency Office. He is a graduate of the U.S. Military Academy and served in various positions with the 20th Engineer Brigade (Combat) (Airborne Corps).

by MAJ Lee A. Peters &
MAJ Kenneth Davidson

TEWTs for Engineer Troops

Engineers get serious about "training th trainers."

"A TOOT?" you may ask. "What in the world is a TOOT?"

Well, it's actually spelled TEWT, and it means tactical exercise without troops. It's the concept of training trainers to be more proficient at training the troops they lead. TEWTs are performance-oriented and follow the Battalion Training Management System (BTMS) principles of holding classroom instruction to a minimum while emphasizing hands-on instruction. If conducted properly, the program will result in better training throughout the unit and increase readiness.

The 972nd Engineer Battalion (Combat) (Corps), USAR, Fort Benjamin Harrison, Indiana, conducted an ambitious and successful TEWT that taught or updated combat engineer and leadership skills to more than 70 NCOs.

The TEWT program was the 972nd's method of correcting training deficiencies observed during the training year, including Annual Training where several units performed marginally.

Some soldiers did not seem to comprehend basic combat engineer tasks.

This was especially evident among the squad and section leaders. They frequently asked for help with basic engineering subjects, or conducted training poorly. Also, returning Basic and Advanced Individual Training students were often more proficient in accomplishing engineer tasks than were their supervisors.

TEWTs were frequently used within the 972nd in the past, usually for training FTX instructors on how to direct specific missions. However, the battalion felt that upgrading combat engineer and leadership skills across the board would benefit all squad and section leaders in the battalion, and the TEWT method was to accomplish this.

The TEWTs required assembling virtually every squad and section leader in the battalion at a training facility; providing the necessary logistical support, including training materials, rations, and transportation; and also providing the key element of competent instruction.

The 972nd's commander contacted the Engineer Team from Army Readiness and Mobilization Region VI at Fort Knox, Kentucky, and discussed the TEWT idea with them. The team felt it could provide the necessary instruction for the project. However, team members emphasized that support from the unit commanders, the battalion staff, and participants would be required for the program to be successful.

Planning the course was the responsibility of the battalion assistant operations officer, who established a list of required actions and responsible parties. Meanwhile, units identified personnel to take part in the instruction. Camp Atterbury, an Indiana National Guard facility south of Indianapolis, was selected as the main training site. Readiness group personnel coordinated subjects and training schedules with the S3.

The classes were taught twice—once Saturday and again on Sunday—for a six-month period. Because of this, a unit or squad lost only one-half of its leaders each drill day.

The subjects taught during the TEWTs included demolitions, mine warfare, route reconnaissance, bridging, NBC and other combat engineer tasks based on ARTEP 5-35 and soldier's manuals (see next page).

The training was conducted in full battle dress under tactical conditions. Leadership was rotated and radiotelephone procedures, safety, NBC, MOPP levels, troop-leading procedures, and basic soldiering skills were integrated throughout.

To measure the relative effectiveness of the training, students received a "Go/No Go" rating for each task performed. These ratings were recorded in each individual's job book. The soldiers finishing the program received a course completion certificate signed by the battalion commander.

Not everything went smoothly. Once a group from one of the companies became lost on the way to Camp Atterbury and missed half of the day's instruction. During another month, the winter weather was so inclement with blowing snow and wind chill in the minus 40-degree (Fahrenheit) range that the training was cancelled and rescheduled for the following month. However, each problem was overcome and used as a lesson learned.

The effectiveness of the program was apparent at the next Annual Training when squads and sections performed at a much-improved level. Their overall performance was reflected in the annual training evaluation. The evaluator said that the 972nd was the finest engineer battalion he had evaluated.

ARTEP 5-35 TASKS

- 6-17 Crater Roads
- 7-3 Breach Obstacles with Explosives
- 7-14 Conduct Route Clearance Operations
- 6-16 Disable Bridges
- 5-15 Conduct Reconnaissance for Obstacle Location
- 5-15 Conduct Hasty Route Reconnaissance
- 5-16 Conduct Deliberate Route Reconnaissance
- 5-19 Conduct Bridge Reconnaissance

The acquired job knowledge that squad and section leaders gained helped them regain confidence and self-esteem. They became enthusiastic leaders who could impart their experience and knowledge to others.

"The program's effectiveness was apparent at the next Annual Training. The AT evaluator said the 972nd was the finest engineer battalion he had evaluated."

Predictably, individual squad members showed increased confidence in their squad leaders.

The TEWT instruction required a trade-off: The first line supervisors were absent from half of their unit's training during the TEWT period. Also, the program was costly in terms of training material, rations, fuel, and reimbursement to the Indiana National Guard for use of their personnel and facility.

To maintain the proficiency now present in NCO squad and section leaders, the battalion has incorporated an active NCO development program for refresher training in basic engineering tasks. Hopefully, this will prevent the need for a large-scale TEWT in the future.

TEWTs can be very effective for improving training in any unit. Careful planning, thorough preparation, and a willingness to overcome problems are necessary. Commanders should consider using this instruction method in planning their unit's training. TEWTs can pay big rewards in improving unit readiness.

MAJ Lee A. Peters, USAR, heads Construction Support Services, Inc., in Indianapolis. He has master's degrees in civil engineering and management from Purdue University and serves as maintenance officer for the 123rd ARCOM. During the TEWT training, he was executive officer of the 972nd Engineers. He served in Vietnam with the 92nd and 169th Engineer Bns. Peters is a registered professional engineer in Indiana.

MAJ Kenneth Davidson, USAR, is an ROTC instructor at the University of Nevada, Las Vegas. He was supervising staff administrative assistant of the 972nd during the TEWTs. He has a master's degree in business administration from Georgia State University and is a graduate of the Administration Officer's Advanced Course.

ENGINEER HOTLINE

Problems, questions, and comments relating to engineer doctrine, training, organization, and equipment can be addressed telephonically to the U.S. Army Engineer School's "Engineer Hotline". The Hotline's auto-answer recorder operates 24 hours a day, seven days a week. Callers should state their name, address and telephone number, followed by a concise question or comment. You'll receive a reply within three to 15 days. **The Hotline is not a receiving agency for formal requests.**

and equipment that a unit is authorized to accomplish its mission; so the first thing an incoming commander should do prior to conducting an inventory is to obtain and closely examine the authorization document for his unit. Every major end item which is authorized to a company is listed on this document, and it is *the company commander's* responsibility to ensure that every item is accounted for at all times.

Additionally, the unit has other items of equipment (e.g., desks, fans, buffers, linen, and beds) which are classified as installation (station) property and are authorized by one of the common tables of allowances (CTAs), the most often cited being CTA 50-909. Both organizational (authorized by MTOE) and station property records are managed and controlled by the property book section of the division materiel management center (DMMC). At some installations, the linen and furnishings for the barracks are managed by the furnishings management office at the installation level, which will maintain the property records for those items. Again, as with organizational property, it is the company commander's responsibility to maintain proper supply company commander is newly assigned to the post and is unfamiliar with local regulations and procedures. Also, the new company commander should familiarize himself with AR 710-2, *Supply Policy Below The Wholesale Level;* AR 735-11, *Accounting for Lost, Damaged, or Destroyed Property;* and DA Pam 710-2-1, *Using Unit Supply System, Manual Procedures.*

An examination of the unit organizational and station property printouts, obtained from the property book section, will provide the latest data on which items of equipment have been issued to the unit. By comparing the organizational printout with the MTOE, the new company commander can determine which authorized items have not been issued to the unit. He can then coordinate with the PBO to ensure that all shortages are, in fact, on request. The PBO will issue DMMC requisition numbers which will allow the company commander to account even for shortage items.

The incoming company commander checks all of the sub-hand receipts to ensure that all the end items for which he is signing are properly sub-hand receipted. Through this type of check *before* the change-of-command inventory, he can identify

> *"The first step is to collect all the references for the components of each end item."*

accountability for the installation property issued to the unit.

Before beginning the inventory, the new company commander should arrange for a briefing by the engineer property book officer (PBO) and someone from the battalion S4 section to bring himself up-to-date on the latest supply procedures and to clear up any questions he may have on supply records and accountability. This briefing will prove especially useful in the possible problem areas early and take steps to resolve them before the inventory starts.

Once all of the major end items have been accounted for, it is time to do the nuts and bolts portion of the change-of-command inventory—the actual inventory of the end items and their components.

The first step in accomplishing this task is to collect the appropriate technical manuals (TMs), supply catalogs (SCs), and other references which prescribe the type and amount of components for each end item. (For example, for the inventory of a Bailey bridge, a copy of TM 5-277 will be needed; the general mechanic's tool kit is covered in SC 5180-90-CL-N26, *Tool Set, General Mechanic's: Automotive.)*

These manuals normally include an illustration and a description of each component. Using such publications is especially critical with the large numbers of new equipment now being introduced into the inventory. GSA catalogs can be especially useful in providing more accurate descriptions and pictures of hand tools than are often provided in TMs and SCs. It is also important that the new company commander use the most recent references so that he is aware of the latest additions or deletions to the component list. DA Pam 310-4 provides the date of the latest published manual and any changes.

To reduce confusion and standardize property records, the Department of the Army now publishes hand receipt manuals for each end item. For example, the hand receipt manual for an M548 cargo carrier is TM 9-2350-247-10-HR, *Hand Receipt Manual Covering Basic Issue Items (BII) and Additional Authorized List (AAL) for Carrier, Cargo, Tracked, 6-Ton: M548;* for the common No. 1 automotive shop set is SC 4910-95-CL-A74-HR. *Hand Receipt Manual Covering Contents of Shop Equipment, Automotive Maintenance and Repair, Organizational Maintenance, Common No. 1 (Less Power).*

These hand receipt manuals identify all the components of an end item as they should appear on the DA Form 2062 hand receipt. Those items not yet covered in DA-level hand receipt manuals may be covered in corps or division manuals which can be obtained locally.

The schedule to perform the actual inventory should be coordinated by the new and old company commanders. (See sample schedule on page 41.) While there are many methods which will work, a suggested method is to schedule inventories by sub-hand receipt for the first half of each day. The other half of the day is dedicated to required paperwork, such as updating component hand receipts, verifying shortages on hand receipt annexes, and preparing relief-from-accountability paperwork. Handling the paperwork in this timely manner prevents an overload of paperwork at the end of the inventory schedule. In most cases, the company will not be able to totally stand-down for the inventory; so such a schedule will provide time for other requirements.

The time needed for the inventory depends on factors such as the unit's size, equipment and external requirements. AR 710-2 prescribes that 30 days be allowed for the inventory; in most cases this will be sufficient, although extensions may be granted in unusual cases. After preparing the schedule, the new and old battery commanders should brief the battalion commander and ensure that the battalion executive officer and the battalion operations officer are aware of how the inventory will affect their areas of responsibility.

When the inventory of each sub-hand receipt is finished, the shortages must be cross-referenced to the hand receipt annex (formerly called the shortage annex) for each end item. The majority of components for the end items will have an expendability code of durable (D); however, some items are classified as non-expendable (N) and expendable (X). The non-expendable hand receipt annex is maintained by the PBO at DMMC.

The company commander must ensure that recent additions/deletions to the component list have been posted to this annex and that the PBO has initialed the annex to validate its accuracy after all changes have been made. The durable hand receipt annex is maintained by the battalion S4 section, and similar actions must take place there.

Hand receipt annexes for expendable items are not required; but, if needed items are not on hand, they should be requisitioned. Also, the departing company commander must see that the latest relief from accountability documents (e.g., reports of survey, statements of charges, etc.) have been posted to the annexes and that copies of both

INVENTORY SCHEDULE

DAY 1
Review authorization document.
Receive briefing from battalion S4 representative.
Obtain unit organizational and installation property printouts.
Compare authorization document with printout; note shortages.
Obtain copies of hand-receipts annexes.

DAY 2
Compare unit sub-hand receipts with printout, ensure that all end items are sub-hand receipted.
Schedule inventory with departing commander; brief battalion commander, executive officer, and operations officer.

DAY 3
Assemble references for inventory.

DAY 4
Inventory heavy equipment.

DAY 5
Inventory heavy equipment.

DAY 6
Inventory tool boxes.

DAY 7
Inventory communications equipment.

DAY 8
Inventory mess.

DAY 9
Inventory maintenance.

DAY 10
Inventory maintenance.

DAY 11
Inventory arms room.

DAY 12
Inventory NBC equipment.

DAY 13
Inventory orderly room, company commander's jeep, and special weapons (as applicable).

DAY 14
Inventory supply.

DAY 15
Inventory supply.

DAY 16
Inventory camouflage equipment set.

DAY 17
Determine shortages and prepare relief-from-accountability paperwork.

DAY 18
Determine shortages and prepare relief-from-accountability paperwork.

DAY 19
Brief battalion commander and sign printout.

DAY 20 Assume command.

possible (for hand tools, for example) since this procedure normally gets the missing item back into the hands of the user more quickly and with less paperwork than other methods. If liability is not admitted, it will be necessary to initiate a report of survey.

The battalion commander should be kept informed during the inventory. He definitely does not want to be surprised by the results of the completed inventory.

The sub-hand receipts should be updated and signed to reflect the results of the inventory as soon as possible. By following the half-day inventory plan previously discussed and with detailed planning, the company commander should be able to update each sub-hand receipt on the same day it was inventoried; then he should double-check all actions for accuracy and completeness. After all necessary relief from accountability actions have been initiated, the new and old company commanders go to the property book section at DMMC and sign the hand receipts which transfer responsibility for all the company's property.

The key to a change-of-command inventory is preparation. Assembling the necessary references before the inventory reduces confusion and saves time. Establishing a realistic schedule allows sufficient time for a thorough inventory and for timely preparation of any necessary paperwork.

A good inventory provides the new company commander with an accurate status of company property and guarantees that there is accountability for all of it, thus setting the stage for continued accurate property accountability throughout the tenure of his or her command.

Every engineer company commander wants to miss the initial scene entirely and be the star actor in this one!

Adapted from an article appearing in the November-December 1983 Field Artillery Journal.

"Sir, Captain Smith reporting as ordered."

"Captain Smith, I have just finished reviewing your report on the results of your change-of-command inventory. I see that you have accounted for every end item with no component shortages—that is a superb achievement! Congratulations on an outstanding job of property accountability."

"Thank you, sir. I was fortunate in that I was able to conduct a very thorough inventory prior to assuming command, and that made the whole job a lot easier."

Dry application of lime underway during a 62nd Engineers' airfield construction project at Camp Bullis.

Military Application of Lime Stabilization

by CPT Joseph M. Seerley &
CPT John D. Norwood

The 62nd Engineers turn a confrontation with 800 feet of unacceptable subgrade into a unique training opportunity.

The 62nd Engineer Battalion (Combat) (Heavy), stationed at Fort Hood, Texas, was tasked by the U.S. Armed Forces Command Headquarters to construct a C130 assault airfield at Camp Bullis, Texas. Camp Bullis is an Army training area north of San Antonio under the direction of Fort Sam Houston.

The project called for the construction of a medium lift airfield capable of handling, during its five-year design life, 100 cycles of a 100,000-pound Air Force C130 Hercules aircraft. A cycle is the landing and takeoff of one aircraft.

To construct the airfield efficiently in minimum time, the battalion consolidated its earthmoving units into a single engineer company (C Team). C Team provided on-site control and consisted of three earthmoving platoons, elements of a direct support maintenance shop, and the headquarters company technical section.

Unacceptable Subgrade

During construction, the unit discovered that an 800-foot section of the proposed runway consisted of highly compressible black clay four to eight feet deep. The soil was unacceptable as a subgrade because its California Bearing Ratio (CBR) was three or less, as determined by inplace CBR. (The design procedures in Army Technical Manual 5-330, *Roads and Airfields*, does not provide for the use of its design chart with an Airfield Index (AI) of less than five, which loosely equates to a CBR of four).

To solve the problem of an unacceptable subgrade, lacking the flexibility of relocating the airfield site and as a learning experience for the unit, the battalion commander formed a special team of eight of the battalion's most technically proficient officers. Their educational backgrounds included engineering, civil engineering, and mathematics. The team relocated to Camp Bullis and conducted a detailed study of various stabilization options. Team members then proposed to the deputy commander of Fort Sam Houston that the area be stabilized with lime.

Lime stabilization is seldom used by military construction units and the procedure required study and research by the battalion's design team.

The procedure finally established is discussed below. Initially, all available data on the soil was gathered. This data is as follows:

Atterburg
Liquid Limit = 73
Plastic Limit = 26
Plasticity Index = 47
Sieve Analysis
Gravel = 0%
Sand = 2.9%
Fines = 97.1%
CBR = 3

Inplace Density/Moisture
= 81 LB/CF
Wc = 29.4%
Penetrometer Readings (every half station)

Depth	*Airfield Index*
6″	4.2
12″	6.3
18″	8.5

The soil was classified by the Unified Soils Classification System as a Highly Plastic, Inorganic Clay (CH) common to the San Antonio area. The above data showed that this soil was an ideal candidate for lime stabilization. During the preliminary soils exploration, local engineering firms were consulted to determine the average lime/soil mix for this type of soil. The average mix was an 8 percent lime solution. This percentage mix was taken as a starting point to calculate design mix. Army technical manuals could have been used for this initial mix design; however, it was felt that in this situation it would be best to contact those with local experience.

Areas For Concern

Two major concerns were identified during the analysis. First, the effect of adding lime on the pH of the soil needed to be determined. It was felt that natural consumption of the lime into the soil might occur if the pH change was too drastic.

Lab studies were conducted to determine the effect of lime on the soil pH. The percentage of lime varied from zero percent to 12 percent. The data is consolidated below.

Percent of Lime	*pH @ 5 Minutes*	*pH @ 24 Hours*
0	6.8	0 to 8.1
6	11.8	12.1
8	11.9	12.0
10	11.8	12.1
12	11.8	12.1

As the data reflects, the pH varied insignificantly at percent mixes of greater than 6 percent. The concern that a natural consumption of lime by the soil would occur was unfounded. Unconfined compression tests conducted on the lime soil mix produced no extraordinary results.

A second concern was to reduce the Plasticity Index (PI) of the soil. The inplace clay had a PI of 47, which indicated a significant water retention property of the soil. If lime stablization was to be effective, the PI had to be greatly lowered, thus reducing the porosity of the soil and its propensity to swell. Lab data

A leased Rototiller is used to reduce soil particle size before lime application. Several days of tilling were required because of the soil's high in-place water content.

"The lime stabilization effort was an overwhelming success. The subbase was altered to yield a soil with outstanding construction properties (CBR=27)."

showed that the PI could be lowered to 15 at mixes of 8 percent and above. Since an 8 percent mix was the most economical mix that satisfied the criteria, it was chosen for design specifications. A CE (Compactible Effort) 55 test was done on the 8 percent lime/soil mix and the following data resulted:

Maximum Compacted Density = 95.8 LB/CF
Optimum Moisture Content = 21.5%

How To Apply?

Once design specifications were determined, a method of application had to be chosen. A dry application of lime was chosen based primarily on the limited availability of slurry dispensing equipment but also because of the poor reactive qualities of a slurry mix with CH soil.

Before the dry lime could be applied, the particle size of the soil had to be reduced. This would ensure proper mixing and the highest degree of uniformity between the soil and lime additive. To accomplish this, a leased commercial roto tiller was used. Because of the high inplace water content of the soil, several days of tilling were required to get the correct particle size. Initial passes were made at a depth of 8 inches and the soil left to dry. After drying, successive passes were made to reduce the size of the clay particles.

Lime was then added dry and mixed by the roto tiller into the soil until a uniform mix was obtained. Water was added using 6,000-gallon water distributors.

The speedy moisture test set should not be used with stabilized soils since the mixture can clog the tester. As a result, a field expedient method was used to determine the initial water content. Denatured alcohol was added to the soil/lime mixture then ignited. This allowed moisture to be burned out of the soil. By weighing samples before and after burning, moisture content was determined.

Once the soil reached optimum moisture content at 21.5 percent water, compaction began. A high-speed, motorized sheepsfoot roller was used to obtain 95 percent of the CE 55 maximum compacted density. Since the lime produced a hydration reaction, the treated area kept moist during a seven-day period.

On the seventh day, Field Moisture/Density (Nuclear Method), In-place CBR, and Penetrometer tests were conducted. The results were:

Average Compaction = 93.5 LB/CF
Average Moisture Content = 28.3%
Inplace CBR = 27
Airfield Index = 15

Based on these results, the lime stabilization effort was an overwhelming success. The very nature of the subbase was altered, yielding a soil with outstanding construction properties (CBR = 27).

The exercise benefitted the 62nd Engineer Battalion and proved that military units can successfully implement stabilization construction techniques.

The successful stabilization project enabled the rest of the construction to proceed on schedule, and the strip was certified for C130 landings by the U.S. Air Force.

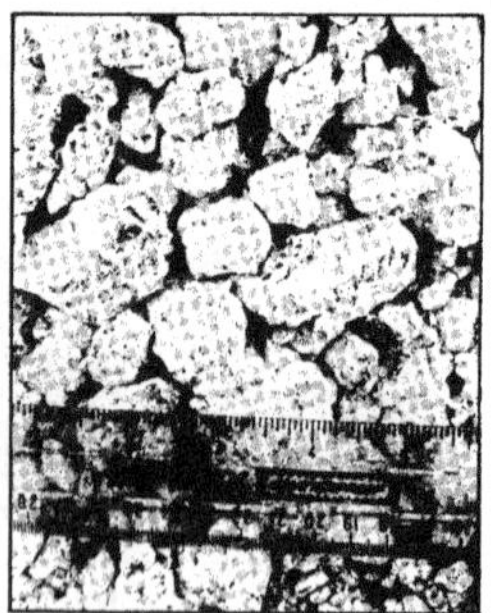

Particle size before (left) and after (right) tilling.

CPT Joseph M. Seerley commanded C Company, 62nd Engineer Battalion (Combat) (Heavy) and was the commander of C Team. He is now attending the Engineer Officer Advanced Course. He is a graduate of the University of California at Santa Barbara. He has served as vertical platoon leader, company construction officer, and civil engineer for the 44th Engineer Battalion (Combat) (Heavy), Korea, and as platoon leader and diving officer for the 801st Engineer Company (Port Construction) (Reserve).

CPT John D. Norwood was the civil engineer, S3, 62nd Engineer Battalion (Combat) (Heavy). He is a graduate of the United States Military Academy and of the Engineer Officer Advance Course. He has served as a vertical and a horizontal platoon leader, company construction officer, and battalion adjutant.

Publications From CERL

A listing of the latest research results from the Construction Engineering Research Laboratory

Each Winter Issue of ENGINEER, beginning with this ie, will carry a list of publications ·oduced by the U.S. Army Con-ruction Engineering Research aboratory (CERL) of interest to ›mbat engineers and to facilities ıgineers.

The list is divided into two sections: ıaterial related to combat engi-ıeering, and material related to facilities engineering. These sections are sub-divided into a list of fact sheets and a list of technical reports/ publications.

Fact sheets are typically short (one or two-page) summaries of CERL's research effort on a given subject. Technical papers/publications are lengthier documents presenting the results of CERL's research on a specific topic.

Fact sheets are available from the Public Affairs Office, U.S. Army Construction Engineering Research Laboratory, P.O. Box 4005, Champaign, IL 61820.

Technical reports/publications are available at a nominal cost from the National Technical Information Center, 5285 Port Royal Road, Springfield, VA 22161, or by contacting the Publications Branch at CERL.

:OMBAT ENGINEERING ACTIVITIES

ıct Sheets are available on the following CERL studies progess on combat engineering activities:

CERL's Work in Support of Army Facilities omponent System (AFCS)—presents CERL's research ıle in improving the AFCS.

Engineer Unit Microcomputer Applications—Disısses the use of microcomputer software applications ır managing construction activities for the 18th ngineer Brigade in Germany.

Engineer Modeling Study—A computer program ısign to determine the effects of combat engineer :tivities on the outcome of a battle.

Foam Applications in Heavy Bridging/Rafting—Use foam composite materials to float vehicles across reams and to repair existing floating bridging systems.

Flotation Bridging/Rafting System for irborne/Airmobile Operations—Evaluation of methods available for floating vehicles across unfordable streams.

Foam Overhead Cover Support Systems (FOCOS)—A rapidly constructed, foam-filled fabric arch used with a top soil covering to protect infantry operators of antitank weapons.

Foam Protective Shelters—Evaluation of theater-of-operations structures to determine which can be best adapted to foam material support systems.

Foam Domes as Expedient Facilities—Use of foam domes in providing housing and storage for mobilization efforts.

Programmable Pocket Calculators for Engineer Troop Units—Use of programmable pocket calculators to support combat engineering activities.

FACILITY ENGINEERING ACTIVITIES

Fact sheets are available on the following CERL research efforts on facility engineering activities:

CERL Publications

Analysis of Industrialized Building Systems Pilot Projects

Appropriate Technologies for Upgrading Army Sewage Treatment Facilities and for New Construction

Building Loads Analysis and System Thermodynamics (BLAST)

Ceramic Anodes for Corrosion Protection

CERL Provides Help for the Director of Engineering and Housing

Characteristics, Control, and Treatment of Leachate and Gas Formation at Military Landfills

Corrosion Mitigation

Composting Toilet

DD Form 1391 Processor

Electrical Consumption Reduction at Army Installations

Energy Monitoring and Control Systems (IEMCS)

Environmental Quality Technology

Habitability Program

Hazardous/Toxic Waste

Improved Roofing Materials and Systems

Improvements to the Integrated Facilities Systems (IFS) Component Inspection System

Industrialized Building Systems in Military Construction

Life Cycle Cost Database for Maintenance and Repair Data

Low-Cost Meters for Solar Energy Systems

Materials Technology

Middle East Base Development

Paint Laboratory

Photovoltaic Power System

Automated Corps of Engineers Concrete Quality Monitor (CE-CQM)

Pipe Corrosion Management System (PIPER)

PAVER—Pavement Management System

Real-Time Weld Quality Monitor

Environmental Technical Information System (ETIS)

ETIS Enhancements

Training Area Maintenance

Solar System Performance Monitoring

Remote Site Waste Treatment

Railroad Maintenance Management System (RAILER)

Quality Control/Quality Assurance (QC/QA)

PORTAWASHER Refuse Container Cleaner/Hazardous Waste Spill Cleanup—Listing of Recent CERL Technical Reports/Publications on Combat Engineering Activities.

Technical Report P-146, "Microcomputer Selection Guide for Construction Field Offices," by F. Grobler, M. O'Connor, and Glen E. Colwell, Jun. 1983, ADA130245.

Technical Report M-323, "Troop Construction in the Mideast," by USACERL and USAWES, Oct. 1982, BO76455.

Technical Report P-131, "Engineer Modeling Study, Volume I: Executive Summary," by John Evans, Se 1982, ADA121166.

Technical Report P-131, "Engineer Modeling Study, Volume II: Users Manual," by Gerald Brown and Hugh Henry, Sep. 1982, ADA121167.

Technical Report P-131, "Engineer Modeling Study, Volume III: CORDIVEN Engineer Module Interface Manual," by Carlton Mills, Sep. 1982, ADA121168.

Technical Report P-136, "User's Manual for MILENG1/UTIL Read-Only-Memory Module of th Combat Engineer Programmable Hand-Held Calculator," by John M. Deponai III, Sep. 1982, ADA120338.

Technical Report P-134, "Software Documentation for MILENG1/UTIL Read-Only-Memory Module," by Laure A. Thomas and John M. Deponai III, Sep. 1982, ADA20317.

Technical Report M-314, "Relocatable Structures for Use in Theaters of Opeations," by A. Kso, M. Frisch J. Lambert, M. Ptak, May 1982, ADA117038.

Special Report M-291, "Concept Paper: The Use of Polyurethane Foam Plastics for Tactical Bridging and Rafting Operations," by A. Smith, Apr. 1981, ADA099033.

Technical Report M-287, "Theater of Operations Construction in the Desert: A Handbook of Lesson Learned in the Middle East," by A. Koa and P. Hadala, Jan. 1981, ADA104389.

Technical Report M-281, "Investigation of the Minimum Deployment Time of a Foam/Fabric Composite Material," by A. Smith, B. R. Culbertson, and R. E. Muncy, Sep. 1980, ADA091658.

Technical Report P-112, "Type II Forward Storage Site Facilities: POMCUS System," by Robert L. Porter, Sep. 1980.
Vol I: ADA092310 Vol II: ADA093672

Technical Report M-272, "Investigation of Rapidly Deployable Plastic Foam Systems," Oct. 1979.
Vol I: System Development, by Alvin Smith, ADA07633:
Vol II: Nonliner Deformation and Local Buckling of Kevlar Fabric/Polyurethane Foam Composites, by Alvin Smith, S. S. Wang, and A. Y. Kuo, ADA076310.

Technical Report M-269, "Foam Overhead Cover Support (FOCOS) System for Dismounted and Mounted TOW Positions," by Alvin Smith, Aug. 1979, ADA075746.

Special Report M-262, "Inflation/Foam/Shotcrete System for Rapid Construction of Circular Arches,' by M. Woratzeck, May 1979, ADA069878.

Sepcial Report M-255, "A Family of Components for the Wood Panelized Prefabricated Building System," by A. M. Kao and T. M. Whiteside, Jan. 1979, DA065659.

ng of Recent CERL Technical Reports/Publications n Facility Engineering Activities:

hnical Report M-334, "Evaluation of Contractor uality Control of Built-Up Roofing," by Myer J. osenfield, Oct. 1983.

ınical Report E-190, "Use of the Building Loads nalysis & Systems Thermodynamics (BLAST) omputer Program to Review New Army Building esigns for Energy Use," by Donald J. Leverenz, ale L. Herron, JoAnn Amber Eidsmore, and Robert E. 'Brien, Oct. 1983.

ɦnical Report N-151, "Oxidation Ditch Technology ɔr Upgrading Army Sewage Treatment Facilities," y J. T. Brandy, C. P. C. Poon, and E. D. Smith, ug. 1983.

ɦnical Report E-186, "Analysis of Facilities' nergy Use Patterns," by Ben J. Sliwinski, and lizabeth Elischer, Aug. 1983, ADA131527.

hnical Report M-333, "Preliminary Investigation of :eramic-Coated Anodes for Cathodic Protection," y E. G. Segan, and A. Kumar, Jul. 1983.

hnical Report M-332, "Electromagnetic Shielding f Full-Sized Structures by Metal-Arc Spraying," by ?. Nielson, Jun. 1983, ADA132883.

hnical Report N-159, "Portawasher: A Self-:ontained Dumpster Cleaning System," by G. Gerdes, and B. Donahue, Jun. 1983, ADA131799.

hnical Report N-157, "Distribution of Water Use at Representative Fixed Army Installations," by John T. Bandy, and Richard J. Scholze, Jun. 1983.

chnical Report N-152, "Users Guide: Simulation Model for Ammunition Plants; Prediction of Wastewater Characteristics and Impact of Reuse/Recycle," by S. Railsback, M. Messenger, R. Webster, and J. Bandy, Jun. 1983, ADA130694.

chnical Report N-155, "Treatment of Landfill Leachate at Army Facilities," by R. A. Shafer, E. D. Smith, J. T. Bandy, P. G. Malone, D. A. Moore, and L. W. Jones, May 1983, ADA132483.

chnical Report E-185, "Use of Simplified Input for BLAST Energy Analysis," by D. Herron, J. Eidsmore, R. O'Brien, and D. Leverenz, May 1983, ADA131261.

chnical Report E-181, "Modification of Cabinet Fans with Inlet Air Guide Fairings to Improve Performance," by William H. Dolan, Apr. 1983, ADA130253.

chnical N-149, "Tracking Hazardous Materials Through Army Installations: A Feasibility Study," by Manette Messenger, Ron Webster, Steve Railsback, and John Bandy, Mar. 1983, ADA129103.

chnical Report N-140, "Particulate Air Pollution Control for Army Coal-Fired Boiler Plants," Mikucki, Mar. 1983, ADA127636.

ecial Report P-143, "A Case Study of Industrialized Building Products and Innovative Building Delivery Techniques used for TACOM Facilities in Warren, MI," by Michael G. Carroll, and Thomas R. Napier, Mar. 1983, ADA128539.

Technical Report E-184, "Electronic Time Switch Evaluation Study," by Lee Thurber, Mar. 1983, ADA127870.

Technical Report E-183, "Analysis of Energy Conservation Alternatives for Standard Army Buildings," by Douglas C. Hittle, Robert E. O'Brien, and George S. Percival, Mar. 1983, ADA129963.

Technical Report M-320, "Military Installation Painting Problems: Survey Analysis and Recommended Solutions," by S. Johnston and A. Beitelman, Jul. 1982, ADA119267.

Technical Report M-310, "Overview of the PAVER Pavement Management System and Economic Analysis of Field Implementing the PAVER Pavement Management System," by M. Y. Shahin, and S. D. Kohn, Mar. 1982, ADA16311.

Technical Report M-312, 'Investigation of Materials of Waterproofing Leaky Corrugated Galvanized Steel-Arch Magazines From the Inside," by Stanley M. Kanarowski, Mar. 1982, ADA115645.

Technical Report M-308, "Insulation Retrofit Under Low-Slope Roofs," by Myer J. Rosenfield and Donald E. Brotherson, Feb. 1982, ADA113802.

Technical Report M-294, "Pavement Maintenance Management for Roads and Parking Lots," by M. Y. Shahin and S. D. Kohn, Oct. 1981, ADA110296.

Technical Report M-283, "Pavement Evaluation and Repair Recommendation Sierra Army, Depot, Amedee Air Strip," by M. Y. Shahin, Nov. 1980, ADA093761.

Technical Report M-280, "Selection of Cooling Water Treatment at Military Installations to Prevent Scaling and Corrosion," by R. Lane and A. Kumar, Jun. 1980, ADA087266.

Technical Report P-107, "Housing Maintenance Contract Guide," by Joyce L. Nay, David W. Brown, et al., May 1980, ADA084539.

Technical Report M-279, "Roofing Repair Materials for Korean Relocatable Buildings—Test and Evaluation," by Robert E. Muncy, May 1980, ADA085188.

Technical Report M-268, "Development of a Pavement Condition Rating Procedure for Roads, Streets, and Parking Lots," by Mohamed Y. Shanin and Starr D. Kohn, Jul. 1979.
Vol I: Condition Rating Procedure, ADA074170.
Vol II: Distress Identification Manual, ADA074171.

Interim Report M-263, "Evaluation of Alternative Reroofing Systems," by E. Marvin, G. Middleton, L. Eubanks, M. Rosenfield, J. Blair, and E. Lindow, Jun. 1979, ADA071578.

Special Report M-256, "Investigation of Materials for Waterproofing Leaky Concrete Ammunition-Storage Bunkers From the Inside," by Stanley M. Kanarowski, Jan. 1979, ADA064731.

Special Report M-257, "Investigation of Techniques for the Rapid Preparation of Painted Wood Surfaces," by P. A. Howdyshell and T. Olsson, Jan. 1979, ADA064813.

Commissioned Officers' Branch

What Shape Are You In?

With increasing frequency, selection boards are asking questio about the physical fitness of the officer corps. Board members oft ask for direct verification of height, weight and body fat percenta for officers at or above the screen weight specified in Appendix AR 600-9, *The Army Weight Control Program*, dated Feb. 15, 19 In addition, board members are correlating the informat contained in Items 3 and 12, Part IVa of DA Form 67-8, *U.S. Ar Officer Evaluation Report*, with the height and weight data Section IV of the Officer Record Brief (ORB). Individuals reporti sudden height increases or weight drops are likely to be viewed wi suspicion by board members.

If you are close to screen weight, it may be in your best interest get a "pinch test." Also ensure that any deviation from publish height and weight standards is adequately explained in Section I of the DA Form 67-8. In addition, if you are in a zone of considerati and there is any significant improvement in your shape, report t information to your assignment officer at MILPERCEN so that change can be made on your ORB.

The selection boards are dead serious about the physical fitness the officer corps.

SC18—Special Operations:

This new additional specialty is concerned with the unconvention employment of individuals and units in a variety of tactical mission Special operations officers are trained to participate in foreig internal defense, unconventional warfare, strike missions ar numerous other activites, both overt and covert, in war or peacetime.

Officers currently holding ASE 5G or SSI 48E have been invited seek redesignation to the new specialty.

Ranger or Special Forces qualification is preferred, but n required. About 83 officers will be assigned to the new specialty ea year.

The prerequisites for SC18 ADSPEC designation:

- Male officer
- Branch qualification (completion of advanced course)
- Airborne qualified

Warrant Officers' Branch

Warrant Officer Training:

In April 1983, a comprehensive study was begun to determine ho the professional development of an engineer warrant officer shoul be accomplished. The approach used in the study was a systemati analysis of engineer warrant officer education and career manag ment by conducting a needs assessment, compiling current data, an conducting an analysis by boards.

The analysis phase was conducted by two boards: specialty tas boards and common warrant officer analysis boards. The objective of the specialty task boards were to produce task lists and jo descriptions by career level for the following MOSs: Utiliti Operations and Maintenance Technician (811A): Engineer Equi ment Repair Technician (621A); Photomapping Technician (811A

Survey Technician (821); Reproduction Technician (833A); and Terrain Analysis Technician (841A).

The objectives of the common warrant officer analysis boards were to perform (1) problem analysis—to determine discrepancies in training (actual vs. projected) and possible solutions; (2) evaluation—to determine the feasibility of those solutions; and (3) action planning—to determine ways to implement solutions into existing training systems for warrant officers.

The types of problems addressed in the study were the current warrant officer education system, prerequisites for appointment, boarding actions for appointment, assignments, ASI management, grading by school qualifications, feeder MOS analysis, civilian education and the role of the engineer warrant officer.

The study was completed on Sep. 30, 1983. The proposals are currently being reviewed and will be published on a later date.

ldiers' Branch

How *should* you prepare for a promotion board? To start with, send for a copy of your Official Military Personnel File (OMPF) and review it from top to bottom to ensure that all data on the fiche is yours and is up to date. Check your photo and make sure your uniform and appearance meet Army standards. Check to see if all your awards and letters are included on your fiche. Anything which has not been entered or needs updating should be taken care of immediately through your PAC.

Physical fitness is heavily emphasized. Make sure you passed your last PT test and make sure the score is on your last SEER.

Training and education also play a major role in the promotion process. Seek leadership positions and leadership schools whenever possible. The NCO who has attended leadership schools is a step ahead.

The Army wants volunteers for language training. Engineer soldiers who are interested must meet the prerequsites of Army Regulation 611-6, *Army Linguist Program.*

Formal foreign language training for the Army is conducted at the Defense Language Institute Foreign Language Center (DLIFLC), Presidio of Monterey, Calif.; at the DLIFLC, Presidio of San Francisco, Calif.; and at the Foreign Service Institute, U.S. Department of State, Arlington, Va.

Personnel who meet the eligibility criteria in AR 611-6 are encouraged to volunteer for language training. Submit DA Form 41871 to MILPERCEN, ATTN: DAPC-EPT-L, 2461 Eisenhower Ave., Alexandria, VA 22331. Each request (DA Form 4187) must include a current DA Form 2, DA Form 2-1, and verification of DLAB score.

For more information on language training, call Ms. Brewers at MILPERCEN, AV 221-8415/0640.

A Personal Viewpoint

by MAJ Lee A. Peters

Military leaders will increase their effectiveness and efficiency as they increase their use of intuition.

Intuition is the ability or power to gain direct knowledge or cognition without rational thought, inference, or deductive reasoning. The great Swiss psychologist Carl Jung called it a sixth sense—a way of gaining information or of making observations—in addition to the five senses of smell, touch, taste, sight, and hearing.

Intuition, which is already used by military personnel, is often called "gut feel" or "hunch." Although military leaders have a vague understanding of what is going on in their minds, they are often fearful of using intuition because it is not empirical and they are unaware of its reliability.

Other leaders use it without realizing what it is or what it does. Platoon leaders who "know" their soldiers use intuition to predict their troops' collective and individual responses to situations, to diagnose problems in the platoon, and to direct actions that motivate the platoon to accomplish its missions.

An aircraft pilot flying nap-of-the-earth lets intuition (the sensor for the subconscious) "feel" the aircraft and its responses while giving the conscious mind the task of watching the terrain. The pilot may let intuition direct the responses to the terrain—"going on automatic."

Intuition has other military applications. For example, it can be used to predict how units will react under stressful situations, to identify what's happening in a member's home life, to operate a tank, to structure combined arms teams, or to diagnose simple enemy movements or to discover a new enemy location.

Eric Bern, in his book *Beyond Games and Scripts*, defines intuition as subconscious knowledge without words, based on subconscious observations without words. Under the right circumstances, he says, it is more reliable and accurate than conscious knowledge based on conscious observation.

In the book, Bern includes, as an example, a psychiatric examination once used for people entering the military. Psychiatrists asked the entrants two simple questions: "Are you nervous?" and "Have you ever seen a psychiatrist?" Using intuitive reactions to the answers, they determined whether a person was psychologically fit for the armed forces. The psychiatrists were 90 percent accurate.

Intuition is the receiver, the antenna, for inductive reasoning. Inductive reasoning uses the proof of a specific case or of a few facts to reach a general conclusion, whereas deductive reasoning uses a series of facts or empirical data to prove a general situation.

Inductive reasoning is the logic of the subconscious. The five senses are the antennae of the conscious and deductive reasoning its logic.

When experience is emphasized by the military, it gives intuition—internalized understanding—a data base that translates into diagnosis, prediction, and action in future situations. The conscious mind may not know that understanding and its internalization have happened until intuition retrieves the data.

Because information voids exist in literature and research on intuition, the subject is often misunderstood. Army leadership publications do not mention intuition. Management literature, however, does recognize it as means of classifying managers. Ralph Stogdill's *Handbook of Leadership* mentions it only as a means of sizing up other people and of determining their place in society.

The military must accomplish the following to fill the informational void and to improve leadership:

- Acknowledge that intuition exists.
- Identify the process of internalizing knowledge.
- Research the use of this internalized knowledge in the intuitive process.
- Help leaders to recognize that they use intuition.
- Develop methodology to determine the reliability and accuracy of intuitions.

Military leaders can perform more effectively if they understand this sixth sense. They should know what intuitive talent they possess, how often they use it, and how reliable and accurate it is. Using intuition will help leaders to better identify priorities for decision making. The accepting intuition as a leadership tool will increase the effectiveness and efficiency of the military.

MAJ Lee A. Peters, USAR, heads Construction Support Services, Inc., in Indianapolis. He has masters degrees in civil engineering and in management from Purdue University and serves as maintenance officer for the 123rd ARCOM. He served in Vietnam with the 92nd and 169th Engineer Bns. MAJ Peters is a registered professional engineer in Indiana.

VOLUME 14 NUMBER 1 SPRING 1984

On the Cover

A CEV from the 522nd Engineer Co., 194th Armored Bde. breaks through a barricade during a training exercise at Ft. Drum. (Photo by SFC Dale Butler.)

FEATURES

DEPARTMENTS

ENGINEER is an authorized publication of the U.S. Army Engineer Center and Fort Belvoir, Va. Unless specifically stated, material appearing herein does not necessarily reflect official policy, thinking nor endorsement by any agency of the U.S. Army. • The words he, him, or his are used to represent personnel of either sex. • All photographs contained herein are official U.S. Army photographs unless otherwise credited. • The use of funds for printing this publication was approved by Headquarters, Department of the Army, on July 22, 1981. • Material herein may be reprinted if credit is given to ENGINEER and to the author. • ENGINEER's objectives are to provide a forum for the exchange of ideas, to inform and motivate, and to promote the professional development of all members of the Army engineer community. • Direct correspondence with ENGINEER is authorized and encouraged. Inquiries, letters to the editor, commentaries, manuscripts, photographs and general correspondence should be sent to: ENGINEER Magazine, ATZA-TD-P Stop 163F, Fort Belvoir, VA 22060. Phone: (703) 664-3082, AV 354. • Subscriptions to ENGINEER are available through the Superintendent of Documents, U.S. Government Printing Office, Washington, D.C. 20402. A check or money order payable to Superintendent of Documents must accompany all subscription requests. Rates are $8.50 for domestic (including APO and FPO) addresses and $10.65 for foreign addresses. Individual copies are available at $4.50 per copy for domestic addresses and $5.65 for foreign addresses. • Second Class postage paid at Fort Belvoir, VA, and additional mailing offices. ISSN 0046-1989.

More Info on 51H Course

Building Supervisors in the Fall 1983 issue was much appreciated in calling the attention of the Engineer community to the 51H NCO professional development course offered at Fort Leonard Wood. However, two major aspects need additional information—the basic intent of the course and how to attend.

We have too long ignored the professional development needs of our noncommissioned officers. CSM Orville Troesch's message in the same issue offers some hope in addressing this problem.

To correct a possible misconception arising from the *Building Supervisors* article, we are *not* offering a technical course of instruction intended to produce proficient building supervisors. The 51H Basic Technical Course (BTC) taught at the 4th Training Brigade's Crusader Academy produces noncommissioned officers who are technically qualified and better prepared to assume the leadership responsibilities required to lead Engineer soldiers. While the skills necessary to supervise construction activities are important, they must be subordinate to those leadership skills required of effective members of the chain-of-command.

Noncommissioned officers attending Basic and Primary Technical Courses at Fort Leonard Wood live and learn in an academy environment designed to prepare them to be the Engineer leaders of tomorrow. Leadership skills, physical fitness, drill and ceremonies, and communications skills training supplement the Academy's technical instructions. Crusader Academy is commanded and staffed by senior noncommissioned officers of the 4th Training Brigade who are technically proficient and proven leaders.

Engineer noncommissioned officers eager to be tomorrow's leaders and set the standards of excellence for Engineer soldiers are welcome at the Crusader Academy and are encouraged to attend. Attendance at the BTC and PTC courses may be by "TDY enroute to a new assignment" or by "TDY and return to current unit." The former option is a matter between MILPERCEN and the soldier, while the latter option involves the soldier's chain-of-command. Reserve Component noncommissioned officers should consult their chain-of-command for attendance procedures. For additional information, contact the Commandant, Crusader Academy, 4th Training Brigade, Fort Leonard Wood, MO 65473 (AV 581-6650/4144).

Preparing Engineer noncommissioned officers in the 51H, 62B, 62N, and 12F MOSs for leadership roles awaiting them is a responsibility we take seriously. Developmenting dynamic leaders, technically proficient in their MOS, is a responsibility we should all take seriously. Our Army depends on it.

COL William M. Shepherd
Commander,
4th Training Brigade
Fort Leonard Wood, MO

52E Update

The *Engineer NCOES* article in Fall 1983 ENGINEER correctly identified the 52E course as a Primary Technical Course. Soldiers, however, must apply according to AR 350-224. The following is a synopsis of the qualifying criteria and instructions for applying.

The Army's Facilities Engineering Support Agency at Fort Belvoir operates a one-year course to teach soldiers how to operate, maintain and rebuild large electrical power plants.

Graduates receive a primary MOS 52E with an additional skill identifier in mechanical, electrical or instrumentation areas.

Applicants must meet the following basic requirements:

- Be in grade E6 or below.
- Have a high school diploma or GED.
- Have a credit for one or more years of high school algebra.
- Have GT/ST and EL scores of 110 or higher.
- Score 70 percent on a basic math and science test available through Army education centers.

Soldiers selected for the one-year course must be prepared for hard work. The American Council on education has recommended that course graduates receive college credit for their work. Graduates also can take the exam for the third-class license offered by the National Institute for the Uniform Licensing of Power Engineers.

Applications are being accepted for the class starting April 1985. For more information call AV 354-5241 or toll-free 800-336-3095, Ex. 5241.

Jo Simpson
Public Affairs Officer
U.S. Army Facilities
Engineering Support Agency

The Wrong Pitch?

You published an article entitled *The Digital Landscape*, by MAJ David Bowen, in your Fall 1983 issue. I applaud MAJ Bowen's efforts to publicize the technology trends in mapmaking and hope that the articl will focus attention on the pos sibilities of tailoring terrain dat displays to commanders' requir ments.

By pitching the article at th general appeal level, however, yo may have invited some unfortunat misinterpretations.

When we put out informatio about systems under developmen let's clearly state up front whethe we're doing it to drum up interest, t educate the readers, or to advertis capabilities that are funded, fielded, and operational.

Richard G. Johnson
MAJ, CE
Honolulu, Hawaii

516th Engr. Co. Makes Good Showing in Edinburgh

The 516th Engineer Company team from Hanau, Germany, scurry to build an MGB during the bridge-building competition in the 37th Annual Edinburgh Tattoo.

The 516th Engineer Co.'s team from Hanau, Germany, participated in a medium girder bridge building competition as guests of the British Royal Engineers in the 37th Annual Edinburgh Tattoo held in Edinburgh, Scotland.

The highlight of this year's Tattoo was the first round-robin competitive building of the medium girder bridge, a most dynamic crowd pleasing engineer performance. With 17 events being for competition, the 516th Engineers won five of them.

The 516th Engineer Co.'s team, of the 559th Engineer Bn., competed against teams from the 11th Field Squadron Royal Engineers and the 104th Field Squadron Engineers, a volunteer army unit similar to our National Guard.

The 516th Engineer Co., is one of only four active duty units (two of them in Europe) in the U.S. Army that have the medium girder bridge. Before going to the Tattoo, they underwent a rigorous 12 week training program which included running, weight lifting, and bridge building under the supervision of SFC Christopher B. Waters, the team's noncommissioned officer in charge.

After arriving in Edinburgh, the teams practiced new bridge building techniques to improve their speed. "We had to change our plans once we got there," Waters said. "We had been building the bridge differently. The other teams knew a few tricks."

Each night the teams competed against each other in constructing a four-bay single story bridge over a simulated 20-foot gap in the arena.

Teams assembled after trucks carried the bridge parts into the arena. On the command, "Go," the bridge parts were dumped and the soldiers scurried to assemble the bridge. The winner was the first team completing the bridge and having all of the team members formed on the "far shore." With a time limit of 11 minutes, the 516th's best time was 4:47.

ENGINEER ROCK-SP4 Joseph Townsend of the 562nd Engineer Company at Fort Richardson, Alaska, sweeps snow off of his unit's unique sign after more than a foot of snow fell. The two-ton rock, the brainchild of 562nd 1SG Patrick Cannon, appeared in front of the company after several persons confused the unit with another engineer company housed in a neighboring barracks. The 562nd Engineers call themselves, "The Rock of the 172nd Infantry Brigade." (U.S. Army Photo by SP5 Jon M. Chelgren.)

New Antifreeze Preservative

A new method of preserving antifreeze has been developed at the Belvoir Research and Development Center that could, according to Army officials, save the military millions of dollars annually.

The liquid chemical extender, scheduled to enter the supply system next spring, should prolong the life of used antifreeze at least four years, says project engineer James Conley.

"Presently the Army's composition based antifreeze should stay effective for at least five years," Conley says. "If used properly and in conjunction with the technical bulletin governing standard use of antifreeze, this additive could extend antifreeze life to ten years."

According to Defense Department procurement figures, the Army is presently spending over $12 million annually on antifreeze replacement. Officials say with proper use of the test kit and reinhibiting extender this figure could be reduced to $2 million.

News & Notes

Generator Control Shelters Save Money and Manpower

At the request of the Army's Facilities Engineer Support Agency (FESA), the Electrical Equipment Division of the center's Engineer Service Support Lab agreed to design and construct 11 generator control shelters. The structures will make it possible for a minimum number of soldiers to operate four 750kw generators in parallel, saving the Army millions of dollars.

The generator shelters, were needed to fill a gap in the Army's mobile generator capabilities and greatly reduce manpower hours.

Under present procedures, eight operators and two supervisors are needed during each shift to operate four separate 750kw generators. The new system will allow all controls to be centralized, and only three people will be needed to operate the consolidated generators, drastically reducing daily manpower needs.

The structures will also allow for operations flexibility, as any combination of the Army's five generator types can be paralleled within the system.

Much of the inital cost-cutting stemmed from adopting standard shipping contrainers to house the control stations instead of designing and building entirely new external structures. Additionally, low-salaried interns and summer hires manually placed the panels inside the shelters. This freed the division's engineers and technicians for other assignments.

Further manpower savings are anticipated when the shelters are used to provide back-up and emergency power and to supplying electricity during routine maintenance operations at large military installations.

Have something for News & Notes? Please send your item (with photographs) to ENGINEER Magazine, ATZA-TD-P, Stop 163F, Ft. Belvoir, VA 22060.

SP4 John A. Kennel, 814th Engineer Company, ties a splint on his buddy's arm at the first aid station during the military stakes in Hanau, Germany.

The 814th Engineers won first place among 40 teams at the competition by completing all of the events in the least time. Events included map reading, assembly and disassembly of the M16A1 rifle, a 2½-ton truck pull, an obstacle course, a boat row, and a first aid station.

S.A.M.E. Awards

The winner of the 1983 Sturgis Award was SFC Eugene Middleton, Co. C, 9th Engineer Bn. (CBT) (CORPS), 7th Engineer Bde., USARUR.

SFC Middleton, a platoon sergeant was cited for his exceptional leadership and technical competence. He and his platoon excelled in a variety of troop exercises and completed several projects supporting the unit's surrounding community.

The Winner of the 1983 Itschner Award was Co. C, 249th Engineer Bn. (CBT) (HVY), 18th Engineer Bde., USAREUR, for their outstanding work during the "GRAF '83" construction period. This range modernization project in Europe is an estimated four-year project costing $55.1 million.

The top engineer Army Reserve unit, according to S.A.M.E. was Co. D, 411th Engineer Bn. (CBT) (HVY), Guam, for their exceptional performance in a variety of construction projects. They were especially commended for their support of schools, churches, and other community centers.

Co. D, 1457 Engineer Bn. (CBT) (CORPS), Utah, earned the Itschner Award as the top Army National Guard unit and also received a C-1 rating for their exceptional training programs. They displayed their "high state of readiness" by winning the Utah State Marksmanship Trophy and the Pershing Plaque for their outstanding marksmanship.

The Wheeler Medal, awarded to an individual making the most significant contribution to military engineering, was presented to John J. Blake at the annual meeting of the Society of American Military Engineers (S.A.M.E.) at St. Paul, Minn.

All three engineering awards are presented each year by S.A.M.E. to honor those individuals and units contributing the most to the Corps mission.

Overstrength MOSs

The chances of career progression (promotions and assignments) are extremely limited in overstrength MOSs. Soldiers in overage MOSs should consider voluntarily reclassifying into shortage MOSs. DA Circular 611-82-3 provides a list of the status of all MOSs. Soldiers interested in voluntarily reclassifying should contact their AG Personnel Management Branch for more information.

Engineer People

Olympic hopeful, 1LT Wayne Dickert, fights the rapids.

Engineer: World Class Boatman

Whitewater rafting may not be the best way to relax for many people, but it is for 1LT Wayne Dickert of the Directorate of Training and Doctrine at Ft. Belvoir.

In fact, Dickert is on the U.S. Canoe and Kayak Whitewater Team and is training for the 1985 World Championships to be held in Garmisch, Germany, this June.

Dickert, 24, started canoeing in college as a YMCA camp counselor. "It's a lot of fun, like a constant roller coaster ride," he says. "The racing has helped my technique. I've gained experience and knowledge."

Dickert has raced for two and a half years, participating in the European Cup and in the Pan American Games competitions.

Dickert says he canoes almost everyday. This spring he begins speed work in his canoe — a Delphin. Delphins are new to the U.S. team, he says. Although they are risky to use because they tip over easier, they are designed for more speed than conventional canoes and kayaks.

"Balance and strength are important (in canoeing)," Dickert explains. "You have to know how to follow the water. You have to know how to use the water."

Dicket says he's also beginning to train with kayaks. He will compete in the U.S. Olympic trials in Lorton, VA., April 9 through 14.

"Kayaks are more stable than a canoe," he says. "But even though they're easier to control, they're faster and do not turn as quick. You also use a two-bladed paddle as opposed to the one-blade you use for a canoe."

Although being in the military allows Dickert little practice time, his chain of command understands his need to train so that he can remain a world class competitor. The Ft. Belvoir area is also advantageous because the U.S. team coaches and other competitors live and practice there.

Soldier-Student: Works Towards 13 Month Associate Degree

While completing two years of college in 13 months is a commendable feat for the average student, it's even more astounding when the student is also a soldier.

SP4 Tom Farmer, a plumber with D Co., 548th Engineer Bn., Ft. Jackson, S.C., is a full-time student at the University of South Carolina. He completed 19 semester hours during the 1983 fall semester and is currently enrolled for 22 credit hours. If successful, Farmer will receive an associate of arts degree in liberal arts in May 1984.

"A lot of people just don't take advantage of their educational opportunities," Farmer says. "Many aren't aware of Army educational programs that are available to them."

Maintaining a 3.60 grade point average, Farmer also enrolls in electronic and electrical military correspondence courses. "The classes I've taken are related to what I'll be doing in my career as a production specialist (52E)," he says. "It includes mechanical and electrical engineering."

He says he plans on using his knowledge while attending the Army's 13-month power engineer school. The "study habits and time management skills" he is developing now will help him through the long course, he says.

As the company's publications, deployment records and legal records clerk, Farmer has no time for studying during duty hours, says CPT Ross A. Burton, Company Commander. He attends classes four nights weekly and studies during weekends, before work in the morning, during lunch, and between classes.

SP4 Tom Farmer studies for his college degree.

by MG James N. Ellis, Commandant, U.S. Army Engineer School

AirLand Battle, A United Effort

We must keep abreast of AirLand Battle Doctrine

The term AirLand Battle Doctrine has become familiar to most engineer NCOs and officers. Leaders at all levels must now make it more than a familiar term. We must study, understand, and train in this new doctrine.

Over the past several years the training and doctrine community has been working hard to develop and publish doctrinal revisions. The Engineer School has been a full partner in this effort. In the coming months, a new series of doctrinal manuals will be published detailing engineer doctrine for the AirLand Battle. This new doctrine is needed because of technological advances and the nature of our potential adversaries.

The U.S. Army is facing a threat in which the potential enemy not only possesses superior numbers but has also closed the technological gap in terms of weapon systems' capability and lethality. The next decade will be marked by a continuing flow of significant changes to the U.S. Army's equipment, organizations, and doctrine. It will be a time when all of us are challenged to not only keep abreast of the demands of our day to day missions but to also read, study, and incorporate the new tactics, techniques and procedures that will allow us to simultaneously exploit the capabilities of our equipment and organizations and the weaknesses of the enemy's.

Several years ago it became clear to the Army's leaders that we could not win future wars from a defensive posture as prescribed in the "active defense" doctrine of a few years past. The only way to successfully operate against a threat that has the capability to employ its attacking fo echelon is to carefully coordinate and synch all elements of the U.S. forces toward creati and seizing the initiative. AirLand Battle doctrine, published in FM 100-5, Operations establishes guidelines for the Army and des how commanders can most effectively use al resources at his disposal. It is a doctrine tha depends upon initiative, depth, agility, and synchronization. The successful commander rely heavily upon these basic tenents of AirI Battle doctrine.

The combined arms team will continue to backbone of our land forces. The outcome o AirLand Battle will depend heavily on how the task force commander coordinates, plan uses the fighting resources at his disposal. engineer plays a key role determining the s of the combined arms team. I challenge eac engineer officer, noncommissioned officer, soldier to ready, study, and understand Air Battle doctrine and its implications and, m importantly, to train with the combined ar team at every opportunity.

This issue of ENGINEER contains a syn the extensive doctrinal effort at Ft. Belvoir have worked very hard to implement AirL Battle doctrine into the major battlefield functions of the combat engineer. Writing publishing a workable doctrine is not an en itself. It must be read, practiced, and impr upon as better ways to accomplish things a discovered. You are the key to this process. welcome your comments and suggestions a depend upon you to determine and help us "what works best."

This is the last issue of ENGINEER wit John Florence as the editor. His efforts hav ENGINEER a readable, informative, and publication. Mr. Florence will be missed. him success in his new job in the Second A Public Affairs Office.

y CSM O.W. Troesch Jr., U.S. Army Engineer Center & School

)octrine—The Key to Quality Training

s NCOs, we must apply the principles of octrine to our daily training and activities

With so many abbreviations and acronyms used in e Army, many of us noncommissioned officers shy vay from learning what these terms really mean and ɔw we can apply them to our daily "Sergeant's usiness."

Consider the terms: AirLand Battle; Army 21; TM)0-5; FM 5-100; battle drills, crew drills; doctrine; ɔctrinal literature and its "application to the modern ıttlefield." And what about mobility, countermobility, ıd survivability?

As noncommissioned officers, we have a great need to nderstand these terms and to be familiar with FM)0-5, *Operations*, and FM 5-100, *Engineer Combat perations*. Both manuals describe the engineer's ıvolvement on the AirLand Battlefield. We must tailor ıd conduct our training to include this AirLand Battle ɔctrine as we prepare to fight and win.

"Doctrine" is merely a philosophy or theory of how to ·ganize and fight. FM 100-5 explains in detail nploying both air and land forces, hence the title \irLand Battle." In addition, it uses "combined arms" ıther than the traditional terms of "combat arms," ɔmbat support," and "combat service support."

It wasn't until recently while in Europe that I really nderstood what combined arms means. During a visit ı a DISCOM (division support command) element, I ɔticed their motto, "Try Fighting the Next War /ithout Us." How true that simple statement is—and ɔw important it is for us as noncommissioned officers ı understand it and to apply it to the doctrine in FM)0-5.

Just as important is FM 5-100, Engineer Combat perations. This manual should become our reference ɔok for everything we do in preparing and conducting ·aining—including FTXs and MAPEXs, as well as ıpporting maneuver units in combined exercises. FM ·100 defines the terms mobility, countermobility, and ırvivability. When used properly, the manual assists ı in defining our responsibilities and role in the irLand Battle and how to apply current engineer ɔctrine to all of our training activities.

Here are brief definitions for mobility, countermobility, and survivability. A more detailed discussion is in the 1984 version of FM 5-100.

a. MOBILITY—As engineers, one of our roles on the battlefield is to permit freedom of movement for our maneuver and combat support elements. We do this by employing obstacles, by locating bypasses to enemy emplaced obstacles, or by neutralizing obstacles quickly and efficiently.

b. COUNTERMOBILITY—Another major role of engineers is to detain, channelize, or disrupt enemy movement by using barriers and obstacles in conjunction with natural terrain.

c. SURVIVABILITY—We take measures as individuals and as units to survive on the battlefield. As engineers, we help to ensure the survival of our fellow soldiers, equipment, and units. Only by surviving on the battlefield can we expect to win.

So how does AirLand Battle, FM 100-5, FM 5-100, and mobility, countermobility, and survivability relate to Sergeant's Business?"

Sergeant's Business is, first and foremost, training soldiers and units for war. It entails a thorough knowledge of weapon systems, maintenance, and units' tactical strengths and weaknesses. To properly conduct Sergeant's Business, we have to understand how our commanders plan to support maneuver forces and fight battles.

The more common definition of Sergeant's Business pertains to garrison type duties such as barracks, formations, PMCS, and common skills training. While not entirely an inappropriate definition, it still does not cover all of the tings you need to know in order to become a proficient engineer NCO.

I suggest that Sergeant's Business is a combination of both definitions with a heavy dose of doctrine.

Once we learn and understand the doctrine of how to fight, we will be able to apply it while training and preparing our soldiers and units. I urge each NCO to be a part of "bridging the gap" by using doctrine in their daily business of running the Army, training our soldiers, and supporting our commanders.

School News

Directorate of Training and Doctrine (DOTD)

TM 5-232 Revision: Training-developers at the Engineer School's Topographic Engine ing Branch are revising TM 5-232, *Elements of Survey.* This revisioı necessary because of new equipment being fielded with ı Topographic Support System. While maintaining the accurε standards of the current manual, the new version will include revis portions of TM 5-441, *Geodetic and Topographic Surveying.* TM 5-4 will become obsolete when the new TM-232 becomes available to trc units. TM 5-242 is scheduled for review in the field in early 1986 a for publication in mid-1987.

ITEP Brochure Available: To aid Engineer commanders in understanding the Individ Training and Evaluation Program (ITEP), the Engineer Sch decided to take the program to commanders via the Engine Commanders' Training Conference held in December 1983. A boc prepared by the SQT Branch was set up in the display area. excellent brochure explaining the ITEP was made available to conference participants to read and distribute to their subordina Copies of this informative brochure are available on request. Write Commandant, U.S. Army Engineer School, ATTN: ATZA-TD- (Mr. Munoz), Fort Belvoir, VA 22060.

Directorate of Evaluation and Standardization (DOES)

USAES Graduates Evaluation: Under the Engineer School's Evaluation Program, DOES develo a new evaluation approach which will provide systematic feedback Engineer school training programs. The emphasis will be on Advanced Individual Training and Primary Technical Courses. engineer units which receive graduates from courses taught at Belvoir and at Ft. Leonard Wood will be affected.

Under this program, DOES will mail surveys to a representat number of recent course graduates and their immediate supervis Responses to the survey will indicate the degree to which Engin School graduates meet the needs of field units. Specific survey for are being developed for each MOS course. Several of these sur forms already developed are currently being validated. When finish the surveys will be sent to field units. These surveys will help Engineer School meet the soldiers' needs by providing an opportun for the soldiers and their leaders to improve Engineer training.

irectorate of raining and Doctrine (continued)

Language Training for Europe-Bound: During his recent trip to Europe, MG Ellis, Commandant of the Engineer School, identified as a problem that facilities engineers and directors of engineering and housing (DEHs) bound for Europe do not receive language training before reporting for duty overseas. The Engineer Proponency Office is requesting that TRADOC coordinate with the Defense Language Institute (DLI) on including FE and DEH personnel in their language training program. Because of the amount of contact DEH and FE personnel have with Europeans, the DLI program will be more beneficial to them than the in-country Gateway Language Program which teaches very basic conversational skills.

irectorate of ombat Developments (DCD)

Countermine Update: The Track Width Mine Roller with an M-60 tank mounting kit was type-classified "standard" during a special in-process review on Nov. 22, 1983. The Belvoir R&D Center sent the roller to the Tank-Automotive Command for production contracting. The roller will be field in for June 1985.

Department of Combined Arms (DCA)

DCA Summary: The Department of Combined Arms (DCA) became a separate training department under the new Engineer School model in October 1983. Aside from transferring logistic instruction to the newly formed Department of Maintenance, DCA remains unchanged. DCA provides instruction in tactics, combined arms operations, combat and threat intelligence, leadership, training management, military history, communicative arts, communications electronics and personnel management.

Many new initiatives will affect DCA this year. These include involvement with the Engineer Captains' Training Team's development of the new EOAC (to be implemented in October 1984;) implementation of the ENCOA common core curriculum, developed by the Sergeant Majors' Academy; implementation of the Lieutenant's Leadership Common Core Curriculum, developed by the Center for Leadership at the Command and General Staff College; and the revision of the Battalion and Brigade Commanders' Pre-Command Course.

School News

Department of Combined Arms (continued)

Pre-Command Course: Personnel within the Department of Combined Arms (DC/ coordinate and conduct the Engineer Brigade Group and Battalic Pre-Command Curse (PCC). Recently, DCA personnel worked coordination with the Director of PCC, at the Command and Gener Staff College (CGSC), in an effort to develop a pre-command cour experience for all brigade, group, and battalion command selectee The thrust of the development effort is to provide them with a cour that will thoroughly and appropriately prime them for success as commander in a combined arms Army. Now, the remainder of tl TRADOC community is involved in the development effort th began at the Engineer School.

Department of Maintenance (DOM)

DOM Summary: The Department of Maintenance was established as the Engine School's third academic department within the Engineer School (January 4, 1984, with LTC Roger C. Strom as director. T department provides Advanced Individual Training instruction power generation equipment repair, utilities equipment repair, a turbine engine driven repair. The department also provid maintenance and logistical management training to officers attendir EOBC, EOAC, the Engineer Senior Officer Course, Engine Warrant Officer Advanced Course, and to the noncommission officers attending the Engineer ANCOC. Besides providir instruction, the department also develops lesson plans offers academ counseling, and provides training evaluation. The department w designated as the worldwide point of contact for engineer maintenanc

Department of Military Engineering (DME)

USAES Systems Software Catalog: The Engineer School has compiled a catalog of available AI software. These programs, the majority of which are written in IB (versus BASIC) language, range from theater of operations road a airfield design to tactical rafting operations planning. The basis f the programs are the current TMs and FMs applicable to the subje material. Requests for copies of the catalog should be sent Commandant, U.S. Army Engineer School, ATTN: ATZA-TE-E Ft. Belvoir, VA 22060.

ENGINEER DOCTRINE FOR THE AIRLAND BATTLE

by COL William C. Burns, LTC Larry Wood, and Mr. Hap Hambric

"Doctrine" is a term that conjures up a diverse collection of images; everything from a martinet blindly following set procedures and rules, to a collection of directives in a dusty book that are seldom used because they bear little relation to the realities facing the commander on the ground. The truth, of course, is that doctrine lies somewhere in between.

U.S. Army doctrine establishes the fundamental principles, procedures and techniques by which our forces operate in order to accomplish the mission. Although doctrine is authorative and represents the best professional judgment available, common sense is necessary in its application. It should be neither followed blindly nor ignored, but studied and understood by the professional soldier.

Doctrine is not static. It must be continually adjusted to take advantage of changes in technology and weapon capabilities. In response to improved target aquisition systems and the lethality of weapons being introduced into both allied and threat force armies, the United States Army has revised its basic war fighting doctrine. The new doctrine, called "AirLand Battle", is presented in the 1982 version of FM 100-5, *Operations*.

AirLand Battle doctrine stresses combined arms operations over large areas. Combat operations to defeat the threat will be conducted in the rear, close-in, and deep battle areas. Relative force size and weapon capabilities dictated significantly increased engineer requirements to ensure the friendly force's freedom to maneuver throughout the battlefield. The requirement to impede enemy movement and to protect key installations also has increased significantly and will continue to increase as threat mobility and weapon lethality improve.

Although much of what a combat engineer must do remains the same, the emphasis on timing, on location, and on certain tasks was altered. It was evident that Engineer Doctrine would have to be extensively updated to meet the challenge posed by the threat force's capabilities, and to accommodate the requirements of our own forces' combined arms operations.

In response, the Engineer School developed the Engineer keystone manual, FM 5-100, *Engineer Combat Operations*. This manual presents the overall doctrinal framework for engineer support to the AirLand Battle. Seven other FM 5-100 series manuals which expand and elaborate the doctrinal framework contained in FM 5-100 are being developed. Together, these eight manuals will contain the fundamental doctrine describing how the engineers will support the combined arms team in the AirLand Battle. Although the doctrine is based upon current equipment and resource constraints, it clearly provides the rationale for equipment development. The following articles on pages 13 to 18 are a synoposis of the significant doctrinal points in the coordinating drafts of the first four of these manuals. These are all points of which the professional combat engineer should be aware. The production schedule for the FM 5-100 series manuals is shown in Figure 1.

The engineers in the field play a key role in doctrine development. First, they must learn the doctrine; secondly, they must teach it to others; and finally, they must practice the doctrine in training. It is the application of doctrine in exercises that validates that doc-

FM 5-100 SERIES PRODUCTION SCHEDULE

NUMBER	SUBJECT AREA	COORD DRAFT PUB	MANUAL PUB
FM 5-100	Engineer Combat Operations	FY82	FY84
FM 5-101	Mobility	FY83	FY84
FM 5-102	Countermobility	FY83	FY84
FM 5-103	Survivability	FY83	FY85
FM 5-104	General Engineering	FY84	FY85
FM 5-105	Topography	FY85	FY86
FM 5-106	ADM	FY86	FY87

Figure 1

ENGINEER'S MAIN BATTLEFIELD MISSIONS

MOBILITY
Countermine
Counterobstacle
Gap Crossing
Combat Roads and Trails
Forward Aviation Combat Engineering

COUNTERMOBILITY
Mine Warfare
Obstacle Development

SURVIVABILITY
Fighting Positions
Protective Emplacement
Protective Support Facilities

GENERAL ENGINEERING
Lines of Communication Construction and Repair
Logistics Facilities Support
Area Damage Control
Construction Material Production

TOPOGRAPHY
Terrain Analysis
Map Production and Distribution

Figure :

trine. The engineer school is heavily dependent on combat engineers in the field to validate and provide changes to doctrine.

FM 5-100, *Engineer Combat Operations*, provides combat unit commanders and their staff with information pertaining to the role of the engineer in combined arms operations. It defines and expands on the engineer tasks, missions, and responsibilities outlined in FM 100-5, *Operations*. Battlefield missions of the engineers are placed in the five mission categories shown in Figure 2.

Before expanding upon the three primary functions—mobility, countermobility, and survivability—a review on how FM 5-100 outlines the engineers' role in conducting of the AirLand Battle is in order.

The key to providing responsive engineer support is two-fold. Firs engineer planning must be inte grated into each stage of develop ment of the maneuver commander' tactical plan. Second, command an control of supporting engineers mus be structured to provide effectiv responsive engineer support to th combined arms team.

Any Suggestions?

No engineer performs his task in isolation. He works as a member of the combined arms team to help the commander accomplish the mission.

Neither can an engineer field manual be written in isolation. The Engineer School retains the primary responsibility for the development of Engineer doctrine. However, extensive planning and coordination is necessary to produce any doctrinal product.

Engineer doctrine is written primarily by the instructors teaching the relevant subject matter. With the Engineer School's responsibility for over 160 field and technical manuals, this is no small task. Before a field manual is published, a coordinating draft is distributed to field units for comments. Each comment is reviewed and incorporated, as appropriate, into the final version of the manual. Since soldiers in units tend to develop unique solutions to common problems, ideas and techniques from the field for accomplishing engineering tasks are important in developing manuals, and training and field circulars. Doctrinal and technical publications are a way to share these good solutions.

If you are not sure where to send your idea, send it to the Engineer School's Doctrinal Literature Management Office, Stop 163, Fort Belvoir, VA 22060. They will ensure that the right people review your suggestion.

Integrate Planning

In the past, many commander tended to develop their scheme o manuever, their fire support plan and their engineer support plan in linear sequence. Warfare concept that place high reliance on maneu ver, in turn place emphasis o effective engineer support. Plannin these three elements, therefore, mus be totally integrated and occu together. To help encourage mor integrated planning, FM 5-100 con tains an entire chapter on enginee staff planning. The intent is fo engineers to provide better infor mation to the commander durin the decision-making process.

One of the significant organ zational changes that affects th engineer's planning is includin brigade and regimental enginee elements in the cavalry regiments separate brigades, and the J-serie heavy division.

In these units, the brigade o

bat, commanders will probably use attachment and operational control more, and use direct support relatively less than before.

FM 5-100 touches on general engineering work within the corps area regarding supporting combat operations. Most general engineering tasks will be done by theater army engineers in support of combat service support operations at echelons above corps. FM 5-104, *General Engineering*, which is being written now, will contain the doctrine for the general engineering.

The need for terrain information on the AirLand Battlefield will be greater than ever before. Major changes are required in topographic engineer support. The concept is to give division and corps level terrain detachments the capability to rapidly meet requirements for terrain and digital terrain data.

A new manual, FM 5-105, *Topographic Operations*, is being developed to provide the topographic unit commander, the maneuver commander, and the maneuver unit's intelligence and operations staff officers with a field reference on terrain analysis and topographic support. Work has just begun on this manual and a coordinating draft is scheduled for delivery to the field in fiscal year 1986.

Infantry & RAP Missions

Although engineers provide the greatest combat power by performing their five functional missions, they retain a secondary mission to fight as infantry.

To assume an infantry role, combat engineer units must be augmented with additional weapons, fire support teams and communications systems. The commander's decision to use engineers as infantry must take into account the long term loss in the overall combat power to the maneuver force because of the lack of engineer mobility, countermobility, and survivability support.

When employed as infantry, combat engineers are best suited for defensive missions but could be effective in the offense in bypass or hasty attacks.

Rear area protection (RAP) is a major concern on the AirLand Battlefield. The rear area begins at the brigade rear boundary and extends through the communications zone (COMMZ). RAP functions include rear area combat operations and area damage control. A command responsibility for RAP must be fully integrated into plans and orders of each echelon from division through echelons above corps.

Engineers will provide support to RAP operations on a task or OPCON basis as prearranged or designated by the appropriate commander. During emergency situations, engineers in the rear may be tasked by rear area commanders to directly support RAP operations regardless of their mission prior to the emergency. This includes not only engineer units within a particular area, but those passing through as well. Engineers at each echelon are integrated into RAP planning and assist the rear area commander and the rear area operations center (RAOC) in planning defenses and in conducting area damage control (ADC) operations. On the AirLand Battlefield, engineers must be prepared to provide their own security in bivouac, on the march, or at work sites. Separate security forces are not expected to be available except at the most critical sites.

There are some changes in engineer support at echelons above corps. The theater army engineer is the senior engineer on the theater army staff. The engineer command commander coordinates and supervises the operations of engineer units which are neither attached nor assigned to other commands within the COMMZ.

MOBILITY

AirLand Battle doctrine emphasizes mobility. It is essential that combat engineers be prepared to preserve the combat freedom of movement for manuever and combat support elements. The traditional

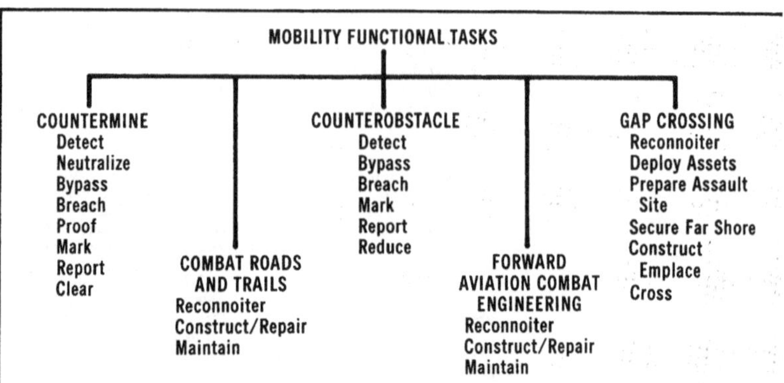

Figure 3

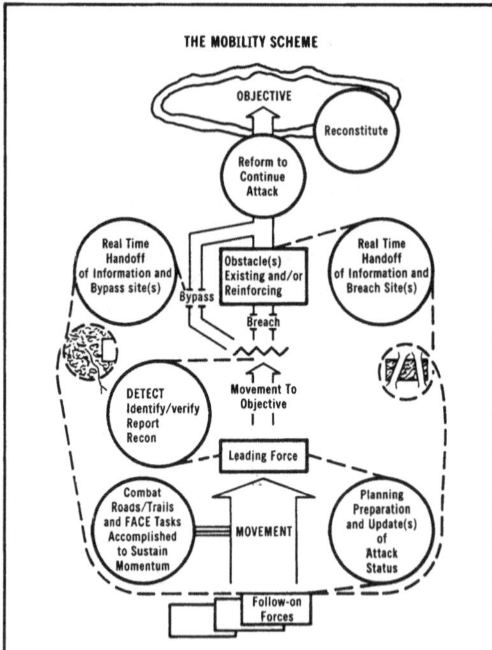

Figure 4

mobility tasks have been placed in five functional mission areas shown on Figure 3.

Throughout the battlefield, the combined arms team and support units can expect to be confronted by a variety of existing and reinforcing obstacles. The latter may have been employed by either friendly or enemy units.

To be successful in overcomin these obstacles, maneuver force com manders must plan for and provid their units with a "mobility system capable of bypassing or neutralizin obstacles quickly and routinel while continuing to provide all othe forms of combat engineer support t the force.

Preplanning and proper use o intelligence is the key to successfu mobility operations. These factor ensure the maneuver task force i properly equipped and prepared t counter obstacles and minefield The maneuver force organized t overcome obstacles contains thre separate forces:

- The support force: Normally th lead element which encounter the obstacle and then deploys t overwatch positions.
- The breaching force: Normall comprised of maneuver and en gineer elements. It conducts th breach and secures the far side o the obstacle.
- The assault force: Comprised o the forces necessary to attack th

objective. This element attacks through or around the obstacle but remains oriented on the objective.

Doctrine developed for overcoming obstacles emphasizes the importance of locating combat engineers and engineer equipment well forward in the formation. When an obstacle is encountered, the leading force will request immediate suppressive fires, move into overwatch positions, and will become the support force base.

Scouts will reconnoiter the limits of the minefield or obstacle, looking for a way to bypass it. The engineers and dismounted infantry will reconnoiter the obstacle to determine neutralizing requirements. If bypassing is possible, this action is taken quickly. If it cannot be bypassed, the minefield or obstacle is hastily breached and the assualt continues. If the hasty attempt fails, a deliberate breach must be conducted.

Obstacles will be overcome one-by-one as they are encountered. Overcoming a complex obstacle and a large defending force will require extensive assets and effort. A simple obstacle or a complex obstacle poorly defended could be overcome using hasty breaching techniques requiring no engineer support except for readily available counterobstacle hardware such as the armored vehicle launched bridge. Larger, more complex or well defended obstacles might require a deliberate breach and will take considerably longer than a hasty breach.

Breaching and neutralizing minefields and obstacles, and crossing wet and dry gaps are a large part of the engineers' mobility responsibility. However, combat road and trail construction, and forward aviation combat engineering (FACE) missions will also place a large demand on the forces' engineers. The philosophy of the AirLand Battle's deep attack will require extensive engineer support to provide the mobility support necessary for units to thrust deep, conduct the attack, and to return safely before being/decisively engaged by the enemy. If the attack is successful in displacing the FEBA forward, the engineers must be prepared to upgrade roads and trails to aid combat support and combat service support mobility requirements.

FM 5-101, *Mobility*, scheduled for distribution to the field in December 1984, describes engineer mobility support to the combined arms team. It summarizes the doctrine and procedures manuever elements and engineers need to form a mobility system capable of overcoming any obstacle on the AirLand Battlefield.

COUNTERMOBILITY

Throughout history, countermobility has played an important role in military conflict. The degree of countermobility success, however, has not always matched the degree of effort expended. The lack of effectiveness of the Maginot Line in World War II is one of many notable examples.

Many factors contribute to making countermobility operations a success or failure. Almost always, the very basic factors are the most critical. Various combinations of time, material and equipment, firepower, terrain, and enemy knowledge and capabilities are normally the factors causing a countermobility effort to succeed or fail.

The advent of AirLand Battle doctrine and technological improvements have significantly changed how, where, and when countermobility efforts will be performed.

AirLand Battle doctrine emphasizes mobility and the ability to maneuver throughout the battlefield. Therefore, maneuver commanders must make conscious and difficult countermobility decisions regarding the need to stop, to delay, and to channelize the enemy, yet still retain the ability to move freely in the future. Naturally, this tradeoff will not occur in every situation, but commanders must carefully consider their own future mobility needs when emplacing obstacles, especially minefields.

Mine Warfare

Mine warfare is changing rapidly, yet the engineer remains the principal advisor to the commander on mine warfare. However, with improved mines and delivery systems, there is a need to clarify the definitions and role of mines in the AirLand Battlefield. We now have two categories of mines: conventional and scatterable.

Conventional mines do not self-destruct and are emplaced by hand or by mechanical mine planters. Conventional mines can be emplaced in classical patterns, or be emplaced randomly if the tactical situation dictates. Scatterable mines are delivered by ground system, artillery, helicopter, or high performance aircraft and contain a self-destruct mechanism.

If properly planned and employed, the family of scatterable mines provides the best of both worlds because they have a preselected self-destruct time. The commander can reap the benefits of a minefield which has slowed, stopped, or channelized the enemy, and then attack through the same area after the mines have self-destructed. Scatterable mines are smaller, more lethal, and can be emplaced remotely and much more rapidly than conventional mines.

With conventional mines, the only decision to be made is whether to mine or not to mine. With scatterable mines, the self-destruct time and the delivery method are additional factors that require decisions. Scatterable mines give the commander the flexibility to employ mines quickly anywhere on the battlefield, to employ them on short notice, and to place them in tactically critical locations based upon enemy movement.

Reporting FASCAM Munitions

Reporting and recording the use of the family of scatterable mines (FASCAM) is particularly important

MINEFIELD EMPLOYMENT AND AUTHORITY DELEGATION

TYPE MINEFIELD	MINEFIELD EMPLOYMENT AUTHORITY
Minefield containing Scatterable mines	Corps commander is the employment authority for all minefields containing scatterable mines within the corps area of operations.
Long duration (24 hours or more)	Corps commander. May delegate employment authority to division level. Division may further delegate to brigade level.
Short duration (less than 24 hours)	Same as long duration except authority may be further delegated to battalion or task force level.

Figure 5

SCATTERABLE MINEFIELD REPORT AND RECORD

LINE	INFORMATION REQUIRED	DATA
1	Approving authority	CDR 3AD
2	TGT/obstacle #	2XXX0157
3	Type emplacing system	ARTY
4	Type mines	AT/AP
5	Self destruct period	08161 OZ - 081900Z Oct 82
6	Aim PT/corner PTs of minefield	MB 01012935
7		
8		
9		
10		
11		
12		
13		
14		
15	Size safety zone from aim point	500M
16	Unit emplacing mines/RPT #	2/48FA/2
17	Person completing RPT	SFC Hollins
18	DTG of report	061645 Oct 82
19	Remarks	N/A

Figure

on a battlefield where the emphasis is on friendly force mobility. Plans for using mines must take into account the future maneuver scheme of the commander. FM 5-102, *Countermobility*, scheduled for publication in fiscal year 1985 will contain a detailed explanation of the employment, recording, and reporting procedures for both conventional and scatterable mines.

Scatterable mines require control, planning, and a rapid and accurate reporting system. Commanders who control scatterable mine use must positively delegate authority to employ the mines based upon the current tactical situation and his future plans. The employment authority and delegation levels are shown in Figure 4.

In addition to positive control, fast and accurate reporting is critically important when using scatterable mines. Figure 4 shows *The Scatterable Minefield Report and Record*. This reporting method is to be used regardless of the mine delivery system. In the example, artillery delivered scatterable mines were used.

Minefield information can be passed quickly by radio, posted to operations maps, and disseminated to units which need the information. The unit emplacing the minefield will initiate the report by radio and follow up with a written copy of *The Scatterable Minefield Report & Record*.

Locations for scatterable minefields should be planned as far ahead of their actual need as possible in advance. Prior planning will help ensure that the logistic requirements are met and that the mines are prestocked. It ensures that mines can be delivered rapidly in response to the tactical situation. Scatterable mines offer great flexibility and, when used in conjunction with other countermobility efforts such as conventional minefields, road craters, and tank ditches, they create tremendous mobility problems for the enemy. More significantly they create command and control problems for the enemy because of the constantly changing obstacle situation facing the enemy commander and his staff.

This aggravation of enemy command and control supports a key precept of AirLand Battle which places great importance on faster friendly assessment and reaction than the enemy assessment and reaction. In short, we "get inside his decision loop."

Even with these advantages, scatterable mines are not the panacea for all countermobility problems; the supply of scatterable mines will be limited and delivery systems will have competing requirements.

Existing and reinforcing obstacles are still important in both defensive and offensive operations. The engineer must identify the existing obstacles and integrate them into the obstacle plan. It is preferable to improve existing obstacles rather than to construct reinforcing ones. Reinforcing obstacles are grouped by design (constructed, demolition, and expedient). Mine warfare and obstacle planning must be accomplished concurrently with the commander's planning for maneuver and fire support.

For AirLand Battle doctrine to succeed, we must be able to disconnect enemy echelons and to provide the "windows of opportunity" necessary to assume the offense. Countermobility efforts that are well planned and well executed are a distinct asset that can strip away the enemy's most vital requirement, that of maintaining momentum and a high rate of combat operations.

The coordinating draft of FM 5-102, *Countermobility*, was sent to the field for comments in fiscal year 1984. The final manual is due to be published in fiscal year 1985.

SURVIVABILITY

Unlike the other engineer battlefield missions, survivability is a principle concern of each soldier regardless of his job or location on the battlefield. Camouflaging personnel and equipment, employing deception, ensuring operations security, and building individual and weapons system protective positions are only a few of the tasks that come under the broad category of survivability.

Although survivability on the battlefield encompasses a wide spectrum of activities, the engineer's responsibilities to the maneuver commander are focused primarily upon building or improving protective positions for fighting vehicles, assistance in hardening command posts, and protecting combat support positions. New engineer equipment such as the armored combat earth mover (ACE), and the small emplacement excavator (SEE) will improve the engineers mobility and capability to support the maneuver commander.

As with mobility and countermobility, each course of action must be evaluated in terms of survivability and recommendations made to the commander regarding the type and level of survivability support required. The commander must establish priorities and determine the percentage of the available engineer effort to devote to survivability. In preparing survivability estimates, the engineer must know the quantity and types of equipment in the unit he is supporting, the capability of his own equipment, and the tactical situation. All types of engineer estimates should begin with an unconstrained assessment, that is, plan what is required without considering limiting factors. This method gives the commander a good feel of what is necessary. It also gives him a baseline from which he can ask for additional engineer support and begin setting priorities. The bottom line is that the maneuver commander cannot make the proper decisions unless he is provided with good estimates and alternatives.

There are several doctrinal guidelines to adhere to when preparing the survivability estimate and establishing priority of effort. They are:

- Field units have primary responsibility for developing, positioning, and initial construction of survivability structures.
- Engineer support is used to supplement the efforts of supported units based on availability and the commander's priorities.
- Engineer support must be concentrated on missions requiring unique engineer skills or equipment.
- The sequence of survivability work is to: use concealment measures, natural cover, construction, and finally, to continuously improve protection.

In addition, the commanders survivability plan must take into account each of the following points, which are critical to allocating effort and establishing priorities:

- Exposure to fire—direct and in direct, tactical air.
- Vulnerability to discovery and location.
- Mobility requirements.
- Protection from tanks.
- Distance from the forward line of troops (FLOT).
- Availability of natural cover.
- Redundancy—the importance of a unique equipment items, the loss of which would degrade other equipment.
- The enemy's engagement priority.

In the defense, substantial effort is required for fighting and protective position construction. General priorities for protective construction in a defensive battle position are:

- Antitank weapons.
- Tank positions.
- Armored personnel carriers.
- Command post position hardening.
- Combat support position hardening, (including, for example, field and air defense artillery, and mortar positions).
- Individual fighting positions, crew-served weapon positions, and covered routes between battle positions.

Although generally thought of as applicable to the defense only, survivability also applies to offensive operations.

During the offensive, protective fighting positions are developed whenever time is adequate, such as during a temporary halt for regrouping and consolidation.

Recommended priorities for protection at a halt in the offense are: antitank weapons, indirect fire weapons, and critical supplies (ammunition and POL). These should be expedient positions with frontal and side protection and make maximum use of the terrain.

Special situations, such as contingency operations, combined operations, and operations in special terrain require special considerations in performing survivability tasks. The planner must account for local support agreements, harsh climate and difficult terrain, shortage of materials, availability of local equipment and use of existing structures.

Performing survivability tasks in mountains, deserts, cold regions, jungle areas, and in urban areas often requires great innovation on the part of the engineers. Construction may be difficult, if not impossible, using conventional methods and equipment. Knowledge must be quickly developed on special construction techniques, such as explosive excavation, or use of snow and ice as construction materials. Knowledge of how to use special terrain features, and the ability to identify and use specific urban structures is critical. Certain existing structures can provide protection to the force with minimum construction by supporting engineers.

Implementation of Specific Positions

After the commander has established priorities, construction of specific protective positions and structures can begin. These positions must be designed, located, and constructed based on the tactical plan as well as cover and concealment requirements. These develop from an analysis of threat weapon and acquisition capability, and by the availability of materials and manpower. Furthermore, position design must consider the physical characteristics of the threat weapon

COL William C. Burns is chief of the Project Management Office, Directorate of Training and Doctrine, U.S. Army Engineer School. He will assume command of the Rock Island Engineer District this summer. COL Burns is a graduate of the U.S. Army War College, has an MBA from Long Island University, a master's degree in operations research from the Naval Post Graduate School, and a bachelor's degree from the U.S. Military Academy. COL Burns is a registered professional engineer in Virginia.

LTC Larry Wood is the Chief of the Doctrinal Literature Management Office at the Engineer School. He has a master's degree from the University of Utah and is a graduate of the Command and General Staff College. He has served with various engineer troop units in Vietnam, Germany and CONUS.

Mr. Hap Hambric is a retired engineer officer. He is a graduate of the Engineer Officer Advanced Course and has a degree in computer science from the University of Southern Mississippi. Mr. Hambric currently serves as a doctrine development analyst in the U.S. Army Engineer School's Doctrinal Literature Management Office.

Engineer Solution

1. Enter Figure 6-7 (TM 5-312) or Figure 7-7 (FM 5-34) with stringer spacing 5′ = 60″. Read up to curve representing class 50-150 and across to vertical scale. Obtain required effective deck thickness (t_{dr} = 7.8″).

2. **Plank Decking**

Generally, if required thickness is greater than 6″, it is more efficient to use laminated decking. Nevertheless, if plank decking is desired it will have to be multilayer plank deck.

Therefore:

t_{act} (actual thickness) = t_{eff} (effective thickness) + 2″
= 7.8″ + 2 = 9.8″ actual thickness required

Selections "**c**" and "**d**" do not provide the thickness required for multilayer plank decking.

3. **Laminated decking**

Lamination percentage required, using 3″ x 10″ material, is calculated as follows:

$$\% \text{ lamination required} = \frac{t_{dr}}{t_{act}}(100) = \frac{7.8}{10}(100) = 7.8\% \text{ lamination required}$$

Answer "**a**" not adequate.

Lamination percentage required, using 4″ x 12″ material, is calculated as follows:

$$\% \text{ lamination required} = \frac{t_{dr}}{t_{act}}(100) = \frac{7.8}{12}(100) = 65\% \text{ lamination required}$$

Answer "**b**", 66 2/3% using 4″ x 12″ material, provides required lamination.

Planning Engineer ARTEP's *(the Easy Way)*

By CPT John A. Durkin

Preparing for an ARTEP (Army Training Evaluation Program) exercise is one of the challenging tasks faced several times a year by all battalion commanders and their staffs. Battalion staffs, however, often lack the time to properly coordinate with each other for planning major events like ARTEPs.

A planning tool that has worked well for ARTEP preparation in the 130th Engineer Brigade is the OMR (Outcomes, Methods, Resources) model. The OMR model is a systematic and simple approach designed to assist commanders and their staffs in planning. It is particularly useful as a staff-training exercise.

The OMR model helps the planner visualize and keep abreast of the planning process. Involving everyone concerned in the planning process, the model uses the "backward planning" approach in which the planners state their desired outcomes first.

Planners must answer the question: "What should our final results or outcomes be?" These results should be defined in specific, measurable terms. The planners then decide on the steps needed to achieve desired outcomes by answering the question: "How are we going to obtain these outcomes?" Finally, the planners consider the materials and resources needed to accomplish the steps by asking, "What resources do we need to carry out our plan?"

This is easy to achieve provided you give it some thought.

The OMR model is best illustrated by an example, the 549th Engineer Battalion's ARTEP planning. The battalion, located in Schwetzinger, Germany, consists of a headquarters and headquarters detachment (HHD) and two subordinate companies—the 541st Engineer Company (MAB), and the 959th Labor Service Company (Ribbon).

First, a planning session was held using the OMR model. The battalion executive officer, the S3, and the remainder of the staff (including staff NCOICs) attended the session. The brigade's organizational effectiveness officer acted as a facilitator and recorder.

Outcomes

The first step was to decide on goals. The staff asked itself, "What do we want to achieve during the evaluation period and how do we measure the terms?" The staff decided that one measure of success would be to evaluate itself and each company on certain tasks.

Each staff member then reviewed the ARTEP manual and isolated the tasks to be evaluated at the company and battalion levels. The lists were consolidated and approved by the battalion executive officer. The end product consisted of a list of tasks to be evaluated and the staff sections to evaluate them. Figure 1 shows part of the list.

The staff also decided to include as goals certain items not specifically outlined in the ARTEP manual. For example, one goal was to have no personal or vehicle accidents and another was to develop standard staff briefings for all future ARTEPs.

COMPANY TASK LIST

		MAB Co	RIBBON Co
(1)	PERFORM COMMAND & CONTROL FUNCTIONS		
1-1	Operate a network control station (NCS)	S3	S3
1-2	Establish and conduct radio communications	S3	
1-4	Install wire communications net	S3	
(2)	PERFORM ADIM & LOGISTICS FUNCTIONS		
2-1	Conduct unit supply operations	S4	S4
2-2	Establish a field kitchen	S4	S4
2-3	Operate a field kitchen	S4	S4
2-4	Supervise equipment maintenance	S4	S4/S3
2-5	Establish a unit motor pool	S4	S4
2-6	Establish a direct support maintenance shop operations		
2-7	Provide internal prescribed load list (PLL) support	S4	S4
2-8	Establish production and quality control procedures for maintenance operations	S4	S4
2-12	Perform field sanitation functions	S1	S1
2-16	Prepare and verify, if possible, casualty feeder report, (CFR), and witness statements on individuals	S1	S1
2-18	Prepare, verify, correct, complete and forward CFR and witness statements on individuals		
2-20	Orient replacements		
2-21	Initiate and maintain personnel data	S1	S1
2-22	Prep personnel daily summary (PDS)	S1	S1
2-23	Provide mail service		

Figure 1

FEBRUARY 1983 MILESTONE LIST

1 Feb	S-1	Request medics; communications (2 radios and 2 CEOIs); transportation from S-4; additional typewriters from S-4
4 Feb	S-3	Request crossing traffic
5 Feb	S-3	Request for telephone
10 Feb	S-4	Request transportation support (503rd)
10 Feb	S-4	Establish water point/refueling point/supply point
11 Feb	S-3	Request divers
11 Feb	S-3	Request air defense support
15 Feb	S-4	Request maintenance support (8592 Engr, 699 Ord.)
18 Feb	S-2	Order maps
20 Feb	S-3	Request river closures
25 Feb	S-3	Request smoke
25 Feb	S-3	Request signal security
25 Feb	S-4	Establish Class I account
25 Feb	XO	In process review
28 Feb	S-1	Request MOS inventory, personnel rosters and TOEs; suspense: 1 April
28 Feb	S-1	Fact sheet to units prescribing unit personnel report
28 Feb	S-4	Request reefer van
28 Feb	S-4	Coordinate with medical facilities

Figure 2

Knowing which tasks were to be evaluated, each staff section could concentrate on training its subordinates. The staffs could also estimate how much equipment support would be required.

Methods

The next step was to decide the best methods to run the evaluation. A scenario was developed by first having the S3 pencil-in the major events on a draft schedule. These included the date and time of deployment, major bridge missions, and rafting operations. Next, the S2 noted aggressor attacks and reconnaissance missions. The NBC NCO recorded NBC attacks and decontamination operations that would mesh with the schedule outlined by the S3 and S2.

The S1 and S4 also listed tasks to be evaluated. The S1 noted where casualties should be assessed so that casualty feeder reports would be forwarded; other personnel actions were also included. The S4 indicated where vehicles should be destroyed so that the units would be forced to requisition replacements during the prescribed resupply times.

The end product was a sensible scenario that included all the tasks developed during the "outcomes" portion of the session. All actions were coordinated and linked to other events in the scenario. All staff sections knew what actions for which they were responsible and how those actions fit into the overall plan.

Resources

The staff then analyzed and listed all the resources and materials required to support the plan. Based on this resource list and the plan, a milestone list was developed for each staff section. Milestones were established for every month prior to deployment. In addition, milestones were developed for items that would occur after the exercise such as the after-action report, letters of appreciation, and the maneuver damage report. Figure 2 shows the milestone list for February 1983.

End Results

By the end of the session, the staff had developed a list of tasks to be evaluated, the scenario, resource requirements, and a milestone list. The agenda is shown in Figure 3. Another benefit of the session was that it helped to promote communication among the staff. During the 549th's practice program, and later during the actual exercise using the ARTEP, the unit performed very well.

AGENDA

0900 — 0945	Introduction — OMR
0945 — 0955	Break
0955 — 1030	ARTEP Task list (each company)
1030 — 1130	Task list for Bn and Staff
1130 — 1230	Lunch
1230 — 1400	Scenario
1400 — 1410	Break
1410 — 1500	Milestone chart

Figure 3

Summary

By using the OMR model as a planning guide, the 549th Engineer Battalion saved much time and developed a well coordinated plan for a practice session using the ARTEP.

The same method was used at the 130th Engineer Brigade headquarters to plan exercises for the brigade's other battalions. Subordinate commanders and S3s were invited to participate in the planning session, and they were instrumental in developing the task lists and milestones.

The OMR model is an excellent planning tool. It encourages staff communication, organization, and involves the entire staff in the planning process. It is effective in planning for events as complex as Reforger exercises or as routine as change of command ceremonies.

CPT John A. Durkin is the S3, 559th Engineer Bn., 130th Engineer Bde., USAREUR. He has a bachelor's degree in chemical engineering and public affairs from Carnegie-Mellon University. He has served as a platoon leader with the 902nd Engineer Co., 11th Engineer Bn. (CBT) (HVY); a company commander with the 13th Engineer Co. (CS); and as the 130th Engineer Bde. organizational effectiveness officer.

EWOS Study Results

Improving Warrant Officer Professional Development

by the Engineer Warrant Officer Study Team, USAES

During 1983, the U.S. Army Engineer School reviewed the status of training development for all warrant officer career fields served by the School. The comprehensive project identified specific problems in Engineer warrant officer professional development and career utilization.

These problems included:

- Performance discrepancies by Engineer warrant officers
- Changes in doctrine affecting the use of Engineer warrant officers.
- Changes in organizational structures imposed by DIVISION 86 affecting warrant officers.
- The introduction of new equipment system and training devices being developed to support force modernization.
- Changes imposed by Army Training 1990 affecting the current training strategy.
- Common warrant officer training and utilization problems generated by identification of collective job/task analysis.

To determine how Engineer warrant officer professional development officers will be accomplished, the Engineer Warrant Officer Study (EWOS) was initiated on April 18, 1983, by the Engineer School's Directorate of Training and Doctrine and the Engineer Proponency Office.

In order to evaluate all the different warrant officer career fields and additional areas of consideration, the study used the consolidated analysis methodology of Criterion Referenced Instruction, Instructional Systems Development, and the Systems Approach to Training. The study was conducted in three phases: a needs assessment, the compilation of data, and analysis of two boards.

Compilation of Data

The results of the survey during the needs assessment were compiled during the compilation of data phase of the EWOS. Also, additional studies and proposals were gathered that affect on Engineer warrant officer professional development. The additional studies and proposals reviewed included the following:

- *The Commissioning of Warrant Officer Study.*
- *The Grading of Warrant Officer Positions Study.*
- *The Enlisted Personnel Management System Study.*
- *The Regular Military Warrant Officer Compensation Study.*
- *Warrant Officer Senior Course Revision.*
- *Warrant Officer Senior Course Position, ASI 4A Proposal.*
- *E7 to CW2 Proposal.*
- *Increased Requirements for Implementation of DIVISION 86.*
- *Army 21.*
- *Force Modernization.*
- *Army Training 1990.*

Needs Assessment

The needs assessment was conducted to verify the job analysis previously conducted by the Review of Education and Training for Officers (RETO) program. Additionally, the needs assessment validated the initial RETO task listing.

To accomplish the needs assessment, the study team evaluated the tasks performed by feeder enlisted MOSs against the warrant officer task list developed under RETO. A condensed task listing was developed, based on the previously validated task listing by the job incumbents under the RETO program and the feeder enlisted MOSs task listing.

This condensed list was used in a survey developed for warrant officer supervisors. In order to determine the importance of how each task was to be performed, the survey was developed with a two part rating. The first part identified the task by level of performance (NCO, warrant officer, or commissioned officer) and the second part determined the significance of warrant officer performance of each warrant officer task.

Analysis by Boards

The analysis of collected data was performed in two separate boarding actions. The first boarding action was the Specialty Task Board. The board was divided into three specialty boards for each of the major career fields: Utilities Operation and Maintenance—MOS 310A; Engineer Equipment Maintenance—MOS 621A; and Topographic Engineering MOSs 811A, 821A, 833A, and 841A. Each Specialty Task Board included several senior warrant officers from each career field.

The board members reviewed data and verified information collected during the needs assessment. Each board then developed a task listing based on the skill levels identified in the supervisor's survey and job incumbent survey. The Specialty Task Board then developed new descriptions based on the identified skill level requirements. The chairmen from the Specialty Task Boards presented their findings and represented their specialty on the Common Warrant Officer Analysis Board.

The Common Warrant Officer Analysis Board consisted of the

following: a chairman; representatives from the Directorate of Training and Doctrine; proponency, National Guard, and USAR personnel; an education specialist; a training systems specialist; the chairman from each Specialty Task Board; and a facilitator.

The Common Warrant Officer Analysis Board's work was divided into problem analysis, evaluation, and action planning. During the problem analysis phase, the board analyzed all data and input from the Specialty Task Board. In the evaluation phase, the problems were refined into specific findings and recommended actions were developed. The recommended actions were further refined and developed into an action plan.

Based on the EWOS, the findings were identified and grouped under these functional areas:

Role of the Engineer Warrant Officer.

- Commissioned officers do not understand the role or proper utilization of warrant officers.
- Engineer warrant officers are uncorrectly used.

Prerequisites.

- Requirements for appointment are too low.
- Appointment requirements are not enforced through field boarding action.
- There is no proponent technical certification prior to appointment.
- Certification is not required for USAR warrant officers before receiving a new MOS.
- The new EMPS is not providing diversified technical management skills.

Field Boarding Actions.

- No guidance is being submitted to board by proponent.
- A warrant officer is not required to sit on appointment boards to ensure applicants are technically certified.

Warrant Officer Education System.

- There is no specific training in "officer skills."
- There is no technical training available for MOSs 310A, 811A, 821A, 833A, and 841A.
- There is no proponent technical certification at entry level.
- Thre is no standardized or required training for either appointment or professional development/promotion.

Utilization.

- There is no correlation between professional development and assignments.
- Warrant officer assignments are not identified by experience level nor grade.
- Additional Specialty Identifier management is not controlled.

MOS Overload.

- Utilities Operation and Maintenance (MOS 310A) has too many diversified feeder MOSs.
- MOSs 310A and 621A have diversified assignment utilization.
- MOS 310A and 621A overlap technical responsibilities.

Civilian Education.

- More technical training is required to support force modernization.
- There are no fully funded college nor other higher education programs for warrant officers.

On September 30, 1983, the findings and recommendations of the EWOS were briefed to Engineer School commandant. Based on the unique problems identified by the EWOS, the commandant approved the recommendations listed below for further staff work.

Establish blocks of instruction in the Engineer Officer Basic and Advanced Courses on how to best use Engineer warrant officers.

Establish better preappointment requirements.

- Preappointment requirements should be increased to require, as a minimum, graduation from the Primary Technical Course or Basic Technical Course (whichever is available) for each enlisted feeder MOS.
- Develop better local appointment board procedures, which includes proponent involvement.

Establish an Engineer Warrant Officer Education System.

- The education system should include entry level/candidate training; advanced level training; and senior level training. These professional development courses should be required for improved career progression.

Establish Grading by School Qualification.

- Grading by school qualification will correlate professional development with assignment utilization by awarding a skill designation to the MOS code for each MOS based on school qualification.
- The skill designation will be coded in TOE/TDA documents to provide better assignment utilization.

Establish a new MOS—Special Purpose Engineer Equipment Repair Technician.

- The new MOS should eliminate the requirement for maintaining the extensive number of equipment systems now under MOS 310A and 621A.

Consolidate Engineer warrant officers under one code structure.

- Using one code structure should eliminate proponency problems and consolidate all Engineer warrant officers under one Military Occupational Area—Engineer Support Operations.

Establish additional Army Educational Review Board positions at major Army commands (MACOM).

- Additional positions should increase the number of warrant officer advanced degree positions to support technical requirements for force modernization.

These proposals are being staffed and will be presented for approval to the Army staff agencies and MACOMs. If approved, implementation will begin in fiscal year 1985.

These proposals were the result of contributions and cooperation from the U.S. Army Engineer School, tenant activities, MACOMs, and staff agencies. The actions based on recommendations in the Engineer Warrant Officer Study will improve professional development of Engineer warrant officers and help them to better support the Engineer mission worldwide.

Engineer Warrant Officer Study Team
CPT Randy Brindle
1LT Gary Ramos
Mrs. Ann Walker
CW4 William Cook
CW3 William Smith
CW2 Carl Burnett

EUROPEAN RANGE MODERNIZATION

Army Engineers Meeting The Challenge

Compiled by 1LT Beverly Barnes

Construction underway on vehicle target pits at Range 42, Grafenwoehr Training Area, Germany.

The 18th Engineer Brigade, USAREUR, and battalions from the 130th and 7th Engineer Brigades, USAREUR, are undertaking the largest troop construction project since World War II at the Grafenwoehr and Wildflecken training areas in Germany. When completed, the project under Colonel (P) Charles E. Williams' command, will provide a modern, extensive training complex for M1 Abrams tank crews and for squads using the M2/M3 Bradley fighting vehicle.

The Project, The Units

The introduction of the M1 Abrams main battle tank and the M2/M3 fighting vehicle into the Army inventory required that training ranges be improved, so that their crews and weapons systems could be adequately challenged. Fourteen ranges at the Grafenwoehr Training Area and the Wildflecken Training Area were identified as needing improvement at a cost of $55.1 million.

From the beginning there were special considerations. The European theater has a relatively short construction season—roughly seven months during which concrete can be placed and heavy equipment can move. An even greater challenge was the need to continue combat readiness training. As a result, range construction time had to be planned so that units on adjacent ranges could keep firing during the project.

Completing the crucial project within the short construction windows available required an engineer task force of unparalleled size. The extensive dud removal and certification process required by German labor unions before civilian workers could enter the impact areas ruled out using civilian contractors. Engineer troops, however, could both clear their work areas and complete range construction tasks. The U.S. Army Europe commander-in-chief, therefore, tasked the 18th Engineer Brigade, the only theater level engineer unit with combat heavy capabilities.

The brigade consists of four combat heavy engineer battalions, a topographic battalion, and a battalion-size civilian service support center of engineer-skilled craftsmen. For the range modernization project, the brigade was augmented by two corps

Contributing Writers
LTC Melvin C. Lynch, 18th Engineer Brigade S3
MAJ Richard C. Herrick, Brigade Maintenance Officer
MAJ Russel P. Baldwin, Operations Officer
CPT (P) Thomas G. Sedelko, Brigade S4 Officer
CPT David M. Patterson, Construction Officer
CPT Robert C. Steiger, Brigade Engineering Plans and Programs
Robert C. Steiger, Analysis Staff
CPT Gary R. Clare, Brigade Engineering Plans and Programs Analysis Staff

combat engineer battalions and two combat support equipment (CSE) companies each year, for an annual strength of approximately 5,000 engineer troops.

In 1983, units participating were the 18th Bridgade's four heavy engineer combat battalions, the 79th, 94th, 249th, and the 293rd; the 649th Engineer Battalion (Topographic) and the 670th Civilian Service Center. Attached to the brigade were the V Corps' 547th Engineer Combat Battalion and the 568th CSE Company, and the VII Corps' 237th Engineer Combat Battalion and 535th CSE Company. Accomplishing the range improvements using troop construction saved millions of dollars compared to the cost of a civilian contract.

Each range has "pop-up" vehicle and personnel targets, moving target systems with remote control target carriers, hull defilade firing positions along the Class 60 course roads, and concrete turnpads at road intersections.

Other new items include electrical sensors that indicate the combat vehicle's location on the range, a new range tower with computerized control systems, a concrete motor park, a cantonment area with two to six billets and a dining facility, a target maintenance building, and a sewage treatment system with a leach field. This scope of work represents 170 kilometers of roads, 75 buildings, 750 culverts, 2,000 targets, and nearly 300 kilometers of buried electrical cable (see Figure 1 for project details).

The task force faced special challenges in the construction area as well as in other areas. Also involved was managing vast amounts of materiel, and special equipment, providing equipment maintenance, operator training, and provisions for support personnel for the soldiers many miles from their home stations.

Construction

The chief challenge of the project was to construct all facilities according to design and with acceptable construction techniques. To accomplish this, a multi-level quality control system was used so that each step of every task was checked three times.

The most important and effective quality control occurred within the platoon at the builder level. Strict quality control measures were stressed at daily battalion meetings and at weekly task force conferences. The battalion operations section consisted of a construction officer or civil engineer and an experienced senior NCO, with a construction supervisor MOS (51H). They conducted daily inspections to make sure that keeping up the construction pace was not emphasized above quality control.

The final quality control level was within the construction element of the task force operations section. The element included two officers; six construction supervisor E7s; construction inspectors; ten surveyors; and two materiel quality specialists. At this level, quality control was given a higher priority than project construction management.

The project quality control effort required two sources for reference and standards. The first was the design and specifications for each facility constructed. Prepared by a civilian architectural firm, these plans were significantly different from those encountered in the United States, since they were based upon German construction codes, called "DINs."

The second reference was a quality

An M1 Abrams tank rolls up to battle position 1 at Grafenwoehr's Range 99.

control annex to the range improvement operations order. This clarified key points, explained certain tests, and helped to tighten construction standards. Published early in the project planning stage, it ensured that planners understood critical standards, and it allowed the battalions to conduct training on construction standards during the winter. A thorough knowledge of both this document and of the project design and specifications was the key to effective quality control.

The 1983 range improvement upgrade project at Grafenwoehr and Wildflecken included a great deal of major construction effort not part of the 1982 program—data cable installation.

The task force installed low voltage and data cable to each target on all the ranges. The power cables required less maintenance because they eliminated batteries. The data cables allowed the Programmable Control Unit (PCU) to communicate instantly with each target, to activate thermal signature and gunfire simulator devices, and to report target operational status. On three of the five ranges, where more than one vehicle could fire simultaneously or where the firing vehicles were out of sight of the control tower personnel, a vehicle sensor system was installed. The system identified vehicle locations to the PCU. This allowed for target exposure control, ensuring that fire was always within the range safety fan, and that vehicles were not accidentally fired upon by other vehicles. The task force installed 261 of these road sensors, using hardware developed for normal traffic sensors.

During the five-month cable installation project, the task force dug over 54 kilometers of trenches and installed over 155 kilometers of high-voltage, low-voltage, and data cable.

Command and Control

Command and control for this huge construction operation presented special challenges to the brigade commander and his staff. Besides being the 18th Engineer Brigade and task force commander, he was also the Karlsrule community commander. Battalion commanders shared similar problems with managing unit operations and still meeting community responsibilities at their home stations.

The management scheme established the deputy brigade commander as the rear detachment commander in Karlsrule for the 18th Engineer Brigade. In addition, a lieutenant colonel became the deputy community commander and handled the community responsibilities.

At Wildflecken, a field grade officer was assigned as range project manager and reported directly to the brigade commander. The brigade's S3 became the deputy task force commander and managed the construction projects of the six battalions at Grafenwoehr and Wildflecken. A communications network gave daily contact between the task force commander and key personnel. To further improve command and control, the task force was provided fixed and rotary wing aircraft.

An unusual command and control situation for task force operations was dealing with the corps reinforcement battalions supporting the project. During the winter, team-building workshops and open-forum conferences were used to create a cohesive team for accomplishing the summer construction activities. Each of the attached units became working members of the task force and cooperative team members in the complex construction effort. After construction began, the commanders continued weekly meetings to discuss progress and problems.

Because of the large interest in the project, a joint visitors' bureau (JVB) was established to coordinate official visits with the units, the 7th Army Training Center, and the training areas. The four-member team handled itineraries, arranged transportation, and secured special clothing (hard hats, wet-weather gear, etc.). The JVB also compiled the project history and kept an extensive photographic file.

Helmets, flack jackets and ground guides were standard safety measures when breaking ground down range.

full view of the up range area of Range 45, Grafenwoehr.

ogistics

Supporting logistical operations atched the large scale of the project in every respect. Facilities for the task force included over 100 barracks, 20 dining facilities, and 15 acres of motor parks with 11 maintenance buildings. A second set of barracks furniture was required for each task force member. Property disposal offices throughout Europe were screened for beds, mattresses, and metal wall lockers. Resources were collected from as far away as England, saving a considerable amount of tax money.

Food service operations continued at six range construction sites, as well as at six troop billeting locations. At each site, lunch and dinner meals included mobile kitchen trailers, and elaborate feeding tents and picnic tables.

A task force field medical facility was established in a converted mess hall and staffed by the Nurenburg Medical Department Activity (MEDDAC). Task force soldiers were treated quickly, properly and returned to duty as soon as possible. While using the facility avoided overbooking the GTA dispensary, the Wildflecken medical facility provided services for the battalion working at WTA.

Transportation was a key aspect of the range improvement project. Commercial buses were contracted each weekend and transported the task force to and from their home stations. Additionally, 18 German buses were used to transport workers to and from the ranges each day, a distance of 20 miles. Twenty-nine leased, nontactical vehicles provided an additional administrative transportation asset around both range areas.

Clearing the ranges of unexploded ordnance, plus handling over 23 tons of demolition materials, required the support of the 10th Combat Engineer Battalion and of an explosive ordnance demolitions team.

To supplement the task force's assigned equipment, 315 items of USAREUR theater reserve equipment, valued at $750 thousand, were released on loan. These items, ranging from vehicle radios to five-cubic yard scoop loaders, were issued by reserve storage activities from places as far away as Belgium and were transported to Grafenwoehr and Wildflecken by the units to which the equipment was assigned.

The task force used over 25,000 gallons of fuel each week. To alleviate a large part of the transportation burden on the organic fuel tankers, the 7th Support Group provided fuel delivery service directly to each range. Rotating through 13th Supply and Service Battalion companies, five 5,000-gallon tankers were available at Grafenwoehr and Wildflecken.

Maintenance

Unique to the maintenance support system for the Grafenwoehr improvement program were direct support maintenance detachments. Traditionally, direct support maintenance is provided under an area support concept, but the task force operated in an area that could not provide the service. Therefore, USAREUR tasked the VII Corps to provide direct maintenance support of Grafenwoehr and tasked the V Corps to provide similar support at Wildflecken.

At Grafenwoehr, a 76-person maintenance detachment established their shop with a cadre from the 71st Maintenance Battalion. Maintenance platoons were drawn from all of the battalions of the 7th Support Group on a two month, rotating basis. The direct support detachment at Wildflecken consisted of 15 personnel who developed a memorandum of agreement with the 94th Engineer Battalion.

Class IX repair parts for the organizational and direct support

COL (P) Charles E. Williams leads the monthly brigade run.

maintenance operations came from the local Grafenwoehr supply support activity (SSA). With a direct line back to the United States, the SSA was able to shorten the shipping time for parts, which benefited the unit's percent zero balance.

Because equipment use during the construction project resembled wartime use and because there was a responsible repair parts system, the resulting Class IX data presented a perfect opportunity for other studies. All requisitions submitted were given a special project code and at the end of the first year of construction the data was used to support the General Support Supply Base for USAREUR engineer equipment.

During work at Grafenwoehr in 1983, the 249th Engineer Battalion, together with a Department of the Army team, collected sample data to develop a combat prescribed load list for heavy engineer battalions. Results of the study should be available in 1984.

Though well supported with maintenance and repair parts, the task force's organic equipment was not entirely suited to meet the strict project construction standards. As a result, some civilian construction equipment loaned to the task force was purchased off-the-shelf through competitive bidding sponsored by the European Distribution and Accounting Agency of the Military Committee, London (EVDAC). The purchased equipment worked well and included gradealls, special entrenchers, and rollers. Operators were trained to use the equipment, but there were problems because of too few mechanics needed to maintain the additional equipment, and from the inability to requisition repair parts through the supply system.

A maintenance contract with civilian firms was let with the task force maintenance officer as the cargo outturn report (COR). Civilian contractors were reminded of their important role in the project, and challenged to develop a sense of urgency. This succeeded with varying degrees. The repairmen took immense pride in their work and proved quite reliable, but they became frustrated when repair parts were not readily available. The training value of this arrangement was that wartime host nation support would parallel this use of off-the-shelf equipment and civilian repair work.

Fiscal Management

The multimillion dollar project presented a fund management challenge within the 18th Engineer Brigade. The project combined many platoon-sized tasks at each range. Major Construction Army (MCA) funds were provided to finance one or more ranges. Fund management was done by giving each construction battalion a limit for TDY and equipment expenditures. Those amounts were further broken down into project spending ceilings. These limitations were based on the battalion's estimate of the work required, coupled with an experience factor applied by the brigade's engineer plans section.

A joint project between the task force and the U.S. Army Construction Engineering Research Lab (CERL) was a microcomputer research project. This assisted in tracking both the construction and the funding status. A weekly progress report (WPR) documented TDY status and equipment hours charged to the project. The WPR also reflected the man-hours worked on each project subtask. A current status of funds earned, funds remaining and of percentage of construction completed was computed for each battalion.

With this data, the brigade resource management office also coordinated reports to European Division and USAREUR central finance and accounting offices for two fiscal years. The problem would have been simpler had MCA funds been involved, but Operation Maintenance Army (OMA) mission funds were required to support related indirect project construction costs. Therefore costs had to be identified as either direct or indirect. Those costs charged to the indirect share had to be allocated to the proper fiscal year since OMA funds were used as a carrier fund to be reimbursed from MCA. Improperly allocating indirect costs would have been either an overstatement or understatement of other OMA costs in one fiscal year and the reverse in the ensuing fiscal year. Active fiscal management procedures were initiated to solve these problems.

Training

The range improvement program proved to be a perfect scenario for cross-training soldiers in various engineer skills because conditions closely compared to those experienced in wartime. During project mobilization and demobilization er 2,000 pieces of equipment were oved to and from the construction tes. Heavy construction equipment as moved by train with the opera-rs in accompanying carrier cars; ghter vehicles were driven from me stations. This movement of-red excellent practice for wartime ployment.

During the project, commanders d staffs were consistently taxed to an missions and to task leaders to ecute those plans. In essence, the ttalions and brigade staff con-cted a seven-month Army Training valuation Program (ARTEP). The ed to rotate troops to different sks made it possible to cross-train uipment operators. Furthermore, e units conducted common skills aining and testing, weapons quali-ation training, and PT testing iring their busy schedules. In dition, the compressed construc-on period and 12 to 15 hour orkdays provided the opportunity work under pressure similar to at of combat.

RANGE IMPROVEMENT PROGRAM SUMMARY

	CY 1982	CY 1983	CY 1984	CY 1985	TOTAL
MCA Costs (Millions)	$14.06	$20.95	$17.45	$2.65	$55.11
Construction					
Gravel roads (Class 30 & 60)	51.0KM	44.7KM	63.1KM	7.3KM	166.1KM
Gravel hardstand	21,000SM	13,300SM	54,040SM	2,100SM	90,430SM
Concrete					
Roads, tankparks & walkways	19,022SM	20,714SM	13,070SM	12,150SM	64,956SM
Culverts	214	217	218	75	724
Defilade firing positions	44	50	100	8	202
Turnpads, ammo pads	30	37	26	9	102
Buildings					
Soule (average size 40' x 60')	16	25	12	6	59
Range towers	6	5	2	1	14
Sewage systems	6	5	2	1	14
Target systems					
Moving targets	4,320M	4,058M	2,820M	700M	11,898M
Vehicle target pits	198	115	129	25	467
Personnel target pits	351	476	562	120	1,509
Data cable trenching	32.75KM	48.40KM	48.21KM	12.00KM	141.36KM
Road sensors	0	259	682	0	941
Chain link fence	746KM	705KM	655KM	1,000M	2,206M

ersonnel

Personnel managers faced prob-ems caused by family separation nd additional TDY costs. They ried to minimize these problems ith various programs and special pportunities.

A morale support program was stablished which included softball, lag football, golf, and bowling. Also, n organization day for all units rovide a welcome break for the task orce. The events included all the ustomary competitions events and a omplete barbeque meal.

Religious services were held on eekends, and the brigade chaplain as available regularly for counsel-ng. He also organized local area rips, including visits to the Dachau oncentration camp outside Munich nd Flossenburg, and trips to the order zone.

Both Grafenwoehr and Wildflec-en Training Areas granted per-nanent party status to task force oldiers, allowing them use of the Class VI stores, post laundries, and heck cashing privileges not afforded o training troops. To better give oldiers access to post facilities, a special bus ran daily from 8 a.m. to 10 p.m. from each unit's area to the main post.

To support the soldier it was necessary to maintain personnel and finance sections at his home station to interface with military personnel offices (MILPO) and finance offices. Processing TDY orders and travel vouchers, and handling mail and distribution increased the amount of work performed by an already geographically separated work force. Furthermore, these sections coordinated personnel in and out-processing and handled limited medical and finance appointments with supporting community units spread across a minimum of 200 miles.

Summary

The challenges presented by the range improvement project have been varied and significant. But with skill and determination, the task force faced each problem and found a solution. Finding new ways of solving old problems and implementing new technology has always been the pride of Army Engineers worldwide. The new ranges at the Grafenwoehr and Wildflecken Training Areas will stand as a monument of the peacetime contribution of Corps of Engineers troops in preserving that peace.

1LT Beverly Barnes is assigned to 649th Engineer Bn. (TOPO). She was attached to the 18th Engineer Bde. as the visitors' bureau officer during the 1983 range improvement project. 1LT Barnes has a bachelor's degree in park management from Texas A & M University and an associate's degree in water and wastewater technology from New Mexico State University. She has completed the Engineer Officer Basic and the Mapping, Charting, and Geodesy Officers' Course.

GRAF '82

by LTC Lawrence L. Izzo

"Graf '82" was the first installment of the four-year plan to modernize USAREUR's training ranges and was concerned wholely with the Grafenwoehr (Germany) Training Area. The six ranges constructed were designed to challenge the crews of the M1 Abrams tank and carried a cost of $15 million.

The scope of Graf '82 presented a monumental challenge. More than 30 miles of gravel roads for tank firing courses and target servicing, 17 moving target systems totaling more than 14,500 feet, 549 concrete target pits, and 44 concrete firing positions were constructed.

Seventeen billets, four dining facilities and five range control towers were also built, along with five target maintenance buildings so targets could be maintained without removing them from the range.

All buildings included heat and electricity, and three included a complete sewage system with septic tanks and a leach field. Five 25,000 square feet concrete motor parks were built for tracked vehicles, plus nine gravel parking areas for wheeled vehicles. In support of these facilities, 13,000 feet of fencing, 1,600 feet of concrete roads, and more than 200 culverts with concrete head walls were installed. To provide power to the target systems, over 20 miles of power cable were buried. Troops did all the trenching and a civilian firm laid the cable and did the splicing and continuity checks.

To support the construction effort, the 18th Brigade assumed responsibility for all material handling operations. Task force operations personnel were responsible for receiving, accounting for, and issuing over 1,000 line items of construction materials to 60 different platoon leaders. They managed the programming and delivery of over 450,000 tons of crushed rock (in seven different commodities) and over 15,000 cubic meters of ready-mix concrete. Material operations personnel tracked procurement and delivery on nearly 300 separate contracts during the project and directly coordinated with numerous German civilian firms to ensure timely deliveries.

Another major challenge was the requirement to clear the downrange portion of the training ranges of all dangerous ordnance before construction began. Over a six-week period, the 16th Engineer Battalion (Combat) surface swept all ranges and located about 10,000 items. Over 3,000 of these were too dangerous to move and were blown in place. The areas where construction cuts were planned had to be earth shocked with demolitions to explode any sensitive ordnance hidden underground. The entire operation required over 50 tons of demolitions and was carried out on a tight time schedule.

The engineer troop task force assembled for Graf '82 consisted of seven engineer battalions. The two combat engineer battalions, one each from V and VII Corps, were the 317th of the 130th Engineer Brigade and the 82nd of the 7th Engineer Brigade. Each battalion was reinforced with a combat support equipment company.

The direct support maintenance element was pieced together fro maintenance units throughout Ge many. Elements of the 18th Enginee Brigade's German civilian lab force, the 6970th Civilian Suppo Center, were also attached to insta heating and electrical lines and build control towers. Surveyors fro the 18th Brigade's 649th Engine Battalion (Topographic) reinforc the combat battalion's organic co struction surveyors and rounded o the task force.

The 18th Engineer Brigade management of the project w highly commendable. All six rang were completed on time. The tro portion of the project was complet for approximately $400,000 und the estimated and budgeted cost. A six ranges were turned over to t Military Committee of the Europe Distribution and Accounting Agen (in London) without constructi deficiencies.

After the project, the 18th Eng neer Brigade continued to provi responsive support to the custome the 7th Army Training Comman by making warranty-type constru tion corrections. The task for accomplishments during Graf ' started the significant role enginee are playing in helping to impro the readiness of the Army in Europ

LTC Larry Izzo was the operatio officer for the 18th Engineer Briga during Graf '82. He now comman the 307th Engineer Bn. (Airborne 82nd Airborne Div., Ft. Bragg, N. A U.S. Military Academy graduat he has completed airborne and rang training, the Command and Gener Staff College, has a master's degree nuclear engineering from the Mass chusetts Institute of Technology an an M.B.A. from Long Island Un versity. He is a registered profe sional engineer in Virginia an served on the physics departme faculty of the U.S. Military Academ

GRAF'82
TASK FORCE ORGANIZATION

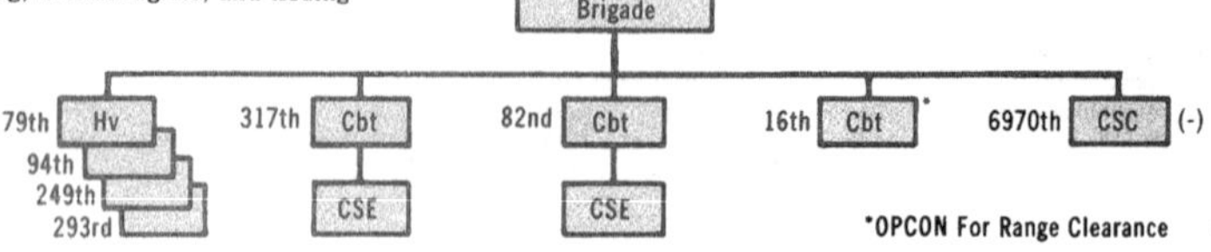

MATERIAL OPERATIONS

by CPT Thomas M. Berger

Among the many problems encountered by the planners of the range improvement program at Grafenwoehr, Germany, was how to request, to store and to issue materials.

Needed for the huge construction project were over 900 different construction materials valued at over $6 million. Besides nuts and bolts, other required items were fluorescent lights and culvert pipes, junction boxes and copper tubing, circulating pumps and shut-off valves, manhole covers and fence poles, 24 Soule building kits, 16,000 cubic meters of concrete, 127 kilometers of electric cable, 62,000 bricks, and 376,000 tons of sand and gravel.

Also required were 12 gradealls, 24 vibratory rollers, 60 plate compactors, 64 circular saws, and 3,500 5-millimeter drill bits, not to mention the hundreds of other types of tools and materials.

But how could a facilities engineer office handle this materials burden? Who was going to take care of receiving, issuing, and storing materials in such vast quantities?

In an agreement with the Directorate of Engineering and Housing (DEH) at Grafenwoehr, the 18th Engineer Brigade established a special team as the agent for the DEH in handling all material actions. Contrary to normal practice, the construction units assumed the responsibility and established a system for receiving, storing, issuing, and accounting for the program's construction materials and tools.

Originally, the material operations team consisted of nine U.S. military personnel and ten civilian support group personnel, but increased to a final strength of 24. They operated a central handling and storage facility in an old German mess hall that was converted into an office and warehouse. Instead of counting potatoes and writing menus in the cook's office, they counted cubic meters of concrete and wrote weekly rock status reports.

In the dining room, plumbing fittings, electrical fixtures, and cans of paint were "served" on written request with 24 hours advance notice. In the old scullery where the master file was located, all receipts and issues for every type of material was recorded on a stockage level card and a running balance was kept. In cold storage were rakes, screwguns, slump tests, and other assorted items. Personnel authorized to receive equipment had cards and signed hand receipts for what they received. Every attempt was made to distribute the tools equally among the units.

In one motor park turned storage yard, no mechanics were seen, but instead there were people stacking lumber, counting conduit, and issuing reinforcing steel. In the other storage area (an old ammunition yard), steel forms were moved by forklift to accommodate landscape dozers and entrenching machines for the winter. All equipment was inspected and serviced before being secured for the season.

In the construction areas, the project officers conveyed material shortage notifications and special needs to the material operations OIC and NCOIC. The material coordinator worked closely with the Army Contracting Agency and civilian firms to ensure that needed items were delivered on time to prevent construction delays. The procurement NCO also purchased various supply items from local stores with imprest funds.

Meeting the immense material requirements of the range improvement program stands as an example of what can be successfully done when a difficult mission is tackled with good planning and team effort.

CPT Thomas M. Berger served with the 79th Engineer Bn. (CBT) (HVY) and was the task force materials officer for the 1983 project. He has a bachelor's degree in electrical engineering from Lafayette College and is a graduate of the Engineer Officer Basic Course and the airborne and ranger schools. CPT Berger is now attending the Engineer Officer Advanced Course.

Engineer Problem

Bridge Design Problem: (Reference: TM 5-312, Chapter 6, or FM 5-34, Chapter 7)

You are designing a semipermanent nonstandard fixed bridge. This two-lane bridge is to have a design class of 100. The stringer spacing will be 5'0" and the available deck material is 4" x 12" and 3" x 10".

QUESTION: Select the best deck design from the following:

a. Laminated: 75 percent using 3" x 10" material.
b. Laminated: 66 2/3 percent using 4" x 12" material.
c. Planked: 2 layers of 4" x 12" material nailed firmly together.
d. Planked: 3 layers of 3" x 10" material nailed firmly together.

Improving your
Platoon Inspections

By MAJ Jonathan A. Jacobsen
and MAJ Jefferson J. Irvin

The pressures may be intense for a platoon leader during his or her first major inspection. If the inspection (such as an Annual General Inspection) is announced, it looms in the distance like an awesome storm cloud. As the inspection date approaches, the first sprinkles of command guidance lead to early preinspections. During the final month, reports from units already inspected buffet the platoon leader like giant hailstones.

Unfortunately, careless handling of inspections frequently negates their usefulness as a fair measure of performance. Soldiers being carelessly inspected are unsure of exactly what is required. No time is allotted for inspection preparation. Those inspected receive no feedback. Standards are often unrealistically high.

However, inspections are your most valuable tool as a platoon leader for gauging the chain-of-command's efficiency. The following steps will ensure that your inspections are fair and, therefore, will guarantee that your inspections are effective.

STEP 1:
Assemble Existing Standards

Assemble the training manuals, field manuals, schedule of components and battalion or company SOPs pertaining to the areas you wish to inspect. Read and thoroughly understand these references. You also should study the results of major inspections pertaining to your areas of interest.

After reading the pertinent references, talk to your company commander, first sergeant, or other experts. If you are planning a maintenance inspection, talk to the motor sergeant. Find out what standards they require. Have the experts demonstrate how they would conduct the inspection, particularly regarding organization and layout. Ask the experts for specific deficiencies which occur repeatedly in your areas of interest and write them down.

STEP 2:
Evaluate Existing Standards

Once you have assembled the published standards and those required by your chain-of-command, put the standards through the following tests. Review the standards first by yourself, then with the platoon sergeant and squad leaders who will ultimately have to enforce the standards. Ask yourself the following questions:

Are the standards necessary? Be sure the standards fit the mission. For instance, painting pioneer tools is an excessive standard. If a standard seems unreasonable, discuss it with your commander.

Are the standards high enough? Frequently the standards listed in SOPs or given by commanders are vague outlines defining a minimum performance level. For instance, "clean the tools" does not specifically address the sharpening, oiling, and cleaning required for good tool maintenance.

Are the standards clear and concise? When you inspect your soldiers, you do not want the standards to be debatable or subject to differing interpretations. Quantify. Be explicit. Do not write a standard like "all tools will be marked." Write standards like "metal hand tools from kits will be etched with 'US' and a code number showing to which kit and platoon the tool belongs" or "wooden-handled tools from vehicles will be stenciled in OD paint with 'US' and the vehicle's bumber number."

Are the standards complete? Make your inspection efficient by issuing a list of all standards you can check during your inspection. This question is critical when the inspection is formal and requires extensive troop preparation. Do not have your soldiers lay out their TA50 one day so you can check the gear for accountability, and again two weeks later so you can check the same gear for serviceability.

Check all pertinent items in a layout at the same time. If this is not physically possible, plan to multiply the number of inspectors (you and the platoon sergeant checking different areas) before you multiply the number of inspections.

Do not finalize your standards without first consulting your NCOs, particularly your platoon sergeant. The NCOs should evaluate each standard, just as you did. Resolve any differences. Frequently the result is a group effort. Then, double check your final standards with your commander, and alter them according to his guidance.

STEP 3:
Plan The Inspection

Your standards now agree with published technical manuals, field manuals, your chain-of-command, and the four questions in Step 2. Next, determine how you are going to perform the inspection.

Will your inspection be announced? If the squad leaders and soldiers are being inspected on routine standards, unannounced inspections are appropriate. If the standards are new or in areas previously ignored or glossed over, start with announced inspections until the basic standards are reached and familiar.

What is the most efficient inspection method? Give instructions to your squad leaders for the inspection which include provisions for:

The Inspection Process

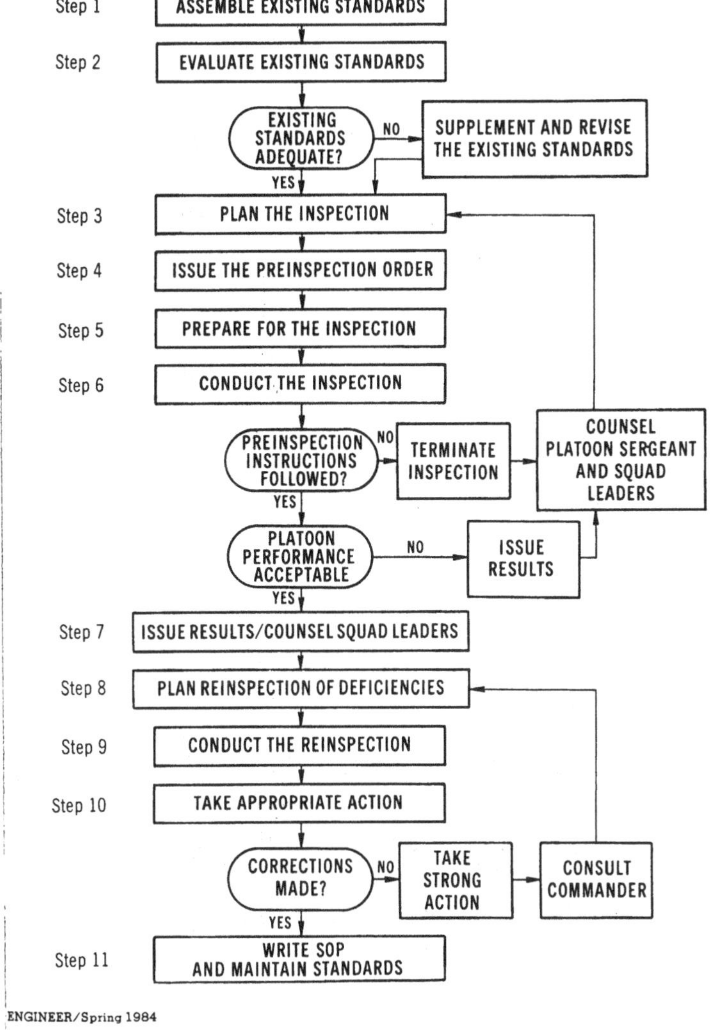

Step 1
ASSEMBLE EXISTING STANDARDS
Step 2
EVALUATE EXISTING STANDARDS
EXISTING STANDARDS ADEQUATE?
NO
SUPPLEMENT AND REVISE THE EXISTING STANDARDS
YES
Step 3
PLAN THE INSPECTION
Step 4
ISSUE THE PREINSPECTION ORDER
Step 5
PREPARE FOR THE INSPECTION
Step 6
CONDUCT THE INSPECTION
PREINSPECTION INSTRUCTIONS FOLLOWED?
NO
TERMINATE INSPECTION
COUNSEL PLATOON SERGEANT AND SQUAD LEADERS
YES
PLATOON PERFORMANCE ACCEPTABLE
NO
ISSUE RESULTS
YES
Step 7
ISSUE RESULTS/COUNSEL SQUAD LEADERS
Step 8
PLAN REINSPECTION OF DEFICIENCIES
Step 9
CONDUCT THE REINSPECTION
Step 10
TAKE APPROPRIATE ACTION
CORRECTIONS MADE?
NO
TAKE STRONG ACTION
CONSULT COMMANDER
YES
Step 11
WRITE SOP AND MAINTAIN STANDARDS

- Consolidating to one location geographically separated items.
- Using layouts based on some logical configuration. Have items laid out in the order listed in the reference you are using as an inspection guide. For instance, tools from kits should be laid out in the order listed in the supply catalog and on kit inventories. A printed drawing of a standardized TA50 layout usually works best.
- Having items to be checked for serviceability ready and near areas where they can be checked. For example, power tools with their cords unwound should be located near outlets.
- Having items such as rifles already disassembled and ready for inspection.

Will your inspection require staggering inspected units? With an expert, practice inspecting a sample unit (truck, TA50 layout, tool box). Time your dry run. Determine if the projected time to inspect the platoon seems excessive. (This is a judgment call. You don't want troops waiting around for hours for an inspection.)

You may either split the standards to be inspected between several inspectors (you, your platoon sergeant, or an expert such as the motor sergeant or supply sergeant) or plan to stagger your inspection of squads at different times or on different days.

How long do your squad leaders need to prepare for your inspection? Determine what blocks of time they require on the training schedule to bring their squads up to standard. These requirements include time for soldier preparation and for both inspection and reinspection by squad leaders. The best source for this information is your squad leaders.

Once you determine the preparation time necessary, go to your commander and negotiate for time on the training schedule, including time for your own inspection and reinspection. Ensure the time blocks you receive do not coincide with major troop diversions such as support details for community or battalion classes.

Does inspection preparation require materials or tools that are hard to get or unavailable? Check with your NCOs. Do they have the paint, the power tools, or the maintenance equipment needed to do the job? Find out where to get the materials and include in your inspection order instructions how to obtain missing items.

Are all references available to squad leaders to make the standards explicitly clear? Make copies of your assembled standards from Step 2. To make a complicated operation more clear, provide a sample inspection/layout at the time you give your inspection instructions.

All the planning in Step 3 must be done with your platoon sergeant and squad leaders. Use their expertise.

STEP 4:
Issue the Preinspection Order

The preinspection order issued to your NCOs should include the following information:

- Specific standards to be achieved (especially regarding the recurring deficiencies which the experts that you consulted said were common). Use a handout, so nothing is "lost in translation."
- The dates and times the squad leaders will have to prepare, inspect, and to reinspect their soldiers.
- The date and time of your inspection, if the inspection is announced.
- The date after which the squads will be expected to be ready for inspection, if the inspection is unannounced.
- Scheduling instructions if inspections are staggered.
- Layout instruction.
- Instructions for obtaining materials used to prepare for the inspection.
- A sample walk-through inspection explaining standards.
- A simple statement that squad leaders' performance ratings are affected by their performance at your inspection.
- A simple statement that all routine business (such as medical appointments or passes) will be routed through the platoon sergeant for

minor corrections were found in the last inspection), do the following:

Double-check to ensure the previous inspections included all personnel and equipment. Invariably the soldier performing special duties or in school is the soldier the chain-of-command ignores. This is probably the soldier with the substandard appearance. Equipment may have been missed because it was lent or at direct support maintenance. If men and equipment were missed in the previous inspections, ensure that they appear at the final inspection.

Give an order for the reinspection of specific deficiencies which is as detailed as the one you gave for the comprehensive inspection. Consider adding the following to your instructions:

- Excusing those who have performed to standard from attending the reinspection. You may give them and the squad leader free time if the entire squad performed well.
- Making more explicit any standards which caused confusion during prior inspections.
- Shortening the time between inspections and reinspection.
- Discussing probable actions for failure to respond to correction.

STEP 9:
Conduct The Re-Inspection

Conduct the re-inspection in the same organized manner as the inspection itself. However, this time you will be inspecting with the previous inspection results in hand instead of the earlier tabulations of standards. Check off the deficiencies that have been corrected.

STEP 10:
Take Appropriate Action

If any of the previously noted deficiencies were not corrected, take strong action. Such action can vary widely; consult your commander for advice and guidance.

Reward those who achieved standards without undue prodding. Again, discuss rewards with your commander.

STEP 11:
Write An SOP

Now that your platoon is at the desired standard, do not assume that level will be maintained without continued effort. Write an SOP to prevent backsliding. The SOP should include:

- The listing of standards from Step 2.
- A regular sequence of unannounced inspections by the chain-of-command ("the platoon leader will inspect at least once a month. . .").
- A record of the platoon's performance to determine platoon rewards and punishments and to track platoon progress.

After the initial flurry of inspections when a new leader takes over, the platoon should be at standard and performing according to SOP in the following areas:

- Vehicle maintenance.
- Tool/tool kit maintenance and accountability.
- Personal appearance.
- Room appearance.
- TA50 maintenance and accountability.
- Weapon maintenance.
- NBC protective equipment maintenance.
- Communications/STANO equipment maintenance and accountability.

This list is obviously incomplete. Solicit additional areas of concern from your commander.

MAJ Jonathan A. Jacobsen is an assistant professor in the Department of Engineering, U.S. Military Academy. He was a platoon leader in the 79th Engineer Bn. (CBT), USAREUR; a company commander in the 307th Engineer Bn. (ABN), Ft. Bragg; and was a project engineer on the Negetv Air Base Project in Israel. MAJ Jacobsen has a bachelor's degree from the U.S. Military Academy and a master's degree from the University of California.

MAJ Jefferson J. Irvin is an assistant professor in the Engineering Department, U.S. Military Academy. He served as a platoon leader and company commander in the 94th Engineer Bn. (CBT), USAREUR. MAJ Irvin has a bachelor's degree from the U.S. Military Academy and a master's degree from Stanford University.

Success through Respect

by 1LT Louis J. Leto

...the ultimate goal of every platoon leader.

A platoon leader must learn the significance of this respect. It is his men who determine his success. It is his men who handle the heavy equipment, place the minefields, and dig the tank ditches. If they succeed, the platoon leader succeeds. If they fail, the platoon leader fails. Soldiers will not risk their lives or strive for perfection for a leader they don't respect.

Only through total dedication to duty and to his men will a platoon leader succeed. Only then will a platoon devote themselves to their leader, and only then will the word "can't" be foreign to them. Only then will they know that they and their platoon leader can do it all.

1LT Louis J. Leto is the assistant editor of ENGINEER Magazine. He has a bachelor's degree in journalism from Temple University. He is an Engineer Officer Basic Course graduate and has served as the assistant adjutant of the 11th Engineer Bn. (C) (H) and as a platoon leader with C Co. of the 11th Engineers.

Hotline Q & A

Q. What does Army doctrine say about the ratio of corps level mechanized combat engineer battalions to wheeled engineer battalions in a fully developed corps?

A. The ratio is normally one corps level mechanized combat battalion and two corps level wheeled engineer battalions per division in a fully developed corps.

Q. The hydraulic jacks with the medium girder bridge have reliability problems. Is there any corrective action planned or under study?

A. The problem with the British-made 15-ton jacks is that the hydraulic release valves have a tendency to leak. Studies indicate that operators often fail to close the valve after use, allowing dirt and sand to get into the seals. This results in hydraulic fluid leaking from the jacks. The Army, however, is buying the link reinforcement set for the medium girder bridge. The set includes a 20-ton hydraulic jack to replace the standard 15-ton jack. However, the operators should take the same precautions with the 20-ton jacks in closing the release valves to avoid future problems.

Q. Is there a new paint for camouflaging vehicles and equipment that is resistant to chemical contaminants? Is the camouflage pattern for vehicles changed?

A. The new camouflage paint, Chemical Agent Resistant Coating, is specifically designed to resist all known chemical agents. This paint, however, demands strict controls in the mixing process as well as in personal safety and application. The paint, therefore, is handled at depot level by specially trained personnel. The camouflage pattern is changed from the four-color pattern to a three-color pattern to improve vehicle concealment.

Q. I completed EOBC in September 1981. Does this meet the requirements for attending the Battalion Training Management Systems (BTMS) Course?

A. Anyone who graduated after June 1982 meets the BTMS course requirements. Anyone graduating before this date must attend a BTMS workshop before receiving a certificate of completion.

Engineer CATS Build in Micronesia

by CPT Randy M. Emory

When most people hear about a "cat-team" operation on Ponape, Micronesia, they either joke about one's choice of pets or ask to see Special Forces credentials.

Actually, "cat-team," or CAT (civic action team), is a self-supporting, 13-man team modeled after the small military construction teams used in Southeast Asia in the 1960s. The current version of these teams were formed to assist the economic development of Micronesia. (Micronesia is under jurisdiction of the Department of Interior (DOI) and has been a U.S. Trust Territory since the end of World War II).

The DOI has delegated responsibility for the civic action program to the Navy because of the Navy's traditional Pacific role and because of its experience with Seabee teams (Navy engineers). Army participation in the program is under operational control of the 30th Naval Construction Regiment (NCR), Guam, with Army participants using Navy equipment and logistic systems.

Part of the Army's contribution to the civic action program was CAT 84-2 which spent eight months (March-November 1981) assisting Ponape (Pone-a-pay), a small island 1,100 miles southeast of Guam and 2,600 miles southwest of Hawaii. (The "84" represents the 84th Engineer Battalion, (Combat) (Heavy) in Scholfield Barracks, Hawaii from which the team came; the "dash 2" indicates the second team of a five-year project.)

The team's mission in Ponape was five-fold: to assist Ponape's economic development with horizontal and vertical construction projects; to conduct on-the-job training for Ponapeans in horizontal and vertical construction; to provide medical assistance using the skills of the team's medical corpsman; to improve the relationship between the U.S. military and Ponape; and to maintain a U.S. military presence in Micronesia.

Starting road building operations through the jungles of Ponape.

Picking The Players

Team selection began in December 1980 under Navy guidelines, followed by 10 weeks of training in Hawaii. With 18 pieces of construction and support equipment, but only a 13-person team, it was imperative to cross-train all team members. After completing training, the team reported to the 30th NCR in Guam for additional training in the Navy supply and maintenance system and to receive its mission. Specific equipment training had to be completed after arriving on Ponape during the week-long overlap with team 84-1.

The major tasks for CAT 84-2 were constructing 2,300 feet of road around Ponape; upgrading and maintaining 13 miles of existing road; completing base camp construction begun by CAT 84-1; and securing projects for team 84-3.

But First...

To understand the Ponape projects, it helps to first understand Ponape. The circular, 126-square mile island is underdeveloped. The capital, Kolonia, is the only part of the island with electricity and water facilities. Half of the island is without roads, and the few existing roads are not maintained. The only asphalt roads are in Kolonia. All others, including the team's new road construction project, are roads capped with coral dredged from the island's surrounding reef. Heavy rains, averaging 21.5 inches a month, make road construction and maintenance a difficult task.

Ponapean culture and language is quite different from ours. This led to difficulties in vocational training and in solving problems during the projects. English is not widely spoken, but there is usually someone in a group that speaks English well enough to translate. Everyone in the government speaks English, but some commonly used American terms are not known by the Ponapeans.

Logistically, very few items were available from the local economy. Resupply came once monthly by Air Force C130s. Items identified by the local government for new projects came by commercial shipping.

Road Projects

The 2,300 feet of new road to be built was designed by the Ponape Transportation Authority (PTA) with specifications similar to our theater of operations (T/O) Class B road, except that the Ponape road would have a 6- to 12-inch coral cap. Construction coral had to be dredged from the island's surrounding reef and placed without being crushed. The team had no crusher, so the coral was smashed by running trucks over the road.

Ponape's soil, a volcanic clay, compounded the problem of the high rainfall. Even worse, the land elevates from the shoreline to a mountain that covers 60 percent of the island; the terrain is obviously very hilly.

Road construction began in April 1981 and immediately there were problems with fill sections. The constant rain and volcanic clay made it impossible to use cut material for fill or to use the D7 bulldozer and other heavy equipment. Dredged coral from the reef was the only effective fill material. One fill section was so large (325 feet long and 21 feet deep) that it could not be completed; an alternate route for the road had to be chosen.

At first, the team's efforts were totally opposed by the PTA commissioner because of right-of-way agreements with land owners. The problem was solved by adjusting the location of the road. The delay was beneficial in one respect, it allowed time to finish dredging enough coral to complete the road.

Since heavy equipment, especially the D7 dozer, was not suited for the environment, the local agriculture station provided an old D6 cable operated dozer with 36-inch wide tracks. The D6 enabled the team to borrow.

During the road project, about 21,000 cubic yards of earth were cut and 4,800 cubic yards of coral placed as fill and cap material. Three culverts were installed, totalling 103 pieces of 2-foot long, 24-inch RCP with rock hardwalls.

The relentless rains were also a constant problem for the other road project, upgrading and maintaining 13 miles of existing road. In fact, it rained at least every four days during deployment, and it rained every day in November.

Vertical Construction

The tremendous rainfall allowed plenty of time to complete base camp construction. The distance from the camp to town, however, meant the team had to provide its own power and potable water.

The rain catchment system designed for the camp proved inadequate for the daily 1,300 gallon demand. The team redesigned the system to take advantage of a small river running 700 feet from the camp by installing 2-inch PVC pipe and erecting five 3,000-gallon water

An old D6 dozer from a Ponapean agriculture station was used for borrowing operations.

bladders. This provided 9,000 gallons of river water and 6,000 gallons of purified water.

Shelters were built to protect from the rain the two 30-kilowatt generators, air compressors, a walk-in refrigerator, water purification equipment, and a welding shop.

Community Relations

Interaction with the Ponapeans, both with projects and socially, was another important aspect of the deployment.

The most vital American-Ponapean contact was through the dispensary at the base camp where the team medic treated over 160 patients per month. The most common diseases for Ponapeans were intestinal parasites and infections in open wounds. In one case, the medic correctly diagnosed an infant's life-threatening skull deformity and helped convince local health officials to send the child to Hawaii for surgery.

Renovating the local high school track for the Liberation Day celebration, clearing home sites, constructing concrete foot bridges and other projects were also part of the civic action program.

Through the vocational training program the team had contact with the Ponapeans and grew to better understand the native culture. The program also helped both sides overcome language and work habit differences, the biggest barriers encountered. In fact, the Ponapean trainees became a valuable asset as workers and as liaison personnel with the community.

For the 13 men from the 84th Engineers lucky enough to serve on CAT 84-2, the duty in Micronesia was the best of both worlds. They were able to employ their skills and training as military engineers, and they had the opportunity to help the Ponapean people improve their standard of living.

Members of CAT 84-2, all from the 84th Engineer Bn., with Ponapean officials (author is on far right).

Quick Compass Conversions

"Now, do I add or subtract the G-M angle from the compass reading to get my grid azimuth?"

Sound familiar? How do you decide if you can't remember the formulas?

by MAJ John C. Jens

New edition maps printed by the Defense Mapping Agency have the formulas printed with the declination diagram. However, most maps currently in use don't have this aid and will not unless the practice is adopted as an international standard. (German maps are well known examples for not having the formulas.)

So, you still have to memorize the formulas right? Or do you use the diagram method in FM 21-26, *Map Reading*? Not so!

Here is a simple method which anyone can use to get the azimuth you want. The only tools you need are those normally used for map reading: a map with declination diagram, a pencil, a straightedge, and a protractor (any of the current GTA 5-2 series will do).

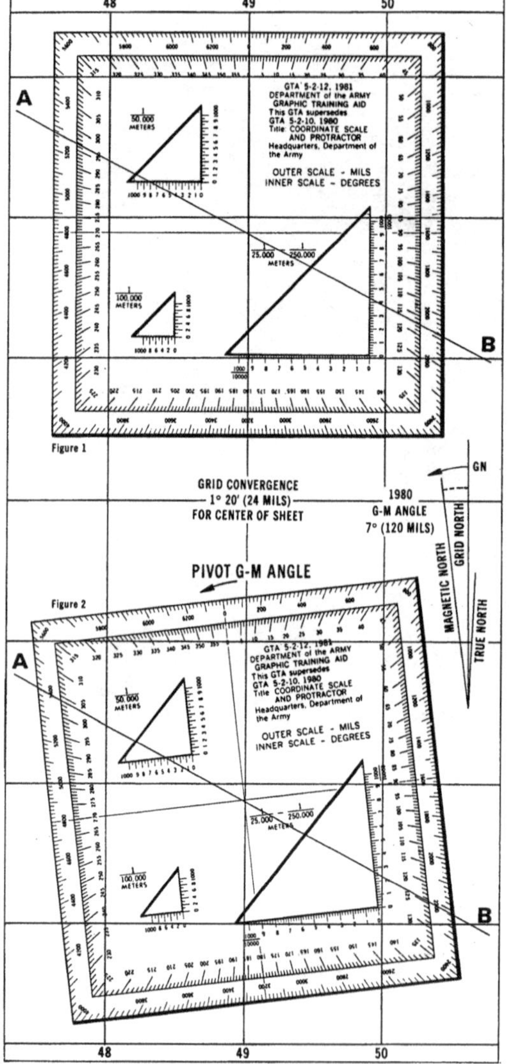

Figure 1

Figure 2

Since this method is best taught by working examples, let's start with an easy one: "Convert grid to magnetic azimuth."

First, you have to locate the azimuth to be converted on the map by drawing the line with a sharp pencil and a straightedge. You have to draw it long enough to cross the entire protractor/scale. For example, in Figure 1, we'll use 297° grid azimuth (GA).

Second, you position the protractor/scale on a north-south grid line, with the 0° mark pointing grid north and with the center cross hairs on the drawn azimuth line (see Figure 1).

Third, examine the declination diagram to see on which side of grid north that magnetic north is located, right or left, and the number of degrees of the G-M angle. In Figure 1 we see that magnetic north is 7° to the left of grid north.

Fourth, now, imagine that your protractor/scale becomes the magnetized needle of a compass. Since the magnetized needle will seek magnetic north, pivot the protractor/scale (your imagined compass) about the center cross hairs in the direction of magnetic north. The number of degrees pivoted should equal the G-M angle (see Figure 2). In our example, the pivot is left 7°.

Last, the magnetic azimuth on your compass reading can now be read directly from the protractor/scale where the line you drew in step one intersects the degree marks of the protractor. Does your answer read 304°, as in Figure 2?

See, I told you it was simple! Remember the key to this method is to imagine that when the protractor/scale becomes a compass needle, the 0° mark seeks magnetic north. Once you've practiced several times you'll be ready to try something a little more difficult: converting a magnetic to a grid azimuth.

The first step in converting a magnetic to a grid azimuth is to draw a line, any line will do, long enough to pass completely across the protractor/scale. Any grid line can also be substituted for this purpose. The line should then be labeled with the magnetic azimuth (MA) reading. For example, 64° MA as in Figure 3.

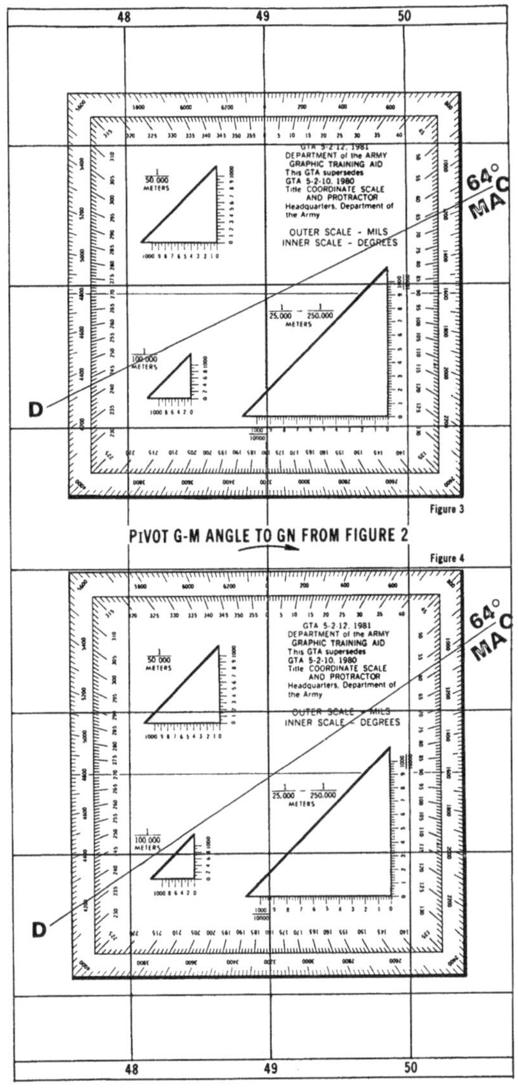

48
49
50
GTA 5-2-12, 1981
DEPARTMENT of the ARMY
GRAPHIC TRAINING AID
This GTA supersedes
GTA 5-2-10, 1980
Title COORDINATE SCALE
AND PROTRACTOR
Headquarters, Department of
the Army
OUTER SCALE - MILS
INNER SCALE - DEGREES
1/50,000 METERS
1/25,000 - 1/250,000 METERS
1/100,000 METERS
64°
MAC
D

Figure 3

PIVOT G-M ANGLE TO GN FROM FIGURE 2

Figure 4

GTA 5-2-12, 1981
DEPARTMENT of the ARMY
GRAPHIC TRAINING AID
This GTA supersedes
GTA 5-2-10, 1980
Title COORDINATE SCALE
AND PROTRACTOR
Headquarters, Department of
the Army
OUTER SCALE - MILS
INNER SCALE - DEGREES
1/50,000 METERS
1/25,000 - 1/250,000 METERS
1/100,000 METERS
64°
MAC
D
48
49
50

Post Support:

It can benefit the supporting unit

by CPT John A. Durkin

Using engineer troops for post support is often a lesson in futility for the facility engineer. Most engineering functions on post are contracted to civilian engineering companies, leaving few projects for the military engineer. A program developed at Fort Gordon, however, has demonstrated a way to effectively use combat engineers, while also helping to improve MOS skills and raise SQT scores.

Company D, 92nd Engineer Battalion (Combat) (Heavy) has provided post support to the U.S. Army Signal School and Fort Gordon since 1970. During that time, D Company was assigned only platoon-size projects. These included renovating two-story World War II buildings for Reserve Component billets, constructing a military police dog kennel and post riding stable, and completing numerous erosion control projects.

Program Drawbacks

The projects maintained unit integrity while supervisors and subordinates learned to work as a team. But there were drawbacks. Few projects effectively used all military occupational specialities (MOSs) within the platoon. Also, the installation lost many manhours of support when there was insufficient platoon-size projects available or when materials did not arrive as planned.

For example, during construction of the riding stables, carpenters were needed throughout the project, and electricians were required during the later phases of construction. The problem, however, was how to use plumbers, truck drivers, and other non-related specialities.

Most of the platoon found that they were merely the labor force until the project was well underway. At that point, those who desired cross training as carpenters or electricians could improve their skills, but when it came to SQT testing, some of these soldiers had no recent experience in their primary skill and, therefore, performed poorly during the hands on component.

A Different Approach

In June 1981, the Directorate of Facilities Engineering at Fort Gordon was reorganized. The move was made so that military engineers might participate in post engineering functions by working along with civilian contractors. For maintenance and repair mission purposes, the post was divided into four maintenance zones and a hospital support division. Two military engineering branches were established to service these zones: A special projects branch, which included welding, carpentry, sheetmetal and locksmith shops, and a roads and grounds branch.

The new method of operation was more conducive to individual and unit training for Delta Company. Dividing the responsibilities lended itself to assigning a squad or larger unit to each zone, branch, or activity. This allowed for engineers to work side-by-side with civilian journeymen while still keeping unit integrity.

To test the idea, one squad was assigned to a zone on a trial basis. The squad leader worked directly with the zone foreman, and the squadmembers worked with civilian journeymen. The results were excellent. The soldiers and civilians had nothing but praise for each other.

Construction projects were assigned to the applicable zones and became the responsibility of the zone foreman. Each foreman reviewed and ordered supplies, assisted the project officer when requested, and ultimately accepted the project for the facility engineer. If delays occurred in the project, the squa continued their individual MO training by assisting a civilia journeyman with routine maintenance and repair projects.

Training Periods

The next step in the new progran was to involve the entire company. 90-day period was established fo providing post support followed b 30 days for company training. Durin the 30-day training period the com pany moved to the field to complet military tasks and to test readiness.

The 90-day post support perio allowed the soldier time to becom familiar with the team projects an gave the civilian jouneymen time t help strengthen the soldier's MO skills. Also, platoon leaders ha sufficient time to plan in detail wh instruction was to be given durin the 30-day field training perio Common skills that needed rei forcing were taught to the enti platoon or company without fear losing key personnel to post details

Since the program began, Fo Gordon has been receiving engine post support and MOSs 51B, C, H, R, and 52G, 64C, and 62J SQT scor have increased nearly 20 perce Also important, company morale a pears to be at an all time high.

LTC Martin C. Fisher is th Director of Facilities Engineerin Fort Gordon, Ga. He holds a bachelor degree in civil engineering from th Virginia Military Institute and master's degree in civil engineerin from Arizona State University. He i a registered professional enginee and a graduate of the Command an General Staff College. He has serve in Germany, Vietnam, Indonesi Cambodia, and Saudi Arabia.

Training Without Straining

Improving strength, ability and endurance will help you pass .e Army Physical Readiness Test. nd, you can prevent injuries in ›ur training program by "training ithout straining."

Soldiers should use their training :ograms to achieve and maintain nproved physical fitness. "Physical tness" is a relative term; we all ›gin conditioning programs with ırying degrees of fitness. Although roup training has its benefits, it is so helpful if training is more ıdividualized and adapted to each ›rson's abilities.

Physical fitness is many things to ıany people. Whatever else it may e, it is generally accepted that tness includes strength, agility and ıdurance.

trength

Many fitness experts feel that to nprove strength one must do at ast one more repetition of any given exercise than was previously done; i.e., 20 pushups today, at least 21 tomorrow. This approach has left many soldiers unable to pass the Army Physical Readiness Test. It is also a potential source of injury.

Few people would attempt to run a given distance—say, a mile—as fast as possible and then come back on succeeding days believing they could improve their times each day. Attempting maximum effort in any strengthening exercise day after day will often result in NO improvement.

In attempting to improve strength regardless of the exercise in question, use the principle of progressive resistive exercise. The following discussion relates to pushups, but is applicable to any strengthening exercise.

First, determine your maximum effort through a self test. If you cannot do even one pushup, you must initiate the exercise with a lesser degree of difficulty, perhaps by doing wall pushups or pushups from the knees instead of full length pushups done on the toes and hands.

Second, reduce your maximum effort by a half or a fourth. If the maximum repetitions you can do is 20, then start with 10 to 15 repetitions. This will be much easier to do. Rest for two or three minutes, perhaps interjecting a stretching exercise as you rest, and then do a second set of 10 to 15 repetitions. Repeat this procedure through three or four sets initially. You now will have done two or three times more repetitions than you did previously, when you did your maximum number of repetitions just once.

On succeeding days, continue the same number of repetitions and sets until this is no longer difficult. Now you can add additional sets. After accomplishing six or seven sets in one exercise period, you may choose to reduce the number of sets back to three while increasing the number of repetitions by 25 percent.

"The key to any training program is to tune in to the body."

Agility

Agility training, which is basically stretching, is different for each individual. Strict numbers of repetitions need not be applied. Follow these principles:

Stretch preventively those areas which routinely are shortened through activities. For example, runners routinely shorten the extensor muscles of the body like the back and hamstrings of the legs.

Stretch these muscles in a manner convenient to you when you feel a need. Do as many repetitions and hold for as long as necessary to achieve the mobility you desire.

Generally speaking, stretching is less critical in warmer weather when you should exercise more slowly for longer periods; for example, run several miles as opposed to a 100-yard sprint. Exercising in colder temperatures increases the need for added stretching before running or other rigorous exercise.

Endurance

In improving endurance, the heart and lungs are the primary areas of focus. To improve the efficiency of the heart and lungs, you should choose an activity that is accessible and enjoyable, one that will satisfy these three basic factors:

Intensity: The activity must successfully elevate the pulse to 70 percent of maximum. To determine maximum intensity, subtract your age in years from 220 and multiply the result by 70 percent. For example, a 40-year old person would want to work at a pulse of 126 beats per minute. At 70 percent of maximum, you'll find yourself breathing normally and not gasping for air. Most people take the pulse at the radial of the wrist or the carotid on the neck.

Duration: The activity must be carried on non-stop for 15 to 20 minutes or more. Some researchers advocate at least a 30-minute exercise period, but anything less than 15 to 20 minutes appears insufficient to produce a "training" effect. Additional time above 20 minutes will produce added training benefits.

Frequency: To improve endurance you should work out at least every second day. If you train more frequently, your results will be better.

Many activities satisfy these requirements for strength, agility, and endurance. Some suggestions are: fast walking, which is recommended for those previously leading a sedentary life, for at least the first three or four weeks or longer; running; swimming; cycling; cross-country skiing; jumping rope; or rowing.

These are but a few suggestions. Choose something you enjoy. If you choose walking, and you plan to progress to running, consider the following points:

Shoes: There are literally hundreds of good walking and running shoes on the market today. In choosing shoes to suit your needs, consider several factors. That portion of the shoe cupping the heel should be firm, molded and padded. Cushioning can be determined only by trying on the shoes, walking, running in them. The heel should be approximately 1/4 inch higher than the front of the

The Balance

by COL (Ret.) Dandridge M. Malone

In the process of developing leaders, there will be one general malfunction. Even with this malfunction the unit will continue to operate, but it won't run smoothly on all cylinders. This malfunction has to do with *balancing.*

Two big factors underlie all we know about Army leadership: accomplishing the mission, and the welfare of the men. Mission and men.

Leaders are always working with these two factors. Whenever and wherever possible, a leader tries to balance them so that both the needs of the mission and the needs of the men are met. But there are times — sometimes in peace, often in war — where the needs of both cannot be met. The balance cannot be kept. A leader must choose one over the other. In these few situations, and the leader must make them few, the mission must come first.

There are those few times when our Army will not, cannot, and should not "be fair." The whole meaning of Army leadership rests on this law: the mission must come first. So does the meaning of "soldier," and "service," and "duty."

In the balancing business, the mission side of the scale requires to but it simply knowing your job in excruciating detail. Without it, an Army leader can never lead for long. Just talk won't work. The troops will know.

The men side of the scale requires the leader to know his soldiers. He must know what's inside of them, what makes them do things or not do things, what turns them on or off, what they can do and what they will do under stress, and when they're afraid, or tired, or cold, or lonely. These are the things he needs to know about his soldiers. They're what tells him how a soldier measures up on the "able and willing" gauge.

You, as a leader, must try to balance between these two requirements — mission needs and men needs. And it is precisely here, in this "balancing" business, where leaders most frequently fail. It is here where young sergeants and young lieutenants have their greatest difficulties and where even old leaders, despite their wisdom, sometimes lose sight of the ultimate purpose of leadership. The problem arises because of the relationship that exists between the soldiers' happiness and satisfaction on the one hand and their productivity and mission accomplishment on the other.

Common sense might tell you that happy, satisfied soldiers will get the job done better. From this, a leader, especially if he's a new sergeant or new lieutenant, might well assume that if he can somehow keep his soldiers happy and satisfied, then they will be more productive, more likely to get the mission accomplished. But the strange chemistry of leadership just doesn't work this way. A thousand scientific studies of leadership, and a thousand lessons of leadership experience, both prove that what seems to be a natural, common-sense assumption is precisely wrong!

In simple terms, mission accomplishment builds morale and esprit far more often than the other way around. When soldiers and units do the things that soldiers and units are supposed to do, that's when morale and esprit are highest. That's why the one best way to build will is to build skill. That's why those new basic training graduates are so fired up about soldiering and about the Army. That's why unit esprit is at its peak when the unit has a good exercise going out in the field.

If soldiers don't know both sides of this leadership scale — the needs of the mission and the needs of the men — in full detail, they'll be forever getting the scale tilted the wrong way. And when that happens, the soldiers' time, or the soldiers' spirit, or the soldiers themselves will be wasted.

There are times, in training, when you may be led astray. You may see cold, wet, muddy troops coming in from a night field exercise at 0200 and say, "Hell, let's let 'em get a hot shower and some sleep; then we'll pull maintenance when it's light enough to see." And there are times just like that in war when a bloody and shot-up company may be stalled in its assault, for the second time, halfway up a hill. You say, "Hell, they just can't do that again. Let's dig 'em in, pound that hill with Red-Leg, and ask battalion for reinforcements." If you love your troops, in the noble way that good leaders do, both these decisions, at the time, may seem to be just common sense. But both are taking the easy way out, and both violate the ultimate purpose of Army leadership.

Now you can, and should, argue this point. But if you're talking about leadership, there's no way you can win. The purpose of leadership is to accomplish a task. And in the final analysis, when the action shifts to the battlefield for which you are now preparing, mission must come first. As you lead, and as you build leaders, this law must be, flat-out, the cornerstone of your foundation.

Reprinted from INFANTRY magazine.

Career Notes

Commissioned Officers' Branch

(202) 325-7504/7505/7506, AV 221

Guide to the OER Support Form: DA Form 67-8-1 is a highly valuable tool for the rated officer an rating officials. It provides the mechanism for the meshing o organizational, professional and personal goals within units an activities. The tool is especially important where time and distanc do not permit close contact between the rated and rating officer (e.g., duty with Reserve Components, remote USACE activitie liaison activities, etc.). In these instances, the rated officer shoul request a personal interview with his rating official to fin agreement on major performance objectives. Mid-course meeting should also be arranged to review progress, re-chart goals or redire efforts. Several helpful hints on the form follow.

Part IIIa, labeled for "duties and responsibilities," is especial critical for non-troop positions. This paragraph should be written i familiar Army terminology. If your position is an unusual on compare your duties to those in familiar Army positions. Avoid littl understood abbreviations, especially in technical material.

In developing your major performance objectives (part IIIb), se a copy of your rater's support form to use as a guide. Your objectiv should be attainable, measureable, and written against objecti criteria.

The third paragraph of the support form, part IIIc, is where yo list your significant contributions. Ensure that your contributio tie-in with your performance objectives. Be objective, yet n humble.

Guide to the OER: Generally, the weight of selection board decisions is with the D Form 67-8. The OER is an articulation of the contributions an potential of the rated officer. The report should be written in cle and solid language. Short, action-oriented declarative sentences a best. Repetitive phrases and adjectives can detract from a report effectiveness. Rating officers need not fill the entire narrati portion of the report to provide a clear understanding of the rate officer's "worth." Once a report is accepted at MILPERCEN f permanent filing, it is very difficult to change. Ensure that what said and what is checked is warranted. Hindsight is inoperative her

Tips for Raters Recheck the job description from Part IIIa of the Support For (DA Form 67-8-1) and ensure it accurately depicts major duties, is i general Army terms, and where required, compares to commo troop positions.

Use the comments portion of Part IVb to explain any anomolies i physical fitness (profile) or military bearing and appearance (such a the results of a pinch test and weight reduction progress to date Address outstanding or weak competencies and similarly addres

Commissioned Officers' Branch (continued)

ethnical traits. The norm is a 1. Give the officer the number he deserves; if he doesn't deserve a 2, 3, 4 or 5, give him a 1.

Use the performance objectives and contributions listed on the Support Form to assist in developing the narrative.

Be logical in commenting on potential for schools and assignments. For example, CSC and battalion command; SSC and brigade-level command. Address leadership potential in the context of command. Problem solving and managerial skills should point to a level of assignment (e.g., unit, division, MACOM, DA).

Tips for Senior Raters

The narrative continues to be the bedrock of this section of the report. Complementary aspects of the senior rater's section of the report are the box check and the senior rater's profile.

Each senior rater needs a profile game plan—a mailbox system if you will—to provide a "mind's eye" point of reference into which officers of each grade can be placed. The vast majority of senior raters continue to spread their box checks. Most appear to be spreading their effective officers across the top four boxes. Senior raters should track their profiles from both an overall and an individual perspective. Losing track of a profile and unknowingly placing an individual lower or higher than in previous reports can have a serious impact on an officer's competitiveness. Profiles should be restarted when conditions or analysis dictate a broadening or contracting of the mailbox system. A phone call to the MILPERCEN Evaluation Systems Officer (AV 221-9659/9570) will restart a profile. Automatic restarting will take place after 100 reports have been rendered for a particular goal.

Senior rates should focus on the potential of the officer being evaluated. Like the rater, this potential should be logically developed and should specify a level of leadership or managerial assignment, and qualifications for additional schooling.

Warrant Officers' Branch

(202) 325-7838/7839, AV 221

MOS 621A Shortage:

The Army has a shortage of Warrant Officers for MOS 621A, *Engineer Equipment Repair Technician.* Qualifications and application procedures are outlined in DA Circular 601-83-2. Warrant Officer Procurement Program - FY 84 dated September 15, 1983.

A warrant officer recruiting team from MILPERCEN is scheduled to visit the following installations and overseas areas: Ft. Gordon, May 7-11; Ft. Polk, May 21-25; USAREAU, June 9-30.

Interested qualified personnel who desires to be a warrant officer are encouraged to attend the recruiting teams' briefing, or to contact CW4 Mullins at MILPERCEN, ATTN: DAPC-OPW, 200 Stovall St., Alexandria, VA 22332. Phone: AV 221-7832/7840.

NCO & EM BRANCH

- **Overstrength MOSs**

See News & Notes, page 3.

ENGINEERING

IE MAGAZINE ARMY ENGINEERS SUMMER

The Division Engineer

A Personal Vi

Because the division Engineer battalion commander's command responsibility will be reduced during wartime, it would be a mistake to misuse his significant role as the division Engineer. Both as a staff planner and as the coordinator for numerous Engineer battalions, he is the key to synchronizing combat units within the division sector.

In a realistic division front, the division Engineer battalion would be fragmented. The line companies in direct support of the brigades would receive all of their missions from their brigades. The general support company will often be sent to reinforce one of the other line companies or it may be tasked to support the cavalry. This leaves only the bridge company under battalion control.

The direct support companies depend on the nearest forward area supply train (FAST) for their logistics support while all Class IV and Class V are doctrinally provided by the maneuver units. The Engineer battalion headquarters maintains operations and logistics status to ensure mission accomplishment and reinforcement as required.

Realistically, the distances involved make any direct involvement difficult, even in logistics support. Consolidating friendly obstacle lists or sitings of enemy obstacles is a major reporting function in the battalion. The battalion headquarters is not significantly taxed, however, with monitoring its own companies.

The division Engineer has two roles. First, he coordinates the efforts of all Engineers working within the division sector. In wartime the division would doctrinally be supported by at least two corps combat Engineer battalions and a combat support equipment company composed of heavy earthmoving equipment. The division Engineer must justify and request the support from corps. These assets may come under either direct support or operational control (OPCON) to the division with new doctrine leaning more toward OPCON, particularly in the attack.

JME 14 NUMBER 2 SUMMER 1984

FEATURES

DEPARTMENTS

The Cover

DAS3 (Decentralized Automated Ser- ...pport Systems) Field System is used in ...ivisional direct support and general ...t units. Especially designed for today's ...the DAS3 significantly aids soldiers in ...idating reports in personnel, supply, ...anagement. (Photo courtesy of Tactical ...ystems, General Electric Company.)

NEER is an authorized publication of the U.S. Army Engineer Center and Fort Belvoir, VA. Unless specifically stated, ial appearing herein does not necessarily reflect official policy, thinking nor endorsement by any agency of the U.S. Army. The he, him or his are used to represent personnel of either sex. All photographs contained herein are official U.S. Army graphs unless otherwise credited. The use of funds for printing this publication was approved by Headquarters, Department of rmy, on July 22, 1981. Material herein may be reprinted if credit is given to ENGINEER and to the author. ENGINEER's ives are to provide a forum for the exchange of ideas, to inform and motivate, and to promote the professional development of embers of the Army engineer community. Direct correspondence with ENGINEER is authorized and encouraged. Inquiries, to the editor, commentaries, manuscripts, photographs and general correspondence should be sent to: ENGINEER Magazine, -TD-P Stop 163F, Fort Belvoir, VA 22060. Phone: (703) 664-3082, AV 354. Subscriptions to ENGINEER are available through uperintendent of Documents, U.S. Government Printing Office, Washington, D.C. 20402. A check or money order payable to intendent of Documents, must accompany all subscription requests. Rates are $11.00 for domestic (including APO and FPO) sses and $13.75 for foreign addresses. Individual copies are available at $3.00 per copy for domestic addresses and $3.75 for n addresses. Second Class postage paid at Fort Belvoir, VA, and additional mailing offices. ISSN 0046-1989.

News & Notes

Bulldozer Blade Kit

The Army's Armor and Engineer Board recently gave the go-ahead for further testing of a bulldozer blade kit for the M-1 Abrams tank developed at the Belvoir Research and Development Center, Ft. Belvoir, VA.

For many years, Army units have mounted bulldozer blades on some of their tanks to clear debris and rubble, improve defensive fighting positions and breach obstacles.

In 1978, Chrysler Defense studied the possibility of adapting the M9 bulldozer kit used with the M60 tank to fit the M1. They recommended designing a new kit that would use moldboard geometry to improve driver vision and system performance and take advantage of the lower profile of the M1 tank. Recommendations also included up-to-date hydraulic components and a quick coupling and release mechanism.

Based on the recommendations of the study, the Center awarded a contract to Barnes and Reinecke, Inc. in 1981 to build a prototype kit which was tested at Ft. Knox the following year. It mounts on the lifting eyes and towing lugs and is powered by the tank's electrical system.

The crew of an M-1 tank uses a dozer blade being developed by the Army's Belvoir (VA) Research and Development Center to clear a path for the tank.

Terrain Analysis Tool Assembly

In the future, combat commanders will rely on automated systems for up-to-date terrain information. Scientists at the U.S. Army Engineer Topographic Laboratories (USAETL) are assembling a prototype terrain data extraction and analysis system which will help make automated topographic support a battlefield reality.

This Terrain Analyst Work Station (TAWS) will use digital techniques to extract, interpret and display terrain data. TAWS takes advantage of recent advances in microcomputer technology, analytical photogrammetry, computer-assisted photo interpretation and geobased information processing. These technologies will eventually allow soldiers in the field to produce and update digital terrain data bases.

The Defense Mapping Agency (DMA) plans to supply digital topographic data for the terrain analysis community and other Army users. DMA data, however, may not always be available for every site where battles may be fought. Combat itself can drastically change the natural landscape, making terrain information that was accurate yesterday obsolete in a matter of minutes. TAWS capabilities can fill the gaps which may exist between the information that's available and the coverage that's needed.

Using TAWS, analysts will be able to extract terrain elevation and feature data from a variety of sources—including maps, charts, aerial photographs and satellite imagery. They can then digitize this information and use it to update existing data bases or create new ones.

ETL scientists are rapidly assembling the hardware and software needed to make TAWS a prototype terrain data management tool. The system's central 32-bit microcomputer will be delivered in May along with two disk drives and related peripherals. Much of the software which will be used for the project has already been developed in the laboratory; contractural efforts are underway to convert these programs to run on TAWS.

Project engineers expect to have TAWS ready for laboratory tests by June 1985.

New Hydraulic Fluid

A fire-resistant hydraulic fluid that will reduce the chances of crew-compartment fires in the Army's combat vehicles is currently under development at the Belvoir Research and Development Center's Materials, Fuels and Lubricants Laboratory.

The need for a hydraulic fluid with increased fire protection was uncovered in an Ordnance School post-battlefield analysis of the 1973 Middle East War. Hydraulic fluid fires in armored vehicles were clearly identified as contributing to the loss of life and equipment. These fires usually occurred where hydraulic systems lines and components were exposed.

Subsequently, the Army replaced its petroleum-based hydraulic fluid (MIL-H-6083) in 1974 with an Air Force/Army developed, synthetic hydrocarbon based substance (MIL-H-46170) that featured improved fire-resistant properties.

However, since the improvement in fire-resistance was marginal, the adoption of MIL-H-46170 was considered an interim solution. To develop a truly nonflammable hydraulic fluid, a completely halogenated material is being used. Tests show that this fluid can be diluted with up to 20 percent of currently-used hydraulic fluid without losing its fire-resistant traits.

Presently, efforts are directed toward developing a fully formulated, nonflammable hydraulic fluid that can be used in existing hydraulic systems. Factors that may affect the eventual fielding of this fluid include the high specific gravity and volatility of the base fluid.

MICROFIX

MICROFIX, a new automated Storage and Retrieval System for mapping information, is being evaluated under a joint effort by the Belvoir Research & Development Center and the U.S. Army Force Command.

MICROFIX will assist the terrain analysts to process, store and retrieve terrain data on a more realistic "Real Time" basis. It will serve as a transition between the manual systems currently in use and the fully automated systems of the future.

Microfix consists of a microcomputer and 10 subsystems that have been certified for field use. Expansion cards enable the central processing unit to control the devices and a 128 kilobyte random access memory card more than doubles the computer's memory giving the system greater data processing capacity.

So far, the Belvoir R&D Center has purchased six of these systems for evaluation at a cost of $35,000 each. These units are currently located at Ft. Bragg, NC; Ft. Lewis WA; Ft. Shafter, Hawaii, the U.S. Military Academy; the Defense Mapping School and the Center's Combined Army Support Laboratory. Operator training has been completed and the results of the evaluation should be ready early next year.

Larger Fuel Storage Tank

A 210,000-gallon collapsible fuel storage tank developed by the U.S. Army Belvoir Research and Development Center, Ft. Belvoir, VA, has been type classified.

Work on the tank began as part of a program to develop large capacity fuel storage containers that can be set up with minimum effort. Standard containers currently available, a 420,000-gallon bolted steel tank and a 1,050,000-gallon hasty storage reservoir, both take considerable time and effort to install and require a great deal of logistics support. The largest collapsible tank currently in the Army's inventory only has a 50,000-gallon capacity.

The new tank will bridge the gap between the 420,000-gallon steel tank and the 50,000-gallon collapsible tank.

A 210,000 gallon collapsible fuel storage tank has been developed for quick supply on the field.

Engineer People

Next Chief of Engineers

MG E.R. "Vald" Heiberg III will become the next Chief of Engineers on Sept. 14, 1984, according to the Department of Defense.

Heiberg, whose nomination by President Reagan was announced on May 11, will succeed LTG Joseph K. Bratton, who will retire from military service on September 30. Heiberg will also be promoted to Lieutenant General when he assumes his title as Chief of Engineers.

Heiberg is currently serving as program manager of the Ballistic Missile Defense Program under the Office of the Army Chief of Staff. He has been assigned to this position since May 1983.

As Chief of Engineers, Heiberg will have the principal responsibility for the development and management of the nation's water resources programs, which include navigation, flood control, hydroelectric power generation, water supply for municipalities and industries, and recreation at Corps of Engineers' projects. In addition, he will be responsible for military construction for both the U.S. Army and the U.S. Air Force in the United States as well as overseas, and will also serve as the executive agent for the Army's worldwide Facility Engineering activities.

Heiberg's previous assignments include: Deputy Chief of Engineers; Director of Civil Works in the Office of the Chief of Engineers; Deputy Chief of Staff, Engineer, U.S. Army, Europe; Military Assistant and Executive to the Secretary of the Army; Chief, Manpower and Structure Team, Planning and Programming Analysis Directorate, Office of the Army Assistant Vice Chief of Staff; and as Special Assistant and Executive Assistant to the Director, Office of Emergency Preparedness under the Executive Office of the President of the United States.

MG E. R. Heiberg III (right) and LTG Joseph Bratton (center) met with former President Jimmy Carter Sept. 15, 1979 in Mobile, AL to discuss damage done by hurricane Frederic that year. At the time of this photo Heiberg was Chief of Civil Works in the Office of Chief of Engineers.

Engineer of the Year

This year's award for the U.S. Army Forces Command Engineer of the year was presented to COL Ralph A. Luther, former director of Engineer and Housing at Ft. Bragg, NC. Luther, who recently assumed duties as engineering officer for the National Security Agency at Ft. Meade, MD, received the award for his service at Ft. Bragg. He credits his selection to a conglomerate of many different positions in the Army which gave him the training and ability to learn new jobs quickly. "I've worked with FORSCOM since I've been here," he said. "I guess the daily relationships that we have here left them with the impression that Ft. Bragg is doing better in the Facility and Engineering business than any other installation within FORSCOM.

COL Ralph A. Luther

Editor's Note:

Training developers at the Engineer School's Topographic Engineering Branch are revising TM 5-232, *Elements of Survey*. This revision is necessary because of doctrinal changes and new equipment being fielded with the Topographic Support System. The new version will include revised portions of TM 5-441, *Geodetic and Topographic Surveying*; TM5-442, *Precise Astronomic Survey*; and the survey specifications published by National Ocean Survey, formerly NOAA. TM 5-441 will become obsolete when the *new* FM 5-232 is published. FM 5-232 is scheduled for review in the field in 1987 with publication in 1988. *(This supercedes any information which has appeared in prior publications).*

Outstanding Citizens Honored

Two members of the Army Corps of Engineers received awards from the Governors of their states.

CSM (Ret) Grady F. Miles, formerly Command Sergeant Major of 2nd U.S. Army, Ft. Gillem, GA, was named as the 1984 Outstanding Military Citizen of Georgia by Gov. Joe Harris.

Dale Brown of the Georgia Intergovernmental Relations Office said that nominees for the award must be stationed in Georgia and have an outstanding record of military and community service. The Governor selects an outstanding military citizen each year from each armed service's active and reserve components.

Miles, who began his 30-year Army career in the Infantry before switching to the Combat Engineers, was honored during ceremonies in the Grand Ballroom of the Omni International Hotel in Atlanta.

His army career includes combat engineer duty in Europe and the United States, as well as 10 years with Special Forces units. A resident of Rex, GA, Miles is active in many activities such as coaching, Boy Scouts, church and the PTA.

The reservist honored was SFC Melvin Kelly of Company C, 926th Engineer Bn. in Huntsville, AL, who was given the Governor's Award by Gov. George C. Wallace in ceremonies at the State Capitol in Montgomery.

Kelley was one of 18 to receive the award, given annually to outstanding enlisted representatives of units in Alabama.

Gov. Wallace said the purpose of the award is to express the appreciation of the citizens of Alabama for the military men and women who preserve freedom around the world.

Selection for the award is based on military bearing, conduct, and outstanding performance of duty. Kelley was also chosen for his leadership ability and his contributions to his unit and community.

In civilian life Kelley is an Equal Opportunity Officer with Ballistic Missile System in Huntsville, AL.

CSM Miles (above) and SFC Kelley awarded as outstanding citizens.

Heiberg continued

Heiberg has also held command assignments in the United States and overseas as Division Engineer with the Corps' Ohio River Division; District Engineer with the Corps' New Orleans District; and as Commander of the 4th Engineer Battalion, 4th Infantry Division in Vietnam.

He is a 1953 graduate of the U.S. Military Academy and has earned three masters' degrees, including one in civil engineering from the Massachusetts Institute of Technology. He is also a graduate of the Army Command and General Staff College and the Industrial College of the Armed Forces.

He has served as one of seven Presidentially-appointed members of the Mississippi River Commission, and has also served as president of the Coastal International Association of Navigation Congresses.

Among his military awards are the Distinguished Service Medal, Silver Star, three Legions of Merit, Distinguished Flying Cross, Bronze Star Medal, seven Air Medals and two Army Commendation Medals.

CLEAR THE WAY

by MG James N. Ellis, Commandant, U.S. Army Engineer School

Goals Achieved, Challenges Ahead

Retaining our basic skills we must adapt to an automated future

This ENGINEER will be the last issue to be published during my term as Engineer School Commandant. Although the past 2½ years have gone by much too rapidly, and perhaps with too many things left undone, we have been able to make significant progress in improving training and equipment, updating doctrine, and in remodeling organizational structure.

For example, the May 1984 publication of FM 5-100, *Engineer Combat Operations*, is now the keystone Engineer doctrinal manual supporting the AirLand Battle. Engineer functional manuals subsequent to FM 5-100 (FM 5-101, *Mobility*; FM 5-102, *Countermobility;* FM 5-1-3, *Survivability;* FM 5-104, *General Engineering;* and FM 5-205, *Topographic Operations*) are scheduled for final publication within the next two years. These manuals will help to ensure the Engineers' ability to fight on the AirLand Battlefield.

The organization of Divisional Engineer Battalions has been remodeled in the Division 86 structure to reflect the demands of AirLand Battle. In addition, a smaller Engineer battalion has been designed to meet the requirements of the new Light Division. In each case, efforts were focused on improving the Engineers' capabilities in providing mobility, countermobility, and survivability to the combined arms team.

But perhaps the most significant progress over the past several years is our improved ability to train the Engineer team. The 12B Basic NCO Course (BNCOC), for example, is one of the best in the Army. Also the new 51H Basic Technical Course (BTC) will soon be joined by a 62N BTC and a 12F BNCOC. Furthermore, these courses are capped by a newly improved Advanced NCO Course (ANCOC), which was started at Fort Belvoir this summer.

Our officers will have a new 20-week Advance Course beginning in October 1984. This course should pose more challenge and provide more educational rewards for each student. I am convinced this will be the best Advanced Course in the Army.

All of these doctrinal and training improvements, as well as improvements in equipment (the Armored Combat Earthmover, the Small Emplacement Excavator and the Ground Emplaced Mine Scattering System, which are all approaching fielded status), are recognized in the series of studies accomplished over the past two years and culminated by the Functional Area Assessment (FAA) and the Mission Area Assessment (MAA) to the vice chief-of-staff, General Max Thurman. Much remains to be done, however, by MG Richard S. Kem as he becomes the Commandant of the Engineer School. I know MG Kem will ensure continued solid progress in the months ahead.

Automation of various Corps activities is one of the many challenges facing MG Kem. This issue of ENGINEER highlights several applications of computer-based automation. As these articles indicate, the Corps of Engineers needs officers and NCOs who are as comfortable with automation as they are with bridges, heavy construction, mines and demolitions. So the challenge of the future is not just MG Kem's, but a challenge to every military and civilian member of the Corps of Engineers to keep abreast of the rapid progress all around them while retaining their current skills.

I've enjoyed my duties as Commandant of the Engineer School more than any job I've had since my commissioning 28 years ago. The highlight of the tour was working at Fort Belvoir and around the world with the finest civilians, soldiers, and officers I've ever seen. I remain convinced that the Engineers will continue to "clear the way."

by CSM O. W. Troesch Jr., U.S. Army Engineer Center & School

NCOs Indebted to School Commandant

As NCOs, we continue to gain a stronger voice in the Corps, but face a more challenging future with automation

As you read or browse through this issue of ENGINEER, the Engineer School and Fort Belvoir will have undergone the traditional change of command ceremony. This ceremony symbolizes the passing of command responsibility from one officer to another and, in this case, the passsing of the duty as the Engineer School Commandant. To MG Richard S. Kem and his family, we bid a warm welcome and a pledge of continued support by the Engineer noncommissioned officers.

To MG James N. Ellis, our outgoing Commandant, the noncommissioned officers owe a great debt. Since the early days of his career when he was commissioned at the United States Military Academy, MG Ellis recognized the need for competent noncommissioned officers in the Engineer Corps. Throughout his years as a platoon leader, company commander, battalion commander and other assignments, he took a personal interest in the NCOs assigned to his command. Now his interest is exemplified in those NCOs who formerly served in his units and now hold key positions of responsibility and trust throughout the force.

Through the turbulent years of the 1960s and early 1970s, MG Ellis never lost faith in the noncommissioned officer corps. Now as the Engineer School Commandant in the 1980s, he was instrumental in helping to rebuild that "time-honored" corps of soldiers who are called the "Backbone of the Army."

In every challenge effecting NCOs and soldiers, his influence and guidance was evident. Through his efforts, NCOs gained a stronger voice in enlisted matters. He helped to add an NCO perspective to the Engineer Corps' changing doctrine. SQTs and related enlisted literature were researched and written, in many cases, by NCOs. NCO courses such as the revised NCO Advanced Course which started in August 1984, were made more innovative and hard-hitting to train Combat Engineer NCO leaders, and became models for other branches to emulate. Although we currently have one Primary Technical Course (PTC) and one Basic Technical Course (BTC) in operation, additional PTCs and BTCs are planned for the future. This will further improve professional development in MOS 62N and 12F technical skills.

NCOs will also face new challenges in automated systems and yet they still must retain their current Combat Engineering skills. The future shows drastic increase in technical equipment and demands all soldiers and NCOs to become experts in these computer systems if they intend to win the AirLand Battle. Thanks to MG Ellis, we now have the opportunity to learn these new systems while still training in our traditional Combat Engineering skills.

All of these accomplishments merely highlight and demonstrate MG Ellis' genuine concern for the Engineer noncommissioned officers' professional development. They will serve as a tribute to his sense of what is good for the Army and its NCOs. For every NCO in the Engineer community, I say thank you. Your efforts have enabled us to "bridge the gap" and make our Engineer family one where excellence is a standard and not an exception.

We wish you and Mrs. Ellis continued success in all of your future endeavors, until we serve together again overseas or here at home.

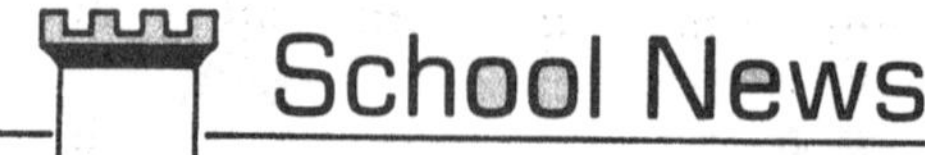

Directorate of Evaluation and Standardization (DOES)

Standardization Program:

The Directorate of Evaluation and Standardization (DOES) i Engineer School manager for the Army Standardization Progr This program identifies tasks or procedures in Army units wh should be standard throughout the Army.

Therefore, if certain tasks are trained and implemented in same manner in all similar Engineer units, soldiers will not required to be retrained in a new unit's method for accomplish the same task. DOES serves as the interface between the Engin School, Engineer units and TRADOC in this area.

If you, as an individual soldier, know of a task or procedure wh should be considered for standardization, please send it to the Di torate of Evaluation and Standardization at Ft. Belvoir.

Professional Development Book:

The Engineer School (USAES) has recently completed distri tion of the Engineer Enlisted Professional Developmental Boo each active Engineer unit. This book covers everything that enlisted Engineer—grades E1 to E9 needs to know for career p ning and professional development. If your unit has not received distribution of this valuable development reference, please cont SFC Wagner, Engineer Proponency Officer, ATTN: ATZA- USAES, Ft. Belvoir, VA 22060. AV 354-2287/4172.

E7 Selection Board Review and Analysis:

After a promotion list is published, the question arises, "W wasn't I selected?" Promotion board members provide a review analysis report to the Soldier Support Center at Ft. Benjamin Ha son and to the commandant of each proponent school after e board. These reports contain observations by the board of w generally was wrong with the records they reviewed.

Here is a brief summary of the major findings: contradict information in promotion packet; poorly written EERs; out-of-d photos; height/weight standards not being met; military educat lacking, and old Article 15s. The Engineer Proponency Office distributed copies of the FY 84 board's report to each active E neer unit worldwide.

Any units not receiving a copy should contact the Engineer P onency Office ATTN; ATZA-EP USAES, Ft. Belvoir, VA 220 Remember, that to the board your record (Official Military Pers nel File) is you. Your file must be accurate and up-to-date. Tak little time out to write for a copy of your file from Ft. Benjam Harrison and make sure it is accurate.

rectorate of aining and Doctrine (DOTD)

5-742 Revision: An updated FM 5-742, *Concrete and Masonry*, should be available to field troops by FY85. Currently under revision by the Engineer School, this manual incorporates the latest information on air-entrainment and mix design.

---

partment of litary Engineering (DME)

COA Preparation: Noncommissioned officers who have been selected to attend the Engineer Noncommissioned Officers Advanced Course should prepare themselves in mathematical and language comprehension skills prior to their arrival at Ft. Belvoir. Upon notification of selection, personnel concerned should contact their Education Center and seek information and guidance on how to upgrade these skills to a 12th grade level. The NCO Student Detachment sends study materials (especially mathematics pamphlets) which will help those who have problems.

It is recommended that personnel who have been selected to attend the course and who have not received the packet at least 90 days before reporting to the course immediately contact the NCO Student Detachment by writing to: Commander, NCO Student Detachment, 3rd Battalion, U.S. Army Engineer School Brigade, Ft. Belvoir, VA 22060, or phone AV 354-6937/2809.

---

epartment of ɔmbined Arms (DCA)

mbat Simulation Center: The Department of Combined Arms, has opened a combat simulation center. The center developed by the Tactics and Operations Division is organized to teach the AirLand Battle doctrine. This is accomplished through war gaming tactical operations of platoons through brigade level units on a realistic terrain board of the Fulda Gap area of Germany.

In addition to the terrain board, three mock M577s with extensions are being built. The M577s will provide the students a realistic combat setting. Control of the terrain board is through a telephone link connecting the brigade and Task Force HQ with the board. A realistic setting is also achieved through taped war sounds, camouflage nets and combat setting.

A computer program is being developed to support the terrain board play. The computer will determine ammunition expenditures and direct and indirect fire engagements, as well as combat support requirements.

For further information contact MAJ Booth at AV 354-2093.

The Automat Engineer Bat

A Glance at the Possibil

by CPT David F. Melcher

The time to automate the Combat and Combat Heavy Engineer Battalions is NOW!

As Engineers we have moved into an era of technology and advanced equipment. However, we have not complimented these gains with equally advanced methods of recording, scheduling and supervising our maintenance activities. We have devised elaborate personnel and training systems, yet we execute them in a painfully slow manner with manual information storage and retrieval. While the rest of society has adopted the microcomputer for running even the smallest enterprise, Engineers are still resorting to older methods which are becoming outdated.

In today's Engineer structure, microcomputers at the battalion level are also becoming a necessity. The large variety of equipment maintained and the size and complexity of its personnel and organization makes the Combat Engineer Battalion ideally suited for automation.

In computer jargon, an "application" is the computer's primary function. There are many applications which are readily obvious for the Engineer battalion. In the logistics/supply area, for example, ordering tools, building materials and ammunition, and maintaining accurate accounts for supplies on-hand, on-order, or backordered can be improved.

Ways of conducting inventories and accounting for personnel and equipment can also be improved. For example, we can achieve better ways to record and order publications. Record-keeping of legal and deployability status is also feasible with a personnel data base management system. Individual training, weapons or physical qualification results, and proficiency testing can be easily maintained for reports and schedules as well as for establishing training priorities.

Possibilities, then, are limitless. Maintenance, for example, is an ideal application for building confidence in an automated system. The risks involved in managing the maintenance process are relatively low, but the potential payoffs are extremely high.

Studies done by F. Warren McFarland of the Harvard Business School show that the variables of project size (relative to the unit's whole operation) can be combined in matrix form to show the relative risks in using a new EDP (electronic data-processing) application. Sounds like a lot of useless jargon, right? But let's examine it again in simpler terms.

The structure of the maintenance function is high since procedures that must be followed are clearly outlined in Army publications. Most data is simply transferred from manual to keyboard. Size is small for preliminary applications (the 2406 Readiness Report) and can be increased as individual successes are achieved. The nature of the system and of its software is not so technical that it cannot be readily adopted by most units. Most applications discussed can be created, debugged and put in place using only existing battalion staff personnel when given proper training with the computer.

This combination of automated

each must be manually identified by scanning reams of forms. This inaccurate screening process usually results in missed or overdue services. If the clerk tries to correct his error with a false entry, the probable result is premature vehicle failure which is even more expensive in terms of labor and parts.

Scheduled services also tie into the parts resupply system because filters, lubricants and bearings must be on hand when the service is due. This cycle could be greatly simplified through automated programming designed to retrieve the required information accurately and timely. This will enable the commander to check that the maintenance operation is functioning properly and that the people required to perform these services are present when needed.

A myriad of other reports which could be better prepared by a computer include parts requests and follow-up actions on deadlined vehicles, maintenance allocation charts and lists of vehicle operators or alternates with the status of their military licensing and driving experiences.

• **Dispatching**

With a microcomputer and an updated database, vehicle dispatching could also be simplified. A simple entry of the operator's name and vehicle bumper number could produce a dispatch and a check on operational status, overdue services, operators qualifications and whether or not the previous dispatch had been closed properly. This sytem could greatly reduce the time it takes to dispatch an entire battalion in the event of rapid deployment for field exercises or alerts.

• **Reordering Function**

In addition to the services application, there is also need for better systems for reordering parts and record-keeping (Prescribed Load List).

Presently, each company PLL clerk manually notes in a bulky card file each time a particular part is used. If it is used three or more times in a quarter, it is added to the Prescribed Load List and stocked within each unit for future use. With current methods and manual bookkeeping, the usual result is that some key parts are overlooked and unit clerks swap parts to cover their oversights, resulting in needless downtime for vehicles.

Automating this function will not guarantee better data entry per se,

TACCS, an off-the-shelf computer and software system for battlefield combat service support missions. (Photo courtesy of Tactical Data Systems, General Electric.)

	High Structure	Low Structure
Low Relative Technology	Large Size Low Risk	Large Low Risk (subject to mismanagement)
	Small size Very Low Risk	Small Very Low Risk (subject to mismanagement)
	Large Medium Risk	Large Very High Risk
High Relative Technology	Small Med/Low Risk	Small High Risk

but it will improve screening stocks on hand with a computerized list rather than a card file. It will also enable the maintenance officer or commander to easily screen his PLL so that he can add parts which are essential to accomplishing his mission. More importantly, a conventional reorder point system used in commercial businesses could even be adapted to trigger prompt action when stocks are low. The applications are only limited by the programmer's or the commander's imagination.

○ Other Intangibles

Although the automated maintenance system can save time, space and paper, the real value in the program is that maintenance clerks, officers and unit commanders are given more time to plan, monitor and check results. Not only do they have more accurate and more timely information at their disposal, they can also get the information they need in order to run an effective maintenance management program.

For the clerk, it permits easier comparison with his peers in like units to see where his records or stocks are flagrantly wrong. It also enables him to devote his time to working with company maintenance personnel to schedule repairs and services.

For the battalion maintenance officer, the computer helps him to

Computers and the Unit Maintenance Programs

Unit Status Reporting

One of the quickest and most visible applications of computerization could be the use of a vehicle status database to generate the 2406 reports. This report is currently prepared daily at each company (four reports in the battalion) and then consolidated manually into a battalion report for the use of commanders and maintenance personnel. It depicts:

1. **Equipment types, authorized and on-hand strength**
2. **Available days for use (drawn manually from another set of forms)**
3. **Specific vehicles that are deadlined and their nomenclature, serial number, reason for nonavailability, dates of nonavailability and part/job order status**

Presently, it takes each company maintenance clerk approximately one hour to update and prepare the report. It takes another hour for battalion personnel to consolidate the report, check it and query company personnel on vehicle status before the reports are submitted to the commanders. In units where typographical errors are frowned on, this process can consume immense amounts of time due to retyping and subsequent checking. With computerized output, the whole process would take roughly one-half hour to update and no time at all to print out. This is because all the information is stored in the databases, and once a change in status is recorded, a report can instantly be printed out. The immediate benefits are:

1. **Quicker report generation**
2. **Legible reports that are easy to check**
3. **Commanders at all levels get the same report**
4. **The system can be designed to include vehicles deadlined for overdue services (not widely done)**

This is just one example of an application that I know would be invaluable to unit commanders and maintenance personnel. The numerous others mentioned are equally invaluable.

Fighting Floods with New Technology

by LTC Stephen E. Shepard

Critical Operation—Structures such as the Steele Bayou Drainage Structure in Mississippi's Yazoo Basin are operated based on information received from the satellite. In a flat area such as the Delta, a few inches in error can mean thousands of dollars in damage. (U.S. Army photo.)

The electronic age, which has crept into the art of flood fighting, is aiding the Corps of Engineers. Automation is converting flood fighting techniques from desperate efforts of sandbags, confusion and prayers to a science of prediction, precision, and immediate response.

Almost annually, the Lower Mississippi Valley has suffered from devastating floods, limiting the socio-economic potential of this fertile, agricultural region.

Although a century of flood control efforts by the Corps of Engineers has greatly reduced flood damage, man has still not succeeded in changing the weather; eliminating floods is still an impossible task.

But recent technological advances have allowed the Corps, working with other federal, state and local groups, to improve its effectiveness in using the flood control works constructed during the past 100 years. These measures have resulted in significant savings by reducing damages and human trauma.

GOES Satellite

A great advance came in 1974 and 1975 when the National Aeronautics and Space Administration (NASA) launched two satellites dubbed MS-1 and MS-2. These first Geo-Stationery Operational Satellites (GOES) were placed in stationary orbit 22,600 miles above the

Pacific Ocean to collect various data such as water resources, agriculture, geology, forestry and meteorology.

In cooperation with NASA, the GOES now helps the Corps of Engineers' Vicksburg District to monitor the 2,300 miles of rivers and streams in its three-state, 68,000-square mile area of responsibility. Based on its need for immediate information concerning rainfall and river levels, the Corps was named a major user of the system, along with several other federal agencies.

Generally, each water resources project is tied hydraulically to all other similar projects. To manage the many reservoirs and flood control structures which protect the thousands of people in urban and rural areas and the vast acres of farmland, the Vicksburg District's hydraulic engineers need data to make accurate, timely decisions.

In less than one second, GOES satellite receives and transmits rainfall and river data from the million-square mile Mississippi River basin to the Corps' Waterways Experiment Station (WES) in Vicksburg. This is a vast improvement over the old days when all river and rainfall information was telephonically transmitted by local gage readers who were at the mercy of damaged phone lines, washed out roads and faulty alarm clocks.

The satellite system is based on a network of automatic battery-powered gages placed in remote areas, under bridges and other strategic locations. The gage batteries are charged by their own solar cell. Some situations are primarily telephonically monitored with the satellite serving as a secondary data transmission system.

One of the major advantages of the satellite system is its "stand alone" capability. Information is automatically transmitted through the satellite to the NOVA computer at WES, which district hydraulic engineers and technicians access to perform instant analysis. Though some local gage readers are still used, the 24-hour information flow and reliability of the satellite system, and the telephone access-satellite system have proven extremely effective in flood fighting.

At present, the district receives its satellite information from the NOVA computer at WES and manually loads it into the district's computer. Plans for system expansion, however, show computers that can compile information directly from the satellite.

Computer Modeling

Information entered into the district's computer is used to develop models for forecasting the rate of flow, rate of rise, and flood crest of streams and lakes in the Vickburg District. The computer modeling system can quickly assimilate such varied information as amount of rainfall (actual and predicted), runoff and river stages, and present it in a usable form.

A Winning Combination

Computer modeling and satellite gages have given the Corps a new advantage in fighting rampant rivers. During the December 1983 flood at Greenwood, MS, the rapidly rising Tallahatchie River threatened to overflow the Fort Pemberton Plug, a major item in the Greenwood protection works. Using satellite information and a computer model, hydraulics personnel were able to accurately forecast the rapidly rising river stages and allow necessary lead for the Greenwood office to successfully implement measures in protecting the plug.

The Corps' modern technology also benefits individuals and small business concerns. During a 1982 flood event, a Mississippi delta catfish farm, an industry highly susceptible to flooding, was threatened by rising water. The owner called the District Hydraulics Branch for information on flood levels.

Using data made available by local gage readers, and the satellite gage system, hydraulic engineers and technicians were able to monitor the river over a 24-hour period and to obtain an accurate prediction. Relying mainly on Corps data, the farmer elected to keep his catfish crop in place rather than undertaking the costly procedure of pond draining and premature harvesting. Accuracy of the forecast was within one-tenth foot and the farmer was spared considerable misery and expense.

Because of the reliability of Corps' information, many people request river information which is not fore-

he OV-1D Mohawk was used to map the extent of flooding, locate seepage under levees, and survey ie District for flood damage. (U.S. Army photo.)

ıfrared photographs to form a comrehensive image.

The OVID offered District experts lofty vantage point to view flood amages, while helicopters from the 21st ARCOM provided for detailed ıspections. Using OH58-A Kiowa ›ur-seater helicopters and the ırger UH1H Iroquois (Huey), the orps maintained a close surveilınce on hundreds of miles of levees nd several flood control structures.

The helicopters were also used for erial photography, assessing flood amages and endangered levees, nd reaching areas inaccessible by round transportation. This llowed Corps Engineers to cover ast areas in hours instead of the ays it would have taken by land onveyance.

essons Learned

Although the new flood fighting chnology has resulted in many lesons learned, one lesson particurly deserves more attention. The formation provided by satellites, omputer models, and aerial reconaissance is only as good as the dividual analyzing the data. omputer-aided forecasts are most seful when tempered by sound dgment based on practical expeence with the rivers.

Often, a forecast based on compur results has been completely revsed because of human interpretaon. An aerial photograph is seless unless the examiner is illed in translating the visual nages into useful data. Even with e timeliness and accuracy of information gathered through the new technology, human judgment remains the critical element in flood fighting. The people of the Vickburg District succeed by applying sound judgments based on vast experience and using the latest technological advances to prevent as much loss and suffering as possible.

LTC Stephen E. Shepard is the Deputy District Engineer of the Vicksburg District. He is a graduate of the Command and General Staff College and has a bachelor's degree in commercial art and engineer management. He also has a master's degree in environmental management from the University of Texas. LTC Shepard previously served as the Readiness Advisor at Fort Sam Houston, the Resident Engineer in Saudi Arabia, and as Project Engineer in the Galveston District.

Hotline Q & A

Q. When disabling a bridge, on which side of the bridge should the Triple Nickle Forty charges be placed (the friendly, enemy or either)?

A. Reference FM 5-25, Chapter 4, section III. The charges are used only on abutments up to five feet thick. Complete demolition and partial demolition under various circumstances require different placement of charges. The Engineer school teaches that for complete destruction - place the "Triple Nickle Forty" charges on both the friendly and enemy sides and for partial destruction - place the charges on the friendly side. The use of charges depends on the target, the time, the commander's requirement and the rule from appropriate manuals.

Q. Smoke grenade launchers on AVLBS and CEVs do not fit properly w/out modification. What is the Engineers School doing to resolve this problem?

When the smoke grenade launchers were used over a year ago, mounting brackets were not issued. These brackets are necessary to install the grenade launchers onto CEVs and AVLBs. Mounting kits, however, are not expected to become available until 1985, and only depot maintenance is authorized to mount smoke grenade launchers on CEVs and AVLBs.

Q. I need to obtain some general purpose barbed tape obstacle (GPBTO) material for training purposes.

GPBTO can be requisitioned material through normal supply. The NSN is 5660-00-921-5516.

Battlefield Environmental Effects Software (BEES)

by Boyd Poush

A warrant officer, who is a terrain team leader, walks into an office and introdu[illegible] himself to the person seated at the desk top computer keyboard.

"I saw the BEES demonstration during Gallant Knight, and I was impressed," he sa[illegible] "Can you show me what else BEES can do?"

An hour later, he departs with 50 feet of computer printouts tucked under his arm. "T[illegible] is just what we need in the field," he says. "I wish the data base covered the whole worl[illegible]

Scenes like this are happening at the U.S. Army Engineer Topographic Laboratories (ETL) and at Army installations and laboratories where BEES (Battlefield Environmental Effects Software) is being demonstrated. BEES, a user-friendly computer program system, is designed to demonstrate environmental effects information available to commanders for planning and conducting military campaigns.

BEES was first demonstrated in 1983 at Fort Bragg, NC, in a training exercise called "Gallant Knight." BEES processed real-time and predicted weather by using information which the Air Force staff weather officer provided. It also processed environmental data provided by the terrain team.

BEES shows how environmental information supports the Corps of Engineers AirLand Battlefield Environment (ALBE) program and the Training and Doctrine Command Demonstration Planning Team. ALBE focuses research and development programs on the Army's realistic battlefield concerns. Under ALBE, both the Materiel Defense and Readiness Command and the Corps of Engineers laboratories are cooperating to create products for field demonstration.

BEES is expected to be incorporated into these demonstration projects. BEES itself is a cooperative project, adapting specialized subprograms developed by other organizations such as the Army Smoke and Aerosol Working Group, the Atmospheric Sciences Laboratory, the Construction Engineering Research Laboratory, and the Night Vision and ElectroOptics Laboratory.

But now, let us return to the team leader and the demonstration he received from ETL geographer Paul Bourget.

The warrant officer reads a computer printout of the BEES 20-program menu. He expresses interest in the Army Construction Engineering Research Laboratory's Military Engineering program. Bourget then "calls up" a list of military engineering functions. The visitor selects the Bridge Classification program which Bourget requests. The computer asks for span length and road width in feet. The visitor supplies the information, and Bourget enters it into the computer. When all the required information has been entered, the computer prints a number that corresponds to a military one-way or two-way load classification.

Next, the visitor chooses the Climatic Statistics and Narratives program. At the computer's direction, he selects a country, region and city from the list which the computer offered. Given a choice of seasons, the visitor selects spring. Immediately, the printer displays statistics in temperature precipitation, winds, obscurants and clouds.

When the visitor chooses the Surface Wind Climatology program from the menu, Bourget removes a 5 1/4-inch flexible disc from the computer and inserts another. Bourget states that each floppy disc is capable of storing 270,000 bytes of information. The Surface Wind Climatology disc, for example, holds 34,000 entries for 62 stati[illegible] in five countries for 10 to 30 y[illegible] periods. The desk top computer n[illegible] used for BEES demonstrations h[illegible] a built-in storage capacity of 572,[illegible] bytes at 8 bits per byte.

The overall BEES concept is n[illegible] restricted to these specificatio[illegible] however. Bourget explains that p[illegible] of the BEES information is bei[illegible] translated into a computer la[illegible] guage for the Army's MICROF[illegible] microcomputer. Although terr[illegible] teams are among the units that w[illegible] soon have MICROFIX system[illegible] BEES programs are also slated to [illegible] included in ETL's Terrain Anal[illegible] Work Station (TAWS) and the D[illegible] ital Topographic Support Syst[illegible] (DTSS) computer programs.

After the new disc is inserted, t[illegible] computer displays the Surface Wi[illegible] Climatology program and giv[illegible] instructions to choose from a list [illegible] countries. The terrain analy[illegible] chooses a country at random a[illegible] then a city within that country. T[illegible] computer gives surface wind av[illegible] ages in various speed categories [illegible] selected hours for each month bas[illegible] on data supplied by the Air For[illegible] Environmental Technical Appli[illegible] tions Center.

The terrain analyst then turns [illegible] the very complex Real-Time Met[illegible] rological Data/Critical Values p[illegible] gram. This program combines t[illegible] weather forecast and terrain ch[illegible] acteristics of a selected area a[illegible] integrates the physical character[illegible] tics of various troops, operatio[illegible] and materiel. With this progra[illegible] the computer can assist the co[illegible] mander in orchestrating the bat[illegible] plan by evaluating the role th[illegible]

ETL Geographer Paul Krause studies map and BEES Classification graphic. (U.S. Army photo.)

Paradrop Climatology program. After accepting ceiling height, visibility and wind speed, BEES quickly responds: Category 1, military free fall—not possible. Category 2, personnel and container delivery system G12—not possible. Category 3, equipment—not possible. Category 4, container delivery stem G13, G14—not possible. In other words, the combination of environmental factors exceeds the critical conditions under which any type of paradrop is possible.

The BEES computer is even programmed to spot operator errors. After Bourget enters arbitrary values to demonstrate a meteorological conversion, the computer first displays the instruction, "reenter data," and then displays the message, "the values are not realistic."

The demonstration ends here, but BEES has still more capabilities, including:

- Army Night Vision and Electro-Optics Laboratory Target Aquisition program
- Army Smoke and Aerosol Working Group Atmospheric Transmission model
- Density Altitude Climatology
- Army Atmospheric Sciences Laboratory KWIK Smoke Obscuration model
- Sunrise, sunset, twilight times
- Moonrise, moonset, moonphase
- Psychometric calculations

BEES is a fast-growing project. With its modular design, it can be quickly updated to include the best subprograms. Environmental effects have always had significant impact on combat. Now we have the means of quickly forecasting the effects for field commanders.

Boyd Poush is a public affairs specialist at U.S. Army Engineer Topographic Laboratories, Fort Belvoir, VA. He has a bachelor's degree in political science from George Washington University and formerly served as a foreign service information officer with the U.S. Information Agency in Indonesia and Yugoslavia. He also served as an aerial imagery interpreter in the U.S. Army.

The Need For The M9 Armored Combat Earthm

by MAJ Donald T. Wynn and CPT Ronald G. Prichard

The M919 Armored Combat Earthmover (ACE), a significant improv operations on the modern battlefield. (U.S. Army Photo.)

Improved weapon systems such as the Abrams tank, the Bradley fighting vehicle, and the Apache attack helicopter require support from associated systems of equal agility, mobility, and survivability. The M9 Armored Combat Earthmover (ACE) has these characteristics.

The evolution of the combat earthmover from World War II to the modern battlefield demonstrates the need for Engineers to provide rapid support in a hostile environment.

The bulldozer was growing in civilian importance when it was first used by the Army during World War II. It proved invaluable for clearing obstacles, breaching ditches, improving fords, filling craters, and increasing mobility.

But as Allied forces began using the bulldozers in combat, they found the operator and the vehicle needed armor protection. The bulldozer's immediate need in combat brought about dozer blades for tanks and armored cabs for bulldozers. The tank dozers were not as efficient or versatile as the armored bulldozers, so division commanders continued to use their bulldozers on the FEBA as much as possible.

Since World War II, the lethality of tank guns and artillery has increased tremendously. For example, a 1944 M4 Sherman tank required 13 rounds to achieve a 50 percent kill probability against a stationary target 1,500 meters away. A 1967 M60 tank required only one round to achieve a 50 percent kill probability. Today, the M1 Abrams tank has an even higher kill probability. The Warsaw Pact developed their weapon systems to a comparable level.

Lethality was also increased by new antitank weapons, such as the TOW and SAGGER. This lethality emphasizes the importance of a combined arms team approach and

ipment within the past few rs. The Soviets, especially, have led systems solely devoted to thmoving on the battlefield. ese new systems are tactically bile and designed to operate in forward modern battlefield.

he U.S. Army has also expressed needs for a mobile combat earthver through the 1981 Engineer tem Program Review (SPR), the ny 86 Study, and the Engineerand Mine Warfare Mission Area alysis (MAA). These studies conled that this needed earthmover st act as a combat multiplier. It st improve the survivability of nbat systems and reinforce the ain to preserve the movement of ndly forces and impede the vement of enemy forces.

he MAA provided a detailed lysis of Engineer missions in an Land Battle to support the comed arms team against the 1992 eat (Figure 1). The MAA study phasized that these Engineer ks must be performed in stride l under fire.

esides the analysis of Engineer sions and task requirements, the A analyzed the Engineers' capaty to deploy, to move, and to sure on the AirLand Battlefield as y perform their mission (Figure

lo single vehicle can perform all types of earthmoving tasks or move in support of the combined arms team (Figure 3). In fact, the Combat Engineer Vehicle (CEV) is the only Engineer vehicle sufficiently mobile and survivable to operate in the forward battle zone. However, it does not possess the required earthmoving capability—a major deficiency.

The M9 Armored Combat Earthmover (ACE) is specifically designed to eliminate this deficiency and provide the combined arms team with a highly mobile, survivable, earthmoving capability in the forward combat zone.

The M9 has the earthmoving capability to perform all the tasks

EARTHMOVING MISSIONS AND TASKS

Mobility Tasks

- **Combat roads and trails**
- **Forward aviation (helipads, forward arming and refueling points, airstrips)**

Counterobstacle Tasks

- **Tank ditch breaching**
- **Gap crossing (preparing sites)**

Countermobility Tasks

- **Obstacle development (digging tank ditches, cutting roads)**

Survivability Tasks

- **Fighting positions (excavating positions, fields of fire)**
- **Protective emplacements (hull defilade positions, command posts, fields of fire)**
- **Protected support facilities (protective berms)**

Figure 1

e ACE will greatly increase Engineers' earthmoving capabilities over the D7 dozer and the mbat Engineer Vehicle (CEV). (U.S. Army Photo.)

The ACE shows its increased mobility capabilities for Engineers in the AirLand Battle. (U.S. Arm photo.)

needed in the forward areas. In addition to many other tasks, the M9 can:

- excavate fighting positions
- clear fields of fire
- cut combat roads and trails
- breach antitank ditches
- dig antitank ditches
- prepare river-crossing access and egress

At the same time the M9 has the characteristics which allow it to survive and move with the combined arms team in the forward combat zone.

- It is armored against indirect artillery and small arms fire.
- It has a smoke screening capability against direct fire weapons.
- It is air transportable in the C-130, C-141, and C-5.
- It provides NBC protection to the operator.
- It is tactically mobile with speeds up to 30 mph.
- It is amphibious.
- It can communicate with the task force.
- It has a night vision capability.

In addition to these characteristics, the M9 is operationally more effective than the D7 dozer it replaces (Figure 3). This advantage was demonstrated in an operational effectiveness study conducted in 1980 by the Engineer School.

The study scenario placed a U.S. battalion-size task force conducting defensive operations against a Warsaw Pact motorized tank regiment. The U.S. defensive operations culminated with a counterattack to reoccupy its initial battle positions before the arrival of the second threat echelon. The U.S. task force was supported first by two M9s a then, in an identical scenario, two D7s. In comparison to the support, the task force supported the M9s: increased average t force movement rate by 67.7 perce improved loss exchange ration 22.44 percent; reduced weapon s tems losses by 22.45 percent; a reduced M1 losses by 32.35 perc

DESIRED EQUIPMENT CHARACTERISTICS

Deployability

Air transportable (C-130, C-141, C-5)

Tactical Mobility

Highly Mobile (moves with maneuver forces)

Amphibious

Night vision

On-board communications

Battlefield Survivability

Armored (survives on lethal battlefield against indirect fire and small arms

Smoke screening capability

NBC protection

Figur

RESENT EARTHMOVING CAPABILITIES

Battlefield Use		System Characteristics		
Counter-Obstacle Tasks	Survivability Tasks	Tactical Mobile	Able To Survive	Air Deployable
No	Yes	No	No	Yes
No	Yes	No	No	Yes
No	No	No	No	Yes
Yes	Yes	No	No	Limited
No	Limited	Yes	Yes	Limited
Proposed Capability				
Yes	Yes	Yes	Yes	Yes

Figure 3

One if the ACE's many capabilities is dumping with its 2 1/2-cubic yard bucket. (U.S. Army photo.)

MAJ Donald T. Wynn is the M9 Project Officer in the Directorate of Combat Developments at the U.S. Army Engineer School. He is a 1971 graduate of the U.S. Military Academy and a 1983 graduate of the Command and General Staff College. He has masters' degrees in applied science and business administration. He is a registered professional engineer in Virginia.

CPT Ronald G. Prichard is Commander, B Company 1st Bn (AIT) at Fort Belvoir. He served as platoon leader and executive officer in the 5th Engineer Bn. (Corps) (Cbt) at Fort Leonard Wood and was a project officer with the Directorate of Combat Developments. CPT Prichard is a graduate of from the U.S. Military Academy, and masters' degrees in engineering management and American history from the University of Missouri-Rolla and George Mason University.

A battalion staff briefs their commander on Engineer operations. (U.S. Army photo.)

Engineer Modeling Progran

by Burnham S. Gould, Jr. and CPT James V. Mudd

Combat Simulation Models Show Importan of Engineers in Fighting Airland Battle

especially important. The Army intends the AMIP to form the basis of all major combat modeling. When completed, it will comprise a new generation of combat models.

The AMIP is a hierarchy of three models sequentially named from small units (highly detailed) to large units (highly aggregated); for example: the Combined Army Support and Task Force Evaluation Model (CASTFOREM); the Corps/Division Evaluation Model (CORDIVEM); and the Force Evaluation Model (FORCEM). (Figure 1 shows the relationship between these models.)

The underlying concept in the system is that combat results will flow from lower level models to higher level models, and scenarios will flow from higher level models to lower level models. Engineer School guidance must ensure that the logical relationships between the models are valid, and that the Engineer functions represented in each model are relevant to the context of the whole hierarchy.

CASTFOREM, a model developed by the TRADOC Systems Analysis Activity (TRASANA) is one model which is near completion. Engineer representation includes close combat activities such as minefield emplacement and breaching, individual items of equipment and weapon systems. TRASANA and the USAES have begun a joint study to debug the Engineer portion of this model and to investigate new Engineer system alternatives.

CORDIVEM, a model developed under Combined Arms Operations Research Activity (CAORA) direction is undergoing testing. The Engineer module in CORDIVEM was developed by the Construction Engineering Research Laboratory (CERL) under the Engineer School's guidance. This module includes a precise method for allocating Engineer resources. Procedures are being developed to better represent Engineer attrition, resource constraints and movement.

FORCEM, a model being developed by the Concepts Analysis Agency (CAA), is in its early stage. Engineer representation will be res-

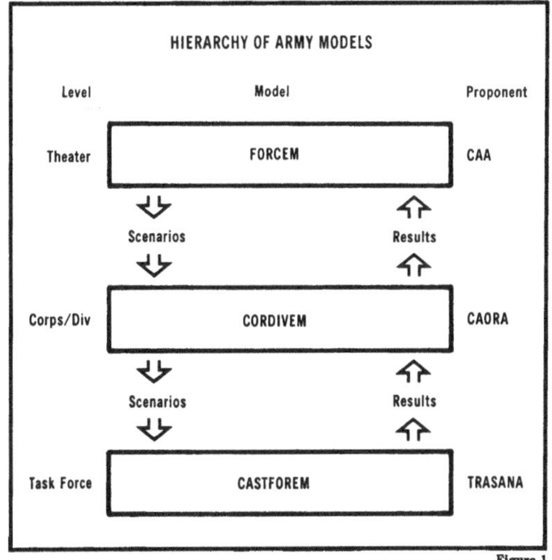

Figure 1

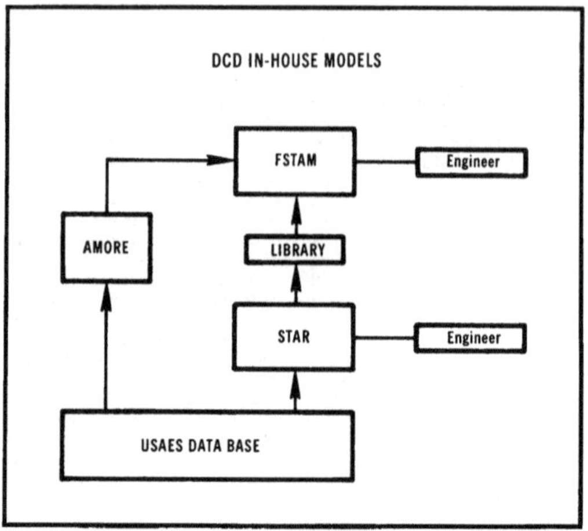

Figure 2

tricted to those activities occurring behind the division rear boundary. CERL is also developing an Engineer module under the Engineer School's guidance to allocate Engineer assets to tasks in priority. This pilot module already has been successfully tested.

Although the models described are extremely important, they are primarily used by the large analytical agencies, such as TRASANA, CAORA, and CAA. However, they are not available to most field analytical cells, such as the Analysis Branch of DCD. This means that DCD must develop its own modeling capability in order to perform quality studies for the Engineer School. Such studies include cost and operational effectiveness of hardware systems, mobility, mission area and functional area of mobility, countermobility and survivability missions, and organizational effectiveness.

Currently, in-house modeling capability is represented by a high resolution analytic model, the Simulation of Tactical Alternative Responses (STAR) Combat Model, and a force design methodology, the Analysis of Military Organizational Effectiveness (AMORE). A Force Structure Trade-Off Analysis Model (FSTAM), where Engineer force contributions can be directly analyzed, is also planned. (Figure 2 shows the relationship between these models.)

The STAR combat model can simulate brigade versus division conflicts. This model has an Engineer module that simulates the effects of minefields and other obstacles on the combined arms battlefield. In August 1982, a memorandum of agreement was signed for the use of the Night Vision and Electro-Optics Laboratory computer facility to use STAR. Since then the STAR combat model has been used to measure the combat effectiveness of several proposed countermine systems. The results were reported in cost and operational effectiveness analysis studies and are being published in Required Operational Capabilities (ROC).

AMORE is a methodology with an associated computer model developed by Science Applications Incorporated (SAI). The Engineer School began using methodology in January 1983 on the School's IBM computer. It provides the ability to measure a unit's robustness, which is defined as resiliency and redundancy. Output from the model shows details of a unit's capability

Automated Construction Management System

by Charles E. Herring

Combat Engineers of the 18th Engineer Brigade have found anaging construction programs sier with the help of a microcomter system called the Automated onstruction Management System CMS).

ACMS is part of a pilot research udy aimed at exploring microcomter applications for Combat Engiers. Using off-the-shelf hardware d software, the U.S. Army Conruction Research Laboratory SA-CERL) was able to minimize ogramming and concentrate on veloping system applications.

To test the ACMS, construction d financial managers at headarters, 18th Engineer Brigade in rmany, are using the system to anage the Grafenwoehr Training nge upgrade project—the largest nstruction effort in Europe, consting of more than 120 individual ojects.

The ACMS enables the user to aintain current records on costs of nstruction projects. For example, uching a button may display the mes of individuals responsible for rious construction tasks. Another tton may show the tasks which ve been completed and when they re completed. The ACMS also speeds the report writing process by compiling data and printing several reports, summarizing the status of construction projects.

According to MAJ Russell P. Baldwin, 18th Engineer Brigade S-3, implementing ACMS was relatively easy. Two clerk-typists assigned to brigade headquarters were trained on-the-job and no formal classroom training was necessary.

The system, itself, consists of five integrated modules. Access to the application modules is provided by a menu program called SUPER-VYZ. The menu presents a list of options from which the user can choose. A menu option may lead to a menu of another module or it may be used to initiate action on a specific function such as "generate reports." The menu system forms a tree structure that is shown in Figure 1. By typing "?" on the keyboard after the menu is displayed on the screen, the user is provided with online help which explains what each menu option does.

Network Analysis Module

The network analysis module will help users track the completion status and scheduling of construction tasks. The module consists of: a powerful Critical Path Method (CPM) program called PMS-11; help files; and utilities for copying and deleting files and for checking file status.

Each project officer develops a network and completes a CPM Input Form. This information is entered into the CPM program which calculates the critical path and generates the following reports: a detailed activity listing; an activity-on-arrow network logic diagram; and a Gantt bar chart (Figure 2). After examining the output, the project officer can perform "what if" analyses by making changes to the network and examining the new results.

Because the ACMS is automated, changes to a CPM are made easily. As work progresses, the actual start and finish dates of the activities may be entered and the updated CPM network generated. In addition, a library of CPMs can be stored for later use in planning to serve as a reference source for project officers.

A summary Construction Status Report is then generated to show the scheduled and actual percent complete, allocated and expended funds, and percent funds expended for each group.

A Monthly Contractor and Troop Construction Report is printed for each battalion and shows the monthly physical and financial progress for each task assigned to that battalion. The Customer Billing Report is produced weekly and lists the allocated funds, costs to date, previous cumulative billing, billing for the current period, and the balance for all projects funded on each construction directive.

The design of ACMS reports are patterned after currently-used Engineering reports. According to MAJ Baldwin, ACMS reports have replaced 99 percent of the reports once prepared manually at the brigade level.

General Application Module

The General Applications Module provides users with two valuable software programs and additional utility menus. First, WordStar, a popular word processing program, can be used for any correspondence

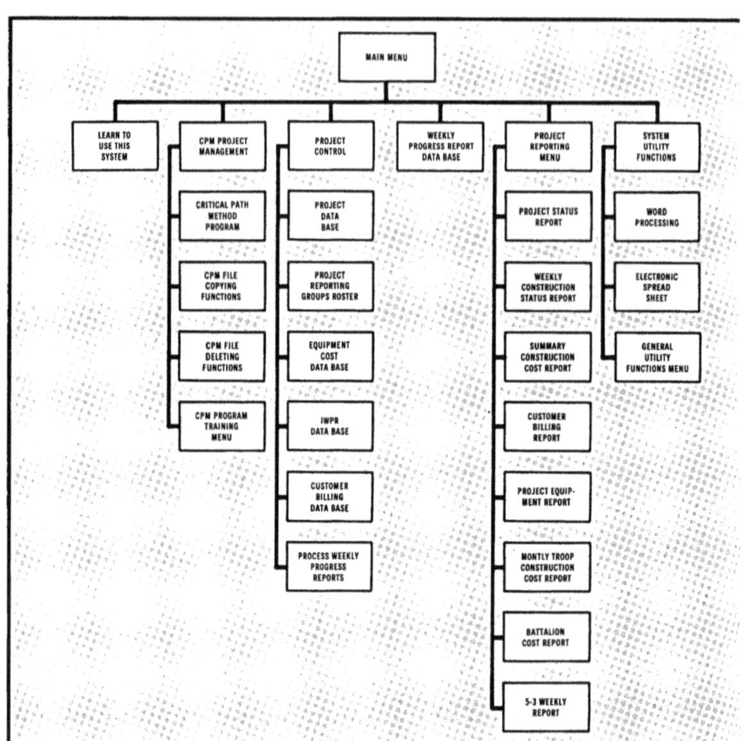

Figure 1. ACMS menu system flow di

associated with construction management. In addition, units without word processing capabilities will have these programs and menus with ACMS.

Second, SuperCalc, an electronic spreadsheet software program, performs any calculations not already programmed into ACMS. Users can also use SuperCalc to keep track of how funds are being allocated within a project.

And third, additional utility menus maintain and duplicate data bases and perform system diagnostics. All of the software systems use current data already stored in the ACMS, making record keeping easier and more accurate.

Advantage of ACMS

Maj Baldwin says that users of the ACXMS at the 18th Brigade have reacted favorably to the system. He adds that personnel at the 18th Engineer Brigade have found that the ACMS helps in three ways.

First, the ACMS significantly reduces the tediousness of the report preparation process. Project officers only have to record raw data on the word processor; the computer performs the vast majority of calculations. This enables construction managers to spend more time in the field supervising their projects.

Second, the ACMS makes it much easier for personnel to keep accurate records. After project information changes are entered into the com ter the new information is im diately disseminated to other us Entering new information will a matically update other report files.

Third, the ACMS quickly prc ces valuable summary reports fı a large volume of data. Manag now have more control over tl projects because summary rep are generated faster. These rep enable a manager to review pha of the project during constructio the entire project after completi In addition, the ACMS can prov a statistical analysis of const tion efficiency for an activity. C

ıe DAS3 van-mounted data processing system allows better control of equipment, spare parts, and maintenance records. (Photo urtesy of Tactical Data Systems, General Electric.)

·quently, managers can make ·tter decisions because they are ·tter informed.

roject Control Module

The remainder of the modules, ith the exception of the General pplications Module, were written ʼ USA-CERL using Base-II, a data ıse management program.

The Project Control Module has ur data bases. The project data ıse stores project information such ı construction directive number, ·oject location, constructing unit, timated cost, allocated funds, and DY rates. Default TDY rates or ıtes specific to a particular location ay be used. Project data (which is ıed for producing a variety of ports) may be entered, changed, or ·leted.

The Equipment Cost Data Base ın record costs for approximately 350 individual line items. Data submitted by the project officer is used to calculate equipment costs charged against individual projects. The 18th Engineer Brigade uses this data base to keep track of the actual equipment hours for over 300 pieces of equipment.

The Customer Billing Data Base is used to produce reports for projects funded under a construction directive. These reports place monetary values on all work completed on these projects. The 18th Engineer Brigade uses the Customer Billing Data Base to summarize the costs of the 120 projects at Grafenwoehr by assigning projects to construction directive numbers. Consequently, the brigade's staff and the brigade's major customer, the 7th Army Training Command, receive an accurate summary of weekly costs.

The Project Groups Data Base is used to define groups of projects for summary reports. For example, the Engineers in the 18th Brigade define project groups according to both the battalions responsible for the projects, and to the firing range in which they are located. This provides flexibility in generating summary reports. All of the battalion's projects for a specific range, or Facility Engineer projects of a certain type or location, can be specified as being part of a particular group for reporting purposes.

Weekly Progress Reporting Module

The Weekly Progress Report (WPR) is the key source data document for project tracking and billing. Each week the project officer submits a WPR to 18th Brigade headquarters. The WPR contains

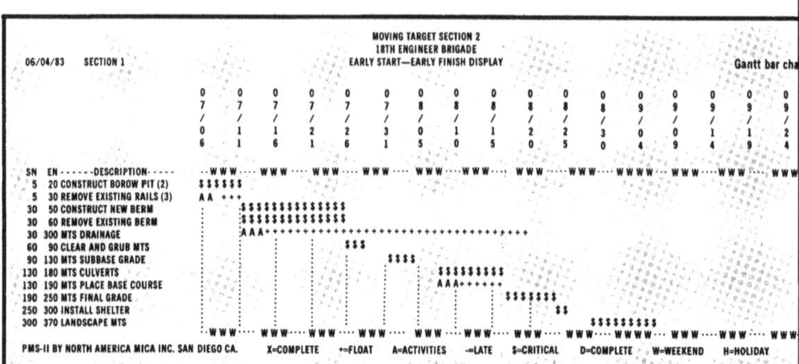

Gantt bar ch

Fig

information on TDY charges, man-hours worked on each activity, and equipment usage. This data is entered into the Weekly Progress Report Data Base. The system performs all required calculations and stores cumulative data for each task. This data is used by the Reports Generation Module to generate summary reports.

Reports Generation Module

This module produces six reports using information provided in the Weekly Progress Reports. A Project Status Report is printed for each active project, showing the current physical progress, cumulative manpower use figures, and financial progress. A copy of this report is sent to the project officer.

The other reports are summary reports for management use. A Weekly Construction Status Report may be produced for each group of projects. The report lists the title, unit, start and completion dates, scheduled and actual percent complete, percent funds expended, and number of days ahead or behind on the critical path for each project.

Future of ACMS

Even though the ACMS was designed for the 18th Engineer Brigade, its modules can be modified to meet other organization's specific needs. The construction management process used in the modules is typical of most Combat Engineer units. Parts of ACMS are being used by the 2nd Engineer Group, Korea; the 20th Engineer Brigade, Fort Bragg; and the 416th Engineer Command, Chicago, IL.

In May 1984, USA-CERL began the development of a "Mission Management System (MMS)" as an interim system to a "Combat Engineer Command and Control System (CECCS)." A generic version of ACMS, applicable to all Engineer units, will be developed as a part of MMS. Some pilot modules of MMS will be field-tested starting in the fall of 1984.

USA-CERL has been tasked to assist the US Army Engineer School (USAES) in developing a command and control system for Combat Engineers. Work on that system will begin in FY85. ACMS version 84.0 is available from the Command and Control Microcomputer User's Group (C[2]MUG). Contact: Chief, CECOM SDSD, ATTN: DRSEL-FL-SDSD (C[2]MUG), Leavenworth, KS 66027. Teleph (913) 684-7550, or AV 552-7550.

Mr. Charles Herring is a progr mer/analyst in the Microcomp and Simulation Team at the Army Construction Enginee Research Laboratory in Ch paign, IL. Herring has a bache degree in physics from the Uni sity of Mississippi and is work toward a master's degree in con ter science at the University of nois at Urbana-Champaign. research at CERL has been in areas of microcomputer appi tions, military engineering, office automation.

Herring is a first lieutenant in Army Reserves and graduated f the Engineer Officer's Basic Co at Fort Belvoir in May 1981.

ENGINEER HOTLINE

Problems, questions, and comments relating to engineer doctri training, organization, and equipment can be addressed teleph nically to the U.S. Army Engineer School's "Engineer Hotline". T Hotline's auto-answer recorder operates 24 hours a day, sev days a week. Callers should state their name, address and telepho number, followed by a concise question or comment. You'll recei a reply within three to 15 days. The Hotline is not a receivi agency for formal requests.

Call commercial (703) 664-3646; WATTS 800-336-3095, extension 36 or AV 354-3646.

MODERNIZATION OF COMBAT CONSTRUCTION EQUIPMENT

by CW3 Ben Fenhagen

Heavy road grader

As a result of the Airborne Airmobile Program and the Commercial Construction Equipment (CCE) Standardization Program, efforts are underway to reduce the number of different makes and models of construction equipment used by the U.S. Army Corps of Engineers.

In the past, the Army's Engineer construction equipment was purchased commercially. Today, many of those items are old, obsolete and logistically unsupportable. To further aggravate the problem, many identical items used by Engineers are available in several makes and models.

One active duty division, for example, has six similar scoop loaders from three manufacturers, four graders from two manufacturers, and five model compressors from two manufacturers. This diversity in construction equipment adversely affects unit readiness by placing additional strain and burden on the logistical support and training base within the Army. The Army, though, recognizes the problem and is moving toward standardizing construction equipment.

Initially, the FAMECE (Family of Military Engineer Construction Equipment) program, a strategy which evolved in the early 1970s, was considered the solution for achieving standardization. FAMECE was an "all purpose" piece of equipment using a common power unit with a variety of earthworking attachments. But after nearly a decade of development and testing, the program was terminated for insufficient funds.

Since 1972 and throughout the full-scale development phase of FAMECE, virtually no funds were committed to buying conventional equipment which was expected to be replaced by the FAMECE. This funding void contributed to the existing construction equipment problem in the Engineer inventory.

After FAMECE was cancelled, the Engineer School analyzed the overall status of combat construction equipment and determined that the need to replace equipment in the airborne and airmobile forces was evident. Major pieces of construction equipment, including loaders, graders, compressors and tractor-towed scrapers, exhibited the worst posture mainly because of overuse, aging and diversity of makes and models.

The analysis also served as a basis for creating two major modernization efforts: the Airborne/Airmobile Program and the CCE Standardization Program. Much of the airborne and airmobile equipment was old at the beginning of FAMECE. BY 1979, many of these items were logistically unsupportable and were degrading unit readiness.

In a joint effort, the Engineer Corps identified the most critical items. These items now comprise the Airborne/Airmobile Program, which consists of loaders, graders, scrapers, water distributors and two sizes of crawler tractors. Contracts for both airborne and airmobile versions were approved in fiscal year 1982. The equipment (conventional commercial items) was altered to meet unique air transportability requirements.

Aside from obvious logistical advantages of new equipment, the program offers additional benefits. It replaces some wheeled tractor-towed scrapers with a modern, self-propelled, elevating scraper. This scraper can be air delivered in a single air drop package or transported in two sorties by a helicopter. Existing scrapers require two air drop packages and possibly five sorties for helicopter transport. In addition, a new increased capacity (2500-gallon) self-propelled water distributor will replace the 900-gallon water bladder, which is generally mounted on a 2 1/2-ton cargo vehicle. Other new features include angle blades for the crawler-tractors and articulated frame steer graders. Both will increase equipment flexibility and productivity.

Still the standardization problem remained unsolved. This significant weakness prompted a DA effort to establish a CCE Standardization Program. This program follows the Airborne/Airmobile Program and is part of a longer term modernization effort.

Since analysis again indicated the need to completely replace key items, it was necessary to list these items by certain limiting factors and by funding constraints imposed by the Army. Some of these factors were mission essentiality, equipment age, density, number of models fielded and logistic supportability. Subsequently, the priority list was used to influence funding. TRADOC and DARCOM developed technical data packages to support procurements scheduled to begin by the middle of the 1980s.

The resulting CCE program basically became a procurement strategy involving competitive multiyear procurements as the key element in achieving standardization. This approach will reduce the number of different makes and models of equipment and reduce the increased logistic burden of documenting, provisioning and training.

With contracts recently approved for the four highest priority ite (loaders, graders, scrapers and compressors), the CCE Standa zation program is now a reality. contracts, awarded to J. I. C Company, Caterpillar Tractor C pany and Ingersoll-Rand in Ja ary and March of 1983, repres orders exceeding 7,000 pieces equipment through 1986. The eq ment under contract is basic from the manufacturer's comn cial product line with modificati to meet military unique requ ments (for example, blackout lig slave receptacles and lifting l and tiedowns).

One of these new contra includes a wheeled loader contr awarded to the J. I. Case Compa for the MW24CIS powered by Case A504BD diesel engine rate 132 horsepower. It is equipped w a 2 1/2-cubic yard multipurp bucket and will replace several m els of like loaders.

Caterpillar Tractor Company v awarded contracts for the grad and tractor-scrapers. The new gr ers, the CAT 130G model powered the CAT 3304 diesel engine, feat articulated frame steering, wh provides greater operator cont and flexibility on the job sites. scraper selected is the 621B s propelled tractor-scraper. It ha 14-cubic yard struck and 20-cu yard heaped capacity powered the CAT 3406 diesel engine. tractor-scraper will replace existi wheeled tractors and tow scrapers.

New trailer-mounted 250 CFM compressors were contracted Ingersoll-Rand. The contr includes complete pneumatic t and compressor outfits and separ trailer-mounted 250 CFM air cc pressors. Field units scheduled receive separate trailer-mounted CFM air compressors, but alrea having complete outfits, w transfer their tools to the new trai and turn in the old trailer and cc pressor. Complete outfits are bei purchased to fill existing shortag The new compressor will be a rot screw type, powered by a Deutz cooled diesel engine.

Each of the new items posses

4-cubic yard scraper

mpressive credentials. Initial fielding of the contracted items will egin by late 1984. Additional items lanned for the multiyear procurement under the CCE Standardization Program include the following: he small emplacement excavator, he T-9 size dozer and the 7 1/2 and 0-ton cranes.

The CCE Standardization Program is a significant achievement modernizing the total force. angible benefits in training and verall logistic support will be evident in future years. The true enefit, however, will be in nproved readiness and capability f Engineers to carry out their role the AirLand Battle.

W3 Ben Fenhagen is assigned to e 557th Maintenance Company in ermany. He was the CCE Project fficer in the Directorate of Combat evelopments at the U.S. Army ngineer School, and has served in rious maintenance management ositions. CW3 Fenhagen has an sociate of science degree and is a aduate of the Warrant Officer enior Course.

Engineer Problem

Specification for a project requires 800 LCY of sand and gravel. The loading unit is a 2½-cubic yard loader, with a cycle time of 50 seconds and an equipment/operating efficiency factor of .65. Hauling units will be 5-ton dump trucks with a cycle time of 12 minutes from the stockpile to the project site (reference FM 5-34, Chap 12-4).

REQUIREMENT 1: How many 5-ton dump trucks will be needed to keep the loader at maximum operations?

REQUIREMENT 2: How many hours will it take to haul the sand and gravel to the project site?

A "team" constructing an M4T6 deck balk bridge with intermediate support. (U.S. Army photo.)

Building A Tea

by Dandridge M. Malo

War isn't a game, but thinking about games can sure help you learn about war.

For example, think about a football team. Think about what it does and how it operates. Then see if you can think of examples that show how a football team is like a unit on the battlefield. That ought to give you a good idea of how teamwork works, on either the playing field or on the battlefield.

But how do you build a team? Well, first, with an overall team-building strategy, and second, using one of those many specific principles of leadership that tell you to train your men as a team.

Fire team leaders build teams with their subordinate soldiers. Squad leaders and above build teams with their subordinate leaders and their teams. In either case, there is one simple overall leadership strategy for building a team. It is an overall way a team operates, not a specific instruction, and it has two requirements.

First, a leader must constantly, on a daily basis, do and say things that will convince each individual team member that he is an essential part of the whole team. He must know that other individuals depend upon him to get their work done and that only with his help will the whole team get its work done.

The second requirement of the strategy is that a leader must do and say things to convince the individual team members that their wants, needs, hopes and goals are tied to the team's performance, output and work. Each individual team member will usually operate in his own best interest. He'll do what he thinks is best for him. That does sound too admirable, but it's a fa of human nature. In building team, a leader has to convince ea team member that the best way him to get what he wants is throu what the team does.

In essence, this team-buildi leadership strategy says:

- Convince each team member that the other team members and the team as a whole are dependent on him.
- Convince him that, even as an individual, much of the whole business of reward and punishment is tied to his team's output and performance.

Building the complex team that battlefield requires is tough. leader can't get it by asking for it by just giving an order. It tak

Work by teams.

Get tasks done by teams, rather than by "details". You, First Sergeant, can do a lot about this. Next time the battalion tasks you to provide a "10-man detail and one NCO," send a fire team with its own team leader *instead* of a detail. Chances are good that half as many men, working as a team, can do twice as much work in half the time. Bet on it. And if you're even smarter, you'll let the team know you bet on them.

Leave teams together.

Whenever there are formations, leave teams together. "Break off and fill it in back there!" may make the platoon formation look better, Lieutenant, but you're breaking up a team. How units work is more important than how they look.

Whenever you, Sergeant, must form your men, brief your men, move your men, work your men, critique your men, feed your men or billet your men, do it the same way as if you had to fight with your men on the battlefield. Do it as a team.

You can tell your troops, "Everyone be at the motor pool at 1300 to clean the tracks." That *may* get them there by 1300, but if you do it that way, Platoon Sergeant, you've just lost one of those valuable daily opportunities to keep working on teamwork. Instead, form your soldiers as a squad in the company area and march them to the motor pool in step. Stand them at ease, give them their instructions with something similar to a brief five-paragraph field order (including mission standards). Supervise the fire team leaders, keeping the whole squad working until the whole job is done. Then call them to formation again, critique their performance as a team, march them back to the company area, and only then release them.

If you, as the leader, can keep your subordinates working and living as a team in their daily activities, the result of those ARTEP drills will automatically improve; and so will that unit we call "the company" when it fights on the battlefield.

Move men on manning boards, not names.

On the wall in the orderly room or in the company commander's office, there should be a manning board. It should look like nothing more than perhaps a chart covered with acetate and filled in with a grease pencil. This chart can be the main tool for building and maintaining teamwork.

The first sergeant and the platoon leaders will make the primary recommendations about who goes where, but the company commander will make the decisions. Never move a name without first thinking about the effect on teamwork and the team. When you rearrange names in an attempt to balance strength figures, you may be doing the same thing the lieutenant does when he evens up his platoon formation. The board may look better, but the unit may not be as effective because you've unintentionally destroyed some of its teamwork power, some of that "extra."

Each time you move a name, what you're really doing is moving a man, and you're moving him out of his family. More importantly, when you move him, you're moving a part of something bigger. If that something bigger is a smooth functioning team, then what you may be doing is taking out the carburetor. And a carburetor can't be replaced with an oil pump. As a general rule, hold manning board moves to an absolute minimum, and always first consider the effect the soldier has on that team.

Talk team language.

There is a simple guaranteed way which all leaders can build teamwork. They should simply start using the team words "we, us, and our," instead of, "I, me, and my." When a leader starts leading by example with his language, his followers will follow. And they'll start talking and thinking more about "us" than about "me". The first two letters in U.S. Army are "US" and the last two are "my." Think about it. It isn't a bad philosophy.

Build team reputation.

Any man worth a damn will work hard to live up to his reputation. So will a team. Whenever a team does something that is both unusual and good, and when the members do it as a team, the leadership of the whole unit should know about it. When this happens three or four times, the word will get back to the team. Then they'll find out that they do have a reputation to live up to.

Reward or punish the team.

Whenever a leader supervises a task that requires a high degree of teamwork (like maybe an ARTEP) he should try to gear his supervision, criticism, reward, and punishment to what the team does more than to what the individuals do. Each individual should clearly understand that what he wants most (or maybe wants least) should depend more on the team rather than on him.

Punishing a whole team is extremely effective, but it should be done very carefully. A whole team should be punished when all the "hands-offs" are too sloppy or too slow, when there's no trust among the parts, or when all the parts get to thinking more about me than about us.

Set the example.

Next to drill, the best thing for building teamwork is that all-powerful, all-purpose leadership tool that has been discussed so many times—the fifth principle of leadership: "Set the example."

If you're a squad leader, you probably want your squad members to believe that the squad's mission is the most important thing. If you do want them to feel this way, then you must show them that for you as the squad leader, the platoon's mission is the most important thing there is.

Also if you're a squad leader, never complain about the platoon's mission or about the platoon leader when you're with your squad. If you do, they're going to follow your example and complain about the squad's mission and about you. Do you want your followers to cooperate, work together, and trust each other? Then show them by example that that's exactly how you work with other squad leaders. From the motor pool to the battlefield, in any situation, followers will do as their leaders do. Good or bad, that's the plain chemistry of followership.

Emphasize differences.

Find out what makes one team different from the other, and keep emphasizing those differences. It may be the kind of work they do, or where they do it, or when they do it—whatever makes them different from other teams. This is another way of telling team members that their team is something special, something different, something important.

Want to build teamwork in your company, Captain? Well, one thing that's always different in any unit is the unit's history. Send a letter through channels and find out what your company did in the last war or two. Then tell the troops about their team at war and how it fought in wars in the past. No lectures, just a talk and some stories. Do this two or three times covering two or three wars and watch what happens with teamwork.

There now, you've got a simple strategy and some simple advice for building a team. All of them are easy, common sense things to do. Will they work? Well, let's return to the football game where we started. Find a team that nearly always wins. Research it a little. Find o[...] how it works internally and wh[...] the coach does to make it wo[...] What you'll find is the same st[...]tegy and most of these same pie[...] of advice that I've provided.

Adapted from the artic[...] appearing in the Novemb[...] December 1983 INFANTR[...] journal.

Dandridge M. Mallone, a reti[...] infantry colonel, has written num[...]ous articles, books, and techni[...] reports. He has a master's degree [...] social psychology from Purdue U[...]versity and has completed seve[...] military schools, including t[...] Armed Forces Staff College. [...] served in staff and faculty assi[...]ments at the U.S. Army Comma[...] and General Staff College, the U[...] Military Academy, and the U[...] Army War College.

Engineer Solution

Requirement 1.

a. First, calculate the loader output. Table 12-4 shows 180 LCY/HR for a 2½-cubic yard loader. Therefore, loader output is calculated as follows:

Loader Basic Production x Efficiency Factor = Loader Production

180 LCY/HR x .65 = 117 LCY/hr

b. Secondly, estimate the hauling requirements.

$$N = 1 + \frac{T}{L}$$

N = number of trucks required

T = travel time (minutes)

L = loading time (minutes)

1. $$\frac{\text{Loader Output}}{\text{Dump Size}} = \frac{117 \text{ LCY/hr}}{5 \text{ cy}}$$

= 23.4 LCY/hr or 23.4 Truck Loads/hr

$$T = \frac{\text{MIN/hr Working}}{\text{\# Loads of material/hr}} = \frac{60 \text{ min/hr}}{23.4\text{/hr}} = 2.56 \text{ minutes loading time}$$

$$L = \frac{\text{Dump Travel Cycle Time}}{\text{Loading Time/Dump}} = \frac{12 \text{ min}}{2.56 \text{ min}} = 4.68 \text{ dumps/cycle}$$

2. Since $N = 1 + \frac{12 \text{ min}}{2.56 \text{ min}}$

N = Extra dump + Dump
= 1 + 4.68 = 5.68 6 days

Requirement 2.

Time it will take to haul materials to the project site is calculated as follows:

$$\frac{\text{Material to be moved}}{\text{Material to be moved/hrs}}$$

$$\frac{800 \text{ LCY}}{117 \text{ LCY/hr}} = 6.83 \text{ Hours}$$

Battalion Command

An After Action

by COL Thomas Jones,
MAJ(P) Lee A. Peters
and
MAJ Kenneth L. Davidson

Battalion Commander, is one of the most revered, demanding nd enjoyable command positions the Army. However, as rewarding nd career enhancing as the posi-on can be, it can also be the water-o of many officers who are nprepared to handle the myriad sks that the job encompasses.

As important as the job is to the ructure and functioning of the rmy, very limited, practical gui-ance is given to a new battalion mmander in the Army Reserve. ossibly the theory is that an officer ho has formerly commanded a mpany, or other such unit and as successful will apply the same arned and inherent skills and be ccessful at battalion level.

Not necessarily! Battalion com-mand comes with a whole different t of demands, responsibilities, and jectives. Many of the things that orked at company level do not rk at battalion and vice-versa.

I was the commander of the 972nd gineer Battalion (Combat), from e 1979 to the summer of 1982. My ttalion was not different from ost other Army Reserve Battal-is. It had a battalion headquar-s and headquarters company at rt Benjamin Harrison, IN, and e units located in three central liana cities.

After my successful command, I lected on why my command was cessful while other commanders, o otherwise had good credentials, re only partially successful, and ne failed miserably. I also pon-ed on what I could have or should ve done to be even more success-in juggling those many com-nd priorities.

rom this thoughtful reflection and from review by former staff members, we developed a list of things which we perceived were items done correctly. We believe that if a new commander followed this "checklist for success" he could start his tenure as battalion commander in a running mode rather than suffering the tribulations of a hit or miss beginning, which may mean dropping some of those juggling priorities and may mean succeeding or failing as a commander.

Checklist for Success

• Fully use your command sergeant major.

The battalion was blessed with a very fine and very active command sergeant major who knew his job. This enabled the commander to use the NCO chain-of-command and to delegate NCO development and training to the sergeant major and to his first sergeants. For example my command sergeant major, CSM Moody, was given total responsibility for the "prep train" program in which the battalion participated. It introduced new soldiers to the Army prior to entry on active duty for initial training.

Using the CSM, as he really should be used, gave the NCOs a flow of formal and informal communication; included them in the functioning and decision making of the headquarters; and, most of all, gave the commander a close supportive and confidential personal resource.

• Completely use the services provided by the Army readiness groups.

For the 972nd this service was offered by the readiness group at Fort Knox and proved very beneficial in most areas. The Engineer team spent many hours at both their home station and at annual training providing expert assistance. The concept of "training the trainers" was used in training exercises without troops (TEWTS) and provided key unit members professional and current training so they could in turn train the personnel within their respective units.

• Use battalion training conferences.

These conferences were held to plan the annual training program for the battalion using the Battalion Training Management System (BTMS). Participants usually included the battalion commander and his staff and the unit commanders along with their first sergeants, training officers, and training NCOs. A lot of preparation took place prior to the conference, a one day meeting held away from the battalion headquarters if possible. At the meeting, the yearly training plan was discussed and the battalion's yearly training circular was published from the results of the meeting.

• Emphasize the importance of the line units.

We had to ensure the staff and the headquarters personnel understood the staff and that their personnel supported the line units. This applied to all areas, including allocating the bulk of the man-day funds and additional training assemblies (ATA) to the line units instead of using them at the headquarters. Also, the staff was frequently sent to the line companies to give assistance instead of being sent to inspect. The feeling of giving help rather than passing judgment was installed within the headquarters personnel.

○ **Stabilize your full-time personnel.**

The people who keep the battalion functioning during the non-drilling hours are your full-time personnel, the unit technicians. In the 972nd, most of the civilian positions were converted to military positions. This military conversion proved to be extremely beneficial. It stabilized the high turnover and allowed personnel to be trained and to become very proficient in their positions.

At annual training the unit administrative supply technicians were consolidated together with the staff administrative specialist in a technician personnel and administrative center at battalion, where they received training and were able to pool their expertise to better serve the soldiers of the entire battalion.

○ **Clearly establish the commander's policies.**

Command policy letters were sent to each unit and staff section. These letters were required to be maintained in a separate, readily available file. They clearly stated the commander's objectives and gave the unit commanders a reference on most key subjects.

○ **Use known personnel qualities, even for short periods.**

Make full use of your personnel's strong points even though you know you will be losing them in the near future. Taking advantage of personnel strong points for even the shortest time periods still gives the unit some reward and can often lead to accomplishing important tasks.

As an example, we had an officer with a strong command background who wanted to join the 972nd, but we knew he would transfer out of the unit within a year. There was a need for a strong commander in one of the line companies, however, to help solve some internal problems. This officer was put in command and used his experience to "straighten-up" the unit. The unit was left in a much improved condition and enabled a capable, but less experienced officer, to take command of a good unit. If the strong qualities of this short term commander were not fully used it may have taken a very long period to correct conditions within the company.

○ **Be willing to take risks with your personnel.**

Allow your leaders to perform on their own as much as possible. Allow them to make mistakes. Be prepared to step in and bring things back under control without accusing individuals if the situation gets out of control. However, do identify the lesson to be learned.

This proved to be a very effective teaching method and also allowed the commander to see fairly quickly what the strong and weak points were within his commanders and staff.

Also, recognize people who do good work, especially under the conditions present in the USAR system. Recognition pays quality dividends to the person, to the unit, and to the commander.

Possible Improvements

One management tool which we used, but later felt that it could have been more effective was the organizational effectiveness (OE). Readiness group Fort Knox organizational effectiveness consultants were invited to work with the battalion and provided very useful feedback on the conditions within the battalion. However, only limited advantage was taken.

New commanders should become familiar with organizational effectiveness and the services which their supporting readiness group is prepared to provide. The benefits are great for limited investments of time and energies.

The following checklist reflects items which we feel are the key areas in helping new battalion commanders to become successful. If a commander follows this guidance he stands a much better chance of a successful command.

Command Philosophy

I operated my command with several open commander's philosophies.

- Don't allow your mistakes to get so serious that you can't correct them. Be astute and committed to saving a man from falling when you see him stumble.
- Set your priorities and hold fast to them. Make sure everyone is working with the same set of priorities.

terable mines (FASCAM) to disrupt the second echelon and to help structure kill zones for deep thrusts of air or ground forces.

Obstacle zones and obstacle-free lanes on the division obstacle overlay depict the commander's vision of how the division sector will be held and provide the guidance which subordinate commanders need to structure the battlefield in their sector. They are equivalent to the coordinated fire lines or restricted fire areas on the fire support overlay. Very few targets appear on the division obstacle overlay. Individual targets are reported from task forces once they are sited on the ground. The final obstacle overlay is a combination of the commander's concept and the subordinate units' plans of execution.

The G-2 must always revise his terrain analysis based on this structured battlefield. If, for example, significant effort has blocked the primary avenue of approach, then it can no longer be viewed as the greatest threat. Forces must be allocated based on the structured battlefield, not the natural battlefield. This is why the critical question the division Engineer must answer is, "From where does the commander want the enemy to come?".

In executing the defense, the division Engineer monitors battlefield preparation. He monitors equipment status and the flow of Class IV and Class V, ensuring that time, and not materials, is the limiting factor in defensive preparation. His critical task is to tell the commander the status of each obstacle system. Although individual obstacles are seldom of consequence at division level, confirming that the terrain has been changed to meet the commander's concept verifies that maneuver units are correctly positioned to fight the battle.

The division Engineer monitors FASCAM emplacement to ensure obstacles in counterattack lanes have detonated prior to friendly movement. By this time the corps Engineer group and battalion headquarters, in coordination with maneuver unit representatives, have already begun to site obstacles on the ground for the next series of battle positions in depth.

How the division Engineer uses his resources to accomplish his missions varies with each division. There is no doctrine. We, at the 1st Engineer Battalion, have found it best for the division Engineer to locate near the division tactical command post (DTAC) when fighting today's battle, while the assistant division Engineer (ADE) is the staff planner at division main command post (DMAIN) for tomorrow's battle. The ADE coordinates with adjacent divisions and with the Engineer brigade supporting the corps. He assesses future requirements and makes requests for additional support.

Once corps Engineers enter the division sector, they coordinate directly with the 1st Engineer Theater Operation Center (TOC), which locates within two kilometers of DTAC and ties into the multichannel switchboard by land line. The TOC tracks the current status of all engineer work within the sector, including unit positions, Class IV and Class V status, equipment status, obstacle execution (defense) and enemy obstacles (offense).

When the division Engineer is not present in the DTAC, a liaison officer (LNO) is positioned there to ensure the current status is available for the close battle, deep battle, and MSRs and positions in depth. The division Engineer returns to DMAIN to advise on Engineer support for significant changes in operations such as initial defensive planning, river crossings or major contingencies.

The division Engineer wears his staff hat far more than his command hat in wartime. He advises and coordinates a brigade-size force of combat multipliers whose capabilities must be fully used if the combined arms team is to fight and win.

LTC Nahas is Commander, 1st Engineer Battalion, 1st Infantry Division (Mech). His previous troop assignments include executive officer of the 2nd Battalion 28th Infantry and S-3 of the 12th Engineer Battalion, both in the 8th Infantry Division (Mech). He is a graduate of the Command and General Staff College and he is a registered professional Engineer in Virginia.

Engineer Command Update

Active Army

7th Engineer Brigade
COL Paul Cerjan
Kornwestheim, Germany

130th Engineer Brigade
COL John Sobke
Hanau, Germany

2nd Engineer Group
COL Ernie Harrell
Camp Coiner, Korea

18th Engineer Brigad
COL Carl Magnell
Karlsruhe, Germany

36th Engineer Group
COL Michael Ward
Ft. Benning, GA

20th Engineer Brigade (C) (ABN)
LTC James Lyle
Ft. Bragg, NC

937th Engineer Group
COL Jerry Hubbard
Ft. Riley, KS

LTC Jerry Sinn
1st Engineer Bn., 1st Inf. Div.
Ft. Riley, KS

LTC Charles S. Thomas
2nd Engineer Bn., 2nd Inf. Div.
Camp Casey, Korea

LTC Hank Miller
3rd Engineer Bn., 24th Inf. Div.
Ft. Stewart, GA

LTC Thomas Farewell
4th Engineer Bn., 4th Inf. Div.
Ft. Carson, CO

LTC Charles Olson
5th Engineer Bn. (CBT) (CORP
Ft. Leonard Wood, MO

LTC Jack LeCuyer
7th Engineer Bn., 5th Inf. Div.
Ft. Polk, LA

LTC Charles Olson
5th Engineer Bn. (CBT) (CORPS)
Ft. Leonard Wood, MO

LTC Jack LeCuyer
7th Engineer Bn., 5th Inf. Div.
Ft. Polk, LA

LTC Leo Laska
8th Engineer Bn., 1st Cav, Div.
Ft. Hood, TX

LTC Charles Cowan
9th Engineer Bn. (CBT) (CORP
Aschaffenburg, Germany

LTC Russ Furhman
10th Engineer Bn., 3d Inf. Div.
Kitzingen, Germany

LTC Charles J. Mills
11th Engineer Bn. (CBT) (HVY)
Ft. Belvoir, VA

LTC David E. Shaver
12th Engineer Bn., 8th Inf. Div.
Dexheim, Germany

LTC Mike Kuehn
13th Engineer Bn., 7th Inf. Div.
Ft. Ord, CA

LTC George Meador
14th Engineer Bn. (CBT) (CORI
Ft. Ord, CA

LTC Mike Norris
15th Engineer Bn., 9th Inf. Div.
Ft. Lewis, WA

LTC Robert J. Greenwalt
16th Engineer Bn., 1st Armd. Div.
Furth, Germany

LTC Pete Sowa
17th Engineer Bn., 2d Armd. Div.
Ft. Hood, TX

LTC Timothy E. Daly
19th Engineer Bn. (CBT) (CORPS)
Ft. Knox, KY

LTC Gary Morgan
20th Engineer Bn. (CBT) (CORI
Ft. Campbell, KY

LTC John Morris
23rd Engineer Bn., 3rd Armd. Div.
Hanau, Germany

LTC Mike Diffley
27th Engineer Bn. (ABN)
Ft. Bragg, NC

LTC Joel Crain
29th Engineer Bn. (TOPO)
Shafter, Korea

LTC Fohn Morgan
30th Engineer Bn. (TOPO)
Ft. Belvoir, VA

LTC Jim Lyles
34th Engineer Bn. (CBT) (HV
Ft. Riley, KS

LTC Philip Shoemaker
39th Engineer Bn. (CBT) (CORPS)
Ft Devens, MA

LTC Rick Shuler
43rd Engineer Bn. (CBT) (HVY)
Ft. Benning, GA

LTC Doug Brown
44th Engineer Bn. (CBT) (HVY)
Camp Mercer, Korea

LTC Hamp Conley
46th Engineer Bn. (CBT) (HVY)
Ft. Rucker, AL 36362

LTC Bill Malone
52nd Engineer Bn. (CBT) (HVY
Ft. Carson, CO 80913

LTC Mike Thuse
62nd Engineer Bn. (CBT) (HVY)
Ft. Carson, CO 80913

LTC Jim Simms
65th Engineer Bn., 25th Inf. Div.
Schofield Bks, HI 96857

LTC Bill Travbel
76th Engineer Bn. (CBT) (HVY)
Ft. Meade, MD 20755

LTC J ohn Wildenberg
78th Engineer Bn. (CBT) (HVY)
Ettleingen, Germany

LTC Milton Hunter
79th Engineer Bn. (CBT) (HVY
Karlsruhe, Germany

LTC Jim Craig
82nd Engineer Bn. (CBT) (HVY)
Bamberg, Germany

LTC Mark Potter
84th Engineer Bn. (CBT) (HVY)
Schofield Bks, HI

LTC Floyd Griffin
92nd Engineer Bn. (CBT) (HVY)
Ft. Stewart, GA

LTC Joe Larremore
94th Engineer Bn. (CBT) (HVY)
Darmstadt, Germany

LTC John Pierce
237th Engineer Bn. (CBT) (HV
Heilbronn, Germany

LTC Mel Lynch
249th Engineer Bn. (CBT) (HVY)
Kneilingen, Germany

LTC John Horne
293rd Engineer Bn. (CBT) (CORPS)
Balmholder, Germany

LTC Church McCloskey
299th Engineer Bn. (CBT) (CORPS)
Ft. Sill, OK

LTC Larry Izzon
307th Engineer Bn. 82nd Abn Div.
Ft. Bragg, NC

LTC Ed Ruff
317th Engineer Bn. (CBT) (CORI
Eschborn, Germany

LTC Clint Willer
326th Engineer Bn. (A ASSLT)
Ft. Campbell, KY

LTC Walt Ivanjack
547th Engineer Bn. (CBT) (CORPS)
Darmstadt, Germany

LTC Fred Ernest
548th Engineer Bn. (CBT) (HVY)
Ft. Bragg, NC

LTC Dan Waldo
549th Engineer Bn. (SVC)
Schwetzingen, Germany

LTC Billy Ricks
559th Engineer Bn. (SVC)
Hanau, Germany

LTC Sam Raines
563rd Engineer Bn. (SVC)
Kornwestheim, Germany

LTC John Mills
565th Engineer Bn. (SVC)
Nevrevt, Germany

LTC Wayne Murphy
588th Engineer Bn. (CBT) (HVY)
Ft. Lewis, WA

LTC Ray Brakham
Composite Engineer Bn.
Ft. Bragg, NC

TRADOC

COL Don Barber
USA Engineer School Brigade
Ft. Belvoir, VA

COL Leo Holland
2nd AIT Brigade
Ft. Leonard Wood, MO

COL William M. Shepherd
4th AIT Brigade
Ft. Leonard Wood, MO

COL Ronald R. Prime
SPT Brigade
Ft. Leonard Wood, M

LTC Frank Reller
1st Battalion, 2nd Brigade
Ft. Leonard Wood, MO

LTC James King
2nd Battalion, 2nd Brigade
Ft. Leonard Wood, MO

LTC Barry Levine
4th AIT Battalion, 2nd Brigade
Ft. Leonard Wood, MO

LTC Tom Jacobus
2nd AIT Battalion, 4th Brigade
Ft. Leonard Wood, MO

LTC Jim Jenkins
3rd Engineer Battalion, 4th Brig
Ft. Leonard Wood, MO

LTC Dave Lindsay
4th Engineer Battalion, 4th Brigade
Ft. Leonard Wood, MO

LTC Hal Alvrod
2nd Battalion, 3rd Brigade
Ft. Leonard Wood, MO

LTC Bill Boutin
5th Battalion, 3rd Brigade
Ft. Leonard Wood, MO

LTC Ken Pryor
2nd Engineer Battalion
Ft. McClellan, AL

LTC Sanford Griffin
3rd Engineer Battalion, USAESB
Ft. Belvoir, VA

LTC John Carny
1st Engineer Battalion, USAESB
Ft. Belvoir, VA

LTC Robert Baker
10th Engineer Battalion, 2nd Brigade
Ft. Jackson, SC

LTC Paschala Aquino
1st Engineer Battalion, 1st Brigade
Ft. Jackson, SC

LTC Michkaud
15th Engineer Battalion, 4th Brigade
Ft. Knox, KY

Army Reserve

2th Engineer Command
3 Robert E. Louque, Jr.
cksburg, MS

416th Engineer Command
MG Maxwell Baratz
Chicago, IL

411th Engineer Brigade
COL Roger L. Kresge
Brooklyn, NY

420th Engineer Brigade
BG Alvin W. Jones
Bryan, TX

th Engineer Group
Cumberland, PA
, Donald D. Emig
th Engr Bn. (CBT) (CORPS) - MAJ(P) James Carrol
th Engr Bn. (CBT) (HVY) - LTC James F Lemp

rd Engineer Group
ahoma City, OK
Paul Revis
th Engr Bn. (CBT) (CORPS) - LTC Jimmie Dyer
th Engr Bn. (CBT) (HVY) - LTC William Long

th Engineer Group
Snelling, MN
, William H. Thom
th Engr Bn. - LTC Allen L. Beeler
th Engr Bn. (CBT) (CORPS) - LTC James Oleson
st Engr Bn. (CBT) (HVY) - LTC John M. Schuster

329th Engineer Group
Brockton, ME
COL Thomas C. Stones
483rd Engr Bn. (CBT) (CORPS) - LTC Eugene Tour
368th Engr Bn. (CBT) (HVY) - LTC Robert Rapp

364th Engineer Group
Columbus, OH
COL James C. Myers
478th Engr Bn. (CBT) (CORPS) - LTC Dennis Grant
983rd Engr Bn. (CBT) (HVY) - LTC Gary Liebenthal

493rd Engineer Group
Dallas, TX
COL Jerry Selly
245th Engr Bn. (CBT) (CORPS) - LTC David Sigler
430th Engr Bn. - LTC Michael L. Griffith
871st Engr Bn. (CBT) (HVY) - LTC John M. Godin

348th Engineer Group
Birmingham, AL
COL Richard B. Burleson
844th Engr Bn. (CBT) (HVY) - MAJ(P) James Sullivan
926th Engr Bn. (CBT) (HVY) - LTC Harry D. Waddle

372nd Engineer Group
Des Moines, IA
COL Max L. Schardein
398th Engr Bn. (CBT) (HVY) - LTC Bruce B. Wands
863rd Engr Bn. (CBT) (HVY) - LTC Jack H. Kotter
972nd Engr Bn. - LTC James L. Bauerle

926th Engineer Group
Montomery, AL
COL Julian F. Botta
467th Engr Bn. (CBT) (CORPS) - LTC Charles Ingram

National Guard

ith Engineer Brigade
3 Roland Bowman
olumbus, OH

30th Engineer Brigade
COL(P) Furman P. Badenheimer, Jr.
Charlotte, NC

35th Engineer Brigade
BG Charles F. Blattner
Jefferson Bks, MO

194th Engineer Brigade
COL(P) Lytle Brown
Nashville, TN

Engineer Group
t, MI
Elon M. Pearson
th Engr Bn. (CBT) (CORPS) - LTC Dougovito
th Engr Bn. (HHD) - MAJ John J. Nelson
th Engr Bn. (HHD) - LTC Edward E Eckart

th Engineer Group
rray, UT
Dee Ray Russon
7th Engr Bn. - LTC Joseph Ford

th Engineer Group
ksburg, MS
L Jerry M. Keeton
rd Engr Bn. (CBT) (HVY) - LTC Dennis R. Self
th Engr Bn. (CBT) (HVY) - LTC Billy R. Barton

th Engineer Group
eville, LA
L Charles R. Lindsey
th Engr Bn (CBT) (HVY) - MAJ Wilson C. Maloz
th Engr Bn. (CBT) (HVY) - LTC Charles Partin
th Engr Bn. (CBT) (HVY) - LTC Edmund Giering
th Engr Bn. (CBT) (HVY) - LTC Lester Schmidt

th Engineer Group
rietta, GA
L Jack D. Cooper
0th Engr Bn (CBT) (CORPS) - LTC Michael Sims
9th Engr Bn. (CBT) (HVY) - LTC Thomas Williams

105th Engineer Group
Winston Salem, NC
COL Harvey L. Poole
505th Engr Bn. (CBT) (HVY)

109th Engineer Group
Rapid City, SD
COL Leroy Beringer
109th Engr Bn. (MAINT) - LTC Robert P. Daane
137th Engr Bn. (MAINT) - LTC Richard P. Gross
153rd Engr Bn. (CBT) (CORPS) - LTC Robert Bensom

134th Engineer Group
Hamilton, OH
COL Raymond E. Trickler
216th Engr Bn. (CBT) (CORPS) - LTC Harlan F. Hess
1138th Engr Bn. (CBT) (CORPS) - LTC Allen Wright
1140th Engr Bn. (CBT) (CORPS) - LTC David R. Moll

176th Engineer Group
Richmond, VA
COL Ralph E. Hickman
276th Engr Bn. - LTC E. Gilman
1030th Engr Bn. (SVC) - LTC Lloyd R. Scott

240th Engineer Group
Waterville, ME
COL Roscoe Tibbetts
153rd Engr Bn. (CBT) (HVY) - MAJ Richard Knight
262nd Engr Bn. - LTC Norm Girouz

308th Engineer Group
Pittsburg, PA
COL Samuel P. Contacoe
429th Engr Bn. (CBT) (HVY) - LTC Mellillo
458th Engr Bn. (CBT) (HVY) - LTC Rodney Ruddock
463rd Engr Bn. (CBT) (HVY) - LTC Walter Ferguson

111th Engineer Group
St. Albans, WV
COL Manual G Goble
1092nd Engr Bn. (CBT) (CORPS) - LTC Casto

164th Engineer Group
Bismark, ND
COL Ronald Affeldt
141st Engr Bn. (CBT) (CORPS) - LTC Robert Schulte
164th Engr Bn. (CBT) (CORPS) - LTC Larry Dennis
231st Engr Bn. (SVC) - LTC Virgil A. Rude

221st Engineer Group
Buffalo, NY
COL Frank J. Ferretti
152nd Engr Bn. (CBT) (HVY) - LTC Richard Fidurski

264th Engineer Group
Eau Claire, WI
COL Elmer O. Simpson
426th Engr Bn. (MAINT) (HHD) - LTC Roger Brill
724th Engr Bn. (CBT) (CORPS) - MAJ Robert Trieland

416th Engineer Group
Walbridge, OH
COL Richard F. Mueller
112th Engr Bn. (CBT) (CORPS) - LTC John Jenkins
612th Engr Bn. (CBT) (CORPS) - LTC David Hering

1169th Engineer Group
Huntsville, AL
COL Andre J. Heritage
151st Engr Bn. (CBT) (CORPS) - LTC David Powell
877th Engr Bn. (CBT) (HVY) - LTC Perry R. Rolfe
1343rd Engr Bn. (CBT) (CORPS) - LTC Joel N. Pugh
145th Engr Bn. (SVC) - LTC Joseph A. Harris

- Beginning with this issue, ENGINEER will publish the "Engineer Command Update" every summer.
- Readers are encouraged to send command updates or any additional information. to ENGINEER. Further unit and command information can be obtained from the "U.S. Army Active National Guard, and Reserve Engineer Units Directory." published in 1984 at Fort Belvoir, VA.

Commissioned Officers' Branch

Restructuring Specialty Code 21:

Letters notifying officers of tentative specialty code designati under the SC 21 restructure were mailed to all officers holding S(during February, March and April. Officers who have not receiv letter should contact CPT George Cooley, Engineer Professio Development Officer at (AV) 221-7426/27.

A system change on the Official Military Personnel File at M PERCEN automatically converted all officers holding additio specialty (ADSPEC) 21 to SC 23 in February. Many of these offi were redesignated to another additional specialty during the re ing of individual records in April and May. (See "Restructuring 21" on page 31 in ENGINEER Winter 1983-84.)

Advanced Civil Schools Board:

The Engineer Branch Advanced Civil Schools Board will mee early September to select officers for FY 85 advanced civil school (Master and PHD level). Officers desiring to be considered sho submit applications in accordance with AR 621-1 to USAMILP CEN, ATTN: CAPC-OPF-E, Alexandria, VA 22332. Fully-fun and partially-funded slots are available in Civil Engineering, O ations Research, Nuclear Engineering, Computer Science/Ar cial Intelligence, Comptrollership, Geodetic Science, and A Studies. Officers with questions should contact CPT George Cor Engineer Professional Development Officer, AV 221-7426.

NCO & Enlisted Soldier's Branch

1984 E7 Selection Board:

The 1984 E7 promotion selection list was based on DA DCSP established selection objectives by MOS. The selection objecti were calculated on projected authorizations and vacancies with intent to minimize overstrength MOSs. The competition within Engineer MOS was keen. The "whole person" concept was used only those determined to be "best qualified" were selected. ' board was extremely interested in primary MOS (PMOS) pr ciency with troops at the E6 level, and in the narrative comme contained in the EER; with both demonstrating performanc present duty and evaluation of potential.

It is anticipated that the FY 84 Selection Boards will use select objectives similar to those used by the 1984 E7 Board. Thus, se tion rates to E8 and E9 are anticipated to be low for CMF 12, 51 81 due to present and projected strengths. The Engineer E7 sele profile is shown on page 41.

1984 ENGINEER E7 SELECTEE PROFILE

	Number Considered	Number Selected	Percent	Education	Age	Time in Service	Time in Grade	EER Weighted Average
Career Management Field 12								
Primary Zone	491	43	8.8	12.2	31.7	10.7	4.3	123.4
Secondary Zone	812	33	4.1	12.3	28.1	7.6	1.6	124.0
Total	1303	76	5.8	12.2	30.1	9.4	3.1	123.7
Career Management Field 51								
Primary Zone	328	76	23.2	12.7	33.5	12.0	4.6	122.7
Secondary Zone	409	39	9.5	12.4	29.4	9.0	2.0	123.8
Total	737	115	15.6	12.6	32.1	11.0	3.7	123.1
Career Management Field 81								
Primary Zone	107	3	2.8	14.3	35.0	11.3	5.0	123.3
Secondary Zone	75	2	2.7	13.5	31.0	8.5	2.5	124.0
Total	182	5	2.7	14.0	33.4	10.2	4.0	123.6
Overall								
Primary Zone	24602	4752	19.3	12.6	33.3	12.2	4.6	123.7
Secondary Zone	25113	2799	11.1	12.5	30.2	9.1	2.0	124.0
Total	49715	7551	15.2	12.6	32.1	11.0	3.6	123.9

Official Photograph: Effective April 2, 1984, official photographs will no longer be a part of the microfiche Official Military Personnel Files (OMPF) for enlisted personnel. The hard copy official photograph will be used by centralized selection boards and career managers. This now requires two copies of your photograph to be forwarded to your local military personnel office for subsequent forwarding to Ft. Benjamin Harrison. The Enlisted Record Examination Center (EREC), Ft. Benjamin Harrison, will forward one copy to your career branch for inclusion in your Career Management Individual File (CMIF). Your photograph is a critical element of your OMPF. Ensure it is of top quality, current, and proper and for fit of uniform, rank, awards and decorations, and service stripes. AR 640-30, paragraph 7, establishes the *minimum* frequency requirements for submitting your photograph.

Three rangers of the 29th Ranger Battalion putting a five section Bangalore Torpedo under obstructing barbed wire prior to charging their objective. Photo taken in England August 1, 1943. (U.S. Army photo.)

Soldiers First, Engineers Second

A Personal Viewpoin

by MG John H. Moellering

Have you ever met a soldier who couldn't remember his drill sergeant in basic training or AIT? Probably not.

Moreover, I've never met one who couldn't remember his drill sergeant's *name*!

Why is that?

It's because the drill sergeant is the soldier's first glimpse of the Army.

He's the role model.

He helped the soldier make the transition from being a civilian to becoming a soldier and assuming the responsibilities inherent to our profession. He taught him to march, to fire a rifle, to don a protective mask, to move under direct fire, and more. He taught him to discipline himself and function as part of a team.

The drill sergeant set the pace and made the soldier adhere to high standards of performance. And that soldier will judge the competence of *every* officer and NCO he encounters in his career by how well they measure up to his drill sergeant's standards.

That's why our focus at Fort Leonard Wood is on excellence. The effectiveness of Army operational units is crucially affected by the habits and techniques soldiers learn in the training base. It is the job of TOE units to create cohesive squads, platoons, and companies. But without fundamentals and discipline, soldiers would never be molded into effective fighting teams.

For years there has been a perception among "up and coming" Army people that an assignment to a training post was a "kiss of death." TOE units were where the action was. Training base assignments were to be avoided at all costs.

Fortunately, today there is a growing awareness by the senior leadership of the Army that assignments in the training base are critically important—in fact, it is not an exaggeration to say that many now realize that training base assignments are as important as TOE jobs.

I've been in command at Fort Leonard Wood for four months now, and I must tell you that I am terrifically impressed by the quality of the officers and NCOs in training units here. The drill sergeants assigned here are some of the best NCOs I've seen in the Army. The commanders—all of whom have been centrally selected just like TOE commanders—can hold up their head with any group I've seen in the Army. There is an electric atmosphere here, one in which standards are high, enthusiasm is rampant and professional excellence is the norm.

If you've never been to a training center before, you ought to come to Fort Leonard Wood and see for yourself. See the confidence of the young enlistee, the raw material that we are receiving into the Army today. See the desire and emotion that he exhibits as he negotiates the most difficult aspects of basic training: bayonet training, the obstacle course, physical training, basic rifle marksmanship, NBC training, and all those basic essentials that comprise soldiership.

See the motivation and enthusiasm with which he approaches everything he does, and experience the thrill of fulfillment with him and his parents on graduation day. If you've ever thought that the quality of American youth has diminished or that patriotism is dead, then just come and sit through a basic training graduation. It will send ch[illegible] down your spine. I guarantee it.

But Fort Leonard Wood is not just [illegible] basic trainees. Some years ago whe[illegible] was commanding the 326th Engin[illegible] Battalion of the 101st Airborne Di[illegible]sion, I arranged to bring two of my li[illegible] companies to Fort Leonard Wood [illegible] much-needed float and fixed bri[illegible] training because of the facilities, equ[illegible]ment and expertise available. It w[illegible] outstanding training which I could [illegible] have duplicated at home station. [illegible] week after I assumed command at F[illegible] Leonard Wood, I stood on one of [illegible] drop zones and watched a company [illegible] the 307th Engineer Battalion, 82d A[illegible]borne Division, jump into Fort Leon[illegible] Wood for a week's worth of nearly id[illegible]tical training to that which I arran[illegible] for my people years ago.

There is a very active and growi[illegible] partnership program between act[illegible] Army FORSCOM units and Fort Le[illegible]ard Wood. We want you to come h[illegible] and take advantage of the great tra[illegible]ing facility we have. We want you [illegible] come and see where the basics [illegible] taught. We want you to experience t[illegible] motivation and enthusiasm of you[illegible] soldiers and drill sergeants.

Why should basic training a[illegible] advanced individual training mean[illegible]

(Continued on page [illegible]

Engineer

LUME 14 NUMBER 3 FALL 1984

the Cover

17-foot rubber assault boats, an advance y of Combat Engineer recruits cross the Big y River at Fort Leonard Wood, MO. (Photo P5 Vicky A. Lipps.)

FEATURES

DEPARTMENTS

INEER is an authorized publication of the U.S. Army Engineer Center and Fort Belvoir, VA. Unless specifically stated, material appearing herein does not necessarily reflect ial policy, thinking nor endorsement by any agency of the U.S. Army. The words he, him or his are used to represent personnel of either sex. All photographs contained herein fficial U.S. Army photographs unless otherwise credited. The use of funds for printing this publication was approved by Headquarters, Department of the Army, on July 22. . Material herein may be reprinted if credit is given to ENGINEER and to the author. ENGINEER's objectives are to provide a forum for the exchange of ideas, to inform and vate, and to promote the professional development of all members of the Army engineer community. Direct correspondence with ENGINEER is authorized and encouraged. iries, letters to the editor, commentaries, manuscripts, photographs and general correspondence should be sent to: ENGINEER Magazine, ATZA-TD-P Stop 163F, Fort Belvoir, 2060-5291. Phone: (703) 664-3082, AV 354. Subscriptions to ENGINEER are available through the Superintendent of Documents, U.S. Government Printing Office, Washington, 20402. A check or money order payable to Superintendent of Documents, must accompany all subscription requests. Rates are $11.00 for domestic (including APO and FPO) esses and $13.50 for foreign addresses. Individual copies are available at $3.00 per copy for domestic addresses and $3.75 for foreign addresses. Second Class postage paid at Belvoir, VA, and additional mailing offices. ISSN 0046-1989.

News & Notes

Lake Allatoona: Project of the Year

Project of the year. (U.S. Army photo.)

Lake Allatoona, located 40 miles north of Atlanta, GA, and one of the most visited lakes in the United States, was selected by the Corps of Engineers as its "Project of the Year."

The selection of the 12,000-acre lake and its recreational and nature facilities was announced by LTG Joseph K. Bratton, then the Corps Chief of Engineers.

Bratton cited the lake's personnel and Mobile District for exceptional efforts in "public involvement, safety education programs, natural resources and environmental protection, and leadership in establishing joint recreation programs with other federal, state and local agencies."

Allatoona, which was completed by the Corps' Mobile District in 1950, attracted eight million visitors las year. It is one of more than 420 Corps lakes nation-wide, and the fourth mos visited.

In addition to its 12,000-acre expans of water, the Allatoona project als encompasses 25,000 acres of adjoinin land, much of it devoted to recreatior wildlife management and natur preservation.

David G. Grabensteder, resourc manager at Allatoona, said he is "e› tremely pleased with the recognitio given to the project and feels that it i a tribute to the hard work of the staf here and the excellent support given to us by the Mobile District."

The Chief of Engineers' Annual Project award was created in 1978 to recognize exceptional managerial achievement at one of the Corps' recreational resource projects. This is the second year that a project managed by a district in the South Atlantic Division has been selected for the award. Last year Hartwell Lake in the South Atlantic Division's Savannah District was selected.

Field Printer Completed

A new electrostatic color printer has been developed to meet the Army's need for a fast, cost effective way to reproduce maps in the field, according to Engineers at the Topographic Laboratories, Ft. Belvoir, VA.

The advanced model of this Quick Response Multicolor Printer (QRMP) developed in Pasadena, CA, is being tested by the Army to produce full-color, full-size (24 x 30-inch) maps from both paper originals and digital data files.

The QRMP matches the print quality achieved by the lithographic presses used in the field today. This new equipment, however, eliminates much of the set-up and production time associated with offset lithograph—and cuts hours off the map reproduction process.

Unlike conventional lithographic presses, the QRMP uses a dry printing process similar to that found in commercial color copiers. The addition of a laser scanner improves the dry copying process and provides the high resolution for reproducing maps.

This combination of color xerography techniques and laser technology allows the QRMP to print maps and other graphic products with the speed and accuracy needed to support combat operations. The printer produces 75 full-color maps per hour.

The QRMP, however, won't be limited to copying maps from paper originals. A digital interface planned for the printer will allow troops in the field to produce maps directly from digital data recorded on tapes or disks. Soldiers will also be able to use the equipment to make quick overlays, overprint new information onto existing maps and copy photographs.

ETL scientists began acceptance tests for the QRMP prototype in late March 1984. Current plans call for fielding the printer early in the next decade.

Paint Test

U.S. Army—CERL has fielded a prototype Paint Test Kit for testing. The paint test will evaluate drying time, hiding power, appearance, gloss, adhesion, cleanability, and other basics. The kits were tested at Forts Sheridan, Campbell, Polk, Gordon, Devens, and Leonard Wood. Installation personnel used these kits this past summer to provide feedback necessary to develop the final paint test kit in FY85.

Marine Explorer Jacques Cousteau Visits Vicksburg Engineer District

COL Dennis J. York explains construction of articulated concrete mats to Jacques Cousteau at the Delta Mat Casting Field. (Photo by Gary Dill.)

COL Dennis J. York, district commander, and LTC Stephen Shepard, deputy commander, Vicksburg, MS, U.S. Army Corps of Engineers, greeted Jacques-Ives Cousteau, international marine explorer, on a recent filming expedition.

York hosted Cousteau and members of his expedition aboard the Corps' patrol boat, *Lipscomb*, for a tour of the Delta Point mat casting fields, various river works, and a briefing session. The *Lipscomb* was undergoing engine tests in the area and participating in the "load-out" of mats in the casting field. York briefed Cousteau on the role of the Army Engineers on the Mississippi River, explaining the methods used and need for the annual revetment and bank stabilization program.

Cousteau appeared impressed with the mat field and other Corps works, according to York. "He about ran us to death. You really had to hustle to keep up with him. He walked up close to where the work was being done on the casting field and was interested in every detail of the job," York said.

The casting field is used in construction of articulated concrete mats for use in the Corps of Engineers annual revetment and bank stabilization program along the Mississippi River.

Following the trip to Delta Point, Cousteau went to the U.S. Army Engineer Waterways Experiment Station to film the model of the Mississippi River Lock and Dam 26, which is north of St. Louis. He also filmed the reconstructed Civil War gunboat, *Cairo*, at the Vicksburg National Military Park and the Corps' 200-acre model of the Mississippi in Clinton, MS.

The purpose of Cousteau's expedition was to understand the river and its role in people's lives and the ecology. The documentary is expected to be broadcasted in nearly 100 nations, in addition to its showing at the World's Fair.

Deputy Chief

MG Norman G. Delbridge Jr., became the new Deputy Commander and Deputy Chief of Engineers of the U.S. Army Corps of Engineers in September 1984.

Delbridge, who had been serving as Assistant Chief of Engineers at the Pentagon since September 1980, succeeded MG Richard M. Wells, who retired from military service on August 31.

As the new Deputy Commander and Deputy Chief of Engineers, Delbridge is the principal assistant and advisor to the Chief of Engineers for the Corps' water resource development and management activities which include navigation, flood control, hydroelectric power generation, water supply for municipalities and industries, and recreation at Corps of Engineers projects. He also assists in management of the military engineering and construction programs for both the U.S. Army and the U.S. Air Force in the United States as well as overseas.

MG Norman G. Delbridge, Deputy Commander and Deputy Chief of Engineers. (U.S. Army photo.)

Delbridge is a registered professional engineer in the State of Iowa, and is a native of Detroit, MI.

by MG Richard S. Kem, Commandant, U.S. Army Engineer School

Engineer Commandant Stresses Training for "Excellence"

Training Our Soldiers is a Top Priority

In assuming command of the Engineer Center and School, I look forward to the opportunity of working with each of you to ensure the effectiveness of the Combat Engineers as members of the combined arms team on the AirLand Battlefield. Training in the Army, and more particularly training Engineers, will form the cornerstone of this effort.

When the Army Policy Council approved the Army Training Rules and Responsibilities Study recommendation on July 24, 1984, training officially became a total Army goal. Although the importance of training to individual proficiency and unit readiness have long been recognized, this significant decision highlights Army leadership commitment to quality training. It formally restates the fundamental role of training in the accomplishment of the Army mission.

As soldiers we must train to mobilize, deploy, fight and win anywhere in the world. Much of what we do through the day is, in fact, training. However, it is the manner in which our officers and NCOs conduct this training, the attitudes displayed, and examples set that spell the difference between ineffectual training and good training.

Two essential characteristics in our approach to this challenge must be interest and professionalism. Interest simply means that we must continually search for ways to make full use of our training opportunities. Leaders must stress performance-oriented training and effective use of resources. Interest implies commitment to a satisfactory level of training 365 days a year to ensure that we will be able to meet the challenges of the modern battlefield. Interest means that the entire leadership cadre participates in the training effort. Although officers focus a greater portion of their time on collective missions and tactical training while the NCOs teach individual training, training at all levels is the business of all.

The second characteristic, professionalism, demands that each officer and NCO constantly improves his level of military awareness and technical skills. The art of military engineering has not changed much over time. The criticality of the tasks themselves remains constant. However, the conditions under which the job must be performed and the standards that must be met have, indeed, changed.

Complex issues such as force modernization, the integrated battlefield, and the Army's new AirLand Battle Doctrine present unique challenges to the Engineer's ability to perform his traditional role. In addition to keeping skills and knowledge current, professionalism also means that trainers present the best possible instruction.

Today's troops are far past the "gee-whiz" stage. They expect training to be challenging and realistic in order to prepare them for critical field situations. All training, at Fort Belvoir, Fort Leonard Wood, and in Engineer units armywide, must concentrate on "Excellence." All of us are responsible for providing the training which will result in mission success both in peacetime and in emergency situations. It is a demanding, full-time, but rewarding job.

The future of our Army depends on how well we develop our junior leaders. These young leaders, both officer and NCO, must be allowed to make mistakes and to learn from them. Effective training is best accomplished in a no-fault environment. Assess each person's capabilities, assign challenging tasks, and then demand more. Today's soldier, more than ever before, looks for competence in his leaders. Young leaders must be allowed to grow in a tactical and technical sense in order to meet the challenge of future years.

This year will see a new emphasis on training. I expect each of you to develop your own training goals—for self-development, for the growth of those you are charged to lead, and for the mission you are expected to accomplish. The effective training and development of the Army's most precious resource, its soldiers, is a top priority.

by CSM Orville W. Troesh Jr., U.S. Army Engineer Center & School

Improved Training for NCOs

CSM Urges NCOs to Take Advantage of New Engineer Courses

With much reluctance, I now write my final chapter as the Engineer School and Fort Belvoir Command Sergeant Major. By the time this article is published, I will have relocated to Fort Sam Houston, TX, assuming the duties of CSM of the 5th U.S. Army.

In this final article, I urge each soldier to continue the dialogue that has been established with the Engineer School in an effort to further improve the training of our Engineer noncommissioned officers and soldiers. Now as I reflect on the past, present and future of the Engineer School, I feel we should be aware of the changes that have taken place and those still to come. Let us begin with the Engineer Noncommissioned Officer Advanced Course.

In August we began an entirely revised ENCOA Course, structured to produce a more complete and hard-hitting Engineer platoon sergeant. The course consists of a five-week block of common NCO subjects and five weeks of common *Engineer* NCO subjects before branching off into various lengths of MOS specific technical training. With the exception of CMF 81 students, most of the ENCOA students will be returned to their units in less time and thus help their unit's readiness.

Our Basic Noncommissioned Officer Course (BNCOC) continues to teach the most current material. An annual instructor's seminar is held each April to update the program of instruction, lesson reference, and support material. In addition, CONUS units will have a new 12F BNCOC available to them at Fort Leonard Wood, MO starting in January 1985. This will ease the training workload on the other 12F BNCOC conducted at Hohenfels, Germany.

In the area of Basic Technical Courses, the Directorate of Training and Doctrine has implemented a 51H30 Construction Supervisor Course which will be held at Fort Leonard Wood in November and December 1984, and will implement a 62N30 BTC for the Engineer Equipment Supervisors. This will provide the much needed training for our skill level 3 CMF 51 NCOs who had not received this type of training at AIT. Attendance is through unit command identification, placement on an order of merit list and submission of a DA Form 4187 to NCO Training Branch at MILPERCEN.

Our Primary Technical Courses are still in operation. The 12C Bridge Section Sergeant Course and 52D20/30 Power Generation Mechanics Courses are conducted at Fort Belvoir. The same procedures for attendance as BTC applies, however, I encourage you to send E5s or even some promotable E4s to the 12C/52D20 course. It is imperative that we train the right NCO at the 12C20/52D20 skill level. In addition, we have added 52D30 BTC at Fort Belvoir available for our more senior generator mechanics (E6s and promotable E5s).

Overall, the Engineer School has made great strides toward enhancing the professional development of our Engineer noncommissioned officers during the past two years. Not only have we developed new courses, we have also improved POIs in existing courses. Instructor quality has been upgraded, and soldier and Army standards are taught and enforced.

You, the field noncommissioned officer, have also contributed. The quality, appearance, knowledge, and physical fitness of students have improved dramatically. You have provided not only constructive criticism but also sound ideas on what is needed in NCO training and how the School could support it. I commend all of you for your efforts and encourage you to provide the same fine support to CSM Charles T. Tucker as he assumes this position, responsibilities and duties.

CSM Tucker comes to you from the U.S. Army Chemical School at Fort McClellan, AL, where he served as Command Sergeant Major.

Together, as a solid Engineer noncommissioned officer support channel, we have constructed the bridge to lessen the gap between the school house and the field and have improved our Corps. To all of you, a fond farewell. I look forward to seeing and serving you again.

Department of Combined Arms (DCA)

ENCOA Course Revision:

The curriculum for the Engineer Noncommissioned Officer Advanced Course (ENCOA) has been revised, and instruction has begun using it. Both the 12 and the 51 series courses have been redesigned to include common core subjects developed by the Sergeant Major's Academy followed by MOS/CMF USAES-developed specific training. These new courses should prove to be challenging, exciting and professionally rewarding and should prepare the Engineer NCO for increased responsibilities.

Directorate of Evaluation and Standardization (DOES)

Follow-up Evaluations:

The Directorate of Evaluation and Standardization (DOES) has been conducting graduate follow-up evaluations of Engineer training. The purpose of these evaluations is to determine if the Engineer School (Ft. Belvoir) and the Engineer Training Center (Ft. Leonard Wood) are training soldiers to perform the critical tasks to an acceptable standard meeting the needs of the field units. The initial evaluation conducted was of the 12B10 (Combat Engineer) One Station Unit Training (OSUT) course. The mail-out evaluation was conducted from January 1984 to June 1984. The results of this evaluation indicated that the 12B10 soldier can accomplish those tasks trained in OSUT and that those tasks are important to the unit's mission. The trainers and training developers are commended for their efforts with this course.

DOES is completing the reports from our evaluations of the 52C10 (Utilities Equipment Repairman), 12C10 (Bridge Crewman) and 52D10 (Power Generation Equipment Repairman) courses. These evaluations are providing valuable feedback to both the trainers and training developers concerning the utility of these courses. DOES would like to thank the soldiers who have supported this evaluation program and encourages support in the future. This program is designed to help provide the best training to Engineer soldiers.

Department of Military Logistics (DML)

Name Change:

The Department of Maintenance (DOM), established as an academic department on Jan. 4, 1984, has been officially redesignated as the Department of Military Logistics (DML). In addition, the Maintenance Management Branch has been redesignated as the Logistics Branch. These changes were made to better convey the overall mission of the training department and to reduce confusion with other Engineer Center maintenance activities.

Directorate of Training and Doctrine (DOTD)

Warrant Officer Training:

Warrant Officer Training Branch is revising and updating all Engineer Warrant Officer training to coincide with TRADOC's Warrant Officer Training System. New courses, depending on the MOS, will vary in length from 7 to 16 weeks and are scheduled to be implemented in June 1985. POC is Officer Training Branch, AV 354-1166/4994.

FM 5-100:

The Army's keystone "How to Fight" manual for Combat Engineers, FM 5-100 was published in May. It presents basic Engineer doctrine and implements the AirLand Battle Doctrine described in FM 100-5. Together, these manuals set forth the concepts for winning the battles and campaigns in modern warfare.

Department of Military Engineering (DME)

SC23 Training:

Officers who are en route to, or assigned to, Directorate of Engineering and Housing positions at military installations or Corps of Engineer District positions will be interested in the Facilities/Contract Construction Management Course being taught by the Department of Military Engineering at Ft. Belvoir, VA. Officers with SC23 should make every effort to attend this course en route to their next assignment.

The FY 85 classes are scheduled to begin January 18, May 24, and Aug. 16, 1985. The course is nine weeks long and is divided into two parts. The first part includes horizontal and vertical construction design, quality assurance, project management, procurement and contract management. The second part is dependent on the officer's assignment.

Officers en route to Engineer Districts will attend local training conducted by the Corps' Huntsville Training Division, while those en route to DEH assignments will attend the Engineer School's Facility Engineering Management Course. Requests to attend the course are made through channels to MILPERCEN Education Branch, ATTN: DAPC-OPA-E. Additional information on the course is available from the SC23 training coordinator, MAJ David White, at AV 354-2628 or 354-3998, Commercial (703) 664-2628 or 664-3998. Correspondence should be directed to the Department of Military Engineering, ATTN: MAJ David White, Ft. Belvoir, VA 22060-5331.

The 12 Bush Combat Engineer

by SGT Debbie Drew

With a mighty shove the 17-foot rubber assault boat is on its way across the narrow Big Piney River. The Combat Engineers are on the move.

12B Combat Engineers perform simulated combat tasks during field exercises. (Photo by Marilyn Fleming.)

Learning about the 17-foot rubber assault boat is only one aspect of the challenging and physically demanding training that Combat Engineers receive during their 13-week One Station Unit Training (OSUT) at Fort Leonard Wood, MO.

OSUT is a program which enables prospective Engineers to complete their basic training and 12B AIT training at the same installation. Soldiers who are male and obtain a score of 85 in CO (combat) may qualify as Combat Engineers.

After seven weeks of basic training, 12Bs participate in an "Essayons" ceremony, similar to a basic training graduation ceremony. ("Essayons," a French term for "Let us try," is the Corps of Engineers' motto.) The ceremony is conducted by the students themselves with permanent party cadre as spectators. The only exceptions are a host commander and a reviewing officer who participate in the ceremony.

The next six weeks are extremely fast-paced; soldiers now learn to be Combat Engineers. The soldiers first learn how to build non-explosive obstacles such as barbed wire barricades. They study rigging, learn various knots and how to use pulleys, and also help to build a three-rope bridge using the knots they have been taught to tie.

The next subject is land-mine warfare. The soldiers are taught how to arm and disarm antitank and antipersonnel mines and are shown mine detection techniques.

The proper use of carpentry tools and power tools is also taught at the 12B OSUT. Every Engineer squad and platoon is issued a tool box (called a pioneer tool box). Besides carpentry tools, the box contains other essential Combat Engineer tools such as shovels, sledge hammers and axes.

Two days of demolition follow the carpentry phase. Here, trainees learn to prime and detonate explosives. Students are shown a demonstration in various special purpose demolitions such as bangalore torpedoes, which are used to create paths through wire obstacles and minefields. A week of training is then devoted to float and fixed bridges.

A highlight of Engineer training is a five-day, four-night tactical training field exercise called "Engineer Week." Soldiers can learn teamwork in applying individual skills they've acquired. They strive to complete missions which they will be required to perform as members of a Combat Engineer company.

During this tactical exercise trainees install and remove minefields, construct wire obstacles, use explosives to create a road crater which is 30 feet long, 10 feet wide and eight feet deep, and learn to rappel. Testing is held after each phase and at the end of the cycle.

Engineer units are located at installations throughout the United States and overseas in Europe, Korea and Panama. They participate in field training exercises to enable them to efficiently perform their mission. When they are not in the field, their specific job depends on the unit to which they are assigned. Combat Engineers frequently help with post construction projects and spend a lot of time maintaining their equipment.

MOS 12B is a large, challenging and rewarding career field for soldiers. Advancement opportunities abound for Combat Engineers because it is a diversified career field and noncommissioned officers are in high demand.

Adapted from an article appearing in the May 1984 issue of *Recruiter Journal*.

SGT Debbie Drew is the editor of Guidon, the newspaper for the U.S. Army Engineer Training Center and Fort Leonard Wood. She has a bachelor's degree in journalism from Southern Illinois University.

PFC Scott Shephard, Company B, 307th Engineer Battalion, 82nd Airborne Division, packs his parachute after a successful jump at Fort Leonard Wood, MO. (Photo by SP4 Thomas Copeland.)

SP5 James Stevens and SP4 Jean Holman, MEDDAC, search their "prisoner," SP4 William Hays, Military Police Command. (U.S. Army Photo.)

New Tracked Vehicle Course Makes Better NCOs

by 1LT John P. Chagaris

1LT Thomas M. Thanos, project officer of the CEV Video Disk Gunnery Trainer, explains the new device to SGT John G. Rappell, section sergeant of SPED platoon, track section, 902nd Engineer Company (AFB) (R). (Photo by 1LT L. J. Leto.)

The Engineer School is helping 12F NCOs to become better trained soldiers. The *way* they're trying to achieve it is through a six-week Combat Engineer Tracked Vehicle Supervisor's Course.

Although the first 12F BNCOC started in West Germany in 1982, it wasn't until last October that it was initiated at Fort Leonard Wood. The course, designed for E4s through E6s, stresses hands-on training. The students are given a diagnostic test at the beginning of the course to determine their proficiency in skill levels I and II, and those who are found deficient in these areas are given additional training.

NCOA instructors teach students the non-technical portion of the course. During the first week, students are taught the Battalion Training Management System, an NCO's general duties and responsibilities; counseling; total physical fitness; preparing a rater's section of an Enlisted Evaluation Report; the Geneva Convention; drug and alcohol abuse prevention; equal opportunity and prevention of sexual harassment; and the Multiple Integrated Laser Engagement System.

Other subjects, such as communications, are taught by 12F instructors. Students learn how to prepare and operate an FM radio set, call for and adjust indirect fire, connect a CEV to a CEV hot loop using the external telephones, and to communicate with an automated CEOI and KTC-600.

Students are also shown how to prepare and submit an NBC-1 (Initial) Nuclear, Biological, and Chemical report during the Nuclear, Biological and Chemical portion of the course. They also study detection and protection from NBC hazards.

During the vehicle maintenance portion, students learn how to inspect organizational maintenance historical records. They also perform daily preventative maintenance on the gunner's and commander's station of the CEV, supervise daily preventative maintenance on a CEV, and learn how to supervise daily preventative maintenance on an AVLB and launching system.

In studying land navigation, students are taught how to interpret a route reconnaissance overlay, conduct a map reconnaissance and participate in a land navigation exercise.

The gunnery phase of the course gives students the opportunity to issue a fire command; prepare a circular range card and a sketch range card; remove, install and operate the M36 periscope; sight and zero the .50 caliber M85 machine gun; sight and zero the main gun; and sight and zero the 7.60 coax machine gun in addition to other gunnery functions.

During the non-gunnery CEV crew functions phase, students supervise various tracked vehicle operations during nuclear warning drills for a CEV. They also learn to supervise abandon tank drills, moving material with the winch and boom, self-recovery tank drills, and towing a disabled CEV using the tow cable.

While also learning about AVLB crew functions, students learn to supervise other soldiers bridging a gap using an AVLB launcher, self-recovery of an AVLB launcher and a nuclear warning drill for an AVLB.

The course is designed to place each soldier into stressful, realistic situations. For example, while supervising an "evade missile drill," a student, as a CEV commander, takes his vehicle onto a live fire move-out range. Within 10 seconds after seeing a smoke cloud, he designates the firing position of an antitank missile, issues correct fire commands enabling the gunner and himself to bring suppressive fire onto the enemy position with their machine guns, and directs the driver to take evasive action.

At the end of this fast-paced six weeks, students take a comprehensive examination covering all of the subjects taught during the course. This is in addition to the tests given after each block of instruction.

The course helps soldiers to become more familiar with the duties of a CEV commander and an AVLB section sergeant. This knowledge will help the soldier when he returns to his unit to lead and train his subordinates and to fulfill the missions assigned to him. The result is a professional, well-rounded NCO who is an asset to his unit and to the Corps.

1LT John P. Chagaris is chief, 12 BNCOC-12F-TRACK at Fort Leonard Wood, MO. He is a 1982 Junior Officer Maintenance Course graduate and has a bachelor's degree from Georgia College.

The new tracked vehicle crew supervisor course helps all Engineers to become more proficient with their tracked wheel equipment. (U.S. Army Photo.)

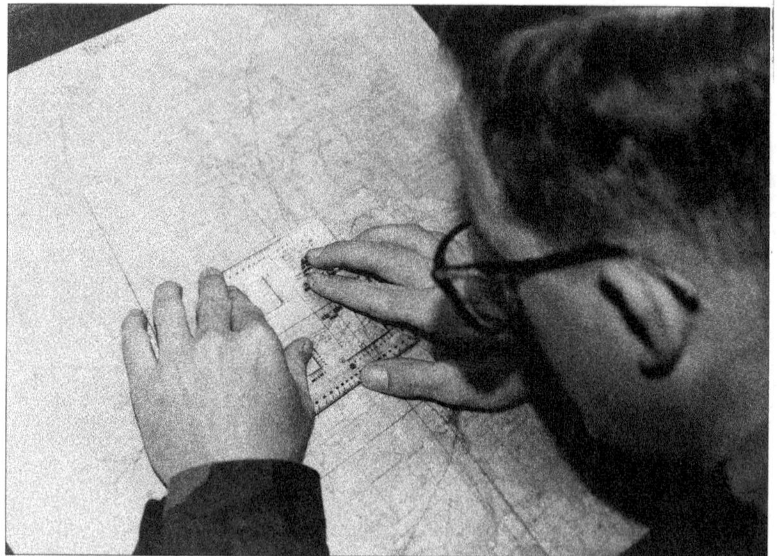

SP5 James Stevens, MEDDAC, finds the PLDC map reading exam challenging. (Photo by SGT Debbie Drew.)

PLDC:

The First Step for NCOs

by SFC Danny L. Bussey Sr.

If NCOs are the "backbone of the United States Army," then Engineer NCOs must be the stronghold of the Corps of Engineers

How do Engineer soldiers develop into noncommissioned officers? How do they learn the necessary skills needed to lead troops? And how do they learn to train other troops?

The first step is the Primary Leadership Development Course (PLDC), which was started at Fort Leonard Wood in December 1983. It is a four-week resident course conducted at NCO academies worldwide. Replacing the Primary Noncommissioned Officer Course (PNCOC) and the Primary Leadership Course (PLC), PLDC provides NCO training to newly appointed or prospective sergeants at skill level II.

The goal of PLDC is to teach these junior leaders to lead others and to build confidence in themselves. It emphasizes leadership in combat situations by placing the students in stressful situations. The course curriculum includes six different areas: leadership, resource management, communications, training management, professional skills, and military studies. Finally, in a 72-hour field exercise, students demonstrate and practice what they have learned throughout the course.

The defensive/offensive operations field exercise is divided into two phases. During the initial phase, students concentrate on establishing a defensive position while preparing for offensive operations. Many tasks throughout the course are taught by the students themselves and are followed by a practical exercise.

Phase II is designed to be a stressful, fast-paced leadership exercise. Students are placed in leadership positions such as first sergeant, platoon sergeant, or squad leader on either the defensive or offensive force. They are evaluated by the cadre for their ingenuity, leadership ability, and overall performance.

Small group instruction is a key feature of PLDC. These groups, consisting of 12 students and two instructors, allow students to give and receive feedback and to share personal experiences with each other. It fosters teamwork and allows collective reasoning in problem solving.

The most current leadership doctrine in FM 22-100, *Military Leadership*, and FM 100-1, *The Army*, is the basis for the leadership instruction at PLDC. The training block includes Principles of Leadership, Character of a Leader, Problems and Decision Making, and Responsibilities and Authority of NCOs. The Battalion Training Management System (BTMS) also requires students to present at least one training session during the field training exercise.

The primary goal during the communication block is to teach junior leaders the necessary skills to better communicate as small unit leaders. They are taught different communication techniques to ensure information is properly exchanged within an organization. The tactical communication instruction during military studies teaches students how to operate an FM radio set and how to use an automated CEOI. They learn to code and to decode messages such as grid coordinates and how to transmit NBC reports.

Also during the military studies, students participate in a practical land navigation exercise and performance examination. Any student who does not receive a "Go" must be retained and retested.

PLDC works on a merit system. Students are given merits for volunteering for details as well as for exceeding uniform standards. They are, however, also given demerits for failing to meet standards. Then, after all of the testing, after all of the field exercises, after all of the physical training, a soldier has taken the first step. He is on his way to becoming a leader, an NCO.

SFC Danny L. Bussey Sr. is the operations NCO at Fort Leonard Wood Drill Sergeant School. He served with the 4th Infantry Division in Vietnam, the 72nd Engineer Company at Fort Benning, and the 237th Engineer Battalion and 15th Ordnance Battalion in Germany. SFC Bussey also has an associate's degree in general studies.

PLDC students cautiously exit a box culvert during their 72-hour field exercise. (Photo by SGT Debbie Drew.)

Command of an Initial Entry Training Company

An Alternate Path to Success

by LTC Barry W. Levine

Not many company grade officers have as much opportunity to directly affect the lives of young soldiers as do Initial Entry Training (IET) company commanders. Because many more command positions exist in TOE units than in IET, the opportunities and the challenges of IET remain hidden from the majority of young officers. Some of these challenges are different from those found in a TOE unit.

Since most junior officers serve in a TOE company at some time, there is a general knowledge and appreciation for this duty. By comparing the challenges and the desirable traits of the IET company commander with those of his counterpart in TOE units, a better understanding of the training company and its path to success can be reached.

Listing the challenges of company command—any company command—is a formidable task. In TOE units the commander must personally set standards for the company. He must motivate his unit in all of its varied activities—from maintenance to field duty to physical training. He must be a leader for his troops, an advisor and a subordinate for the battalion commander, a trainer for the officers in his company, and the Engineer to supported units. Just as important, he must be a member of the community and a good citizen.

The IET commander has all of these same challenges to varying degrees. The standards he sets for his company must be extremely high, but attainable. These are the standards first encountered by new recruits and, since these standards affect these soldiers throughout their careers, the impact on all other Army units is significant. Because it is easier to begin and maintain high standards than to attempt to raise them later, IET companies must rigorously establish and enforce the highest standards to ensure TOE units receive quality soldiers.

The challenges in motivating cadre and trainees are different from those in a TOE unit. An IET unit operates in cycles. All of the work, time and effort that made the last cycle great are gone with each new cycle. There is a new group of civilians to turn into soldiers, and they may not respond to the same techniques as did the last group of trainees.

The company cadre—the drill sergeants—must also remain highly motivated cycle after cycle. These highly trained, professional NCOs look to the company commander for direction. After a few cycles, even the most professional NCO or officer might become a bit complacent and may not put the same enthusiasm and extra effort into training as he did in the beginning. It rests with the company commander to avoid this trap and to motivate his subordinates so that training does not suffer.

In IET, training is the only mission. Instead of taking ARTEPs, there are frequent tests to ensure that the trainees meet Army standards in every phase of training. These tests are graded and the results carefully scrutinized at all levels of command. Because of this, much time and effort goes into preparing trainees for the tests and into analyzing the results.

The traits of a soldier taken for granted in TOE units (saluting, shining shoes, recognizing rank, wearing the uniform) are all taught in IET. As in TOE units, there never seems to be enough time to completely prepare.

Two major challenges in TOE units, which are much less formidable in IET units, are maintenance and logistics. On the other hand, there is a very small company staff which is provided to deal with maintenance and logistics. But the requirements for sound leadership are the same wherever one is assigned. Soldiers are soldiers. They have a right to expect professional leadership regardless of the mission.

In a TOE unit one seldom has a chance to profit from earlier mistakes. Any company commander embarking on a mission relies on his own experience on similar missions as well as the experiences of his key personnel. The cyclic nature of IET allows a company commander to perfect his company's actions in a particular area. To be able to profit from one's own successes and mistakes and not merely write an after action report for one's successor is satisfying.

Another difference seen in IET is the profound change which occurs during each cycle in a group of soldiers for whom one has responsibility. The change from civilian to soldier is significant and is always a source of immense job satisfaction.

Even though the challenges of IET and TOE command sometimes may differ, the traits required of all commanders regardless of the type of company are identical. While there can be no finite and definitive list of traits which make a commander, some must be present in any good commander.

The first, and perhaps the most important, is integrity. An IET commander must be completely honest and trustworthy. He is setting the example for the soldiers who will comprise the Army of the future. Other traits which produce successful IET company commanders are initiative, attention to detail, moral and physical courage, self-confidence, humility, adaptability, sound judgment, and maturity.

Of course, these same traits produce good TOE company commanders, good general officers, good bank presidents and good U.S. Congressmen. Each trait is applied a bit differently in the IET environment, but the requirement is the same as in any field of endeavor.

Considering the challenges which exist in IET and the traits which produce successful commanders, it is evident that experiences gained in an IET assignment are in some ways different but in most ways similar to that available in a TOE unit. Both paths can lead to success for those who deserve it.

Officers who have had experience in TOE units are better able to produce properly trained soldiers when assigned in IET. Officers who have had experience in IET can better understand the soldiers coming to their TOE units and thus can quickly make them productive soldiers. As always, success is not a function of which unit an officer is in, but how he performs in that unit.

LTC Barry W. Levine commands the 4th Battalion, 2nd Training Brigade at Fort Leonard Wood, MO. Among other assignments, he has served as a company commander in the 65th Engineer Battalion in Vietnam; Director of Engineering and Housing at Grafenwoehr and Garmisch, Germany; executive officer of the 237th Engineer Battalion; and as a faculty member at the Defense Systems Management College. LTC Levine is a graduate of the United States Military Academy, the Command General Staff College, and the Defense Systems Management College. He also has a master's degree in engineering physics form the University of California—Davis.

Engineer Problem

You are located in a remote part of a developing country. Pit privies and latrines are currently the only provisions for handling human waste. Your unit was just tasked to build a 2,500-man base camp for continuous operations in this remote area. Since facilities are not available, your commander decided that a sewage lagoon will be a simple and economical solution to the water-treatment requirements. Sufficient land and construction capabilities are available for a sewage lagoon construction. The soil absorption rate is 30 min/inch and the water table level is 14.7 feet.

Based on the following information supplied by Army Medical Services and general Army standards, design a lagoon for a 2,500-man base camp.

a. Water flow from supported population

$$Q_p = \frac{40 \text{ gal/day}}{\text{man}}$$

b. Pipe infiltration

$$Q_i = \frac{2 \text{ gal/min}}{1{,}000 \text{ ft of pipe}}$$

c. Flow due to rainfall (Q_r), evaporation (Q_e), and seepage (Q_s) are negligible.

d. Pipe length within the base camp L_p = 1250 ft

e. Biological Oxygen Demand (BOD)

$$\text{BOD} = 0.20 \text{ lbs } \frac{O_2/\text{man}}{\text{day}}$$

f. Design BOD, Surface Loading Factor

$$\text{LF} = 60 \text{ lbs } \frac{O_2/\text{acre}}{\text{day}}$$

g. Retention time

T_r = 60 days

ENGINEERS TRAINING FC

Combat Support Boat (above) carries bridge building equipment to soldiers (below), who prepare to launch the M4T6 Pontoon. (Photos by SFC Dennis O. Lindsey.)

Troops launch an M4T6 (Photo by SFC Dennis O

XCELLENCE

Helicopter (above) delivers a Bridge Erection Boat. (Photo by SFC Dennis O. Lindsey.)

Engineers haul M4T6 long balk, which is used by Engineers as decking on fixed or float bridging. (Photo by SFC Dennis O. Lindsey.)

A crane atop Bonnet Carre spillway lifts one of the 7,000 "needles" to begin opening one of its bays. (U.S. Army photo.)

High Water, Hard Decisions

The 1983 Bonnet Carre Spillway Operation

by MG William E. Read (RET) and Dr. Michael C. Robinson

The Bonnet Carre Spillway was opened by the U.S. Army Corps of Engineers for the seventh time in its 52-year history, on May 20, 1983. To the spectators who observed the event, the operation seemed a simple, routine process. Once again water was diverted from the Mississippi River into Lake Pontchartrain to protect New Orleans and downstream parishes from undue risk of flooding.

The fact is, though, the Bonnet Carre operation entailed a complex, highly disciplined public works management process. The decision-making scenario involved Corps officials and other professionals pooling their talents to arrive at a tough decision. Will predicted Mississippi River stages and discharges subject the main flood protection system to unacceptable stress and require the relief Bonnet Carre provides?

Louisiana is far from the Mississippi River's source that trickles out of Lake Itasca in Minnesota. However, on its way to the Gulf of Mexico, North America's greatest river gathers the runoff of 31 states—a drainage basin that ranges from the Continental Divide, northward to Canada, and as far east as the Appalachians.

The Missouri, Illinois, Ohio, and Arkansas rivers as well as hundreds of smaller streams directly or indirectly discharge into the Mississippi. Lower Louisiana forms the spout of this 1,246,000-square mile, funnel-shaped drainage basin that encompasses 41 percent of the continental United States. Therefore, during major floods, such as the 1983 event, the river's enormous hydraulic forces severely test this area's flood control works as well as the skills and ingenuity of Corps and other professional emergency managers.

The Bonnet Carre spillway is but one important feature of the Mississippi River and Tributaries Project (MR&T) which was authorized by Congress in 1928. This still incomplete system of levees, floodways, channel improvements, and other elements provides flood protection along the Mississippi's main stem, as well as to portions of tributary basins in the Lower Mississippi Valley. The main stem features of the MR&T project are designed to safely convey the project flood to the Gulf.

The entire MR&T project is under the direction of the Mississippi River commission (MRC) located at Vicksburg, MS. Operational responsibility for Bonnet Carre rests with the Corps' New

Water flows from the Mississippi River through a few of Bonnet Carre's 350 bays to Lake Pontchartrain to protect New Orleans and downstream Louisiana parishes from flooding. (U.S. Army photo.)

Orleans District (NOD). However, the decision of whether to open the spillway is the responsibility of the MRC president, after consultation with the Chief of Engineers in Washington, D.C.

The spillway is located on the east bank of the Mississippi River, 32 river miles north of New Orleans. The structure was built by the Corps following the disastrous record flood of 1927. It is designed to protect New Orleans and other downstream areas by diverting Mississippi River flows from upstream New Orleans into Lake Pontchartrain and finally into the Gulf of Mexico.

The spillway was completed in 1931 and its guide levees were finished the following year. The 7,000-foot long structure contains 350 bays or openings separated by concrete piers. Each bay is closed by twenty 8 x 11½-inch timbers called "needles." They are either 10 or 12 feet long depending on the elevation of the weir crest. Cranes atop the spillway lift the individual timbers during operations. Guide levees confine the flow along the 5.7 miles from the Mississippi River to Lake Pontchartrain. The floodway gradually widens from 7,700 feet at the river to 12,400 feet at the confluence with the lake.

As flows began to approach project flood magnitude in the main stem below Old River during April, the possibility of a Bonnet Carre operation became a major concern of the MRC, the NOD, and non-Federal interests.

During the first two weeks of May, Corps employees monitored weather and stage predictions, evaluated New Orleans' need for temporary flood protection at certain locations, considered the affects of Bonnet Carre flows on shellfish in Lakes Pontchartrain and Borgne and studied the probable impacts of storm surges from the Gulf on river stages at New Orleans. They also poured over laws and regulation governing the spillway's use, and con sulted with local interests on leve conditions and the influence of hig stages on navigation activities.

These activities took place as othe floodfighting efforts were underwa throughout the Lower Mississipp Valley.

The prospect of a Bonnet Carre oper ation weighed heavily on Corps offi cials' minds because of environmenta considerations. Diverting a great dea of fresh water into Lakes Pontchartrai and Borgne would reduce salinit

Water pours through one of Bonnet Carre's 350 bays. (U.S. Army photo.)

A crane atop Bonnet Carre Spillway pulls an 8 x 11½-inch timber "needle" from a bay. (U.S. Army photo.)

levels and further damage the shellfish harvest already seriously affected by record spring rains. In the long run, nutrients from the Mississippi River water would improve the shellfish industry, but the immediate impact would be largely adverse.

On May 12, a meeting was held at the New Orleans District between Corps officials and representatives of various federal and state agencies that manage fishery resources in Louisiana and Mississippi. All parties agreed that if Bonnet Carre had to be opened the Corps would provide ample notice so that the agencies could lessen the impact, prepare to conduct samplings, and monitor the affects of the event.

By May 15, the National Weather Service predicted a peak stage of 18.0 feet for May 29 for the main stem at the Carrollton gage in New Orleans. (The authorized grade for the flood control system is about 25 feet there.)

During the 1983 flood, permanent protection through the entire New Orleans reach existed only for a river elevation of 19 feet on the Carrollton gage. Above that elevation, reaches of increasing lengths for higher stages require temporary construction to provide the authorized freeboard.

Temporary flood control works were being added at areas with deficient grade that would provide the city protection for a river stage of 21 feet on the Carrollton gage. Relying on hastily constructed temporary protection to convey long duration floods through metropolitan New Orleans is at best very risky.

To further assess conditions, the MRC President and various MRC and NOD staff and local levee board officials inspected the temporary protection on May 16 and consulted with local officials on navigation-related and other issues.

Thus, after considering a host of hydrologic, structural, navigational, legal and other factors, the need and schedule for operation of the Bonnet Carre Spillway was decided. Discussion between the MRC and NOD ensured that all factors were considered and appropriate alternatives weighed.

On May 18, the MRC President, after consulting with the Chief of Engineers, accepted the District Engineer's recommendation to open Bonnet Carre on May 20 when the river was expected to reach a flow of 1.25 million cubic feet per second (cfs) and to limit the river discharge to no more than 1.30 million cubic feet past New Orleans during the flood. This range in discharges (1.25 to 1.30 million cfs) was considered a practical necessity due to inability to precisely measure river flows or control the spillway discharge.

This flow corresponded to a 17-foot stage on the Carrollton gage, based on the stage-discharge relationship of that time. Subsequently, the stage at New Orleans never exceeded 17.2 feet but would have exceeded 19 feet without the spillway's operation.

Two weeks prior to the decision to operate the spillway, the New Orleans District began to implement a comprehensive plan to ensure that the spillway was ready. Test bay openings were performed to familiarize work crews with proper procedures and verify that all equipment was in good working condition.

A general reconnaissance of the guide levees was made and roadways along their crests were judged capable of facilitating inspection during the spillway's operation. Contacts were made with the Louisiana Office of Emergency Preparedness as well as the Red Cross, and all interests with property in the floodway were advised to remove it.

Furthermore, liaison was established with owners of pipelines, bridges, and powerlines that cross the floodway. Finally, the U.S. Coast Guard was asked to close a ship anchorage area near the spillway, and the Corps' picket boat, *Beinville*, was stationed near the site to prevent wayward tows from being drawn into it.

Thus, by the middle of May most preparations had been already made for the spillway operation. The first "needles" were removed from 70 bays on May 20 and by May 24 all 350 bays were in full operation. Based on the preliminary stage-discharge relationship, the maximum flow through the structure was approximately 260,000 cfs, which corresponded to about a 2-foot stage reduction at and below New Orleans. (Subsequent detailed analysis of the stage-discharge rela-

Corps Writers Assistance Program

"High Water, Hard Decisions: The 1983 Bonnet Carre Spillway Operation" was published in the December 1983 *Louisiana Engineer,* the publication of the Louisiana Engineering Society, located in Baton Rouge, LA. This story was brought to the attention of ENGINEER through the Corps Writers Assistance Program (CWAP), a newly formed program in the Headquarters, United States Army Chief of Engineers office.

The program gives Corps employees encouragement, assistance and recognition for writing articles centered around the Corps, and helps by placing their articles in magazines as well as by discussing book publishing opportunities. HQUSACE Chief of Public Affairs awards a Certificate of Merit for Journalistic Achievement to those who have articles published.

Although submission of Corps-based articles is not required before publication, authors (both published and unpublished) are encouraged to contact the CWAP office for assistance. For further information, anyone interested should call Ms. Lu Christie DuCharme, Public Affairs Specialist, Public Affairs Office, Department of the Army, Office of the Chief of Engineers, DAEN-PAI, Washington, DC 20314. Her phone number is (202) 272-0011, AV 285-0011.

MAJ Skip Morrow, executive officer, 3rd Battalion, 3rd Brigade, and CPT Robert Lentz, Commander, E Company, 2nd Battalion, 3rd Brigade discuss the Junior Officer Skill Sustainment Program. (Photo by SP4 Thomas Copeland.)

Developing Our Junior Officers

by COL Samuel J. Ady

Have you ever found yourself as the only officer of your branch assigned to your unit? That being the case, have you ever tried to get adequate branch training? Not so easy, is it? Especially for a junior officer.

Unless their training center is co-located with a service school or has tenant TOE units, many junior officers who are assigned to training units often cannot practice their branch skills as do their contemporaries who are assigned to line companies. While some officers lead infantry platoons, tactically employ tanks, or conduct RSOPs (reconnaissance, selection, and occupation of position), others find themselves totally isolated from their branch.

But in order to make amends, the 3rd Basic Training Brigade at Fort Leonard Wood, MO, is introducing a new program which provides junior officers the opportunity to practice their branch skills. The program is called the Junior Officer Skill Sustainment and Development Program and it has three major goals:

- to develop and sustain war-fighting capability among junior officers during their tours with the training base;
- to develop junior officers using technical equipment and resources beyond the capability of training battalion commanders;
- to keep junior officers, serving with the training base, reasonably competitive with their contemporaries in TOE units.

To meet these objectives, two subprograms were instituted. These programs are in addition to the normal battalion professional development programs and systems for common skills testing. These are the Branch Counselor Program and a cross-fertilization program for company commanders.

Currently, there are 47 junior officers (excluding chaplains) in the 3rd Brigade. They are represented by several branches: Infantry with 23 officers; Armor and Field Artillery each have 8; Engineer is represented by 1; Quartermaster has 1; Air Defense Artillery has 4, and Adjutant General Corps has 2 officers.

In order to give each junior officer access to a senior, knowledgeable branch officer, five field grade branch counselors have been appointed, one from each of the first four branches and a fifth officer to be responsible for all others.

It is critical that the counselor be an experienced, branch qualified field grade officer. Battalion commanders often have neither the time to devote to the intensive management nor the experience and expertise to advise officers of other branches on branch related skill development or appropriate career management.

Within the 3rd Brigade the five battalion commanders represent Military Intelligence, Engineer (two), Field Artillery, and Armor branches; yet the greatest number of junior officers are Infantry. Fortunately, there are sometimes field grade infantry officers in battalion executive officer and brigade staff positions who can be called upon to serve as branch counselors.

Counselors are formally appointed by letter from the brigade commander and operate across battalion boundaries. They are required, however, to keep each battalion commander advised of the branch skill development plan which is devised by each of his junior officers, problems encountered, and the progress of each officer. They are also required to brief the brigade commander semiannually on the status of each of these junior officers. Shortly after arrival to the brigade, each junior officer receives a letter from the brigade commander advising him of the Branch Counselor Program and the name of his counselor.

The Branch Counselor Program has two primary objectives. The first objective is to maintain and increase officers' branch proficiency while assigned to the training base. In close coordination with each officer, counselors formulate a specific program tailored to the needs of the officer.

The program includes hands-on training with branch units, which normally involves temporary duty. It may also involve association with reserve components, enrollment in correspondence courses, use of Fort Leonard Wood resources, and some in-house unit development.

The major problems associated with the program are the lack of time and, as always, TDY funding. Funding is particularly important because TDY is one of the few ways to obtain hands-on training (particularly, collective training) with TOE units.

The second objective is to educate the officer on planning his career and to assist him in the effort. He is informed of his next promotion window, the officer educational system through senior service college (including the time of his eligibility), the alternate specialty program, the requirement for branch qualification as a junior officer, the necessity for submitting periodic preference statements, and other matters related to career progression and development.

In early 1984, LTG Charles W. Bagnal, the TRADOC Deputy Commanding General for Training, and MG Maurice O. Edmonds, TRADOC Deputy Chief of Staff for Training, were briefed on this program. They agreed to provide funds exclusively for junior officer TDY to gain practical field experience with TOE units.

Since the program started, nine lieutenants have participated in field exercises with TOE units for 12 to 28 days and another seven are scheduled during the next several months. Because each TDY is carefully planned, the average cost has been about $350 per trip.

Two armor lieutenants recently participated in tank gunnery with the 4th and 1st Engineer Battalions at Fort Riley. Four other infantry, armor, and field artillery lieutenants served with the 1st Engineer Battalion as scout platoon leaders, tank platoon leaders, and as members of a fire support team. These officers gained experience that was impossible to obtain at Fort Leonard Wood.

The 1st Infantry Division has been especially helpful in this program by publishing a policy directive. Their directive assigns internal staff responsibility to ensure that the program is administered effectively and that junior officers gain the maximum benefit from the training. The 4th and 5th Engineer Battalions at Fort Knox as well as other units at Forts Sill and Hood are also making significant contributions.

Our officers are eager for this training. They want to learn and practice their branch skills. It is a credit to TRADOC that this need has been recognized and that funds have been provided. Equally important, FORSCOM units have done a superb job in providing rigorous field training during each trip.

In addition to the branch-related TDY trips, more than 85 percent of the junior officers are enrolled in a rigorous series of correspondence courses, as well as taking advantage of branch-related, hands-on training. A sizeable number are enrolled in advanced courses of either their branch or another branch to sharpen their combined arms skills, and almost all are enrolled in tactical refresher and maintenance courses. Branch counselors provide advice and assistance in the selection of these courses and monitor each officer's progress.

The second major brigade-level subcomponent in the program encourages cross-training among company commanders. The rationale for the program is that junior officers can often become so involved in the daily business of running their units that they fail to see and learn what is happening in other units. In some cases they work hard, thinking they are meeting high standards, however, their standards are only mediocre.

The program forces them out of the small universe of their own companies and teaches them how to profit from the ideas and practices (both good and bad) of their contemporaries.

In order to accomplish this goal, five

ENGINEER HOTLINE

Problems, questions, and comments relating to Engineer doctrine, training, organization, and equipment can be addressed by telephone to the U.S. Army Engineer School's "Engineer Hotline." The Hotline's auto-answer recorder operates 24 hours a day, seven days a week. Callers should state their names, addresses and telephone numbers, followed by a concise question or comment. You'll receive a reply within three to 15 days. **The Hotline is not a receiving agency for formal requests.**

Call commercial (703) 664-3646; WATTS 800-336-3095, extension 3646; or AV 354-3646.

company commanders (one from each battalion) have lunch with the brigade commander every two or three weeks. These are working luncheons and last from 1½ to two hours. They are relatively informal and included a healthy interchange among junior officers and between the company commanders and the brigade commander.

Each company commander then visits a specific company in another battalion for at least one-half day within a certain period. He is given a list of things to accomplish during the visit and a list of questions which may be useful to ask his fellow company commanders during the visit.

The program forces the visiting commander out of his company, introduces him to standards in another company, allows for an exchange of ideas, and introduces him to other commanders on a professional basis. During the year each brigade company commander will have visited units five times and will have himself been visited approximately five times.

The program's short-term objective is to increase professionalism within the brigade. The long term objective is to teach each junior officer the habit of profiting from the ideas, techniques and standards of contemporaries and, consequently, accelerating his own growth process as he advances in rank.

The Junior Officer Skill Sustainment and Development Program is not a cure-all for sustaining officers in their branch skills while in the training base, but does accomplish important objectives:

- it gives each junior officer 1½ to four weeks of field training with a TOE unit of his branch;
- it forces the officer to devise a plan with a milestone schedule on how he is going to maintain his branch skills while stationed at the training base;
- it introduces him to the correspondence course system and forces him to take a fairly rigorous schedule of courses;
- it provides him with a field grade officer from his branch to advise him on career matters;
- it forces company commanders to begin acquiring the habit of profiting from the ideas of their contemporaries.

The program has been successful and will continue to succeed in the future only through the collective efforts of the officers and NCOs in the 3rd Basic Training Brigade, TRADOC, and the FORSCOM units who provide such truly outstanding support.

COL Samuel J. Ady commands the 3rd Basic Training Brigade at Fort Leonard Wood, MO. He has served in Vietnam as an advisor in 1963 and with the headquarters of the 1st Infantry Division from 1967 to 1968. Among other assignments, COL Ady has also served as executive officer and S-3 of the 4th Battalion, 3rd Artillery, 1st Armored Division and as G-3 of the Southern European Task Force in Vicenza, Italy. He has a bachelor's degree in political science from Loyola College and a law degree from Harvard. COL Ady is also a graduate of the Command and General Staff College and of the Army War College.

SFC Ronnie Guy reports to his company commander, CPT Robert Lentz. (Photo by SP4 Thomas Copeland.)

A New Way to Brea

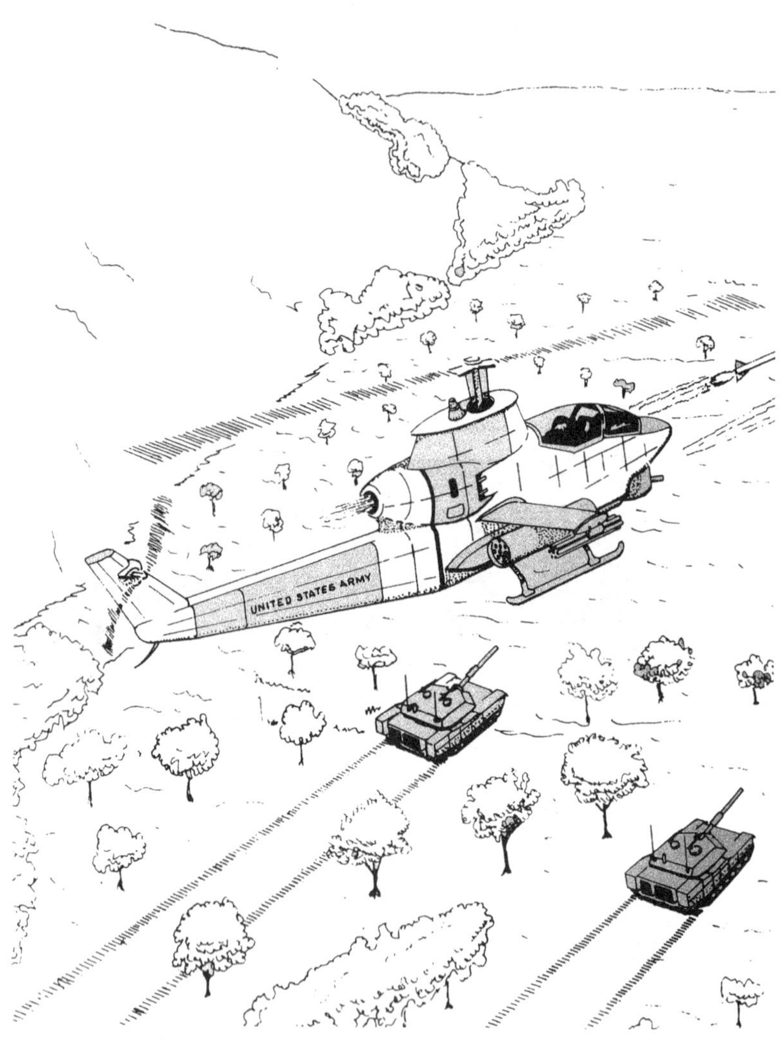

inefields

by: Harry N. Hambric and MAJ Edwin L. Booth

The lack of viable counterobstacle doctrine has long been a problem for an armed force desiring unimpeded battlefield maneuver.

When we examine the U.S. Army's requirements in this area, we find that there are five basic missions:

- counterobstacle missions such as negotiating craters;
- countermine missions such as clearing or breaching minefields;
- gap crossings missions such as river crossings, tank ditches, and overbridging existing structures;
- force mobility tasks such as constructing combat roads and trails;
- forward aviation Combat Engineering tasks (FACE) to construct landing zones and strips, low altitude parachute extraction system (LAPES) sites and forward arming and refueling points (FARPS).

In reviewing each of these missions we find that our capability to accomplish counterobstacle, gap crossing, mobility and FACE tasks are sufficient to provide U.S. forces with all the support necessary to operate on the AirLand Battlefield. Countermine missions, however, are another matter.

For years, the methods we have used in breaching minefields have been so inefficient that they not only threatened the lives of our soldiers, but the success of important missions as well.

Modern technology and knowledge of potential adversaries require that we base our countermine requirements on a threat that routinely employs current mine delivery systems as part of a combined arms effort. The Warsaw Pact, as well as other countries trained by them, have well learned the lessons of mine warfare from World War II. They have continued to build on this knowledge by using information gained from the numerous conflicts and battles since then.

A simple review of the mine and countermine equipment available to threat forces reveals that they have substantial amounts of current hardware to both install and breach minefields. Threat force commanders have combined this equipment with viable doctrine and tactics to allow either system to be located well forward in the battle area. They have gone so far in their development of doctrine, that special combined arms teams or detachments are formed to install minefields and obstacles, or to breach those in their path.

The serious student of military science has little difficulty in recognizing that a U.S.-equipped force encountering a Warsaw Pact minefield on today's battlefield would experience serious difficulty. The mines by themselves would have a small impact and could be overcome with existing technology and doctrine. Combined, however, with the direct and indirect fires available to the defender, they would be capable of quickly and substantially degrading the combat effectiveness of an attacking U.S. force.

The threat commander has the capability to quickly locate, target and mass indirect fires anywhere within his sector. This capability requires that an attacker must overcome minefields rapidly. Loss of momentum by the attacking force gives the defender an opportunity to catch it in a devastating "fire sac" as well as gaining time to call forward reinforcements.

Current U.S. Army doctrine for overcoming minefields stresses "bypassing" the minefield. If bypassing is not possible, either a "hasty" or "deliberate" breach must be conducted.

If the defender has made the mistake of leaving a tactically sound by-pass, there is no requirement for countermine activities and the assault can continue. When there is no alternative but to cross the minefield, a breach is conducted.

A "hasty" breach is defined as one which uses assets organic to the force and is accomplished without loss of momentum. Although a hasty breach is accomplished as fast as possible, it may take hours.

A "deliberate" breach occurs when a hasty breach has failed or when the tactical situation dictates. The deliberate breach requires a build-up of substantial combat power and will usually be conducted by Combat Engineers brought forward for the mission. A deliberate breach may take several hours or even days depending on the strength of the defenders and magnitude of the minefields and other obstacles.

Because of the threat's ability to locate and target our forces quickly, a hasty breach taking longer than 30 minutes or a deliberate breach will receive severe opposition. The longer it takes to accomplish the breach, the greater the opposition—the greater the attacker's casualties.

Current U.S. Army combined arms doctrine specifies that an attacking force be organized into three elements: a support force to suppress the defenders with direct and indirect fires and obscure the breaching mission; a breaching force to conduct the breach, mark the lanes and secure the far side; and an assault force to continue the attack against the objective.

The breaching force will have tank-mounted mine rollers for detection and proofing; line changes for breaching lanes; or as most Engineers and infantrymen are aware, the mine detector and probe.

Although there are other items such as plows and fuel air explosives, they are not available now and there is no assurance that they will be available in time for the next war.

Some U.S. commanders, realizing that they cannot rely on a capability that does not exist, have developed expedient breaching methods such as pushing disabled vehicles through the minefield, aiming unmanned vehicles at the objective, using Engineer equipment to scrape the ground, or employing indirect fires in an attempt to provide a safe lane. Some commanders have given serious thought to "bulling" through a minefield to maintain momentum and escape the effect of massed fires.

Even with our current hardware and doctrine there is little doubt that crossing a defended minefield is a dangerous undertaking. There is also no doubt that until we provide a better means through equipment, techniques or doctrine, enemy minefields will dangerously impede mission accomplishment.

As mentioned earlier there are items which are developed and waiting to be called forth. Other systems and concepts using special sensors and electronics to detect and neutralize minefields are being studied, but some require major technology breakthroughs before they can be available for actual battlefield use.

Because of limited advances in the countermine arena we can expect that our force's capability to breach minefields on today's battlefield will be at or below what we had in World War II!

Perhaps some relief to this problem can come from existing equipment or weapon systems. The question is: "Which ones, and how can we employ them to provide the capability we need?"

One such proposal is to consider the combat power of attack helicopters. These helicopters can carry 76 2.75-inch free flight rockets.

There are currently two warhead options which may be suitable for breaching a path through minefields. One is the 17-pound high explosive warhead, and the other is the flechette warhead. By launching the rockets at a predetermined air speed, altitude and aircraft attitude in quick sucession as specified in FM 17-40, *Helicopter Gunnery*, a narrow, but long "beaten area" is produced. Mines close to this path would be detonated or destroyed by the 17-pound warhead explosion.

Flechettes from the other warhead would penetrate the mine case and damage internal components but may not detonate the mine.

Perhaps with minor modifications flechettes could be made even more effective by making them pyrophoric or capable of providing the flame necessary to initiate the mine's explosive charge.

At this time we do not have the techniques or a doctrine, or for that matter, assurance that this concept would be effective. If it were proven effective, it would be the only system ever available which could provide U.S. forces with the capability to conduct a truly hasty breach through a conventional or FASCAM minefield.

Explosive Warhead Rockets

In considering the results from actually using these proposals, we can see where they might be effective. The 17-pound warhead rockets would be fired in pairs. The helicopter's firing attitude and altitude, its speed, and launch sequence of the rockets could be correlated to cause the rockets' path to form a clear lane of a specific width and length.

Width of the lane would be based on the effective radius of the warhead to detonate, destroy or clear mines from the lane. The length of the lane provided by a single aircraft would depend on aircraft speed, launches per second and the number of rockets fired. The deeper the minefield depth, the greater the number of firing runs which would be required to breach the entire depth.

The effect of the rockets on the minefield could be as follows:

- Mines close enough for sympathetic detonation would, of course, explode. The combined force of the rocket and mine explosion may destroy or detonate other nearby mines.

- Through the forces transmitted from the ground, mines not detonated may be displaced or crushed. By shifting the mine from the horizontal position, more force would be required to activate the fuze mechanism. In addition, the ground would be disturbed and could conceivably be so loose that the mine would sink into the ground without exploding. An undesirable factor resulting from this is that some mines may become *sensitized*.
- Mounds of debris covering the mine would also transfer a vehicle's weight over a greater area so that the fuze does not receive sufficient pressure to activate.
- Mounded dirt and debris would also expend some of the explosive force even if the mine did detonate, thereby decreasing the damage probability.
- Mines with anti-handling devices would be disturbed and might detonate.
- Magnetically fuzed mines might also explode when quickly shifted. They would be vulnerable to being displaced, detonated, covered by debris or rolled into craters resulting from explosions.
- The resulting path (lane) from warhead explosions would be readily visible because of the close proximity of the linear crater path.
- The entrance and end of the cleared path could be designated by using perhaps a "marking" rocket which emits a colored smoke. White Phosphorous (WP) would not be feasible because it would mask the clear lane.
- Resulting mounds and craters would preclude the effective use of proofing devices such as rollers, but the self-bridging capability of armored vehicles would allow them to stay on mounds and other debris. This practice would drastically reduce the probability of detonating a mine.

Flechette Rockets

Flechette rounds would be employed in the same manner as the explosive warhead. They would be employed at an airspeed, altitude, aircraft attitude and range which would create a thin, long, beaten area in which flechettes would cover the beaten area in any density desired.

The current flechette would have a low probability of detonating a mine, but two or three of them hitting a mine could damage the fuze or firing chain.

In addition to breaching conventional or FASCAM minefields in a unit's path, this concept, if feasible, could be the answer to a major problem which all armies have today—extricating friendly units from air or artillery-delivered mines which have been placed directly on them. A friendly force in this situation could button up and have attack helicopters fire directly onto them. Safe lanes could be quickly breached without damage to the force.

A warhead containing 2,500 flechettes could cover a 20-foot x 20-foot area with six flechettes per square foot. Firing the rockets in pairs would place twelve flechettes in each square foot. This would allow a helicopter with 76 rockets to breach a 20-foot x 760-foot lane with a high probability of damaging any mine in the lane.

Combined High Explosive and Flechette Warheads

An alternative concept would have each pair of rockets contain one high explosive (HE) warhead and one flechette warhead. This would provide a high probability that any mines in the lane would be damaged by the flechettes and exploding warhead. This concept would also provide an instant means for marking the cleared lane using the craters formed by the HE rounds.

For this reason the concept of using a mix of one HE and one flechette appears to offer advantages over firing just flechettes. Not only will the lanes be marked by craters, but the craters and resulting spoil will provide loose soil in the same manner as using purely HE warheads. The possibility of affecting each individual mine, however, increases with each flechette round used.

Certainly there is some question of the danger involved in a proposal such as this. However, when you compare it with our present breaching capability, it provides us with capabilities we have not had before. That is, the ability to maintain force momentum, the ability to safely counter air or artillery-delivered mines, and the ability to combine breaching and marking into a single operation without exposing soldiers.

The important factor is that U.S. forces would be able to plan for and cross large mined areas much quicker than the critical 30-minute time limit. This would prevent them from being exposed to the full force of the threat's direct and indirect fires.

Doctrinal Implications

Minefields would be breached in minutes rather than hours. This factor would allow the force commander to count on a much larger portion of his force to be intact when he reached the objective.

In addition, the speed with which the objective could be reached would prevent enemy reinforcement. By the time enemy fires could be brought on the attacker, it would be too late. The two forces would be so close to each other that effective supporting fires would be difficult and dangerous to deliver.

The use of air-delivered, free flight rockets in a minefield breaching role is just an idea; and there are certainly many who could argue against it. There are also many who may consider it to be a good idea, particularly since this method of delivering free flight rockets with a high degree of reliability can be trained on using existing techniques. Good or bad, it is an idea which may get other people thinking.

U.S. forces have some of the best combat vehicle systems in the world. Their speed and survivability will be worthless if they spend valuable minutes or hours waiting for a minefield to be breached.

Somewhere there is a better way to breach minefields and we need to find this technique before the next battle. The concept of using free flight rockets launched from attack helicopters, a system already available to the force, may be the answer.

Mr. Harry N. Hambric is a doctrine development analyst at the U.S. Army Engineer School. He has written several articles on mobility, as well as participating in writing the key engineer publications (FM 5-100, ***Engineer Combat Operations****, FM 5-101,* ***Mobility****, and FM 5-103,* ***Survivability****. Mr. Hambric is a retired Combat Engineer officer and is currently employed with the Directorate of Training and Doctrine, U.S. Army Engineer School.*

MAJ Edwin L. Booth is the Armor-Aviation representative at the U.S. Army Engineer School. His recent assignments include Aviation Advisor in Montana, and Armor and Infantry Company Commander. MAJ Booth is a recent graduate of the U.S. Army Command and General Staff College.

Another Side of "Authority"

by MAJ Lawrence R. Sadof

CPT Robert Lentz, commander, E Company, 2nd Battalion, 3rd Brigade, stresses importance of personnel and weapons readiness. (Photo by SP4 Thomas Copeland.)

Obedience to authority is essen to the system of military discipline as we know it toda

Obedience is one of the basic tenets of our military heritage. It can often mean the difference between success or failure on the battlefield. Yet, obedience to authority can have another dimension, a dimension which all of us who carry the baton of leadership must be aware of constantly.

The concepts of responsibility and authority, the "Siamese twins" of command, have been the subject of many penetrating and incisively written analyses during the past several years. Generally, responsibility has been defined as the obligation to perform assigned activities, while authority has been described as the right to perform or command.

We have all heard it said, "A commander is responsible for all his unit does or fails to do," which simply means that true responsibility cannot be delegated. It follows that if one is given responsibility for a mission, he must also be given the authority to carry it out. In the military, rank is bestowed upon those who are given more responsibility and more authority.

Beginning with basic officer or enlisted training, obedience to authority is ingrained in our thought patterns and in our responses. Such Pavlovian reactions are reinforced throughout our careers. However, although obedience to authority (sometimes even blind obedience) is often required by our profession, there are potential pitfalls which mandate further analysis.

In their book, *In Search of Excellence*, Thomas J. Peters and Robert H. Waterman, Jr. describe some experiments which Stanley Milgram conducted to illustrate how people can blindly obey those in positions of authority.

"*Milgram brought adult subjects off the street into a Yale lab and asked them to participate in experiments in which they were to administer electric shock to victims. (In fact, they were not doing so. The 'victims' were Milgram conspirators and the electric shock devices were bogus.) Initially, Milgram had the 'victims' placed in one room and the shock givers in another.*

Following instructions given to them by a white-coated experimenter (the authority figure) the shock giver turned the dial which went from 'mild' to 'extremely dangerous.' On instruction shock givers administered the electricity, and all went 'all the way' in administering shock. One hundred percent followed orders, although in earlier written tests (where there was no authority figure present) over 90 percent predicted they would not administer any shock whatsoever.

Milgram added embellishments. He connected the rooms with a window, so the shock giver could see the 'victim' writhe in pain. He added victim 'screams.' Still 80 percent went to 'intense' on the dial and 65 percent went to 'extremely dangerous.' Next he made the victims appear to be 'homely 40-year-old female accountants.' He took the experiments out of the university and conducted them in a dreary downtown loft. He had the shock giver hold the victim's hand on the electric charge plate. All these steps were aimed at breaking down the subject's acceptance of the white-coated experimenter's authority. None worked well. People still by and large accepted authority."

Milgram's experiments have great meaning to those of us in uniform. The results force us to examine the consequences of authority from the perspective of both a subordinate and a superior. As superiors, we try to give clear and concise orders which we often expect to be followed without delay. Such obedience is essential to success on the battlefield. At other times, though, we simply may be doing no more than giving general direction, providing guidance or making policy.

In our own minds we are delegating and decentralizing authority, while expecting our subordinate staff and commanders to develop and execute the specifics. We expect our subordinates to provide feedback if something is extremely dangerous, wrong, irregular, or even illegal or immoral. Still, we must remember that we are the "authority figure"—Milgram's man in the white coat.

We want our subordinates to provide feedback instead of being "yes men." This expectation by itself will not ensure that this goal is accomplished. The command climate we establish is the key mechanism to ensure that our subordinates provide valuable and needed information.

We can say we want feedback, but our reactions when we receive it (especially if it is unfavorable) speak for themselves. How often have we heard our superiors say that they do not want "yes men" only to be subsequently scolded by these same superiors when we state our honest convictions. If we commanders do not establish a climate of genuine trust which allows feedback, we are little more than extensions of the rigid white coated authority figure in Milgram's experiments.

As subordinates, we are trained for total response and obedience to our superiors. We must always be aware, though, of our internal clock that tells us right from wrong. During the post World War II Nuremberg Trials, many of the accused justified their actions because, they were simply "following orders of those in higher authority."

The basic question then is, when do our internal controls override the actions that have their origin in higher authority? This is obviously a complex, not easily answered question. On one end of the spectrum we extol obedience to those in authority, but on the other end we see a need for a safety mechanism with internal controls, a sensitivity to what is right or morally correct.

Obviously all of us will draw this line differently. We must differentiate right from wrong and wrong from illegal or immoral. Many times, we as subordinates, receive orders which we feel are wrong—yet they are not illegal nor immoral. Remember that when we were in the role of superior, we expected our subordinates to tell us if the orders we gave them were dangerous or wrong. Now that we are in the role of subordinate, do we not owe our superiors that same consideration?

What happens if these orders are illegal or immoral? We still owe our superiors the same feedback. Yet, failing to execute orders which we feel are wrong is far different from failing to carry out an illegal or immoral order.

Obviously issues are not normally so simple or clearcut, nor will questions of legality or morality be solved here.

The key point is that we are all involved with complex issues involving the use of authority, as either a subordinate or superior. As Milgram's experiments imply, authority means power, and we always must be aware of this and its potential for abuse or misuse. Whether as a leader or follower, each of us must use our internal balancing mechanisms, lest we become real life players acting out Milgram's experiments.

One other aspect in Milgram's experiments warrants comment. When Milgram gave written tests (where the authority figure was not present) over 90 percent of those tested predicted they would not administer any shock whatsoever. However, this obviously changed with the "appearance" of the white coat authoritarian figure who commanded obedience and respect. This respect for those who "appear" to be authoritative is evident in the following excerpt from John Molloy's well read book, *Dress for Success*:

"*Take the raincoat for example. Most raincoats sold in this country are either black or beige . . . Intuitively I felt that the beige raincoat was worn generally by the upper-middle class (authority figure) and black by the lower-middle class.*

First, I visited several Fifth Avenue stores that catered almost exclusively to the upper-middle class customers . . . The statistical breakdown was four to one in favor of beige raincoats. I then checked stores in the lower-middle class level and found that almost the reverse statistic applied. They sold four black raincoats to each beige raincoat.

. . . On rainy days I hired responsible college students to stand outside subway stations in determinable lower-middle class neighborhoods and outside determinable upper-middle class suburban commuter stations. The students merely counted black and beige raincoats. My statistics held up four to one in favor of beige in upper-middle class neighborhoods and exactly the opposite in lower-middle class neighborhoods."

Molloy conducted similar experiments throughout the United States and hypothesized that,

" . . . *Since raincoats were an intrinsic part of the American environment, they had in all probability conditioned people by their predominance in certain classes and automatic (Pavlovian) reactions could be expected.*

In short, when someone met a man in a beige raincoat, he was likely to think of him as a member of the upper-middle class, and when he met a man in a black raincoat, he was likely to think of him as a man in the lower-middle class."

We in the military also have our beige raincoats, be they the scrambled egg of a field grade officer's hat or the wide-brimmed hat of the drill instructor. Our raincoats indicate authority instead of socioeconomic standing. While symbols of rank, position and authority are not necessarily bad, we must, however, recognize that they do exist, and the trappings of our authority can be used or abused, either intentionally or more often than not, unintentionally.

In carrying out our responsibility, we are often required to play many roles, be that of a stern taskmaster, an allocator of resources, an arbitrator. As we carry out our varied responsibilities, we must be aware of potential problems that might occur as we switch from one role to another.

Such problems were graphically illustrated in experiments conducted by Philip Zimbardo at Stanford. Zimbardo advertised in a newspaper in Palo Alto, CA, an upper-class community, for volunteers in a role-playing experiment. The volunteers were taken to a "wallboard" prison in the basement of the Stanford University psychology building and randomly assigned roles as "guards" or "prisoners."

Within hours the randomly assigned "guards" were acting as guards and the randomly assigned "prisoners" were acting as prisoners. By the end of the first day the guards were behaving brutally—both physically and psychologically. By the end of the second day two of the prisoners had to be released from the experiments because they were on the verge of a psychotic breakdown. "Warden" Zimbardo, afraid of his own behavior as well as that of others, stopped the experiment four days into the ten-day protocol.

We are all products of our environment and we all are required to play various roles in uniform. Once again, we must rely on our internal balancing mechanisms to control actions that have their origin in authority.

The proper use of authority, as we carry out the myriad of complex functions associated with our responsibilities, cannot help but make every one of us better leaders. Although our superiors are the ones who judge our leadership abilities and our potential, we are often successful because of the actions of those whom we lead and exercise authority over.

It has been said that, "No man is a leader until his appointment is ratified in the hearts and minds of his men.' A conscientious effort by all of us o how we use our own authority with it explicit as well as implicit conse quences cannot but help to make u better leaders not only in the heart and minds of those for whom we work but more importantly, in the heart and minds of those who work for us

Everyone of us who carries th leadership baton must ensure that w understand the implications of ou responsibilities and, more importantly all the sides and dimensions of th authority that comes with it.

MAJ Lawrence R. Sadoff is the execu tive officer of the Office of the Chief o Engineers. Among other assignments he was a company commander in th 8th Engineer Battalion, 1st Caval Division, and in the 503rd Enginee Battalion. He was also the Deputy Dis trict Commander of the Corp of Engi neers Albuquerque. A graduate with th highest distinction at the Naval Colleg of Command and Staff in 1981, M Sadoff is also a U.S.M.A. graduate an has master's degrees in civil enginee ing from the University of Illinois an in business administration fro Southern Illinois University. He is registered engineer in Virginia.

Let BTMS Work For You

by CPT Bryan L. Page

The Battalion Training Management System (BTMS) and its implementation poses unique problems for all Training and Doctrine Command units. Due to its unique structure and mission, each unit has to develop a program to serve its own needs.

As a commander of a Combat Engineer One Station Unit Training (OSUT) company, I was among the first to find a thousand reasons why BTMS should not apply to my company. However, after attending a Training Manager's workshop, I was surprised to discover that it was nothing more than "common sense training."

Upon completing the workshop, I was eager to develop a system which would benefit both the noncommissioned officers and our training mission. The system would have to train NCOs to reenter the FORSCOM units fully proficient in their respective MOS. Additionally, the system needed to be easily manageable, self-generating, and capable of providing reliable feedback.

The first step in developing our BTMS program was to determine training objectives and to ensure that they coincided with our ARTEP requirements. Since the company is in the only Combat Engineer Training Brigade in the Army, we used ARTEP 5-35, *Combat Engineer Battalion, Corps*, as a basis to develop these objectives and to establish the standards.

Once these goals were established, we had to determine how we would make them work for our unit. But before accomplishing this, we had to determine our current combat readiness status.

Unlike a TOE unit, the training company has no formal means of determining combat readiness such as ARTEP exercises, and, therefore, has to rely on other forms of evaluation to find its combat proficiency status.

Since BTMS in a training company is aimed at the permanent party cadre only, the system which determines our proficiency status had to be modified.

First, we closely examined the individual, and not the platoon or squad. A process of personal interviews, reviewing SQT results, and administrating self assessment surveys was used, listing every sub-task of every mission established as a training or ARTEP objective. It required individuals to take stock of their own ability and report proficiency as being either trained, needing practice, or untrained for each individual task.

Special care was taken to define standards for these three categories to ensure the survey was valid. After collecting the data, the results were compiled into one easily read chart. From it, strengths and weaknesses could be identified and long-range BTMS plans were formulated.

The long-range plan was broken into four phases, with each phase covering one training cycle (normally 15 weeks) of an Engineer OSUT company. Once the major missions listed in ARTEP 5-35 were broken down and listed in the long-range plan, it was time to turn attention to the short-range plan for Phase I.

This told us we needed to train and evaluate the basic skills necessary to survive in a combat environment. With that in mind, efforts were concentrated on command and control procedures, unit movement and security operations, intelligence gathering operations, and infantry operations. Each major mission was further broken down into sub-tasks, and classes were developed and given through the company's NCO professional development/ BTMS program.

At the end of Phase I, an evaluation was conducted to determine the effectiveness of the unit's training program while allowing modification or adjustments for future plans. This was conducted during a five-day, four-night Engineer Week exercise in which the drill sergeants removed their campaign hats and assumed platoon sergeant and squad leader roles. They were evaluated on their ability to perform under pressure while completing various missions, such as conducting an ambush patrol, establishing a tactical bivouac, performing defensive and offensive operations, and conducting reconnaissance patrols. The sergeants were also judged on their ability to care for and motivate their soldiers.

The short-range plan for Phase II called for continued reinforcement of the basic survival skills, while focusing on mobility and countermobility missions. Second only to the ability to survive, these two missions are required to enable a Combat Engineer unit to fulfill its role.

As in Phase I, the major missions were broken into sub-tasks, and classes were developed and taught in such areas as calculation and placement of explosives and installation of tactical minefields. Again, our evaluation was conducted during an Engineer Week exercise. That week, however, marked a new awakening for the company. We were no longer satisfied with just meeting the standards, we were setting future standards for all Combat Engineers.

To accomplish this, we planned a more realistic Engineer Week by locating existing unsafe bridges on Fort Leonard Wood. Permission was given from the Directorate of Engineering and Housing to remove three such bridges through demolition use.

A target folder was developed for each of the bridges indicating the amount and placement of all demolition charges. These were placed according to the target folder by soldiers-in-training under the careful supervision of their drill sergeant squad leaders. The realism involved provided one of the most effective means to train the company's NCOs while giving the trainees the "hands-on" experience they might never have had under normal training circumstances.

At the conclusion of the Engineer Week, individual and company combat readiness was reevaluated, and we were surprised at the progress shown. From this it was determined that basic survival skills should never be taken for granted and must be constantly evaluated.

The short-range plan was modified for Phase III to reflect the continued evaluation of all survival skills, while focusing the main emphasis on fixed bridging operation. As with the previous phases, the major mission was broken into sub-tasks.

Classes were developed and given in such areas as erecting a Bailey crib pier, constructing a Bailey bridge, and constructing an M4T6 Dry Span. As before, it was the company's goal to provide the most realistic training possible.

We elected to construct a 100-foot section of Bailey bridge on an unprepared site to meet this goal. This in itself was a major undertaking, since the transportation, construction, and disassembly of the Bailey bridge "in the wild" had never before been accomplished by a Combat Engineer training unit. A Bailey crib pier was also constructed under the existing bridge, upgrading its classification from class 30 to class 65. This particular achievement had never before been accomplished on Fort Leonard Wood by any military unit, either training or TOE.

The assets to transport the bridge on five-ton dump trucks were not available, thus requiring bridge trucks and pallets. Because cranes were not available, we were dependent on the trucks' own capabilities. Special tie-downs were designed and built by the company to secure the loads during the lifting and hauling operations.

The pallets made loading and unloading the bridge easier, while allowing a greater load capacity than the standard five-ton dump truck. In addition to the support it provided during the hauling operation, the bridge truck proved to be a highly versatile piece of equipment because of its boom and wrench, used during the Bailey crib pier construction.

After careful examination of the Engineer Week evaluation results, we made minor adjustments to Phase IV, where we planned to place our emphasis on float bridging. Our short-range plan not only had to be constantly upgraded, but the long-range plan also had to be projected. For training units this can become very difficult due to the constant turnover of key personnel. However, if flexibility is built into this system, it can survive drastic changes.

Our BTMS plan has shown us that the program will work in a TRADOC unit with slight modifications to allow training unit usage.

CPT Bryan L. Page is Commander, Company E, 1st Engineer Battalion, 2nd Engineer Training Brigade (OSUT). He has served as a platoon leader and executive officer with the 237th Engineer Battalion (CBT) in Hielbronn, Germany, and as Training Standards Officer in Fort Leonard Wood, MO. He is an Engineer Basic Course and Advanced Course graduate and has a bachelor's degree from Missouri Southern State College.

Hotline Q & A

Q. I would like to know when is the best time to seal asphalt?

A. If there are no cracks in the pavement, a seal coat is not necessary, since the asphalt will provide waterproofing. Apply the seal coat if there are superficial cracks or tears in the pavement.

Q. What is the date of the Engineer Conference that is held each year in early December in Crystal City, Arlington, VA? Are there any restrictions on attendance?

A. The date for the conference is 30 November through 2 December 1984. The Conference is limited to Commanders and CSMs/SGMs of Engineer Battalions, Groups, Brigades, and Commands.

Q. How can I obtain a subscription to ENGINEER for official use in my office?

A. The U.S. Postal Service requires that you furnish ENGINEER with the following:

a. A request in writing stating that you wish to receive ENGINEER (your official letterhead must appear on the request).

b. A list of all duty positions for each copy requested.

c. A signature at the bottom of the request.

d. Specify number of copies.

Once we receive this letter with the required information you will be placed on ENGINEER's distribution list.

MG John H. Moellering commands the U.S. Army Engineer Training Center and Fort Leonard Wood, MO. A 1959 West Point graduate, he has commanded Engineer troops and served in various staff positions with the 1st Cavalry Division in Korea and the 24th Infantry Division in Germany. In Vietnam he was S-3 of the 937th Engineer Group (Combat) in the Central Highlands. He later commanded the 326th Engineer Battalion, 101st Airborne Division (Air Assault) at Fort Campbell, KY. He has also served as Assistant Division Commander of the 9th Infantry Division, Fort Lewis, WA.

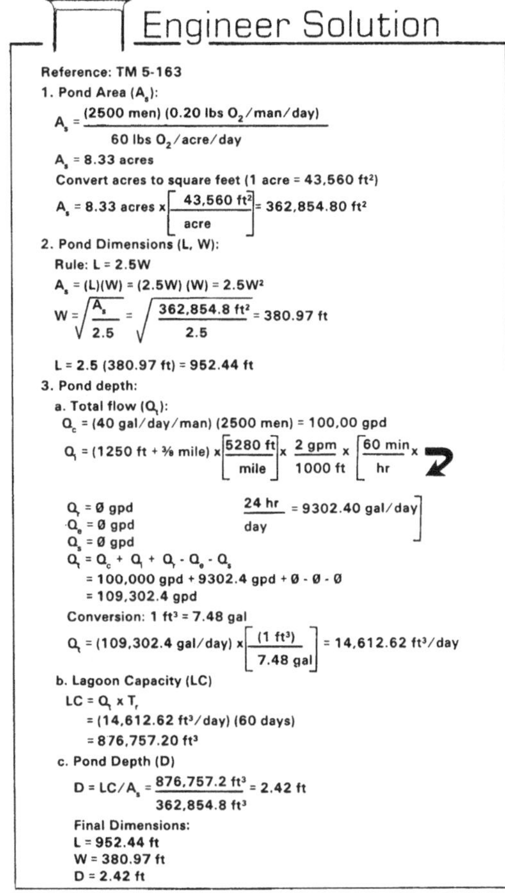

Engineer Solution

Reference: TM 5-163

1. Pond Area (A_s):

$$A_s = \frac{(2500 \text{ men})(0.20 \text{ lbs } O_2/\text{man/day})}{60 \text{ lbs } O_2/\text{acre/day}}$$

$A_s = 8.33$ acres

Convert acres to square feet (1 acre = 43,560 ft^2)

$$A_s = 8.33 \text{ acres} \times \left[\frac{43{,}560 \text{ ft}^2}{\text{acre}}\right] = 362{,}854.80 \text{ ft}^2$$

2. Pond Dimensions (L, W):

Rule: L = 2.5W

$A_s = (L)(W) = (2.5W)(W) = 2.5W^2$

$$W = \sqrt{\frac{A_s}{2.5}} = \sqrt{\frac{362{,}854.8 \text{ ft}^2}{2.5}} = 380.97 \text{ ft}$$

L = 2.5 (380.97 ft) = 952.44 ft

3. Pond depth:

a. Total flow (Q_t):

Q_c = (40 gal/day/man) (2500 men) = 100,00 gpd

$$Q_i = (1250 \text{ ft} + 3/8 \text{ mile}) \times \left[\frac{5280 \text{ ft}}{\text{mile}}\right] \times \frac{2 \text{ gpm}}{1000 \text{ ft}} \times \left[\frac{60 \text{ min}}{\text{hr}} \times \frac{24 \text{ hr}}{\text{day}} = 9302.40 \text{ gal/day}\right]$$

Q_r = Ø gpd

Q_e = Ø gpd

Q_s = Ø gpd

$Q_t = Q_c + Q_i + Q_r - Q_e - Q_s$

= 100,000 gpd + 9302.4 gpd + Ø - Ø - Ø

= 109,302.4 gpd

Conversion: 1 ft^3 = 7.48 gal

$$Q_t = (109{,}302.4 \text{ gal/day}) \times \left[\frac{(1 \text{ ft}^3)}{7.48 \text{ gal}}\right] = 14{,}612.62 \text{ ft}^3/\text{day}$$

b. Lagoon Capacity (LC)

$LC = Q_t \times T_r$

= (14,612.62 ft^3/day) (60 days)

= 876,757.20 ft^3

c. Pond Depth (D)

$$D = LC/A_s = \frac{876{,}757.2 \text{ ft}^3}{362{,}854.8 \text{ ft}^3} = 2.42 \text{ ft}$$

Final Dimensions:

L = 952.44 ft

W = 380.97 ft

D = 2.42 ft

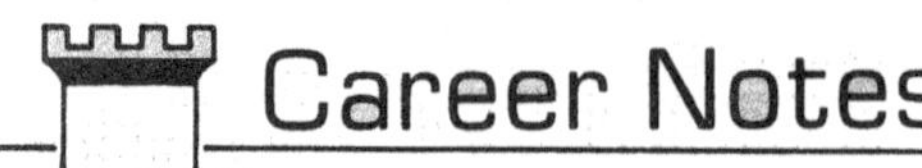

Warrant Officers' Branch

Voluntary Indefinite Status:

In accordance with AR 135-215, "*Officer Periods of Service on Active Duty*," upon completion of initial tour of obligated service, the authority to apply for VI status is suspended for all warrant officers except those managed by the Surgeon General and the Judge Advocate General.

Warrant officers managed by MILPERCEN will no longer be authorized to apply for VI status. However, this change in policy does not interfere with an officer's right to apply for integration into the Regular Army (RA).

The policy and procedures were updated for warrant officers by MILPERCEN due to an upcoming change in the VI status policy for all officers. Officers other than RA will be considered for VI status during the third and seventh years of officer service.

Warrant officers do not have to be in a VI status to apply for RA. They must have two years of warrant service on current tour, but may still be an obligated volunteer (OBV) at the time of application for RA.

Centralized board selection of personnel applying for VI status will be part of the process. Since virtually all warrant officers apply, it has been determined that warrant records will be automatically reviewed, making the application process unnecessary.

A yearly circular will be published announcing the names of all warrant officers who will be considered by the VI status selection board. Those who do not want to continue on active duty beyond their normal ETS will notify MILPERCEN and then will separate with no further action required. For those considered by the centralized selection board, a notification of selection or non-selection will be forwarded through the local commander to the individual officer.

The warrant officer's commander must concur before VI status is awarded. Commanders will be permitted to recommend disapproval of a board-selected VI status and return the action to MILPERCEN for final determination. Declination of VI status by the individual officer will constitute a request for voluntary separation at ETS.

By going to a centralized selection process for VI status, the Army will assure that each officer is given fair, consistent, and equal consideration for career status. In addition, a large administrative workload of paperwork progressing through command channels and MILPOs will be eliminated. The Army will be able to select the best quality officers in the right numbers to meet its needs.

Questions may be directed to CW4 Edward Cole at MILPERCEN, AV 221-7839, commercial (202) 325-7839.

NCO & Enlisted Soldiers' Branch

Where Would You Like to Go:

Is your DA Form 2635 (Enlisted Preference Statement) up-to-date? Does it reflect your current desired area of assignment? Is the dependent data correct? Are personal considerations such as family requirements for special medical or educational facilities included in the remarks sections?

While sometimes referred to as a "dream sheet," the Enlisted Preference Statement was developed to establish a direct line between the soldier and the career managers at MILPERCEN. This information helps the career manager consider the soldier's desire for assignments, schooling, types of duty, and areas of preference.

Also, check your areas of preference on your DA Form 2 or 2A. Do they agree with your Enlisted Preference Statement? If they are in disagreement, or not submitted in the first place, your assignment manager cannot possibly anticipate your personal preferences. Unfortunately, the majority of soldier inquiries received by the Engineer Branch are assignment related and are received after an assignment has been completed, instead of before.

By no means do current preference statements ensure you will get your "dream" assignment. The priorities established by the Army often override personal preferences, however, when they are known they are always considered as an important part of the assignment process. CSMs should encourage members of their units to use these preference statements.

Equal Opportunity Advisors:

The Army needs Equal Opportunity advisors in PMOs 12B (Combat Engineer), 12C (Bridge Crewman), and 51H (Construction Foreman). NCOs may apply if they meet the following qualifications:

- currently serving in grade E-6 (P) or E-7
- have been selected to attend ANCOC or already graduated
- qualified in their PMOS
- eligible for worldwide assignment
- meet height/weight standards
- passed the Army Physical Readiness Test

Volunteers who are accepted will attend 16 weeks of training at the Defense Equal Opportunity Management Institute, Patrick Air Force Base, FLA. All graduates will be awarded Skill Qualification Identifier "Q" and will be assigned to Engineer units in CONUS or overseas.

For more information, contact your local MILPO or personnel staff NCO. For MOS 12B and 12C, ask for SFC Richard Markle at AV 221-7710 or commercial (703) 325-7710. For MOS 51H, ask for SFC John Lane at the same numbers.

MINEN

A Personal

The true test of a technical manual is its usefulness in a practical field situation. A true test of TM 5-349, *Arctic Construction*, came when the 23rd Engineer Company (CBT) (HVY), Fort Richardson, was tasked to build the main supply route for the joint training exercise, "Brim Frost '83" in central Alaska.

Site Selection

The first task was to bridge the Delta River. This required choosing a site for an ice bridge. Site considerations are covered in the "Ice Bridges" section of TM 5-349.

Additional site considerations used by CPT Chris Turletes, commander of the 23rd, included aligning the ice bridge with the prevailing wind direction, insuring that streams or creeks were not entering immediately upstream from the site, removing obstructions upwind, and placing snow berms downwind. His additional criteria are included in "*Ice Bridging*," Pamphlet 350-2 of the 172nd Infantry Brigade (February 1983) that was necessitated by the lack of a specific guidance in TM 5-349.

Approaches

"Preparation of Approaches" suggests using a timber ramp from the ice bridge to frozen fill on the banks. This ignores the fact that ice forming at the banks usually expands off the river and becomes supported by the banks. The overhanging ice creates a weak spot because of the hinge effect.

This problem was dealt with in "Brim Frost '83" by breaking the hinge ice and making the ramps of icecrete: crushed ice, aggregate, snow, and water. This newer method of approach-ramp construction must be included in a rewrite of TM 5-349.

Ice Profile

The next step in ice bridging is profiling the ice which TM 5-349 addresses in general terms only. The reader is left guessing where to place the profile holes, how to estimate the load-bearing capacity for different types of ice, and what to do with ice frozen solid to the river bottom or unsupported by water.

The load-bearing capacity for ice is given in table XIV of TM 5-349. Unfortunately, this table does not say which type of ice these minimum thicknesses are for and does not give correction factors for other types of ice. The *Ice Bridging* pamphlet gives the load class formulas and also has a table listing certain military vehicles with the corresponding minimum ice thicknesses required for certain types of ice.

The Delta River crossing posed many problems. The four major river channels had conditions varying from solid ice to the river bottom to 40 inches of ice over 4-foot air voids. At the beginning of construction, the water flow was subterranean. The *Arctic Construction* manual does not mention these possible problems, much less offer solutions.

Captain Turletes consulted Edward F. Sheehan, long-time resident, geologist, and Senior Test Manager with the Cold Regions Test Center at Fort Greely, AK. Mr. Sheehan said that the subterranean flow was normal, but that it would not continue all winter.

This information led to the following solution: two crossing sites were prepared, one on the ground-supported ice sheet and one weaving from sandbar to

TED STATES ARMY
INEER CENTER
FORT BELVOIR, VA

IANDER/COMMANDANT
Richard S. Kem

TANT COMMANDANT
Ralph T. Rundle

F OF STAFF/DEPUTY
LLATION COMMANDER
Peter D. Stearns

IAND SERGEANT MAJOR
Charles T. Tucker

CTOR OF TRAINING
DOCTRINE
Don W. Barber

OF PUBLICATIONS
ley Georges

R
lyn Fleming

GING EDITOR
Louis J. Leto

TANT EDITOR
ald Schmoldt

RIBUTING EDITOR
D. Shields

N DIRECTOR
mas Davis

RIAL ASSISTANT
Jean Tate

he Cover

is German-laid minefield won't hold up
d forces invading France as 1Lt Merle
tein makes a final sweep on June 13,
. Notice the mines that have already
recovered (U.S. Army Photo).

FEATURES

DEPARTMENTS

EER (ISSN 0046-1989) is an authorized publication of the U.S. Army Engineer Center and Fort Belvoir, VA. Unless specifically stated, material appear-
ein does not necessarily reflect official policy, thinking nor endorsement by any agency of the U.S. Army. The words he, him, or his are used to represent
nel of either sex. All photographs contained herein are official U.S. Army photographs unless otherwise credited. The use of funds for printing this
tion was approved by Headquarters, Department of the Army, on July 22, 1981. Material herein may be reprinted if credit is given to ENGINEER
the author. ENGINEER's objectives are to provide a forum for the exchange of ideas, to inform and motivate, and to promote the professional develop-
f all members of the Army engineer community. Direct correspondence with ENGINEER is authorized and encouraged. Inquiries, letters to the editor,
ntaries, manuscripts, photographs and general correspondence should be sent to: ENGINEER Magazine, ATZA-TD-P Stop 291D, Fort Belvoir, VA
5291. Phone: (703) 664-3082, AV 354. ENGINEER may be forwarded to personnel in military units. Address changes should be sent to ENGINEER.
iptions to ENGINEER are available through the Superintendent of Documents, U.S. Government Printing Office, Washington, D.C. 20402. A check
ey order payable to Superintendent of Documents, must accompany all subscription requests. Rates are $11.00 for domestic (including APO and FPO)
ses and $13.75 for foreign addresses. Individual copies are available at $3.00 per copy for domestic addresses and $3.75 for foreign addresses. Second
postage paid at Fort Belvoir, VA, and additional mailing offices.

Engineers Save Historic Sit
Clean Hawaiian Habitation

Working in the heat and blowing dust of South Point, HI, the 25th Infantry Division's 65th Combat Engineers worked from August 15 to September 7 to clear debris from an ancient Hawaiian habitation cave (photo by SP4 Robert P. Lindsay).

Engineers from HHC, 65th Engineer Bn. Schofield Barracks, HI, preserved a portion of Hawaiian history recently.

From August 15 to September 7, the squad of Engineers cleaned an ancient Hawaiian *habitation cave* at South Point, on the southern tip of the Hawaii.

The habitation cave area of South Point was the site of the first Hawaiians' landing in the islands, according to SGT Terrence Whitfield, HHC, 65th Engineer Bn. During WW II, however, the Army Air Corps used the cave area as an airfield. After the war, when the airfield was deactivated, barb wire, fuel drums, and other debris were discarded into the caves.

"The 65th Engineers became involved in the cleaning project through the Hawaiian Home Lands Department," explained Whitfield. "The Department preserves lands owned by the original Hawaiians in much the same way as Indian reservations preserve Indian lands."

When the original Hawaiians came to South Point, they found several cave-like holes in the countryside called lava tubes. These are formed when the surface of a lava flow cools, allowing molten lava in the center to flow out. This forms a tunnel or "tube." According to Whitfield, the first visitors to Hawaii used these as shelters or homes.

In the future, a microprocessor-controlled backhoe and manipulator arm, mounted on a cross-country vehicle, may be used to improve the safety and efficiency of Combat Engineers (U.S. Army photo).

while, would have the capacity to lift and stack a pallet of ammunition at angles up to 90 degrees when fully extended. When close in, this could be increased to as many as four pallets—all while the driver remains in the safety of the cab.

Data from initial tests currently underway will also form the basis for using artificial intelligence in other types of construction and materials handling equipment.

Link Reinforcement Kit

In October 1984, the Engineers of the 559th Engineer Bn. were once again leaders in their field, as the 516th Engineer Co. became the first unit in Europe to construct a medium girder bridge (MGB) with a link reinforcement kit.

At the field construction site in Hanau, Germany, the Engineers were found adding more than the usual number of bays to the bridge under construction.

According to SSG Gary Layton, a section sergeant with the 516th, the reinforcement kit allows them to build a 22-bay double story bridge that can handle a Class 60 load. "Without the kit," he said, "a Class 60 bridge could only be 12 bays long, and 22 bays could only handle a Class 16 load."

Mr. Charles Lynn, chief of a New Equipment Training Team that was available from the Field Services Activity of St. Louis, MO, discussed how the integration of new engineering equipment such as the link reinforcement kit begins with research, development and testing at Ft. Belvoir, VA. "Then we get the responsibility to manage the unit's training," he said. He further added that the instructors training the Engineers were from the manufacturers of the MGB.

Assisting Mr. Lynn was SFC Gary Stayon from Ft. Belvoir. He further described how it was the New Equipment Team's mission to ensure that products are designed that can be properly used by troops in the field.

"As a 12C, my work primarily concerns bridging," Stayon said. "For instance, the original third roller assembly used with the link kit kept faltering. Consequently, my team convinced the civilian Engineer to redesign the roller assembly, so that we no longer experience any problem in this area."

The majority of the Engineers' actual training was done by Mr. Bob Farrar, an Englishman from Fairey Engineering LTD of Stockport, England, the designers and manufacturers of the MGB.

A man of dry English wit and distinct British colloquialisms, Mr. Farrar was always found in the midst of the soldiers he was training, showing them in detail the proper assembly of the reinforcement apparatus. He noted that it takes about three bridge builds to get a unit well acquainted with the reinforcement kit.

Engineers of the 516th Engineer Co. "heave ho" as they adjust the link reinforcement apparatus, visible below the medium girder bridge (photo by SP4 Paul Graveline).

CLEAR THE WAY

by MG Richard S. Kem, Commandant, U.S. Army Engineer School

The American Military Engineer: A Proud Heritage

As an American military Engineer, you possess a multifaceted heritage that reaches as far back as Europe during the Renaissance. The Engineers of that creative period recognized no dichotomy between military and civil engineering. They moved easily from combat engineering to the design and construction of civil structures such as canals, cathedrals, and fortifications. For example, Francesco di Giorgio Martini of Siena, a Renaissance master known for his painting, sculpture and architecture, was responsible for his hometown's water supply and invented the star-shaped bastion. Another, Aristotle Fiorviante of Bologna, built one of the cathedrals in Moscow's Kremlin and laid pontoon bridges for armies on the march.

All of the elements of this 15th century tradition are reinforced by our unique American heritage as military Engineers. As Combat Engineers, we trace our descent to the earliest hours of the U.S. Army at Bunker Hill and to the original company of sappers and miners who led the way through the British fortifications at Yorktown. Although technology has changed dramatically since then, their mission remains ours—mobility, countermobility, survivability. We are still sappers—"clear the way."

Also, since the American Revolution, we have been constructors of military fortifications; and that military construction mission has grown through the years, particularly since World War II. Finally, Army Engineers have been instrumental in developing civil society since the early 19th century. This started with clearing obstacles from rivers, building the major highways of the period, as well as the exploration, survey, and mapping of our nation's westward expansion. This led to major national responsibilities in water-resource development and major programs to construct facilities for our space program, to modernize the postal system, and in significant overseas construction.

Because of this diverse background, it is appropri that this historical issue offers articles across breadth of our mission—combat engineering, milit construction, and our civil works engineering and c struction for the nation. The lead article tells h Combat Engineers "cleared the way" in the Europ theater during World War II. A second provides origin of the Corps of Engineers civil works missi and another, "The Fort Leonard Wood Museum," t us how some of this heritage is captured and preser for us and future generations of Engineers.

We look to this rich and varied past for many r sons. Those of you who attended the commemorat at Fort Belvoir's 40th anniversary of the Battle of Bulge experienced first-hand some of the pleasu and uses of our history. The talks by Engineers w fought in the Bulge not only taught us much abc leadership in battle, but were inspiring and enterta ing as well.

The content of this issue illustrates many ways which we draw on this heritage. In the first place, c past explains the origins of our current missions. F example, the article on the builders of America's inf structure traces the expansion of Engineer parti pation in the development of public works such as ra roads, canals, and highways.

Finally, our heritage as American military En neers should provide us a source of pride. The w time achievements of American military Enginee show what an Engineer organization, with its ro in such a wide variety of military and civil engine ing accomplishments, can do.

Understanding our roots, fully appreciating t major contribution our forebearers made in buildi our great nation and contributing on the battlefie to its defense, is necessary. Necessary to apprecia that you are a part of a great organization and a gre tradition; and that you carry a heavy responsibili to continue that tradition—in the peacetime Army, the AirLand Battlefield, serving our Natic Essayons!

CSM Charles T. Tucker, U.S. Army Engineer Center & School

esterday's Engineers, Today's Inspiration

ıst Engineers Show the eaning of "Soldier"

pleases me that my first opportunity to write dge the Gap" would be for a historical issue. n we think about the history of the Army and of Corps of Engineers, we actually think of our tage. We may think of the Continental Army at ey Forge, Saratoga, and Yorktown. We may also k about the soldiers who gave their lives at nandy, the Bulge, Pork Chop Hill, and Saigon.

ıe point is that as Engineers, we must first ember our heritage as combat soldiers. Many ıs throughout history, Engineers were forced to their shovels and pick up their weapons. We see ime example of this in the article, "WWII: ineers in the European Theater." Engineers were d to defend against an overwhelming enemy force Trois-Ponts, even though other American troops ordered to retreat.

en at the Normandy landings, Engineers faced ıtless enemy fire and suffered perhaps more alties man-for-man than any other unit. Without r courage and determination, the American forces well have faced utter disaster.

ıis is illustrated in a book by Janice Holt Giles. *The Damned Engineers*," she explains how LTC er led the German offensive at the Battle of the ge and tried to maneuver his panzers against an ıumbered enemy. But every time he tried to move anks across a bridge, he found that it had been n up by Engineers. The story goes that all he kept ng upon discovering the bridges was, "The ned Engineers." Again, we see the significant role h American military Engineers have played in history.

All of these examples should remind us of our first duty—to be a professional soldier. Our prime mission on the battlefield is to defeat the enemy. If dropping our shovels and leaving behind our bulldozers is what we have to do to defeat our enemy, then that is what we do. The fact was true on June 6, 1944, and it still stands today.

The AirLand Battle requires all soldiers to work together. It demands that we recognize our mission in supporting the maneuver forces and executing this task in the most proficient and professional manner possible. It means reorganizing and fighting as infantry, should it become necessary. As Engineers, we must realize this. If we don't win the first battle, we may very well lose the war.

The American military Engineer has played a major role in this country's history and continues to do so. Not only was he instrumental against Hitler's final desperate attempt to defeat the Allies, but he also planted the seed for this country's infrastructure. Troops continually work within our communities improving roads, dams, bridges, and buildings. They constructed the first railroad tracks so that Americans could travel easier, faster, and safer. They did all this and were proud of their work.

So, what do I ask of all noncommissioned officers and soldiers? Remember that as Engineer soldiers, you can be just as proud of your heritage as any other soldier. Remember the key role Engineer soldiers have in the Army. Remember what your predecessors have done and use that to inspire your soldiers. Educate your soldiers as to whose footsteps they are following. That inspiration and dedication is what we need in the AirLand Battle.

Strongest Man in the Army

SSG Tom Benoit, a soldier assigned to the 11th Engineer Bn, Ft. Belvoir, VA., claims to be the strongest man in the Army.

In his competition, Benoit usually opens by squatting 722 pounds at least five times. Then he moves to 766 pounds and finally maxes with 805 pounds, squatting each of these weights three times. He then benchpresses 505 pounds and dead-lifts 665 pounds.

In the 14 months that Benoit has been powerlifting, he's won over 33 medals. In a recent meet at Gettysburg, PA, held last August, Benoit deadlifted 665 pounds. That was the first time he had ever lifted that much weight. He placed first in the dead-lift and bench press competitions, and he also received a medal for best lifter in the 270 pound body weight class.

Right before a lift, Benoit usually gets his adrenalin flowing by having someone slap his face or by hitting his head against the weight bar. "I'm a super-aggressive person, so when I work out with weights, it's like I'm at war."

He enters only four competitions a year. He says that if he competed in any more, his body wouldn't be able to take the stress. "You need time in between to prepare for meets," he said.

Benoit works out at a private gym in

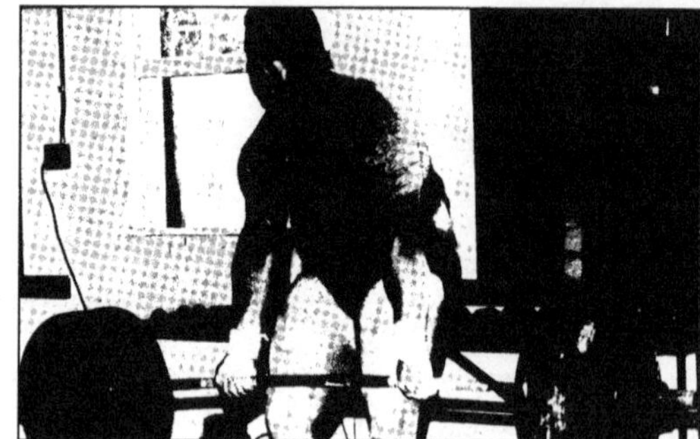

SSG Tom Benoit, who claims to be the strongest man in the Army, shows the strength that he hopes will give him the world champion powerlifter title (U.S. Army photo).

Marlow Heights, MD. He says he feels that having the right atmosphere is very crucial. He credits his success to his personality. "I love all sports and I'm very aggressive. Powerlifting is the only sport I've found that's individualistic. It's not like team sports, where you have to depend on a team's total effort. My way a person can be as good as he wants to be."

In his upcoming meet in February 1985 at the Armed Forces Championship Meets, Benoit intends to walk away with a few more medals. With proper weight training, working out at the gym three times a week, and proper diet, he says he could be the world champion powerlifter by 1988.

Have something for Engineer People? Please send your item (with photographs) to ENGINEER Magazine, ATZA-TD-P, Stop 291D Ft. Belvoir, VA 22060-5291.

German Friendship Award Given to CSM

The former Engineer School Command Sergeant Major was named first military recipient of the Federal Republic of Germany Friendship Award in recognition of his efforts to foster good German-American relations.

CSM Orville W. Troesch Jr. received the award from German Charge d' Affaires Theodor Wallau during a recent ceremony at the German embassy in Washington, D.C.

Troesch, who was honored for his endeavors in supporting and sustaining friendship between Germany and the United States, served 12 years in Germany during a 26-year Army career. While assigned in Germany, he was actively involved in partnership activities, joint training ventures, and social events.

In 1983, during the 300th anniversary celebration of German immigration to the United States, Troesch organized activities in support of those festivities. Throughout his tenure at Ft. Belvoir, he assisted military families departing or returning from assignments to Germany.

Troesch was recently reassigned to Ft. Sam Houston, TX, as Command Sergeant Major of the Fifth Army Garrison.

(DCA)

Engineer Officer Basic Course (EOBC) students will soon receive additional leadership training, as well as courses in the communicative arts.

The officers, who are being trained to become professional Engineer platoon leaders, will also be given additional night training and orienteering. More time will be devoted to the Engineer Stakes and the Common Training Test, and the final ARTEP/FTX has been changed to emphasize the role of the Task Force Engineer as both a platoon leader and a planner who integrates with a task force staff.

The EOBC cadre, which is organized into three training companies, recognizes the need to improve certain fundamental tasks for these new Engineers. It encourages feedback from Engineer commanders on the EOBC curriculum results.

Standardization (DOES)

The Engineer School and five university ROTC detachments are now affiliated in an agreement signed Aug. 15, 1984. The five are Iowa State University, Johns Hopkins University, North Carolina State University, Penn State University, and the University of Missouri-Rolla.

The program's goal is to increase the number of engineer and science students who participate in ROTC and to ultimately increase the number who will choose Engineer commissions. This program is in its first year, with only the Corps of Engineers and the Signal Corps participating. The universities were chosen based on three criteria:

- Sound engineering school
- Strong ROTC detachment
- History of commissioning relatively few Engineer officers

The program will be examined later for possible expansion into more universities, as well as expanding the program for other Army branches.

At the Engineer School, the Engineer Proponency Office was given the program responsibility. By agreement, the Professor of Military Science at each of the universities is to be an Engineer officer. This branch assignment will occur on the next possible assignment rotation date.

The program will provide the Professors of Military Science with a direct line to the Engineer School for assistance in instructing and informing ROTC students about the Army branches, in particular the Corps of Engineers.

The Engineer School will assist the ROTC program by providing slide shows, pamphlets, and other audio-visual material that will help to publicize the Corps of Engineers as a service choice.

Directorate of Training and Doctrine (DOTD)

62N30 Basic Course:

The Construction Equipment Supervisor Basic Technical Course (62N30) began October 15 at Fort Leonard Wood, MO. The five-week, three-day resident course teaches the basic supervisory management and technical skills which are required for planning and executing construction projects at the section level.

The 62N30 BTC is available to active Army or Reserve Component soldiers who are qualified in MOS 62E, 62F, 62G, 62H, or 62N and have their commander's approval.

First priority will be given to promotable E5s or E6s who are assigned to skill level 3 positions for which the training is designed. Second priority will be given to E5s or promotable E4s who, because of unit shortages, are assigned to E6 positions.

Time restrictions and the technical subject matter required the course to be taught in three phases. First, a diagnostic test is given at the beginning of the course to identify any deficiencies in prerequisite skills and to provide the curriculum for remedial training. This training will be conducted outside the normal academic day and will prepare each student for future BTC classes during the course.

Next, each student will learn a variety of subjects including equipment utilization and maintenance, interpretation of planning documents, production rate estimation, job planning, schedule development, safety and quality control procedures, personnel supervision, and personnel management.

Finally, the course will end in a three-hour comprehensive test to evaluate the soldier's knowledge of all the skills taught. This system of instruction will enable the soldier to return to his unit better qualified to resume his leadership position.

Soldiers desiring to attend the 62N30 BTC should initiate the request on DA Form 4187 through their company commander in accordance with DA Pam 600-8. The POC for further information is 1LT Bostian, General Engineering Branch, Ft. Belvoir, VA 22060-5291, (703)664-1997/4834 or AV 354-1997.

Functional Review:

The second Engineer Functional Review (EFR) was presented to the Headquarters, Department of the Army (HQDA), Deputy Chief of Staff for Personnel (DCSPER) May 30, 1984. The Engineer School Commandant uses these annual reviews to express the total personnel requirements and problems for the Engineer community.

The Engineer Functional Review is used as a management tool to ensure that soldiers are trained to man new materiel systems and can support the Engineer force structure. The review examines new material systems and new or restructured organizations to identify their total personnel requirements. This enables the proponent to identify personnel issues which, if not resolved, could slow the fielding of new systems and organizations or could hamper unit readiness.

Several personnel issues, identified in the May 1984 EFR, were women's limited opportunities for early career progression in the Engineer force, the critical shortfall of Army divers, the shortage of Engineer warrant officers, and the lack of requirements for MOS 53B (Industrial Gas Production Specialist) in either the active or reserve forces.

The Engineer Proponency Office has now assigned directorates within the USAES to solve these issues. If required, outside agencies such as other proponents, the Soldier Support Center—National Capitol Region, MILPERCEN, or the Army Staff will be asked to assist in problem solutions.

A continuing program called the Engineer School Branch Training Team (BTT) has been established by the Directorate of Evaluation and Standardization to maintain open communications with Engineer units worldwide.

The Team, made up of representatives from the Engineer School and the Engineer Training Center at Ft. Leonard Wood, provides briefings on current actions and answers questions the unit may have. The BTT goal is to visit each active duty component Engineer battalion, group and brigade every two years, and reserve units as scheduling permits.

Typically, Engineer School members include individuals from the Directorates of Combat Developments and Training and Doctrine, as well as the training departments.

Both the Engineer School and the unit benefit from the Branch Training Team program since the visiting team receives feedback from the field and communications are improved. The unit also benefits from the information it receives.

Contact the Directorate of Evaluation and Standardization at (703) 664-3668, AV 354-3668 for further information.

The Engineer School has adopted the New Equipment Systems Training Development Management Model (NESTDMM) handbook. This manual was developed to provide training developers, combat developers, and trainers with a management model and procedural guide for meeting training development requirements while acquiring new equipment systems.

The NESTDMM handbook will give managers and project officers a comprehensive guide which outlines responsibilities and interactions that should occur between the different USAES organizations as they relate to the Life Cycle Management Model (LCMM).

Completion of this handbook was made possible through the joint efforts of various branch representatives within the Engineer School who participated in numerous work sessions. Distribution of these handbooks began in October 1984. If you wish to receive a copy, contact Ms. Commie Brown, New Equipment Systems Office, (703) 664-2456, AV 354-2456.

Engineers
in the
European Theater

D-Day, June 6, 1944: 57,500 American and Allied troops mass together on the Normandy beaches to make Operation Overlo: the largest single assault ever launched . . . and the Enginee led the way.

by Dr. William C. Baldwin and Dr. Barry W. Fowle

Normandy Landings

On June 6, 1984 the United States and its western Allies celebrated the 40th anniversary of the landings on the Normandy beaches. Those landings began a drive that led to Germany's surrender less than one year later. Contributing mightily to the effort were United States Army Engineers who participated in every part of that offensive.

Although Allied forces had already landed in North Africa, Sicily, and southern Italy earlier in the war, none of these landings had been as large as Operation Overlord, which was a direct assault on Hitler's vaunted Atlantic wall.

The First Canadian Army and the Second British Army under the command of Field Marshal Bernard L. Montgomery landed on three beaches on the eastern coast of Normandy, while the First United States Army under LTG Omar Bradley landed on two western beaches, code-named Omaha and Utah. Although the Allies had carefully planned the operation, the outcome of the assault was uncertain.

Omaha was the most formidable of the two American beaches. It stretched for almost 8,000 yards between two sections of coastline dominated by rocky cliffs. At low tide, the beach had a 300-yard tidal flat of hard-packed, gently sloping sand which could support Allied landing craft. Behind this tidal flat lay a rocky shingle and a level shelf of sand and grass. Inland from the shelf, the ground rose steeply into bluffs from 100 to 125 feet high. Five small valleys, which cut through these bluffs to the beach, were the exits through which American troops, vehicles, and supplies had to pass (Figure 1).

The Germans, recognizing that Omaha was a possible invasion site, began to fortify the beach. They erected hedgehogs, ramps, and "Belgian gates"; placed stakes, minefields, barbed wire; dug antitank ditches; and studded all of these obstacles with mines.

Realizing that the valleys were the key to defending the beach because they provided exits for American troops, vehicles, and supplies, the Germans fortified them with pill boxes, dugouts, and interlocking trenc They established artillery and mo positions which could blanket beaches with deadly, accurate fir

The Germans decided to defeat invasion attempt on the beaches th selves and, therefore, prepared no p tions further inland.

The American plan for assaul Omaha required the Air Force and Navy to bombard the beach prior t Hour. Landing just behind the f wave of American infantry, gap ass teams would create gaps through surviving German beach obstacle

Each of the 16 gap assault teams composed of 28 Engineers from 146th and 299th Engineer Com Battalions, a naval combat demoli squad, and a tank dozer. Eight sup teams and two command teams wc closely follow the assault teams.

Each of the assault and sup teams carried 1,000 pounds of eq ment including explosives, demoli accessories, mine detectors, and markers. Each man in the team car a 75-pound load, including 40 pou of explosives; and each team had 1, pounds of extra explosives in rub boats.

After the gap assault teams clea the initial passages through the be obstacles, troops from the 5th and Engineer Special Brigades wo enlarge these gaps and begin unl

Off the beach and driving forward, Engineers build roads on the coast of northern France near Cherbourg, June 8, 1944. Ships of the invasion fleet hover in the background (U.S. Army photo).

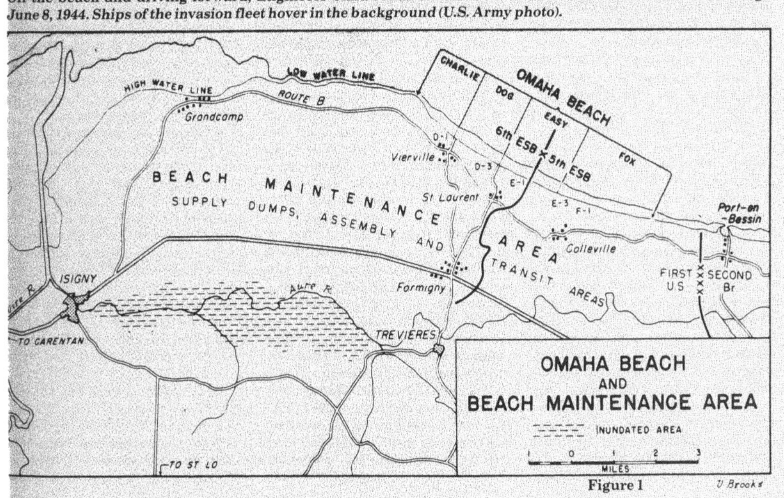

Figure 1

Photograph, taken several months after D-Day, shows a general view of beach defenses near Fort de Foucarville in th Utah Beach area (U.S. Army photo).

ing supplies and moving them inland. The 37th, 149th, 336th, and 348th Engineer Combat Battalions which formed the nuclei of the special brigades' battalion beach groups, also included quartermaster, ordnance, chemical, signal, medical, and military police personnel.

Although American planners anticipated that these Engineers might have to fight as infantry in the first phases of the landing, they did not anticipate the enormous confusion or the stiff German resistance that confronted the American troops on D-Day.

Since the preliminary air and naval attacks on the German beach defenses had little effect, the first waves of American assault troops faced intense German small arms and artillery fire. Most of the first-wave troops landed east of their assigned beaches, and few landed on time. Of the 16 gap assault teams, 9 landed ahead of schedule and only 5 landed on their assigned beach.

The intense German fire forced many infantry troops to take refuge among the beach obstacles which the gap teams were trying to destroy. Unable to clear soldiers from the obstacle area it had wired, one team was heading toward the shingle for cover when a German mortar shell detonated the charges, killing or wounding 19 of its members and as many infantry. By 7 a.m. as the rising tide drove American soldiers inland, the gap assault teams had only cleared five narrow lanes through the German obstacles.

As more men and vehicles crowded onto the beach, the teams had to devise new methods for removing obstacles. They discovered that it was easier and safer to remove the mines attached to the obstacles and use the tank dozers and, later, armored bulldozers to shove the obstacles aside. Later in the day, two landing craft demonstrated that they could ram their way through the disarmed obstacles. This technique became standard practice.

Also at 7 a.m. the first special brigade Engineers landed 10 minutes early and found the situation little improved from H-Hour. Because it was impossible for them to land and move supplies, the battalion beach group Engineers joined the gap assault teams in removing beach obstacles, aiding the wounded, and reinforcing the ragged fire line that was forming behind the shingle pile.

With German small arms and artillery fire still intense, artillery shells hit a landing craft carrying the first wave of 90 men from the 147th Engineer Combat Battalion and caused 45 casualties. This forced the rest of the Engineers to jump into neck-deep water without most of their equipment. The success of the landing now depended on getting the troops from the beach to the bluffs, where they could suppress German fire.

Elements of the 37th Engineer Combat Battalion then landed near Exits E-1 and E-3 (Figure 1) and immediately joined the infantry in attacking German strong points. Gathering a leaderless infantry company, 1LT Robert P. Ross led them and his Engineer pl toon against two German machine gu emplacements. This make-shift for captured the positions, killing defenders.

A German minefield located on shelf of land between the shingle an the bluff still kept American soldie pinned on the beach. Working und heavy German fire, six Engineers fro the 37th cleared and marked what w probably the first foot trail from th beach to the bluffs. All six we wounded. While the Engineers clear additional paths through the min fields, the officers of the 37th guid the infantry through the lanes to le exposed positions at the foot of th bluffs.

Although scattered groups of soldie began moving from the beach and u the bluffs, the tidal flat becam increasingly littered with equipme and vehicles which threatened to bloc the exits. Privates Vinton W. Dove an William Shoemaker, bulldozer oper tors of the 37th Engineer Battalio worked under heavy German fire du ing the next several hours, movin wreckage and obstacles from the beac clearing a passage for vehicles throug the loose rock of the shingle, and fil ing antitank ditches at the foot of th bluffs.

As the infantry gradually subdue the German strongpoints at Exit E- the 37th and 149th Combat Enginee built access roads from the beach to th exit. By 1 p.m. tanks and artiller could move from the beach through th

were not as strong as those at Omaha. During the night preceding D-Day, assaults by the 82nd and 101st Airborne Divisions had further weakened and disrupted German defenses.

The assault plan for Utah, like that for Omaha, required Army-Navy gap assault teams to land shortly after the first infantry units and create passages through the beach obstacles.

As a result of several miscalculations, the entire Utah assault force landed 2,000 yards south of the intended landing site at a beach that was less heavily defended. Although German artillery fire caused numerous casualties, they were light compared to those at Omaha. The teams quickly cleared the initial gaps, and by 9:30 a.m. the entire beach was free of obstacles.

While the teams were clearing the obstacles, other units from the 237th Engineer Battalion were creating gaps in the seawall and clearing passages through the sand dunes. Fortunately, the best causeways across the flooded area were near the landing site.

One company of the 237th destroyed several obstacles near Exit 2 and accompanied an infantry battalion as it advanced inland. In the middle of this causeway, the Germans had destroyed a culvert. While the infantry waded to the other side, the 237th Engineers, assisted by the 238th, built a 30-foot treadway bridge; and by early afternoon, Exit 2 was open.

As the infantry and Engineers were clearing Exit 2, another force, including two companies of the 49th Engineer Combat Battalion, moved south from the beach toward Exit 1. Under small arms and artillery fire, the infantry moved inland to join the 101st Airborne troops, while the Engineers attacked German positions protecting the sluice gates that had created the water barrier behind the beach. The Engineers captured the gates on D-Day; and the next day they seized another stronghold, capturing 59 prisoners and 17 tons of ammunition. During the next several days, 49th Engineers held these positions on the southern flank of the beachhead and drained water from the flooded area behind the beach.

While Engineers from the combat battalions moved inland with the advancing troops, members of the 1st Engineer Special Brigade remained on the beach, improving the exits and clearing the obstacles. By nightfall on D-Day, the 531st Regiment had cleared a new beach and opened another causeway leading inland.

By the end of D-Day, American forces at Omaha and Utah had overcome most of the German beach defenses and were advancing inland. Engineers on the beaches now faced the formidable task of establishing the supply lines that would support American forces as they fought to break out of the Normandy beachhead and advance across northern France.

Battle of th[illegible]

Although D-Day gave the Western Allies a beachhead in northern France, almost two months of bitter fighting had passed before the forces were able to force their way out of the hedgerow country. After the breakout, Allied armies raced across France, liberated Paris, and headed toward the German frontier.

The rapid pace of the advance, however, placed a severe strain on Allied logistics. The logistical problems, along with bad weather and stiffening German resistance, slowed the offensive. By mid-December, American armies had reached the Roer River inside Germany and the West Wall along the Saar River in eastern France. Between these two fronts lay the Ardennes—a hilly, densely forested area.

In 1944, units of five American divisions and a cavalry group held the 85-mile long Ardennes front. Three of these divisions mostly consisted of new soldiers who had recently arrived on the continent, while the other two divisions had been badly mauled in the bitter fighting in the Huertgen Forest.

The shortage of American troops forced Allied commanders to man portions of the front lightly. In addition, the bad terrain within the Ardennes and the belief that the German army was near exhaustion had convinced the commanders that the sector was relatively safe.

After months of retreat, however, Hitler decided on a bold gamble to regain the initiative in the west. Under cover of bad winter weather, he and his generals massed 25 divisions opposite the Ardennes and planned to crash through the thinly-held American front, cross the Meuse river, and drive to Antwerp.

Before daybreak on December 16, the German army launched this last desperate offensive, taking the American divisions in the front lines by surprise. One of these American divisions, the 106th, was a new unit. Its Engineer combat battalion, the 81st, had spent the early part of December repairing roads and removing snow in the division's sector. Behind the 81st was the 168th Engineer Combat Battalion which had been operating quarries and sawmills.

The massive German assault interrupted these routine tasks. Both battalions found themselves fighting as infantry in a brave but futile attempt to stem the German assault. On the morning of December 17, as German troops were cutting off and surrounding the regiments of the 106th, the division ordered LTC Thomas J. Riggs Jr., commander of the 81st, to establish defensive positions east of the important crossroads at St. Vith.

Reinforced by the 7th Armored Division, elements of the two Engineer battalions under Riggs held their position against determined German attacks until December 21.

During that afternoon, a heavy German assault, led by tanks and accompanied by intense artillery, rocket, and mortar fire, overran the exhausted American defenders. Riggs ordered his men to separate into small groups and attempt an escape to the rear. The Germans captured most of the survivors, including Riggs.

As the American front collapsed, GEN Eisenhower and his subordinates summoned their slender reserves. But while these troops were moving into position, the American commanders had to rely on rear-area troops already in the Ardennes.

Many of the units along the front were corps and Army Engineer battalions, scattered throughout the area in company, platoon, and even squad-sized groups. Engineers, who had been engaged in road maintenance and sawmilling, suddenly found themselves manning road blocks and preparing defensive positions in the face of powerful German armored columns. Against a more powerful enemy force, these 18 Engineer battalions were very instrumental in delaying an offensive whose only hope for success lay in crossing the Meuse quickly.

LTC Jochen Peiper, a Nazi SS officer, led one of the armored columns racing toward the Meuse. His route took him near Malmedy and toward the village of Trois-Ponts, the headquarters of the 1111th Group.

When the 1111th Group commander learned on December 17 of the German breakthrough, he sent LTC David E. Pergrin, the 26-year old commander of the 291st Engineer Combat Battalion, to organize defenses. Although most of the American troops in the area were fleeing, Pergrin decided to hold his position in spite of the panic and confusion. He ordered his Engineers to establish roadblocks and defensive positions around Malmedy.

During the afternoon of the 17th, Engineers manning a roadblock heard gunfire coming from a crossroads just south of their position. Shortly thereafter, four terrified American soldiers staggered up to the roadblock. They brought the first news of the "Malmedy Massacre" in which Peiper's soldiers had captured and murdered 85 American soldiers.

After the German armored column bypassed Malmedy, it headed towards Trois-Ponts, where, Company C of the 51st Engineer Combat Battalion had established positions. The 51st, also part of the 1111th Engineer Combat Group, had received orders to defend the village and prepare its bridges for demolition. Another detachment of the 291st wired one bridge south of the village; and Company C, reinforced by an antitank gun and a squad of armored infantry, prepared its positions.

When Peiper's tanks approached, the Engineers demolished the main bridge leading into the village. Although the river separating Trois-Ponts from the German column was shallow enough for infantry to ford, it was an effective barrier to tanks.

By the evening of December 18, the small American force at Trois-Ponts had come under the command of MAJ Robert B. Yates, executive officer of the 51st, who had come to the village expecting to attend a daily staff meeting.

Fearing that the Germans would discover the weakness of his force, Yates tried to deceive the enemy. Dur-

Engineers fought as infantry roughout the bulge formed by the ɜrman offensive. Engineer officers e LTC Pergrin and MAJ Yates sisted on holding their positions even hen other American troops were fleeg to the rear. The delays which Engineers imposed, often at the cost of heavy casualties, gained some of the time that Allies needed to rush reinforcements into the area. Gradually, the Americans and the British stopped the penetration and pushed the Germans back.

The Battle of the Bulge vividly demonstrated that Engineer troops, located in an apparently quiet sector well behind the front lines and engaged in routine, rear-area tasks, could not forget their secondary mission of fighting as infantry.

Bridging the Rhine

The Rhine River was probably the largest and most challenging naral obstacle facing the Engineers in rope. The width of the 320-mile ver, from Basle to the Netherlands, ries from 700 to 2,000 feet. There are fords in the river, even at low tide. ıring flood periods, the river level ries as much as 25 feet and often ɔods as much as a mile or more to the vees on either side.

Elaborate planning for crossing the ver began as early as August 1944. ngineer units and infantry assault oops conducted an extensive training ogram behind the lines. Engineers made studies of the approaches and exits before selecting actual crossing sites.

Consideration in selecting sites was given to location of airfields for air support, location of construction materials, and the effect of weather including ice floes and floods. Once everything was ready, the 12th U.S. Army Group with its First, Third, and Ninth U.S. Armies and the 6th U.S. Army Group's Seventh Army began crossing operations.

First Army

After months of training and planning, the 9th Armored Divison made the first crossing of the Rhine River in the III Corps area entirely by accident. On March 7, 1945, CCB, 9th Armored Division was surprised to find the Ludendorf Railway Bridge at Remagen still standing. Its commander, BG William M. Hoge, then immediately ordered its capture. Although badly damaged, the bridge provided one-way traffic until it finally collapsed a week later. Tanks and other vehicles were able to cross the Rhine on the existing bridge instead of by storm boats as previously planned. Rapidly the bridgehead began to expand.

hotograph shows the collapsed Ludendorf Bridge across the Rhine River at Remagen, Germany (U.S. Army photo).

Engineer Remembers WWII

by 1SG Mike Zimmerman and 2LT Greg Steggerda

It was the first trip abroad for many in the 224th Engineer Battalion, Iowa Army National Guard, deployed in West Germany for REFORGER '84· But SFC Robert Popejoy had been there before.

"About 39 years ago, I was very near where we are standing now," stated Popejoy. He entered the military just after his 18th birthday as a voluntary replacement in the 97th Infantry Division, the most-traveled American combat organization in World War II, and arrived in Germany just after the famous Battle of the Bulge.

From there he moved with his unit, B Company of the 387th Infantry Regiment, to an area east of Bastogne where they witnessed the round-the-clock bombing of Dusseldorf by Allied bomber groups based in England.

"That was something else," Popejoy said. "There were dozens of planes in the air, both day and night, making their runs. At night, search lights tried to single them out, and then German 88s (sophisticated anti-personnel, anti-aircraft weapons) would try to hit them."

Next, the unit pushed on through Bonn, down to Remagen. "Although the Allied forces had tried to blow up the bridge there, it was still standing, as I recall. Later it collapsed," he said.

The B Company crossed the Rhine River on a float bridge, moving north into the German industrial area known as the Ruhr Pocket. Pushing on, the 97th moved across country through Germany into Czechoslovakia, to a small town near Pilzen. It was there that Popejoy participated in a history-making patrol.

"I was with the rifle squad as a machine gunner; we had advanced to within 100 yards of the town when we came under fire and were driven back about a thousand yards to a church. Artillery was called in," Popejoy relates, "and the patrol managed to disengage. Moving back to our line, we saw a sniper in a tree, and PFC Mozzetta hit him. That was the last shot."

SFC Robert Popejoy looks over familiar terrain (photo by 1SG Mike Zimmerman).

Having logged over 30,000 miles with his WWII unit, across two continents and through two theaters, Popejoy has seen many things that are difficult to imagine. From Dusseldorf to Hiroshima and Nagasaki, he has learned of the destruction of war and the resilience of soldiers in combat.

SGT Popejoy was discharged in 1946 and a year later joined the Iowa Army National Guard as a private. In 1965, with 21 years of service, he retired.

Was it peer pressure, or could it be his desire to wear a 25-year ring? Only SFC Popejoy knows why. But, in 1972 he again joined the Guard, at the rank of Staff Sergeant, with the 224th Engineer Battalion.

"I guess I'm what the young fellas call a short-timer," said Popejoy. He retires in December, 1985. "However, right now I'm enjoying my return to Germany."

1SG Mike Zimmerman, 135th Public Affairs Detachment, Iowa Army National Guard, is a professional photographer.

2LT Greg Steggerda is a press officer with the 135th Public Affairs Detachment, Iowa Army National Guard. He is a journalism student at Dordt College.

The Victor Treadway Bridge, the longest tactical bridge in the world, crosses the Rhine River at Henningen, Germany (U.S. Army photo).

ings. Plans required Ninth Army's XVI Corps to make the assault crossing in the northern sector of its zone, and the XIII and XIX U.S. Corps to pass through its bridgehead.

Ninth Army began its Rhine River crossing at 2 a.m. March 24, 1945, after one of the war's heaviest artillery barrages. The 258th Engineer Combat Battalion ferried the 30th Infantry Division assault troops across in four hours; and the 79th Infantry Division crossed just as quickly, supported by the 149th and 187th Engineer Combat Battalions. Equipment and supplies were not only crossing the Rhine the same day, but in less than seven days, 10 floating bridges were completed.

On March 26, the Corps Engineers reorganized and sent the 1103rd and 1153rd Engineer Combat Groups forward to support the attack east of the Rhine. The next day, the 1148th Engineer Combat Group reverted to the control of Ninth Army, and the Army Engineers took control over all Engineer work west of the east bank. By April 10, the major portion of Ninth Army's combat elements had crossed the river, and traffic began to decline. Most of the traffic had passed over the Wesel bridges, constructed by units of the 1117th Engineer Combat Group.

Third Army

The Third Army plan required crossings near Mainz with Frankfurt and Darmstadt as the targets. The Army Engineer established a special staff section which formulated the Engineer plan and made estimates of needed equipment and material. He established schools to train Engineer units for the Rhine crossing and to train the naval unit in the use of LCVPs (Landing Craft, Vehicle Personnel) and LCMs (Landing Craft, Mechanized) on rivers.

Toul, France became the assembly point of stocking the equipment needed for bridging the Rhine River. Third Army assembled a huge fleet of trucks to move equipment from the storage dumps at Toul, Esch, and Arlon to the Rhine, a 300-mile round trip since some direct roads were not yet cleared and streams were not bridged.

While both XII and XX Corps initially were scheduled to make the crossing, only XII Corps was assigned the mission. XII Corps made the crossing near Nierstein where a good network of roads intersected, and hills and a town masked Engineer approaches to the river on the west bank.

The 1135th Engineer Combat Group directed the operation using 100 storm boats and motors, 300 assault boats and motors, and already assigned equipment of 500 boats and 100 motors.

Approximately 18 Engineer units were attached to the 1135th Group to support the crossing which started at 10 p.m. on March 22, with the 204th Engineer Combat Battalion paddling the 11th Infantry across in assault boats. By dawn most of the 5th Infantry Division had crossed.

During the night, the 150th Combat Engineer Battalion began work on a Class 40 M-2 treadway bridge at Oppenheim, just north of Nierstein. Although artillery fire and the Luftwaffe harassed construction, air cover and anti-aircraft fire prevented extensive damage. At daybreak the Engineers moved the assembled parts to the crossing site and began work on the bridge. By 6 p.m. the bridge was taking traffic.

In addition to the treadway bridge, the heavy pontoon company of the 88th

Heavy Pontoon Battalion began constructing Class 40 rafts at Nierstein for ferrying operations. Sixty-five tanks and tank destroyers plus hundreds of other vehicles, rations, gasoline, and ammunition were ferried across the bridge the first day.

The 87th Engineer Heavy Pontoon Battalion began a heavy pontoon bridge at Nierstein on the 23rd; and by 1:30 the next morning, the 1,280-foot Class 24 bridge opened for traffic. By 7 a.m. it had been reinforced to carry Class 40 loads. Furthermore, Engineers started another treadway at Oppenheim on March 24 which opened by noon the next day.

Five divisions passed over the three bridges by March 27 with supplies and necessary supporting troops; the entire 6th Armored Division crossed in 16¾ hours. During the assault phase from March 21 to March 31, 60,000 vehicles crossed the bridges at Oppenheim.

While XII Corps crossed the Rhine, VII Corps prepared to cross the Rhine in the Great Gorge which runs from Bingen to Ober Lahnstein. The cliffs, depth of the river, and current created difficult conditions for ferrying troops or building bridges.

Corps assigned the 1134th Engineer Combat Group to support the crossing and to ferry the 87th Infantry Division across at the main crossing site at Boppard and Rhens. At Boppard, the 159th Engineer Combat Battalion, supported by the 991st and 1012th Engineer Treadway Bridge Companies, erected an M-2 steel treadway bridge. Engineers started construction at 8 a.m. on the same day as the assault crossing and completed the 1,044-foot Class 40 bridge by 9:30 a.m. the next day.

On the night of March 25, VIII Corps began crossing operations at St. Goar and Oberwesel. The Germans strongly resisted the crossing at St. Goar, and operations were shifted to Oberwesel where nearly a whole division was ferried across in 48 hours. By March 27 the division cleared the east bank of the St. Goar area while the 243rd Engineer Combat Battalion, supported by the 1010th and 1012th Engineer Treadway Bridge Companies, began an 828-foot steel Class 40 treadway bridge and completed it 36 hours later.

Meanwhile, XXth Corps made the fourth Third Army crossing of the Rhine at Mainz, which was also strongly resisted. The first waves of the 80th Infantry Division were secretly paddled across in assault boats on March 28 while succeeding waves crossed in powered assault and storm boats. But by March 29, 24 hours after the first crossing, Engineers completed a 1,896- foot M-2 steel treadway bridge. Built by the 160th Engineer Combat Battalion and the 997th Engineer Treadway Bridge Company, it was the longest tactical bridge across the Rhine River.

By March 30, the date marking the end of the assault phase of the Rhine operations, the Third U.S. Army controlled the entire west and east banks of the Rhine River from Oppenheim to Koblenz except for one small pocket from Eltville to Winkel.

Seventh Army

Seventh Army crossed the Rhine River on March 26, 1945, in an area from Oppenheim to a point between Mannheim and Speyer. XV Corps conducted the assault on a two-division front with a width barely exceeding nine miles. The 540th Engineer Combat Group supported the 3rd Infantry Division crossing on the right, and the 40th Engineer Combat Group supported the 45th Infantry Division cross

ADSEC En

The Advance Section (ADSEC) Engineers of the Communications Zone (ComZ) took charge of road maintenance in early July 1944. After the Allied breakthrough at St. Lo on July 26, ComZ Engineers began work on the road net within the French border. Fortunately, the Germans had not destroyed many of the small bridges, concentrating instead on the longer spans. Unfortunately for the Americans, however, the road net was inadequate for military use.

As a result of the heavy traffic and bad weather, roads sometimes disappeared in the mud. Engineers, however, were able to temporarily repair roads by using corduroy, timber plank, pierced steel planks, and crushed stone. Later, while the weather grew warmer and the roads began to thaw, Engineers applied more crushed stone and used more corduroy construction.

There was an excellent road system within northern France. Engineers maintained 2,878 miles of road during

1945, Engineers used 6,871 prisoners of war to repair roads in the ComZ. From July 1944 through May 1945, Engineer troops performed about one-half the road work while POWs performed one-third, and civilians one-sixth.

Engineer work on bridges and roads in the ComZ was extensive. From June 6, 1944 to July 1, 1945, ComZ Engineers constructed 237 bridges at least 40 feet in length. In addition, ComZ Engineers maintained 7,688 miles of roads. Of that number, 6,903 miles were in France, 658 miles were in Belgium, 30 miles were in Holland, and 97 miles were in Luxembourg.

The Engineer mission of constructing and maintaining roads and bridges in the ComZ was vital to the success of the troops on the front line. Without an efficiently functioning road network, vital ammunition and equipment would be in short supply in the combat zone.

Until the major ports in Holland were captured and the rail systems rebuilt, forwarding supplies to the front lines depended on the road network from Normandy to the front line. Engineer construction and maintenance of the road network in ComZ allowed the successful forwarding of those vital supplies and the rapid defeat of Germany.

From the Normandy landing on June 6, 1944, to the surrender of Germany on May 8, 1945, Engineers played a key role in the campaigns of the U.S. Army in the European Theater of Operations.

Engineers were among the first troops to land on the Normandy beaches; and throughout the campaign, Engineer troops performed important functions in every part of the theater. On the front line, Engineers built bridges, cleared minefields and other obstacles, repaired and maintained roads, and assisted in assault crossings.

Although most of the Engineers' work at the front contributed to the forward progress of American armies, Engineers were prepared to fight as infantry also. This was evident through their training and ingenuity to resist enemy counterattacks at the Battle of the Bulge.

Behind the front lines, Engineers helped to operate the vast and complex logistical network necessary to support the American advance. The construction and maintenance of roads, railroads, bridges, hospitals, warehouses, and other facilities placed heavy demands on Engineers.

When Germany surrendered in May 1945, there were more than 325,000 U.S. Army Engineers in the European Theater. All of them had reason to be proud of their contribution to the Allied victory.

Dr. William C. Baldwin is a historian with the Historical Division, Office of the Chief of Engineers. He has written a history of the U.S. Army Engineer Studies Center which will be published in 1985 and received his Ph.D in military history from the University of Michigan.

Dr. Barry W. Fowle is a historian in the Historical Division, Office of the Chief of Engineers. He retired from the Army in 1971 as a lieutenant colonel after 23 years of service and attended the University of Maryland where he received his Ph.D in history.

ENGINEER HOTLINE

Problems, questions, and comments relating to Engineer doctrine, training, organization, and equipment can be addressed by telephone to the U.S. Army Engineer School's "Engineer Hotline." The Hotline's auto-answer recorder operates 24 hours a day, seven days a week. You should give your name, address and telephone number, followed by a concise question or comment. You'll receive a reply within three to 15 days. **The Hotline is not a receiving agency for formal requests.**

Call commercial (703) 664-3646; WATTS 800-336-3095, extension 3646; or AV 354-3646.

A WWI

The Fort Leonard Wood museum allows both military and civilians to experience the history of Fort Leonard Wood during World War II and tells the story of the early development of the fort. In November 1940, after first considering an unsuitable Iowa site, the War Department announced that Pulaski County had been chosen as the site of an $8 million Army training camp.

Construction soon began on what was to become one of the nation's largest military installations. Suddenly, 32,000 workers swarmed over the quiet Ozark countryside hoping to find good-paying jobs in those late years of the Depression and challenged surrounding communities to provide housing, recreational facilities, and law enforcement.

Despite many difficulties, buildings appeared at an astonishing rate (1,600 in less than six months), and the post was transferred from the contractors to the War Department in June 1941.

um:

by Robert K. Combs

Leonard Wood was to be used as intended by the Mobilization Act of 1935. The buildings and training facilities were designed to accommodate a maximum of 45,000. During the early war years, more than 40,000 troops from various branches were continuously in training at Fort Leonard Wood with as many as 56,000 during the peak periods of WW II.

Additional facilities assigned in December 1942 were constructed for a prisoner-of-war camp. The 3,000 German and Italian prisoners were used as laborers to build stone bridges, walks, chimneys, and culverts which still exist.

Approximately 320,000 soldiers had received training at the post when Fort Leonard Wood was deactivated in March 1946 and left in caretaker status. The land was leased to a rancher, and cattle roamed freely over the fort while a portion of the post was used during summer each year for National Guard training.

Currently, one building is open to the public, and the museum is planning to restore a complete World War II mobilization complex of twelve buildings.

The Q-9, or regimental commander's quarters had basic luxuries such as a private bath, bedroom, and sitting room.

The company supply building, when restored, will contain complete stocks of World War II issue items such as sheets, blankets, and gas masks, as well as some of the smaller vehicles, a ¾-ton weapons carrier and the famous Willys Jeep.

The company dayroom will be restored on the exterior, but the interior will be renovated for use as a temporary exhibits gallery.

The mess hall, one of the most ambitious projects, was modernized during the 1950s. The interior will have to be totally recreated to include three coal-fired ranges, the ever-popular potato peeler, and exhibits on military cooking, with examples of various field stoves, mess kits, and rations.

Originally the 63-man barracks was a drafty wooden box that slept 53 enlisted men and 10 noncommissioned officers on single cots. Coal was used for heat during the winter, and the original coal-fired hot water heater and furnace have been installed. Bunks, footlockers, rifle racks, and wall racks were the only furniture in the barracks.

The asphalt floor tile and the battleship-gray linoleum have been removed to expose the original tongue-and-groove wood flooring. Wall racks have been replaced, and the latrines restored to include the correct "whiz" showerhead, stainless-steel mirrors, and wooden toilet seats.

Most Army museums discuss the combat history of the war, but few ever mention training, the backbone of the Army. The Fort Leonard Wood museum preserves this unique and basically unaltered World War II mobilization compound.

Robert K. Combs has been the curator of the Fort Leonard Wood Museum since 1982. He has a bachelor's degree in history from San Francisco State University and a master's degree in museum studies from John F. Kennedy University in California. Mr. Combs served his internship at the Smithsonian Institute in Washington, D.C. and was a historical museum technician at the Presidio of San Francisco.

Basic trainees enter a restored WWII barracks to view the uniforms and historical displays at the Fort Leonard Wood museum (photo by Robert K. Combs).

Engineers from Fort Stewart and the Savannah District inspect the historic Blackwell Bridge (photo by Jon Jordan).

The 67-year-old Blackwell Bridge . . . saved from a watery grav

ıckwell ridge:

,tructure Through Meth

by Jack Wilson

"Even the flotation scheme, which was 10 times less expensive than a move over land, was outside the budget," said John Hager of the district's structural section. By checking around Corps, "we found eight unused dredging pontoons in Mobile District," he added.

Fort Stewart's 3rd and 92nd Engineer Battalions agreed to provide their manpower and expertise to relocate the bridge—with the Savannah District doing design work and procuring materials and supplies for the venture. The battalion commanders agreed that the salvage operation would provide the Engineer troops with an exceptional training experience.

In the spring of 1983, the 92nd Engineers spent almost a month at the new bridge site constructing embankments for the bridge, placing gabion walls, and building access roads. In the fall they returned to complete the new site work, driving piles and placing concrete caps for the bridge abutments.

Meanwhile at the old site, the 3rd Engineers removed the old bridge decking, attached the eight 19-foot dredging pontoons, and added bracing to the bridge structure.

Pontoons were set on 25-foot timber crib walls which were built on each abutment. A 35-foot lifting beam was then set on top of the pontoons. Cables were threaded around the main-end pins and lifting beam, and then the beam was jacked up, raising the bridge.

In January, after the lake rose and lifted the pontoons, the 3rd Engineers maneuvered and towed the bridge 12 miles across the newly forming lake to a temporary location to await future rising of the lake's water in June—when the bridge was towed another 5 miles to its new location.

The operation involved guiding the bridge through the channel, between and over tree stumps only inches under the water. If the water level had been too high, the structure would not have been able to pass under a railroad bridge. On the day before the operation, district resource management personnel hurried to top trees in the bridge's path, remove floating debris, and set out buoys marking the channel that the bridge would take.

The Engineers used special Army bridge boats which are highly maneuverable, equipped with twin Saber diesel engines, and propelled by water jets. When fully loaded, they draw only 26 inches of water.

'The Engineers did a professional job in moving the bridge," said MAJ John Seibert, Savannah District Deputy Engineer for civil works. "I was especially impressed with the timeliness of personnel in getting the new job done," he said.

The January bridge-moving operation is believed to be the first attempt to move a bridge that size by water.

Lifting the bridge out of the water by cranes onto its newly constructed abutments was a precision job, as well as an exercise in caution. No one was absolutely certain if the old bridge could survive such a lift, according to Jim Parker, Public Affairs Officer. Now at its new home, Blackwell Bridge stands as a landmark for future generations to enjoy as a bit of American Engineering history.

Jack Wilson is a writer-editor in the Public Affairs Office of the Savannah District, U.S. Army Corps of Engineers. He was a public affairs specialist at Fort Stewart, GA for 10 years. A former journalist with the U.S. Navy, he served with the Polaris Submarine Squadron 14 in Holy Lock, Scotland, and with Submarine Flotilla Two Public Affairs Office in Groton, CT. He is a graduate of Mercer University in Macon, GA.

"A PROUD HERITA

While there was no formal organization to monitor the evolution of doctrine, tactics, or equipment, Engineer officers initiated changes on their own. Railroads, river crossing, route preparation, and fortifications were improved as Engineer units improvised and adapted to keep pace with the war. The seacoast blockade renewed interest in harbor defense, and in 1864 the Board of Engineers on Fortification was again established. Its mission was to survey all harbors, design fortifications, and supervise their construction.

The conclusion of the Civil War brought a change in the system of training Engineers. The Corps of Engineers lost responsibility for the Military Academy, but recognized that specialized education for Engineers was required. The Engineer School of Application at Willets Point, NY was organized to fill that need. Besides serving as the center for educating Engineer officers, this school became the source and test center for new organizations, tactics, and equipment. The Essayons Club, an organization of officers and students, served as a forum in which new developments were discussed.

The military emphasis of Engineers continued to be fortifications and harbor defense and was strengthened by the report of a Congressional committee in 1885. The Endicott Board found that the seacoast defenses of the United States were woefully inadequate due to recent developments in ordnance and years of neglect. A joint board of Engineer and Ordnance officers was created to address the problem. This Board on Fortifications and Ordnance provided for seacoast defenses and related developments until it was dissolved in 1920.

The Spanish American War found the entire Army organization understrength and poorly organized for its new global mission. The Corps was enlarged to three battalions with one battalion permanently on station in the Philippines. The Engineer School was transferred to Washington Barracks (now Fort McNair) which had more room and was closer to the Chief of Engineers' office.

Technology was changing rapidly because of the internal combustion engine, and the Engineers recognized that they would have to keep pace. The first organization specifically charged with monitoring equipment developments was created in 1911. This Board on Pontoons and Engineer Equipment was comprised of officers from the school and from the staff of the Chief of Engineers and served as an "on-call" advisory body to the Chief. Due to its ad hoc nature, this board accomplished little before the United States entered World War I.

The Engineer School served as the intellectual center for Engineering developments. Through several publications such as *Professional Papers, Occasional Papers*, and the *Professional Memoirs*, Engineers discussed their role in the new type of warfare which was evolving in Europe. Engineers went into battle in France in 1917 with organizations and doctrine which they adopted from the Allies who had more experience in trench warfare. Engineer equipment, however, remained relatively unchanged from what had been used in the Civil War, and WWI proved this equipment inadequate.

During WWI, the Engineer School relocated to Camp A. A. Humphreys (now Fort Belvoir) in order to provide adequate space for training officers and enlisted men. While Engineer officers universally recognized the inadequacies of their equipment and doctrine, the Army was concerned with demobilization after the war. It was 1921 before a formal organization was created to remedy those deficiencies.

The Board of Engineer Equipment consisted of three officers appointed by the Chief of Engineers and one officer from the Engineer School. It was charged with the design, development, construction, and testing of Engineer equipment. (The 13th and 29th Engineers, assigned to Camp Humphreys, conducted the actual equipment testing.) This board focused its attention on float-bridging equipment, searchlights, and water-purification equipment. While this board represented a tremendous advancement in efforts to improve Engineer capabilities, membership on the board was an additional duty for all the officers. As a result, its accomplishments were limited.

The Board of Engineer Equipment was replaced by the Engineer Board in 1933. The Engineer Board, with a permanent staff, was able to expand the scope of equipment evaluations. This board examined all tool kits, river-crossing equipment, and construction equipment; and it focused attention on the new areas of mines, countermines, and obstacles. When the military units of the Corps began to expand before World War II, they encountered no difficulty with equipment, for the Engineer Board had done a superb job with its evaluation process.

World War II saw the creation of many new types of Engineer organizations and tremendous changes in missions of Engineer units. Some of the new Engineer missions included: amphibious landings, aviation facility construction, and (from the Quartermaster Corps) responsibility for base construction. During the war, the Engineer Board grew in size and scope. It monitored and accelerated equipment research and development programs for Engineers (occurring at a variety of locations), and initiated changes in doctrine and organization.

After WWII, the Engineer Board continued in its role (with a much decreased staffing) until 1951. Tremendous technological strides had taken place during the concentrated war effort; and organizations, doctrine, and equipment became more sophisticated for the entire Army. The Corps of Engineers evaluated its organization for research and development and restructured it to provide for earlier exploitation of technology.

The Engineer Board was dissolved and replaced by the Engineer Developments Board. This new board absorbed part of the equipment mission of the old Engineer Board and took responsibility for organizations, doctrine, and technique from the school, but it remained part of the school. The remainder of the equipment development mission fell to the Engineer Research and Development Laboratory (ERDL) which had been created in 1947 and grew out of the sections of the Engineer Board which had actually designed, constructed, and tested equipment.

This new organization was inadequate, and in 1955 the Engineer School was reorganized again. The ERDL was separated from the Engineer School and evolved into what is currently known as the Mobility Equipment Research and Development Command. The Engineer Developments Board became the Engineer Combat Developments Group. This new agency established the foundations of the current organization. Its three sections, known as Projects A, B, and C, later became the Studies, Materiel, and Organization and Doctrine Divisions.

The entire Army reorganized in 1962, and the combat development activities of all branches were consolidated under the Combat Developments Group which was located at Fort Belvoir. The Engineer Combat Developments Group became the CDC Engineer Agency. Its mission and structure remained the same for the duration of CDC's existence. One of the major initiatives of the Engineer Agency was the Universal Engineer Tractor. The fact that the CDC Engineer Agency was no longer in the Engineer School, but part of a consolidated combat development community, created many problems. The Engineer Agency had to be responsive to both the Chief of Engineers and the Commander of CDC.

While there were problems, a benefit was that combat developments activities were clarified while the Engineer Agency was part of the CDC. Responsibility for preparing Tables of Organization and Equipment (TO&E) and Basis of Issue Plans (BOIP) became a part of the Organization Branch. The Material Division accepted responsibility for proponency of Engineer equipment from ERDL in addition to testing and evaluation for all developmental systems. The Studies Division began war gaming and conducting operations research to evaluate Engineer mission areas. The last area of responsibility was the preparation of doctrine and literature.

Point Engineers:

uilders of America's RASTRU T RE

by MAJ Mark Vincent

westward, requirements for east-west transportation also grew. The early roads, railroads, rivers, and canals became the nation's first engineered infrastructure.

As the need for such works grew, so did the demand for civil Engineers. The Army's need for Engineers was recognized during the American Revolution and did not disappear when the British were defeated; fortifications to protect harbors, cities, and other defenses were still required. So, for similar reasons, the Army's requirement for Engineers paralleled that of the civilian economy.

In 1800, the nature of constructing masonry fortifications, other defenses, and lines of communication was comparable to constructing buildings, highways, and other public works. In fact, so little distinction existed between civil and military engineering that it was said "that nothing is so easily converted to civil use, as the science common to both the profession of a civil and military Engineer."

The Army's Engineer staff during the late 1700s consisted primarily of such foreign-trained officers as Richard Gridley and Thaddeus Kosciuszko. While well respected, their presence

often sparked resentment among native-born, self-made Engineers. The need for a source of trained Engineers in this country was a practical and political concept held by many.

President George Washington was a supporter of a school for military Engineers, but he doubted the constitutionality of the idea. Although the Army itself was small, a pervasive argument for creating an academy was that its Engineers' "utility would extend beyond military works to whatever respects public buildings, roads, bridges, canals, and all such works of a civil nature."

West Point

Although Congress authorized the construction of coastal and harbor fortifications in 1794, it was not until 1802, at the insistence of President Thomas Jefferson, that an academy at West Point was authorized with the purpose of training a Corps of Engineers. With its founding, West Point became the only engineering school in the country, a distinction it held for almost 20 years.

The curriculum at West Point evolved into a program that produced Engineers. By 1816, instruction included military and civil architecture, and permanent as well as field fortifications. In 1823, the first course titled "Civil Engineering" was taught. By 1824, studies included elementary parts of buildings; orders of architecture; and construction of buildings and arches, bridges, canals, and other public works. In 1826 the courses were expanded still further to include roads, tunnels, railroads, artificial harbors, and inland navigation.

During this era, most Engineers already in practice had little formal education, but instead developed skills from experiences as apprentices and from individual study. According to Daniel Calhoun in his book, *The American Civil Engineer,* the nature of training at the academy caused the Board of Visitors to report that "the pupils of West Point will deliver the country from the quack engineering which has, in diverse instances, inflicted deep wounds upon our system of internal improvements."

Coastal Defense

For a decade, the new Corps and its West Point graduates devoted efforts almost exclusively to coastal defenses. However, the role of the Corps grew rapidly in proportion to the swelling ranks of its academy graduates.

In 1816, the Army established a Board of Engineers for Fortifications within the Corps of Engineers. This board devoted increasingly greater portions of its personnel to civilian projects with some relevance to Army needs. Engineer surveys broadened from coastal areas to include rivers, harbors, and even canals.

Surveying

President James Monroe recommended that the Corps prepare surveys and plans for canals between Chesapeake Bay, Lake Erie, and the Ohio River in 1823. That involvement led to the General Survey Act of 1824 which authorized the President to use Army officers together with civilian Engineers to survey roads and canals of national importance. That legislation actually formalized the introduction of Army Engineers into civil engineering.

The General Survey Act thrust West Point graduates into the tasks of mapping, exploring, and surveying for which they are well known. The Stephen Long expedition that plotted the courses of the Platte, Arkansas, and Canadian rivers included John R. Bell (1812), J. D. Graham (1817), and W. H. Swift (1819).

Benjamin Bonneville (1815) conducted an expedition from 1832 to 1834 that first accurately mapped the hydrography of the territories west of the Mississippi River. While western exploration was most prominent, West Point Engineers were dispatched to the limits of all our frontiers.

Waterways

River and harbor works soon became a major duty of the Corps of Engineers. Harbor work on the coast extended beyond fortifications to the planning of breakwaters and management of harbor improvements. Rivers and lakes were surveyed for navigability; and reports were prepared recommending ways to remove snags and rocks, construct dikes, or bypass falls with canals. Other responsibilities included planning and building lighthouses, beacon lights, bridges, and even aqueducts.

one of the earliest rational methods of analysis of stresses in trusses.

The Haupt lattice truss design was named for its inventor. Haupt's reputation as chief Engineer or superintendent of several railroads during the 1850s resulted in his recall into service in 1862 as a general in charge of building, maintaining, and operating the railroads for the Union during the war.

Many other graduates were committed to lives of service with private railroad companies. Possibly West Point contributed more to railroads through its civilian Engineers than through the military Engineers who remained Army officers. By 1903, 212 West Point graduates had become president, superintendent, or chief Engineer on railroads or other public works.

Public Works

West Point graduates were also prominent leaders of that part of the infrastructure including municipal engineering and buildings. George S. Greene (1823) made noteworthy contributions to urban water supply by helping to develop systems for New York City and Washington, D.C. Montgomery Meigs (1836) was also involved with water supply, but he is best known for the design and construction of the dome and wings of the United States Capitol Building.

The time from 1820 to 1860 has been called the most sensitive period of national growth. The Federal government, through its Corps of Engineers, tried to satisfy the extraordinary demands by its citizens for Engineering assistance. The rank of Engineering graduates of West Point met those needs. The almost limitless opportunities within the embryonic nation drew graduates from the service to other positions, both private and public, and spread the talents of the Engineers.

The combined successes that those Engineers achieved in developing the early elements of our first infrastructure—the roads, harbors, railroads, and other public works—earned them a special place in our history. Never before or since that era has one group so positively influenced the shape of the building of America as did the Civil Engineers of West Point.

MAJ Mark Vincent is an assistant professor of civil engineering at the United States Military Academy. A 1973 USMA graduate, he has commanded an assault bridge company in USAREUR, instructed at the Engineer School, and served as a project manager and engineer in the Seattle District. Vincent has a master's degree in civil engineering from the University of Illinois and is a registered professional engineer.

Your platoon has been ordered to install a standard pattern minefield. Given the following requirements, determine the total number of mines, number of regular strips, number of antihandling devices, and total manhours.

Given:

Desired density	**AT = 3 APF = 4 APB = 2**
IOE representative cluster composition	**AT = 2 APF = 2 APB = 2**
Front	**250m**
Depth	**300m**
Antihandling devices	**10%**
Type mines available	**M14, M15, M16A1**

REFERENCES: FM 5-34; FM 20-32, Mine/Countermine Warfare; ERRATA information provided by Engineer School.
(Problem submitted by SSG Gene R. Shelnutt, Department of Military Engineering).

Survival Guide to NTC

by CPT James G. Liwsk

So, you're going to the National Training Center! Everywhere you turn these days, you hear that name . . . another war story from the guys at the club. Another article describing the numerous pitfalls. Another memo from the battalion commander emphasizing his "concern."

With all the attention focused on NTC, you want to make sure that your platoon does the best possible job of supporting your task force. The question you ask yourself is . . . how?

Part of that "how" has been developed at the Engineer School. Due largely to the efforts of CPT Dave Dunaway (Unit Training, DOTD), the Engineer School has produced an *Engineer NTC Train-Up Package* that presents a coherent training strategy for success at the NTC. The package consists of three parts.

Part one contains a discussion of the significant recurring problems in the Engineer support at the NTC, a list of key skills obtained from a Battalion Management Training System (BTMS), analysis of the NTC mission and terrain, and suggestions to assist you in supporting maneuver units more efficiently.

Engineer Employment Considerations

- **Task organization based on Engineer work requirements**
- **Single point of contact**
- **Normal association**
- **Centralized control**
- **Integral part of Combined Arms Team**
- **Early involvement in planning**
- **Engineer effort forward**
- **Engineers as terrain experts**
- **Engineer construction equipment moves slowly**
- **Once Engineers are committed as infantry, no further Engineer effort can be expected**

Part two addresses Engineers as part of the Combined Arms Team. A sa ple briefing is included to assist you starting an early and effective workir relationship with the brigade and tas force commanders and their staff Done well, the briefing will allo Engineer platoon leaders to establis credibility and give the task force a appreciation of Engineer capabiliti and specific information on how th can fully integrate Engineer effor into Combined Arms operations.

Task Force Support To Engineers

- **Intelligence from scouts**
- **Incorporation of Engineers into troop-leading procedure**
- **Early warning orders**
- **Logistical support (particularly class IV and class V)**
- **Labor support for constructing and breaching obstacles**
- **Cooperation on obstacle-breaching battle drill**
- **Team locations**
- **Tactical Operations Center (TOC) locations**
- **Engineer vehicles that task force cannot fix**
- **Class IV recovery plan**
- **Bulldozers operating at night**
- **Withdrawal routes for the teams and Engineers**
- **Priority of repair at unit equipment repair points (UERP)**
- **Priority of obstacle construction start time**
- **Task force collection points for medical evacuation and maintenance (UERP)**
- **Replacement time lag for destroyed vehicles**
- **Routine for replacing destroyed vehicles**
- **Informs when brigade will pull assets: bulldozers and swing platoon**

Part three contains "off-the-shel materials which will assist your pre aration for effective Combined Arn Operations at the NTC. It contai training tips, emerging doctrine, ar a variety of other materials.

It's truly an impressive packag What makes it unique, however, is tl Engineer briefing mentioned in pa two.

The Engineer briefing is an integr part of the package. It provides tl starting point to sell yourself and tl Engineer capabilities that you supe vise to the maneuver force commande The briefing is prefaced by a sho introduction by your battalion or con pany commander. The entire briefin takes about 30 minutes, not includin time for questions. It's an ideal top for a professional development class f sk force officers or any other suitable eeting to prepare for the NTC.

The briefing covers topics such as:

Command/Support Relationships

Engineer Employment Considerations (See chart)

Obstacle Employment Principles

Engineer Assets

Mobility, Countermobility, Survivability Missions

Engineer Planning Factors and Work Rates

Family of Scatterable Mines (FASCAM)

Task Force Support to Engineers (See chart)

Engineer Platoon Leader Responsibilities (See chart)

Engineer Platoon Sergeant Responsibilities

An M-1 tank provides a smoke screen for advancing friendly forces during NTC training at Fort Irwin, CA (U.S. Army photo).

Engineer Platoon Leader Responsibilities

- **Receive the warning order**
- **Move the platoon**
- **Reconstitute: sleep; evacuate casualties; resupply ammunition, fuel, and basic load; recover and repair vehicles; rezero MILES; maintain personal hygiene; provide food for troops**
- **Forage class IV from battlefield**
- **Establish a hasty platoon defense**
- **Go to the after action review**
- **Liaison with the company XOs who have picked battle positions**
- **Liaison with XOs for primary obstacle line**
- **Write the operations order with staff**
- **Organize reserve obstacles and closures**
- **Receive full operations orders**
- **Coordinate with S4 for class IV**
- **Coordinate with the fire support officer**
- **Meet the class IV drop on the ground**
- **Coordinate with Engineer swing platoon**
- **Coordinate with Engineer support platoon**
- **Maintain the platoon (coordinate I, III, V, IX)**
- **Fill out casualty feeder report**
- **Send courier with casualty reports**
- **Receive replacements**
- **Contact team commanders to start obstacle work**
- **Coordinate resupply of class IV**
- **Inspect obstacle construction**
- **Escort and control all bulldozers in area**
- **Submit all obstacle reports to the task force**
- **Prepare and submit minefield reports**
- **Conduct leader's reconnaissance of Engineer withdrawal and battle positions**
- **Provide security on obstacles**
- **Provide anti-reconnaissance**

The list of topics discussed is extensive. In fact, you'll probably learn something yourself from reviewing the briefing.

The best part of this briefing is the clear, concise way it presents the many varied Engineer considerations in support of a task force. It establishes you as the Engineer "expert" and gives you needed exposure and credibility as a critical member of the commander's staff. This facet has been an annoying problem experienced by your predecessors at the NTC.

Dedicated use of the package along with careful research of the briefing topics will help cement your position as part of the team; and that's half the battle!

That's the *Engineer NTC Train-Up Package* . . . problems identified, resources listed, and an Engineer briefing to help get you on-board with the task force.

So, if you're going to the National Training Center, or even if you just want to get a better handle on Engineer support of a task force, get a copy of the *Engineer NTC Train-Up Package*—your survival guide to NTC.

Requests for copies of the *Engineer NTC Train-Up Package* should be forwarded to:

U.S. Army Engineer School
ATTN: ATZA-TD-U-D
Fort Belvoir, VA 22060-5291
AV 354-2070/2286

CPT James G. Liwski, a graduate of the United States Military Academy, is assigned to the Unit Training Division, DOTD, at the Engineer School. He was the assistant operations officer and platoon leader with the 9th Engineer Battalion in Germany.

SFC Jeffrey Singer's expression depicts the seriousness of the drill sergeant's job (U.S. Army photo).

a Close Look at Drill Sergeant School

by SP4 Thomas Copeland and SP5 Kathleen Ellison

"This is probably one of the toughest schools a noncommissioned officer can attend," said MSG Samuel Clark, chief instructor at the Fort Leonard Wood Drill Sergeant School. "Not everyone can be a drill sergeant. Only the best soldiers out of each career field are selected."

Between 450 and 500 drill sergeants are presented with their distinctive "brown round" hats each year. Only 10 percent of the students do not graduate from the school usually because of reasons ranging from medical to academic.

Formerly, the attrition rate was as high as 25 percent, and because of this the school supervisors were prompted to add a three-week drill sergeant orientation phase to the regular eight-week course.

"The orientation phase introduces the candidates to different levels of instruction," said SFC Jesus Gomez, senior course manager. Here we teach classes on subjects like uniform regulations, drill and ceremony, trainee treatment, and the role and responsibility of the NCO. Many of these courses may be repeated in the actual course, but presenting this material to them before starting the actual course greatly increases their chances of graduating and their ability to be a good drill sergeant.

"Another thing that separates our school from other drill sergeant schools is that we have a group-paced format rather than a self-paced one," Gomez added. We noticed that the self-pace class people were looking out only f themselves. With our group class ev ryone learns at the same pace. If som one is having difficulty with one su ject, another student will help him that the class can go on," Gomez sai

Classes include basic rifle markma ship, stress management, leadersh and physical training.

"During the summer the first form tion is at 5 a.m., and the day lasts unt 4:30 p.m. In the course of eight week the drill sergeant candidate must su cessfully complete 103 course mo ules," according to Clark.

For most candidates, the cour proves both mentally and physicall demanding. "During the three-wee ientation phase," said SFC Allen lark, master fitness trainer and assisnt chief instructor, "we give the candates a complete diagnostic test. It vers height, weight and a diagnostic ysical training test. During that ree weeks we get everyone up to out the same physical readiness level d able to easily pass the Army iysical Readiness Test.

"When the actual course starts, we e the level they were at as a starting ock. From there we push them to eir fullest. We have them run more an they ever thought they could. ıre, there's a point where the human dy can't go any further. But there is so that little *something* down there at drives you to do that last effort," lark said.

The academic portion of the course is so challenging. Everything the candiıtes learn will not only be passed on new soldiers, but they must be able do it professionally and proficiently. verything the trainee does, the drill ergeant candidate does.

"I think being a drill sergeant brings restige and job satisfaction to the NCO," Clark said, "At the end of the basic training cycle, the drill sergeant can see the improvement in the people he's had to train and turn into soldiers."

"I was kind of sad when I first got here," said SFC Leonard Wilson, a candidate in his fourth week, who had been selected by the Department of the Army. "But once I got here it was all right. With more than 18 years in (the Army), it was something that I still hadn't done. Being that it was a new challenge, I went for it."

"The course is very challenging. You really learn a lot that you may have taken for granted. It is different when you have to teach someone something that you have learned," Wilson said, who before coming to the school was a mortar platoon leader at Fort Riley.

"I volunteered for the school," said, SGT Jeffrey Thomason, a former crane operator at Fort Bragg. "I've always liked the overall appearance that you had to maintain and the respect that you get from it. The PT hasn't been too tough on me so far, although the oral presentations were pretty stressful at times."

I called my branch at DA and told them I wanted to go (to Drill Sergeant School), and so they sent me here," said the former Fort Hood atomic demolitions munition platoon sergeant. "The drill sergeant is the first impression of the Army these young soldiers have when they first come in. He provides them a role model, someone to emulate."

Students said the school does what it can to help them through the course. Many said the group pace was a great help.

The requirements listed in Army Regulation 614-200, Section II, state that male candidates must be in grades E5 through E7. Female candidates must be in grades E4 through E7. Candidates must possess a high school diploma or GED equivalent and have demonstrated leadership ability. Upon graduation, drill sergeants have a two-year stabilized tour, with an option for another year.

Biographical information on SP4 Copeland and SP5 Ellison was not available at the time of publication.

Drill sergeants enforce the highest standards during basic training at Fort Leonard Wood (U.S. Army photo).

Construction and Maintenance of Delta Creek Airstrip

by MAJ Thomas A. York

Delta Creek Airstrip was constructed by the 562nd Engineer Company, 172nd Light Infantry Brigade (Separate), at a remote site on a dry creek bed. The airstrip, 30 miles west of Delta, AK, was built in the summer of 1982 to support Brim Frost '83, a major Army field exercise in January and February.

This was a joint operation with the 23rd Engineer Company (CBT) (HVY) which assisted in developing the road network, clearing bivouac sites, and providing general maintenance support of the airstrip. The runway length was 4,000 feet with 500 feet of clear zone on each end.

Design Criteria

The airstrip was designed to be a medium-lift, support-area strip that would require minimum maintenance for two months. It had to support aircraft with a maximum gross weight of 130,000 pounds and included:

- a minimum runway length of 3,500 feet and runway width of 60 feet;
- a parking apron for four C-130 Hercules;
- a refueling apron to support two C-130s or "bladder birds" that could distribute fuel to ground fuel storage;
- a helicopter refueling area to support four helicopter refueling pads.

Orientation of the airstrip was based on two considerations: the prevailing winds and the cleared approach and departure zones. Approach zones had to allow aircraft to head into prevailing winds. A 50:1 ratio was maintained for the height of obstacles in the approach and departure zones. For example, a one-foot tree must be 50 feet from the end of the runway clear zone.

The airstrip was oriented to avoid forested approach and departure zones, thus overriding the consideration for prevailing winds. This decision became costly when aircraft with troops and equipment were diverted to a paved airstrip in Delta Junction for two days during the exercise airlift. The prevailing crosswinds had made landing of fully loaded aircraft too dangerous.

The airstrip required less than 2 percent slope from end to end, less than 1.7 percent slope from centerline to shoulder, and 2 percent moisture content. The C-130s needed airstrip soil that could support 75 psi on impact. Penetrometer readings were taken on diagonals across the airstrip at 50-foot intervals and consistently gave 150 psi readings. The sieve analysis results showed that the soil was poorly graded gravel with a California Bearing Ratio (CBR) of 30.

Site Selection

A relatively level site was needed to minimize the amount of earth that had to be moved to meet slope requirements. All equipment and personnel were brought in and resupplied helicopters because no existing roa lead to the area.

Heavy Engineer construction equi ment could not be used because t CH-54B skycranes could lift a ma imum of 22,000 pounds. A D-5 bu dozer was the largest that could airlifted into the site.

A gravel airstrip was preferr because it could be used year-rou with few drainage problems. An a strip built in marshlands or swam would only be suitable for winter co struction and use.

A nearby water source was necessa to provide water for compaction.

The site had to permit proper orie tation of the runway allowing for p vailing wind direction and clear approach and departure zones.

A primary consideration was that t airstrip would be surrounded by a mi city of 10,000 soldiers and various fu medical, food, ammunition, and mai tenance support packages. This e tailed a vast road network and ar that would support bivouac sites hi den from view and required the int gration of the road with forest cove

A year-round water source was nec sary to support construction in t summer and to provide water for pe sonnel in the winter. The Delta Cre River has meandering six to eight-fo streams that were two to three fe deep in the summer. The strea ecame subterranean flows in the inter, an action that was not nticipated.

Valuable time was lost because a two-ile winter road had to be constructed December to reach a nearby lake at would become the primary water urce. A water-purification unit capa-e of 420 gallons per hour produced ater (over 40,000 gallons during the ercise) from this lake. Two-inch cot-n water-distribution hoses were insu-ted inside six-inch fuel hoses during xtreme cold.

onstruction

The airstrip and surrounding road etwork were constructed in two onths using a John Deere 570-A road ader and 450-C bulldozer, two Cater-illar D-5 bulldozers, a 13-wheel com-acting roller, two 2½-ton dump trucks, nd a jeep.

Communications rigs, medical eams, and daily helicopter support ere also added to the construction ackage. A 500-gallon water tank was laced in the bed of one of the dump ucks modified with a spray bar to be sed in the compaction process. Heli-copters provided fuel for all operations by sling-loading in 600-gallon fuel blivets.

Clearing and grubbing operations took about one week. Cut and fill operations with compaction took the remainder of the time. Delays were caused when the Air Force recommended widening the strip from 150 to 300 feet. The extensive work dedicated to the surrounding road network and bivouac sites caused significant delays to the original estimate of two weeks.

Maintenance of equipment and resupply of repair parts for low-density construction equipment were continual problems. A skycrane lift in early September replaced deadlined equipment with new equipment including an additional D-5 bulldozer and two new 2½-ton dump trucks.

Penetrometers and nuclear densometers were used to test the density of the poorly graded gravel during the initial site selection and during the compaction process.

Fill operations required some innovative ideas because lifting equipment such as 2½-cubic yard scoop loaders were too heavy to be flown in by sky-crane. A ramp was constructed that allowed the bulldozers to push gravel from a borrow pit into awaiting dump trucks.

Construction was hampered by problems with helicopter support. Bad weather, damaged multileg slings, and limited weekend availability for National Guard skycranes caused planning problems. The total dependence upon air resupply kept planners busy adjusting critical path networks.

The project took 62 days, used 3,900 gallons of diesel fuel and 1,400 gallons of gasoline, and cost $4,000 for repair parts. During the compaction process, 120,000 gallons of water with glacier silt were added to fill the voids in the top six-inch compacted layer.

When completed, the airstrip was 5,000 feet long and 300 feet wide. The runway was 4,000 feet long and 150 feet wide. The end-to-end slope was 0.67 percent.

Maintenance and Use

Two months later, a similar construction team followed a freshly cut road (the width of one D-7 blade) into the airstrip to clear an accumulated two-

A D-5 bulldozer performs grubbing and clearing operations for the Delta Creek Airstrip and surrounding road network (photo by MAJ Thomas A. York).

Parking aprons and refueling areas for helicopters and C-130s appear on the outline of the airstrip (photo by MAJ Thomas A. York).

foot snowfall. Skycranes were scheduled as backup mobility for some of the heavy equipment if the road couldn't be opened by December 10 due to maintenance, hot springs, or Air Force bombs that were found on a bombing range in one area of the main supply route.

The main supply route was opened on schedule; and the snow removal of the airstrip, road network, and bivouac site took approximately seven days. Scoop loaders did the work of bulldozers in clearing new roads in forested areas.

On January 6, the unit convoyed ten dump trucks and logistics vehicles to the airstrip for final preparation. The first C-130 was scheduled for a January 11 touchdown. Avalanches in the Paxson area 60 miles south of Fort Greely delayed the convoy for 24 hours.

The airstrip was opened on time with a 150 foot width cleared. Snow berms were kept below ten feet so that C-130s would not hit their wing tips during a possible skid or turn. The berms were lowered by driving D-5 bulldozers over them.

Temperatures were below -40°F, and the unit had its highest number of cold-weather injuries during this period. The equipment was kept running for 24 hours. Turbochargers were being damaged on the diesel trucks because operators were not manning the trucks at all times and keeping the RPMs up to 1,500. Operators needing sleep could not stay in their vehicles because of possible carbon monoxide poisoning.

During the extremely cold weather, maintenance was cumbersome, minds became tired and did not reason clearly, and hidden problems in machinery emerged. Only one maintenance tent was available, and it could support only one piece of equipment at a time. Herman Nelson heaters (40,000 BTUs per hour) were critical, but suffered periodic service problems.

Scoop-loader tires were going flat when they were off-loaded from low boy tractors or from railroad flat cars. Parachutes covered the tires with pumped in heat and made the tires pliable so they could be repaired.

Maintenance of the airstrip was relatively easy. When ruts developed, gravel and water mixtures were placed in the ruts and frozen. Spalling of rocks below the six-inch compacted surfaces began to appear after the 200th aircraft had landed. The refueling parking apron was bermed in case of fuel spills which did not occur.

The C-130s that were loaded over 27,000 pounds used the entire runway for takeoff and sometimes did not leave the ground until they were in the clear zone. Blowouts were a major concern due to the gravel airstrip. The only incident occurred at Elmendorf Air Force Base and was attributed to the gravel at Delta Creek Airstrip.

When the last aircraft departed Delta Creek Airstrip on Feb. 12, 1983, over 400 C-130s had safely landed. landed.

MAJ Thomas A. York is the Deputy Commander, U.S. Army Engineer District, Pittsburgh. He was the Assistant Inspector General, 172nd Infantry Brigade at Fort Richardson, AK, and commanded A Company, 10th Engineer Battalion, and the 562nd Engineer Company while stationed there. He also held command and staff assignments in Germany and Korea. MAJ York has a bachelor's degree in engineering management and a master's degree in civil engineering from the University of Missouri and is a graduate of the Command and General Staff College.

mafrost and promote roadbed stabilization. A recent study by CRREL shows that the use of membrane encapsulated soil layers (MESL) is effective in road construction in an arctic or subarctic environment.

Building Materials

Utilities, buildings, and airfields cannot be left out of a new arctic construction manual. Many studies have evaluated the use of snow and ice as building materials and the effects of insulation and aerodynamic considerations for all types of construction. An excellent source of information concerning utilities construction would be the underground utilidor (utility corridor) built in permafrost at Barrow, AK.

Since 40 percent of all landmass in the northern hemisphere is in the subarctic or arctic, its military significance must not be overlooked. History shows that the subarctic can be a theater of war (Norway, Finland, U.S.S.R.). The Army Engineer must have an updated and accurate manual to provide the know-how to support the mobility and survivability of the Army's Combined Arms Team.

CPT William J. Stein is a deputy division chief and project inspector at Letterkenny Army Depot, Chambersburg, PA. He was a platoon leader in the 23rd Engineer Company (CBT) (HVY) and the training support branch chief at Fort Richardson, AK, where he was an assistant G-3 coordinating Air Force tactical support for the Brim Frost exercise. CPT Stein is a graduate of the Engineer Officer Advanced Course and has a bachelor's degreee in mechanical engineering from the University of Missouri at Rolla.

Hotline Q & A

Q. I need the latest reference manual, film, or television tape for Engineer River Crossing Operations.

A. FM 90-13 or ETM 350-100 covers Engineer River Crossing Operations. DA PAM 108-1 answers questions about available films.

Q. I need to know the NSN and supply catalog for short, medium, and long picket fences. I also need the NSN for general, barbed tape obstacle, and information on how to obtain it.

A. U-shaped pickets come in two sizes: 60-inch (NSN 5660-00-370-1587) and 30-inch (NSN 5660-00-270-1589). This information can be found in CTA 50-920, Section II, Expendable Items and in the Army Master Data File. GPBTO can be requisitioned through normal supply channels. The NSN is 5660-00-921-5516.

Q. What is the classification of the M-10 5-ton truck with a water distributor mounted on the rear?

A. The vehicle classification is as follows: Overall weight 20,050 lbs (empty), 28,383 lbs (full). Vehicle classification is 15 empty (E), 21 cross-country (C), 25 highway (H). Additional information can be obtained from TM 5-3825-221-5 and TM 5-3825-227-12. Information on the 5-ton truck may be obtained in TM 9-2320-260-10-1.

Q. Where are the 160 radios to be mounted on the new 510-M929 squad vehicles?

A. Radios in squad vehicles, particularly the M929 Series Vehicles are currently being tested and evaluated at U.S. Army Tank-Automotive Command at (TACOM). It is expected that the results will have been completed by Dec. 3, 1984, and the requested information will be made available at that time. The tested mount is located between the operator and passenger seats on the rear panel.

Q. We are trying to determine a way to winterize graders for snow removal. Does the Army have a temporary cab canvas-type window?

A. At the present time there is no standard winterization kit in the supply system. However, a commercial kit can be purchased from Safety Cab Co., Fresno, CA, and it was used for graders sent to Alaska. The phone number for the Safety Cab Co. is: (209) 268-5545. The AMC Systems Manager at TACOM, AV 786-7349, can be called for further assistance.

This is ENGINEER's second annual listing of publications produced by the U.S. Army Construction Engineering Research Laboratory (USA-CERL).

The list is divided into two sections: material related to Combat Engineers and material related to Facility Engineers. These sections are subdivided into a list of fact sheets of current USA-CERL research efforts and a list of technical reports/publications produced since October 1983.

Fact sheets are typically short summaries of USA-CERL's research on a given subject. Technical reports and publications are lengthier documents presenting the results of USA-CERL's research on a specific topic.

Fact sheets are available from the Public Affairs Office, U.S. Army Construction Engineering Research Laboratory, P.O. Box 4005, Champaign, IL 61820-1305.

Technical reports and publications are available at a nominal cost from the National Technical Information Service, 5285 Port Royal Road, Springfield, VA 22161, or through the Defense Technical Information Center, Cameron Station, Alexandria, VA 22314. When ordering publications from NTIS or DTIC, please use the ADA numbers listed. Additional information on these publications can be obtained by writing to the USA-CERL Publications Branch.

COMBAT ENGINEERING ACTIVITIES

Fact sheets are available on the following USA-CERL studies in progress on Combat Engineer activities:

Engineer Unit Microcomputer Applications — Discusses the use of microcomputer software applications for managing construction activities for the 18th Engineer Brigade in Germany.

Engineer Modeling Study — A computer program designed to determine the effects of Combat Engineer activities in the outcome of a battle.

Flotation Bridging/Rafting Concepts for River Crossing Operations — Evaluation of methods available for floating vehicles across nonfordable streams.

Foam Overhead Cover Support Systems (FOCOS) — A rapidly constructed foam-filled fabric arch used with a topsoil covering to protect infantry operators of antitank weapons.

Photovoltaic Power Systems — Test results on a photovoltaic power system for a permanent military facility.

Modular Solar Domestic Hot Water Systems — A two component system for DOD barracks buildings.

Computerized Evaluation of Utility Plans (CEUP) — Computer programs that analyze the electrical and water distribution and sanitary sewerage collection systems on military installations for their adequacy in supporting future construction and base mobilization.

Computer-Aided Engineering and Architectural Design System (CAEADS) — Automated design tools used by designers (architects, engineers, specifiers, estimators) through the 35 percent level of the building design process.

Systematic Evaluation of Architecture (SEARCH) — Reviews architectural plans against measurable criteria found in design guidance and Army and Engineering regulations.

SKETCH — Permits computer entry of single-line floor-plan drawings for automatic generation of double-line drawings in production of plots and criteria evaluation.

Habitability Program — Procedures and design information to assist installation personnel in providing input for improving constructed facilities.

Construction Management Microcomputers — Provides the area engineer an opportunity for improvements in construction scheduling and resource allocation using microcomputer technology.

Decision Support System/Directorate of Engineering and Housing — Microcomputer-based information management system to assist DEH in managing installation facility engineering activities.

Facility Space Planning System — Procedures for identifying space planning requirements for administrative offices and managing space planning activities to meet future needs.

Industrialized Building Systems — Use of industrialized building systems to provide more facilties for the construction dollar in less time.

One and Two Step Facility Acquisition — Procurement processes which incorporate performance specifications and allow contractors to submit a design proposal along with the bid for new facilities.

Facilities Technology Application Tests (FTAT) — A 5-year program which demonstrates the use of over 35 technologies is available through Corps of Engineer research laboratories in support of the Directorate of Engineering and Housing. Technologies will be demonstrated in areas of energy, environmental quality, buildings, and pavements and roads.

Training Ranges — Planning and management of training ranges designed to accommodate new weapons systems.

PORTAWASHER — High-pressure cleaning system for sanitizing dumpsters, washing heavy equipment, cleaning latrines, and recovering liquid spills at half the cost of traditional procedures.

Sanitary Landfill Leachate Control — Provides guidance for identifying and solving installation leachate problems from abandoned and existing refuse disposal sites.

Army Sewage Treatment Alternatives — Alternatives for upgrading existing trickling filter sewage treatment plants.

Hazardous/Toxic Waste Management Information System — Provides identification of those chemical substances both listed and defined by the Resource Conservation and Recovery Act (RCRA).

Composting Toilet Technology — A waterless, odorless, low-maintenance waste treatment alternative to pit latrines and vault and chemical toilets that requires no chemicals and creates no polluting discharge; may be a practical alternative to present remote-site technology (at training and firing ranges) and for mobilization application.

Installation Compatible Use Zone (ICUZ) — A program to prevent noise-sensitive development in high-noise areas through cooperative efforts of installations and adjacent communities.

Vehicle Maintenance and Consolidated Washing Facilities — A revolutionary approach to control water pollution originating in vehicle exterior cleaning and maintenance areas.

Early Warning Analysis System (EWAS) — Allows MACOM and installation environmental planners to identify potential problem areas at the "what if" stage of planning with both tabular and mapped output.

Integrated Noice Contour System (INCS) — Provides MACOM and installation environmental planners with contours showing the noise impact of installation activities.

Environmental Technical Information System (ETIS) — Analyzes environmentally related impacts resulting from DOD programs.

Civil Works Computer-Aided Environmental Legislative Data System (CW-CELDS) — Aids planners in certifying compliance with 15 environmental statues as mandated by Office of Management and Budget.

Mobilization Facilities Planning System — Evaluates the capability of an installation to respond to mobilization tasking or other crisis response.

Training Range/Facility Management — Methods to manage training ranges and facilities assets while maintaining environmental conservation.

Stationing Analysis Model (SAM) — Systematic process for comparing installation facility assets with projected unit force and equipment demands.

Water Conservation/Recycle Technology — Application of water conservation technologies for use at military installations.

Acoustic Noise Warning System — A microphone and "smart" monitor to alert the range control officer when operational noise levels exceed an established limit.

PCB Transformer System — Provides guidance to Army DEH's on regulations and options for use of transformers containing PCB in the insulating field.

Technical Report N-178, "Noise From Traffic and Noise Barrier Performance: A Prediction Technique," by Kenneth McK. Eldred, Richard Raspet, and Paul Schomer, July 1984, ADA144287.

Technical Report N-69, "Economic Impact Forecast System (EIFS) II: User's Manual, Updated Edition," by D. P. Robinson, J. W. Hamilton, R. D. Webster, and M. J. Olson, May 1984, ADA117661.

Energy Research

Technical Report E-197, "Summary of USA-CERL Research on Control of Heating, Ventilating, and Air-Conditioning Systems," by Douglas C. Hittle and David L. Johnson, July 1984, ADA145530.

Technical Report E-190, "Use of the Building Loads Analysis and System Thermodynamics (BLAST) Computer Program to Review New Army Building Designs for Energy Efficiency," by Donald J. Leverenz, Dale J. Herron, JoAnn Amber Eidsmore, and Robert E. O'Brien, October 1983, ADA134487.

Technical Report E-188, "Energy Impact Analysis of the Military Construction-Army Building Delivery System," by D. Leverenz, D. Herron, A. Stumpf and A. Eidsmore, October 1983, ADA135277.

Technical Report E-189, "An Estimate of Process Energy Consumption in DARCOM," by Ben J. Sliwinski, October 1983, ADA135418.

Technical Report E-187, "Energy Conservation Strategies for Army Installations," by D. C. Hittle, January 1984, ADA137918.

Technical Report E-191, "Wind Power Generation Design Considerations," by Elizabeth Elischer and Larry M. Windingland, December 1983, ADA138841.

Technical Report E-192, "Procedures for Acceptance Testing of Solar Energy Systems," by D. L. Johnson and D. M. Joncich, April 1984, ADA141839.

Technical Report E-195, "A Photovoltaic Power System for the Holman Guest House, Fort Huachuca, AZ," by D. M. Joncich, May 1984, ADA142646.

Technical Report E-194, "Development of a Modular Solar Domestic Hot Water System for Department of Defense Barracks," by D. M. Joncich and R. E. Kirts, May 1984, ADA142678.

Technical Report E-196, "Investigation of Power Factor Controller Applications," by Mary B. Chionis and Ben J. Sliwinski, July 1984, ADA144466.

Technical Report E-193, "Evaluation of Microcomputer Energy Analysis Programs," by Linda Lawrie, William Klock, and Donald Leverenz, July 1984, ADA144684.

Facility Systems Research

Technical Report P-146, "Microcomputer Selection Guide for Construction Field Offices, Updated Edition," by M. J. O'Connor, T. Kruppenbacher, and G. Colwell, September 1984, ADA146615.

Technical Report P-166, "The Application of Artificial Intelligence to Contract Management," by Timothy Kruppenbacher, August 1984, ADA146681.

Technical Report P-162, "ADP Documentation and Specifications for Microcomputer Applications to the Military Construction Process (MICRO)," by Carl E. DeLong, August 1984, ADA146738.

Technical Report P-141, "Housing Operations Management Systems (HOMES) Volume I: Executive Summary," by Robert Blackmon, August 1984, ADA146936.

Technical Report P-164, "Economic Analysis Models for Evaluating Costs of a Life Cycle Cost Data Base," by L. Murphree and R. Neathammer, September 1984, ADA146801.

Technical Report P-144, "Development of a Facility Management and Improvement Manual for Army Service Schools," by Robert L. Brauer, Cynthia McNeilly, and Kim Groesbeck, March 1983, ADA135145.

Technical Report P-150, "Strategy for Development of an Expedient Facilities Catalog," by R. L. Schneider and Ed Goodale, December 1983, ADA136616.

Technical Report P-155, "The Microcomputer Knowledge Base: Introduction and User Instructions," by Frank Mabry, William Hohensee, and Gregory Norris, January 1984, ADA137694.

Technical Report P-149, "A Model for Training Range Planning Data," by R. L. Brauer, Martin Koch, Hugh Henry, and Samuel T. Brooks, April 1984, ADA141140.

Technical Report P-157, "A Concept Description for a Directorate of Engineering and Housing Decision Support System (DEH DSS)," by Allen W. Moore, Janet R. Randle, Simon J. Kim, and Robert E. Buhts, August 1984, ADA145075.

Engineering and Materials Research

Technical Report M-355, "A Review of Metallic Surface Treatments for Corrosion Mitigation," by V. Hock, J. Rigsbee, and J. Boy, September 1984, ADA146701.

Technical Report M-358, "Recommended Aluminum Pipe Welding Procedures for Corps of Engineers Construction," by Robert Weber, September 1984, ADA146712.

Technical Report M-333, "Preliminary Investigation of Ceramic-Coated Anodes for Cathodic Protection," by E. G. Segan and A. Kumar, August 1983, ADA133440.

Technical Report M-334, "Evaluation of Contractor Quality Control of Built-up Roofing," by Myer J. Rosenfield, October 1983, ADA135672.

Technical Report M-336, "Construction of Aluminum Standing-Seam Roofing at an Army Facility," by Myer J. Rosenfield, November 1983, ADA136401.

Technical Report M-335, "Criteria for Evaluating Impact Damage Resistance of Exterior Insulation and Finish Systems," by Alvin Smith, Robert E. Muncy, and Steven C. Sweeney, November 1983, ADB079523.

Technical Report M-339, "Fixity of Members Embedded in Concrete," by Fernando Castilla, Phillippe Martin, and John Line, February 1984, ADA138862.

Technical Report M-337, "Development of Concepts for Corrosion Assessment and Evaluation of Underground Pipelines," by A. Kumar, E. Meronyk, and E. Segan, April 1984, ADA140633.

Technical Report M-344, "Deformation and Fracture Maps for Polymer-Foams, Solid Polymers, and Polymer-Composites," by M. E. Ashby and P. W. R. Beaumont, April 1984, ADA141197.

Technical Report M-345, "An Investigation into Polymer Design and Synthesis for Infrared Energy Absorption," by Alvin Smith, May 1984, ADA141265.

Technical Report M-342, "Evaluation of Commercial Magnetic Descalers," by Debbie J. Lawrence, May 1983, ADA143020.

Technical Report M-346, "The Effects of Minor Constituents in Calcium Silicate Insulation on the Corrosio[n] of Underground Heat Distribution Systems," by E. G. Segan, D. W. Blackmon, and C. March, June 1984, ADA143378.

Technical Report M-351, "Evaluation of the Pavement Condition Index for Use on Porous Friction Surfaces," by Starr D. Kohn and Mohamed Y. Shahin, July 1984, ADA144521.

Technical Report M-347, "Investigation of Tri-Service Heat Distribution Systems," by Ellen G. Segan and Ching Ping Chen, June 1984, ADA145181.

Technical Report M-343, "Construction of Experimental Polyvinyl Chloride (PVC) Roofing," by Myer Rosenfield, April 1984, ADA145406.

THE DIFFERENCE

by Dandridge M. Malone

A major malfunction in the development of company-level leaders will certainly occur when the leadership of a unit does not put enough effort into recognizing, emphasizing, and using *the difference*.

Of 169 soldiers in a full-strength company, 43 are officers and 126 are not. And that's *the difference*. There is a line between them.

The line is totally unimportant [in] terms of making the 43 better indiv[id]uals than the 126. Any one of the 1[69] can be as good as any other. The li[ne] is extremely important, though, [in] terms of making it possible for t[he] officers to lead the unit.

Any organized effort involving two [or] more people must have someone [in] charge. There must be leaders a[nd]

strengthen, to clarify *the difference* between those who are part of the leadership and those who are not. The better the leadership of the unit does this separating, the better the unit will be led.

Adapted from an article appearing in the September-October 1982 issue of INFANTRY journal.

Dandridge M. Malone, a retired Infantry Colonel, has published many articles, books, and technical reports. He has a master's degree in social psychololgy from Purdue University and completed the Armed Forces Staff College. He has served in staff or faculty assignments at the U.S. Army Command and General Staff College, the U.S. Military Academy, and the U.S. Army War College.

Engineer Solution

A. To determine the number of mines needed:

1. Number of IOE clusters
   Front (250m) ÷ 9 = 28

2. Mines in IOE IOE cluster composition (2-2-2) x 28	AT = 56	APF = 56	APB = 56
3. Mines in mainfield Front (250m) x desired density (3-4-2)	AT = 750	APF = 1000	APB = 500
4. Subtotal of mines	AT = 806	APF = 1056	APB = 556
5. Compute 10% for mine rejections	AT = 81	APF = 106	APB = 56
6. Total mines needed	AT = 887	APF = 1162	APB = 612

B. To determine the number of strips needed:

1. Add desired density AT 3 + APF 4 + APB 2 = 9
2. $\frac{3}{5}$ x total desired density (9) = 5.4
3. 3 x AT desired density (3) = 9
4. Number of strips
   (highest number from lines 2 and 3) = 9

C. To determine the number of antihandling devices:

1. AHD (given 10%) x AT mines
   .10 x 887 = 89

D. To determine the total manhours needed:

$$\frac{\text{Total AT mines}}{4} + \frac{\text{Total APF mines}}{8} + \frac{\text{Total APB mines}}{16} \times 1.2$$

$$\frac{887}{4} + \frac{1162}{8} + \frac{612}{16} \times 1.2$$

222 + 146 + 39 x 1.2 = 489MH

Note: Most figures are rounded up to the next whole number.

Commissioned Officers' Branch

Officer Retention Program:

On December 1 the Army began using centralized DA-level boards to select other than Regular Army officers for Conditional Voluntary Indefinite (CVI) and Voluntary Indefinite (VI) status.

LTC Dennis Dalton, chief of MILPERCEN's Officer Personnel Management Branch, said, "these boards will be responsible for the qualitative management of the officer corps. They are needed to maintain the necessary strength limits in both high and low density branches."

Officers with 2½ years of service who wish to apply for CVI should submit their applications through their chain of command to their career management divisions. The application should include a statement that the officer understands that CVI status may include a branch transfer. The officer will also be required to list three under-strength branches in order of his preference.

The revised system also gives officers the opportunity to voluntarily request re-branching when they apply for CVI status. Applications which contain branch transfer volunteer statements will be processed in the same manner as normal requests for branch transfers under existing regulations. Officers approved for voluntary branch transfers will be considered for CVI status in their new branch.

Centralized boards will consider applications along with other applicants from the same year group. This will ensure that the process is applied fairly to officers with both three and four-year obligations.

Officers who are approved for CVI status will be extended on active duty through their eight years of service, unless they are separated sooner or released from active duty under appropriate regulations," Dalton said.

"Officers who are disapproved for CVI status will be reassigned to the reserve components after they complete their active duty obligated tour," he added.

Centralized boards will screen the files of officers who have applied for CVI status. The board's review will be based on the officer's performance and potential, and on recommendations from the chain of command and the officer's career management division.

Dalton said the board will then list, by branch, the files of officers approved for CVI status. The board will then determine if rebranching is required to properly align branches. If necessary, a proportional number of officers in the top, middle, and lower third of the list will be transferred from over-strength to under-strength branches. During re-branching, MILPERCEN will consider officers' preferences and criteria provided by branch proponents (such as military and civilian education level) as much as possible.

All officers approved for VI will be allowed to remain in the Army until selected for 04 and integrated into the Regular Army, unless separated sooner under other regulations.

Engineer Branch will hold its last FY85 Advanced Civil School Board on March 1, 1985. Applications should be sent to U.S. Army MILPERCEN, ATTN: DAPC-OPF-D, 200 Stoval St., Alexandria, VA, 22332. For further information, call CPT Corley, AV 221-7504/7506.

listed Soldiers' Branch

Are you confused about whether you are a crane operator, a forklift operator, or maybe both? Well, here's the latest scoop on MOS 62F, crane operator reclassification, from the Engineer Proponency Office.

Two years ago the Directorate of Training and Doctrine (DOTD) submitted a request to MILPERCEN recommending that forklift operations should be deleted from MOS 62F. At that time, the job title for that MOS was "Lifting/Loading Equipment Operator."

This decision was made because, of 1,700 MOS 62F personnel in the field, only one-third were working within Engineer units. The other two-thirds were assigned to either ordnance, transportation, or quartermaster units as forklift operators.

This was an unacceptable situation for the Corps of Engineers for two reasons. First, once individuals were assigned to one of those other branches, they usually stayed there, separated from and lost to the Engineers; and second, because they were in other than Engineer units, it was difficult to keep them proficient in their MOSs due to their limited duties. Crane operations, the main focus of the MOS, was not available for training purposes.

In January 1984, MILPERCEN published five reclassification guidelines for the 62F MOS:

• Personnel and positions associated with Rough Terrain Forklift (RTFL) operation in ammunition units will be reclassified to MOS 55B and further identified with additional skill identifier, B1 (Rough Terrain Container Handling Operations).

• Personnel and positions who operate RTFL equipment in Transportation Terminal units will be reclassified to MOS 57H and further identified with ASI B1.

• Personnel and positions which are a part of the operation of RTFL equipment in supply units will be reclassified into MOS 76V and further identified with ASI B1.

• Personnel and positions associated with the operation of container cranes will be reclassified into MOS 57H and further identified with ASI G1 (Terminal Crane Operations).

All other MOS 62F positions and personnel are scheduled to remain unchanged. MILPERCEN has also revised the MOS 62F job title from Lifting/Loading Equipment Operator to Crane Operator.

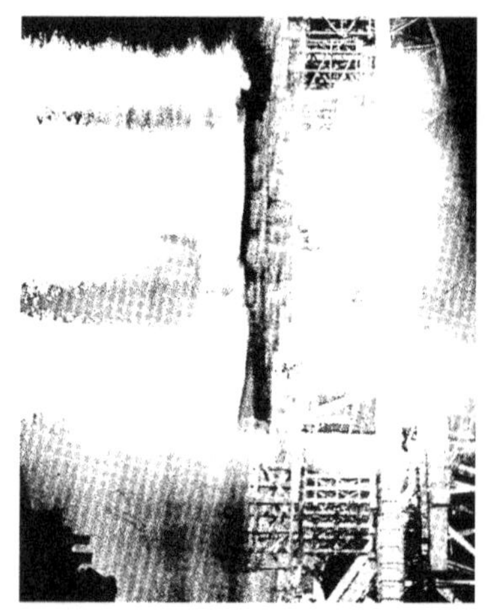

Total Force . . . Essayons

A Personal Viewpoint

by MSG John M. Hall

As General Wickham stated: "We face a more complex and diverse threat and must continue the forward-looking doctrine with an expanded role for the Reserve forces," the 464th Engineer Battalion headquartered in Schenectady, NY, continues to *train as we will be required to fight.*

When I was first assigned as a full time manning, active army operations sergeant to a reserve Engineer battalion, you might say I had several reservations . . . long hair, poor uniforms, and week-end drills to train an Engineer battalion to fight in Europe and accomplish a CAPSTONE mission.

Well, after several months of evaluation and training, I found that these reserve force soldiers are as well-trained and capable of accomplishing their mission as active units, given the limited training time and limited amounts of funds, ammunition, equipment, and—most important—time to train. Needless to say, I had my work cut out for me and went to work using all the knowledge and experience that I have obtained over the years.

As the year went along, I found that these soldiers wanted the same things as the active force. They wanted to be challenged with training that was tough and demanding. This we have done and will continue to accomplish. Here is what this battalion, as a reserve unit, has accomplished and continues to accomplish:

- Built a timber-trestle bridge for the Vanhornsville, NY school system.
- Have crew-served weapons and demolition firing for the entire battalion at Fort Drum, NY.
- Have battalion-wide STX/CPX for the commanders and staff, under the CAPSTONE mission doctrine.
- Have a sustained 11-day annual training period at Fort Drum, NY, with company ARTEPs evaluated by the ARTEP Branch, Fort Belvoir, VA, and 1st Army with success and mission accomplishment.
- Have annual weapons-qualification and hand-grenade training at West Point, NY.
- Have regular joint training with the 3rd Field Engineer Regiment (Canadian Army).
- Have an overseas deployment for 10 days in the mission area with visits and reconnaissances to the actual mission areas.
- Have battalion quarterly training meetings, commanders conferences, and BTMS reviews.
- Participate in MAPEX '86 with the entire corps CAPSTONE units and active forces.
- Have smoke operations and decontamination operations for the AT-85 training period at Fort Drum, NY with company ARTEPs.
- Attend all Commander and CSM CAPSTONE conferences and keep the units current on doctrine and how to fight in the Combined Arms areas.

Finally, this unit, which is a part of the 1209th U.S. Army Garrison and the 98th Division (Training) in peacetime, and the 329th Engineer Group for CAPSTONE will help rebuild the Engineer training area at Fort Drum, NY. A tall order for a reserve Engineer unit, however, *we will accomplish the mission.*

Yes, this battalion is capable of accomplishing its wartime CAPSTONE mission with limited resources and knows how to fight under the most current and up-to-date doctrine and CAPSTONE mission guidance. It truly is a pleasure, as well as hard work, to be a part of the Total Force and to understand that the 70 percent reserve Engineer force is capable and willing to fight when and if called upon to do so. Our motto for this year is TOTAL FORCE . . . ESSAYONS.

MSG John M. Hall was the Engineer Office NCOIC to the British Army of the Rhine and Northern Army Group, 5th Ordnance Brigade Staff Element in Moenchengladbach, Germany. His other assignements in Germany were the 275th Engineer Company in Stuttgart, the 237th Engineer Battalion in Heilbronn, and the 78th Engineer Battalion in Ettlingen. MSG Hall was also assigned to the U.S. Army Engineer School and attended Virginia Tech and the Combat Engineer Advanced Course.

LTC John M. Paris III commands the 464th Engineer Battalion (CBT) (CORPS), 1SG Ogden Tuttle is the Command Sergeant Major.

D STATES ARMY
EER CENTER
'ORT BELVOIR, VA

DER/COMMANDANT
ard S. Kem

IT COMMANDANT
ph T. Rundle

STAFF/DEPUTY
TION COMMANDER
er D. Stearns

ID SERGEANT MAJOR
arles T. Tucker

R OF TRAINING
TRINE
n W. Barber

PUBLICATIONS
eorges

leming

G EDITOR
J. Leto

T EDITOR
chmoldt

TING EDITOR
es M. Althouse

IRECTOR
Davis

L ASSISTANT
Tate

ks to 1LT Gayleen Branden-
her help in coordinating and
is issue.

ver

en G. Strong ensures that EOBC
e' technically competent by
m the proper construction of a
medium girder bridge (photo by
).

FEATURES

DEPARTMENTS

News & Notes

Fuels and Lubricants

There is good news and bad news in the recent status report by Maurice LePera of the Belvoir R&D Center on the Army's efforts to improve management of packaged fluid, lubricant and grease products entering the military supply system.

The bad news is that a proliferation of proprietary products, now in excess of 25 percent, continues to plague logistical and supply personnel, impair readiness, and increase military costs.

The good news is that DARCOM/AMC Regulation 750-11, *Maintenance and Supplies–Use of Lubricants, Fluids and Associated Products,* can remedy the problem. All that Army equipment managers, specification writers, and program managers have to do is to adhere to it.

The regulation's biggest bonus is that it establishes the Belvoir R&D Center as the Army Material Command focal point on proper selection and use of the packaged products it governs. In this role, the Center's Fuels and Lubricants Division provides the coordination and approval necessary to ensure that lubricant orders and technical manuals contain only current standardized product specifications.

Guidance in the regulation prohibits random introduction of proprietary products. It curtails former procedures that have allowed contractors and developers to specify them.

The regulation accomplishes this by requiring justification for use of nonstandard products as opposed to those qualified in accordance with military and federal specifications or purchase descriptions; imposing MIL-STD-836, *Lubrication of Military Equipment,* on all designs, developments, and acquisitions; and insisting that all procurement requests, solicitations, and contracts have lube-order/technical manual approval before first unit acceptance.

If DARCOM/AMC Regulation 750-11 is followed, according to Mr. LePera, the next news on long-term management of packaged lubricants and fluid will be all good.

D5B Dozer Parachuted

A 15-ton D5B dozer belonging to C Company, 27th Engineer Bn. (CBT) (ABN) 82nd Airborne Division, floats to the ground at Camp Blanding, FL. The airborne earthmover is the first D5B to have ever been dropped during actual operations (photo by CPT Peter Eschbach).

A claim for a "first time ever" was entered recently as a D5B bulldozer was parachuted during an exercise at Camp Blanding, FL.

Performing this "first" was the 27th Engineer Bn. (CBT) (ABN) of the XVIII Airborne Corps at Ft. Bragg, NC. While the D5B dozer, which weighs 15 tons, has been dropped in the past under test conditions, a spokesman said this was the first time it had been done during an actual training exercise.

The exercise, called Dragon Team 1-85, involved an emergency deployment readiness exercise (EDRE) which moved the Engineers from Ft. Bragg to Camp Blanding. There, the 27th, along with other elements of the Airborne Corps, parachuted personnel and equipment onto a small sand-covered drop zone.

After the landing, the D5B dozer was used to construct a field landing strip

Engineers in the Combined Arms Team will be the theme of the Fall issue of ENGINEER. Readers are encouraged to submit manuscripts and photographs. Our copy deadline is May 17, 1985.

Engineers can build the ribbon bridge in shallow water because of the new boat's 22-inch draft (U.S. Army photo).

Bridge Erection Boats

The Army's Belvoir Research and Development Center has awarded a contract worth more than $12 million to the American Development Corporation of North Charleston, SC, for the production of 96 ribbon bridge erection boats. The award is the first installment of a multi-year purchase of 554 boats, with an option to buy 262 more.

Constructed of welded aluminum and powered by two diesel engine-driven water jets, the 25-foot boat features a 22-inch draft and a top speed of 31 mph. It can be transported to the crossing site and launched by the same vehicle that carries the ribbon bridge.

The ribbon bridge's modular design reduces the logistical problems associated with the old M4T6 bridge which took 260 men five hours to erect a 400-foot span. With the ribbon bridge, 50 men can build the same span in less than an hour. Delivery of the boats should begin next fall and be completed in 1989.

Engineers Clear Hurricane Debris

For most people, a trip to Wilmington, NC, means relaxing and basking in the sun at one of the area's numerous beaches.

However, for some soldiers of the 264th Engineer Co.; A Co., 27th Engineer Bn.; and A Co., 548th Engineer Bn. at Ft. Bragg, a trip to Wilmington meant 15 days of hard work clearing fallen trees and debris caused by Hurricane Diana.

The task force consisted of 39 soldiers and 22 pieces of equipment, including scoop loaders and five-ton dump trucks.

Working from sunrise to sunset six days a week, the soldiers found little time to indulge in activities offered by the resort area. However, they expressed no concern about the lack of recreational opportunities.

"It feels great to be operating my equipment," said SP4 Rob Leak, a scoop loader operator from the 27th Engineer Bn. He added that it was a good opportunity to practice with the clamshell attachment for the scoop loader, which is used for grasping trees and brush.

According to Felix Cooper, New Hanover County Manager, the assistance was greatly needed to reduce the county's financial burden. He explained that the county was not prepared to fund such a large clean-up operation.

Camouflaged vehicles rumbling through the streets were welcome sights to local residents who had debris to be removed. "This is fantastic," commented one happy resident. "I really appreciate all the work the Army is doing."

Some local elementary school students even approached the soldiers and asked them for autographs. "This made the troops feel like real heroes," said MAJ. Charles Simons, the officer in charge.

PFC Kenneth Hauer clears trees (photo by PFC Dennis McMahon).

CLEAR THE WAY

by MG Richard S. Kem, Commandant, U.S. Army Engineer School

Leadership . . . Tactical Proficiency . . . Technical Competency

The Triad of Engineer Success

As our Army better organizes itself to fight the AirLand Battle, the courses which train our Engineer leaders are being structured to provide the leadership, technical, and tactical skills needed to win. Our recently improved Advanced NCO Course (ANCOC) and the new Engineer Officer Advanced Course (EOAC) made the Engineer School the forerunner in providing high-quality training for company grade leaders. It is important that these courses do this, since few branches require such a wide range of abilities from their leaders as do Engineers.

Today our technical challenges stem primarily from automation and equipment modernization. The Army in general and the Corps of Engineers in particular are ever more dependent upon high-technology hardware such as computers to accomplish their missions in both peace and war. To do our jobs, Engineers must understand the benefits and the constraints of automation. Further, as new Engineer combat equipment is fielded, we must learn to effectively employ it and to properly maintain it.

Keep in mind that these are tasks above and beyond those we presently encounter. We must surely continue to maintain our capabilities in Combat Engineering and in designing and building the facilities necessary to support the Combined Arms Forces in the Theater of Operations, just as we have done in the past. But technical competence is only one of the traits we require.

We must also be adept at performing tactical tasks. AirLand Battle doctrine provides a demanding, dynamic operational framework in which Engineers have great responsibilities. The newly structured light and heavy divisional Engineer battalions create formidable challenges on that battlefield. Scarce Engineer resources dictate that we must be especially skillful in knowing when, where, and how to use our assets in supporting the maneuver commanders. Tactical proficiency is a vital trait, then. However, it is also insufficient by itself.

Competence in blending tactical precepts wi technical skills may be the most important trait can have. Our full understanding of how all th knowledge and many skills are woven together to for the fabric of our jobs is essential. Military leade throughout history have been confronted with th problem. But never before have leaders been requir to master so many diverse skills or so much technic knowledge. This is the crux of the problem for t Engineer School: how do we teach our leaders all th they need to know and train them to do all the tas required of them, while keeping them out of the A my mainstream for a minimum of time? Our favorab experience with the revised EOAC makes us thi that we might have the answer.

After two weeks of training in our leadership fu damentals, the 14-week core phase of the new EOA devotes six weeks of instruction to tactics, followed b six weeks of technical engineering. Some periphera topics are included in the training during the last 1 weeks, so the new course provides fewer hours for ta tics and engineering than did the old. It is the qual ty of training—not the quantity—which is importan however. This is where the new course greatly ou paces the old.

The revised EOAC emphasizes small-group exercise where knowledge and skills must be successfully in tegrated by the students to complete their assigne tasks. It was not often that the prior course made ou officers think and act with this broadened perspectiv This simultaneous application of the students' leade ship, technical, and tactical skills creates the energ that makes the new course a superior training veh cle. Those who are best trained to combine these skil will win the AirLand Battle.

Incorporated with other engineering topics in th issue of ENGINEER is an article about the revise EOAC. The article should be read especially by thos officers who will return to Fort Belvoir within the ne few years to attend the Advanced Course. Also, seni Engineer leaders will find it useful to know wh training recent EOAC graduates in their units ha received.

CSM Charles T. Tucker, U.S. Army Engineer Center & School

oday's NCO: Leader, Student, Teacher

nly through strong leadership, technical competence, and ctical proficiency will soldiers follow NCOs onto the battlefield

oday's senior Engineer NCO plays a very impor- nt role in supporting the AirLand Battle. He must t only be able to provide the maneuver commander th mobility, countermobility, survivability, and neral engineering; but he must also ensure that his en are properly trained and proficient in their jobs well.

But with all of the roles which the Engineer NCO ust play in today's Army, he must remember that e role of senior trainer is probably the most impor- nt. Regardless of his MOS, the NCO must be pre- ıred to execute all of the technical Engineer tasks ıd still train his soldiers to the highest standards.

Coupled with tactical competence, technical profi- ency is essential in a successful leader. Only if you, NCOs, are technically proficient in your specialties ıd know how to survive on the battlefield will your ldiers follow you, fight for you, and perhaps even sk their lives for you. These main ingredients (tech- cal proficiency and tactical competence) must be ended together to make effective leadership. And en all three must be interwoven to comprise the iad of success.

Soldiers must understand that it isn't enough, how- er, to be technically proficient in engineering tasks. ıey also must be able to apply these skills in various ructured organizations. To have an NCO move from combat heavy Engineer battalion to a corps Engi- ıer unit and then to a mechanized divisional Engi- ıer battalion, and to expect him to apply his skills best improve the organization's effectiveness has ways been one of our greatest challenges as Engi- ıer NCOs.

With the Advanced Noncommissioned Officer ourse at Fort Belvoir, the Field Engineering Branch the Department of Military Engineering accepted e challenge of providing the technical skills which l NCOs need. The new instruction program adopted the Engineer School enables our senior NCOs to receive training on common engineering tasks. This training teaches skill level four tasks and reinforces the skill level one, two, and three tasks by showing the NCOs how to organize and manage these skills. They are instructed on techniques which are used in performing these tasks. They are also provided with technical instruction on the equipment which they may encounter and how to properly employ this equipment.

Therefore, the Engineer common core teaches NCOs more than just standards. It provides ideas and alter- natives in meeting these standards. As Engineers, the individual NCOs must add their own ingenuity and resourcefulness and make the finest product from the tools they have been given.

With an ever-changing environment and with new equipment constantly being introduced into the Ar- my's inventory, it is no longer just a wise move for an NCO to learn about this new equipment. Now it is a necessity. For example, the article, "Beefing Up the MGB," which appears in this issue shows how this bridge has had to undergo changes to withstand the weight of new vehicles and equipment such as an M-1 Abrams tank. Our soldiers, especially 12Cs, will be trained and totally proficient with changes such as the new Link Reinforcement Set. There is simply no room for incompetence on the AirLand Battlefield.

Another article about a new obstacle breach course shows us other ways in which we can be more efficient in the Combined Arms Team. It is vital that our sol- diers are fully trained in tasks such as this. CPT Harshbarger shows us how important time, speed, and agility are and that we, as Engineers, must make breaching obstacles another one of our specialities.

Success on the AirLand Battlefield is by no means an easy task. Engineer NCOs must not only ensure their soldiers can fight, but they must also make cer- tain their soldiers are totally proficient in their MOSs. Leadership, technical proficiency, and tactical com- petency are the vital ingredients for that success.

School News

Department of Combat Developments (DCD)

Counterobstacle Vehicle: Contractor testing of two Counterobstacle Vehicle (COV) test beds began in March at Ft. Indiantown Gap, PA. The test bed design is based on the hull and chassis of the M88A1 recovery vehicle and is intended to provide a future replacement for the Combat Engineer Vehicle (CEV).

The COV will have excavating, bulldozing, lifting, hauling, and breaching capabilities to provide a rapid and effective means of completing both countermine and counterobstacle missions. Countermine tasks will be performed by a track-width mine roller or plow, a full-width mine plow with automatic depth control, or a towed projected line charge. A Vehicle Magnetic Signature Duplicator (VEMASID) can be used for magnetically fuzed mines.

For counterobstacle tasks, the COV will be equipped with one or two arms with digging, lifting, grappling, pavement breaking, tree cutting and auger attachments, and a heavy-duty winch and dozer blade converted from the full-width plow.

Test bed delivery to the government is scheduled for late May, to be followed by testing and evaluation ending in April 1986.

Department of Combined Arms (DCA)

Army Writing Program: Because tomorrow's Army must have leaders who can read well, think critically, and express their thoughts with precision and clarity, the Army Chief of Staff recently approved an Army writing program. Its goal is to ensure that all officers, warrant officers, and NCOs possess effective communications skills.

The Directorate of Combined Arms has established a writing office to coordinate the Engineer School's writing program. This contains diagnostic testing, remedial training, and core curriculum instruction in communicative skills, which include not only oral and written abilities, but also the reading comprehension necessary for effective communication.

Beginning in March, EOBC will have 16 hours in this new program, EOAC will have 24 hours, and ENCOA will include self-paced instruction as part of its curriculum.

A staff of military and civilian educators has designed a writing program that blends the best education resources available in the local community with a series of reading, writing, and speaking requirements that use military situations to reinforce instruction.

The Engineer School POC for this program is MAJ McLaughlin, AV 354-2274, commercial (703) 664-2274.

OBC Changes:

The EOBC Training Detachment has made significant changes in the five-day field training exercise (FTX) for its student officers.

The new ARTEP-based FTX stresses independent actions and decision making by a task force Engineer in a maneuver battalion.

EOBC students take part in weekend training with the 16th Bde. (SEP) Virginia Army National Guard, at Ft. A.P. Hill as one of these changes. The Brigade provides one AVLB and one CEV, with crews, to add realism to the FTX platoon missions.

ield Circular:

Field circular, "*The Task Force and Brigade Engineer*," has been scheduled for distribution at the end of the fourth quarter by the Tactics and Operations Division of the Department of Combined Arms (DCA). The new circular will define the duties and responsibilities of staff Engineers at task force and brigade levels.

Through this, the Engineer School hopes to better integrate Engineers into Combined Arms operations by discussing staff planning. In addition, both field Engineer and maneuver units have requested clarification of the Engineer staff officer's role.

Both active and reserve units provided information, and further comments can be given to CPT Milt Seekings at AV 354-3280, commercial (703) 664-3280.

The new circular will be distributed automatically to all active duty and reserve units.

New Branch Created:

The Tactics and Operations Division is organizing an Engineer Operations Branch, which will be responsible for developing and writing doctrinal literature pertaining to Engineer tactical operations. The new branch is being organized because of revisions to the School Model '83 realignment.

Directorate of Training and Doctrine (DOTD)

51T Basic Technical Course Selected:

An Air Force Career Development Course, CDC 55350, *Engineering Assistant*, has been selected as an interim technical engineering supervisor basic technical course for MOS 51T. This correspondence course is available to active Army and Reserve Component E6 soldiers in MOS 51T and to E5 soldiers in MOSs 51G, 81B, and 82B.

The course consists of eight subject-area volumes and will be used primarily as a merger training for 51T soldiers and cross-training for the soldiers in the feeder MOSs. Subject area volumes include: *Introduction to Civil Engineering*; *Applied Mathematics*; *Surveying*; *Soils Analysis*

Directorate of Training and Doctrine (continued)

51T Basic Technical Course Selected: (continued)

and Testing; *Pavements Analysis and Testing*; *Drafting*; *Engineering*; and *General Contingency Responsibilities*.

All volumes are to be completed in 12 months and require a satisfactory grade on an end-of-course examination in order for students to receive credit. An Army Correspondence Course Program catalog or any Army education office should be referred to for enrollment instructions.

Engineer Doctrine Update Planned:

Engineer doctrine is due for a major update starting in FY 85. FM 5-101, *Mobility*, has been forwarded to the DA printer with a release date to the field in early spring. Keystone manuals which will follow during the summer and fall are FM 5-102, *Countermobility*; FM 5-103, *Survivability*; and FM 5-104, *General Engineering*.

FY 86 will see continuing emphasis on getting doctrine to the field with scheduled publication of FM 5-205, *Engineer Topographic Operations*; FM 5-541, *Military Soils Engineering*; FM 5-25, *Explosives and Demolitions*; FM 5-34, *Engineer Field Data*; FM 5-210, *Military Float Bridges*; and FM 20-32, *Mine/Countermine Operations, Company Level*.

Supporting drills and field circulars for FY 85 publication are TC 5-101, *Mobility Drills*; TC 5-102, *Countermobility Drills*; and two new field circulars, *Brigade Engineer/Task Force Engineer* and *Airfield Damage Repair*. For FY 86, the schedule calls for publication of TC 5-103, *Survivability Drills; TC 5-104, General Engineering Drills*; and TC 5-105, *Topography Drills*.

Topographic Engineers Obtain New Training Products and Classes:

Many new training products and classes will be available to Topographic Engineers in FY 86 and FY 87, according to the Topographic Element of the Directorate of Training and Doctrine.

Both TM 21-33-1, *Vegetation Analysis*, and TM 21-33-2, *Surface Configuration*, will be fielded in FY 86. The coordinating draft of FM 5-10, *Topographic Operations*, will be ready in the third quarter of that year. Coordinating drafts of TM 5-240, *Compilation and Color Separation of Topographic Maps*; TM 5-245, *Photo Lithography*; and TM 5-232, *Elements of Survey*; are planned for FY 87.

The SQT 83F4, *Lithographer*, will be tested for the first time in FY 85. Three SQTs will be tested for the first time in FY 86. These are 81C4, *Cartographer*; 81Q, 2, 3, and 4, *Terrain Analyst*; and 82D4, *Topographic Surveyor*.

Many TEC and ACCP lessons will be fielded in the next two fiscal years in each of those MOSs, including TEC lessons on the operation and maintenance of the Heidelberg press and other new equipment in the topographic support system.

Many graphic training aids (GTAs) will be ready in FY 86, including a protractor that can be used with USGS maps, proportionate scales,

Azimuth-Bearing/Grid Magnetic Azimuth Conversion Charts, and *Perform Maintenance on the Heidelberg Offset Press.*

Resident courses in advanced lithography (BTC) will be offered in FY 86, and Topographic common core ANCOC courses will be available in FY 87. The Topographic Engineering Branch is now under operational control of the Defense Mapping School and has been designated the U.S. Army Topographic Element, DOTD.

Either CPT Davis or CW4 Maxwell can be contacted for further information at AV 354-1831, commercial (703) 664-1831.

be

Operators of the newly introduced Bridge Erection Boat—Shallow Draft (BEB-SD) will be awarded the 12C Additional Skill Identifier (ASI) according to recommendations made by the Engineer School.

Because training requirements for the new boat have proved more demanding than those for the boat it replaced, a three-week course will be given, open to selected 12C10 OSUT graduates, beginning in 1988. In the meantime, plans are being developed to award the ASI to presently qualified operators.

Since the BEB-SD was originally developed as the United Kingdom Combat Support Boat (UKCSB), two Engineer School NCOs have attended the six-week Royal Engineering School's Craft Operator Specialist Course in Great Britain, before developing the new course.

The newly introduced BEB-SD is a transportable hydrojet-propelled aluminum hull boat used to maneuver floating bridge components. Introduced into the system in 1981, it has replaced the 27-foot diesel-powered bridge erection boats in most Army units. While the old 27-footer is still used in reserve units, it is gradually being replaced by the new boats.

TRADOC has approved the recommendation for the ASI, and DA approval is expected in October 1985.

The Engineer School Secretary has been reorganized to form both a Central Resource Management Office and a Support Division. The consolidation between DOTD and the three training departments brings G-1 and G-4 functions under one contact point.

The School Secretary continues to manage the School library and the Academic Records Division. The new Central Office will handle budget and manpower programming and determine the number of instructors needed for each School course.

The School Secretary's Support Division will add the Text Distribution Warehouse. That division will also do maintenance coordination and coordinate between all School elements and Ft. Belvoir on major logistics actions.

All School directorates will remain the same, although there will be some reorganization with the Directorate of Training and Doctrine, the Department of Combined Arms, and the Department of Military Engineering. The directorates and the departments are listed below with their AUTOVON (354) numbers.

- Directorate of Training and Doctrine, COL D. Barber, 2188
- Directorate of Combat Development, COL T. Vander Els, 4177

Directorate of Training and Doctrine (continued)

School Secretary Reorganized: (continued)

- Directorate of Evaluation and Standardization, COL D. Karrer, 366
- Department of Combined Arms, COL J. Fesmire, 2907
- Department of Military Engineering, COL P. Chinen, 2628
- Department of Military Logistics, LTC. R. Strom, 3144
- School Secretary, LTC M. Bowe, 2413
- POC for the Engineer School Secretary, CPT Woodward, 3771 or 321

These changes, which are being made to further meet School Mod '83 guidance, should be completed by April.

Department of Military Engineering (DME)

PE and EIT Study Materials:

Study materials for the Professional Engineer (PE) and Engineer i Training (EIT) exams will be distributed by the U.S. Army Engine School until current stocks are exhausted. A recent comparison to co mercially available material showed that the Engineer School's materi needs considerable revision. In the future, the Engineer School will con tinue to provide assistance to students with exam applications. Th National Society of Professional Engineers has provided a selec bibliography of study materials and home-study courses. Thi bibliography can be obtained by sending a written request to: The Com mandant, USAES, ATTN: DME, Professional Engineer Program Cooı dinator, Ft. Belvoir, VA 22060-5331.

Concrete Mobile:

Several reports have come to the Engineer School of field units hav ing trouble with the M-919 Concrete Mobile. While many difficultie are caused by incorrect operation or maintenance, some units have foun unique problems in placing concrete.

If you have a problem that goes beyond the scope of normal operations help is available from the Structure and Utilities Branch. You can con tact them through the Engineer Hotline, AV 354-3646, commercial (70 664-3646. Correspondence should be directed to the Department o Military Engineering, ATTN: ATZA-TE-SU, Ft. Belvoir, VA 22060-5331

ADSPEC 23 Training:

CAPT Charles Wilkins (USMC), chief of the Structures and Utilitie Branch, has been named coordinator of the Facilities/Contract Construc tion Management Course, which is designed to prepare officers fo assignments with Corps of Engineer districts or installation Directorate of Engineering Housing.

Those interested in the course should call CAPT Wilkins at A 354-2797/3806; commercial (703) 664-2797/3806. Requests to attend th course are made through channels to MILPERCEN Education Branch ATTN: DAPC-DPA-E, 200 Stovall St., Alexandria, VA 22332-0400.

Letters to the Editor

The Division Engineer—Counterpoint

I must commend LTC Nahas on his article entitled *"The Division Engineer, A Personal Viewpoint"* which appeared in the ENGINEER Summer 1984 issue. It was an excellent attempt to outline the responsibilities for the Division Engineer on today's battlefield. However, there were several areas brought out in the article that deserve further discussion.

Contrary to LTC Nahas' stated viewpoint, the Division Engineer battalion commander's command responsibility will not be reduced during wartime. In fact, I would strongly argue that his command responsibilities will be far more demanding in wartime than in a peacetime environment. The Engineer battalion commander wears two hats both in wartime and peacetime. While he may have difficulty in exercising command and control (C2) in wartime due to the positioning of his battalion on extended battlefields, the requirement to maintain C2 remains an absolute if the Engineers are to contribute to influencing the battle.

While based on the Engineer Estimate, each brigade may receive a Direct Support (DS) Engineer company (the key word here being *may*), the Engineer battalion commander never relinquishes command or control of his subordinate DS Engineer companies. They remain his responsibility and can (if not fully committed) in fact receive missions directly from him in addition to receiving missions and priorities from the supported brigade.

The days of "fire and forget" Engineer support where Engineers are fragmented and piecemealed into ineffectiveness must be terminated given the fact that Engineer requirements will almost always exceed capabilities. Engineer personnel and equipment must be actively commanded by the Engineer battalion commander to ensure that Engineer support is always maximized. The maximum Engineer effort starts with the Division Engineer's Engineer Estimate prior to hostility and continues throughout the battle.

The Division Engineer has both the brigade and S-3 sections and in the heavy and motorized divisions a brigade Engineer section to assist him in planning for Engineer support activities. In addition, he may receive the assistance of an Engineer group or corps battalion to provide additional Engineer planning.

While the Division Engineer provides basic guidance on Engineer activities, to include the division commander's priorities of effort and other tactical considerations, it is the staff that produces the actual estimate and ensuing operation orders. This frees to a great extent the ability of the Division Engineer to don his other hat as commander, allowing him to exercise his command and control responsibilities. Point/Counterpoint.

MAJ Dana Robertson
Program Manager,
Survivability
Army Development and
Employment Agency
Fort Lewis, WA

Caption gets NO GO—Magazine gets GO

One of the many keys to becoming a successful leader is to "know your men and your equipment." It is with this in mind that I direct your attention to the caption in the lower right on page 17 of your Fall 1984 issue of ENGINEER. The soldiers pictured are carrying "normal balk." Long balk does not exist. The three types of M4T6 balk are tapered, short, and normal.

I'm not trying to be critical, but having spent two years on the trail at Fort Leonard Wood, I quickly learned that the best way to teach soldiers how to correctly perform a task is to show them first. Identifying M4T6 components is a task included in the C.E.T. at TA 204, and any soldier who identifies "normal balk" as long balk would receive a NO GO for that task.

I do, however, enjoy reading ENGINEER; and I find it extremely informative. Keep up the good work.

SSG David M. Barnes
U.S. Army, Engineer
HQ, 2nd Engineer Group

Engineer Command Update

ENGINEER will publish its annual Engineer Command Update in the Summer 1985 issue. Readers are encouraged to submit the names of commanders and command sergeants major of Engineer brigades, groups and battalions to:

ENGINEER Magazine
ATTN: ATZA-TD-P Stop 291D
Fort Belvoir, VA 22060-5291

Force Structure Management and Equipment

Change . . . but Not Engineer Standards

by LTG E. R. Heiberg III
Chief of Engineers, U.S. Army

Both because of my position and my personal concerns, I am especially interested in changes that affect Army Engineers. I review here some recent developments that are important for you to know about. I also will highlight a few areas that remain unchanged.

After extensive studies of its force structure over the past year, the Army has decided to keep most of its Engineers. The Army was seriously considering cutting Engineer forces by 22,000 before the Army Vice Chief of Staff hosted a force structure functional area assessment last November. However, after reviewing the Engineers' role and mission, the Army decided it could not afford to lose so much Combat Engineering support. As a result, the Engineers will lose significantly less than first considered, although there will be some painful cuts. The Engineer troop ratio of active component (AC) to reserve component (RC) will continue to be about 30 to 70.

Several changes resulted from the assessment. Some AC Engineer units —primarily utility detachments—will be inactivated to allow for high priority Army initiatives. Other AC companies from corps combat battalions and combat heavy battalions will be moved to the RC as roundout units. In addition, there will be some conversion of selected RC Engineer units as a result of revised allocation rules. For example, some dump truck companies will convert to panel bridge units.

The AC Engineer strength is unlikely to grow under the Army's imposed AC strength of 781,000. Where there is a shortage of Engineer forces, one of our future challenges is to offset this through host nation support or contracting. This involves finalizing host nation agreements and ensuring that contracts are in place. This is a difficult challenge, but it has to be met if we are to ensure adequate Engineering support.

Another area of change is in the way the Army manages its officers. In an effort to meet the future needs of the Army, the Officer Personnel Management System (OPMS) will be fine-tuned to emphasize branch—a return to pre-1974 policy. The recent OPMS study will mean a number of changes to Engineer officers over the next three to five years.

Engineer officers will be managed and developed only by the Engineer branch. Engineers, therefore, will not serve in areas such as maintenance management and material services management which become areas of concentration within the Ordnance branch and the Quartermaster branch. By the same token, officers from other branches will not be developed in Engineer areas of concentration.

In order to meet Army field grade requirements in each branch, some officers will branch transfer at the thi and eighth years of service. Office from overstrength branches will tran fer to the Engineer branch and t Combat Support Arms and Comb Service Support branches. Among t combat arms, only the Enginee require more field grade officers as th officers are promoted. All the othe combat arms decrease their requir ments as the officers in those branche gain seniority. For the Engineers, th is highlighted by the large comman opportunities for lieutenant colone and particularly colonels. And th need is further emphasized by th Engineers' challenge to produc qualified Directors of Engineering an Housing at field grade levels.

Officers will no longer be required t have two specialties. The OPMS stud found that the current system tak qualified officers away from Comb Support and Combat Service Suppo assignments just when the need f these officers is increasing. Under th new system, branches with multip specialties will have those specialti consolidated. Our current Engine specialties will become four areas concentration within the Engine branch.

The current specialty code 21, Con bat Engineer, will become areas of co centration 21A (General Engineer) an 21J (Combat Engineer). Specialty cod 22 (Topographic Engineer) will becom

and civilians, trained in managing large construction projects should the nation ever have to mobilize in a national emergency. That strategic reserve cadre across the United States and overseas also provides a "bank" of Engineer-related skills we would need in an emergency: real estate and procurement specialists, lawyers, fiscal and administrative experts, and a host of others.

Engineer equipment is an area that is changing for the better, although sometimes progress is slow. We are seeing new equipment, both tactical and construction, entering our Engineer units, both AC and RC. Some of our forward battalions are receiving the M-113 Armored Personnel Carriers made available as the infantry and cavalry receive the new M-2/M-3 series of Bradley Fighting Vehicles. Testing of the M-9 Armored Combat Earthmover is underway. A small emplacement excavator (SEE) is in production. And new mine/countermine equipment continues to be supported by Army dollar decisions. I expect the Army's need for modernized Engineer forces to continue to be recognized in the years ahead.

I challenge all Engineers to continue to bring your best to the job. Continue to maintain our high standards of excellence, professionalism, and integrity. I also ask that you support each other. Share your enthusiasm and energy with other Engineers as well as with your staffs and co-workers. We need to nurture a sense of responsibility for the Engineer Family and the whole Army Family. To have an Army that works, each of us must be committed to each other's success.

LTG E. R. Heiberg III challenges Engineers to maintain standards of excellence, professionalism, and integrity (photo by Donald R. Jones).

Announcing the 118th Annual Engineer Dinner and Castle Celebration

118th Annual Engineer Dinner
Friday, May 17, 1985
MacKenzie Hall, Fort Belvoir, VA
Officers Only
Mess Dress Blues, Whites
or Tuxedo with Black Bow Tie
RSVP Protocol Office
(703) 664-3036; AV 354

The 1st Castle Celebration
Thursday, May 16, 1985
MacKenzie Hall, Fort Belvoir, VA
Active, Reserve Component, and Retired
Engineer Officers and their Spouses
Informal Civilian Attire
Reservations by Mail
Contact Protocol Office

Airfield and Base Camp Construction in Honduras

by CPT Don C. Young

Over 300 aircraft used the parking aprons and taxiway of the San Lorenzo airstrip constructed for Big Pine II A major problem during construction was the basic soils equation of DIRT + WATER=MUD (photo by 1LT Samue Burkett).

Central America has become a major news-breaking area in the past several years. Millions of U.S. dollars are budgeted for this area annually. The rise of Cuban activities in Nicaragua and Grenada has certainly opened many Americans' eyes to the security threat from Soviet intervention into Central America. Honduras, approximately the size of Tennessee, has become an important ally in Central America due to its location and political status.

The 46th Engineer Battalion (CBT) (HVY) from Fort Rucker, AL, constructed two C-130 medium-lift dirt airstrips and three base camps during the 179-day Joint Service Exercise AHUAS TARA II (Big Pine II) in Honduras. Three Engineer task forces were formed to accomplish these five missions at San Lorenzo, Comayagua, and Aguacate. Each site encountered a variety of construction problems, and the task forces developed interesting techniques to overcome these problems throughout the exercise.

- Non-standard mill lumber.
- Excess water during the wet season.
- Limited availability of civilian construction equipment repair parts.
- Mountainous terrain and substandard road conditions.
- Limited availability of standard U.S. Code electrical and plumbing materials.
- Lack of specific plans from the host nation.
- Lack of topographic maps and information.
- Long acclimatization period required for soldiers.

Airfield Construction

The San Lorenzo airstrip project was located two miles north of the San Lorenzo base camp. Construction began Sept. 15, 1983 during the heavy rain season. Daily rainfall caused mucky soil conditions that cut equipment utilization time to less than half a day.

The airstrip design criteria was taken from TM 5-330, *Roads, Airbases and Heliports in the Theater of Opera-*

tions. All transverse and longitudinal grades were set at maximum values achievable to ensure effective drainage from the heavy rainfall. Parallel V-type drainage ditches carried the runoff to trapezoidal open-channel ditches at each end of the airfield. These open-channel ditches carried the runoff to existing stream beds.

Clearing, grubbing, and stripping operations were done with bulldozers and scrapers. Approximately 30,000 cubic yards of organics were moved before hauling fill for the runway, and 15,000 compacted cubic yards of CH-SC type soil fill were cut from the drainage areas and used to build the runway.

The runway supported its first C-130 landing on Nov. 10, 1983. Over 300 sorties of C-130 and C-7 aircraft used the airstrip before the end of the exercise (ENDEX). The runway sustained minimal landing and takeoff damage. An access road, taxiway, and parking apron were completed by Dec. 20, 1983. Their dimensions were modified slightly to fit onto the available land space.

Major problems encountered during the San Lorenzo airstrip project included working with the basic soils equation of DIRT + WATER = MUD and keeping critical pieces of Engineer equipment operational. Late afternoon rainstorms (daily at 1600–1800 hours) caused extremely mucky soil conditions even with site drainage established daily. The sun would dry out the top layer by midday, allowing the crews to work until the next rainstorm.

Bulldozers were primarily required to strip the organics because of the lack of traction with the scrapers. The bulldozer push-method was used whenever scraper traction was satisfactory. Soil stabilizing additives such as lime, to dry out the mucky soil, were not available in-country. The large quantity of lime required for this airstrip project would not have been cost-effective if sent from the United States.

Lack of repair parts for Engineer construction equipment caused problems throughout the exercise. Turn-around time using normal exercise maintenance channels was too long, and in-country construction equipment dealerships could not provide parts. Besides cannibalizing repair parts, the only other requisition system was to telephone Fort Rucker, AL, and order the required parts. The rear-detachment maintenance element would immediately acquire the parts and send them on the next available supply plane to Central America.

The most critical piece of Engineer construction equipment was the high-speed compactor/motorized sheepsfoot roller which is essential for compacting each layer of fill. Because there are only three compactors organic to a combat heavy Engineer battalion, a major construction problem occurs when the battalion is working on more than one airfield or earthmoving project simultaneously.

A high-speed compactor/motorized sheepsfoot roller was the most critical piece of Engineer construction equipment at the two airstrips in Honduras (photo by 1LT Samuel Burkett).

Equipment breakdown and lack of spare parts caused construction delays by having to shuttle compactors from one site to the other. As a result, a change of the Modified Table of Organization and Equipment (MTOE) was submitted at the end of exercise to add a minimum of three additional high-speed compactors with transport-hauling capabilities (tractor-trailers).

The Aguacate airstrip project was located in the mid-northeastern sector of Honduras, approximately 70 kilometers west of the Nicaraguan border. No prior planning had been done by the Honduran civil engineers for this airstrip. Therefore, the S-3 construction section researched, designed, coordinated, and laid out the airstrip design according to TM 5-330.

The major missions for the Aguacate task force were to build the runway through subbase, establish a base camp, and install a 10,000-foot PVC-pipe waterline. The short time of the exercise prevented the completion of the runway as it was originally designed. However, a clay cap was installed to render the subbase runway C-130-capable as built.

Again, all transverse and longitudinal grades were set at the maximum values allowed to assure effective drainage from the heavy rainfall. Construction began Oct. 6, 1983 with the stripping of organics through swamps, farm fields, streams, and rice paddies along the designated airstrip centerline. Approximately 200,000 cubic yards of cut (organics) and fill (GP-type soil) were hauled to finish the subbase of the airstrip by the end of the exercise.

The mountainous terrain surrounding the Aguacate airstrip made drainage construction extensive. The drainage plan included four culverts that were installed underneath the airstrip to carry runoff and stream water away from the project. Two 36-inch diameter, single barrel, reinforced concrete culverts and two 36-inch diameter, triple barrel, reinforced concrete culverts were placed underneath the airstrip. Upstream and downstream soil-cement sandbag headwalls were built at each culvert site.

An efficient, field-expedient method of installing 4-foot concrete culvert sections was brainstormed by SGT David Coleman of C Company, 46th Engineer

Engineers from the 46th Engineer Battalion install culvert sections at a triple-barrel site to carry runoff and stream water. To save time, materials, and money, the Engineers also constructed a trapezoidal channel to carry water from the runway (photo by 1LT Samuel Burkett).

Battalion (CBT) (HVY). Instead of using the traditional method of lifting each section with a crane and pushing the section into place with manpower, a 2½-cubic-yard bucket loader with a multi-purpose (four-in-one) bucket was modified by securing a 4 x 8-inch post in the bucket with a chain and binder.

In essence, a field-expedient forklift was created that increased the installation rate of 36-inch diameter concrete culverts from 2.5 sections per hour (crane method) to over 6 sections per hour. Therefore, with each culvert length averaging between 220 and 280 feet, a significant amount of construction time was saved during the culvert-installation activities.

An extensive open-channel ditch was cut around the northeastern end of the airstrip to carry a large wet-season stream away from the runway. A trapezoidal channel was designed according to TM 5-330 standards with the deepest cut about 21 feet into the hillside. Construction of this open-channel ditch saved construction time, materials, and cost that would have been expended to install another triple-barrel culvert site underneath the airstrip to carry stream runoff.

Base Camp Construction

The vertical construction platoons were tasked to build a number of base camps at San Lorenzo, Aguacate, and Comayagua. The facilities included clearing hospitals, AAFES post exchanges, road culverts, ammunition storage points, mess halls, bunkers, obstacles, helipads, observation towers, latrines, shower facilities, orderly rooms, and offices.

Each base camp development plan centered around the construction of tropical buildings, nicknamed CAT-HUTs or C-HUTs for Central American Tropical Huts. Approximately the size of a G.P. medium tent, each building cost about $1,500 in materials to build in Honduras and will certainly outlast any canvas tent in tropical climates. The battalion aid station conducted a series of inside temperature tests comparing a G.P. medium tent and a C-HUT. In almost every case, the inside temperature of a C-HUT was 20 to 25 degrees cooler during tests in the heat of the day.

The basic C-HUT unit (16 x 32 feet) was considered a squad level construction mission. It normally took a vertical construction squad six to seven days to complete one C-HUT from footers to the tin roof. However, prefabrication yards were set up to build doors, steps, stud walls, and roof trusses that were hauled to the building sites as needed.

With a prefabrication yard in operation, it normally took a vertical construction squad two to four days to complete one entire C-HUT. However, one vertical construction squad from B Company completed an entire C-HUT in one day at Comayagua base camp. On several days, the vertical squads were broken down into technical advisor teams to assist in self-help construction of C-HUTs by other supporting units.

The overall design of the C-HUTs

proved very effective for a tropical climate. The design improved living conditions immensely and allowed for easy expansion. However, several modifications were made to ease construction and improve living conditions. Recommended modifications included lowering the wall height from 8 to 7 feet, placing roof trusses every 8 feet on-center instead of 4 feet on-center, and installing canvas rolls above screens for use during rain and dust storms. During the entire six-month deployment, less than 30 percent of the battalion personnel lived in C-HUTs. The G.P. medium tents were home for the soldiers located at Aguacate and Comayagua.

AHUAS TARA II provided a unique opportunity for the battalion to train, survive, and build in the austere conditions of Honduras. A remarkable improvement in leadership skills, operator skills, maintenance, and MOS qualification at all levels was realized.

Training Summary

- Movement from CONUS.
- Equipment operator skills.
- Maintenance operations.
- Convoy procedures.
- Secure communications equipment.
- Water purification.
- Construction and topographic survey.
- Soils analysis.
- Vertical construction skills.
- Reconnaissance of roads, airfields, and bridges.
- Survivability.
- Command and control operations.

Despite internal and external problems, the battalion accomplished all assigned missions and provided a smooth transition for the follow-on Engineer unit, the 864th Engineer Battalion (CBT) (HVY) from Fort Lewis, WA.

CPT Don C. Young is the commander of the 586th Engineer Company (AFB) at Fort Benning, GA. He led the Quality Control Team attached to the Mobile District and 1st/7th Special Forces Group during the construction of the Regional Military Training Center near Trujillo, Honduras. He redeployed to Honduras with the 46th Engineer Battalion (CBT) (HVY). CPT Young completed the Engineer Officer Advanced Course and has a degree in civil engineering from Vanderbilt University.

CPT Young wishes to thank the following people for their assistance in gathering information: CPT Michael Flanagan, 1LT Samuel Burkett, 1LT John Gunter, 1LT Michael Rorex, 1LT James Balocki, SFC Lewis Hamilton, and Blake Peck.

Top, soldiers align girders on C-HUT footers. A squad from B Company completed an entire 16 x 32-foot building in a record time of one day. Bottom, completed C-HUTs at one of the base camps provide effective shelter in tropical climates (photos by 1LT Samuel Burkett).

Leadership Development in *EOAC*

by MAJ Don Riley
CPT Mark Buck
CPT Richard Crocker
CPT Jerome Rosperic
CPT Joseph Schroedel

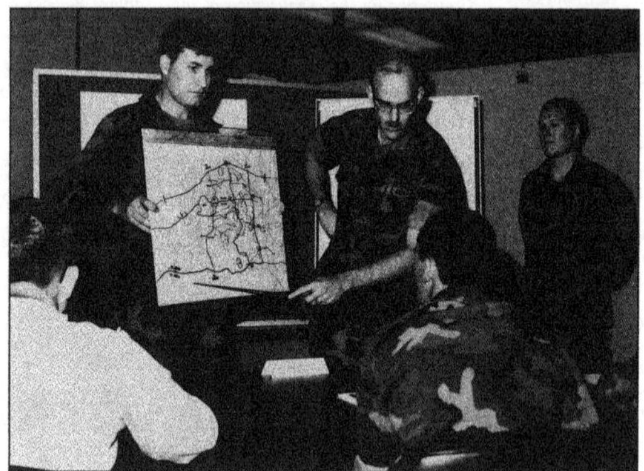

Captains Mike Candelaria, Jay Parker, and Billy Fortner give a student briefing on their scheme of maneuvers to their team and Team Leader (U.S. Army photo).

At his periodic counseling session, CPT J's Team Leader encouraged him to work on his ability to think on his feet and act quickly. This need became evident in CPT J's last briefing when he relied heavily on his briefing charts.

When CPT J's next chance to brief came, he was sure that he would impress the team with his well-prepared overhead slides. His briefing went well until his Team Leader turned off the overhead projector and asked him to proceed.

CPT J was surprised, stumbling for a few moments. But he pressed on, knowing why he was confronted with this situation and realizing that his teammates' expectations of him were high since he was one of the few with company command experience.

The open critique which followed helped to reassure all on the team that they were there to help each other and that open, honest feedback is one of the best aids to learning a skill. This was a meaningful learning experience for both CPT J and all of his teammates. An opportunity was provided for a team member to practice his leader skills, for team members to reflect more on their own capabilities and limitations, and to promote team cohesion through candid evaluations.

In the Winter 1983 issue of ENGINEER, CPT Ralph Graves described the development strategy for the new Engineer Officer Advanced Course (EOAC). Driving this strategy was the Engineer School's need to better develop professional officers and leaders as described in the key manuals, FMs 100-1, 100-5, and 22-100. The mission—train leaders to fight and win.

It's tough to do this training in the classroom, but many positive steps can be taken to develop the skills and attributes needed in our leaders. The small-group instruction and exercises, total fitness, team building, and Team Leaders are all integral parts of our leadership development program. These efforts build upon the leadership instruction presented by the Leadership Branch in the first weeks of the course.

The key to the program is the *reinforcement, application,* and *appraisal* of leader skills and attributes within the small-group environment.

Course Design

The design of a leadership development program began with a study of the most current standards, doctrine, and research to determine the *leader skills* (what we must ***do***) most critical to our training objective—to fight and win. The number of skills was limited to allow for efficient management of the program and to give adequate feedback to the student (Figure 1). These skills were integrated through training, application, assessment, and individual plans for improvement; and feedback is given at each step.

The design of the program to develop *leadership attributes* (what we must **be**) was tougher—how do you reinforce qualities like honesty, creativity, and flexibility? The keys are honest feedback from both the Team Leader and team members, Team Leaders and instructors who set the example, and a classroom environment which promotes these qualities. Attributes were selected in much the same way as leader skills. A worksheet with attribute definition and appraisal criteria was then developed to appraise team members.

However, the real impact is made in the *small-group exercises* designed to integrate leader, tactical, and technical skills. These exercises were examined to determine which situations best presented the student with an opportunity for application and practice. A plan was then developed detailing in which lessons the skills would be trained, applied, and appraised.

Figure 1.
Leader Skills

Take risks
Act quickly
Make decisions
Write effectively
Contribute to teamwork
Use initiative
Motivate subordinates
Manage time
Communicate effectively
Think on feet
Solve problems
Manage stress
Conduct briefings

Also, *team building* is reinforced throughout the program. This both improves the potential for the team members to learn and places them in a very realistic team environment. To promote team building, careful consideration was given to all course requirements, lesson sequence, composition of work and briefing teams, and physical and competitive activities.

To support leadership development, the *total fitness* program was designed around basic instruction in personal and unit conditioning, lifestyle improvement, physical training, and personal programs for improvement based on a battery of assessments, all oriented to developing leaders to fight and win.

Leader Skills

Besides ensuring understanding of the course subject material, the Team Leaders assess student development of leader skills during small-group exercises, leadership and fitness lessons, and physical training activities.

The strategy to develop these skills follows a competency model developed by the Army Organizational Effectiveness School. Students are initially informed of the criteria, shown examples of good and poor skill application, and instructed (formally or informally) in each skill. Following an initial assessment, students practice the skills within the context of the course curriculum. Additional opportunities to practice and reevaluate the skills precede the final step—applying the skills in future assignments.

For example, one element of "thinking on your feet" is recognizing a change in the situation. This "change" may be prompted by the Team Leader as in the example of CPT J. Individual student weaknesses form the basis for this prompting. Standard appraisal criteria are then used to provide students with immediate feedback as one focus for periodic counseling and eventually as input to the ***Academic Evaluation Report.***

Leadership Attributes

The leadership-attributes assessment is closely related to the leader-skills appraisal. Attributes are qualities which make us what we are, and good leadership depends both on the development of leader skills and the internalization of leadership attributes. We develop the skills through practice and feedback; improvement in leadership attributes is fully the student's responsibility. His observed weaknesses are identified by both his Team Leader and peers and remain his responsibility.

An assessment considers 23 leadership attributes, each with five descriptors which characterize a particular level of behavior. A carefully worded definition explains each attribute and its accompanying descriptors, for example, "judgment" (Figure 2).

The assessment is used both by the Team Leaders and peers. Usually there is a close correlation between assessments made by several students of the same individual. In any case, the information is provided to the student for his personal use. Further advice is provided to those who are interested.

The students are very receptive to the feedback. They usually agree with the assessments made, although they may have not previously recognized that aspect of their behavior. Also, they have shown a desire to improve both their leader skills and attributes as leaders.

Small-Group Exercises

After receiving initial instruction in a given subject (such as tactics and

Figure 2.
Judgment

The ability to see the essential elements of a problem, logically weigh facts and possible solutions, assess priorities, and base sound decisions upon these considerations.

5. Sound	Shows consistently sound, well-founded, logical judgment even in difficult situations.
4. Reliable	Can generally be relied upon to produce sound judgment in most circumstances.
3. Measured	Sometimes unsound. Apt to overlook some aspects.
2. Hazy	Has difficulty in marshalling facts, determining possible solutions, and making logical decisions.
1. Unreliable	Inclined to rush into hasty, illogical conclusions without full consideration of all the facts.

(This format was suggested by MAJ Rod McKinnon, Australian Exchange Officer to the Engineer School, who worked on a similar project at the Australian Command and Staff School.)

engineering) in the more traditional fashion of a lecture, the students move to their team rooms for practical application. Often the team is broken down into smaller work groups. Role-playing as a commander, an S-3, or a brigade Engineer allows for realistic application. The primary instructor (the author of the exercise) provides technical expertise. The Team Leader functions in two roles, that of facilitator of the exercise and instructor.

In most exercises, the students develop two products—a written assignment and a military briefing. The students also brief and critique each other.

Our experiences with the small-group instruction show that greater learning takes place in small groups. The students prefer to work and learn in the team environment. They learn to rely on each other's experiences, and they exhibit greater enthusiasm and effort (including those students who already have a good grasp of the material and who often participate less in other methods of instruction). Some of the best learning occurs as a result of the peer interaction within the team.

Team Building

In EOAC, we build team cohesion through efforts to develop bonds of mutual trust, respect, confidence, and understanding. This begins by selectively composing teams of officers who represent a cross section of typical Engineer assignments and education. The varied background of a team presents a challenge in group dynamics, but greatly increases the potential for learning through the sharing of experiences. Additionally, the students have responsibility for team administrative matters providing a structure to promote team cohesion.

The Team Leader guides and coaches the team. He *guides* the team through the successive stages of team development. He provides the initial structure for the team, assists in establishing initial norms, sets standards of performance, and establishes systems for feedback. As a *coach*, he meets with each team member periodically; and he uses a combination of his observation the student's academic performanc and peer evaluations to provide mea ingful feedback to the student. Fami iarity with the course content and th student's values and goals allows th Team Leader to place the student i situations which reinforce strength and overcome weaknesses.

Also, the small-group exercises ar designed to facilitate team buildin Different team members are placed i charge of subgroups for graded an ungraded exercises. The added comp nent of a group grade requires the st dent leader and team members to wor together and reflects how well the st dent leader organizes and motivate the team members. The student leade gains an appreciation of group dyna ics and how it contributes to tea building. Every opportunity is taken t translate this experience to teamwor in units and how to build a team spiri in units.

Competitive athletic events an social activities during the course hel to speed the development of team coh sion. After these activities, team me bers are friendlier, less inhibited in th classroom, and more candid in thei comments.

This deliberate effort to build teams is evident in the improvement in stu dent learning of both the subject mat ter and the benefits and constraints o working together as a team.

Total Fitness

The abilities to lead, think clearly and act decisively are enhanced by the leader's total fitness. In EOAC, the

Teammates work together to solve an engineering design problem (left to right) CPT Ken Collier (AR), CPT Ron Young, CAPT Lee Moran (USMC), CPT Rich Jennings, and MAJ Ibraham Hassan (Jordan) (U.S. Army photo).

rudiments of total fitness (mind, body, and spirit) are presented cognitively (lectures, readings, and class discussions) and experientially (practical exercises, physical exercises). The basic framework of the instruction uses simple equipment; standard facilities; and current Army manuals, pamphlets, and training guidance.

The students receive instruction for improvement at a personal level and guidance for applying the same techniques to soldiers in their future commands. All the instruction is practical and simple. The honest assessments, plans for improvement, and final results are easy for students to use in their future units.

Physical fitness is assessed in the first week of instruction. Each student takes the Army Physical Readiness Test (APRT), measures his flexibility, and determines his blood pressure and pulse rate. With this data, he assesses his current level of physical fitness. He then develops an exercise plan which incorporates mandatory EOAC physical activities with the team and additional individual activities emphasizing a balanced program of endurance, strength, and flexibility.

Goals for improvement are set, student progress is monitored, and an evaluation is made at the end of the course. Students must score at least 50 aerobic points during each of the final twelve weeks of the course and are strongly encouraged to set high goals for the final APRT.

Instruction is presented on the basics of exercise, flexibility, exercise considerations, and unit fitness. Organized physical training includes relay races, water polo, exercise circuits, parcourses, basketball, soccer, guerilla drills, team runs, and volleyball.

Health is also emphasized during the first weeks of the course. Students have their body fat content measured; analyze the composition and caloric content of their diets; have their blood tested for cholesterol, uric acid, glucose, and tryglyceride levels; take a total life stress assessment; and evaluate their risks of heart attack in relation to their lifestyles. With his Team Leader, each student assesses and evaluates his state of health, plans any needed improvements, sets goals, and monitors his progress.

Instruction is presented on nutrition, weight control, cardiovascular fitness, and stress management. Students are given practical guidance on diet and stress reduction techniques. At the end of the course, a subsequent blood test helps to measure any effect of lifestyle changes.

The physical fitness plan and lifestyle improvement begin progress towards *lifetime* total fitness for each student, thereby developing more effective leaders for the Army.

Results of the new course will take time to measure, and the Engineer School's Directorate of Evaluation and Standardization has begun an extensive program to evaluate the course and its graduates.

However, we are confident that by presenting opportunities for the students to apply leader skills; to form and work together as teams; to improve their total fitness; to receive feedback on their performance and observed attributes; and to make assessments, set goals, and measure progress, the new EOAC provides a great opportunity for leadership development.

MAJ Don Riley is a graduate of the U.S. Military Academy and has a master's degree in engineering from the University of California, Berkeley. He served with the 7th Division at Fort Ord, CA; the U.S. Army Engineer District, Far East; and the General Staff, U.S. Army Engineer School.

CPT Mark Buck is a graduate of the U.S. Military Academy. He served with the 54th Engineer Battalion in Germany and the 3rd Battalion at Fort Belvoir, VA.

CPT Richard Crocker is a graduate of Penn State University. He served with the 19th Engineer Battalion in Germany, was a Facilities Engineer in Kitzigen, Germany, and served with the 30th Engineer Battalion at Fort Belvoir, VA.

CPT Jerome Rosperich is a graduate of OCS and the Combined Arms and Services Staff School. He served with the 10th Engineer Battalion in Germany and the Directorate of Training and Doctrine at Fort Belvoir, VA.

CPT Joseph Schroedel is a graduate of the U.S. Military Academy and has a master's degree in civil engineering from the University of Illinois. He served with the 20th Engineer Brigade at Fort Bragg, NC, and the 82nd Engineer Battalion in Germany.

(The authors were Team Leaders for EOAC Class 1-85, Department of Military Engineering, U.S. Army Engineer School.)

ENGINEER HOTLINE

Problems, questions, and comments relating to Engineer doctrine, training, organization, and equipment can be addressed by telephone to the U.S. Army Engineer School's "Engineer Hotline." The Hotline's auto-answer recorder operates 24 hours a day, seven days a week. You should give your name, address and telephone number, followed by a concise question or comment. You'll receive a reply within three to 15 days. **The Hotline is not a receiving agency for formal requests.**

Call commercial (703) 664-3646; WATTS 800-336-3095, extension 3646; or AV 354-3646.

Correction

The article, "Developing Our Junior Officers," by COL Samuel J. Ady incorrectly stated " . . . the 4th and 1st Engineer Battalions at Fort Riley," and " . . . the 4th and 5th Engineer Battalions at Fort Knox" (Fall 1984, page 24). This should have read " . . . the 4th Armored Battalion of the 37th Armored Regiment and the 1st Battalion of the 63rd Armor," and " . . the 4th Battalion of the 5th Infantry and the 5th Battalion of the 41st Field Artillery."

Tim Ketchum discusses productivity and efficiency with students attending the Facilities Engineering Management Course at the Engineer School (U.S. Army photo).

Preparing for Your DEH Assignment

by Tim Ketchum

Is there a DEH assignment in your future? Are you prepared to move into one of the most challenging jobs in the Army today?

You say you are. You've had the right assignments along the way. You've had the normal schooling—EOBC, EOAC, possibly graduate school. You've gotten your company command under your belt and have served at various positions in several Engineer units. All these previous assignments have developed your leadership abilities and have given you confidence in dealing with soldiers in a military environment.

But has your previous experience prepared you for the challenges of being a director of engineering and housing or an operations officer with the DEH? Chances are, if your career has followed the normal progression, the answer to that question is no.

Why aren't you ready? What's so different about the DEH business than the other assignments you have had?

To begin with, in today's monetary terms, the DEH is big business. Looking at a standard size CONUS installation, the DEH controls an average yearly budget of $45 million. This accounts for about 50 percent of the base operations money spent on that installation. The DEH work force comprises about 30 percent of base operations personnel.

Aside from the sheer magnitude of the job and the responsibilities, there are several other new problems you will encounter. One of the most frustrating of these, especially when coming from a military environment, is dealing with a predominantly civilian work force. In a typical DEH organization of 300 to 400 people, there may only be two or three people wearing the green suit.

Now you are confronted with the civil service system. Your first reaction would be to treat the organization like any military one and assume you have great flexibility in dealing with personnel matters. But soon you are bogged down in the rules and regulations on hiring and firing, rewards and discipline, promotion, merit pay, hiring freezes, grievances, and all the other factors which affect your ability as a manager to get the job done.

Associated with the challenges of a civilian work force is another organization you have not had to deal with in the past, and that is the employees' union.

When you look at how the DEH accomplishes its mission, you will find that over half the work is performed by civilian contractors. You have now moved into a new dimension of time and space, the twilight zone of procurement rules and regulations. You are challenged by trying to get the lowest bidder on a job to give you a quality product on time. You are introduced to new players in the game: contracting officer, legal counsel, and small business administration. You are able to increase your vocabulary with new terms such as *termination for default, cure notice, cost-plus award fee,* and *change order.*

Just when you thought there could be no more challenges left, you face another problem unique to the DEH—customer satisfaction.

For every project you get, every work order that comes across your desk, there is someone out there—the customer, the user—who wants that job done yesterday. You have to be a good juggler, balancing your limited resources of money and people against the unlimited requirements of your customers and the desires of your commander.

The most highly visible part of the DEH is the H . . . Housing. Under the previous facilities engineering organization, the FE was responsible for the maintenance and repair of family housing. Under the DEH organization, the management of the housing function has been added. Providing adequate housing is essential to the quality of life for the soldiers and their families.

These are just some of the challenges awaiting a new DEH. It is obvious that the more preparation you can make before assuming your new job, the faster you can take control and the less on-the-job training you will require. If one of your previous assignments was in a Corps of Engineer District, you are probably better prepared than individuals who have spent all their time in troop units.

What training is available? The U.S. Army Engineer School offers a three-week Facilities Engineering Management Course (FEMC), a DEH Executive Course, and seven different housing management courses. You should attend FEMC before starting your assignment. This course will provide you with the latest guidance in the DEH business and valuable contacts with the various functional experts. Other training available at your own installation includes supervisor courses which familiarize you with the civil service system and contracting courses which will give you the basics in government procurement.

For additional information on the DEH courses available at the USAES, call AV 354-4195, FTS 544-4195, or commercial (703) 664-4195.

Mr. Tim Ketchum is the Chief, Engineering and Housing Management Division, Department of Military Engineering, at Fort Belvoir, VA. He has worked in the Directorate of Engineering and Housing, Military District of Washington and for the Office of the Chief of Engineers, Housing Division, and the Facility Engineer Support Agency. A former Engineer officer, Mr. Ketchum has associate degrees in data processing and business management from Northern Virginia Community College, a bachelor's degree in civil engineering from Virginia Tech, and a master's degree in engineering administration from George Washington University. He is a registered professional engineer in Virginia.

Hotline Q & A

Q. My question deals with the triangular tank ditch. We have information from an Engineer pamphlet which states that the spoil is placed on the enemy side of the tank ditch. Does it go on the friendly or enemy side?

A. The spoil is placed on the enemy side of the tank ditch and not on the friendly side because of the factor of work effort required in construction. If the spoil were to be placed on the friendly side of the ditch, it would require the digging team to lift the spoil over the 1.5 meter high wall of the friendly side. In addition, the spoil reduces the traction of approaching enemy tanks and affords good soil cover for antitank mines. This information can be found in FM 5-15, *Field Fortifications;* FM 5-34, *Engineer Field Data;* and the Engineer pamphlet, *Tank Ditches,* dated May 1982.

Q. I would like to know when ARTEP 5-35, *Engineer Combat Battalion, Corps,* will be available.

A. ARTEP 5-35 was fielded February 1985. It can be ordered from the U.S. Army AG Publications Center, 2800 Eastern Boulevard, Baltimore, MD 21220.

Q. I am trying to find the NSN for the overhead foxhole covers. How can I order them?

A. The NSN is: 4200-00-444-7118. The covers can be obtained through normal supply channels.

Q. We have received the link reinforcement set for our MGB. However, we have not received any guidance as to how to employ it, nor can we find any information in any DA pamphlets about this kit.

A. TM 5-5420-212-12-1, *Link Reinforcement Set for the Medium Girder Bridge (LRS),* is available through normal channels. An additional chapter covering the LRS will be included soon in TM 5-5420-212-12, *Medium Girder Bridge.* A mobile training team from Ft. Belvoir, the office of Non-Resident Training, can also be requested for Army Reserve or National Guard units. The AUTOVON number is 354-3008, commercial (703) 664-3008.

Engineer Platoon Leader *at* NTC

by CPT David R. Frick

You graduated from EOBC three months ago in the top 20 percent of your class. You took a quick 30-day leave to *relax* and then reported to your unit ready to start work with the "Real Army."

After a hasty introduction, your new company commander briefed you on all your additional duties, told you that you would be taking over second platoon, and said that the company would be leaving for Fort Irwin, CA, to provide support to 3rd Brigade at the National Training Center.

It's now the fourth day of a 14-day rotation through the training center. Since the exercise kicked off, the task force that your platoon is supporting has conducted a night attack, a deliberate daylight attack, and is currently preparing to defend to retain a battle position. So far, your platoon has not been actively involved in any of the operations.

The S-3 has approached you several times for information he needed to write the Engineer annex to the task force operations order; but for the most part, you just attend the briefings, try to understand where your platoon fits into the order of movement, and then follow the vehicles in front of you to the objective. You are beginning to wonder when you will get a "real mission" so you can show these tread-heads what the Engineers can really do.

At 0330 you receive word to attend a warning order briefing at the task force TOC in 30 minutes. As you arrive, the S-3 is going over the general situation: The task force has received a reflex mission and will conduct a hasty attack NLT 0800. The various members of the staff go through their portions of the briefing as you settle back and mentally wonder how you're going to get all your vehicles topped off with fuel before 0800.

After the artillery finishes their portion of the briefing, you expect the S-3 to stand up and tell everyone what the Engineer mission is. Normally in an offensive operation like the one just received, the S-3 will say something about the priority of Engineer effort as being to "provide mobility support as required" and then move on to coordinating instructions.

However, this time it's different. Instead of the S-3, the task force commander gets up and explains that for the last two operations, the task force has been criticized in after-action critiques concerning its utilization of Engineers. The ADC will be observing the attack in the morning, and the task force WILL function as a cohesive and coordinated Combined Arms unit. The TF commander proceeds to outline the type and size of threat-force obstacles to be expected and then turns to you and says, "What do the Engineers say about how we should breach obstacles in a situation like this?"

You stumble to your feet as your mind races for an answer to his question. Your momentary silence provides an opportunity for others in the TOC to bring up their own questions.

"Shouldn't we be attaching a squad of you guys out to each of the company teams?"

"Who actually controls you anyway?"

"What exactly can you do that the grunts can't do?"

Engineers must coordinate with their supported maneuver units. The minefield emplaced by Engineers is being closed by the withdrawing Cavalry unit (U.S. Army photo).

Sadly enough, the situation described here has occurred more often than we as Engineers would care to admit. The reasons it occurs are many, and the solutions are neither simple nor easy to implement. The purpose of this article is to focus some attention on key areas and identify some actions that will assist the platoon leader in overcoming or at least minimizing some of the problems.

To begin, the role of the Engineer platoon leader must be clearly understood. Unlike his infantry or armor counterpart, the Engineer platoon leader has two separate roles that he must fill:

- **Platoon Leader**—That of leader, manager, and supervisor of a small unit.
- **Staff Officer**—That of Engineer advisor and "expert" on the task force staff.

Understandably, this is a tremendous responsibility for anyone with the experience and knowledge of a second lieutenant to be expected to fulfill. The task is made even more difficult because most maneuver commanders and S-3s are not proficient in planning for the use of Engineers.

The result is that many times at NTC, Engineer support is relatively ineffective. Obstacles are not placed to support the tactical plan and are easily bypassed. Obstacle breaching and fighting position construction is conducted by maneuver forces alone when the bulk of the effort should be performed by Engineers.

So, how can a lieutenant with six months time in service have any impact on task-force operations in a realistic combat environment? Several points outlined below can contribute to Engineer performance at the task-force level and are within the power of the lieutenant to implement.

Be technically and tactically proficient. Know what your platoon's capabilities are in providing mobility, countermobility, and survivability support in a Combined-Arms operation. You're not expected to be a walking field or technical manual, but you should have a firm grasp on what your platoon's mission is and what its capabilities and limitations are. You also need to be aware of how the maneuver force plans to fight.

Here again, you are not expected to be an expert tactician, but you should be able to intelligently assess the effects of Engineer effort in the overall tactical plan. Characteristics and capabilities of U.S. weapon systems should come as second nature. Becoming proficient in this area requires a lot of individual effort on your part. EOBC gave you a basis to serve in a wide variety of Engineer assignments. Once you find yourself attached to a combat unit, the responsibility falls to you to ensure that you are professionally competent.

Seek out and insist upon joint train-

ing with your supported maneuver unit. Engineers cannot expect to train in a vacuum and then function effectively when thrown together with a combat arms unit at the last minute. Get to know the commanders that you will be working for. Understand how they operate and what they expect of you. Let them know who you are and what you can and cannot do for them.

Practice drills with your supported units and within your platoon for certain actions that are expected to occur on the battlefield. For example, your platoon may want to have breaching teams established with individual roles and actions defined and equipment identified. This ensures that everyone knows what is expected and eliminates a lot of planning and preparation time when actually in the field.

Take an active part in the task force planning and briefing sessions. Don't hold back and wait to be tasked with something to do. Seek out the S-3 and offer to write or assist in writing the Engineer annex and obstacle plan for the task force operations order. You are the Engineer expert and have much to contribute to how the commander plans his operations.

Use your subordinates effectively. Your platoon sergeant has a tremendous amount of experience that is there for the asking. Use him and your squad leaders effectively and don't try to do everything yourself. While you're involved with the planning process (which will occupy a large part of your time), let the platoon sergeant run the platoon. Provide guidance and follow-up supervision as appropriate.

Develop a "leader's book." Compile a list of commonly referred to data and checklists that will assist you in the performance of your mission. You can't carry all your FMs and TMs to the field, so just include the information that you feel will be critical. The idea is to have something readily available that will jog your memory and keep you from forgetting important responsibilities.

As the senior Engineer in a battalion-size unit, you have a tremendous responsibility to fulfill. You must make the effort to become proficient in your profession as quickly as possible. Most commanders will understand your situation and will assist you as much as possible. However, there is no excuse for incompetence. Remember, what you lack in experience must be made up in motivation.

CPT David R. Frick is an instructor assigned to the Field Engineering Branch, Department of Military Engineering, at the Engineer School, Fort Belvoir, VA. He has served in Engineer troop and staff assignments in Germany and CONUS. CPT Frick has a bachelor's degree in chemistry from The Citadel and a master's degree in business administration from Boston University.

The siting and construction of fighting positions is another example of the close coordination required between Engineers and their supported maneuver units. The tactical commander knows where to position his weapon systems while the Engineer knows how to construct the positions (U.S. Army photo).

The Subject Matter Expert Program

by MAJ David T. White

The Subject Matter Expert Program, which may not be understood outside of the TRADOC command, is an effort by the TRADOC schools to improve the quality of the doctrinal manuals and other training products exported to the field. The U.S. Army Engineer School wholeheartedly supports this program.

The Subject Matter Expert Program is designed to simplify, standardize, and institutionalize the responsibilities for writing and staffing doctrinal and training publications, answering questions from the field, and accomplishing other tasks related to particular Engineer subject areas.

A Subject Matter Area (SMA) is an area or topic that is considered so important by the Engineer School that it has made a concerted effort to institutionalize the expertise. The School has identified various departments and directorates to maintain the required expertise. The training departments are responsible for the majority of the subject matter areas.

Within the three training departments, the SMAs have been assigned primarily to the instructional divisions or branches. In most cases, the SMAs are closely related to the subjects in which the branch provides instruction in one or more of the resident courses. The SMAs for the three training departments are shown in Figures 1, 2, and 3.

A Subject Matter Expert (SME) is an instructor within the branch who has responsibility for a particular SMA. The SME could be an officer, an NCO, or a civilian. The SME has been assigned by the branch chief as the point of contact or action officer for all tasks related to the SMA. The SME is expected to continually update and build on his expertise in the subject area.

This program is of tremendous benefit to the Engineer in the field. He now has an identified point of contact within the Engineer School for all the subjects that might concern him. The areas cover the spectrum of leadership, tactical, and technical subjects.

The instructors/SMEs in the branches divide their time appropriately to handle both teaching the subject and authoring doctrinal literature or training products related to the subject. The project could be an FM, ARTEP, SQT, POI, or some other training product. The number of soldiers in the training departments at the Engi-

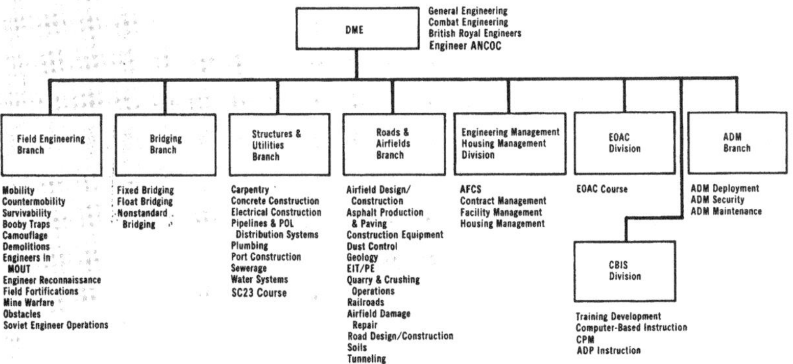

FIGURE 1. Department of Military Engineering Subject Matter Areas.

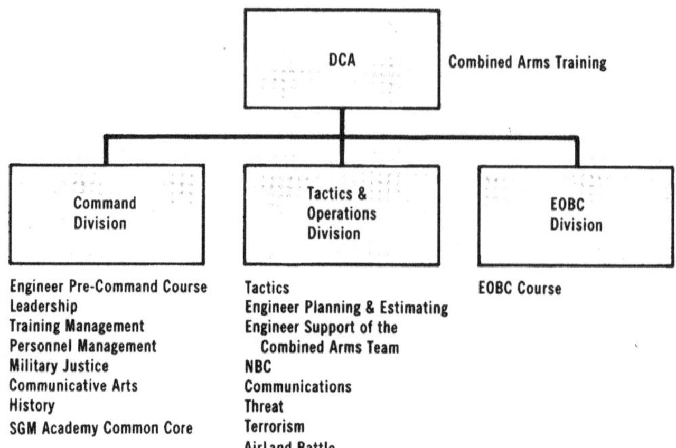

FIGURE 2. Department of Combined Arms Subject Matter Areas.

neer School that exclusively instruct has been dramatically reduced through this program.

Since all of this work is related, quality is improved in all areas. The key to the concept is the continuous interaction with the field in the classroom. The instructor/SME is constantly getting feedback from the students enroute from Engineer assignments all over the world. The feedback—plus the reference effort made by the instructor/SME—improves both the instruction at the School and the doctrine and training products the School produces.

The U.S. Army Engineer School has published Fort Belvoir Regulation 10-1 to publicize this program to the Engineer community. It details all of the Engineer SMAs and the responsible agencies. Requests for this regulation should be sent to the Directorate of Evaluation and Standardization, ATZA-ES, Fort Belvoir, VA 22060-5271 or call (702) 664-3668 (AV 354-3668).

Questions, comments, or concerns on any of the SMAs can be directed to the appropriate department.

- Department of Military Engineering responsibility can be sent directly to the department, ATTN: ATZA-TE, Fort Belvoir, VA 22060-5331 or call (703) 663-2628/3998 (AV 354-2628/3998).
- Department of Combined Arms responsibility can be sent directly to the department, ATTN: ATZA-TC, Fort Belvoir, VA 22060-5341 or call (703) 664-2907/2093 (AV 354-2907/2093).
- Department of Military Logistics responsibility can be sent directly to the department, ATTN: ATZA-TM, Fort Belvoir, VA 22060-5351 or call (703) 664-3144/3303 (AV 354-3144/3303).

MAJ David T. White is the Assistant Director, Department of Military Engineering, at the Engineer School, Fort Belvoir. He is an Armor officer who graduated from the Armor Officer Advanced Course in 1978 and the Facility/Contract Construction Management Course in 1983. He has been selected to attend the Command and General Staff College. MAJ White has served in Engineer assignments at Fort Bragg and in Armor assignments in Europe and at Fort Hood. He has a bachelor of science degree in Civil Engineering from West Virginia University.

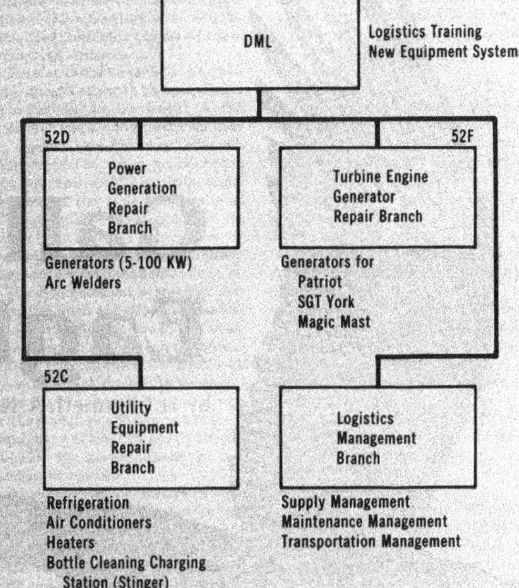

FIGURE 3. Department of Military Logistics Subject Matter Areas.

Past in Review

Starting with the Summer 1985 issue, ENGINEER will feature "Past in Review." This new department will focus on significant people and events in the Corps of Engineers throughout American history. Readers are encouraged to send manuscripts and photographs to ENGINEER. Please include author's biographical sketch, address, and telephone number. Photos and manuscripts can be returned upon request.

Gallant Eagle '84

by 1LT Kenneth A. Kennedy

Units from the 1st Infantry Division got a taste of Engineer handiwork at 0400 hours on Sept. 8, 1984. Facing them was a desert Maginot Line that stretched from one side of the Valley of Death to the other.

As Gallant Eagle '84 continued, the value of solidly constructed, well-placed obstacles became apparent. While the infantry and field artillery chalked up estimated casualties caused by "notional firepower," the Combat Engineers of the 101st Airborne Division (Air Assault) demonstrated the effectiveness of *real* combat multipliers.

Gallant Eagle '84, a joint readiness exercise sponsored by the U.S. Central Command, involved units from the XVIII Airborne Corps, the 1st Infantry Division, and elements of the Air Force. The battle was fought in several training areas throughout the Mojave Desert in southern California, each command playing off a similar OPFOR scenario.

Planning

The 101st received the Corps OPLAN on July 31, 1984, but planning had begun long before. A brigade task force with all its supporting elements was deployed from Ft Campbell, KY. The brigade's supporting Engineers were supplemented at NTC by units from the 20th Engineer Brigade to increase the amount of "heavy" equipment available for operations. For most of the exercise, the task force had the support of thirteen bulldozers, seven scoop loaders, four scrapers, and over 400 Engineers (not the normal task force complement).

The obstacle plan designed by the Brigade Engineer, CPT Roy Hightower, called for immense amounts of Class IV barrier material. The plan consisted of five linear, cross-compartment obstacle traces that ran two to three kilometers across the valley. An in-depth terrain analysis, CPX, and on-the-ground reconnaissance (TEWT) beforehand confirmed the feasibility of the plan.

Time would be a major factor. What work rates could the bulldozers maintain in desert soil? How long could man and machine operate efficiently in a very hot, dry and dusty environment? As final preparations were completed, the Brigade Engineer made a final tabulation of the necessary Class IV amounts: 4,000 rolls of concertina, 212 rolls of barbed wire, 5,000 pickets, and 10,000 simulated mines.

Transporting the barrier material

over 2,000 miles would be a problem in itself. The 2½-ton dump trucks organic to an air assault Engineer battalion would have to be loaded with Class IV material instead of the normal complement of squad tools and personal gear. If the mines had been actual training mines instead of sandbags, transportation planning would have been even more constrained. This illustrates the fact that the Engineer obstacle plan is likely to be limited by transportation of barrier material, rather than by available manpower.

Deployment

Heavy Engineer equipment was deployed by rail in mid-August from Fort Campbell to Georgia, then transported by ship 3,000 miles to California. The bulk of the task force equipment, including the Engineer tactical vehicles, was sent directly to California. The remainder of the Engineer tools and equipment was loaded into MILVANS and convoyed to the NTC. The medium-lift helicopters of the task force self-deployed, while others used MAC for support.

Finally, the troops of the task force were transported by military and civilian aircraft with the final flights arriving on September 3. Logistic support teams at key points coordinated billeting and made medical and dining arrangements for soldiers involved in the loading and unloading operations.

Obstacle Construction

The task force commander, COL Harding, gave the release to begin obstacle preparation on September 3. Four days later, five linear traces lay across the Valley of Death. Each trace consisted of concertina-filled antitank ditches (11 kilometers total length), simulated minefields, and nonstandard concertina obstacles.

The plan called for tank ditches to be dug concurrently with the installation of minefields by the troops. A D-5 bulldozer and a scoop loader working in tandem were the most efficient. Work rates of 25 meters per hour were accomplished with this combination. Because of the underlying rocks at NTC, it would be advantageous to use heavy bulldozers (D-7 or D-8) with rippers to precede the smaller bulldozer/scoop loader combination.

The Engineers cut a standard rectangular ditch and deposited the soil on the friendly side bank. The situation did not allow for much experimentation, but consideration should be given to a tank ditch with an angled enemy side (rather than perpendicular to the ditch floor). This would make it much more difficult for enemy tracked vehicles to cave-in the banks and bridge the obstacle.

Whenever possible, the traces were tied into small hill masses on the valley floor and wadiis running off the Tiefort Mountains and Furlong Ridge. Gaps left in the traces were later closed with cratering charges once all forward ground units had withdrawn to the rear. The closed gaps had to be reinforced with additional material later due to the energy-absorbing characteristic of the loose, desert soil.

Maintenance problems that did arise during construction seemed more related to extended use and vehicle age than environmental factors. However, tires did receive excessive wear traversing rocky terrain. Filters and wheel seals were replaced frequently. Hydraulic system failures were a major problem—bursting hoses were commonplace.

Because of the low density of Engineer equipment, many of the parts needed during the exercise could not be procurred through the supply system, but had to be fabricated or locally procurred. One solution to the problem involved using a Class A agent to procure repair parts commercially. This solution is particularly effective at the NTC where the nearby city of Los Angeles has many vendors of heavy equipment parts.

Once the countermobility operations had been nearly completed, several survivability positions were constructed for the task force TOW and DRAGON weapon systems. The lack of overhead-cover materials was overcome by using portable fighting shelters—preformed fiberglass shells reinforced with a covering of sandbags.

The Exercise

Although the exercise officially began on September 5, the OPFOR main attack started at 0400 hours on September 8 as a mechanized team from the 1st Infantry Division began probing the 101st sector. After several smoke-filled minutes, they withdrew east. The defenses were as formidable as the 1st Infantry Division commander had suspected. A full-scale attack the next day eventually breached all of the obstacle traces. The 101st Infantry, in conducting an Air Assault delay, slowly withdrew to the rear of the battle area.

An M-88 tank recovery vehicle tows two threat force vehicles which have been "destroyed" by friendly fire during exercises at the NTC, Fort Irwin, CA (photo by MAJ Robert Somers).

At MOPP Level 4, this soldier looks for enemy mines with a mine detector (photo by MAJ Robert Somers).

According to one Engineer platoon leader, "We sat on top of one of the hills overlooking the valley and watched the smoke pop (simulating the explosion of the mines), but the OPFOR tanks kept coming." It is reasonable to assume that any obstacle requiring 35 minutes to breach would be highly successful when covered by *real-life* direct and indirect fire.

At this point, the task force established an air assault defense in preparation for air assault deep attack against two objectives in the enemy rear. This was especially challenging because the air assault was conducted under the cover of darkness. Once the objectives were taken, friendly forces in the south linked-up with the air assault forces, concluding the exercise.

Engineers from the 20th Engineer Brigade performed several successful missions during the exercise, including an airstrip-denial mission and an airstrip-construction mission.

Endex was called at 1000 hours on September 10. Following a number of "hot washes" and after action reviews, redeployment began. Previous arrangements and prior experience made planning for the redeployment much easier.

Lessons Learned

The Engineers came back from NTC with much information about operations in the desert. Many of the points stressed by LTC John Mennig (*"Getting Up To Speed,"* ENGINEER, Fall 1983) were confirmed. Some of the comments made by the Engineer units in their after-action review include:

- The logistics burden was eased through the use of containerized deployment system drops and helicopter slingloading.
- Mines should be surface-laid in nonstandard patterns. Using simulated mines, however, does not adequately give realistic installation time or manpower requirements.
- Antitank ditches where rock is lying three feet below the surface of the ground require the use of bulldozer with rippers.
- Concertina must be solidly anchore to the ground, thereby preventin easy removal with rope and grap pling hook.
- Prefabricated position shelters ar necessary when no natural cove materials are available.
- Obstacle gaps should be turned ove to the infantry immediately. Thi frees Engineers to continue work o Engineer tasks.
- Maintenance units deploying wit the task force must be able to servic heavy Engineer equipment. Als they should have the capability t fabricate hoses and fittings fo hydraulic systems.
- Aircraft-lifting capability is greatl diminished in the desert—especiall at midday.

The principle lesson learned durin Gallant Eagle '84 was that light, ai assault infantry, when supported by a detailed and well-executed obstacle plan, can be effective against mechanized forces in a desert environment.

1LT Kenneth A. Kennedy is the liaison officer for the Assistant Division Engineer of the 101st Airborne Division (Air Assault) at Fort Campbell, KY. He is a graduate of the United States Military Academy.

Although the D-7 dozer clears obstacles and digs tank ditches, the M-9 ACE would greatly improve Enginee capability which is vital on the AirLand Battlefield (photo by MAJ Robert Somers).

Beefing Up the MGB

by 1LT Steven W. Chandler and SGT David J. Mohan

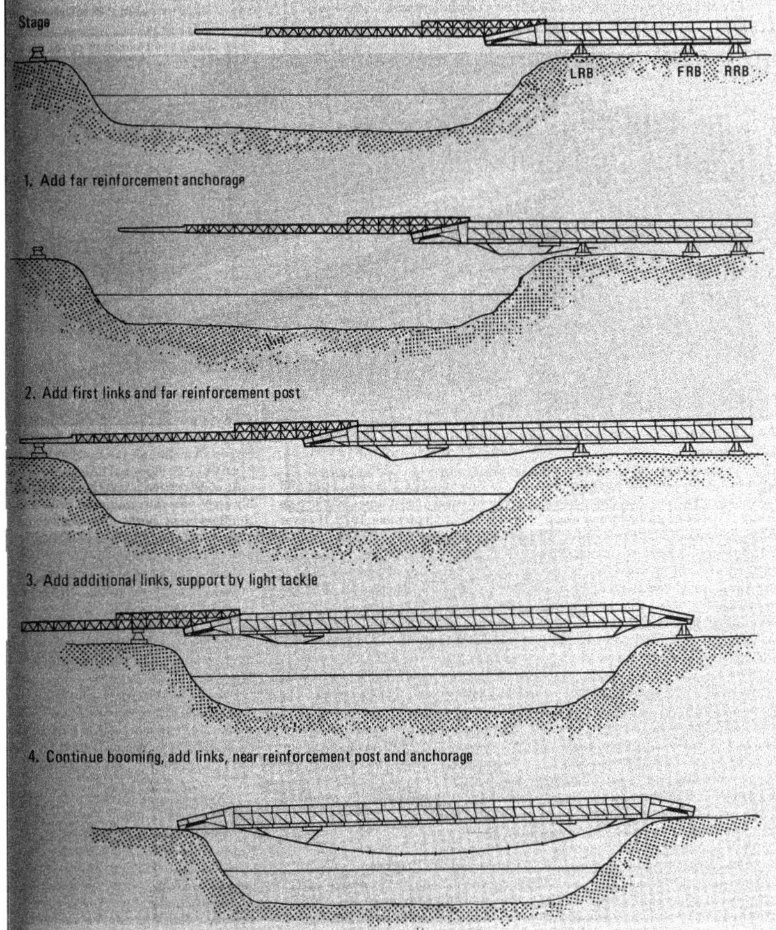

1. Add far reinforcement anchorage

2. Add first links and far reinforcement post

3. Add additional links, support by light tackle

4. Continue booming, add links, near reinforcement post and anchorage

5. Complete launch and jack down, release light tackle

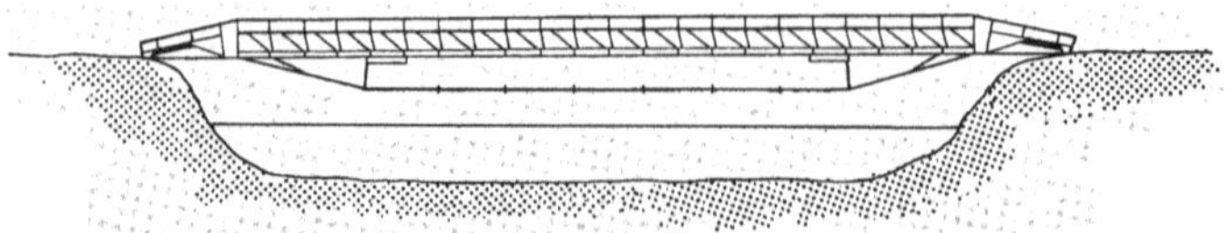

6. Reinforcement posts pulled towards vertical and pinned

Illustrations courtesy of Fairey Engineering LT

The Link Reinforcement Set provides a good shared-load distribution, unlike the Cable Reinforcment Set (U.S Army photo).

Since its introduction more than a decade ago, the Medium Girder Bridge (MGB) has gained rapid acceptance throughout NATO as a tactical fixed-bridging asset of unequalled simplicity, reliability, and speed of construction. As a complement to the proven Bailey M-2 panel bridge, the MGB rounds out our inventory of standard fixed bridges and will undoubtedly see extensive service for years to come.

Developed by Fairey Engineering of Great Britain, the MGB permits the rapid construction of Class 60 spans as long as 103 feet (31.4 meters) without the need for intermediate supports. In recent years, however, the U.S. Army and its NATO allies have produced new families of armored vehicles with military load classifications nearing Class 70 (the M-1 Abrams tank, for example). This fact, coupled with the desire to increase the maximum unsupported gap-crossing capability of the MGB, prompted efforts to provide a means of quickly and easily reinforcing the bridge.

To this end, the U.S. developed and type-classified the Cable Reinforcing Set (CRS) in September 1978. It never went into production, however, because the system proved unwieldy. The CRS was difficult to construct, and funds for procurement were not available. Additionally, the cables themselves supported a major portion of the load, thereby preventing a good shared-load distribution.

Further efforts on the CRS were dropped when Fairey Engineering developed the Link Reinforcement Set (LRS). The set alleviates the problems observed with the CRS and extends the single span Class 60 capability of the MGB to 163 feet (49.7 meters). It also provides a Class 70 capability up to 145 feet (44.2 meters).

Construction Process

As the far end of the bridge passes over the launching roller beam (LRB), the far reinforcement anchorage is pinned to the first bottom panels (Figure 1).

As construction proceeds, the assembly crew adds the remaining links and reinforcement posts and anchorage. Light tackle is used to temporarily suspend the links until tension is applied.

Upon completion of the launch, the bridge is jacked down and the tackle released. During the decking and ramping drill, the reinforcement is tensioned using Tirfor jacks attached to the reinforcement post mechanisms. The reinforcement posts are then pulled nearly vertical and pinned. The effect is a slight upward bowing of the center of the bridge, with a portion of the load being transmitted through the links.

Construction Time

Fairey Engineering contends that installation of the LRS will not appreciably increase building times of a comparable unreinforced bridge. However, practical experience shows that construction times should be increased approximately 10 percent for trained troops.

Fielding Plan

The LRS worked well during the test phase after a slight modification of the rollers. A contract was let in February 1983 for seven sets, with an additional 18 sets scheduled for procurement by FY 86.

Each MGB company will be authorized two Link Reinforcement Sets. The first seven sets have been issued to the 264th Engineer Company (MGB), at Fort Bragg, NC; 516th Engineer Company (MGB), Hanau, Germany; 38th Engineer Company (MGB), Kornwestheim, Germany; and the U.S. Army Training Center, Engineer, Fort Leonard Wood, MO.

1LT Steven W. Chandler is a fixed bridge instructor at the U.S. Army Engineer School. He was a platoon leader and company executive officer with the 902nd Engineer and HHC companies of the 11th Engineer Battalion (CBT) (HVY) at Fort Belvoir, VA. He is a graduate of EOBC and has a master's degree in systems management from the University of Southern California.

SGT David J. Mohan, reassigned to Germany, was a fixed and float bridge instuctor at the U.S. Army Engineer School. He was previously assigned to the 10th Engineer Battalion, Kitzingen, Germany, and is a graduate of PNCOC, BPTC, and ITC.

Engineer Problem

Your unit has to construct five tank turning pads that are to be 18 x 36 feet each (see illustration below). The concrete mix proportions for a one cubic yard batch are:

Cement	786 lbs or 8.4 sacks
Water	275 lbs or 33 gallons
Fine aggregate	893 lbs or 8.1 cubic feet
Coarse aggregate	1,971 lbs or 20.8 cubic feet

1. Determine the amounts of materials required for this task.
2. The fine aggregate has 4.5 percent free surface moisture. The coarse aggregate has one percent free surface moisture. Adjust the mix proportions for the moisture on the aggregates.
3. You are to mix the concrete using 16-S mixers. Adjust the mix proportions accordingly.

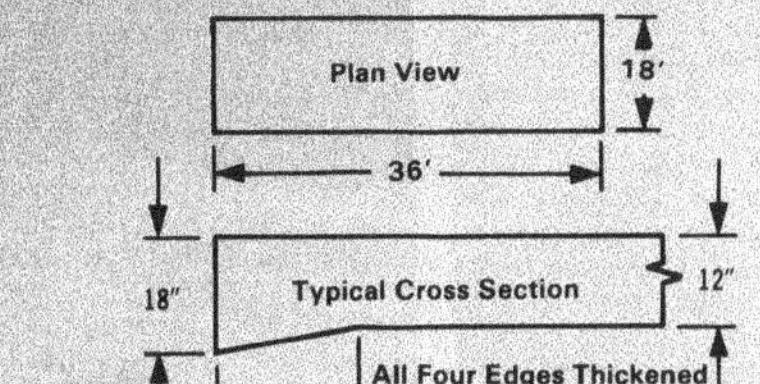

REFERENCES: FM 5-35; TM 5-742

(Problem/Solution submitted by CPT Robert J. Irby, Department of Military Engineering).

The U.S. Army and its NATO allies have produced new families of armored vehicles precipitating the need for a good bridge reinforcement system (U.S. Army photo).

Dismounted Complex Obstacle Breach Course

by CPT Kenneth A. Harshbarger

AirLand Battle doctrine has changed the priority of battle tasks and focused training on mobility operations. These operations require well-trained, coordinated and integrated Combined Arms teams. The teams are physically and mentally trained to use the element of surprise and initiative in breaching the depth of defensive obstacle systems. Time, speed, and agility are essential to synchronize combat firepower and mobility of forces through barriers.

Although bypassing an obstacle is still the desired course of action, breaching an obstacle will sometimes yield preferred results by avoiding threat kill zones and friendly force channelization.

The Dismounted Complex Obstacle Breach Course was constructed by the 2nd Engineer Battalion to train dismounted Combined Arms forces on obstacle-breaching and lane-marking operations. The course represents anticipated defensive obstacle systems that troops could encounter during dismounted breaching operations. The course consists of ten obstacles emplaced in depth, four enemy bunkers, six demolitions pits, and one safety bunker.

After an obstacle is detected, the advancing Combined Arms force is organized into four separate elements:

- The ***breaching force*** which breaches and marks a foot path through the course. This force is composed of Engineers.
- The ***assault force*** which neutralizes and destroys enemy forces in the breach area and on the objective. The assault force can include Engineers along with the infantry.
- The ***support force,*** composed of infantry, which provides over-watching fire and command and control of the operation.
- The ***Engineer deliberate breaching force*** which widens and remarks the initial breach to allow vehicle traffic.

The course is divided into six obstacle system zones. Each zone must be breached and secured before a force continues to the next zone. The course provides realistic battlefield conditions that include both smoke and opposing forces. Soldiers are required to wear an armor vest and MILES equipment.

As the breaching and assault forces breach and secure a zone, the support force maneuvers through the course providing direct and indirect fires for the breaching operation. The Engineer deliberate breaching force then follows, widening the lanes.

Concealed by smoke, the breaching force marks a lane through the minefield (photo by CPT Kenneth A. Harshbarger).

The breaching and assault forces enter the *Initial Obstacle System Zone* and breach a footpath through an enemy minefield consisting of antitank and antipersonnel mines 50 meters in depth. The breaching force must breach and mark a lane through the minefield while concealed from enemy observation and fire by darkness or a smoke screen. As the breaching force marks a lane through the obstacle, the assault force maneuvers through the zone.

The *Forward Obstacle System Zone* consists of a triple standard concertina fence and a seven-foot electric cattle fence. Still concealed by night or under a smoke screen, forces breach and mark both obstacles.

Next, the *Main Obstacle System Zone* presents a series of dragon's teeth and rock obstacles distributed 75 meters in depth. The breaching force breaches and marks a dismounted lane through the obstacles, while the support force maneuvers to provide cover. Meanwhile, at the start of the course, the deliberate breaching force begins to widen the lane for vehicles to pass through the enemy minefield.

The *Rear Obstacle System Zone* consists of a seven-foot electric cattle fence, a triple standard concertina fence, an antitank ditch, and two enemy emplacements. The support force provides direct and indirect fire to clear the enemy bunkers. Afterwards, the breaching force breaches and marks a dismounted lane through the wire entanglements and negotiates the antitank ditch which is mined and booby-trapped to prevent the assault force from using the ditch as a fighting position. At this point, the deliberate breaching force widens the forward zone for vehicle traffic.

The *Defensive Obstacle System Zone* consists of an enemy minefield 50 meters in depth and a 10-foot antitank wall with two enemy emplacements. The support force and assault force neutralize the enemy bunkers before the breaching force breaches the minefield and negotiates the antitank wall. A lane through the minefield is breached and the antitank wall negotiated to allow the assault force to continue forward.

The *Final Obstacle System Zone* consists of a triple standard concertina fence. A dismounted lane through the wire entanglements is breached and marked. Then, the breaching force, the assault force, and the support force maneuver through the lane and set up a perimeter securing the far side of the obstacle system.

At this time, the deliberate breaching force breaches one of the dragon's teeth and one rock obstacle using reinforced-concrete breaching charges. They then mark a vehicle lane through the Main Obstacle System Zone. The training exercise ends with the destruction of the dragon's teeth and rock obstacle.

Well-coordinated and integrated Combined Arms mobility operations are necessary for successful AirLand Battle operations. Success requires detailed planning and rehearsals in assembly areas before such an operation begins. The 2nd Infantry Division identified the need for a dismounted Combined Arms force obstacle-breathing and lane-marking course. It was constructed by Company C, 2nd Engineer Battalion in Korea. The Army now has a Dismounted Complex Obstacle Breach Course for soldiers and leaders to use for training.

CPT Kenneth A. Harshbarger is a graduate of the Engineer Officer Advance Course and commands Company C, 2nd Engineer Battalion, in the Republic of Korea. CPT Harshbarger has served as a platoon leader, company executive officer, and S-4 staff officer in the 326th Engineer Battalion, Fort Campbell, KY.

Note: Complex obstacle breaching doctrine for heavy divisions is outlined in FM 71-2J (Draft), **The Tank and Mechanized Infantry Battalion Task Force,** and FM 5-101, ***Mobility.*** *Light unit breaching doctrine is still under development. This article is one way a unit trains for dismounted obstacle breaching as an expedient method to meet training needs.*

The 10-foot antitank wall is no problem to the breaching force in the Defensive Obstacle System Zone (photo by CPT Kenneth A. Harshbarger).

Soldiers breach and mark triple standard concertina and an electric cattle fence in the Forward Obstacle System Zone (photo by CPT Kenneth A. Harshbarger).

Reserve Engineers

The Total Army Team is alive and well, as exemplified by the 416th Engineer Command's increasing Engineer support of the Eighth U.S. Army (EUSA) in the Republic of Korea. Through the CAPSTONE program, the 416th Engineer Command (ENCOM)—the largest Engineer organization in the force structure with over 8,000 Engineers—has acquired global responsibilities. The area of operations ranges from the Persian Gulf to Korea and the Western Pacific. If hostilities were initiated, ENCOM's commander, MG Max Baratz, would become the EUSA Engineer.

Engineer Needs

The Eighth U.S. Army and its Republic of Korea allies have a common goal, the maintenance of peace in Northeast Asia. General Robert W. Sennewald, former Commander of U.S. Forces Korea (USFK), has stated that these forces must be able to take the fight to the enemy in depth should South Korea be attacked by North Korean forces.

The small, tough EUSA force combined with other U.S. armed forces and Republic of Korea forces provides an effective deterrent to aggression with a high state of combat readiness. However, because of its economy-of-force profile, EUSA relies on the availability of other active and reserve forces should the growing North Korean military threat break into open hostilities.

The ability to swiftly reinforce EUSA with combat, service support, and logistical units is an essential part of the total deterrence. The lean EUSA force is reflected in its limited availability of Engineering support, both unit and non-unit.

In early 1983, after discussions with the USFK/EUSA Engineer on how the ENCOM's broad range of Engineering skills and depth in personnel could assist in their missions, the Third U.S. Army approved the involvement of the 416th in Korea. Discussions culminated later that year in a formal agreement to provide continuing ENCOM support for USFK/EUSA Engineer activities.

Initial efforts focused on several areas including:

- Reinforcing USFK/EUSA Engineer personnel.
- Taking the lead in the preparation of the Civil Engineering Support Planning components.
- Providing Engineering support for the USFK POL system.
- Establishing a USFK program for the continuation of peacetime maintenance support during hostilities.
- Preparing the 416th ENCOM for deployment to the Republic of Korea.
- Establishing and maintaining close communications/liaison with the USFK/EUSA.

MAJ Keith Wedge examines an igneous basalt rock outcrop during a geologic evaluation of a suspected North Korean infiltration tunnel site (U.S. Army photo).

Since that formal agreement, 416th ENCOM support has increased at a steady rate. One indicator of this growth is the number of Reserve Engineer person trips to the Republic of Korea. Starting with zero person trips in FY 82, the rate has grown to 65 person trips in FY 85.

Engineer Tasks

Although the 416th has become

PACOM, U.S. Central Command, and WESTCOM.

RS&D Planning

The 416th ENCOM has established a facility master planning team to identify and plan the RS&D sites and facilities to receive and process designated EUSA reinforcements essential to EUSA's wartime operations. ENCOM planners are identifying alternative facility sites and developing required facility lists, by type and quantity, for a variety of potential troop populations.

The RS&D master planning efforts cover a wide range of Engineering disciplines necessary for programming an installation for today's Army and tomorrow's needs. The final product of this effort will be detailed master-planning documents that will guide construction of required facilities.

Geologic Support

A team of 416th ENCOM geologists and geotechnical experts directly supports EUSA's Tunnel Neutralization Team (TNT) whose job is detecting North Korean Peoples Army efforts to tunnel beneath the Demilitarized Zone. The 416th continually works on specialized geologic evaluations of suspected infiltration sites. The analysis is aimed at characterizing each site geologically before site testing by a geophysical work crew.

These crews bore holes and insert subterranean geophones and cameras to listen and look for signs of tunnel construction. ENCOM team geologic analysis is designed to establish the required number of holes and their locations and to recommend optimal depths for geophone and camera monitoring.

In these days of economy of active forces, expanding global responsibilities, and need to maximize the combat arms deterrence, it is essential to mobilize our Total Engineer Force to defense objectives.

MAJ Kurt Carlson and SP4 Tatia Payne examine a microwave/signal facility at Camp Long, Korea (U.S. Army photo).

As the 416th ENCOM's direct support of "front line" comands grows, its title "Reserve" has increasingly become simply a payroll designation. With hundreds of professional engineers, architects, and other specialists at their disposal, the 416th ENCOM and other Reserve Engineers stand ready to make major contributions to the Total Army efforts.

MAJ Gary L. Groat is a staff officer with Headquarters, 416th Engineer Command (USAR), Chicago, IL. He was an advisor in the Construction Directorate, Military Assistance Command Vietnam (MACV) and a company commander with the 24th Engineer Battalion in Germany. As a project manager with the Washington, D.C. office of De Leuw, Cather, and Company (a part of the Ralph M. Parsons Corporation), he specializes in transportation planning. MAJ Groat has a bachelor's degree in architecture from the University of Illinois, a master's degree in science from the University of Wisconsin, a postgraduate diploma from Edinburgh University (Scotland), and graduated from the Command and General Staff College.

by MAJ Gary L. Groat

rea

History and Military Engineering Design:

An 18th Century Example

by MAJ Steven H. Myer and
MAJ Jefferson J. Irvin

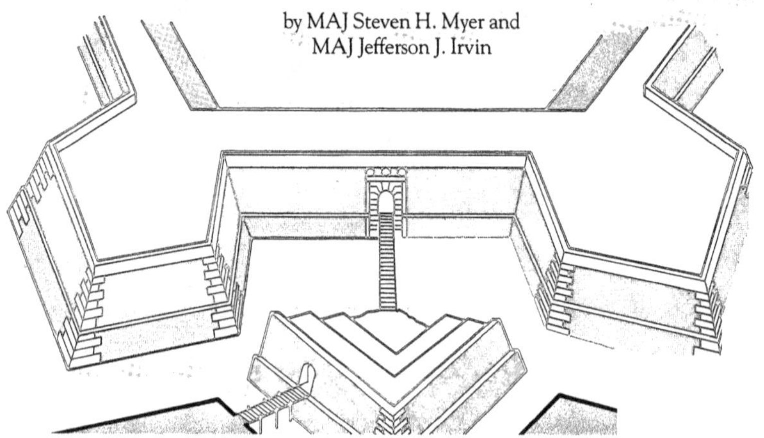

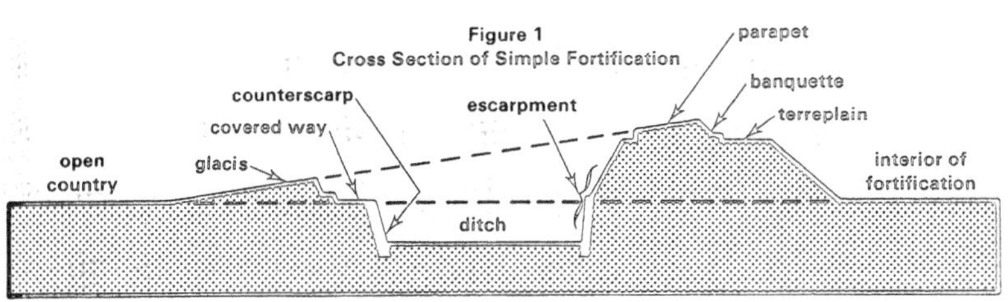

This article applies the principles of design of French 18th century fortification to modern field fortification and obstacle design, but it has the broader purpose of advocating history as a fertile source of design ideas. The first example provides a short illustration of using history to discover principles useful in design and sets the stage for the more involved 18th century example.

The Belgian fortifications near Liege did not perform well during the German onslaught of August 1914, despite having been designed by one of the 19th century's leading fortification theorists, General Brialmont. The forts, built in the late 1880s, gave inadequate protection against 1914 artillery; the concrete walls were too thin, were not reinforced with steel, and were made from a weak concrete mix. The forts were sited poorly, so that German siege artillery could bombard from positions out of sight of the defenders. Ventilation within the forts was so poor that men asphyxiated during the smoke and dust of battle.

In addition, when the German shells began dropping around the forts, the garrison was cut off from access to its food supply and latrines. Noting the latrine problem, the Belgian General Leman said: "Brialmont's military genius had an academic bent, and he forgot that his works were made for human beings. He left out of account a natural function of mankind which does not cease during bombardment: quite the reverse" (*The Architecture of War* by Keith Mallory and Arvid Ottar).

This tale of disaster taught soldiers in 1914 that fortresses required strong concrete walls, inner battlement latrines, and inner battlement storehouses. The tale provides today's soldier with more enduring principles of design. Defense must remain current with enemy technology. The human needs of the defending soldier must be met under battle conditions. A study of 18th century fortification highlights some similarly derived universal principles.

The 18th century fortification radically differs from the more familiar, earlier castle. The high towers and masonry walls of the castle became obsolete when accurate cannon were developed. The lower profile and thick, earth-filled walls of the 18th century fortress have interesting modern implications.

Attacker's Viewpoint

Assume you are an attacker attempting a frontal assault against a fortress (Figure 1). You charge across 80 yards of bare ground (the glacis) subjected to grazing fire from infantry on the covered way and artillery fire from the ramparts. If you successfully storm the covered way, the jagged fortress outline ensures that infantry and artillery on the ramparts can now hit you with enfilading fire along your attacking lines.

Your men have to either jump down 12 feet into the ditch or jam through narrow staircases, covered by defensive fire, into the ditch. The ditch is also enfiladed by fires from walls on the jagged fortress outline. At the opposite end of the ditch, you have to climb a 30-foot wall to the ramparts on 40-foot ladders you somehow transported to the ditch. The defenders have prepared covered routes for counterattack forces, which can assault you any time along the hazardous path from covered way to rampart.

Dimensioning

Let's look first at what determined the thickness of protective berms and the dimensions of the obstacles: the ditch and parapet. The thickness of the parapet was set at 18 feet because a 24-pound shot from enemy cannon penetrated 15 feet into a berm. Berm protection from direct fire and overhead protection from indirect fire must exceed in thickness the penetrability of enemy shells.

In 1700, the fortifications were designed and built by persons other than the individual soldiers manning the ramparts. This is not true today. The contemporary soldier designs and constructs his own individual position. He needs to know that the required thickness of the berm in front of the individual foxhole is equal to the length of an M-16 for the purpose of stopping the enemy equivalent of a .50 caliber shell.

Soldiers need to understand the difference in safety between compacted and loose berms and between piled rocks, loose sand, and tight clay. Foxholes must be taught as fairly complex structures designed for maximum protection and utility, not as camouflaged pits. The same type of information and emphasis must be applied to design and construction of hull-down positions for APCs and tanks.

The development of 18th century ditch and escarpment dimensions were also set by enemy breaching capability. Escarpment heights exceeded practical ladder dimensions. Ditch dimensions were set by balancing two factors: making the ditch deep enough to protect the base of the escarpment from plunging fire and making the ditch wide enough to exceed enemy expedient bridging.

Modern obstacles should also be explicitly tailored to enemy breaching capability, and recent obstacle design

instruction includes referencing critical values. For example, FM 5-102, *Countermobility*, states:

- ditches 3 meters wide exceed a tank's self-bridging ability;
- cross-country slopes of 45 percent reach the upper limits for tanks;
- vertical steps 1.5 meters high stop tanks;
- trees with diameters of 20 to 25 centimeters and spaced 3 to 5 meters apart stop tanks.

Such data are vital obstacle design aids, but may be seductively oversimplified. Simplicity was acceptable in the 18th century fortress where the terrain constituting the field of battle was largely unvarying and man-made. The fields of fire (glacis) were graded and cleared by hand. Also, the opposing weapons system did not change for two centuries. The terrain of our battlefields changes radically, and our primary adversary changes weapons systems at least each decade.

First, consider how the variability of local conditions affects design. Trees 20 to 25 centimeters wide and less than 5 meters apart will stop a tank. Logically, if you reduce the diameter and increase tree density, you might still have a viable obstacle. Similarly, if your enemy had to make a run uphill into your stand of trees, lesser diameters and spacing might be adequate. Enemy vehicle approach speed may be important.

A computer fed such data should be able to provide estimates that could be transformed into design charts and consolidated on a card like the demolitions card. The charts would force consideration of important factors that might otherwise be ignored. How many Combat Engineers would bother to place charges at a breaching distance up from the ground, if that factor did not appear in the calculations? That simple improvement in placement halves the required explosives.

Likewise, if a tank attacking at high speed can breach your obstacle by bulldozing, leaping, or shearing, that is useful information. You then have a strong incentive to precede your obstacle by something which will slow a tank down. Charts that illustrate the reinforcing action of slope, soil, and tree density will greatly aid obstacle siting, particularly for deliberate barriers in long-range planning.

Second, consider how changes in technology affect design. The prime threat to the 18th century fortress was the muzzle-loaded 24-pound cannon. The cannon was inaccurate at ranges exceeding 200 yards. The length of the glacis, the maximum exposed fortress wall length, the lengths of ditch segments, and so on were all set at less than 200 yards. These dimensions did not change in design for 200 years because for 200 years, no new cannon substantially improved on the existing 24-pound cannon.

The Russians produce a new tank every 10 years, and therefore critical obstacle dimensions must be adjusted for each new generation. The T-62, for instance, is configured so that its leading edge precedes the tread. Its step-climbing ability is limited by the slope of the forward edge of the chassis to 55 degrees. The leading edge of the T-72 is the tread, and it can climb vertical steps much easier. The T-72 is heavier and can generate more force at its leading edge and thus should be able to shear trees and bulldoze obstacles easier than the T-62.

It would be interesting to know how tank type affects data like those given in FM 5-102, which are unlabeled by tank type. The differences may or may not be significant. In any case, tagging such data to a specific generation of weapons system automatically would provide flags when the data are outdated.

Sequencing

Sequencing of obstacles was as important as dimensioning in the 18th century example. The reason the 30-foot escarpments of the 18th century fortification were difficult to assault is not that 30 feet exceeds the maximum ladder length. The attacker's problem was that a 40-foot ladder could not be transported safely across the open areas to the ditch and escarpment. In other words, the rearward obstacle (the vertical escarpment wall) was shielded from breach by the forward obstacle (the long, cleared fields of fire of the glacis). This principle has interesting implications. The sequencing of obstacles should be set to progressively inhibit the enemy's capability to breach rearward obstacles.

Imagine a tank ditch preceded and followed by minefields. The enemy's main breaching capability for minefields consists of vehicle-mounted mine rollers and plows. The enemy assaults through the lead minefield behind the rollers and plows. The lead vehicles are stopped by a properly designed ditch because their rollers and plows substantially hamper the bulldozing and rocking action needed to breach a ditch.

Following tanks are forced to fan out

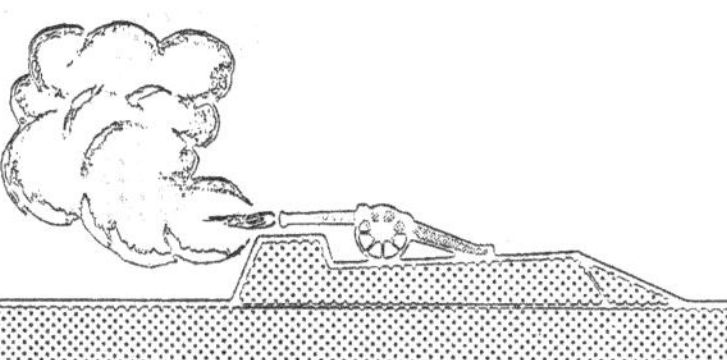

to cross the ditch. When these tanks do bulldoze their way across the ditch, the rollers and plows are no longer leading, and the assaulting force takes many more mine-induced casualties in the minefield after the ditch. Logically, the highest concentration of mines should be placed along the forward edge of the ditch, far enough back so the ditch is not partially filled or breached when the mines are exploded. This protects the ditch from breach and catches tanks forced to leave the protective trails of the rollers and plows.

Cleared fields of fire preceding the ditch serve the same purpose as the 18th century glacis. The cleared area greatly inhibits the transport of breaching equipment to the tank ditch. Priorities of fire set to eliminate AVLBs first (as was done by the Israelis on the Golan Heights in 1973) protect the integrity of the ditch as an obstacle.

The main point here is that intelligent sequencing of obstacles can create a barrier much more difficult to breach than the simple sum of the barrier components. Design hinges on thorough knowledge of enemy breaching tactics and technology and the application of this knowledge in the creative siting and sequencing of obstacles.

Masking

Finally, 18th century obstacle masking techniques can be used to postulate improvements to an obstacle. Imagine that you were standing on the leading edge of the glacis in the open country (Figure 1). You could see nothing of the ditching that protects the fortification; you could only see the gun embrasures on the main ramparts. The progressive rise of the glacis masked the location and geometry of the obstacle system: the ditches. The attacking commander was forced to perform daring, detailed reconnaissances before initiating siege maneuvers.

In this day of satellites and aerial reconnaissance, hiding a tank ditch from an enemy division commander is probably not possible. Hiding the ditch from an individual tank driver is possible. Assume the tank ditch spoil is piled on the enemy side of the ditch and graded towards the enemy, in the manner of the glacis, and made to look like surrounding land (or vice-versa). If you do not have time to seed the spoil, tear up the area ahead of the spoil.

The attacking tank column, under fire, not being able to see the far edge of the ditch, will not be able to judge where the ditch is cut. The column hits the ditch. The lead tanks cannot cross with their roller attachments; and the following tanks, having been drawn in, must run diagonally instead of straight through the high-density mine zone near the ditch. The increased length of the diagonal path increases the chance of a mine casualty. Additionally, a tank commander who cannot see a ditch is also less likely to approach at speeds necessary to bulldoze or leap the ditch.

Low berms graded towards the enemy and preceding point obstacles can be employed in the same way. The spoil from a crater, or destroyed bridge abutment, can be shaped to hide from an approaching attacker the far edge of the gap created. However, just like the glacis in 18th century fortification, the berms must be covered by commanding fires. Otherwise, the berms provide cover to the attackers.

A few important points should be reiterated. In the 18th century, the fortress was static, and the individual soldier had no design responsibilities. The king's chief military engineer derived the fortress layout and dimensioning from a coldly rational analysis of the explosive power, breaching ability, and assault tactics of the enemy forces.

Today, the same knowledge is needed to design our own field fortifications and obstacles, but now squad leaders are frequently designers. Engineer squad leaders must be experts on enemy attack formations, breaching technology, the penetrability of enemy munitions into protective shelters, and the reinforcing effects of combined obstacle structure and terrain. Forcing consideration of these additional factors in obstacle design prevents possibly disastrous over-simplification and aids creativity.

As a final note, this discussion is meant to encourage the search through history for ideas applicable to current design.

MAJ Steven H. Myer is an assistant professor of mathematics at the U.S. Military Academy and served as a platoon leader in the 127th Infantry Battalion, 25th Infantry Division in Hawaii. He was company commander, 1/504th Infantry and assistant G-3 OPS in the 82nd ABN Division at Fort Bragg, NC. MAJ Myer has a bachelor's degree from the U.S. Military Academy and a master's degree from Stanford University.

MAJ Jefferson J. Irvin is an assistant professor of geography and computer science at the U.S. Military Academy. He served as a platoon leader and company commander in the 94th Engineer Battalion in Germany. MAJ Irvin has a bachelor's degree from the U.S. Military Academy and a master's degree from Stanford University.

Fusion for the AirLand Battle

Engineer Echelons, Corps and Below

by MAJ Michael A. Lytle and 1LT Mark T. Banigan

The Army is undergoing rapid and revolutionary change in both force structure and doctrine. FM 100-5, *Operations*, August 1982, provides the authoritative statement of the U.S. Army's combat doctrine in the form of AirLand Battle.

This doctrine seeks to exploit the full potential of U.S. forces by blending two concepts—attacking the entire enemy force to its full depth and synchronizing all available combat means. To ensure unity of effort and success in combat, all three areas of engagement (deep, close-in, and rear) must be considered part of one battle.

AirLand Battle doctrine provides the foundation for the U.S. Army to examine future concepts. These ideas and notions permit the Army to move forward deliberately—developing doctrine, designing forces, and obtaining resources from which to field these forces.

Much rethinking and retooling is already evident within the Corps of Engineers, as doctrine and combat developers anticipate present needs and future fighting capabilities. Frequently in the dynamics of organizational change, as evolutionary concepts and new dimensions become accelerated, certain subcomponents are overshadowed. The realm of intelligence and electronic warfare (IEW), as a component of the Combat Engineer package, may be receiving little or no attention.

Recent opportunities for the Engineer community to comment on the merit of branch coding the Engineer battalion S-2 position, either as Engineer or Military Intelligence, were only an inkling. Larger, unanswered questions loom! That is to say, where is the clear and coherent refinement of the perceived inadequacies in Engineer-Intelligence and Electronic Warfare (E-IEW) support, doctrine, organization, operation, and procedures at echelons, corps and below (EAB)?

Intense concern for these matters at the 420th Engineer Brigade (CORPS) led to the creation of a self-directed, experimental test-bed, which over the past two years has been studying and attempting to define and remedy this doctrinal void. Engineer and IEW rela-

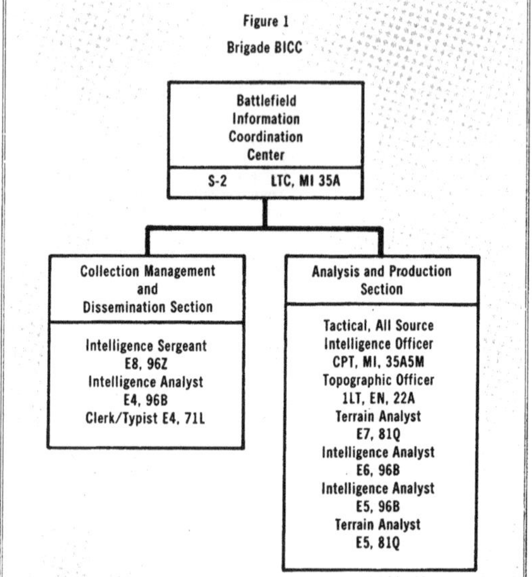

Battlefield Information Centers (BIC) at the Engineer groups, absent a brigade support element from the MI group (CEWI) as is now assigned to certain other combat, combat support, and combat service support units in the corps and to provide the S-2 with the IEW assets required.

Located at the tactical operation centers of these Engineer units and staffed by assigned MI-trained personnel of modified S-2 staff sections, these

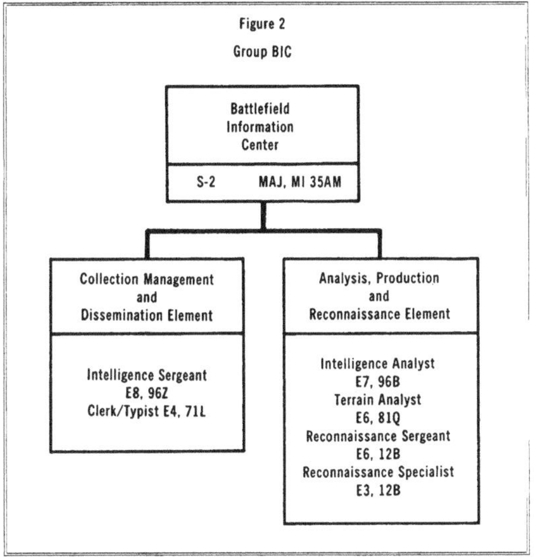

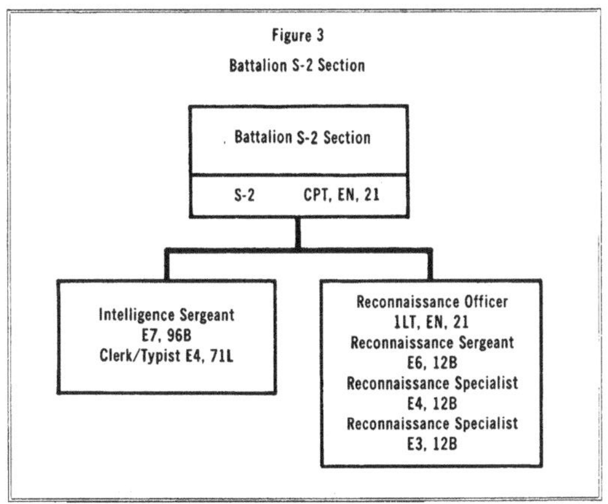

Centers would give the S-2s the capability to fully realize their role in the IEW system. In actual practice, Army-wide, BICCs and BICs provided the detailed control and coordination of intelligence collection, production, and dissemination. They have been suitably described as "management enhancers" which actually extend the capabilities of the S-2 sections, while liberating the S-2 from extensive routine and detail, to better develop and manage the overall intelligence activities.

Third, increased recognition must be given to the need for closer E-IEW linkages and information interdependency with the Corps' All-Source Analysis Center and Division TOC Support Element. The magnitude of collection, analysis, and production requirements generated from Intelligence Preparation of the Battlefield (IPB) at Engineer echelons, corps and below, for instance, is integral to such a linkage.

Finally, serious study is required to clearly define and articulate vertical and horizontal E-IEW system architecture, communications requirements, and dynamic flow at EAB for the eventual adoption of sound doctrine.

FM 34-1, *Intelligence and Electronic Warfare Operations,* August 1984, clearly illustrates the fusion process.

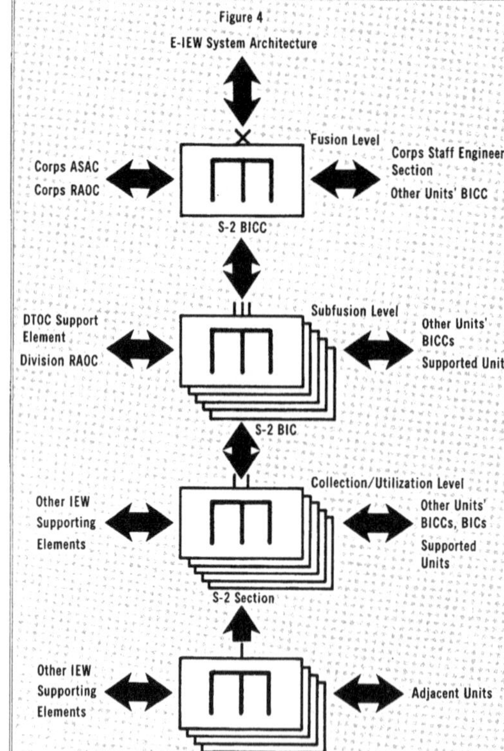

For our purposes, the most attention must be placed in IEW at the Engineer brigade level, as the greatest fusion of tactical and strategic intelligence occurs at echelons above corps (EAC) or at corps. Here, strategic intelligence received from EAC integrates with the tactical intelligence for use by the corps commander and for dissemination to other tactical levels. At the same time, tactical intelligence for use at strategic levels is integrated, formulated, and transmitted by the corps.

Engineer-derived or dependent tactical intelligence, IPB products, and other source data centrally place the Engineer brigade in the information/intelligence flow at EAB, and a major contributor as a corps major subordinate command.

The Engineer brigade's role in IEW outweighs in volume, time dimension, and area of interest that of the groups or battalions and calls for a greater density of specialist talent for its BICC. The brigade BICC and groups BICs generally vary only in size, scope, and depth of functions, with the exception of a reconnaissance-collection capability retained at the group BIC.

Their peacetime mission is IEW support, contingency planning, and training directed to the brigade or group's mission within the corps. During tension phases, these centers begin increased collection and analysis missions to satisfy the commander's Priority Intelligence Requirements (PIR). During hostilities, the centers interface with the doctrinal EAB-IEW system architecture, supporting the battle coordination—deep, close-in, rear, or in combination.

As described in FM 34-1, whether in static, tension, or hostility phases, the brigade BICC or groups BICs serve to:

- Develop and coordinate collection planning.
- Prepare and transmit tasking messages and requests for information to satisfy collection management.
- Develop and maintain various data bases for S-2 formal intelligence estimates.
- Process intelligence.
- Disseminate combat information and intelligence.
- Provide intelligence support to EW, operations security (OPSEC), and tactical cover and deception (TC&D).

As mentioned, the evolution and eventual refinement of E-IEW system architecture requires radical modification of existing S-2 staff section TOEs to create the necessary brigade BICC, group BICs, and vertical dimension to the system.

The 420th studies support the adoption of the organization schemes at Engineer brigade, group, and battalion (Figures 1, 2, 3).

Modified TOEs for Engineer units EAB are mediating factors in the development of the larger E-IEW picture. The 420th studies of corps operations, viewing the requirements for situation development, target development, the intelligence cycle, and the existing corps IEW functional resources which are linked into an interlocking organization at each level of command to provide IEW/OPSEC/TC&D support, give rise to a type E-IEW functional structure.

The 420th studies synthesized the E-IEW design which allows the Engineer unit S-2s to support their commanders; see deep; reduce battlefield uncertainty; develop targets and situations; identify vulnerabilities; provide support to command EW, OPSEC, and TC&D; and provide that Engineer units are prepared for the next battle (Figure 4).

"Hip pocket" or "shoe string" doctrinal developments in the field, at the Engineer brigade, may be incomplete and certainly contain many limitations. Diligent study and deliberate action is needed to fill the E-IEW doctrinal void in the AirLand Battle force and what lies beyond in merging fighting capabilities. Yet, the initiative and experimentation on those problems provide a prototype, a foundation for further steps by those carrying the standard for Engineer proponency.

MAJ Michael A. Lytle (MI, USAR), the Special Assistant to the Chancellor (Federal Relations), the Texas A&M University System, is a policy scientist with specializations in national and international security affairs and legislative processes. He is S-2, 420th Engineer Brigade (CORPS), Bryan, TX. MAJ Lytle has been awarded an additional specialty of Combat Engineer.

1LT Mark T. Banigan (EN, USAR), is a telecommunications marketing representative in Austin, TX, and a graduate of Texas A&M University, the Engineer Officer Basic Course, and the Motor Officer Course. He is with the S-3 Plans Section, 420th Engineer Brigade (CORPS).

Engineer Solution

1. Materials required:

a. Determine project volume for one turning pad.

V = (18')(36')(1') + ½(3')(.5')(96') = 720 cubic feet
= 26.7 cubic yards

b. Add waste factor: WF = 10 percent for projects requiring 200 cubic yards or less of concrete.

Adj. V = (26.7)(1.1) - 29.3 cubic yards

c. Materials required:

Cement: (786 lb/cy)(29.3 cy) = 23,030 lbs or 245 sacks

Fine aggregate: (893 lb/cy)(29.3 cy) = 26,165 lbs or 13 tons

Coarse aggregate: (1,971 lb/cy)(29.3 cy) = 57,750 lbs or 29 tons

Water is used for mixing, cleaning, and preparing forms. As a rule, 8 gallons per sack of cement will provide adequate water for these operations.

2. Mix proportion adjustments for free surface moisture.

a. Determine the weight of water on the aggregates.

Fine aggregate: (893 lbs)(0.045) = 40 lbs

Coarse aggregate: (1,971 lbs)(0.01) = 19.7 lbs

Total weight: 40 lbs + 19.7 lbs = 59.7 lbs

b. Reduce the mixing water.

275 lbs - 59.7 lb = 215.3 lbs/cy of concrete or 25.8 gallons

c. Adjust aggregate quantities.

Fine aggregate: 893 lbs + 40 lbs = 933 lbs/cy of concrete

Coarse aggregate: 1,971 lbs + 19.7 lbs = 1,990.7 lbs/cy of concrete

d. Adjusted mix proportions (for one cy of concrete):

Cement: 786 lbs or 8.4 sacks

Water: 215.3 lbs or 25.8 gallons

Fine aggregate: 933 lbs

Coarse aggregate: 1,991 lbs

3. Adjust the cubic yard mix proportions for a 16-S mixer (batch capacity = 16 cf).

Cement: $\frac{16}{27} \times 8.4 = 5$ **sacks or 468 lbs**

Water: $\frac{16}{27} \times 275 = 163$ **lbs or 19.6 gallons**

Fine aggregate: $\frac{16}{27} \times 993 = 588$ **lbs**

Coarse aggregate: $\frac{16}{27} \times 1,991 = 1,180$ **lbs**

NOTE: If reduced cement quantity was not a whole number of sacks, reduce the amount to the next whole sack and adjust the other components accordingly.

Career Notes

Commissioned Officers' Branch

Post-Advanced Course Assignments:

A recent policy change in post-advanced course assignments will mean that officers attending advanced courses in 1985 will know not only where they are going, but what their next job will be. The change, announced by Army personnel planners, will make this information available during the 10th week of the course the officer is attending. Currently, officers learn of their projected assignment locations before arriving at school.

The new policy will also identify their duty positions or types of unit to which they will be assigned halfway through the course, officials of the Military Personnel Center's Officer Distribution Management and Mobilization Branch said.

"Revision of the Officer Advanced Courses means we have to identify an officer's next projected assignment for training purposes," said Diana Lueker, program manager for the Officer Advanced Course Advanced Assignment Program.

When the schools such as the new EOAC begin to add branch-specific modules to the advanced courses, some officers will stay in school longer than others. The newly revised officer advanced course is 20 weeks long. Also, there will be from one to six weeks of intensive, job-specific, follow-on training available after EOAC," she said.

About six weeks before the advanced course begins, officers will be asked to tell the Army where they would like to be assigned after training. Approximately two months before courses begin, assignment managers will write to officers concerning their tentative assignments.

"Branch assignment managers who visit within the first two weeks of each advanced course will talk with the officers and make changes, if any, to the original assignment," Ms. Lueker said.

Shortly thereafter, requests for orders will be sent to gaining commands. These will decide which type of unit or duty position each officer will be assigned. The schools will then decide what follow-on training is needed for the officers to do their jobs.

Details of the new policy are listed in a November message sent to major commands. Officers should visit their local military personnel officers for more information or contact CPT Dwight Durham at MILPERCEN, ATTN: DAPC-OPF-E, 200 Stoval St., Alexandria, VA 22332-0400. The telephone numbers are AV 221-7504/7505/7506, commercial (202) 325-7504/7505/7506. Officers may also contact CPT Thomas Milo at AV 354-2184/1048 or commercial (703) 664-2184/1048 before arriving at Ft. Belvoir.

Corrected Number:

The correct number for officers to call to get a copy of the new pocket guide for officer record briefs is AV 221-8140. The pocket guide was issued January 11.

NCO & Enlisted Soldiers' Branch

Article 15 Transfers:

The chance for some NCOs to have an Article 15 moved from their performance fiche to their restricted fiche of their Official Military Personnel File (OMPF) will expire Oct. 31, 1985.

Non-commissioned officers who were in grade E-6 or above on Nov. 1, 1982, must make their request to the Department of Army Suitability Evaluation Board (DASEB) before Oct. 31, 1985. After October 31, NCOs can only petition the Army Board for the Correction of Military Records (ABCMR).

Robert R. O'Connor, Chief, Personnel Actions Branch, United States Army Enlisted Records and Evaluation Center, Ft. Benjamin Harrison, IN, said, "Considering the publicity given this administrative mechanism to help the soldier improve his or her record before review by DA Promotion Selections Boards, the argument that the applicant was not aware of the opportunity to make an earlier request of the DASEB may be difficult to 'sell' to the ABCMR."

If a request is denied, a copy of the letter is entered on the performance fiche to show the selection board that the NCO has made some attempt to improve his record. The procedures for petitioning the DASEB and its address are contained in paragraph 3-43, AR 27-10, *Military Justice*.

O'Connor said the letter, in military format, should be directed to the DASEB from the NCO. The letter does not have to go through channels. "Preferable, the letter should be accompanied by letters of support from the NCO's commander or supervisor and any other signed documents attesting to outstanding performance and professional development," O'Connor added. The letter should state why the soldier feels the intent of the non-judicial punishment has been served and why it is in the Army's best interest to transfer the Article 15.

The board normally returns petitions without action unless at least one year has passed and one non-academic evaluation has been received since the Article 15.

Toll-Free Number:

The toll-free number established last year to aid enlisted soldiers in contacting the Information and Assistance office located in the Enlisted Personnel Management Directorate at MILPERCEN has changed. Soldiers seeking personnel assistance should now call 1-800-255-ARMY.

SFC Dana L. Seegel designed and submitted last issue's Engineer Problem/Solution. Although the problem was mathematically correct, readers should remember that mine warfare doctrine allows only five total mines in the IOE with one antitank mine. The problem was intended as a practice exercise only.

A Personal Viewpoin

by MAJ Charles Kersha

"Whenever one surveys the forces of the battlefield," wrote S.L.A. Marshall in his masterpiece, *Men Against Fire*, "it is to see that fear is general among men, but to observe further that men are commonly loath that their fear will be expressed in specific acts which their comrades will recognize as cowardice. The majority are unwilling to take extraordinary risks and do not aspire to a hero's role, but they are equally unwilling that they should be considered the least worthy among those present."

It is, therefore, in Marshall's view, "vital that an army should foster the closest acquaintance among its soldiers, that it should seek to create groups of friends, centered if possible on someone identified as a 'natural' fighter, since it is their 'mutual acquaintanceship' which will ensure no one flinches or shirks. When a soldier is known to men who are around him, he has reason to fear losing the one thing he is likely to value more highly than life—his reputation as a man among other men."

Cohesion among soldiers has long been recognized as one of the most potent forces of the battlefield. Soldiers do not fight for the flag, their country, and the mission; soldiers fight for those they trust. Even after a combat-weary soldier has suffered the loss of comrades and leaders; is worn by fear and fatigue; has been subjected to bombs, bullets, and artillery; is out of ammunition, food, and water; and has survived all other fearful things associated with combat; the element that sustains his will to fight is cohesion. His motivation lies in the belief that no matter how bad the situation gets, his buddies in the foxholes on his left and right will not cut and run, but will sacrifice their lives to protect his flank.

Cohesion in military units exists on several planes. Soldiers bond vertically to their leaders and laterally to their comrades. They also develop unit loyalties. However, the cohesion that sustains units in combat develops at the lowest echelons of the unit, at the squad and fire team level.

All levels of cohesion are important. Each acts as a contributing vector that enhances mission accomplishment. But none is more important or as powerful as that developed in the foxhole.

"In the course of the airborne landings in Normandy during World War II," reported Marshall, "some units landed together while others were widely scattered. As the soldiers assembled on the ground, two types of groups emerged. One type was composed generally of soldiers known to each other, and the other type was composed generally of soldiers unknown to each other. Almost without exception, the soldiers in groups formed primarily of those unknown to each other contributed nothing to the success of the airborne invasion. This was despite their being from elite airborne units and despite their depending upon group effort for personal survival."

Just being members of the same unit, even one having an elite status and esteemed heritage, is not enough. Shared rigorous or dangerous experience fosters the development of group cohesion. And by groups, we mean face-to-face association that only rarely transcends the fire team or squad unit. And, within limits, the more dangerous the experience, the more rapidly cohesion develops.

Otto Skorzeny, Hitler's chief commando, recognized the importance of shared experience to small group cohesion and to mission when he stated, "If you need men for a dangerous mission, ask for volunteers. From these select the best. Train them in fellowship and fortitude and they will follow you into any danger, even to certain death."

Sharing dangerous activities is s ficient to make a soldier feel that is part of a group, but it is r necessarily sufficient for the rest of t group to feel the same way toward hi For the latter to happen, the soldi must also share in the mundane acti ities of the group as well as th dangerous ones. A wise leade therefore, ensures that personnel combat units change as little as poss ble, so that comrades in peacetim maneuvers shall be comrades in wa

In 1800, Sir John Moore wrote i *Regulations for the Rifle Corps*, "Havin formed his company he (the captai will then arrange comrades. Every co poral, private, and bugler will select comrade of the rank differing from h own, i.e. front rank and rear rank, an is never to change him without the pe mission of the captain. Comrades ar always to have the same berth i quarters and, that they may be as littl separated as possible in either ba racks or the field, will join the same fil on parade, and go on the same dutie with arms."

As MG Norman D. Cota, commande of the 28th Infantry Division durin World War II, observed, "Soldiers hav a right to go into battle as members c a trained unit flanked by friends an associates and if possible led by leader who have trained with them and whon they have come to trust." Smart leader understand the significance of thi thought to unit performance and trai their units accordingly.

MAJ Charles Kershaw, an Infantr officer, is stationed with the 193r Infantry Brigade in Panama. He was a instructor in the Command and Leade ship Branch, Department of Combine Arms, at the Engineer School.

ITED STATES ARMY
GINEER CENTER
D FORT BELVOIR, VA

COMMANDER/COMMANDANT
MG Richard S. Kem

ASSISTANT COMMANDANT
COL Ralph T. Rundle

CHIEF OF STAFF/DEPUTY INSTALLATION COMMANDER
COL Peter D. Stearns

COMMAND SERGEANT MAJOR
CSM Charles T. Tucker

DIRECTOR OF TRAINING AND DOCTRINE
COL Don W. Barber

CHIEF OF PUBLICATIONS
Stanley Georges

EDITOR
Marilyn Fleming

MANAGING EDITOR
1LT Louis J. Leto

DESIGN DIRECTOR
Thomas Davis

EDITORIAL ASSISTANT
SP4 Jean Tate

Special thanks to LTC John B. Cunningham Jr., Bruce Barclay, CPT Joseph Miano, and the Department of Military Logistics.

n the Cover

PFC Anthony Q. Miller, C. Company, 11th Engineer Battalion, checks the radiator of his 5-ton dump truck during command motor stables (photo by 1LT L. J. Leto).

FEATURES

DEPARTMENTS

GINEER (ISSN 0046-1989) is an authorized publication of the U.S. Army Engineer Center and Fort Belvoir, VA. Unless specifically stated, material appear- herein does not necessarily reflect official policy, thinking nor endorsement by any agency of the U.S. Army. The words he, him, or his are used to represent sonnel of either sex. All photographs contained herein are official U.S. Army photographs unless otherwise credited. The use of funds for printing this lication was approved by Headquarters, Department of the Army, on July 22, 1981. Material herein may be reprinted if credit is given to ENGINEER to the author. ENGINEER's objectives are to provide a forum for the exchange of ideas, to inform and motivate, and to promote the professional develop- nt of all members of the Army engineer community. Direct correspondence with ENGINEER is authorized and encouraged. Inquiries, letters to the editor, mentaries, manuscripts, photographs and general correspondence should be sent to: ENGINEER Magazine, ATZA-TD-P Stop 291D, Fort Belvoir, VA 60-5291. Phone: (703) 664-3082, AV 354. ENGINEER may be forwarded to personnel in military units. Address changes should be sent to ENGINEER. scriptions to ENGINEER are available through the Superintendent of Documents, U.S. Government Printing Office, Washington, D.C. 20402. A check noney order payable to Superintendent of Documents, must accompany all subscription requests. Rates are $11.00 for domestic (including APO and FPO) resses and $13.75 for foreign addresses. Individual copies are available at $3.00 per copy for domestic addresses and $3.75 for foreign addresses. Second ss postage paid at Fort Belvoir, VA, and additional mailing offices. POSTMASTER: send address changes to ENGINEER, ATZA-TD-P, Stop 291D, Fort voir, VA 22060-5291.

PV2 Krzysztof Lopata, a Polish defector, now enjoys being a bridge specialist with the 5th Engineer Bn. at Ft. Leonard Wood, MO (photo by Steve Gaynor).

Polish Defector Joins Ranks

A 22-year-old Polish defector who escaped from his homeland and waited nine months in an Austrian refugee camp to come to the U.S. is stationed at Ft. Leonard Wood as a Combat Engineer.

PV2 Krzysztof Lopata, assigned to D Co., 5th Engineer Bn., grew up in Bielawa, a town of 40,000 residents in southwestern Poland.

He developed anti-Soviet feelings as a high school student. "For 15 years, I believed what the communists told me about America was true," Lopata said. "Every time I read a book about the U.S., I got a feeling they were lying about America."

In 1980 when Poland was suffering a severe food shortage, Lopata and many of his countrymen grew tired of Soviet propaganda which kept promising things would get better for the Polish people, while the communists continued to take 70 percent of the national product from Poland, according to Lopata.

"That was the reason we didn't have anything. We got what was left after they took it from us. They didn't provide for us first," said Lopata bitterly.

He joined the country's politically active labor union, Solidarity, at age 18. Lopata worked for the underground putting anti-Soviet posters on walls. He was also involved in strikes and demonstrations to free political prisoners.

Once while walking home from a party with a friend, Lopata was arrested by Polish police. He was charged with fighting with civilians and told he would spend a few months in jail until a court date was set for him.

Lopata spent about six months in jail, "the worst time of my life," he commented. "I was given minimal food—just enough to survive." He was allowed out of his cell only a half hour a day for exercise. He and other prisoners discussed defecting to other countries.

Lopata was finally released after his parents paid money to authorities. But he lost his job and was not allowed to attend school because he was con-

Engineers Awarded

SSG James A. Kochara, B Co., 249th Engineer Bn. (CBT)(HVY), was the winner of the 1984 Sturgis Award. Serving as a squad leader, SSG Kochara was cited for leadership and technical competence during the 1984 Grafenwoeher Range Upgrade Program.

The 1984 Itschner Award for active Engineer units was awarded to B Co., 249th Engineer Bn. (CBT)(HVY). The unit was especially recognized for its efforts in GRAF '84 providing quality construction, significant cost savings, and training for its soldiers.

The 141st Engineer Co., NDARNG, and the 409th Engineer Co., WAUSAR, earned the 1984 Itschner Award for national guard and reserve units. Both units were recognized for their outstanding unit readiness, training, and work in community projects.

These awards are given annually to those individuals and units contributing most to the Corps of Engineers.

Other nominees for the awards were as follows:

Sturgis Award

EUSA
SFC Thomas E. Logan
C Co., 44th Engineer Bn.

TRADOC
SFC Paul C. Ondesko
HHC, 2nd Engineer Bn.

WESTCOM
SSG Franklin O. Reffitt
B Co., 65th Engineer Bn.

FORSCOM
SFC Roger D. Grant
36th Engineer Group

Itschner Award

EUSA
B Co., 802nd Engineer Bn.

TRADOC
C Co., 4th Engineer Bn.

WESTCOM
C Co., 65th Engineer Bn.

FORSCOM
B Co., 326th Engineer Bn.

SSG James A. Kochara (above) discusses work requirements with a fellow platoon member during the GRAF '84 construction project.

Below, soldiers of B Co., 249th Engineer Bn., place concrete. The job site was always busy when concrete was delivered; cylinder tests were completed and flexural beams were tested to ensure a quality product was constructed (U.S. Army photos).

Past in Review

Amphibian Engineers in World War II

by Dr. William C. Baldwin, Historical Division, O.C.E.

Loaded with combat troops, landing craft of the 542nd Engineer Boat and Shore Regiment head for Red Beach, Tanahmerah Bay, New Guinea, on April 22, 1944 (U.S. Army photo).

In 1944, GEN Douglas MacArthur described the war in the Southwest Pacific as "an Engineer's war" because of the Engineer contributions to the success of air and amphibious operations. The role that Engineers played in supporting the air war against Japan is relatively well known, but the contribution of Army amphibian Engineers is less familiar.

From the beginning of World War II, the United States knew that it would have to conduct many landing operations against Germany and Japan. To support these missions, the Corps of Engineers created the Engineer Amphibian Command (EAC) at Camp Edwards, MA. The EAC trained and equipped six Engineer Amphibian Brigades, which were later renamed Engineer Special Brigades. The 1st Special Brigade participated in the Allied landings on the North African coast and later supported the amphibious operations in Sicily and southern Italy. In June 1944, the 1st, 5th, and 6th Engineer Special Brigades operated Omaha and Utah beaches during the Normandy Invasion.

In Europe the special brigades were primarily shore Engineers, but in MacArthur's Southwest Pacific Area (SWPA), the 2nd, 3rd, and 4th Special Brigades were both boat and shore units. Each special brigade in SWPA had three Boat and Shore Regiments which landed men, equipment, and supplies, and also transported them in a fleet of small Engineer-operated landing craft.

During 1942 and 1943, MacArthur's forces moved along northern coast of New Guinea in a series of hard-fought overland and shore-to-shore amphibious assaults. In October 1943, the 2nd Engineer Special Brigade landed Australian troops near the strategically important village of Finschhafen. A detachment of the brigade's 532nd Boat and Shore Regiment remained on the beach to help the Australians defend it from seaborne counterattack.

As dawn approached on October 17, the defenders heard the faint sound of boats gliding toward the beach. PVT Nathan Van Noy Jr. and CPL Stephen Popa rushed to their .50-caliber machine gun position just a few yards from the water line.

Slowly, the silhouettes of Japanese landing barges came into view. The Australians and American Engineers farther up the beach opened fire, but Van Noy, the gunner, waited until the barges dropped their ramps. As the Japanese stormed onto the beach, Van Noy opened fire, killing many of the invaders. A hail of Japanese grenades shattered Van Noy's leg and wounded Popa. In spite of their wounds, the two Engineers continued to fire.

After the Allied troops had repulsed the Japanese raid, they found Van Noy dead, his finger still on the trigger of his empty machine gun, and Popa severely wounded. Popa received a Silver Star and Van Noy became the first Engineer enlisted man in World War II to receive the Medal of Honor.

The Engineer Special Brigades participated in many of the remaining campaigns in the Pacific, including Leyte, Luzon, and Okinawa. In both Europe and the Pacific, these specially trained and equipped Engineer units made an important contribution to the success of American amphibious operations.

Suggestions for further reading:

BG William F. Heavey, *Down Ramp! The Story of Army Amphibian Engineers*

HQ Army Forces, Pacific, Office of the Chief Engineer, *Engineers of the Southwest Pacific 1941-1945,*Volume IV: *Amphibian Engineer Operations*

"Past in Review" is ENGINEER's new historical department regularly sponsored by the Historical Division, O.C.E.

Idaho National Guard...Par for the Course

Members of the maintenance and heavy equipment sections, 129th Engineer Co., Idaho Army National Guard, are assisting with the construction of the Nampa Public Golf Course.

"The National Guard agreed to assist with the project after voters there rejected a bond election to finance the project. It's an all-volunteer, community effort," said Mr. Mike King, assistant city engineer. "We couldn't do this without the help of the National Guard. It would take 10 years to move all the earth the Engineers are moving in the eight days they are working here."

"With our two front-end loaders, two 5-ton dump trucks, a caterpillar, and a road grader, we are moving 10,000 cubic yards of dirt to make way for roads, sand traps and small lakes," said SSG Michael A. Dela Garza, project NCOIC.

Using front-end loaders and 5-ton dump trucks, Engineers from the Idaho Army National Guard incorporate military skills into the excavation work for a community golf course project (photo by SSG Lucia M. Lammers).

According to King, several local business are donating their specialty items to complete the project. "A gas station is donating diesel for the National Guard equipment; and there's everything from trees and grass seed to well drilling and free architectural plans for the club house to local farmers contributing their time and equipment," said King. "The Army National Guard will have contributed over 1,250 man-hours to the $1.2 million project once it is completed."

The construction platoon of the 129th Engineer Co. may become involved with the construction of footbridges and detail work of the lakes and ponds, according to King.

New Engineer Units in the National Guard

A new company-sized unit is being activated into the Minnesota Army National Guard. The new C Company of the 142nd Engineer Bn. (CBT)(HVY) will be based at Camp Ripley, MN. It will be capable of performing general engineering tasks such as construction and maintenance of heavy equipment, pipeline systems, roads, utilities, structures, airfields, and bridging. Its wartime mission is to support an Army corps or division engaged in combat.

The headquarters of the 142nd Engineer Bn. is being established in Fargo, ND, as part of the North Dakota Army National Guard (NODAK). The NODAK Guard is also activating A Company at Grand Forks and B Company at Wahpeton. D Company will be part of the Michigan National Guard in Augusta. These units are being activated as a result of the deactivation of an Engineer Battalion in Ft. Drum, NY.

Engineer School to Move

The Secretary of the Army has approved plans to move the U.S. Army Engineer School from Ft. Belvoir to Ft. Leonard Wood in 1989.

Relocating the School, along with the 902nd Engineer Co. (AFB), should save the Army more than $23 million annually, Army officials said. This effort will consolidate and standardize the training of Engineers and reduce equipment and manpower duplication now existing because of the separate locations. The move will also improve training by lifting the restrictions caused by the Ft. Belvoir urban area. New facilities will be constructed , and existing facilities will be converted to accommodate expanded training requirements for Engineers.

For further information, contact LTC James P. King, director of the Engineer Center Transition Office at Ft. Leonard Wood (AV 581-2272). COL Don W. Barber, DOTD, is the point of contact at Ft. Belvoir (AV 354-2188).

by MG Richard S. Kem, Commandant, U.S. Army Engineer School

Maintenance and Peer Leadership

The military audience must receive the maintenance message.

Peer leadership in maintenance management is an often overlooked resource that can bring significant results.

Maintenance is a very great nail that anchors everything we strive to accomplish.

Maintenance is a simple process involving equally simple functions, yet we seem to have inordinate difficulty accomplishing it. And when "The General" talks about maintenance, we don't always hear what he is saying. But when our peers speak . . . we listen.

Can you remember the commencement speech given at the graduation from your last military course? Probably not. The advice of someone with many years of experience is often ignored because it often sounds like a "war-story" from an old soldier who has lost touch with today's Army. No wonder the Chief of Engineer Branch advises all EOBC students to "plan on getting dirty, greasy, and muddy" with their soldiers during their early assignments.

At times, I feel my credibility is questioned when talking to company commanders about maintenance. They say, "Yes, Sir," but they are suspicious because it has been many years since I was in charge of a unit motor pool. My credibility, however, improves when I talk to pre-command course colonels who are about to become brigade commanders.

Peer leadership in maintenance mangement is an often overlooked resource that can bring significant results. If you have not faced the situation before, the chances are that one of your peers has. Instead of sending the battalion maintenance officer or battalion XO to "fix" Company X's problems, have the company commander spend time discussing his problems with the commander of Company Y who is doing well with his maintenance. Done with patience, this can have an amazing effect.

The contents of this issue stress other ways o achieving success. In his article, *"Maintenance Management,"* LTC Strom emphasizes the importance o defining roles and coordinating functions.

Capitalize on recent experience when placing people in staff positions. A former company commander can put his experience to good use as a BMO. Although a former company commander can be useful in many staff positions, the BMO is the position most in need of his skills.

The same situation exists in a formal training environment. A seasoned captain who has commanded a company lends great credibility to both basic and advanced officer classes. Such an officer is a tremendous resource for his peers, and everyone can make good use of his experience in maintenance. The important thing is that he communicates his ideas and that his peers forget their pride and listen to him.

Other articles in this issue discuss formal training in maintenance. One article shows how Engineers in the 52F MOS receive the technical training to repair gas turbine engine driven equipment. Another identifies the problem of providing training for the utilities equipment repairer, then offers two solutions.

Remember the poem that blames the fall of Britain on a nail? Maintenance is a very great nail that anchors everything we strive to accomplish. The military audience must receive the maintenance message, and this audience will be more receptive when that message comes from a peer whose recent experience validates what he is saying.

y CSM Charles T. Tucker, U.S. Army Engineer Center & School

NCOs Face a Dual Role in Maintenance

Good maintenance does not just happen. It requires rior planning and strong leadership. In fact, leaderhip is more important in maintenance than any other rea supervised by NCOs.

NCOs face a dual role in today's Army—that of eacher and supervisor. This means they must be xperts with their equipment and know everything bout it. That is, what its purpose is, how to use it, nd what the maintenance standards are.

In addition, NCOs must teach their soldiers how to naintain their equipment and ensure that the equipnent is, in fact, being maintained. They must ensure hat these repairs and other services are within the apability of their men and that these factors are nade known to second and third echelons.

NCOs must spend considerable time in mainteiance-related functions and feel comfortable in this irea. They must understand the system and expect heir subordinates to know and understand how the ystem applies to particular skill levels or job responibilities. Some of the particular areas that the NCO hould stress are outlined as follows:

Record Keeping: Good record keeping is a must. The key to a successful maintenance program is accuate records properly using the Army's Maintenance Management System (TAMMS).

PLL (Prescribed Load List): Spend money to supoort your maintenance program. You cannot afford to und slow-moving items. Maintenance NCOs must eview the PLL to ensure that the repair parts are ommand-supported and that excess is not being naintained at any time.

Use of Publications: NCOs must ensure their 12 eries are current. Maintaining our equipment is very omplex in some cases. Personnel cannot be expected o remember the step-by-step process for accomplishng maintenance functions. NCOs must ensure that he proper manuals are available and their personiel use them correctly to guide them through these steps.

Scheduled Maintenance Periods: This means NCOs must be present and guide their subordinates hrough the proper maintenance steps.

Scheduled Maintenance Services: This means accomplishing scheduled maintenance services as outlined in the appropriate TMs.

Oil Analysis Program: This program is probably one of the most cost-effective programs we have in the Army. NCOs must ensure that their program is workable and responsive.

Equipment Calibration Program: NCOs should establish a system that provides a means of ensuring that equipment is being calibrated on a scheduled basis.

Installation of Repair Parts: Repair parts should be safeguarded and installed immediately upon receipt.

Obtaining and Using Maintenance Personnel: There is a shortage of assigned Engineer maintenance personnel (62B). The NCO support chain must be aware of this shortage and follow up on the status of obtaining replacement personnel in a timely manner. In today's environment where personnel shortages exist, NCOs are prone to borrow from the motor pool to meet their personnel requirements. NCOs should make sure mechanics are doing mechanical work, which is what they are trained to do.

OJT Program: The NCOs have the responsibility to train their maintenance personnel. Many of the maintenance personnel reporting to units are just out of the Army school system and are nothing more than apprentices.

Dispatching Procedures: NCOs must establish control of their equipment. This is done by establishing a good dispatch program.

If all NCOs maintain good daily maintenance management procedures, such as those I have just outlined, we can improve our maintenance posture and reduce operating costs tremendously. This is especially important for Engineers because of all the heavy equipment required to execute our mission. We may not like maintenance, but keeping our equipment running properly is surely better than having our Engineer equipment stall out in the middle of a battlefield.

Kiss of Death . . . Knock of Opportunity

I have just read the Fall 1984 issue of your magazine and wish to make a brief comment about LTC Barry W. Levine's article entitled *"Command of an Initial Entry Training Company."*

As the former commander of a Combat Support Company in a TOE armor battalion and later a TDA cavalry troop which was organized under the "One Station Unit Training" concept, I must agree that commanding an initial entry training organization can be an outstanding alternative for officers wanting to command. The training command was the highlight of my career.

Two facets of such a command stand out as elements of a training assignment. First is the nearly absolute high standard of performance by the training cadre. The caliber of drill instructors cannot be underestimated. Sure there may be ups and downs, but nowhere else is a young commander likely to have nearly hand-picked people. Second is the training command which is the place where the young officer can actually see and measure the results of his efforts, his policies, his leadership. Nothing can top the feeling of getting a Christmas card from parents you have never met thanking you for the positive effect your training had on their son.

As LTC Levine stated, the best system for supplying company grade officers to IET positions is to get them with TOE experience. That way they have a better sensing of the quality of their training and the standards that will be expected in the field. In my experience we usually found that the training center had higher expectations of performance, discipline, military bearing, and stamina than the units who ultimately received our soldiers.

An officer assigned to IET should never think that his career has received the "kiss of death" as I had been led to believe. Rather, he or she should think of it as the knock of opportunity.

CPT James C. Allard
Public Affairs Officer
HQ, 2nd Support Command (CORPS)

Building a Better Knife Rest

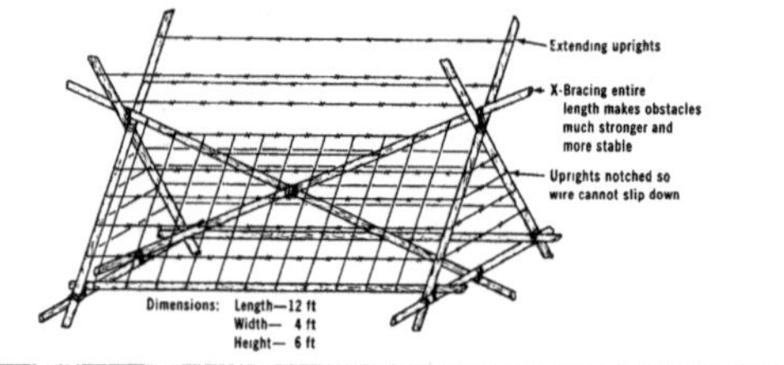

This worked for us. During our annual training (AT) held at Camp Ripley, MN, in January 1985, our squad was tasked to build obstacles to support an infantry company. After we had built the "knife rest" (FM 5-34, *Engineer Field Data*, Figure 4-26), I noticed some of its shortcomings, so I set out to design a modified version.

One of the shortcomings of the knife rest is it can easily be moved by a breaching party due to its height and weight. Also, in cold climates, obstacles must be frozen to the ground so they cannot be moved. The knife rest has virtually no area on the ground to be frozen in.

The modified version can be built by the same number of people and uses almost the same amount of wire. The X-bracing in the center makes this obstacle much stronger and more stable. It also allows the obstacle to be built higher (6 feet as opposed to 1.2 meters) making it harder to breach and less affected by the depth of the snow. Being a higher obstacle, it will not have to be raised as often.

The two bottom braces give a larger area to freeze in, in cold climates and make the obstacle more stable. Poles may be placed across these bottom braces (crisscrossed) and frozen in to make this obstacle impossible to move. Extending the uprights about 6 feet above the X-bracing would cause the breaching party to be climbing at a backwards angle in order to climb over it. Also, the "V" formed by these uprights is a natural saddle for concertina wire.

Because it is very stable, it can withstand being transported many times with little damage. We notched the uprights where the wire mated them; plus we wrapped the wire around them to keep the wire in place and impossible to move. As I said, this worked for us.

SGT Richard Routon
Assistant Training NCO
890th Engineer Company
Tennessee Army National Guard

NOTE: Although SGT Routon's design is a modified version of the knife rest in FM 5-34, the following facts should be noted.

- The design does not address construction using metal. With a metal frame, the knife rest can be used as an effective underwater obstacle.
- The knife rest is not easily removed if it is covered by fire and under friendly observation at all times.
- The design may have just been suitable for one exercise.

Built any bigger and better knife rests lately? How about another new wire obstacle or a new way to demolish a bridge? ENGINEER invites you to share your *Engineer Ingenuity* with the rest of the Engineer community.

Directorate of Combat Developments (DCD)

Mobility Update:

The robotic obstacle breaching assault tank (ROBAT) should be fielded by late FY 87. It will consist of an M-60 chassis modified to accommodate a track-width mine roller or plow, two top-mounted mine-clearing line charges, and a clear-lane marking system. It may be operated manually or by remote control. Contracts will be awarded soon for the remote control system and the logistics support package.

Bridging Update:

The light assault bridge (LAB) has been developed to meet the needs of the light infantry division and rapid deployment forces. The LAB is a lightweight, double-fold scissors bridge designed to span a 23-meter gap. It is trailer-mounted, military load Class 30. It is also air transportable in a C-141 aircraft and can be moved, launched, and retrieved by a variety of vehicles, 5-ton and over. Prototype testing will begin between late FY 86 and early FY 87.

Countermobility Update:

The tactical explosive system (TEXS) is a new antitank ditching system composed of off-the-shelf components. It combines blasting agent ingredients, a mixing and pumping unit, a small emplacement excavator (SEE) with trencher attachment, and 4-inch PVC pipe to produce a ditch 13 meters wide and 3 to 4 meters deep. Emplacement time is significantly less than conventional construction time using bulldozers and bucket loaders. The system is expected to be fielded by early FY 88.

Directorate of Evaluation and Standardization (DOES)

Graduation Follow-up Evaluations:

For the past year, DOES has been conducting graduate follow-up evaluations of Engineer MOS training. Evaluation results are being sent to units participating in the evaluations and appropriate Ft. Belvoir and Ft. Leonard Wood organizations. The next group will be surveyed during the last quarter of FY 85 (by early September). This group includes:

- 62H10 Concrete/Asphalt Equipment Operator
- 52F10 Turbine Engine Driven Generator Repairman
- 52G10 Transmission and Distribution Specialist

This directorate thanks those who have already contributed to these evaluations and hopes to receive continued support from other Engineers in the field.

Defense Mapping School (DMS)

Construction Draftsman Course Redesigned

The Construction Drafting Division, Department of Cartography and Applied Graphics, has totally redesigned Construction Draftsman (81B10) training. The 12-week resident course teaches enlisted and selected civilian students apprentice-level skills necessary to perform construction drafting tasks. The course is divided into three four-week phases.

The first four weeks provide the students with the basics required to draft engineering drawings. Students learn the use of standard drafting instruments, orthographic sketching, projected and pictorial drawing techniques, and the dimensioning of engineering drawings. After this phase, the students can complete single and multiview detail drawings and pictorial asemblies.

During the second phase, the students learn those skills necessary to draft architectural working drawings. This phase includes architects' and metric scales manipulation, architectural detailing practices, material estimating, and metric conventions. The students will complete foundation plans; floor plans; wall sections; building details; electrical, heating, ventilating, or air conditioning plans; and plumbing plans.

During the last four weeks, the students learn structural and civil engineering drafting skills. This includes drafting of structural detail drawings that communicate the designer's intent, plus roadway drawings, earthwork volumes, and mass curves to develop critical paths used in construction management. Students learn to prepare charts and graphs during this phase.

The complete revision of the course enables the Defense Mapping School to provide a better trained soldier for the field units.

Department of Military Engineering (DME

Bridge Erection Boat

Procedures to air transport the bridge erection boat, shallow draft, may soon be available for the field, according to MAJ Christopher P. Werle, Chief of Bridging Branch at the Engineer School. Meanwhile, a list of procedures acquired from the 82nd Airborne is being compiled for the next ENGINEER. Any unit needing help before then should contact MAJ Werle at (703) 664-2378 (AV 354).

Directorate of Training and Doctrine (DOTD)

MGB Link Reinforcement Set

Our Winter 1984–85 "News and Notes" featured an article about the link reinforcement set (LRS). As stated, the LRS can maintain a Class 60 load while extending the gap-crossing capabilities of the MGB from 109 feet (33.2 meters) to 163 feet (49.7 meters). The additional construction material, however, increases manpower and construction time requirements. The chart below illustrates how the LRS affects a double-story, single span MGB.

Double-Story, Single Span MGB

	Normal Set			With LRS		
Number of Bays [1]	13	18	22	13	18	22
Personnel (NCO/Enl)	1/24	1/24	1/24	1/32	1/32	1/32
Daytime[2, 3]	1½ hr	1¾ hr	2 hr	2 hr	2¼ hr	2½ hr
Nighttime[2, 3]	2 hr	2¼ hr	3 hr	2¼ hr	2¾ hr	3 hr

[1]Number of bays does not include two end bays each.

[2]Increase time by 20 percent for untrained troops.

[3]Increase time by 30 percent for inclement weather.

The manpower requirements for installing the LRS is eight additional soldiers, divided into two four-man teams, one team on each side of the bridge. All LRS components are portable, but will require one additional truck and trailer to carry nearly 10,000 pounds of materials.

Note that there is little increase in construction time. This is because all LRS components can be installed simultaneously with the construction of the MGB superstructure.

FM 5-102 Countermobility

FM 31-10, *Denial Operations and Barriers,* was superceded by FM 5-102, *Countermobility.* Distribution began in March 1985 for the new manual which can be acquired through normal publication channels.

Other coordinating drafts being disseminated to the field are as follows:

FM 5-34, *Engineer Field Data*	4th Quarter, 1985
FM 5-105, *Engineer Topographic Operations*	3rd Quarter, 1985
TC 5-103, *Survivability*	1st Quarter, 1986
TC 5-104, *General Engineering Drills*	3rd Quarter, 1985
ARTEP 5-25J, *Engineer Units: ABN, AMBL, INF DIV AND SEP (Div 86)*	April 1985
ARTEP 5-64J, *Engineer Bridge Companies, Corps*	April 1985

ctrinal Literature

New developments in the doctrinal arena have been officially announced with the publication of the new TRADOC Regulation 11-7, *Operational Concepts and Army Doctrine.* The regulation reemphasizes the concept that service school instructors are the subject matter experts within their functional areas and the principal writers of Army doctrine. The regulation further states that, with the exception of joint manuals, all doctrinal field manuals and drill training circulars will be coordinated as field circulars. This procedure provides a faster means of disseminating interim doctrine and training material to the field.

The Engineer School is developing field circulars on the Brigade/Task Force Engineer and on Airfield Damage Repair to satisfy perceived needs for published guidance in those areas. Other field circulars will be developed as input from the field dictates.

News

To correct identified weaknesses in the training system, it has become necessary to expand the ARTEP to make it a total training strategy for each element within a unit. This is accomplished by formatting the ARTEP into a series of mission training plans (MTP), each designed to provide a complete training guide for a specific echelon within a unit. Each ARTEP consists of a training matrix, training plans, detailed training and evaluation outlines, drills, situational training exercises (STX) as applicable, and unit test guidance. This design represents evolutionary progress and a natural extension of the ARTEP philosophy—a training program designed to prepare us today to fight on the AirLand battlefield tomorrow and win.

First production models distributed to the field will be MTPs for the Engineer battalion, light infantry division, and Engineer battalion, armored infantry (MECH) division. Each battalion will have an MTP for their headquarters company and battalion staff, one for the Engineer company, and one for the Engineer squad and platoon.

The coordinating drafts for these publications should be completed by Oct. 1, 1985; and the final drafts should be prepared for DA publication by July 1, 1986. By 1989, all ARTEPs, as we know them, should be converted to more than 50 echelon-oriented MTPs.

The Engineer School welcomes all suggestions and recommendations for improving these publications. Please send your comments to Commandant, U.S. Army Engineer School, ATZA-TD-D, Ft. Belvoir, VA 22060-5291.

ENGINEER recently distributed a readership survey to units randomly selected from our mailing list. Please complete these surveys and return them as soon as possible. The results help us to evaluate our magazine and to publish the material which our readers like to see.

ENGINEER welcomes articles, photographs, ideas, and comments at any time from all our readers.

How much do you know about the Noncommissioned Officer Education System? The following quiz was given at a recent TRADOC Commander's Conference. If you are qualified on the subject of NCOES and AR 351-1, then you should be able to answer all of these questions correctly.

1. When does an NCO become skill level 5 qualified?
   a. Upon graduation from Sergeants Major Academy.
   b. Upon graduation from First Sergeants Course.
   c. Upon promotion to master sergeant (E8).
   d. Upon selection for promotion to master sergeant (E7)(P).

2. At which organizational level must an order of merit list be established and maintained for PLDC and BNCOC?
   a. Company.
   b. Battalion and brigade.
   c. Battalion and separate company.
   d. Division.

3. Which is one of the main objectives of NCOES as outlined in AR 351-1 (Individual Military Education and Training)?
   a. To familiarize soldiers with their leadership responsibilities at various skill levels.
   b. To improve unit readiness and collective mission proficiency of NCOs and subordinate soldiers.
   c. To improve individual technical proficiency.
   d. To provide a formal training base for each skill level.

4. Who has first priority to attend the Primary Leadership Development Course (PLDC)?
   a. Those E5s who have not attended PNCOC.
   b. Soldiers selected for promotion of E5 and E6s and E5s who have not previously attended an NCOES leadership course.
   c. E4s who, because of unit NCO shortages, are performing in E6 and E5 leadership positions.
   d. Soldiers, regardless of position, who the local commands have recognized as needing training.

5. Which of the following is a prerequisite a soldier must meet to be placed on an order of merit list?
   a. Passed the Army Physical Readiness Test within the past 12 months.
   b. Be recommended by the unit first sergeant.
   c. Passed the SQT within the past six months.
   d. Be trained (initialed off) on 70 percent of all MOS tasks in the individual soldiers job book within the past six months.

6. When is a soldier qualified to wear the numeral 2 on the NCO professional development ribbon?
   a. Upon completion of Basic NCO Course.
   b. Upon graduation from Primary Technical Course.
   c. Upon graduation from First Sergeants Course.
   d. Upon graduation from Advanced NCO Course.

7. How are soldiers selected to attend advanced Noncommissioned Officers Course (ANCOC)?
   a. MACOM commanders are responsible for submitting nominees to MILPERCEN who will select attendees, based on availability of allocations for each MOS.
   b. DA selection board, centrally managed by MILPERCEN, will select soldiers to attend ANCOC from a list of nominees submitted by MACOMs.
   c. DA selection board, centrally managed by MILPERCEN will select soldiers to attend ANCOC.
   d. DA selection board, centrally managed by MILPERCEN, will select soldiers to attend ANCOC from a list of soldiers that have submitted a request for schooling.

8. Which soldiers have second priority for attending NCOES resident school courses?
   a. Soldiers who have been assigned to the unit less than 90 days.
   b. Soldiers who are pending assignment to or occupying a duty position within their PMOS in grades higher than their present grade.
   c. Soldiers undergoing supervised-on-the-job-training.
   d. Soldiers who have requested enrollment in correspondence course programs.

What is the normal length of basic NCO courses?
   a. Four-week core with one week add-on option by local commander.
   b. Eight-week core with one week add-on option by local comander.
   c. Course length varies by MOS. Local commanders are permitted to extend POI by one week.
   d. Six weeks in length with one week add-on option by local commander.

10. How soon after being promoted to E5 or E6 must a soldier be sent to the appropriate PTC/BTC?
   a. MILPERCEN will automatically select the soldiers for attendance within 30 days of the date the soldier attains E5/E6 promotion list status.
   b. Commanders will nominate to MILPERCEN those active component soldiers qualified to attend resident PTC and BTC within 30 days of the date the soldier attains E5/E6 promotion list status.
   c. MILPERCEN will automatically select the soldiers for attendance within 90 days of the date the soldier attains E5/E6 promotion list status.
   d. Commanders will nominate to MILPERCEN those active component soldiers qualified to attend resident PTC and BTC within 60 days of the date the soldier attains E5/E6 promotion list status.

11. How are NCOs selected to attend the First Sergeants Course?
   a. Based on projected vacancies, MACOM commanders select all active component NCOs that attend the First Sergeants Course.
   b. MILPERCEN will select the First Sergeants Course attendees from a list of nominees submitted the the MACOMS.
   c. An annual DA selection board, centrally managed by MILPERCEN, will select NCOs to attend the First Sergeants Course.
   d. Based on programmed quotas, MACOM commanders will select First Sergeants Course attendees, who will be sent TDY to the course; and, MILPERCEN will select attendees for TDY enroute (PCS).

Maintenance Management

by LTC Roger C. Strom

Soldiers of HHC, 11th Engineer Battalion (CBT)(HVY) carefully use appropriate manuals to ensure this M-880 5/4-ton truck is properly lubed (photo by 1LT L. J. Leto).

If there is one area in which the Army has failed over the years, it must be in its training of maintenance management. While we often see success in maintenance programs, that success is usually attributable to individual effort rather than a systematic approach to maintenance training.

Nobody likes maintenance! There is little glamour in the motor pool, and the drama of the backline holds no one's interest for long. Maintenance isn't fun the way a construction project can be. But without it, nothing works . . . and higher headquarters wants to know what is wrong almost on a daily basis.

A battalion commander is faced with the myriad challenges of an Engineer battalion. "Get your maintenance up," says the brigade commander, and off the battalion commander charges.

Some Myths about Maintenance:

Myth 1: Absolute command participation in motor stables will improve the unit's overall maintenance posture.

Fact: That's dead wrong! Having the entire chain of command at motor stables just confuses things.

Myth 2: The most important link in the maintenance chain is the operator.

Fact: That's also wrong! Operators come and go; it's the first-line supervisor who's usually around the longest.

Myth 3: If you teach a junior officer how to do what the mechanic does and how to fill out forms properly, he will be a better maintenance manager.

Fact: Wrong again! Teach a lieutenant how to manage, not how to fix. If he learns how to pack wheel bearings, he will be frustrated when he doesn't get to do it on the job. And if he does succeed in packing a wheel bearing, the mechanic will sit back and let him do the rest of the job.

Myth 4: The OR rate is the most important measure of maintenance effectiveness that, when combined with PLL zero balances, provides a quantifiable measure of success.

Fact: OR rates are indicators of past trends; the result of efforts made. The evaluation measurement of OR rate performance fosters a climate wherein integrity can be easily threatened. Measuring PLL lines at zero balance leads to parts remaining in the bins instead of going on the vehicle they were intended for. Likewise, it may become easier to drop a line rather than reflect it at zero balance and suffer the commander's wrath.

Proper management of maintenance is nothing more than the correct analysis of functions to be performed and ensuring that the wherewithal to perform the functions is available. Yet, it is in this statement that a paradox arises. If maintenance management is basically so simple, why is it likewise so difficult to accomplish?

As mentioned before, maintenance is not fun. Because it is not fun, the tendency exists to concentrate on form and appearance rather than function. How many inspections concentrate on the fringe file and stockage lists, ignoring the fact that the PLL clerk does not know how to use a -20P manual? If a scheduled application of a lube order is properly documented, is the mechanic or operator ever questioned as to the timing of the service or how long it took to do the job?

Success in maintenance management is knowing who does what, with what, when, and how. No vehicles are repaired by filling out a form; no part is ordered and placed on a vehicle by merely completing a requisition. Likewise, the fault noted on DA Form 2404 cannot be corrected if the part, properly requisitioned and received, is not put on the vehicle for want of time to get the vehicle into the shop.

Proper maintenance management follows most of the principles of the AirLand Battle with great facility. The most important principle is, however, synchronization. Synchronization in maintenance management means ensuring that the different actors know their roles and the roles of those they come in contact with in the maintenance process.

1LT Brendan J. O'Shea, platoon leader, spot-checks the maintenance on a 5-ton dump truck to ensure proper PMCS procedures are followed (photo by 1LT L. J. Leto).

The ***operator*** must know that he has certain responsibilities for maintenance of his vehicles. He must be shown that there is a manual that outlines these responsibilities and that the most important part of the manual is the PMCS checks. He must be aware that a form exists to facilitate the transfer of information derived from the PMCS; that this form is the DA Form 2404.

Further, he must know that the form must be given to a mechanic if he, the operator, cannot correct all of the faults noted. Finally, the operator must understand that his job is not finished until all of the shortcomings are corrected; he cannot consider his responsibilities fulfilled until the vehicle is operational without fault.

The ***mechanic*** must diagnose what is wrong with the vehicle once the operator has identified a fault. He must know the operator's responsibilities as well as his own. He must be able to know what is available to him to aid in his diagnosis and how to use the manuals, test equipment, and measuring devices that can correctly pinpoint what is wrong.

Once the mechanic has diagnosed the cause of the fault, he must be able to determine what parts and tools are needed to fix it. He must further determine if it is within his capability to accomplish the repairs. He must know how to pass on the information as to parts he requires to the PLL clerk and must be able to give the PLL clerk all the necessary elements of information for him to expeditiously requisition them.

The ***first-line supervisor*** has the most important responsibility in the preventive maintenance cycle. It is his responsibility to oversee the operator and to deal with the motor sergeant. Because operators change from time to time, it is the first-line supervisor who provides continuity and oversight and training to the operator that is assigned. He must keep track of several vehicles and is in a position to see if systemic problems are preventing proper maintenance from occurring.

What is the ***officer's*** role in maintenance and management? Whether the platoon leader, executive officer, or commander and regardless of echelon, the officer must be a facilitator of information exchange and marshal of resources. He ensures that information passes efficiently among the players and that they know what to do with the information once they get it; and he must provide the necessary resources of time, personnel, and equipment to accomplish the necessary repairs. If this synchronization occurs, success is assured.

There are some successful painters who are not artists. They paint by copying parts of various images into a larger composition that becomes original by its choice of images. By reducing the function of painting into a composite set of brush strokes and color selection, they create complex works that considered as a whole might be beyond them.

Good maintenance management does the same thing. It takes a complex situation and defines the roles and functions of each element within the picture. Through identification and definition of these roles, an effective maintenance management program can be developed much in the way the non-artist produces a painting.

LTC Roger C. Strom is the Director of the Department of Military Logistics at the U.S. Army Engineer School. He has commanded a combat heavy Engineer battalion. LTC Strom has a master's degree in logistics management from Ohio State and is a graduate of AFSC.

by Charles Vickers

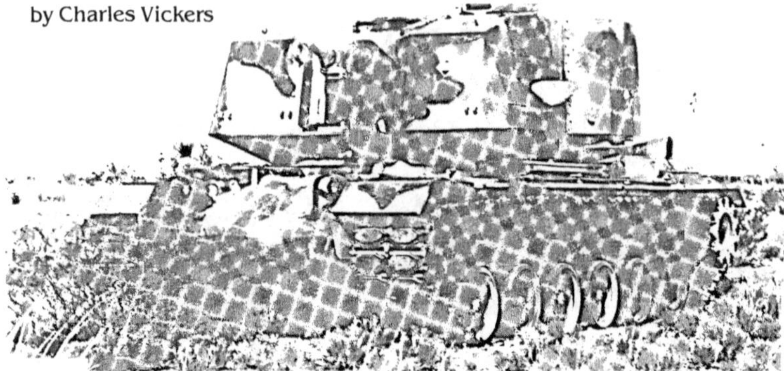

The prime power unit of the DIVAD will soon become a maintenance duty of the 52F MOS. The air defense gun system is officially named "SGT York" in honor of SGT Alvin C. York, the WWI infantryman who received the Medal of Honor for his actions during the Meuse-Argonne battle of 1918. DIVAD is the first major Army weapon system named for an enlisted soldier (photo courtesy of Ford Aerospace).

Many of the newest advances in the Army's Electrical Power Equipment Development Program feature gas turbine engine driven equipment. In addition to use in missile systems, the turbine engine driven generator set has many other applications to meet the demands of today's military environment.

The extent of the many new systems in the program created a new MOS on Oct. 1, 1983 when the Army approved a split from the 52C MOS. As a result, all turbine engine driven equipment and Antenna Mast Group maintenance would now be performed by the 52F MOS—Turbine Engine Driven Generator Repairer.

The duties of this new MOS were defined in AR 611-201, Change 20, as performing or supervising organizational, direct, and general support maintenance functions of turbine engine driven generator sets and prime movers. When the split of MOSs occurred, a program of instruction (POI) for 52F10 was developed and in May 1983 approved by the commander of TRADOC. Based on a 36-hour instruction week, this course was to be slightly longer than 11 weeks.

The AIT students' need for basic skills and knowledge, in addition to the technical training on turbine equipment, resulted in the development of a basic electricity block of training which would introduce the students to electrical schematics and the proper use of electrical test equipment. This 60-hour block was developed by the instructors assigned to the 52F Branch in the Department of Military Logistics at the Engineer School. An annex of maintenance management was also developed and included in the POI. Its purpose was to teach the students to use technical manuals and to prepare maintenance forms and records.

This new course, the Turbine Engine Driven Generator Repairer Course, initially included an annex on the Pershing 1A Missile Power Station. This annex was deleted from the POI in December 1984 when Pershing 2 was fielded and training requirements for a turbine engine power station were no longer required. At the present time, the Turbine Engine Driven Generator Repairer Course includes annexes on the Medical Unit, Self-Contained Transportable (MUST) Utility Pack and Patriot Missile Peculiar Equipment which includes an Antenna Mast Group.

The Patriot Mast System, used in support of the Patriot System, is

An additional skills identifier is assigned to individuals who maintain the MAGIC MAST hydraulic and pneumatic systems. Although this equipment has no turbine engine, maintenance is assigned to the 52F MOS (photo courtesy of GTE).

pneumatically and hydraulically operated. It has no turbine engine, but maintenance of this equipment was assigned to the 52F MOS. A 100-hour block of instruction on the Antenna Mast Group was developed by 52F Branch instructors. This block will be added to the POI given to all MOS 52F personnel in AIT who have received orders for follow-on assignments to Fort Bliss, TX, and USAREUR units through FY 85. An additional skill identifier, C-9, will be assigned to individuals going to units authorized Antenna Mast Groups.

The Turbine Engine Repairer will soon be maintaining two of the newest items in the Army's inventory of turbine engines and generator sets. First, the DIVAD Gun System or SGT York, with a turbine engine as the prime power unit, has gone into production. AIT student training should begin in the 4th quarter of FY 85. Also, the Aviation Ground Power Support Unit will soon be added to the 52F MOS training. This 10 KW, 28 VDC generator set will be used for aircraft starting, checkout, and maintenance.

The fast growing family of gas turbine engine driven equipment has made this new 52F MOS attractive and one of the most sought after career fields in the today's modern Army.

Mr. Charles Vickers is Chief of the 52F Branch, Department of Military Logistics, U.S. Army Engineer School. He has served as a training instructor in the Pershing Missile Equipment and MUST Hospital Training Sections. He has been with the Engineer School since 1968. Mr. Vickers is a veteran of 21 years in Marine Corps Aviation.

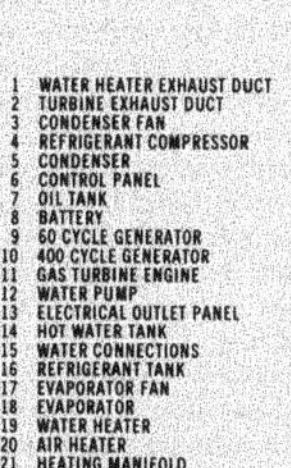

The MUST field hospital utility element is a 52F responsibility (illustration courtesy of Garrett-Airesearch).

Job Task Training for the 52 Charlie

by Richard Kilgore

The unit commander in today's Army is tasked with providing training to maintain the overall job proficiency of soldiers in a variety of technical fields. The commander's unit training programs usually do a good job in the common task area and a fair job in training for those technical tasks that relate to the unit's mission. Training on other technical MOS tasks all too often is either disregarded or leaves much to be desired. Because of a lack of equipment, tools, and subject matter experts, this training is usually difficult to formulate and deliver at the unit level.

The Skill Level 1 Utilities Equipment Repairer (MOS 52C10) is typical of an MOS with this problem. The soldier with this specialty is tasked with a broad range of responsibilities in the maintenance of utilities type equipment used by the Army. His duties vary from operation/maintenance of the Bottle Cleaning and Charging Station (BC/CS, AN/TAM-4) to performance of direct and general support maintenance on air conditioning and refrigeration equipment.

It is rare for a soldier in the 52C10 MOS to be assigned to a position that provides experiences in all of the skill areas. Interviews with utility equipment repairers returning from the field to attend the Utility Equipment Repairer Primary Technical Course (662-52C20) indicated that some soldiers have never practiced their trade and that the majority have been limited to work experiences in only a portion of their overall job responsibilities. At least two problems created by this situation are readily evident:

- Erosion of unused job skills leading to unsatisfactory job performance in future assignments.
- Poor performance on the Skill Qualification Test (SQT).

It is the commander's responsibility to provide training that will sustain and upgrade the soldiers' technical skills, but what can he do if unit resources prevent him from providing that training?

First, the commander should review the training publications (soldier's manual, training guide, and job book) and determine which tasks are actually being performed by his 52C10 soldiers and which are included in his unit training plan for the soldier. From this action the commander can develop a list of tasks that require training. He then should determine if he has the required assets to conduct any of this training within the unit. If so, the training should be incorporated into his unit training plan.

In those situations when a lack of equipment or an absence of subject matter experts precludes unit level training of a particular task, the commander should explore the possibility of providing this training through outside sources. Two possible approaches can provide additional skills training for the 52C10 soldier:

- Cooperative training.
- Exchange training.

Let's examine the basic mechanics of each of these programs.

Cooperative Training

The first method, cooperative training, has been used successfully in public schools for many years. With this program, an agreement is reached with an employer who uses similar job skills to act as an on-the-job trainer. Trainees under the supervision of qualified personnel from the employer organization are used in job actions related to required skills training. Program monitoring and coordination is the responsibility of the organization requesting the training, while evaluation of performance is the responsibility of the trainer organization.

Directorate of Industrial Operations and Directorate of Engineering and Housing are recommended as employers for this action because they are normally involved in a wide variety of utility equipment maintenance tasks that are similar or identical to tasks of the 52C10 MOS.

Exchange Training

The second method, exchange training, involves the actual exchange of soldiers between Army units that have dissimilar missions, equipment assets, and subject matter expertise. This approach to training is especially relevant when training involves operation/maintenance tasks on equipment such as the Bottle Cleaning and Charging Station or the Power Plant, Utility, MUST. To establish this type of program, the commander should screen units in the same geographical area to determine asset availability and then work out an exchange agreement with the other commander.

Regardless of the method of training, command initiative is required. To ensure that training objectives are met and that the program is beneficial from a manpower/production standpoint, agreement for training programs of these types must be carefully developed. Written guidelines, which both parties agree to, should include provisions for the maintenance of training records required by the soldier training publications. Length of training periods will have to be flexible to ensure the required training is provided without causing an adverse effect on mission performance of the involved organizations.

I have experienced the positive effects of a program similar to those I have described. While on active duty as a battalion-level, Missile Engineer equipment repair supervisor, I recognized a skills-retention problem for the 62C series soldier (duties similar to the 52C today) when assigned within CONUS. To alleviate this problem, an oral agreement was reached with the Facility Engineer and the DS/GS support unit to team 62C soldiers with qualified civilian mechanics to perform all Engineer-related maintenance and repair operations performed at the firing batteries of the battalion.

Within a year of establishing the program, the 62Cs under my supervision had assumed responsibility for performance of over 50 percent of support-category site maintenance and had been provided work experience and training that sustained and upgraded their MOS job skills. In addition to the training benefits provided to the 62C soldiers, the supporting organizations were recipients of many hours of free maintenance.

Establishing programs of this type will be a "hard sell." Positive effects of the program for the trainer organization, manpower gains, military-civilian cooperation, and a back-up source of qualified personnel in emergencies are a few of the selling points that the commander could present during initial stages of program development.

Training is a primary responsibility of the unit commander. The commander has little difficulty providing common skills training and mission-related technical training; however, the responsibility does not end there. All MOS job skills must be trained. The training alternatives described here are a means to improved training and proficiency in the 52C10 MOS field, and the potential exists for adoption of these alternatives to other technical MOS categories.

Mr. Richard Kilgore is a training instructor in the 52C Branch, Department of Military Logistics, U.S. Army Engineer School. After serving 21 years in the military, he retired as an Engineer Maintenance NCO.

Permissive TDY for House Hunting

Commanders may grant soldiers permissive TDY for house-hunting connected with a PCS move.

Housing officials must verify that government housing is not available, or if it is available, verify that it is not required to be occupied.

Soldiers may take one house-hunting trip for each set of PCS orders. They may be granted one of the following options:

- Up to seven days of permissive TDY after they receive notification of PCS orders, but before the scheduled departure from the losing duty station.
- Up to five days of permissive TDY in conjunction with PCS travel and leave.
- Up to five days of permissive TDY at the new duty station.

The soldier should contact the housing officials at the gaining installation, following the procedures in Chapter 12 of AR 630-5, "Leaves and Passes."

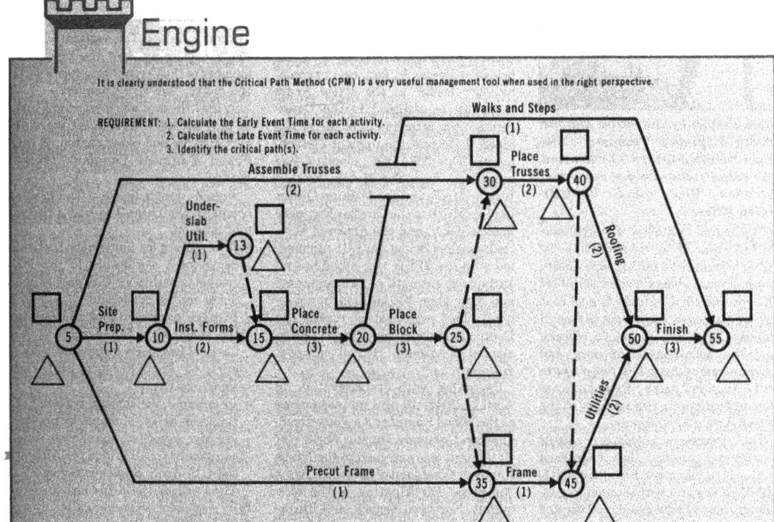

THE DEUCE

by CPT Kevin Brice

A joint effort by the 902nd and the 1438th Engineer Company (Missouri National Guard) constructed this 44-bay ribbon bridge across the Arkansas River (photo by CPT Kevin Brice).

Operation Pontonier, the dynamic, fast-paced demonstration of Army bridging and rafting capabilities, is one of many events sponsored by Fort Belvoir and the Engineer School that exhibit Engineer equipment to foreign dignitaries, VIPs, Engineer officers, and the surrounding military and civilian community. The responsibility for this and many other show-case demonstrations is the mission of the 902nd Engineer Company.

The "Deuce" is a separate assault float bridge company that is attached to the 11th Engineer Battalion (CBT) (HVY). It is a unit with a unique organization, proud history, and multifaceted mission.

What's on the schedule for classes this week?

On Tuesday we have a soils exam; Thursday, a concrete P.E.; and on Friday afternoon, we have something called "Operation Pontonier."

What's "Operation Pontonier?"

I'm not sure but I think it's some sort of bridging demonstration. I've heard it's pretty good though!

The 902nd is more than a ribbon bridge company. In fact, every type of military bridge in the active Army inventory is assigned to the Deuce through the attachment of the SPED (Special Purpose Equipment Detachment). This TRADOC element has everything from the Mobile Assault Bridge (MAB) and the Medium Girder Bridge (MGB) to the Combat Engineer Vehicle (CEV) and the Armored Vehicle Launched Bridge (AVLB). Augmented with the SPED, the 902nd has an authorized strength of 212 personnel and more than $40 million in equipment. This organization makes the Deuce uniquely equipped for its unparalleled Engineer School support mission.

Beginning with its activation in April 21, 1942, the unit was designated as the 902nd Engineer Air Force Headquarters Company. During World War II, the unit was assigned to the Ninth Engineer Command of the Ninth Army Air Force. Participating in the Normandy, Northern France, and Rhineland Campaigns from June 6, 1944 to March 21, 1945, the 902nd built 301 airfields in France, Belgium, Holland, Luxembourg, Austria, and Germany.

For its service during World War II, the 902nd Engineer Air Force Headquarters Company was awarded the Meritorious Unit Commendation for exceptionally meritorious conduct from April 1, 1944 through May 8, 1945. Today, the 902nd maintains a tie to the past by proudly wearing the distinctive unit crest which symbolizes its history. The horizontal perforated steel planking and blue coloring represent the unit's ties with the Army Air Corps as airfield builders. The vertical shovel and red coloring show the unit is a member of the Corps of Engineers with the motto, "We Will Conquer."

In 1947 the unit was inactivated, and on May 26, 1967, it was reactivated at Fort Belvoir and redesignated as the 902nd Engineer Company (Float Bridge).

Since its designation as a float bridge company, the Deuce has had a threefold mission.

- To be poised for immediate tactical deployment world-wide to provide combat mobility for U.S. and Allied forces on the battlefield.
- To make significant contributions to the image of the U.S. Army and the Corps of Engineers by providing support to Fort Belvoir and the community.
- To enhance the combat training of Engineer School students by providing the expertise, manpower, and equipment for all bridge training at the U.S. Army Engineer School.

Always ready, the 902nd has successfully responded whenever called upon. In July 1970, the 902nd was alerted to

Operators and equipment from the 902nd prepare to demonstrate the Army's river-crossing capability. The Deuce is unique in that it maintains every type of military bridging equipment in the active Army inventory (staff photo).

provide two 180-foot M4T6 bridges at Great Bridge, VA. The bridges were constructed and maintained for civilian use across the Albemarle and Chesapeake Canal. Over 170,000 vehicles crossed these bridges without mishap; and daily for 38 days, the center sections of both bridges were removed to allow water traffic to pass through the canal.

In the aftermath of Hurricane Agnes in June 1972, the 902nd performed emergency rescue and rafting operations in Fairfax, Alexandria, and Occoquan VA; in Pittston, Laceyville and Lancaster, PA; and in Ellicot City, MD. The 902nd also provided emergency bridging at Hilton Head, SC, in March 1974 and at Siloam, NC, in June 1975.

In January 1983, when an Air Florida Airlines jet plunged into the frozen Potomac River, the 902nd provided an emergency floating platform to facilitate rescue operations. Most recently, the Deuce constructed a Bailey Bridge across Dogue Creek near the Walker Gate entrance of Fort Belvoir to allow repair of the existing bridge.

Last July, the Deuce deployed to Fort Chaffee, AR, to participate in Scarlet Sabre II. This major CAPSTONE FTX with the Missouri National Guard allowed the 902nd to practice its alert procedures, POM processing, and deployment to simulated POMCUS sites near Fort Chaffee. After drawing equipment, the unit deployed as a member of the 135th Engineer Group. During the exercise the Deuce combined its forces with the 1438th Ribbon Bridge Company to provide for three deliberate river crossings of the Arkansas River. The success of this exercise graphically demonstrated that the Deuce is capable of performing its world-wide deployment mission.

At Fort Belvoir, the most well known of the 902nd's demonstrations is Operation Pontonier. Last year special pontoniers were given for the civilian aides to the Secretary of the Army, a group of officers from the Mexican Army, and for the annual Fort Belvoir's Retiree Open House.

The Operation Pontonier "float-by" presentation demonstrates the phases of a deliberate river crossing while displaying the Engineer equipment used during each phase. The use of helicopters from the Military District of Washington and the Pennsylvania National Guard and demolitions and pyrotechnics create a realistic look at U.S. river-crossing capabilities.

Although the equipment and special effects are highlighted, the professional performance of the men in the Deuce is what makes Operation Pontonier possible. Last year the Honorable John O. Marsh, Jr., Secretary of the Army, wrote to GEN William Richardson, TRADOC Commander, that the "superb performance" of these Engineers was the highlight of the 30th Annual Conference for the civilian aides to the Secretary of the Army.

Other unique contributions of the 902nd include several static displays. Last year equipment was displayed at Andrews Air Force Base for the Armed Forces Day Celebration, at the Fairfax County Fair, and at the Fort Belvoir's Annual Retiree Open House. In these displays the bulk of the equipment supplied by Fort Belvoir comes from the 902nd and the SPED. The 902nd plans to display equipment again this year at the Armed Forces Day Celebration and the Fairfax County Fair.

The 902nd Engineer Company's primary mission is to support the training at the Engineer School:

- This includes more than 16,500 man-hours each year in support of Engineer School "white sheets." (White sheets list the support requirements needed by the School.)
- Training on the Ribbon Bridge, the Mobile Assault Bridge (MAB), the Light Tactical Raft (LTR), the M4T6 Fixed and Float Bridges, the Medium Girder Bridge (MGB), and the Bailey Bridge is all provided with 902nd assets.
- All Engineer Officer Advanced and Basic Course students, all Engineer NCO Advanced Course students, and all 12C Bridgeman's Primary Technical Course students receive training provided by the Deuce.

The training support mission of the 902nd goes far beyond the main gate of Fort Belvoir. Every summer a large contingency of the 902nd travels 600 miles north to the United States Military Academy at West Point to assist with cadet summer training. Last summer, the SPED supported this high-visibility training while the rest of the company was at Fort Chaffee. This year, 2nd platoon will provide the support.

Throughout the year, the 902nd Engineer Company provides continuous, professional support to the Engineer School at Fort Belvoir, the Center for Excellence.

CPT Kevin Brice commands the 902nd Company, 11th Engineer Battalion (CBT)(HVY). He was an instructor in the Bridging Branch, DME, at the Engineer School and served as platoon leader, company executive officer, and the adjutant of the 317th Engineer Battalion in Germany. CPT Brice has a bachelor's degree in civil engineering from the University of Wisconsin and has completed the Engineer Officer Advanced Course. He is a registered professional engineer in Wisconsin.

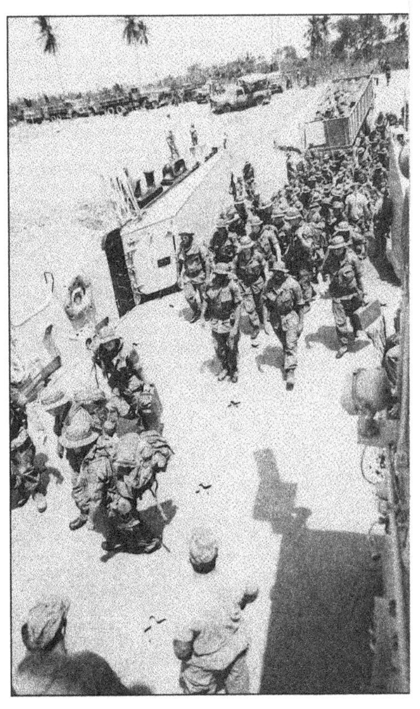

lazing Trails hru Panama

Photo essay by CPT Daniel B. Miles Jr.

Missouri and Louisiana National Guard Engineers cleared and surfaced 27 kilometers of roadway during Blazing Trails. Over 9,500 soldiers from eight states participated in the Combat Engineer exercise.

I want to share with you some information I received and lessons I learned while serving in MILPERCEN. Much of what I say here is not controlled at Engineer Branch level; but it is reality, and I sincerely want all of you to understand *the rules* as they are being applied.

We tell all EOBC students to first plan on being soldiers, troop leaders that is, and not be concerned about working in the civil engineering arena yet. The Corps of Engineers exists to provide support to the Combined Arms Team on the battlefield. The essence of being a combat arms officer is leadership; this must be learned and practiced as a lieutenant. *Don't* plan on working in your undergraduate civilian major field; *do* plan on getting dirty, greasy, muddy, and professionally satisfied while leading our combat soldiers during your early assignments.

Branch Qualification

The term, "branch qualification," identifies those officers who have met certain minimum qualifications:

- Initial troop-leading experience.
- Resident EOAC (completing EOAC only by the nonresident method requires Branch approval).
- Company command.

Once officers are branch qualified, they may be selected for assignments such as ROTC instructor duty, recruiting company command, reserve advisor duty, U.S. Army Corps of Engineers (USACE) civil/military construction positions, instructor duty at the Engineer School or at another branch's school, attendance at advanced civil schooling (ACS), or command of a separate company.

Most of our Engineer officers become branch qualified after commanding a company during their second troop tour (following EOAC). However, some officers do command during their initial troop assignment and become branch qualified upon graduation from EOAC. While Engineer Branch recommends that all officers go to a second troop-type assignment after EOAC—to broaden their perspective of the Army and to give them a better professional development base for a long career in the Corps of Engineers—Army requirements do not always permit us to do that.

Can you apply for ACS if you are branch qualified after EOAC?

Yes.

Might Engineer Branch send you to one of the assignments mentioned previously if you are branch qualified after EOAC?

It is quite possible; however, we would prefer to send you to a second troop assignment.

When one becomes branch qualified is not as critical as *how* one becomes branch qualified. Your performance as a troop-leading lieutenant and as a company commander is extremely important to having a viable Army career ahead of you.

Upward Mobility

All promotion rates used here are for "first-time-considered" officers .

- Promotion rate to **captain** is 92 percent. Most lieutenants will get promoted unless they have some major deficiencies in their performance record.
- Promotion rate to **major** is 80 percent. Some captains who are fully qualified for promotion will not be selected. To be selected, you must have commanded a company and performed all of your jobs exceedingly well. Your company command reports are critical in making this promotion selection.
- Promotion rate to **lieutenant colonel** is 70 percent. You *must* be a Command and Staff College (CSC) graduate (Military Education Level 4—commonly referred to as MEL 4). It does *not* matter if you attended in residence or if you took Command and General Staff College (CGSC) by the nonresident method.

Each officer will be considered four times for selection to resident CSC. If you are not selected by the second consideration, you should start one of the CGSC nonresident courses immediately. Don't wait until the last minute as many officers have unfortunately done.

If you complete CGSC by the nonresident method and then get selected for the resident course, this simply expands your options. You can request attendance at one of the sister schools (or CGSC), or you can waive attendance. Waiving attendance at resident CSC is not normally recommended, but it is an option. A letter is placed on your performance microfiche stating you were selected for resident CSC and waived attendance because you had completed the nonresident course.

In addition to being a MEL 4, selection for lieutenant colonel requires that your performance must have been outstanding, not just adequate, in nearly every job you have done.

Career Goals

Success, as reflected by career goals, must be tempered by the realities of today's Army. A realistic career goal today is the expectation of being promoted to lieutenant colonel. While this may be different from the situation 10 years ago, it certainly reflects what is happening now. The promotion system necessarily causes officers to be nonselects. That does not mean they are not solid performers; in fact, most of the officers that have not been selected for promotion are doing outstanding work. Unfortunately, as we ascend in rank, the probability of non-selection increases.

Objectively analyzing your performance and establishing realistic career goals is a trying experience. I urge you to consult others (perhaps your commander, maybe peers, and certainly your assignment officer at Branch) for advice, guidance, and ideas.

Advance Civil Schooling

Each year, Engineer Branch sends officers to Advanced Civil Schooling (ACS) for master's degrees (usually in engineering and related fields). Selection is made by a board conducted by Engineer Branch and is based primarily on potential for future service as demonstrated by manner of performance.

This ACS board meets in September and March of each fiscal year. Your application is good *only* for the fiscal year in which you apply. If you are not selected by the September Board, you will automatically be reconsidered in March.

Your time in service and time in grade as a captain, coupled with your own realistic goals, should indicate whether or not you should apply for ACS. Army policy dictates that ACS must always be followed by a required utilization tour of three consecutive years. Very, very few of these utilization tours are with Engineer troops.

Spending from one to two years in ACS followed by a three-year utilization tour, plus possibly one year in CSC, could add up to six years away from soldiers. If this six-year period coincides with your years as a major, you have substantially reduced the probability of being selected for lieutenant colonel command.

Is going to ACS followed by a three-year district tour or a teaching assignment at West Point a good idea?

Yes, of course it is!

Can it be a bad idea or hinder your career?

Yes, depending on what your career goals are and where you are with respect to time in service and time in grade.

Unfortunately, many officers do not realize this until it is too late. Engineer Branch has absolutely nothing to do with the three-year utilization policy; this is required by law.

Let's say you have completed your three-year ACS utilization assignment and are coming out of CSC with one, two, or three years left as a major. Because of the stabilization criteria under which we operate, Engineer Branch has only one opportunity (PCS move) to get you to an installation or MACOM where troops are located. We do not and cannot assign you to a particular unit; that is the installation commander's prerogative.

The major's assignment office will do all he can to get you to a place where troops are located if that is your desire. However, he must satisfy a MEL 4 distribution plan that requires "X" number of CSC graduates go to certain MACOMs. Very few of these requirements may be with Engineer soldiers. On the other hand, if you are able to get a master's degree during your off duty time or while in a permissive TDY status of less than six months, you will not owe the Army a three-year utilization tour and you will have all six years (at least two assignment locations) as a major to try to get with Engineer troops.

Is having a master's degree required to get selected for lieutenant colonel?

No, absolutely not! It does open up additional assignment possibilities, but it doesn't even come close to the importance of being a CSC graduate.

Lieutenant colonel and lieutenant colonel command seem a long way off when you are a relatively young captain, but this is when you must plan for your future. Draw yourself a time line and plot out where you are and where you would like to go. Your assignment officer will be happy to discuss it with you.

Lean and Mean

AR 600-9! Army policy is very clear about not being overweight. Do everything humanly possible to get within the screening table height and weight limits and do not rely on the pinch test. Certainly, though, some body builders and weight lifters must rely on the pinch test; in such cases, your rater must make a comment concerning your height and weight in Part IV b. of your OER. Ensure that he does!

My recommendation remains . . . *get within the table standards!* If you are overweight or fail the PT test, you will not be selected for promotion/schooling regardless of your manner of performance.

Photograph

The hard-copy photograph is absolutely essential to your file. The importance of your photograph cannot be overemphasized. (Some would argue that it has become too important—I will not address that issue here, but you must understand that the photograph is critical.) Its use spans the entire spectrum of personnel actions: promotion boards; school boards; nominations for ROTC, USAREC, and IG positions; and nominations for special high-level positions within DA, DoD, JCS, and the federal government. In almost any selection/nomination action, the first items examined in officers' files are their photographs.

Your photograph should show you as a neat, well groomed soldier . . . no wrinkles in your uniform, no "high water" trousers, correct brass (not GS or IG), and only authorized awards and decorations. I recommend no mustache.

Although the AR requires a photo only every four years, I suggest you get a new photo upon promotion and ensure that before a scheduled board, the photo in your file is not more than one year old. The more current the better because you are showing the board members how you look now and that you are proud of it instead of showing them how you looked four years ago.

The photo must reinforce the height and weight data on your IRB (Individual Record Brief—formerly known as the ORB, Officer Record Brief) and your latest OERs. (If these items do not agree, you are asking for trouble.)

Individual Record Brief

The IRB represents a single page summation of your career and background. Before any field grade promotion board, your local Military Personnel Office (MILPO) will ask you to conduct an IRB audit and sign a promotion board IRB verifying that everything is true and accurate. Carefully review all the IRB entries and correct any errors neatly—that is what the signed IRB system is for! Most critical is your height and weight data, military education level, and your assignment history. Your MILPO will forward this *signed* and *validated* IRB to MILPERCEN for inclusion in your file which goes before the board.

Your assignment officer will do all he can to ensure your file is accurate and complete, but he is obviously concerned about many officers. The ultimate responsibility rests with you; you have only one officer to be concerned about.

Truth and/or Consequences

It is important that you realize that Army requirements still "drive the train." While your assignment officer sincerely wants to accommodate everyone's preferences, it is virtually impossible. We are all professional soldiers and must periodically "lean forward in the foxhole" to meet the needs of the Army. Believe me, your assignment officer does not enjoy sending you to a job or location that you do not want!

Problems, questions, and comments relating to Engineer doctrine, training, organization, and equipment can be addressed by telephone to the U.S. Army Engineer School's "Engineer Hotline." The Hotline's auto-answer recorder operates 24 hours a day, seven days a week. You should give your name, address and telephone number, followed by a concise question or comment. You'll receive a reply within three to 15 days. **The Hotline is not a receiving agency for formal requests.**

Call commercial (703) 664-3646; WATTS 800-336-3095, extension 3646; or AV 354-3646.

NIGHT CROSSING

by LTC Richard V. Gorski and 1LT William Vickers

Soldiers practice connecting MABs during daylight hours to prepare themselves for more challenging conditions of nighttime operations in MOPP IV (staff photo).

For some time the 2nd Armored Division had been in contact with the enemy. Intelligence reports of a decisive and successful battle against elements of the 1st Shock Army began to emerge. A warning order alerted the division that it would soon be maneuvered against other forces elsewhere. The 17th Engineer Battalion's Echo Company knew that it would play a major role in the upcoming operation.

The terrain facing the division was crisscrossed with small streams and rivers. Most permanent bridges had been demolished earlier during the war. Clearly, river-crossing operations would have a great impact on the results of any engagement. The side with the more efficient, better trained mobile bridging assets would have a great advantage.

As Echo Company escalated its preparations for the coming battle, the S-2 reported extensive enemy use of chemical weapons. Enemy intelligence was excellent and would be watching carefully for any movement of our Mobile Assault Bridges. Since the enemy controlled the skies during daylight, the division would have to move at night to escape detection.

A night river-crossing under total blackout conditions . . . possibly in a chemically contaminated environment . . . could Echo Company pull it off? . . .

Fortunately, this scenario was just the fictitious build-up to one phase of exercise Hardened Steel VII, the 2nd Armored Division's annual spring exercise. But the mission was real: construct two MABs in MOPP IV in total blackout.

Our division commander, MG John W. Woodmansee Jr., had issued a warning order for this mission after the previous spring's exercise. Operating and constructing a Mobile Assault Bridge isn't easy under the best of conditions. Doing it in either MOPP IV or in total blackout is difficult enough. Putting it all together in complete chemical protective gear and in total blackout is a task that the MAB's designers probably never envisioned.

With a year to get ready, we needed a training program that would sustain our high level of proficiency through the inevitable personnel changes and develop crew proficiency and confidence rapidly and safely. Echo Company designed such a program to be ready for a blackout MOPP IV crossing in stages: daylight bridge construction and rafting procedures; daylight operations wearing protective masks; night bridge construction and rafting procedures; and ultimately, night operations in MOPP IV in total blackout.

Because Fort Hood's famous Cowhouse Creek is too narrow and too shallow to support MAB operations, most of the training took place in Belton Lake, the man-made reservoir created by the damming of Cowhouse Creek near the Fort Hood reservation. Calm-water MAB operations on a lake don't simulate moving water operations on a typical fast-moving German river, but in Texas you use the water that God gives you and you're thankful for that!

Initial training took place in the heat of summer. MAB crewmen practiced driving their rigs into the water, maintaining a tight formation, throwing the ropes used to pull the rigs together, connecting the rigs into rafts, maneuvering the rafts, and finally landing the rafts onto the shore. Because time is precious when constructing a bridge, all the exercises emphasized teamwork and were geared towards saving time.

And teamwork was the key. Individual MAB rigs had to enter the water smoothly and stay in formation. As rigs were called in by the raft commander, a deckhand on each rig threw a rope to his counterpart on the adjacent rig, wrapped it quickly around the capstan, and used the rotating capstan to tighten the ropes and draw the rigs together.

Practice ensured that the rope was caught on the first attempt so that no time would be wasted pulling a missed rope out of the lake. As the ropes were drawn tight, the crewmen carefully controlled the speed of the capstans so that the rigs would slide together smoothly. After inserting the hydraulic pin connectors and checking them for secure fit, the raft commander called in the next MAB rig to hook up.

After individual rigs had been hooked together to form a raft, the raft commander began maneuvering the raft into position to form a bridge. If the raft commander missed the precise landing spot on each shore, the bridge would be off the centerline of the crossing site. If the ramps failed to hit the landing site on the first pass, the raft would sweep past the landing site and lose valuable time maneuvering back into position.

There were usually about 18 to 20 crews in the company at any one time; seven or eight crews and their rigs were needed to complete each bridge. Cross-training in crew skills meant each drill had to be repeated several times to ensure proficiency. Moreover, although most of our training was done by platoon and stressed section integrity (there are two MAB sections in each platoon), cross-section and cross-platoon training was required to prepare us for any eventuality.

Once we had achieved a reasonable level of proficiency—and this took quite a lot of practice—we did it again, this time wearing chemical protective masks.

Working in protective masks immediately caused problems. Aside from the obvious difficulties of limited vision and reduced ability to communicate, the troops couldn't fasten their steel helmets over their masks. Unfortunately, a few helmets were lost in the river before a clever sergeant convinced his lieutenant to store the steel pots in the cabs of the MABs.

Impaired peripheral vision was not so easy to correct. The raft commander had to learn to look at each marine drive operator in turn to be able to tell if all marine drives were being operated correctly. Engine noise and the ever-present wind compounded the problem of communications between raft commander and marine drive operators. The raft commander had to be especially clear and concise with his verbal instructions, use exaggerated hand and arm signals, and act without hesitation. Otherwise, operators would become confused and unsure of their actions.

By comparison to what was to come, the training so far was easy.

We had practiced before, performing night crossings in total darkness without cab lights, running lights, or even flashlights. A single MAB could easily become misoriented in the darkness; therefore, each crew chief was carefully briefed on his position in the formation in the water. He had to keep the MAB in front of him in sight and be ready to hook up when his turn came, yet he could not get too close or he would limit the other rig's maneuvering room.

Other minor problems caused by limited visibility were solved one by one through attention to detail, discipline, and practice. For example, usually the hydraulically actuated pins which hold the raft together are checked visually by the raft commander. Since we couldn't use any lights and fluorescent paint and tape were useless, we learned how to physically feel for the correct placement of the pins. This involved some potential danger and discomfort to the raft commander which we just had to acccept.

Operating the MABs at night and with M-17 protective masks turned out to be less difficult than we had expected. The practice without masks at night and with masks during the daylight had paid off. Crew confidence was amazingly high. Raft commanders would run along the bridge roadway until they could stand directly in front of and communicate with particular operator.

Of course constructing a bridge is only half the battle. Getting traffic across the bridge is an integral part of the effort—and doing it at night creates some special problems.

Previous river-crossing exercises had taught us the importance of well trained ground guides. Keeping traffic moving quickly and steadily at night absolutely requires well trained ground guides.

Vehicles equipped with night vision devices, like the M-1 Abrams and the M-2 Bradley, can see a ground guide's hand and arm signals without any additional light. Other vehicles require that the ground guides have a light in each hand so that their signals are visible. In either case, the ground guides have to use standard hand and arm signals that are known to the vehicle drivers, and their hand and arm movements have to be bold and exaggerated.

The ground guide's position is also critical. He can hamper the vehicles he is guiding if he is too close to them. If he's too far away, the drivers can't see

Under the cover of darkness and protected by their MOPP equipment, soldiers of the 17th Engineer Battalion, 2nd Armored Division, work to connect their MABs to provide the maneuver brigades the means to cross a water obstacle (U.S. Army photo).

him. Several guides on a bridge are necessary. By keeping their distance and handing off vehicles from one guide to the next, the guides can keep the traffic flowing at near-daylight rates. We found that one of the most important roles of the officer who was the bridge site commander was to watch the efficiency of the ground guides and ensure that correct procedures were being followed.

We also found that we could wear AN/PVS-5 night vision goggles (NVGs) over our M-17 protective masks. Some ground guides had great difficulty at first coping with the severe tunnel vision effect, but like everything else, practice instilled confidence. With the NVGs, the ground guides could see the oncoming traffic as well or better than the traffic could see them.

Previous night-bridging missions had proved the value of chem lights. By putting a chem light inside a C-ration box or a tin can, the light is visible from only one direction. We would use lights like this to mark the landing sites so that raft commanders could see in the dark exactly where to position their bridge ramps. We would also use them to mark the bridge site's approach and exit roads.

Chem lights would also be used by the ground guides. By holding the chem lights in their foil wrappers so that just their tips were exposed, the lights would not be visible outside the bridge area, and they would not blind vehicle operators using night vision devices.

We found that chem lights made identification of key personnel a snap. Using "100-mile-an-hour" tape, we taped a chem light to our left sleeves just below our shoulders. By taping over the chem light and leaving only narrow bands of light showing, we could easily identify leaders—one light band for NCOs, two for junior officers, three for senior officers. By doing the job carefully, we solved two problems: how to identify key personnel at night in MOPP IV and how to prevent those leaders from being too visible under night vision devices.

. . . in the bivouac area we anxiously awaited word from battalion S-2 about what was happening on the front lines. The MABs were well concealed under heavy camouflage. Although we were in the division rear and occupying a fairly secure area, we kept our perimeter security alert. We didn't want any surprises from OPFOR airborne forces.

Finally the word arrived. Division had successfully counterattacked and destroyed an enemy division. As part of our move to another part of the corps area, the division would conduct a retrograde operation. The move would have to be done at night for concealment. We were cautioned that several areas had been chemically contaminated during the battle and that all the permanent bridges were destroyed.

Echo Company's mission: construct two bridges across Cowhouse Creek after dark and cross the division before daylight. And since the crossing areas had been hit with chemical weapons early that day, conduct the entire operation in MOPP IV!

This was it! All that training would finally pay off. The bivouac area was humming with activity. The air of restlessness that had permeated Echo Company during the past days was replaced with one of excited anticipation. Personal equipment was scrutinized by the practiced eyes of the section sergeants. MOPP gear was checked one final time for serviceability. At the pre-operation briefing, final instructions were issued.

Plans were finalized and the crews thoroughly briefed. We stressed attention to detail, light and noise discipline, MOPP IV procedures, and safety. We had to be ready to cross traffic at 2100.

At precisely 1900, 1st Platoon emerged from its perimeter and 2nd Platoon followed 15 minutes later. As each checkpoint was passed, the platoon leader reported his position by radio. At the final checkpoint before the crossing area, the convoys pulled over, dispersed, and assumed MOPP IV. Light was fading rapidly. At 1930 the first MAB splashed into the water on schedule.

The first three interior bays went together without incident. The next two were a struggle. Time and again the bridge commander would bring the MABs close, the capstans would scream with their coils of rope, but the pins would not slide into place. Sweat poured off the men on the ropes, pooling in irritating puddles at the base of their protective masks.

Finally, after we tried every trick in the book, the pins grudgingly slid into place, and the process of closing the bridge began. First, the two free interior ends were brought together, and ropes were thrown to form a "V" in the middle of the river. By raising the ramps, throwing the MAB marine drives into full throttle reverse and then lowering the ramps, the ends of the bridge were slipped into place. The exhausting process had taken almost 1 1/2 hours.

It was now 2055. The troops had worked up quite a sweat under their MOPP gear. The cool night air cut easily through their protective suits.

Then we felt the rumbling of tons of Abrams tanks. Next came the distinctive sound of road wheels picking up and laying down track. Before we knew it, they were upon us and crossing. The 2AD was here.

Ground guides worked smoothly and carefully. Shifts moved in and out with the precision of a drill team. By morning it was over. The retrograde was complete.

The division had called for a total blackout crossing in MOPP IV. Echo Company had delivered!

LTC Richard V. Gorski is attending the U.S. Army War College. He previously commanded the 17th Engineer Battalion at Fort Hood, TX. LTC Gorski is a 1966 U.S.M.A. graduate and has a master's degree in civil engineering from Stanford University. He is a registered professional engineer in California.

1LT William Vickers is a platoon leader in the MAB Company of the 17th Engineer Battalion, Fort Hood, TX. He completed EOBC and the Atomic Demolitions Course at Fort Belvoir, VA. 1LT Vickers has a bachelor's degree in civil engineering from the Virginia Military Institute.

THE OBSTACLE PLANNING SIMULATION

by John M. Deponai III
Dr. James E. Snellen
CPT Rick Jones
CPT Leo J. Fontana

The time is 0730Zulu, CPT Brown breaks into a cold sweat. His Engineers, in support of a Combined Arms task force in defense, have been frantically emplacing obstacles and digging-in weapon systems. This is according to an obstacle plan he designed in response to the maneuver commander's concept of the operation. CPT Brown knows that within the next 8 to 16 hours, the battle south of Bad Hersfeld, West Germany, will begin. . . .

As CPT Brown leans back in his chair, the computer screen flashes with the arrival of the "Red" forces. Now he will see just how effective his obstacle plan really is, using the Obstacle Planning Simulation at the U.S. Army Engineer School.

The Obstacle Planning Simulation (OPS) is a computer-based, interactive, video exercise that models the effects of Combat Engineer efforts on a battlefield. It was developed as a practical exercise to be used at the Engineer School to give students experience in survivability and countermobility missions.

OPS is a two-phased exercise. In Phase One, the player modifies battlefield terrain with an obstacle plan of his or her own design. Engineer resources are limited. The player is guaranteed a minimum of two blocks of simulated time, each representing four hours of Engineer effort, but may get a maximum of four blocks of time to implement an obstacle/survivability plan. Thus, as in real life, priority of work is critical to the success of the battle plan.

Phase Two is the battle. Once the battle begins, the player observes the effectiveness of individual obstacles and the obstacle plan in general. One of five significantly different, doctrinally sound enemy attacks is directed against the "Blue" force defensive position. The paths of the attacking "Red" forces are programmed into the model.

Map Display

The map shown on the computer terminal (Figure 1) is an abstraction of an area 6 km by 12 km in West Germany, south of Bad Hersfeld. OPS is designed to take into account the effects of terrain in vehicle movement rates and line-of-fire/line-of sight. However, it will not allow the player to emplace nonsense obstacles, such as a bridge demolition where there is no bridge!

"Blue" force units are represented by letter designations in small squares on the screen. The attacking "Red" forces which move into the screen during Phase Two of the simulation appear as inverse video letters (Figure 2). Letters represent different weapon systems so the player can be selective in preparing fighting positions and can distinguish one "Red" force unit from another.

Simulation Model

OPS is modeled after the Dunn-Kempf Simulation. In contrast, OPS does not model effects of artillery and does not require more than one player. OPS allows a single user to enter an obstacle plan at a computer terminal, then observe its effectiveness as the "Red" force attacks across the map screen. Both enemy and friendly fires can be observed as OPS models weapon ranges, simulates the effects of obstacles and fighting positions, and uses probability tables to access casualties much the same way Dunn-Kempf does.

During Phase One, the player may choose from a variety of defensive works and obstacles as shown in Figure 3. Reusable assets are noted in the upper corner of the display with expendable assets below. As the player makes a selection, assets required for that particular task are noted, and the player may place that obstacle on the map screen if sufficient assets are available.

Future Developments

Future versions of OPS will enhance its utility as a training tool. By May 1985, Engineer School instructors will have the capability to design their own scenarios, to vary map type and scale, and to tailor "Blue" and "Red" force composition and size. This scenario editor will be used to demonstrate the value of obstacles and fighting positions, the importance of capitalizing on weapon range superiority (stand-off distance), and effects peculiar to different terrain types. A more detailed statistical analysis than the "Combat Losses" shown in Figure 2 will also be available. In October, OPS will have the additional option of allowing the player to interactively maneuver the "Blue" forces during Phase Two while the "Red" forces attack.

Thus, CPT Brown and the officers who follow him to the Engineer School will be able to take advantage of a unique training tool. OPS will allow Combat Engineers to experiment with obstacle placement and gain a greater appreciation for the factors that affect obstacle planning.

More Information

Information on the technical aspects of OPS is available in *Obstacle Planning Simulation (OPS): Introduction and User Instructions* by John M. Deponai III and James E. Snellen. This technical report, P-85/08 (January 1985) ADA 149468, was published by the Construction Engineering Research Laboratory (CERL). It can be ordered from the National Technical Information Service, 5285 Port Royal Road, Springfield, VA 22161.

For more information on OPS at the Engineer School, contact the Field Engineering Branch, DME, at AV 354-3411, commercial (703) 664-3411.

John M. Deponai III leads the Military Engineering Team at the U.S. Army Construction Engineering Research Laboratory (CERL), at Champaign, IL. He graduated from the United States Military Academy and

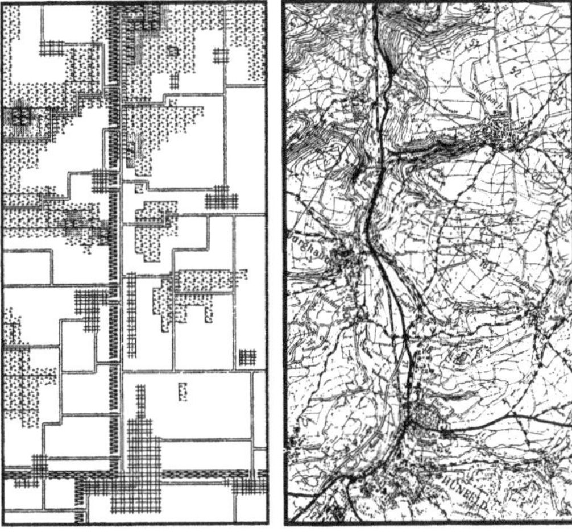

Figure 1. The topographic map of the battlefield (right) is portrayed by the computer screen (left).

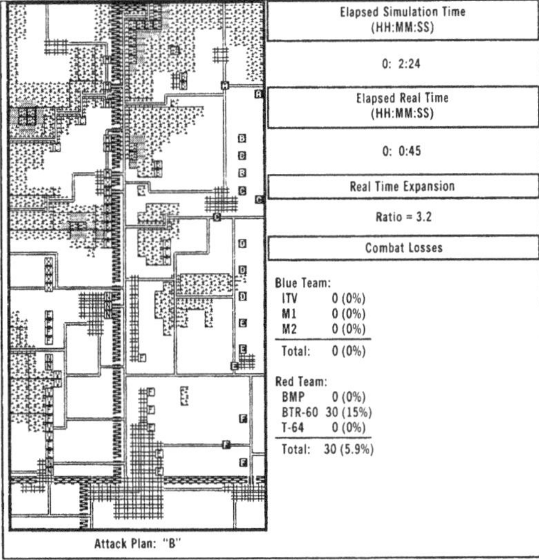

Figure 2. The Phase Two screen shows "Red" Forces attacking from right to left (inverse video) over the terrain map. NOTE: The right side of the screen shows simulation time which approximates the time an attack would actually take. Real time represents the time a player spends observing the attack. Expansion is the ratio of real time to simulation time. Combat losses show the number and type of vehicle casualties and a percentage of the total.

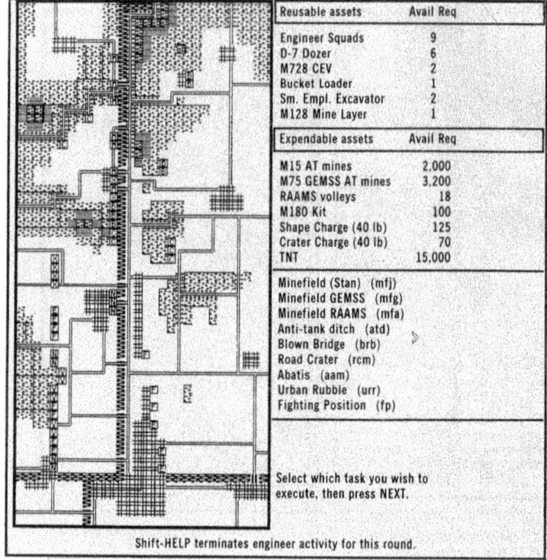

Reusable assets Avail Req
Engineer Squads 9
D-7 Dozer 6
M728 CEV 2
Bucket Loader 1
Sm. Empl. Excavator 2
M128 Mine Layer 1
Expendable assets Avail Req
M15 AT mines 2,000
M75 GEMSS AT mines 3,200
RAAMS volleys 18
M180 Kit 100
Shape Charge (40 lb) 125
Crater Charge (40 lb) 70
TNT 15,000
Minefield (Stan) (mfj)
Minefield GEMSS (mfg)
Minefield RAAMS (mfa)
Anti-tank ditch (atd)
Blown Bridge (brb)
Road Crater (rcm)
Abatis (aam)
Urban Rubble (urr)
Fighting Position (fp)
Select which task you wish to execute, then press NEXT.
Shift-HELP terminates engineer activity for this round.

Figure 3. The computer display during Phase One portrays the assets available to emplace selected obstacles or fighting positions.

served over eight years as a Combat Engineer. Mr. Deponai received his master's degree from the University of Illinois.

Dr. James E. Snellen is a research programmer at the Microcomputer Systems Laboratory at the University of Illinois at Urbana. He has a master's degree from California State College at Long Beach and a doctorate from the University of California at Davis.

CPT Rick Jones is an instructor in the Field Engineering Branch, Department of Military Engineering, at the U.S. Army Engineer School. He was previously assigned to the 23rd Engineer Battalion in Hanau, Germany. CPT Jones graduated from the Engineer Officer Advanced Course and Virginia Military Institute.

CPT Leo J. Fontana is a project officer in the Technology Training Branch, Department of Military Engineering, at the U.S. Army Engineer School. He was previously assigned to the 78th Engineer Battalion (Combat) in Ettlingen, Germany. CPT Fontana is a graduate of the United States Military Academy.

Engineer Solution

Walks and Steps (1)
Assemble Trusses (2)
Under-slab Util. (1)
Site Prep. (1)
Inst. Forms (2)
Place Concrete (3)
Place Block (3)
Place Trusses (2)
Roofing (2)
Finish (3)
Utilities (2)
Precut Frame (1)
Frame (1)

Problem/Solution submitted by 1LT Robert J. Smith, DME, Engineer Management Branch

Exterior line crew, Jimmy Robertson and Herbert Hudgins, perform recovery operations to restore power knocked out when a plane crashed into Building 550 at Defense Depot Memphis (photo by Willie Jones).

The Facilities Engineer in a Defense Logistics Agency

by MAJ Roger L. Gorres

It all starts with a call from the Engineer assignments officer at MILPERCEN. "You're being nominated for a Facilities Engineer (FE) position in the Defense Logistics Agency (DLA)."

You hold your reply, and he asks, "Are you still there?"

By now you have recovered enough to say, "What is DLA?"

The conversation then encompasses the role and mission of DLA and how it serves the other Department of Defense organizations. The initial conversation ends with your needing to reply to MILPERCEN by a certain date, accepting the duty. Still in a state of surprise, you make urgent phone calls to your superiors, your former commanders, and others trying to learn the status of a position called Chief, Facility Engineering Division, Defense Depot Memphis.

The next day you receive a phone call from the present Engineer officer in the slot and have many of your questions answered—and new ones formed. So you call back the assignments representative and calmly say that you will take the job, little realizing that you have just agreed to perform the toughest duty in your military career to date.

When your name hits the installation commander's desk, he talks to the present FE and several of your previous commanders to receive a commander-to-commander report of your abilities. While this is taking place, you are reviewing your decision and wondering if you have made the right choice, even though it is considered a joint service assignment. This is all forgotten when the next phone call informs you that you have been accepted and must report on a certain date, after going through the Facilities Engineering Management Course (FEMC) at Fort Belvoir, VA.

Your time is busy as you leave your organization; go to the FEMC; take a short vacation; receive an orientation from the Director of Installation Services and Environmental Protection, HQ, DLA, Cameron Station, VA; and finally arrive at your new home. The outgoing FE and his family warmly welcome you, as do the other military members of the depot.

As the FE introduces you around, you quickly realize that 99 percent of the work force is civilian. You also observe that the FE is a very **busy** individual, but you dismiss this as the usual urgency suffered by all officers preparing to depart a duty station. You even accompany him on an emergency call at 0200 concerning an air conditioning problem for the base computer facility. He shows you the emergency procedures to follow for the myriad utility requirements of the 642-acre complex (109 buildings, 33 miles of paved road, 26 miles of railroad track . . . total 1985 replacement cost of more than $837 million).

Toward the close of the two-week transition period, the FE spends more of his time preparing to leave, and you start sitting in ***the chair***. You make some initial decisions of minor importance and begin to feel that this job will be easy. After all, your official duty hours are from 0730 to 1600.

The old FE departs early on a Saturday morning, and the weekend is uneventful; so you approach Monday morning with a relaxed attitude. Then it happens. From the time the work bell rings until the office closes, you are BUSY. You make more decisions the first day than on any other day you can recall, including the worst days of your company command time. By the end of the first month, it starts to dawn on you just how BIG a job you have. Now you understand the old FE's last comment, the one about his inability to describe the difficulty of the job. You begin each day with the renewed determination and the desire to learn more, but you're grateful that the old FE left you with the work planned for the next four months.

Even with a 90-man, highly dedicated work force and no difficulty in obtaining funds for your work, you soon realize that you will never accomplish 100 percent of your requirements. There is just too much to do, and not enough time to do it in; so you concentrate on the most important 90 percent, an ability that must be acquired quickly.

The variety of work and complexity of decisions you must make are never-ending challenges. One minute you are in a telephone conversation with DLA headquarters concerning an $8 million MILCON (military construction) project, and the next minute you have an emergency phone call from security concerning a fire in a building.

You deal with your District Engineer, tenant commanders, architectural engineering firms, various EPA (Environmental Protection Agency) offices, and many other organizations. The realization soon sets in that *the buck stops at **your** desk.*

As time passes, you start to measure it in units of weeks because of the pace. The days are just too short to use as a guide. Some start at 0530 with physical training, and others end at 2200 hours with work on your Army War College's National Security Course Correspondence Program (to maintain the military education level of your counterparts **not** assigned to DLA).

Despite the workload, there is an unexpected benefit of your assignment that also comes to your attention at the six-months self-evaluation. That is the fact that you are always able to be at home with your family at night. This is a real treat, and they begin to enjoy your being there. The joy of seeing your wife and children each night and being able to plan time together—without last minute changes—is great!

Two Memphis firefighters extinguish plane crashed through the roof of a D (photo by Willie Jones).

tence says more than you can imagine. Those who have been in DEH assignments know what it means, but realize that it is impossible to convey to non-FE types.

If anyone is interested in doing such a job, there is more to consider. An example of what may happen at a moment's notice follows.

THE PHONE CALL (Every FE or DEH gets one, don't they?) comes in at 0100 on a Friday night. It has been a hectic week; the 40-hour official work week has really been 60 hours. You know the instant the security desk sergeant says his first word ("Major, . . .") that ***this is your PHONE CALL.***

"Major, an airplane has just crashed into Warehouse XYZ, and the building is on fire."

One second you were sound asleep, and the next second you are wide awake, mentally analyzing the exact location of the building and its utility connections, while simultaneously dressing in record time.

You and the first fire truck meet at the crash site, and you're stunned at what you see. You leave the scene 16 hours later, feeling ***years*** older, with three airline personnel dead and the building and contents loss approaching $10 million. However, the DLA mission of receiving, storing, and shipping continues with little or no delay; and except for one fifth of one building destroyed, the installation is fully operational by Monday morning.

This is a brief synopsis of what a DEH in DLA (it's still called an FE) assignment is like. Some things are certain: You will never be bored, never run out of something to do, and never have enough time to do all that is required. If you are a major who wants the challenge of being the DEH (and not the operations officer) and don't want to wait until promotion for such a position, an assignment in DLA could be just what you are looking for.

MAJ Roger L. Gorres is Chief of the Facility Engineer Division, Defense Depot, Memphis, TN. He was previously assigned to the 547th Engineer Battalion, Darmstadt, Germany; the 14th Engineer Battalion (Combat), Fort Ord, CA; and the U.S. Army Readiness Group, Fort Snelling, MN. MAJ Gorres is a graduate of the Engineer Officer Basic and Advanced courses, the Command and General Staff College, and the Army War College's National Security Course. He has a bachelor's degree in industrial engineering from North Dakota State University and a master's degree in business administration from the College of St. Thomas in St. Paul, MN.

Q. Can I plug into the Engineer School computer system with my home computer?

A. Dial-in access to the Engineer School computer system is scheduled to begin at the end of September. Computer software must be compatible with PLATO and will include lessons in general and military engineering, other military topics, and the Obstacle Planning Simulation (OPS). Computer courses delivered at Ft. Belvoir will also be available at education centers in CONUS. For further information, contact CPT Leo Fontana, (703) 664-3953, AV 354.

Q. What is the National Stock Number (NSN) for staples and tie wire used in constructing triple-strand concertina wire obstacles?

A. There is no NSN for the staples or tie wire. There is, however, a Federal Stock Number under Class 5315 and 9505, respectively. Staples can be fabricated locally, and #10 gage smooth wire can be used for tie wire.

Q. What is the Basic Initial Issue (BII) for the bridge transporter in a ribbon bridge platoon?

A. The BII for the M-812 is found in TM 5-5420-209-12, *Improved Float Bridge (Ribbon Bridge).* See pages B-4, C-1, and C-2.

Q. Where can we order copies of ***Engineer Enlisted Professional Development?***

A. The publication has recently been reprinted and is available through the Engineer Proponency Office, ATZA-EP, Ft. Belvoir, VA 22060-2591. For further information, contact SFC Bob Wagner, (703) 664-3760, AV 354.

A Living Genie

by LTC Robert H. McDonald

The view of the valley below was absolutely breathtaking, especially after our German guide pointed out that we were over 500 feet above the valley floor. Perched cautiously below the roadway surface on one of the bridge piers, we paid close attention to our guide's instructions, crawled back to the security of solid ground under our feet, and departed. This was not a "budget special" tour of Europe, but an orientation visit with a wallmeister team.

Historical Perspective

The wallmeister, translated literally as "rampart master," is a highly specialized engineer of the German Army (Bundeswehr) who is a gold mine of information for fellow NATO Engineers. In performing his mission of territorial defense, he follows in the proud footsteps of his predecessors centuries ago.

Fortification specialists have always been key members of armies. One of the oldest examples of their work is the Great Wall of China, while the Porta Nigra (Black Gate) in Trier remains as one of the best examples of Roman fortifications in Germany. During the Middle Ages in Germany, the Festungsbaumeister (fortress construction master) supervised the building of fortified castles and the construction of town defensive works. The term "wallmeister" was used as early as 1693 when Prince Frederick III mentioned these craftsmen in his *"Standing Orders for Fortification Measures in the Fortress."*

Wallmeister Training

Originally passed down from master to apprentice, wallmeister training was formalized in a school founded in Berlin in 1886. Several similar schools were established in other German cities between 1886 and 1914. In 1922, the various training locations were centralized and consolidated at the German Army Engineer School in Munich, where wallmeister training continues to this day.

While training of the wallmeister before 1886 concentrated on the construction of massive defensive works, the Berlin school broadened the course of instruction, and wallmeisters who served in the Reichswehr (World War I) or the Wehrmacht (World War II) received a more diversified curriculum like that currently presented to wallmeisters. The course now includes training in terrain reinforcement, obstacles and explosives, and weapons-system capabilities so that the wallmeister may be a true source of Combat Engineering expertise. This training in purely military areas follows a two-year Engineering Technician's course that includes subjects such as technical drafting and construction of permanent structures. To keep abreast of new developments and share their work experiences, wallmeisters annually attend a week-long advanced technical course.

The modern wallmeister is a true specialist with no real counterpart in the U.S. Army. Typically, he is a senior Engineer noncommissioned officer who volunteered for wallmeister duty and was selected based on past duty performance and technical expertise. A wallmeister receives no special pay for his job. Like his peers in active Bundeswehr units, he is paid based on his rank and service time.

After his selection, the wallmeister attends the Bundeswehr Engineer School in Munich for his specialized schooling. Upon completion, he is sent to his first wallmeister assignment, based both on where vacancies exist and on his personal desires. Once assigned, he can expect to stay in that location for ten years or more, depending on the time remaining until his mandatory retirement at age 53 or until his enlistment term expires. The benefits to the Bundeswehr of such a long service in one location are as great as they are to the wallmeister and his family.

Wallmeister Team

A wallmeister team has three members. The team chief is normally an active military E8 or E9 who is in a career military status and likely to be a wallmeister until he retires. The other military member is normally an E7 who is either in a career status (and may become a team chief upon a vacancy in his team or another team) or is a long-term enlistee who serves on the team until reaching the end of his 10 or 15-year enlistment. The third member of the team, the driver, is a government civilian who commonly is also a Bundeswehr reservist.

Wallmeister teams normally operate from an office on a Bundeswehr kaserne, but they are under the supervision of an Engineer officer at the Military Region Command (Verteidigungsbezirkskommando—VBK). The VBK staff engineer office sets work priorities and serves as the official link between the team NCOs and the Bundeswehr for personnel actions and other military matters.

The VBK, in turn, reports to the Military District Command (Wehrbereichskommando—WBK), which is subordinate to either the Northern or Southern Territorial Command whose mission is basically providing territorial defense rather than functioning as a major maneuver force headquarters.

Thus, while they are active-duty Engineers, wallmeisters are associated not with the active forces but with the home-defense element of the German military. This reporting chain shows why one of the paramount qualities considered in selecting an NCO for wallmeister duty is his ability to be a self-starter who thrives on working independently.

Members of a typical wallmeister team display their vehicle and equipment used to support their mission of territorial defense (photo courtesy of the German Military District Command (WBK) IV).

Typical Team

The team we visited is typical. HauptFeldwebel (Master Sergeant—HFw) Alfons Messner, team chief, has nearly 29 years of military service. Almost 17 of those were spent in various troop assignments or at the Engineer School in Munich. He has been a wallmeister for 12 years (the last 10 at his present location in central Germany) and expects to stay in his job for the remaining seven years until his retirement. The other sergeant was not present during our orientation visit. Since his 15-year enlistment term ends soon, he was on a job-hunting trip. The civilian driver has been with the team for four years and was a driver for the German Air Force before that. He is also an NCO in the Bundeswehr reserves. (As team drivers go, he is a relative newcomer. The driver for an adjacent wallmeister team has been driving for team members for just over 25 years.)

The modest team office consists of two rooms. One room is used by the team NCOs for paperwork and storing vast amounts of information. Plaques of appreciation for their support to various U.S. Army Engineer units on past exercises hang on the wall and are proudly pointed out to visitors. The other room is for the team driver and for the lockers in which they store extra clothing and equipment.

Introductory Briefing

HFw Messner enthusiastically gave us an overview briefing on his team's sector (which includes two counties in central Germany and follows their political boundaries), the types of obstacles found in it, obstacles being planned, demolitions storage sites, and how his team relates to the Territorial Command and can assist U.S. units.

He showed us copies of completed target folders for obstacles and explained the maps illustrating the target location, where its explosives are stored, routes between the storage site and target, cross-sectional drawings indicating where the explosive charges should be placed for optimal results, and blank forms used by the executing unit to report the extent of damage achieved. HFw Messner stated that in all cases the planned damage is the minimum amount required to produce an obstacle. Total destruction is not desired since it would considerably increase the time and cost necessary for the Germans to place the road or bridge back into use after hostilities. For each target he also maintains a folder outlining the target dimensions, estimated time and explosives needed to create the desired obstacle, and approximate cost to repair or replace the target.

He also showed us the engineer resource data books he maintains. These list local civilian firms which have such commodities as asphalt or concrete, lumber, gravel, or construction equipment.

Information on rivers and streams in his sector is also available to any unit for use in planning river crossings. Gathering this data integrates a curious mixture of modern technology (stream widths are measured using a sophisticated hand-held optical distance measurer) and basic Combat Engineering (stream velocity is commonly measured by throwing a stick into the stream and timing it over an estimated distance).

He told us that the team usually works in the office one day a week and travels the other four days checking various sites and updating information on engineer resources, waterway conditions, and target folder data. While there is no set schedule for these checks, his team normally visits each site in the sector at least monthly. During these visits, the team checks for damage or vandalism and also performs basic maintenance on the target demolition chambers or catwalks by greasing hinges or cleaning out accumulated dirt or rust. Only occasionally does he see his supervisor.

Most of their contact is by telephone or through his reports.

Team Van

Following the thorough office orientation on the duties of the wallmeister team, HFw Messner ushered us out to the team's transportation, an ordinary Volkswagen van that has been adapted by the team to support its work. The van has a worktable with drawers to serve as a field desk. Various hooks, boxes, and nooks hold the rest of the team's equipment—surveying stadia rod, measuring tapes, tools for removing demolition chamber covers, spare coveralls, wading boots, plus grease and cotton plugs to prevent water and dirt from clogging the demolition chamber cover openings. The van is a complete, yet compact, mobile work area organized with typical German precision.

Job Requirements

While the wallmeister is not assigned to the combat forces, his job not only requires close coordination with such forces, but makes him an unparalleled source of engineer information for Allied Nations as well as the Bundeswehr. For example:

- He must be an expert on the emplacement of obstacles in his sector to significantly assist in territorial defense.
- He must know the terrain and its tactical significance.
- He must know the types and capabilities of Bundeswehr munitions and equipment.
- He must know the local civilian sources of engineer resources in addition to any military sources within his sector.
- He must maintain a solid rapport with local political officials and civilian personnel involved with transportation systems, navigable waterways, power generation, communications, heavy construction, and industrial facilities within his sector.
- He must be familiar with the resources and planned obstacles in adjacent sectors.

In addition to being an information repository, the wallmeister assists Allied and Bundeswehr Engineers in planning obstacles—from site selection and determining the optimum type of obstacle to assisting in preparing necessary documentation for placing the target on a NATO list. If requested, wallmeisters normally will participate in unit field training exercises, lending their technical expertise and giving unit Engineers practical experience in coordinating host-nation support.

Typical Obstacles

During our visit, we were shown a stretch of public highway where a steel post obstacle can be installed quickly. With a river on one side and a steep slope on the other, this site appeared capable of being a very effective means of impeding enemy movement over the highway. Called a schachtsperr (beam post obstacle), the obstacle is created by placing steel I-beams (weighing nearly 500 pounds) into a prepared shaft in the roadway. The beam, rising nearly five feet above the road surface, is virtually impossible to remove from the shaft once emplaced, according to HFw Messner. In keeping with tactical doctrine, these shafts are built in rows, would have concertina wire placed among the beams and would be covered by fire. He explained that while this obstacle is more expensive to construct than demolition types, it is popular near urban areas since it is nonexplosive.

HFw Messner also showed us typical planned obstacle sites. We saw a railroad bridge and a highway bridge, each marked with the emplacement location for explosive charges to do effective, yet minimal damage to the structure. Each site has catwalks installed to assist troops in emplacing the charge and has routes marked for running the fuse or electrical wiring to the charge. We also saw a prechambered road crater site which is similarly engineered with a demolition chamber and fusing route requiring minimal troop time and effort to create an effective obstacle.

Demolition Storage

The wallmeister also monitors the storage of demolitions earmarked for barrier use. We were shown such a storage site, impressive not only for its size but also for the planning evident in the storage of the explosives themselves:

- All explosives and ancillary firing devices (blasting machine, fuse, detonating cord, and blasting caps) for a particular target are grouped together.
- Each grouping contains a complete inventory of the items stored for the target and a complete set of any tools a troop unit would need to gain access

Korea

by LTC William D. Brown

4P3 is an unlikely name for a troop construction project recently visited by the Chief of Engineers. Behind the unassuming title of 4P3 lies a most important effort to enhance the combat strength of the 2nd Infantry Division in Korea. An artillery fire support base, 4P3 is located just south of the Imjin River, only seven miles from North Korea. There, B Company, 44th Engineer Battalion (CBT) (HVY) completed what is perhaps the most interesting and challenging project undertaken this year in the 2nd Engineer Group.

B Company, commanded by CPT Don Curtis, deployed to 4P3 in March 1984 and bivouacked there in a tent city while constructing the facilities needed to support M-198 155mm howitzer batteries which will occupy the firebase on a rotational basis.

The complex includes six artillery firing positions, twelve wooden guard towers around the perimeter, three gate-guard buildings, ten 20×48-foot wood-frame billets, two latrines, a 40×64-foot dining facility, and a 20×48-foot administrative building. Other facilities, including two single-bay maintenance buildings, two fire direction control bunkers, interior roads and drainage, and perimeter fencing, were completed earlier under a CDIP (Combined Defense Improvement Program) initiative monitored by the Far East District.

While B Company was on site at 4P3, a great variety of challenges were met and overcome. The austere living conditions found the soldiers occupying G.P. medium tents from the very cold March weather to the rainy July conditions and on into the August heat, until the company moved into some of the just-completed billets. The nearest dining facility was at Camp Giant several miles away, while recreational facilities were even farther away.

With no designs available for firing positions, Engineers built and tested a prototype. The concrete firing pad was enlarged to accommodate self-propelled howitzers (photo by SP4 Tedric Garrison).

The construction itself was challenging since the company had no recent experience in this type of project. A design did not exist for the artillery firing positions. Thus, the platoon leaders and company commander, with the assistance of the battalion operations officer, prepared a design, built a prototype, and had the supported artillery battalion do a proof test with an M-198 155mm howitzer to verify the design. Based on this experience, the concrete firing pad was enlarged and the design modified to support self-propelled howitzers.

Flexibility and adaptability characterized other aspects of the construction as well. The standard theater-of-operations design for the guard towers would have required the guards to climb a ladder to reach the tower. Believing that an exterior stairway would make access easier and quicker, the 44th Engineer Battalion's S-3 design section modified the plans to accommodate a stairway, although this proved to be more complicated to build.

Engineer ingenuity was also required to find a way to place the concrete footers for several of the towers which were sited in areas inaccessible to wheeled vehicles. This problem was solved by using a D-7 bulldozer to very carefully tow the "old faithful" 16-S mixer into position to accomplish what the M-919 concrete mobile truck or commercial truck could not.

Although the project provided construction training and earned B Company recognition from the many visitors at the site, the company pushed hard to complete the remaining work on schedule, redeploy to its home base at Camp Nimble, and then immediately launch into its fall ARTEP. Once again, the men of the 44th Engineer "Broken Heart" Battalion lived up to their motto, *Builders of Freedom.*

LTC William D. Brown is the commander of the 44th Engineer Battalion (CBT)(HVY), Camp Mercer, Korea. He was a staff officer in the Program Analysis and Evaluation Directorate, Office, Chief of Staff, Army; Executive to the Chief of Engineers, OCE; and Executive Officer, 20th Engineer Battalion (CBT), Fort Campbell, KY. LTC Brown completed the Project Manager Course, the Defense Ssytems Management College, Command and General Staff College, and the Engineer Officer Advanced Course. He has graduate degrees in nuclear engineering from MIT and in operations research from George Washington University.

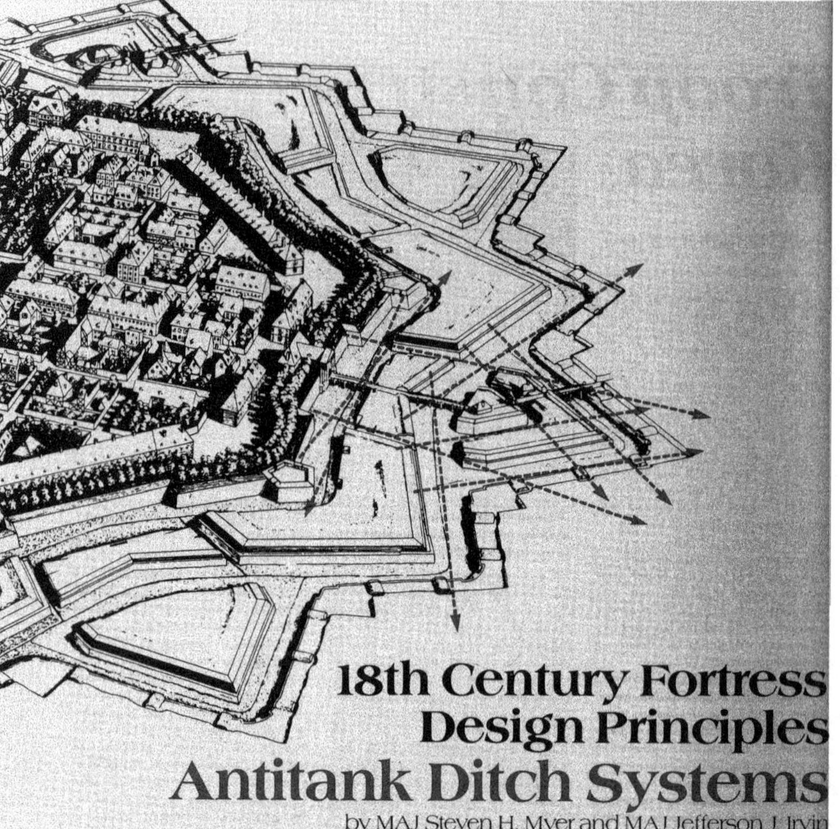

18th Century Fortress Design Principles Antitank Ditch Systems

by MAJ Steven H. Myer and MAJ Jefferson J. Irvin

Illustration of Neuf Brisach is from **The History of Fortifications** *by Ian Hogg. Copyright 1982, St. Martin's Press Inc., New York.*

In *"History and Military Engineering Design: An 18th Century Example"* (Spring, 1985), we argued that the profile of an 18th century European fortification yielded some general principles applicable to obstacle design. The plan view of the same fortification also reveals some useful ideas. From a vantage point overhead, the baroque fortress appears as a series of detached fortifications projecting from an intact main perimeter. Each outer fortification and the main perimeter are protected by interconnected linear obstacles: the fortress ditch system.

This article first discusses the principles governing the layout of this ditch system, highlighting the inherent advantages of the linear obstacle. It then gives an example of how these advantages can be exploited in the design of antitank ditch systems for antiarmor defense.

Neuf Brisach (shown above) is one of of the border fortifications built for France during the reign of Louis XIV. (This fortification is an easy day's excursion from Karlsruhe or Stuttgart.) The main fortress perimeter is the polygon delineated by the double row of trees. Firing platforms for 24-pound cannon point outwards from the lines of trees. Beyond the main perimeter are the detached forts. The raised edges on the outer sides of these forts are also firing platforms for cannon.

The shaded areas between the forts and main perimeter comprise the ditch system. The ditch walls on the outer (towards the enemy) side of each ditch are 12 feet high. The walls on the inner side of the ditches, which generally lead vertically up to the raised gun platforms, are 30 feet high. The ditches were thus difficult to enter on the enemy side (a 12-foot drop) and virtually impossible to scale on the friendly side. The layout of these outer forts and heir encircling ditches was a strict eometric exercise directed towards aximizing the effectiveness of the inear ditch obstacles.

The portion of the fortification over-iew overmarked with defending artil-ery lines of fire shows the following:

1. Every ditch segment was directly nfiladed by a rearward or adjacent ar-illery platform. Cannonballs fired rom this platform bowled along the itch length, caroming off hard mason-y ditch walls if fired slightly off line.

2. If an outer fortification was taken, here was a ditch behind that fortifica-ion, between it and the next rearward ayer of forts. This ditch, like all itches, was enfiladed by defensive fire. ecause the outer forts were open to he rear and lower than the more nward forts, the outer gun platforms ere themselves enfiladed by rear-ard, commanding fires. The enemy hus received no relief when he took an uter fort; he remained in crisscrossing ones of enfilading fire. The system was a rational series of linear obstacles in epth.

A brave enemy could storm the open area preceding the ditch system, bet-ting against the ability of the defend-ing infantry and artillery to hit iso-lated, scattered, moving targets. Once into the ditches, the attacker had a problem. He stood directly in the preset line of fire of defending cannon.

This is the significant advantage of a linear obstacle. It greatly reduces the difficulty of defensive target acquisi-tion. The easiest example to cite as a modern equivalent is the deployment of barbed wire in infantry defense. We employ concertina directly along the final protective lines of machine guns.

Linear obstacles also aid in the mod-ern antiarmor defense. We will first explain why minefields do not possess the advantages of linear obstacles, and in contrast why antitank ditches do. Then we will give a simple example exploiting the lessons of the 18th cen-tury fortress ditch system in the design of antitank ditch systems.

An effective minefield in an armor kill zone serves one major purpose: it forces enemy lead tanks to lower and use rollers and plows. This substanti-ally slows the enemy column, prolongs the time the column spends in the kill zone, and allows more targets to be suc-cessfully engaged. The TOW gunner, however, must still search through a three-dimensional fan of fire for indi-vidual moving targets; and the enemy has some capacity to take evasive action moments before TOW missile impact.

A proper antitank ditch is designed like its 2½-century-old French counter-part. It is painful to enter and difficult to exit. The attacking tank must labor-iously collapse the forward and rear ditch banks through time-consuming dozing and rocking motions. During this period of breach, if the ditch is aligned along TOW principal directions of fire, the TOW gunner is bowling along a lane in much the same man-ner as the artillerist on the late medieval French rampart.

The ditch need not be directly point-ing towards the TOW position, as this would be an invitation for enemy artil-lery or air strikes. The ditches need only be aligned so the angle is within the TOW's main fan of fire. The ditch alone reduces the target search from three to two dimensions. The more the ditch alignment approaches the TOW direction of fire, the more the search becomes one dimensional, and the more the flank of the trapped tank is exposed. For the breaching period, the ditch fixes the moving target. There is no evasive action.

The following example of task force antiarmor defense in sector is taken from the *Antiarmor Handbook* pub-lished by the 7th Infantry Division in February 1982 (pages 3-1 to 3-10). The handbook discusses the considerations surrounding the choice of TOW and platoon positions and the designation of armor kill zones. These locations are shown in Figure 1. An antitank ditch

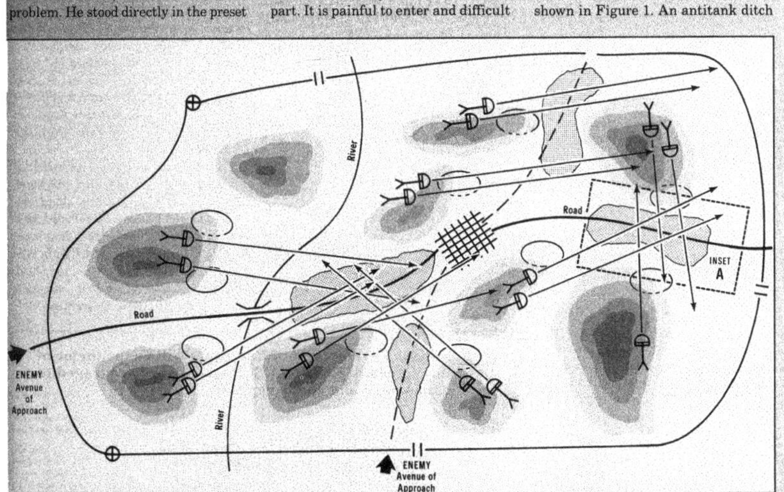

FIGURE 1. Overview of inset A (from Antiarmor Handbook)

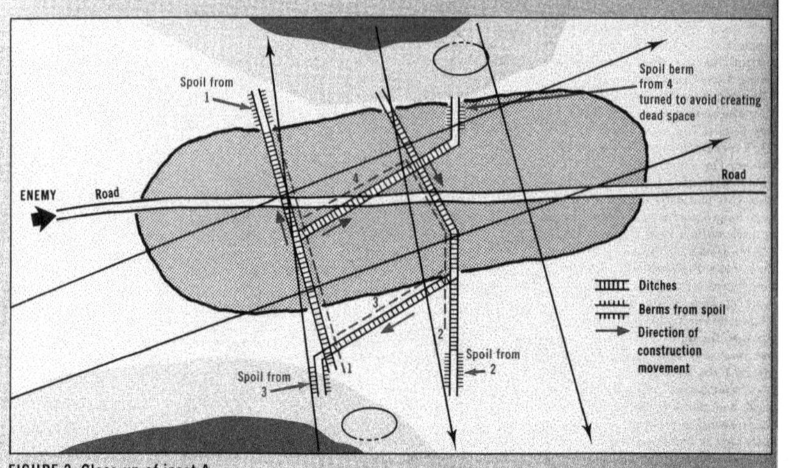

FIGURE 2. Close-up of inset A

system for the armor kill zone marked "A" is shown in a close-up in Figure 2. Note the following concerning the design of this system:

1. The rough pattern of the design is that of a pound sign, or crosshatching. This pattern has advantages in construction, as earthmovers can dig and dump in continuous loops. One set of 290M tractors can circuit, cutting ditches 3 and 4. Spoil berms are placed roughly parallel to defensive fires, creating no dead space, but forming additional obstacles.

An interesting variation would be to create at the end of the ditch segment two closely spaced parallel berms. The rearward berm would be higher than the forward, with the space between covered by enfilading fire. Tanks climbing over the first berm would plunge nose down into the base of the second: an antitank ditch above ground.

The leading edge of the ditch system should be sited on the reverse slope of a slight rise in terrain to mask the obstacle from approaching tanks. If this is not possible, the spoil from ditch segment 3 would be spread in front of the obstacle to mask the leading edge.

2. The crosshatching pattern is possibly broken (Figure 2) and oriented slightly askew from the lines of fire of intersecting pairs of TOWs. As mentioned before, this prevents the use of ditch orientation as a pointer to TOW locations.

3. The crosshatching creates "detached forts" in a manner similar to the 18th century pattern. Once the first ditch is breached, a second and possibly third ditch segment must be breached. The observant enemy tank commander would head for the ditch segment intersections to avoid multiple ditch breaches. These areas of intersection would be saturation mined.

This article serves several purposes. First, it demonstrates that history provides useful, frequently simple examples of the application of basic military principles. Second, it shows the inherent advantages of linear obstacles like antitank ditches over area obstacles like minefields. Both slow down the enemy, but the linear obstacle fixes the enemy along lines of fire. This advantage is worth the expenditure of considerable additional effort. Finally, it gives a simple procedure for basic antitank ditch pattern design, along the lines of logic defined by the French in the early 1700s.

MAJ Steven H. Myer is an assistant professor of mathematics at the U.S. Military Academy and served as a platoon leader in the 1/27th Infantry Battalion, 25th Infantry Division in Hawaii. He was company commander, 1/504th Infantry and assistant G-3 OPS in the 82nd ABN Division at Fort Bragg, NC. MAJ Myer has a bachelor's degree from the U.S. Military Academy and a master's degree from Stanford University.

MAJ Jefferson J. Irvin is an assistant professor of geography and computer science at the U.S. Military Academy. He served as a platoon leader and company commander in the 94th Engineer Battalion in Germany. MAJ Irvin has a bachelor's degree from the U.S. Military Academy and a master's degree from Stanford University.

Professional Development of Engineers will be the theme of the Winter issue of ENGINEER. Readers are encouraged to send manuscripts and photographs to:

ENGINEER Magazine
ATTN: ATZA-TD-P, Stop 291D
Fort Belvoir, VA 22060-5291

ACTIVE ARMY

7th Engineer Bn., 5th Inf. Div.
Ft. Polk, LA
LTC John Behrens
CSM Robert Strickland

8th Engineer Bn., 1st Cav., Div.
Ft. Hood, TX
LTC Steve Page
CSM George Ramirez

9th Engineer Bn., (CBT)(CORPS)
Aschaffenburg, Germany
LTC Pete Hines
CSM Donald Schmidt

10th Engineer Bn., 3rd Inf. Div.
Kitzingen, Germany
LTC Russ Furhman
CSM Dennis Watters

11th Engineer Bn., (CBT)(HVY)
Ft. Belvoir, VA
LTC Charles J. Mills
CSM William Crisp

12th Engineer Bn,. 8th Inf. Div.
Dexheim, Germany
LTC Carl Jensen
CSM Colin Hargrove

13th Engineer Bn,. 7th Inf. Div.
Ft. Ord, CA
LTC Mike Kuehn
CSM Roscoe Harshaw

14th Engineer Bn. (CBT)(CORPS)
Fort Ord, CA
LTC George Meador
CSM James Coley

15th Engineer Bn., 9th Inf. Div.
Ft. Lewis, WA
LTC Mike Norris
CSM John Ramsey

16th Engineer Bn., 1st Armd. Div.
Furth, Germany
LTC Robert J. Greenwalt
CSM Dallas Bailey

17th Engineer Bn., 2nd Armd. Div.
Ft. Hood, TX
LTC Pete Sowa
CSM Marvin Williams

19th Engineer Bn. (CBT)(CORPS)
Ft. Knox, KY
LTC Jim Gnage
CSM Langford Clay

20th Engineer Bn. (CBT)(CORPS)
Ft. Campbell, KY
LTC Gary Morgan
CSM Tom Singleton

23rd Engineer Bn., 3rd Armd. Div.
Hanau, Germany
LTC Dick Kanda
CSM Donnie Stoneking

27th Engineer Bn. (ABN)
Ft. Bragg, NC
LTC Mike Diffley
CSM George Shaw

29th Engineer Bn. (TOPO)
Ft. Shafter, HI
LTC Bob Kerby
CSM Robert Marshall

30th Engineer Bn. (TOPO)
Ft. Belvoir, VA
LTC Gene Hazel
CSM John Sewell

34th Engineer Bn. (CBT)(HVY)
Ft. Riley, KS
LTC Jim Lyles
CSM James Mangram

39th Engineer Bn. (CBT)(CORPS)
Ft. Devens, MA
LTC Philip Shoemaker
CSM Donald Boxall

43rd Engineer Bn. (CBT)(HVY)
Ft. Benning, GA
LTC Rick Shuler
CSM Edmund Armstrong

44th Engineer Bn. (CBT)(HVY)
Camp Mercer, Korea
LTC Doug Brown
CSM Delnora Rector

46th Engineer Bn. (CBT)(HVY)
Ft. Rucker, AL
LTC Hamp Conley
CSM Douglas Harris

52nd Engineer Bn. (CBT)(HVY)
Ft. Carson, CO
LTC Mike Collmeyer
CSM Bernd Dela-Cruz

54th Engineer Bn.
Wildflecken, Germany
LTC Jack MacNeil
CSM Arthur Browning

62nd Engineer Bn. (CBT)(HVY)
Ft. Hood, TX
LTC Mike Thuss
CSM Robert Sullivan

65th Engineer Bn., 25th Inf. Div.
Schofield Bks, HI
LTC Phil Carroll
CSM Matthew Lee

76th Engineer Bn. (CBT)(HVY)
Ft. Drum, NY
LTC Bill Traubel
CSM Charles Adams

78th Engineer Bn. (CBT)(CORPS)
Ettleingen, Germany
LTC John Wildenberg
CSM William Cleveland

79th Engineer Bn. (CBT)(HVY)
Karlsruhe, Germany
LTC Jess Gatlin
CSM Ivan Wentworth

82nd Engineer Bn. (CBT)(CORPS)
Bamberg, Germany
LTC Jim Craig
CSM Merlyn Pence

84th Engineer Bn. (CBT)(HVY)
Schofield Bks, HI
LTC Denny Cochrane
CSM Preston Thompson

92nd Engineer Bn. (CBT)(HVY)
Ft. Stewart, GA
LTC Floyd Griffin
CSM Irones Bryant

94th Engineer Bn. (CBT)(HVY)
Darmstadt, Germany
LTC Joe Larremore
CSM Wash Knoten

237th Engineer Bn. (CBT)(CORPS)
Heilbronn, Germany
LTC John Pierce
CSM Joseph Oliver

249th Engineer Bn. (CBT)(HVY)
Knielingen, Germany
LTC Mel Lynch
CSM Eugene Roberts

293rd Engineer Bn. (CBT)(HVY)
Balmholder, Germany
LTC John Glass
CSM Edward Price

299th Engineer Bn. (CBT)(CORPS)
Ft. Sill, OK
LTC Jim VanEpps
CSM Franklin Zorn

307th Engineer Bn., 82nd Abn. Div.
Ft. Bragg, NC
LTC Bob Flowers
CSM Bobby Ewell

317th Engineer Bn. (CBT)(CORPS)
Eschborn, Germany
LTC Jim Cooper
CSM James Terrell

326th Engineer Bn. (CBT)(AVLB)
Ft. Campbell, KY
LTC Jeff Wagonhurst
CSM Walton Woodall

536th Engineer Bn.
Panama
LTC Larry Winchester
CSM John Lobash

547th Engineer Bn. (CBT)(CORPS)
Darmstadt, Germany
LTC Steve Winsor
CSM Robert Thames

548th Engineer Bn. (CBT)(HVY)
Ft. Bragg, NC
LTC Bruce Malson
CSM Clarence Blackburn

549th Engineer Bn (SVC)
Schwetzingen, Germany
LTC Dan Waldo
CSM David Moore

559th Engineer Bn. (COMP)
Hanau, Germany
LTC Billy Ricks
CSM Richard Wilson

565th Engineer Bn. (COMP)
Nevrevt, Germany
LTC John Mills
CSM Kenneth Wojczynski

588th Engineer Bn. (CBT)(HVY)
Ft. Lewis, WA
LTC Wayne Murphy
CSM Thomas Carr

649th Engineer Bn. (TOPO)
Schwetzingen, Germany
LTC Samuel Schwartz
CSM Robert Turner

Composite Engineer Bn.
Ft. Bragg, NC
LTC Tim Pratt
CSM Wade Gattes

802nd Engineer Bn. (CBT)(HVY)
Camp Humphries, Korea
LTC Robert Froude
CSM Sam Moore

TRADOC

3rd AIT Bde.
Ft. Leonard Wood, MO
COL James E. Brayboy
CSM Leroy N. Mello

4th AIT Bde.
Ft. Leonard Wood, MO
COL Fred Edwards
CSM Russell E. Fultz

SPT Bde.
Ft. Leonard Wood, MO
COL Jude Patin
CSM Eugene A. Rasmussen

1st Bn., 2nd Bde.
Ft. Leonard Wood, MO
LTC Dick Hoover
CSM Edward O. Strunge

2nd Bn., 2nd Bde.
Ft. Leonard Wood, MO
LTC Jim Raymond
CSM Roy Duffield

4th AIT Bn., 2nd Bde.
Ft. Leonard Wood, MO
LTC Don Holzwarth
CSM James Williams

2nd AIT Bn., 4th Bde.
Ft. Leonard Wood, MO
LTC Tom Jacobus
CSM Timothy E. Arnold

3rd Engineer Bn., 4th Bde.
Ft. Leonard Wood, MO
LTC Jim Jenkins
CSM Domer Richter

4th Engineer Bn., 4th Bde.
Ft. Leonard Wood, MO
LTC Dave Lindsay
CSM Paul Fulwood

2nd Bn., 3rd Bde.
Ft. Leonard Wood, MO
LTC Hal Alvord
CSM Wayne A. Utley

5th Bn., 3rd Bde.
Ft. Leonard Wood, MO
LTC Bill Boutin
CSM Roy C. Burton

1st Engineer Bn., USAESB
Ft. Belvoir, VA
LTC John Carey
CSM Joseph C. Alexander

3rd Engineer Bn., USAESB
Ft. Belvoir, VA
LTC Al Jansen
CSM Jerry Coughill

NATIONAL GUARD

ALABAMA

1169th Engineer Group (CBT)(CORPS)
Huntsville, AL
COL Andrew J. Heritage
CSM Frank M. Birmingham

145th Engineer Bn.
Centreville, AL
LTC Joseph A. Harris
CSM Alex M. Latham

151st Engineer Bn. (CBT)(CORPS)
Fort Payne, AL
LTC David E. Powell Jr.
CSM Robert T. Turner

877th Engineer Bn. (CBT)(HVY)
Hamilton, AL
LTC John A. Nichols III
CSM Norman K. Emerson

1203rd Engineer Bn. (TOPO)
Dothan, AL
LTC Dwight W. Tew
CSM Marion M. Spivey

1343rd Engineer Bn. (CBT)(CORPS)
Athens, AL
LTC Joel N. Pugh
CSM Billy G.Swanner

31st Engineer Co.
Fayette, AL
MAJ John F. Parker
1SG Jesse C. Rainey

166th Engineer Co. (AFB)
Centreville, AL
CPT Jackson W. Pow
1SG John N. Nichols Jr.

167th Engineer Co. (AFB)
Demopolis, AL
CPT Arthur D. Evans
1SG Joseph A. Langford

168th Engineer Co.
Eutaw, AL
CPT Jeffrey Clary
1SG Bennie L. Abrams

1204th Engineer Co. (CARTO)
Slocomb, AL
CPT Otis Corbin Jr.
1SG David H. Avery

1205th Engineer Co. (SURVEY)
New Brockton, AL
CPT James M. Morris
1SG Charles E. Goodson

ARIZONA

258th Engineer Co. (CSE)
Phoenix, AZ
CPT Thomas T. Galkowski
1SG Thomas Matthew

259th Engineer Co. (CSE)
Phoenix, AZ
CPT David Freeland
1SG Bruce Ward

ARKANSAS

875th Engineer Bn. (CBT)(CORPS)
Jonesboro, AR
LTC William L. Stanley
CSM Charles T. Purvis

239th Engineer Co.
Clarksville, AR
MAJ Ronald S. Chastain
1SG James A. Carter

CALIFORNIA

132nd Engineer Bn.
Sacramento, CA
LTC Ronald W. Cross
CSM Gerry D. Reese

579th Engineer Bn. (CBT)(CORPS)
Santa Rosa, CA
LTC Jerrold L. Jurrin
CSM John David

112th Engineer Co.
Chico, CA
CPT Michael F. Hau
1SG John Whittier

CONNECTICUT

192nd Engineer Bn.
Putnam, CT
MAJ Richard E. Blake
CSM Gerald S. Bennett

242nd Engineer Bn. (CBT)(CORPS)
Stratford, CT
MAJ Joseph T. Wojtasik
CSM John Bodnar III

248th Engineer Co.
Norwich, CT
CPT Carl A. Blackstone
1SG John J. Sigersmith III

250th Engineer Co. (MGB)
Danielson, CT
1LT Richard A. Donais
1SG Joseph O. Gadbois

FLORIDA

153rd Engineer Co.
Lake City, FL
MAJ Richard G. Donoghue
1SG Richard T. Patterson

269th Engineer Co.
Live Oak, FL
CPT Ronald T. Duguid
1SG James G. Gaskins

GEORGIA

265th Engineer Group
Marietta, GA
COL John R. Paulk
CSM King D. Laviner

560th Engineer Bn.
Columbus, GA
LTC Benjamin W. Grinstead
CSM Morris E. Stafford

878th Engineer Bn. (CBT)(HVY)
Augusta, GA
LTC Thomas R. Williams
CSM Donald L. Hartley

1148th Transportation Co.
Augusta, GA
CPT Bobby J. Donaldson
1SG Wayne E. Henderson

HAWAII

227th Engineer Co.
Honolulu, HI
CPT Kerry K. Oshiro
1SG James Ilae Jr.

IDAHO

116th Engineer Bn. (CBT)(CORPS)
Lewiston, ID
MAJ Michael P. Whiles
CSM Gordon J. Hubbard

248th Engineer Bn.
Idaho Falls, ID
LTC Forrest P. Hanson
CSM Clifford C. Carlson

129th Engineer Co.
Payette, ID
CPT Randy J. Dillon
1SG Fredrick J. Egurrola

ILLINOIS

233rd Engineer Co.
Joliet, IL
MAJ John G. Zupancic
1SG Harlow A. Peues

INDIANA

113th Engineer Bn.
Valparaiso, IN
LTC Charles F. Burns
CSM (Vacant)

1313th Engineer Co.
Edinburgh, IN
1LT James A. Fritsche
CSM Ancil D. Ballinger

IOWA

224th Engineer Bn.
Fairfield, IA
MAJ Roger C. Roskens
CSM Dale L. Blodgett

KANSAS

891st Engineer Bn. (CBT)(CORPS)
Iola, KS
MAJ James E. Lee
CSM Chester C. Johnston

KENTUCKY

201st Engineer Bn. (CBT)(CORPS)
Ashland, KY
MAJ Bruce W. Pieratt
CSM Edwin F. Conley

LOUISIANA

225th Engineer Group (CONST)
Cape Beauregard, LA
COL Charles Lindsay
CSM Riley Woods

205th Engineer Bn. (CBT)(HVY)
Bogalusa, LA
LTC Wilson Maloz Jr.
CSM Howard Jordan

527th Engineer Bn. (CBT)(HVY)
Bossier City, LA
LTC Charles M. Partin
CSM Robert Bott

528 Engineer Bn. (CBT)(HVY)
Monroe, LA
LTC Edmund Giering III
CSM Fred Lindsay

769th Engineer Bn. (CBT)(HVY)
Baton Rouge, LA
LTC Fred Palmer
CSM Clarence Thibodeaux

2223rd Engineer Bn. (MAINT)
Baton Rouge, LA
LTC Donald Bringol
CSM Earl Picard

256th Engineer Co.
Opelousas, LA
CPT Michael Richardson
1SG Herbert Prudhomme

2228th Engineer Co.
Bunkie, LA
CPT Joseph Kutch
1SG Roger D. Swan

MAINE

240th Engineer Group
Waterville, ME
COL Roscoe Tibbetts
CSM Raymond A. Young

133rd Engineer Bn.(CBT)(HVY)
Portland, ME
MAJ Donald Laflin
CSM Fred Desarno

262nd Engineer Bn.
Bangor, ME
LTC Norman Giroux
CSM Richard Graves

MARYLAND

121st Engineer Bn. (CBT)(CORPS)
Ellicott City, MD
LTC Maurice W. Partin
CSM John H. DuVall Jr.

MASSACHUSETTS

101st Engineer Bn.
Reading, MA
LTC John J. Hannon
CSM Paul S. Rouillard

181st Engineer Co. (CSE)
Whitman, MA
CPT Brian E. Gilmore
1SG David B. Martin

MICHIGAN

46th Engineer Group
Flint, MI
COL Elon M. Pearson
CSM David R. Daly

107th Engineer Bn.
Ishpeming, MI
LTC James P. Dougovito
CSM William A. Eckloff

207th Engineer Bn.
Bay City, MI
MAJ Michael L. Paluda
CSM (Vacant)

507th Engineer Bn.
Wyoming, MI
LTC Edward E. Eckart
CSM Dale A. DeMarr

1432nd Engineer Co. (MGB)
Wyoming, MI
1LT Marvin R. Deur
1SG Donald J. Roberts

1433rd Engineer Co.
South Haven, MI
CPT Dennis L. Knappen
1SG Alfred L. Edmonds

1435th Engineer Co.
Bay City, MI
CPT James R. Anderson
1SG Phillip A. Wagner

1436th Engineer Co.
Muskegon, MI
CPT Edwin S. Braden
1SG Joseph R. Schwartz

1437th Engineer Co. (AFB)
Sault Ste Marie, MI
CPT Robert H. Beauprey Jr.
1SG Howard G. Sanderson

MINNESOTA

682nd Engineer Bn.
Roseville, MN
LTC Kurt H. Hoehne
CSM Allan K. Knutson

MISSISSIPPI

168th Engineer Group
Vicksburg, MS
COL Jerry Keeton
CSM Marvin Smith

223rd Engineer Bn. (CBT)(HVY
West Point, MS
LTC Dennis Self
CSM Royce E. Fulgham

890th Engineer Bn. (CBT)(HVY
Gulfport, MS
LTC Woodrow Lyon
CSM Barnard A. Harrington

MISSOURI

35th Engineer Bde.
Jefferson Barracks, MO
BG Waylen E. Jobe
CSM Claude J. Huskey

135th Engineer Group
Cape Girardeau, MO
COL Robert A. Harry
CSM Herschel L. Hunt

110th Engineer Bn.
Kansas City, MO
LTC Harlan L. Hess
CSM Sherman Todd

203rd Engineer Bn. (CBT)(HVY
Joplin, MO
LTC Andrew J. Hager Jr.
CSM Philip H. Chew

880th Engineer Bn.
Jefferson Barracks, MO
LTC Donald R. Sievers
CSM Harold V. Munson

1138th Engineer Bn.
Jefferson Barracks, MO
COL Ronald Weiscoptf
CSM William Leeper

1140th Engineer Bn.
Cape Girardeau, MO
COL David R. Moll
CSM Paul R. Summers

220th Engineer Co.
Jefferson Barracks, MO
CPT Norman D. Charleville
1SG Guy N. Swiger

134th Engineer Group (CBT)(CORPS)
Hamilton, OH
COL Jack D. Arnett
CSM James T. Dougherty

416th Engineer Group (CBT)(CORPS)
Walbridge, OH
COL Richard F. Mueller
CSM Carl S. Bicanovsky

112th Engineer Bn. (CBT)(CORPS)
Brook Park, OH
LTC Louis V. Leo
CSM Clarence W. Smith

216th Engineer Bn. (CBT)(CORPS)
Portsmouth, OH
LTC Lynn V. Coriell
CSM Larry D. Rase

372nd Engineer Bn. (CBT)(CORPS)
Kettering, OH
LTC Roger E. Rowe
CSM Thomas G. Brown

512th Engineer Bn.
Cincinnati, OH
MAJ Chester Lewis
CSM Albert F. Spiller

612th Engineer Bn. (CBT)(CORPS)
Walbridge, OH
LTC Vivan Duffy
CSM James A. Robarge

26th Engineer Co. (ACR)
Brook Park, OH
CPT Timothy J. Harmon
1SG Richard Gadke

OKLAHOMA

120th Engineer Bn. (CBT)(HVY)
Okmulgee, OK
LTC Alfred F. Westrope
CSM Larry E. Edmonston

245th Engineer Co.
Muskogee, OK
CPT William D. Fillman Jr.
1SG Eugene N. Foster

OREGON

1249th Engineer Bn. (CBT)(CORPS)
Salem, OR
LTC Fred R. Flint
CSM Donald W. Knapp

162nd Engineer Co.
Lake Oswego, OR
CPT William V. Clement
1SG Robert M. Cule

PENNSYLVANIA

103rd Engineer Bn.
Philadelphia, PA
LTC James J. DiBella
CSM John F. Hoke

876th Engineer Bn. (CBT)(CORPS)
Johnstown, PA
LTC Charles Bechtel
CSM Terry L.Lienhardt

PUERTO RICO

130th Engineer Bn. (CBT)(CORPS)
Camp Tortuguero
Vega Baja, PR
MAJ Emilio Diaz-Colon
CSM Angel Birriel

RHODE ISLAND

243rd Engineer Bn.
Warwick, RI
MAJ James T. Dunn
CSM Jean T. Vanti Jr.

861st Engineer Co.
East Greenwich, RI
CPT Herbert J. Andrade
1SG Ronald A. Cunha

1118th Engineer Co.
Woonsocket, RI
CPT Albert Guarnieri Jr.
1SG Arthur W. O'Rourke

SOUTH CAROLINA

122nd Engineer Bn.
Edgefield, SC
MAJ Frank H. Chapman
CSM Donald G. Robinson

122nd Engineer Co.
Saluda, SC
1LT William C. Derrick
1SG Kenneth D. Miller

125th Engineer Co.
Camden, SC
CPT Xanthan W. Polk
1SG Jerry W. Strawbridge

SOUTH DAKOTA

109th Engineer Group
Rapid City, SD
COL Richard P. Gross
CSM John W. Mechling

109th Engineer Bn.
Sturgis, SD
LTC Robert D. Daane
CSM Norman L. Pudwill

137th Engineer Bn.
Wagner, SD
LTC Lawrence L. Weiss
CSM James L. Selers

153rd Engineer Bn.
Huron, SD
LTC Robert M. Benson
CSM Robert L. Stratton

200th Engineer Co. (ABR)
Chamberlain, SD
CPT Michael J. Dacy
1SG Ronald E. Globke

211th Engineer Co. (MGB)
Lemmon, SD
CPT Harold D. Irland
1SG John Jund Jr.

214th Engineer Co.
Hot Springs, SD
CPT David A. Oerlline
1SG Phillip G. Knapp

842nd Engineer Co. (CSE)
Spearfish, SD
1LT Charles R. Gray
1SG Harold D. Haivala

854th Engineer Co.
Wagner, SD
CPT Norbert L. Mohnen
1SG Vernon J. Sip

TENNESSEE

194th Engineer Bde.
Nashville, TN
BG Lytle Brown III
CSM Billy J. Law

230th Engineer Bn.
Martin, TN
LTC Allen Strawbridge
CSM Samuel J. Fugua

155th Engineer Co.
Waverly, TN
CPT Robert M. Stooksberry
1SG Charles Cullum

212th Engineer Co. (CBT)(HVY)
Monteagle, TN
CPT Larry L. Owens
1SG C. D. Fenstermacher

913th Engineer Co.
Union City, TN
CPT Terry M. Smyth
1SG Frank L. Mandrell

2998th Engineer Co.
Martin, TN
CPT Ken R. Parks
1SG Joseph D. Smith

TEXAS

111th Engineer Bn.
Abilene, TX
LTC Clifford B. Barkley
CSM Tommy W. Ivison

386th Engineer Bn. (CBT)(CORPS)
Houston, TX
LTC Alvin J. Haley
CSM Eston L. Boehm

VERMONT

45th Engineer Co.
Rutland, VT
CPT Paul M. Liberty
1SG Robert F. Knight

131st Engineer Co. (CSE)
Burlington, VT
CPT Dale R. Norton
1SG John J. McCarthy

VIRGINIA

176th Engineer Group
Richmond, VA
COL Thomas T. Thompson
CSM Gay W. Davis

276th Engineer Bn.
Richmond, VA
LTC Larry E. Gilman
CSM James C. Bishop Jr.

1030th Engineer Bn.
Gate City, VA
MAJ Claude A. Williams
CSM Billy T. Gilreath

237th Engineer Co.
Fredericksburg, VA
CPT Kenneth E. Lankey Jr.
1SG Winston Ward

1031st Engineer Co.
Gate City, VA
CPT Robert L. Sparks
1SG Billy Larke

WASHINGTON

286th Engineer Co.
Bellingham, WA
MAJ Donald L. Adderley
1SG Arnold H. Wahl

WEST VIRGINIA

111th Engineer Group
Saint Albans, WV
COL Eldridge R. Casto Jr.
CSM Joseph J. Sale Jr.

1092nd Engineer Bn. (CBT)(CORPS)
Parkersburg, WV
LTC John R. Mathews
CSM Denver L. Guthrie

119th Engineer Co. (CSE)
Clarksburg, WV
CPT James B. Henderson
1SG John H. Sandy

193rd Engineer Co.
Oak Hill, WV
CPT William H. Miller
1SG Thomas M. Powell

WISCONSIN

264th Engineer Group
Eau Claire, WI
COL Michael L. Downey
CSM Palmer Johnson Jr.

426th Engineer Bn.
Onalaska, WI
LTC James Nelson
CSM Willis B. Fernholtz

724th Engineer Bn. (CBT)(CORPS)
Superior, WI
MAJ Robert G. Treland
CSM Thomas L. Meronek

32nd Engineer Co.
Onlaska, WI
CPT Wayne E. Wright
1SG Richard Roth

229th Engineer Co.
Prairie du Chien, WI
CPT Wayne D. Sharp
1SG Gerald J. Zuhlsdorf

273rd Engineer Co.
Onalaska, WI
CPT Bill G. Koch
1SG James E. Schwaegerl

WYOMING

133rd Engineer Co. (CSE)
Laramie, WY
CPT Martin R. Gill
1SG Wayne Anderson

he commanders and command sergeants major for all active units were obtained formation on National Guard units was supplied by individual states. The Army Reserv ts is scheduled for the Fall issue. Readers are encouraged to send any additional GINEER.

Commissioned Officers' Branch

Revised OPMS:

The revised Officer Personnel Management System (OPMS) will gradually change the officer corps from a dual specialty system to one in which officers will be managed, developed, and promoted by branch and/or functional area. The revised OPMS will affect many facets of the current system.

One major change will be the consolidation of multiple specialties into a single branch (Figure 1). For the Engineer community, that equates to converting specialty codes 22 and 23 to "areas of concentration" within Engineer Branch.

NEW DESIGNATION		PREVIOUS DESIGNATION	
		21K	General Engineer
General Engineer	21A	21G	General Army Support Engineer
		21A	Combat Engineer
		21B	Construction Engineer
Combat Engineer	21J	21E	Battlefield Support Engineer
		21J	Combat Engineer
Topographic Engineer	21C	21D	Topographic Engineer
		22A	Topographic Engineer
		21C	Engineer Management Officer
		21F	Garrison Support Engineer
Construction Engineer	21D	21H	Specialized Support Engineer
		23A	Facility Management Engineer
		23B	Contract Construction Management Engineer

Figure 1. Evolution of Engineer Specialty Codes.

As outlined in *Commanders Call* (October 1984), major features of the revised system include:

- One branch per officer.
- Multiple career paths (single, dual, and sequential).

Many Engineer officers will single track within Engineer Branch. To provide the flexibility to develop individual officers within their abilities and to meet the Army's and the Corps of Engineers' needs, some Engineer officers will also be developed in a functional area by either dual or sequential tracking (Figure 2).

The officers under the current OPMS (generally senior captains and field grade officers) will be grandfathered if they are equally qualified in both of their currently held specialties. This means that, for example, an officer who holds specialties 21 and 53—and is determined to be qualified in both—will retain those specialties.

Officers qualified in specialties 21 and 23, or 21 and 22, will single track in Engineer Branch, as they currently are doing, and retain classification code 21.

Officers not qualified in their currently designated additional specialty may be able to single track within Engineer Branch, dual track by selecting another functional area, or sequentially track and serve in

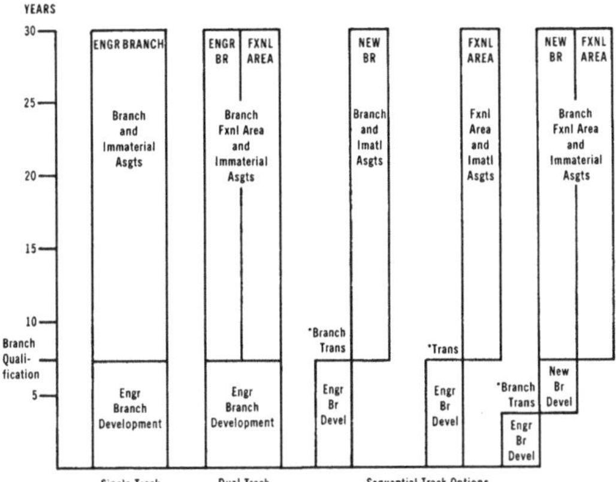

NOTES: 1. Branch includes assignments and development in one or more areas of concentration.

2. Branch immaterial (USAREC, ROTC, Instructor, Protocol, IG, OESO, Community Commander) - All Branches.

3. Combat Arms immaterial (Reserve Advisor, Chief of Staff, Instructor) - IN, AD, AV, AR, FA, EN.

4. Logistics immaterial (Logistics Officer, G-4, Instructor, Reserve Advisor) - OD, QM, TC.

* These transfers do not necessarily occur at only the 7 and 3 year points, but are shown here for illustration.

Figure 2. Typical Career Patterns for Engineer Officers Under Revised OPMS.

only a functional area as their qualifications and Army requirements permit.

Some officers currently holding specialties in two branches may retain both or be designated into a single area of concentration within the second branch. For example, an officer qualified as a 21/81 (Petroleum Engineer) might be designated as 21/92F, the new branch and area of concentration code for petroleum management within the Quartermaster Corps.

These are some of the difficult options being considered by MILPERCEN in developing the transition plan. Individual qualifications will be reviewed and the desires of the officers affected will be solicited before a decision is made on reclassification. Full implementation of the revised classification system is expected in FY 87.

Officers in Year Group 79 are scheduled to have additional specialties designated in late 1985. Not all officers will receive a second specialty, but those who do are expected to be designated into functional areas rather than into specialties of other branches.

Commissioned Officers' Branch (continued

(continued)

The revised classification system will enhance and strengthen the branch concept which has been diminished under the current system. This "rollup" of specialties 21, 22, and 23 into one branch code within Engineer Branch is similar to the "rollup" which occurred in Military Intelligence and Aviation Branches and the Ordnance, Quartermaster, and Signal Corps. The new management structure will improve the Army's ability to manage and develop its Engineer officers.

Engineer Branch Chief

MAJ John Basilotto is acting Chief of Engineer Branch, Office of Personnel Management, at MILPERCEN. LTC Jim Simms takes over the branch in September.

Warrant Officers' Branch

Qualified Personnel Needed

Engineers need qualified personnel to apply for warrant officers in the following fields:

621A Engineer Equipment Repairs Technician
821A Survey Technician
841A Terrain Analysis System Technician

For more information, contact CW4 Edward Cole, AV 221-7839.

Warrant Officers Training Program

Applicants for warrant officer must complete a "triple check" evaluation under the new Warrant Officers Training Program before being assigned to their first unit. The new Warrant Officers Training Program abolished direct appointments on Oct. 1, 1984.

The "triple check" process consists of the following.

First, the applicant must be approved by a centralized board drawn from MILPERCEN and the different proponents.

Second, once selected, the service member must complete the Warrant Officer Entry Course (WOEC). This training consists of almost seven weeks of mandatory MOS immaterial training in leadership, ethics, communications, military history, Army structure, and other common core subjects. WOEC is conducted in a high stress, OCS-type environment at Ft. Rucker, AL; Aberdeen Proving Ground, MD; and Ft. Sill, OK.

Individuals must have a current physical examination which allows them to undergo rigorous physical training.

Individuals must pass a *standard* Army physical readiness test without modification (activities like bicycling or swimming may not be substituted).

Individuals over 40 years of age must have "over 40" PT clearance.

Third, candidates in Engineer MOSs will receive their technical training at Ft. Belvoir, VA, or Ft. Leonard Wood, MO. The Engineer School is responsible for certifying the individual is qualified for appointment in his or her MOS based on diagnostic examinations and completion of a resident technical course.

Soldiers interested in applying for warrant officer appointment should refer to DA Circular 601-84-4, *WO Procurement Program FY 85*. For more information, contact CW4 Edward Cole (703) 325-7839, AV 221-7839.

NCO and Enlisted Soldiers' Branch

Promotion Point Worksheet

The U.S. Military Personnel Center announced that the revised Promotion Point Worksheet (DA Form 3355) for promotion to E5 and E6 was fielded in April 1985. Scheduled for implementation in May and June, the form emphasizes physical fitness, self-discipline, professional competence, and a commitment to self-improvement and achievement. The commander's recommendation for promotion will also be a part of the form.

Duty performance points awarded by the commander were decreased from 200 to 150 points. Promotion board points were also decreased from 250 to 200 points.

The standards and points awarded for other areas such as education, SQT training, and time in service and time in grade were also changed or eliminated.

Master Bridge Builder Dies

Sir Donald Coleman Bailey, 83, inventor of the Bailey Bridge, died recently in Bournemouth, England. Bailey spent much of his early life creating small models of bridges from pieces of wood. He drew the original design of his reknown structure on an envelope and sold it to the British War Department in 1941 for 12,000 pounds ($48,000).

Bailey's idea for his particular design came when he sensed the need for bridging narrow water barriers. The bridge was ideally suited for the terrain and streams encountered in Europe during WWII. Except for the major rivers, most water obstacles had steep banks; yet they were within the limits of the design. The usual cluster of village housing at destroyed crossing sites restricted any mechanical lifting, hence only manpower could be used. Additionally, there were mountain sidecuts, canals, and railroad overpasses requiring passage.

"Without the Bailey Bridge we would not have won the war," Field Marshal Montgomery once said. "It was the best thing in that line we ever had."

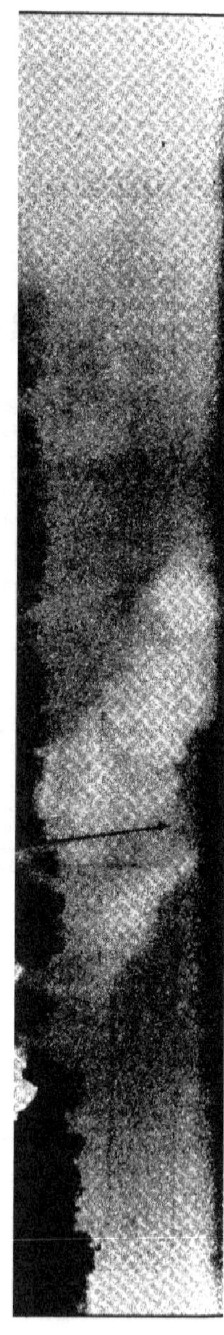

Initiative—The Key Ingredient

A Personal Viewpoint

by CPT William Scully

The other day while I was instructing an EOBC class, a student was wrestling with many of the new terms, acronyms, and jargon that he was encountering. He was confused about a term called "AirLand Battle." He said that he really did not know what it was and asked me to explain it to him.

Without going into the tactics involved, I said that AirLand Battle doctrine extended the main battle area to incorporate the full scope of the battlefield—forward, rearward, and vertically. More important, however, from the human dimension, it reversed the defensive posture mentally to one fully incorporating the spirit of the offense. I took a moment to digress and tell the class how I felt about this new doctrine and what must be done to make it work.

It is very important to me that the AirLand Battle doctrine was developed. The doctrine gives soldiers the psychological advantage of initiative associated with offensive operations. My belief is supported by the age-old cry of the football sportscaster who complained that the defense was on the field all day, and thus it was inevitable that they wore down to defeat.

The defense no longer has to worry about wearing down, and the offense can have a little fun focusing their efforts in putting some points on the board. We must have leaders who will take initiative and capitalize on the offensive opportunities provided by the AirLand Battle. To have leaders who will demonstrate initiative means we must do two things.

First, our Army must be able to recognize dynamic leaders who have the ability to *take charge*. Second, the Army must develop other leaders to the point that they can employ this new doctrine. The answer is to structure a leadership climate that will thrive on initiative and innovative spirit.

The Army is constraint oriented. At the company commander level, success is judged too much by a person's ability to cope with a myriad of checklists (i.e., IG reports, SOPs, readiness reports, inventory) and not enough with the ability to take charge, create, and succeed. The saddest part of all is that not enough attention is paid to the bottom line—mission accomplishment.

Instead, the success factor is based upon partial successes which are checked-off along the way. In this case, the sum of the parts does not equal the whole. ARTEPs, FTXs, and even the NTC have become a G-2 game and not honest displays of ability. Commanders enter these exercises understanding what they must accomplish in order not to lose—instead of focusing on all-out fighting to *win!*

The Army as a whole must encourage more dynamic leaders—more self-starters. The AirLand Battle was not made for the Jim O'Leary's (Jim's name has been changed to protect the innocent) of the world.

Who is Jim O'Leary? He is a kid who played high school sports with me. He was never cut from a squad, and he started on a few teams. The problem with Jim was also the thing that made him a success. Jim had "coach's eyes." That's right, no matter what sport he played, he always sought the coach's approval after every play. He would back-pedal down the basketball court looking at the bench to check the coach. He would look in from the infield or over at the sidelines.

It is true that the coach felt some security in putting Jim on the playing field, but you could never get the big play from him. He never created any real advantage because he lacked the assertiveness or the innovation to take charge on his own volition. What he did well was minimize the losses . . . not create the win.

AirLand Battle embodies the spirit of the offense. It must have leaders who can create the advantage even at times when there is none, or to initiate action in the absence of instruction. Jim O'Leary was ultimately unsuccessful because when the game got heated, there was never enough time to check with the coach; and he didn't know what to do.

The stakes of the AirLand Battle demand that our leaders are better than Jim O'Leary. The good news is that we have people who fit the bill. The bad news is that the leadership climate does not allow them to come into the spotlight. The leadership climate that will produce winners in the AirLand Battle is mission oriented, observes more than it directs, and rewards initiative on site.

A German general once explained to me how the German army trains its armor leaders. The system works on a series of mission-type orders in which the young leader is given the mission and must develop his own solution. The general explained that "initiative" was the key. The observers watched to ensure that the young leader took action. Even if the action was doctrinally unsound (this could be coached), it was better than no action at all. A shrug of the shoulders by the young leader helped choose another career for him.

For maximum effectiveness of our force under the AirLand Battle doctrine, the American Army must do more to create an environment as described by that German general. The organization must sift out the "shoulder shruggers," and it must watch, develop, and reward those who *take charge*. This climate must start in

(Continued on page 15)

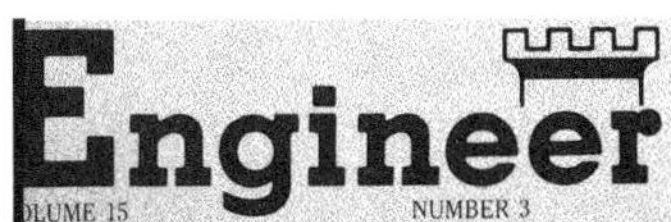

)LUME 15 NUMBER 3 FALL 1985

THANKS, LOU!

Special thanks to LTC James W. Shoff II, CPT Richard J. Cashman, and the Department of Combined Arms.

On the Cover

Soldiers of today continually train to become the effective leaders of tomorrow. Teamwork, one of the many facets of leadership, is necessary as these engineers hustle to connect a short ramp to an MGB during Operation Pontonier (U.S. Army photo).

FEATURES

DEPARTMENTS

NGINEER (ISSN 0046-1989) is an authorized publication of the U.S. Army Engineer Center and Fort Belvoir, VA. Unless specifically stated, material appear-g herein does not necessarily reflect official policy, thinking nor endorsement by any agency of the U.S. Army. The words he, him, or his are used to represent ersonnel of either sex. All photographs contained herein are official U.S. Army photographs unless otherwise credited. The use of funds for printing this iblication was approved by Headquarters, Department of the Army, on July 22, 1981. Material herein may be reprinted if credit is given to ENGINEER id to the author. ENGINEER's objectives are to provide a forum for the exchange of ideas, to inform and motivate, and to promote the professional develop-ent of all members of the Army engineer community. Direct correspondence with ENGINEER is authorized and encouraged. Inquiries, letters to the editor, mmentaries, manuscripts, photographs and general correspondence should be sent to: ENGINEER Magazine, ATZA-TD-P Stop 291D, Fort Belvoir, VA 2060-5291. Phone: (703) 664-3082, AV 354. ENGINEER may be forwarded to personnel in military units. Address changes should be sent to ENGINEER. ibscriptions to ENGINEER are available through the Superintendent of Documents, U.S. Government Printing Office, Washington, D.C. 20402. A check money order payable to Superintendent of Documents, must accompany all subscription requests. Rates are $11.00 for domestic (including APO and FPO) ddresses and $13.75 for foreign addresses. Individual copies are available at $3.00 per copy for domestic addresses and $3.75 for foreign addresses. Second lass postage paid at Fort Belvoir, VA, and additional mailing offices. POSTMASTER: send address changes to ENGINEER, ATZA-TD-P, Stop 291D, Fort elvoir, VA 22060-5291.

A survey party on elephants passes a bulldozer working on the Ledo Road in northern Burma. The 500-mile road was constructed by U.S. Army engineers during World War II to connect northeastern India with the Burma Road leading into southwestern China (U.S. Army photo).

Past in Review

The Ledo Road

by Dr. William C. Baldwin
Historical Division, O.C.E.

After the Pearl Harbor attack, the Japanese empire spread rapidly into southeast Asia. By May 1942, Japanese forces conquered most of Burma and threatened India. Because Japanese troops already controlled the Chinese coast, their conquest of Burma severed the last ground lines of communication between China and the western Allies.

During the early years of the war, American leaders believed that China could become a major theater in the war against Japan but would require huge infusions of military equipment and supplies. With Japan in control of southeast Asia, the Allies had to airlift supplies across the vast Himalayan range that separated India from China. Many doubted that this hazardous air route could transport the enormous quantities of supplies that China needed.

In late 1942, the Allies planned an offensive that would clear the Japanese from northern Burma and allow the construction of an overland line of communication to China. American engineers would build a road from the town of Ledo in northeastern India to connect with the old Burma Road which led to southwestern China. Construction of the 500-mile Ledo Road through the remote and inhospitable jungles and mountains of north Burma was one of the largest and most demanding tasks given to U.S. Army engineers in World War II.

Primative roads already existed for the southern half of the route, but the first 275 miles of the road passed through uncharted jungles and mountains. In November 1942, three engineer units, which had received only part of their equipment, began work under the command of COL John C. Arrowsmith, who told his troops to put the leading piece of equipment ahead as fast as possible and build the best road they could to keep up with it.

Work progressed rapidly until the monsoons came in April 1943. Throughout the summer, torrential rains washed out bridges and collapsed embankments. The combination of rain and worn-out equipment stopped progress on the road as engineers struggled to save what they had already built.

In the fall of 1943, COL Lewis A. Pick, later Chief of Engineers, took charge of the project. Gradually, more engineer units and equipment arrived to work on the road; local labor and Chinese army engineers assisted. During early 1944, COL Pick had to provide combat support to Allied troops who were pushing the Japanese out of north Burma. In February work stopped because the roadhead was too close to Japanese lines, and in May the monsoons again brought progress to a halt.

With north Burma recaptured and the monsoons over, the road moved forward rapidly in late 1944. One engineer battalion built 104 bridges totaling 5,105 feet in three months, and a light pontoon company built a 1,200-foot pontoon bridge over the Irrawaddy River. In late January 1945, COL Pick left Ledo with a large convoy and, after several delays, reached Kunming, China, on February 4 amid great celebration. The Ledo Road, dubbed *Pick's Pike* by the soldiers and officially named the Stilwell Road, now provided a ground link to China.

U.S. Army engineers provided almost half of the labor required to build the Ledo Road. Their existence, according to the official history of the theater, was a "grim monotony of rain, damp, heat, mud, mildew, mold, insects, isolation, boredom, and physical effort in an obscure corner of the world." Their work, however, produced one of the major engineer accomplishments of World War II.

Suggestions for further reading:

Leslie Anders, *The Ledo Road: General Joseph W. Stilwell's Highway to China* (Norman: University of Oklahoma Press, 1965).

Karl C. Dod, *The Corps of Engineers: The War Against Japan, US Army in World War II* (Washington, D.C.: Government Printing Office, 1966).

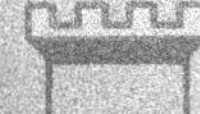

Letters to the Editor

The DEH Management Course in Europe

In support of Mr. Ketchum's article, *"Preparing for your DEH Assignment,"* ENGINEER, Spring 1985, I want to urge attendance at "functional" training courses for personnel enroute to DEH, or DEH-equivalent, assignments in Europe.

The Facilities Engineering Management Course (FEMC), a general overview of the DEH business, and the DEH Executive Management Course, current issues facing the DEH, provide a preparatory base necessary for enhanced job performance and are offered at the United States Army Engineer School (USAES), Fort Belvoir, VA. In Europe, at their Munich facility, the 7A Combined Arms Training Center (7A CATC) offers the DEH Management Course, which provides the USAREUR perspective of the DEH business. This course complements the USAES DEH training.

Particular emphasis should be placed on attendance at the FEMC, with an eye toward a well-rounded DEH Training Program including all three complementary courses. To this end, review by DA of current assignment procedures was requested, so that appropriate training can be scheduled enroute.

C. Cary Jones
Assistant Deputy Chief of Staff
Engineer (Engineering & Housing)
HQ, U.S. Army, Europe, and Seventh Army

Bailey Bridge . . . A Back Breaker

I read with some interest an article from the May 6th edition of the *Philadelphia Inquirer* regarding the recent death of Sir Donald Bailey. I think it might be of interest to other members of the Army engineer community considering the role that the Bailey Bridge has had in the Corps of Engineers. I would think that just about every engineer soldier, officer, enlisted and NCO alike, has had the opportunity and challenge of assembling a Bailey Bridge.

However, having been a Bailey Bridge platoon leader for over a year as a second lieutenant and having humped with the 500-plus pound panels and 800-plus pound stringers along with my troops, I would take issue with the comment that its components "could be carried easily by a few men."

MAJ Timothy P. Drozd
U.S. Army ROTC Instructor Group
University of Pennsylvania

Note: See tribute to Sir Donald Bailey in ENGINEER, Summer 1985.

112th and 121st Vital to Normandy Landing

I would like to note an omission made in your winter edition article, *"WWII Engineers in the European Theater."* The Normandy Landings section of that article failed to note this battalion and the 121st Engineer Combat Battalion. The 112th and 121st closely followed the 146th Engineer Battalion and preceded the Engineer Special Brigades ashore.

Besides eyewitness accounts from former members of this organization, I have attached three items taken from this organization's history files to support this letter. Enclosure number one is a landing diagram with the 112th highlighted. Enclosure two is a portion of the 146th Engineer Combat Battalion's Field Order Number 1 noting the missions of some of the 112th units on Omaha Beach. Enclosure number three is an extract from a letter by the 1121st Engineer Combat Group noting the actions by the 112th Engineer Battalion.

The actions of this battalion at Omaha beach earned it the Presidential Unit Citation (see enclosure four).

While I'm aware that not every engineer unit can be mentioned, the vital role as assault engineers with the 116th Infantry could hardly be overlooked when it is placed with the roles of the 5th and 6th ESBs. The 146th Engineer Battalion lost nearly 40 percent of its troops and 80 percent of its equipment upon landing. I would strongly suggest that this battalion played a vital role on that historic day that deserves a notation in your magazine.

LTC Louis V. Leo
HQ, 112th Engineer Battalion (CBT)(CORPS)
Ohio Army National Guard

Engineer Unit Designations

I just finished reading the Summer issue of ENGINEER Magazine and was impressed with the Engineer Command Update.

One of the questions that arose in my mind was whether ENGINEER Magazine has ever published a series of articles on how the various engineer units obtained their unit designations. I have seen a similar series of articles on the division-sized units in the SOLDIERS Magazine over the last three years.

I believe that such a series of articles on engineers would be informative and a significant teaching tool for our younger engineer officers and soldiers. If such an article has already been published, or a book has already been written on the subject, I would appreciate knowing about it.

Winston V. Coley
CPT, EN
USAR

Note: ENGINEER has not printed such articles. Readers, can you help provide the information?

News & Notes

Assault Bridges to be Evaluated

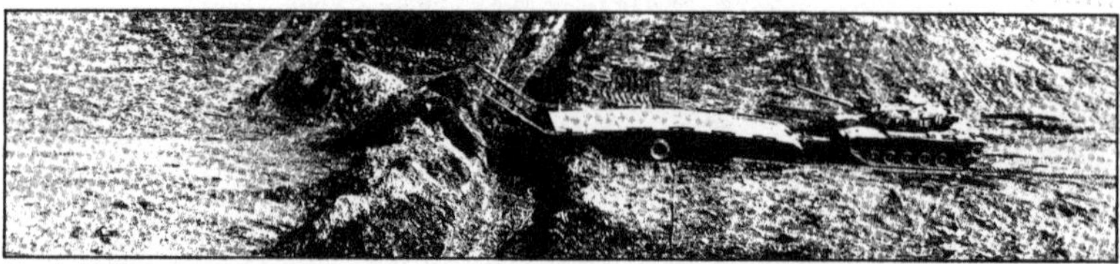

New bridging systems to support the Army and Marine modernization programs will be tested during the next 18 months. This Class 70 assault bridge can breach terrain gaps of 30 feet and can be split down the middle for easier transport by air, sea, or rail.

The Combat Systems Test Activity (CSTA) at the Aberdeen Proving Ground, MD, will test new bridging systems for the Army and Marine Corps during the next 18 months. Actual test sites, however, will be at Fort Lewis, WA, and installations in Pennsylvania.

According to Nancy Troccoli, CSTA test director, plans are being developed for a heavy assault bridge (HAB) and a light assault bridge (LAB) for the Army and a trailer-launched bridge (TLB) for the Marine Corps. Both the HAB and the TLB are Class 70 bridges, making them capable of supporting the heaviest tank in the Army inventory (63-ton M1A1 Abrams). The LAB, a Class 30 bridge, is intended for light engineer units not equipped with heavy tanks.

According to Byron Hawley, Troop Support Division, the new systems will improve battlefield mobility, enabling commanders to overcome "channelizing" effects of obstacles.

"By taking advantage of deep gullies, streams, and destroyed bridges . . . an enemy commander can channel forces opposing him into areas where his defenses are best. The bridges we're developing will allow our forces to cross these obstacles quickly and reach areas where the enemy's defense is weaker. The bridges will also enhance our ability to conduct retrograde movements when the situation requires," he said.

New Tool Ideas Wanted

The Army has established a new entry point within the Army Materiel Command for new tool ideas or suggestions for minor items of equipment. This is to assist and encourage tool users to submit their suggestions to the Army's maintenance community for evaluation and possible acquisition.

The new screening point is:

Commander
USAMC Materiel Readiness
Support Activity (MRSA)
ATTN: AMXMD-MD
Lexington, KY 40511-5101

New ideas may also be sent to MRSA through SMART channels. That address is:

Commander
U.S. Army Logistics Center
ATTN: ATCL-CST (SMART)
Ft. Lee, VA 23801-6000

The M998 series high mobility multipurpose wheeled vehicle (Hummer) is one of two replacements for the M151 ¼-ton truck. The Hummer, which is being fielded now, is equipped with an air-conditioning unit that will be maintained by engineers in the 52C MOS. The 15 varieties of the Hummer include two cargo/troop carriers, eight weapons carriers, three ambulances, and two communications carriers (photo courtesy of the LTV Corporation).

Engineers Help Feed Hungry Children

Over 2,000 children at six feeding centers in Gao, Mali, now get two meals a day instead of one, thanks to the 565th Engineer Battalion which built an M4T6 assault bridge to transport grain (photo by SP4 Craig Beason).

U.S. Army combat engineers are bringing food to thousands of hungry children in drought-stricken Mali, on an M4T6 assault bridge they built and now operate.

A 15-man detachment from the 565th Engineer Battalion, 7th Engineer Brigade, Karlsruhe, West Germany, built the tactical pontoon raft near the southern Sahara village of Gao and began to ferry truckloads of grain across the Niger River on May 24.

The grain, which is donated by the U.S., France, Switzerland, Holland, and Denmark, is distributed from 160 Red Cross feeding centers in the district most affected by the two- year drought.

"The extra grain brought in the raft allows us to double the amount of food we give out," Red Cross nutrition advisor Pascal Villenueve said. Instead of one meal a day, the six feeding centers in Gao now feed about 2,000 children twice daily.

Supplies to the town dwindled while the ferry that normally connects Gao with seaports to the south was being repaired in the capital city of Bamako. The ferry can't make the 550-mile return trip until the Niger River rises, which normally happens by September. The engineers will operate their raft until then.

Before the Army raft was built, few trucks made the three-day journey from ports in Benin, Senegal, Togo, and Ivory Coast where the donated grain arrives. The ones that did were delayed two days at Gao while their shipments were off-loaded by hand into small dugout canoes and paddled across the river.

This method cost the drivers about $100 daily, and one ton in fifty was lost to spillage or theft. The U.S. alone has donated 17,000 tons of grain to Mali in 1985. Much of that sat at the seaports until word of the raft reached the truckers there.

The engineers used C-130s to deploy the equipment from the capitol to the remote desert town of Gao, and 20 Malian soldiers helped the Americans transport the bridge by truck to the raft site. An Air Force airlift team packed the three C-141 loads at Ramstein, reloaded the equipment at Bamako for nine C-130 flights to the smaller Gao airport, and helped off-load there.

Once the raft reached the river, the engineers built the five-float M4T6 raft in less than two days, working through sandstorms and daily temperatures of over 135 degrees. "Twelve soldiers laid on all the deck plating in four hours," 1SG Douglas Masterson said. "That's good time for twice that many people."

The Malian Army gets its training and some equipment from the Soviets, French, and West Germans. This is the first time Malian and American soldiers have worked together and is the largest American presence ever in the country.

(SP4 Craig Beason, 7th Engineer Brigade)

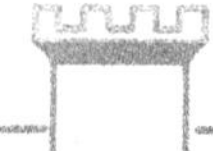

News & Notes

Dealing a New Deck

A new design for bridge decks that could reduce the weight of the Army's future bridges by 20 percent was developed by the Belvoir R&D Center.

Catherine Kominos, an engineer in the Engineer Support Laboratory, began work on the deck design as an independent research project after her branch chief suggested that she experiment with a membrane and shell structure as a design for a bridge deck.

Bridge mobility is directly related to the weight of the bridge components, and the heaviest part of the bridge is its deck. Traditionally, military bridges were designed as deck-floor beam systems which carried vehicle loads to truss girder support systems. Deck surfaces were flat and carried only local loads. Following World War II, engineers began to design deck surfaces which were part of the support structure, creating a composite deck structure.

"We knew that a membrane structure was the most efficient means of weight distribution, but there was no record of its being used in either civilian or military bridge structures," Kominos said.

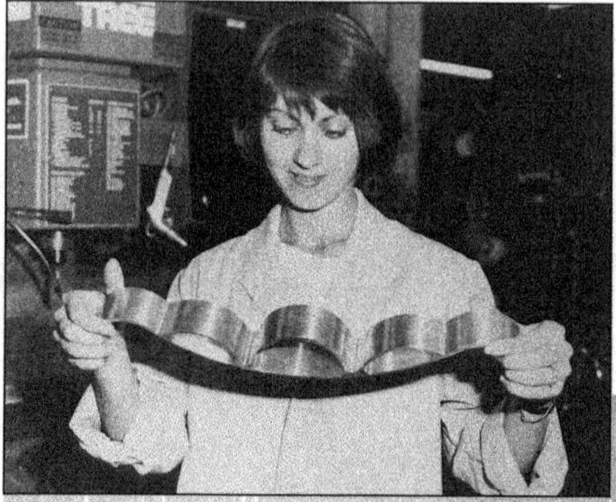

Catherine Kominos examines a completed model of her new bridge design. If tests are successful, this concept could reduce the weight of Army bridges by almost 20 percent (photo courtesy of Belvoir R&D Laboratories).

The new design consists of a curved membrane stiffened by a series of opposing curved shells which formed the deck surface. The structure would reduce the weight of the bridge by eliminating the top cord of the bridge deck. Computer tests show that the design could "theoretically support a Class 70 vehicle," Kominos added.

After further testing and producing models, the Belvoir R&D Center plans to let a contract for producing 10-foot sections for initial evaluations later this year.

Fort Bragg . . . or Bussed

It began as a training mission . . . B Company, 27th Engineer Battalion was to parachute into Fort A. P. Hill, VA; march one mile to an airstrip; destroy it with explosives; and return to Fort Bragg, NC, by helicopter. Engineers of the 82nd Airborne Division would then rebuild the landing zone.

What the 27th Engineers didn't know was that fate had other things planned for them. Almost everything that could go wrong, did.

Trouble first started when the engineers' transportation to Fort A. P. Hill was delayed for two hours because of mechanical problems with the C-130 Hercules aircraft. The airplane was eventually fixed, but high winds over the drop zone forced the paratroopers to cancel their jump.

The engineers did, however, airdrop 500 pounds of tools and 1,200 pounds of explosives on two of the several passes made over the drop zone.

After landing at the Richmond, VA, airport, the engineers returned to the drop zone by bus where they picked up their equipment and marched to the airstrip.

Upon arriving at the airstrip, the paratroopers learned they were unable to use their explosives because an extension on the midnight deadline to destroy the runway could not be granted.

Determined to complete their mission, the engineers used their picks, shovels, posthole diggers, and a lot of muscle to crater the airstrip during the night. They also showed ingenuity in using a D-7 bulldozer to destroy the runway. As the sun began to rise, Company B's crew completed their mission with a total of 30 potholes, each measuring approximately 5 x 5 x 4 feet, dug into the airstrip.

But the ordeal was not over for the soldiers. The final straw was drawn when inclement weather approached Fort Bragg. The CH-47 Chinook helicopters scheduled to fly the paratroopers home were grounded, once more leaving them to travel by bus.

CPT Minihan, Company B commander, later credited his troops for a job well done. "They continued to drive on and get the job done when things began to go wrong." **(PFC Ruben Maestas, PAO, Fort Bragg, NC)**

Mapping on Video Disc

A microcomputer-controlled video disc system assembled by the Engineer Topographic Laboratories provides a unique mission-planning tool (photo courtesy of ETL).

Video disc technology may soon help commanders map out their battle plans. Scientists at the U.S. Army Engineer Topographic Laboratories (ETL) have assembled a microcomputer-controlled video system which makes it easy to store, retrieve, and display maps and manage other military information.

Army groups in West Germany observed how the system works when ETL researchers demonstrated the equipment at the USAREUR Military Engineering Conference in Berchtesgaden. After the conference, they conducted hands-on sessions for officials at USAREUR Headquarters in Heidelberg, the 1st Armored Division in Ansbach, and the 649th Engineer Battalion in Schwetzingen.

"We wanted to show how the microcomputer/video disc combination could be used to manage large amounts of mapping and tactical data," said Rob Lambert, an ETL project engineer who demonstrated the system in Germany.

The system has a microcomputer, a video disc player, a television signal decoder, and a touch-panel controlled television monitor. ETL scientists wrote software programs and designed a special video to demonstrate the military planning applications of this equipment. The demonstration disc contains maps, aerial photographs, and three-dimensional terrain views for selected areas in Germany.

Microcomputers can increase the data management capabilities of video disc systems. By teaming the two technologies, ETL scientists have created a unique mission-planning tool.

Operators can take military symbols stored on a magnetic disc and arrange them over the recorded map displays to show the location of friendly and enemy forces. They can use the resulting "situation maps" to keep track of troop units by adding, deleting, or moving symbols as the battle progresses.

Users can also call up climate information and weapons data stored in the microcomputer. Climatological listings describe the temperature, precipitation, and ground conditions expected in the field. Weapons data files catalog the contents and capabilities of U.S. and enemy arsenals; photographs of these weapons systems are included on the video disc. An "order of battle" program breaks each army down into smaller units and shows their locations and strengths. These programs can support a variety of planning functions.

ETL's demonstration system is a first step in exploring the mapping applications of video disc technology. Researchers are examining other aspects of this technology which might be useful to the military. These studies may eventually pay off in improved techniques for managing and manipulating mapping and tactical data.

by MG Richard S. Kem, Commandant, U.S. Army Engineer School

Engineers: Key Members of the Combined Arms Team

We Must Train Our Young Leaders to Meet the Challenge

Warfare on the modern battlefield will be characterized by highly mobile forces equipped with lethal and highly technical weapons systems. To win on this battlefield, we need capable leaders. Combat power must be synchronized and brought to bear on enemy weaknesses at decisive times and places. AirLand Battle doctrine, therefore, requires that modern techniques and technology can be exploited to the greatest extent possible. This can only be accomplished through competent leadership. But the questions may arise, "Can leaders be trained? Can they be taught to be competent, especially in such adverse conditions as the modern battlefield?" The answer is a resounding yes!

In the Spring 1985 issue of ENGINEER, I emphasized three main ingredients of success—leadership, technical competency, and tactical proficiency. Again, I reiterate the importance of leadership. We have a responsibility to train our young leaders to be strong, aggressive, and competent. We owe them that training. We must make them all they can be for the sake of their soldiers, their Army, and their country.

History is replete with episodes in which engineers played a major role in determining the outcome of major battles. Engineers have repeatedly proven themselves to be key members of the Combined Arms team. Our goal, then, must be to continue being an assured combat multiplier. We must clearly understand the full scope of the battlefield, including the maneuver commander's concept. We must know his unit's capabilities and use our assets to complement the effectiveness of the maneuver force. Therefore, our most important mission at the Engineer School is to prepare the future task force engineers to meet this challenge.

The training which lieutenants receive at EOBC is the beginning of this process. The article, *"Final Exam in EOBC,"* by MAJ Bowen and CPT Dyer shows our progress in providing realistic and challenging training in scenarios similar to those that will be encountered by the lieutenant in support of a task force. Task force engineers need to be as conversant in all factors o METT-T as the maneuver commanders they support. In addition, the engineer lieutenant must know how to get the most out of his men and equipment. The Engineer School plays an important role in developing young officers; but engineer commanders must continue the training process, stressing the importance o dynamic leadership.

The task force engineer should participate in the planning phase of all operations. After-action reports from the National Training Center reveal that the task force engineer is frequently not a participant in the task force planning process and often does not attend operations order briefings. This lack of coordination almost always results in mission failure.

The normal associations that foster the teamwork among the maneuver commander, his staff, and the engineer platoon leader begin in garrison and are essential for working well in combat. Engineer commanders must ensure that their platoon leaders attend maneuver battalion training meetings and participate in CPXs, FTXs, and other training exercises to develop their tactical sense and to foster team spirit. Only then will engineers become fully integrated and truly become combat multipliers.

The task force engineer must also be imaginative, innovative, completely reliable, and have a desire for action. The article, *"The Will to Lead,"* by MAJ Benham and MAJ Kershaw describes how the task force engineer must develop an accurate understanding of himself, his subordinates, and the situation if he is to impose his will successfully in adverse conditions.

The task force engineer plays a key role in the engineer support of the Combined Arms. We have a responsibility to ensure that he is well prepared and totally integrated into all aspects of the Combined Arms team.

by CSM Charles T. Tucker, U.S. Army Engineer Center & School

NCOs: The Passport to Effective Training

The NCO Is the Heart of the Army's Training Concept

All NCOs are trainers. A trainer is a role model, mentor, instructor, coach, and leader. This requires substantial time and effort. Usually, NCOs train their soldiers independently—unsupervised and unobserved by the chain of command. Consequently, the most critical evaluators of the trainers' performances are the NCOs themselves.

All trainers have one objective: To develop the best possible soldier with the available time and resources. Obviously the emphasis is on developing a soldier's technical and leadership skills for combat. To develop these two skills, NCOs must concentrate primarily on the soldier's ability to successfully accomplish individual tasks. They must also teach their soldiers how important unit cohesion is for mission accomplishment. Individuals do not win wars; squads, platoons, and companies do.

NCOs must be professional in all respects. Your credibility is directly related to your knowledge, technical expertise, conduct, conditioning, appearance, and demeanor. You should be knowledgeable of small unit tactics, basic weapons, MOS expertise, equipment, vehicles, and the capabilities and vulnerabilities of the opposing force.

As an NCO trainer, you will demand high standards of conduct from your soldiers. Conversely, you must always demonstrate these same high standards.

First, profane language should not be used. It rarely contributes to increased learning or effective training.

Second, soldiers are going to make numerous and repeated mistakes as they learn. Be patient in training slow learners.

Third, never demean, belittle, or embarrass your soldiers.

Fourth, you are a trainer and not one of the students. You must maintain *distance*. Only you can judge the correct measure of distance depending on your experience and confidence level as well as the group personality of your soldiers.

Fifth, you cannot afford to be a prima donna. Always be willing to set the example, fully participate in all activities, and share the hardships as well as the triumphs.

Finally, do not jeopardize your effectiveness as an NCO trainer with marginal weight, uniform, haircut, or improper footwear. Do you carry yourself erect? Do you salute smartly? Do you communicate in a military, effective, and respectful manner? Do you appear professional, or do you take shortcuts? If after some introspection you find yourself deficient in some areas, you must dedicate yourself to improvement.

There are many responsibilities inherent in training soldiers. Here are some of the most important:

- Use your training time effectively. Have a contingency plan, present hip pocket training, always carry abbreviated lesson plans for two or three subjects.
- Plan ahead and in detail. Use every minute, involve all soldiers, develop detailed checklists for field problems.
- Document soldier performance in detail.
- Improve your counseling techniques and approach to developing soldier performance.
- Know your soldiers.
- Be accessible to your soldiers.
- Enforce safety.
- Enforce personnel and property accountability.

The NCO is the heart of the Army's concept for training. Your individual skills and knowledge, your professional manner, and your ability to counsel and develop the students in your class or soldiers in your platoon all contribute to your effectiveness as a trainer. Never be satisfied with your present level of performance. Your responsibilities to the young officers you may train in EOBC and to the soldiers you may lead in a combat engineer platoon demand nothing less than your best effort, all of the time.

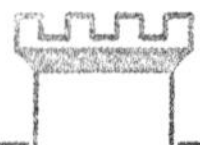

School News

Directorate of Evaluation and Standardization (DOES)

Engineer Orientation Team:

The Engineer Orientation Team (EOT) will visit engineer units during FY 86 in an effort to improve communications with these units. The team will conduct presentations about current developments within the Engineer School and gather feedback on the effectiveness of various school products.

Although dates for these visits were not available at publication time, the units below are on the agenda for EOT visits. In addition, engineer units in Europe are scheduled for visits during April 1986.

Ft. Carson, CO	Ft. Stewart, GA
Ft. Riley, KS	Ft. Benning, GA
Ft. Devens, MA	Ft. Rucker, AL
Ft. A. P. Hill, VA	Ft. Ord, CA
Ft. Knox, KY	Ft. Lewis, WA

Department of Military Engineering (DME)

EOAC Computer Literacy Instruction:

An additional 13 hours of computer literacy instruction was recently added to the EOAC curriculum. The 20 hours of training which students receive now includes word processing, spreadsheets, and database management applications.

Instruction is divided into two phases. The first phase consists of six hours of classroom instruction and a one-hour test covering basic computer terminology and applications. The second phase consists of two hours of classroom instruction, but also includes eleven hours of hands-on training with microcomputers and their applications. This material is taught concurrently with the computer-assisted instruction (CAI) which students receive throughout the course on the Engineer School's PLATO computer-based instructional system.

For more information, call CPT Leonard Whitehead at the Training Technology Branch. His telephone number is (703) 664-3953, AV 354.

Field Engineering Update:

Input from the field has indicated that although engineer lieutenants graduating from EOBC are technically proficient in such skills as installing minefields and emplacing obstacles, they are deficient in integrating these obstacles into an overall plan. This makes them less efficient as task force engineers.

In response, the Field Engineering Branch has increased the course hours taught at the basic course in an effort to integrate the technical skills of mobility, countermobility, and demolitions with tactical expertise. Conducted in close conjunction with Combined Arms instructors, the objectives of the increased course hours are the following:

- Future platoon leaders become proficient mangers and supervisors of field engineering skills such as obstacle emplacement and mine warfare.
- Future platoon leaders learn to perform better as viable Combined Arms members by seeing the overall plans of the battlefield and by properly representing the engineers to the task force maneuver commander.
- New lieutenants learn how to use their NCOs better and how to delegate tasks. (For this reason, the primary field engineering instructors will be NCOs.)

Professional Engineers Exam Guide:

A new *Guide to Registration for Professional Engineers* has been published by the U.S. Army Engineer School. Subjects covered are: benefits of registration, requirements for registration, overseas exam locations, organization of exams, preparation for the exam, addresses and phone numbers of all state boards, examples of military experience that are accepted by some boards, and a selected bibliography of preparatory study material.

Requests should be addressed to the Commandant, USAES, ATTN: PE/EIT Coordinator, ATZA-TE-RA, Fort Belvoir, VA 22060-5331.

New Director:

This department recently welcomed COL Peter O'Neill as its new director. COL O'Neill is the former chief of the Engineer Management Division, MILPERCEN, and a recent graduate of the Industrial College of the Armed Forces.

Already having spent two tours at Fort Belvoir, COL O'Neill has also served in Vietnam; Germany; Fort Carson, CO; the Corps of Engineers District in Philadelphia; and the Office of the Chief of Engineers.

Directorate of Training and Doctrine (DOTD)

Cableman's Handbook:

The Lineman's and Cableman's Handbook (ISBN 0-07-035678-5), recently replaced TM 5-765, *Electric Transmission and Distribution,* and will be issued free to users once. Units authorized the 52G MOS should send names of their property book officers, DODAAC (Department of Defense Activity Access Codes), and document number to: U.S. Army Engineer School, ATZA-TD-P, Stop 291D, Fort Belvoir, VA 22060-5291.

Brigade Slice Observations at NTC

by MAJ Robert G. McKeever and MAJ Robert L. Somers

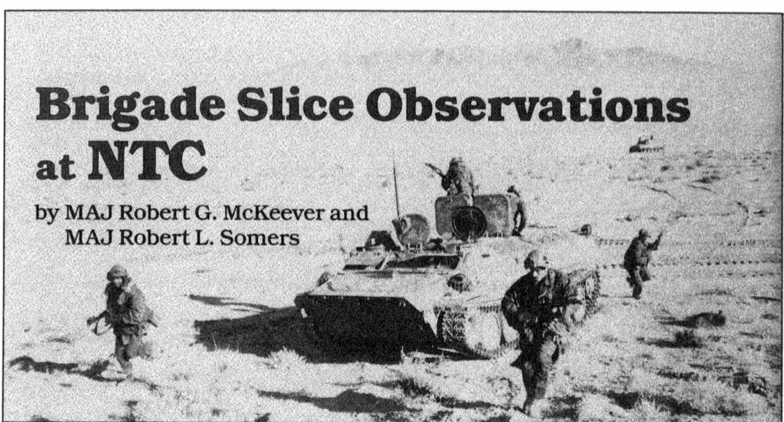

Opposing force (OPFOR) soldiers participate in recent brigade slice operations at the NTC. The OPFOR is equipped with a Soviet MT-LB for this exercise. During brigade slice operations, engineers are concerned mainly with command and control, planning and coordination, and offensive and defensive execution (U.S. Army photo).

Recently, the National Training Center started observing operations above the task force level. This effort, the Brigade Slice Observation Program, has been conducted by personnel assigned on a temporary duty basis from the various TRADOC schools. Objectives of the program included exploring ways to improve training for brigade and brigade slice elements, determining methods for feedback to brigade players and support assets, and providing feedback to the service schools.

Responsibility for conducting these observations soon will transfer to a team of 13 subject matter experts permanently assigned to the NTC. The engineers are represented on this team by MAJ Mel Saxton, who worked with us during four rotations. This article will focus on the organization and operation of the brigade slice observations, as well as on the observations made of brigade engineer operations during the four rotations.

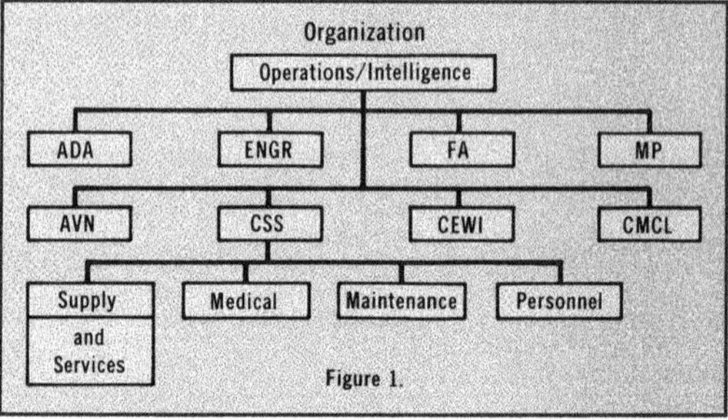

Figure 1.

Organization

In the brigade slice observation (Figure 1), combat service support (CSS) personnel operated as a team and conducted a separate CSS after action review (AAR). Their efforts were, of course, focused on the combat trains of the battalion task force and on the brigade support area (BSA). Combat arms and combat support arms personnel operated semi-independently (transportation was the major limiting factor) and reported to the operations observer. The findings were then integrated and condensed into the interim and final AARs. In addition, the team members performed individual coaching and immediate feedback functions. Finally, they prepared the take-home package for the brigade.

Operation

Most of the brigade slice observers had not visited NTC before, establishing a requirement for a brief orientation period before the rotation began. Early in the rotation (Figure 2), the subject matter experts observed their respective functional areas, coached, and provided feedback. Comments were consolidated, integrated, and condensed into interim and final AARs. NTC operations groups personnel formed the link between the brigade and battalion operations and coordinated with the observers/controllers for observations from the battalion task forces.

The engineer approach (Figure 3) focused on command and control, planning and coordination, and offensive and defensive execution. Key brigade engineer missions were identified (Figure 4) and were considered in formulating observations.

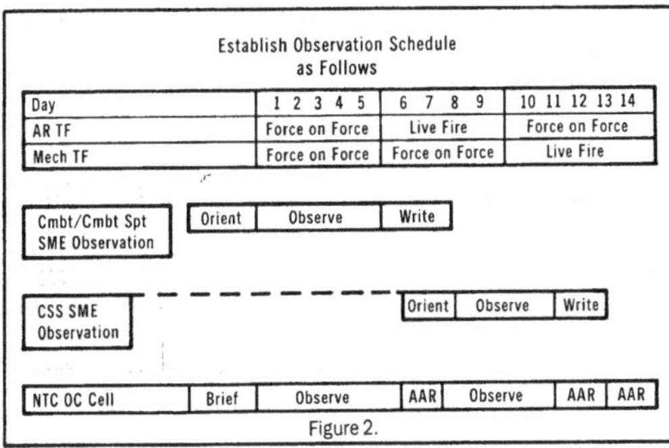

Figure 2.

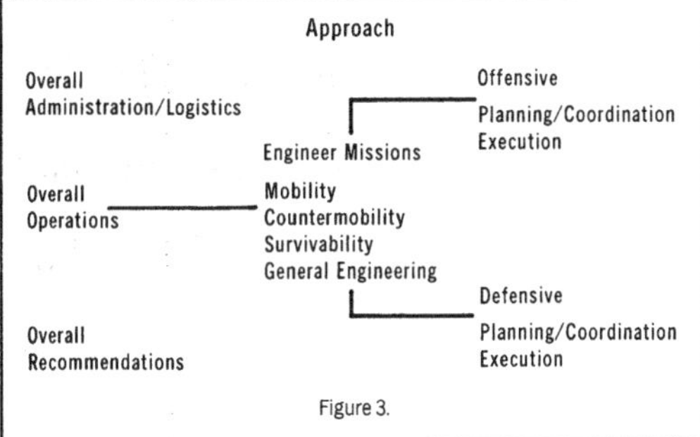

Figure 3.

Brigade Engineer Observations

This section will give brief observations followed by specific examples. In keeping with NTC practice, names and units will not be disclosed.

1. A functional brigade engineer section is critical and must be supported with its proper fill of people and equipment. The grade of 04 for the engineer provides the maneuver commander with a qualified combat engineer expert who can support the scheme of operations. Dual-hatting the company commander or downgrading the brigade engineer position is not a solution.

The brigade engineer section must also be supported with transportation and communications equipment commensurate with the unit to which assigned. For mechanized and armor units, the engineer should have the use of an M-577 with at least two radios.

2. Planning the execution of obstacles is weak, and reporting and recording of minefields is poor. For example, a unit not reporting an emplaced minefield caused an adjacent friendly unit to suffer casualties in the minefield. In another example, a unit failed to record and report a minefield and entered its own minefield, not once, not twice, but three times. The use of Figures 5 and 6, *Minefield Reporting* and *Deploying Scatterable Minefields,* would correct this problem.

3. Coordination, command and control, is weak. Specific examples are numerous. One engineer platoon attached to a task force went 36 hours without support from its attaching unit. This resulted in hungry soldiers and vehicles with no fuel. Not uncommon was the sight of a dozer sitting idly by on a trailer for six hours while the crew waited in the cab for further instructions.

4. Engineer assets at all levels are poorly preserved. A ¼-ton truck provides the brigade engineer with absolutely no protection from small arms or shrapnel; yet he needs to go forward for reconnaissance, planning, and coordination with the task force engineer. When forward, the survivability of the brigade engineer is probably defined in terms of minutes. Manuever commanders consistently did not provide security for the engineers working in front of their sectors, usually resulting in heavy losses or total annihilation for the engineers.

5. Priority of engineer missions is flexible. Different commanders will rank missions in a different order. For example, on one defensive mission, a commander's priorities of engineer tasks were as follows: countermobility, survivability, and mobility. On a similar defensive mission from a different rotation, the commander's priorities were survivability, mobility, and countermobility. Both missions succeeded, in part, because each commander's priorities for the engineer tasks supported his own scheme of maneuver.

6. Engineer equipment requires special consideration at brigade level to ensure continuous operations. One task force lost its engineer platoon, including equipment, to enemy artillery before the task force defensive positions were complete. However, the brigade engineer was able to task additional assets to assist the maneuver commander in completing his obstacles. Without the intervention of the brigade engineer, the mission would certainly have failed. This special consideration applies no less to equipment down due to maintenance problems.

7. Maneuver units are generally not involved in obstacle construction. Engineers should assist, supervise, and operate equipment for the supported unit (FM 71-2J, *Task Force Operations*). Manuever units should heavily exercise their responsibility to prepare obstacles and defensive positions for themselves. By doing so, the maneuver forces free engineers to construct additional obstacles. On one mission, the engineers worked alone on survivability positions for the maneuver force and then worked on obstacles. Insufficient time remained before the battle for the engineers to construct survivability positions for themselves.

Engineer Brigade Slice
Considerations and Key Brigade
Engineer Missions

1. Keep the maneuver commander abreast of all engineer operations in the brigade area of operations.

2. Provide engineer input (annex) to all brigade and task force OPLANS and OPORDS.

3. Task engineer assets under brigade control to accomplish engineer missions in accordance with maneuver commander's scheme of operations.

4. Collect and disseminate (as required) engineer essential elements of information (i.e., gap crossing data, route classification, bridge data, trafficability data).

5. Plan and advise maneuver commanders on FASCAM employment.

6. Plan and advise maneuver commanders of barriers and target installation and execution.

7. Ensure engineers have required logistical support in the area of operations.

8. Keep accountability of key engineer supplies in the brigade area of operation such as FASCAM, mines, and demolitions.

Figure 4.

8. Engineer ARTEPs do not promote Combined Arms activity. As such, engineer commanders should actively seek opportunities to train with maneuver forces. Also, the forthcoming ARTEP Mission Training Plans (AMTPs) will integrate engineer tasks into maneuver arms training, further improving engineer performance and survivability.

9. Engineers are a viable and valuable member of the Combined Arms team. This point was illustrated at least once each rotation when the planning and coordination for obstacles, maneuver and fire support produced highly successful kill zones in and around obstacles.

The brigade engineer is the focal point of all engineer activities in a brigade. The brigade slice observation process begun at NTC can provide valuable information and lessons learned to be used in improving our performance. There are as many ways for a brigade engineer to operate as there are brigade engineers. The experience and lessons of the past are currently being synthesized into FC 5-100-1, a new field circular on the brigade engineer.

Countermobility is a primary engineer mission on the AirLand battlefield. The Soviet MT-LB is one vehicle which engineers must engage (U.S. Army photo).

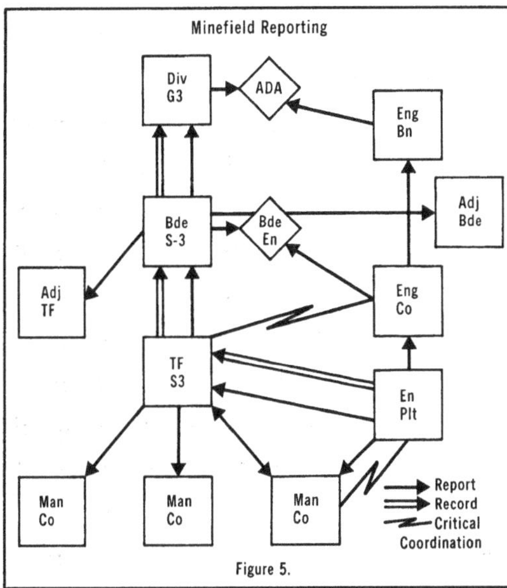

Figure 5.

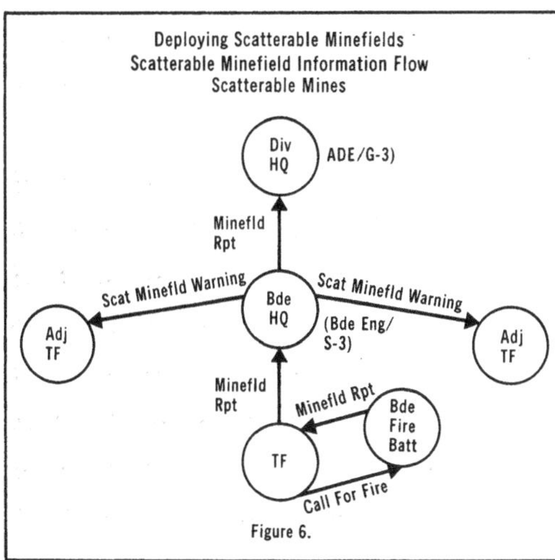

Figure 6.

MAJ Robert G. McKeever is the section chief of the new Doctrinal Foundations Section, Department of Combined Arms, USAES. He has had varied assignments in Germany, Korea, and the United States and is a 1972 ROTC graduate from Indiana University of Pennsylvania. He has a master's degree in geoenvironmental studies from Shippensburg State College.

MAJ Robert L. Somers is the chief of Field Engineering Branch, Department of Military Engineering, USAES. He has held command and staff assignments in Germany and the United States. A graduate of both the U.S. Military Academy and the Command and General Staff College, MAJ Somers obtained his MBA from Central Michigan University.

Initiative— The Key Ingredient A Personal Viewpoint

(continued from inside front cover)

the precommissioning sources, be extended through the schools such as Fort Belvoir, Fort Benning, and Fort Knox, and show itself at the National Training Center and Reforger.

Truly creating this atmosphere requires bold and courageous changes in many leaders in our system who are more comfortable in micromanaging. If we are going to experience the true synergy derived from developing innovative leaders, then we must be brave enough to change our mind set. The net result will be an AirLand Battle doctrine which not only looks good on paper, but will be stamped indelibly in the hearts and minds of our leaders.

CPT William Scully, formerly an instructor in the Command and Leadership Branch, Department of Combined Arms, USAES. CPT Scully is a 1977 graduate of the U.S. Military Academy and has an MBA from American University.

TRAINING TASK FORCE ENGINEERS

CPT ROBERT A. O'BRIEN III

Engineer platoon leaders serving in divisional engineer line companies have to perform one of the most demanding junior officer roles on the entire battlefield. While leading their platoon, they also normally serve as task force engineers. Because of this, engineer battalion and company commanders, as well as task force commanders, must place significant emphasis on training, monitoring, and supporting the platoon leader/task force engineer.

The engineer company commander trains the task force engineers subordinate to him. With his battalion and task force commanders, the company commander develops the training program to meet the needs of the task force. When developing the task force engineer training program, the company commander should consider at least the following:

- Understanding the task force commander.
- Getting into the decision flow.
- Conducting staff coordination.
- Building confidence and mutual respect.
- Briefing the task force commander.

Understanding the Task Force Commander

The task force engineer must begin to think like the task force commander. Remember that the task force commander has at least 15 years of military experience. Specifically, the task force engineer must learn the doctrine. There is no substitute for studying FMs 71-1 and 71-2J, *Tank and Mechanized Infantry Battalion Task Force* and *Task Force Operations,* and the task force field standing operating procedures (FSOP). Along with this, he must know the task force equipment and its capabilities, the number of tanks or IFVs it has, the maximum effective range of its weapon systems, and the capabilities of its vehicles.

The task force engineer must also understand detailed operational graphics and keep his own overlay current with the task force commander's. FM 101-5-1, *Operational Terms and Graphics,* is the reference. Using good graphics to discuss operations overlooking the terrain and asking questions based on METT-T, OKOCA, and the five-paragraph field order will result in the task force engineer's better understanding the task force commander's intent.

Keeping communications with the task force commander is essential. This may be by radio, telephone, messenger, or any means available. The essential thing is to KEEP COMMO. The task force engineer should also frequent the same places as the task force commander and update him on the engineer operations in sector.

The task force engineer must know engineer doctrine and capabilities as well. The FM 5-100 series is now available and must be studied. A thorough knowledge of mobility/countermobility/survivability is vital. The task force engineer must learn about his organic equipment as well as that which may be attached to him. He also needs to know the threat equipment and capabilities. Then, with the help of his battalion and company commanders, he must work with the task

port or reinforce the terrain with available or projected assets. He also provides mobility/countermobility advice on route selection. The task force engineer and the S-2 establish the priority intelligence requirements (PIR) of engineer significance to be directed to the scout platoon leader. The task force engineer must also report the results of any engineer reconnaissance in sector to the S-2.

S-3: The task force engineer must translate all of the information resulting from the S-2 coordination into an engineer plan that supports the concept of the operation. He should be a key link between terrain analysis and battle planning by reinforcing to the task force commander the significance of choke points and terrain and water obstacles in both the offense and the defense.

The task force engineer recommends task organization inputs to the S-3 on paragraphs 3a, mobility/countermobility/survivability; 3b, subunit missions; and 3c, coordination instructions, and helps develop the obstacle plan for the operations order. He ensures the inclusion of priority of work, link ups, rally points, logistic release points, locations of primary and fallback positions, follow-on missions, and evacuation times. He must also continually stress that obstacles in the attack or defense are covered by direct and indirect fire. In addition, he advises the S-3 on deception and FASCAM missions.

Before attacks, the task force engineer must learn from the S-3 of intended battle positions or defense sectors on the objective in order to preplan the logistics needed for a hasty defense. Those supplies and equipment will then be ordered and may be moved forward in conjunction with the attack so that they will not delay preparation of defensive positions once they are selected. He must also coordinate hasty and deliberate marking and reporting of breach or bypass lanes through enemy obstacles.

In the defense, the task force engineer must coordinate obstacle turn-over procedures, safe lanes through obstacles, and obstacle marking techniques. He must ensure that the obstacle plan is integrated into the task force surveillance and patrol plan to guard against breaching by the enemy during darkness. He must also coordinate for work-site security to be provided by the maneuver unit. Security elements *must* be positioned between the work parties and the enemy to prevent enemy weapons systems from engaging the critical and vulnerable engineer assets at maximum effective range. Just overwatch is not sufficient.

S-4: The task force engineer coordinates with the S-4 to ensure that logistics are projected, requisitioned, and acquired in a timely manner. Together they must ensure that logistics release points and Class IV and V prestock points (task force run) are established and SOPs are developed to ensure the proper functioning of these systems. The S-4 must also be made aware of the Class III requirements for supporting engineers.

Scouts: The scout platoon leader and the task force engineer must coordinate to ensure that PIR concerning engineer matters are met. The task force engineer will normally send an engineer representative with the scout platoon reconnaissance effort to assist in collecting and reporting intelligence. Important are:

- Trafficablity.
- Existing natural, cultural, and man-made obstacles.
- Routes, roads, fords, AVLB sites, and bridges.
- The locations of stockpiles of engineer assets.

FSO: The task force engineer and the FSO coordinate to determine the availability of Class V to support engineer operations. Obstacles should appear on the fire support overlay to ensure that indirect fire is plotted to cover them. RAAM and ADAM missions must be carefully analyzed and planned and must be included on both the fire support plan and the obstacle overlay.

S-3 (Air) or ALO: Obstacles must appear on overlays given to supporting aviation so that gunship and close air support (CAS) pilots will know where to expect clusters of targets. Air-delivered FASCAM must be planned and coordinated.

Building Confidence and Mutual Respect

Company commanders can help to develop confidence and credibility in the task force engineers they train. Through officer professional development (OPD) classes, task force engineers can become more proficient in doctrine and staff functions. There are at least a few ideas for OPD classes contained in this article.

Becoming an active participant in task force regular staff, training meetings, and OPDs will help to develop a solid relationship. Get task force engineers involved in the task force training management cycle. Monitor this closely to ensure that brigade, task force, and engineer battalion and company training cycles mesh. Train together whenever possible. The more the task force and the task force engineer see of each other, the better.

Task force CPXs, TEWTs, and MAPEXs are other good sources of education. Training his own platoon will also give the task force engineer a realistic picture of the time and effort expended in tasks that provide mobility/countermobility/survivability support to the task force.

Briefing the Task Force Commander

The only way to become proficient at briefing is to brief, brief, and brief. Use FM 101-5 and the five-paragraph field order as guides. Establish an SOP with the task force commander on what he wants in a briefing. Always include a mission statement (Sir, my mission is . . .). Also consider the following:

- Priority of work (mobility/countermobility/survivability).
- Obstacle overlays including FASCAM for both offensive and defensive operations.
- The execution matrix (time vs task).
- The survivability plan for each company/team and weapon system (don't forget ADA, FA, and engineer assets).
- The engineer equipment, weapons, and personnel status.

Obstacle delay times are of interest as well. While the task force engineer will quality-control the construction of obstacles, the key to long delays at good obstacles is effective direct and indirect fire. Great obstacles not covered by fire can be rapidly breached. FM 5-102, *Countermobility;* FM 20-32, *Mine/Countermine Operations at the Company Level;* and FM 71-2J, *Task Force Operations,* are the references for obstacles.

The Engineer School is doing its part to improve task force engineer training. A field circular on the duties of the brigade task force engineer is scheduled to be published in the fourth quarter of FY 85. The program of instruction for the Engineer Office Basic Course is also being analyzed to determine what else potential task force engineers should be taught.

The task force engineer has finally gained the full attention that the position deserves. Through proper training and emphasis on the part of engineer platoon leaders, company and battalion commanders, and maneuver commanders, the task force engineer will soon truly be the task force commander's engineer expert on the battlefield.

CPT Robert A. O'Brien III is an ROTC instructor at Seton Hall University. Before that he was a project officer, Department of Combined Arms, USAES. Also, he was a platoon leader, 842nd Engineer Company, South Dakota National Guard, and commanded Company B, 1st Engineer Battalion, Fort Riley, KS. CPT O'Brien was twice a company commander at the NTC. He graduated from EOBC, EOAC, and has a bachelor's degree from the University of Nevada-Reno.

Engineer Matrix

Obstacle control and security must be coordinated in addition to a matrix. Experience has shown that obstacle handover and position security, while being the most critical, are habitually mismanaged. A matrix, by itself, will not suffice.

by 1LT Charles A. Radke

It is 0100 hours, and moonrise is still two hours away. You've been driving through blackness for over an hour with no lights and few terrain features to guide on. Soon you'll be at the task force TOC (tactical operations center), and the time to switch from engineer platoon leader to TOC staff officer will be at hand.

Although you are the junior officer at the TOC, the knowledge you have as a task force engineer is vital to the success of the operation. The task force commander expects you to be the expert on all engineer aspects of the operation. He also expects you to prepare the obstacle plan and to write the engineer annex to the operations order. Even so, the subdued castle you wear on your shirt collar does not guarantee that you can meet his expectations.

In most cases, you will have the largest platoon in the task force. Often the assets you control will outnumber the personnel in one of the maneuver company teams. You will have control over your platoon and the additional heavy nd armored equipment attached to our platoon. Additionally, the task rce will place any corps level engi-eers under your control. With all these eople and their equipment at your dis-osal, the engineer contribution to the peration can be awesome.

Still, these assets must fit into the oncept which the task force com-ander has outlined. In the early tages of the planning phase, the task rce engineer outlines his suggestions o support the operation. Upon appro-al, these suggestions become the plan; nd it's the task force engineer's task to ut the plan into writing.

As in all orders, the need for brevity is alanced by the need for the engineer to :onvey his intent. In an offensive opera-:ion, the five-paragraph field order will often suffice. However, when this format s used in a defensive operation, the written explanation of subunit mis-sions becomes long and hard to inter-pret. This is due primarily to the ntense engineer effort required in a lefensive operation.

One solution to this problem is to adopt a matrix to substitute for some of the written portions of the order. This nethod makes the order easier to read and usually takes less space than a engthy mission statement. It also allows the engineer to include addi-tional information in the order without reducing its clarity.

Those engineer operations most often addressed in a task force operations order include three different areas of possible engineer effort: mobility, coun-termobility, and survivability. The task force engineer will most likely concen-trate his defensive efforts on counter-mobility and survivability and leave most of the mobility tasks to the supporting engineer forces.

Concentrated on countermobility and survivability operations, the engineer assets can become the biggest combat multiplier on the battlefield. In order to use all the assets available to produce the optimum effect, careful planning of the operation becomes the first step to success. The plan will deal with the use of men, machines, and material as well as allocation of the time available for each of these assets.

Use of manpower will usually include your platoon members, available man-power from the task force, and any addi-tional engineer soldiers allocated to the task force from higher levels. Planning to get them to the right place at the right time is easier if the matrix is used. It shows their priorities in conjunction with all other assets which affect their mission.

Class IV will be used by all units within the task force and transported by a variety of haul assets. When the engineer makes the plan for the distri-bution of the Class IV, he adheres to priorities for obstacle emplacement. Using a separate column on the matrix greatly reduced the need for lengthy coordination with other staff sections.

With the men and material taken care of, machines, the most productive asset, need close attention. These pieces of heavy equipment must be put to work as soon as possible. As in all other defensive planning steps, the use of heavy equipment needs to be organized. Usually the dozers go to one battle posi-tion to dig in tanks while the backhoe goes to another to dig in dismounted infantry. The trick is to keep the assets together as much as possible, but con-stantly productive. Again, use the matrix to outline what the heavy equip-ment does. List the missions in order of priority and make sure all the task force leaders understand how the assets are being used.

The objective of a written order is to ensure that the commander's intent is understood by everyone in the chain of command. The objective of the matrix is to convey this intent, but to do it in an easily understood manner. Attempts to communicate the information included in the matrix would take many written pages and make it very difficult to pick out a specific event or coordination point. Usually the need for brevity causes a degradation of the written plan.

The matrix used at the National Training Center fits the bill for plan-ning of all engineer assets and respon-sibilities, according to observers/con-trollers. The matrix has withstood the test of actual use and can make the task of the engineer planner many times easier.

1LT Charles A. Radke is the executive officer of the 522nd Engineer Company, Fort Knox, KY. He was a platoon leader in the 194th Armored Brigade, Fort Knox, and served as the task force engineer for the 4/54th Infantry at the NTC. 1LT Radke has a degree in mathe-matics and computer science from the State University of New York at Albany and was commissioned as an engineer officer through ROTC. He has been selected to attend the Armor Officers Advanced Course.

Task Force Engineer/Combined Arms Integration Package

A copy of the newly revised *Task Force Engineer/Combined Arms Integration Package* is being sent to all engineer units. The package focuses on task force engineers. The Directorate of Evaluation and Standardization plans to update the package every quarter by publishing lessons learned (or when new lessons are identified).

For additional copies, write: Commandant, U.S. Army Engineer School, ATTN: ATZA-ES-E, Stop 271, Fort Belvoir, VA 22060-5271. Platoon leaders scheduled for rotations at NTC as task force engineers may call CPT Craig Tavani at (703) 664-3668, AV 354 for additional information.

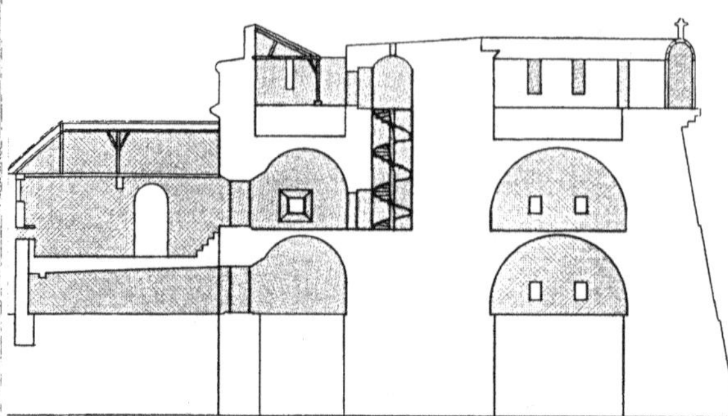

18th Century Fortress Design Principles:

Modern Point Obstacles

by MAJ Steven H. Myer and MAJ Jefferson J. Irvin

We applied the basic principles of the 18th century system of fortification to the design of modern obstacles in two previous articles (ENGINEER, Spring and Summer). In this final article, we will discuss the dimensioning and layout of the inner fortress communications (gates, bridges, stairs) of the same 18th century defensive system and apply them to today's principles governing point obstacles.

Specifically, the design of the fortress provides insight into answering the following questions.

- Given bridges of varying classifications (i.e. Class 30, Class 60) passing over a stream, which bridges should be demolished first and which left open to handle inner battlefield movement of friendly forces?
- What types of fail-safing techniques can we employ in designing critical, command-executed point obstacles?
- How does siting of a point obstacle affect its effectiveness?

As stated in our last article, the 18th century European fortress was designed as a series of linear obstacles in depth (Figure 1). An attacker had to cross several ditches, bordered on each side by high masonry walls, before reaching the inner fortress positions. The ditches were laid out in a jagged pattern, allowing cannons on the inner fortress wall and the platforms of the detached outworks to fire along the length of each ditch segment. Crossing the ditches was therefore a difficult operation for an attacker.

For the defender, inner fortress movement was much simpler. How was the fortress designed to allow easy movement of friendly men and materiel between the various fortress components without making the attacker's job easier? The defenders supplied, resupplied, and counterattacked using gateways and passageways through the main inner wall, bridges over the ditches, and stairs. The dimensions and positions of these features pertain to our questions concerning point obstacles.

Capacity of Lines of Communications

The dimensions of the bridges, passageways, and stairs were convenient for movement of the friendly troops or equipment. Artillery passages were 10 to 15 feet wide, with maximum inclines of 1/6. Infantry passages were 4 to 6 feet wide. These choices seem obvious.

Less obvious is the simple fact that infantry passages, either stairs or narrow ramps, could not pass artillery. Look again at Figure 1. The forward edge of the fortress (the covered way) was manned by infantry. The only access to this outer edge passed through narrow stairways. This meant that if enemy infantry successfully stormed part of the outer fortress edge, and then one of the detached forts, the enemy would still not be able to move his own artillery across the ditch to the secured fort. There were no artillery passages breaking through the continuous outer edge of the outer fortress ditch.

A modern analogy to the infantry on the covered way is a unit being used as a screening or covering force. Assume the unit's largest vehicle is Class 30. Leaving a four-lane Class 60 bridge intact to retrieve a delaying unit would be equivalent, in our fortress example to having ramps 16 feet wide leading from the covered way to the detached forts. The Class 60 bridge is too big for its purpose and is an invitation to high-speed enemy approach. A bridge more suited to the purpose, if available, should be chosen for the unit withdrawal; and the Class 60 bridge should be destroyed.

Redundant Safeguards

Critical fortress communications were designed with many redundant safeguards. The critical passageways (tunnels) through the main rampart are called posterns. The design of a postern, given in D. H. Mahan's 19th century text, *An Elementary Course in Permanent Fortification,* is described below.

"The most important postern is the one leading from the parade (plain inside the main perimeter) to the main ditch. This generally receives a width of 12 feet. . . . For greater security from surprise, its outlet is at least 6 feet above the bottom of the ditch, this difference of level being overcome by means of a tem-

porary ramp. . . . Besides two strong doors at the two ends of the postern, there is a partition of masonry about midway between the two ends, which is pierced with a doorway of the same size as the doorways of the ends, and closed by a strong door which, as well as the partition wall, is loop-holed for musketry.

In cases where the postern forms the main entrance to the work, an arched chamber is placed at one side of it, at the outlet, which serves as a guard room for a few men, to secure the outlet from surprise. The wall between this chamber and the postern is loop-holed, so that fire can be brought to bear on the doorway of the postern. . . ."

Note the successive layering of features designed to seal the passageway. Removing the ramp makes storming or ramming the entrance from the ditch difficult. The entrance, exit, and midpoint are sealed by doors, each covered by musket fire. These expensive precautions against surprise attack were taken because the fortress is like a turtle. Once you pass through the hard outer shell, the insides are soft. The area within the main perimeter was unprotected once an enemy gained access. The main perimeter had no defenses against an attack from the rear.

The modern equivalents of the postern leading from the parade to the main ditch are the critical road communications through a defense. The entrances and exits are our point obstacles. Bridges crossing major rivers and mountainside road crater sites are examples of these point obstacles.

These critical obstacles require an entire series of precautions to ensure completeness of their execution. Obstacle demolition must—like the fortress postern—provide layered safeguards. Typical precautions include installing dual firing systems, electric and non-electric, for each set of demolitions.

The fortress tunnel hints at some additional precautions. We can provide a steep drop at the enemy end of a bridge by cratering the end of the abutment and installing easily removed ramps. We can demolish floor slabs at intervals along a bridge and install easily removed temporary floors. In extremely important cases, we can demolish the bridge span nearest the friendly bank and replace the span with tactical bridging. Then, if all the demolitions on the bridge fail, we can remove the enemy end ramp, remove the temporary flooring, and retrieve the tactical bridging. Another extreme option is to demolish the bridge before the last friendly unit crosses, pre-position enough tactical rafting to handle the remaining non-amphibious vehicles, and let the remaining amphibious vehicles swim across the stream.

Siting Point Obstacles

The positions of the inner fortress passageways provide insight into how the careful siting of a point obstacle enhances its effectiveness. Look at Figure 1. Note the following principles are employed in siting the main gate and the bridges leading from the gate.

1. Forward passages are always covered by rearward friendly fires.

2. Passages are protected from enemy fires because the areas forward of the passages are blocked by the series of detached, triangular-shaped forts (outworks).

3. Openings in the main perimeter are placed in the recessed part of the perimeter. This allows overlapping friendly fires to rake the front of the opening.

4. There is no opening on the sides of the detached forts allowing communication between laterally adjacent forts. Openings only appear in the rear of the forts. This prevents a captured fort from compromising the communications or security of adjacent forts.

All these principles apply to point obstacles today. We use the first principle when we site obstacles so they can be covered by friendly fire. We use the second when, in the defense, we clearly assign road communications security to specific units. We do not draw our unit boundaries along roads (and along the road's bridges). We ensure clear assignment of coverage of major avenues of approach.

The third principle gives useful advice. Assume you have six bridges crossing a stream in your sector (Figure 2). You decide that three, including contingencies, are needed. Which bridges should be demolished early and which retained for use in counterattacks or withdrawal? Using the third principle, the best choices for retention are those

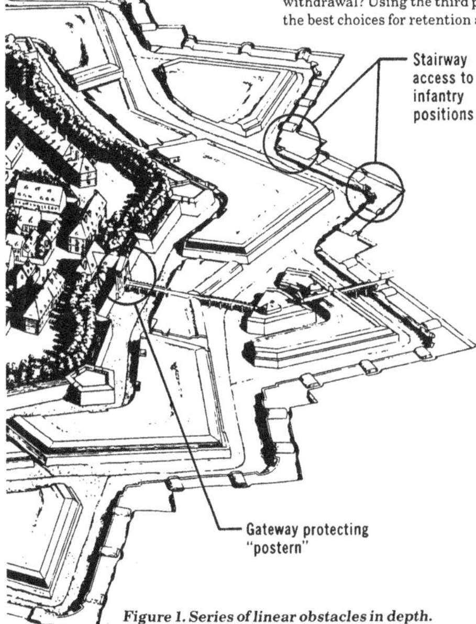

Figure 1. Series of linear obstacles in depth.

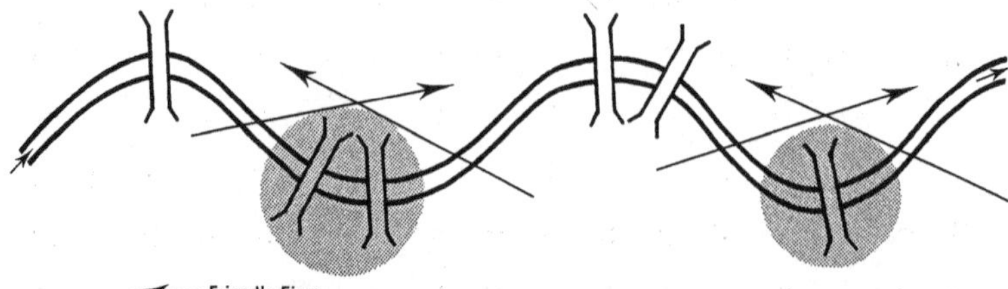

Figure 2. Sector of six bridges crossing a stream.

circled. At these sites, fires from the friendly bank overlap across the area leading to the far abutment.

The fourth principle is also familiar. We routinely assign supplementary positions in our defenses to handle attack from unexpected or secondary avenues of approach. This principle advises that communications along the supplemental avenues (which are required for friendly lateral movement early in a battle) must be prepared for command-executed demolition. Apparently harmless bridges pointed at a flank may not be harmless if the adjacent position is lost.

We have proposed little that is new. The 18th century fortress is a visual reminder of many important principles pertinent to planning inner battlefield road communications.

- Size communications to the need.
- Fail-safe critical command-executed obstacles with many redundant precautions.
- Where choices between communications routes exist, cut off the routes which are difficult to cover by fire or cannot be protected from enemy fire.
- Prepare to cut off lateral communications in case an emergency arises.
- Meet your needs, but deny the enemy his.

These three articles apply the basic principles of 18th century fortifications to the modern battlefield and, by example, demonstrate the lessons that history can provide us. History examined with our minds attuned to today's challenges can provide insights into basic principles, simplified models to order and structure today's more complex problems, and even lessons that can be directly applied to the battlefield. Whether strategy, tactics, leadership, or any aspect of our profession, history is a valuable, but too often forgotten source of wisdom. READ IT.

MAJ Steven H. Myer is an assistant professor of mathematics at the U.S. Military Academy and served as a platoon leader in the 1/27th Infantry Battalion, 25th Infantry Division in Hawaii. He was a company commander with the 1/504th Infantry and was the assistant G-3 OPS in the 82nd ABN Division at Fort Bragg, NC. MAJ Myer has a bachelor's degree from the U. Military Academy and a master's degre from Stanford University.

MAJ Jefferson J. Irvin is an assista professor of geography and compute science at the U.S. Military Academy. H served as a platoon leader and compan commander in the 94th Engineer Ba talion in Germany. MAJ Irvin has bachelor's degree from the U.S. Milita Academy and a master's degree fro Stanford University.

Engineer Problem

Your squad is tasked to control traffic at a bridge crossing in the division rear. The bridge is a single-lane timber trestle with a wheeled vehicle classification of 27. Two vehicles approach your bridge. One is a standard combination 10-ton tractor, pulling a 25-ton lowboy with a D7E on top. Its load classification was previously determined by a corps level ERP as 33. The other vehicle is a combat loaded 2½-ton cargo truck pulling a loaded bolster trailer. The load classification of this vehicle has not been determined. Will your bridge support these vehicles, and if so, what type of crossing should they make?

(You collect the following data to support your calculations.)

W_T (2 ½T) = 5,530 lb **A_T = Average tire contact area (trailer) = 30 in²**

W_T(load) = 2 tons **P_T = Tire pressure (trailer) = 55psi**

N_T = Number tires (trailer) = 4

REFERENCES: FM 5-34; FM 5-36; FM 5-12B2/3/4

Problem/Solution submitted by 1LT Michael Mazzuki, Directorate of Evaluation and Standardization.

Do you have any challenging Engineer Problems? We are looking for original Engineer Problems and Solutions that can be solved by using appropriate engineer references. Your problems should be checked for technical and doctrinal accuracy, and should strengthen combat engineer skills. ENGINEER Magazine
ATTN: ATZA-TD-P, Stop 291D
Fort Belvoir, VA 22060-5291

Daily GPAC Operations

The approach of using a modified LOGPAC procedure has enabled the 8th Engineer Battalion to overcome logistical support difficulties in the field. FM 5-100, *Engineer Combat Operations,* states that logistical support for the forward elements of an engineer battalion is provided in varying degrees by the supported maneuver units, depending upon the command and support relationships specified in the tasks organization and coordinating instructions.

An engineer battalion should attempt to enforce doctrinal support responsibilities of the supported units and should use existing logistic channels from the division support area (DSA) and the brigade support area (BSA) before operating an in-house LOGPAC operation.

by CPT Paul A. Petzrick Jr.

In early 1984, the 8th Engineer Battalion (CBT) was confronted by two major problems affecting the way it conducted field support operations. Companies routinely spent significant amounts of time returning to the rear to obtain support; and staff visits to companies were conducted in a haphazard, disorganized manner. Often key personnel were absent from the battalion trains when needed to coordinate with higher headquarters.

Further compounding these problems, the recent organizational changes of the Army of Excellence made it necessary for the battalion headquarters to substantially increase its role in providing supply and service support to organic companies.

To assist in resolving these problems, the battalion adapted and modified the Logistics and Administrative Package (LOGPAC) procedures used by maneuver units.

The LOGPAC is a supply and service package from the battalion trains that meets elements from the company trains at designated rendezvous points. It has a flexible organization that can be tailored to meet various situations. During a recent exercise, the LOGPAC ranged in size from a jeep with trailer to a column consisting of two 5,000-gallon fuel trucks, two 5-ton trucks with flatbed and refrigerator trailers, a 2½-ton truck, and a 5/4-ton truck.

Supervision is essential for efficient LOGPAC operations. A responsible NCO or officer must accompany every LOGPAC. Besides serving as the commander of the LOGPAC, he serves as a liaison between the battalion trains and companies. He is one of the few persons to conduct actual face-to-face coordination with the companies. Since the bulk of the LOGPAC is normally logistics, it may be helpful for the LOGPAC commander to come from the S-4 section.

The LOGPAC uses a flexible cycle of preparation, planning, and execution to support sustained operations. The execution phase of the cycle occurs at night and is followed by the preparation phase. Individual staff sections plan continuously. Their efforts culminate in a daily staff planning meeting.

The planning meeting is held before the uploading of supplies for that night's LOGPAC. The S-1, S-4, maintenance, medical, and communications officers or their representatives should attend. The meeting is intended to determine exact transportation requirements, pass information, select the LOGPAC commander, and resolve problems. If the availability of vehicles is limited, augmentation from other sources, such as DISCOM or bridge company trucks with pallets, may be necessary. Tactical issues, such as the situation, route selection, and rendezvous points, are determined and operational plans developed.

Upon departure, the LOGPAC moves directly to a designated linkup point and sets up. The transfer of supplies to the companies should be timed to ensure that departure from the battalion trains area is after dusk. As companies arrive, they are met by guides and escorted through the LOGPAC site. Accountable supplies and paperwork, mail, and other items requiring special handling are verified by the LOGPAC commander before each company departs the area. A representative from each staff section accompanies the LOGPAC to conduct customer service. Delivery of replacement personnel and evacuation of personnel returning to the rear also takes place. As soon as all units are serviced, the LOGPAC returns to the battalion trains.

The preparation phase consists of three distinct elements. Maintenance of vehicles and identification of potential maintenance losses occurs as early as possible so that sufficient time is available to arrange for necessary augmentation. It is also essential that personnel routinely involved in the LOGPAC, such as drivers, get adequate rest. In addition, staff sections conduct routine business with support agencies during this phase. Vehicles and personnel required for these actions may impact on sustaining the LOGPAC as previously mentioned.

The LOGPAC's key advantages are its flexibility and efficiency. Supplies are pushed forward, allowing companies to maintain their focus on engineering missions without the burden of supply and support issues. Consolidation of supplies allows for a more efficient use of trains personnel and vehicles and enhances security for vehicles going forward. The LOGPAC enables the battalion to provide maximum support to the companies and sustain it with minimal effort.

CPT Paul A. Petzrick Jr. is the G-1 Plans Officer for V Corps, Frankfurt, Germany. He was the Organizational Effectiveness Staff Officer, 130th Engineer Brigade, Hanau, Germany, and the S-4, 8th Engineer Battalion, 1st Cavalry Division, Fort Hood, TX. Commissioned from the U.S. Military Academy, he has served in infantry and engineer troop assignments in the U.S. and Germany.

The Final Exam in EOBC

by CPT Duane A. Dyer and MAJ David R. Bowen

The Captain in battle dress uniform with helmet, load-bearing equipment, and camouflage spoke first:

"I am the task force S-3. At 0530 hours, the United States was invaded by elements landing from the two Soviet fleets off our eastern seaboard. One force has gone ashore in southern New England; and the other has landed near Newport News, VA. In accordance with prepared contingency plans, your platoon has been mobilized to support my task force which is part of 1st Brigade, 52nd Infantry Division."

The blurry-eyed lieutenants sat in the auditorium of Humphreys Hall at Fort Belvoir and listened as various staff officers poked at maps, gave briefings, and recited required reports. This was the day before the final FTX for the Engineer Officer Basic Course (EOBC). The training company had just been plucked from the physical training field without notice. The opening scenario suddenly became real. Two weeks before "D-Day," the EOBC students had received build-up intelligence briefs. Now, this was war!

Priming a shaped charge, 2LT Jay P. Still and 2LT Michael L. Rogers prepare to detonate explosives to create a hasty road crater. Demolitions is one of the many challenging tasks for EOBC students during an FTX at Fort A.P. Hill, VA (photo by 1LT L. J. Leto).

The final FTX for EOBC students emphasizes coordinated staff planning and independent actions of a task force engineer.

The New FTX

The high point of EOBC is not graduation, but the final FTX which acts as a final "field" examination and evaluates the lieutenants' technical and tactical skills gained through previous classroom instruction. Doctrine, theory, and class notes are now put into practice where it counts—the field.

In the past, each EOBC training company had planned, coordinated, and controlled its own FTX. Not only was there duplication of effort, but often not enough planning was done; and an important exercise became disorganized. The company commander was unable to adequately advise, check, and inspect his platoons—his primary mission.

In late 1984, the final FTX was rewritten and standardized so that the problems of planning, coordination, and control at the company level were eliminated. The new FTX is designed to be more realistic and incorporates five phases: lead-in scenario, D-Day briefing, initial actions, main exercise, and recovery (Figure 1).

Using a European scenario of defend-hold-counterattack, the EOBC students build up to the FTX; and then they conduct it. The FTX itself is five days long, starting on a Thursday and ending on a Monday. The FTX is conducted at Fort A.P. Hill, VA. The lead-in scenario begins 15 days before the FTX on D-Day −10; the D-Day briefing is the day before moving to Fort A.P. Hill; and recovery is on Day 5.

Lead-In Scenario

The lead-in scenario provides a realistic background to the FTX and follows a buildup to open hostilities between the United States and the Soviet Union. Each day (−10 through −1), information is provided to the EOBC students to set the stage for the increasing tensions. On D-Day, the United States is invaded.

Sun	Mon	Tue	Wed	Thur	Fri	Sat
			Lead-In Scenario (Fort Belvoir) -10	-9	-8	
	Lead-In Scenario -7	-6	-5	-4	-3	
	-2	-1	D-Day	Initial Actions 1	Field Training (Fort A.P. Hill) 2	3
Exercise 4	Recovery 5					

Figure 1. Five-phase FTX.

D-Day Briefing

Not knowing that the invasion has occurred, the EOBC officers start the day at 0600 with PT. Shortly after they begin their physical exercises, an EOBC trainer arrives and moves the platoons into the auditorium where they are given the D-Day briefing. The EOBC officers are informed of the invasion and told that they have been mobilized as Company A, 52nd Engineer Battalion, to support an armor-heavy task force (TF) organized under a J-series TOE. The briefing is conducted with EOBC cadre representing the following command and staff positions:

TF S-1
TF S-2
TF S-3
TF S-4
Brigade Engineer
Engineer Company Commander
TF Commander

The EOBC students are restricted to Fort Belvoir and told to report the next morning (Day 1) with their baggage ready to go to war.

Initial Actions

On Day 1, the lieutenants are issued their weapons and NBC protective masks and clothing and transported to Fort A.P. Hill where they pick up prepositioned equipment and vehicles. They are briefed by their training company commander and given their first missions. From this point, until FTX completion, subsequent missions and other messages are sent to the platoons by radio or briefed at the Task Force Tactical Operations Center (TF TOC).

Main Exercise

Each platoon is controlled as if it were directly attached to the task force. Each platoon leader assumes the role of task force engineer and reports directly to the S-3 or commander through the TF TOC. The engineer company commander (EOBC training company commander) advises his student officers, but does not assist them. He acts as an ARTEP evaluator throughout the FTX. Essentially the EOBC officer is "on his own."

The lieutenant is responsible for everything his platoon does (or does not do) when he or she is the platoon leader. The platoon must accomplish all missions assigned as well as plan for all logistics support such as requesting Class IV barrier materials or feeding tactically in the field. Engineer equipment is available to the task force engineer from an entire company of the 11th Engineer Battalion (CBT) (HVY) which supports every EOBC FTX.

Twice daily, operations/staff meetings at the TF TOC keep the commander, his S-3, the engineer company commander, and the platoon leaders informed. Each platoon leader is required to brief the activities of his platoon at this time. Prepared overlays, operational situation reports (OPSITREPs), and periodic intelligence reports (PERINTREPs) are used to make each briefing more realistic. The operations/staff meetings give the lieutenants an idea of how such meetings are conducted. Additionally, lieutenants from each platoon work in the TOC to gain an appreciation for task force staff procedures.

The chain of command in each platoon changes every 12 hours, and both the new and old command chains attend the meetings in the TOC. This "constant" chain of command change does cause some minor continuity problems; however, missions are designed for the 12-hour time frame. Also, mission completion is not the aim of the FTX—excercising good leadership skills with technical proficiency in a stressful environment is the main goal.

Evaluation

Evaluation and critique are constant. The EOBC training company commander (FTX engineer company commander) and the EOBC trainers accompany their lieutenants throughout the entire FTX and provide periodic critiques to keep all platoon members informed of what is being done correctly and what needs to be improved.

Each EOBC trainer uses ARTEP task evaluation checklists to record the platoon's progress; EOBC trainers rotate among the platoons to ensure an objective analysis is being conducted. Mission accomplishment is only a small part of the evaluation—organization, coordination, proper use of troop-leading procedures, delegation of tasks, attention to detail, safety, and leadership are the major elements being emphasized and appraised.

The TF TOC maintains a status board of all missions assigned and completed by the platoons (Figure 2). Mission accomplishment, the ARTEP checklists, and cadre input all contribute to the platoon's evaluation. Competition between the platoons is keen. How well each platoon progresses through the FTX determines the "winner." As incentive, the best platoon may be able to terminate the exercise early or receive other benefits, such as being excused from PT for a week upon return to Fort Belvoir.

Future

Future plans for the EOBC final FTX include alerting the training company and moving to a holding area, tactical road marching to Fort A.P. Hill, an assault river crossing of the Rappahannock River, and an air assault on an objective. As part of the alert procedure, a modified EDRE (Emergency Deployment Readiness Exercise) is also being planned.

The final FTX is challenging, competitive, realistic, and above all an excellent training opportunity for new engineer platoon leaders to demonstrate their technical skills and leadership potential. The FTX is demanding and, at times, stressful—it was specifically designed to be conducted under these conditions. The EOBC training detachment's mission is to train young officers to be confident in themselves and to be professionally competent as combat engineer platoon leaders. The final FTX is a major catalyst in accomplishing this mission.

CPT Duane A. Dyer is an instructor in the Tactics and Operations Division, Department of Combined Arms, USAES. He was an EOBC platoon trainer and has served with the Albuquerque District, Corps of Engineers, and the 10th Engineer Battalion, Third Infantry Division. An EOAC graduate, CPT Dyer has been a combat engineer platoon leader, a bridge company commander and executive officer, an assistant S-3, and a brigade engineer. He graduated from the University of Maine at Orono with a degree in forest management and was commissioned through the Maine Army National Guard OCS.

MAJ David R. Bowen commands the EOBC Training Detachment at Fort Belvoir. He has led a platoon and commanded a mechanized infantry company and a squadron of the Royal Australian Survey Corps. MAJ Bowen has been a staff officer at battalion, brigade, division, and DoD level. He completed his graduate studies at Arizona State University and was an assistant professor at the U.S. Military Academy. MAJ Bowen is a graduate of the Infantry and Engineer Officer Advanced Courses, the Command and General Staff College, and the Armed Forces Staff College.

Day	First Platoon	Second Platoon	Third Platoon
	(All Move to Fort A.P. Hill; Issue Vehicles and Equipment)		
1	M4T6 Dry Span Reconnaissance Target Folders	Reconnaissance Target Folders Bailey Bridge	Construct Log Crib Construct Road Crater Bridge Demo
2	Construct Log Crib Construct Road Crater Decontamination Bailey Bridge	M4T6 Dry Span Hasty Minefield Decontamination Assault River Cross	Reconnaissance Target Folders Hasty Minefield Decontamination
3	Bridge Demo Remove Minefield Assault River Cross	Construct Log Crib Construct Road Crater Bridge Demo	Destroy Log Crib Fill Road Crater Bailey Site Layout Assault River Cross
	Blocking Positions		
4	Destroy Log Crib Fill Road Crater Road Improvement Construct Heliport	Destroy Log Crib Fill Road Crater Remove Minefield Construct Culvert	M4T6 Dry Span Remove Minefield Construct New TOC
	(All Move To Fort Belvoir)		
5	Recovery	Recovery	Recovery

Figure 2. FTX master schedule.

Engineer Solution

1. 2½-ton w/trailer

Temporary classification of wheel vehicles is 85 percent of the gross vehicle weight (in tons). A 2½-ton truck pulling a bolster trailer is considered a standard combination since the weight on the trailer is distributed to the axles of the truck. The temporary classification of the combination is 85 percent of the sum of their weights. The weight of the truck is taken from its data plate, and the weight of the combat load was estimated. The weight of the trailer and its load are unknown, but it may be estimated using the tire pressure and contact area. With the data provided and the estimation formula found in FM 5-34, it follows that:

$$W_T \text{ (bolster trailer \& load)} = \frac{(A_T)(P_T)(N_T)}{2{,}000}$$

$$= \frac{(30)(55)(4)}{2{,}000} = 3.3 \text{ tons}$$

Therefore, the load classification of the combination is

$$C = .85\ (2.77T + 2T + 3.3T) = 6.86 \text{ or } 7 \text{ tons}$$

The 2½-ton with bolster trailer can make a normal crossing (100 feet between vehicles, maximum speed of 25 mph).

2. 10-ton combination

The 10-ton combination exceeds the bridge classification for a normal crossing. Caution crossing of a nonstandard fixed bridge is 1.25 times the normal classification. In this case, 27 x 1.25 = 33.75, safeside round to 33. Therefore, with the approval of the tactical commander, the 10-ton combination can make a caution crossing (50 meters between vehicles, maximum speed of 8 mph, no stopping, accelerating, or shifting gears while crossing).

NOTE: The third type of crossing, risk crossing, would not apply in this situation since the timber trestle bridge is not a standard military bridge.

Broken Heart International Airfield

The Broken Heart Battalion got its name during the Korean War when hastily deployed combat engineers left their wives and sweethearts behind in the U.S. "Broken Heart" was their code name during the Inchon landing led by GEN Douglas MacArthur.

by LTC William D. Brown and 1LT Blake Middleton

Broken Heart International—an unusual name for an engineer mission completed by C Company, 44th Engineer Battalion (CBT) (HVY) in support of Team Spirit '85, a major training exercise held annually in the Republic of Korea. The name was given to the airfield by the 44th "Broken Heart" Engineer Battalion.

Located 60 miles south of Seoul, the medium-lift forward area airfield was constructed using M-19 matting, a system of interlocking aluminum panels. The airfield featured a 3,500-foot runway, a parallel 3,500-foot taxiway, and associated parking and warmup aprons. A similar airfield constructed to support Team Spirit '84 resulted in using the M-19 airfield as a major port of entry and exit for troops participating in Team Spirit '85.

C Company, commanded by CPT John Bailie, was tasked to build the airfield; and 2LT Kun M. Yi was given the primary responsibility for the construction. Planning began several months before actual construction. A complete support structure had to be developed for the operation to accommodate construction and to sustain the company. Coordination was required to:

- Arrange movement of over 2,000 tons of matting by rail and contract truck haul to the worksite.
- Set up shower, laundry, and water supply operations.
- Provide FM and AM communications with the home station at Camp Mercer.
- Plan for rations and refrigeration support.
- Develop a bivouac site.

An advance party, comprised mainly of the earth-moving platoon, was dispatched to Yoju a week ahead of the main body to do preparatory earthwork for the matting operation. The airfield site, a peanut field 10 months of the year, is comprised of sandy soil which proved to be a training challenge for SFC Stephen Walls, the project NCOIC. The layout of the airfield, selected by the Air Force, necessitated extensive earth-moving operations along the entire length of the runway—eventually totaling over 6,000 cubic yards of cut and fill.

This effort was complicated by the unseasonably mild weather which caused an alternate thawing/freezing cycle, resulting in poor drainage due to large ice lenses throughout the soil. The ice lenses were a perplexing problem as they drew moisture from surrounding soil and caused large soft spots where compaction was impossible. Efforts to remove these ice lenses were hampered by the weather which alternately brought rain then snow, warm temperatures then numbing cold.

A solution was found in TM 5-330, *Planning and Design of Roads, Airbases, and Heliports in the Theater of Operations.* Bulldozer teams used rippers to cut grooves parallel to the runway surface. Ice lenses then began to form in these uncompacted areas which drew the water from under the compacted runway surface. Though not a "school solution," the procedure effectively solved the problem.

The main body arrived on site and began to lay the first of over 39,000 panels (4 feet x 4 feet) required to complete the project. As panel crews worked, the earth-moving equipment from C Company and the other line companies, as well as the 802nd Engineer Battalion, prepared the laying surface. The "matlayers" of C Company, with support from the battalion's 30th Korean Service Corps Company and a Republic of Korea engineer platoon, placed over 2,250,000 pounds of metal and completed the laying operation in only 12 days.

Although the M-19 matting provides temporary landing facilities and requires frequent repairs, Broken Heart International Airfield held up well during over 410 sorties of C-130s. One minor repair was completed in under three hours without affecting landing operations. The entire experience provided training for the battalion and ensured the smooth deployment of forces into and out of Korea.

The bivouac site provided heated GP medium tents with M-19 flooring, showers, Korean and English movies at night, flag-raising ceremonies at work call, plus reliable and secure communications with battalion.

The dismantled airstrip is now history, but the skills and the leadership experiences have enhanced the combat readiness of the "Broken Heart" Battalion and once again demonstrated its role in the defense of the Republic of Korea.

LTC William D. Brown commands the 44th Engineer Battalion (CBT)(HVY), Camp Mercer, Korea. He was a staff officer in the Program Analysis and Evaluation Directorate, Office, Chief of Staff, Army; Executive to the Chief of Engineers, OCE; and executive officer of the 20th Engineer Battalion (CBT), Fort Campbell, KY. LTC Brown completed the Project Manager Course, the Defense Systems Management College, CGSC, and EOAC. He has graduate degrees in nuclear engineering from MIT and in operations research from George Washington University.

1LT Blake Middleton is assigned to the staff of the U.S. Military Academy at West Point. He was a platoon leader and construction officer in C Company, 44th Engineer Battalion (CBT)(HVY), Camp Mercer, Korea. 1LT Middleton has a bachelor's degree from Montana State University.

The Will to Lead

by MAJ Philip Benham and MAJ Charles Kershaw

Throughout history, distinguished military leaders have proved effective at imposing their will. The importance of this quality of leadership, especially in the face of adversity and its attendant risks, is emphasized by Clausewitz. He contended that the success of a leader's effort is the product of two inseparable factors—the total means at his disposal and the strength of his will. A leader with ample means at his disposal who lacks the resolve to act and to compel others to follow, as did George B. McClellan in opposing Robert E. Lee, will, as Clausewitz predicted, fail. And failure on the battlefield is catastrophic.

History is replete with examples of leaders coercing their soldiers into battle. John Keegan in *Face of Battle* describes instances of French leaders under Napoleon pushing against the backs of soldiers using their halberds horizontally in both hands to keep men in place. On the Western Front in World War I, battalions appointed squads of "battle police" to prevent stragglers from seeking refuge in the trenches during an attack.

These coercive measures will undoubtedly be inadequate, however, on the AirLand battlefield of tomorrow. The accelerated pace of operations, lethality, and decentralized nature of the AirLand battlefield will require more sophisticated and diverse methods for imposing one's will. The defiant "Nuts!" of Anthony C. McAuliffe to the German request for surrender at Bastogne will continue to serve as the legacy of confidence and courage of the commander imposing his will, but the conditions for the successful imposition of one's will extend to the careful consideration of the following factors:

- Know your situation.
- Know your subordinates.
- Know yourself.

Know Your Situation

Commenting on the dearth of good generals, Marshal Saxe observed wryly that not knowing what they (good generals) do, they (the less adept ones) do what they know. The commander who is to impose his will successfully has to be aware of what he must know about his situation. Too narrow and limited a view of the requirements for success can prove disastrous.

Writing of the German army's failure on the Eastern Front in World War II, Field Marshal Erich von Manstein derided Hitler's inability to realize that any long-range offensive operation called for a steady buildup of troops over and above those committed in the original assault. Hitler's inability to understand that any long-range offensive operation called for a steady buildup of troops over and above those committed initially resulted in heavy losses to the German army. As Hitler himself later acknowledged, it also contributed to his loss of control over his generals.

Poor assessments of tactical situations detract from one's tactical competence. They also indicate an insensitivity to the needs of one's troops. Frequently this condition results in orders given and not executed properly. In some instances, orders are regarded as impossible; and the consequence is often disobedience, a clear manifestation of failure in imposing one's will.

Know Your Subordinates

Cohesiveness and competence perhaps are the two most important qualities units need to perform well under adversity. Cohesiveness and competence provide the confidence that subordinates and leaders need to confront adversity and its attendant risks with expectations of succeeding.

As Henry Boetlinger indicated in his article, *"Is Management Really an Art?"*

veterans play a key role in building confidence in military units. Veterans, using the wisdom that typically accrues from experience, serve as role models for less experienced troops. They frequently establish the behavioral norms for the unit, and they reinforce the value of performance standards to mission accomplishment.

What's key for the leader here is the value of experience. Knowing the capabilities of your troops is essential. Where deficiencies exist, leaders successful at imposing their will "build veterans" to create the bond of trust necessary to confront the adversities of combat. The validity of this point has been confirmed by many. MG Norman S. Cota, who commanded the 28th Infantry Division in World War II, summed up his thoughts on the subject this way:

"Men have a right to go into battle as members of a trained unit flanked by friends and associates and, if possible, led by leaders who have trained with them and whom they have come to trust."

The regrettable incidents of troop rebellion during the latter stages of the Vietnam War stem in part from the few opportunities leaders had to "build veterans" before confronting the adversities of combat. The conflict between the survival ethic and the duty ethic precluded the confidence that some units needed to perform. Few small unit leaders knew their men before they were required to rely on them.

Know Yourself

In *The Power of Personality in War,* MG Baron von Freytag-Lovinghoven remarked that the most capable officers develop their own powers of understanding through constant, critical examinations of the past and present. They may well start with historical profiles of great leaders. They must then be extended, however, to an introspective analysis of one's personal attributes and the degree to which they are compatible with the values of the profession and the requirements of command.

The list of attributes describing the consummate military leader is justifiably long. Thus, any reflection on one's own capability to lead is necessarily a complicated and time-consuming task. The examples of history suggest two attributes in particular which seem important—competence and consideration. The first needs little emphasis here; the second, however, may require some elaboration.

The brillance of Robert E. Lee's leadership is well documented. Perhaps his most distinguishing characteristic which served him so effectively on the battlefield was his consideration for others. To his officers, as Douglas Southall Freeman described him, ". . . he was sensitive to their hardships and unfailing in his consideration for them."

For the men in the ranks, Lee's continuing concern for their welfare was extraordinary. On many occasions he personally administered to the physical and psychological needs of his men. So effective was Lee that, as Freeman again describes it, one soldier remarked, ". . . the rest of us may have developed from monkeys; but I tell you none less than God could have made such a man as 'Marse Robert.' "

The essence of effective military leadership is the ability to impose your will. That ability is derived from an accurate understanding of your situation, your subordinates, and yourself. By combining tactical and technical competence with genuine consideration for others in building the confidence and cohesiveness characteristic of high-performing veterans, leaders can impose their will successfully despite the conditions of adversity posed by future battle.

MAJ Philip Benham is an assistant professor of management at Bucknell University and an Individual Mobilization Augmentee (USAR) instructor with the Command and Leadership Branch, Department of Combined Arms, USAES. His active duty experience included service in Vietnam and company command with the 5th Engineer Battalion (CBT). MAJ Benham has a bachelor's degree from the U.S. Military Academy and master's and doctoral degrees in business administration from the University of Colorado.

MAJ Charles Kershaw was chief of the Command and Leadership Branch, Department of Combined Arms, USAES. MAJ Kershaw is assigned to the 193rd Infantry Brigade in Panama.

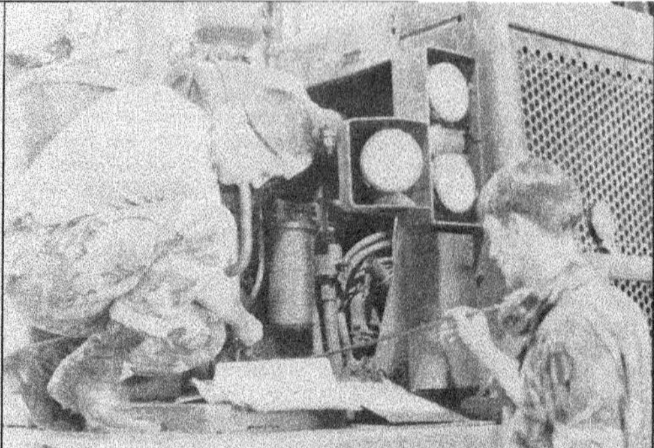

Trainees perform before-operation services on a 621B scraper, one of the newest pieces of equipment in the Army's system. The training for soldiers in the 62B10 MOS has been extended from over five weeks to nine weeks (photo by Ray Crosby).

Engineer Construction Equipment Repairer

by CW3 Melad Smith Jr.

An MOS Under Change

A complete analysis of the 62B MOS identified the need for several changes for the construction equipment repairer.

- Restructuring the 62B MOS in skill levels 1 through 4.
- Selecting a different training mode and extending the AIT course.
- Discontinuing the 62B20 Primary Technical Course (PTC) taught at Fort Leonard Wood and converting it to nonresident instruction.
- Designing a new Basic Technical Course (BTC) for 62B30, beginning in FY 87.
- Analyzing the need for resident training for skill level 4 soldiers.
- Revising Soldier Training Publications (STPs) and extension training material.

Restructure

A Memorandum of Understanding (MOU) to restructure the 63 CMF to include the 62B MOS was signed by MG Richard S. Kem, Engineer School Commandant, and MG William E. Potts, Ordnance School Commandant, in February 1985. This MOU allows 62B soldiers to progress from skill levels 1 through 4. The 52C, 52D, and 52F MOSs will no longer feed into the 62B MOS at skill level 4, but will feed into the new 52X MOS (Figure 1).

Restructuring the 62B MOS will go into effect in March 1986. This will increase unit readiness by ensuring the senior maintenance NCOs are technically proficient as construction equipment maintenance supervisors.

62B10

The training requirement for 62B10 soldiers was extended from over five weeks to nine weeks. The new course will use a "lock-step" instruction mode and will include shop operations, engines, scheduled services, power trains, hydraulics, maneuver of equipment, and welding. This course is scheduled to begin by October 1985.

62B20

This PTC was expanded from four to six weeks. The curriculum is highly technical and includes repair of diesel engines, power trains, mechanical systems, and special purpose engineer equipment. This course applies to both active duty and reserve component soldiers. An Army Correspondence Course Program (ACCP) is being prepared for skill level 2 soldiers to replace the resident course at the end of FY 86.

62B30

Analysis of the 62B MOS, supported by surveys, also indicated a critical need for a BTC for the first line supervisor. The Course Administrative Data (CAD) was approved by TRADOC for a six-week course to be implemented in October 1986 at Fort Leonard Wood, MO. A learning analysis is being prepared for the highly technical course.

The BTC will concentrate on maintenance management and operations and will provide the skill level 3 soldiers with the skills they need to become maintenance supervisors. The curriculum includes advanced troubleshooting of engineer equipment systems, equipment inspection procedures, and maintenance operations and management as it applies to engineer units.

The course will also develop an NCO's skills and knowledge for training his soldiers in engineer equipment repair. Finally, it will align 62B soldiers more with other career management progressions within the 63 CMF.

E8	63Z50 Mechanical Maintenance Supervisor			
E7	62B40		Special Purpose Equipment 52X40 Repair Supervisor	
E6	62B30	52C30	52D30	52F30
E5	62B20	52C20	52D20	52F20
E4	62B10	52C10	52D10	52F10
	Construction Equipment Repairer	Utilities Equipment Repairer	Power Generation Equipment Repairer	Turbine Engine Generator Repairer

Figure 1. MOS restructure diagram.

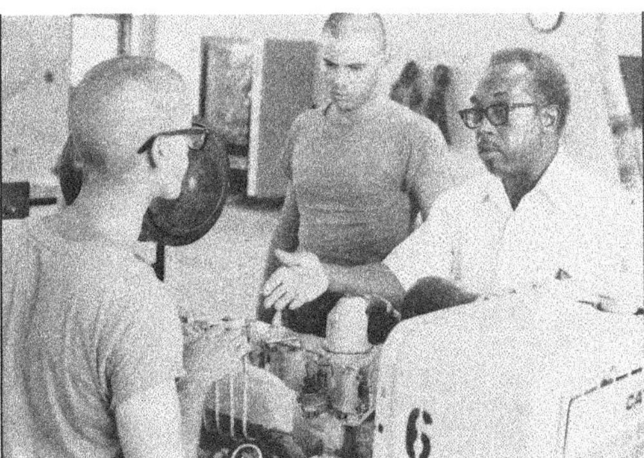

Artie Wright, 62B10 instructor, explains adjustments on a CAT engine to two of his students at Fort Leonard Wood, MO (photo by Ray Crosby).

62B40

The Engineer School is analyzing the 62B40 tasks to determine the need for resident technical training at skill level 4. Once the analysis is complete, a board will convene to determine the extent of technical training needed. Meanwhile, skill level 4 soldiers may attend ANCOC at Aberdeen Proving Grounds in Maryland.

Soldier Training Publications

Several new Training Extension Course (TEC) lessons are being developed for 62B10 soldiers at the rate of one per quarter. These will include hydraulics, cooling systems, and electrical systems.

A job book was also developed for the 62B. A new 62B soldier's manual for skill level 1 and a soldier's manual/trainer's guide for skill levels 2 through 4 were published in draft form, and recommended changes were received from the field. The soldier's manuals are undergoing a final edit by the Publications Division at the Engineer School. All such publications, to include job books, are scheduled to be fielded in September 1985.

Implementing the new 62B AIT course, developing the nonresident course materials, restructuring the 62B MOS, and developing the STPs will help to streamline and improve training in the MOS.

Anyone interested in additional information on training and development for the 62B should write or call: Training Development Field Office, USAES, Building 465, Fort Leonard Wood, MO, 65473-5895 (AV 581-1174).

CW3 Melad Smith Jr. is chief of the 62B Training and Development Team at Fort Leonard Wood. He previously served as the 3rd forward detachment commander of the 15th Maintenance Company, 19th Maintenance Battalion, 3rd Support Command. CW3 Smith has a bachelor's degree in political science/history from Austin Peay State University and a master's degree in human resource development/public administration from Webster University.

Writer's Guidelines

Do you have any articles, photographs, or artwork to submit to ENGINEER? Here are some tips.

TOPIC: We focus on combat engineering; however, any articles of interest to engineers are welcome. Write your articles in active voice and be as concise as possible. Please give your article a title, too.

LENGTH: Let your subject dictate length; generally, articles should be two to six pages, double spaced.

PHOTOGRAPHS AND ARTWORK: Besides photographs and artwork which supplement articles, photographers and artists should submit any work that may be of interest to engineers. Your photos should be 5x7 black and white, glossy. (We can also use good quality color slides.) Please include a caption and photo credit. Drawings should be legible, but do not have to be camera ready.

DEPARTMENTS: We are always looking for items for our departments:

- Letters to the Editor.
- Engineer Ingenuity.
- Engineer People.
- News and Notes.
- Personal Viewpoint.

ENGINEER PROBLEM: Please submit your challenging, but not too hard Engineer Problems. Problems should be referenced to a manual, but must be original. They should be checked for accuracy and should strengthen combat engineer skills as well.

COVER LETTER: When submitting material to ENGINEER, enclose a cover letter with your name, address, and phone number. Also, please include biographical information such as military and civilian education and past and present assignments.

If you have any questions, please call us.

(703) 664-3082, AV 354.

External Air Transport Procedures For Bridge Erection Boat

Pending the publication of FM 55-450-1, *Army Helicopter External Load Operations,* the following procedures should be followed for rigging and externally transporting the bridge erection boat, shallow draft.

First, safety tie the beach legs, securing the pins on the diving platform. Then secure the hydrojet compartment hatches with the nylon cord and the engine compartment hatches with a tiedown strap, load binder, and D-ring (Figure 1).

Next, safety tie the mast retaining pin, secure the map locker, secure all lights on the mast with tape, tape all windows and lights on the cab, ensure the cab is secured to the floor of the forward compartment (Figure 2), and attach the small clevis assemblies to the lifting eyes. These preparation steps should take two soldiers 20 minutes.

You are now ready for rigging.

First, place the apex fitting centered on the engine compartment hatches. Route the outer sling legs to the front lifting eyes (bow) and the inner sling legs to the rear lifting eyes (stern).

Next, loop the chain end of each sling leg through the clevis at its corresponding lifting eye and insert link #46 of each chain in its own grab hook. Now loop each chain end of the other sling legs through the clevis assemblies at its corresponding lifting eye and insert chain link #3 in its own grab hook.

Secure the free-running end of the chain with tape and pull up the apex fitting. Then trace all sling legs to the cab with one turn and tape. Take up all remaining slack in the sling legs and place the apex on the engine compartment hatches. Rigging this load should take two soldiers approximately 10 minutes.

You are finally ready for hook-up. The hook-up man should stand on the engine compartment hatch near the center.

Note that these instructions are applicable for the CH-47C at speeds not exceeding 80 knots. When hooked to the aircraft in flight, the load's long axis should be approximately 75° to the direction of flight. The 25,000-pound capacity sling set may also be used to rig this load by placing link #3 in the grab hook for sling legs 1 and 2, and link #35 in the grab hook for sling legs 3 and 4.

Materials needed for this operation are as follows:

- 2-inch wide adhesive tape.
- Type II nylon cord.
- 15-foot tiedown strap with load binder and D-ring.
- ¼-inch cotton webbing.
- Small clevis assembly. (Shackle provided with boat may be used in lieu of clevis assembly.)

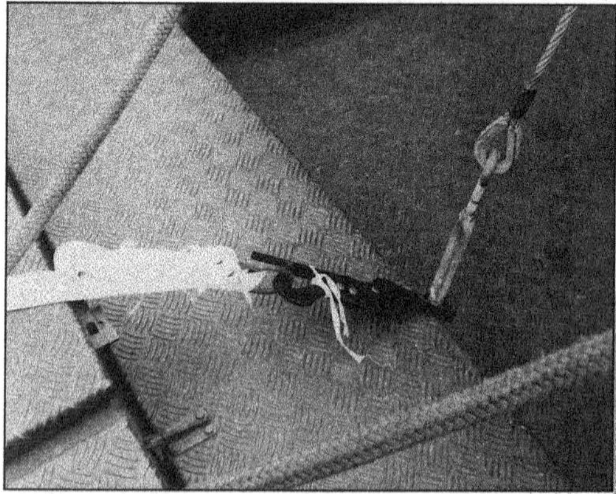

Figure 1. Secured hydrojet and engine compartment hatches.

Figure 2. (Top) Cab secured to floor of forward compartment. (Bottom) Side view of bridge erection boat ready for air transport.

Hotline Q & A

Q. I have a letter from Fort Leonard Wood, MO, which authorized the use of calculators during last year's 12B and 12B40 SQTs. I would like information on the use of calculators during the SQT.

A. The letter of approval referred to the 1983 SQT, not the 1984 or 1985 SQTs. USAES does not allow calculators to be used unless they are necessary to perform the task, but the school is negotiating with USATSC to allow their use on future engineer SQTs.

Q. In FC 5-102, *Mine Warfare*, dated January 1985, brigade commanders have the authority for hasty protective minefield emplacement. ARTEP 5-115, *Engineer Combat Battalion, Heavy*, also dated January 1985, says that battalion commanders have the authority for hasty protective minefield emplacement. Which is correct?

A. FC 5-102 is the correct reference. The brigade commander is the authority for hasty protective minefield emplacement. But, the authority may be delegated down to battalion or company level on a mission basis.

Q. Is the school evaluating the issue of reinstating chaplains in the heavy division engineer battalions?

A. Due to personnel constraints, USAES cannot reinstate chaplains in the heavy division engineer battalions. However, the issue is being evaluated.

Q. What is the minimum area required on the far shore to conduct bridging operations for rafting and mobile assault bridges?

A. There is no minimum area requirement on the far shore for rafting or bridging. Far shore area requirements are normally governed by the size of the crossing force, the nature of the terrain, and the tactical objectives for the assault force. A bridgehead line and release points will be established accordingly.

Q. When is the new ARTEP 5-500, *Engineer Cellular Teams*, scheduled for publication?

A. The new ARTEP 5-500 is scheduled for February 1987.

Q. How can we identify good crossing sites for training analysis overlays?

A. Good characteristics of river crossing sites include road networks into the near shore area and away from the far shore area, good bank conditions with a slope of less than 10 percent, and minimal river obstacles such as sandbars and submerged, dead trees. In addition, the water current should be under 10 feet per second; and, if possible, there should be cover and concealment for engineer regulating points and engineer equipment parks.

TOC Operations Revisited

by LTC John W. Braden Jr.

In the Winter 1980-81 ENGINEER magazine article, *Molding an Effective Tactical Operation Center,* I presented some considerations to improve command and control of engineer units in the field. The feedback from that article has been very encouraging. Now, I would like to supplement that article with a checklist that may further assist your organization in this important area.

Certainly there will be variations among engineer units as to how each organizes its Command Post (CP) or Tactical Operations Center (TOC). For purposes of this article, however, I will use a style that assumes the following is part of a Standing Operating Procedure (SOP) and that the checklist is directive in nature.

Organization

YES NO

References. As a minimum, are the following references on hand? FMs 3-10, 3-10-1, 3-12, 3-22, 3-50, 3-87, 5-15, 5-20, 5-25, 5-30, 5-31, 5-34, 5-35, 5-36, 5-100, 5-101, 5-102, 5-103, 5-104, 20-32, 21-41, 30-5, 90-2, 90-3, 90-4, 90-5, 90-6, 90-10, 90-10-1, 90-13, 90-14, 100-2-1, 100-2-2, 100-2-3, 100-5, 100-5-1, 101-10-1, 101-10-2, and TMs 5-210, 5-277, 5-312, 5-330, 5-725. (Circle any that are missing. Note that the list is **not** all inclusive.) ___ ___

Supplies and Equipment. Do you have the following items? Flashlights, spare batteries, range cards, spare microphones, fuel and water cans, trash bags, light bulbs, overlay paper, acetate, grease pencils, alcohol-base pens, tape of various types, map tacks, unit symbols, manifold paper, rags, stapler and staples, paper clips, envelopes, correction fluid, string, stencils and duplicating fluid, carbon paper, pens and markers, battery or gasoline lanterns with spare lantern parts, document protectors, two-prong fasteners, hole punches, candles, matches, tire chains, chemical lights, tow cable, minefield marking signs, camouflage sticks, first aid kit, rope. (Circle any that are missing. Note that the list is **not** all inclusive.) ___ ___

Blank Forms. Do you have the following forms? DD Form 173; DA Forms 1155, 1156, 1171-R, 1248, 1249, 1250, 1251, 1252, 1355, 1355-1, 1594, 2496; blank target folders; Joint Tactical Air Reconnaissance and Surveillance Request Forms. (Circle any that are missing. Note that the list is **not** all inclusive.) ___ ___

Maps.

1. Is the situation map (SITMAP) on hand and does it provide sufficient coverage of the area of operations (perhaps 1:50,000 coverage of the battalion's area and 1:250,000 coverage of the Corps' area)? ___ ___

2. Are there standard overlays for use by each staff section? ___ ___

3. If special maps are available of the area (road and bridge maps, trafficability maps, special products by division and corps topographic units and detachments), are these on hand? ___ ___

YES NO

Journal. Is a staff journal set up to control incoming and outgoing messages and to record operational events? (One way to set up a journal is to staple manila folders together into a three-piece logbook with two-prong fasteners at the top of each section. Mark the left section "INCOMING" and the right section "OUTGOING." Fasten DA Form 1594 into the center section.) ___ ___

Standing Operating Procedures. Is there sufficient quantity to provide copies of the SOP to units that may be attached or placed under your operational control (OPCON)? ___ ___

Mission Status Boards. Is there some means to keep track of missions: location, type, unit assigned, unit supported, progress? (Note that these boards should look much like your mission status reports required by SOP.) ___ ___

Reports Book. Is there a binder prepared which contains all required report formats so that when, for example, an NBC-1 report is submitted, the journal clerk can turn to the NBC-1 section and copy the incoming message directly onto a preprinted form rather onto scrap paper, the wall, or his hand? ___ ___

Duties and Responsibilities. Are these clearly defined by SOP and are shifts specified? ___ ___

Amenities. Do you have the following items? Soap, paper plates, plastic ware, paper towels, cups, toilet paper, sugar and creamer packets, tools, heat tablets, insect repellent, igloo containers. ___ ___

Operations

Staff Journal (DA Form 1594).

1. Is the journal being posted with consecutively numbered events (to preclude confusion by having two events with the same number)? ___ ___

2. Are all incoming and outgoing messages being logged into the journal—with the journal number on the message—and (is "hard copy") fastened into the folder rather than being loose in the TOC/CP? ___ ___

3. Does the "ACTION TAKEN" column of the DA Form 1594 actually reflect some action taken such as "Posted on the SITMAP," "Notified 1st Platoon," "Sent forward to Brigade," "See Message # ___" rather than "Logged" or something else that doesn't indicate any action? ___ ___

SITMAP.

1. Does the SITMAP have the friendly situation, enemy situation, and logistics information posted or available via overlays? ___ ___

YES NO

2. Does the SITMAP have the missions posted on it? (One way to do this is to use the system shown below.) ___ ___

. T1234 (RC) 1/C
a b c

. = mission location
/ = mission initiated
✳ = mission completed
a = mission number
b = mission (road crater)
c = unit assigned (1st Platoon, Co. C)

Missions.

1. Once missions are received, are they being checked and analyzed at the TOC/CP as opposed to being "stovepiped" straight down to subordinate units? ___ ___

2. Is the TOC/CP working to stay on top of missions by requiring updates and taking action if nothing is heard or is it content to find out how a mission went only after the troops return? ___ ___

3. Are TOC/CP personnel knowledgeable as to personnel and equipment assets committed and available? VERY IMPORTANT ___ ___

4. Are required reports to higher headquarters being made as specified by SOP and/or by the OPORD? ___ ___

5. If multiple requirements are received and/or if requirements appear to exceed capabilities, is there an effort to ascertain priorities? ___ ___

6. If it appears that a mission cannot be completed within the specified time (and this should usually be determined during mission analysis), are efforts made to influence the action (lay on more troops and/or equipment or find ways to increase efficiency) or does the TOC/CP wait until late and then report the bad news and request an extension? ___ ___

7. Does the TOC/CP use warning orders or other means to enable subordinate or supporting units to begin troop-leading procedures and thereby maximize their time for mission execution? ___ ___

Nuclear, Biological and Chemical (NBC).

1. Are chemical alarms set upwind of the TOC/CP? ___ ___

2. Is there a metal-on-metal alarm set up near the TOC/CP to enable TOC/CP personnel to warn other personnel in the area? ___ ___

3. Do TOC/CP personnel have their personal chmical-biological defense equipment and their spare protective garments and mask filters? ___ ___

YES NO

4. Are there spare batteries for chemical alarms and radiometers and are there spare refill kits for chemical detectors? ___ ___

5. Is there a trained chemical detection team among TOC/CP personnel? (Recommend this team be formed from among the SS clerks and drivers.) ___ ___

6. Does the TOC/CP actively seek the latest effective downwind message and expeditiously pass this information on to subordinate and supporting units? ___ ___

7. Does the TOC/CP analyze enemy NBC capabilities and possible intentions and recommend a mission-oriented protective posture to the commander? ___ ___

8. Are there personnel for each shift who are trained to prepare NBC-3 reports, plot downwind chemical hazards, and make radiation fallout predictions? ___ ___

9. Are operation exposure guide (OEG) analyses being performed? Is the radiation status (RS) of subordinate units being monitored, and do TOC/CP personnel know the prescribed point at which further exposure is prohibited without higher authority? ___ ___

10. Are at least 20 each "GAS," "BIO," and "ATOM" NBC working signs on hand? ___ ___

Command, Control, and Communications.

1. Command and Control.

A. Has an alternate TOC/CP been designated and does this alternate have the redundant maps, plans, references, and other equipment to perform the TOC/CP mission? ___ ___

B. Have liaison officers (LNO) been identified and is there a package of material (maps, radio, telephone, references, date sheets, administrative items) for each LNO to carry with him?
Note: The LNO may also require his own transportation. ___ ___

C. Is the TOC/CP configured for a "JUMP" capability, to include designated personnel and equipment? ___ ___

D. Has a rally point or reconstitution point been designated in the event the TOC/CP is overrun or otherwise disbanded or separated? ___ ___

2. Communications.

A. Does the TOC/CP have a complete copy of the CEOI to include operations codes, authentication tables, command and staff packets, and supplemental operating instructions? ___ ___

YES NO

B. Do all stations have proper and compatible communications security (CONSEC) keying material for all nets? ___ ___

C. Does the communications-electronics staff office have additional copies to provide LNOs and attached or OPCOM units? ___ ___

D. Are radio communications minimized via use of messengers and couriers, wire, arm and hand signals when moving or maneuvering, and authorized brevity codes? (Note that use of International Morse Code is also of value in this area, although not taught to most operators.) ___ ___

E. Are all TOC/CP personnel knowledgeable of procedures to deal with meaconing, jamming, intrusion, and interference? ___ ___

F. Is there a plan to respond to situations of total or temporary radio outages? ___ ___

G. Are TOC/CP personnel knowledgeable of procedures to protect radio equipment from electromagnetic radiation when given warning of friendly use of nuclear weapons? ___ ___

H. Do TOC/CP personnel use proper procedure when making a scheduled frequency and call-sign change? (Note that most supplemental operating instructions *do not* require existing stations to reenter the net.) ___ ___

I. Are the TOC/CP vehicles prewired to facilitate rapid establishment/reestablishment of wire communications? ___ ___

Equipment. Are TOC/CP personnel trained and licensed to operate and maintain the vehicles, generators, radios, light sets, lanterns, and other TOC/CP equipment? ___ ___

Operations Security (OPSEC).

1. Physical Security.

A. Is access to the TOC/CP controlled? ___ ___

B. Are all personnel rehearsed on actions to take in the event of a ground or air attack on the TOC/CP? ___ ___

2. Information Security.

A. Are the sign-countersign, access rosters, and badges being used to identify personnel, verify clearances, and ascertain need-to-know? ___ ___

B. Are classified papers and maps inside the TOC/CP covered when not in use and are there clearly labeled containers for classified waste? ___ ___

C. Upon displacement of the TOC/CP, is there an effort to ensure that trash or other waste is not left which would reveal information about the unit? ___ ___

YES NO

3. Signal Security.

A. Are antennas erected away from the TOC/CP and are remotes used to maintain distance from emitters? ___ ___

B. Are directional antennas being used? ___ ___

C. Are radio operators using proper prowords and keeping transmissions brief? ___ ___

D. When operating in an unsecure mode:

(1) Is authentication being required? ___ ___

(2) Are authorized operations codes being used vice clear text or pseudocodes? ___ ___

4. Deception and Countersurveillance.

A. Are camouflage and concealment procedures being followed? ___ ___

(1) Are nets at least 18 inches above vehicles, tents, and equipment? ___ ___

(2) Are glass and mirrors covered? ___ ___

(3) When using the Woodland Camouflage Screen System, is the proper side being used to conform to the season/general background? ___ ___

(4) When using fresh vegetation, is the vegetation being changed regularly? ___ ___

(5) Is there an effort to preclude vehicle tracks or communications wire from identifying the location of the TOC/CP? ___ ___

B. Are noise and light discipline being maintained? ___ ___

C. Are efforts being made to reduce the infrared signature of the TOC/CP? ___ ___

D. Are helipads and vehicle parks located at a distance from the TOC/CP? ___ ___

LTC John W. Braden Jr. is the deputy commander of the 7th Engineer Brigade in Europe. He has served in engineer units in the United States, Germany, and Vietnam, and commanded the 20th Engineer Battalion, Fort Campbell, KY.

LTC Braden graduated from the Command and General Staff College and the U.S. Army War College and was an instructor at the U.S. Army Engineer School. He has a bachelor's and a master's degree in civil engineering from Purdue University and is a registered professional engineer in Virginia. Besides Specialty 21 (Engineer), LTC Braden holds Specialty 54 (Operations, Plans and Training).

NATIONAL GUARD

.ANSAS

9th Engineer Co.
nporia, KS
ЛAJ Eugene Kramer
SG Dale Putnam

2nd Engineer Co.
ichita, KS
PT Dave Wheeler
SG Johnny Newman

ЮRTH DAKOTA

4th Engineer Group
ismarck, ND
OL Virgil A. Rude
SM Donald T. Marx

141st Engineer Bn. (CBT)
Valley City, ND
LTC Robert E. Schulte
1SG Lloyd A. Nelson

164th Engineer Bn. (CBT)
Minot, ND
CPT John L. Hocking
CSM David C. Cichos

231st Engineer Bn.
Grand Forks, ND
LTC Gereld F. Gurnholz
CSM Dewey J. Garceau

816th Engineer Co.
Fargo, ND
CPT Thomas L. Wilson
1SG Harlan C. Muehler

957th Engineer Co.
Grafton, ND
CPT Allen L. Nygard
1SG Thomas R. Spicer

UTAH

115th Engineer Group (CBT)
Murray, UT
COL Dee R. Russon
CSM Donald Nielsen

1457th Engineer Bn. (CBT)(CORPS)
American Fork, UT
LTC Joseph Ford
CSM Gayle Whatcott

116th Engineer Co. (CSE)
Springville, UT
CPT Clark Christensen
1SG Marvin Baker

117th Engineer Co. (AFB)
Lehi, UT
1LT Craig Morgan
1SG Max Smith

118th Engineer Co. (AFB)
Tooele, UT
CPT Michael Johnsen
1SG Donald Wickham

ARMY RESERVE

'IRST ARMY

11th Engineer Bde.
rooklyn, NY
3G Roger L. Kresge
SM Ronald P. Busz

)8th Engineer Group
ittsburgh, PA
OL Samuel P. Contacos
SM Donald D. Lewis

15th Engineer Group
lew Cumberland, PA
COL Donald K. Emig
CSM Anthony W. Lippert

29th Engineer Group
rockton, MA
COL Bruce B. Ellsworth
CSM Richard R. Bourbeau

30th Engineer Bn. (CBT)(CORPS)
Vorchester, PA
LTC James J. Carroll Jr.
CSM Lynwood J. Vogel

65th Engineer Bn. (CBT)(HVY)
chuylkill Haven, PA
LTC James F. Lent
CSM Kermit B. Tolbard

68th Engineer Bn. (CBT)(HVY)
Лanchester, NH
LTC Robert H. Ropp
CSM Arthur E. Starkweather

29th Engineer Bn. (CBT)(HVY)
Jniontown, PA
MAJ Jeffrey L. Barton
CSM Rudolph V. Bartuch

58th Engineer Bn. (CBT)(CORPS)
ohnstown, PA
LTC Rodney D. Ruddock
CSM Richard P. Philage

463rd Engineer Bn. (CBT)(HVY)
Wheeling, WV
LTC Joseph Miker Jr.
CSM Donald L. Showalter

464th Engineer Bn. (CBT)(CORPS)
Schenectady, NY
LTC John M. Paris III
CSM Ogden Tuttle

469th Engineer Bn. (CBT)(HVY)
Jersey City, NJ
LTC William Mercurio
CSM vacant

479th Engineer Bn. (CBT)(CORPS)
Watertown, NY
LTC David Bent
CSM Laurence T. Graves

483rd Engineer Bn. (CBT)(CORPS)
New Bedford, MA
LTC Thomas R. Meler
CSM John E. Macedo

854th Engineer Bn. (CBT)(HVY)
Kingston, NY
LTC Anthony R. Kropp
CSM Edward C. Dougherty

SECOND ARMY

412th ENCOM
Vicksburg, MS
MG Robert E. Louque Jr.
CSM Charles A. Rule

348th Engineer Group
Birmingham, AL
COL Richard B. Burleson
CSM Lindsey R. Hadley

926th Engineer Group
Montgomery, AL
COL Julian F. Botts
CSM James H. Lamon

391st Engineer Bn. (CBT)(CORPS)
Greenville, SC
LTC Eskel N. Miller III
CSM Ronald H. Owensby

448th Engineer Bn. (CBT)(HVY)
Ft. Buchanan, PR
LTC Luis M. Garcia
CSM Julio Fuentes

467th Engineer Bn. (CBT)(CORPS)
Memphis, TN
LTC Charles A. Ingram
CSM John M. Nichols

478th Engineer Bn. (CBT)(CORPS)
Ft. Thomas, KY
LTC Dennis L. Grant
CSM William L. Eggemeier

841st Engineer Bn. (CBT)(CORPS)
Miami, FL
LTC Joseph L. Budreau III
CSM Alvin G. Baughns

844th Engineer Bn. (CBT)(HVY)
Knoxville, TN
MAJ Morris G. Herndon
CSM Harold E. Berry

926th Engineer Bn. (CBT)(HVY)
Birmingham, AL
LTC H. Inge Waddle Jr.
CSM Roland Barnwell

FOURTH ARMY

416th ENCOM
Chicago, IL
MG Max Baratz
CSM Dave Moore

364th Engineer Group
Columbus, OH
COL James C. Myers
CSM Lauren H. Calvin

372nd Engineer Group
Des Moines, IA
COL May L. Shardein
CSM William S. Gates

385th Engineer Group
St. Paul, MN
COL William Thom
CSM Ronald Levendoski

367th Engineer Bn.
St. Paul, MN
LTC Alan L. Beeler
CSM Mike Danberry

389th Engineer Bn.
Dubuque, IA
LTC Bruce B. Wands
CSM Lloyd L. Smith

397th Engineer Bn.
Eau Claire, WI
MAJ Michael Metcalf
CSM Richard Madsen

863rd Engineer Bn. (CBT)(CORPS)
Aurora, IL
LTC Jack H. Kotter
CSM Donald C. Phillips

961st Engineer Bn. (CBT)(HVY)
Milwaukee, WI
MAJ David D. Parkinson
CSM Conrad H. Dazer

972nd Engineer Bn.
Ft. Benjamin Harrison, IN
LTC James L. Bauerle
CSM Willard D. Gibbons

983rd Engineer Bn.
Toledo, OH
MAJ John C. Blanchard
CSM Kenneth R. Garrett

FIFTH ARMY

420th Engineer Bde.
Bryan, TX
BG Alvin W. Jones
CSM Jess Phillips

353rd Engineer Group
Norman, OK
LTC Clifford Cantrell
CSM Gayland Griffin

493rd Engineer Group
Dallas, TX
COL Jerry L. Selby
CSM Wayman Hemphill

245th Engineer Bn.
Baton Rouge, LA
LTC Ronald Gentry
CSM Robert L. Bundick III

430th Engineer Bn.
Tomball, TX
LTC Michael Griffith
CSM Robert E. Smith

489th Engineer Bn.
Little Rock, AR
MAJ Woodrow Cummins
CSM Thomas Terryman

871st Engineer Bn.
Austin, TX
LTC John M. Gosdin
CSM J. R. Langerhans

980th Engineer Bn.
Wichita Falls, TX
LTC William A. Long Jr.
CSM Charles W. Peterson

SIXTH ARMY

244th Engineer Bn. (CBT)(HVY)
Aurora, CO
MAJ Donald V. Labrot
CSM Paul E. Nesselroad

321st Engineer Bn. (CBT)(CORPS)
Boise, ID
LTC Glen L. O'Dell
CSM Gregory P. Gleason

820th Engineer Bn. (CBT)(CORPS)
San Pablo, CA
LTC William W. Applegate Jr.
CSM Lynn G. Datwyler

ACTIVE ARMY

588th Engineer Bn.
Ft. Polk, LA
LTC Wayne Murphy
CSM Charles D. Crim

3rd Engineer Bn., USAESB
Ft. Belvoir, VA
LTC Al Jansen
CSM Terry A. Cougill

864th Engineer Bn.
Ft. Lewis, WA
LTC Steve Young
CSM Charles Nobles

Individual Army headquarters provided the names of commanders and command sergeants major for Army Reserve units. The state headquarters supplied information on National Guard units. Readers are encouraged to send any additional information to ENGINEER.

by CPT Micheal A. Lansing

The newly implemented, centralized Conditional Voluntary Indefinite (CVI) selection process raises new challenges for commanders in their Other than Regular Army (OTRA) officers' professional development. Unlike RA officers who remain in a career status as long as they are competitive for promotion, OTRA officers must compete for voluntary indefinite status.

The first step in obtaining career status is getting selected by the CVI centralized selection board. This board, consisting of a representative from each of the combat, combat support, and combat service support branches, convenes to select only the best OTRA officers for continuing active duty. Unlike lieutenant and captain promotion boards, which select officers on a fully qualified basis, the CVI selection board uses criteria that select only the best qualified officers. This distinct difference in selection criteria makes it critical to document OTRA officers' duty performance.

It is paramount that all commanders fully understand the CVI process, the criteria for selection, and the impact of the initial and subsequent OERs for their OTRA officers. Failure to comprehend the impact of the CVI process may deny a deserving young officer the opportunity to further develop on active duty.

To apply for CVI consideration, officers must meet certain minimum requirements and be willing to make some tough choices to obtain career status. CVI applications are forwarded through command channels once the officer meets these requirements:

- Have served at least two years active federal commissioned service (AFCS) on the current tour.

- Submit the CVI application before the 27th month of AFCS. This requirement applies to both a three-year and four-year OBV (obligated volunteer) officer.

More important, the officer must state a willingness to accept a branch transfer as part of the awarding of CVI status. During professional development counseling, commanders should explain to their OTRA officers that rebranching junior grade officers is necessary to meet Army officer requirements at the captain and field grade levels. Of course, those officers wanting to volunteer for branch transfer to underaligned branches should be encouraged to state their desires on their CVI applications.

A separate DA board is convened to determine required branch transfers to meet Army needs. This board chooses a proportional number of top, middle, and lower-third officers from the CVI selection results to enter underaligned branches. Therefore, it is imperative that commanders counsel their Reserve officers so even the top performers may be chosen for mandatory rebranching. Subsequently, it is vital that all officers give careful consideration before indicating their preferences for branch transfer. The choice may have long-term consequences.

The recently released CVI results clearly demonstrate the board's highly competitive nature. Only 78 percent of the officers were selected for retention, and in some branches the selection rate was only 59 percent. Those officers not selected for retention will have to separate within 90 days of written notification or at the end of their initial obligated tour, whichever is later.

Officers must understand there are no regulatory provisions for appeals or reconsideration, unless there is a material positive change to their Official Military Personnel File (OMPF). In addition, active duty extensions will not be granted pending results of a request for reconsideration or awaiting the outcome of an OER appeal.

Once an OTRA officer has been selected for CVI status, commanders should know that the first year is a probationary period. In addition to incurring a one-year active duty service obligation, the OTRA officer is on probation. To the commander, this means that any misconduct, failure at an Army-sponsored school, or downturn in duty performance is reason for revocation of CVI status. If CVI status is revoked during the probationary period, the officer will separate from active duty within 90 days.

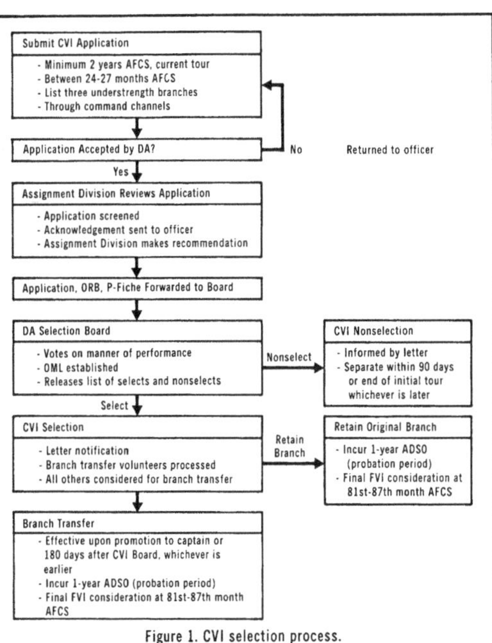

Figure 1. CVI selection process.

The Army demands high standards of performance from all its officers, whether RA and OTRA. The CVI selection process is one tool the commander has to ensure that only the best qualified OTRA officers are permitted to serve on active duty in a career status. Acts of misconduct, integrity issues, and failure to meet APRT and height and weight standards are obvious discriminators.

Commanders, however, must ensure that officers who are slow to develop, but show potential, have their duty performance documented to clearly indicate the officer's potential. In light of the CVI board's competitive nature, OERs designed to "get an officer's attention" will likely deny him continued active duty.

The CVI process is the most competitive process a junior OTRA officer faces. A commander with a complete understanding of the process and its impact toward achieving career status will have met the command challenge of mentor and coach. To do otherwise is a disservice to our quality OTRA officers.

CPT Micheal A. Lansing is the personnel management officer in the Combat Support Arms Division, MILPERCEN. He has served as a recruiting company commander; a military police company commander; the battalion adjutant of the 716th Military Police Battalion at Fort Riley, KS; and a platoon leader with the 3rd Armored Division. CPT Lansing graduated from the Military Police Advanced Course and has a bachelor's degree in history from Wheaton College and a master's degree in systems management from the University of Southern California.

Career Notes

NCO and Enlisted Soldiers Branch

Enlisted Preference Statement:

The *Enlisted Preference Statement* (DA Form 2635) has often been called the "dream sheet." In the real world, however, career planning by soldiers and their families can often result in assignments to at least one of those locations indicated on the preference statement.

The preference statement, dated August 1984, also contains vital information which can help soldiers in choosing assignments. When preparing their preference statements, soldiers should seek counsel from the PAC NCO, PSNCO, MILPO NCO, commander, or command sergeant major. Soldiers should also ask themselves the following questions before speaking to any of these persons and before completing the DA Form 2635.

- Is my grade and MOS authorized at the locations I choose?
- When should I submit the preference statement?
- What type of assignment should I ask for to gain experience in my MOS?
- Are dependent schools available?
- Is there a military hospital nearby?
- Are there civil service employment opportunities for my spouse?
- What programs and locations are available for exceptional family members?

AR 614-200, *Selection of Enlisted Soldiers for Training and Assignment,* and DA PAM 600-8, *Military Personnel Management and Administrative Procedures,* contain detailed procedures for completing the preference statement; soldiers are advised to thoroughly acquaint themselves with these publications.

The preference statement plays an important role in the personnel assignment system. When correctly submitted, it improves soldiers' opportunities for assignment to desired locations.

Engineer Ranger Training:

The Engineer Career Management Branch at MILPERCEN is seeking combat engineers (12B) to volunteer for ranger training. This anticipated shortage of ranger-qualified engineers is a result of the new light infantry divisions.

Soldiers who wish to volunteer for ranger training should apply through command personnel channels to the Engineer Branch, MILPERCEN. The basic qualifications and application procedures are outlined in Chapter 6, AR 614-200, and in DA PAM 600-8. The only exception to these procedures is that those selected engineers will not be reassigned to ranger battalions. However, a special qualification identifier (SQI) will be awarded: SQI G (Ranger) or SQI V (Ranger-Airborne).

Any questions should be directed to SGM Welsh at the Engineer Branch, MILPERCEN. His telephone number is (202) 325-8326, AV 221.

Initial EERs Eliminated:

Soldiers will no longer be rated three months after they are promoted to E5, MILPERCEN officials announced. The requirement for initial EERs was eliminated on May 1.

MILPOs are accepting initial reports with a "thru" date of April 1985 or earlier, but any reports with a "thru" date later than this are being returned as unauthorized.

All other provisions of AR 623-205, *Enlisted Evaluation Reporting System*, are still in effect.

MILPERCEN officials also said that some units may still not be aware that the Army-wide EER weighted average was eliminated on January 1, 1984. The last EER weighted average was published in December 1983, and some units may still be using it or calculating a local EER average.

Officials said the EER weighted average was misleading because it was based on EER scores collected over a five-year period. It also contributed to inflated EER scores, which caused DA selection boards to emphasize the narrative sections in the selection process.

MILPERCEN has prepared an instructional package to teach soldiers and raters the proper preparation of EERs. A copy may be obtained by writing: Commander, MILPERCEN, ATTN: DAPC-MSE, 200 Stovall St., Alexandria, VA 22332-0400. For more information on EERs, call MSG Hendrix at (202) 325-9610, AV 221.

Revised Promotion Worksheet:

A revised promotion worksheet (DA Form 3355) was recently adopted into the Army personnel system for soldiers being recommended to E5 or E6, or already on these respective promotion lists, MILPERCEN officials said.

The revised form emphasizes physical fitness, self-discipline, professional competence, and a commitment to self-improvement and achievement. The form also allots more points for commanders' evaluations, SQT scores, military education, weapons qualification, and APRT scores. However, points are no longer awarded for time in service, time in grade, and high school completion.

Promotion points are now computed annually instead of semi-annually. The next recomputations will be in February 1986 for soldiers on an E5 promotion list and in May 1986 for those on an E6 list. These recomputations will occur during the same months every following year. However, soldiers will still be allowed to reappear before promotion boards earlier than the scheduled recomputations in order to add points for recent achievements.

New Recruitments:

The 299th Engineer Company, a new ribbon assault bridge company, was activated on July 20 at Fort Belvoir. Many positions in this Army Reserve unit are still available to engineers. Anyone interested should contact 2LT Umana-Williams at (703) 664-2739 or MSG Wicker at (703) 664-2525.

Soldiers from the 135th Engineer Group use a pile driver to construc bridge at the Rio Pabo bridge site in Panama. Engineers from t Missouri National Guard built six bridges in the 9½ miles of ro constructed during Blazing Trails '85 (photo by CPT Lynda Mann).

Engineers to the Rescue

A Personal Viewpoint

by CPT Marc E. Marszalek

A terrorist attack on the American Embassy in Beirut killed 63 people in April 1983. Many of the dead were not extracted from the rubble until days later. In September 1983, over 200 marines were killed and 81 injured after terrorists bombed their headquarters. Cranes and bulldozers excavated the twisted concrete and steel while marines dug down toward the survivors with their bare hands.

The increase of terrorist bombings, the destructive forces of modern warfare, and natural disasters have escalated the need for emergency rescue operations. At present, the Corps of Engineers is not properly equipped to remove injured and trapped people from collapsed structures. Bulldozers and cranes chewing at rubble is not an effective nor safe rescue technique, and a major earthquake in California or a terrorist bombing of the Pentagon would tax local rescue resources beyond their capability.

Currently, disaster recovery teams from the Corps of Engineers handle natural disasters, and engineer units responsible for area damage control at corps level handle warfare destruction recovery operations. However, according to MAJ Riley Jacobs, Directorate of Combat Developments, USAES, the training and unique equipment needed to rescue casualties from rubble is not available within the Army.

Engineers need rescue teams to carry out this task in the United States and overseas. We must integrate newly formed rescue teams into present organizations with the ultimate goal of saving lives. Specialized training and equipment are key factors.

Training

Successfully rescuing people from collapsed buildings requires fast and precise hand-intensive labor which can only be developed through special training.

Special training for the rescue team leader in areas like civil or structural engineering will expedite decisions at the disaster site. Evaluating the balance, material composition, and structural soundness of the remaining structure will enable the leader to make decisions for bracing the remaining structure and removing debris without weakening the building and causing further collapse.

Most of the officers in the Corps have these required skills associated with civil engineering. Engineer officers receive special training in leadership, rigging, vertical structure design, utilities, and many other important skills at EOBC and EOAC. With this special training, the team leader can direct tasks to the team members and local labor.

In addition to training and skills related to civil engineering, rescue team leaders and members need more advanced training in medical treatment. The Medical Services Corps provides classes in which team members can learn about burns, fractures, internal injuries, and other medical areas. Students learn the effects of heavy weights on people and how to remove debris without causing further injury.

If the rescue team leader understands how the body works during times of stress and traumatic injury, he can make educated decisions when rescuing injured persons from rubble. He must see that they are given immediate first aid treatment and quickly evacuated from the danger area.

Also critical for the rescue team is knowing how local fire fighting teams function and deploy. The fire departments of large American cities provide training in rescue techniques, In these classes, the team can learn ladder safety and the use of new rescue equipment: power cutoff saws, hydraulic spreaders and cutters, life lines and belts, and pumps and ventilators.

The heavy rescue course developed by California's Heavy Rescue Committee Fire Service Training and Education Program was created for the Federal Emergency Management Agency. The course objectives include:

- Information on basic types of building construction and their collapse characteristics from various causes.
- Information on different equipment used during heavy rescue operations.
- Methods for using heavy rescue equipment.
- Methods of improvising rescue equipment using available materials.

This course, modified to meet Army requirements on or off the battlefield, would be an excellent way to educate rescue teams.

Rescue team training must also include rapid deployment, quick hand-intensive excavation, and the use of specialized equipment. The team must be lightly equipped and easily air-transportable. Most disasters will not occur within driving distance of the rescue team.

Training by many diverse programs and concentrating on modern specialized equipment form the structure and objective of the rescue team—to save lives. However, the special training required for rescue missions will prevent the team from performing other engineer-related tasks such as countermobility or survivability. A rescue team in a corps battlefield rear area performing area damage control would be ineffective if reorganized as infantry. Their specialized training in noncombat areas and lack of combat equipment would be fatal.

Equipment

Combat heavy battalions are tasked with emergency rescue operations.

(continued on page 42)

VOLUME 15 NUMBER 4 WINTER 1985-86

Special thanks to Lee M. Rivas, the Directorate of Evaluation and Standardization, and the Engineer Proponency Office.

On the Cover

The Sapper Leader Course (page 12) trains engineers to fight as light infantry. The 13th Engineer Battalion masters air assault. (U.S. Army photo).

FEATURES

DEPARTMENTS

ENGINEER (ISSN 0046-1989) is an authorized publication of the U.S. Army Engineer Center and Fort Belvoir, VA. Unless specifically stated, material appearing herein does not necessarily reflect official policy, thinking nor endorsement by any agency of the U.S. Army. The words he, him, or his are used to represent personnel of either sex. All photographs contained herein are official U.S. Army photographs unless otherwise credited. The use of funds for printing this publication was approved by Headquarters, Department of the Army. Material herein may be reprinted if credit is given to ENGINEER and to the author. ENGINEER's objectives are to provide a forum for the exchange of ideas, to inform and motivate, and to promote the professional development of all members of the Army engineer community. Direct correspondence with ENGINEER is authorized and encouraged. Inquiries, letters to the editor, commentaries, manuscripts, photographs and general correspondence should be sent to: ENGINEER Magazine, ATZA-TD-P, Stop 291D, Fort Belvoir, VA 22060-5291. Phone: (703) 664-3082, AV 354. ENGINEER may be forwarded to personnel in military units. Address changes should be sent to ENGINEER. Subscriptions to ENGINEER are available through the Superintendent of Documents, U.S. Government Printing Office, Washington, D.C. 20402. A check or money order payable to Superintendent of Documents must accompany all subscription requests. Rates are $11.00 for domestic (including APO and FPO) addresses and $13.75 for foreign addresses. Individual copies are available at $3.00 per copy for domestic addresses and $3.75 for foreign addresses. Second Class postage paid at Fort Belvoir, VA, and additional mailing offices. POSTMASTER: send address changes to ENGINEER, ATZA-TD-P, Stop 291D, Fort Belvoir, VA 22060-5291.

News & Notes

New Camouflage Fits Soldier's Pocket

Soldiers using the new individual camouflage net vanish at will. Buttoned together, these nets help conceal units of battalion, brigade, and division size. The nets become a combat multiplier by adding the element of surprise to the light infantry soldier (Belvoir R&D photo).

A small, lightweight camouflage net developed by Belvoir R&D Center was used successfully in Korea during Team Spirit '85. The individual concealment cover (ICC) is a solid color net (5 feet by 7 feet) made of incised, rip stop nylon.

Each unit weighs less than a pound and can be folded to fit into the pocket of a soldier's uniform. The nets can be joined together to form a larger cover to conceal fighting positions, weapons emplacements, and soldiers.

The nets were developed in response to Army doctrine for the future which calls for a new kind of soldier—light and mobile. During the Team Spirit exercise, the ICC was used by elements of the 7th Light Infantry Division for concealment before a surprise attack.

Work is underway on improved versions of the net for use in desert, woodland, and snow. The ICC is being developed under a quick response program at the request of the 9th Infantry Division and the Army Development and Engineering Agency (ADEA).

Foam Bridging and Rafting for a Fast-Moving Army

The U.S. Army Construction Engineering Research Laboratory (CERL) is developing foam applications for bridging and rafting operations—applications that can get troops and vehicles quickly and safely across unfordable streams and rivers.

- Foam can be transported in small containers and then expanded up to 30 times its original volume to build a bridge or flotation system.
- When needed in the field, polyurethane foam can be mixed by hand or with high speed mixers.
- Once formed, foam flotation devices are lighter and easier to handle than comparable conventional bridging and rafting systems.

Two flotation systems are designed to move people across water. The foam footbridge consists of 20-foot by 3-foot bridge sections lashed together. Each section can support 1,200 pounds. The foam-filled reconnaissance boat is the same size as the inflatable boat currently used by the Army. The three-man boat resists puncture, will not sink, and supports up to 700 pounds.

CERL researchers have also developed foam flotation systems for vehicles. The utility truck rafting system consists of two cylinders (11 feet long, 25-1/4 inches in diameter) attached to the sides of a 1/4-ton truck. Each cylinder weighs 100 pounds, yet can support up to 2,200 pounds in water. A larger version, the MLC20 rafting system, uses two 500-pound cylinders which can support up to 13,000 pounds in water. With both systems, troops use a guide rope and tow rope to pull the vehicles across water. The floats can be detached and used again.

Footbridge sections and flotation cylinders get Army troops and vehicles safely and quickly across unfordable streams or rivers (CERL photo).

Future plans include developing a vehicular bridge for military load classes 5 through 30 and a rafting system for vehicles up to military load class 70.

Water Detection Team Supports Bright Star '85

U.S. forces participating in maneuvers in the Middle East this summer got some help from the Army Corps of Engineers' newly formed water detection response team.

Seven civilian scientists from the Engineer Topographic Laboratories, Fort Belvoir, VA, and Waterways Experiment Station, Vicksburg, MS, located well-drilling sites for Army, Navy, and Air Force units participating in Bright Star '85. They identified three well sites, two in Egypt and one in Jordan, for the combined joint training exercise involving the United States, Egypt, Jordan, Somalia, and Oman.

The team will support future military operations as well as training exercises. It will identify and develop equipment and techniques which terrain teams and well-drilling units can use to detect subsurface water, according to Allan DeWall, an ETL geologist who manages the detection team and served as team leader for the Bright Star mission. The team will be ready to support U.S. forces in emergencies and will also act as a referral service.

Finding groundwater is particularly difficult in arid regions. Evaluating well sites involves interpreting geological factors, analyzing geophysical data, and making complex technical judgments—tasks which drilling detachments are neither trained nor equipped to handle. Military planners, however, count on wells to provide over 15 percent of the water needed for soldiers and equipment deployed in arid regions. The water detection team will help drilling crews meet this goal.

Tony Dardeau and Dwain Butler, Waterways Experiment Station, set rods for an electrical resistivity survey at a potential well site west of Cairo. Team members and other civilians wore uniforms during Bright Star '85 (Engineer Topographic Lab photo).

Two Light Infantry Divisions Reactivate

Two engineer units now support light infantry divisions reactivated this fall. The 41st Engineer Battalion, Fort Drum, NY, is part of the 10th Mountain Division. The 229th Engineer Battalion, Fredericksburg, VA, supports the 29th Infantry Division—the only National Guard unit of the Army's five light infantry divisions.

The light division, one of the Army's latest tactical developments, has fewer troops and less equipment than a standard infantry division. It relies more on agility, stamina, and cunning than on firepower. The division can deploy rapidly to trouble spots and sustain itself for 48 hours anywhere in the world. It clears and defends urban areas or hostile terrain, provides antitank defense, conducts raids and heliborne operations, and protects rear areas.

Wanted . . . Computer Programs

The U.S. Army Engineer School is developing automated computer programs which will aid engineer command and control functions. Presently, engineer tasks are being analyzed and selected for inclusion in the Engineer Command and Control and Digital Topographic Support systems.

If your unit is using computer-based applications authored by unit members or adopted from other sources, please contact CPT Leo Fontana, AV 354-3953 or write to: Commandant, U.S. Army Engineer School, ATTN: ATZA-TE-TT, Fort Belvoir, VA 22060-5331. Your programs may be used as a prototype for applications Corps-wide.

News & Notes

The Pyramid Project

"People come up to me on the street and ask me what it is we're building and when we will be finished with it," said SGT Mark Dorminey of C Company, 307th Engineer Battalion, 82nd Airborne Division.

The project is an outdoor amphitheater built in South Camp on the Sinai Peninsula where soldiers of Task Force 1-508 stay when they aren't occupying observation posts or check points. Dorminey and four other men from C Company are engineers who volunteered to be part of the U.S. battalion currently stationed in the Sinai as members of the Multinational Force and Observers (MFO).

The amphitheater is used as a movie theater and stage for the bands and entertainment tours that visit South Camp. The audience sits in the semicircular tiers and enjoys entertainment in the atmosphere of the Red Sea just beyond the stage. The rough cutting of the tiers and stage area was done with explosives and a bulldozer, and all fine cutting was done by hand. According to Dorminey, "This is basically a pick and shovel job; we aren't allowed the luxury of earthmoving equipment."

In its early stages of construction, the project was halted because it was feared that the added weight to the shelf of land could cause that area to drop off into the sea, explained 1LT Craig LaBelle, a platoon leader from the 307th Engineers at Fort Bragg, NC. "SP4 Rowsey has some land surveying experience. Based on his survey results and some tests of the earth's firmness in the area, we determined that the theater even with a capacity crowd would not be hazardous," he said.

The engineers were assisted by a squad of infantrymen from one of the line companies that were on a break from their sector duties. "We can feel a sense of accomplishment from our work here," said one soldier from A Company. "This isn't like building a fighting position that we work hard on and then have to tear down. This is something that will be here for a long time. We can take pride in having contributed to it," he said. **(SGT Ken Hudson, 82nd Airborne)**

Fiberglass Cover Protects Against Aerial Attack

The fiberglass overhead cover developed by CERL will protect Army fighting positions against aerial explosive rounds. Weapons systems like the TOW antitank weapon are particularly vulnerable because they are prime targets for enemy fire.

Four 32-pound corrugated fiberglass sections (59 inches by 40 inches) are fastened together to form a complete arch. This forms the necessary support for a protective layer of soil or sandbags to shield personnel from shrapnel. The soil-covered arch can be camouflaged for further protection.

CERL researchers designed the arch so that sections can be closely stacked and easily transported. Future plans include evaluating other materials and designs that will reduce the structure's weight and size, yet increase its load-bearing capacity.

Fiberglass overhead covers provide foundations for protective layers of soil or sandbags (CERL photo).

Letter To The Editor

The article in News and Notes, *Engineers Help Feed Hungry Children,* (Fall, 1985) contains erroneous information in the last paragraph. ("This is the first time Malian and American soldiers have worked together.")

Prior to 1964, an airborne team (US) trained a Malian parachute company. From June 1964 to June 1965, a 20-man team (MTT Y69) trained the Malian engineer company in vertical and horizontal construction, ordnance and engineer equipment maintenance, surveying, and rock crusher operations. The 20-man team was replaced by a 5-man team in June 1965.

The mobile training teams were assembled at Fort Bragg, equipped at Fort Belvoir, and the liaison officer at that time was MAJ Fred Lenoach (CPO Training Officer).

An additional interesting fact is that MTT Y69 also trained the Malian engineers on a light tactical raft on the Niger River at Bamako.

Twenty years ago the road from Abidjan, Ivory Coast, was partially paved (150 miles); and heavy truck traffic was hauling all the import-export materials that could not be hauled by rail from Dakar, Senegal, to Bamako.

Walter S. Lockard, Chief, 52D10, Department of Military Logistics, USAES.

Past in Review

Eleventh Engineers in World War I

by Dr. William C. Baldwin, Historical Division, OCE

Members of Company D, 11th Engineers (Railway) work near the Meuse River. They were among the first Americans to fight in France during World War I (U.S. Army photo).

On April 6, 1917, the United States declared war on Germany and entered World War I. Britain and France, America's new allies, requested immediate engineering assistance in building, maintaining, and operating railroads in France. The War Department responded by quickly organizing nine new regiments of railway engineers.

Two months before the outbreak of war, the Chief of Engineers, BG Willliam M. Black, had begun forming a reserve engineer regiment in New York City. Using the slogan, *First to France—Join the Engineers*, the First Regiment, Reserve Engineers, opened its recruiting office in early May and soon filled its ranks. To avoid confusion with the First Engineers of the regular Army, the War Department redesignated the new unit the 11th Engineers in July 1917 and made it the first of the new railway regiments. The present 11th Engineer Batallion (CBT)(HVY) traces its lineage to this unit.

The 11th Engineers (Railway) trained at Fort Totten, NY, during June and set sail for Europe on July 14. Three American engineer regiments, including the 11th, were attached to the British army in France. On September 5, 1917, a German artillery shell wounded two soldiers of the 11th Engineers. These engineers were the first battle casualties of the American Expeditionary Force (AEF) in France.

In mid-November, the regiment joined in the British preparations for the Cambrai offensive. Amid great secrecy, the 11th Engineers helped move and unload the primitive tanks that the British had massed for the offensive. The attack made some gains initially, but like most offensives on the Western Front, soon bogged down. The 11th Engineers supported the British advance by building and repairing rail lines.

On November 30, two and a half companies of the 11th, along with some Canadian engineers, began constructing a rail yard just behind the British front lines. Sporadic German artillery fire interrupted their work. German shelling was routine, but this fire suddenly became a barrage of gas and artillery shells.

The officers ordered a withdrawal, but the engineers were already caught up in a surprise German counterattack. Some hid in dugouts to escape the shelling and found themselves trapped behind the German advance. Others used their picks and shovels to fight the advancing infantry. Most of the American engineers got back to their camp where the rest of the regiment had taken up defensive positions to help the British stop the counterattack. Six of the 11th Engineers were killed, eleven were wounded, and thirteen were taken prisoner.

GEN John J. Pershing, commander of the AEF, wrote that Cambrai deserved special attention because "it was here that American troops (11th Engineers) first participated in active fighting." Engineers of the 11th received three Distinguished Service Crosses and three British decorations. The regiment was credited with campaign participation in the Battle of Cambrai, the first campaign credit given to American units in World War I. A quarter of a million U.S. Army engineers eventually served in World War I, but the men of the 11th Engineers (Railway) were among the first American soldiers to fight in France.

Suggestions for further reading:

V.T. Boughton, *History of the Eleventh Engineers*, United States Army.

William Barclay Parsons, *The American Engineers in France.*

CLEAR THE WAY

by MG Richard S. Kem, Commandant, U.S. Army Engineer School

Rapid Modernization:

The Army Must Answer the Demands of New Technolog

All of us have been exposed to the many initiatives which our Army continues to develop in creating a force which is the best equipped and the best trained. The primary focus of the rapid modernization is to ensure that our Army is successful in either peace or war.

Our mission is among the most varied and important of any branch. To guarantee that our efforts will be fully and successfully coordinated throughout the complex Army organization, a special concept has been established. To fulfill that concept, each branch school commandant has been designated as the proponent for a number of functions within his branch since the reorganization of the Army in the early 1970s.

As commandant of the U.S. Army Engineer School, I am the proponent of the Engineer Branch. As branch proponent, I am responsible for the development of concepts, doctrine, tactics, techniques, procedures, organizational designs, material requirements, training programs, training support, personnel requirements, education requirements, and other engineer matters as they pertain to the total Army.

In addition to the branch proponency, I am the personnel specialty proponent for engineers. Specialty proponency from the Army staff agencies was transferred to the field by the Army Chief of Staff in 1981. It focuses on coordinating personnel policy throughout the Army. The entire life-cycle issues are followed from structure and acquisition to separation. My role is to articulate our professional needs which consist of a wide spectrum of concerns. Our goal is to have a competent and professional engineer force and provide it with the greatest opportunities for development, education, and advancement.

Although the other specialty proponency issues are important, let me concentrate on personnel professional development. This vital issue affects all of us throughout our careers. Requirements are continuously developed throughout our careers to ensure that the necessary skills are identified and will be attained when needed. Training and education requirements are analyzed with regard to assignment priorities; patterns of professional development are established for our career fields (officer, warrant officer, and enlisted); and qualification standards are reviewed and established for each of our specialties. Likewise, functional area and special skill requirements are identified.

Currently, we are working on a number of significant engineer professional development issues. The Total Warrant Officer Study (TWOS), the Enlisted Personnel Management System (EPMS) Review, and the Officer Personnel Management System (OPMS) Review are examples of ongoing personnel policy actions which will affect us all.

In addition, the Army must answer the demands of new technology. This occurs at a time of extensive force modernization. We must maintain an active role in obtaining the best qualified individuals and sustaining our professional force through training and education. Engineers have always excelled in technical and decision-making skills. We must ensure that we continue to provide the opportunities for future developments.

I hasten to add that leadership skills are cultivated and exercised as an integral portion of professional development. Historically, the Corps has provided the Army with capable leaders who have met the challenge in both peace and war. Certainly we must never forget the important role we play in the Army and the nation as we continue to develop officers, NCOs, and civilians who can meet the challenge.

As you know, this is the Army's year of leadership. I believe that, as never before, the engineers have major roles in leadership both within and outside the Corps. Ours is a branch of unique opportunities, and we are working hard to maintain our lead by pursuing proponency issues. Essayons!

by CSM Charles T. Tucker, U.S. Army Engineer Center & School

Professionalism:

An NCO's Viewpoint

Professionalism. We always hear the term, but what does it mean really?

Professionalism means unique. It means special talent. It means pride in yourself, your work, and your troops, and dedication to the same.

Professionalism means you are better at your job than anyone else, but you share your knowledge. It means you are an expert, an artist, and a specialist. It means you are never satisfied with the status quo. You have pride in what you do, but try to do it better. You have pride in your troops, but try to make them better. You have pride in your unit, but strive to improve it.

A professional is that drill sergeant you despised at boot camp, yet you came to respect and admire. In fact, you tried to outdo him. Nothing he could do or say could break you. No challenge he gave could stop you. Before you knew it, he made you a soldier.

Professionalism means duty before self. It means putting your soldiers before yourself. It means putting your leaders before yourself. It means putting your unit before yourself. It means refusing to enter the chow line until every one of your soldiers has been served first. It means you are willing to die for those troops and, perhaps, they are willing to die for you. It's that platoon sergeant at Vietnam who went back through the jungle to look for you when you were separated from your unit. It's that private manning the perimeter who dies protecting his unit.

A professional is the squad leader who kept his composure when your platoon was ambushed. He feared the battlefield, but overcame that fear. He did not leave soldiers to die, but risked himself to save them. He knew how to fight, but knew when to stop. When hope was gone, he hoped. When all was lost, he found answers.

Professionalism means integrity and loyalty—to yourself, to your leaders, and to your troops. It means stepping forward when your troops fail, but stepping aside when they shine. It means adopting a code of ethics and sticking by it when others don't.

A professional knows when to push and knows when to comfort. He knows when to act and knows when to watch. He knows when to lead and knows when to follow. He knows when to work and knows when to joke. He enjoys his work and so do his troops. His enthusiasm is contagious. He sparks drive, intensity, and determination. He is renowned, yet removed.

A professional is that first sergeant who worked nights and weekends to finish the paperwork so you could get your award. But he's the same first sergeant who denied you a weekend pass when you failed a barracks inspection. He's the platoon sergeant who attended night school to further his education and, at the same time, helped you to study for your high school diploma. But he's the same platoon sergeant who put you on 30 days extra duty when you missed a formation.

A professional accepts criticism. He admits his faults, yet strives to erase them—and does. He offers criticism, but offers it soundly, tactfully, and intelligently. He shows you your faults, but compliments your strengths. He tells you when you're wrong, but takes the time to tell you when you're right.

A professional sets goals—challenging goals. He's that platoon sergeant who challenged you to your limit; yet when you reached it, you found you could do better. He told you to build that bridge in 30 minutes, yet you did it in 20 minutes (under MOPP IV conditions).

A professional accepts himself, knows his troops, and studies his enemy. He's the engineer who continues forward when everyone else stalls, yet he clears the way and assures their progress during the attack. He is confident and optimistic. He will outdo his troops and strive to better his leaders. He's that battalion command sergeant major everyone calls "Pops," yet he runs circles around you on the PT track.

Professionalism. What is it?

It's duty, honor, country—all of the time. Professionalism is an NCO—a soldier, an engineer. Work at it.

School News

Directorate of Training and Doctrine (DOTD)

Plumbing Course Revised:

The 51K10 Plumbing Specialist Course has been revised to enhance performance-oriented training and provide a greater challenge to the student.

Each soldier is now required to construct a complete plumbing system from a given construction plan. This is done in four phases using the same work station for each phase of construction. Previously, the phases were performed in different work areas. Upon completion of the system, the soldier will understand how the quality of work done on each phase affects the completed system.

The course is taught in the new Brown Hall vertical skills building at Fort Leonard Wood, MO.

FC 5-104-1, Airfield Damage Repair:

Airfield Damage Repair (Pavement Repair), a joint Army-Air Force publication, was distributed in October 1985. The Field Circular (FC 5-104-1) is a user's manual for the field. It gives U.S. Air Force techniques for emergency repair and U.S. Army techniques for work that goes beyond emergency repair.

The point of contact for more information is chief of Roads and Airfields Branch, Department of Military Engineering, AV 354-2527.

Defense Mapping School (DMS)

APPS IV Training Package:

The Defense Mapping School has converted Room 203A, Wheeler Hall, into a high-tech computer center by installing two APPS IVs (Analytical Photogrammetric Positioning System), a high-resolution graphic display system, a powerful VAX 11/750 minicomputer, and comprehensive software.

The Department of Topographic Sciences will be using the APPS IV to train Rapid Strike Planning System (RSPS) operators in support of the Tomahawk cruise missile program. This APPS IV training package allows DMS instructors and students to work with modern high-technology systems.

The first two-week APPS IV operators course was completed by students in August. Upon graduation from this course, students will continue their RSPS training at other locations and then serve a tour at one of the theater mission planning centers which control the Tomahawk cruise missiles.

Department of Military Engineering (DME)

Scatterable Minefield Estimations:

Several requests have come to the Engineer School from field units regarding scatterable minefield requirement estimations. FM 5-102, *Countermobility*, Appendix D, gives a quick method of determining the number of mines/rounds for ADAM, RAAMS, GEMSS, and M56 systems.

A simplified (step-by-step) method for determining scatterable minefield requirements estimations is given in the *Engineer Officer's Handbook for Scatterable Mine Systems*. This handbook can be obtained by sending a written request to: Department of Military Engineering, ATTN: ATZA-TE-FE, Fort Belvoir, VA 22060-5331. POC is CPT Ronald Young, (703) 664-3411, AV 354.

Math Pretest for BNCOC:

Before attending the MOS 12B (combat engineer) BNCOC, all soldiers must pass a two-part math pretest. Since it became mandatory in January, the pretest and basic skills education program (BSEP-II) have reduced the number of academic failures in the course.

The pretest consists of a common portion of 35 questions and a 12B portion of 40 questions that evaluate the soldier's ability in 10 math skills essential to the course. If a soldier misses two of four questions in a given math skill, he will have to use the BSEP-II module for that skill.

A soldier may fail up to three blocks in the common portion and one block in the 12B portion without retaking the entire exam. He must retake the blocks he missed. All soldiers must pass the math pretest before attending BNCOC.

The math pretest is available for review by the chain of command (E-7 and above) at local education centers.

Department of Combined Arms (DCA)

Topographic Instructor:

To fully integrate topographic operations with department instruction, a topographic instructor/writer has been assigned to the Department of Combined Arms.

Presently teaching map availability and terrain analysis to EOAC students, the instructor will be evaluating existing programs of instruction (POI) to see where topographic operations can be included. To this end, input from the field is desired and may be sent to: Commander, U.S. Army Engineer School, ATTN: ATZA-TC-T (CPT David Jones), Fort Belvoir, VA 22060-5341. CPT Jones can be reached at (703) 664-2986, AV 354.

Department of Combined Arms (continued)

Doctrinal Literature Update:

DCA has produced and distributed two publications during the last quarter to update engineer doctrine. Training Circular (TC) 90-13-1, *Deliberate River Crossing Planning,* is designed as a guide for engineer planners in division level deliberate river-crossing operations.

Field Circular (FC) 5-100, *The Brigade/Task Force Engineer,* establishes doctrine on the employment of the brigade engineer section and the task force engineer. It lays down the functions and responsibilities of the brigade engineer and the task force engineer and contains sufficient detail on how they operate to guide development of standing operating procedures.

Reserve Component Advisory Staff (RCS)

Reserve Component Advisors:

The Reserve Components Advisory Office at the U.S. Army Engineer School is staffed with an ARNG advisor, LTC John B. Cunningham Jr., and a USAR advisor, LTC James W. Shoff II. They advise the Commandant and his staff on Reserve Component (RC) matters and act as POC for RC members. The phone numbers for their office are: 1-800-336-3095 (extensions 4166/4434/5921), commercial (703) 664-4166, AV 354.

EOAC-RC:

The Engineer Officer Advanced Course for Reserve Components (EOAC-RC) consists of seven two-week modules. Officers attending the course should report on Sunday for classes beginning on Monday. Uniform for the classes is BDUs. Quotas for EOAC-RC must be obtained from ARPERCEN, Engineer Branch, for USAR officers and through channels to National Guard Bureau for ARNG officers. The Reserve Component advisors at the Engineer School have no control over quotas, nor do they issue them.

ADT Phases:

The 2071st USAR School, Owings Mills, MD, will conduct the ADT Phases of EOAC (Phases II, IV, VI, and IA) at Fort Belvoir between June 1 and June 13, 1986.

EOAC-RC Class Schedule FY 86
(14 Weeks/2-Week Modules)

Class	Module	Report Date	Availability Date
1-86		27 OCT 85	15 FEB 86
	1	27 OCT 85	9 NOV 85
	2	11 NOV 85	23 NOV 85
	3	24 NOV 85	7 DEC 85
	4	8 DEC 85	21 DEC 85
	5	5 JAN 86	18 JAN 86
	6	20 JAN 86	1 FEB 86
	7	2 FEB 86	15 FEB 86
2-86		8 DEC 85	29 MAR 86
	1	8 DEC 85	21 DEC 85
	2	5 JAN 86	18 JAN 86
	3	20 JAN 86	1 FEB 86
	4	2 FEB 86	15 FEB 86
	5	17 FEB 86	1 MAR 86
	6	2 MAR 86	15 MAR 86
	7	16 MAR 86	29 MAR 86
3-86		2 FEB 86	10 MAY 86
	1	2 FEB 86	15 FEB 86
	2	17 FEB 86	1 MAR 86
	3	2 MAR 86	15 MAR 86
	4	16 MAR 86	29 MAR 86
	5	30 MAR 86	12 APR 86
	6	13 APR 86	26 APR 86
	7	27 APR 86	10 MAY 86
4-86		16 MAR 86	21 JUN 86
	1	16 MAR 86	29 MAR 86
	2	30 MAR 86	12 APR 86
	3	13 APR 86	26 APR 86
	4	27 APR 86	10 MAY 86
	5	11 MAY 86	24 MAY 86
	6	26 MAY 86	7 JUN 86
	7	8 JUN 86	21 JUN 86
5-86/6-86		27 APR 86	2 AUG 86
	1	27 APR 86	10 MAY 86
	2	11 MAY 86	24 MAY 86
	3	26 MAY 86	7 JUN 86
	4	8 JUN 86	21 JUN 86
	5	22 JUN 86	4 JUL 86
	6	6 JUL 86	19 JUL 86
	7	20 JUL 86	2 AUG 86
7-86		8 JUN 86	13 SEP 86
	1	8 JUN 86	21 JUN 86
	2	22 JUN 86	4 JUL 86
	3	6 JUL 86	19 JUL 86
	4	20 JUL 86	2 AUG 86
	5	3 AUG 86	16 AUG 86
	6	17 AUG 86	30 AUG 86
	7	1 SEP 86	13 SEP 86

EOAC-RC Class Schedule FY 86
(14 Weeks/2-Week Modules)
(continued)

Class	Module	Report Date	Availability Date
8-86		20 JUL 86	25 OCT 86
	1	20 JUL 86	2 AUG 86
	2	3 AUG 86	16 AUG 86
	3	17 AUG 86	30 AUG 86
	4	1 SEP 86	13 SEP 86
	5	14 SEP 86	27 SEP 86
	6	28 SEP 86	11 OCT 86
	7	13 OCT 86	25 OCT 86
9-86		1 SEP 86	6 DEC 86
	1	1 SEP 86	13 SEP 86
	2	14 SEP 86	27 SEP 86
	3	28 SEP 86	11 OCT 86
	4	13 OCT 86	25 OCT 86
	5	26 OCT 86	8 NOV 86
	6	9 NOV 86	22 NOV 86
	7	23 NOV 86	6 NOV 86

EOAC Class Schedule FY 86
(20 Weeks)

Class	Report Date	Availability Date
1-86	24 OCT 85	1 APR 86
2-86	5 DEC 85	13 MAY 86
3-86	30 JAN 86	24 JUN 86
4-86	13 MAR 86	5 AUG 86
5-86	24 APR 86	16 SEP 86
6-86	24 APR 86	16 SEP 86
7-86	5 JUN 86	28 OCT 86
8-86	17 JUL 86	9 DEC 86
9-86	28 AUG 86	3 FEB 87

EOBC/EOBC-RC Class Schedule FY 86

Class	Report Date	Graduation Date
1-86	20 OCT 85	24 FEB 86
2-86	5 JAN 86	6 MAY 86
1-86 (RC)	5 JAN 86	5 MAR 86
3-86	9 FEB 86	10 JUN 86
4-86	16 MAR 86	15 JUL 86
5-86	27 MAY 86	26 SEP 86
2-86 (RC)	27 MAY 86	23 JUL 86
6-86	13 JUL 86	12 NOV 86
7-86	12 AUG 86	11 DEC 86
8-86	28 SEP 86	13 FEB 87

Sapper Leader Course

A New Rope to Climb

by CPT Michael J. Grove

The UH-1H banks hard to the right and accelerates down the final approach along the shoreline. As the butterflies begin to surface, the soldier receives the signal to unhook the safety belt and prepare to execute. The helicopter lurches as the speed decreases.

The soldier pushes the rucksack out and follows it to the water's surface. After recovering from the impact of the water, the lightfighter pulls his rucksack to the shore and prepares to move out on his combat mission. A scene from ranger school? No. It is the Sapper Leader Course for the members of the newly formed or newly forming light engineer battalions.

The helocasting operation just described is one of the many exciting and demanding blocks of training. The Sapper Leader Course was conceived to prepare members of the new light engineer battalions to better support their new light infantry divisions. The course is divided into four phases: the confidence phase, the engineering phase, the battle drill phase, and the situational training exercise phase.

Symbolic of the course was the 20-foot rope that hung in the barracks area. This obstacle was negotiated before breakfast, lunch, and dinner. It represented the difficulty of the course and became a symbol of the strength we would gain and the team building we would undergo. At the beginning of the course, little more than half of the students could negotiate the rope all the way to the top. Students failed for several reasons: lack of upper-body strength, improper technique, or fear of heights. As the course progressed, our class went farther and farther up the rope.

During the confidence phase, physical training was stressed as well as other confidence building skills critical to light forces. During this phase the students learned and practiced rappelling, helocasting, helicopter rappelling, hand-to-hand combat, and RB-15 movement. The difficulty of the course was increased by the severe heat and humidity of July at Fort Leonard Wood, MO, the home of the Sapper Leader Course.

The confidence phase also provided training on both hand-to-hand and bayonet fighting. The way the cadre handled these blocks of instruction indicated the professionalism and innovation that made the course such a worthwhile experience. Instead of starting from the basics, they took off from our levels attained at the Rites of Passage Course conducted at Fort Ord, CA. The Sapper Leader Course cadre taught us kicks, punches, street fighting and other tricks picked up from collective experience in ranger battalions, special forces, and other units. The way they treated us and

Expedient poncho rafting trains soldiers f[or] engineer missions in hostile environments.[...] the light infantry, engineers will take to w[ar] what they can carry on their backs (photo [by] Steve Gaynor).

The 28-day Sapper Leader Course stresses physical stamina, technical expertise, and troop leading skills under simulated combat conditions (photo by Steve Gaynor).

gave us more than the basics made us yell louder, throw harder, and feel more special—another foot up the rope.

Instruction on rappelling was both a great confidence builder and a valuable movement tool for light forces. Several classes were given on buddy rappelling, litter rappelling, and helicopter rappelling. It was the first time that many students had used these advanced techniques. One NCO insisted he could not do the buddy rappel, but the cadre refused to let him fail. With the entire class at the bottom of the cliff screaming encouragement, the instructors skillfully talked the student down the rope and then made him do it on his own to standard. He was obviously still terrified, but we as a unit were stronger because he had conquered his fears and learned an important technique in casualty evacuation.

One of the most exciting days was insertion training at the Lake of the Ozarks. In the morning the students participated in several helicopter rappels, and in the afternoon each man performed at least four helocasts. For individuals who were not strong swimmers and afraid of heights, this was a double horror show. These soldiers getting ready to board the helicopters were portraits of fear; but after the first jump into the water, the war stories were flying hot and heavy and people were running back from the beach to jump again. The day ended with RB-15 training, and the class was ready for the engineering phase—another foot up the rope.

The engineering phase provided demolitions training that was extensive and extremely valuable. The instructors from the Sapper Leader Course had attended the special forces demolitions course and brought back much information. The two most worthwhile concepts were the cherry knot and the dual detonating assembly. The advantages of these techniques are that they significantly reduce the time it takes to set up a complete firing system and they enable a soldier to set up a firing system safely and quickly in complete darkness.

We used these techniques on a night mission where the patrol moved down a stream using poncho rafts. When the demolitions team reached the target, a bridge, all they had to do was place the charges, attach them to a ring main by pulling the running end of the cherry knot, and attach the dual detonating assembly with a square knot. Safe, simple, and effective. Considering the importance of night operations to light forces, this knowledge is invaluable.

We also learned about several special-purpose charges: platter, satchel, soap dish, and dust initiator charges. We got hands-on experience with each.

Mountaineering was also given special attention. Expert instructors gave extensive rigging and climbing classes that will be extremely beneficial to the light engineer. Some of the NCOs who had problems with rappelling did extremely well climbing, and the soldier that had difficulty with the buddy rappel went right up the mountain. We also discovered that some mountaineering equipment can be adapted to other techniques that will help us and the division become more mobile.

Air assault operations were covered. We did extensive work with preparing and hooking up sling loads, aerial resupply, and helicopter insertions. Team building was becoming more evident as the two air assault corporals in the class shared their skills. The fact that the corporals volunteered their

Light engineers can respond rapidly to a wide variety of threats anywhere in the world. The light infantry is 100 percent air-transportable, is equipped to defeat tanks, and can sustain itself in rough terrain (photo by Steve Gaynor).

expertise was not earth-shaking, but the fact that everyone else was eager to listen showed the unifying effect that the course was having. The actual hooking of a sling load was a unique and valuable experience that provided still more war stories. Imagine what the pilot of the helicopter thought when one of the students wanted to cut the sling load and gave the pilot the patrolling hand and arm signal for danger area ahead.

We received extensive instruction on patrolling techniques during the course and incorporated them into all facets of training. Troop leading procedures were stressed as each hands-on portion of the training was conducted on a mission basis. The patrolling classes were given in a field setting by former members of the ranger battalions with emphasis on walk-throughs and practical exercises. Besides the patrolling techniques, the course provided an excellent preparation for light force operations because we moved almost always on foot. With this phase behind us, we were prepared for the next foot of the rope, the battle drill phase.

During the battle drill phase, the instructors concentrated on training to standards. We performed each of 16 tasks to a set of drill standards; if we didn't perform a task properly, we would do it again. The drills ranged from neutralizing a bunker to crossing a danger area. This phase was physically challenging as we found out on the first night when we got 40 minutes of sleep in the patrol base before stand to.

The drills accomplished several things. First, they established a standard way to perform 16 combat-essential tasks so the unit increases its combat power and its ability to work comfortably with different maneuver units. Another benefit of the drills was that they helped in team building, as each member of the patrol had to count on every other man to perform his job. You could feel the bonds of loyalty and respect being formed.

An example of this is how the soldiers came together for the one-rope bridge drill. Throughout the course, the strong swimmers had been looking out for the weak swimmers; this bond gave the weak swimmers the confidence to cross the river. Even one soldier rescued by the far shore lifeguard on an earlier operation was

The Sapper Leader Course teaches the use of explosives, equipment, and other materials available to engineers operating on foot (photo by Steve Gaynor).

all backgrounds that should not be missed. The Army gave the light engineers a rope to climb; and the Sapper Leader Course gave them the strength, technical knowledge, and desire to get to the top. Sappers . . . lead the way!

CPT Michael J. Grove is the commander of C Company, 13th Engineer Battalion at Fort Ord, CA. He was the student OIC of the first certified class of the Sapper Leader Course at Fort Leonard Wood, MO. CPT Grove is a graduate of the U.S. Army airborne and ranger courses and has a degree in engineering from the U.S. Military Academy.

Units wishing to attend the Sapper Leader Course must submit requests through their appropriate MACOM to TRADOC for approval. For more information, the POC at Fort Leonard Wood is CPT Matthew Bogart, AV 581-3195. At Fort Belvoir, call CPT David Depastina or Donita McGeary, AV 354-2684.

Sapper

by Dr. Charles Hendricks
Historical Division, OCE

The illustration is from *A Manual of Seigecraft and Fortification* by Sebastien LePrestre de Vauban, Copyright 1968, The University of Michigan Press, Ann Arbor.

A sapper, according to *The Oxford English Dictionary*, is "a soldier employed in working at saps, the building and repairing of fortifications, the execution of field-works, and the like." The same dictionary states that the word *sap* may mean "the process of undermining a wall or defensive work," "the process of constructing covered trenches in order to approach a besieged place without danger from the enemy's fire," or "a covered trench made for the purpose of approaching a besieged place under the fire of the garrison."

The English word *sap* was used in this military sense as early as 1591 by an English ambassador to the French court who was reporting on the siege of Rouen during the French wars of religion. The ambassador spelled the word *zappe* and *sappe* after the Italian and French words from which it derived. Although the Italian word *zappa* had long been used to denote a garden hoe, it was first applied to a military trench early in the sixteenth century.

The art of military engineering changed rapidly after gunpowder was introduced into European warfare in the fifteenth and sixteenth centuries. Before that time, armies could attack Europe's forts and fortified cities either by storming the walls or by denying provisions to the defenders through a lengthy siege.

Sixteenth-century commanders discovered that they could have trenches or tunnels dug to the walls of a fort and there emplace large explosive charges that would destroy those walls. As European manufacturers developed heavy bronze and cast-iron artillery pieces, commanders gradually began using trenches to bring their big guns within range of the besieged fort without exposing them to direct fire from the emplaced batteries of the fort. The trenches used for mining or advancing artillery were called *saps*, and the men who dug them became known as *sappers*. The men who placed the explosive mines under the walls of fortifications were called miners.

The French army in 1679 created the first permanent company of miners in Europe, more than a century and a half after explosive mines had been introduced into the warfare of that continent. Although initially organized under engineer officers, the French army's companies of miners were subsequently placed under artillery command. In 1720 a squadron of sappers and miners led by a sergeant was incorporated into each of the 40 companies of the French Royal Artillery Regiment. The squadron of sappers and miners comprised 27 men in each 84-man company. The sappers were placed in a separate company in each of the five battalions of this regiment in 1729.

The French army removed the sapper companies from its artillery regiment in 1758 and made them separate companies. They were placed under the Corps of Engineers in May 1759, but returned to the Artillery Corps in 1760. In 1776 a company of sappers was again added to each battalion of the Royal Artillery Regiment. In short, while sapper organization varied considerably in the French army during the eighteenth century, the sappers were normally under artillery command, although they might be given engineer direction during actual siege operations.

In the eighteenth-century French army, engineer officers did not normally command troop units. The French engineer captain Philippe Maigret complained about this as early as 1725, arguing that "engineers are

Technological Enrichment Program

by
MAJ Richard J. Treharne

The Technological Enrichment Program (TEP) offers newly commissioned second lieutenants an opportunity to earn master's degrees in emerging technologies at prestigious colleges and universities. The TEP students are on active duty and draw full pay and allowances. The Army also pays for their tuition, fees, books, and supplies. After graduation, TEP officers are awarded a functional area and serve consecutive utilization tours. Most TEP officers can expect branching in the engineer, signal, or ordnance corps. Upon graduation, TEP officers have a three-for-one active duty service obligation (ADSO), not to exceed six years.

The TEP selection board meets each November and can select up to 30 participants. Seventeen second lieutenants entered graduate programs as TEP-sponsored students in FY 84; 30 in FY 85. For FY 86, the TEP selection board will consider applicants for graduate programs in the following fields:

- Artificial intelligence
- ADPS-engineering
- Astrodynamics
- Chemical engineering
- Composite materials
- Computer science
- Electrical engineering
- Electronic engineering
- Industrial engineering
- Instructional technology (computer-based instruction)
- Metallurgy
- Operations research systems analysis (ORSA)
- Physics
- Robotics (automated manufacturing)

Who Qualifies?

Participants may be:

- Senior ROTC cadets graduating during spring commencement.
- Senior lieutenants graduating in spring who were commissioned under the early commissioning program and can be brought to active duty.
- Officer candidates assigned to the 5th Student Battalion (OCS), Fort Benning, GA.

Applicants must have a bachelor's degree and at least a B grade point average. They must be commissioned on active duty before attending graduate school.

To Apply

Applicants should apply for TEP on DA Form 1618-R. The form must be forwarded through their professor of military science or commander of the 5th Student Battalion (OCS) to: Commander, MILPERCEN (DAPC-OPA-E), 200 Stovall Street, Alexandria, VA 22332-0400, with the following enclosures:

- A copy of their undergraduate and any graduate level transcripts.
- A narrative addressing their career intentions, desires, and qualifications for TEP participation.
- The names of colleges and universities where the applicant has applied or has been accepted for graduate school.

Applications are endorsed forward by the professor of military science or the 5th Student Battalion (OCS) commander. The endorsement must include the ROTC cadet's summer camp results (TRADOC Form 958) or the officer candidate's standing on the order of merit list and distinguished military graduate status.

The selection board will determine appropriate institutions and fields of study for all officers selected. Individuals who are chosen must gain admission to their designated graduate program in time to begin their studies in the FY of selection. The Army is only interested in sending students to premier institutions for the selected field of study. Applicants should not view TEP solely as a means to stay at their undergraduate institution or remain near friends and family.

After commissioning and spring commencement, TEP officers attend the Officer Basic Course, then graduate school. Following graduate school, they complete an initial four-year utilization tour, the Officer Advanced Course, and a second utilization tour. They are considered for doctoral programs following the second utilization tour and then serve consecutive utilization assignments for the duration of their careers. Most assignments are within the Army Materiel Command, the Corps of Engineers, and the Training and Doctrine Command.

TEP is governed by AR 621-1, *Training of Military Personnel at Civilian Institutions*. Additional information can be obtained by writing Commander, MILPERCEN (DAPC-OPA-E) or by calling (202) 325-8101, AV 221.

MAJ Richard J. Treharne currently serves as the civilian education officer in OPMD, MILPERCEN. He is a graduate of the FAOAC and the Command and Staff College. He has a bachelor's degree from Iowa State University in industrial administration and an MBA from Campbell University.

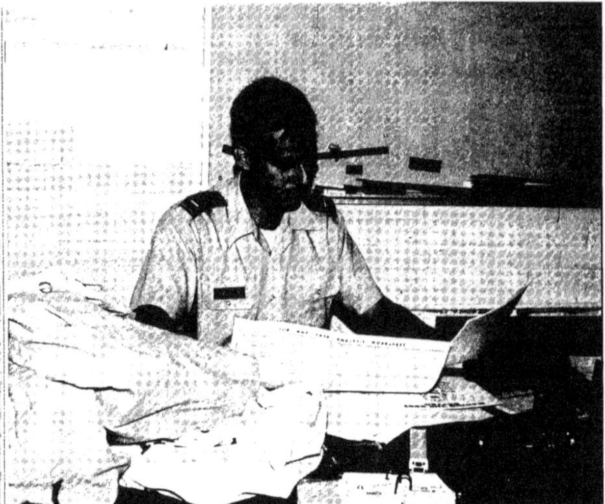

1LT Walter Andersen reviews thousands of surveys returned to the Directorate of Evaluation and Standardization. Comments from a soldier and his supervisor on how his performance is affected by engineer training are used to evaluate courses at the Engineer School (photo by L.J. Leto).

The Engineer Graduate Follow-Up Training Evaluation

or

How Many Surveys Can You Handle?

by Dave Abraham

Mail call at battalion headquarters, and the distribution clerk drops a bulky package on your desk. As the battalion S-3, you recognize yet another survey package from the Engineer School, probably the third your office has received in the past month. What do those guys at the Directorate of Evaluation and Standardization (DOES) at the Engineer School do anyway, just send out surveys?

Well, you're partly correct. The surveys piled on your desk do represent one of the most important elements of our job. In the course of a year, we send out thousands of surveys to hundreds of locations around the world. Our ability to effectively evaluate current engineer training depends primarily on receiving data from as many soldiers in the field as possible.

Each year, DOES, in conjunction with other departments of the U.S. Army Engineer School (USAES), identifies 20 to 30 engineer training courses for external evaluation. This evaluation process, known as the Graduate Follow-Up Program, is used to determine the adequacy of the training received by soldiers in all engineer training courses through analysis of the soldier's performance in the field.

The Graduate Follow-Up Program uses the surveys to answer three primary questions:

- Can the soldier perform the tasks for which he was trained?
- Does he actually perform the tasks in his current assignment?
- Are the tasks the soldier was trained for actually necessary to fulfill the mission of the unit?

The first two questions are asked of the engineer course graduate and his supervisor. The last question is answered only by his supervisor.

Occasionally we have the opportunity to administer the surveys directly to the troops (such as Engineer Orientation Team visits), but most often we must rely on mailing the surveys to the battalion operations officer. To improve our survey return rate, we ask that the S-3 distribute the surveys, have them completed, and return them, en masse.

The survey forms, when properly completed and returned to DOES, are fed into our computer. From the computer analysis and any additional soldier's or supervisor's written comments or complaints, we can determine whether the engineer training is meeting its objectives and the needs of the field.

Upon completion of each engineer training evaluation, we send a report to all units included in the initial survey. Each report includes the significant findings, conclusions, and recommendations arising from the study. This information is used by the Engineer School to modify programs of instruction and various manuals.

Included in the report you receive will be a task-by-task printout which is helpful in developing individual training plans for your soldiers. The information included in the report will document any areas that need either increased or decreased emphasis.

So, when that next packet of surveys makes it to your in-basket, you can help improve the quality of the Army's engineer training by getting those surveys to the right people. Consider it an investment in your unit's future.

Dave Abraham is an operations research analyst in the Directorate of Evaluation and Standardization, USAES. He has a bachelor's degree in mathematics from St. Vincent College and worked as a computer performance analyst with the Air Force.

romotion Boards

The selection was based upon a review of each soldier's official photo, personnel qualified record (PQR), DA Forms 2A and 2-1, *Personnel Qualification Record* (parts one and two), and the contents of the soldier's official military personnel microfiche and records containing enlisted efficiency reports (EER), MOS/SQT evaluation results, and recent hard-copy EERs.

Correspondence to the board president was also considered. However, letters to the board president which did not depict factual information were not given much consideration.

Those soldiers selected were the best qualified by virtue of their demonstrated performance, potential value to the Army, and ability to absorb and apply their military and civilian education in positions of greater responsibility throughout the Army. The promotion board placed special emphasis on leadership, physical fitness and appearance, professional development and reports, EERs, and official and commendatory files.

Leadership

Leadership rates the highest for E-7s who want to get to the top. Successfully performing in a TOE leadership position such as first sergeant or operations sergeant at the battalion level or as a platoon sergeant was an overriding factor in the promotion of E-7s, especially if the soldier had repetitive assignments in such positions.

Credit toward promotion was also given for outstanding performance as a drill sergeant, as well as duties with the Reserve Components, recruiting commands, and as an instructor at a service school, if the soldier did not remain in these positions for long periods of time. On the other hand, soldiers were penalized who, in the opinion of the board, were avoiding tough jobs by remaining in the same type of non-leadership duty for long periods of time. When the promotion board did not find the requisite number of qualified primary zone CMF 12 soldiers to recommend for promotion, additional highly qualified secondary zone soldiers were recommended. It was apparent that NCOs in CMFs 12 and 51 needed to seek leadership positions.

The competition for "fully qualified" and "best qualified" classifications was intense. Many of the soldiers labeled as "not best qualified" in the engineer CMFs had not successfully served as a platoon sergeant.

A number of soldiers (in all CMFs) who had been assigned outside of their CMF for more than one tour in such duties as recruiter or Reserve Component advisor had difficulty upon returning to the CMF. But, successful service in these types of assignments clearly complemented the overall professional development of the soldier and made a favorable impression on the board.

- There was not a sufficient number of CMF 12 soldiers to meet the primary zone promotion objective.
- There is a large pool of talented, hard-charging secondary SFCs in CMF 12.
- Many SQT scores were low or not available for CMF 51 and 12 soldiers.
- Many secondary zone soldiers had out-of-date photographs or none at all.
- CMF 51 is experiencing an inordinate number of soldiers with profiles and/or ANCOC incompletion.
- The commendatory portion of CMF 51 soldier files was somewhat lacking.
- EER duty titles and descriptions require improvement.
- Greater emphasis is needed to complete the record EERs.
- Civilian education and GT improvement were adequate.
- Many soldiers are not taking advantage of the opportunity to remove potentially derogatory information from their official military personnel records.

Figure 1. Board Conclusions.

Tips for Promotion
(Requirements for NCOs and officers are similar.)

NCO	Officer
• SQT preparation.	• Officer record brief.
• Photograph.	• Official military personnel file.
• Physical condition.	• Photograph.
• Military education.	• Letters to the board.
• Commendatory data.	• Height/weight standards.
• EER duty titles and job descriptions.	• Civilian education.
• Complete record EER.	• Military education.

Figure 2. Board Recommendations.

Physical Fitness and Appearance

Physical fitness in terms of APRT pass or fail on the EER did not appear to be a problem. In the cases where a failure was noted on the most recent EER, the soldier was severely penalized. There seemed to be an inordinate number of profiles in CMF 51. In most cases, Military Medical Review Board (MMRB) data was not available for review for those soldiers with a P3 profile. This is an Armywide problem because MMRB data is not reaching the promotion boards.

Weight problems were also evident, especially in CMF 51. Soldiers appearing to be overweight in their photographs and records were carefully examined to determine if they exceeded the Army standard. Only a small percentage of records had the completed pinch test data. In far too many instances, the board found either outdated pinch test data or soldiers who exceeded the body fat percentage.

Often, the soldier verified he was a certain height and weight. Yet, during the same time frame, the rater's certification on the EER indicated a different height and weight for the soldier. Soldiers who did not meet the height and weight requirements of AR 600-9, *The Army Weight Control Program*, were not selected for promotion.

In addition, the board put heavy emphasis on the soldier's having a current photograph and presenting a good military appearance. Records missing photographs had a negative impact as did photographs that were not recent or that contained deficiencies. The deficiencies included incorrect length of the blouse, sleeves, and trousers.

Photographs also revealed many soldiers with mustaches that did not meet the Army standard. All of these were viewed as an indication of apathy and a failure on the part of the soldier.

Although Army regulations only require a photograph every five years for a senior NCO, a more current photograph is an indication of professional pride and initiative. In most cases, soldiers in the primary zone had an up-to-date photograph. However, far too many soldiers in the secondary zone lacked an up-to-date photograph.

Professional Development and Reports

With the exception of CMF 51, most engineers have successfully completed ANCOC. Very few of those who had not attended had taken the opportunity to enroll in the nonresident course. Honor graduates of such courses were given an advantage. Likewise, soldiers who failed any military course of instruction were penalized.

The GT scores were not a significant discriminator. The board was favorably impressed with those soldiers who had taken the initiative to be retested to raise their GT scores above 106. The panel also noted that some soldiers have started their college education, yet have not taken the initiative to retest and raise their low GT scores.

Generally, any education beyond high school was viewed with favor except in those cases where soldiers had concentrated their efforts on civilian education and had failed to achieve the military education standard. The board was impressed by those soldiers who exceeded the military education course standard, but there was some evidence that a large number of soldiers in CMF 12, CMF 51, and MOS 52E ceased their college work once they were selected for E-7. Soldiers in CMF 81 appeared to be more active in acquiring both military and civilian education.

Most CMF 81 SQT scores were current and respectable. However, there

for soldiers in CMFs 81 and 12 were in excellent condition. This gave the board an in-depth view of the whole soldier. DA Forms 2A and 2-1 were in satisfactory condition. They provided helpful explanations for comments in files such as "not allowed to reenter the drill sergeant program" or indicated why a recruiter incentive award was revoked.

The results of any selection for promotion can be no more valid than the information upon which the board bases its judgment. For that reason, it is important for NCOs to ensure that their personnel records are current and accurate before they are reviewed by a selection board.

If soldiers prepare their records with the same attention to detail as if they were preparing themselves to appear in person, they would greatly enhance their chances for selection. If NCOs take care of their records, their records will take care of them.

In order to prepare for promotion, a copy of the *Engineer Enlisted Professional Development* informational pamphlet may be obtained by writing to the Engineer Proponency Office, U.S. Army Engineer School, ATTN: ATZA-EP, Stop 248, Fort Belvoir, VA 22060-5248.

SFC Carl V. McKinzey is assigned to the Engineer Proponency Office, USAES, Fort Belvoir, VA. He has served as an instructor in mine warfare and a drill sergeant at Fort Leonard Wood, MO, and was a platoon sergeant and squad leader in Germany. SFC McKinzey received his associate's degree from Columbia College, MO.

Engineer Problem

You command an engineer construction support company deployed to a theater of operations to support friendly forces fighting there. You need high-quality aggregate to help upgrade the main supply route (MSR) through the COMM-Z. Engineer reconnaissance teams found an abandoned basalt quarry located conveniently close to the MSR. The enemy used the quarry until friendly forces overran it last week. You arrive at the site to find a staggered pattern of blastholes as shown below. The holes are drilled vertically to a depth of 47 feet, the bottom 7 feet of which is subdrilling.

QUESTION 1: If you decide to use the existing hole pattern, what volume of aggregate should you obtain from a proper explosive excavation?

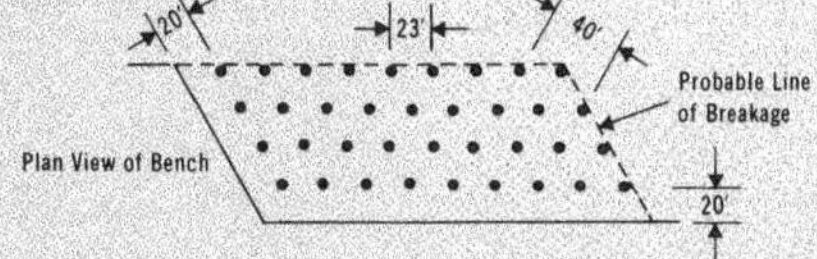

You have access to some local commercial explosives of the same type and quality as found in the U.S. Due to the lack of delay electric blasting caps (DEBC) and for the sake of safety (no caps in the blastholes), you elect to fire the shot in echelon using detonating (det) cord and millisecond (MS) delay cord connectors. The shot will be initiated with two instantaneous electric blasting caps (EBC) taped lengthwise to the det cord at the same point. The holes will be bottom primed (primer resting directly on the bottom of the hole).

QUESTION 2: How much detonating cord and how many MS connectors should you obtain to properly rig the shot?

REFERENCE:

TM 5-332, *Pits and Quarries;* Chapter 6.

Engineer Problem/Solution submitted by CPT Randy R. Rapp, EOAC Team Leader, Department of Military Engineering.

On July 30, 1864, a group of coal miners from Schuylkill County, Pennsylvania accomplished one of the "most extraordinary feats of military engineering up to that time—the explosion of a mine under the fort blocking the Union advance toward Petersburg and Richmond, Virginia."[1] However, only a few short hours later, the improper employment of engineer officers and working parties would later be determined to be one of the primary reasons for the failure of the Union attack at the Battle of Petersburg.[2]

The Battle of Petersburg provides the student of military engineering a unique contrast. On one hand, the success of the Union mine should have arguably provided the means for a stunning Union victory. After all, a 500-yard gap existed in the Confederate line after the explosion. On the other hand, the failure of the Union engineers in clearing friendly and enemy obstacles following the explosion contributed enormously to the Northern defeat.

This action, called the *Battle of the Crater*, has been examined in great depth by many military historians. The most common lessons gleaned from this battle center on leadership, the employment of surprise, and the use and effect of a mass-destruction weapon. However, this battle provides a striking historical example of a problem facing all engineer officers today. This problem revolves around the inherent conflict involved between the engineer officer's roles of both an advisor and a leader under the AirLand Battle doctrine.

This problem will be examined during both the successful and unsuccessful engineer phase of the Battle of Petersburg. In addition, a combination of solutions will be developed to specifically aid junior grade engineer officers in forging favorable relationships with their supported maneuver commanders.

The 48th Pennsylvania Regiment of Volunteers, commanded by LTC Henry Pleasants, had become weary of the siege at Petersburg and the resulting casualties incurred during the summer of 1864. On June 23, LTC Pleasants overheard two enlisted men say, "We could blow that damned fort out of existence if we could run a mine shaft under it."[3]

This idle discussion fell on fertile ears since Pleasants was a registered anthracite mining engineer from Pottsville, Pennsylvania. He had extensive experience in the art of tunneling and had been the senior assistant engineer in the construction of the Sand Patch Tunnel for the Pittsburgh and Connellsville Railroad.[4] In addition, the 48th Pennsylvania Volunteers consisted of 85 enlisted men and 14 officers who were professional miners before the start of the war.[5]

During the next two days, LTC Pleasants made tentative plans and drew a preliminary sketch of the enemy positions under which he proposed to construct the mine. On June 25, he briefed BG Robert Potter, the 2nd Division commander, on his plan to excavate a mine, fill it with gunpowder, and blow a hole in the Confederate lines.[6] Potter relayed the request to the IX Corps commander, LTG Burnside, who gave his immediate approval to commence work.[7]

At this time, MAJ James Duane, the acting chief engineer of the Army of the Potomac, was advising MG George Meade, commander of the Army of the Potomac, against the project. Duane stated that "such a length of mine had never been excavated in military operations and could not possibly succeed."[8] In particular, he felt that inadequate shoring materials were available; and the mine was too long to be properly ventilated.[9] Given these difficulties, Meade is said to have consented to, rather than approved the project, if, for no other reason than to keep the men occupied during the siege.[10]

The work on the mine progressed rapidly, and each succeeding difficulty was confronted and overcome by the ingenuity of the former coal miners. The completed mine measured 512 feet in length and required the removal of

The En

ADVIS

A Study of t

by CPT

over 18,000 cubic feet of material.[11] The engineering effort accomplished by LTC Pleasants and the difficulties he encountered while trying to obtain support from the Army of the Potomac are extremely interesting, but are not relevant to the development of the basic topic of this article.[12]

Early in the morning of July 30, 1864, the mine was exploded after having been charged with 8,000 pounds of gunpowder. The ensuing crater tore a huge gap in the Confederate line and killed over 270 men outright. The resulting hole measured 170 feet long, 60 feet wide, and 30 feet deep.[13] For a length of 500 yards, the Southern line

Officer

:ADER

: Petersburg

ɔrook

was unoccupied as a result of the massive explosion.

In order to proceed into the second phase of the battle, the initial orders issued by MG Meade concerning the engineer effort required subsequent to the explosion of the mine must be examined. Recognizing the need to maintain the momentum of the initial assault, Meade ordered Burnside to "prepare his parapets and abatis for the passage of the columns and have pioneers equipped for work in opening passages for artillery and for destroying enemy abatis."[14] The order went into great depth on the intended use of the engineers and also stated that each corps was to place its pioneers well forward in order to quickly neutralize enemy obstacles hindering the advance.

In addition, MAJ Duane was detailed to assign an engineer officer to each corps staff who would act as the corps engineer during the battle. The assignment of these engineer officers was left completely to the discretion of MAJ Duane.[15]

MG Meade's orders were quite specific in nature concerning the employment of engineers. This was due to the preponderance of obstacles which each side had constructed in front of their lines. Abatis, parapets, and trenches had been constructed in depth; and the Union obstacles had to be prepared for the passage of the IX Corps during the night before the attack.

Following the explosion of the mine, BG James Ledlie's 1st Division led the IX Corps attack over the high parapets and abatis of the Union works; neither of which had been removed by Burnside's engineers.[16] MG Burnside did not prepare his own obstacles for passage, in direct violation of orders, because he feared that it would give the Confederates advanced warning of the pending attack. In addition, Ledlie placed his engineer units and pioneers at the rear of his attacking brigades which seriously hampered their responsiveness.[17]

The corps engineer detailed to IX Corps was 1LT William Benyaurd who had no previous dealings with MG Burnside. During the course of the battle, he remained with Burnside and simply advised the general on the employment of the engineer units. Unfortunately, 1LT Benyaurd's advice was ignored by MG Burnside. When it was obvious that the lack of engineer effort forward was holding up the advance, Benyaurd failed to go to the front in order to assume command of the forward work parties. In fact, Benyaurd remained at the IX Corps headquarters for the majority of the battle and never did personally observe the action that day.[18]

History has documented the ensuing failure and slaughter of the Union forces who had their advance broken by the myriad of obstacles in their path. Even though the Union Army obtained the initial important element of surprise, their continuity of attack had been broken and led GEN Grant to state, "The effort was a stupendous failure."[19] This failure resulted from a set of complex variables, but only the issues relating to the utilization of LTC Pleasants and 1LT Benyaurd will be examined further.

During the successful phase of the battle, that part leading up to and including the explosion fashion of the mine, Pleasants acted in a fashion comparable to a division engineer in today's Army. He was the principal engineer advisor to BG Potter during the construction of the mine and also was the regimental commander of the unit tasked to build the mine. In this instance, the relationship between the engineer officer's role as an advisor and leader worked to perfection. Pleasants was able to keep Potter completely informed as to the capabilities and possible employment of his soldiers.

In addition, after completing his advisory role, Pleasants was allowed the freedom to remain constantly with his unit, adding his personal leadership, engineering knowledge, and supervision to the task of constructing the mine. This is perhaps the primary reason for the success of the project.

The second phase of the battle shows the results of an improper relationship between the maneuver commander and his supporting engineer officer. Even though the ranks and force structure differ, this phase is analogous to today's engineer company commander advising a maneuver brigade commander. During the assault, MG Burnside ignored the advice of his corps engineer officer and additionally would not let him personally supervise the employment of the corps' engineer assets.[20] These decisions proved disastrous for Burnside's IX Corps as has already been discussed.

An analysis of these decisions results in some definitive conclusions in support of the current brigade engineer concept in today's AirLand Battle doctrine. As the second phase of the Battle of Petersburg points out, maneuver commanders are historically inclined to require their engineer support officer to be physically nearby in order to provide instant advice on the employment of the engineer effort. This perceived requirement made it physically impossible for the engineer company commander to break away from his supported brigade in order to personally lead and supervise his platoons at critical points in a battle.[21]

A perfect example of this was exhibited when 1LT Benyaurd could not receive MG Burnside's permission to go forward to lead the engineer effort in attack, even though it was critical that he do so. Under current doctrine, an engineer major will become the brigade engineer and will assume the duties of the engineer staff officer responsible for advising the commander on engineer asset employment and utilization. This will free the engineer company commander to lead forward and thus personally influence the performance of his unit.[22]

The second lesson to be learned from this phase of the battle is that the brigade engineer has to be of the rank, persuasion, and experience to stand up to the maneuver commander when it relates to advice concerning the employment of engineer assets. It is very probable that 1LT Benyaurd's advice was ignored partially because MG Burnside was not in the habit of taking advice from a somewhat inexperienced lieutenant . . . even if the advice was sound.

This type of incident remains a common occurrence on major combined arms exercises where junior grade engineer officers, acting as brigade engineers, give somewhat timid advice to brigade commanders who are three to four ranks higher than themselves. The result of the inequity in rank and experience can degrade the overall effectiveness of the entire combined arms operation. This makes it imperative that today's brigade engineer be at least a senior captain or major who has successfully commanded an engineer company.

In addition, the position cannot be perceived as a place to "retire" captains and majors who are not performing well in engineer maneuver battalions. Obviously, the successful performance of a brigade engineer is critical to the accomplishment of the brigade's mission. The failure of Burnside's corps ultimately rests with himself, but conjecture lets one envision more favorable results if a strong willed, higher ranking, more experienced engineer officer had been available to act as the IX Corps engineer during the attack at the Battle of the Crater.

The lessons derived from this battle can also be applied to a lower level of the engineer support relationship. Specifically, the modern engineer lieutenant is not afforded the luxury of having a dedicated engineer staff officer within his supported maneuever battalion. Therefore, he must assume the roles of both advisor and leader. As in the case of 1LT Benyaurd, the improper balance of these somewhat conflicting duties can lead to a disaster for an entire operation.

A combination of the following solutions will aid the junior grade engineer

At this point, the engineer battalion ommander's role becomes critical. It his duty to come to terms with each ıpported maneuver commander, who ill hold the same rank, as to the use of e engineer officer in his task force. ıis interaction should set the tone for e use of the engineer lieutenant as an lvisor before a battle and as a leader ıring the actual employment phase. TC Pleasants used this strategy durg his mining operation and thus was ble, after an initial advisory role, to ssume total control over his mining roject.

The final resolution of the problem etween an engineer's role as an adisor and leader rests solely on the houlders of the engineer lieutenant. e must do everything within his ›wer to personally convince the aneuver battalion commander that e belongs at the head of his platoon, ading them from the front when the ituation dictates it. Only there can he irectly influence the performance of is men.

However, he must be careful in maintaining constant communication with his supported commander so that he can provide instant engineering advice when required. The communications link is vital since the engineer lieutenant might possibly lose sight of the overall operation once the strings holding him to the battalion commander's side become stretched.

Obviously the degree to which an engineer lieutenant is employed in his dual role as an advisor and leader rests ultimately with the supported commander. His orders must be carried out explicitly by the supporting engineer officer, regardless of his personal opinions and feelings. The maneuver commander will determine the final utilization of the engineer officer.[26]

In conclusion, the Battle of Petersburg provides a striking example of both the effective and ineffective utilization of engineer officers. The efficient use of engineers on today's modern battlefield has not changed drastically in over 100 years. The Army still needs engineer leaders for the front lines and engineer advisors for the headquarters.

The degree to which a maneuver commander accepts engineering advice and the degree to which he permits his engineer to lead will greatly influence the outcome of future conflicts under the AirLand Battle doctrine just as it influenced the Battle of the Crater in 1864.

CPT William J. Sandbrook is working on joint master's degrees in systems engineering and business administration at the University of Pennsylvania and the Wharton School. A U.S. Military Academy graduate, he has completed airborne and ranger training and the Engineer Officer Advanced Course. CPT Sandbrook was a cavalry platoon leader in the 2/2 Armored Cavalry Regiment and a company commander in the 82nd Engineer Battalion in Bamburg, West Germany.

"*The Engineer Officer: Advisor or Leader; A Study of the Battle of Petersburg*" won first place in the 1984 Military History Writing Awards for the Center of Military History in Washington, D.C.

Suggestions for further reading:

Bernard, George S. *The Battle of the Crater.* Petersburg, Virginia: Fenn and Owen, 1892.

Catton, Bruce. *A Stillness at Appomattox.* New York: Doubleday, 1954.

Crafts, W.A. *The Southern Rebellion.* Boston: Samuel Walker and Company, 1867.

Notes

1 Henry Pleasants Jr. and George H. Straley, *Inferno at Petersburg* (Philadelphia: Chilton Company, 1961), p. 1.

2 *Report of the Joint Committee on the Conduct of the War* (Washington, D.C. : The U.S. Government Printing Office, 1965), Vol. I, p. 215.

3 Pleasants, p. 48.

4 Pleasants, p. 11.

5 Pleasants, p. 54.

6 Pleasants, p. 51.

7 Alfred H. Guernsey and Henry M. Alden, *Harper's Pictorial History of the Civil War* (New York: The Fairfax Press, 1975), p. 697.

8 Pleasants, p. 66.

9 Larry George, "Battle of the Crater: A Combat Engineer Case Study," *Military Review*, February, 1984, p. 38.

10 Raymond O. Miller, "A Stupendous Failure," *Military Review*, July, 1960, p. 32.

11 James F. Bell, "A Lesson in Nuclear Effects," *Military Review*, July-August, 1961, p. 47.

12 Pleasants, pp. 59-120. (A detailed account of the engineering effort accomplished by LTC Pleasants can be obtained in this reference.)

13 Frank B. Case, "The Petersburg Crater and Nuclear Weapons," *Military Review*, November, 1960, p. 23.

14 *War of the Rebellion: A Compilation of the Official Records of the Union and Confederate Armies* (Washington, D.C. : The U.S. Government Printing Office, 1892), Vol. XL, p. 43.

15 Miller, p. 36.

16 Miller, pp. 37-38.

17 George, pp. 42-43.

18 George, p. 42.

19 Miller, p. 31.

20 George, p. 46.

21 The requirement imposed on the engineer officer to remain physically near the maneuver commander was experienced by me during all maneuver exercises involving the Second Armored Cavalry Regiment between 1980-1983 in West Germany.

22 William C. Burns and others, "Engineer Doctrine for the AirLand Battle," *Engineer*, Spring, 1984, pp. 12-13.

23 George, p. 46.

24 Field Manual 5-100, *Engineer Combat Operations* (Washington, D.C. : The U.S. Government Printing Office, 1979), pp. 2-9.

25 George, pp. 41-42.

26 Field Manual 100-5, *Operations* (Washington, D.C. : The U.S. Government Printing Office, 1982), pp. 7-3 and 7-4.

The Engineer Proponen Offic

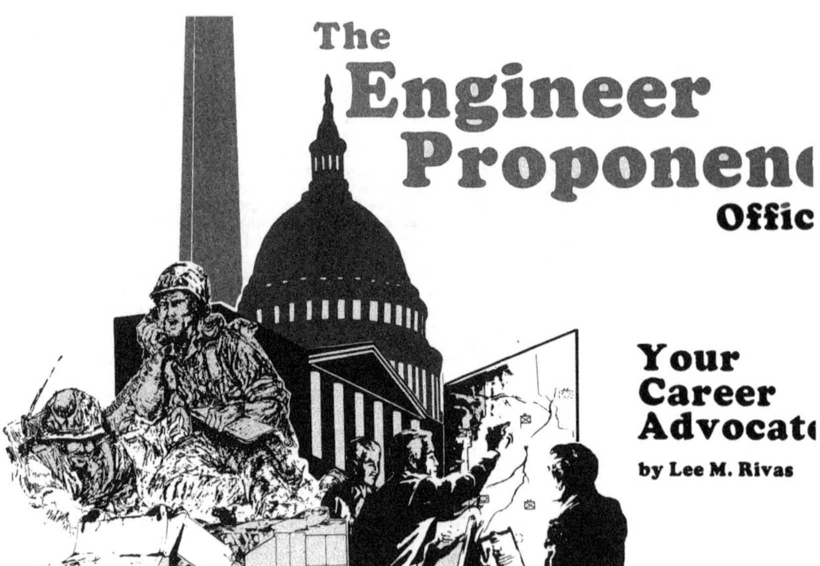

Your Career Advocat

by Lee M. Rivas

"What's proponency?"

That's the first question people usually ask when they hear about the Engineer Proponency Office. If you consult the Army's standard dictionary, ***The American Heritage College Edition****, you'll find that, like much of the jargon the Army is fond of using, proponency isn't listed. However, a terse definition of the parent word cuts to the heart of the matter:*

Proponent: One who argues in support of something, an advocate.

The proponency office is the engineer community's advocate to HQDA DCSPER for changes in personnel management policies and programs that affect the Corps of Engineers. The staff works on behalf of the Engineer School Commandant to identify solutions to problems that affect the careers of engineer officers, warrant officers, and enlisted personnel. They evaluate:

- Force structure
- Acquisition
- Training and education
- Distribution
- Deployment
- Sustainment
- Professional development
- Separation

The figure provides a more detailed listing of the proponency office's responsibilities.

Here are highlights of a few of the on going initiatives currently shaping the military engineering profession.

Commissioned Officers

The newly revised Officer Person Management System (OPMS) v gradually offer more engineer offic the opportunity to single-track th careers within the engineer branch concentrating on professional devel ment in one of the three engin specialty codes:

- Combat engineer
- Topographic engineer
- Construction (facility/contract ma agement) engineer

Warrant Officers

As part of the Army's Total Warr Officer Study, the warrant offi management system is being restr tured to better define the professi and system of appointments and properly manage the force. All w rant officers will be automatically tegrated into the regular Army up promotion to CW3. Positions are to grade coded to provide promotion p gression and improve utilization. Cr tion of a master warrant (CW5) ser is recommended for the future. T proponency office provides the engineer warrant officer representative on the USAMILPERCEN Warrant Officer Accession Board.

Enlisted Specialties

Many impractical grade structures exist within the engineer MOSs. These MOSs are being reviewed and realigned whenever feasible to provide soldiers in all specialties a fair, competitive chance at promotion.

The handbook, *Engineer Enlisted Professional Development*, published by the proponency office, offers advice for engineer soldiers on how to get selected for promotion and advanced schools. The booklet consolidates information gathered from numerous promotion boards and Engineer School experts.

For a copy of the book or information on personnel issues that affect engineer specialties, contact the Engineer Proponency Office, ATTN: ATZA-EP, Stop 248, Fort Belvoir, VA 22060-5248, or phone (703) 644-3760, AV 354.

Lee M. Rivas is the deputy chief, Engineer Proponency Office, USAES. Mr. Rivas has a bachelor's degree in business and management from the University of Maryland and is working on a master's degree in management and supervision from Central Michigan University.

Proponency Office Responsibilities

IAW AR 600-3

Structure
- Analyzes spaces on TAADS
- Recommends changes to TOE
- Analyzes SGA in TOE/TDA units and recommends changes as required
- Recommends classification criteria
- Forecasts future needs

Acquisition
- Recommends accession criteria
- Performs job task analysis of branches/functional areas
- Recommends procurement numbers by year/branch
- Recommends criteria for selected recall programs
- Recommends percentages of company grade to be assigned branches

Training and Education
- Identifies training criteria
- Identifies civilian education
- Develops and revises training
- Recommends standards for service school instructors
- Validates/revalidates AERB positions
- Recommends selection criteria for DA centralized boards
- Ensures functional area/branch training agrees with commissioned officer professional development

Distribution
- Accesses against authorizations
- Accesses by grade for schooling
- Identifies functional areas required
- Recommends changes to policy for assignments, details, and transfers
- Recommends initiatives to counter space imbalanced MOS (SIMOS)

Unit Deployment
- Evaluates unit distribution/home basing related to regimental system
- Evaluates effects of mobilization on personnel management systems

Sustainment
- Establishes/maintains communication with constituents
- Represents professional interests of constituents
- Fosters a positive attitude toward personnel system and programs
- Evaluates continuation/retention rates of functional areas
- Recommends MOS changes to improve health of branches
- Recommends changes to retention
- Recommends percentages by grade for functional areas

Professional Development
- Establishes professional development patterns
- Analyzes training and education requirements vs assignment priorities
- Determines qualification standards for each branch
- Identifies functional area skills required
- Identifies special skills required

Separation
- Recommends selected shortage specialties as an exception to elimination policy
- Recommends minimum qualification standards at selected grades by branch
- Recommends changes to retirement policies
- Recommends minimum time of service for military or civilian training or education prior to separation

Field Circular Helps Heavy Force

Field Circular 71-4, *Combined Arms Live Fire Exercise (CALFEX)*, provides a list of planning considerations for integrating all members of the combined arms team and a detailed formula for resource coordination i emplacement guidance, and safety diagram procedures. The publication also includes four sample scenarios, a sample LOI, and control plans.

Distribution was made in October to all members of the close combat (heavy) force to battalion/squadron level. Units may obtain additional copies by writing to: Commander, U.S. Army Armor Center, ATTN: ATZK-DPT-NRT (AWTS), Fort Knox, KY 40121.

Series Presents Official Army History of the Vietnam War

The authoritative history of the Vietnam War is being published in a 20-volume series by the U.S. Army Center of Military History. The books, to be printed over a 10-year period, cover the Army's involvement from its early advisory years to 1973 when the American troops left Vietnam.

Each book will include a comprehensive index including names, military titles, geographic locations, major Army functions, and commands down to the division level. The series features illustrations, maps, charts, and photographs. Special books will focus on the massive logistics support of the war, pioneering technologies, intelligence, and communications.

For more information, write to Superintendent of Documents, Mail Stop: MK, Washington, DC 20401 and ask for Priority Announcement List N-534.

Dear Friends at Home

The letters and diary of Thomas James Owen reveal the life and duties of a volunteer engineer during the Civil War. Union forces needed far more engineers than the regular Army could furnish. Volunteer engineers supported operations ranging from constructing pontoon bridges under fire to building fortifications for siege operations. *Dear Friends at Home* conveys the author's reactions to the extreme conditions of wartime, from the rigors of combat to the boredom of camp life.

The book from the Historical Division, Office of the Chief of Engineers, was edited by Dale E. Floyd. It may be ordered from the U.S. Government Printing Office, Department SSMC, Washington, D.C. 20402.

Hotline Q & A

Q. What is the FSN for staples and tie wire used in constructing triple-strand concertina wire obstacles? Last summer the Hotline Q&A said no NSN existed, but there was a FSN.

A. The DME Field Engineering Branch investigated further and discovered NSNs for both staples and tie wire. Here are the numbers:

Staples:

Size	*NSN*
⅝	5315-00-664-7035
¾	5315-00-664-7038

Wire:

Gage	*NSN*
9"	9505-00-833-6433
12"	9505-00-180-7212
14"	9505-00-180-7204

Q. I was unable to find any reference to barrier free zones in the new FM 5-100 series. Has any information been published on the barrier free zone concept? What is the exact definition of barrier free zone, barrier restricted zone, and barrier zone?

A. Authority to designate these zones is usually held at field army/corps level, and the scope of the barrier free zone is determined by the authorizing commander. This action is under consideration by HQ Allied Forces, Central Europe. The Northern Army Group is in favor of the new designations, but the Central Army Group opposes them. The NATO Combat Engineer Working Party Terminology Group has the definitions under study and worked on them during its September 1985 meeting in Munich. The definitions are:

Barrier free zone—No executed barriers. The force can maneuver in combat formations throughout the sector with the exception of existing natural and cultural obstacles.

Barrier restricted zone—Selected barriers executed. The force can maneuver in specific portions of the sector for operations such as counterattack.

Barrier zone—No restriction on obstacles except for designated reserve targets.

Q. According to an ARTEP evaluator, my company was advised not to use the JD-410, tractor utility, during foxhole digging. I understand that engineers do use heavy equipment for that kind of construction. Can you send me some kind of verification on that point?

A. It is the commander's option to use his equipment according to the priorities of the unit's mission.

Q. Can the AVLB be rail-loaded standing on its side?

A. The bridge cannot be rail-loaded on its side. The cross bracing and scissor cylinder must be removed. Also, the hinge pins should be removed and each ramp loaded separately. The procedure for loading the bridge is found in FM 5-12F1/2, task number 051-226-0305.

Q. I need information concerning tactical employment of ring-mounted 50-caliber machine guns. Our TOE has changed to issue us ring mounts and take away our tripods. How do you employ these ring-mounted 50s in a perimeter defense?

A. Tripod M75577 is needed for perimeter defense. TOE 05115 is being redesigned to include M75577 tripods. References for ring mounts are TM 9-1005-245-14, TM 9-1005-213-10, and TM 23-65.

Engineer Solution

ANSWER 1: 24,500 cubic yards.

The plan area of the likely zone of breakage will form a parallelogram defined by the open faces of the bench and the innermost blastholes.

Length of the zone	(23 ft x 9)	=	207 ft
Width of the zone	(20 ft x 4)	=	80 ft
Area of the breakage zone	(207 ft x 80 ft)	=	16,560 sq ft
		=	1,840 sq yd

Blasthole subdrilling is that portion of the hole which extends below the quarry floor. A bench tends to break more evenly at the quarry floor if subdrilled holes are used in the shot.

Bench height	(47 ft - 7 ft)	=	40 ft = 13.3 yd

The volume of aggregate that you should obtain from the shot:

(1,840 sq yd x 13.3 yd) = 24,500 cu yd

ANSWER 2:

To figure how much det cord and how many MS connectors are needed, you should have designed the echelon delay firing system as depicted below. Note that sound blasting practice emphasizes redundancy in all types of circuits. As a result there are two cord paths to any echelon.

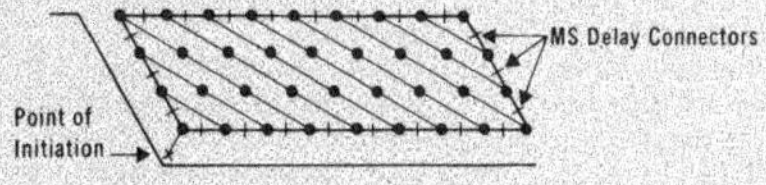

By inspection, 22 MS det cord delays are required.

The det cord lying on the surface and connecting the blastholes (the trunk lines) must have a total length of 22 hole spacings (around the perimeter), plus 24 staggered spacings (diagonally across the pattern).

Trunk line length:

(23 ft x 22) + (40 ft x 24) = 1,470 ft

You should add 10 percent to this amount for slack, plus an extra foot for the overlap at each MS connector. Also, a foot of cord should be provided to tie a diagonal line to the perimeter line at the point of intersection. Diagonal trunk lines intersect the perimeter at 20 locations.

Minimum length of det cord required for the trunk line:

1,470 ft + (1,470 ft x 10%) + (1 ft x 22) + (1 ft x 20) = 1,660 ft

The det cord extending into the blastholes (the down lines) must reach the primers. Each bottom primed hole requires 47 feet. To this amount, you should add 2 feet for slack, 1 foot for connecting to the trunk line, and 1 foot for securely attaching the cord to the primer.

The minimum length of det cord required for the 36 down lines:

(47 ft + 2 ft + 1 ft + 1 ft) x 36 = 1,840 ft

The total quantity of det cord required:

1,660 ft + 1,840 ft = 3,500 ft

Practicalities may demand that you obtain more than this quantity. You must allow for splicing of two lengths of det cord where one roll of cord ends and another begins. Each splice requires about 2 feet of cord. You need enough det cord to reach from the open corner blasthole to the point of initiation.

National Guard *Blazes Trails*

by CPT Lynda Mann

Central America has surfaced as a challenging area for National Guard training exercises. One such exercise, Blazing Trails '85 set in the isolated Azuero Peninsula of Panama, truly tested the road-building mettle of the combat engineers from Missouri.

The Reconnaissance Mission

In November 1984, CPT Clyde A. Vaughn, project engineer of the 135th Engineer Group, and eight other men from the Missouri National Guard were dropped into the wilds of the Azuero Peninsula on a reconnaissance mission for Blazing Trails '85· They came via a CH-47 Chinook helicopter with two jeeps, two trailers, and enough provisions for two weeks. Their task was to observe the area during the wet season (the Azuero gets more than 150 inches of rain during a five-month period) and to determine the best location for the Missouri Guard to build their portion of the road.

According to MAJ Charles Friend, 880th Engineer Battalion, "They couldn't have dropped us in a worse place!"

Ten-foot-high grasses, swamps, and flooding rivers required difficult passages to be made on horseback. The water was often so high that the horses carrying their riders had to swim across creeks. The first impression, which proved correct, was that the road couldn't go over the mountaintop as planned.

'We looked 'over the terrain and knew the road had to go through a nearby saddle," Vaughn said. "Otherwise we'd have to move 100,000 yards of dirt, and 20 percent would be the best grade we could get."

The Base Camp

In January 1985, CPT Vaughn and SSG Mike Phillips returned to the Azuero with two Panamanian Defense Force (PDF) personnel to establish the Missouri base camp.

According to Phillips, "At that time we didn't speak very much Spanish, and they didn't speak any English. But they were really good soldiers, so the communication gap really wasn't there."

Vaughn and Phillips met a local landowner, Roy McKone, a Canadian expatriate of 44 years. McKone spoke fluent English, and he immediately offered one of his rice fields as a base camp location. The agreement was sealed on a handshake.

While McKone finished his rice harvest, Vaughn and Phillips aligned the base camp. They determined entrances, streets, and airstrip locations. A few days later, LTC Tom Seavers, commander of the 880th Engineer Battalion, arranged for a priority load of two bulldozers, two loaders, and a dump truck to be delivered to a port near the base camp.

Vaughn and Phillips unloaded the equipment and cut the port road to accommodate future port activities and then stripped out the base camp. Engineers had to take the first four inches off the rice field so the residue would not burn. Next, they located a water point, cut a road, and made a borrow pit for the rock haul. Once the 880th arrived and the base camp was under way, the port was cut in, and Vaughn turned his attention to the road design.

Designing the Road

The whole sequence of building the road included road location (design), surveying, earthwork computations, earthwork, and final grading—but most important was road location.

The old road went straight up a mountain and then crossed a river several times. According to Vaughn, "It was doubtful that we could build anything along that route that would last beyond two rainy seasons."

The combat engineers talked with residents and local elected representatives about where the road should go for the sake of the people. They also considered the engineering requirements such as drainage structures and the location and availability of Class IV materials. In order to avoid going over the mountaintop, the engineers stepped into high ground and bypassed a swamp.

It was a major construction effort to

Engineers constructing bridges in Panama often had to fabricate parts due to the shortage of materials and stringers. Here, a crane lifts a Bailey Bridge to its pilings at Rio Marillo (photo by CPT Lynda Mann).

get to the saddle. It took two weeks and required diverting the headwaters of a stream into another valley. Vaughn said, "You couldn't possibly do this in the United States. The years that it would take to get the easements and the ground leased would be prohibitive."

One of the greatest challenges was an area dubbed *Monkey Mountain*. This area was a large vertical drop in a very short space. To get the desired 12 percent grade, the engineers designed a straightforward massive cut and fill which would require taking 65 feet from the top of the mountain. The resulting road base on this section was 30 feet wide with 20-foot shoulders on each side.

Drainage Structures

The Missouri National Guard also built 49 drainage structures and 6 bridges in the 9½ miles of road. This included 3 combination Bailey Bridges and 3 timber trestles, a combination of 9 low water crossings, 38 low water crossings with culverts, and 2 box culverts.

The Missouri engineers really had to adapt to change. Often the Bailey Bridges were fabricated. PLT SGT George Arth, Company C, 110th Engineer Battalion, cut bearing plates to place between the wood pilings and the bridges. "We've had difficulty getting materials, and stringers were at a premium," Arth said. "We took panels and turned them on their sides, welded channel iron to them, and made fabricated stringers. I think it will be just as strong as what would normally be there—it might even be something to look at for the future," he added.

Low water crossings, although unhandy, were often the answer because there would be so much water coming through the structures, they did not have enough culverts to carry it all, and the gaps were not deep enough for a bridge.

In many cases, natural drainage was diverted to avoid a drain structure or to create a larger one. In each case, watershed was calculated to determine if the pipe could handle additional water flow from another natural drain. A smooth transition was necessary to be sure the new drain did not cut back into its old channel.

The availability and timeliness of delivering materials also affected the design of the road. According to Vaughn, "Rather than there being, for example, a 12-foot or 15-foot fill with an area that we could easily have kept balanced, we had to fill it 5 feet because of the availability of only 48 feet of pipe for a concrete culvert."

Almost all drainage and culverts used 36-inch and 48-inch pipe. The road was designed with a basic 36-inch culvert because of the Azuero rainfall.

According to Phillips, "In the United States you're not talking about anything like 36-inch culvert, but here it's necessary. It's just unbelievable the amount of water that flows through these valleys."

Construction Rotations

Blazing Trails demanded that earthwork continue every day in order to complete the mission on time. Units were on the ground for 10 days, so while they were deploying and getting oriented, personnel assigned for the duration of the exercise operated the equipment and built the road. There was always a smooth transition when duration personnel were replaced by the current rotation units.

A major factor to the mission's success was the planning done by the 135th Engineer Group. As each rotation arrived, the engineers knew exactly what to do. They never stopped building the road. As a result, exercise participants were able to improve their engineer skills. According to Vaughn, "When they leave here, they are experts because they've never moved as massive an amount of dirt as they've moved here."

Benefits of the Experience

Because of the road, good things will come to Azuero—utilities, medical care, education—things to raise the standard of living. But it meant a lot to the combat engineers, too.

Blazing Trails '85 displayed the capabilities of the National Guard. They mobilized outside of the country and completed a huge mission. Every type of unit received excellent training.

"The number of ARTEP tasks we have accomplished is unbelievable," Vaughn said. "We now need to sit down and really define tasks—like driver's training. We don't drive vehicles under these conditions and terrain anywhere in the U.S."

"Very few people have this kind of opportunity," he added. "It's the most rewarding thing I've ever done. It will be on record from now on that the combat engineers from Missouri came through this part of the Azuero Peninsula and built this road. And the people will never forget what the National Guard has done here."

CPT Lynda Mann is the community relations officer of the 100th Public Affairs Detachment, Texas Army National Guard. She served 11 years on active duty, including an assignment with the 9th Infantry Division. CPT Mann established the Organizational Effectiveness (OE) program for NATO/SHAPE in Belgium and managed the OE program for the 21st Support Command, Kaiserslautern, West Germany.

She is working on her dissertation toward a PhD in human resource development from the University of Texas and is now attending the Command and General Staff College at Fort Leavenworth, KS.

The Evolution of Doctrine:

Development of Engineer Tactical Doctrine and Equipment 1939-1944

by MAJ Stanley J. Murphy and MAJ F. Marion Cain III

The situation of LTC Floid A. Davidson's 1st Battalion, 110th Infantry Regiment, was most discouraging. The time was early morning September 15, 1944. Their mission was to capture Hill 553, a Siegfried Line strongpoint along the Heckhuscheid-Uettfeld Highway. Without tank support, the infantry could make no headway against the German pillboxes. Five rows of concrete dragon's teeth and a roadblock prevented the tanks from closing in on the pillboxes.

Not until 1700 did the engineers and tanks arrive. Under cover of fire from tanks and towed tank destroyers, 10 unarmed engineers, each carrying 50 pounds of TNT, began to creep slowly, carefully toward the roadblock. As they inched forward, tension mounted, passing almost electrically to the waiting infantrymen and tankers.

Reaching the roadblock at last, the engineers found six steel I beams embedded in concrete caissons on either side of the road. Several large, portable iron tetrahedrons reinforced the obstacle. Working swiftly, they placed their charges. An hour and a half after they started their perilous task, the charges were set. Activating the charges, the engineers jumped to their feet and "ran like hell to the rear." The roadblock disintegrated with a roar.

Acting on cue, the tanks advanced and fired pointblank at the pillboxes. The infantry went forward on the run. Forty-five minues later, Hill 553 was secure. It yielded 17 pillboxes and 58 prisoners. After almost three days of mounting casualties and frustrations, the 110th Infantry in a quick, coordinated assault at last gained a significant objective within the Siegfried Line.[1]

World War II saw the use of obstacles, minefields, and barriers on a scale never before imagined. To cope with these obstacles to mobility, the U.S. Army Corps of Engineers rapidly developed new equipment and doctrine to support maneuver forces. This required a change in emphasis from constructing bunkers and field fortifications in support of World War I attrition warfare to breaching minefields and other obstacles in support of World War II maneuver warfare.

Like the Army of the mid-1980s, the Army of the late 1930s was also struggling with the problems of changing from a doctrine based on attrition to a doctrine based on maneuver. Therefore, a discussion of the development of tactical doctrine and equipment during the early years of World War II provides valuable insight into the development of contemporary tactical doctrine and equipment. This article examines one aspect of the evolution of tactical doctrine by the U.S. Army Corps of Engineers—the development of mobility doctrine and equipment from 1939 to 1944.

Background

The Japanese attack on Pearl Harbor in December 1941 caught the U.S. Army Ground Forces in the process of transitioning from a small peacetime army to a vast mechanized force. During this period, responsibility for developing mobility doctrine and training was vested in the Engineer School at Fort Belvoir, VA. The Engineer Board was responsible for developing equipment, and the Ordnance Department was responsible for procurement and production.[2]

Many senior officers, including GEN Malin Craig, U.S. Army Chief of Staff from 1935 to 1939, and GEN Leslie McNair, Chief of Staff, Army Headquarters from 1939 to 1940 and later Commander of the Army Ground Forces from 1942 to 1944, thought the new style of mobile warfare required only limited mobility support, primarily for emergency road repair. In fact, in the 1936 reorganization of the infantry division, GEN Craig recommended divisional engineers be deleted from the new triangular division.[3]

Search for a New Mobility Doctrine 1939-1942

Mobility in the Old Army

Throughout the 1920s and 1930s, few substantial changes were made in the methods of providing mobility support to the infantry division. The infantry division of the interwar years was primarily the square division, a large, cumbersome organization of over 22,000 men designed for the attrition warfare of World War I. Since most of the division's vehicles were horse- or mule-drawn and the infantry either walked or rode the train, there was little need for mobility support. The major function of the division's engineer regiment was to construct fortifications (survivability) using picks and shovels. In 1930, hand labor was supplemented by the addition of horse- or mule-drawn wagons, road graders, and scrapers.[4]

Reorganization

Seeking to increase the division's ability to maneuver, the new triangular division was organized in 1936. The organization had 13,552 men and contained three infantry regiments. The square division engineer regiment of 816 men was reduced to a battalion of 518. Convinced that the triangular division did not need significant mobility support, the strength of the divisional engineer battalion was further reduced to 420 men by 1939.

This marked the low tide of mobility support to the division. Many argued that proper reconnaissance would enable the division to detour around destroyed bridges and other obstacles. There seemed, therefore, little need for divisional engineers in maneuver warfare.

This concept was swept aside when Germany invaded Poland in September 1939. Analysis of German army operations in Poland revealed a larger number of engineer troops were required to provide mobility support for motorized and mechanical forces. Subsequently, in December 1939, the General Staff approved increasing the strength of the divisional engineer battalion to 520 men.[5]

In addition to changing the strength of the divisional engineer battalion, improvements were also made in equipping the battalion. In the fall of 1939, the Engineer Board used the 5th Engineer Battalion to test a 4 1/2-ton dozer by comparing its performance to a slip scraper pulled by a mule team. In the test, the dozer moved 16 times as much earth as the animal-drawn scaper. The test results were so impressive that before the end of the year, 7 1/2-ton dozers were authorized for divisional combat engineer battalions.[6]

Impact of the German Blitzkrieg

The German Blitzkrieg through France in 1940 also had a tremendous impact on the development of U.S. Army mobility doctrine and equipment. Throughout late 1940 and early 1941, several articles appeared in the *Infantry Journal* and *The Military Engineer* describing the importance of mobility support to breach obstacles, assault fortified positions, and conduct river-crossing operations.[7]

In 1940, maneuvers also provided another opportunity to demonstrate the need for increased mobility support. For the first time, it became standard practice to attach a platoon of engineers to infantry regiments. As a result, the strength of the engineer battalion increased to 734 men over the objection of GEN McNair who advocated only a single company of 175 men for divisional engineers.[8]

During the 1941 maneuvers, it became common practice to attach two platoons of engineers to each of the division's regimental combat teams. Based on the increased realization of the need for mobility support, the divisional engineer battalion strength was further increased in January 1942.

Impressed by the ability of German engineers to breach obstacles and assault fortified positions, the Engineer School conducted a series of tests in 1941 and 1942, stressing mobility support to armor and infantry units by breaching obstacles and supporting the assault of a fortified position using the Siegfried Line as a model. The purpose of these tests was to evaluate current Army doctrine and techniques and make recommendations.[9]

The Engineer School's final report, published in September 1942, reached several conclusions. First, assaulting obstacles and fortified positions required specially trained soldiers. Another key finding was that infantry, as well as engineer troops, should receive demolitions training. The report concluded that the infantry division organization was not suited to breaching and assaulting fortified positions and that present U.S. doctrine in FM 100-5 was sound, but needed clarification.[10]

In addressing specific assault techniques, the report stated the use of hand-placed charges would be successful against isolated obstacles. However, this method would not be successful against obstacles covered by fire from mutually supporting emplacements. The test committee thought that success would depend largely upon the ability of artillery and air force to suppress enemy fire and that use of smoke would significantly reduce casualties.[11]

A revised version of FM 5-6, *Engineer Field Manual – Operations of*

Engineers remove the detonator of a teller mine found on the beach at Nettuno, Italy, February 6, 1944. Americans created special mine training centers to counter the Germans' large-scale use of mines. Other methods of breaching obstacles included hand-placed charges, removal by hand, artillery fire and bombardment, bridging, and direct fire from tanks (U.S. Army photo).

Engineer Field Units, published in April 1943, established countermine and counterobstacle doctrine for the remainder of the war. FM 5-6 discussed five methods of breaching obstacles: hand-placed charges, hand removal, artillery fire and aerial bombardment, bridging, and direct fire from tanks or tank destroyers. The manual emphasized hand-placed charges as the most efficient method for breaching minefields and all other obstacles. Minefields could also be breached by hand removal using probes to locate the mines and then digging them out or exploding them one by one. Artillery fire and aerial bombardment was not considered a reliable method, and direct fire from tanks was only effective against some obstacles. FM 5-6 also stressed the importance of reconnaissance and the use of smoke to mask breaching operations.[12]

FM 5-6 and FM 100-5 stated that assault of a fortified zone would be conducted in four phases by a combined arms team consisting of infantry, armor, artillery, and engineers. Phase I was reduction of the enemy outpost system. Phase II was breaching a gap through the obstacles. In Phase III the gap was extended, and in Phase IV mobile forces would pass through the gap and continue the attack. Assault units would require specialized training, and special units should be organized to breach a major fortified position.[13]

An infantry battalion supported by attachments from tank, tank destroyer, artillery, engineer, and chemical units would conduct the assault. The assault would be preceded by a heavy preparation and aerial bombardment. As preparatory fires shifted to enemy reserves and counterbattery fire, direct fire from tank and tank destroyer units would suppress enemy fire and cover the assault and breaching detachments as they moved forward. Using smoke to conceal their movements, the breaching detachment would breach a gap through the obstacles. The assault detachment would then move through the gap and assault the fortification using a combination of hand-placed charges, hand grenades, antitank rockets, flamethrowers, and rifle grenades.[14]

Final Reorganization of Combat Engineer Battalions

In early 1943, the strength of the divisional combat engineer battalion was reduced from 745 to 647 officers and men. The battalion consisted of a headquarters company and three line companies. This reduction in strength was part of a general cut in the strength of the infantry division. The 1943 reorganization was the last major change in troop strength and organization of the divisional combat engineer battalion.[15]

During this period, the armored engineer battalion of the armored division was also reorganized. In early 1943, GEN McNair insisted the strength of the armored engineer battalion be reduced by more than 40 percent. He argued that since tracked vehicles could move easily cross-country, less mobility support was required to construct and maintain roads. Therefore, the treadway bridge company was removed from the division and placed under Corps control. Under the September 1943 reorganization, the armored engineer battalion was reduced from a strength of 1,174 to a strength of 693. This organization remained relatively unchanged throughout the remainder of the war.[16]

Improvements to Mobility Doctrine 1943-1944

The Impact of Combat Experience

Not until 1943 did actual combat experience overseas begin to influence development of mobility doctrine and equipment in the U.S. Army. Up to then, development of mobility doctrine and equipment was based primarily on theoretical work, observations, and tests conducted by the Engineer School and the Engineer Board.

By 1943, evidence began to pile up from the Russian Front and the British experience in North Africa. Throughout the year, *The Military Engineer* ran a series of articles on various aspects of combat engineering from the Russian Front. One of these articles by LT B. Marchenko of the Soviet army specifically addressed breaching German obstacles. LT Marchenko's article stressed the need to breach obstacles quickly to reduce the exposure of friendly units to enemy fire. He also discussed the importance of conducting a detailed reconnaissance, usually at night, to determine the exact nature and location of the obstacles prior to the assault. LT Marchenko's article recommended engineers accompany the lead elements in the assault. Breaching methods included hand removal of mines or detonating with explosives. Wire obstacles could be cut by hand or blown with demolitions.[17]

Retreating German units began employing obstacles in increasing numbers to slow down the advance of attacking units. In North Africa, Rommel placed large numbers of antipersonnel and antitank mines to impede British attacks. Later in Italy, retreating enemy forces went to great lengths to modify terrain with obstacles to slow the Allies' advance. GEN Eisenhower remarked that retreating Germans "... made certain that every culvert and bridge on the miserable roads were blown out; every shelf road cut into the steep mountain sides was likewise destroyed."[18]

Combat in North Africa in early 1943 revealed that not enough attention was focused on training for placing and removing mines. Present practice was for only engineer units to receive training in mine warfare. However, the large-scale use of mines by the Germans required that everyone be able to breach minefields. As a result, special mine training centers were established. Before deploying overseas, each combat unit sent a quota of officers to a one-week course in laying hasty minefields and breaching German minefields. Engineer officers received an additional week of instruction which included laying and marking deliberate minefields and disarming enemy mines.

Stressing the importance of realistic training prior to combat, CPT Robert Rigg published an article in the October 1943 issue of *The Military Engineer* describing a training course in the removal of mines. The mile-long course contained 11 obstacles with mines and booby traps. Realism was enhanced by connecting the mines and booby traps to 1/4-pound blocks of TNT buried off to the side of the obstacle. Another interesting fact is that CPT Rigg was not an engineer but a cavalry officer and the training course he recommended was established not for an engineer unit but for the 106th Cavalry.[19]

Countermine and counterobstacle techniques were becoming important not only to engineers but to other combat units as well.

Development of Mobility Equipment

Clearance of land mines and other obstacles presented many significant

1LT C.A. Post, attached to a combat engineer unit in France, prepares to detonate two German teller mines, November 15, 1944 (U.S. Army photo).

problems, and the Corps of Engineers pursued several lines of investigation. Basically, mines and obstacles may be cleared by either explosive or mechanical means. By 1943, the greatest progress in clearance techniques was in the area of explosives. Late in 1941, the Engineer Board conducted detailed experiments in the Tennessee Valley to determine the best types, amounts, methods of placement, and relative effectiveness of various explosives. Further tests were conducted at Aberdeen Proving Ground, MD, on antitank obstacles such as log blocks, tetrahedrons, hedgehogs, and log posts.

Explosive Methods

The Engineer Board determined that satchel charges of 25, 50, and 75 pounds were effective against large concrete obstacles such as dragon's teeth, while line charges, such as the bangalore torpedo, were effective for breaching lanes through minefields and wire obstacles.

The bangalore torpedo, invented by a British Army officer in Bangalore, India, before World War I, was a metal tube filled with explosives. After several tests, the Engineer Board, with the assistance of DuPont, American Can Company, and Republic Steel Corporation, designed a prefabricated bangalore torpedo five feet long, two inches in diameter, and containing 8 1/2 pounds of ammonium nitrate.[20]

Meanwhile, soldiers were still being trained to breach minefields by loosening mines with a probe and either removing them by hand or exploding them with TNT. This was a very slow and dangerous method, especially under fire. Although several bangalore torpedoes could be joined together to breach a minefield, the lane was only one to two meters wide, not enough for a vehicle.

In January 1943, the Engineer Board began testing a Canadian line charge called the snake. Similar to today's M157, the snake was designed to be assembled in the field out of enemy view, then pushed out into the minefield by a tank. When detonated, the snake cleared a path sufficient for vehicles. Although assembly was time-intensive, the tank protected the breaching team from small-arms fire.[21]

In addition to line charges, the Engineer Board investigated several other explosive methods for breaching minefields such as artillery fire, bombs, and rocket-propelled charges. All these methods worked up to a point, but explosives always left sensitive mines on the edges of the cleared lane. These sensitive mines were extremely difficult to remove and became very dangerous. Bombs larger than 250 pounds left a large crater which also became an obstacle to mobility. Consequently, by mid-1943, the Engineer Board and the Ordnance Board began to seriously investigate mechanical or pressure methods.[22]

The snake was used to clear a path wide enough for vehicles. It was assembled out of the enemy's view, and a tank pushed it into the minefield. The closeup (top left) shows a detail of the snake, a Canadian line charge similar to today's M157. A medium tank (bottom right) rolls down a snake-cleared minefield (U.S. Army photos).

Mechanical Methods

Throughout 1942 and 1943, the Ordnance Board experimented with several different types of disk rollers as a method of breaching minefields. These devices consisted of a number of large steel disks mounted on a medium tank. The tank pushed the disks through the minefield, detonating mines in its path. Major limitations of the rollers were their extreme weight and slow speeds. They also tended to break down frequently. Over 15 devices were tested before one model, the T1E3, proved more satisfactory than the rest. Named the Aunt Jemima, the T1E3 was fielded by early 1944.[23]

As early as January 1942, the Engineer and Ordnance Boards experimented with bulldozer blades mounted on medium tanks. Various straight and V-blades were developed and tested by LaPlante-Choate Company and LeTourneau Corporation. However, by the spring of 1943, a satisfactory solution had not been found.

Meanwhile, reports from the Pacific and North Africa emphasized the requirement for an armored vehicle to provide mobility support to front-line units where the operator was often exposed to enemy fire. Since the tank dozer was still in the developmental stage, another method had to be found.

The concept of armored bulldozers was suggested back in 1942, but steel plate was too scarce in the summer of 1942 to be diverted for this purpose. By mid-1943, the situation had changed, and the Engineer Board designed an armored cab for bulldozers. The cab was constructed of 1/2-inch steel plate and could be assembled in the field. The armor plate protected the dozer operator against bullets smaller than .30 caliber, but it was heavy and tended to overload the tractor. Cabs also reduced operator visibility and efficiency. By the summer of 1944, armored cabs were in the field.[24]

This medium tank is equipped with a T1E3 mine exploder. The Ordnance Board tested several types of disk rollers. However, they were heavy, slow, and frequently broke down (U.S. Army photo).

By late 1943, LeTourneau Corporation developed a successful tank dozer. This model employed a hydraulically controlled straight blade mounted on a medium tank. Its earth-moving capabilities compared favorably with those of a D-8 tractor. The LeTourneau tank dozer performed well under a series of demanding tests, easily overcoming obstacles previously classed as rendering direct assault useless. Rushed into production, the tank dozer was deployed to Italy by the spring of 1944.[25]

Impressed by the improvements in equipment and techniques for breaching minefields and other obstacles, the Office of the Chief of Engineers (OCE) directed the Engineer School to take advantage of Engineer Board test facilities to test techniques and doctrine and to bring tactical considerations to bear upon the Board's work. The School decided that unless U.S. Army doctrine changed, the infantry would precede the arrival of the tanks and must be prepared to breach obstacles using simple expedients such as wire cutters and ramps. Wide gaps through obstacles were not needed until the tanks arrived. Furthermore, vehicle lanes could not be provided until the infantry silenced the enemy's fire.[26]

Obstacles, minefields, and barriers in World War II created a demand for new equipment to support maneuver warfare. The Army experimented with various straight and V-shaped blades on tanks (U.S. Army photo).

The armored bulldozer protected the operator and provided mobility support essential after the German invasion of Poland and the Blitzkrieg through France. However, the armor plate overloaded the tractor and the cab reduced visibility (U.S. Army photo).

Encouraged by the successful tests of the tank dozer, the Engineer Board decided to develop a more versatile engineer armored vehicle. Based on a medium tank chassis, the engineer armored vehicle included a dozer blade, a trailer for carrying extra demolitions, a doozit (device for mechanically placing explosives), and substituted a rocket launcher for the 75-mm main gun. This vehicle was reasonably efficient and afforded good protection to its operator, although the rocket launcher was accurate only at short ranges and the launcher and doozit were vulnerable to enemy fire.

The engineer armored vehicle was successfully tested in the spring of 1944. However, procurement was blocked because the vehicle did not fit into the organization and doctrine of the Army. The Engineer Board concluded the vehicle could only be absorbed in the armored engineer battalion. The Engineer School recommended forming special units similar to the British approach. The Office of the Chief of Engineers thought the vehicle should be placed in all divisional engineer units. Consequently, the engineer vehicle was not deployed in time to participate in the fighting in Europe. On V-J Day, two engineer armored vehicles with crews and instructors were at the port of embarkation ready to deploy overseas.[27]

Throughout the prewar years, the Office of the Chief of Engineers resisted pressure from many senior officers to reduce the strength of the divisional engineer battalion below 300. During this period, they also struggled to field new mobility equipment replacing man power—first with horse power and then with machine power.

Initially, developments in organization, doctrine, equipment, and training were based on results of maneuvers and field tests. Later, lessons gleaned from analyzing German army combat operations were used to modify original concepts and theories. Finally, recent combat experience in the Pacific and North Africa was used to further refine doctrine, equipment, and training.

As a result, by D-Day 1944, the U.S. Army was equipped with a variety of mobility equipment to include: bangalore torpedoes, snakes, mine detectors, mine rollers, armored bulldozers, and tank dozers. Nevertheless, none of these methods was entirely satisfactory. The armored engineer vehicle had completed development, but disagreements over how and where it should be employed delayed fielding until the end of the war. The tank dozer was the closest approach to an engineer assault vehicle capable of providing mobility support to frontline units under fire.[28]

During the late prewar years of 1936 to 1941, the Office of the Chief of Engineers struggled to convince the Army that mobile warfare did not decrease the need for mobility support, but actually increased it. Throughout a period of seven years from 1936 to 1943, the U.S. Army tried to adapt the organization of the division to meet the demands of mobile warfare by testing new organizations, incorporating new equipment, and developing new doctrine.

Initially, development of mobility doctrine was largely theoretical and based on experience gained in World War I and more recent maneuvers in Louisiana and North Carolina. Later, mobility doctrine was influenced by the success of the German Blitzkrieg. Development of mobility doctrine and equipment during 1943 and 1944 was primarily guided by actual combat experience of Soviet, British, and American armies on the Eastern Front and in North Africa and Italy.

FM 5-6 and FM 100-5 emphasized the use of firepower to breach obstacles and assault fortified zones. These manuals did not discuss the use of mobility to bypass or outflank obstacles or fortified positions. The assault and breaching detachments were expected to lead the attack with only supporting fire and smoke to protect them from enemy fire and to breach enemy obstacles using hand-placed explosives.

Even though the 1941 tests by the Engineer School clearly showed that hand-placed charges would not succeed against obstacles covered by fire from mutually supporting positions, FM 5-6 and FM 100-5 did not mention the use of any mechanical methods of breaching obstacles or the need to provide the breaching detachment with armor protection.

GEN McNair's insistance on a lean, flexible organization played a key role in limiting the mobility support available to the division. McNair's concept was reinforced by his belief that tracked vehicles would require less mobility support as they traveled cross-country. This decision often came back to haunt U.S. Army units when obstacles and terrain restricted movement of tracked vehicles to roads.

American industry played a vital role in the development of mobility equipment for the U.S. Army. The military establishment simply did not have the necessary experience or technology to develop sophisticated mobility equipment such as the mine detector, bangalore torpedo, snake, and tank dozer.

Throughout the development process, the U.S. Army placed too much emphasis on perfection instead of set-

Soldiers place a bangalore torpedo under barbed wire, England, August 1943. Line charges were effective for breaching lanes through minefields and wire obstacles (U.S. Army photo).

tling for equipment capable of clearing sufficient obstacles to get a large percentage of vehicles through. This held up equipment development and delayed production. The result was that fewer items were available in the field.

Combat units deploying to Europe in the summer of 1944 were not adequately equipped to breach obstacles under fire. Despite extensive testing and development, the U.S. Army failed to develop a really satisfactory (quick and safe) method of breaching minefields under fire. The roller and and bangalore torpedo were simply the best of the lot.

Training could be changed rapidly based on actual combat experience, for example, correcting deficiencies in mine warfare training based on North African experiences. Equipment changes, however, took longer. When a particular item of equipment did not perform as expected in the field, it could not be quickly modified by the CONUS industrial base to meet actual field requirements. Therefore, a great deal of emphasis had to be placed on innovation and initiative in the field.

World War II witnessed the development of specialized mobility equipment and doctrine on a scale unforeseen and unpredicted in the preceding years of peace. The greater part of this specialized mobility equipment was actually developed after the majority of combat units deployed overseas. Consequently, there were initially no units specifically trained to employ most of this equipment. Furthermore, the number of officers and men in the European Theater familiar with the doctrine, capabilities, and limitations of this specialized mobility equipment was negligible.[29]

Experience and doctrine drive the development of equipment. The U.S. Army had not experienced Dieppe. None of their landings in North Africa and southern Europe had been heavily opposed. Doctrine emphasized the use of hand-placed demolition charges to clear obstacles, not the use of specialized equipment. Therefore, when the Engineer Board began to study the problem of clearing obstacles, they failed to evaluate the real strength of defenses and miscalculated the ability of the individual soldier to breach obstacles under fire.[30]

The eminent military historian Michael Howard once said, "It is the challenge of military science in an age of peace to prevent doctrines from becoming too badly wrong."[31] The final test of an army's doctrine is the battlefield. Perhaps there is no greater challenge to a peacetime army than the development of a viable doctrine for future war.

AirLand Battle doctrine is the U.S. Army's operational concept to meet the challenges of future war. However, AirLand Battle is not fully implemented. Problems still exist in applied doctrine, equipment, training, organization, and tactics. This is not to say that AirLand Battle should be discarded. On the contrary, this doctrine has established an ideal that should be strived for continually.

Like the Army of the late 1930s, we are struggling with the problems of changing from a doctrine based on attrition to one based on manuever. An understanding of the problems associated with the development of mobility doctrine and equipment during the early war years may prevent us from making some of these same mistakes.

MAJ Stanley J. Murphy is an instructor/doctrine writer at the U.S. Army Command and General Staff College. He received a bachelor's degree from the University of Oregon and master's degrees in civil engineering and systems management from Texas A&M University and the University of Southern California respectively.

He has served in a variety of command and staff positions in engineer units in Vietnam, CONUS, Germany, and Korea; most assignments have been in divisional engineer battalions.

MAJ F. Marion Cain III is a student in the Advanced Military Studies Program at the U.S. Army Command and General Staff College. He received a bachelor's degree in civil engineering from the Citadel, a master's degree in civil engineering from the University of California at Berkeley, and a master's degree in military art and science from the U.S. Army Command and General Staff College.

His key assignments include engineer platoon leader, 82nd Airborne Division, Fort Bragg, NC; company commander and assistant S-3, 62nd Engineer Battalion, Fort Hood, TX; project officer, Middle East Division, Saudi Arabia; and S-3, 2nd Engineer Group, Korea. MAJ Cain is a registered professional engineer in Virginia.

The Impact of Dieppe on the Development of Mobility Equipment

In August 1942, British and Canadian forces conducted a large-scale amphibious raid on the occupied French coastal city of Dieppe. This first attempt to land forces in Europe was a disaster. The raiding force of approximately 5,000 men suffered over 3,000 casualties. Over 1,000 of these casualties occurred on the beach before the raiders could breach the German obstacle system. The raiders encountered a formidable array of obstacles including steel spikes, barbed wire, concrete walls and blocks, antitank ditches and mines—all covered by persistent enemy fire.[1]

From this experience the Allies learned many valuable lessons. One was that engineers cannot consistently perform deliberate tasks under fire unless they are given armored protection. In March 1943, therefore, the British army converted the 79th Armored Division into an experimental formation and ordered its commander, Major General Sir Percy Hobart, to devise and develop specialized armor and equipment to breach enemy obstacles.[2]

Rather than design one vehicle to accomplish several tasks, the British thought each type of obstacle required a special antidote. Therefore, every conceivable method of breaching every known German obstacle was worked out on full-scale models at the division training base at Oxford, England. The 79th Division then designed and manufactured prototypes in the division's own workshops.[3]

One of the best known pieces of specialized armor developed by the British was the crab or flail tank. This vehicle consisted of 43 chain flails fastened to a rotating drum mounted on the front of an M4 series medium tank. The crab was an improvement upon the earlier model scorpion flail developed by the British during the North Africa Campaign. By rotating the drum, the chains flogged the ground in front of the tank and detonated mines buried in its path.[4]

Another important British armored vehicle was the Armored Vehicle, Royal Engineers (AVRE). Designed around a Churchill tank chassis, the AVRE carried a crew of six engineers and could fire a shaped charge round 80 yards from a 12-inch spigot mortar mounted in the turret. This versatile vehicle could carry several devices to enhance friendly mobility. Among these were:

- Fascine: a 7-foot diameter bundle of chestnut paling which was carried in the AVRE and dropped in ditches and craters.
- Bobbin: a 70-foot roll of prefabricated matting mounted on the AVRE and rolled across patches of boggy ground to permit the AVRE and other vehicles to cross.
- Skid Bailey: a 60-foot Bailey Bridge mounted on skids and pushed in place by the AVRE.[5]

The British also developed the ark. This armored vehicle consisted of a Churchill tank with the turret removed and trackways installed along the top of the hull. The ark simply drove itself into the ditch or gap to be bridged, providing a 54-foot span. Other vehicles could then cross over the gap.[6] Other vehicles developed by the 79th Armored Division included the searchlight, flamethrower, and amphibious tanks, as well as armored personnel carriers.

In practice, the British system of consolidating specialized armor in a single unit worked quite well. These vehicles were used extensively during the Normandy landings to breach German defenses and were in great demand after D-Day. During the remainder of the war, it became the practice not to commit specialized ar-

The crab or flail tank used 43 chains on a rotating drum to flog the ground and detonate mines. The British developed a different vehicle for each type of obstacle unlike the Americans who used one vehicle for several functions (U.S. Army photo).

mor unless the 79th Division staff was involved in planning the operation. This ensured effective utilization of a scarce resource.[7]

Furthermore, specialized armor remained with the supported unit only long enough to accomplish its mission. The equipment was task-organized for each mission and then returned to the 79th Division base which was equipped with special maintenance shops to repair and rebuild damaged or worn equipment.[8]

The 79th Division continued to improvise and solve problems even after deploying to the continent. The division headquarters was always close to Montgomery's headquarters to facilitate command and control, and the division commander roamed the battlefield ensuring his specialized armor was properly utilized.[9]

The British army developed completely different doctrine and equipment than the U.S. Army. The British experiences at Dieppe and in North Africa taught them early that unprotected, exposed troops could not breach obstacles under fire without exceptionally high casualty rates. For this task the British developed special-purpose armored vehicles.

Instead of integrating this specialized equipment into regular units, a special organization was created to centralize control of the equipment, doctrine, and training. Centralized control was necessary because there was not enough time to retrain the entire army in the use of this specialized equipment.

During World War II, the British realized that a specialized type of vehicle was required to breach each particular obstacle. The result was a proliferation of many different specialized vehicles. The American approach, on the other hand, was to combine several different functions in one vehicle. Since the U.S. Army often insisted on nearly perfect performance, its mobility equipment took longer to develop and was more complicated to maintain than British mobility equipment.

Two radically different systems for the employment of mobility equipment evolved during the war. The British, a year before D-Day, designed the 79th Armored Division as a special equipment division with the mission of developing, testing, training, and employing specialized mobility equipment in combat. There was no counterpart to this unit in the U.S. Army. Instead, mobility equipment was added to conventional tactical units. The British system was more effective because their system provided combat units with specially trained troops accompanying the special equipment. The American system did not.[10]

Notes

[1] Blanche C. Coll, Jean E. Keith, and Herbert H. Rosenthal, *The Corps of Engineers: Troops and Equipment (U.S. Army in World War II, The Technical Services)*, 1958, p. 472.

[2] Chester Wilmot, *The Struggle for Europe*, 1952, p. 181.

[3] K. J. Macksey, *Armoured Crusader: A Biography of Major General Sir Percy Hobart*, 1967, p. 261.

[4] U.S. Forces European Theater, *Study No. 52: Armored Special Equipment*, February 21, 1946, p. 7.

[5] USFET, *Study No. 52*, p. 43.

[6] Ibid, p. 43.

[7] Macksey, *Armoured Crusader*, p. 300.

[8] Ibid, p. 311.

[9] Ibid, pp. 301-302.

[10] USFET, *Study No. 52*, p. 3.

Engineers to the Rescue
A Personal Viewpoint

(continued from inside front cover)

- Air-operated lifting cushions (2.7-ton, 18.3-ton, 54-ton)
- Jacks, mechanical and hydraulic (6 to 10 ton capacity)
- Cutting scissors (pneumatic, manual, hydraulic)
- ORBIFON, high-sensitivity microphone to detect voices to a depth of 25 meters
- Polyurethane supports to assist jacking devices
- Miscellaneous tools (axes, pry bars, rope, pulleys)

Figure 1. Equipment for light rescue operations.

- Hurst and Lucas cutting and spreading systems
- Gas cutting system (oxygen/acetylene)
- KOBRA engine drill
- Chain and disc saws
- Ladders
- Air-mover ventilators
- Lighting systems
- TIRFOR heavy lift rigging system
- Dehydration pumps to drain water

Figure 2. Equipment for heavy rescue operations.

Yet, these units are not equipped to remove injured or trapped persons from collapsed structures. These battalions do have cranes, dump trucks, bulldozers, and air compressors which are fine for heavy work, but clumsy for the precision work of moving massive beams and clearing rubble in passageways. The specialized equipment needed does not exist in the combat heavy battalions.

An example of a rescue team with specialized equipment is the Israeli Civil and Home Defense Corps (CHDC). This equipment, which has been successfully used for many years, is configured around three main groups:

Light rescue trailer or wagon. A 2.5-ton cargo trailer is outfitted with equipment for light rescue operations (Figure 1). The equipment is compact, portable, and can generally be carried by one person.

Heavy rescue trailer. In addition to the equipment in the light rescue trailer, the heavy rescue trailer also has a small gas generator, a portable light set, and additional pneumatic cutting tools and manifolds or air-circulating devices (Figure 2).

Heavy equipment. The most versatile heavy equipment is the American-produced Bobcat, a small rubber-tired loader capable of accepting several front-end attachments. In the CHDC rescue system, the Bobcat has a pneumatic pavement breaker attached to the front boom. Because of its small size, the Bobcat can be placed inside a structure to perform clearing operations.

All the components of the Israeli rescue system are off-the-shelf and have been obtained from a variety of worldwide sources. Each item has been selected for its simplicity, durability, and suitability. All this equipment is air-transportable. The CHDC has developed an excellent rescue set that is combat tested. This equipment should be adapted by the engineers without further development or testing.

Rescue teams must also have help from local and battalion assets. Most fire departments have hydraulic ladders. The lifting capacity for heavy lifts can be supplied by follow-on assets from the combat heavy battalion: scoop loaders, forklifts, and 25-ton cranes.

Most of this equipment can be purchased in the United States, and many tools listed are already in the Army supply system. A squad-sized rescue team should have:

- Two 5-ton dump trucks with winches which can pull the Bobcat and its attachments and the heavy equipment trailer.
- An M-880 contact maintenance truck which can carry light sets, saws, generators, compressed air cascades, and compressors. It can also pull the light equipment trailer.

A Bobcat, which can be a great asse to the team, is not in the Army suppl system. The Bobcat can supply th power required for the jobs that jack and hands cannot do swiftly. It can f into tight locations to clear rubbl quickly, yet it will perform its intende mission smoothly and carefully, no like a D-7 dozer or scoop loader. Rescue teams must carefully employ the equipment to reduce further injury to the casualties.

The Case Uni-Loader 1845B should be selected for engineer rescue teams. It can be equipped with an auxiliary hydraulic tool attachment similar to the one equipped on the new small emplacement excavator (SEE). Stanley Corporation makes many tools already in Army stocks that could be attached to this auxiliary. Breaking hammers, hydraulic lifting equipment, and saws for cutting steel and wood beams could be added to the rescue sets as well.

The hand-operated hydraulic jacks and hydraulic cutting scissors, in the CHDC sets, could be adapted to fit an auxiliary hose from the Bobcat. This would reduce manual fatigue and provide sleek movement.

In addition to the preceding equipment, the air-operated lifting cushions in Figure 1 could have adapters so the air compressor can supply air directly to the cushions through half-inch air lines. If air lines are not practical, the self-contained air cylinders could be used. The compressor mounted on the truck could be hooked to a cascade

ENGINEER recently distributed a readership survey to units randomly selected from our mailing list. Please complete these surveys and return them as soon as possible. The results help us to evaluate our magazine and to publish the material which our readers like to see.

ENGINEER welcomes articles, photographs, ideas, and comments at any time from all our readers.

system to refill compressed air cylinders. The air-operated lifting cushions are important to the rescue missions.

The need for a properly equipped rescue team exists now. If one life is saved, the expense for the equipment and training will be worthwhile. How many marines in Beirut could have been saved if the United States had a well-trained and well-equipped rescue team standing by?

Deployment

These rescue teams and their equipment should be placed in combat heavy battalions usually assigned to corps-level headquarters. The AirLand Battle doctrine stresses the rear battle and magnifies the importance of rear area damage control. Because the corps is tasked with this mission, developing a rescue team organization into the combat heavy battalion is logical. In its TOE, the combat heavy battalion does have the heavier equipment required to supplement the rescue team's efforts, but not the specialized equipment.

The Corps of Engineers civil works districts in the United States and overseas perform many emergency operations. During wartime, the districts will have increased responsibilities. Even today, several sets of equipment could be used for relief during natural disasters. The Corps must ensure that the rescue teams are centrally located to better cover areas that may call for their services and to reduce the expense of organizing a team everywhere one is required.

This is the very reason why deployment in the civil defense network would be prohibitive. In the United States during wartime, the civil defense network will perform many tasks including recovery of injured people from damaged buildings. If a nuclear war occurs, this task is incomprehensible.

A study called *Civil Defense Rescue Requirements Following a Nuclear Attack* explains why equipping and manning enough rescue teams is impractical. In the first 15 minutes following an attack on a single metropolitan city, there would be 15,000 people trapped in debris. The study calculates that 150,000 man-hours and 600,000 rescue workers would be required. The specialized rescue team would be insignificant. During natural disasters, the Corps of Engineer districts and the Army could provide the support that the civil defense would require.

The Corps of Engineers must meet its tasked requirements or surrender responsibility. Developing and deploying specialized rescue teams will ensure that the Corps of Engineers will continue to accomplish its assigned tasks. Since emergency recovery operations may be required anywhere at any time, the Corps of Engineers must be prepared now.

Training team leaders and procuring off-the-shelf equipment to outfit several rescue teams must start as soon as possible. The Corps of Engineer's mission and the ultimate goal of the rescue team is to save lives.

CPT Marc E. Marszalek is assigned to the 299th Engineer Battalion (CBT) at Fort Sill, OK. He served in engineer troop and staff assignements in CONUS and was the hazardous material/safety officer and civil engineer in an engineer district in Saudi Arabia. CPT Marszalek has a bachelor's degree in industrial occupational safety and health from the University of Wisconsin at Whitewater and is a Certified Hazard Control Manager (CHCM). He is actively involved in SAME, ASSE, and other professional organizations to promote the safety profession.

Engineer Command Update

98th Division (Training)
Rochester, NY
MG Norbert J. Rappl
CSM Henry W. Curtis III

Training Group, 98th Division
Rochester, NY
COL Lee Cornaire
CSM Lawrence Davis

1st Bde. (Engineer OSUT & GST)
Schenectady, NY
COL Francis G. MacFarland
CSM Richard Peabody

1st Bn., 389th Regt., 1st Bde.
Glens Falls, NY
LTC Richard I. Bryant
CSM Howard C. Allen

2nd Bn., 389th Regt., 1st Bde.
Utica, NY
LTC Barrett L. Gates
CSM Thomas F. Rathbun

3rd Bn., 389th Regt., 1st Bde.
Mattydale, NY
LTC George T. Hiltebrant
CSM Clarence P. Countryman

4th Bn., 389th Regt., 1st Bde.
Schenectady, NY
LTC John E. Fitzgerald
CSM Anthony L. Caputo

2nd Bde. (Engineer OSUT)
Buffalo, NY
COL David Maul
CSM Ray Olsen

1st Bn., 390th Regt., 2nd Bde.
Buffalo, NY
LTC Bernardo O. Romanoski
CSM Dominick Futia

2nd Bn., 390th Regt., 2nd Bde.
Batavia, NY
LTC Dennis Demeyer
CSM Robert Ward

3rd Bn., 390th Regt., 2nd Bde.
Niagara Falls, NY
LTC Ronald Mis
CSM Joseph Daniels

1st Bn., 391st Regt., 2nd Bde.
Buffalo, NY
LTC Bohdan Bejger
CSM John Lindner

2nd Bn., 391st Regt., 2nd Bde.
Newark, NY
MAJ Laurence Feasel
CSM James Shaw

3rd Bde. (Engineer OSUT)
Ithica, NY
COL Michael R. Wilton
CSM Clarence Michaud

3rd Bn, 391st Regt., 3rd Bde.
Norwich, NY
LTC James Moravec
CSM Edward C. Gregoire

1st Bn., 392nd Regt., 3rd Bde.
Corning, NY
LTC Edward Castellana
CSM Gordon Bauman

2nd Bn., 392nd Regt., 3rd Bde.
Horseheads, NY
LTC James Cochran
CSM James Ruscitto

3rd Bn., 392nd Regt., 3rd Bde.
Binghamton, NY
LTC William Hammett
CSM Richard Romano

770th Engineer Co.
Penn Yan, NY
CPT Robert Cyranna
1SG Roger Morey

Active Army

522nd Engineer Co.
Fort Knox, KY
MAJ William B. Rynearson
1SG Herman L. Mitchell

The names of commanders and command sergeants major were provided by Headquarters, 98th Division. Readers are encouraged to send any additional information to ENGINEER.

Correction: The 204th Engineer Battalion, New York Army National Guard, is located in Binghamton.

Career Notes

Commissioned Officers Branch

Expanded Information Program:

Engineer Branch, Officer Personnel Management Division, MILPERCEN, mailed Engineer Bulletins 1 and 2 to all engineer commands. These bulletins contain information concerning promotions, assignments, military and civilian education, and career programs. Current plans are to publish the bulletin quarterly.

Several personnel update messages also were sent to engineers in key positions. These messages provide information concerning engineer officer personnel matters. Messages are released monthly.

Engineer Branch Chief:

LTC John Basilotto is now Chief of Engineer Branch, Officer Personnel Management Division, MILPERCEN.

Professional Registration:

Registration as a professional engineer (PE) for qualified engineer officers to enhance their credibility and professional stature with the civilian engineering community has been a goal for several years. Registration as a PE for an engineer is similar to the recognition a lawyer receives for passing his bar exam. A person taking the PE exam is required to have engineer work experience and education and possess the engineer-in-training (EIT) certificate.

As a positive step in promoting the PE registration, all officers starting fully funded advanced civil schooling in engineering or related fields will be required to take the engineer-in-training (EIT) exam. Engineer officers who began studying engineering in FY 84 or FY 85 and who are currently in school are encouraged to take the exam if they have not already done so. AR 621-1, *Training of Military Personnel at Civil Institutions*, is being revised to incorporate this change.

U.S. Army Register:

The U.S. Army Register will no longer be sent automatically to organizations which were on the special distribution list, according to MILPERCEN officials.

The register is now designated DA PAM 600-100. Organizations must use DA Form 12-9C, *Requirements for Classified DA Administrative Publications*, to request it from the Baltimore Publications Center, 2800 Eastern Boulevard, Baltimore, MD 21220.

The register which lists all active duty and retired Army officers is published annually by MILPERCEN.

Warrant Officers Branch

Warrant Officer Education:

The Army's goal is for all warrant officers to have MOS-related associate degrees by their 15th year of service. Education and experience are major factors when an officer is being considered for schooling and assignments.

Comments from the last CW3/CW4 selection board showed that maintenance warrant officers fell well below the norm in both military and civilian education levels. Selection rates for the Warrant Officer Senior Course were higher among officers who had attained the DA education goal.

If you have not attended the Warrant Officer Advanced Course (WOAC), you should remember that the only time MILPERCEN can send you to the WOAC is in conjunction with PCS orders. You should ask your commander about TDY funds to attend the school on a TDY and return basis. One other option is to take the Warrant Officer Advanced Course by correspondence.

You should review DA PAM 600-11, *Warrant Officer Professional Development*, Chapter 5, "Warrant Officer Education System," and consider all the options available to you regarding civil schooling. You should apply for schooling after two years on station. Don't wait until you are being considered for assignment. Keep in mind, however, that the degree completion is available on a "best qualified" basis.

Ask MILPERCEN

Q. I'm an E-4. Why can't I get a homebase assignment when I go to Korea? My wife and daughter need a place to stay while I'm over there.

A. The Department of Defense directive authorizing the Homebase/Advanced Assignment Program (HAAP) applies uniformly to all services and specifically identifies the authorized grades as E-5 through E-8 and O-1 through O-5. The program applies to soldiers being assigned to dependent-restricted areas only. If a soldier is entitled to move his or her family at government expense, that family can still be moved to a designated CONUS location while the soldier is serving overseas.

Q. I did not get 125 on my last EER. Can I still get promoted to E-7?

A. It basically depends on your MOS, your overall performance record, and the current trend in promotions. In a critically under-strength MOS, a relatively low EER score might still allow an individual to be promoted. An overstrength MOS has less promotion opportunity; fewer selections are made from only the very best qualified.

Q. Why was my joint domicile assignment disapproved? I know there are openings?

A. Joint domicile assignments are approved only when valid requirements exist for the MOS and grade of both service members. In addition, both members must meet the particular requirements for the respective vacancies.

If you have questions to ask MILPERCEN, call (202) 325-8856, AV 221.

CPSIA information can be obtained
at www.ICGtesting.com
Printed in the USA
LVHW081429061218
599201LV00024B/214/P